Contents

Notes

LONDON STAGE IN THE 20th CENTURY covers year by year in chronological order all the London premieres of world playwrights, all the major classic and modern revivals, and all the major visitors from five continents.

DATES: Dates are based on information in programmes and advertisements.

DIRECTORS: Directors, as we understand the role today, have been termed stage managers and producers in the past; but to avoid confusion, since the earlier terms now have different meanings in the theatre, all productions are described as having a director.

RSC: The Royal Shakespeare Company's base is in Stratford-upon-Avon. The company has regularly transferred productions to West End theatres. Between 1960 and 1982 its London home was the Aldwych Theatre. During this period they also performed at The Warehouse (now the Donmar) and in the West End. In 1982 the RSC moved into new premises in the Barbican, which has a main stage and The Pit. The company continued to transfer productions to the West End. Artistic directors: Peter Hall (1960–68), Trevor Nunn (1968–1991), Adrian Noble (1991–2003).

NT: All National Theatre productions were at the Old Vic theatre from 1963 to 1974 while the company waited for the new building to be built. The company moved to their present home on the South Bank in 1976. There are three theatres: Olivier, Lyttelton and Cottesloe. Artistic directors: Laurence Olivier (1962–1973), Peter Hall (1973–1988), Richard Eyre (1988–1997), Trevor Nunn (1997–2003).

OLD VIC: The Old Vic Theatre was bombed during World War II in 1940 and did not re-open until 1950. During some of that period The Old Vic Company performed at Streatham and The New Theatre, London.

ENGLISH STAGE COMPANY. Founded by George Devine, opened at Royal Court in 1956.

THEATRE WORKSHOP, founded by Joan Littlewood, opened at Theatre Royal Stratford from 1953.

ACKNOWLEDGEMENTS: I should like to express my appreciation to all the staff of the Theatre Museum, London, to all the staff of the Westminster Central Library, London, and to Richard Mangan of Mander and Mitcheson for their invaluable help.

1900–1909

1900

Jan 9. Cyril Maude as Mr Hardcastle, Winifred Emery as Kate Hardcastle, Paul Arthur as Marlow and Miss A M Victor as Mrs Hardcastle in Oliver Goldsmith's **She Stoops to Conquer** at Waldorf. George Giddens was very funny as Tony Lumpkin.
—The dearth of good new plays has at any rate one good advantage. It induces managers to revive some old ones. *The Times*

Jan 10. Herbert Beerbohm Tree as Bottom in Shakespeare's **A Midsummer Night's Dream** directed by Herbert Beerbohm Tree at Her Majesty's. Music by Felix Mendelssohn. Mrs Tree as Titania, Julia Neilson as Oberon, Louise Freear as Puck, Lewis Waller as Lysander, Dorothea Baird as Hermia. As always with Tree's Shakespearian productions the emphasis was on the scenery rather than the poetry. The revival was famous for its woodland, its wild flowers, its thickets full of blossom and its live rabbits. "The comedy," said Era, "can only be described as bewitching."

Feb 1. George Alexander in Anthony Hope's **Rupert of Hentzau** at St James's. This sequel to the popular *The Prisoner of Zenda* failed because the public didn't want to see Rupert killed and his body lying in state.

Feb 3. Edmund Payne in **The Messenger Boy** at Gaiety. Musical comedy. Book by Alfred Murray. Music by Lionel Monckton and Ivan Caryll. Lyrics by Adrian Ross and Percy Greenback. The messenger is sent up the Nile with the wrong letter. He disguises himself as a dancing Dervish and as a resuscitated mummy.

Feb 15. F R Benson in Shakespeare's **Henry V** at Lyceum.
—Vigorous declamation and keen intelligence hardly atone for ill-treatment of the blank verse line, hard monotony of voice and absence of passion. *Illustrated London News*
—Not one of the parts was played with any distinction. MAX BEERBOHM *Saturday Review*

Feb 19. Mrs Patrick Campbell in Hermann Sudermann's **Magda** at Royalty. Her performance in 1896 had been a miserable failure. Now it was hailed as a triumph, praised for its artistry, power and variety, and compared favourably with Bernhardt and Duse. The revival ran for five months.

Feb 22. Frank Benson Company in Shakespeare's **A Midsummer Night's Dream** at Lyceum. Isadora Duncan played a fairy.

Mar 1. F R Benson in Shakespeare's **Hamlet** at Lyceum. The play was acted in its entirety in two parts at 3.30 and 8.00.
—I thank Mr Benson for giving us Hamlet in halves – so that we need not see it all. *Illustrated Sporting and Dramatic News*

Mar 4. Frank Benson as Jack Absolute in Richard Brinsley Sheridan's **The Rivals** at Lyceum.
—Not only is the actor's own Captain Absolute a triumph of aridity but he seems to have succeeded in desiccating the whole of the company. The Lydia Languish (Mrs Benson) is afraid to languish and Mrs Malaprop (Miss Denvil) slurs almost apologetically over her malapropisms. *The Times*

Mar 15. F R Benson in Shakespeare's **Richard II** at Lyceum. The play had not been seen in London since 1857 when Charles Kean played the king. Many thought it was Benson's best performance. "His temperament stands him in good stead," said *The Times*. "He has a turn for acerbity, for sarcasm, for querulous peevishness."

Mar 27. Sydney Valentine as Sir Anthony Absolute, Paul Arthur as Captain Absolute, Winifred Emery as Lydia Languish, Mrs Charles Calvert as Mrs Malaprop and Cyril Maude as Bob Acres in Richard Brinsley Sheridan's **The Rivals** at Haymarket. The actors playing the juvenile leads were in their second youth.
—It seems ungracious to complain of any defect in the Mrs Malaprop of Mrs Charles Calvert so monumentally, so enormously droll as it is; but it must be hinted that Mrs Malaprop with all her absurdities was a fine lady, which Mrs Calvert is not. *The Times*

Apr 14. Mrs Lewis Waller as Tess of the D'Urbevilles and Whitworth Jones as Angel Clare in H A Kennedy's adaptation of Thomas Hardy's novel, **Tess**, at Coronet. Max Beerbohm said there was only one way to do it better and that was not to do it at all.

Apr 19. Charles Wyndham in the first performance in English of Edmond Rostand's **Cyrano de Bergerac** at Wyndham's. Mary Moore as Roxane.
—The English actor has neither the voice nor the training, nor the temperament required by the impersonator of so gallant a part. There is nothing orotund or heroic in his diction or bearing in his gesture or figure. *Illustrated London News*

Apr 25. Miriam Clements and Ellis Jeffreys in Maurice Hennequin and Antony Mars's **Kitty Grey** at Vaudeville. J S Pigott's English version was much more sentimental than the French original. The coquette was no longer a coquette.

Herbert Tree and Mrs Tree in Midsummer Night's Dream

Apr 26. Arthur Bourchier and Miss Compton in R C Carton's **Lady Huntworth's Experiment** at Criterion. Lady Huntworth masquerades as a cook in a country vicarage. A E Matthews played the curate.

Apr 28. Allan Aynesworth and Evelyn Millard in David Belasco's **Madame Butterfly** at Duke of York's. Adaptation of a story by John Luther Long. Puccini, alerted by Covent Garden, came from Milan especially to see the play and immediately set about acquiring the rights. The opera was premiered in 1904.

May 2. Yorke Stephens as Valentine, Mabel Terry-Lewis as Gloria and James A Welch as the Waiter in Bernard Shaw's **You Never Can Tell** at Strand. Six matinee performances. Young Modern Woman falls in love with an impoverished, social-climbing dentist and is instantly transformed into a sentimental woman. Shaw admitted he had set out to write a commercial play. "I was ashamed of its laughs and popularities," he said.
—Mr Shaw remains ineffectual because he has too much intellect... incorrigible ideologue though he is, he is also a delightful humorist and the actions of the puppets he presents are enormously droll. *The Times*

May 5. Robert Taber and Lena Ashwell in **Quo Vadis?** at Adelphi. Adaptation of Henryk Sienkiewicz's novel by Hugh Stanislaus Stange. The critics said the melodrama was tawdry, the stage craft feeble, the dialogue inept and the references to Christianity claptrap.
—The critics should remember that what seems vulgar to them does not seem vulgar to the public and what seems vulgar to them is really a very potent means of bringing religion home to the public. MAX BEERBOHM *Saturday Review*

May–Jun. Eleanora Duse in a season of plays at Lyceum: Arthur Wing Pinero's **The Second Mrs Tanqueray**, Gabriele D'Annunzio's **La Giaconda**, Victorien Sardou's **Fedora**, Hermann Sudermann's **Magda** and Alexandre Dumas's **La Dame aux Camélias**.
—Her knowledge of the technique of the stage is unlimited. Her gesture is perfect. Her power of facial expression quite unique. Technically, without a doubt, she is the greatest living actress. But with it all there is something lacking. It is great acting, but it is always acting. It is wonderfully clever; it is never quite convincing. *Daily Mail*

1900 World Premieres

New York
David Belasco's *Madame Butterfly*
Eugene Brieux's *Damaged Goods*

Stockholm
August Strindberg's *To Damascus I*
August Strindberg's *Easter*

Munich
Frank Wedekind's *The Marquis of Keith*

Oslo
Henrik Ibsen's *When We Dead Awaken*

Paris
Edmond Rostand's *L'Aiglon*

Births

Eduardo de Filippo, Italian actor, director

Marlene Dietrich, German actress, singer
Tyrone Guthrie, British director
Lotte Lenya, German singer
Kurt Weill, German composer

Deaths

Arthur Sullivan (*b.* 1842), British composer
Oscar Wilde (*b.* 1854), Irish playwright

History

—Assassination of King Umberto I of Italy.
—Relief of Mafeking in Boer War
—Boxer Uprising in China
—Paris Exhibition

May 29. George Arliss, Gerald du Maurier, Mrs Patrick Campbell and Winifred Fraser in Edmond Rostand's **The Fantasticks** at Strand. Parody of old-style romantic drama.

May 30. Herbert Beerbohm Tree in a new version of Washington Irving's **Rip Van Winkle** at Her Majesty's. Rip wakes after 20 years to find his wife is dead, his house derelict and the world completely changed. The supernatural did not convince.
—His performance was full of external charm, elaborate artistry, and expressive pantomime. But the actor's voice is too metallic and monotonous, his emotional methods are too theatrically sentimental, to render the long-winded rodomontade of the final passages genuinely impressive. *Illustrated London News*

Jun 13. John Martin Harvey as Sydney Carton in **The Only Way** at Prince of Wales Theatre. Premiered in 1899 Freeman Wills's dramatisation of Charles Dickens's *A Tale of Two Cities* secured his position as a leading actor-manager. He made the role his own and the exquisite pathos of the farewell ("It is a far, far better thing that I do...") was indelibly engraved on the collective memory of theatregoers. His performance was so popular that he was still playing Carton in 1939 when he was 67.

Jun 16. Ellen Terry as Olivia, Henry Irving as Dr Primrose and Fred Terry as Squire Thornhill in **Olivia** at Lyceum. W G Wills's adaptation of an episode in Oliver Goldsmith's *The Vicar of Wakefield*. Terry, at 53, was a bit old to be playing a young lady just out of her teens.

Jun 16. Dion Boucicault's **The Streets of London** at Prince's. The destitute rich are driven to begging on the streets and subsisting on the charity of the poor. The sentimental melodrama mixed social observation, Christian sermon and spectacle. The play was famous for its "sensational" scene – a burning house. The title was changed according to the city in which the play was being performed.

Jun 19. Henry Irving as Corporal Gregory Brewster in Arthur Conan Doyle's **Waterloo** at Drury Lane. Doyle's one-act adaptation of his short story, *The Straggler of Waterloo*, was a character study of the only surviving member of the battle on the last day of his life.
—The whole performance does not involve one gesture, one line, one thought, outside the commonest routine of automatic stage illusion. Bernard Shaw *Saturday Review*

Jun 19. Cyril Maude and Winifred Emery as Sir Peter and Lady Teazle in Richard Brinsley Sheridan's **The School for Scandal** at Haymarket. Constance Collier as Lady Sneerwell. Emery was the definitive Lady Teazle of her generation.

June 20. Charles Wyndham in Henry Arthur Jones's **The Liars** at Wyndham's. Love and morality, duty and honour. A man "sold his honour, his fame, his country, his duty, his conscience, his all for a petticoat" (i.e. he made love to a married woman). He paid the price and was banished to darkest Africa.

Jun 30. Henry Irving as Mathias in Leopold Lewis's **The Bells** at Lyceum. Probably the most famous of all Victorian melodramas. Premiered in 1871, it ran for 151 performances and brought Irving lasting fame. His agonised cry of "The Bells! The Bells!", even to this day, still remains part of theatregoers' collective consciousness, a remarkable testimony to the mesmerism of Irving's acting. The most celebrated scene was the phantom trial when, under hypnosis, the highly respected burgomaster re-enacts the stages leading to his murdering a Polish Jew for his money.

Jul 1. Janet Achurch as Candida, Charles Charrington as Rev Morell and Harley

Granville Barker as Marchbanks in Bernard Shaw's **Candida** at Strand. Ellen Terry had turned the play down.
—Candida, between you and me, is the Virgin Mother and nobody else. Bernard Shaw *in a letter to* Ellen Terry
—The Stage is not for sermons – not my Stage – no matter how charming – how bright – how clever – how trenchant those sermons might be...It's an incident – nothing more. All the world is crying out for deeds – for action! Ellen Terry *in a letter to* Bernard Shaw

Jul 7. W S Penley as the Rev Robert Spalding in Charles Hawtrey's farce **The Private Secretary** at Great Queen Street. The quasi-clerical whimsicalities had been booed at its premiere in 1890 and had only become a box-office success when it was reported in the press that the leading actress had dropped one of her petticoats whilst she was on stage and had had to throw it into the wings. The long-suffering curate – with his band-box, his parcels, galoshes, orange, bath-bun and catch-phrase, "D'you know? – quickly endeared himself to audiences and became one of Penley's most famous roles, second only to his Lord Fancourt Babberley in *Charley's Aunt*.

Jul 17. Henry Irving as Shylock and Ellen Terry as Portia in Shakespeare's **The Merchant of Venice** at Lyceum. Shylock – played as a gaunt, dignified Levantine – was one of Irving's great roles. The most famous scene was an interpolation. The curtain came down on the elopement of Lorenzo and Jessica during a Venetian carnival. Seconds later the curtain went up to reveal an empty stage and Shylock returning home over the bridge. He knocked on the door of the deserted house three times, the sound echoing throughout the theatre.
—I look upon Shylock as the type of a persecuted race; almost the only gentleman in the play, and the most ill-used. Henry Irving
—For absolute pathos, achieved by absolute simplicity of means, I never saw anything in the theatre to compare with his Shylock's return home. Ellen Terry *The Story of My Life*

Jul 18. Mabelle Gillman in **The Casino Girl** at Shaftesbury. Musical. Book by Harry B Smith. Music by Ludwig Englander. Pretty scenes, dancing girls, American soubrettes and picturesque Arabs.

Jul 24. Henry Irving in Charles Reade's **The Lyons Mail** at Lyceum. Napoleonic melodrama: one of the most popular productions in Irving's repertoire. He played two roles: the saintly Lesurques and the villain Dubosc.

Aug 21. Marie Tempest in **English Nell** at Prince of Wales. Dramatisation by Anthony Hope and Edward Rose of Hope's novel, *Simon Dale*. This, the first of two plays about Nell Gwynn to open within ten days of each other, was considered the best. Frank Cooper played King Charles II.

Aug 30. Julia Neilson as Nell Gwynn and Fred Terry as King Charles II in J Hartley Manners's adaptation of Paul Kester's **Sweet Nell of Old Drury** at Haymarket. It had neither literary nor historical merit. Neilson was beautiful, sprightly and gracious but she was never Nell Gwynn.
—A handsomer pair of lovers never trod the boards or raised rubbish to the plane of pure delight. A E Wilson *Edwardian Theatre*

Sep 1. George Alexander in Sydney Grundy's **A Debt of Honour** at St James's. Barrister breaks off a ten-year-old liaison with a devoted mistress to marry an heiress.

Sep 6. Herbert Beerbohm Tree as Antony in Shakespeare's **Julius Caesar** at Her Majesty's. Lewis Waller as Brutus, Robert Taber as Cassius and Murray Carson as Caesar.
—Although not qualified by voice or physique to play Antony, he still makes the great Forum speech a very effective, if flashy, piece of oratory, punctuated as it is by the interruptions of an admirably managed and realistic stage-crowd. *Illustrated London News*

Sep 27. H B Irving and Violet Vanbrugh in J M Barrie's **The Wedding Guest** at Garrick. Ménage à trois. Arid discussion.

Oct 9. Lena Ashwell and Charles Wyndham in Henry Arthur Jones's **Mrs Dane's Defence** at Wyndham's. The hysterical protests finally gave way to sobbing confession. The long and humiliating cross-examination in the third act established Ashwell's reputation as one of London's leading actresses.

Oct 18. Arthur Bourchier, Weedon Grossmith and Ellis Jeffreys in Robert Marshall's **The Noble Lord** at Criterion. The Prime Minister and the Opposition woo the same feminist with political promises. This political skit on the Women's Rights Bill was acted for comedy when it should have been acted for farce.

Oct 25. Gerald du Maurier, Mrs Patrick Campbell and Frederick Kerr in Frank Harris's **Mr and Mrs Daventry** at Royalty. Husband begs his wife's lover to give her up but she has no desire to return to him and tells him she is carrying her lover's child. The husband kills himself. The play was based on a scenario by Oscar Wilde. Clement Scott in *The Daily Telegraph* described it as "the drama of the dustbin". A B Walkley, in *The Times*, said "It goes as near to indecency as anything we remember on the stage." The bad notices did not affect the box office. The public believed that Wilde was the author and that Harris had merely lent his name.

Oct 31. Herbert Beerbohm Tree as Herod and Eleanor Calhoun as Salome in Stephen Phillips's **Herod** at Her Majesty's. Phillips's verse, though likened by some critics to Christopher Marlowe and John Webster, tended to be decorative rather than dramatic. Tree said it was "a grand play to go bankrupt on."

Nov 3. **The Three Musketeers** at Lyceum. Henry Hamilton's adaptation of Alexandre Dumas's novel. Superficial costume drama was robustly acted. Lewis Waller as D'Artagnan, William Mollison as Richelieu, Lily Hanbury as Milady, Norman McKinnel as Louis XIII and Eva Moore as Gabrielle de Chalus.

Nov 10. George Grossmith senior in **The Gay Pretenders** at Globe. Historical burlesque. Book by George Grossmith. Music by Claud Nugent. Lyrics by Walter Rubens. The Pretender to the English throne was Perkin Warbeck. The future Henry VIII was not amused.
—The reception of the piece was what is kindly called ambiguous and the author and composer were decidedly prudent in declining to come before the curtain. *The Times*

Nov 27. Cyril Maude, Allan Aynesworth and Sybil Carlisle in Captain Robert Marshall's **The Second in Command** at Haymarket. Maude had a big success in this sentimental comedy set in the Dragoon Guards. The uniforms were supplied by military tailors, not theatrical costumiers.

Dec 11. Frank Mills and Mrs Patrick Campbell in Max Beerbohm's **The Happy Hypocrite** at Royalty. Regency Rake falls in love with a beautiful and innocent maiden, who cannot love him back because he is so very ugly. He buys a mask to hide his face and wins her by false pretences, only to discover he's beautiful after all. The mask and face have become one. George Arliss played the Hawker of Masks. Beerbohm described his play as "a fairy tale for tired men."

Dec 15. W S Penley in Brandon Thomas's **Charley's Aunt** at Great Queen Street. Thomas (who had played Colonel Sir Francis Chesney in the original production) wrote the role of Lord Fancourt Babberley in 1892 especially for Penley. The farce

ran for four record-breaking years. 1,466 performances later, Penley's energy was unimpaired. Brandon was always insistent that this most famous of all drag roles had nothing whatsoever to do with female impersonation and that the actor playing him should never be effeminate.
—Mr Penley's make-up for the part of Donna Lucia D'Alvadorez is something to be seen, laughed at and long remembered. So, too, is Mr Penley's face with its wondrous variety of comic expressions. *Era*
—I hoped to go down to fame as a great actor. If I go at all it will be as the author of *Charley's Aunt*. BRANDON THOMAS

Dec 16. Janet Achurch and Laurence Irving in Bernard Shaw's **Captain Brassbound's Conversion** at Strand. The much-travelled Lady Cicely Waynflete has the vitality and humanity of an English nanny and treats everybody (brigands, Arabs and Brassbound) as if they were all little boys. Shaw said his play was a spoof on the sort of "melodramatic tosh Irving used to put on at The Lyceum."

Dec 19. Ellaline Terris as Alice in Lewis Carroll's **Alice in Wonderland** at Vaudeville. Book by H Savile Clarke. Music by Walter Slaughter. Seymour Hicks as Mad Hatter.

Dec 23. Lewis Waller in Shakespeare's **Henry V** at Lyceum. Lily Hanbury as Chorus. William Mollison as Pistol. Magnificent spectacle. Waller's female fans – known as KOW (Keen on Waller) – would shout, yell, clap, stamp and hold up the action for minutes at a time.
—The martial mien, the stately presence, the quiet humour, the fiery eloquence of the warrior-king are all made evident. Considered even as a feat of sustained elocution, sonorous, emotional, musical, Mr Waller's performance would be noteworthy; but it is something more –an impressive and arresting impersonation. *Illustrated London News*

Dec 23. Scottish singer-comedian **Harry Lauder** became a star overnight at Gatti's. He was a last-minute addition to the bill so his name did not appear in the programme. He sang "Tobermory", "Calligan" and "The Lass of Killiecrankie."

Dec 26. George Grossmith in Dr Heinrich Hoffmann's **Shock-Headed Peter** at Garrick. Adaptation by Philip Carr and Nigel Playfair. The Frankfurt doctor had produced the "pretty stories and funny pictures" for his three-year-old son in 1845. The stories were caricatures of the cautionary tales of his time.

1901

Jan 2. Frank Benson's Company in a season of Shakespeare's plays at Comedy: **The Taming of the Shrew**, **The Merchant of Venice**, **Coriolanus**, **As You Like It**, **Richard II** and **Hamlet**. Mrs Benson as Kate, Rosalind and Ophelia. Genevieve Ward as Volumnia. Ward's stateliness, incisiveness and elocution were highly praised.
—The method is the same, the Bensonian method of rough-and-ready interpretation, the method that substitutes earnest scholarly behaviour for heaven-born fitness and hearty vigour for a chiselled finish... Mr Benson's Shylock inspires many feelings but awe is not among them. His vindictiveness is rather petulant than deadly. *Era*

Jan 16. Oscar Asche as Shylock and Eleanor Calhoun as Portia in Shakespeare's **The Merchant of Venice** at Comedy.

Jan 22. Theatres closed at death of Queen Victoria.

Feb 5. Herbert Beerbohm Tree as Malvolio, Lily Brayton as Viola, Maud Jeffreys as Olivia and Lionel Brough as Sir Toby Belch in Shakespeare's **Twelfth Night** at Her Majesty's. The garden with its terraced hedges and statues was copied from *Country Life*. Malvolio was accompanied by four miniature Malvolios who aped his every move. One of the biggest laughs was for Tree's comic timing in a near-spectacular fall down a magnificent flight of steps.

Feb 6. Louie Pounds and H Lytton in Arthur Sullivan and Edward German's musical **The Emerald Isle** at Savoy. Book by Basil Hood. Sullivan had composed only two numbers before he died.

Feb 13. Marie Tempest in Charles Reade's **Peg Woffington** at Prince of Wales. Melodrama based on the life of the 18th century actress
—To play the part of Peg Woffington, to carry an imperfect and artificial piece practically on one's shoulders, requires a more finished and sympathetic method, greater ease and authority, and a sweeter and more winning style than Miss Tempest at present possesses. *Era*

Feb 21. The Apollo Theatre opened with Dave Lewis and D L Don in Ludwig Englander and Harry B Smith's musical **The Belle of Bohemia**. Wealthy brewer and travelling photographer look so alike they are mistaken for each other. The comedy flagged.
—Its American concocters appear to have imagined that mere qualities will atone for poor

Lewis Waller as Henry V

1901 World Premieres
Moscow
Anton Chekhov's *Three Sisters*
Stockholm
August Strindberg's *The Dance of Death*
Berlin
Frank Wedekind's *Spring Awakening*
Amsterdam
Herman Heijermans's *The Good Hope.*

Births
John van Druten, American playwright

Odon von Hovarth, Austro-Hungarian playwright

Deaths
Richard D'Oyly Carte (*b.* 1844), British impresario

History
—Death of Queen Victoria
—Accession of Edward VII
—Assassination of US President McKinley
—Succession of Theodore Roosevelt

Sarah Bernhardt in Edmond Rostand's L'Aiglon

quantity of entertainment, that the repetition of what is hackneyed has only to be thorough enough to afford real pleasure. *Illustrated London News*

Feb 27. Gerald du Maurier and Mrs Patrick Campbell in Arthur Wing Pinero's **The Notorious Mrs Ebbsmith** at Royalty. Free-thinking feminist throws the Bible into the fireplace only immediately to plunge her hands into the flames to retrieve it. Many critics thought Mrs Campbell's performance was subtler and more potent than it had been at the premiere in 1895.

Mar 29. Harley Granville Barker as Napoleon and Margaret Halstan as The Strange Lady in Bernard Shaw's **The Man of Destiny** at Comedy. Young Napoleon is outmanoeuvred in a battle of wits over some French letters. He has two fine speeches: one on fear, the other on English Imperialism. Shaw was the first to acknowledge that his one-act play was hardly more than a bravura piece to display the virtuosity of the two principal performers. It was originally intended for Ellen Terry and Henry Irving but they never acted it.
—Mr Shaw's tense, energetic and imaginative little piece is one of the cleverest he has ever written... Mr Granville Barker played Napoleon with care and intelligence but without all the desirable authority. *Era*

Mar 30. Florence St John, Decima Moore and Phyllis Rankin in **Florodora**. Book by Owen Hall. Music by Leslie Stuart, Ernest Boyd-Jones and Paul Rubens. Floradora was the name of an island and a perfume. This popular musical, premiered in 1899, closed after 455 performances. Hit number: "Tell me pretty maiden are there any more like you?"

Apr 11. George Alexander and Eva Moore in Henry Vernon Esmond's **The Wilderness** at St James's. A woman marries a man for his money, only to find she loves him and not her penniless lover. The wilderness is London society.

Apr 15. Henry Irving and Ellen Terry in Shakespeare's **Coriolanus** at Lyceum. Both actors were miscast. He didn't have the youth and vitality. She didn't have the physique or the disposition of a Roman matron. The beautiful designs were by Laurence Alma Tadema.
—Oh, how bad it makes one feel to find they all [the critics] think my Volumnia 'sweet' and I thought I was fierce, contemptuous, over bearing. ELLEN TERRY *The Story of My Life*

Apr 22. The Imperial Theatre opened with Lily Langtry as Marie Antoinette in Pierre and Claude Berton's **The Royal Necklace**. Lumbering pseudo-historical drama.

Apr 24. Seymour Hicks and Ellaline Terriss in Basil Hood's **Sweet and Twenty** at Vaudeville. Two brothers are in love with the same girl.

Apr 25. Charles Hawtrey and Fanny Brough in F Anstey's **The Man from Blankley's** at Prince of Wales. Young peer calls at the wrong house and discovers his former sweetheart is a governess. The comedy, based on a story in *Punch*, relied for its laughs on the eccentricities of the characters, the naïvety of their conversation and the burlesque acting of the cast.

May 11. John Martin Harvey and Mrs Patrick Campbell in Maurice Maeterlinck's **Pélleas and Mélisande** at Royalty. Five matinees. Pseudo-medieval fantasy. James Barrie, the playwright, thought Mrs Campbell was "beyond comparison, better than she has ever been in anything else."
—Her beautiful delivery of the words, the vague dreamy manner in which she moves through the scenes and her extremely picturesque appearance – all make up an impersonation of rare physical grace, distinction and poetic charm. *The Times*

May 12. Stage Society. Oscar Asche as Kersten Bernick in Henrik Ibsen's **The Pillars of Society** translated by William Archer at Strand. Bernick, the highly successful and highly respected ship-builder, has the cheek to justify his blatant self-interest and

ruthless opportunism as acts of philanthropy for the community. Archer in a programme note pointed out that the play had been performed 1,200 times in Germany, but only twice in England.
—Bernick ought to wring the soul with anguish and pity. In this Mr Asche did not quite succeed. *The Times*

May 16. Charles Wyndham and Mary Moore in Henry Arthur Jones's **The Case of Rebellious Susan** at Wyndham's. A wife discovers her husband is having an affair. Everybody advises her to patch it up, not to make a fuss, to shut her eyes, to forgive, and to forget. She, however, decides to pay him back in kind, arguing that wives should be allowed to be as unfaithful as their husbands are. The question is whether she did or did not take her revenge with a young man whilst she was on holiday in Cairo. Her husband would dearly like to know, but she refuses to tell him.
—My comedy isn't a comedy. It's a tragedy dressed up as a comedy. HENRY ARTHUR JONES

May 23. Mrs Patrick Campbell in Jose Echegarz's **Mariana** at Royalty. Violent, gloomy Spanish melodrama. James Agate said Campbell's performance was one of the great acting experiences of his life. Max Beerbohm dismissed the play as "Foolish melodrama by a distinguished and much-lauded foreigner whose very name we are afraid to pronounce."

Jun – Jul. Sarah Bernhardt in a season of French plays at Her Majesty's: Alexandre Dumas's **La Dame aux Camélias,** Racine's **Phèdre** and Victorien Sardou's **La Tosca**. Phèdre was thought by many critics to be her greatest achievement.

Jun 3. Sarah Bernhardt as the 20-year-old Duc de Reichstadt in Edmond Rostand's **L'Aiglon** at His Majesty's. Four hours of patriotic rhetoric. Napoleon's delicate son wastes away from ill-health and neglect. Obsessed by his father, he dreams of re-establishing the Bonaparte Empire with himself at its head. One of Bernhardt's biggest successes in London, Paris and New York.
—Fury and weakness alternate in amazing contrast, and no one can dash from softness to a shriek with such skill and fervour as Sarah Bernhardt. At one moment there is the hand of velvet and in the next the claw of a panther. *Black and White*
—The trouble is that to every one she looks like a woman, walks like one, talks like one, is one. That primary fact upsets the whole effort, mars all illusion. MAX BEERBOHM *Saturday Review*

Jun 10. Henry Irving as Napoleon and Ellen Terry as the ex-washerwoman in Victorien Sardou's **Madame Sans Gene** at Lyceum. Weak plays produce weak performances. Terry was not on form. King Edward VII, a regular theatregoer, was not the only one to think that Irving should have played Wellington and not Napoleon.

Jun 17. Marie Studholme, Gertie Millar, Edmund Payne and George Grossmith in **The Toreador** at Gaiety. Musical comedy. Book by James T Tanner and Harry Nicholls. Music by Ivan Caryll and Lionel Monckton. Gertie Millar's debut. She sang "Keep Off the Grass" and "Cora, Cora, Captivating Cora, Just a Little Bridesmaid that is All."

Jul 9. Coquelin Aîné as Cyrano and Sarah Bernhardt as Roxane in Edmond Rostand's **Cyrano de Bergerac** at His Majesty's. The play was a rebellion against the excessive realism of the problem plays. 29-year-old Rostand, in love with theatre and hankering after some long lost chivalric ideal, looked back to the 17th century, as the elder Dumas had done before him. In a dazzling mixture of rhyme and rapier, he played up the romanticism to provide a verbal and visual firework display. For sheer theatrical bravado, of an unashamedly old-fashioned kind, Rostand's heroic comedy is hard to beat. Cyrano, poet, soldier, duellist, a swashbuckling, hot-headed, extraordinarily courageous Gascon – immortalized by a grotesque nose – scorns all that is ignoble and mediocre. Coquelin, eloquent, flamboyant, witty, charismatic, had the panache and his death scene was heartbreaking.

Jun – Jul. Rejane in a season of French plays at Globe: Victorien Sardou's **Madame Sans Gene**, Adolphe Daudet's **Sappho** and Henri Becque's **La Parisienne**.

Aug 24. Norman McKinnel as the convict and A E George as the Bishop in **The Bishop's Candlesticks** at Duke of York's. Norman McKinnel's adaptation of a scene from Victor Hugo's *Les Miserables*. The Bishop tells the gendarmes that Jean Valjean could not have stolen the candlesticks because he had given them to him.

Aug 27. Marie Tempest in **Becky Sharp** at Prince of Wales. Adaptation of William Makepeace Thackeray's *Vanity Fair* by Robert Hichens and Cosmo Gordon-Lennox. "It succeeded," said *The Times*, "in exhibiting Miss Tempest rather than Becky Sharp."

Sep 7. Mrs Patrick Campbell in Arthur Wing Pinero's **The Second Mrs Tanqueray** at Royalty. A woman with a past commits suicide. The play had made both Pinero's and Mrs Campbell's name in 1893. The critics refused to see anything more in it than an effective commercial piece.
—Nothing could have been more successful. Mrs Campbell's strong and subtle portraiture of the hapless Paula came straight home to the audience with all the force and poignancy of truth. WILLIAM ARCHER *World*

Sep 7. Evie Greene in **Kitty Grey** at Apollo. Musical version of the Hennequin and Mars play. Lyrics by Adrian Ross. Music by Augustus Barratt, Howard Talbot and Lionel Monckton. The production was a triumph for Edna May, who sang "Give Back Your Heart To Me."

Sep 9. William Gillette and Maude Fealy in Arthur Conan Doyle and William Gillette's **Sherlock Holmes** at Lyceum. An old-fashioned sensational melodrama of incriminating royal letters and blackmail was fashioned from three of Doyle's stories. First seen in New York in 1899, it was never that good; but it succeeded because the most famous detective in the world was making his stage debut. When Gillette was writing the play he sent a telegram to the author, asking: "May I marry Holmes?" Doyle wired back: "Marry him or murder him or do what you like with him." Three months after its London opening there was a popular send-up, *Sheerluck Jones or Why D'Gillette Him Off* at Terry's Theatre. Gillette would go on acting Holmes for the next 36 years. It was the play, not the novel, which popularised the deerstalker.
—The more enthusiastic the admirer of the book the more deeply will he be disappointed with the drama – if this crude series of exciting incidents can be called drama. *Era*

Sep 21. Fay Davis and Oscar Asche in Arthur Wing Pinero's **Iris** at Garrick. Iris is very nearly strangled by her lover. *Punch* thought Asche's performance verged on the laughable.
—It has remarkable and unholy power and the influence is scarcely to be resisted. It leaves us, however, tearless and resentful, and to a certain extent perplexed. Do women such as Iris exist we ask ourselves? *Athaenum*
—Iris is a very powerful, very painful play, the most characteristic specimen of Mr Pinero's art, a piece of literature and at the same time a piece of solid, throbbing drama. *The Times*

Oct 3. Seymour Hicks in **Scrooge**, and adaptation of Charles Dickens's *A Christmas Carol* by J C Buxstone, at Vaudeville. *The Illustrated London News* thought Hicks would have been admirable if only he had adopted the voice of an old man and had avoided hysteria.

Oct 5. Alfred Barron and Louise Freear in **A Chinese Honeymoon** at Strand. Book by George Dance. Music by Harry Talbot. The first musical to run for over 1,000 performances. Chipee Chop (a naval officer) falls in love with Fi Fi (a waitress.) In China those who kiss evidently have to marry. The high spots were the cockney music hall numbers. Freear sang "I want to be a lidy".

Oct 24. Herbert Beerbohm Tree, Lily Hanbury, Lily Brayton and Mrs Tree in Clyde

Fitch's **The Last of the Dandies** at His Majesty's. The dandy was Count D'Orsay. The play, a series of picturesque tableaux, was decorative nonsense, lacking wit. Tree was far too solemn and slow.

Nov 27. Edna May in Hugh Morton and Gustave Kerker's **The Belle of New York** at New Century. Salvation Army lass becomes heir to a fortune. The musical fared better in London than it had in New York; its success was due, in no small part, to the loveliness of the English chorus girls. Phyllis Dare took over from May

Dec 18. Seymour Hicks and Ellaline Terriss in **Bluebell in Fairy Land** at Vaudeville. A dream play for children by Seymour Hicks and Walter Slaughter. Bluebell was a flowergirl. Terriss sang "The Honeysuckle and the Bee." Hicks played Dicky, the crossing-sweeper. It was this production which stimulated James Barrie to write *Peter Pan*. He had wanted Hicks to play Captain Hook.

Dec 26. Dan Leno in **Blue Beard** directed by Arthur Collins at Drury Lane. Leno was acknowledged by the public and the profession to be the greatest music hall comedian of his day.
—I defy anybody not to have loved Dan Leno at first sight. He had the saddest eyes in the whole world. That's why we all laughed at Danny because if we hadn't we'd have cried ourselves sick. MARIE LLOYD
—He had, in a higher degree than any other actor that I have ever seen, the indefinable quality of being sympathetic. I defy anyone not to have loved Dan Leno at first sight. MAX BEERBOHM

1902

Jan 4. John Hare as Benjamin Goldfinch in Sydney Grundy's adaptation of Eugène Labiche's **A Pair of Spectacles** at Criterion. Lovable old Goldfinch puts on his brother's spectacles and becomes a cynic who sees knaves and tricksters everywhere. Era described Hare's performance as "a masterpiece of histrionic high finish."

Jan 5. Fanny Brough as Mrs Warren, Madge McIntosh as Vivie and Harley Granville Barker as Frank in a private performance of Bernard Shaw's **Mrs Warren's Profession** at Lyric. Shaw wrote the play in 1893 "in order to draw attention to the truth that prostitution is caused not by female depravity and male licentiousness, but simply by underpaying, undervaluing and overworking women so dreadfully that the poorest of them are forced to resort to prostitution to keep body and soul together." Shaw made it clear that it was the very towns which were in the hands of the brothel trade who always prosecuted to keep his play off the stage. Faced with the choice in the 1860s of working in a factory, being a scullery maid, a waitress or a barmaid and earning starvation wages, Mrs Warren made her decision and now manages four classy and highly profitable brothels in Brussels, Ostende, Vienna and Budapest. The life-style suits her and she says she would be a fool to give it up. There were no public performances of the play until 1925.

Jan 7. The first revival of Oscar Wilde's **The Importance of Being Earnest** at St James's. George Alexander as John Worthing, W Graham Brown as Algernon Moncrieff, Margaret Halstan as Gwendolen Fairfax, Lilian Braithwaite as Cecily Cardew and M Talbot as Lady Bracknell. *The Illustrated London News* said it was "exhilarating champagne farce."

Jan 18. Evie Greene and Huntley Wright in **A Country Girl or Town and Country Life** directed by George Edwardes at Daly's. Musical comedy. Book by James T Tanner. Music by Lionel Monckton. Lyrics by Adrian Ross and Percy Greenbank and Paul Rubens. The country girl marries an aristocratic nincompoop. There were long waits on the first night because the scenery had not been delivered.

Jan 25. Lewis Waller as Bonaparte and Lily Langtry in Paul Kester's **Mademoiselle Mars** at Imperial. Royalist is saved from execution twice. Langtry went to Paris for her costumes and hat, but didn't bring back any French accents for the cast.

Jan 26. Winifred Fraser in Harley Granville Barker's **The Marrying of Ann Leete** at Royalty. Written in 1899 when he was 22, the play deals with class distinction, political jobbery, social rebellion and the role of women in society. Ann refuses to be a political pawn and decides to follow in her brother's footsteps and marry beneath her. She proposes to the gardener. The dialogue, complex and not always easy to follow, is fragmentary, full of half-heard conversations. A B Walkley in *The Times* admired its cleverness, humour and observation but found there was "no trace of constructive talent, no skill in building up the framework of a drama, no coherency, no clearness."
—Granville-Barker calls this piece a comedy. It might be more suitably termed a practical joke. *The Times*

Jan 27. Johnston Forbes-Robertson, Gertrude Elliott and Ben Webster in Madeleine Lucette Ryley's **Mice and Men** at Lyric. Philosopher in the 18th century trains an orphan girl to be his ideal wife, only to lose her to a dashing young captain.

Jan 28. Arthur Bourchier and Jerrold Robertshaw in Anthony Hope's **Pilkerton's Peerage** at Garrick. Pilkerton wants to be a peer. The Prime Minister's secretary, who might be able to help, wants to marry Pilkerton's daughter.

Feb 1. Herbert Beerbohm Tree and Constance Collier in Stephen Phillips's **Ulysses** at His Majesty's. Ulysses is Useless said the wags.

Feb 27. Gerald du Maurier and Annie Hughes in Arthur Law's **The Country Mouse** at Prince of Wales. Transferred to Criterion and then back to Prince of Wales.
—The delightful comedienne Miss Annie Hughes delivers piquantly the barbed comments of the seeming innocent, but after a while the monotony of a character never developed and humanised becomes painfully apparent. *Illustrated London News*

Mar 6. Henry Ainley and Evelyn Millard in Stephen Phillips's **Paolo and Francesca** at St James's. George Alexander as Giovanni. Phillips was compared to Swinburne and Tennyson and hailed as the greatest poet since Elizabethan times. His success led to a vogue for poetic plays. 23-year-old Ainley's romantic good looks were admired much more than his acting. Alexander's acting came as a revelation

1902 World Premieres
Moscow
  Maxim Gorky's *The Lower Depths*
Dublin
  W B Yeats's *Cathleen Ni Houlihan*
  W B Yeats's *The Pot of Broth*

Births
Ralph Richardson, British actor
Flora Robson, British actor
Richard Rodgers, American composer
John Steinbeck, American playwright, novelist
Donald Wolfit, British actor

Deaths
Emile Zola (*b.* 1840), French novelist, playwright

Honours
Knight: Charles Wyndham, manager

History
—Boers surrendered
—Guglielmo Marconi sent first transatlantic telegraph message
—Enrico Caruso made his first gramophone record

The chariot race in **Ben Hur**

to those who knew him only as a leading man in plays by Oscar Wilde and Arthur Wing Pinero.

Mar 20. E W Garden, Robertha Erskine, Beatrice Farrar, Charles Rock and Herbert Standing in Georges Feydeau's **The Girl from Maxim's** at Criterion. Philandering and religious mania in Paris. First production of a Feydeau farce in London.

Apr 2. Rosina Brandram, Robert Evett and Agnes Fraser in Edward German's musical **Merrie England** at Savoy. Book by Basil Hood. Queen Elizabeth loves Sir Walter Raleigh, who loves Bessie Throckmorton, a lady-in-waiting. Hit song: "The Yeomen of England".

Apr 3. Robert Tauber as Ben-Hur and Basil Gill as Messala in William Young's adaptation of General Lew Wallace's **Ben-Hur** at Drury Lane. The most thrilling spectacle in London. The public came for the chariot race. (The horses galloped on a moving platform.) The actors at the end of the race took a curtain call alone, which seemed a bit unfair on the horses.
—The scene has, of course, no acting value whatsoever. It is no more connected with dramatic art than would be climbing a greasy pole or a discharge of fireworks. *The Times*

May 4. Janet Achurch as Ellida Wangel in Henrik Ibsen's **The Lady from the Sea** at Royalty. Laurence Irving as The Stranger. Romance, melodrama and mysticism. Who would be a carp in a stagnant fishpond when she could be a mermaid and live in the ocean? Ellida is haunted by memories of a Finnish seaman whom she "wed" when he threw their joined "wedding" rings into the sea. She waits for him to come back and claim her. Ibsen drew on Hans Christian Andersen (the play was originally called *The Mermaid*) Wagner's Flying Dutchman, Motte Fouque's Ondine (later to be dramatised by Jean Giraudoux) and Nordic folklore of drowned sailors haunting the living.

May 6. John Hare and Irene Vanbrugh in Arthur Wing Pinero's **The Gay Lord Quex** at Duke of York's. Quex turns the tables on a scheming manicurist, who has constantly tried to compromise him, only to retract when he finds she has spirit. *The Times* thought the play was spoiled by certain lapses of taste.

May 10. Hilda Moody, Edna May and Madge Crichton in **Three Little Maids** at Apollo. Musical comedy. Book by Paul A Rubens. Music by Howard Talbot. Lyrics by Percy Greenback. Three country girls come to London and find three beaux. The girls sang a "naughty" song, 'She Was the Miller's Daughter.' Transferred to Prince of Wales.

Jun 10. Herbert Beerbohm Tree as Falstaff, Ellen Terry as Mistress Page and Mrs Kendall as Mistress Ford in Shakespeare's **The Merry Wives of Windsor** at His Majesty's. Oscar Asche as Ford. Henry Kemble as Dr Caius. The first night audience – "the jolliest I ever saw," said Terry – were surprised that "such thwacking, rough-and-tumble, Rabelaisian horseplay" could be by Shakespeare. They did not seem to mind that Terry did not know her lines and read from printed pages (which were scattered about the stage) and that the actors had to prompt her. "The audience crooned with pleasure," reported *The Standard*, "and filled up all the blanks."
—We do not remember ever having seen a performance of the play which was so immensely enjoyed by the audience and one which amused them so much. *Era*

Jun 11. Elizabethan Stage Society. Edith Wynne Matthison in **Everyman** directed by William Poel and Ben Greet at Imperial. Tina Brandt as Knowledge. Poel as God. Long neglected, this was a major revival of the 12th century morality play in which Everyman pleads with the Devil to give him one more one day. All the allegorical figures were strongly characterised.
—That talented young actress Miss Edith Wynne Matthison impersonates with rare poetic charm and emotional sensibility. *Illustrated London News*

Jun 14. Herbert Beerbohm Tree as Svengali and Lily Brayton as Trilby in Paul M Potter's **Trilby** at His Majesty's. Highly successful adaptation of George du Maurier's novel. Trilby falls under the mesmeric spell of Svengali who trains her voice and she becomes a famous singer. When he dies she loses her voice. Tree though the play was "hogwash" but it proved to be the biggest money-maker of his career and it enabled him to put on his Shakespearian productions.

Jul 3. Johnston Forbes-Robertson in Shakespeare's **Hamlet** at Lyric.
—Here is a Hamlet of overpowering charm, sweet graciousness and sunny geniality. Tragic intensity and sardonic humour are lacking; but what true feeling, what dignity, what urbanity! *Illustrated London News*

Jul 3. Henry Irving gave a reception on stage at Drury Lane to the 800 representatives of the colonies and the Indian Empire who were visiting London for the coronation of King Edward VII.

Jul 12. Coquelin Aîné in a season of plays by Molière at Garrick: **Le Bourgeois**

H B Irving and Irene Vanbrugh in The Admirable Crichton

Gentilhomme, Tartuffe, Les Précieuses Ridicules, L'Avare, Le Depit Amoureux. Coquelin acted Tartuffe so broadly – quite contrary to modern tradition – that audiences barely recognised the charlatan. The other plays were more traditionally performed.
—There is not a gesture in it, not an accent, not a shoulder-shrug or a plumed hat that is not part of the ritual; we see just what Molière's public saw, hear just what they heard. *The Times*

Jul 19. Henry Irving and Ellen Terry in Shakespeare's **The Merchant of Venice** at Lyceum. Their final appearance together.

Aug 19. Marie Tempest and Leonard Boyne in Cosmo Gordon-Lennox's **The Marriage of Kitty** at Duke of York's. Adaptation of the novel *La Passerelle* by Freddie Gresac and Francis de Croiset. A man intends to marry Kitty only so that he can inherit her fortune. Once married he intends to divorce her and marry a widow. Kitty has other plans.

Aug 30. George Alexander as Francois Villon, Lilian Braithwaite as Katherine de Vaucelles and Henry Ainley as Noel de Jolys in Justin Huntley McCarthy's **If I Were King** at St James's. Romantic melodrama. Alexander appeared in full armour on a white horse.

Sep 17. Ellaline Terriss and Seymour Hicks in J M Barrie's **Quality Street** at Vaudeville. Romantic fairy tale set during the Napoleonic Wars: tender, quaint and very sweet. Phoebe waits ten years for her Valentine. When he returns he finds she has changed into an unattractive teacher. She dresses up as her sister and attends the Officers' Ball where she flirts outrageously with everybody.
—It is acted with pathos and grace too exquisite for words on the part of Miss Ellaline Terriss. S R LITTLEWOOD *Morning Leader*
—More than once the sentiment threatens to degenerate into wallowing sentimentality. *Star*

Oct 2. Constance Collier in Hall Craine's **The Eternal City** at Her Majesty's. Didactic rather than dramatic. Brandon Thomas, who was cast as the Pope, played him as such as a doddery, senile old fool that he offended a great number of Roman Catholics.
—Such a farrago as this could not possibly be a vehicle for great acting. But all concerned do what they can: that is to say, they show abundant energy and strike picturesque postures. *The Times*

Oct 25. Lewis Waller in Newton Booth Parkington and Evelyn Greenleaf Sutherland's **Monsieur Beaucaire** at Comedy. Beaucaire is a prince disguised as a barber.

Waller's debonair gallantry and his swordsmanship was what his fans came to see and, whenever he needed money, he would revive the production. Beaucaire was his favourite modern role.

Nov 4. H B Irving as Crichton, Irene Vanbrugh as Lady Mary, Gerald du Maurier as Ernest, Henry Kemble as Lord Loam and Pattie Brown as Tweenie in J M Barrie's **The Admirable Crichton** at Duke of York's. Lord Loam, a socialist peer, despises class distinctions and once a month he entertains his servants on equal terms. Crichton, his conservative butler, disapproves. For him the most beautiful thing in the world is a haughty aristocratic English house with everyone in his place. Disdain is what he looks for from his superiors. He argues that in civilised communities, there must always be masters and servants and that equality is against nature. So when they are all shipwrecked on a desert island, the social barriers are not swept away. The class structure remains. The only difference is that the roles are reversed. Crichton becomes the master and the aristocrats are his servants.
—I think *The Admirable Crichton* is quite the best thing that has happened, in my time, to the British stage. MAX BEERBOHM *Saturday Review.*
—As delightful a play as the English stage has produced in our generation; always fresh and enchanting, yet always giving *furieusement a penser. The Times*

Nov 15. The Girl from Kay's at Apollo. Book by Owen Hall. Music by Cecil Cook. Lyrics by Adrian Ross and Claude Aveling. The musical was based on a French play by Leon Gandillot without his permission. Gandillot sued and won. Comedian Willie Edouin had a big success playing a silly American and his "I'm not rude, I'm rich" became a popular catch-phrase. Transferred to Comedy.

Dec 2. Cyril Maude and Evelyn Millard in Robert Marshall's **The Unforgiven** at Haymarket. A virtuous lady's reputation is at risk.

Dec 12. Charles Wyndham as Mr Puff in Richard Brinsley Sheridan's **The Critic** at Lyric. H B Irving as Sir Fretful Plagiary. The play was heavily cut.

Dec 15. Johnston Forbes-Robertson in Shakespeare's **Othello** at Lyric. Herbert Waring as Iago. Gertrude Elliott as Desdemona. Lena Ashwell as Emelia. Ben Webster as Cassio.
—Somewhat lacking in volcanic force; we get a series of explosions rather than one overwhelming eruption. *The Times*

Dec 26. Dan Leno and Fred Emney in **Mother Goose** at Drury Lane. Leno as a nymph in flaxen curls and gauzy drapery was a sight to behold.

1903

Jan 21. Fred Terry and Julia Neilson in Robert George Legge's **For Sword or Song** directed by Louis Calvert at Shaftesbury. A poetical musical play. Music by Raymond Rose. Scenery by Gordon Craig. Vladimir has a taste for music. His family thinks he should be fighting battles and murdering people. *Era* said Neilson's "feminine notes were inconsistent with her appearance as a strapping young man."

Jan 22. Constance Drever in Edward German's musical **A Princess of Kensington** at Savoy. Book by Basil Hood. 1000 years ago Kensington Gardens was the home of fairies. The princess was the daughter of Oberon. Walter Passmore played Puck.

Jan 25. G S Titheradge in Henrik Ibsen's **When We Dead Awaken** at Imperial. First performance of Archer's translation. Ibsen's last play is a deeply personal statement about himself and his art. A world-famous sculptor has lost his passion. Burnt-out, grumpy, restless, he feels guilty that he chose fame rather than happiness, and art rather than life. He finds the artistic vocation is "empty, hollow and fundamentally meaningless" but knows he must keep working until the day he dies. Most critics had difficulty with the symbolism and the heightened prose. *The Referee* found it "depressingly obscure, deplorably dull."
—The dialogue so often verges on the grotesque that the unprivileged listener is more inclined to doubt the author's earnestness. *Lloyd's Weekly News*

Feb 7. Johnston Forbes-Robertson, Gertrude Elliott, Aubrey Smith, Nina Boucicault and Sydney Valentine in George Fleming's adaptation of Rudyard Kipling's **The Light That Failed** at Lyric. Painter goes blind. His model, driven by jealousy, destroys his last painting. Transferred to New.
—Nobody who saw it will forget the tragedy of that blind figure, feeling his way about the studio and fingering that destroyed masterpiece. W MACQUEEN-POPE *Ghosts and Greasepaint*

Feb 17. Herbert Beerbohm Tree as Prince Dimitry Nehludof in Michael Morton's adaptation of Leo Tolstoy's novel, **Resurrection**, at His Majesty's. "As drama," said *The Times*, "it belongs unmistakably, to the category of second best."

Mar 2. Violet Vanbrugh and Arthur Bourchier in Henry Arthur Jones's **Whitwash-**

1903 World Premieres
Munich
  Arthur Schnitzler's *Reigen* (abridged)
Nuremberg
  Frank Wedekind's *Pandora's Box*
Dublin
  J M Synge's *In the Shadow of the Glen*
  J M Synge's *Riders to the Sea*

Births
Tallulah Bankhead, American actor
Beatrice Lillie, British comedian

Notes
—Plans for a National Theatre formulated in a book written by Harley Granville Barker and William Archer
—Abbey Theatre founded by W B Yeats and Lady Gregory with financial support from Annie Horniman

History
—Wright Brothers first to fly in a powered heavier-than-air machine
—Henry Ford established Ford Motor Company
—Mrs Pankhurst formed The Women's Social and Political Union.
—Madame Curie won Nobel Prize
—Inauguration of the Tour de France

ing Julia at Garrick. Scandal in a cathedral town. What sort of marriage did the widowed Julia have with the late Duke?

Mar 7. Edith Cole in Walter Melville's **The Worst Woman in Town** at Adelphi. Old-fashioned melodrama.

Mar 12. Charles Wyndham and Mary Moore opened New Theatre with a revival of Louis N Parker and Murray Carson's **Rosemary: That's For Remembrance**. Middle-aged squire falls in love with an eloping bride.

Mar 14. Sybil Arundale in Sydney Jones's musical **My Lady Molly** directed by Sidney Ellison at Terry's. Book and lyrics by George H Jessop. Lyrics by Sidney Jones, Percy Greenbank and Charles H Taylor. Molly disguises herself as a boy.

Mar 15. Stage Society. A E George and H Nye Chart in St John Hankin's **The Two Mr Wetherby's** at Imperial. Wives treat their husbands badly.

Mar 17. Cyril Maude as Lord Ogleby in George Colman and David Garrick's **The Clandestine Marriage** at Haymarket. Mrs Charles Calvert as Mrs Heidelburg. Allen Aynesworth as Sir John Melville. Lionel Rignold as Mr Sterling. Beatrice Ferrar as Miss Sterling. A E Matthews as Brush.
—All the physical disabilities of the old beau [Lord Ogleby] are dwelt upon with almost repulsive elaboration; while the noble, generous and kindly nature of the man, and his gallant attempt to keep the flag flying are handled unsympathetically and his debonair gaiety and 'grand style' are not done justice to. *Era*

Mar 17. George Alexander and Eva Moore in Rudolf Bleichmann and Wilhelm Meyer-Forster's **Old Heidelberg** at St James's. Alexander, over forty, thought he was far too old to be playing the young romantic Prince. Moore played the innkeeper's daughter.

May 30. Herbert Beerbohm Tree as Svengali and Dorothy Baird as Trilby in Paul M Potter's **Trilby** at His Majesty's.

Apr 3. Lyceum put up for sale, but since the highest bid was only £244,000, the property was withdrawn.

Apr 15. Ellen Terry and Oscar Asche in Henrik Ibsen's **The Vikings** directed by Edward Gordon Craig at Imperial. Costly failure. W B Yeats found Craig's scenery distracting. Terry said it was "a fine play to have made a failure with."

Apr 24. Herman Heijermans's **The Good Hope** at Imperial. The Dutch playwright (1864 – 1924) who had written a number of social-realistic dramas, which preached a socialist message, was compared to Ibsen, Hauptmann and Chekhov. The play was an attack on the deceit and corruption of ship-owners, who put profit above safety and exploited and sacrificed the lives of poor fishermen. The play had a huge impact in Holland and the laws regarding ships and shipping were changed.
—I wish that some of our so purely artistic dramatists could, through their coldly observant eyes, see life as clearly and steadily as it is seen through the somewhat flashing eyes of Heijermans. MAX BEERBOHM *Saturday Review*
—I flatter myself that I was able to assume a certain roughness and solidity of the peasantry in *The Good Hope* but although I stumped about heavily in large sabots I was told by the critics I walked like a fairy and was far too graceful for a Dutch fisherwoman! ELLEN TERRY *The Story of My Life*

Apr 30. Henry Irving in Laurence Irving's adaptation of Victorien Sardou's **Dante** at Drury Lane. Irving looked like Dante but the play was so poor that the critics thought the Danteists would be creating another circle of hell especially for the authors.

The cast of Broadway's first legitimate American black musical, In Dahomey

May 9. John Martin Harvey as Napoleon in Lloyd Osbourne and Austin Strong's **The Exile** at Royalty. Harvey did not convince.
—He seemed like a gentle, agreeable, sentimental, ambitious, old man, such as you might meet at any moment in the smoking room of any room of any club in London. Max Beerbohm *Saturday Review*

May 9. Edna May, Marie Studholme and C P Huntley in **The School Girl** at Prince of Wales. Musical comedy. Book by Henry Hamilton. Music Leslie Stuart. Convent girl runs away to Paris.
—Seldom has the sweet virginal charm of Miss Edna May's style been so effective. The ingenuousness of the pretty school girl and her bright intelligence and her natural acuteness are suggested by Miss May with delightful simplicity and fascinating grace. *Era*

May 12. Charles Wyndham, Mabel Terry-Lewis and Mary Moore in Hubert Henry Davies's **Mrs Gorringe's Necklace** at Wyndham's. The necklace is stolen. The thief commits suicide. Moore played the silly, chattering Mrs Gorringe. Transferred to New.

May 16. Aida Walker, Bert A Williams and Abbie Mitchell in **In Dahomey** at Shaftesbury. First black American musical. Book by Jesse A Shipp. Music by William Marion Cook. Lyrics by Paul Lawrence Dunbar. Cook not only conducted, he also sang along with the cast.
—The terrible difficulty that composers of my race have to deal with is the refusal of American people to accept serious things from us. William Marion Cook quoted by *Tatler*
—There is an electrical energy about its coloured interpreters, about their choral singing, their dancing, their naïve fooling, which, whether due or not to racial temperament, is certainly very refreshing. *Illustrated London News*

Jun 7. Ben Webster as Cashel Byron in Bernard Shaw's **The Admirable Bashville** at Imperial. Rich young lady loves a prize fighter. Her footman loves her. The play was written by Shaw to prove that he could write in blank verse just as badly as Shakespeare could. The joke is in the dreadful bathos of the dialogue. Cashel Byron's argument against being a gentleman is the most Shavian speech. Bashville's bitter soliloquy of rejected love is the most Shakespearean. The play was written at speed to protect the stage copyright of his novel, *Cashel Byron's Profession*, which was about to be pirated in America.

Jun 18. Cyril Maude, Ellis Jeffreys and Beatrice Farr in Hubert Henry Davies's **Cousin Kate** at Haymarket. Kate falls in love with a man who turns out to be her cousin's fiancée. The acting was better than the play.
—The clever, brilliant female novelist, petted by society, pretty, fashionable, and yet affectionate and true, was depicted by Miss Jeffreys with a winning charm, a delicacy of sentiment and a vividness and variety which were irresistible. *Era*

Jun 25. Réjane in Lucien Sardou's **Divorçons** at Garrick.

Jul 8. Henry Irving as Shylock in Shakespeare's **The Merchant of Venice**.
—That magnificent embodiment retains all the marvellous intensity and romantic mystery of Sir Henry's original conception. But it is far deeper, more terrible, and more impressive…a truly weird and awesome impersonation. *Era*

Aug 31. E S Willard in Louis N Parker's **The Cardinal** at St James's. Italian Renaissance melodrama. The cardinal (E S Willard) pretends to be mad so as to get a murderer (Herbert Waring) to confess his crime in the presence of concealed witnesses and thus save the hero (A S Homewood) from execution and allow him to marry the heroine (Alice Lonnon).

Sep 2. Eva Moore and Allan Aynesworth in H V Esmond's **Billy's Little Love Affair** at Criterion. Farce and melodrama. Billy is a girl.
—It is a pity to find a playwright who has so often shown graceful fancy and refreshing naturalness condescending to what is tawdry and meretricious. *Illustrated London News*

Sep 10. Herbert Beerbohm Tree in Shakespeare's **Richard II** at His Majesty's. A scene was specially introduced so that Tree could ride on a white horse and the citizens of London could boo Richard.
—This is a character which suits Mr Tree to perfection. The curious blend of the man of shrinking effeminacy and philosophical irony, the dreamy languor interrupted by half bouts of crazy speculation – all these things the actor brings out with completeness to make his Richard the most haunting figure he has yet given us. *The Times*

Sep 17. Weedon Grossmith and Margaret Halstan in Cecil Raleigh's **The Flood-Tide** directed by Arthur Collins at Drury Lane. A parody of Drury Lane melodrama.

The *Illustrated London News* said it was "first-rate cynical entertainment". The high spot was the spectacle of the flooding of a Cumberland valley.
—[Weedon Grossmith] acted with the quiet but irresistible drollery which he always exhibits, his demure yet incisive humour displayed in every scene. *Era*

Sep 25. Gerald du Maurier, Nina Boucicault and John Hare in J M Barrie's **Little Mary** at Wyndham's. Little Mary was a stomach. Boucicault's seriousness helped to maintain the play's plausibility.

Sep 30. The shareholders of the Lyceum met to consider a scheme to convert the theatre into a music hall. The motion was carried 33 to 13.

Oct 6. Cyril Maude and Lena Ashwell in W W Jacob's **The Monkey's Paw** at Haymarket. Grand Guignol. The possessor of the paw can have three wishes.
—Mr Jacob's story is the most cheerless and morbid thing we have had on the stage for some time and it is not likely to be welcome to the large class of playgoers who come to the theatre for cheerfulness, brightness and fun. Nevertheless its tragedy and gloom are impressive in their eeriness. *Era*

Oct 7. Eleanora Duse in a season of plays at Adelphi: Gabriele D'Annunzio's **Francesca da Rimini**, Hermann Sudermann's **Majda** and Henrik Ibsen's **Hedda Gabler**.
—So delicate are many of her effects – fleeting shades of facial expression that even in a theatre no larger than the Adelphi – they run the risk of passing unperceived. To make matters worse the stage was very dimly lit. *The Times*
—For this actress never stoops to impersonation. I have seen her in many parts, but I have never (you must take my evidence for what it is worth) detected any difference in her. To have seen her once is to have seen her always. She is artistically right or wrong according as whether the part enacted by her can or cannot be merged and fused into her own personality. MAX BEERBOHM *Saturday Review*

Oct 8. H B Irving and Irene Vanbrugh in Arthur Wing Pinero's **Letty** at Duke of York's. Aristocratic profligate pursues girl clerk. Max Beerbohm dismissed it as "Nothing but the lowest and most piteous kind of journalese."

Oct 17. Halbrook Blinn as Napoleon and Evie Green as the Duchess in Ivan Caryll's musical **The Duchess of Danzic** at Lyric. Book by Henry Hamilton based on Victorien Sardou's *Madame Sans-Gêne*. The grand opera story was set to light opera music; the result was there was more drama than comedy.

Oct 26. Gaiety opened with Gertie Millar, George Grossmith, Edmund Payne, Gabrielle Ray and Marie Studholme in **The Orchid**. Musical comedy. Book by James T Tanner. Music by Ivan Caryll and Lionel Monckton. Lyrics by Adrian Ross, Percy Greenback and Paul Rubens. A valuable South American orchid is lost. A duplicate is bought for £5.
—Miss Gertie Millar distinguished herself most by her exquisite and charming manner, alike as actress, singer and dancer. Her performance last night brought her within the very front rank of her profession. *Daily Telegraph*

Nov 29. James Welch in Maxim Gorky's **The Lower Depths** at Court. Premiere of Laurence Irving's translation. One performance. Transferred to Great Queen Street for one performance.
—The production of it seemed to me a mistake because it consisted of nothing but its hideous and revolting details. There was no form, no meaning in the thing; and therefore no excuse for it – no effect from it except the effect of purely physical disgust. MAX BEERBOHM *Saturday Review*

Dec 1. Arthur Bourchier and Violet Vanbrugh in Dion Boucicault's version of Charles Dickens's ghost story **The Cricket on the Hearth** at Garrick. The production concentrated on the sentimental rather than the fantastic.

Dec 28. Herbert Beerbohm Tree in David Belasco and John Luther Lang's **The Darling of the Gods** at His Majesty's. Tree played a cunning Samurai chieftain. It was the picturesque Japanese scenery, not the drama, which made the performance a success. *The Daily Graphic* said it was the "quaintest and most original entertainment London had ever seen."

1904

Jan 19. Cyril Maude and Ellis Jeffreys in Henry Arthur Jones's **Joseph Entangled** at Haymarket. A matrimonial scandal in which husband, wife and friend are, nevertheless, all entirely innocent.

Jan 20. Weedon Grossmith and Eva Moore in Robert Marshall's **The Duke of Killiecrankie** at Criterion. Farcical romance. Transferred to Wyndham's.
—The play is slight farce, innocent of attempt at ingenuity of construction or plausibility of intrigue, but noteworthy for the quantity of jokes. *Westminster Gazette*

Jan 23. Henry Granville Barker as Pierrot and Thyrza Norman as Prunella in **Prunella or Love in a Dutch Garden** at Court. "Play in three acts for grown-up children" – sweet, innocent and charming. Pierrot elopes with Prunella, abandons her and then regrets it. She forgives him. Pierrot is seen in various guises: seigneur, philosopher, poet and rascal.
—A blend of the quaint, the sentimental, and the weird; elegant prose, dainty rhymes, songs not sung but said to music; the whole tone *fumamburlesque*. *The Times*

Jan 27. Brandon Thomas and Irene Rooke in Basil Hood's **Love in a Cottage** at Terry's. Officer is so poor he hesitates to ask the daughter of an impecunious earl to marry him.

Feb 10. Kate Cutler and George Fuller Golden in **The Love Birds** at Savoy. Musical comedy. Book by George Grossmith. Music by Raymond Rose. Lyrics by Percy Greenbank. The love birds were husband and wife. Lottie Venne scored a success playing a grass widow who couldn't remember what her husband looked like. The lack of any memorable songs did not help. "As to plot," said *The Times*, "it seems almost bad form to mention such a thing in connection with a musical comedy. The players are far more important."

Feb 11. Lewis Waller and Mrs Patrick Campbell in John Davidson's **Queen's Romance** at Imperial. A version of Victor Hugo's *Ruy Blas*. Mrs Campbell complained that, whereas she always addressed the blank verse to him, Waller always addressed the blank verse to the auditorium.

Feb 16. Arthur Bourchier and Violet Vanbrugh in Bernard Miall's **The Arm and the Law** at Garrick. Adaptation of Eugène Brieux's *La Robe Rouge*. Two Basque peasants taking their revenge on the local magistrate offered plenty of opportunities for histrionic acting.

Feb 18. Ben Webster and Muriel Wylford in Somerset Maugham's **A Man of Honour** at Avenue. Barrister marries barmaid. The misalliance ends in the wife's suicide.

Mar 5. Sybil Arundale and Rutland Barrington in **The Cingalee** directed by George Edwardes at Daly's. Musical comedy. Book by James T Tanner. Music by Lionel Monckton. Lyrics by Adrian Ross and Percy Greenbank. Hit songs included Huntley Wright and Grace Leigh singing the "Monkey Duet", Isabel Jay singing "My Heart's At Your Feet" and Barrington singing "There's Nothing Much More To Say."
—The pity is that managements fail to take advantage of the sheep-like character of their audiences and lead the silly public into a taste for something better. The authors and musicians would benefit, too. All the clever people who concoct these entertainments are obviously suffering from a lack of stimulus. *The Times*

Mar 23. Arthur Bourchier and Violet Vanbrugh in Alfred Sutro's **A Marriage Has Been Arranged** at Garrick

Mar 26. A season of Irish plays at Royalty. John Millington Synge's **In the Shadow of the Glen**. A woman courts a tramp and a young shepherd over her husband's dead body. But the husband, an impotent old man, whom she had married for his farm, cows and sheep, is only shamming death to test her fidelity. He orders her out of the house. The shepherd, finding her destitute, deserts her. The tramp offers to look after her. Synge had presumed that the Irish wouldn't mind being laughed at, but audiences were offended by the black comedy and slur on Irish women. **Riders to the Sea** is a miniature epic. The grief-stricken Mauray (a symbol of Ireland and all her mothers), has already lost her husband, her father-in-law, and five sons, all drowned at sea. She is resigned to the death of her last boy and refuses to bless him when he leaves the house against her will. The language of Synge's plays was based on the rural speech he had heard on the islands of Aran. The season also included two plays by W B Yeats, **The King's Threshold** and **A Pot of Broth**, and Padraic Colum's **The Broken Soil.**

Apr 8. Thyrza Norman as Julia in Shakespeare's **The Two Gentlemen of Verona** directed by Harley Granville Barker at Court. The play was thought to be of academic interest only. Barker cast himself as Speed, the clown.

Apr 14. George Alexander and Lilian Braithwaite in Frederick Fenn and Richard Pryce's **Saturday to Monday** at St James's. A number of unwanted people descend on a widow in the country just when she and a former admirer want to be on their own...

Apr 17. C M Hullard as Mirabell and Ethel Irving as Millamant in William Congreve's **The Way of the World** at Court. Nigel Playfair as Witwoud. The critics thought that Irving had given new life to a dead play.

Apr 26. Kate Rorke as Candida, Norman McKinnel as Morell and Harley Granville Barker as Marchbanks in Bernard Shaw's **Candida** at Court. Six matinees. Morell, complacent, pompous and naïve, has no idea how much he owes to his wife Candida until she spells it out to him. Marchbanks, the lovesick poet, full of youthful arro-

1904 World Premieres

Moscow
Anton Chekhov's *The Cherry Orchard*.

St Petersburg
Maxim Gorky's *Summerfolk*

Dublin
J M Synge's *Riders to the Sea*

Births

George Balanchine, American choreographer
Cecil Beaton, British designer
John Gielgud, British actor
Witold Gombrowicz, Polish playwright
Graham Greene, British novelist, playwright
Moss Hart, American playwright, director
Harold Hobson, British critic

Christopher Isherwood, British novelist, playwright
Oliver Messel, British designer
Anna Neagle, British actor
Glen Byam Shaw, British actor, director

Deaths

Anton Chekhov (*b*.1860), playwright
Dan Leno (*b*.1860), comedian

Notes

—Granville Barker-J E Vedrenne season began at Court and continued until 1907.
—Abbey Theatre founded in Dublin
—Royal Academy of Dramatic Art founded by Herbert Beerbohm Tree at His Majesty's.

---

gance and torment, is a typical figure of the 1890s. In the auction he offers her his weakness, his desolation and his heart's need. Candida, a liberated modern woman, is tempted to become Marchbanks's mistress so that he might learn from a good woman what love really is.
—Miss Kate Rorke was Candida to perfection in her capacity, promptitude, width of mind and patronising kindliness; but she left out Candida's smiles, her irony, her maternity, and the charm of her perfect self-control. DESMOND McCARTHY *New Statesman and Nation*

May 3. Arthur Bourchier and Violet Vanbrugh in W S Gilbert's **Harlequin and the Fairy's Dilemma** at Garrick. Jessie Bateman played a fairy who was going to lose her job if she couldn't find any young lovers.

May 14. John W Ransone and Arthur Donaldson in **The Prince of Pilsen** directed by George Marion at Shaftesbury. Musical comedy. Book by Frank Pixley. Music by Gustave Luders. American-Dutch brewer is mistaken for a German Prince. The chorus saved the show.

May 18. Ruth Vincent and Laurence Rea in André Messager's **Veronique** at Apollo. Book by A Vanloo and G Duval. Adaptation by Henry Hamilton. Lyrics by Lilian Eldée and Percy Greenback. Opera-comique. Bride-to-be disguises herself as a flower-girl to spy on her husband-to-be on his last bachelor night.

May 25. Ellis Jeffreys, Fred Kerr and Cyril Maude in Roy Horniman's **Lady Flirt** at Haymarket. Adaptation of a French play by Paul Gavault and Georges Berr. Unaddressed love-letter gets into the wrong hands

May 26. Ben Webster in Gilbert Murray's translation of Euripedes's **Hippolytus** at Lyric. Harley Granville Barker's impassioned elocution as the Henchman was singled out for special praise.

Jun 14. Farren Soutar in **Sergeant Brue** at Prince of Wales. Musical farce. Book by Owen Hall. Music by Liza Lehmann. Lyrics by Hickory Woods. The sergeant joins forces with a convicted thief.

Jul 1. Sarah Bernhardt and Mrs Patrick Campbell in Maurice Maeterlinck's **Pelléas et Mélisande** at Vaudeville. Music by Gabriel Faure. Two performances. The actresses were far too old. A Dublin critic said "they were old enough to know better." Max Beerbohm refused to see them, saying the casting was sensationalism. The actresses played pranks on each other on stage. Bernhardt broke a raw egg into Campbell's outstretched hand.

Aug 8. Eleanor Robson, Gerald du Maurier and Henry Ainley in Israel Zangwill's **Merely Mary Ann** at Duke of York's. The American actress scored a big success as a boarding-house maid who becomes a Duchess.

Aug 30. Cyril Maude and Jessie Bateman in W W Jacobs and Louis N. Parker's **Beauty and the Barge** at New. Girl runs away to find love on a barge. Bright and breezy. The curtain-raiser was Jacobs's **The Monkey's Paw**. Transferred to Haymarket.
—Mr Cyril Maude, whose skipper in make-up, in voice, in semi-blustering, semi-deprecating manner, is a triumph of comic portraiture. *Illustrated London News*

Sep 14. William Haviland as Prospero, Herbert Beerbohm Tree as Caliban and Violet Tree as Ariel in Shakespeare's **The Tempest** at His Majesty's. No poetry but a spectacular shipwreck. Viola Tree flew on wires and sang "Where the bee sucks there

suck I" as she flew. The Epilogue was cut and Caliban was left all on his own at the end staring out to sea.
—The play which now enthrals the uncritical audience is Shakespeare's only in name and title. *Blackwood's Magazine*
—I claim that an artist works primarily for himself – his first aim is to satisfy his own artistic conscience. HERBERT BEERBOHM TREE

Sep 19. Oscar Asche and Irene Vanbrugh in J B Fagan's **The Prayer of the Sword** at Adelphi. Young medieval Italian monk (Walter Hampden) breaks his vows to help a damsel in distress (Vanbrugh) but fails to stop her being poisoned by her arch-enemy (Asche).

Oct 6. Lewis Waller and Evelyn Millard in Sarah Barnwell Elliott and Maud Hosford's **His Majesty's Servant** at Imperial. H V Esmond as Charles II. Strictly for Waller's fans. "Nothing more than tawdry, sham romance," said *The Illustrated London News*, "every incident of which reeks of stalest melodrama."

Oct 12. Dion Boucicault and Lettice Fairfax in Arthur Wing Pinero's **The Wife Without a Smile** at Wyndham's. Initially subtitled "a comedy in disguise" it ran for 174 performances, the run due to its notoriety. Actresses had refused to appear in it. Audiences came to see the doll. Some thought the doll should be burned publicly by the common hangman. There were boos from the gallery. The doll was suspended from the ceiling and tied to the sofa in the room above. The moment anybody made love on the sofa, the doll jigged up and down. The more it jigged the greater the ardour. One critic likened the play to the "unclean antics of monkeys in the zoo." Pinero claimed that he hadn't meant to suggest sexual intercourse, only hugging and kissing. Nobody believed him.

Oct 31. Arthur Bourchier and Violet Vanbrugh in Alfred Sutro's **The Walls of Jericho** at Garrick. Australian sheep farmer lambastes English society for its selfishness and insists that his wife comes and lives with him in Queensland. Transferred to Shaftesbury.

Nov 1. Louis Calvert as Broadbent, Harley Granville Barker as Father Keegan and Ellen O'Malley as Nora in Bernard Shaw's **John Bull's Other Island** at Court. Six matinees. "My way of joking is to tell the truth," said Shaw. "It is the funniest joke in the world." Broadbent, an English civil engineer, comes to Ireland with his best friend and partner to buy out the peasants and build a hotel and golf course. He argues that "Home Rule will work wonders under English guidance" and is accepted to stand for the Irish seat in parliament. William Archer, writing in *World*, thought it "a brilliant piece of dramatic literature."
—No Englishman could deny the truth of Broadbent. Indeed no thoroughbred Englishman would want to deny the truth of Broadbent. That is the cream of the joke. MAX BEERBOHM *Saturday Review*
—Mr Louis Calvert's Broadbent was a masterpiece of acting. It is seldom that a character so thoroughly homogeneous in gesture, voice, and carriage is seen on the stage. DESMOND McCARTHY *New Statesman and Nation*

Nov 15. Marie Tempest and Allan Aynesworth in Cosmo Gordon-Lennox's **The Freedom of Suzanne** at Criterion. Silly woman wants a divorce but first she needs evidence of her husband's cruelty. The play fell apart after the first act. 177 performances.
—The general public thinks more of persons than of plays and we should not be surprised if the delightful acting and popular personality of Miss Marie Tempest more than answered all objections. *Era*

Nov 19. Marion Terry as Mrs Erlynne, Ben Webster as Lord Windermere, Lilian Braithwaite as Lady Windermere and C Aubrey Smith as Lord Darlington in Oscar Wilde's **Lady Windermere's Fan**. "Compared with some of our modern pieces," said *The Era*, "*Lady Windermere's Fan* is a fount of purity and freshness." Nevertheless, the dialogue ("He shall have the worst scandal there has been in London for years. He shall see his name in every vile paper") must have brought back memories of Wilde's trial for gross indecency.

Nov 29. Oscar Asche as Petruchio and Lily Brayton as Katharine in Shakespeare's **The Taming of the Shrew** at Adelphi. Asche also played Sly. Immensely popular, the production toured all over Britain. Hesketh Pearson, in *The Last Actor Managers*, described the production as "a breathless, knockabout, rampageous show." Over 1500 performances.

Dec 17. Adrienne Augrade, G P Huntley, Fred Emney and Aubrey Boucicault in **Lady Madcap** directed by J A E Malone at Prince of Wales. Musical comedy. Music by Paul A Rubens. Book by Paul Rubens and Nathaniel Newham-Davis. Lyrics by Paul A Rubens and Percy Greenbank. The lady, well-known for telling fibs, escapes from her locked bedroom to entertain the officers of the East Anglia Hussars. Augarde sang "He loved her little dog, so don't you see he really must have loved her equally." French tenor Maurice Farkoa sang a risqué song, "I Like You in Velvet." Madge Crichton took over from Augarde. 354 performances

Nina Boucicault as Peter Pan with Hilda Trevelyan and Gerald du Maurier as Captain Hook
···

Dec 23. Thyrza Norman and Harley Granville Barker in Laurence Housman and Harley Granville Barker's **Prunella** at Court. This whimsical, exquisite, bitter, Pierrot play failed. The mistake was to have put it on at Christmas when it was in direct competition with J M Barrie's *Peter Pan*.
—Surely one of the most delicate and purely delightful fantasies that has graced the London stage. A E WILSON *Edwardian Theatre*

Dec 24. London Coliseum, the first theatre to have a revolving stage, finally opened, the opening having twice been delayed. There were four shows a day: Noon, 3 pm, 6 pm, and 9 pm. The American Sisters Meredith sang an Indian love song. Madge Lessing sang "Goodbye Little Girl, Goodbye". Eugene Stratton blacked-up and sang "Lily of Laguna", one of his most popular "coon songs". The finale was a Derby sketch with real horses and jockeys racing against the revolving stage. In the first week over 67,000 people came. At one performance a horse fell into the orchestra pit and the jockey was killed.

Dec 27. Nina Boucicault as Peter and Gerald du Maurier as Captain Hook in J M Barrie's **Peter Pan or The Boy Who Wouldn't Grow Up** at Duke of York's. Romantic fantasy, gooey sentiment and Edwardian spectacle plus patriotism and a bit of religion. ("To die will be an awfully big adventure.") Peter Pan wouldn't grow up because he wanted to be a boy and have fun. Barrie had intended Peter (an amalgam of the five Llewellyn Davies boys he had adopted) to be acted by a boy, but the licensing laws did not allow children to perform after 9 p.m. Actresses continued to play Peter right up to 1982. Barrie and his producer, Charles Frohman, were so worried that nobody would clap when Tinker Bell died, that they arranged for the orchestra to lead the applause. They need not have bothered. The audience clapped spontaneously. Captain Hook is a parody of a stage villain: part blood-curdling, lip-smacking relation of Robert Louis Stevenson's Long John Silver (a leg and an arm between them); part highly educated, cigar-smoking scoundrel in a Victorian melodrama; part Shakespearean ham (shades of Macbeth and Richard III); part Restoration fop with his extraordinary oaths ("Split-me-infinitives!" and "No, bicarbonate of soda!"); and part music hall comedian. Du Maurier used to imitate such actors as Henry Irving, Beerbohm Tree and Martin-Harvey. He was so frightening that children were carried screaming from the theatre. A production ran every Christmas until the outbreak of World War 2. Novelist Anthony Hope at the premiere was not impressed: "Oh, for an hour of Herod!" he begged.
—To our taste Peter Pan is from beginning to end a thing of pure delight. A B WALKLEY *The Times*
—So true, so natural, so touching that it brought the audience to the writer's feet and held them captive there. *Daily Telegraph*.

—Mr Barrie is not that rare creature, a man of genius. He is something even more rare – a child, who by some divine grace, can express through an artistic medium, the childishness that is in him...Mr Barrie has never grown up. He is still a child, absolutely. But some fairy once waved a wand over him, and changed him from a dear little boy into a dear little girl. MAX BEERBOHM *Saturday Review*

1905

Jan 5. Fred Terry as Sir Percy Blakeney and Julia Neilson as Lady Blakeney in Baroness Orczy's **The Scarlet Pimpernel** at New. Horace Hodges as Chauvelin. Sir Percy is the ideal English gentleman and sportsman – the sport being the rescue of French aristocrats from the guillotine. The production was regularly revived during the 1900s. Terry would still be playing Sir Percy in his seventies.
—Wildly, crudely melodramatic...It is exciting, flamboyant, sensational in an amateurish way. *Illustrated London News*

Jan 21. Lewis Waller in Shakespeare's **Henry V** at Imperial.

Jan 24. Herbert Beerbohm Tree as Benedict and Winifred Emery as Beatrice in Shakespeare's **Much Ado About Nothing** at His Majesty's. The production had a long and irrelevant lighting sequence showing the passing of the night.
—Mr Tree is more at home in the skirmishes of repartee than in the love passages to which as yet he brings no convincing fervour. *Illustrated London News*

Feb 28. Harley Granville Barker, Gertrude Kingston and A G Poulton in Bernard Shaw's **How He Lied To Her Husband** at Court. Vaudeville farce of the French school is anglicised and given a neat twist. The husband is outraged when a young poet denies he is in love with his wife. "So she is not good enough for you, is she?"

Mar 11. King Edward VII attended a performance of Shaw's **John Bull's Other Island** at Court and laughed so much that he broke the chair he was sitting on.

Mar 21. Rosina Filippi in Gerhart Hauptmann's **The Thieves Comedy** directed by Harley Granville Barker at Court. A German peasant steals a deer and a fur coat. Her husband steals some logs. They get away with it.
—As the Frau, Miss Rosina Filippi showed herself an admirable comedian and gave an example of interpretation such as our stage has seldom witnessed. So good is the entire performance we regret that the piece may not be mounted for a run. *Athenæum*

—In Germany the drama is taken seriously, and the citizens go to the theatre with their wits about them, in England the theatre is regarded simply as a place for fatuousness. MAX BEERBOHM *Saturday Review*

Mar 23. Herbert Beerbohm Tree in Shakespeare's **Hamlet** at His Majesty's. Something new for Tree: a production without scenery. W S Gilbert in the 1890s had described Tree's Hamlet as "funny without being vulgar" and said that his performance offered an admirable opportunity to decide whether Shakespeare or Bacon had written the play. "Open their burial places," he said, "and see which of them had turned in his grave."

Apr 4. H B Irving in Shakespeare's **Hamlet** at Adelphi. Lily Brayton as Ophelia. Many thought Irving was the best Hamlet of his generation.
—It is a little dry and hard, a little deficient in personal magnetism and human charm and sympathy. But is replete with distinction and never degenerates into mere cheap and easy effects. *Era*

Apr 5. Irene Vanbrugh, Ellen Terry and A E Matthews in J M Barrie's **Alice Sit-By-The-Fire** at Duke of York's. 17-year-old girl, who bases life on what she has seen in the theatre, imagines that her mother is having an affair. Her mother humours her. Barrie wrote the role of the mother especially for Ellen Terry. Max Beerbohm thought that Terry was too exuberant, too impulsive and that the play was not big enough for her.
—Although it was made for me, it didn't fit me. I sometimes felt I was bursting at the seams! I was accustomed to broader work in a larger theatre. ELLEN TERRY
—Each night she [Terry] would give a different rendering of her part, handling it according to the inspiration she got from the particular audience. As audiences varied so did her performance. A E MATTHEWS

Apr 11. Edythe Olive as Cassandra, Edith Wynne Matthison as Andromache and Marie Brema as Hecuba in Euripides's **The Trojan Women** at Court. Gilbert Murray's translation was a major breakthrough for the revival of Euripides.
—Miss Matthison's depiction of the dignity and distress of Hector's widow was superb and her expression of wild wretchedness and deadly despair was intensely affecting, drawing visible tears from many in the house. *Era*

Apr 22. Lewis Waller and Evelyn Millard in Shakespeare's **Romeo and Juliet** at Imperial. Millard was melodramatic. Mary Rorke was a bad-tempered Nurse.
—Mr Waller's stirring, trumpet-tongued declamations and sheer surrender to hysteria afford his audience a delightfully electrical shock. *Illustrated London News*

Apr 29. Henry Irving in Alfred, Lord Tennyson's **Becket** at Drury Lane. Irving, who had been ill, was received with great warmth by the audience who clapped, cheered and waved their hats and handkerchiefs. Every scene in which Becket appeared was greeted with shouts of approval. Irving's performance dominated the play, intellectually and spiritually.

Apr 29. Mabel Green and Adrienne Augarde, Robert Evett, Ambrose Manning and Huntley Wright in Andre Messager's musical **The Little Michus** directed by George Edwardes at Daly's. Book by A Vanloo and G Duval. English version by Henry Hamilton. Lyrics by Percy Greenbank. Two girls are brought up as sisters, but one is a foster child. The question is which? 400 performances.

May 1. Harley Granville Barker as Valentine in Bernard Shaw's **You Never Can Tell** directed by Harley Granville Barker at Court. Sydney Fairbrother as Gloria and Louis Calvert as the Waiter were singled out for special praise.
—Mr Bernard Shaw's plays have at length become the vogue... Society chuckles over the caustic Irishman's wit as if for all the world it thoroughly understood and revelled in his sallies. *Illustrated London News*
—His plot is at the mercy of his ideas; and his ideas being what they are, get a delicious sensation of irresponsible frolicking amid serious things. *The Times*
—How delightful is William the waiter! How beautiful Mr Calvert played him. DESMOND MCCARTHY *New Statesman and Nation*

May 2. Lena Ashwell in Hugh Morton's **Leah Kleschna** at New. A thief is caught red-handed; released by her victim, she determines to go straight.

May 3. William Collier, Arthur Roberts and James Welch in Richard Harding Davis's **The Dictator** at Comedy. A New Yorker masquerading as the President of a Central-American Republic is liable to be shot by the real President. John Barrymore made his first London stage appearance.
—*The Dictator* is acted with brio and alertness that are distinctly American. Mr Collier is about the best comedian that America has sent us during the last decade. *Era*

May 21. Harley Granville Barker as John Tanner and Lillah McCarthy as Ann Whitefield in Bernard Shaw's **Man and Superman** at Court. In the battle of the sexes Tanner and Whitefield are in the same league as Beatrice and Benedict and Millamant and Mirabell. Despite his articulacy, audacity and massive intellect, Tanner

1905 World Premieres
St Petersburg
  Maxim Gorky's *Children of the Sun*
New York
  David Belasco's *The Girl of the Golden West*
Dublin
  J M Synge's *The Well of the Saints*
Vienna
  Frank Lehar's *The Merry Widow*
Dresden
  Richard Strauss's *Salome*
Cologne
  Henrik Ibsen's *The Dance of Death*

Births
Lillian Hellman, American playwright
Jean-Paul Sartre, French playwright

Deaths
Henry Irving (*b.*1838), British actor, buried at Westminster Abbey

Notes
—Edward Gordon Craig published *The Art of Theatre*
—Aldwych Theatre built
—RADA moved to Gower Street
—The whole cast of *Mrs Warren's Profession* were arrested in New York on a charge of disorderly conduct. Released on bail, they were acquitted at the trial.

History
—Revolution in Russia
—Bloody Sunday in St Petersburg
—Mutiny on the Battleship *Potemkin*
—Massacre on the Steps of Odessa
—Suffragette Mrs Pankhurst jailed
—Roald Amundsen discovered magnetic pole
—Albert Einstein published his first theory of relativity

cannot escape Whitefield's predatory clutches. He says he has no intention of being "beaten, smashed and non-entized" into marriage, but he's fighting a losing battle and knows it. Tanner can shatter creeds, idols and hypocrisy; but he can't shatter Whitefield in her role of Modern Woman, part coquette, part boa-constrictor. Her mother thinks it will serve her right if she marries him. Barker made up to look like Shaw. Edmund Gwenn had a big hit as Henry Straker, the chauffeur. The premiere excluded the *Don Juan in Hell* scene.
—May be cordially commended to the attention of all playgoers who do not leave their brains along with their wraps in the cloak-room. *The Times*
—In dealing with this most intractable of plays Mr Shaw has established an indefeasible right to be counted among our acting dramatists of the humorous school. *Athenæum*

May 30. Gertie Millar, Edmund Payne and George Grossmith in **The Spring Chicken** at Gaiety. Book by George Grossmith. Musical version of *Coquin de printemps*. Music by Ivan Caryll and Lionel Monckton. Lyrics by Adrian Ross and Peter Greenbank. From May to September a married advocate, normally the epitome of bourgeois respectability, becomes a reckless womaniser. Grossmith singing "I Adore Them All" and Grossmith and Payne singing "Over Forty and Under Forty" were the high spots.

May. Eleanora Duse in a season of plays at Waldorf: Arthur Wing Pinero's **The Second Mrs Tanqueray**, Hermann Sudermann's **Magda**, Henrik Ibsen's **Hedda Gabler** and Alexandre Dumas's **La Dame aux Camélias**.
—[Hedda Gabler] As in every other part she plays, she behaves like a guardian angel half-asleep at her post over humanity. Her air of listlessness, in this instance happened to be apt, but otherwise she showed not a shadow of comprehension of her part. MAX BEERBOHM *Saturday Review*
—This great actress makes her effects, not by being natural, but by seeming natural. *Referee*

Jun 3. John Martin Harvey and N de Silva in John Rutherford's **The Breed of the Treshams** at Lyric. English Civil War melodrama. John Rutherford was the *nomme de plume* for two American women, Evelyn Greenleaf Sutherland and Beulah Marie Dix. Harvey's performance as 'The Rat' was so excessive that the authors complained he was prostituting their play.

Jun 12. Réjane in Victorien Sardou's **Madame Sans Gene** at Terry's. Her greatest role.
—Here is a washer woman to the very life in tones of voice, in swing of body, in pose and walk and gesture, in breezy humour and engaging frankness. *Illustrated London News*

Jun 15. Henry Irving in Arthur Conan Doyle's **Waterloo** at His Majesty's. Irving's last appearance in London.

Jun 19. Charles Hawtrey in Richard G Anthony's **Message from Mars** at Avenue. Sentimental message about selfishness.

Jul 10. Herbert Beerbohm Tree as Fagin, Hilda Trevelyan as Oliver Twist, Constance Collier as Nancy and Lyn Harding as Bill Sikes in **Oliver** at His Majesty's. Adaptation of Charles Dickens's novel by Comyns Carr. Transferred to Waldorf and then transferred back to His Majesty's.
—Mr Tree has shown us nothing so grim and lurid as his Fagin, which is, in its line, unsurpassable and, may, perhaps, claim to be a masterpiece. *Athenæum*
—This grim, sardonic ghastly creature is made by an actor a very nightmare of lurid villainy, a thing to haunt one's dreams, an achievement in the sphere of the bizarre and the fantastic

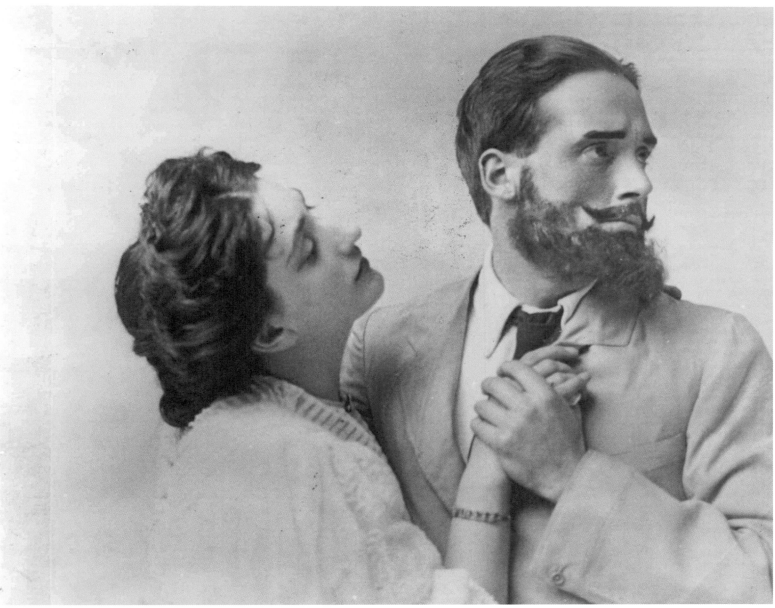

Harley Granville Barker and Lillah McCarthy in Man and Superman

worthy of the great magician whose imagination gave the monster birth. *Illustrated London News*

Aug 28. Florence Smithson and Courtice Pounds in **The Blue Moon** at Lyric. Musical comedy set in Burma. Book by Harold Ellis. Music by Howard Talbot and Paul Rubens. Lyrics by Paul Rubens. Variation on *The Geisha*.
—The main interpretation is neither seismic nor soporific – merely rather dull. *Illustrated London News*
—It is one of the most consistently bright and most unfailingly vivacious "entertainments of the stage" that has been seen in London for sometime. *Era*

Aug 31. Isabel Jay in Howard Talbot's musical **The White Chrysanthemum** at Criterion. Book by Leedham Bantock. Book and lyrics by Arthur Anderson. Heroine follows a naval officer to Japan and disguises herself as a geisha.

Sep 7. George Alexander in Hall Caine's **The Prodigal Son** at Drury Lane. The stage version of Caine's novel abandoned the original idea that the prodigal's sins were past redemption.
—Mr Caine is one of those sensationalists who must go from climax to climax of emotion and it must strike twelve at every hour. *Illustrated London News*

Sep 26. A E Matthews in St John Hankin's **The Return of the Prodigal** directed by Harley Granville Barker at Court. Cynical and amusing critique of middle-class materialism. The black sheep of the family, packed off to Australia, returns home, having squandered all his money. He is totally unrepentant. He doesn't like work and threatens to take himself off to the workhouse if the family doesn't cough up a decent allowance for the rest of his life. Since his father has political ambitions and his younger brother has social ambitions, they agree to be blackmailed. The prodigal,

who has a keen and bitter self-knowledge of his worthlessness, talks of drowning himself. Hankin drowned himself in 1909 and much of the dialogue in Act IV, with hindsight, can be read as his suicide note. *The Daily Mail* dismissed the play as "twaddle, twaddle, twaddle."
—We venture to think *The Return of the Prodigal* would be extremely popular in Berlin. It is just the type of play that is appreciated by German audiences; the ordinary English theatregoer likes his dramatic fare a little more highly flavoured, and does not concern himself so much about probability and the natural sequence of events. *Era*

Sep 28. Florence Smithson, Billie Burke and Carrie Moore in Howard Talbot and Paul Rubens's musical **The Blue Moon** directed by Robert Courtneidge at Lyric. Book by Howard Ellis revised by A M Thompson. Lyrics by Percy Greenbank and Paul Rubens. Smithson sang "I'm a little maid, dark, demure and dreamy".

Oct 7. Harley Granville Barker, Dorothy Minto and Matheson Lang in Henrik Ibsen's **The Wild Duck** at Court.
—If the play is a masterpiece of any kind, it is assuredly only one of pedantry and priggishness…unquestionably a piece for a study than for the stage. *Daily Telegraph*

Oct 11. Arthur Bourchier as Shylock and Violet Vanbrugh as Portia in Shakespeare's **The Merchant of Venice** at Garrick.
—Mr Bourchier's conception of Shylock is free from that worst of modern heresies, the idea that there is any full sense a tragic character or an object of sympathy. [Irene Vanbrugh's] staccato delivery is hardly suited to the sustained music of Shakespeare's blank verse. *Athenæum*

Oct 14. Lewis Waller in Alfred Sutro's **The Perfect Lover** at Imperial. Sentimental drama. The perfect lover is a perfect fool.

17

—[Alfred Sutro] works out his situation and chooses the character not in direct reference to life but with a wary eye on popular demand. *The Times*

Oct 17. William Gillette in Conan Doyle's and William Gillette's **Sherlock Holmes** at Duke of York's. 16-year-old Charlie Chaplin played Billy, the pageboy.

Oct 24. Charles Wyndham, Marion Terry, Mary Moore, A Vane-Tempest and Eille Norwood in Hubert Henry Davies's **Captain Drew on Leave** at New. Drew flirts with a married woman who takes him seriously. Transferred to Wyndham's.
—Miss Marion Terry acts with inexpressible charm as Martha and renders her dalliance so sympathetic and moving that we are disposed to condone its silliness. *Athenæum*

Oct 25. H B Irving and Eva Moore in Henry Havelock's **Lights Out** at Waldorf. Exposure of the rigid and inhumane German code of military honour: a father kills his unmarried pregnant daughter and then himself to save face.

Nov 2. Herbert Beerbohm Tree as Dr Thomas Stockman in Henrik Ibsen's **An Enemy of the People** at His Majesty's. "The intellectual aspects of his character," said *The Athenæum*, "were subordinate to the physical."

Nov 7. Thalberg Corbett in Harley Granville Barker's **The Voysey Inheritance** at Court. Voysey is a solicitor and his inheritance has come from his father who had speculated with his client's capital. The dilemma he faces is whether to perpetuate the dishonesty in order to put the accounts straight or to make a clean breast of the affair and go to prison. As a commentary on the Edwardian upper middle class society and its hypocrisy, callousness and vulgarity, the play was a damning indictment. The outburst in Act V ("But do you think the world today couldn't do without us? ... We and our like have ceased to exist at all") made audiences uncomfortable. William Archer described *The Voysey Inheritance* and Barker's *Waste* as "two of the greatest plays of our time."
—It has fresh and rare observation, subtle discrimination of character, sub-acid humour, an agreeable irony, and a general air of reality. *The Times*
—He is too purely intellectual to be perfect. Max Beerbohm *Saturday Review*

Nov 28. Louis Calvert as Undershaft and Hazel Thompson as Barbara in Bernard Shaw's **Major Barbara** at Court. Who is better placed to look after the poor? The Salvation Army or a millionaire munitions manufacturer? Undershaft argues that he much prefers his workers to be sober, honest, happy, unselfish and godly because his

Louis Calvert and Harley Granville Barker as Major Barbara

profits are then larger. He is not in the least ashamed of his wealth. He has no conscience about what he does, because for him poverty is by far the greater crime. Shaw gave Undershaft all the best arguments and came down, surprisingly, on the side of capitalism and the governing classes. ""I am the government of your country," says Undershaft. "You will do what pays us. You will make war when it suits us, and keep peace when it doesn't...When I want to keep my dividends up, you will discover that my want is a national need."
—*Major Barbara* is a play to be heard, to be seen, to be read. It will raise discussion and arguments galore. We need such drama. J T Grein *Sunday Times*
—There is wit enough to make the fortune of half-a-dozen ordinary plays. The question is whether there is wit enough to save a three hours' discussion in the theatre. We doubt it. *Pall Mall Gazette*
—Its offences against good taste and good feeling are of a kind not to be readily forgiven. But against these defects are to be set the merits of much brilliant if unconvincing dialogue, a great deal of brutal humour and of an interpretation which must really be pronounced admirable all round. *Morning Post*
—There are no human beings in *Major Barbara*; there are only animated points of view. William Archer *World*

Dec 6. Charles Hawtrey, Fanny Brough and Cosmo Gordon-Lennox in Cosmo Gordon-Lennox's **The Indecision of Mr Kingsbury** at Haymarket. Kingsbury, forced to choose between his mother and a merry widow, invites the two women to discuss what he should do. Based on a French play by Georges Berr.

Dec 26. **Cinderella** at Drury Lane. The Tiller Girls danced for the first time.

1906

Jan 13. Evie Greene and Gabrielle Ray in **The Little Cherub** at Prince of Wales. Musical comedy. Book by Owen Hall. Music by Ivan Caryll. Lyrics by Adrian Ross. Peer who loathes the stage is won over by the charm of an actress.

Jan 16. Harcourt Williams as Orestes, Edith Wynne Matthison as Electra and Edyth Olive as Clytemnestra in Euripides's **Electra** at Court. Translation by Gilbert Murray.
—Miss Matthison's performance was full of intelligence, but woke neither terror nor compassion in the audience. So, again, Mr Harcourt Williams as Orestes used his fine voice without restraint and seemed to think tragic effects could be gained by shouting. *Illustrated London News*

Jan 24. James Welch in Henry Arthur Jones's **The Heroic Stubbs** at Terry's. Stubbs was a romantic and idealistic bookmaker who worshipped a society beauty.

Jan 25. Herbert Beerbohm Tree in Stephen Phillips's **Nero** at His Majesty's. Luxury and decadence in Ancient Rome: a mixture of spectacle and rhetoric.

Feb 1. Irene Vanbrugh and George Alexander in Arthur Wing Pinero's **His House in Order** at St James's. Wife is sacrificed to her husband's devotion to the memory of his first wife. She is surrounded by smug, snobbish, hypocritical relations who make her life a misery. She finds some incriminating letters which would destroy the first wife's reputation. Her brother-in-law persuades her not to act, saying she can only attain real happiness by self-renunciation.
—This is great drama. To other authors we may turn for brilliant pamphlets or exquisite fairy tales but for great drama we still have to go to Mr Pinero. William Archer *World*

Feb 12. Harley Granville Barker in Harley Granville Barker's **The Voysey Inheritance** at Court.

Mar 3. Lewis Waller in Arthur Conan Doyle's **Brigadier Gerard** at Imperial. Absurd melodrama set in the Napoleonic era concerning the retrieval of some all-important papers.
—With Mr Waller to play the dare-devil hussar and Miss Millard his countess it will be readily understood that there is no lack of panache. *The Times*

Mar 12. Henry Ainley as Orestes and Edith Wynne Matthison as Electra in Euripides's **Electra** at Court.
—Perhaps only a Bernhardt or a Siddons could thrill us as we should be thrilled in the part of Electra. Miss Wynn Matthison's performance was full of intelligence; but woke neither terror nor compassion in the audience. *Illustrated London News*

Mar 14. John Hare, Kate Rorke and Charles Groves in Sydney Grundy's adaptation of Eugene Labiche's **A Pair of Spectacles** at Comedy.

Mar 19. Seymour Hicks and Ellaline Terris in **The Beauty of Bath** at Aldwych. Musical comedy. Book by Seymour Hicks and Cosmo Hamilton. Music by Herbert E Haines. Lyrics by Charles H Taylor. Beauty is in love with an actor. His brother, a

George Alexander (far left) and Irene Vanbrugh (centre) in **His House in Order**

naval officer, is in love with her. When they are both dressed in sailor suits she pretends she can't tell them apart.
—*The Beauty of Bath* is certainly the brightest, the most elaborate and the prettiest thing of its kind that has been seen in town for a long while. *Era*

Mar 20. Ellen Terry as Lady Cicely Wayneflete and Frederick Kerr as Captain Brassbound in Bernard Shaw's **Captain Brassbound's Conversion** at Court. Edmund Gwenn as Drinkwater. Lewis Casson as Sid el Assif. Shaw wrote the play for Ellen Terry, who was not impressed: "I don't like the play one bit. Only one woman in it. How ugly it will look and there will not be a penny in it." But when she came to play it, she adored "the adventure". This was not surprising. The play itself may have been nothing special; but the part was everything. Lady Cicely is a typically Shavian heroine who gets her own way because nobody dares to refuse her. The character was a joke at Terry's expense. She had difficulty remembering her lines and passages from the script where left about the set. Shaw claimed she said whatever came into her head and that it was often better than his script.
—Two qualities there are in Miss Terry that no amount of nervousness can mar. Nothing can obscure for us the sense of beauty and her buoyant jollity. It is this latter quality that explains the unique hold she has on the affections of the public. MAX BEERBOHM *Saturday Review*
—It doesn't answer to take Bernard Shaw seriously. He is not a man of convictions. That is one of the charms of his plays – to me at least. One never knows how the cat is really jumping. But it *jumps.* ELLEN TERRY *The Story of My Life*

Mar 20. Oscar Asche as Angelo and Lily Brayton as Isabella in Shakespeare's **Measure for Measure** at Adelphi. There were many critics who thought this was Asche's best Shakespearian performance.

Mar 20. Cyril Maude as Dr Pangloss in George Colman the younger's **The Heir-at-Law** at Waldorf. First produced in 1797. Pangloss was a pompous, avaricious pedant. The five acts were compressed into three acts.
—He seems to have made the character completely his own and has so polished every detail that it stands forth as one of the most remarkable examples of which the modern stage can boast. *Era*

Mar 26. Henry Ainley in Euripides's **Hippolytus** translated by Gilbert Murray at Court. *Era* thought Ainley had excelled himself as Hippolytus: "This young actor is, we feel certain, destined ultimately to hold a high place on the English stage."

March 27. Ellen Terry's stage jubilee.

Apr 11. Edna May in **The Belle of Mayfair** at Vaudeville. Musical comedy. Book by Basil Hood, Charles H E Brookfield and Cosmo Hamilton. Music by Leslie Stuart. Belle of Mayfair, Belle of New York, it's all the same thing. Camille Clifford sang the popular "Why Do They Call Me A Gibson Girl." Courtice Pounds sang a song which compared a marriage with a ride in a motor car. Phyllis Dare got the lead role when Edna May walked out of the show. 416 performances
—Miss May's appearance is angelic and her style is calm and virginal. She has that valuable stage asset, a distinct personality. Even her method of singing is original, and the combination of West End manner and an Eastern American accent is all that can be of bewitchery. *Era*

Apr 21. Isabel Jay and Hayden Coffin in **The Girl Behind the Counter** at Wyndham's. Musical comedy. Book by Leedham Bantock. Lyrics by Leedham Bantock

and Arthur Anderson. Music by Howard Talbot. General's daughter turns shop girl. Isabel Jay sang "I Mean to Marry a Man".

Apr 24. W Graham Browne as Pierrot and Dorothy Minto as Prunella in Laurence Housman and Harley Granville Barker's **Prunella** at Court. *The Times* thought that Minto was "an almost perfect representative of the Prunella of the earlier scenes in whose demure simplicity there was no touch of a fatal self-consciousness."

Apr 26. Violet Vanbrugh and Arthur Bourchier in Alfred Sutro's **The Fascinating Mr Vanderveldt** at Garrick. Vanderveldt was a bounder. Bourchier was far too heavy an actor for so lightweight and flippant a comedy.

May 5. Else Gademan as Rebecca West in Henrik Ibsen's **Rosmersholm** at Great Queen Street. Hans Andressen as Rosmer. W Klein as Kroll
—The construction of the play and the development of the drama is as masterly as anything that Ibsen ever did, and it has been absent too long from the London stage. *The Times*

May 12. Gerald du Maurier in E W Hornung and Eugene Presbury's **Raffles** at Comedy. Based on Hornung's novel, *The Amateur Cracksman.* The first of the crook plays with the villain as hero. Raffles, English gentleman, cricketer and thief, practises burglary only for the sake of burglary. Dion Boucicault was cast as the not-too-clever American detective.
—Mr Gerald du Maurier is the life and soul of the play, his quiet and casual style of acting being admirably effective. *The Times*
—It was badly written, poorly constructed, and the love interest was puerile, considered by later standards; but the pace and excitement of it left the 1906 audiences breathless. DAPHNE DU MAURIER *Gerald, A Portrait*

May 12. Norman McKinnel, Lena Ashwell and Henry Ainley in Claude Askew and Edward G Knoblock's **The Shulamite** at Savoy. Brutal Boer, who mistreats his wife, is murdered by his overseer. The unhappy ending was rewritten after the first night so that the wife could marry the overseer.

May 17. Lewis Waller as Othello, H B Irving as Iago, Evelyn Millard as Desdemona and Henry Ainley as Cassio in Shakespeare's **Othello** at Lyric.
—The convenience of the divorce court has a tendency to make marital revenge seem superfluous. Othello is ethically out of date. *Era*

May 29. Herbert Beerbohm Tree in **Colonel Newcome** at His Majesty's. Michael Morton's adaptation of W M Thackeray's *The Newcomers.* "Should Mr Tree be allowed to play Colonel Newcome?" asked *The Daily Mail* headline. There were lots of letters in the press objecting to the casting, but William Archer thought Tree was physically quite perfect.

Jun 12. Benefit night for Ellen Terry to celebrate her jubilee. Twenty-two members of the Terry family appeared, included brother Fred and sisters Marion, Minnie and Kate. Also participating were all the leading members of the British theatrical profession plus Duse, Rejane, Coquelin aîné and Caruso.

Jun 20. Denise Orme, Huntley Wright, Fred Emney and W H Berry in **See-See** at Prince of Wales. Musical comedy. Book by Charles Brookfield. Music by Sidney Jones. Lyrics by Adrian Ross. Additional Music by Frank E Tours. Additional lyrics by Percy

1906 World Premieres
Berlin
Bernard Shaw's *Caesar and Cleopatra*
Frank Wedekind's *Spring Awakening*
New York
William Vaughn Moody's *The Great Divide*
Dublin
W B Yeats's *Deirdre*

Births
Samuel Beckett , Irish playwright

Clifford Odets, American playwright

Deaths
Henrik Ibsen (*b.*1828), Norwegian playwright

History
—The verdict on Alfred Dreyfus reversed
—SOS adopted as international distress signal
—Ford Motor Race at Le Mans
—San Francisco earthquake

Matheson Lang and Lily Brayton in Tristram and Iseult

Greenbank. Hang-Kee (Wright) wants to marry Lee who is engaged to Yen who is in love with See-See (Orme). "Too many jokes and too little wit," said *The Times*.
—When the comedians have elaborated their parts and Miss Orme has learned to act as well as she sings *See-See* will be the brightest as well as the prettiest musical in town. *Illustrated London News*

Jul 9. Henry Ainley as Valentine and Lillah McCarthy as Gloria in Bernard Shaw's **You Never Can Tell** at Court. First Louis Calvert, then Edmund Gwenn, played the Waiter.

Sep 1. Ellen Terry as Hermione, Charles Warner as Leontes and Mrs Tree as Paulina in Shakespeare's **The Winter's Tale** at His Majesty's. Basil Gill as Florizel. Violet Tree as Perdita. O B Clarence as Clown. Terry had made her stage debut 50 years earlier as the boy, Mamillus.

Sep 3. Cyril Maude, Gertrude Kingston, Lottie Venne and Alfred Bishop in Clyde Fitch's **Toddles** at Duke of York's An adaptation of Tristan Bernard and André Godferneaux's *Tripplepatte*. Peer is totally incapable of making up his mind, even when he is in the mayor's office and about to get married. One of Maude's biggest successes. Transferred to Wyndham's and then the Playhouse.
—As a purely comic creation the performance must be classed as a little masterpiece. It is as exquisitely finished as a bit of Dresden china. WILLIAM ARCHER *World*

Sep 4. Matheson Lang and Lily Brayton in J Comings Carr's **Tristan and Iseult** at Adelphi. Based on Thomas Malory's *Morte d'Arthur* and Richard Wagner's opera. Oscar Asche as King Mark. The writing was never as good as the acting.
—Something to kindle the imagination, to occupy the intellect, to flatter our sense of the beautiful. J T GREIN *Sunday Times*
—Mr Carr's verse in the most strenuous situations never rises above the pretty in literature. E S BAUGHAN *Daily News*

Sep 20. Henry Ainley in Hall Caine's **The Bondman** at Drury Lane. Two men are in love with the same woman: the story becomes a clash between the pagan ideal of revenge and the Christian ideal of love. The production had live cattle on stage and a sulphur mine was blown up, accompanied by Rachmaninoff's *Prelude*.
—I am bound to record that there is a vigour, a sort of slap-dash grandiosity with which he [Hall Caine] imposes himself upon the public to whom he appeals. WILLIAM ARCHER *Tribune*
—His plays seem to us of poor intellectual texture, crude in method, garish and as noisy as a brass band. A B WALKLEY *The Times*

Sep 25. Irene Rooke, Norman McKinnel and A E Matthews John Galsworthy's **The Silver Box** directed by Harley Granville Barker at Court. What is the difference between a rich Liberal MP's son (A E Matthews) who steals a prostitute's purse and a poor charwoman's out-of-work husband (Norman McKinnel) who steals a cigarette case? The difference is that the son gets off scot-free while the husband goes to prison and hard labour for a month. Galsworthy's sympathies were with the working man and his decent wife, but he did not sentimentalize the criminal and went out of his way to establish the brute he was. Galsworthy was most satirical at the expense of the rich mother who wants her son to lie. William Archer thought Galsworthy's indictment was "all the more telling because it is studiously unemphatic and unrehetorical." Irene Rooke was infinitely moving as the charwoman
—We can boast of a new playwright, we can boast of having seen acting equal to the best on the continent. Let us take heart. There is life in the old British theatre yet. J T GREIN *Sunday Times*
—One of the grimmest, most realistic and most powerful studies of actual life... As a picture of what is most sordid in middle-class respectability, it need not have been disowned by Ibsen. *Athenaeum*
—[Norman McKinnel] gave us the real living man, never exaggerated as is often the case with low-class types on the stage. *Daily Graphic*

Sep 29. Lily Elsie, Connie Ediss and George Grossmith in **The New Aladdin** directed by George Edwardes at Gaiety. Musical extravaganza. Book by James T

Tanner. Lyrics by W H Risque, Adrian Ross and Percy Greenbank. Music by Ivan Caryll. Fantasy and travesty. Grossmith played the Genie and the French star Gaby Deslys, making her London debut, played a character called Charm of Paris and sang "Sur La Plage" in a bathing suit with great success.

Oct 17. Lewis Waller and Evelyn Millard in Henry Hamilton and William Devereux's **Robin Hood** at Lyric.
—Its primitiveness is the secret of its popularity. Mr Waller's transcendent bravery and disregard of odds are in the best style of melodrama, but they are accompanied by a tendency to the didactic. *Athenaeum*

Oct 23. Dennis Eadie, Ben Webster and Edmund Gwenn in St John Hankin's **The Charity That Began At Home** at Court. Young man persuades a wealthy middle-aged woman (Florence Haydon) to invite people to her house who in normal circumstances she would shun. The *Daily Mail* thought if Hankin were to stop writing about "drawing-room chatterers" he might write an excellent comedy.

Oct 23. Oscar Asche, Lily Brayton and Genevieve Ward in Rudolf Besier's **The Virgin Goddess** at Adelphi. The Goddess Artemis decrees that Artis and all her people must die unless Haepheston kills the beautiful Queen Althea whom he loves and who loves him. Besier had said he wanted his drama to be judged as an acting play not as a literary *tour de force*. His hybrid-Greek drama was written in second-rate blank verse, which was neither classical, nor romantic.
—Its note was stately and dignified. If it was never sublime it was never ridiculous but preserved a fine means of rhetorical vigour. ANTHONY L ELLIS *Star*
—Miss Genevieve Ward's acting in the role of the blind clairvoyant Queen-Mother proves her once more (who can forget her Volumnia?) to be our only great tragedienne. *Illustrated London News*

Nov 20. Harley Granville Barker as Dubedat and Lillah McCarthy as Jennifer in Bernard Shaw's **The Doctor's Dilemma** at Court. One of the best satires on the fallibility and arrogance of the medical profession. "We're not a profession but a conspiracy," says one doctor. The self-absorbed, callous, bungling physicians, with their pet theories and favourite cures, are portrayed as "ignorant, licensed murderers," performing useless, indiscriminate and highly lucrative operations. The play was written in answer to a challenge that Shaw could not write a comic death scene. "Life," he said, "does not cease to be funny when people die any more than it ceases to be serious when people laugh." The death scene was variously described by the critics

as daring, admirable, clever, offensive, theatrical (a term of abuse), vulgar, lacking in feeling, harrowing, pathetic and almost tragic. "What is an operation?" asks one doctor and answers his own question: "Manual labour."
—Judged as a whole, the work is a piece of capital fooling, which the lover of wit, frolic and unreason is bound to see. *The Globe*
—Mr Shaw seems to provide an entertainment which excites, interests, disappoints, enraptures, and offends everybody. Tastes differ; but this play must surely have a strong peculiar flavour to affect different palates so violently, making some critics grimace, some smile, and bringing tears to the eyes of others. DESMOND MACCARTHY *Speaker*
—We hold that the death of Louis Dubedat is a bungling, ineffective, theatrical touch and must have disgusted many members of the audience and certainly left the rest indifferent. *Daily Mail*

Dec 8. Gilbert and Sullivan's Savoy Operas at Savoy.

Dec 9. Gerhart Hauptmann's **The Weavers** at Scala. Early and highly influential example of agit-prop realism. Hauptmann was the first playwright to put the proletariat on the stage and to make the crowd rather than any individual the hero. The script (written in 1892 and based on Hauptmann's grandfather's first-hand experience of the Silesian weavers' unsuccessful revolt in 1844) took a documentary, fly-on-the-wall approach, observing the weavers in the work place, at home, in the pub, and finally on the rampage, attacking and plundering the factory owner's house, forcing him and his family to flee for their lives. Hauptmann's anger was directed against the bosses for exploiting the workers and against government and Church for standing by and doing nothing about it. The old man, who thinks that the weavers should kow-tow to management and wait for their reward in heaven, is shot by a stray bullet.

Dec 11. Arthur Bourchier and Violet Vanbrugh in Shakespeare's **Macbeth** at Garrick.
—Mr Bourchier gave us the rugged soldier, the man of honour, the man of weak will and delirious notion; he failed to give us the poet, the man of nerves or the play actor. *The Times*

Dec 18. Pauline Chase in Barrie's **Peter Pan** at Duke of York's. Gerald du Maurier as Captain Hook. Chase would continue to play Peter every Christmas until 1913.

Dec 26. Seymour Hicks and Ellaline Terris opened Hicks Theatre with a revival of **The Beauty of Bath**.

Dec 27. Herbert Beerbohm Tree and Constance Collier in Shakespeare's **Antony and Cleopatra** at His Majesty's. Lyn Harding as Enobarbus. Tree rearranged the text to suit the scenery. The audience kept calling for Harding during Tree's curtain call. Tree had to put the houselights up to stop the applause.

1907

Jan 29. James Welch and Audrey Ford in Charles Marlowe's **When Knights Were Bold** at Wyndham's. Variation on Mark Twain's *A Yankee at the Court of King Arthur*.
—The duel scene alone would make the fortune of a music hall turn. Only the unflagging vivacity of the principle performer [James Welch] prevents the farce from going to pieces. *Play Pictorial*

Jan 31. Isabel Jay and G P Huntley in **Miss Hook of Holland** at Prince of Wales. Chatter by Fred A Rubens and Austen Hurgon. Jingles and tunes by Paul A Rubens. Distiller's daughter in Amsterdam boosts her father's sales by inventing a liquor which contains 61 different ingredients.

Feb 5. Ben Webster in Bernard Shaw's **The Philanderer** at Court. The subject is marriage, "that worst of blundering abominations, an institution, which has outgrown and not modified." The action was based on something that actually happened. Jennifer Patterson, Shaw's discarded mistress, burst in on him and Florence Farr while they were enjoying the hurly-burly of the chaise longue. "I did not pursue women," said Shaw. "I was pursued by them…I found sex hopeless as a basis for permanent relation and never dream of marriage in connection with it." Lynne Wynne Matthison played the woman who refuses to marry the philanderer.
—The play, like all artistic work which has aimed primarily at being up-to-date, strikes us now as old-fashioned. It is a product of the early eighteen-nineties, when Ibsen first arrived as a moral prophet on out shores and people went about trying to "realise themselves." DESMOND MCCARTHY *New Statesman and Nation*
—Mr Shaw we all know can be delightfully amusing; he can also be very dull. *The Philanderer* is an example of Mr Shaw in a dull, unskilful and not particularly refined mood. *Daily Mail*

Feb 10. Evelyn Weeden, Clare Greet and Maudi Darrell in St John Hankin's **The Cassilis Engagement** directed by Madge McIntosh at Court. Mrs Cassilis's son has become engaged to a working-class girl. She feigns approval and invites the girl and her mother to stay with them, knowing full well that the girl will get bored to death

with country life and that her mother will make enough social gaffes to sink any further thoughts of marriage. Maudi Darrell (a music hall artiste, making her debut in a straight play), livened things up when she gave a defiant rendering of a vulgar music hall song, "Stop That Ticklin'".

Feb 16. Henry Ainley as Valentine, Lillah McCarthy as Gloria, Edmund Gwenn as Waiter and Henrietta Wilson as Mrs Clandon in Bernard Shaw's **You Never Can Tell** directed by Harley Granville Barker at Savoy.

Mar 5. Mrs Patrick Campbell in Henrik Ibsen's **Hedda Gabler** at Court. Trevor Lowe as Tesman. James S Hearn as Judge Brack. Laurence Irving as Lovborg. Hedda became one of Campbell's regular standbys. Max Beerbohm thought her only fault was that she was too beautiful.
—Played by Mrs Patrick Campbell with a sinister yet fascinating intensity of realism absolutely unique upon the English-speaking stage. *People.*

Mar 8. George Alexander and Eva Moore in Alfred Sutro's **John Glayde's Honour** at St James's. Wall Street financier neglects his wife. She takes a lover.

Mar 19. H G Pellisier's **Follies** at New Royalty. Sophisticated revue. Six black and white pierrots and pierrettes burlesque the latest theatrical fashions. Three hours of hilarity, according to *The Times*.

Apr 4. Herbert Beerbohm Tree as Shylock in Shakespeare's **The Merchant of Venice** at His Majesty's.

Apr 6. Marie Tempest in Clyde Fitch's **The Truth** directed by Allan Aynesworth at Comedy. The heroine has a hereditary tendency to lie.

Apr 8. Irene Rooke, Norman McKinnel and A E Matthews in John Galsworthy's **The Silver Box** at Court.

Apr 9. Dorothy Minto, Agnes Thomas, Edmund Gwenn, Wynne Matthison and C Aubrey Smith in Elizabeth Robins's **Votes for Women** at Court. A dramatic tract. Mrs Pankhurst's slogan was Votes for Women and Chastity for Men. Robbins was on the governing committee of the Women's Social and Political Union and its members came to cheer the play. The second act, representing a Trafalgar Square rally, with a crowd of 48 actors, was particularly convincing.

Apr 17. C Hayden Coffin in Edward German's **Tom Jones** at Apollo. Book by A W Thompson and Robert Courtneidge. Lyrics by Chas H Taylor. Henry Fielding's virile 18th-century novel was turned into a pretty and insipid musical.

Apr 27. Madge Carr-Cook in Alice Hegan Rice's **Mrs Wiggs of the Cabbage Patch** adapted by Anne Crawford Flexner at Terry's. Homely American comedy offered a popular and sentimental picture of the poor.

Apr 29. A E Matthews in St John Hankin's **The Return of the Prodigal** at Court. Mathews's delicate humour was perfect for the impudent prodigal.

May 1. Gerald du Maurier in Winchell Smith and Byron Ongley's **Brewster's Millions** at Hicks. American farce. Brewster is left two million on the condition he spends it within a year without resource to gambling.

May 15. Edmund Payne, Gertie Millar and George Grossmith in **The Girls of Gottenberg** at Gaiety. Musical comedy. Book by George Grossmith and L E Berman based on Carl Zuckmayer's *The Captain of Kopenik*. Lyrics by Ivan Caryll and Lionel Monckton. Music by Adrian Ross and Basil Hood. Grossmith was cast as a German cavalry officer and sang "The girls all call me Otto for they know that my heart never closes if things are getting hotto."

May 22. Marion Terry as Mrs Arbuthnot, Herbert Beerbohm Tree as Lord Illingworth and Ellis Jeffreys as Mrs Alonby in Oscar Wilde's **A Woman of No Importance** at His Majesty's.
—Mr Tree's style has ripened and matured since *A Woman of No Importance* was produced and the air of leisured ease and cynical calmness with which he played Lord Illingworth in 1893 is even more perfectly polished and perfected. *Era*

May 28. Aubrey Smith, Marie Löhr and A E Matthews in Michael Morton's **My Wife** at Haymarket. Adaptation of Mlle *Josette, Ma Femme* by Paul Gavault and Robert de Charvay. Guardian marries his teenage ward on the condition that he divorces her in ten months time so that she can marry the man she really loves. The play made Löhr's reputation.

Jun 3. Martin Harvey in John Rutherford's **The Breed of Treshams** at Adelphi. "He has added greatly to its comic and grotesque side," said *Era*. "The impersonation is now one of the most weird, eccentric, droll and yet terrible things imaginable."

1907 World Premieres

Stockholm

August Strindberg *Ghost Sonata*
August Strindberg's *Dream Play*
August Strindberg's *The Pelican*
August Strindberg's *The Storm*

Dublin

J M Synge's *The Playboy of the Western World*
Lady Gregory's *The Rising of the Moon*

Paris

Georges Feydeau's *A Flea in her Ear*

Births

Peggy Ashcroft , British actor
W H Auden, American poet, playwright
Daphne du Maurier, British playwright
Christopher Fry, British playwright
Laurence Olivier, British actor

Deaths

Alfred Jarry (*b.*1873), French playwright

History

—Baden-Powell formed Boy Scouts
—Guglielmo Marconi opened transatlantic radio service
—Zulu uprising ended
—Pablo Picasso painted *Les Demoiselles d'Avignon*

Jun 4. Robert Loraine as Don Juan, Norman McKinnel as Devil, Lillah McCarthy as Donna Ann and Michael Sherbrooke as Statue in Bernard Shaw's **Don Juan in Hell** and Dion C Boucicault and Irene Vanbrugh in Bernard Shaw's **The Man of Destiny** at Court.

—It needed all the elocutionary ease and graceful diction of Mr Robert Loraine's Don Juan and the truculent declamation of Mr McKinnel's Devil to give the talk last Tuesday even the sense of dramatic monologue.. Miss Vanbrugh was very arch as the lady who almost fools the future conqueror of Europe but Mr Dion Boucicault with his thin voice and his small measure of authority in no sense realised Napoleon. *Illustrated London News*

—It is rather outrageous of the Court management and very foolish of Mr Shaw to fancy that it is possible to induce a sane audience to attend a wearisome hotchpotch of shoddy metaphysics, a kind of glutinous porridge of Schopenhauer and Nietzsche and Shaw. *Referee*

Jun 4. Arthur Bourchier and Violet Vanbrugh in Alfred Sutro's **The Walls of Jericho** at Garrick.

Jun 8. Lily Elsie as Merry Widow, Joseph Coyne as Prince Dalio and George Graves as Baron Popoff in Franz Lehar's **The Merry Widow** at Daly's. Operetta. Book by Basil Hood. Lyrics by Adrian Ross. This glamorous, frothy *fin de siècle* escapism had had an enormous success in Vienna in 1905 and its success was repeated in London, New York and Buenos Aires (where it played in 5 languages simultaneously.) Fashionable women wore The Merry Widow broad-rimmed hat. "The Merry Widow Waltz", infectious, haunting, tender and slightly erotic, was repeated endlessly. Coyne, a poor singer, spoke his lyrics. Lehar was initially appalled, but, such was Coyne's success, that Lehar decided that in all future productions the lyrics should always be spoken.

— Miss Elsie danced with an abandon which was as entrancing as it was surprising.
B W FINDON *Play Pictorial*

Jun 10. Irish National Theatre season at Great Queen Street. W G Fay, Maire O'Neill and Sara Allgood in J M Synge's **The Playboy of the Western World.** Christy, a simple, lonesome, frightened lad in County Mayo, whom nobody heeded, is transformed into a rollicking, popular playboy because everybody believes he has killed his da. The Dublin audience at the premiere at the Abbey in 1907 did not take kindly to the portrait of Ireland, the wild language, the glorification of patricide and the aspersions on Irish women. The riots lasted almost a week and made the Abbey Theatre and Synge famous.

Jun 11. Irish National Theatre season at Great Queen Street: J M Synge's **Riders to the Sea**, Lady Gregory's **The Jackdaw**, and W B Yeats's **The Shadowy Waters**.

Jun 12. Irish National Theatre season at Great Queen Street: W B Yeats's **The Hour Glass** and **On Baile's Strand**, Lady Gregory's **The Rising of the Moon**, **The Coal Gate** and **Hyacinth Valley**.

Jun 13. Irish National Theatre season at Great Queen Street: Sara Allgood in W B Yeats's **Kathleen Ni Houlihan**. Patriotic piece. Kathleen is Ireland (in the guise of an

Joseph Coyne and Lily Elsie in **The Merry Widow**

old crone) calling her young to their death. Bridegroom deserts his bride and enlists for the wars in France in 1798.
—There was some excellent acting, especially among the ladies of the company, though we could have wished for a little more variety in their productions; not that there was not a large choice, but that with few exceptions, one play seemed exceedingly like another.
EVELINE C GODLEY *Annual Register 1907*

July 30. George Giddens as Pinglet in Georges Feydeau and Maurice Desvallieres's **A Night Out** at Criterion. English adaptation of *Hotel Paradiso* by Charles Klein. Giddens had had a big success when he had played Pinglet in 1896, but the farce wasn't so funny this time round.

Aug 27. Marion Terry and Doris Keane in Henry Arthur Jones's **The Hypocrites** at Hicks. A young woman is seduced and becomes pregnant. An idealistic priest rails against society.

Aug 31. Matheson Lang and Ruby Miller in a new version of Hall Caine's **The Christian** at Lyceum. Melodrama. A priest makes it his life's work to rescue prostitutes. The critics had loathed Caine's adaptation of his novel when it was premiered in 1898. The public loved it. The critics continued to loathe it. The public continued to love it.
—We were struck with the fine voice of and presence of Mr Matheson Lang and regret his success insomuch as it may lead to further employment in this kind of work. *The Times*
—If we must have popular drama which misrepresents life, it can do its patrons no harm that such drama should be frankly propagandist, especially for so good a cause as sexual purity. *Illustrated London News*

Sep 4. Oscar Asche and Lily Brayton in Laurence Binyon's **Attila** directed by Oscar Asche at His Majesty's. The blank verse was acted on one monotonous fortissimo note.

Sep 8. Norman McKinnel in Shakespeare's **King Lear** at Theatre Royal, Haymarket.
—Mr McKinnel's lungs are magnificent and he has a true ear for the rhythm of the verse. But his voice lacks variety, and is not in itself of a beautiful quality. And his presence, though impressive, is not regal. MAX BEERBOHM *Saturday Review*

Sep 11. Seymour Hicks, Ellaline Terris, Zena Dare, Fred Emney and Sidney Fairbrother in **The Gay Gordons** at Aldwych. Musical comedy. Book by Seymour Hicks. Music by Guy Jones. American heiress masquerades as gypsy. Peer masquerades as common soldier.

Sep 14. Eric Lewis as Sir Peter Teazle, Lilian Braithwaite as Lady Teazle and Henry Ainley as Joseph Surface in Richard Brinsley Sheridan's **The School for Scandal** at St James's.
—Mr Henry Ainley's version of Joseph is also contemptuous of tradition. Joseph in his hands is a gay and debonair young rascal with hardly a touch of the smugness with which the man of sentiment is credited. *The Times*

Sep 24. Wynne Matthison and Dorothy Minto as mother and daughter in John Galsworthy's **Joy** at Savoy. 36-year-old mother is torn between her love for a commonplace swindler and her love for her 17-year-old daughter. "Am I to live all my life like a dead woman because you're ashamed?" she asks. Galsworthy argued that marriage was not sacred and that people were free agents. He practised what he preached. He had been having a discreet ten-year liaison with his cousin's wife. The critics found the subject matter "unpleasant", "unpalatable" and "indecent."

Oct 7. Lily Brayton and Henry Ainley in Shakespeare's **As You Like It** at His Majesty's. Rosalind was a minx. Orlando was a lusty male. The comedy was robust and larky. The set had 2,000 pots of ferns, moss-covered logs and cartloads of autumn leaves. Oscar Asche was Jaques.

Oct 8. Queen's Theatre opened with Ellis Jeffreys and Fred Kerr in Madeleine Lucette Ryley's **Sugar Bowl**. Young lady, socially neglected, invites a diplomat to pay court to her in public during the season without any commitment on his part. Naturally, he falls in love with her. Jeffreys was so attractive that it wasn't believable that she had no suitors. *The Times* dismissed it as "a trivial, unconsciously absurd, entirely harmless evening's pastime."

Oct 9. Lena Ashwell and Norman McKinnel in Anthony P Wharton's **Irene Wycherley** directed by Norman McKinnel at Kingsway. Irene is unhappily married to a brute, who is having an affair with the wife of a colonial who shoots him dead. Irene is thus free to marry a nice engineer whom she adores and who adores her.
—A piece of great acting. Indeed from beginning to end, Miss Ashwell's performance was the finest thing she had done. H M WALBROOK *Pall Mall Gazette*
—Mr McKinnel, wonderfully impressive though he is as the husband increases the impression of violence by his rather too melodramatic outbursts. But violent or not, Mr Wharton's drama is a remarkable achievement for a young man. *Illustrated London News*

Oct 10. Marie Tempest in Alfred Sutro's **The Barrier** at Comedy. Romantic and irrational behaviour among the upper classes: more like a penny novelette than a faithful representation of life.
—Everything that Miss Tempest stands for in theatrical art – veracity, spontaneity, absence of gush – is absent from the theatrical art of Mr Sutro. She is out of her element playing here; he is out of his element in writing for her. *The Times*

Oct 14. Matheson Lang as Dick Dudgeon, Edith Wynne Mathison as Judith Anderson, C Rann Kennedy as Pastor Anderson and Harley Granville Barker as General Burgoyne in Bernard Shaw's **The Devil's Disciple** at Savoy. Set during the American revolution of the 1770s, it had all the ingredients of a popular 19th century melodrama: will-reading, abused orphans, a mother's curse, mistaken identity, arrest, heroic self-sacrifice, court martial and last minute reprieve at the gallows. Shaw said his "shameless pot-boiler" did not contain one single passably novel incident. Harley Granville Barker also played Dudgeon. Transferred to Queen's.
— [Matheson Lang's] performance is virile and intellectual and he gives us the very man that Dick Dudgeon was, in every detail, except the all-important detail of pace. MAX BEERBOHM *Saturday Review*

Oct 15. Mary Moore, Charles Wyndham, Sam Sothern and Elaine Inescourt in Hubert Henry Davies's **The Mollusc** at Criterion. A pretty, frivolous, selfish woman puts all her energy into doing absolutely nothing. But will she snap out of her compulsive lethargy when she catches a pretty governess in her husband's arms? A triumph for Moore.

Oct 22. Edyth Olive in Euripides's **Medea** at Savoy. Translation by Gilbert Murray. Hubert Carter as Jason. Lewis Casson as Messenger. Popular with suffragettes.

Oct 26. Ethel Irving and W Graham Browne in Somerset Maugham's **Lady Frederick** directed by W Graham Browne at Court. Maugham's first big success. Young man's infatuation for an older woman is cooled when she allows him to see her, dishabille, putting on her make-up. Considered dated and mechanical, shallow and silly, it was the epitome of "the well-made play"–already a term of abuse in 1907.

Nov 7. King Fordham as Mirabell and Ethel Irving as Millamant in William Congreve's **The Way of the World** at Royalty. Mrs Theodore Wright as Lady Wishfort. Nigel Playfair as Witwoud. Max Beerbohm thought the play as dead as a doornail.

Nov 12. George Alexander and Irene Vanbrugh in Henri Bernstein's **The Thief** at St James's. Adaptation by Cosmo Gordon-Lennox. Audiences in Paris, London and New York were shocked (and delighted) by Bernstein's portrait of a grasping materialistic society.
—The youthful lover of the young married woman is a product of Paris and has nothing in common with the English youth of nineteen. Lads of that age in this country give their thoughts to football and cricket and a clandestine intrigue with the wife of their father's friend is utterly foreign to their habits and mode of thought. B W FINDON *Play Pictorial*

Nov 24. Harley Granville Barker as Henry Trebell and Aimée de Burgh as Amy O'Connell in Harley Granville Barker's **Waste** at Imperial. Private performance. Written when Barker was scarcely 30, it was banned because the Lord Chamberlain objected to the "extremely outspoken references to sexual relationships" and to "a criminal operation." The play, a scathing analysis of political compromise, was an indictment of the cynical manoeuvres of government and the hypocrisy of the Church. Henry Trebell's potentially brilliant career is ruined when a married woman, who is separated from her husband, dies, aborting the child he had fathered on a one-night stand. The scandal proves useful to destroy both the man and his policies. Hounded out of the party, he shoots himself. The play was not publicly performed until 1937.
—The subject matter of *Waste*, together with the sincere realism with which it is treated, makes it, in our opinion, wholly unfit for performance under ordinary conditions before a miscellaneous public of varying ages, moods and standards of intelligence. A B WALKLEY *The Times*
—That the Lord Chamberlain should have stood between this play and the public is surely not very material except in so far as the act showed the irresponsible power of the censorship. That is to say that it is altogether anomalous and bad that the purview of a great and popular art should be subject absolutely to limitation by one man. *Stage Year Book 1908*

Nov 25. Johnston Forbes-Robertson and Gertrude Elliott in Bernard Shaw's **Caesar and Cleopatra** at Savoy. Written in 1898, it was modelled on the fashionable pseudo-historical dramas of the day and conceived on a grand scale. The deliberate anachronisms underlined that there had been no progress since Caesar's time. Shaw said he wrote Caesar specifically for Forbes-Robertson "because he is the classic actor of our day, and had a right to require such a service from me" and because "he is the only actor I know who can find the feeling of a speech from its cadence."
—We think [Forbes Robertson] misses some of the humour of this Caesar, taking some of the irony in all seriousness, and generally aiming too steadily at an effect of impressiveness. The result is an occasional heaviness. *The Times*
—Much of the satire is nearly as good as Gilbert's, and certainly it is not easy to resist the

impression that the whole thing is nothing more than a huge joke at the expense of ancient history. *Yorkshire Post*

Dec 27. Herbert Beerbohm Tree and Constance Collier in Shakespeare's **Antony and Cleopatra** at His Majesty's. It was more of a pageant than a play. Tree gave Cleopatra five children. When Collier complained it was impossible to be romantic with five children they were reduced to two. The most spectacular scene was Cleopatra's entrance as the Goddess Isis, when she was dressed all in silver. *The Graphic* thought play was incoherent and almost incomprehensible to anyone who had not read it.

Dec 30. Robert Loraine as Bluntschli, Lillah McCarthy as Raina and Harley Granville Barker as Sergius in Bernard Shaw's **Arms and the Man** at Savoy. Revived for the first time since its premiere in 1894 when there had been a lone booer. "My dear fellow," said Shaw, "I quite agree with you, but who are we two against so many?" His anti-romantic comedy is set during the Serbo-Bulgarian war of 1885–1886. War, the dream of patriots and heroes, is as hollow a sham as love.
—The play is champagne and for sheer gaiety of mood must take rank as a little masterpiece. *The Times*
—It is a brilliant thing, the play; but shrill in tone, and narrow in outlook and shallow, as compared with the work of Mr Shaw in his maturity. MAX BEERBOHM *Saturday Review*

1908

Jan 5. Sicilian Players. Giovanni Grasso and Mimi Aguglia in Luigi Capuana's **Malia** at Shaftesbury. Love, jealousy and hate. London had not seen such intensity of fierce, ungovernable passions. "Aguglia's grimaces," said *The Times*, "seemed more simian than human."

Jan 28. Harley Granville Barker's **Waste** was banned by the Lord Chamberlain. Its copyright was secured by one performance at Savoy. The cast included H G Wells, St John Hankin, Laurence Housman, Gilbert Murray, Bernard Shaw, William Archer and Granville Barker.

Feb 7. Sicilian Players. Mimi Aguglia and Giovanni Grasso in G Verga's **Cavalleria Rusticana** and Giuste Zenopole's **La Zolfara** at Shaftesbury.

Feb 10. Sicilian Players. Mimi Aguglia in Gabriele d'Annunzio's **La Figlia di Jorno** at Shaftesbury. "A comparatively calm Briton might, indeed," said H M Walbrook in *Pall Mall Gazette*, "be excused for thinking it grossly overdone."

Feb 12. Lena Ashwell in Cicely Hamilton's **Diana of Dobson's** at Kingsway. Charming comedy with a dash of socialism. Diana is a shop assistant in the hosiery department of a high-class emporium where she works a fourteen-hour day and earns five shillings a week, out of which she has to provide her own clothes. A distant cousin unexpectedly leaves her £300. She determines to have some fun and blows it all in one month on pretty clothes and travel. Masquerading as a widow she is made much of because everybody believes she is an heiress worth £3,600 a year. Hamilton, who described herself as a feminist rather then as a suffragist, had a life-long commitment for improving the options for women's financial security and self-esteem. Diana was the mouthpiece for millions of inarticulate, exploited, bullied and patronised shopgirls.

Feb 13. Sicilian players. Giovanni Grasso in P Giacometti's **Morte Civile** at Shaftesbury. Convict returns home to find that his wife still hasn't forgiven him for killing her brother. English audiences were not used to seeing a grown man perpetually blubbing on stage. They also found his death by poison, and all its attendant facial and bodily contortions, a bit too harrowing.
—No one could fail to respect the power and sincerity of the actor; but this photography of the horrible and the morbid may really be carried too far. H M WALBROOK *Pall Mall Gazette*

Feb 19. Sicilian players. Mimi Aguglia in G Verga's **La Lupa** at Shaftesbury. The she-wolf fancies her step-daughter's husband, but he doesn't fancy her. A happy ending was provided for West End audiences. The spontaneity of the company was much admired in some quarters.
—It would be a mistake to suppose that they are not self-conscious. They can pass in a moment from pathos to farce; they bow to applause in the middle of a scene; and despite the tempestuous energy they put into their acting, they show plainly their recognition that it is only playacting. *Era*

Feb 25. A deputation was made to the government by 71 authors and playwrights who complained that the powers of censorship should not be in the hands of one single officer. The protesters included James Barrie, Harley Granville Barker, John Galsworthy, St John Hankin, Henry James, Henry Arthur Jones, Somerset Maugham, Gilbert Murray, Arthur Wing Pinero and Bernard Shaw.

Feb 28. Sicilian Players. Mimi Aguglia and Grasso in Guimera's **Feudalismo** at

Shaftesbury. Auguglia played a long soliloquy with her back to the auditorium and she still held the audience's attention.

Mar 3. F R Benson, George R Weir and Helen Haye in G E Morrison's adaptation of Cerventes' **Don Quixote** at Coronet. Benson, even in Quixote's most absurd moments, was never a buffoon. He cut a noble figure and looked as if he had just stepped out of a painting by Velasquez. Many critics thought it one of his best performances.

Mar 7. Gertie Millar and Robert Evett in Oscar Straus's **A Waltz Dream** at Hicks. Musical comedy. Book by Felix Doerman and Leopold Jacobson. Lyrics by Adrian Ross. Lieutenant, who has been forced by royal command to marry a German princess, falls in love with the leader of an Austrian ladies band. Not much plot but plenty of tunes. The most popular songs were "The Waltz Dream" and "The Gay Lothario." The cast included the opera singer Mary Grey.

Mar 14. Matheson Lang and Nora Kerin in Shakespeare's **Romeo and Juliet** at Lyceum. The production was aimed at audiences who would normally give Shakespeare a miss. They roared with laughter when the star-cross'd lovers kissed.

Mar 25. Fire at Drury Lane. Third time unlucky. The theatre had already burned down in 1678 and 1809. The auditorium was saved by the fire curtain. The damage was confined to stage and flies.

Mar 26. Charles Hawtrey and Lotte Venne in Somerset Maugham's **Jack Straw** at Vaudeville. Archduke masquerades as a waiter in a London hotel and then in a hyper-snobbish country house. He marries the daughter of the house, making only one condition, namely that her ghastly relatives should never visit them.
—With his magnetic personality, his incomparable humour and unfailing charm [Charles Hawtrey] was a great comedian. He became adept in stage prevarication in a style quite his own, never flurried, always natural, quiet and persuasive. SOMERSET MAUGHAM

Apr 4. Herbert Beerbohm Tree as Shylock and Alexandra Carlisle as Portia in Shakespeare's **The Merchant of Venice** at His Majesty's. Tree went even further than Irving had done when Shylock returns home to find that Jessica has gone. Tree banged on the door again and again, shouting, "Jessica!" Then he dashed into the house, going from room to room, still shouting. Finally, he emerged and collapsed as he caught sight of a distant gondola in which Lorenzo was eloping with his daughter.

Apr 13. Winifred Mayo in Gerhardt Hauptmann's **Hannele** at Scala. Translation by William Archer. Child brought up in the slums dreams of heaven. Cecily Hamilton played her mother. H R Hignett was her schoolmaster and Saviour.
—It must, in fairness to our theatrical managers, be admitted that *Hannele* is scarcely a play that clamours for production. Its story is too harrowing, its presentment of the terrestrial and the celestial too realistic and perhaps its lesson a little too pronounced for the average playgoer. H M WALBROOK *Pall Mall Gazette*

Apr 27. Marie Tempest and W Graham Browne in Somerset Maugham's **Mrs Dot** at Comedy. Incorrigible schemer sets her heart on the fiancé of another woman. A comedy of manners in which the manners were bad and the epigrams were cynical.
—If Somerset Maugham as a dramatist is a charmer, Miss Marie Tempest is a charmeuse; between the pair of them the critic, along with the general public, capitulates in unconditional surrender. J T GRIEN *The Times*

Apr 30. John Hare and Nancy Price in Arthur Wing Pinero's **The Gay Lord Quex** at Garrick.

May 8. George Alexander and Mabel Hackney in Arthur Wing Pinero's **The Thunderbolt** at St James's. A provincial family, blatantly insincere and downright malicious, squabbles over their dead brother's estate.
—I cannot flatter myself that it has failed from any other cause than that it is composed of material for which the public has no fancy. ARTHUR WING PINERO
—We think it a masterpiece in its way, the peculiar way of Mr Pinero, the way of telling a story with the directness and rapidity and sledge-hammer force. It is an evening of first class acting. *The Times*

May 12. Henry Ainley, Robert Loraine and Fanny Brough in Bernard Shaw's **Getting Married** at Haymarket. "There is no subject on which more dangerous nonsense is talked and thought than on marriage," said Shaw. "There will be," he added, "nothing but talk, talk, talk – Shaw talk." Twelve people sit around and express their different attitudes to marriage in a series of lively conversation pieces which expose the silliness of the Edwardian divorce laws. The groom and bride decide not to get married. He backs down when he learns that he will be legally responsible for his wife's actions. She backs down when she realises she couldn't divorce him, not even if he committed murder. Many critics thought the play virtually unactable and that the only way to perform it would be to overact.
—This play is my revenge on the critics for their gross ingratitude to us, their arrant

1908 World Premieres

Moscow
Maurice Maeterlinck's *The Blue Bird*
New York
Edward Sheldon's *Salvation Nell*
Paris
Georges Feydeau's *Occupe Toi D'Amelie*
Dublin
Lady Gregory's *The Workhouse Ward*
Bernard Shaw's *Shewing Up of Blanco Posnet*.
Manchester
Stanley Houghton's *The Dear Departed*

Births

Arthur Adamov, Russian playwright
Rex Harrison, British actor
Robert Morley, British actor
Michael Redgrave, British actor
William Saroyan, American playwright

Max Wall, British comedian

Deaths

Victorien Sardou (*b.*1831), French playwright

Notes

—Miss Horniman bought and refurbished Gaiety Theatre, Manchester and ran a repertory there from 1908–1917

History

—Wright Brothers patented flying machine
—Great Suffragette rally
—Olympic Games in London
—Prohibition in Georgia and Carolina
—Jack Johnson defeated Tommy Burn

Philistinism, their shameless intellectual laziness, their low tastes, their hatred of good work, their puerile romanticism, their disloyalty to dramatic literature, their stupendous ignorance, their susceptibility to cheap sentiment. BERNARD SHAW *in an interview with The Daily Telegraph*

May 19. Campaign for a National Theatre opened with a meeting at Lyceum.

May 25. Lillah McCarthy in John Masefield's **Nan** at New Royalty. Nan's father was hung for stealing a sheep. This miscarriage of justice is compensated for by a cash payment. When Nan's lover, who had deserted her, hears she now has money, he returns. She kills him with a carving knife. The scene was described by one critic as "by no means calculated to send a thrill of aesthetic pleasure through any company of well-consorted playgoers." Nan drowns herself.
—Mr Masefield cannot be entirely acquitted of needlessly prolonging the agony. *The Times*

June 9. Lewis Waller and Evelyn Millard in Somerset Maugham's **The Explorer** at Lyric. Should a man be bound by a promise which jeopardises the happiness of the woman he loves for the sake of a ne'er-do-well? Maugham created a record with four plays running at the same time in the West End. Bernard Partridge, the *Punch* cartoonist, drew a picture of Shakespeare biting his nails in front of a hoarding advertising *The Explorer*, *Jack Straw*, *Lady Frederick* and *Mrs Dot*. *The Explorer* was the most serious and the least successful of the quartet. Maugham rewrote the last act and it still didn't work.

Jun 16. Cyril Maude, Winifred Emery, Lilian Braithwaite and C Aubrey Smith in William Price Drury and Leo Trevor's **The Flag Lieutenant** at Playhouse. Reckless self-sacrifice. The lieutenant lets his best friend take credit for his brave deed, thus putting his own reputation at risk.

Sep 1. Johnston Forbes-Robertson as The Stranger and Gertrude Elliott as The Slavey in Jerome K Jerome's **The Passing of the Third Floor Back** at St James's. Christ-like figure takes a room in a squalid Bloomsbury boarding house and converts the disreputable lodgers (cheats, prostitutes, bullies, cowards, rogues) with the milk of human kindness. Preaching a Christian message, he sees nothing but good in them. Theatregoers were evidently prepared to put up with the preaching for the sake of Forbes-Robertson's elocution but most people thought Jerome would have done better to have given the public a little more drama and a little less sermon.
—This tenth-rate writer has been, for many years, prolific of his tenth rate-stuff. But I do not recall, in such stuff of his as I have happened to sample, anything quite so vilely stupid as *The Passing of the Third Floor Back*...Well, I suppose blasphemy pays. MAX BEERBOHM *Saturday Review*

Agnes Thomas, Johnston Forbes Robertson and Gertrude Elliott in *The Passing of the Third Floor Back*

Sep 3. Gerald du Maurier as John Shands and Hilda Trevelyan as Maggie in J M Barrie's **What Every Woman Knows** directed by Dion Boucicault at Duke of York's. Shands is caught burgling and offered £300 to complete his education on the condition that at the end of three years he marries Maggie.

—What every woman knows is that behind every successful man there is a woman without whom he would not be the success he is. The man likes to think he has done it all by himself and the wife smiles and lets it go at that. It's her only joke. JAMES BARRIE.

—This beautiful little bit of humanity is most beautifully played by Miss Hilda Trevelyan, who was last night the darling, the acclaimed idol of a house excited to the highest pitch of enthusiasm. *The Times*

Sep 5. Henry Ainley as Faust, Herbert Beerbohm Tree as Mephistopheles and Marie Löhr as Marguerite in Goethe's **Faust** at His Majesty's. A new version by Stephen Phillips and Comyns Carr. Tree was a striking figure in green armour. The spectacle, predictably, was its most successful feature. Tree, who loved to play pranks on his fellow actors, screwed down a chalice to the table. Ainley, who had to drink a fatal potion, was forced to drink it like a horse.

Oct 14. Fanny Ward in Jerome K Jerome's **Fanny and the Servant Problem** at Aldwych. Fanny, a chorus girl, marries into the aristocracy only to find his servants are all her relations. The butler is her uncle, the housekeeper is her aunt and the maidservant is her cousin.

Oct 15. H B Irving and Dorothy Baird in Charles Reade's **The Lyons Mail** at Shaftesbury. One of the most popular Victorian melodramas. The play was based on a real mail robbery in France in 1796. Henry Irving (H B Irving's father) had had a big success in the dual role of two look-alikes: the innocent Lesurques and the guilty Dubosq. For some critics Irving lacked his father's magnetism.

—We missed, however, the awful strength with which Henry Irving made the garret scene so appalling, the diabolical power which seemed to add feet to his stature and make him gigantic, a terrifying figure with a livid face that had Hell in every line of it. H M WALBROOK *Pall Mall Gazette*

Nov 10. Lillah McCarthy as Dionysus, Esme Percy as Pentheus and Winifred Mayo as Argave in Euripides's **Bacchae** directed by William Poel at Court. Translation by Gilbert Murray. Percy had a piping voice and a mincing gait.

—Imagine a sound midway between the howling of dogs locked out in the yard by night and the intoning of the Commination Service by curates with very bad colds in the head, and you will have some notion of the noise made by these Maenadi. MAX BEERBOHM *Saturday Review*

Nov 11. George Alexander and Irene Vanbrugh in Alfred Sutro's **The Builder of Bridges** at St James's. A woman deceives an engineer. *The Illustrated London News* said that Sutro "provides dramatic effects only by distortion of human nature."

Nov 25. Lewis Waller in Shakespeare's **Henry V** at Lyric Theatre. No English actor in living memory had played the role better. The performance was hailed as a superb, patriotic trumpet-call.

Nov 27. Mrs Patrick Campbell in W B Yeats's **Deirdre** and Euripides's **Electra** at New. Florence Farr as Clytemnestra. Vernon Steele as Orestes. Scenery and costumes by Charles Ricketts.

—[Mrs Patrick Campbell] was more impressive as Electra but even here one was conscious of eccentric poses, curious vocal tricks and occasional lapses from tragic dignity. *Illustrated London News*.

Dec 1. H G Pellisier's **Follies** at Apollo. Revue. The actors, who wore Pierrot costumes, looked like a seaside concert party, but their songs, sketches and performances had a West End sophistication.

— [Pelissier] was the perfect compère – his commentaries were ripples of mirth and laughter, sly, malicious, and wonderfully witty. His audience command was a thing to wonder at. W MACQUEEN-POPE *Carriages at Eleven*.

Dec 6. Lillah McCarthy, Amy Lamborn, H A Saintsbury and Nigel Playfair in St John Hankin's **The Last of the de Mullins** at Haymarket. A mother's refusal to marry the father of her child was the basis for a bitter attack on society's smug hypocrisy.

Dec 19. Ellen Terry in **Pinkie and the Fairies** directed by Herbert Beerbohm Tree at His Majesty's. Lyrics by Graham Robertson. Music by Frederick Norton. Marie Lohr was a blasé Cinderella. Viola Terry was a very sleepy Sleeping Beauty.

1909

Jan 7. Fred Terry and Julia Neilson in William Devereux's **Henry of Navarre** directed by Fred Terry at New. Plenty of opportunity for the cast to appear in a variety of picturesque costumes.

"One more step and he's dead!" Fred Terry (behind chair) and A E Hanson in Henry of Navarre

Jan 9. Marie Tempest in Somerset Maugham's **Penelope** directed by Dion Boucicault at Comedy. Young wife wants a divorce when she learns of her husband's affair. On the advice of her father, she hides her feelings, pretends indifference, and does all in her power to throw the pair together. Maugham wrote the play for Marie Tempest. *The Athenæum* said she had never been more arch, more roguish, more fascinating.

Jan 23. Gertie Millar in **Our Miss Gibbs** directed by George Edwardes at Gaiety. Musical comedy. Lyrics by Adrian Ross and Percy Greenbank. Music by Ivan Caryll and Lionel Monckton. Shop girl loves bank clerk, who is actually a lord. The shop was called Garrods and the stage set was practically a replica of Harrods. Hit numbers included Millar singing "Moonstruck" dressed as a Pierrot and George Grossmith singing "Yip-I-Addy-I-Ay", a song which Edwardes had originally wanted to cut.

Jan 27. Lawrence Grossmith and Charles Rock in **An Englishman's Home** directed by Gerald du Maurier at Wyndham's was billed as having been written by "A Patriot" and showed Germans invading Britain and killing Englishmen in their homes. The Secretary of State for War declared that it was excellent propaganda. There was a rush to join the Territorials. The Patriot was Major Guy du Maurier, elder brother of Gerald, later killed in World War I.
—The author of *An Englishman's Home* has certainly performed a valuable patriotic service. H M Walbrook *Pall Mall Gazette*

Feb 3. Arthur Bourchier in Henri Bernstein's **Samson** at Garrick. Self-made millionaire takes revenge on his wife's aristocratic lover by bringing about his financial ruin.

Feb 18. Johnston Forbes-Robertson and Gertrude Elliott in Henry James's **The High Bid** at His Majesty's. A captain, mortgaged up to the hilt, is being blackmailed to change his politics and marry the blackmailer's daughter. He is given a new lease of life by the arrival of a rich American widow, who helps him to see, for the first time, the beauties of his 15th-century house. The *Evening Standard* said the play was "sheer delight."

Feb 20. Robert Loraine as Marlow, Ethel Irving as Kate Hardcastle and George Giddens as Tony Lumpkin in Oliver Goldsmith's **She Stoops to Conquer** at Haymarket.
—Mr Loraine surprised everybody by the clever manner in which he played the part... though shy he was never actually awkward, and though comical he never became ridiculous. *Era*

Feb 27. Marie Dressler in **Philopena** and **The Collegettes** at Aldwych. Two musical comedies. Book and Lyrics by Edgar Smith. Music by Maurice Levi. Dressler had had a big success on the London variety stage and the critics thought she deserved something better than this so-called "farrago of fun, fancy and foolishness" in which she appeared in two roles: as a millionaire's daughter with social ambitions and as a caricature of a chorus girl.

Mar 9. Norman McKinnel and Fisher White in Galsworthy's **Strife** directed by Harley Granville Barker at Duke of York's. The strike is only kept alive because the leader of the strike and the chairman of the board are at loggerheads. Fighting for a mere principle, neither man is willing to surrender or compromise. The strike drags on until both sides have lost and everybody is in exactly the same position they were in before the strike began. The suffering had been totally unnecessary. Galsworthy refused to take sides though there was never any doubt where his sympathies lay. McKinnel and White were highly praised. Transferred to Haymarket and then Adelphi.
—He has done much more than write a play; he has rendered a public service. *The Times*
—Perhaps the best thing I can say is that I feel proud to think it was written by an Englishman and acted by English men and women. *Globe*

Mar 13. Matheson Lang in Shakespeare's **Hamlet** at Lyceum. Acted for melodrama to please an audience who would not normally go to a play by Shakespeare.

Mar 20. Charles Hawtrey, Kate Cutler and Fanny Brough in Somerset Maugham's **The Noble Spaniard** at Royalty. Victorian farce adapted from the French of Grenet-Dancourt. Pretty widow longs for a romantic suitor with raven locks and whiskers. *The Times* said that Cutler made "a delightful Victorian roguey-poguey in ringlets."

Mar 28. Two plays at Aldwych. Mary Jerrold and Nancy Price in George Calderon's **The Fountain**. A satire on philanthropy in the East End. Edmund Gwenn in Margaret M Mack's **Unemployed**. A tramp dies of starvation whilst two middle-class people chatter about unemployment.

Apr 4. Herbert Beerbohm Tree and Marie Löhr as Sir Peter Teazle and Lady Teazle in Richard Brinsley Sheridan's **The School for Scandal** at His Majesty's. Basil Gill as Joseph Surface. Robert Loraine as Charles Surface. Suzanne Sheldon as Mrs Candour. Ellis Jeffreys as Lady Sneerwell. Tree was not the decrepit old man of tradition, but a man of dignity and strength. Loraine had all of Charles's high spirits and bravado but it was generally felt that Löhr was far too inexperienced to be playing Lady Teazle.

—Basil Gill as Joseph Surface lacks any pretence at subtlety; but delivers all the sentiments with unction; he is more like a good man feigning to be wicked than a hypocrite mouthing morality. *Athenæum*

Apr 8. The Lord Chamberlain refused to sanction a performance of the medieval **Passion Play** by the English Drama Society.

Apr 13. Nigel Playfair in Cicely Hamilton and Christopher St John's **How The Vote Was Won** at Royalty. Feminist propaganda was given one performance. The play showed what might happen if women didn't get the vote. The army might have to be employed as waitresses in restaurants. Playfair delivered a long speech in support of the suffragist claims. The audience, predominantly female, cheered. Transferred to Court for one performance.

Apr 13. Weedon Grossmith and Miss Compton in R C Carton's **Mr Preedy and the Countess** at Criterion. Farce. Preedy was presumed to be the Countess's lover when he was nothing of the sort. The comedy came from the temperamental and social contrast between the two characters. Preedy was overpowered by his social inferiority. The actors were amusingly matched.
—Of course Mr Grossmith is a 'worm', drolly deferential, drolly embarrassed, drolly spirited when the worm turns. And of course Miss Compton is drolly phlegmatic, drolly slow, drolly dry and drolly monumental. *The Times*

Apr 18. Ashton Pearse and Gillian Scaife in Elizabeth Baker's **Chains** at Court. One performance. Young clerk, fed up with life in suburbia, intends to escape to Australia until he learns that his wife is pregnant. He remains in England, complaining bitterly that marriage shouldn't tie a man up as if he were a slave.

Apr 23. The establishment of a Shakespeare Memorial Theatre was decided upon.

Apr 28. Florence Smithson, Dan Rolyat, Phyllis Dare and Harry Welchman in **The Arcadians** at Shaftesbury. Musical comedy. Book by Mark Ambient and A M Thompson. Lyrics by Arthur Wimperis. Music by Lionel Monckton and Howard Talbot. Nobody is allowed to lie in Arcady. One offender is dispatched to London where he opens a restaurant. Smithson sang "Arcadia is Ever Young", The Pipes of Pan" and "The Joy of Life."

Apr 30. Herbert Beerbohm Tree in Henrik Ibsen's **An Enemy of the People** at His Majesty's. Tree and the rest of the cast were uncertain of their lines on the first night.

May 27. Arnold Bennett's **What the Public Wants** directed by Harold Robertson Grimston at Royalty. Ironic skit on the press.

Jun 8. Irish National Theatre Society. J M Synge's **The Well of the Saints** directed by W B Yeats at Court. The illusions and vanity of two elderly, ugly, blind beggars are cruelly shattered by the unwelcome miracle of sight. Synge's dialogue was remarkable for the ferocity with which the Irish peasants were portrayed.

Jun 15. Lewis Waller and Evelyn D'Alroy in Arthur Conan Doyle's **The Fires of Fate** at Lyric. Romantic melodrama: white women in the desert find themselves at the mercy of fanatical Arabs. Transferred to Haymarket.

Jun 20. Violet Vanbrugh and Grace Lane in Clyde Fitch's **The Woman in the Case** directed by Allan Aynesworth at Garrick. Wife pretends to be a prostitute in order to save her husband from the electric chair for a crime he did not commit.

Jun 21. Herbert Beerbohm Tree as Falstaff, Constance Collier as Mistress Ford and Iris Hoey as Mistress Page in Shakespeare's **The Merry Wives of Windsor** at His Majesty's. Tree's performance said *Era*, has "mellowed with time and improved with repetition and it stands as a monumental example of Shakespearean acting."

Jun 30. F R Benson in Shakespeare's **Richard III** at His Majesty's. Genevieve Ward as Margaret. Benson had had a big success in the role at Stratford-Upon-Avon. *The Times* thought that he was "a little too plaintive and lacks the necessary demoniacal quality."

Jul 6. Dawson Millward, Henry Ainley, Gertrud Kingston, Dorothy Minto and Mrs Patrick Campbell in Mrs George Cornwallis-West's **My Borrowed Plumes** at Globe.
—The play proved to be nothing more than a modest, amateurish venture, revealing no special faculty for dramatic construction and giving no special promise of future achievement. B W Findon *Play Pictorial*

Jul 9. Bernard Shaw's **Press Cuttings** directed by Bernard Shaw at Court. Topical revue sketch on the government's inability to cope with the suffragette movement. The Lord Chamberlain refused a license because it burlesqued public figures such as Balfour, Asquith, Kitchener and Milner. The PM can only move around the capital

The train crash in The Whip

1909 World Premieres
Budapest
Ferenc Molner's *Liliom*

Honours
Knights
Beerbohm Tree, British actor-manager
Arthur Wing Pinero, British playwright

Births
Robert Helpmann, British dancer, choreographer, actor, director
Eugène Ionesco, French-Romanian playwright
James Mason, British actor
Stephen Spender, British poet, playwright

Deaths
Coquelin aîné (*b.*1841), French actor
Clyde Fitch (*b.*1865), American playwright

St John Hankin (*b.*1869), British playwright
J M Synge (*b.*1871), Irish playwright

Notes
—Birmingham Rep founded by Barry Jackson in 1913
—Sergei Diaghilev successfully launches his ballet company, Ballets Russes, in Paris
—Authors wanted to abolish censorship. Theatre managers thought that were it to be abolished there would be a serious risk of a gradual demoralisation of the stage.

History
—Death of King Edward VII
—Accession of King George V
—Revolution in Constantinople
—Robert E Peary reached North Pole
—Bleriot flew across Channel

disguised as a woman. The army advises him to shoot all the suffragettes, pointing out that it would be more humane than sending them to Holloway Prison where they would be forced fed.

Jul 15. E L Calkin in Sophocles's **Electra** directed by George A Foss at Court.

Aug 25. Prime Minister Asquith stated that a joint committee of the two Houses would be appointed to inquire into Censorship.

Aug 30. Gerald Du Maurier in Francis de Croisset and Maurice LeBlanc's **Arsene Lupin** at Duke of York's. Lupin was a sharp-witted gentleman thief in the Raffles mould and therefore a perfect role for Du Maurier's characteristically nonchalant style.

Sep 2. Lyn Harding, Irene Vanbrugh and Eric Maturin in Arthur Wing Pinero's **Mid-Channel** at St James's. A wife, who is willing to forgive her husband's infidelity, finds that he is not prepared to forgive her infidelity. She does the only theatrical thing possible in such circumstances. She throws herself off the balcony.
—But for the most part *Mid-Channel* is a sheer horror...to regard the play as an 'entertainment' in any generally accepted sense of the words is impossible. H M WALBROOK *Pall Mall Gazette*

Sep 8. Norman McKinnel in Shakespeare's **King Lear** designed by Charles Ricketts and directed by Frank Vernon at Haymarket. Twenty-six scenes were reduced to thirteen. Some members of the audience were so shocked when Gloucester's eyes were put out that they wanted to leave the theatre.
—The fact remains that nothing short of inspiration can make *King Lear* with all its splendour an acceptable acting play to a modern public. B W FINDON *Play Pictorial*

Sep 8. Henry Ainley, Herbert Beerbohm Tree and Mrs Patrick Campbell in Eugene Brieux's **False Gods** at His Majesty's. Translation by J B Fagan. An Egyptian extravaganza: it was like *Aida* without Verdi. Campbell thought her costume made her look like "an elderly wasp in an interesting condition."

Sep 9. Fanny Brough, Jessie Bateman, Cyril Keightley, Basil Gill and Nancy Price in **The Whip** by Cecil Raleigh and Henry Hamilton directed by Arthur Collins at Drury Lane. This popular drama of sporting life had not only live jockeys but also live horses and a live pack of hounds, plus a superb reproduction of a hunting banquet, a motor car accident and a sensational railway crash. "Never," said *Era*, "has the annihilation of a horsebox by a locomotive been represented so plausibly."

Sep 11. Arthur Bourchier, Ethel Irving and Athene Seyler in Alfred Sutro's **Making a Gentleman** at Garrick. Father, deserted by his children, seeks consolation from an orphan he has adopted.

Sep 16. Laurence Grossmith and Viva Birkett in F Anstey's **The Brass Bottle** directed by Frederick Kerr at Vaudeville. A genie is let out of the bottle after three thousand years and causes a young architect a lot of embarrassment.
—This piece is, in fact, the drollest and most audacious farce that has been seen in London for a long time and its success was complete. H M WALBROOK *Pall Mall Gazette*

Sep 25. Joseph Coyne, Gabrielle Ray and Robert Michaelis in A M Willner and H Grünebaum's **The Dollar Princess** at Daly's. Musical comedy. Book by Basil Hood. Lyrics by Adrian Ross. Music by Leo Fall. Millionaire recruits his servants from the facsimiles of the English aristocracy.

Sep 30. Robert Loraine and Marie Löhr in Somerset Maugham's **Smith** directed by Dion Boucicault at Comedy. A young man decides that Smith, a maid, is the ideal woman for him to marry.
—Miss Löhr speaks with all the preciseness of the student of elocution, that is to say she pronounces every word so deliberately that one seems to hear a precieuse instead of a parlour maid. J T GRIEN *Sunday Times*

Oct 8. Herbert Beerbohm Tree unveiled a bronze memorial tablet of the Globe Playhouse affixed to premises in Southwark on the site of Shakespeare's Theatre.

Oct 12. Charles Quartermaine, Norman McKinnel and Christine Silver in Rudolf Besier's **Don** directed by Norman McKinnel at Haymarket. Poet rescues woman from her brutal husband, a Plymouth Brother, who beats her for the glory of God.
—Mr Norman McKinnel impersonated the Plymouth Brother with a masterly blend of realism and reserve. H M WALBROOK *Pall Mall Gazette*

Oct 13. Lewis Waller as Raleigh and Winifred Emery as Queen Elizabeth in William Devereux's **Sir Walter Raleigh** at Lyric. Melodramatic caricature of history.
—[Lewis Waller] voice, his manner, his virility and his tenderness are irresistible. He fights like a lion, loves like a Romeo and outwits wickedness like an archangel. *Evening Standard*

Oct 21. Charles Hawtrey and Mary Blayney in Monckton Hoffe's **The Little Damozel** directed by Charles Hawtrey at Wyndham's. The damozel who discovers that the husband she loves was bribed to marry her. Transferred to Prince of Wales and then transferred back to Wyndham's

Oct 25. Subscription list for a Shakespeare Memorial Theatre was opened. The sum to be raised was £500,000.

Nov 9. Herbert Beerbohm Tree as Svengali and Viola Tree as Trilby in Paul M Potter's **Trilby** at Her Majesty's.
—[Audiences go] not to see the play but to see the wonderful vitalising Svengali, genius, bon viveur, unprincipled scoundrel as he is, hypnotising the audience even as he hypnotised the poor heroine of the play. It is perhaps the weirdest of all Sir Herbert Tree's impersonations; the repetition only adds to the fascination of its might and power. *Era*

Nov 9. H B Irving in Charles Reade's **The Lyons Mail** at Queen's Theatre. King Edward VII invited Irving to perform his father's famous dual role of the innocent Lesurques and the guilty Dubosq at Windsor.
—The genius of the son is at all events the same as the father in this respect that he turns what in the hands of many good actors would be mere melodrama into a vivid and real tragedy. *The Times*

Nov 11. Mona Limerick and Clare Greet in J M Synge's **The Tinker's Wedding** at His Majesty's. Posthumous premiere. Irish lass, a wild-eyed beauty, wants to get married and be respectable. Since her partner is not keen, she threatens to go off with another tinker. His mother is appalled that they should be wasting good money on marriage when the money could be spent on something worthwhile like booze. Lady Gregory didn't think Dublin audiences were ready to see a priest beaten up, even if he was a corrupt priest robbing poor sinners of their gold. The story was based on an incident that had taken place in County Wicklow a few years earlier. The play was dismissed as an abominable libel on the Irish priesthood and was not performed in Ireland until 1971. Edmund Gurney played the priest.

Nov 12. Matinee by the Actresses's Franchise League and the Women Writers' Suffrage League in **A Pageant of Famous Women** at Drury Lane. The women included Charlotte Corday, Joan of Arc, Nancy Oldfield and Florence Nightingale. The performance lasted over four hours.

Nov 13. Frances Dillon and Frederick Ross in Eric Mayne's version of Mrs Henry Wood's **East Lynne** directed by Ernest Carpenter at Lyceum. Lachrymose-sentimentality for unsophisticated audiences. The novel, a big success in 1861, was dramatised in 1874. Jiffin (Herbert Willis), formerly a staunch Conservative, was transformed into a comically militant trade unionist. There is one line of dialogue which has been endlessly mocked by the theatrical profession ever since the play was first staged: "Dead – and never called me mother!"

Nov 25. Herbert Beerbohm Tree in Louis N Parker's free adaptation of Rene Fauchois's **Beethoven** at His Majesty's. A failure financially but memorable for Tree's transformation. His make-up was a *tour de force*. He looked amazingly like Beethoven.

Nov 30. George Alexander as John Worthing, Allan Aynesworth as Algernon Moncrieff, Mrs Patrick Campbell as Gwendolen and Helen Rous as Lady Bracknell in Oscar Wilde's **The Importance of Being Earnest** at St James's. The revival was intended as a stopgap. It ran for 8 months.
—The fashion of inverted aphorism has passed away. But the humour is as irresistible as ever. It is certainly the best farce of our time. H Hamilton Fyfe *World*

Dec 2. Christine Smiltou in Sophocles's **Electra** at Terry's. Acted in Greek.

Dec 5. Fred O'Donovan as Posset, Sara Allgood as the prostitute, Arthur Sinclair as the Elder and Sydney J Morgan as the Sheriff in Bernard Shaw's **The Shewing-Up of Blanco Posset** at Aldwych. Horse thief is put on trial in America's Wild West. Shaw offered his "sermon in crude melodrama" to Tree but he turned it down, objecting to lines such as "God is a sly one who plays cat and mouse with you." The censor, who also objected to the blasphemy and the prostitute, refused to pass the play and the production had its premiere at the Abbey Theatre in Dublin in 1909. The Irish company was presented in London by the Incorporated Stage Society, a private club, and therefore outside the jurisdiction of the Lord Chamberlain. The Dublin and London critics thought the censor looked foolish.
—The whole performance was characterised by that unselfish art for which the Abbey Theatre players are famous, all of them thinking of the character and the play, and none of them seeking applause or seeming to be conscious of an audience. It is not often we see a whole company acting in that way in London. H M Walbrook *Pall Mall Gazette*

Dec 7. Lydia Yavorska in Henrik Ibsen's **Hedda Gabler** at His Majesty's. Acted in Russian.

Dec 8. Olive Walter and Pauline Gilmer in Maurice Maeterlinck's **The Blue Bird** at Haymarket. Translation by A Teixeira De Mattos. Boy and girl go in search of the blue bird, a symbol of happiness which is never caught. Some critics feared that this exquisite children's fantasy might be a little too deep and spiritual for English children. "Some persons see mystic meanings in the piece, but I," said Maeterlinck, "I see none."

Dec 9. Lady Tree as X and Lydia Yavorskia as Y in August Strindberg's **The Stronger Woman** at His Majesty's. The stronger woman says nothing and lets the other woman do all the talking.

Dec 13. Bransby Williams as Fagin in **Oliver** at Broadway. Walter Dexter and F T Harry's adaptation of Charles Dickens's novel. Williams was famous for his Dickensian monologues and impersonations of Henry Irving as Fagin and Herbert Beerbohm Tree as Trilby.

Dec 27. Ben Webster in Arthur Conan Doyle's **The House of Temperley** at Adelphi. Hearty melodrama set in the Regency era. The appeal of the production was in the realism of the boxing bouts and the crowd watching them.

Dec 27. Marie George as Aladdin, Wilkie Bard as Widow Twankey and George Graves as Abanazer in **Aladdin** directed by Arthur Collins at Drury Lane. "Better than ever" said *The Times*.

1910–1919

Oedipus Rex

1910

Feb 21. Dennis Eadie and Edyth Olive in Galsworthy's **Justice** directed by Harley Granville Barker at Duke of York's. The play, premiered the same day as the State Opening of Parliament, was propaganda for prison and penal reform. A young clerk forges a cheque and is sentenced to three years penal servitude and solitary confinement. The trial was the most accurate yet seen on stage. The most famous scene – the prisoner pacing up and down his cell – took place in total silence. Its horrors made a deep impression on audiences. Winston Churchill, then Home Secretary, saw the play four times and announced that he would institute a programme of prison reform.

Feb 23. C M Lowne, Miriam Lewes and Lena Ashwell in Bernard Shaw's **Misalliance** directed by Bernard Shaw at Duke of York's. Debate on parents and children: "Talk, talk, talk. It never stops." A modern young woman, bored by conventional family life, is prepared to marry a man she does not love because he has brains. She quickly changes her mind when a dashing aviator literally drops in from the sky. She orders her father to "buy the brute" when the chap says he can't afford to marry her. "Arrant nonsense," said *The Standard*. "Absolutely his worst play," said *The Globe*. "The debating of a lunatic asylum without a motion and without a chairman," said *The Times*.
—I find that his great mind has gone astray, coerces the public by the fetiche of his name to sit in the theatre in torture, to listen to tittle-tattle about everything and nothing in particular for three and a half hours with no profit, no illumination, no palliation by purpose or by action. *Sunday Times*
—Brilliant but disgusting ... everyone wishing to have sexual intercourse with everyone else ... let us hope that future historian will not take this play ... as really representing English society as a whole at the beginning of the twentieth century. BEATRICE WEBB

Feb 24. Arthur Bourchier and Frances Dillon in Somerset Maugham's tragic comedy, **The Tenth Man** directed by Harold Robertson Grimston at Globe. The fall of a Titan of finance.

Mar 1. Edmund Gwenn and Lena Ashwell in J M Barrie's **The Twelve Pound Look** directed by Dion Boucicault at Duke of York's. One-act anecdote: a pompous and ostentatious vulgarian is about to be knighted when his first wife unexpectedly returns after a 14-year absence to explain she didn't walk out on him for another man, but left him because she had been suffocated by his financial success, his lack of ideals, his ignoble view of women and his boring friends. "Sheer delight," said the *Athenæum*.

Mar 12. Fred Terry and Miriam Lewes in Baroness Orczy and Montague Barstow's **The Scarlet Pimpernel** at New. Full houses were always guaranteed whenever Terry revived this production.

Mar 9. Sydney Valentine, Dennis Eadie, Mary Jerrold and May Whitty in Harley Granville Barker's **The Madras House** at Duke of York's. The conversation was intellectual, civilised, subtle, detached and cold. The text was diffuse, inconclusive and ambivalent. The plot – the sale of high-class fashion house and a drapery business – was of no dramatic interest. Instead there were a number of scenes on the theme of the status of women in society and the attitudes of men towards their wives, daughters, mistresses, mothers and female employees. Women, whether they were middle class or working class, married or single, were deprived, degraded, exploited and abandoned.
—Its author dazzles you with his brilliance and annoys you – whether deliberately or unconsciously we cannot guess – by too frequent passages of ugliness and now and then, bad taste. *The Times*

Mar 21. Giovanni Grasso in Shakespeare's **Othello** at Lyric. Hesketh Pearson said, "There was no restraint in Grasso's performance; a sweeping, tornadic display of primitive and almost epileptic passion."

Apr 2. Herbert Beerbohm Tree as Antony, Lyn Harding as Brutus and Henry Ainley as Cassius in Shakespeare's **Julius Caesar** at His Majesty's.
—Sir Herbert Beerbohm Tree's Antony is one of his best things. His handling of the mob is masterly and the well-drilled, intelligently acted mob helps to make the whole scene impressively convincing. *The Times*

Apr 5. Irene Vanbrugh as Rose Trelawny, Dion Boucicault as Sir William Gower, Charles Maude as Gower and Dennis Eadie as Tom Wrench in Arthur Wing Pinero's **Trelawny of the 'Wells'** at Duke of York's. Sentimental Victorian backstage story first performed in 1898. Rose Trelawny, an actress at Sadler's Wells Theatre, becomes engaged to a swell and abandons the profession for a rich life in Grosvenor Square, which proves so boring that she quickly returns to the stage. Her fiancé turns actor and they are reunited in a play by a new playwright in a refurbished theatre under a new management. Pinero's affectionate comedy was rooted in a major turning-point in British theatre. The theatre was The Prince of Wales and the actress-manager was

Mary Wilton, who later married Squire Bancroft. The playwright was based on T W Robertson (1829–1871) who wrote miniature realistic dramas of contemporary domestic life, so miniature and domestic that they came to be known as 'the cup-and-saucer plays of the bread-and-butter school.' Robertson wanted his stage characters to talk and behave naturally on the stage.

Apr 13. Laurence Houseman and Harley Granville Barker's **Prunella** at Duke of York's. Pierrot play. Music by Joseph Moorat. Whimsical fantasy.

Apr 14. Charles Hawtrey, Dorothy Minto and Charles Maude in George Paston and W B Maxwell's **The Naked Truth** at Wyndham's. Young man cannot restrain himself from telling his mother, his girl friend, his uncle, his mistress and a company of directors, unpalatable truths about themselves. Transferred to Prince of Wales.
—Mr Charles Hawtrey's famous excellencies – his perfect polish, his unconsciousness and his absolutely natural and easy style and bearing – are invaluable. *Era*

Apr 20. Elizabethan Stage Society. Winifred Rae and George Ellis in Shakespeare's **The Two Gentlemen of Verona** directed by William Poel at His Majesty's. Poel had a penchant for casting women in male roles. Rae played Valentine.
—I am disappointed, very disappointed indeed. Of all Shakespeare's heroes Valentine is one of the most romantic, one of the most virile. I have chosen you out of all London for this part, but so far you have shown me no virility whatsoever. WILLIAM POEL at rehearsal quoted by W BRIDGE ADAMS quoted by ROBERT SPEAIGHT *Shakespeare on Stage*
—Though Miss Winifred Rae did her best in the circumstances; she was hopelessly handicapped by the injudicious arrangement. *Era*

May 17. Dennis Eadie and Hilda Trevelyan in Elizabeth Baker's **Chains** directed by Dion Boucicault at Duke of York's. The chains of marriage. "I cannot imagine," said Modred in *The Referee*, "that such a play should attract anybody outside that inconsiderable circle of ardent playgoers who imagine that to be dull is to be intellectual."

May 28. Martin Harvey in Shakespeare's **Richard III** at Lyceum. Harvey was a good-looking villain with no visible hunchback.
—His pretty appearance and gay attire mock at his own descriptions of his deformity and make them seem unreal. His courtship is that of a D'Artagnan rather than an ogre. The strength, the implacable will, the devilish brutality of the man are missing. *Athenæum*

May 30. Irish National Theatre. Maire O'Neill in J M Synge's **Deirdre of the Sorrows** directed by W B Yeats at Court.
—The playwright has devoted rather too much to the literary and too little to the dramatic side of the tragedy. *Illustrated London News*
—[Maire O'Neill] has a voice full of beautiful tones for pathetic emotion and the rare mystic temperament which makes the Irish players so attractive to us. *The Times*

Jun 1. Irish National Theatre. Arthur Sinclair, J A Rourke and Fred Donovan in Lady Gregory's **The Rising of the Moon** directed by W B Yeats at Court.

Jun 3. Irish National Theatre. Fred O'Donovan and Arthur Sinclair in Lady Gregory's **The Workhouse Ward** directed by W B Yeats. Two bed-ridden workmen quarrel all the time, yet when a relation of one of them comes to take him away from the workhouse, he refuses to be parted from his companion. Acted in a double-bill with Lady Gregory's **Kathleen Ni Houlihan** with Sara Allgood.

Jun 3. Irish National Theatre. Fred O'Donovan as Christy, Maire O'Neill as Pegeen, Sara Allgood as Widow Quinn in J M Synge's **The Playboy of the Western World** at Court.

Jun 4. H A Saintsbury as Sherlock Holmes in Arthur Conan Doyle's **The Speckled Band** at Adelphi. Blood-curdling fun. Audiences came to see a snake sliding down a bell-rope to kill a sleeping woman in her bed. Lyn Harding played the villain and, naturally, it was he who was killed by the snake. Transferred to Globe.

Jun 4. Huntley Wright and Phyllis Dare in **The Girl in the Train** directed by Edward Royce at Vaudeville. Musical comedy. Book by Victor Leon. Music by Leo Fall. Lyric by Adrian Ross. Adapted from the German. A judge and an actress are compromised when they share a sleeping compartment on a train.

Jun 5. James Hearn and J Fisher White in Ashley Dukes's **Civil War** directed by Frank Vernon at Aldwych. A denunciation of the social system. Landowner and anarchist clash but find themselves united in opposition to their respective son and daughter marrying.

Jun 17. Irish National Theatre. Marie O'Neill, Arthur Sinclair, J A Rourke and J M Kerrigan in J M Synge's **In the Shadow of the Glen** directed by W B Yeats at Court.

Jun 25. Martin Harvey and Miss N de Silva in John Rutherford's **The Breed of the Treshams** at Wyndham's.

1910 World Premieres

Moscow
Maxim Gorky's *Vassa*

Budapest
Ferenc Molnar's *The Guardsman*

Stockholm
August Strindberg's *The Great Highway*

Manchester
Stanley Houghton's *The Younger Generation*

Births
Jean Anouilh, French playwright
George Devine, British actor, director
Jean Genet, French playwright

Deaths
Lottie Collins (*b.*1866), British singer
Leo Tolstoy (*b.*1828), Russian novelist, playwright

Notes
— The Shakespeare Memorial National Theatre committee convened.
— Frank Benson received the Freedom of the Borough of Stratford for having run the annual Festival.
— Charles Froham began an experiment of repertory theatre at Duke of York's over a three-month period. The experiment was a financial failure.
— Lord Chamberlain refused to license Laurence Housman's *Pains and Penalties* because of references to King George IV which lead to a censorship committee being reconvened.

History
—Death of King Edward VII
—Accession of King George V
—Dr Crippen hanged for murder of Belle Elmore
—Count von Zepplin's airship, *Deutschland*, flew with paying passengers
—The tango gained popularity in USA and Europe
—Enrico Caruso made first wireless broadcast

Aug 30. H G Pelissier's **The Follies** at Apollo.

Sep 1. Arthur Bourchier as King Henry, Violet Vanbrugh as Queen Katharine, Herbert Beerbohm Tree as Cardinal Wolsey, Henry Ainley as Buckingham and Laura Cowie as Anne Bullen in Shakespeare's **King Henry VIII** at His Majesty's. Though the text was heavily cut, the pageantry still went on for four hours on the first night. Bourchier, manly, breezy, was Holbein's portrait come to life, but not very kingly. Tree (who addressed the audience rather than the other characters) dominated the action.
—Tottering in speech and bearing [Herbert Beerbohm Tree] was like a column broken by the undulation of an earthquake. J T GRIEN *The Sunday Times*

Sep 3. Gerald du Maurier and Lilian Braithwaite in George Paston's **Nobody's Daughter** directed by Gerald du Maurier at Wyndham's. George Paston was the *nom de plume* of Miss E M Symonds. An illegitimate child is brought up by a humble store-keeper. Her parents are not pleased when they learn she wants to marry a chauffeur.

Sep 10. C H Workman, Constance Drever and Roland Cunningham in Oscar Straus's **The Chocolate Soldier** translated and directed by Stanislaus Stange at Lyric. Book by R Bernauer and L Jacobson. The operetta was based on Shaw's *Arms and the Man*; but since it was totally lacking in any satiric bite, Shaw threatened to take legal proceedings if it were stated or even remotely implied that the work was a musical setting of his play and that he was in any way a party to it. The production was billed "with apologies to Mr Bernard Shaw for an unauthorised parody of one of his comedies." When he saw the operetta he described it as "putrid opera buffe in the worst taste of 1860" and "the degradation of a decent comedy into a dirty farce." Shaw had every reason to be annoyed. Such was its success that it drove *Arms and the Man* off the stage in the early part of the century as surely as Alan Jay Lerner and Frederick Loewe's *My Fair Lady* drove *Pygmalion* off the stage in the 1950s. The production was advertised with a cartoon of a Balkan soldier pointing an accusing finger at the public: "You have not seen *The Chocolate Soldier*." Kitchener and Uncle Sam would shortly pinch the idea for the famous World War I poster: "Your Country Needs You!" *The Chocolate Soldier* has been described as the last waltz before ragtime. Its most famous number "Hero Supreme, Man of My Dreams" has the most haunting refrain.

Oct 3. Clarence Whitehill in Ambroise Thomas's opera **Hamlet** conducted by Thomas Beecham at Covent Garden. Libretto by Jules Barbier and Michel Carré. *The Times* regretted that so much care and expense had been lavished on something which was not likely to be heard very often.

Oct 11. Gertrude Kingston in Aristophanes' **Lysistrata** directed by Cavendish Morton at Little. The women of Athens in 411BC go on a sex strike to stop a war. The script was considerably toned down.
—There is nothing to shock the most fastidious modesty. If the truth be told the piece as modified proves a rather tame and schoolgirlish affair. *Athenæum*

Oct 15. Irene Vanbrugh, Dennis Eadie, Edmund Gwenn and Lillah McCarthy in Somerset Maugham's **Grace** directed by Dion Boucicault at Duke of York's. One code for the landed gentry (its original title) and another code for their employees.

—The pathetic note is there right enough, but it is mostly muffled – or I should rather say, outvoiced – by the theatricality of the structure. J T GRIEN *Sunday Times*
—I knew that I must interest, move and amuse, and I heightened the note. [*Grace* and *Loaves and Fishes*] were neither frankly realistic nor frankly theatrical. My indecision was fatal. The audiences found them rather disagreeable and not quite real. SOMERSET MAUGHAM *The Summing Up*

Oct 20. Oscar Asche and Lily Brayton in Stanley Weyman's **Count Hannibal** adapted and directed by Oscar Asche at New. Robust, romantic cape-and-sword melodrama set at the time of the Massacre of St Bartholomew. Transferred to Garrick.

Oct 21. Beryl Faber and Dawson Millward in Cosmo Hamilton's **Mrs Skeffington** at Queen's. Farce. Major pretends a woman is his wife in order to save another woman's reputation. "Perhaps," said *The Athenæum*, "the piece would gain in plausibility if it were taken at a quicker pace."

Nov 10. Gertie Millar, Joseph Coyne and George Carvey in **The Quaker Girl** directed by J A E Malone at Royal Adelphi. Musical comedy. Book by James T Tanner. Music by Lionel Monkton. Lyrics by Adrian Ross and Percy Greenbank. Famous French dressmaker transforms old Quaker dress into a Paris fashion. The Quaker girl, disowned by her family, turns mannequin. Hit number: "Come to the Ball".

Nov 14. Laurence Irving in **Unwritten Law** at Garrick. Irving's adaptation of Fydor Dostoyevsky's *Crime and Punishment*. Transferred to Kingsway.
—Perhaps [Laurence Irving] is a little too flamboyant and conventional in his representation of a character, which has been transformed here into the average revolutionary student and has lost some of its individuality to become a mere type; but nevertheless his Rodion may be described as the most virile and impressive work of his career. *Athenæum*

Nov 24. Harley Granville Barker and Suzanne Sheldon in Bernard Shaw's **The Dark Lady of the Sonnets** directed by Herbert Trench at Haymarket. Costumes by Charles Ricketts. Two matinees. Meeting between Shakespeare and Elizabeth I. The Bard pleads for a National Theatre. The Queen is impressed by his argument and says she will see her Lord Treasurer. Shakespeare is appalled: "Then am I undone, madam; for there was never yet a Lord Treasurer that could find a penny for anything over and above the necessary expenses of your government, save for a war." The joke about Shakespeare getting all his best lines off an illiterate beefeater and much of Lady Macbeth's sleepwalking scene from over-hearing the Queen worrying about the execution of Mary ("Who would have thought that woman to have had so much blood in her?") was laboured. The play was written specifically to help the funds for a National Theatre.
—Having seen Mr. Barker in the part, we have no desire to see anybody else assay it. He suggested something like intellectual distinction, imaginative energy, and conscious power. H M WALBROOK *Pall Mall Gazette*

Dec 5. Statue of Henry Irving was unveiled next to National Portrait Gallery.

Dec 8. English premiere of Richard Strauss's **Salome** conducted by Thomas Beecham and directed by Louis Verande at Royal Opera House, Covent Garden. Based on Oscar Wilde's play. Ernst Kraus as Herod. Aino Ackte as Salome. Clarence Whitehill as the Prophet. The critics described the opera as "a stupid travesty of the real thing", "decadent melodrama gorgeously embroidered with splendid hyperbole" and "brilliant fungus sprung from a decaying genius."

Dec 26. London Palladium re-opened as music hall. Martin Harvey in Robert Barr and Sydney Lewis Ransom's **The Conspiracy**, a one-act drama, which was part of a variety bill. A Ruritanian king joins the conspirators who are plotting his overthrow. Harvey, accused of slumming, pointed out that Bernhardt had appeared at the Coliseum in a variety bill, so why shouldn't he appear at the Palladium? The bill included comedienne Nellie Wallace.

1911

Jan 19. Arthur Playfair, Marie Löhr and Lilian Braithwaite in Arthur Wing Pinero's **Preserving Mr Panmure** at Comedy. Pretty governess is kissed by the master of the house (an act of gross impropriety) but she refuses to say who has kissed her, thus incriminating all the men and throwing the whole household into confusion. The play was uneven. It was almost as if Pinero had written a serious "problem play" and then changed it into the sort of farce he used to write ten years earlier.

Feb 1. George Alexander and Ethel Irving in A E W Mason's **The Witness for the Defence** at St James's. Wife shoots her husband while they are in India and is ostracized when she returns to England.
—Ethel Irving is perhaps the most gifted in the matter of facial expression; she can show the emotions to such perfection that it is almost impossible to believe that she commands them, and that they are really no more than extremely clever acting. *Sketch*

1911 World Premieres
Berlin
Carl Sternheim's *Knickers*

Births
Max Frisch, Swiss playwright
Terence Rattigan, British playwright
Tennessee Williams, American
playwright

Death
W S Gilbert (*b.*1836), British
playwright

Honours
Knight
George Alexander, British actor-
manager

Notes
—Grock, the Swiss clown, appeared
at Coliseum from 1911 to 1914

History
—Siege of Sydney Street
—Emiliano Zapata deposed Dictator
Dias in Mexico.

Feb 2. Fred Terry and Julia Neilson in Boyle Lawrence and Frederick Mouillot's **The Popinjay** directed by Fred Terry at New. Terry played a dissolute King who is about to throw away his right and his heirs' rights to the throne. The Queen threatens to throw herself and their son into the street below unless he does what she commands.

Feb 14. Lydia Yavorska as Nora in Henrik Ibsen's **The Doll's House** at Royalty. Yavorska was Princess Bariatinsky. She had learned English so that she could play Nora in London. The critics thought her Russian accent actually helped her performance.

Feb 21. Harley Granville Barker's **Rococo** directed by Harley Granville Barker at Court. One-act farce. Middle-class suburban family fight (literally) over a hideous vase, an heirloom. The characterisation was cartoon-thin and it was not difficult to guess what would happen to the vase.

Feb 22. Weedon Grossmith and Donald Calthrop in Margaret Mayo's **Baby Mine** directed by Weedon Grossmith at Criterion. Farce involving triplets. The comedy worked on the principle of the more babies the louder the laughter. Transferred to Vaudeville.

Feb 22. Oscar Asche as Falstaff, Lily Brayton as Mistress Ford and Constance Robertson as Mistress Page in Shakespeare's **The Merry Wives of Windsor** at Garrick. Frenetic pantomime set in winter.
—[Oscar Asche] humour is dry and not unctuous; he lacks the geniality which should mark Falstaff even in his decline; we miss the gusto and brain-power. *Athenæum*

Feb 23. Mabel Hackney, Geraldine Olliffe and Laurence Irving in David Belasco's **The Lily** at Kingsway. Adaptation of a French play by Pierre Wolff and Gaston Leroux. Two daughters – one brave, the other meek – finally round on their dictatorial father.

Feb 24. Robert Loraine and Ellis Jeffreys in Somerset Maugham's **Loaves and Fishes** directed by Dion Boucicault at Duke of York's. Ambitious parson courts a rich widow and intrigues to get a bishopric. Maugham's satire, written in 1903, had initially failed to find a management willing to risk it. Nine years on the public still did not want to see a clergyman being mocked on stage and the play ran for only 48 performances.
—It should be acted as a rollicking farce and then its absurdities might have passed muster. *Play Pictorial*

Mar 22. Mrs Patrick Campbell and Arthur Wontner in Rudolf Besier's **Lady Patricia** directed by Herbert Trench at Haymarket. The fascinating, infuriating and charming Patricia gave Mrs Campbell plenty of opportunities to burlesque herself.

Mar 28. Norman McKinnel as Solness and Lillah McCarthy as Hilda Wangel in Henrik Ibsen's **The Master Builder** directed by Harley Granville Barker at Little. Translation by Edmund Gosse and William Archer. McKinnel stressed the architect's bourgeois origins.

Mar 29. Gerald du Maurier, Nina Sevening and Irene Vanbrugh in Charles Haddon Chambers's **Passers-By** directed by Gerald du Maurier at Wyndham's. Sentimental tearjerker for sentimental audiences. A woman has a child out of wedlock and is reunited with the father. The long arm of coincidence was stretched. Meanwhile a waif, who is taken in by a rich young man, is outraged to find that he is expected to do the housework.

Apr 18. Lewis Waller and Madge Titheradge in E G Hemmerde and Francis Neilson's **Butterfly on the Wheel** at Globe. The butterfly was broken on the wheel of the Divorce Court. ("It's not what you do, it's what people say you do that makes mischief.") Titheradge's performance put her in the front rank of her profession. Norman McKinnel was the ruthless cross-examiner.

Apr 19. Oscar Asche, Lily Brayton and Ben Webster in Edward Knoblock's **Kismet** at Garrick. Music by Christopher Wilson. Designs by Joseph Harker. Oriental spectacle. Asche turned Hajj into a grim comedian and cut a long prayer to just four words ("Glory be to Allah"). Knoblock was furious. "You'll get a laugh," he said. "I hope so," replied Asche.
—[Edward Knoblock] offers everything in the way of a romantic story except style. He should not have tried to compete with the poet who wrote the Song of Solomon. *Athenæum*

Apr 19. Lillah McCarthy in Bernard Shaw's **Fanny's First Play** at Little. Shaw's first commercial success, produced anonymously, ran a record 622 consecutive performances, longer than anything else he had written. Fanny is a rebellious freethinker, who had joined the Fabian Society when she was up at Cambridge. Her play is an attack on middle-class morality and the substitution of custom for conscience. Fanny's father, who has not come to terms with the 19th century, let alone the 20th century, and dresses in the clothes of the 18th century, is deeply shocked that his daughter should have written "a modern play" and is even more shocked by her argument that parental guidance is a disaster and that the young need to break down the barriers and escape the stifling restrictions of Victorian home life. The description of the state of British prisons had a special resonance for the suffragettes who filled the theatre. The comedy ends with an epilogue in which the critics of the day review Fanny's play and this allowed the original actors to guy the mannerisms of William Archer, A B Walkley and E S Baugham. Shaw had dismissed his play as a pot-boiler, but later in a letter to his biographer, Hesketh Pearson, he wrote: "I do not waste my time writing pot-boilers: the pot must be boiled and even my pot au feu has some chunks of flesh in it."
—One of the most amusing plays he has ever written, one of the most audacious of all his attacks. H M WALBROOK *Pall Mall Gazette*

Apr 20. Charles Hawtrey in Gladys Unger's **Better Not Enquire** directed by Charles Hawtrey at Prince of Wales. Adaptation of French play by Alfred Capus and based on the motto: "Whoever the man a woman marries she must expect to be deceived and had better not ask questions." The English translation lacked the necessary Gallic sparkle.

May 20. Lily Elsie and Bertram Wallis in Franz Lehar's **The Count of Luxembourg** at Daly's. Operetta. Book by A M Willner and Robert Bodanzky. Adaptation by Basil Hood. Lyrics by Adrian Ross and Basil Hood. The satire at the expense of the money-grabbing bourgeoisie (with their money-will-buy-anything mentality) was kept under wraps. The music had an unexpectedly melancholy edge. Elsie and Wallis waltzed up and down an elaborate staircase. *The Daily Chronicle* said it was "a voluptuous dream of luscious music and dazzling light."

May 28. Stage Society. Katharine Pole as Ranevsky, Harcourt Williams as Trofimov, Herbert Bunston as Lopahin, Mary Jerrold as Varya, Franklyn Dyall as Gaev and Nigel Playfair as Pischtchik in British premiere of Anton Chekhov's **The Cherry Orchard** directed by Kenelm Foss at Aldwych. Translation by Mrs Edward Garnett.
—Cannot but strike an English audience as something queer, outlandish, even silly... They all seem children who have never grown up. Genuine comedy and scenes of pure pathos are mixed with knockabout farce. The players did their best; it was not their fault that the entertainment was not entertaining. *The Times.*
—A slice of life comedy, but the life was very foreign and the slice was rather big. *Westminster Gazette.*
—It gave the impression of somebody who had entered a lunatic asylum and taken down everything the lunatics had said. HENRY ARTHUR JONES

June. The inauguration of the King George Pension Fund for actors and actresses at the Coronation Performance at His Majesty's.

Jun 30. Diaghilev's Ballets Russes season with Anna Pavlova, Adeline Genee, Vaslav Nijinsky and Tamara Karsavina at Covent Garden.

Jul 4. Graham Moffat and Kate Moffat in Graham Moffat's **Bunty Pulls the Strings** at Haymarket. The Scottish comedy was acted in broad Scottish dialects. The sentimental plot (set in 1860) was of no consequence. The production was admired for its quaint humour, its naturalism and the truthfulness of its observation. The eminently practical Bunty was charmingly played by Kate Moffat.

Sep 2. Vernon Steele and Phyllis Neilson Terry in Shakespeare's **Romeo and Juliet** directed by Fred Terry at New. The "two hours' traffic of our stage" lasted four hours.
—We should have liked [Vernon Steele] better if he had once or twice conveyed the impression of behaving naturally. *The Times.*
—There is no sex abandonment about this Juliet. *Athenæum*

Sep 5. Herbert Beerbohm Tree and Violet Vanbrugh in Shakespeare's **Macbeth** at His Majesty's. Tree was not the traditional bloodthirsty murderer. The production was slow and monotonous. 15 different scene changes meant that the play lasted four hours.
—It was weightier and more restrained and it had more body, volume than any of his earlier Shakespearian characterisations. *Morning Post*

—Sir Herbert did not suggest nor did he at any point give one the impression of the physically brave and skilful soldier. *Daily News.*

Sep 9. Cicely Courtneidge, Nelson Keys, Florence Smithson, Dan Rolyat and Harry Welchman in **The Mousme** (**The Maids of Japan**) directed by Robert Courtneidge at Shaftesbury. Musical. Book by Alex M Thompson and Robert Courtneidge. Music by Lionel Monckton and Howard Talbot. Lyrics by Arthur Wimperis and Percy Greenback. Two sisters are in love with two Japanese officers.

Sep 12. Gerald du Maurier and Athene Seyler in Alfred Sutro's **The Perplexed Husband** directed by Gerald du Maurier at Wyndham's. A tea merchant's silly wife turns suffragette and parrots feminist jargon. The satire was heavy-handed.

Sep 14. Evelyn d'Alroy and Cyril Keightley in Cecil Raleigh and Henry Hamilton's **The Hope** at Drury Lane. Sporting melodrama. Hope is a horse. The spectacle included a ball in India, an earthquake in Italy followed by a fire, and a race from the Derby. The horses were on a turntable and they rode towards the audience.

Sep 21. Cyril Maude and Winifred Emery in Austin Strong's **Rip Van Winkle** directed by Cyril Maude at Playhouse. An entirely new version. Real dwarfs were engaged. The scene when Rip is reunited with his old sweetheart was as actor proof as it had always been, but Maude was not happy with his performance. "I realised too late," he said, "that the comedy, the fun of it, was poor and I saw that as Rip I was not going to be able to be funny."
—It is a wonderful piece of acting, a perfect fantasy, because it is perfectly real. *Daily Telegraph*

Sep 23. Arthur Wontner, Marie Löhr and John Hare in Pierre Wolff's **The Marionettes** directed by Dion Boucicault at Comedy. Translation by Gladys Unger. Neglected wife wins over callous husband. Stale comedy for stale audiences.

Sep 28. Robert Loraine as John Tanner, Pauline Chase as Ann Whitefield, Ion Swinley as Octavius and Edmund Gwenn as Straker in Bernard Shaw's **Man and Superman** directed by Robert Loraine at Criterion. This production was the start of Shaw's popularity with the general public. Loraine was high-spirited, breezy, impudent and eloquent. His crisp delivery was perfect for the long speeches.

Oct 7. Marie Tempest and Graham Browne in Arnold Bennett's **The Honeymoon** directed by Dion Boucicault at Royalty. Love or patriotism? Airman has to decide whether to go on his honeymoon or take part in a race over Snowdon and beat his German rival. The actors failed to disguise the thinness of the plot and the characterisation.

Oct 14. Marion Terry as Mrs Erlynne in Oscar Wilde's **Lady Windermere's Fan** at St James's. Lilian Braithwaite and Norman Trevor as Lord and Lady Windermere. Dawson Millward as Lord Darlington.
—Wilde mastered the tricks of the stage in five minutes and never troubled about the rules; and so we get a play that is at once very stagey and clumsy, perfectly planned and feebly constructed. *The Times*
—Yet when the dialogue is discounted, how artificial the plot, how familiar, yet laboured, its devices! *Athenæum*

Oct 27. Defying the Censor, The New Players Society gave a private performance of Oscar Wilde's **Salome** at Court. Adeline Bourne as Salome. Herbert Grimwood as Herod.
—It is pretentious – morbid – epileptic ... it was a sorry spectacle, fit only for sexless women and "pussy cat" men. MORAG *Penny Illustrated Paper*
—When all is said and done I think we may take it that we have now seen the first and last of Salome. MODRED *Referee*

Nov 4. E Dagnall, Ethel Dane and George Grossmith in Jose G Levy's **The Glad Eye** directed by E Dagnall at Globe. Adaptation of *Le Zebre* by Paul Armont and Nancey. Spiritualism and farce. Transferred to Apollo, then to Strand.

Nov 6. Victoria Palace opened with a variety bill and continued to present variety bills and revues until 1934.

Nov 8. Austen Milroy as D'Artagnan in **The Three Musketeers** at Lyceum. Broad humour and lurid melodrama. Ethel Warwick, playing Milady, hammed it up to roars of applause. Bassett Roe was Richelieu.

Nov 11. Basil Dean opened Liverpool Repertory Theatre.

Dec 2. Holman Clark as Luka in Maxim Gorky's **The Lower Depths** at Kingsway. Life in the Russian slums. Powerful political statement. Translation by Laurence Irving.
—Gorky relies too much on rhetoric and his interpreters almost all indulge in too noisy a method of declamation. *Athenæum*
—The one perfect performance comes from Holman Clark, sweet-tempered and charming as the philosopher tramp. *Illustrated London News*

—Fortunately we have had the Christmas festivities to help us over the depression caused by the sordid drama in Gorky's work. *Playgoer and Society*

Dec 4. Harcourt Williams and Margaret Halstan in Bernard Shaw's **How He Lied to Her Husband** directed by Harcourt Williams at Palace. The one-act play was part of a music hall bill. "The whole thing is delicious," said *The Times*.

Dec 11. London premiere of **The Miracle** directed by Max Reinhardt and designed by Stern at Olympia Hall. Wordless mystery spectacle by Karl Vollmoeller. Music by Engelbert Humperdinck. Cast of 1,800. Natasha Trouhanowa as Nun. Maria Carmi as Madonna. Max Pallenberg as Spielmann. Audiences of up to 30,000 sat on tiers three sides of The Hall, which had been transformed into a Gothic cathedral with stained glass rose windows, massive pillars and a soaring roof. The stage was filled with nuns, priests, choristers, peasants and the sick waiting for a miracle. The sheer size was impressive but there were longueurs in between the pageantry.

Dec 21. Reginald Owen as St George of England in Clifford Mills and John Ramsey's **Where the Rainbow Ends** at Savoy. Music by Roger Quilter. Billed as "a patriotic play for children every self-respecting child can safely take its parents." Two boys and their sisters fly on a magic carpet to Dragon Wood where St George kills the dragon. The children were played by Philip Tonge, Esme Wynne, Sydney Sherwoood and Dot Temph. Noël Coward was cast as a malicious pageboy who was cruel to the children's pet lion.

Dec 26. The Princes Theatre opened with **The Three Musketeers**, which transferred from Lyceum.

1912

Jan 15. Martin Harvey as Oedipus, Lillah McCarthy as Jocasta and Louis Calvert as Creon in Sophocles's **Oedipus Rex** directed by John Kurkamp and Max Reinhardt at Covent Garden. Translation by Gilbert Murray adapted by W L Courtney. The singing was supervised by the choirmaster of Westminster Abbey. Harvey was the first actor to act Oedipus in England since Betterton in 1679. There was more Reinhardt than Sophocles. The production was too colossal for the play. The actors were upstaged by the 300-strong crowd moaning, howling, wailing and waving their arms as they surged down the aisles through the auditorium. Harley Granville Barker worked with McCarthy (his wife) three hours every day helping her with the verse and getting rid of unnecessary gestures. The Censor tried to ban the performance on account of the incest.
—[Martin Harvey] has cut the bonds that fettered his genius and made himself with one stroke immortal. His Oedipus is an undying achievement that men will remember till their remembrance ends. JAMES DOUGLAS *Morning Leader*
—His treatment of the verse was cruel; it came out as prose not easily understood. *Daily Sketch*

Jan 31. Norman McKinnel in Githa Sowerby's **Rutherford and Son** at Court. This gripping, granite-like Edwardian family drama, set in the North of England during a period of industrial strife, had a feminist agenda, which made it popular with the suffragette movement. Rutherford, the boss of a glass factory, has two sons, neither of them wants to come into the business. His true heir, the only man he respects, is his loyal foreman; but the man, servile and compromised, is unable to rise above his working class station. He even thinks Rutherford is right to sack him when his affair with Rutherford's daughter is discovered. All the men are weak and ineffectual and only the women have the moral courage to stand up to him.
—A playwright of uncommon promise and a play, which though a little ragged on its technical side and somewhat harsh in style, deserves to be described as a powerful and conscientious piece of work, showing marked intelligence and ability. *Athenæum*

Feb 12. George Grossmith in **The Sunshine Girl** at Gaiety. Musical comedy. Book, music and lyrics by Paul A Rubens. Book by Cecil Raleigh and Arthur Wimperis. The tango routine set off a tango craze in London.

Feb 12. Herbert Beerbohm Tree as Svengali and Phyllis Neilson-Terry as Trilby in Paul M Potter's **Trilby** at His Majesty's.

Feb 17. Marie Löhr, Allan Aynesworth and Vernon Steel in Arthur Wing Pinero's **"Mind-the-Paint" Girl** at Duke of York's. The sordid private lives of Edwardian chorus girls and their aristocratic clientele did not appeal to the gallery who groaned out loud during the performance.

Feb 20. Arthur Wontner and O P Heggie in Macdonald Hastings's **The New Sin** directed by Clifford Brooke at Royalty. The sin is to remain alive when your family would benefit from your death.

Feb 28. Basil Gill, Francis Dillon and Marie Polini in Frederick Melville's **The Monk**

Henry Ainley, C Hayden Coffin and Evelyn Millard in Twelfth Night

Martin Harvey as Oedipus Rex

1912 World Premieres
Budapest
Arthur Schnitzler's *La Ronde*
Berlin
Bernard Shaw's *Androcles and the Lion*

Births
Wendy Hiller, British actor
William Douglas Home, British playwright
Eugene Ionesco, French playwright

Deaths
August Strindberg (*b.*1849), Swedish playwright

Notes
Lilian Baylis in charge of the Old Vic 1912–1929
Andre Charlot revues ran from 1912 to 1937

History
—Robert Falcon Scott reached South Pole one month after Roald Amundsen
—*Titanic* sank
—Woodrow Wilson US President
— Start of Balkan War
—First non-stop flight from Paris to London
—First issue of *Pravda*

Apr 18. Arthur Wontner as Ben-Hur and Reginald Owen as Messala in Lewis Wallace's **Ben-Hur** dramatised by William Young and directed by Joseph Brooks at Drury Lane. Thrilling spectacle (and a bit of religion) with enormous crowds, camels, rafts at sea, songs, dances, and a chariot race. The stage moved rapidly under the horses' feet and the scenery revolved behind them.
—Its sentiment is chocolate-box and its archaeology is merely absurd, its story is rather silly, and its taste deplorable. And yet there is a rough-and-ready straightforward effectiveness which is not to be denied. *The Times*

Apr 22. Norman McKinnel in K G Sowerby's **Rutherford and Son** returned to the Court.

Jul 2. First Royal Command Music Hall at Palace. Cast included Harry Tate, Little Titch, Vesta Tilley, George Robey, Harry Lauder and Marie Lloyd. Anna Pavlova danced The Dying Swan.

Jul 2. Edyth Goodall in Stanley Houghton's **Hindle Wakes** directed by Lewis Casson at Playhouse. Houghton belonged to the Manchester school of realism and his study of Lancashire provincial industrial life created something of a scandal because of its reversal of Victorian values. The heroine was very much the modern woman revolting against man-made laws and man-made conventions. After she had spent a weekend with the boss's son everybody thought that he should make "an honest woman of her" by ditching his fiancée and marrying her. She would have none of it: "You're a man and I was your little fancy. Well, I'm a woman and you were my little fancy." Transferred to Haymarket.
—The acting of Miss Horniman's Company was most refreshingly human. They never troubled about stage tradition, but simply consulted the book of nature. Owen Seaman *Punch*

Aug 31. Edmund Gwenn and Hilda Trevelyan in Sydney Blow and Douglas Hoare's **The Little Miss Llewellyn** at Vaudeville. A version of *Le Mariage de Mlle Beulemans* by Frantz Fonson and Fernaud Wicheler set in Wales.

Sep 3. Lyn Harding as Drake and Phyllis Neilson-Terry as Queen Elizabeth in Louis M Parker's **Drake** directed by Herbert Beerbohm Tree at His Majesty's. Spectacular patriotic pageant with quasi-historical characters.
—It is a call to the spirit of patriotism to the English people. We see England in the vigorous days of Elizabeth faced by a great peril and rising to meet it with dauntless courage. It has a moral for the present day and will surely make a popular appeal to the spirit of the race. Herbert Beerbohm Tree
—Miss Neilson-Terry plays her so charmingly as to suggest the reflection that, if the real Elizabeth had been anything like her, the whole course of English history would have been altered. *The Times.*

Sep 5. Arthur Playfair, Robert Averell, Yvonne Arnaud and Margaret Paton in **The Girl in the Taxi** directed by Philip Michael Farady at Lyric. French musical. Book by George Okonowski. English version by Frederick Fenn and Arthur Wimperis. Music by Jean Gilbert. The action was set in rowdy Paris. French actress Yvonne Arnaud, making her London debut, made her reputation. "Suzanne, Suzanne, We Love You To A Man!" The waltz tune was so melodious that the audience was whistling it by the interval.

Sep 7. Edward Maurice and Arthur Wontner in Harley Granville Barker's **Voysey Inheritance** at Kingsway.

Sep 16. Sarah Bernhardt in a six-week season of plays at Coliseum as part of a variety bill. Act II of Victor Hugo's **Lucrèce Borgia**. Act II of Racine's **Phèdre**. Act IV in Emile Moreau's **Elisabeth**, **Reine D'Angleterre** and Sous Terreur's **Une Nuit de Noël**.

and The Woman at Lyceum. Costume melodrama. The hero when cornered immediately produced his cross. The soldiers, Christians to a man, immediately dropped their muskets.

Mar 5. O B Clarence in Rudolf Besier's adaptation of H G Wells's **Kipps** directed by Louis Calvert at Vaudeville. The story of a simple soul was reduced to farce and Kipps was merely ludicrous.

Mar 9. Dennis Eadie, Mary Jerrold and Haidee Wright in Arnold Bennett and Edward Knoblock's **Milestones** directed by Frank Vernon at Royalty. Three generations: a family drama set in 1860, 1885 and 1912. Times change but human nature remains the same. The only unhappy member is the girl who broke off her engagement and repented ever after.
—It's a long time since anything has given us so much simple, sweetly sorrowful pleasure in the theatre as the old maid by Miss Haidee Wright. *The Times*

Mar 19. Lillah McCarthy as Iphigenia and Godfrey Tearle as Orestes in Euripides's **Iphigenia in Taurus** directed by Harley Granville Barker at Kingsway.
—The present production is a triumph of stage-management and acting. There are superb pictures and the treatment of the chorus is quite masterly. Miss McCarthy's Iphigenia is a great piece of acting that will add even to her reputation. *Sketch*
—Mr Tearle was a worthy Orestes; he looked like a Greek, and spoke like a man. *The Times*

Apr 9. Herbert Beerbohm Tree in Shakespeare's **Othello** at His Majesty's. Most critics thought Tree should have played Iago, a role taken by Laurence Irving, who was more impish than devilish. Phyllis Neilson-Terry was Desdemona.
—Essentially an intellectual and introspective actor he can but simulate a display of animal ferocity; he cannot give passion full rein and carry the playgoer away by the compelling power of his emotion. *Athenæum*

Apr 11. Marie Tempest, Norman Trevor, Graham Browne, Charles V France and Ernest Mainwaring in Anthony P Wharton's **At the Barn** at Prince of Wales. Musical comedy actress captivates the hearts of three golf-playing bachelors. An excellent vehicle for Tempest.

Sep 21. Henry Ainley as Leontes, Lillah McCarthy as Hermione and Cathleen Nesbitt as Perdita in Shakespeare's **The Winter's Tale** directed by Harley Granville Barker at Savoy. The scenery was by Norman Wilkinson. Barker returned to the basic principles of Elizabethan and Jacobean staging. Faithful to the text (only six lines were cut) he deliberately set out to shock the audience visually with vivid colours. The Sicilian costumes were inspired by Giulio Romano. Bohemia was pure Warwickshire. The speech was swift. The critics were divided, many presuming that the actors would loathe it and hate being in it. A B Walkley in *The Times* said it was "post-Impressionist Shakespeare."
—Never before had Shakespeare's splendid rhetoric, his glamour of resistless verse, the true and vivid illusion upon which he alone and so successfully relied, reached me in a London theatre. JOHN PALMER *Saturday Review*

Oct 3. Gerald du Maurier, Marie Löhr and Dawson Millward in Hubert Henry Davies's **Doormats** at Wyndham's. Silly wife treats her artist-husband like a doormat. The play collapsed in the third act.
—The moment Mr Davies tries to go below the surface and to sound the depths of passion, the artificiality of the puppets becomes apparent. *Illustrated London News*

Oct 19. Gertie Millar and Joseph Coyne in **The Dancing Mistress** at Adelphi. Musical comedy. Book by J T Tanner. Lyrics by Adrian Ross. Music by Lionel Monckton. Millar danced in a rose-colored sand-storm and Coyne sang "Bring Her Along."

Oct 23. At the Savoy Hotel on her 69th birthday **Sarah Bernhardt** was presented with a national Tribute signed by 100,000 persons.

Nov 4. At Southwark Cathedral the unveiling ceremony and dedication of the Shakespeare Memorial took place.

Nov 15. Henry Ainley as Malvolio, Lillah McCarthy as Viola, Evelyn Millard as Olivia and Leon Quartermaine as Sir Andrew in Shakespeare's **Twelfth Night** directed by Harley Granville Barker at Savoy. The scenery was by Norman Wilkinson. Set in a black and white Italianate Elizabethan court, all traditional comic business was eliminated. Malvolio was an idealised Puritan prig. The production was received with universal acclaim and Barker was confirmed as the leading director of the day. John Masefield, in a letter to Barker, said it was the most beautiful thing he had ever seen on the stage.
—A performance of sheer delight, wonder and surprise. The traditions of a lifetime torpedoed into infinity. *Play Pictorial*
—Mr Ainley scores the greatest victory of his career – one of the finest performances of our time. *Illustrated London News*

Nov 19. Stanley Drewitt, Ada King and Nigel Playfair in Stanley Houghton's **The Younger Generation** directed by Stanley Drewitt at Haymarket. Middle-class children rebel against their teetotal, chapel-going, narrow-minded, puritanical parents.
—The characters are all absolutely true to life and the actors and actresses concerned stand out clearly as actual men and women of real flesh and blood. *Tatler*

Nov 25. Edmund Maurice in John Galsworthy's **The Eldest Son** directed by Harley Granville Barker at Kingsway. Baronet swears to disinherit his son (Guy Rathbone) if he marries a lady's maid (Cathleen Nesbitt) whom he has got pregnant. The son wants to do the right thing, but she turns him down when she realises he doesn't love her.
—Mr Galsworthy is terribly in earnest. Unfortunately he is in earnest about other things than dramatic art. Indeed his earnestness can hardly be said to bear any relation to art at all. *Manchester Guardian*

Dec 12. Elizabethan Stage Society. Shakespeare's **Troilus and Cressida** directed by William Poel at King Hall, Covent Garden. Edith Evans, still an amateur, made her debut as Cressida, and played her as a fashionable, languid Elizabethan Court Lady. Esme Percy was an effeminate Troilus. William Poel was an exquisite Pandarus. Hermione Gingold wailed as Cassandra. Thersites was played by Elspeth Keith as an Elizabethan Scottish clown. Since Poel did not have enough men, Aeneas and Paris were also played by actresses. The Greeks were dressed as Elizabethan soldiers. The Trojans were dressed as Renaissance soldiers. Transferred to Stratford-on-Avon in 1913.

Dec 23. Ethel Levey, Shirley Kellogg and Dorothy Minto in **Hullo, Ragtime** at London Hippodrome. Book by Max Pemberton and Albert de Courville. Music by Louis Hirsch. This revue made ragtime popular in Britain.

Dec 26. Louis Calvert as Broadbent, Harcourt Williams as Larry Doyle, William Poel as Keegan and Ellen O'Malley as Nora in Bernard Shaw's **John Bull's Other Island** at Kingsway.
— It is a play that never grows old. Its gleams of poetry, its hard-hitting pronouncements, its political and racial understanding, and its shrewd not too devilish wit makes it an enduring delight. *The Times*

1913

Feb 4. Vaslav Nijinsky, Tamara Karsavina, Alexander Kotchetovsky in **Petroushka** at Covent Garden. Music by Igor Stravinsky. Libretto and décor by Alexandre Benois. Choreography by Michel Fokine.

Feb 13. Laurence Irving as Skule, Basil Gill as Haakon and Ion Swinley as Peter in Henrik Ibsen's **The Pretenders** directed by E Lyall Swete at Haymarket. Picturesque.
—Here are three great, hairy, shaggy, woolly men out of some fierce Norwegian past, talking not the accustomed fustian of the romantic drama but sound hard-bitten English.
A B WALKLEY *The Times*

Feb 15. Birmingham Repertory Theatre, founded by Barry Jackson, opened with Shakespeare's **Twelfth Night**.

Feb 17. Vaslav Nijinsky as the faun in **L'Après Midi d'un Faune** at Covent Garden. Libretto and choreography by Vaslav Nijinsky. Music by Claude Debussy and décor by Leon Baskt. Languid faun is playing with his flute when he spies nymphs bathing. The nymphs – with their flattened profile positions and their rigid, heavy, angular limbs – looked as if they have just stepped off a Minoan frieze. There was uproar at the premiere in Paris in 1912 when at the climax Nijinsky spread himself on a scarf he had stolen from one of the nymphs and simulated masturbation. The scandal divided the city into two camps: *Le Monde* led the anti-group, Auguste Rodin led the pro-group. There was no mention of any masturbation in London.

Feb 18. Iris Hoey in **Oh! Oh!! Delphine!!!** at Shaftesbury. Book by Hugh Morton. Music by Ivan Caryll. French farce: husband lends his wife to her former husband. Walter Passmore sang "Everything's at home except your wife" and Dorothy Jarden had a big success in the "Venus" Waltz.

Feb 25. Winifred Emery, Dion Boucicault, Hilda Trevelyan and Edmund Gwenn in Arthur Wing Pinero's **The Schoolmistress** directed by Dion Boucicault at Vaudeville. Farce. A respectable schoolmistress takes to singing in comic opera in order to supplement her income to pay her husband's debts.

Posters for Oh! Oh! Delphine

1913 World Premieres
Vienna
Bernard Shaw's *Pygmalion*
Berlin
Carl Sternheim's *Burger Schippel*

Births
Albert Camus, French playwright
Benjamin Britten, British composer
Anthony Quayle, British actor

Deaths
H G Pellisier (*b.*1874), founder of *Follies*
Stanley Houghton (*b.*1881), British playwright

Honours
Knight
Johnston Forbes-Robertson, British actor

Notes
—Inez Bensusan mounted a season of women's plays at Coronet
—British Drama League inaugurated.

—Florrie Forde sang *It's a Long, Long Way to Tipperary*
—First Charlie Chaplin film
—Film censorship imposed in Britain
—Sir Robert Harcourt MP introduced a private members Bill to seek the abolition of theatre censorship. The theatre managements opposed the bill
—Tango Teas at Queen's Theatre. The stalls seats were removed and replaced with dance floor, tables and chairs. Afternoon tea was taken while watching tango demonstrations.

History
—300 Istanbul Armenians intellectuals arrested and murdered
—Start of Balkan War
—King George of Greece assassinated
—Serbia declared war on Bulgaria
—Woolworth Building opened in New York
—The Kaiser banned the tango in Berlin

Mar 23. Henry Ainley and Wish Wynne in Arnold Bennett's **The Great Adventure** at Kingsway. Famous painter dies and is buried in Westminster Abbey. Only he didn't die. His valet died and he let the doctor think it was him.

Mar 26. Gladys Cooper, Gerald du Maurier, Owen Nares, Lady Tree, Arthur Wontner, Ellis Jeffreys and Donald Calthrop in Clement Scott and Benjamin Charles Stephenson's **Diplomacy** directed by Gerald du Maurier at Wyndham's. The play, a highly popular adaptation of Victorien Sardou's *Dora*, premiered in 1878, was brought up to date with telephone and motor car.
—Miss Cooper has hitherto been a dainty player of dainty parts; last night the opportunity came to her of showing something bigger and she took the opportunity splendidly. *The Times*

Mar 27. Holman Clark, Frederick Ross, Ernest Hendrie, Christine Silver and Sheila Hayes in **The Yellow Jacket** directed by H Benrimo at Duke of York's. Book by George C Hazelton and J H Benrimo. Music by William Furst. Chinese play staged in the Chinese manner. A dainty little fable, quaint and charming.

Mar 28. James Welch in Sydney Blow and Douglas Hoare's **Oh! I Say!!** at Criterion. Farce. Stanley Houghton's **The Dear Departed** was the curtain raiser.

Apr 2. Laurence Irving and Mabel Hackney in Melchior Lengyel's **The Typhoon** adapted and directed by Laurence Irving at Haymarket. Young Japanese spy murders a French cocotte. A patriot takes the blame for his crime. The spy, once his mission is accomplished, commits hara-kiri.

Apr 14. Johnston Forbes-Robertson and Gertrude Elliott in Bernard Shaw's **Caesar and Cleopatra** at Drury Lane. "So perverse, so ingenious, so very nearly persuasive and yet so exasperating," said *The Illustrated London News*, whilst *Era* doubted "if any other actor has ever caused the greatness of Caesar to be so fully realised."
—Mr Shaw has now reached to the proud position where the British public laughs at whatever he says, almost before he says it, lest they should subsequently stand convicted of having missed a joke. *The Times*

May 3. Norman McKinnel and Fisher White in John Galsworthy's **Strife** at Comedy. "A great play," said *Punch*.

May 5. Johnston Forbes-Robertson as Shylock and Gertrude Elliott in Shakespeare's **The Merchant of Venice**. Elliott was an arch Portia.
— [Johnston Forbes-Robertson] is of far too gentle a temperament to realise the more atrocious phases of his character … His Shylock is picturesque rather than bizarre, humanly pathetic rather than passionately Jewish or tragic. *Illustrated London News*

May 10. Martin Harvey as Petruchio and N de Silva as Katharine in Shakespeare's **The Taming of the Shrew** at Prince of Wales. High-spirited but ill-advised. Harvey was not masterful and de Silva was compared unfavourably with Ada Rehan.
—As for my own conception of Petruchio I see in him one of the greatest gentlemen Shakespeare ever drew. MARTIN HARVEY

May 17. Gertie Millar, G P Huntley and W H Berry in **The Marriage Market** directed by Edward Rose at Daly's. Musical comedy. Book by Gladys Unger. Music by Victor Jacobi. Lyrics by Arthur Anderson and Adrian Ross. Millionaire's daughter (Sari Petrass) masquerading as a farm girl finds herself married off to a cowboy

Johnston Forbes Robertson in **Hamlet**

Lilian Braithwaite and Matheson Lang in Mr Wu

(Robert Michaelis). Millar, "the most chic and dainty of comediennes", had a big success doing the hornpipe and polyglot. 423 performances.

May 19. Johnston Forbes-Robertson in Shakespeare's **Othello** at Drury Lane. J H Barnes as Iago. Gertrude Elliott as Desdemona.
—The cry of "Blood! Blood!" comes strangely from so ascetic, so merely rhetorical an Othello. *Illustrated London News*

May 24. Edyth Goodall in Bayard Veiller's **Within the Law** directed by Herbert Beerbohm Tree at Haymarket. The best way to stop habitual stealing in an Emporium would be to pay the girls sufficient wages to enable them to live in some degree of comfort.
—In this play we have a return to the type of drama which usually spells "money". Whatever may be the trend of a section of "producers" and authors, we rarely find their efforts attended with financial success. People like "thrills", not morbid studies of the seamy side of life, and *Within the Law* provides them. Hence it success! *Play Pictorial*

Jun 6. Johnston Forbes-Robertson's farewell performance in Shakespeare's **Hamlet** at Drury Lane. The play ended on the line, "The rest is silence," which he spoke. The applause went on for 3 minutes and 21 seconds.
—His Hamlet was great. We all admit that. He is the Hamlet of our time. J T GREIN *Sunday Times*

Jun 27. A special matinee performance of Dion Boucicault's **London Assurance** at St James's Theatre with Herbert Beerbohm Tree, Godfrey Tearle, H B Irving, James Welch, Henry Ainley, Arthur Bourchier, Charles Hawtrey, Dennis Eadie, Weedon Grossmith, Irene Vanbrugh, Phyllis Neilson-Terry and Mary Tempest. In the presence of the King and Queen in aid of King George Pension Fund.

Aug 28. M. Lou-Tellegen as Dorian Grey, Franklyn Dyall as Lord Henry Wotton and Arthur Scott Craven as Basil Halward in a dramatisation of Oscar Wilde's novel **The Picture of Dorian Grey** by G Constant Lounsbery at Vaudeville.
—Lou-Telligan's beautiful face, pure Greek in outline, and his tall graceful figure lend themselves admirably to the part and his accent is so slight that after the first few minutes it becomes unnoticeable. *The Era*
—No doubt M. Lou-Tellegen has a face and figure which many people admire. On the other hand, many people – well, won't. *The Times*

Sep 1. Leon Quartermaine as Emperor, Ben Webster as Captain, O P Heggie as Androcles and Lillah McCarthy as Lavinia in Bernard Shaw's **Androcles and the Lion** directed by Harley Granville Barker at St James's. Shaw described the play (first produced in Berlin 1912) as a religious harlequinade suitable for children of all ages. It is not suitable for young children at all. He uses the fable as a basis for a semi-serious, semi-humorous debate on Christianity. The script was an antidote to the sentimentality of the religious dramas of the day. Shaw complained that the laughter of the first night audience interrupted the smooth progress of the play. The critics didn't like it, dismissing it as offensive, insulting, nasty, infantile, crude, repulsive and blasphemous.

Sep 2. Herbert Beerbohm Tree as Jacob in Louis N Parker's **Joseph and His Brethren** directed by Louis N Parker at His Majesty's. This was the first Biblical play to be licensed since the establishment of the Censorship and it was Tree's greatest spectacular triumph. There were live sheep, live donkeys and a live camel. The Old Hebrew chants were accompanied by ancient Egyptian instruments.
—But though the crude and the sublime are strangely blended in his scheme and Joseph's character is left curiously vague, and there is little to stir the imagination in this pageant, it is splendid as a pageant. *Illustrated London News*

Sep 4. Double bill by J M Barrie at Duke of York's. John Hare and Mrs Patrick Campbell in **The Adored One, A Legend of the Old Bailey**. A mother pushes a man out of a train when he refuses to shut the window. **The Will**. Portrait of a man (Sydney Valentine) at three stages: firstly, the tender young husband; secondly, the hard, self-made businessman; and finally, the tragic realisation that financial success has brought him no happiness.

Sep 11. Madge Fabian in Cecil Raleigh and Henry Hamilton's **Sealed Orders** directed by Arthur Collins at Drury Lane. The admiral's wife has gambling debts to pay, so she steals her husband's sealed orders and sells them to an agent of a foreign power.

Sep 13. Charles Hawtrey in W H Post's **Never Say Die** at Apollo. Farce. A man told that he is going to die very shortly marries a girl but only so that he can leave her his money so that she can marry a penniless artist. But he does not die and they remain married.

Sep 25. Harry Welchman, Alfred Lester, Cicely Courtneidge and Ava Blanche in **The Pearl Girl** at Shaftesbury. Musical comedy. Book by Basil Hood. Lyrics by Hugo Felix. Music by Howard Talbot. Jack Hulbert, straight from Oxford University, made

his professional debut. The ladies of the chorus showed how pearls at popular prices could be worn with as much effect as the genuine article. 254 performances.

Oct 16. Irene Rorke and Milton Rosmer in John Galsworthy's **The Fugitive** directed by Milton Rosmer at Court. A wife, who finds her husband physically repulsive, is pestered by so many men in the workplace that she finally commits suicide. Galsworthy never liked the play. Transferred to Prince of Wales.

Oct 18. Joseph Coyne, Gracie Leigh, Phyllis Dare, Edmund Payne and Ina Claire in **The Girl from Utah** directed by Philip Faraday at Adelphi. Musical comedy. Book by James T Tanner and Paul A Rubens. Lyrics by Adrian Ross, Percy Greenbank and Paul A Rubens. Music by Sydney Jones and Paul A Rubens. A shop proprietor is mistaken for a Mormon.

Nov 7. Franklin Dyall as the Stranger in G K Chesterton's **Magic** at Little. Spiritualism versus materialism. A fantasy.

Nov 22. Jean Aylwn in Jose G Levy's **Who's the Lady?** at Garrick. Adaptation of *Madame Le President* by Maurice Hennequin and Pierre Veber. Alwyn had "a deliciously light touch", but some of the other actors, according to *The Illustrated London News*, were "too stolidly British in their style."

Nov 25. Nina Boucicault, Cathleen Nesbitt, and Godfrey Tearle in J M Barrie's **Quality Street** directed by Dion Boucicault at Duke of York's. Soldier returning from the Napoleonic wars does not recognise his former sweetheart. The revival was so successful that, come Christmas, *Peter Pan* could only play matinees.
—Eleven years have gone by and the play has lost none of its freshness and charm...this pretty, fantastic story captures all hearts. *Sphere*

Nov 27. Matheson Lang and Lilian Braithwaite in Harry M Vernon and Harold Owen's **Mr Wu** directed by Matheson Lang at Strand. Oriental melodrama set in Kowloon. Lang had come back from a tour of the Far East, obsessed with the idea of playing a real Chinaman. He based his performance on the mannerisms of the First Secretary to the Chinese Legation. Wu was a powerful, Oxford-educated mandarin and he tried to persuade a mother to sacrifice her honour in order to save her son from death. She poisoned him with a nice cup of tea. Wu, a fine combination of ferocity and imperturbability, was Lang's most famous role and he called his memoirs *Mr Wu Looks Back.*
—With his icy dignity, his perfect self-control, his lovely clothes and surroundings, his complete lack of nerves, scruples or bowels of mercy, his exquisite manners, his immense wealth and power, and his exact sense of revenge, he is a fine study of the qualities which English people do not possess. FILSON YOUNG *Pall Mall Gazette*
—The play will be remembered; it will go beyond London and these isles. Its exotic flavour is not merely the product of the theatrical greenhouse. It has character of its own – a backbone of knowledge. J T GREIN *Sunday Times*
—For ferocity of theme, for the impressiveness, atmosphere and fine character acting there has been nothing like Mr Wu on the stage within the memory of the playgoer. *Lloyd's*

Dec 1. Yavorska in John Pollock's adaptation of Leo Tolstoy's **Anna Karenina** at Ambassadors. Yavorska wore a succession of lovely dresses and lots of furs. Lachrymose.
—The last two acts gave plenty of opportunities to Mme Yavorska for emotional acting; but we noticed nothing in her performance we had not seen before and nothing that could preserve our interest. *The Times*

Dec 1. Leon Quartermaine as Ekdal, Harcourt Williams as Gregers Werle, Gladys Wiles as Hedvig, and H O Nicholson as Old Ekdal in Henrik Ibsen's **The Wild Duck** at St James's.
—Mr Quartermaine occasionally creates the impression that he is playing with his tongue in his cheek, which is a little irritating to worshippers of Ibsen who would like to see the works of the master treated with reverential seriousness. *Era*

Dec 13. Annie Saker, Alfred Paumier and Graeme Campbell in Walter Howard's **The Story of the Rosary** at Princes. Two Austrians are in love with the same woman. The hero ends up in a labour camp. He manages to escape and return in the nick of time, just as his wife, thinking he is dead, is about to take vows. He kills the villain. The rosary was a present on the night of their marriage.

Dec 23. Godfrey Tearle as Captain Hook and Pauline Chase as Peter Pan in J M Barrie's **Peter Pan** at Duke of York's. Slightly was played by 14-year-old Noël Coward.

1914

Jan 1. George Alexander in Henri Bernstein's **The Attack** directed by John Reynders at St James's. Adaptation by George Egerton. MP's early indiscretions are exposed. The *Athenæum* said it was "an orgy of sentimentality."

Jan 17. Herbert Beerbohm Tree, George Relph and Marie Löhr in David Belasco and John Luther Lang's **The Darling of the Gods** at His Majesty's. Love and honour among the warriors of Ancient Egypt. Reality and common sense were sacrificed throughout to spectacular display.

Jan 25. Yiddish People's Theatre. Harold Chapin in Israel Zangwill's **The Melting Pot** at Court. Acted for the first time in English. The fusion of all races, Jews not exempted, so as to produce the true American.

Jan 27. Esme Percy in Shakespeare's **Hamlet** directed by William Poel at Little. Percy's affectations and antics were extraordinary.
—The rapidity he [William Poel] advocates is all for the good – if only we had players capable of speaking fast and distinctly. But it seems we have none, for none in the company is always audible. *The Times*

Feb 2. First performance at Covent Garden of Richard Wagner's **Parsifal**.

Feb 5. Robert Loraine, Ethel Irving, Fred Kerr and Alfred Bishop in C Haddon Chambers's **The Tyranny of Tears** at Comedy. Wife weeps to get her own way. *The Times* thought it was a little classic: "one of the brightest, deftest, sanest and most humorous comedies of our generation."

Feb 6. Nigel Playfair as Bottom, Lillah McCarthy as Helen, Ion Swinley as Lysander and Arthur Whitby as Quince in Shakespeare's **A Midsummer Night's Dream** directed by Harley Granville Barker at Savoy. The scenery was by Norman Wilkinson. The fairies were gilded from head to foot and looked like Cambodian gods. Oberon and Titania's costumes had long, translucent, shimmering trains. The mortals looked Byzantine. Donald Caltrop, the first grown man to play Puck, wore flaming scarlet clothes, baggy trousers and a large flaxen wig with red berries. "A revelation," said *The Observer*. "A Shakespearian nightmare," said *The Daily Mail*.
—Shakespeare slaughtered to make an intellectual and post-impressionistic holiday. *Saturday Review*

Feb 16. Three matinees of Eugène Brieux's **Damaged Goods** directed by Kenelm Foss at Little. *Play Pictorial* thought the subject matter – syphilis and its effects on marriage – too gruesome and repugnant and the theatre no fit place for it.

Feb 23. Allan Aynesworth and Sam Sothern in Cyril Harcourt's **A Pair of Silk Stockings** at Criterion. Husband hides in a wardrobe in an attempt to bring about a reconciliation with his wife.

Feb 26. Irene Vanbrugh and Godfrey Tearle in Somerset Maugham's **The Land of Promise** directed by Dion Boucicault at Duke of York's. Variation on *The Taming of the Shrew*. Refined heroine immigrates to Canada and marries a backwoodsman. She rebels against his suppression. *The Times*, "deeply moved and intensely repelled," recommended the play to women.

Mar 10. Oscar Asche and Lilly Brayton in Edward Knoblock's **Kismet** directed by Oscar Asche at Globe. *The Athenæum* said that "his sturdy ferocity and bombast as the truculent beggar have lost nothing of their pungency."

Mar 30. Milton Rosmer and Irene Rooke in John Galsworthy's **The Mob** transferred from Manchester to Gaiety. "I hate and abhor war of all kinds," wrote Galsworthy in his diary, looking back to the gung-ho imperialism of the Victorians. A Member of Parliament resigns because Britain is waging a war against a small nation. He continues to speak out against the government and the press at public meetings. The nation expects him to be silent when British lives are being lost. His wife, who has three brothers at the front (one of them is killed), tries to bribe him with sex to give up his principles. He refuses and destroys his parliamentary career and his marriage. Accused of blasphemy and branded a traitor, he faces a violent mob.
—I never got to like it very much – it lacks I don't quite know what. Still it's not as bad as some of the Press tries to make out. JOHN GALSWORTHY *in a letter to Professor Murray*

Apr 11. Herbert Beerbohm Tree as Professor Higgins, Mrs Patrick Campbell as Eliza Doolittle and Edmund Gwenn as Doolittle in Bernard Shaw's **Pygmalion** directed by Basil Dean at His Majesty's. "It is," wrote Shaw in his Preface, "impossible for an Englishman to open his mouth without making some other Englishman despise him." Professor Higgins, an ill-mannered 20th century Pygmalion, takes a flower girl out of the gutter and determines to pass her off as a duchess within six months, never giving a thought as to what might become of her after the experiment is over. It was the first time "bloody" had been heard on the stage. On the first night there was a sharp intake of breath, followed by a stunned silence and then a roar of laughter. The audience laughed so much they almost wrecked the play. Shaw objected to the romantic ending Tree insisted on giving the production. "I cannot conceive a less happy ending to the story of Pygmalion than a love affair between the middle-aged, middle class professor and a confirmed bachelor, with a mother fixation, and a flower girl of eighteen," said Shaw. "My ending makes money and you ought to be grateful," said Tree. "Your ending is damnable," said Shaw, "and you ought to be shot." The theatre was far too big

1914 World Premieres
Berlin
  Carl Sternheim's *The Snobs*

Births
Marguerite Duras, French playwright
Alec Guinness, British actor
Joan Littlewood, British director
Dylan Thomas, Welsh poet, playwright

Deaths
Brandon Thomas (*b.* 1856), British playwright

History
—Assassination of Archduke Franz Ferdinand at Sarajevo
—World War I began
—Battle of Mons
—Battle of the Falkland Islands

and Tree and Campbell were not ideal casting. He was 60 and she was 49. *The Daily Express* took a Charing Cross flowergirl to see the play. She was evidently shocked by the language. The Theatre Management Association asked Shaw to delete the offending word. "Not bloody likely!" he replied and resigned from the Association.
—Mrs Patrick Campbell swears on stage and cultured London roars with laughter. *Daily Sketch headline*
—You will be able to boast you are the first dramatist to use this word on the stage! But, really, was it worth while? There is a whole range of forbidden words in the English language; a little more of your courage and we suppose they will be heard, too. And then goodbye to the delights of really intimate conversation. *The Times*

Apr 15. Augustus Yorke as Potash and Robert Leonard as Perlmutter in Montague Glass's **Potash and Perlmutter** at Queen's. Highly popular American-German Jewish comedy about two constantly bickering partners in the garment industry. The success was due to their characterisation rather than the plot.

Apr 16. Yvonne Arnaud in **Mam'selle Tralala** at Lyric. Musical comedy. Book by Arthur Wimperis and Harley Carrick. Music by Jean Gilbert.
—A more dainty lady could hardly be imagined than Miss Yvonne Arnaud made of Mam'selle Tralala. Her singing was as charming as ever. *Era*

Apr 21. Gladys Cooper and Dennis Eadie appeared in a number of roles in Edward Knoblock's **My Lady's Dress** directed by Frank Vernon at Royalty. The creation of a dress was told in three sections: *1)* The Material. *2)* The Trimming. *3)* The Making. The action moved from the slums of London to Italy, France, Holland, Siberia and back to a fashion house in London.

Apr 23. Gerald du Maurier and Marie Löhr in Alfred Sutro's **The Clever Ones** directed by Gerald du Maurier at Wyndham's. Man pretends to be an anarchist to win a girl's affections. Edmund Gwenn played her philistine father.

Apr 27. New Constitutional Society for Women's Suffrage. Bessie Hatton as Mrs Alving, Fisher White as Pastor Manders, Leon Quartermaine as Oswald and Dorothy Drake as Regina in Henrik Ibsen's **Ghosts** translated by William Archer and directed by Leon M Lion at Court.

May 5. Eva Moore and H V Esmond in H V Esmond's **The Dangerous Age** at Vaudeville. 40-year-old widow falls in love with a 22-year-old. The dangerous age is 40.
—*The Dangerous Age* makes a very charming entertainment, a patchwork of humour and pathos ingeniously woven together; of which the humour was as fresh and jolly as anything I've heard on the stage, and the pathos put me in greater danger of being caught blubbering like a seal than I have ever been before. OWEN SEAMAN *Punch*

May 10. Guy Rathbone as Vanya, Herbert Grimwood as Astrov and Gillian Scaife as Sonia in Anton Chekhov's **Uncle Vanya** at Aldwych. Sonia emerged the leading role.
—A very strange play it is, utterly opposed to all our English notions of playmaking, a play with unity of mood but without unity of action. *The Times*

May 13. Cyril Maude in Horace Hodges and T Wigney Percyval's **Grumpy** at Criterion. Grumpy, a cantankerous and seemingly senile lawyer, who solves a crime mystery, was one of Maude's most remarkable character sketches and transformations. Ann Trevor was the heroine. James Dale played a thief.

May 14. Hilda Moore as Mrs Cheveley, George Alexander as Lord Goring, Arthur Wontner and Phylis Neilson-Terry as Sir Robert and Lady Chiltern in Oscar Wilde's **An Ideal Husband** at St James's. Robert Ross, Wilde's literary executor, attempted to bring the play up to date with references to eugenics, motor cars and golf. *The Illustrated London News* thought the play was still *vieu jeu*.

May 21. Mrs C Hayden Coffin gave an "at home" in aid of the Performing Animals Defence Committee which was in favour of complete abolishment of performing animals on the stage whether they were kindly or badly treated, arguing that "any-

Mrs Patrick Campbell in George Bernard Shaw's Pygmalion

thing which prevents an animal from leading a natural life was in itself cruel." Among those who were present were Mr and Mrs Granville Barker.

May 25. Edward Sass and Gillian Scaife in Israel Zangwill's **Plaster Saints** at Comedy. Clerical sinner argues that repentant sinners make the best pastors.

May 29. Laurence Irving and his wife, Mabel Hackney, drown in the wreck of *The Empress of Ireland*.

Jun 3. Marie Tempest and Graham Browne in Robert Marshall's **The Duke of Killicrackie** at Playhouse. Burlesque romance. Duke carries off wife to Highlands to tame her. Transferred to Garrick.

Jul 9. H B Irving and Miriam Lewes in Stephen Phillips's **The Sin of David** at Savoy. Update of the Biblical story. A commanding officer sacrifices a capable soldier for his own ends.

Jul 14. Bessie Hatton as Mrs Alving, Dorothy Drake as Regina in Henrik Ibsen's **Ghosts** at Court. The performance was to commemorate the lifting of the ban. Leon Quartermaine's Oswald was highly praised.
—One leaves the theatre feeling that one has come to grip with the great things of life, that one has a clearer understanding of essentials, a deeper sympathy with suffering, and a more fervent desire to strike, in however a tiny way towards progress and enlightenment. *Era*

Aug 19. Herbert Beerbohm Tree in a revival of Louis N Parker's **Drake** directed by Louis N Parker at His Majesty's. During the interval the audience sang the national anthems of the Allies.

Sep 1. Gerald du Maurier and Ethel Levey in Hubert Henry Davies's **Outcast** at Wyndham's. Woman refuses offer of marriage preferring to be his mistress. Du Maurier was his effortless natural self. Levey, who usually appeared in musical comedy, was making her debut in a straight play and was a bit less subtle.

Sep 3. Marie Löhr and Donald Calthrop in J M Barrie's **Little Minister** directed by Dion Boucicault at Duke of York's. The perfect romance to take the audiences' minds off the war.

Sep 8. Lillah McCarthy and Godfrey Tearle in C Haddon Chambers's **The Impossible Woman** at Haymarket. The impossible woman was a famous pianist, monstrously rude and egotistical. The play was based on Anne Sedgwick's novel, *Tanto*.

Sep 30. Oscar Asche and Lily Brayton in **Mameena** at Globe. Adaptation of Rider Haggard's *Child of Storm*. Ear-splitting spectacle offered primitive passion in the Bush and Zulus war dancing.

Oct 5. Lilian Baylis's first production at Old Vic. The complete cycle of Shakespeare's First Folio began with William Stack as Petruchio and Hutin Britton as Katharine in **The Taming of the Shrew** directed by Hutin Britton. The cycle was completed in 1923.

Oct 10. Laurette Taylor and A E Matthews in J Hartley Manners's **Peg O' My Heart** directed by Hartley Manners at Comedy. The American actress Taylor made her London debut in her husband's sentimental comedy drama which had run for over 600 performances in New York. She had not been on the stage ten minutes, said *Play Pictorial*, before she had won all hearts with her captivating personality. The play transferred to Globe in 1915 and then to Apollo and then to St James's. Only the Zeppelin raids put an end to the run.

Oct 17. Alice Delysia in **Odds and Ends** directed by Charles B Cochran at Ambassadors. Revue. Book by Harry Gattan. Music by Edward Jones.

Oct 27. Phyllis Dare in Paul Rubens and Austen Hurgon's **Miss Hook of Holland** at Prince of Wales. Miss Hook is courted by a bandmaster and a military captain. Alfred Wellesley had a big success as her alcoholic father, the owner of a distillery, who loses the recipe of liquor cream.

Oct 28. Gertie Millar and Robert Michaelis in **A Country Girl** at Daly's directed by Edward Royce. Musical. Book by James T Tanner. Music by Lionel Monckton. Lyrics by Adrian Ross and Paul Rubens.
—It is a brilliant revival brought up to date, of an evergreen musical comedy, English to the core, and fresh and fragrant in melody and sentiment. *Era*

Nov 14. Herbert Beerbohm Tree as Falstaff, Owen Nares as Prince Hal and Basil Gill as King Henry in Shakespeare's **Henry IV Part 1** at His Majesty's. Tree revived the play because "it voices the national spirit of the time and makes its appeal to chivalry and patriotism." Matheson Lang played Hotspur with a stammer.
—Sir Herbert Tree had not quite that exuberant joviality which is necessary to recommend a

modern audience to Falstaff's grossness. His mutilation of Hotspur's dead body might surely have been omitted from the last act. *Athenæum*
—Surely, it may be taken for granted that if Shakespeare had intended his Hotspur to stammer aggressively in the delivery of blank verse he would have given some more definite instruction to that effect. EVELINE GODLEY *Annual Register*

Nov 16. Frank Cellier as Shylock and Florence Glossop-Harris as Portia in Shakespeare's **The Merchant of Venice** at Princes. Cellier was at his best in the trial scene. Glossop-Harris was at her best in the scenes at Belmont.

Nov 19. Elsie Janis in Arthur Wimperis's **The Passing Show** at His Majesty's. Music by Herman Finck. Clara Beck sang "I'll Make a Man of You", one of the most popular recruiting songs of World War 1.

Nov 20. Arthur Williams in H J Byron's **Our Boys** at Vaudeville. Byron's comedy returned to the theatre where it had had its premiere in 1875. It was a mistake to try and modernise it.

Nov 25. Thomas Hardy's **The Dynasts** directed by Harley Granville Barker at Kingsway. Written 1904 – 1908. Epic drama of the war with Napoleon in three parts: *1)* Trafalgar. *2)* The Peninsula. *3)* Waterloo. The production in 19 acts and 130 scenes echoed "the nation's hopes for success and fears of defeat." Henry Ainley was The Reader.
—It is the most highly imaginative production ever seen on the English stage and must make an overwhelming appeal to all but the most unimaginative. *Era*

Nov 28. Godfrey Tearle, Allan Aynesworth and Ellis Jeffreys in Major W P Drury and Major Leo Trevor's **The Flag Lieutenant** directed by E Lyall Swete at Haymarket. Love and duty in war: naval hero refuses to split on his pal.

Dec 10. Dennis Eadie and Isobel Elsom in J E Harold Terry and Lechmere Worrall's **The Man Who Stayed Home** directed by Eille Norwood at Royalty. Farce. German spies lie low in an East Coast boarding house. Transferred to Apollo.
—Schoolboy adjectives such as "ripping" and "topping" and "jolly good" appear to be the most applicable. *Illustrated London News*

Hilda Moore and Gerald Du Maurier in Raffles

Dec 23. Gerald du Maurier in a revival of E W Hornung and Eugene Presbrey's **Raffles** at Wyndham's.

Dec 24. Owen Nares as David in an adaptation of Charles Dickens's **David Copperfield** at His Majesty's. Herbert Beerbohm Tree was moving as Peggotty but, surprisingly, not amusing as Micawber.

Dec 25. Frank Benson in Shakespeare's **Henry V** at Shaftesbury. A patriotic call to arms.

1915

Jan 2. Fred Terry and Julia Neilson in **Mistress Wilful** at Strand. Adaptation of Frank Barrett's novel by Ernest Hendrie. Romantic melodrama. Mistress Wilful is the illegitimate daughter of King Charles II.
—Mr Fred Terry, as the husband, patient under exasperation, fierce in passion, gives us, as often, an idea how fine a romantic actor he might be with worthy material. *Illustrated London News*

Jan 16. Carlo Liten, the Belgian tragedian, and M G de Warfaaz in Emile Verhaeran's **Le Cloitre** at Kingsway. Tragedy in a monastery: a fanatical monk is driven mad by remorse for the murder he committed.
—It is a powerful but gloomy play, full of intense sincerity, written in beautiful blank verse and contains great nobility of thought. *Era*

Jan 25. Jean Francois Fonçon's **La Kommandatur** at Criterion. Belgian play dealing with German occupation. The heroine stabs an odious Hun in the heart.

Feb 11. H B Irving and Fay Davis in Horace Annsley Vachell's **Searchlights** at Savoy. War changes people. Irving played a cold and melancholy father who became a nice old man. His illegitimate son (Reginald Owen), a wastrel, became a hero at Mons. The War also changed attitudes to illegitimacy.
—Although it enjoyed a considerable run – no doubt due to the clever impersonation of Mr H B Irving as the principal character, it was not a good play, being distinctly the product of a novelist rather than a dramatist. *Annual Register 1915*

Mar 23. O B Clarence and Helene Haye in J M Barrie's **The New Word** at Duke of York's. Barrie's sentimental tribute to British reserve at times of emotional crisis. A mother's only son goes off to war. She says she wouldn't have had one son stay at home, though she had had a dozen boys. Acted in a double-bill with **Rosy Rapture, The Pride of the Beauty Chorus** with Gaby Deslys. Lyrics by F W Mark. Music by Hermann Darewski and Jerome D Kern. Deslys was a very energetic dancer and exhausting to watch.

Apr 3. Edyth Olive and Aimée de Burgh in Vane Sutton-Vane's **The Blow** at Little. A mother discovers that committing murder produces social problems if your daughter is about to be married.

Apr 12. Réjane in Gaston Leroux and Lucien Camille's **Alsace** at Court. Alsatian marries a German girl: a crude patriotic war melodrama in which all the French were very nice and all the Germans were perfectly beastly.
—What the authors fail to achieve in the way of subtlety and finesse the art of Réjane provides. *Illustrated London News*

Apr 14. George Alexander, Nina Boucicault, Madge Titheradge and Owen Nares in Hartley Manners's **Panorama of Youth** at St James's. Amatory difficulties. "It uses all the familiar shop-soiled phrases," said *The Times*. "Indeed his dialogue throughout is sheer stereotype... you know you're not really in England but in Stageland."

Apr 20. Henry Ainley, Sydney Fairbrother and Godfrey Tearle in Horace Annesley Vachell's **Quinney's** directed by E Lyall Swete at Haymarket. Quinney, the art dealer, was one of Ainley's most flamboyant character studies.
—Humour, tender, dignity, pathos, a fine sense of "character" and an equally fine presence, have combined to put Henry Ainley in the very front rank of his profession. *Sketch*

Apr 24. Winifred Barnes and Donald Calthrop in Paul Rubens's musical **Betty** directed by Edward Royce at Daly's. Book by Frederick Lonsdale and Gladys Unger. Earl marries a kitchen maid to spite his father and then refuses to consummate the marriage.

Apr 28. George Grossmith and Julia James in **Tonight's the Night** at Gaiety. Musical comedy. Book by Fred Thompson. Music by Paul Rubens. Lyrics by Rubens and Percy Greenbank. Hit songs: "Please Don't Flirt with Me" and "Take Me Up To Town Tonight."

Apr 29. Edyth Goodall and Arthur Wontner in Elmer Reizenstein's **On Trial**

1915 World Premieres
Moscow
Leonid Andreyev's *He Who Gets Slapped*

Births
Arthur Miller, American playwright
Frank Sinatra, American singer

Deaths
James Elroy Flecker (*b.*1884), British playwright
Lewis Waller (*b.*1860), British actor

Notes
Sarah Bernhardt had her right leg amputated

History
—Gallipoli campaign
—Sinking of *Lusitania*
—Nurse Cavell executed
—Ku Klux Klan reborn
—Einstein propounded theory of relativity
—Premiere of D W Griffiths's film, *Birth of A Nation*

directed by Felix Edwardes at Lyric. American melodrama. The courtroom scenes were interspersed with flashbacks. Goodall played two roles: the victim and the wife of the defendant.

May 3. Réjane in Victorien Sardou's **Madame Sans Gene** at New. Réjane's greatest role. Transferred to Court. *Era* thought that her "performance had gained, if it were possible, in power, in humour, in pathos."

May 4. Herbert Beerbohm Tree, Arthur Bourchier and Violet Vanbrugh in Pierre Frondaie's **The Right to Kill** (**L'Homme Qui Assassina**) at His Majesty's. Based on novel by Claude Farriere and translated by Gilbert Cannon and Frances Keyzer. The melodrama, set in Constantinople, was not melodramatic enough. "We were not thrilled," said *The Daily Telegraph*. "We were not excited."
—Versatility is one of the greatest of Sir Herbert Tree's many gifts. He is an actor of many parts. He can play the king and the criminal, the lover and the cynic, youth and senility, the sensualist and Don Quixote. *Era*

May 7. Charles Frohman, theatre manager, died in the sinking of the *Lusitania*.

Jun 1. Martin Harvey as Satan in the late Stephen Phillips's **Armageddon** at New. N de Silva played Joan of Arc. Anti-German propaganda in blank verse. A complete failure.
—I don't know Satan really well in a personal sense so I cannot say whether Mr Harvey was a good imitation of him. But I gather the master of hell wears fewer clothes than his subordinates and talks enormously louder than anybody else. E V LUCAS *Punch*

Jun 3. Henry Irving, Holman Clark and Lady Tree in Eden Phillpotts and Macdonald Hastings's **The Angel in the House** directed by Holman Clark at Savoy. Absurd egoist persuades a family to do his bidding. Irving, tongue in cheek, played the part with unflinching gravity.

Jun 8. Marie Löhr in Edward Knoblock's **Marie-Odile** directed by Herbert Beerbohm Tree at His Majesty's. Wartime story. A novice in a convent is so innocent that she thinks the handsome corporal is Saint Michael and the baby that follows is a miracle. The critics wondered where on earth you could find such an innocent girl.
—[Marie Löhr] made an adorable figure in her novice habit, and even more to the mundane eye when she took off her veil. *The Times*

Jun 9. Gerald du Maurier, Lewis Waller and Madge Titheradge in May Martindale's **Gamblers All** at Wyndham's. Titheradge played an inveterate and reckless gambler who gets involved in forgery. Du Maurier played her husband who follows her to the casino and gets arrested in a police raid. Waller played the decent moneylender who sorted everything out. *The Times* reported that a woman in the stalls had been heard to say that it was such a nice play because there wasn't a word in about the War in it. Martindale died on June 18.

Jun 11. Constance Collier, Lilian Braithwaite and Arthur Bourchier in Keble Howard's **The Green Flag** at Vaudeville. A nice woman (Braithwaite) triumphs over a malicious woman (Collier). No sex is actually going on behind the closed bedroom door.

Jun 18. Morris Harvey, Iris Hoey, Gaby Deslysia and Leon Morton in Harry Grattan's **More** at Ambassadors. Revue.

Aug 24. Fred Emney, Tom Stuart and Louise Tinsley in **Shell Out** directed by Robert Marks at Comedy. Revue. Book by Albert de Courville and Wal Pink. Music by Herman Darewski. Emney was very funny as an old lady climbing a stile.

Aug 28. William Taylor in Willard Mack's **Kick-In** directed by Noel Arnold at Vaudeville. Brutal policeman is foiled by kindly criminals. The ensemble work of the American cast was much praised. Kick-in was American slang for shake hands.

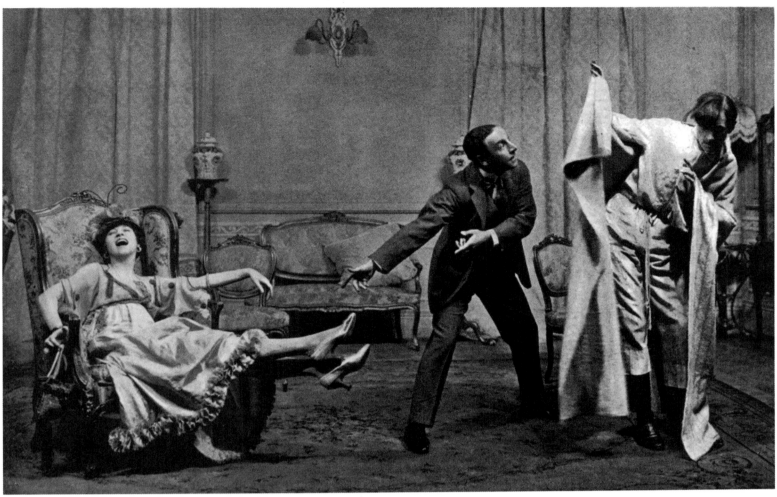

Ruby Miller, George Desmond and Ernest Thesiger in A Little Bit of Fluff

Sep 1. George Alexander and Irene Vanbrugh in Arthur Wing Pinero's **The Big Drum** directed by Arthur Wing Pinero at St James's. Unsuccessful author sells 25,000 copies of his novel. His fiancée bought them all.

Sep 4. George du Maurier and Marie Löhr in George Pleydell's **The Ware Case** at Wyndham's. Murderer, on trial, escapes justice. He confesses his crime to his wife and then takes poison – the only course open to a gentleman.
—Marie Löhr forces the hysterical note too much so that when the worst crisis comes, she has no reserves of emotional distress to produce. *Athenæum*

Sep 30. Arthur Chesney, Mary Jerrold, Robert Shaw and Margaret Halstan in W Strange Hall's **The Stormy Petrel** at Criterion. Farce. An independently minded young lady, having said she doesn't want to marry a middle-aged squire, changes her mind.

Oct 6. Doris Keane and Owen Nares in Edward Sheldon's **Romance** directed by A E Anson at Duke of York's. Young clergyman in love with an opera singer discovers the romance of religion and eroticism. Keane, said A B Walkeley in *The Times*, "has a rich temperament, a real personality and irresistible charm."

Oct 21. Percy Hutchison in Carlyle Moore's **Stop Thief!** directed by Percy Hutchison at New. American crook play. Thief poses as detective. His accomplice poses as a lady's maid.

Oct 23. Lily Elsie and Malcolm Cherry in Louis N Parker's **Mavoureen** at His Majesty's. Sentimental history. Sweet Irish girl runs away from home, disguised as a young man, and lands a job on the London stage and ends up at the court of King Charles II.
—When a nation is fighting for its existence it is well that it should be reminded of its noblest traditions. *Punch*
—Certainly, Lily Elsie was charming, especially when she showed a leg or rather legs, and so shapely were they that some may cherish a grudge against a convention that allows her to show them thus publicly only on the stage. *Athenæum*

Oct 27. George Desmond and Ernest Thesiger in Walter W Ellis's **A Little Bit of Fluff** directed by Walter W Ellis at Criterion. Farce. 1,241 performances. Thesiger never missed a performance.

—To relieve the monotony of saying the same things night after night, one is tempted to introduce new business and new "gags" and the inevitable result is that an actor begins to play the part to amuse himself instead of the audience. At the end of our long run the management paid me the compliment of saying that I never varied my performance by a hair's breadth, but the effort nearly drove me mad. ERNEST THESIGER *Practically True*

Nov 2. Phyllis Dare, Godfrey Tearle and W H Berry in **Tina** at Adelphi. Musical comedy. Book, music and lyrics by Paul A Rubens. Book by Harry Graham. Music by Haydn Wood. Lyrics by Percy Greenback. The daughter of a cocoa manufacturer falls in love with a violin player who is, naturally, a bankrupt duke in disguise. Berry played the girl's father.

Nov 30. Bert Coote and Terry Twins in Harry Grattan's revue **Samples!** at Vaudeville.

Dec 6. Matheson Lang as Shylock and Hutin Britton as Portia in Shakespeare's **The Merchant of Venice** at St James's Transferred to Strand.
—Mr Lang's Shylock is picturesque rather than majestic... a splendid voice gives poignancy to his appeals; but there are few reserves about this Jew; he is a romantic not tragic figure. *Illustrated London News*

Dec 9. Henry Ainley and Clare Greet in Horace Annesley Vachell's **Who is He?** at Queen's. An eccentric was mistaken for a criminal. The story was very freely adapted from Mrs Belloc Lowndes's novel, *The Lodger*.

Dec 29. O B Clarence and Mercia Cameron in **The Starlight Express** at Kingsway. Adaptation from Algernon Blackwood's novel, *A Prisoner in Fairyland*. Music by Sir Edward Elgar. A superabundance of didactic talk.

1916

Jan 6. George Alexander and Genevieve Ward in Clifford Mills's **The Basker** at St James's. The basker is an indolent duke who wants to get rid of all his money and of all his responsibilities.
—Every playgoer capable of distinguishing the art of acting from parlour game must be

1916 World Premieres
Paris
Paul Claudel's *Partage du Midi* (private performance)
Rome
Luigi Chiarelli's *The Mask and the Face*
New York
Harold Brighouse's *Hobson's Choice*

Births
Peter Weiss, Czech playwright, director, novelist, painter

Deaths
Janet Achurch (*b.*1864), British actor
Henry James (*b.*1843), American novelist, playwright

Notes
—Government imposed entertainment tax
—Jazz swept US
—Thomas Beecham wartime season began at Covent Garden

History
—Battle of the Somme
—Battle of Jutland
—Easter Rebellion in Dublin
—Italy joined war against Germany
—Dada movement founded in Zurich
—Rasputin murdered
—Sir Roger Casement executed
—Premiere of D W Griffith's film, *Intolerance*

delighted to welcome Miss Genevieve Ward back to the stage. She has not lost a jot of her authority, of her feeling for style, of her general air of high intelligence. *The Times.*

Jan 24. Terry Twins (Charles and Frank) in Harry Grattan's revue **Samples** at Vaudeville.

Jan 29. Basil Gill and Madge Titheradge in George Potter's **Tiger's Cub** directed by H A Saintsbury at Garrick. Romance in Alaska. Transferred to Queen's.

Feb 8. Irene Vanbrugh, Lillah McCarthy and Nina Sevening in Somerset Maugham's **Caroline** directed by Dion Boucicault at New. Society comedy on the theme that the things we yearn for lose their fascination once they are within reach. Grass widow finds that when she really is a widow, the last thing she and her lover want to do is to get married. During the final rehearsals Maugham discovered that the last act was not as funny as he had imagined it and rewrote it in 24 hours.
—Thanks to the consummate art of Miss Irene Vanbrugh you forget that Caroline is a puppet and revel in every phase of her frivolity. *Illustrated London News*
—The dialogue of *Caroline* is by far the best that he [Maugham] has written; in fact, by far

the best that has been heard on the London stage since the days of Wilde's plays. *The Annual Register 1916*

Mar 11. Rosalie Toller and Malcolm Cherry in **Kultur at Home** by Rudolf Besier and Sybil Spottiswoode at Court. English girl and Prussian officer find they are incompatible.

Mar 16. Hilda Trevelyan and Gerald du Maurier in J M Barrie's **A Kiss for Cinderella** at Wyndham's. Tweeny-maid dreams she is Cinders and a policeman is her Prince.
—It is quaint and funny, and dear and tender and wistful in the way which only Barrie can be all these things. It may not be the best Barrie but it is the Barrie that touches the heart and disarms criticism. *Era*

Mar 22. H B Irving in Walter Hackett's **The Barton Mystery** at Savoy. The murder mystery was half genuine and half bluff and it combined farce and melodrama. Irving played a clairvoyant who was a charlatan and enjoyed gulling the gulls.

Mar 24. Sybil Thorndike in **Everyman** directed by Ben Greet at Old Vic. Greet played the Messenger and Doctor. Thorndike's sincerity and earnestness made her performance both moving and impressive.

Mar 30. Arthur Bourchier as a highwayman and Miriam Lewes as Orange Moll in John Huntly McCarthy's **Stand and Deliver** at His Majesty's. Romantic melodrama. Bourchier was not a natural for the bold, reckless, dashing hero.

Apr 1. Molly McIntyre in Catherine Chisholm Cushing's **Kitty Mackay** at Queen's. American Cinderella story set in a pseudo-1845 Scotland with lots of pseudo-Scottish characters in kilts, drinking whisky and quoting from the Bible and Robbie Burns. American actress McIntyre, repeating her Broadway success, was sweet and winning. Jean Cadell played a dour matron.

Apr 4. Dennis Eadie in Louis N Parker's **Disraeli**, directed by Louis N Parker at Royalty. Disraeli purchases shares in the Suez Canal. Parker excused his inventions, saying, "The Suez Canal was purchased without any romantic or sentimental frills, but stocks and shares are dull stuff unless they be gilt-edged."
—Dennis Eadie's make-up is wonderful and he is able to lend his Disraeli's superficial charm and attractiveness. Treat the play as spectacle and the man as such and you will enjoy the setting and admire the actor's tour de force. *Illustrated London News*

Joe Nightingale, Edyth Goodall, Hilda Davies, Lydia Bilbrooke and Norman McKinnel in **Hobson's Choice**

Apr 10. Marie Löhr, A E Matthews and Lady Tree in James Forbes's **The Show Shop** at Globe. American farce: life in the theatre backstage with Matthews as a stupid amateur actor and Tree going way over the top as a stage-struck mama who is determined her daughter shall act. The English cast sounded very English.

Apr 19. The Bing Boys Are Here at Alhambra. Revue. Music by Nat D Ayer and lyrics by Clifford Grey. George Robey and Violet Lorraine sang "If You Were the Only Girl in the World".

Apr 23. Shakespeare's Tercentenary performance took place at Stratford-upon-Avon. Moscow Arts Theatre "sends greetings to great country of great Shakespeare."

Apr 23. Henry Ainley as Antony, H B Irving as Cassius and F R Benson as Caesar in Shakespeare's **Julius Caesar** at Drury Lane. Benson, still covered in blood, was knighted by King George V in the royal box during the interval. Since there was no sword available, an aide had to dash to a shop to get one.

May 5. A Shakespeare Pageant. A matinee at Drury Lane. The pageant began at 1.30 and finished just after 7.00. Practically the whole profession took part, including Ellen Terry as Portia, Charles Hawtrey as Falstaff and Mary Anderson as Hermione. A wreath was laid at the foot of a pedestal on which was mounted a bust of Shakespeare.

May 8. Martin Harvey in Shakespeare's **Hamlet** at His Majesty's. In his curtain-call speech Martin Harvey made reference to our 'darling' Shakespeare.
—The epithet was not quite so silly as you might think, for he had been playing a darling Hamlet. A darling Hamlet, you understand is a Hamlet all favour and prettiness; a Hamlet who turns all his vowels into musical notes, and drops his consonants whenever he can because they interrupt the melody; a Hamlet who returns to England in a perfect duck of a bonnet; a Hamlet who immensely enjoys his own death-scene, turning up his eyes ecstatically while the organ swells louder and louder as in the last act of Faust. A B WALKLEY *The Times*

May 13. José Collins in **Happy Days** at Daly's. Musical comedy. Book by Seymour Hicks. Music by Sidney Jones. Music and Lyrics by Paul Rubens. Lyrics by Adrian Ross. A royal marriage begins with quarrels and ends with love.
—Miss José Collins who with her attractive voice and picturesque personality proves herself a very real acquisition to our musical comedy stage. *Illustrated London News*.

May 29. Renée Kelly in Jean Webster's **Daddy Long Legs** directed by Violet Melnotte at Duke of York's. Orphan rejects the young man she loves thinking she should marry her guardian who had paid for her education. She does not know that her guardian and the young man are the same person. Kelly, vivacious, winsome and charming, had a great success.

May 30. Henry Ainley in Horace Annesley Vachell's **Fishpingle** directed by E Lyall Swete at Haymarket. Fishpingle, the family butler, turns out to be the squire's illegitimate half-brother.

Jun 5. Alice Delysia, Dorothy Minto, Leon Morton and Morris Harvey in **Pell Mell** directed by Frank Collins at Ambassadors. Revue. Minton sang "What did Cleopatra do to make Mark Antony laugh." High spot: Fragonard impression acted in dumb show.

Chu Chin Chow, musical tale of the East: Pantomimic banality

Jun 22. Norman McKinnel as Hobson, Edyth Goodall as Maggie Hobson and Joe Nightingale as Willie Mossop in Harold Brighouse's **Hobson's Choice** at Apollo. The best-loved comedy of the Manchester school of sentimental realism celebrated Victorian middle-class values, such as hard work and thrift. Initially, it was turned down by all the London theatre managers, who had a prejudice against regional writers and it didn't arrive in the West End until after its highly successful premiere in New York in 1915. The action is set in Salford in the 1880s, when Maggie, already an old maid at thirty, is working in her father's shoe shop. She decides that if she is not to remain on the shelf for the rest of her life she will have to marry her father's bootmaker. Maggie was modelled on Brighouse's sister and the shop was based on the shop his mother had taken him as a boy to get his boots. The censor only allowed the wedding night scene at the end of Act III so long as no member of the public complained. Transferred to Prince of Wales. 228 performances.
—To us these people speak our same language in a different manner. They brace us up like a touch of the north-west wind. Their spontaneous humour, without a breath of artifice or aforethought, sounds new and fresh. Compared with the usual London article it is like the country cheek blooming next to paint and powder. *The Times*
—Not for a long time have we seen a play so refreshing in qualities, so full of human nature and commonsense and humour told so simply and yet so brilliantly. *Era*

Jun 29. Lee White, Beatrice Lillie and Betty in **Some (more samples!)**. Revue. Music by Jas W Tate. Betty was a child actress.

Aug 24. W H Berry and Nellie Taylor in **High Jinks** at Adelphi. Musical comedy. Book by Frederick Lonsdale. Music by Paul A Rubens, Jerome Kern and James W Tate. Lyrics by Percy Greenback, Clifford Grey and Clifford Harris and Valentine. High Jinks was the name of a perfume. "The music," said *The Illustrated London News*, "is worthy of the perfume – it is insidious, heady, exhilarating." Berry and Violet Blythe had a big hit singing "What is Life Without Love."

Aug 31. Oscar Asche and Lily Brayton in **Chu Chin Chow** written and directed by Oscar Asche at Her Majesty's. Music by Frederick Norton. Based on Ali Baba and The 40 Thieves, it was a triumph for the designer and producer. The actors played a supporting role to the lavish Oriental picturesqueness. Part musical, part farce, part pantomime and shaped like a revue, it was the perfect show for troops on leave. Asche had an agreement with the management that if *Chu Chin Chow* played to £50,000 in twenty weeks they would pay him over and above his author's royalty 20% of the takings in excess of £1,500. They never thought it would happen. The play became an institution and ran for 2,238 performances, longer than the war. Asche earned £200,000 in royalties. Herbert Beerbohm Tree thought *Chu Chin Cow* was "scented hogwash."
—Never have we felt more keenly and exasperatingly the banalities of mere staging and cheap wit. *Athenæum*

Sep 4. Madge Lessing and H V Esmond in Pierre Veber's **The Girl from Ciro's** adapted by Jose C Levy at Garrick. French farce set in the *demi-monde* of Paris.

Sep 4. Gerald du Maurier, Nina de Boucicault and Rosalie Toller in Dion Clayton Calthrop's **The Old Country** at Wyndham's. American millionaire comes to England to put things right for his mother. She had been ostracized by the village when she was unmarried and pregnant. She thinks the village was right to do so. "We're history," says the village, "You're trash." The millionaire returns to the US.

Sep 5. Marie Löhr, Irene Vanbrugh, Allan Aynesworth and Dion Boucicault in A E Thomas's **Her Husband's Wife** directed by Dion Boucicault at New. American comedy. Hypochondriac wife, convinced she is going to die, determines to find a new wife for her husband.

Sep 6. Gladys Cooper, Malcolm Cherry and Weedon Grossmith in Paul Dickey and Charles Goodheart's **Misleading Lady** directed by Felix Edwardes at Playhouse. American comedy fashioned in *The Taming of the Shrew* manner with the hero tying his wife up by a dog's chain and she retaliating by breaking his head with a telephone. Grossmith played an escaped lunatic who thinks he is Napoleon. *The Annual Register* thought he gave "a truly wonderful performance, comic and pathetic by turn."

Sep 7. H B Irving and Kate Moffat in J M Barrie's **The Professor's Love Story** directed by E Holman Clark at Savoy. A man in his forties discovers that his pretty secretary is far more attractive and charming than electricity; but thinks he is too old to be loved by her. Premiered in 1894 Barrie had always wanted Irving's father to play the love-sick and absent-minded professor.

Sep 12. Augustus Yorke and Robert Leonard in Montague Glass and Roi Cooper Megrue's **Potash and Pellmutter in Society** directed by Lee Colmer at Queen's. Yorke and Leonard were back with more American-Jewish wit.

Sep 19. George Grossmith and Leslie Henson in **Theodore and Co** at Gaiety. Musical comedy. Book by H M Harwood and George Grossmith. Music by Ivor Novello and Jerome Kern. Lyrics by Adrian Ross and Clifford Grey. Theodore and Co are all gamblers. Henson was a huge success.

Oct 1. H V Esmond, Ellis Jeffreys and Dawson Millward in Walter Hackett and Horace Annesley Vachell's **Mr Jubilee Drax** at Haymarket. Spoof detective story.

Oct 18. Dennis Eadie, Marie Löhr and Mary Jerrold in Edward Knoblock's **Home on Leave** at Royalty. A woman is involved with three men: her husband (a drug-addict), her lover (a cad) and her ex-sweetheart (a sweetie back from the frontline.)

Nov 6. Nelson Keys, Arthur Playfair and Stanley Logan in **Vanity Fair** directed by J A E Malone at Palace. Revue. Book by Arthur Wimperis. Music by Herman Finck. High spots were two exquisite tableaux: *The Romance of the Dragon Fly* and *The White City*. "They are," said *Play Pictorial*, "irresistible in their appeal to a refined and cultivated taste."

Nov 23. The St Martin's theatre opened with George Graves and Gertie Millar at Houp la! Musical comedy. Book by Fred Thompson. Book and lyrics by Hugh E Wright. Music by Nat D Ayer and Howard Talbot. Lyrics by Percy Greenback. Millar was an equestrian in a circus. Graves was her business manager. The show's two big hits were Millar singing "The Fool of the Family" and Madeleine Choiseule singing "L'Amour est bon."

Dec 6. Gerald du Maurier and Mabel Russell in Gladys Unger and A Neil Lyons's **London Pride** at Wyndham's. Cockney in the front line exchanges his identity with a soldier who was killed so that he can come home and see his girl.

1917

Jan 25. George Alexander in Louis N Parker's **The Aristocrat** at St James's. French aristocrats being guillotined are always good for the English box-office.
—[George Alexander] brings out the pathos and single-mindedness of the character with a depth of sincerity that could not be bettered. *Era*

Feb 1. Charles Hawtrey and Winifred Barnes in Monckton Hoffe's **Anthony in Wonderland** at Prince of Wales's. Anthony sees a cowboy film and then has a dream in which he is transplanted to the Wild West. The dream was played for typical Hawtrey comedy. His grief when he wakes to find it all been a dream was unexpectedly real and the sincerity and intensity of his acting took audiences completely by surprise. Hoffe took Hawtrey to court for engaging Barnes without his approval.

Feb 1. George Robey and Daphne Pollard in **Zig Zag** at New Hippodrome. Revue. Pollard, an American comedienne, did a weird dance on an electric carpet. Robey was very funny mistaking a theatre box for his bedroom. The finale, with zig-zagging ladders all in black, white and gold, was striking.

Feb 10. José Collins and Arthur Wontner in **The Maid of the Mountains** at Daly's directed by Robert Evett. Musical. Book by Frederick Lonsdale. Lyrics by Harry Graham. Music by Harold Fraser-Simson. The militia arrest the lover of a brigand and then promise to release her if she betrays him. The musical was a spectacular wartime success and hailed as the most brilliant, tasteful show of its kind yet seen under George Edwardes' management. Songs included "Love Will Find A Way", "Bachelor Gay", and "Live for Today". Collins became a big star. 1,353 performances.

Feb 14. Alfred Paumier and Annie Saker in Walter Howard's **Seven Day's Leave** directed by Walter and Frederick Melville at Lyceum. Spy story. The heroine swims to a buoy a mile off shore to lure a German submarine to its destruction. One of the most popular productions of the war, it played for 711 performances.
—Radiates honest, undisguised sentiment intersected by a strong thread of patriotism and showing here and there a skilful woven note of religious fervour. *Era*

Feb 24. Joseph Coyne and Violet Loraine in **The Bing Girls Are There** at Alhambra. Revue. Loraine sang "Let the Great Big World Keep Turning."

Mar 3. Marie Löhr and Dennis Eadie in Michael Morton and D Niccodemi's **Remnant** directed by Wilfred Eaton at Royalty. Street waif brings happiness to one and all.
—Miss Löhr's chief gift is to be sweet. It is the chief gift of many women, bless them, off as well as on stage, but Miss Lohr out sugars them all. *The Times*

Mar 14. Madge Titheradge, Norman McKinnel, Lilian Braithwaite and George Tully in Harold Terry's **General Post** directed by Percy Hutchison at Haymarket. The war removes social barriers. A tailor is a brigadier, whilst his lordship is only a private. "A brilliant and witty comedy," said *The Daily Mail*. "Amusing, dramatic, charming, exciting," said *The Daily Express*.

Mar 16. Lillah McCarthy and George Elton in Ashley Duke's adaptation of Anatole France's **The Comedy of A Man Who Married a Dumb Wife** directed by C B Williams at Ambassadors. Husband takes his dumb wife to the doctors. The operation

Arthur Wontner and José Collins in The Maid of the Mountains

1917 World Premieres
Milan
  Luigi Pirandello's *Right You Are (If You Think You Are)*
Munich
  Georg Kaiser's *From Morn to Midnight.*
New York
  Eugene O'Neill's *The Long Voyage Home*
Atlantic City
  Somerset Maugham's *Our Betters*

Births
John Whiting, British playwright

Deaths
Herbert Beerbohm Tree (*b.*1853), British actor-manager

Notes
—Premiere of *Parade* in Paris. Choreography by Léonide Massine. Libretto by Jean Cocteau. Music by Erik Satie. The dancers performed in the street, desperate to attract audiences into the theatre.

History
—US joined war against Germany
—October Revolution in Russia
—Royal family assumed name of Windsor
—US voted in favour of Prohibition
—Mata Hari executed

is so successful that when she comes home she can't stop talking. He begs them to reverse the operation. When he is told they can't, he insists they make him deaf.

Mar 17. Reginald Bach in Eugène Brieux's **Damaged Goods** (*Les Avaries*) translated by John Pollock and directed by J B Fagan at St Martin's. Advertised as The Great Play on the Social Evil. (The evil was venereal disease.) Banned by the Lord Chamberlain, a Society was specially created to perform it.

Mar 24. The revue **Hanky Panky** finally opened after four postponements at New Empire. Book by Hartley Carrick and Worton David. Music by May Darewski. Lyrics by George Arthurs. Phyllis Monkman appeared in a ballet. Phyllis Dare sang in a gondola. Joe Nightingale did male and female impersonations. Robert Hale drilled an awkward squad.

Mar 29. Gaby Deslys and Stanley Lupino in **Suzette** directed by Austen Hurgon at Globe. Musical comedy. Book by Austen Hurgon and George Arthurs. Lyrics by George Arthurs. Music by Max Darewski. The money spent on Deslys's headdresses – some so high as almost to double her height – cost a fortune.
—Mlle Deslys is the same as ever (only more so) in her performance. Her mouth is still as wide and is constantly open; her English is still so broken as to save one the trouble of trying to understand it. And her dancing is still so vigorous, as wild-animal, as exciting as ever. *The Times*

Apr 7. Jean Cadell in J M Barrie's **The Old Lady Shows Her Medals** at New. "I have," wrote Barrie to his adopted son, George Llewellyn Davies, who was at the Front during World War 1, "lost all sense I ever had of war being glorious. It is just unspeakably monstrous to me." A few days later he received a letter informing him that George had been killed. Barrie wrote his one-act war play to raise money for the victims of the war and their families. A lonely, elderly charwoman (Jean Cadell), husbandless and childless, is unable to brag, like other charwomen, about what her menfolk are doing in France. She pretends to have a son at the front, having found his name in a newspaper. The soldier (C H Mulcaster) turns up on leave and is, initially, furious at her deception; but, since he is an orphan, he decides to put her on probation. After a couple of days he allows her to become his surrogate mother. He returns

to the front and is killed. The final image is of the charwoman proudly grieving. The play opened the same week the United States entered the war and was one of Barrie's biggest successes.
—It is the sort of performance which would make the "lasting reputation" of any actress in any other country except the one, where an actress to be really famous has to be elegant and beautiful and "look too sweet for anything". *Tatler*

Apr 26. Lee White, Clay Smith and Beatrice Lillie in Harry Grattan's **Cheep** at Vaudeville. Revue. Songs by Clay Smith, R P Weston and Bert Lee. Lee White wore a three penny dress composed of six copies of a halfpenny evening newspaper, which was gradually torn up by three men. The funniest sketch was a quartet of musicians.

Apr 28. Darragh as Mrs Alving, Basil Sydney as Oswald and Charles Groves as Pastor Manders in Henrik Ibsen's **Ghosts** at Kingsway. The ban was finally lifted; but the actors weren't good enough.

May 5. Phyllis Monkman, Miss Teddie Gerrard, Arthur Playfair, Jack Hulbert and Laura Cowie in **Bubbly** at Comedy. Revue. Book by John Hastings Turner. Music by Philip Braham. One of the high spots was Hulbert and Monkham dancing together, pretending to be in love and saying sweet things to each other, when in fact they were being incredibly rude. When Hulbert went on active service his place was taken by Walter Williams.

May 26. Ida Adams and Eille Norwood in Earl Derr Biggers' **Inside the Lines** directed by Bernard Hishin at Apollo. Spy play set in Gibraltar.

Jun 8. Lewis Sydney, Tom Stuart and Phyllis Bedelle in **Smile** at Garrick. Revue. Book by Albert de Courville and Wal Pink. Music by Frederick Chapelle.

Jun 8. Ethel Irving, O B Clarence and C M Hallard in St John Hankin's adaptation of Eugene Brieux's **The Three Daughters of M. Dupont** at Ambassadors. One daughter is a prostitute. Another daughter is a spinster who has turned to religion. The third daughter has married a man she does not love and who won't give her children. Ethel Irving as the unhappy wife scored the greatest triumph of her career.
—Tornado of acting, the like of which is very seldom seen in an English theatre. *Daily Express*
—Miss Ethel Irving worked up to an outburst of uncontrollable passion that fairly swept the audience off their feet. It was the irresistible appeal of a great artist. *Daily Mail*
—In the third act Miss Ethel Irving literally over-powered the audience. That was no mere acting; it was a woman's heart leaping to her lips – it was life in revolt against the bondage of law. *Sunday Times*

Jun 26. John Galsworthy's **The Foundations** directed by Wilfred Eaton at Royalty. Galsworthy's warning that the nation would return to its bad old ways the moment the war had ended.

Aug 14. Arthur Bourchier as Old Bill in Bruce Bairnsfather and Arthur Eliot's **The Better 'Ole** at Oxford Theatre. Tom Wootwell as Bert. Sinclair Cotter as Alf. Billed as 'a fragment from France in Two Explosions, Seven Splinters and a Gas Attack' the show was based on a popular cartoon character by Bruce Bairnsfather and set in the trenches of France. Old Bill, having destroyed a bridge, is arrested for disobedience and faces the firing squad for carrying incriminating papers. Instead of being shot, he is awarded the Croix de Guerre.
—In the depths of his nature, Old Bill stands equally for peer and peasant, his rough figure idealises the national sentiment, the unostentatious sense of duty, the abnegation of self, which dominates officer and private. He commands the tears of laughter as well as those of pathos.

C M Hallard and Ethel Irving in *Three Daughters of M. Dupont*

He fills us with the milk of human kindness as well as with the meat of human courage.
Play Pictorial

Aug 22. Alice Delysia and Leon Morton in **Carminetta** at Prince of Wales. Musical comedy. Book by Andre Barde and C A Carpentier adapted by Monckton Hope. Music by Emile Lessailly. The heroine was the daughter of Carmen and Don Jose. Delysia disguised as a British officer had the most popular number with a refrain: "Oh, bless you, damn you, Cliquot, you make the world go round." Transferred to Princes.

Aug 25. Iris Hoey and Dennis Eadie in F Tennyson Jesse and H M Harwood's **Billeted** directed by Wilfred Eaton at Royalty. Grass widow sends herself a telegram, saying her soldier husband has been killed in the war, only for him to return home on leave.

Sep 4. Ellis Jeffreys in Henry Arthur Jones's **The Pacifists** directed by Henry Arthur Jones at St James's. Jones's parable was dedicated to "the tribe of Wordsters, Pedants, Fanatics and Impossibilists who so rabidly pursued an ignoble peace that helped to provoke a disastrous war and are still seeking to bring about the tragedy of a delusive and abortive peace."

Sep 6. Joseph Coyne, Winifred Barnes and Stanley Lupino in Jose Levey's musical **Arlette** at Shaftesbury. English Book by Austen Gurgon and George Arthur. Music by Jane Vieu, Guy le Feuvre and Ivor Novello. Impecunious prince contemplates marrying an American heiress but decides to give up the throne and marry a commoner. Novello wrote the catchy number "Didn't Know The Way To."

Sep 14. W H Berry in **The Boy** at Adelphi. Musical based on Arthur Wing Pinero's *The Magistrate*. Book by Fred Thompson. Music by Lionel Monckton and Howard Talbot. Lyrics by Adrian Ross and Percy Greenback. Berry played the magistrate. Donald Calthrop played the step-son who leads him astray.

Oct 10. Charles Hawtrey, Ellis Jeffreys and Mary Jerrold in C Haddon Chambers's **The Saving Grace** directed by Charles Hawtrey at Garrick. The saving grace of the hero, an egotistical, roguish waster, was his humour. Noël Coward was cast as a silly ass.

Oct 16. Mrs Patrick Campbell in Bayard Veiller's **The 13th Chair** directed by Albert de Courville at Duke of York's. 12 people at a New York séance are investigating a murder when one of their number is murdered. Campbell played the medium with a French accent.
—Not for long have we had such a genuinely sensational drama, or one more cleverly constructed, the spectators remaining throughout on tenterhooks of expectancy. *Daily Telegraph*

Oct 16. Gerald du Maurier and Hilda Moore in J M Barrie's **Dear Brutus** at Wyndham's. The fault dear Brutus is not in our stars but in ourselves that we are underlings. A group of people, on midsummer's eve, are given a second chance. They have the opportunity to find out what would have happened, if they had they not taken that "wrong turning" years ago and for which they have blamed the paucity of their lives. John Gielgud said Du Maurier's performance was "a masterpiece of understatement, acted with a mixture of infinite charm and regretful pathos." Arthur Hatherton played Lob.
—Whether *Dear Brutus* is too delicate for the times we live in I do not know, but this I do know – that no play running at the present moment is nearer to the big hearts of the men and women who frequent the crowded amphitheatre of this sad old world. ARKAY *Tatler*

Oct 22. Owen Nares and Renée Kelly in J H Benrimo and Harrison Rhodes's **The Willow Tree** directed by J H Benrimo at Globe. The hero is faced with a choice: love in Japan or duty in England. Dreamy, fragile, soporific, the play was a Japanned version of Pygmalion and Galatea. The actors were required to do more posing than acting.

Nov 3. Percy Hutchison in Byron Ongley and Winchell Smith's **Brewster's Millions** directed by Percy Hutchison at Queen's. There was a great deal of shouting and rushing in and out of innumerable doors. Hutchinson was indefatigable.

Nov 21. Randle Ayrton, Aubrey Smith, Lennox Pawle and Fisher White in Harold Owen's **Loyalty** at St James's. Described as "a new play of present day life" and set between June 1914 and September 1918, it wasn't a play at all but a series of arguments designed to produce patriotic feeling. There was a grim description of atrocities in German POW camps. The pacifists were caricatured to such an extent that it was impossible to take them seriously, thus negating Owen's argument against them.

Nov 26. Russell Thorndike as John, Sybil Thorndike as Constance, Ben Greet as Hubert and Agnes Carter as Prince Arthur in Shakespeare's **King John** directed by G R Foss at Old Vic. London was under bombardment. The line "This England never did nor never shall/Lie at the proud foot of a conqueror" got a roar of approval from the audience. The quotation was put over the proscenium arch for the duration of the War.

Dec 24. Fay Compton in J M Barrie's **Peter Pan** directed by Dion Boucicault at New. E Holman Clark was Captain Hook.

Dec 29. Leslie Henson and Davy Barnaby in **Yes, Uncle** at Prince of Wales. Musical comedy. Book by Austen Hurgon and George Arthurs. Music by Nat D Ayer. Lyrics by Clifford Grey. Hit song: "Would You Believe It". 626 performances.
—Mr Henson is the life and soul of the piece, the arch-reveller in its revels, resourceful, chameleon-like, bubbling over with ideas and humour. *Illustrated London News*
—With a comedian such as Mr Leslie Henson in the cast it may safely be assumed that ample scope will be slowed for the exercise of his particular bent of humour, irrespective of its absolute relevance to the plot. B W FINDON *Play Pictorial*

1918

Jan 7. Ben Greet and Sybil Thorndike as Sir Peter and Lady Teazle in Richard Brinsley Sheridan's **The School for Scandal** directed by G R Foss at Old Vic.

Jan 14. Ben Greet as Malvolio and Sybil Thorndike as Viola in Shakespeare's **Twelfth Night** directed by G R Foss at Old Vic. *Era* said Greet was droll and Thorndike was "charmingly dramatic and winsomely appealing."

Jan 21. Lillah McCarthy in Bernard Shaw's **Annajanska, The Bolshevik Empress** at London Coliseum. His "revolutionary romancelet," written barely a month after the Bolshevik revolution, was performed as a variety turn between a ballet and a music hall act with a beautiful white horse and highly trained dogs. Annajanska comes to save the revolution, not the royal family. She says she wants anything that will make the world less like a prison and more like a circus. Shaw said the play was a chance for a favourite actress to make a dazzling impression.

Jan 26. Marie Löhr in Somerset Maugham's **Love in a Cottage** directed by Allan Aynesworth at Globe. The action was set in a hotel on Lake Como. Löhr played a rich woman who dressed up as Pompadour for a fancy dress ball. She had to learn how

1918 World Premieres
Rome
  Luigi Pirandello's *The Rules of the Game*
Dusseldorf
  Georg Kaiser's *Gas*
New York
  Winchell Smith and Frank Bacon's *Lightnin'*
  Eugene O'Neill's *Moon of the Caribbes*

Births
Ingrid Bergman, Swedish actor
Leonard Bernstein, American composer
Alan Jay Lerner, American lyricist

Deaths
George Alexander (*b.*1858), British actor-manager
Edmond Rostand (*b.*1868), French playwright
Frank Wedekind (*b.*1864), German playwright

History
—Murder of the Russian Imperial family
—World War I ended
—House of Commons voted to admit women as MPs
—Spanish Flu killed more people than the war

(D'Annunzio's *La Citta Morte*) translated by Arthur Symons and directed by W G Fay at Court. The translator and the actors were defeated by the text.
—The horror of the part possessed Mr Farquharson so thoroughly as to twist him into the most ungainly postures. *The Times*

Feb 27. Ellen Terry celebrated her 70th birthday by acting the trial scene from Shakespeare's **The Merchant of Venice** at the Coliseum. Bernhardt sent her best wishes.

Mar 4. Sybil Thorndike as Imogen in Shakespeare's **Cymbeline** directed by G R Foss at Old Vic.

Mar 11. **Romance** reached 1,000 performances.

Mar 30. Arthur Wontner and Madge Titheradge in Austin Page's **By Pigeon Post** directed by Arthur Hardy at Garrick. War melodrama. German spies are wearing French uniforms.

Apr 8. Irene Vanbrugh in A A Milne's **Belinda** at New. Husband returns to the wife he left twenty years earlier to discover that he had fathered a daughter.

Apr 10. C Aubrey Smith, Kyrle Bellew and Sam Livesey in Eugene Walter's **The Knife** at Comedy. American medical ethics melodrama: can a man of science ever be justified in experimenting for the good of humanity on the body of the most terrible criminal? Smith was the vivisector. Livesey was the villain. Transferred to Queen's.

Apr 11. Gladys Cooper went into management at The Playhouse and appeared with Charles Hawtrey, Ellis Jeffreys and Stanley Logan in Fred Jackson's **The Naughty Wife** directed by Charles Hawtrey and Gilbert Miller. Apparently complacent husband helps his wife and her lover to elope and even places his Long Island bungalow at their disposal. He then invites the lover's fiancée to join them.
—We now import from America not only American plays of American life and of an American type, but also plays which the Americans have themselves imitated from Paris. We apparently no longer equal to the miserable business of bowdlerising and adapting French farce for London consumption. London, which once supplied New York with English plays, now goes to New York for plays which are not even American. *Saturday Review*

May 15. Beatrice Lillie and Walter Williams in Ronald Jeans and Harry Grattan's revue **Tabs** at Vaudeville. Music by Ivor Novello.
—The name of Harry Grattan should go down to posterity as the revue writer par excellence who understood his art. *Era*

May 30. Iris Hoey, George Tully and Eric Lewis in Douglas Murray's **The Man from Toronto** directed by Charles Hawtrey at Duke of York's. Girl masquerades as a parlour maid in order to get her man.

futile riches were and give them up to marry a nice doctor. "I'm giving up ashes," she declared modestly, "and gaining treasure in Heaven". The play was not published.
—[Marie Löhr] has the one indispensable quality for success on the London stage – a charming prettiness which she uses with excellent effect in the many changes of becoming costume for which her thoughtful author has provided. *Punch*

Feb 5. A E Matthews in James Montgomery's **Nothing But The Truth** directed by Charles Hawtrey at Savoy. Adaptation of Frederick Isham's novel. Popular farce. Hero tells nothing but the truth for 24 hours. His candour is absurd.

Feb 14. Fred Kerr, Helen Ferrers, Ben Webster and Isobel Elsom in Arthur Wing Pinero's **Freaks** at New. An idyll in Suburbia. Are circus freaks any more freakish than the so-called normal people who live in suburbia? Laura Cowie, who played an illiterate contortionist, had the best role. The dwarfs were played by children.
—Amusing, harmless, sentimental, at one moment, sincerely pathetic, at some others rather wordy – in short Pineroish. *The Times*

Feb 16. George Robey and Violet Lorraine in **The Bing Boys on Broadway** at Alhambra. Revue.

Feb 21. Clara Butterworth in **The Lilac Domino** directed by William J Wilson at Empire. Book by Harry B Smith. Music by Charles Cullvier. A triumph for Butterworth.
—Not since *The Chocolate Soldier* has such a tuneful and exquisitely orchestrated score been heard in our midst. *Tatler*

Feb 25. Robert Farquharson, Barbara Everest and Edith Evans in **The Dead City**

Jun 1. Arthur Playfair, Charles Hawtrey and Marie Hemingway in **Tails Up** at

Horton Cooper, Alice Moffat, Matheson Lang and Alfred Brandon in **The Purple Mask**

Comedy. Book by John Hastings. Music by Philip Braham. Lyrics by David Burnaby and Hugh E Wright. Jack Buchanan sang Ivor Novello's "Any Little Thing with Phyllis Monkman."

Jun 20. Rex London in Georges Feydeau's **You Never Know, Y'Know**, an adaptation of *La Puce à l'oreille* by Martin Henry and Hanneford Bennett at Criterion. The French farce was castrated for English audiences. There was no revolving bed.

Jun 21. Marie Löhr and Lottie Venne in R C Carton and Justin Huntley McCarthy's **Nurse Benson** at Globe. Nurse falls in love with wounded soldier who has won the VC. His outraged mama gets her dismissed. High spot was a very funny scene with Fred Kerr and Gregor Elton as two elderly gents: a case of mistaken identity, played up to the hilt, voices raised, and Kerr getting very angry.

Jun 26. Lawrence Leonard in **Soldier Boy!** at Apollo. Musical comedy. Book by Rida Johnson Young and Edgar Wallace. Music by S Rombeau and Frederick Chappelle. Lyrics by Clifton Crawford, Douglas Furber and Wal Pink. Officer in the French army pretended to be a dead soldier so that his blind mother and sister can be spared the news of his death. Naturally, he fell in love with the sister and the soldier wasn't really dead. Winifred Barnes sang "The Lonely Princess".

Jun 28. James Barrie double bill at Wyndham's. Gerald du Maurier, Will West, Helen Morris in **La Politesse**. Two hungry cockney soldiers break into a farmhouse in occupied France but when they discover the couple have been married only a couple of hours and he has to return to the front they opt to sleep in the pig sty. Johnston Forbes-Robertson, Lilian Braithwaite, Faith Celli and Gerald du Maurier in **The Well-Remembered Voice** directed by Joseph Coyne. Father at a séance chats with his son who was killed during the war. Plays about spiritualism were popular during World War 1.

July 8. Annie Saker and Alfred Paumier in Walter Howard's **The Story of the Rosary** at Lyceum. Revival of a popular success. The actors repeated the performances they had given in 1913, but the location and the characters names had been changed because of the War.

Jul 10. Matheson Lang and Alice Moffatt in Armant Charles Latour's **The Purple Mask** directed by Matheon Lang at Lyric. Adaptation of *Le Chevalier au Masque* by Paul Armant and Jean Manouissi. Romantic adventure acted with panache. French conspirator, a dashing royalist, outwits everybody in Paris in 1804. Latour was Lang's pseudonym. Transferred to Princes and then to Scala.

Jul 11. Leon M Lion and Ethel Irving in Marion Bower and Leo M Lion's **Chinese Puzzle** at New. Lion played a mandarin. *The Times* said his performance "will please all amateurs of the grotesque."

Jul 30. Eva Moore, C Aubrey Smith, Joyce Carey and Leslie Howard in Arnold Bennett's **The Title** directed by Wilfred Eaton at Royalty. Husband doesn't want a title, but his wife does. A superannuated theme was rejuvenated by the acting. "The war is changing my ideas," says the husband. "I'm dashed if I don't join the Labour Party and ask Ramsey Macdonald to lunch."
—As a theatrical piece Mr Bennett's play is unpretentious and simplicity itself. He neither startles nor intrigues. He provides good characterisation and pointed dialogue. *Play Pictorial*

Aug 1. Dennis Eadie in Walter Hackett's **The Freedom of the Seas** at Haymarket. Sub-lieutenant outwits the villains who are sending codes to U-Boats. Sydney Valentine, cast as a boozy skipper, had the most fun.

Aug 5. Percy Hutchinson and Ruth Mackay in Clifford Mill's **The Luck of the Navy** at Queen's. The naval hero wrote the key word to his secret orders on the photograph of the woman he loved, only to discover she was a spy.

Aug 28. Alfred Lester and Dorothy Brunton in **Shanghai** at Drury Lane. Musical. Book by Isidore Witmark and William Carey Duncan. Adaptation by Laurie Wylie. Music by Isidore Witmark. Spectacular. The high spot was the dancing of Ivy Shilling.

Aug 29. H V Esmond and Jessie Winter in H V Esmond's **The Law Divine** at Wyndham's. Young soldiers come home on leave to find their father is being unfaithful to their mother. She is to blame. She has been so busy in her war effort that she has neglected him. She decides it is time for a second honeymoon.

Sep 2. Gertrude Elliott in Max Marcin and Charles Guernon's **Eyes of Youth** at St James's. American country girl visualised the future and saw herself as a penniless, faded governess, an opera diva who took to drink and a wife involved in a sordid divorce case. Showcase for Elliott: she was at her best as the diva. The production adopted the flashback technique of cinema.

Sep 18. Doris Keane, Basil Sydney and Athene Seyler in Avery Hopwood's **Roxana** at Lyric. Roxana finds that the husband, she had told everybody was dead, is alive and well in Florida.

Sep 25. Ellis Janis and Owen Nares in **Hullo! America** at Palace. Book by J Hastings Turner. Music by Herman Fink and Clifford Grey. Maurice Chevalier took over from Nares.

Oct 2. Sam Livesey and Gladys Mason in Walter Melville's **The Female Hun** at Lyceum. An unlikely war tale: a general shot his wife dead when he discovered she was spying for the enemy. His butler turned out to be a spy as well.

Oct 21. Ernest Milton and Gwen Richardson in Shakespeare's **Macbeth** at Old Vic. —Macbeth is far more, certainly, than "a Scottish gentleman in difficulties" – a criticism once delivered upon Macready. But he [Ernest Milton] is inclined to turn flesh and blood to abstraction and to underline the poetic passages which should be allowed to fend for themselves. *Era*

Oct 25. The Queen and Princess May attended a centenary matinee at Old Vic and watched scenes from Shakespeare and grand opera.

Oct 27. In defiance of the censor the New Players Society gave a private performance of Oscar Wilde's *Salome* at Court. Maud Allan as Salome, George Relph as Herod. Ernest Milton as Jokanaan. *The Stage* said the play was "little more than a mass of luscious verbiage" and that it was not fit for the stage. Noel Pemberton Billing, MP, attacked Allan's performance, which led to a case of libel, which escalated into a full-blown trial. He argued that one of the reasons why Britain was not winning the war was because of the wholesale corruption of the nation by plays such as Oscar Wilde's *Salome*. He said that the Germans had compiled a dossier of 47,000 people who had been corrupted.
—A very impure work, impure in theme, impure in atmosphere and charged with sickly voluptuousness. *Stage*
—Miss Maud Allan as Salome gave an artistic and delicate performance, although occasionally her delivery became a little monotonous. Graceful and interesting as was her Dance of the Seven Veils it did not represent her art at its highest point. *Era*

Oct 29. Leah Bateman as Viola, Herbert Waring as Malvolio, Arthur Whitby as Sir Toby Belch and Miles Malleson as Sir Andrew Aguecheek in Shakespeare's **Twelfth Night** directed by J B Fagan at Court. *The Morning Post* said it was the best revival of the play in the last 40 years.
It is a pleasure to see Shakespeare so admirably interpreted with such taste, with such regard for the meaning of the text and respect for the heart of the poet's work. *Sunday Times*

Nov 19. Marie Löhr in Edmond Rostand's **L'Aiglon** at Globe. Translation by Louis N Parker. First performance in English.
—Miss Löhr gave a magnificent performance as the weak young Duke. Let it rank among the finest pieces of individual acting seen on the English stage. *Era*

Dec 20. Nelson Keys, Walter Williams, Margaret Bannerman, Gertrude Lawrence and Caleb Porter in **Buzz-Buzz** at Vaudeville. Revue. Book by Arthur Wimperis and Ronald Jeans. Music by Herman Darewski.

Dec 24. Nigel Playfair opened the modernised Lyric, Hammersmith with A A Milne's **Make Believe.** A revue and pantomime for children's. Music by C E Burton. Lyrics by Georges Dorlay.

1919

Jan 14. The Stage Society. Hubert Carter and Margaret Halstan as Lord and Lady Brute in John Vanbrugh's **The Provok'd Wife** at King's Hall. Ethel Irving as Lady Fancyful. Mary Clare as Belinda.
—These revivals set one's mouth watering. Is it not time – in a weary world of revues and movies – that some bold spirit had a shot at discovering the lost art of high comedy? *The Times*
—What good purpose does the Stage Society achieve in reviving such plays as Vanbrugh's *The Provok'd Wife*? It is bawdy literature and that it is cleverly written does not enhance its claim on the attention of posterity. If it truly reflects the morals of the period, then the inquisitive sociologist can peruse it in the sanctity of his study. *Play Pictorial*

Jan 22. Ernest Milton in Shakespeare's **Hamlet** directed by George R Foss at Old Vic.

Jan 27. Tom Powers, Beatrice Lillie and Helen Rous in **Oh! Joy** at Kingsway. Book by Guy Bolton and P G Wodehouse. Music by Jerome Kern. Lyrics by Julian Frank and Clifford Grey. A young man's rooms are invaded by a bevy of girls. Lillie's grotesque antics had nothing to do with the plot.

1919 World Premieres
New York
James Montgomery, Joseph McCarthy and Harry Tierney's *Irene*

Births
N F Simpson, British playwright

Deaths
Leonid Andreyev (*b.*1871), Russian playwright
H B Irving (*b.*1870), British actor-manager
Charles Wyndham (*b.*1837), British actor-manager

Honours
Knight
Martin Harvey, British actor-manager

CBE
George Robey, British comedian

Notes
—Arnold Bennett and Nigel Playfair managed Birmingham Repertory Theatre
—Geoff Whitworth founded British Drama League

History
—Foundation of the League of Nations
—Ernest Rutherford split atom
—Benito Mussolini established Fascist Party
—Mary Astor became first woman MP
—Jack Dempsey became World Heavyweight Champion

Jan 29. Leslie Banks, Nigel Playfair and Herbert Marshall in Stanley Houghton's **The Younger Generation** directed by Stanley Drewitt at Lyric, Hammersmith. The grimness, the humour and the irony were as strong as ever.

Feb 12. Dick Bernard and Howard Lang in Samuel Shipman and Aaron Hoffman's **Uncle Sam** directed by Clifford Brooke at Haymarket. American wartime propaganda. Two German-Americans: one is an American patriot, the other still hankers after the Fatherland.

Feb 19. William Rea in John Drinkwater's **Abraham Lincoln** directed by John Drinkwater transferred from Birmingham Repertory Theatre to Lyric, Hammersmith. Lincoln's life from 1860 to his assassination in 1865. One critic dismissed it as "an amalgamation of bad history, worse drama and intellectual snobbery." Drinkwater (acting under the pseudonym John Darnley) played a treacherous member of Lincoln's cabinet.
—It is a little high-brow and none the less welcome for that in these days when the drama is as low-brow as are some ladies' hats. *The Times*

Mar 8. Owen Nares, Norman McKinnel, Emily Brooke and Margaret Halstan in Horace Annesley Vachell's **The House of Peril** directed by Owen Nares at Queen's. Drawing-room melodrama: two German murderers are on the loose in a French spa.

Mar 17. Arthur Whitby and Mary Grey as Sir Peter and Lady Teazle in Richard Brinsley Sheridan's **The School for Scandal** directed by J B Fagan at Court.
—Miss Mary Gray has high spirits and charm but she is too buxom, too sophisticated to suggest the country hoyden learning to be a woman of the world. *Illustrated London News*

Mar 25. George Robey in **Joy Bells** at New Hippodrome. Four hours, nineteen scenes, no interval. Robey's wartime sketch was the hit of the show.

Mar 27. Fay Compton, C Aubrey Smith, George Relph, Eva Moore and Helen Haye in Somerset Maugham's **Caesar's Wife** directed by Wilfred Eaton at Royalty. The story was suggested by Madame de Lafayette's *La Princesse de Cleves*. Young wife, who is married to a diplomat 20 years her senior, falls in love with his young secretary. Maugham was full of admiration for Compton's grace, tenderness and beauty.
—Miss Fay Compton represents her as a child of nature – perhaps, rather too petulant a child. The petulance is in the part, no doubt, but the actress seems inclined to emphasise it. It is a skilful, forceful performance; also it is a little hard. *The Times*

Mar 28. Robert Loraine and Mrs Patrick Campbell in Edmond Rostand's **Cyrano de Bergerac** directed by Robert Loraine at Criterion. Loraine had the presence, the audacity and the physical energy, but not always the voice.

Apr 3. Arthur Wontner, Mary Moore and Mary Merrall in Gladys Unger's **Our Mr Hepllewhite** directed by Frank Vernon at Criterion. Young woman is so shocked to find that her family actually approves of her marriage to a tradesman that she decides to marry somebody of her own class.

Apr 12. Basil Sydney and Doris Keane in Shakespeare's **Romeo and Juliet** directed by Basil Sydney at Lyric. Ellen Terry as Nurse. Leon Quartermaine as Mercutio.
—Miss Keane takes no pleasure in Shakespeare's words, is content to let half of them be inaudible, and to utter the rest – or rather to let them clip out – in a harsh, strained (we had almost said cracked) monotonous voice that turns poetry into prose. *The Times*

Apr 19. Marion Green and Maggie Teyte in **Monsieur Beaucaire** directed by J A E Malone at Princes. Romantic opera set in Bath in the early 18th century. Book by Frederick Lonsdale based on story by Booth Tarkington. Music by André Messager. Lyrics by Adrian Ross. Beaucaire was the Duc d'Orleans, the future king of France, disguised as a barber.
—Since the great Sullivan days light opera has fallen on evil times. We applaud Messager's efforts to direct this very delightful form of art away from the primrose path that led to everlasting revue. *Daily Mail*

Apr 21. Donald Calthrop, Mary Glynne. Stephen Ewart, G H Mulcaster and Margaret Shelley in William Le Baron's **The Very Idea** at St Martin's. Comedy about eugenics.
—The characters have all been given far too healthy minds to treat eugenics as anything but a drawing-room subject. *Era*

Apr 30. Lillah McCarthy, Claude King and Ernest Thesiger in Arnold Bennett's **Judith** directed by Wilfred Eaton at Kingsway. The Biblical legend, which mixed patriotism and eroticism, was given a semi-modern treatment; but the satiric and the emotional passages didn't hang together. The outstanding features of the production were the costumes of Charles Ricketts; but audiences were disappointed that Holofernes's decapitated head was not on view.

May 1. Royal Opera House opened for the first time since the War with Nellie Melba in Puccini's **La Bohème**, conducted by Thomas Beecham.

May 20. George Grossmith, Leslie Henson, Phyllis Dare and Yvonne Arnaud in **Kissing Time** at Winter Garden. Musical comedy. Book by Guy Bolton and P G Wodehouse. Music by Ivan Caryll. Lyrics by Clifford Grey. "Mr Grossmith," said *The Times*, "sings, dances and makes love in the most charming fashion."
—The vast majority of London theatregoers were content with almost anything – provided that it was sufficiently light and frivolous in character. *The Annual Register 1919*

Jun 10. Norman McKinnel in Lennox Robinson's **The Lost Leader** directed by J B Fagan at Court. The leader was Charles Parnell. The propaganda was sincere but ineffectual.

Jun 10. Marie Löhr in Edmond Rostand's **L'Aiglon** translated by Louis N Parker at Globe. Lyn Harding as Flambeau.

Jun 12. Owen Nares and Renée Kelly in Edward Childs Carpenter's **The Cinderella Man** directed by Guy F Bragden at Queen's. New York comedy. He's a poor poet. She's the rich girl who lives next door.

Jul 12. Charles Glenney, Herbert Ross and Arthur Lewis in Austin Strong's **Three Wise Fools** at Comedy. Judge, doctor and financier, bachelors in their dotage, are livened up by the presence of a girl.

Aug 26. Marie Löhr, Arthur Wontner and Norman McKinnel in Robert Hichens's **The Voice from the Minaret** at Globe. A man, forced to choose between the Church and a married woman, chooses the Church. Six years later, when he is a vicar, they resume their affair.

Aug 28. Beatrice Lillie, Odette Myrtil and Phyllis Titmuss in **Bran Pie** at Prince of Wales. Revue. Best sketch: Jack Hulbert and Alfred Lester as master and servant in 1915 and 1919: a reversal of roles

Aug 30. Gladys Cooper, Charles Hawtrey, Lottie Venne, Malcolm Cherry in Somerset Maugham's **Home and Beauty** directed by Charles Hawtrey at Playhouse. The comedy had been premiered in Atlantic City under the title of *Too Many Husbands*. World War 1 war widow has married her husband's best friend only to find her husband isn't dead after all. The wife is a vain and selfish woman and the two husbands can't wait to ditch her. The slight plot is eked out with two topical jokes. The first is a revue sketch in which a cook interviews her prospective employers. She insists that they light the kitchen fire before she comes down in the morning and says she expects a cup of tea and a thin slice of bread and butter to be brought to her before she gets up. The other joke is at the expense of the divorce laws. A solicitor explains the method of proving adultery without actually committing adultery and introduces a formidable elderly spinster (Jean Cadell), who has made a profession out of being a correspondent and has appeared in all the best divorce cases. No impropriety takes place. She plays cards with the gentlemen. Maugham wrote *Home and Beauty* in a sanatorium in 1919 whilst he was recovering from tuberculosis. "If I were a stern critic," he said, "I should feel it my duty to point out that the play is finished by the first act."
—One is tempted to call Mr Maugham's farce exquisite. It has style, wit, elegance and at the same time the sheer fun that all farces should have, but fun of the choicest sort, quiet fun. It is a little masterpiece of quiet merriment. *The Times*

Sep 3. Emily Brooke, Mary Jerrold, George Tully and A E Matthews in John

Gladys Cooper in Home and Beauty

L'Hobble's **Daddies** at Haymarket. Orphans manage to convert dire-hard bachelors into paternal figures. Sentimental American comedy.

Sep 8. Gerald du Maurier, Viola Tree and Leon Quartermaine in Alfred Sutro's **The Choice** at Wyndham's. The choice is between duty and love. An employer dismisses a man for drunkenness and incurs the danger of a strike. He also incurs the disapproval of the nation. The sacked man was a former soldier who had been gassed during the war. His fiancée is so appalled by his behaviour that she marries his secretary.
—Mr Gerald du Maurier finds a part admirably suited to his crisp, incisive style, and his power of suggesting unexpressed emotion. WILLIAM ARCHER *Star*

Sep 9. Oscar Asche and Violet Lorraine in **Eastward Ho!** at Alhambra. Spectacle: the most spectacular transformation was the ruins of a Phoenician temple restored to its former glory.

Sep 11. Cronin Wilson and Dorothy Dix in Richard Walton Tully's **Bird of Paradise** at Lyric. Picturesque Hawaii, its folklore and songs in the early Nineties. American married a native princess. He degenerated into a drunkard. She threw herself into a volcano to appease the god Pele. The crater in full eruption was the high spot.

Sep 12. Frederick Ross and Sybil Thorndike in Louis N Parker and George R Sims's **Great Day** directed by Arthur Collins at Drury Lane. Music by J M Glover. Wife, believed to have been killed in an air-raid, returned just as her husband was about to remarry. The most spectacular scenes were the furnace of a great steel works and the Seine bursting its banks.

Sep 13. W H Berry in **Who's Hopper** at Adelphi. Musical comedy. Book by Fred Thompson based on Arthur Wing Pinero's *In Chancery*. Music by Howard Talbot and Ivor Novello. Lyrics by Clifford Grey. Hopper is pursued by three women: his wife, his supposed wife, and a publican's daughter.

Sep 17. Alice Delysia, Harry Welchman and Marie Burke in **Afgar** at London Pavilion. Eastern extravaganza. Girls in a harem go on strike. There had been rumours before the show opened that there was impropriety. Producer C B Cochran assured everybody that any impropriety in the French original had been removed and the production was "above reproach."

Sep 25. Walter Catlett and Dorothy Brunton in **Baby Bunting** at Shaftesbury. Musical comedy. Book by Fred Thompson and Worton Davies. Music by Nat D Ayer. Lyrics by Clifford Grey. Based on Harry Nicholls and William Lestocq's *Jane*. The American comedian gave an amusing demonstration of dancing from country green to ballroom to ballet. He had a big success.
—Ones only regret is that he was not discovered for home consumption a year or two ago. He would have been an invaluable asset during the dark days. *The Times*

Oct 4. Maurice Moscovitch as Shylock in Shakespeare's **The Merchant of Venice** at Court. Moscovitch, a young Jewish actor, spoke in Dutch while the rest of the cast spoke in English. Mary Grey was Portia. Miles Malleson was Launcelot Gobbo. *The Annual Register* described Moscovitch's performance as "a creation of extraordinary freshness and interest, wholly individual in conception and arresting in execution."
—[Shylock] is overwhelmingly alive and grotesquely deadly, an obsession, a nightmare. Ugh! (An interjection which in the circumstances is the highest possible compliment)... Shylock is a terror. We do not excuse, but begin to understand, pogroms. *The Times*

Oct 6. H F Maltby, Gordon Ash and Alice Mansfield in H F Maltby's **The Temporary Gentleman** at Oxford Theatre. Satire on snobbery. A lower middle-class clerk is made an officer during World War 1, there being a shortage of officers. After the war is over he is expected to return to his former station in life. "A remarkably fine play," said *The Morning Post*, "the best and truest war play we have had."

Oct 17. Oscar Asche in **Chu Chin Chow** established world record, celebrating 1,466 performances at His Majesty's. This spectacular wartime entertainment was loosely based on *Ali Baba and the Forty Thieves*. A slave girl saves the day by pouring molten liquid into the forty jars and stabbing the robber chief to death. Songs included "Anytime's Kissing Time" and "The Cobbler's Song". Audiences would come again and again to see the show. One family had a standing order for six stalls every month. Asche admitted that it was a strain playing the same role indefinitely.

Nov 10. Katharine Cornell as Jo in Marion De Forest's adaptation of Louisa M Alcott's **Little Women** directed by Jesse Bonstelle at New.
—[Catherine Cornell's] acting is conspicuous for vivacity, high spirits and variety. On the other hand it lacks the air of spontaneity requisite to create the impression that it is really the outcome of natural impulse. *Era*

—*Little Women* will continue to make unsophisticated playgoers laugh and cry for months to come. *Queen*

Nov 11. Cyril Maude and Connie Ediss in Sydney Blow and Douglas Hoare's adaptation of Martin Swayne's novel **Lord Richard in the Pantry** at Criterion. Farce. Impoverished lord, hunted by the police, disguises himself as a butler. The cook fancies him.

Dec 26. Martin Harvey in Shakespeare's **Hamlet** at Covent Garden. Miriam Lewes as Gertrude. Fred Ross as Claudius. Nina De Silva as Ophelia. *The Times* did not think Harvey had the physical force to fill the theatre. The supporting actors were not up to a West End standard.

Maurice Moscovitch as Shylock in **The Merchant of Venice**

Mira Nirska and Chorus of Totem Poles in Rose Marie

1920–1929

1920

Jan 5. Irene Vanbrugh and Ben Webster in A A Milne's **Mr Pym Passes By** directed by Dion Boucicault at New. Pym, an absent-minded old gentleman, leads a married couple to believe they are bigamists.
—The author's only trouble is that he will always be looking for humour. He is a young man who refuses to take anything with consistent seriousness. *Sunday Times*

Jan 9. Henry Ainley as Antony, Basil Gill as Brutus, Milton Rosmer as Cassius, Clifton Boyne as Caesar, Claude Rains as Casca and Lilian Braithwaite as Portia in Shakespeare's **Julius Caesar** directed by Stanley Bell at St James's. Since Antony was portrayed as the noblest Roman of them all, the scene with Octavius, which showed him being ignoble, was cut.

Jan 29. Ruth Draper made her London debut at Aeolian Hall. American monologist. Character sketches. Bare stage, no scenery, no prop; but the stage felt peopled.

Feb 2. Frank Benson in Shakespeare's **Hamlet** at St Martin's. Esme Biddle as Ophelia. Hamlet was a 62-year-old post-graduate at Elsinore.
—[Frank Benson] really seems to be thinking it out there and then, philosophising as he goes along – a notable achievement with passages so hackneyed. But in his more violent moments he is apt to sing his lines and he prolongs his vowels into a kind of undulation. *The Times*

Feb 5. Matheson Lang, Hilda Bayley and Dennis Neilson-Terry in C M Harding and Matheson Lang's **Carnival** directed by Matheson Lang at New. Melodrama: an insanely jealous actor becomes homicidal whilst playing Othello.
—To combine the first act of *Pagliacci* and the last act of *Othello* with a carnival scene as a connecting link is a theatrical conception which is both ingenious and captivating. *Play Pictorial*

Feb 10. Ellis Jeffreys, Donald Calthrop, Sydney Fairbrother, Joyce Carey and Leslie Howard in **The Young Person in Pink** directed by Ben Webster at Prince of Wales. Duchess's daughter is adopted by a dealer in second-hand clothes.

Feb 11. Matheson Lang as Othello and Arthur Bourchier as Iago in Shakespeare's **Othello** directed by Matheson Lang at New. Hutin Britton as Emilia. Hilda Bayley as Desdemona. Lang's performance consolidated his position among the first rank of Shakespearian players. Bourchier indulged in some hammy Mephistophelian laughter. The play was performed every Wednesday afternoon.
—After each performance we gave of the play at the New Theatre I used to feel spiritually battered and bruised as though I had been through a mental football match. MATHESON LANG *Mr Wu Looks Back*

Feb 23. Sybil Thorndike as Hecuba in Eurpides's **The Trojan Women** directed by Lewis Casson at Holborn Empire.

Feb 24. Edyth Goodall as Ethel Monticue and Ben Field as Mr Salteena in Daisy Ashford's novel **The Young Visiters** directed by J V Bryant at Court. A child's vision of grown-ups in an Edwardian world was first published in 1919. Many people thought wrongly that it had been written by J M Barrie. The adaptation was charming and the actors played it totally straight. But *The Young Visiters* without Ashford's spelling is almost like *Hamlet* without the Prince.

Mar 1. Sybil Thorndike, Nicholas Hannen and Lewis Casson in Bernard Shaw's **Candida** directed by Lewis Casson at Holborn Empire.

Mar 8. Sybil Thorndike and Nicholas Hannen in Eurpides's **Medea** directed by Lewis Casson at Holborn Empire. Raucous passion. Thorndike had a great deal of sympathy for Medea: "I don't believe in complete evil. I think in a way Medea was justified," she said. "She had given up everything and done awful things to help Jason...She had the most terrible time."
—The effect of the two Greek performances was explosive. None of the critics had seen tragic performances of this calibre since the war. W A DARLINGTON *Daily Telegraph*

Mar 15. Tamara Karsavina in J M Barrie's **The Truth About the Russian Dancers** at Coliseum. The one act play was written especially for Karsavina, the Russian ballerina, who was appearing with the Ballets Russes.

Mar 25. Alfred Lester, Thorpe Bates and Evelyn Laye in H J W Dam and Ivan Caryll's **The Shop Girl** directed by Seymour Hicks at Gaiety. The shop girl turned out to be a missing heiress. Premiered in 1894, the show had been overhauled. The band of the Brigade of Guards appeared on stage. Laye, singing and dancing with great charm, was everything that a Gaiety leading lady should be.

Apr 5. Irish-American actress Peggy O'Neil and Ion Swinley in Gayer Mackay and Robert Ord's adaptation of Gertrude Page's **Paddy the Next Best Thing** directed by Robert Courtneidge at Savoy. A girl is the next best thing to a boy.
—Miss Peggy O'Neill suddenly showed she could be very funny when she was not too busy being "Irish" and noisy. *The Times*

Apr 6. Dawson Millward and Mary Merrall in Harold Brighouse's **Other Times** directed by V Sutton-Lane at Little. A contrast between life in the present (1920) and in the future (1960).

Apr 7. Edith Day and Robert Hale in **Irene** directed by Thomas Reynolds at Empire. Musical version of James Montgomery's *Irene O'Dare*. Music by Harry Tierney. Lyrics by Joseph McCarthy. Poor girl marries into rich family. Edith Day, who had

Henry Ainley in Julius Caesar

1920 World Premieres

New York
Bernard Shaw's *Heartbreak House*.
Eugene O'Neill's *The Emperor Jones*.
Atlantic City
Eugene O'Neill's *Anna Christie*
Berlin
Arthur Schnitzler's *La Ronde*
(complete)
Warsaw
Solomon Anski's *Dybbuk*
Brno
Georg Kaiser's *Gas II*

Notes

—1920–1925 Robert Atkins directed every play in the First Folio except *Cymbeline*
—Birmingham Rep staged *Cymbeline* in modern dress
—Everyman Theatre founded by Norman MacDermott

History

—Prohibition became national in US
—Joan of Arc canonised
—Formation of Communist Party in England
—White Russians defeated in final battle of Russian Civil War
—Bloody Sunday in Ireland

created Irene on Broadway in 1919, repeated her success in London. Hit song: "Alice Blue Gown".

Apr 20. Norman McKinnel, Fred Kerr and Henry Caine in H M Harwood's **The Grain of Mustardseed** directed by Stafford Hilliard at Ambassadors. A witty political satire. There is a wide difference between what the politicians think the people want and what the people actually want. McKinnel was the new man, who wanted to change things. Kerr was the cynical Leader of the House. Caine was a sceptical chauffeur.

Apr 21. Athene Seyler as Rosalind and Ivan Samson as Orlando in Shakespeare's **As You Like It** directed by Nigel Playfair at Lyric, Hammersmith. Seyler was a giggling, hoydenish chatterbox. Herbert Marshall as Jacques gave an almost sinister quality to the Seven Ages of Man speech. Nigel Playfair played Touchstone.
—When [Athene Seyler] was gay she was ravishing, but when she grew tender she was the pattern and quintessence of all lovers. *Spectator*

Apr 21. Edmund Gwenn, Athole Stewart and Helen Haye in John Galsworthy's **The Skin Game** directed by Basil Dean at St Martin's. Galsworthy's first commercial success was a fight between gentry and *nouveau riche*. Hornblower (Edmund Gwenn), a self-made northern businessman, is an obstinate, thick-skinned, pushy, self-seeking opportunist, who has a total disregard for people and places. He sets out to destroy Hillcrist (Athole Stewart), an act of revenge for the snubs he has received; but the revenge rebounds on him. The gentry win because they choose to fight dirty, resorting to blackmail and exposure. The play was recognised as an allegory on the Great War with Hillcrist representing Britain and Hornblower representing Germany. 'Skin game' was American slang for unscrupulous conduct.

Apr 22. Fay Compton, Robert Loraine, Ernest Thesiger, Mary Jerrold, Norman Forbes and Arthur Whitby in J M Barrie's **Mary Rose** at Haymarket. Freudians had a field day. Young girl disappears for thirty days and then disappears again for twenty-five years, only to return unchanged, and totally unaware that she's been away. Fay Compton's Rose was beautifully childlike. The Island That Likes To Be Visited is Death. The play's success must have been in part because it gave comfort to an audience who had lost husbands and sons in The Great War. When Barrie was a child, he was left-handed but had been forced by his parents to write with his right hand. While he was writing *Mary Rose* his right hand swelled up and he wrote with his left hand for the first time in 50 years. Alfred Hitchcock always wanted to film the play.
—Anything curious or uncomfortable about *Mary Rose* arises from it having been a product of the left hand. It seems to have a dark and more sinister outlook on life and is trying at present to make a woman knife her son. J M BARRIE
—Mr Ernest Thesiger, who seems to touch nothing that he does not adorn, gave a fine rendering of as charming a character as ever came out of the Barrie box – the superstitious, learned, courteous crofter's son, student of Aberdeen University, temporary boatman and (later) minister. JOSEPH THORP *Punch*

May 3. Laurette Taylor in J Hartley Manners's **One Night in Rome** at Garrick. There was a riot on the first night and cat calls, rude epithets, packets of snuff pellets and stink bombs were hurled at the stage. The curtain had to be brought down. Taylor, <u>making her London debut</u>, had another 'first night' a few days later when her reception was better, but the play wasn't any better.

NO. 1917 in "Peg O My Heart"

May 11. Sacha Guitry and Yvonne Printemps made their London debut in Sacha Guitry's **Nono** directed by Sacha Guitry at Aldwych. 40-year-old abandons his boring mistress for another boring mistress.
—Polish of acting is a special prerogative of the French. It is second nature to them, and with these players the smoothness, the shine, the grace, the flexibility of their performances eclipse all the nature and many vulgarities of the story. *Sunday Times*

May 15. José Collins, Claude Flemming, Bertram Wills and Mark Lester in **A Southern Maid** directed by Robert Evett at Daly's. Musical comedy. Book by Dion Clayton and Harry Graham. Lyrics by Harry Graham and Douglas Furber. Music by Harold Fraser-Simson. Additional numbers by Ivor Novello. The story concerned a vendetta in Santiago. James Agate observed there was plenty of resemblance but no essential difference between *The Southern Maid* and *The Maid of the Mountains*. Hit songs included "Love's Cigarette" and "Dark Grows the Sky."
—[José Collins] is fortunate enough to combine two great gifts, a voice which very often matches grand opera level and a power of dramatic expression which makes one wish to see her now and again in a straight play. *The Times*

May 17. Anna Pavlova in **Giselle** at Covent Garden.

Jun 5. Frederick Ranalow as Macheath, Sylvia Nelis as Polly, Violet Marquesita as Lucy and Frederic Austin as Peachum in John Gay's **The Beggar's Opera** directed by Nigel Playfair at Lyric, Hammersmith. Additional music by Frederic Austin. Charming, pretty, witty and tuneful, the production was a great success. Ranalow, a fine singer and a fine actor, was highly praised for his diction and finesse. Playfair refused all offers of a transfer to the West End. James Agate felt it was all too pretty and that it needed some 18th century grubbiness and the shadow of the gibbet.

June 6. **Vesta Tilley's farewell** at the Coliseum. Ellen Terry paid tribute and presented her with a book containing more than a million of her admirers' signatures.

Jun 24. Godfrey Tearle, Madge Titheradge and Basil Gill in Robert S Hichens and Mary Anderson's **The Garden of Allah** directed by Arthur Collins at Drury Lane. Crude story of crude passions in the Sahara Desert. A Trappist monk breaks his vow and falls in love. On the first night the gauze curtain failed to come down and the sandstorm covered not only the actors but also the audience.

Jul 14. Albert Chevalier in Arthur Shirley and Albert Chevalier's **My Old Dutch** directed by Walter and Frederick Melville at Lyceum. A coster's life is told in the songs that Chevalier had sung for over twenty years. Homely humour and sentiment.

Jul 21. Kate Cutler in Noël Coward's **I'll Leave It To You** directed by Stanley Bell at New. A man promises to leave his fortune to the member of the family who makes the most money
—Freshly written and brightly acted, the piece betrays a certain striving after ultra-comic effect. Mr Noël Coward, who is not yet 21, is almost too successful in making the younger nephew a most objectionable boy. But Miss Kate Cutler is perfect as the children's absurdly young mother. *Daily Mail*

Aug 9. Charles V France, Basil Rathbone, Haidée Wright, H R Hignett and Lady Tree in Somerset Maugham's **The Unknown** directed by Viola Tree and Wallett Waller at Aldwych. A vicar tells a woman that World War 1 was due to the loving kindness of God, who wished to purify the nation by suffering. The mother (whose only son died in the war) asks: "Who is going to forgive God?" Audiences were uncomfortable with the profanity. Maugham defended his right to discuss religion openly on the stage. *The Guardian* agreed and said that every clergyman should see the play.

Aug 18. Mary Nash in Jules Eckert Goodman's **The Man Who Came Back** at Princes. The *Daily Mirror* thought it was the most thrilling drama that had been seen in the last ten years. Mary Nash, according to another critic, was "an artist capable of setting the heartstrings of the most callous quivering."

Aug 28. Faith Celli and Harold French in H De Vere Stacpoole's **The Blue Lagoon** directed by Basil Dean at Prince of Wales. Adaptation by Norman MacOwen and Charlton Mann. Romance in the South Seas: a series of episodes, some of them without dialogue. The impressive scenic effects were drawn from Victorian theatre. The 20-foot idol was part Easter Island, part Jacob Epstein. The lead roles were played by children in the opening scenes.

Sep 1. Sybil Thorndike in Pierre Rehm's **C.–H.–Q. Love** directed by Lewis Casson at Little. Grand Guignol. Translation by Sewell Collins.
—It is nasty without any redeeming artistic feature, save the acting of Sybil Thorndike as the cocotte. Its environment savours of the lavatory, and its morals of the brothel. *Play Pictorial*

Sep 9. Matheson Lang and Lillah McCarthy in E Temple Thurston's **The Wandering Jew** directed by Matheson Lang and A W Tryer at New. Play in four phases: 1) Jerusalem on the Day of the Crucifixion. 2) Syria in the time of the First Crusade. 3) Sicily in the 13th Century. 4) Spain in the Middle Ages. Picturesque longueurs with rhetoric but without poetry.
—The sense of inexorable fate is lacking; we are not made to feel the man before us is always the same doomed wretch. *The Times*

Sep 18. Leslie Henson, Phyllis Monkman, Margaret Bannerman and Stella St Audrie in **A Night Out** directed by Tom Reynolds at Winter Garden. Musical adaptation

63

of Georges Feydeau's *L'Hotel de Libre Eschange* by George Grossmith and Arthur Miller. Music by Willie Redstone. Lyrics by Clifford Grey. Henson was a great asset.

Sep 23. Ethel Irving as Tosca, Lyn Harding as Scarpia and Gerald Lawrence as Cavaradossi in Victorien Sardou's **La Tosca** at Aldwych.

Sep 28. E Holman Clark, Leon M Lion and Lauderdale Maitland in Ernest Hutchinson's **The Right to Strike** at Garrick. With a major strike going on in the country the play was topical. A doctor is murdered by the strikers; the doctors in the district decide not to attend the strikers, their wives and children.

Oct 2. Maurice Moscovitch in **The Great Lover** by Leo Ditrichstein and Frederick and Fanny Hatton directed by Felix Edwardes at Shaftesbury. The great lover was an opera singer who lost his voice.

Oct 4. Ernest Milton as Shylock and Florence Saunders as Portia in Shakespeare's **The Merchant of Venice** directed by Robert Atkins at Old Vic.

Oct 7. W H Berry and George Grossmith in **The Naughty Princess** directed by J A E Malone at Adelphi. Opera bouffe adapted from Andre Barde's *La Reine Joyeuse*. Book by J Hastings Turner, music by Charles Cuvillier, lyrics by Adrian Ross. The high spots were a great waltz and an Egyptian fancy dress party.

Oct 18. Arthur Wontner and Lottie Venne in A A Milne's **The Romantic Age** directed by Arthur Wontner at Comedy. Whimsical events in the country on midsummer's day. The heroine is disillusioned when she discovers that the man she took to be a medieval hero works in the Stock Exchange. Transferred to Playhouse.

Oct 21. Brember Wills in John Galsworthy's **The Little Man** directed by John Galsworthy at Everyman. Farcical morality play. Wills played the little man who was the only person on a crowded train who was willing to look after an abandoned baby who was believed to have typhus. Acted in a double-bill with John Galsworthy's **The Foundations**.

Oct 30. Marie Löhr, Ellis Jeffreys, Basil Rathbone, Henry Vibart and Allan Aynesworth in Victorien Sardou's **Fedora** directed by Louis N Parker at Globe. Fedora was a role identified with Sarah Bernhardt, a difficult act to follow.

Nov 2. James K Hackett and Mrs Patrick Campbell in Shakespeare's **Macbeth** directed by Louis Calvert at Aldwych.
—Her sleepwalking scene is not exquisitely pathetic – and indeed her sleepwalking is rather too wide-awake. *The Times*

Nov 11. Evelyn Laye in **Betty in Mayfair** at Adelphi. Musical based on John Hastings Turner's novel, *Lilies of the Fields*. Music by H Fraser Simson. Lyrics by Harry Graham.

Dec 1. Maggie Tyte in **A Little Dutch Girl** at Lyric. Musical comedy. Book by Seymour Hicks and Harry Graham. Lyrics by Harry Graham. Music by Emmerich Kalman. Princess disguises herself as a little Dutch girl in order to win the heart of a shy prince.

Dec 19. Arthur Sinclair, Sara Allgood, Roy Byford and Nan Fitzgerald in Bernard Shaw's **O'Flaherty VC** at Lyric, Hammersmith. An Irish youngster joins the army to get away from his termagant mum. She thinks he is fighting the British and is furious when she finds he is fighting for them. During World War 1 Shaw had wittily offered his one-act anti-war tract as a recruiting pamphlet. It had had its premiere on the Western Front in 1917.

1921

Jan 8. Gladys Cooper in Maurice Maeterlinck's **The Betrothal** directed by Harley Granville Barker. Sequel to Maeterlinck's *The Blue Bird*. Sets by Charles Ricketts. Cooper's face remained completely hidden until very nearly the end of the play.

Jan 21. The Dolly Sisters in **The League of Notions** by John Murray Anderson and Augustus Barratt directed by Frank Collins at New Oxford. Billed as an "Inconsequential process of music, dance and dramatic interlude."

Feb 21. Felix Aylmer as Ridgeon, Nicholas Hannen as Dubedat and Muriel Pratt as Mrs Dubedat in Bernard Shaw's **The Doctor's Dilemma** directed by Edith Craig at Everyman.

Feb 27. Jean Cadell, H K Ayliff, Baliol Holloway and Adela Mavis in G K Munro's **At Mrs Beam's** directed by Allan Wade at Kingsway. Mrs Beam ran a Notting Hill boarding house full of rogues and sycophants. A thief bullies and beats his wife, who

tries but fails to seduce a young man. Cadell was hilarious as the inquisitive, malicious, gossiping old spinster. *The Times* thought the play brilliant but objected to all the kissing: "Salacity may be a fact of life, but it is not therefore suitable for the footlights."

Mar 3. Ernest Thesiger, Fay Compton, Lottie Venne and Allan Aynesworth in Somerset Maugham's **The Circle** directed by J E Vedrenne at Haymarket. 35-year-old MP, a fussing prig, has been married for three years and is much more interested in his career and antique furniture than he is in his wife. When he was five years old, his mother ran off with a married man, his father's best friend. The scandal wrecked both men's political careers. It now looks as if his wife is about to repeat his mother's mistake and bolt with a breezy, young rubber planter. His initial reaction is to give her a good hiding. The elopers of the past, Lady Kitty and Lord Porteous, are an amusing and grim warning to any young couple intending to elope; but Maugham, having led the audience to believe that the wife will be a good wife and stay with her husband, lets her go off with her lover. The gallery, morally outraged, booed.

Mar 14. Lilian Braithwaite, Malcolm Keen and Meggie Albanesi in Clemence Dane's **A Bill of Divorcement** directed by Basil Dean at St Martin's. Wife obtains divorce from her husband on the grounds of insanity. (Madness was a taboo subject on the London stage.) Just as she is about to remarry, he returns cured. What is she to do? The action takes place twenty years hence when the recommendations of the Royal Commission of Divorce have become law. A P Herbert in the *Westminster Gazette* described it as a great play.

Mar 29. Gerald du Maurier in **Bulldog Drummond** by "Sapper" directed by Gerald du Maurier at Wyndham's. Thick-ear drama (a popular alternative to highbrow drama and sex drama) offered adventure for schoolboys of all ages: drugged wine, doctored cigarettes, disguises and fights.
—Mr Gerald du Maurier played the devil-may-care, lion-hearted, do-any-mortal-thing-for-the-girl-he-loved Drummond. He could play such a part standing on his head and make it real. *Tatler*

Apr 4. 76-year-old Sarah Bernhardt's farewell in Louis Verneuil's **Daniel** at Shaftes-

Dolly Sisters in League of Notions

1921 World Premieres

Rome
Luigi Pirandello's *Six Characters in Search of an Author*
New York
Eugene O'Neill's *Anna Christie*
Eugene O'Neill's *The Emperor Jones*
Prague
Karel Capek's *RUR*
Munich
Bertolt Brecht's *In the Jungle of the City*

Births

Friedrich Dürrenmatt, Swiss playwright
Ray Lawler, Australian playwright

Deaths

Lady Bancroft (*b.* 1839 Ann Wilton), British actor
Georges Feydeau (*b.* 1863), French playwright

Honours

Knight
Martin Harvey, British actor-manager

Notes

—Arthur Schnitzler (1862–1931) wrote *Reigen* in 1896, a sharp and sophisticated sexual merry-go-round, and never intended it to be staged. It was first performed in a university club, which was closed by the public authorities. Schnitzler didn't allow it to be performed again in Berlin until 1921. Two months into the run there were riots in the theatre and the producer and the actors were arrested and put on trial for obscenity. The trial lasted six days. The theatre won the case. In the same year in Vienna there were more riots. 600 people stormed the theatre throwing stink bombs and eggs covered in tar, smashing glass panes and seats, and clubbing the audience. The riot only ended when stage-hands turned fire hydrants on the mob. The police banned further performances. Schnitzler refused to allow the play to be performed in Europe and made his son, Heinrich, promise to keep the ban for the next 50 years.

History

—Adolf Hitler elected President of National Socialist German Workers Party
—Benito Mussolini declared himself leader of National Fascist party
—Marie Stopes opened first birth control clinic

bury. Daniel was a delicate boy poet who had taken to drugs. The long applause was a tribute to a much-loved actress and her endurance and pluck. (She had continued to act after her leg had been amputated.) Verneuil was her grandson by marriage.

Apr 21. Godfrey Tearle in Shakespeare's **Othello** directed by J B Fagan at Court. Basil Rathbone was a handsome, smooth, insinuating, intellectually superior Iago. Madge Titheradge as Desdemona was out of her depth.
—We cannot but wish that he [Godfrey Tearle] would not be in a hurry to begin roaring, and that he would not begin *fff* but aim at a gradual crescendo effect. *The Times*

May 27. J M Barrie's unfinished thriller, **Shall We Join the Ladies?** directed by Gerald du Maurier celebrated the opening of the Royal Academy of Dramatic Arts Theatre. The all-star cast included Dion Boucicault as the host and Fay Compton, Charles Hawtrey, Sybil Thorndike, Cyril Maude, Lady Tree, Ronald Squire, Leon Quartermaine, Lillah McCarthy, Nelson Keys, Madge Titheradge, Johnston Forbes-Robertson, Irene Vanbrugh, Marie Löhr as the guests. Norman Forbes was the police officer. Hilda Trevelyan was the maid. Gerald du Maurier was the silent, imperturbable butler. The host, in answer to calls for a speech, informs them that one of them had poisoned his brother in Monte Carlo two years previously. He produces a pair of handcuffs from under the table and invites them all to listen to their beating hearts. The play ends with "a dreadful scream off-stage" (screamed by Mrs Patrick Campbell). Whenever Barrie was asked who the murderer was he would invariably reply, "I wish I knew." According to Cynthia Asquith he did tell Queen Mary but she took the secret with her to the grave. It has also been said that he confided in a couple of friends that the host had done it, but when the rumours began to circulate, he denied ever having said any such thing. Barrie never got past the first act. In the published text he disarmingly wrote that "the brilliancy of the cast excused the proud author of giving the play in full." It was said he didn't know how to end it, but the truth is that he was writing it as a 21st birthday present for his adopted son, Michael Llewellyn Davies, when Michael, then up at Oxford, drowned in the Thames with his friend, Rupert Buxton, a month before his majority. (There were suspicions that it might have been mutual suicide.) Barrie found it impossible to continue writing the play.

May 30. Gladys Cooper and Henry Ainley in Lord Dunsany's **If** directed by Nigel Playfair at Ambassadors. Middle-class suburban couple find themselves transplanted to an Oriental setting.

Jul 6. William Rea in John Drinkwater's **Abraham Lincoln** directed by John Drinkwater at Lyceum. Rea's performance was as good as it had always been, but it was the meeting between the two generals, as acted by Victor Tandy as Ulysses Grant and Harcourt Williams as Robert E Lee, which made the most impression.

—Of all the plays produced in London during the last few years *Abraham Lincoln* is the only one that merits the epithet "great". *Daily Telegraph*
—There cannot be much wrong with our theatre-going public when a throng of many thousands can be found to hang on every word of a play of the calibre of *Abraham Lincoln*. *News of the World*

Jul 22. Chu Chin Chow closed after 2,238 performances.

Aug 28. The Co-Optimists at Royalty. Pierrot entertainment: skull caps, ruffles, pom-poms. The company included Stanley Holloway. Transferred to Palace.

Aug 31. Matheson Lang in Giovacchino Forzano's "fantastic play", **Christopher Sly**, directed by Matheson Lang and A W Tyrer at New. Forzano's Sly wasn't Shakespeare's ignorant drunkard, but a poet, a dreamer and a lover, who drank. He also had a soliloquy which went on for 25 minutes. thought it was "a beautiful piece of romantic acting."

Sep 1. Gladys Cooper and Leslie Faber in Channing Pollock's **The Sign on the Door** directed by Channing Pollock at Playhouse. Melodrama. Wife takes the blame for a murder in order to shield her husband.

Sep 10. Dorothy Dickson, Leslie Henson and George Grossmith in Jerome Kern's musical **Sally** directed by George Grossmith at Winter Garden. Book by Guy Bolton. Lyrics by Clifford Grey. Sally is a dish-washer who becomes a celebrated dancer. She is befriended a waiter, who is, of course, a Grand Duke in disguise. The score included "Look for the Silver Lining." The Butterfly ballet to music by Victor Herbert was particularly admired.

Oct 15. Oscar Asche and Lily Brayton in Oscar Asche's **Cairo** directed by Oscar Asche at His Majesty's. The elaborate pageant ("a mosaic in music and mime") had a Bacchanalian orgy in the Cecil B De Mille manner which caused a great deal of comment. The curtain came down on a frenzied dance and then went up to show the exhausted dancers lying in picturesque confusion on the steps of the palace.

Oct 18. Brember Wills as Captain Shotover, Edith Evans as Lady Utterword, Mary Grey as Hesione Hushabye, Ellen O'Malley as Ellie Dunn, James Dale as Hector Hushabye, Alfred Clark as Boss Mangan and Eric Maturin as Randall Utterword in Bernard Shaw's **Heartbreak House** directed by J B Fagan at Court. Begun in 1913, but not finished until 1919, Shaw described the play as "a fantasia in the Russian manner on English themes." It was his favourite play. He saw it as a sort of national fable. In the same way that the orchard in *The Cherry Orchard* is Russia, so the house in *Heartbreak House* is England. The leisured Edwardian classes, bored and morally lethargic, are, as they freely admit, useless, dangerous and ought to be abolished. They can't wait for the Zeppelins to drop more bombs. "It's splendid!" they cry. "It's like an orchestra. It's like Beethoven! What a glorious experience: I hope they'll come again tomorrow night." The first night was spoiled by a technical hitch which resulted in the performance lasting 3 hours and 50 minutes. The 17-year-old John Gielgud found the play dull, badly constructed and boring, though he had to admit there were some brilliant remarks and ideas. The play did not have any real success until World War 2.
—Mr Shaw is gloriously an artist in his sense of the importance of ideas, and in his sense of a subject, but he is without artistic respect for unity of effect. It seems he does not care about it ... His high spirits are a wonderful gift, but they master and distract him, and they have seriously damaged this fine play. DESMOND MacCARTHY *New Statesman*
—The old captain of Mr Brember Wills was magnificently distraught – Ibsen and Shaw, Whitman and General Booth rolled into one. JAMES AGATE *Sunday Times*
—Miss Evans, who never appears in any play without astonishing me by the range of her powers and the complete absorption of her personality in the part she interprets, was a soft and lovely and utterly materialistic and self-satisfied woman of the decadent world. *Westminster Gazette*

Nov 3. Robert Loraine and Madge Titheradge in Sacha Guitry's **Deburau** at Ambassadors. Translation by Harley Granville Barker. Deburau was the great French mime of the 1840s. The role was more suited to Guitry than Loraine and the production was dismissed as superficial, sentimental and commonplace.

Nov 16. Godfrey Tearle, Ruth Maitland, Mary Odette and Mollie Kerr in Monckton Hoffe's **The Faithful Heart** directed by Leon M Lion at Comedy. Sailor has an affair with a barmaid whilst on leave and fathers a child. Years later, just as he is about to marry, he learns that he had fathered a daughter. Since his fiancée won't accept her, he decides he would be better off with the barmaid. Transferred to Queen's.

Nov 17. Philip Merivale as Shakespeare and Haidée Wright as Queen Elizabeth in Clemence Dane's **Will Shakespeare** directed by Basil Dean at Shaftesbury. Will catches Kit Marlowe (Claude Rains) with Mary Fitton (Mary Clare) in a Deptford pub and accidentally kills him. Finton deputises for the boy actor who had been going to play Juliet at the premiere of *Romeo and Juliet* – an idea which was developed in the 1998 film, *Shakespeare in Love*. Basil Dean said Merivale acted

Shakespeare as a man who had already given up life's struggle before he had even left Stratford.

Dec 15. Edna Best and Ernest Thesiger in J M Barrie's **Peter Pan** directed by Lichfield Owen at St James's. Barrie told Thesiger that the important thing to remember about Captain Hook was that he had been educated at Balliol.

Dec 20. Norman McKinnel in A A Milne's **The Truth About Blayds** directed by Dion Boucicault at Globe. The truth is that a famous 90-year-old poet has not written any of the poems which made him famous.
—[A A Milne] appeals frankly to the cultivated minds in his audience … It is all so delicate and fragile that it might have been ruined if it had not fallen into the right hands for production. *Nation*

Dec 24. Beatrice Lillie and Jack Hulbert in **Pot Luck** at Vaudeville. Revue. Book by Ronald Jeans and Dion Titheradge. Music by Philip Braham, R P Weston and Bert Lee.

1922

Jan 23. Arthur Wontner and Eva Moore in Mary Roberts Rinehart and Avery Hopwood's **The Bat** by directed by Collin Kemper at St James's. Who is the Bat? American crime mystery: robbery and murder. Every so often the stage would be plunged into darkness. Wontner played the detective.

Feb 1. Philip Merivale and Phyllis Neilson-Terry in J B Fagan's **The Wheel** directed by J B Fagan at Apollo. Colonel's wife, having had a fling with a captain in the Himalayan kingdom of Bhutan, decides it best to stay with her boring husband.

Feb 25. Charles Austin in **Rockets** at Palladium. Book by Charles Henry. Lyrics by Ernest Melvin. Music by Herman Darewski and L A Tunbridge. The Palladium was normally a variety theatre. This was its first attempt at revue. The funniest sketch had Charles Austin as a harassed dad and his family missing train after train after train.

Feb 26. Franklyn Dyall as the Father and Muriel Pratt as the Step-Daughter in Luigi Pirandello's **Six Characters in Search of an Author** directed by Theodore Komisarjevsky at Kingsway. The half-finished characters, abandoned by their author, interrupt a rehearsal, searching for a director and actors capable of responding truthfully to their story of lechery, incest, prostitution, drowning and suicide. The play is an intellectual debate on illusion and reality and the very nature of theatre itself. Are the tragic six characters (the father filled with self-disgust, the grief-stricken mother, the hysterical stepdaughter, the silent children) any less real than the shallow actors, who want to play them in a crudely theatrical manner? The characters are fixed in time. They are what they are forever, with no possibility of change, constantly reliving their nightmare. *The Times* said it was "an amusing parlour game for metaphysicians." At the premiere in Rome in 1921 a furious audience had chased Pirandello down the street and he had escaped only by jumping into a taxi.

Mar 1. Owen Nares, Laura Cowie and Jean Cadell in Arthur Wing Pinero's **The Enchanted Cottage** directed by Arthur Wing Pinero at Duke of York's. Couple, who only got married in order to console each other, find true love in a cottage.
—[Pinero] has no natural genius for magic and it is too late in his career for him to apprentice himself to the fairy business. OWEN SEAMAN *Punch*

Mar 6. Russell Thorndike as Peer and Florence Buckton as Ase in Henrik Ibsen's **Peer Gynt** directed by Robert Atkinson at Old Vic. Translation by William and Charles Archer. First production in England.
—So long as it is possible for poetic drama to sweep its hearers from breathless silence into great tumultuous cheering there need be no despair for the theatre. *The Times*

Mar 8. Ernest Milton, Eric Maturin, Dawson Millward and Meggie Albanesi in John Galsworthy's **Loyalties** directed by Basil Dean at St Martin's. Rich young Jew, enjoying a Christian weekend in the country, is robbed of nearly a thousand pounds and since he feels he is only valued for his money, he wants it back. His host finds his behaviour "infernally awkward" and would prefer no fuss, no scandal. The public school bullies stick together and the unwritten code of gentlemen becomes synonymous with racial prejudice. The thief finally confesses and does "the decent thing" and shoots himself. Basil Dean thought Milton's performance as the Jew was the finest of his career. The company's ensemble work was highly praised. The pro-

Ernest Milton in **Loyalties**

1922 World Premieres
New York
 Eugene O'Neill's *The Hairy Ape*
Milan
 Luigi Pirandello's *Henry IV*
Berlin
 Ernst Toller's *The Machine Wreckers*
Leipzig
 Bertolt Brecht's *Baal*
Gottenburg
 August Strindberg's *To Damascus III*
Prague
 Karel Capek's *The Makropulous Secret*
Brno
 Karel and Josef Capek's *The Insect Play*

Births
Paul Scofield, British actor

Deaths
Marie Lloyd (*b.* 1870), British music hall star

Notes
BBC began transmissions
Marx Brothers make their first appearance in Europe at Coliseum

History
—Mahatma Gandhi imprisoned
—Tomb of Tutankhamun discovered

gramme informed the audience that the Lord Chamberlain had asked for "bloody" to be removed from the text. Audiences wondered why it was all right for Shaw to say "bloody" on the stage in Pygmalion in 1914 but not all right for Galsworthy in 1922. Acted with J M Barrie's **Shall We Join the Ladies?**
—The spirit of team-work will do for the London theatre what the actor-manager system did for it in the past. *Sunday Express*

Mar 19. Edith Evans as Cleopatra and Ion Swinley as Marc Antony in John Dryden's **All for Love** directed by Edith Craig at Shaftesbury. Staged in Restoration costume. Antony wore tights and curls.
—Miss Edith Evans has been betrayed by her costume into making of Cleopatra neither a Queen nor a woman of great passion but a lady of the court, indeed a pitiable, fluttering lady all tears and futile protests. It affects her intonation and weakens even her gestures. *The Times*

Mar 21. Arthur Bourchier and Kyrle Bellew in Arnold Bennett's **The Love Match** directed by Frank Vernon at Strand. Domestic discord.
—Mr Arnold Bennett takes himself very seriously as a dramatist; probably if he thought less of the importance of being Arnold B. he might write better plays ... He needs a guiding hand, someone to point out to him the North Star of dramatic climax. Action-action-action is what is wanted on the stage, not talk-talk-talk, which is what he gives us in *The Love Match. Play Pictorial*

Mar 22. Seymour Hicks in André Picard and Yves Mirande's **The Man in Dress Clothes** adapted and directed by Seymour Hicks at Garrick. Count is reduced to beggary but is too proud to ask his wife for some of the millions of francs he has settled on her.

Mar 27. Gertrude Kingston, Felix Aylmer, Mabel Terry-Lewis, Harold Scott, Milton Rosmer and Aubrey Mather in Bernard Shaw's **Getting Married** directed by Norman MacDermott at Everyman.
—The play is all talk but it is brilliant talk; and however serious in intention the dialogue is rampageously gay. DESMOND McCARTHY *New Statesman*

Apr 13. Ralph Lynn, Robertson Hare, Tom Walls and Mary Brough in Will Evans & Valentine's **Tons of Money** directed by E Holman Clark at Shaftesbury. Married couple, deep in debt, decide the best way to get some much-needed cash would be to impersonate a dead relative. The first of the Aldwych farces was a typical, but a poor, example of the genre. It ran for 723 performances.

Apr 13. Edyth Goodall in Edward Percy's **If Four Walls Told** directed by Reginald Denham at Royalty. Village drama: a woman knowingly lets her husband go to his death and then repents.

Apr 20. Willette Kershaw, Cowley Wright, Ellis Jeffreys in Robert McLaughlin's **Decameron Nights** adapted by Boyle Lawrence and directed by Arthur Collins at Drury Lane. Music by Herman Finck. Garish spectacle.

Apr 23. Henry Kendall and Louise Hampton in Harold Brighouse's **Zack** directed by Tristan Rawson at Comedy. Zack is a weakling and bullied by everybody.

Apr 25. Mary Odette and Ernest Thesiger in John Galsworthy's **Windows**, directed by Leon M Lion at Court.
—The play completely baffles me. Mr Galsworthy describes it as a comedy (for realists and others) but what he meant by it I cannot imagine. It is full of fun and wit and the situation is novel but I do not know whether Mr Galsworthy is making fun of the "idealists" or the "others" or himself. ST JOHN ERVINE *Observer*

May 1. Sybil Thorndike as Hecuba in Euripides's **The Trojan Women** directed by Lewis Casson at Palace.

May 30. Lyn Harding as Svengali and Phyllis Neilson-Terry as Trilby in Paul M Potter's **Trilby** directed by Cecil King at Apollo.
—*Trilby* has passed beyond the range of criticism; it is one of the Victorian things which the Georgian generation of playgoers accepts as sacrosanct. Mr Lyn Harding's Svengali has not the macabre, Semitic touch of Sir Herbert Tree used to lend the character but it is none the less a vigorous and impressive study. *Illustrated London News*

Jun 3. Gladys Cooper and Dennis Eadie in Arthur Wing Pinero's **The Second Mrs Tanqueray** at Playhouse. With her hair scraped back to accentuate her beauty, Cooper looked great. She made Paula harder, more petulant and less sympathetic. Mrs Patrick Campbell said she did not recognise the role she had created 29 years previously.

Jun 7. Henry Ainley, Allan Aynesworth, John Deverell and Athene Seyler in A A Milne's **The Dover Road** at Haymarket directed by Charles Hawtrey. Wealthy bachelor traps eloping couples and keeps them on a week's probation.
—Perhaps the most original feature in Mr Milne's treatment of the situation is his almost total disregard of the element of sex, which is popularly supposed to play some part in the relationship of lovers. OWEN SEAMAN *Punch*

Jul 12. The Lyceum reopened after a five-month closure with Edmund Gwenn as Bill in Bruce Bairnsfather's **Old Bill, MP**, directed by Seymour Hicks. Bairnsfather appeared as himself.

Aug 11. A W Baskcomb in **Snap** directed by Herbert Mason at Vaudeville. Revue by Ronald Jeans and Dion Titheradge. Music by Kenneth Duffield.
—It is one of the great secrets of Mr Baskcomb's success is that he can play a great variety of parts in a single performance, and while the characters are utterly different he can yet bring to them his own individuality which makes each piece of work a little gem of its kind. *The Times*

Aug 22. Cyril Maude and Binnie Hale in Ben Travers' **The Dippers** directed by Charles Hawtrey at Criterion. The Dippers were a dancing act. Maude played a man who was mistaken for a professional dancer.

Aug 26. Madge Titheradge, Norman McKinnel and Hugh Wakefield in Arthur Wimperis's adaptation of Alfred Savoir's **Bluebeard's Eighth Wife** directed by Stanley Bell at Queen's. A rich man is so crude in his courtship that his wife-to-be decides to teach him a lesson. She pretends she has had sex with another man. Transferred to Globe and then to Comedy.

Sep 2. C V France, Henry Kendall, Malcolm Keen and Meggie Albanesi in Somerset Maugham's **East of Suez** directed by Basil Dean at His Majesty's. European marries Chinese half-caste. Spectacular melodrama.

Sep 7. Fay Compton in Rudolf Besier and May Edginton's **Secrets** directed by Norman Page at Comedy. Family saga from 1865 to 1922. Fay Compton remained sweetly angelic throughout. Sentimental drama for sentimental theatregoers.

Sep 19. Dorothy Dickson, George Grossmith and Heather Thatcher in Jerome Kern's musical **The Cabaret Girl** directed by George Grossmith at Winter Garden. Book and lyrics by P G Wodehouse and George Grossmith. Witty and tuneful. The high spot was "Dancing Time".

Sep 25. Laura Cowie in John Drinkwater's **Mary Stuart** directed by John Drinkwater at Everyman. Harcourt Williams as Darnley. Randle Ayrton as Bothwell.
—Though we may have been wrong in supposing Mary to have been a voluptuary we hardly think Mr Drinkwater can be right in presenting her as a sentimental highbrow. *The Times*
—Obviously Miss Laura Cowie cannot in the title role give us the real Mary Stuart but there is distinction, colour, charm in her acting, despite the hampering influence of the precocity of the author. *Illustrated London News*

Oct 7. José Collins in Oscar Straus's **The Last Waltz** directed by Charles Hawtrey at Gaiety. Musical comedy without comedy. Collins sang the waltz song and "The Mirror Song" with consummate ease.

Oct 16. Sybil Thorndike in Euripides's **Medea** directed by Lewis Casson at New. Translation by Gilbert Murray. Leslie Faber as Jason. Lewis Casson as the Messenger.
—Her performance never falls short of its full tragic effect and is remarkable not only for its force but for the intellectual insight it exhibits. *The Times*

Oct 25. Beatrice Lillie in Morris Harvey and Harold Simpson's **The Nine O'Clock Revue** directed by Dion Titheradge at Little. One of the most popular numbers was Lillie as a suffragette singing "The Girls of the Old Brigade".

Oct 30. Irene Vanbrugh, Scott Sunderland and Martin Lewis in Arthur Wing Pinero's **Mid-Channel** directed by Leon M Lion at Royalty. Middle-aged couple take separate holidays. The wife is willing to forgive her husband his affair, but he is not willing to forgive her affair. She commits suicide by jumping off a balcony. *Era* said of Vanbrugh's performance: "We remember no finer piece of acting either on the English stage or any other stage. It is perfection – there is no other word for it."

Oct 31. Frank Denton and Mary Glynne in John Willard's **The Cat and the Canary** directed by Percy Moore at Shaftesbury. Homicidal maniac (with claw hands) is on the loose in a country house. The first in a series of American comedy-thrillers designed to scare the living daylights out of the heroine.

Nov 2. H St Barbe West as Mr Verloc in Joseph Conrad's **The Secret Agent** directed by Benrimo at Ambassadors. Too much talk. Alfred Hitchcock was more successful with his film version. "Mr Conrad is a great novelist," said *The Times*, "but not yet a great dramatist."

Nov 13. Sybil Thorndike and Robert Farquharson in Percy Bysshe Shelley's **The Cenci** directed by Lewis Casson at New. First public performance. Thorndike has, said one admirer, "the loveliness of Brynnhilde going into battle."

Nov 17. Violet Vanbrugh, Marie Löhr and Godfrey Tearle in Alfred Sutro's **The Laughing Lady** directed by Charles Hawtrey at Globe. Divorcee meets her brutal cross-examiner after the case is over.

Dec 22. Doris Clayton, Clara Butterworth and Courtice Pounds in **Lilac Time** directed by Dion Boucicault at Lyric. Musical based on the life and music of Franz Schubert. Book and lyrics by Adrian Ross. Songs included "Under the Lilac Bough", "Three Little Girls" and "Yours is My Heart".

Dec 23. Arthur Bourchier as Long John Silver in J B Fagan's adaptation of Robert Louis Stevenson's **Treasure Island** directed by J B Fagan at Strand.

Dec 30. Lilian Davies as Polly and Pitt Chatham as Macheath in John Gay's **Polly** adapted by Clifford Bax and directed by Nigel Playfair at Kingsway. Sequel to *The Beggar's Opera*. Set in the West Indies. Macheath was blacked up and led a band of pirates.

1923

Jan 31. Lydia Lopokova, Léonide Massine and George Robey in **You'd Be Surprised** at Covent Garden. The audience was indeed very surprised that Robey was appearing at the Royal Opera House in "a jazzaganza".

Jan 31. Owen Nares in **If Winter Comes** at St James's. Adaptation by A S M Hutchinson and B Macdonald Hastings of Hutchinson's best-selling novel. A girl refuses to disclose the name of the father of her child. She commits suicide. The wrong man gets the blame.

Feb 1. Kate Cutler, Herbert Marshall and Muriel Pope in Noël Coward's **The Young Idea** directed by Robert Courtneidge at Savoy. A comedy of youth inspired by Bernard Shaw's *You Never Can Tell*.
—Mr Coward is not only witty, but is also clever at covering up his wit. JAMES AGATE *Saturday Review*

Feb 15. Tallulah Bankhead and Audrey Carten in Hubert Parsons's **The Dancers** at Wyndham's. Parsons was a pseudonym for Gerald du Maurier and Violet Tree. Bankhead's solo dance made her reputation. Walter Maqueen-Pope said there had been nothing like her since Lily Langtry.
—[Tallulah Bankhead] has a quality of Yankee audacity and beauty combined with a smartness and breeding that would make her especially desirable in belted Earl circles. *Theatre*
—Some of us wish that Sir Gerald would sometimes do something better than a good Wyndham's play. But perhaps that's a little too ingenious of us. JOSEPH THORP *Punch*

Feb 21. Jean Cadell, Raymond Massey, Franklin Dyall and Hilda Moore in G K Munro's **At Mrs Beams'** directed by Franklin Dyall at Everyman. Boarding house comedy. Cadell repeated the big success she had had in 1921 as the gossiping spinster. "A masterpiece of acting," said *The Times*. "If the word 'genius' was not so misused we would apply it to this performance." Transferred to Royalty.
— [G K Munro's] peculiar power is his concrete grip of actualities. He pins down his figures and mercilessly dissects them. They stand revealed in their futility. J T GREIN *Illustrated London News*

Mar 24. Gladys Cooper in Hermann Sudermann's **Magda** at Playhouse. There were those who thought Cooper was better than Eleanor Duse.

Mar 31. Foster Richardson and Winifred O'Connor in a very free adaptation of John Gay's **Polly** directed by Chas B Williams at Chelsea Palace.

—So many false steps were being made all around her that at times she [Winifred O'Connor] seemed quite out of the picture, when the truth was that she was often the only one who was actually in the picture at all. *The Times*

Apr 10. Pauline Lord as Anna in Eugene O'Neill's **Anna Christie** directed by Arthur Hopkins at Strand. Ballad-like melodrama. When Mat (Frank Shannon), a strapping Irish stoker, claims Anna as his bride, as if she were a piece of furniture, she turns on him and her father (George Marion): "You can go to hell both of you. Nobody owns me. No man can tell me what to do. I am my own boss." Mat, who has never known a really decent woman in his life, is shattered when he learns she was a whore. "Will you not believe me that loving you has made me clean?" she pleads. The happy ending, which satisfied Broadway audiences in 1921, didn't satisfy O'Neill and he went on tinkering with the play, long after it had won the Pulitzer Prize. Pauline Lord recreated her Broadway performance.
—When the chance was here Miss Pauline Lord took it with amazing delicacy and power. Her performance cast over the theatre a spell now very rare, for it held beyond the emotion it immediately created. *The Times*

Apr 10. Herbert Marshall in Frederick Lonsdale's **Aren't We All?** directed by Stanley Bell at Globe. Wife unexpectedly returning home from abroad, catches her husband kissing a vamp. She refuses to forgive him. Her father-in-law determines to expose her hypocrisy by telling everybody about her own flirtation in Egypt. She in turn takes a terrible revenge on him and announces his engagement to an old flame in *The Times*. Lonsdale thought it his best play.

Apr 18. Charles Hawtrey and Lottie Venne in Somerset Maugham's **Jack Straw** directed by Charles Hawtrey at Criterion. Hawtrey repeated his successful double act of jocular, amicable Grand Duke disguised as dignified bearded waiter and Venne repeated her success as a parvenu, but the play fifteen years on didn't seem as good as it had done.
—Miss Lottie Venne, when one reckons the length of her public service, her comic genius and her enduring vitality, is easily the most remarkable actress of our time. *Era*

Apr 24. Leslie Banks and Basil Rathbone in Karel and Josef Capek's **RUR** (Rossum's Universal Robots) directed by Basil Dean at St Martin's. The word robot was coined by Karel from a word for toil and drudgery. Machines in human form kill off humans until there is only one left. The savage commentary on the soulless alliance between science and commercialism was hailed as one of the most original productions ever seen on the stage. Leslie Banks was a grim figure of metallic menace. "If the British playgoer does not want it," said Sydney W Carroll in *The Sunday Times*, "he does not deserve catering for at all."

May 5. Claude Rains, Elsa Lanchester, John Gielgud and Angela Baddeley in Karel and Josef Capek's **The Insect Play** directed by Nigel Playfair at Regent. Satire on mankind opened with butterflies flirting and fox-trotting. Their sexual activities were severely curtailed in the English translation. Gielgud as a poet butterfly looked very pretty. "I am surprised," he said. "that the audience did not throw things at me."
—Unparalleled effort in rampant lunacy...a futuristic satirical phantasmagoria without beauty, truth or balance. SYDNEY W CARROLL *Sunday Times*

May 6. Herbert Marshall, Raymond Massey and Edward Rigby in Ernest Toller's **The Machine Wreckers** translated by Ashley Dukes and directed by Nugent Monck at Kingsway. Set in the North of England at the time of the Luddite movement, circa 1816, the play begins with a debate between Lord Byron (defending the starving workers) and Lord Castlereagh (speaking for the bosses) on whether a parliamentary bill should be passed which will allow any person who destroys a weaving machine to be hanged. Castlereagh's message is expediency not sympathy: "The weak must go to the wall." Toller lectured and harangued the audience; the propaganda was heavy-going and repetitive. The production came to life only in the final quarter of an hour.

May 19. Carl Brisson, Evelyn Laye and George Graves in Franz Lehar's **The Merry Widow** directed by Fred J Blackman at Daly's.
—Evelyn Laye, without eclipsing her predecessor, was in every way her equal – she sings, acts, moves charmingly, and she has a pair of eyes so lustrous, so full of light and tenderness that they cast a spell on the house. *Illustrated London News*

May 28. Foundation stone of The People's Theatre laid at Pavilion, Whitechapel. First season included Bernard Shaw's **You Never Can Tell**, Henrik Ibsen's **Ghosts**, Emile Zola's **Thérèse Raquin** and H Weirs-Jennsen's **The Witch** translated by John Masefield. Young girl (Phyllis Relph) unhappily married to a priest (Campbell Gullan) falls in love with his son (Ernest Milton) by a former wife. She is transformed into a witch and burnt at the stake.

May 29. Henry Ainley in John Drinkwater's **Oliver Cromwell** directed by John Drinkwater at His Majesty's. A series of tableaux. Much of the dialogue was taken verbatim from old documents, but Drinkwater left out the grim and repellent side of his character.

1923 World Premieres

New York
Bernard Shaw's *Saint Joan*
Elmer Rice's *The Adding Machine*
Dublin
Sean O'Casey's *The Shadow of a Gunman.*
Vienna
Bertolt Brecht's *Baal*
Paris
Jules Romain's *Doctor Knock*
Birmingham
Bernard Shaw's *Back to Methuselah*

Births

Brendan Behan, Irish playwright
John Mortimer, British playwright

Deaths

Meggie Albanesie (*b.* 1899), British actor
Sarah Bernhardt (*b.* 1844), French actor

Notes

—J B Fagan founded Oxford Playhouse

History

—Atakurk proclaimed Turkey a Republic
—Adolf Hitler's *Mein Kampf* published
—5,000 speakeasies operating in New York

—Cromwell, idealised in this fashion, becomes a bravura part and Mr Ainley brings to it the right sort of bravura acting, though a little too easy in his rhetoric at times. *Illustrated London News*
—This brilliant and charming writer has unfortunately been encouraged since *Abraham Lincoln* to the belief that he has a flair for drama. *Era*

May 30. Fred Astaire and Adele Astaire in **Stop Flirting** directed by Felix Edwardes at Shaftesbury. Musical comedy. Book by Frederick Jackson. Music by William Daly, Paul Lannin and George Gershwin. Transferred to Strand.

May 31. Florence Mills in **Dover Street to Dixie** directed by Frank Collins at London Pavilion. Anglo-American revue. In the first half, the company was all white; in the second they were all black. Mills scored a big success.

Jun 5. Edna Best, Meggie Albanesi and J H Roberts in J Hastings Turner's **The Lilies of the Field** directed by Basil Dean at Ambassadors. Two sisters are rivals for the prize of a visit to London. A clergyman will decide who wins. The final performance of Meggie Albanesi who died at 24, following an abortion.

Jun 20. Felix Aylmer, Claude Rains, Leo G Carroll, Gordon Harker and John Gielgud in John Drinkwater's **Robert E Lee** directed by Nigel Playfair and John Drinkwater at Regent. Drinkwater having dramatised the American Civil War from a Northern perspective in *Abraham Lincoln*, now looked at events from a Southern perspective. Aylmer gave Lee a melancholy dignity.

Jun 29. Baliol Holloway in Ben Jonson's **Volpone** directed by Allan Wade at Regent. Rupert Harvey as Mosca.

Aug 2. Gladys Cooper in André Picard's **Enter Kiki** adapted by Sydney Blow and Douglas Hoare at Playhouse. Ambitious chorus girl sets her sights on becoming a theatre manager's wife or his mistress. A somewhat degraded picture of stage life, said *Era*. "It may be true of Paris; we are quite sure it is untrue of London – or at any rate wildly exaggerated."

Aug 25. Hermione Baddeley in Charles McEvoy's **The Likes of 'Er** directed by Esme Percy at St Martin's. Life in the slums. Child actress Baddeley had a big success smashing all the crockery.

Sep 4. Noël Coward and Gertrude Lawrence in Noël Coward's revue **London Calling**, directed by Herbert Mason at Duke of York's. Lawrence sang "Parisian Pierrot". The Sitwells were not amused by a skit at their expense.

Sep 5. Leslie Henson and Dorothy Dickson in Jerome Kern's musical **The Beauty Prize** directed by George Grossmith at Winter Garden. Book by George Grossmith and P G Wodehouse.
—On the whole the narrative is an arid desert in which the music of Mr Jerome Kern makes only an occasional oasis. *The Times*

Sep 7. George Arliss in William Archer's **The Green Goddess** directed by Maude T Howell at St James's. Melodrama set in a remote region beyond the Himalayas.

Sep 12. Margaret Bannerman and Constance Collier in Somerset Maugham's **Our Betters** directed by Stanley Bell at Globe. Written in 1915, it was not performed until 1923 and then only in a censored version. Maugham portrayed the American expatriates in London as trivial, transitory, worthless, heartless, vulgar snobs, whose only redeeming quality were their bank balances. They married into the aristocracy for a title and the English married them for their money. Since fidelity was not expected between husbands and wives, they had nothing to do but spend their time

in tawdry affairs. The kept boy (a liar, a gambler, an idle spendthrift, constantly sulking) had two very funny scenes. The first was when he persuaded his rich, fat, old mistress to buy him a motor car. The second was when she, having just caught him with another woman, begged for his forgiveness. The programme carried a note to the effect that owing to the rumours, which had circulated when the play was produced in America, Maugham wanted to make it clear that the characters were entirely imaginary. But the boy (called Anthony Paxton) was a portrait of Gerald Haxton (Maugham's own boyfriend), while the boy's mistress was a grotesque parody of himself.
—Mr Maugham's new comedy is like its heroine, clever, cynical and shameless. Straight-laced playgoers will affect to be shocked by it. *The Times*

Sep 17. Frederick Cooper, Frederick Leister, Gladys ffolliott and Diana Hamilton in Vane Sutton-Vane's **Outward Bound** directed by Vane Sutton-Vane at Everyman. Modern morality play set aboard an ocean liner is a microcosm of society. Everybody travels first class. "We're all dead, aren't we?" asks a neurotic young man who drinks too much. "We're sailing for heaven or hell – it's the same place," replies the steward, pouring him another drink. The passengers have a bit of difficulty getting used to the idea that they are dead. The crooked financier and the snobbish aristocratic old lady (who was once a tart) are damned and going to hell. The nice char and the nice vicar (who doesn't know why he should have died so young) are on their way to heaven. The neurotic young man is saved at the last minute by an act of kindness and is re-united with his old mum (a charwoman) though he doesn't know she is his mum. Two would-be suicides are rescued in the nick of time by their dog turning off the gas and breaking the window. They get off the liner. Glib, sentimental, silly and often unintentionally funny, the production was, nevertheless, every so often, chilling and moving. Transferred to Garrick.

Sep 19. Sybil Thorndike as Imogen and Robert Farquharson as Iachimo in Shakespeare's **Cymbeline** directed by Lewis Casson at New. Lawrence Anderson was very funny as Cloten.
—Miss Thorndike gives the impression of having swallowed the character in one gulp and of looking round the stage for something with which to be effective. JAMES AGATE *Sunday Times.*

Cathleen Nesbitt and Henry Ainley in Hassan

Sep 20. Henry Ainley, Basil Gill, Leon Quartermaine, Malcolm Keen, Laura Cowie, Frank Cochrane and Cathleen Nesbitt in the late James Elroy Flecker's **Hassan and how he came to make the golden journey to Samarkand** directed by Basil Dean and choreographed by Michel Fokine at His Majesty's. An Arabian Nights mixture of spectacle, poetry, cruelty, irony and beauty.
—*Hassan* is that rare thing, a work of genius; not faultless, but of an overwhelming, almost dismaying, vitality. There is a splendour, a prodigality in Flecker's outpouring of himself in this borrowed but entirely congenial and perfectly adapted Oriental mood which gives the experience, seldom attained by the sophisticated playgoer, of a genuine excitement of the theatre. JOSEPH THORP *Punch*

Sep 22. José Collins in Reginald Arkell and Fred de Gresac's **Catherine** by directed by Matheson Lang at Gaiety. Music by Tchaikovsky. Not Catherine the Great but rather Catherine the peasant who became the Empress. Bertram Wallis played Peter the Great.

Oct 9. Eille Norwood in J E Harold Terry and Arthur Ross's **The Return of Sherlock Holmes** directed by Eille Norwood at Princes. Since the play was based on a number of stories by Arthur Conan Doyle, Holmes has to deal with a number of criminals at the same time. H G Stoker as Watson.

Oct 13. Sybil Thorndike and Mary Merrall in Henry Arthur Jones's **The Lie** directed by Lewis Casson at New. Two sisters: one pretends her illegitimate baby belongs to the other.
—Miss Thorndike and Miss Merrall give able and lavish displays of emotional fireworks in parts that call for little else. *The Times*

Oct 19. Milton Rosmer in Arnold Bennett's **What the Public Wants** directed by Milton Rosmer at Everyman.

Nov 4. Henry Kendall, Leslie Faber, Richard Bird and Frances Carson in Harry Wall's **Havoc** directed by Leo G Carroll at Regent. Two officers in World War I, great friends, fall out because of their love for the same woman. The rejected lover takes his revenge by sending his rival to almost certain death. Transferred to Haymarket.

Nov 7. Ion Swinley and Florence Saunders in Shakespeare's **Troilus and Cressida** directed by Robert Atkins at Old Vic. Hay Petrie as Thersites. The Old Vic was the first theatre to have presented a complete cycle of Shakespeare's plays.
—We may hope, look forward now to a return to plays done more for pleasure's sake than for duty's. *The Times*

Nov 21. John Deverell as Algernon Moncrieff, Leslie Faber as John Worthing and Margaret Scudamore as Lady Bracknell in Oscar Wilde's **The Importance of Being Earnest** directed by Allan Aynesworth at Haymarket. Modern dress production.
—Time has taken the curl out of the epigrams, and they cannot be brought up to date merely by the ladies of the cast wearing the latest from Curzon Street ... It can do his reputation [Leslie Faber's] no harm to point out that for light fantastic comedy he has no talent. *Observer*

Dec 20. Evelyn Laye in **Madame Pompadour** directed by Fred J Blackman at Daly's. Book by Frederick Lonsdale. Musical. Book and lyrics by Harry Graham. Music by Leo Fall. Historical pageant. Bertram Wallis played King Louis.
—Miss Evelyn Laye looks as pretty as a piece of Louis Quinze porcelain; she has dainty, coquettish ways and she sings attractively. *Illustrated London News*

1924

Jan 2. Binnie Hale and Stanley Lupino in **Puppets!** directed by Dion Titheradge at Vaudeville. Revue. Book by Dion Titheradge. Music by Ivor Novello. Hale gave imitations of Evelyn Laye, José Collins and Beatrice Lillie.

Jan 16. Richard Bird, Henry Kendall and Frances Carson in Harry Wall's **Havoc** directed by Leslie Faber at Haymarket. The horrors of World War I. Bird played a shell-shocked young soldier. Kendall played a blinded major. Carson played a vamp.

Jan 23. Marie Tempest and Elizabeth Irving in J M Barrie's **Alice-Sit-By-the-Fire** directed by Stanley Bell at Comedy. The vogue for make-believe had passed.

Jan 31. Madge Titheradge and Frank Cellier in Somerset Maugham's **The Camel's Back** directed by H F Maltby at Playhouse. Wife decides to teach her priggish husband a lesson. She pretends he is mad and calls in a doctor.

Feb 1. Ralph Lynn, Tom Walls and Will Deming in Roi Cooper Megrue and Walter Hackett's **It Pays to Advertise** directed by Tom Walls at Aldwych. American farce. Bogus soap business: "Thirteen Soap – Unlucky for Dirt."

Feb 5. Athene Seyler and Franklin Dyall in Luigi Chiarelli's **The Mask and the Face** translated by C B Fernald and directed by Norman MacDermott at Everyman. Italian count feels that marriage is a pact for life and that a woman who breaks her vow should pay with her life. So when he discovers his wife has been unfaithful to him he kills her. He stands trial for murder and thanks to the brilliance of his lawyer (who happens to be his wife's lover, though he does not know this) his sentence is reduced. Actually, he hasn't killed her at all. The Italian legal system is not amused and he is threatened with arrest. Since the period of imprisonment would be far longer than a sentence for murder, the Count and his wife decide to run away together. One of the first Italian plays to deal with reality and illusion. Premiered in 1916 in Rome it launched the Teatro del Grottesco.

Feb 7. Robert Loraine as Mirabell and Edith Evans as Millamant in William Congreve's **The Way of the World** at Lyric, Hammersmith. Nigel Playfair's fantasticated production was declared to be "the most deliciously witty thing in London" and "a rattling, jigging, almost jazzing revival." Evans entered in full sail, with her fan spread and streamers out. Loraine matched her in elegance and ease of manner.
—[Edith Evans] is a brilliant, sparkling, charming Millamant, a coquette who plays with her own heart as well as Mirabell's; yet never in her most provoking moments lets you forget she has one. *Morning Post.*
—Miss Edith Evans is the most accomplished of living and practising English actresses...She has a wider range than any other artist and is unrivalled alike in sentimental and heartless comedy. JAMES AGATE *Sunday Times.*
—*The Way of the World*, in spite of the eulogies of the critics, has never failed to lead to bankruptcy. NIGEL PLAYFAIR *History of Lyric Hammersmith*.

Feb 17. Baliol Holloway as Horner and Isabel Jeans as Marjery Pinchwife in William Wycherley's **The Country Wife** directed by Allan Wade at Regent. The first performance since 1748. *Era* said that Isabel Jeans had never done anything better.

Feb 18. Bernard Shaw's **Back to Methuselah** directed by H K Ayliff at Court. "Are you mad?" Shaw asked Barry Jackson, artistic director of Birmingham Repertory Theatre, when he requested his permission to stage the British premiere. Shaw (who had written the play shortly after World War I) said it was his Ring cycle and that it was either a world classic or it was nothing. The cycle of five plays begins with Adam and Eve and then is set in 1921, 2170, 3000 and 31, 920. The subject is longevity and the argument is that man will continue to live longer and longer because life at present is too short for him to take it seriously and to profit by the experience. Shaw thought it was his best play, an opinion nobody who has sat through its tedium has ever shared. The production was spread over five nights.

Feb 20. Ion Swinley in Goethe's **Faust** directed by Robert Atkins at Old Vic. George Hayes as Mephistopheles. The *Faust* audiences had seen when Henry Irving and Herbert Beerbohm Tree played the leading role was based on Gounod's opera. Atkins's production aimed at something which was more faithful to Goethe.

Mar 6. Leslie Banks and Hermione Baddeley in John Galsworthy's **The Forest** directed by Basil Dean at St Martin's. Diamonds and slave-trade. Englishmen in Central Africa fight a losing battle against the forest.

Mar 8. Gladys Cooper, Lady Tree, Irene Vanbrugh, Norman Forbes in Victorien Sardou's **Diplomacy** directed by Gerald du Maurier at Adelphi.

Mar 11. Cedric Hardwicke, Melville Cooper, Evelyn Hope and Maud Gill in Eden Phillpotts's **The Farmer's Wife**, directed by Barry Jackson at Court. The farmer proposes to three women before he realizes that he should have proposed to his housekeeper in the first place. "You'd never know I was breaking you in," he assures her. The humour, the aphorisms, the metaphors and similes were drawn from Devonshire

Robert Loraine and Edith Evans in The Way of the World

country life. Originally written in 1912 and produced at Birmingham in 1916, Phillpotts never saw the play. At each centenary he would give a party for the cast, which he never attended.

—I never see a good provincial repertory team at work without strengthening my conviction that this is the way the business of acting should be done. Joseph Thorp *Punch*

—Sweet and wholesome humour that is typically English. Probably that is why the play is so popular. *Theatre World*

Mar 13. Godfrey Tearle, Allan Jeayes, Henrietta Watson and Franklyn Bellamy in Frederick Lonsdale's **The Fake** directed by Godfrey Tearle at Apollo. Altruistic murder. A drunkard is killed by a friend of the family who feels sorry for the man's wife.

Mar 16. Stage Society. Brember Wills as Mr Zero in Elmer Rice's **The Adding Machine** directed by A E Filmer at Strand. Expressionistic fable dedicated to all the guys who didn't get a "square deal" from either President Roosevelt or God. Zero is a clerk, who has given twenty-five years to his firm. The only time his boss speaks to him is to sack him. Automation has made him redundant. Zero shoots his boss, is convicted, and goes to heaven where he works in a new office until he is told that he has to go back to earth and start his humdrum, anonymous life all over again. Zero's defence in court is a moving indictment of the dehumanized 20th century and the retrograde mentality it produced. Rice was at its best when he was being satirical and at his most embarrassing when the action was set in the graveyard and in the Elysium Fields, and he was imitating William Saroyan.

Mar 23. Nicholas Hannen in Allan Monkhouse's **The Conquering Hero** directed by Milton Rosmer at Aldwych. Anti-war play. Shell-shocked soldier returns from the front to berate his family for celebrating his homecoming. Transferred to Queen's and then to St Martin's.

Mar 26. Sybil Thorndike in Bernard Shaw's **Saint Joan** directed by Lewis Casson under Bernard Shaw's instruction at New. Designed by Charles Ricketts. O B

Clarence as Inquisitor. Ernest Thesiger as Dauphin. Eugene Leahy as Cauchon. Lyall Swete as Warwick. Robert Horton as Dunois. Jack Hawkins as the Page. Chronicle in six scenes and an epilogue draws freely on history and legend. The Inquisitor has a great exit line after condemning Joan to death: "It is a terrible thing to see a young and innocent creature crushed between these mighty forces, the Church and the Law … Oh, quite innocent. What does she know of the Church and the Law? She did not understand a word we were saying. It is the ignorant who suffer." *The Daily Telegraph* said Saint Joan "might have been written for Miss Thorndike." *The Daily Express* said she had never given a better performance.

—It was the greatest achievement of her career. All the simplicity, the sublime tenacity of faith and passion for a cause, was shown clearly and vividly. A E Wilson *Star*

—Miss Thorndike did her best to tear down her extravagant mannerisms to the simple dignity of the role she was taking. But she has these last few years so played up to the gallery, so indulged all her worst proclivities that she will need a longer course of spiritual mortification before she can play a poetic character simply. As it was, whenever she got on to the high pedal she was intolerable. *Athenæum*

—The Dauphin was beautifully played by Mr Thesiger, who showed beneath his astonishing grotesqueries the pity and pathos of all weakness. James Agate *Sunday Times*

—[Bernard Shaw] can lay you flat and knock all the conceit out of you without making you feel humiliated. *Sybil Thorndike*

Apr 16. José Collins in **Our Nell** directed by Arthur Bourchier at Gaiety. Musical whitewash of Nell Gwynn, stodgy and humourless. Book by Louis N Parker and Reginald Arkell. Music by Harold Fraser-Simson and Ivor Novello. Lyrics by Harry Graham and Reginald Arkell. Arthur Wontner as Charles II. Novello wrote a stirring marching song, "Our England", which was popular with military bands and British Fascists who liked it so much they wanted to adopt it as their anthem.

—The first song to raise the enthusiasm of the audience to Gaiety first night pitch was *Our England*, which seemed a judicious mixture of Shakespeare, *God Save the King* and *Keep The Home Fires Burning*. It was sung by José Collins as Nell Gwynn, who also for then occasion had become a symbol of patriotism, a sort of Cockney Joan of Arc. *Evening News*

Sybil Thorndike in Saint Joan

Apr 26. Shakespeare's **Hamlet** directed by Robert Atkins at Old Vic with Ion Swinley playing the matinee and Ernest Milton playing the evening performance. Swinley was a virile, mature man of action. Milton was young, gentle, hesitant, and romantic.

May 12. Jack Buchanan and June in **Toni** directed by Herbert Bryan at Shaftesbury. Musical. Book by Douglas Furber and Harry Graham. Music by Hugo Hirsch. Lyrics by Douglas Furber. Farcical comedy. Englishman helps a European princess sort out her political problems. Buchanan saved the show with his wit, singing and dancing.

May 15. Brian Aherne, Mary Clare and Franklin Dyall in Leon Gordon's **White Cargo** directed by Ida Molesworth at Playhouse. In a far-flung post of the British Empire, a half-caste vamp attempts to poison her husband when she learns that marriage is a life contract. Billed as "Vivid play of the Primitive Unvarnished Life of the Tropics," it offered malaria, whisky, sex and quinine. The censor insisted Mary Clare put on more clothes. Transferred to Fortune and then to Princes.

May 21. Alfred Lester, Sonnie Hale and Billy Leonard in **Punch Bowl** directed by Alfred de Bear at Duke of York's. High spot was a Punch and Judy ballet to music by Norman O'Neill. Transferred to His Majesty's.

May 24. John Gielgud and Gwen Ffrangcon-Davies in Shakespeare's **Romeo and Juliet** directed by H K Ayliff at Regent. Ffrangcon-Davies got the praise. Gielgud got the brickbats.
—Mr Gielgud's body from his hips down never meant anything throughout the evening. He has the most meaningless legs imaginable. Ivor Brown *Observer*

Jun 3. Marie Tempest and Frederick Ranalow in **Midsummer Madness** at Lyric, Hammersmith. Book by Clifford Bax. Music by Armstrong Gibbs.

Jun 9. Ivor Novello and Isabel Jeans in David L'Estrange's **The Rat** directed by Constance Collier at Prince of Wales. The Story of an Apache. The Rat is redeemed by a woman. David L'Estrange was a pseudonym for Novello and Collier.
—No cliché in the way of phrase has been omitted and no tag of sentiment neglected. James Agate *Sunday Times*
—As a work of art the value of *The Rat* is about ninepence, at a liberal estimate, but as a box office attraction I should think it ranks at about £1,500 a week. *London Opinion*

June 27. Phyllis Dare, Harry Welchman and A W Baskcomb in **The Street Singer** directed by E Lyall Swete at Lyric. Musical. Book by Frederick Lonsdale. Music by H Fraser-Simson. Lyrics by Percy Greenback. Duchess disguises herself as a singer.

Sep 11. Margery Hicklin, Jack Hulbert, Leslie Henson and Heather Thatcher in **Primrose** directed by George Grossmith at Winter Garden. Musical comedy. Book by George Grossmith and Guy Bolton. Lyrics by Desmond Carter. Music by George Gershwin. An old-fashioned, pre-war sumptuous production lasted four hours. There was a fabulous staircase stretching from footlights to the roof.

Oct 9. Colin Keith-Johnston as Adam, Gwen Ffrangcon-Davies as Eve, Edith Evans as Serpent and Scott Sutherland as Cain in Bernard Shaw's **Back to Methuselah** directed by Barry Jackson at Court.
—It is an extraordinary imaginative effort, but not an artistic success; the proportions are wrong. Some profound things are said by the way and not a few absurd ones. Desmond McCarthy *New Statesman and Nation*

Oct 21. Norman McKinnel in John Galsworthy's **Old English** directed by E Lyall Swete at Haymarket. Based on Galsworthy's short story, *A Stoic. The Times* thought McKinnel's portrait of an old man on his last legs was "a masterpiece of imaginative acting in the grand style."

Oct 23. Elsie French, Frank Cochrane, Elsa MacFarlane and Nigel Playfair in Richard Brinsley Sheridan's **The Duenna** directed by Nigel Playfair at Lyric, Hammersmith. The comic operetta enjoyed seventy-five nights when first produced in 1775 but it never held the stage so well again outside of the 18th century. The lyrics have wit. Two scenes – the irate father giving orders to his household and the Duenna entertaining her Jewish suitor – hint at the brilliance that was to come in *The School for Scandal*. A scene which might have caused offence to Roman Catholics was omitted.

Nov 9. The Fellowship of Players. Ernest Milton in Shakespeare's **King John** directed by Stanley Drewitt at Strand. An orgy of shouting. Milton's John was a melodramatic rogue, a drawling simpleton. Norman V Norman's Bastard, acted with great gusto and humour, made a bigger impression.

Nov 25. Lilian Braithwaite and Noël Coward in Noël Coward's **The Vortex** directed by Noël Coward under direction of Norman Macdermott at Everyman. Shallow, silly woman craves admiration and flattery. She makes a vulgar scene and humiliates herself with her lover, a boy half her age, who happens to be the ex-boyfriend of her son's fiancée. The 24-year-old Coward said he wrote the play to give himself a whacking good part. The idea of an upper-class boy upbraiding his mother for her immorality so revolted the stage censor that he wanted to ban the play. Nor did he care for Coward's portrait of a hedonistic society, idle, bitchy and decadent, "swirling about in a vortex of beastliness." The play was a smash hit, making Coward's name as playwright and

Noel Coward and Lilian Braithwaite in The Vortex

actor. Gerald du Maurier, the leading member of the acting profession, was horrified. "The younger generation," he observed, "are knocking at the door of the dustbin."
—There's a great deal of morality in that drama. I disapproved of elderly ladies having young lovers. NOËL COWARD.

Dec 7. The Stage Society. Laura Cowie, Leon Quartermaine, Allan Jeayes and Eileen Beldon in Ashley Duke's **The Man with a Load of Mischief** directed by A E Filmer at New. The Man is an inn where an opera singer (Cowie), fleeing from her lover (the Prince Regent, no less) meets a nobleman's valet (Quartermaine), who successfully woos her. The valet, both in mind and character, is infinitely superior to his ignoble master (Jeayes). Ashley Duke's elegant conversation piece was hailed as a modern masterpiece and revived at the Haymarket in 1925.

Dec 24. Tubby Edlin and Ambrose Thorne in an adaptation of W A Darlington's novel, **Alf's Button** directed by Holman Clark and E Dagnall at Prince's. Alf is a descendent of Aladdin. Edlin, droll and tearful, and Thorne, hale and hearty, made a good double act.

Dec 26. Gwen Ffrangcon-Davies as Titania and Robert Harris as Oberon in Shakespeare's **A Midsummer Night's Dream** directed by Basil Dean at Drury Lane. Christmas spectacular with a large choir, 21 fairies and 5 gnomes. Music by Mendelssohn. Ballet by Michel Fokine. D H Petrie as Puck. Edith Evans as Helena. Athene Seyler as Hermia. Leon Quartermaine as Lysander. Wilfrid Walter as Bottom. Frank Cellier as Quince. H O Nicholson as Starveling. Miles Malleson as Snout. Clifford Mollison as Flute. Mary Clare as Hippolyta. Allan Jeayes as Theseus. The play had not been produced at Drury Lane in nearly 100 years. Evans was so disappointed with her performance that she decided to go to the Old Vic to learn how to play Shakespeare.
—His people were not shadows of a dream, but grossly realistic personalities, who moved about principally in a scene which reminded me more of the steps of the Albert Memorial than a wood not far from Athens. B W FINDON *Play Pictorial*

1925

Jan 29. Ian Hunter, Cecily Byrne, Edna Best and Cathleen Nesbitt in Frederick

Lonsdale's **Spring Cleaning** directed by Basil Dean at St Martin's. Satire on post-war society. Young husband, disapproving of his wife's decadent friends, invites a prostitute to dinner, pointing out that she only does for a living what they do for pleasure.

Feb 19. John Barrymore in Shakespeare's **Hamlet** directed by John Barrymore at Haymarket. Malcolm Keen as Claudius. Constance Collier as Gertrude. Fay Compton as Ophelia. "I want him to be so male," said Barrymore, "that when I come out on the stage they can hear my balls clank." He was the most successful American in the role on the London stage since Edwin Booth.
—He began far better than he went on. He has undoubted grace and intelligence but he does not improve an unShakespearean voice by sad over-emphasis. The king spoke him clean off the stage. *Sunday Express*

Feb 21. Lilian Davies in Frederick Lonsdale's **Katja, The Dancer** directed by Fred J Blackman at Gaiety. Gene Gerrard and Ivy Tresmand sang "Leander" and took eight calls before the show could proceed.

Mar 5. Dorothy Green as Mrs Malaprop, Douglas Burbidge as Captain Absolute, Isabel Jeans as Lydia, Claude Rains as Faulkland, Nigel Playfair as Acres and Angela Baddeley as Lucy in Richard Brinsley Sheridan's **The Rivals** directed by Nigel Playfair at Lyric, Hammersmith.
—The best performance was given by Mr Claude Rains whose Faulkland was a fine, spirited piece of comic acting … Miss Isabel Jeans was deliciously languid and charmingly affected as Lydia. *Era*
—[Dorothy Green's] faults of diction are delivered with an over-emphasis which misses all the unconscious humour which should make you laugh in the delivery. There is no unction or spontaneity in her acting, and she throws her Malapropisms at you like an "Irish bouquet." YORRICK *Theatre World*

Mar 11. Binnie Hale, George Grossmith and Joseph Coyne in Vincent Youmans's **No, No, Nanette** directed by William Mollison at Palace. Quintessential American 1920s flapper musical. Book and lyrics by Frank Mandel, Otto Harbach and Irving Caesar. Binnie Hale became a star overnight and everybody sang "Tea for Two" and "I Want to Be Happy".
—*No, No, Nanette* is the happiest musical comedy London has seen for years. It is spontaneous, harmonious, delicious; it prances, bubbles, makes rings of joy like a dog let loose in a field; it goes with a lilt and a swing and a scamper. HERBERT FARJEON *Sunday Pictorial*

John Barrymore in **Hamlet**

1925 World Premieres

New York
George S Kaufman's *Cocoanuts*
Sidney Howard's *Lucky Sam MacCarver*
Vincent Youmans's *No, No Nanette*

Births
James Saunders, British playwright

Honours
Knight
Barry Jackson, British director
Dame
Ellen Terry, British actor
Nobel Prize for Literature
Bernard Shaw

Notes
—Charleston became popular
—Josephine Baker was a sensation in Paris in *La Revue Nègre* at Théâtre des Champys-Elysées
—Mae West and Broadway cast of her play, *Sex,* were arrested in New York

History
—Monkey Trial of John T Scopes for teaching Darwinian evolution in school in USA
—Premiere of Charlie Chaplin's *The Gold Rush*
—Premiere of Sergei Eisenstein's *Battleship Potemkin*

Mar 18. Matheson Lang, Isobel Elsom and Edmund Willard in Rafael Sabatini's **The Tyrant: An Episode in the Career of Cesare Borgia** directed by Matheson Lang at New. Historical romance. "It brings back," said Yorrick in *Theatre World*, "the thrill of colour and adventure to our drab and clock-ruled world."

Mar 20. Billy Merson, Edith Day and Derek Oldham in **Rose Marie** directed by Felix Edwardes at Drury Lane. Musical. Book and lyrics by Otto Harbach and Oscar Hammerstein 2nd. Music by Rudolf Friml and Herbert Stothart. Romance in the Canadian Rockies.(Yoo-oo-oo is the Indian Love Call.) The critics thought it "a conglomeration of pretentious piffle." The public loved it. High spot was the *Totem Tom Tom* dance.

Mar 21. Gladys Cooper in Arthur Wing Pinero's **Iris** at Adelphi. The play was set in the Twenties when it would have been better to revive it as a period piece.
—The impression of pain is no doubt in the playwright's scheme but it is made all the sharper by the actress. Of course it is a beautiful performance – Miss Cooper has done nothing better – but the very beauty of it only intensifies your pain. *The Times*

Apr 21. Edna Best and Tallulah Bankhead in Noël Coward's **Fallen Angels** directed by Stanley Bell at Globe. The critics said it was vulgar, disgusting, outrageous, shocking, nauseating, vile, obscene and degenerate, all of which were excellent for the box office. The sight of two respectable, married women getting spectacularly drunk while waiting for a former French lover was thought to be particularly degrading. The *Daily Express* described them as 'suburban sluts.'

—Glitters with the phosphorescence of decay. Shows not a nasty mind but a juvenile preoccupation with nasty things. JAMES AGATE *Sunday Times*

Apr 25. Ernest Milton in Shakespeare's **Hamlet** in its entirety directed by Robert Atkins at Old Vic. The performance began at 1 p.m. and ended at 6 p.m.
—His mannerisms were less noticeable this time. He was quicker for one thing and did not dwell too long over certain words, rolling and loving them as he does sometimes. *Era*

Apr 30. Alice Delysia, Douglas Byng, Nigel Bruce, Ernest Thesiger and Hermione Baddeley in Noël Coward's revue **On with the Dance** directed by Frank Collins at London Pavilion. The high spots were two ballets by Léonide Massine: *The Rake* was based on William Hogarth's engravings. *Crescendo* "attempted to shatter the gentle tranquillity of *Les Sylphides* by the insistent clamour of modernity."

May 12. Olga Lindo as Sadie Thompson and Malcolm Keen as Rev Davidson in Somerset Maugham's **Rain** directed by Basil Dean at Garrick. Adaptation by John Colton and Clemence Randolph. The prostitute and the preacher made for a sordid, sub-tropical drama. The local colour was laid on thickly and the rain was incessant. 750 gallons of water were precipitated from the flies at each performance. Tallulah Bankhead had hysterics outside Dean's offices when she learned Dean had cast Lindo in the leading role.
—There is nothing your average pit and gallery like so much as the fury of hysteria and the actress who can achieve it becomes their idol. Miss Olga Lindo can, and is duly idolised. *The Times*

May 28. Anton Chekhov's **The Cherry Orchard** directed by J B Fagan transferred from The Oxford Playhouse to Lyric, Hammersmith. Mary Grey as Ranevsky. O B Clarence as Firs. John Gielgud as Tusenbach. Audiences and critics unused to Chekhov were divided. Some thought the play "one of the dramatic masterpieces of all time", "flawless in artistic form", "an oasis just now in a desert of jazz", "a great play"; others found it "dull, stupid, stuff" and saw "no reason why this fatuous drivel should be translated at all."

Jun 2. Evelyn Laye and Alec Fraser in Brammer and Gruenwald's comic opera **Cleopatra** adapted by John Hastings and directed by Oscar Asche at Daly's. Music by Oscar Straus. Lyrics by Harry Graham. It wasn't very Egyptian. Laye and Fraser sang "I'm Your Slave."
—What matter, therefore, if our one and only Evelyn did get occasionally a trifle off the note, or mouthed her words like sweetmeats – which they are, as they fall in faultless elocution from her lips? YORRICK *Theatre World*

Jun 8. Marie Tempest, W Graham Browne, Athole Stewart and Hilda Moore in Noël Coward's **Hay Fever** directed by Noël Coward at Ambassadors. Four self-centred egoists and their unfortunate guests have a stressful weekend in the country.

Helen Spencer, Athole Stewart, Ann Trevor, Patrick Susands, W Graham Browne, Hilda Moore, Robert Andrews and Marie Tempest in Hay Fever

The family are insufferable Bohemians and liable to turn any situation into instant theatre. "You're the most infuriating set of hypocrites I've ever seen," says one of the guests. "This house is a complete feather-bed of false emotions" Coward based his comedy on his own experience when he was the weekend guest of the American actress Laurette Taylor and her husband, Hartley Manners, and had to suffer their appalling manners and acrimonious party games. Dashed off in three days, Coward said *Hay Fever* was far and away one of the most difficult plays to perform that he had ever encountered; but this has never stopped countless revivals, professional and amateur.

—As a piece of brilliant, impudent and sustained fooling the play is very pleasant entertainment and well enough "made" to delight a Frenchman. JAMES AGATE *Sunday Times*

—There is no real plot, nor wit, and the humour is rather that of a decorous clown-scene, but it is very funny. The first act, especially so. The second act, too. ARKAY *Tatler*

Jun 11. Fay Compton, Leon Quartermaine, Frank Cellier and Joyce Kennedy in Ashley Dukes's **The Man with a Load of Mischief** directed by E Lyall Swete at Haymarket. The critics likened Dukes to Marivaux.

—It is an exquisite little work of art, romantic in its total significance, perfect in its symmetry, and of the most delicate workmanship. A E WILSON *Star*

Jun 12. George Merritt, Alexander Field, Leslie J Banks, Felix Aylmer, Harold Scott, and Roger Livesey in Eugene O'Neill's **The Long Voyage Home** directed by Norman MacDermott at Everyman. Swedish seaman, who hasn't been home in ten years and has had enough sea to last him all his life, is drugged, robbed of all his money and press-ganged into service yet again. Acted in a double bill with Eugene O'Neill's **Diff'rent** with Ion Swinley and Roger Livesey directed by Norman McDermott.

Jun 20. Seymour Hicks and Madge Titheradge in Ferenc Molnar's **The Guardsman** directed by Seymour Hicks at St James's. Lovelorn actor attempts to seduce his actress wife in the guise of a guardsman to test her faithfulness. The question is who gives the most convincing performance? The husband as the guardsman? Or the wife pretending she cannot see through the disguise? They are both actors, liars by profession. She says she recognised him all the time; and for his own peace of mind he has to believe her and admit he is a second-rate actor. The play was booed.

—All those who love the stage should voice their protests against a policy of indiscriminate "free imports" such as that responsible for the production of such Hungarian sexualities. *Play Pictorial.*

—The audience everywhere in the world laughed at a perfectly agonising play of mine. FERENC MOLNAR.

Jun 23. Frederic Ranalow as Macheath in John Gay's **The Beggar's Opera** directed by Nigel Playfair at Lyric, Hammersmith. Sara Allgood as Mrs Peachum. Kathlyn Hilliard as Polly. Miles Malleson as Filch. The once infamous and immensely popular "Newgate Pastoral" was first performed in 1728, when its popularity was due to audiences enjoying the musical burlesque of Italian opera and opera singers and the satire at the expense of the notoriously corrupt Prime Minister, Sir Robert Walpole, and his Whig administration. Highwaymen and whores were a perfect mirror reflection for the lives of the politicians.

Jul 15. Ernest Milton in Luigi Pirandello's **Henry IV** directed by A E Filmer at Everyman. Italian aristocrat, taking part in a historical pageant, dressed up as Henry IV, falls from his horse and is knocked unconscious. When he comes to he is convinced he is Henry IV (1050–1106), the German Emperor, famous for his great charm and dangerous temper, who was twice excommunicated by the Pope. The aristocrat's family maintains the deception by converting part of his villa into a medieval castle and hiring actors to impersonate his retinue. For the next twenty years they continue the masquerade for his "mad" benefit. The role was an excellent showcase for Ernest Milton's talents. Pirandello wrote the play shortly after his wife was committed to an asylum in 1919.

Jul 22. Tom Walls, Ralph Lynn, Robertson Hare, Mary Brough and Yvonne Arnaud in Ben Travers's **A Cuckoo in the Nest** directed by Tom Walls at Aldwych. This production marked the real beginning of the famous Aldwych farces in the 1920s. A reluctant married man is forced to share a bedroom in an inn with a married woman. The monocled, knuckle-biting Ralph Lynn was the supreme silly ass.

—Mr Ben Travers has performed – a rather significant, and in these days, rare feat, that of treating what is known as a delicate situation without prurience or vulgarity. JOSEPH THORP *Punch*

Aug 25. Colin Keith-Johnston in Shakespeare's **Hamlet** directed by H K Ayliff at Kingsway. Frank Vosper as Claudius. Modern dress production, known as The Jazz Hamlet. The Prince wore plus-fours and smoked a cigarette. Ophelia wore a jumper and a short skirt. The Gravedigger wore a bowler hat. "A complete success," said *The Daily Telegraph*.

Aug 31. Robert Harris, Raymond Massey and Carleton Hobbs in J R Ackerley's **Prisoners of War** directed by Nigel Playfair at Playhouse. The first 20th century British drama to deal with homosexuality. The play is set in a Swiss hotel, where a group of officers are interred and waiting for repatriation. It records the sexual ten-

caption to come

sions among the young inmates, for whom the army was simply an extension of their lives at public school. Ackerley, who wrote the initial draft when he was a POW in Switzerland during World War 1. He confessed in his autobiography that the highly strung hero was a portrait of himself.

Sep 2. Eric Maturin, Norman McKinnel and Tallulah Bankhead in Michael Arlen's **The Green Hat** directed by Nigel Playfair at Adelphi. Arlen's novel didn't work on stage. "Over-nourished, over-dressed, over-laundered, and over-sexed," said James Agate in *The Sunday Times*. Bankhead hated the play, hated her role and mumbled her lines.

Sep 7. Gwen Ffrangcon Davis as Tess and Ion Swinley as Clare in Thomas Hardy's **Tess of the D'Urbervilles** directed by A E Filmer at Barnes. Ffrangcon-Davies, far too delicate, just didn't look like a farm labourer. Transferred to Garrick.

Sep 10. Paul Robeson in Eugene O'Neill's **The Emperor Jones** directed by James Light at Ambassadors. Jones, a former porter on a Pullman car, a thief, a jailbird and twice a murderer, is now a military despot in the West Indies. The natives he has betrayed for so long, finally revolt and drive him into the jungle. He believes he has a charmed life and that he can be killed only by his own silver bullet. The play, expressionistic in style, is a long monologue, tracing his physical, mental and verbal disintegration: a journey backwards to savagery. The enveloping forest, in its massed, oppressive, pitched blackness, is a major character in its own right. The production laid emphasis on the visuals (ghosts from his past, visions of slavery, pagan ritual sacrifice) and the sound effects (the incessant throb of the tom-toms.) Robeson's magnificent physique, his voice and the sheer power of his acting were highly praised. "Magnificent," said *The New Statesman*. "Superb," said *The Times*. "One does not need a very long racial memory to lose oneself in such a part," said Paul Robeson. English audiences stayed away. The play was preceded by Eugene O'Neill's **The Long Voyage Home**. Milton Rosmer played the Swedish sailor, who is doped, robbed and shanghaied.

Sep 22. Gerald du Maurier, Gladys Cooper, Ellis Jeffreys and May Whitty in Frederick Lonsdale's **The Last of Mrs Cheyney** directed by Gerald du Maurier at St James's. Mrs Cheyney is a shop girl turned professional thief. Caught in her hostess's bedroom, she prefers to be exposed and arrested rather than be seduced by "an unmitigated bounder." The bedroom scene is Victorian melodrama. The beginning of the third act (a last-minute addition, written when the play was already in rehearsal) has the rich panicking at the thought of scandal and willing to acquiesce to blackmail. It is the best scene in the play. The rest is stale and artificial and was redeemed only by the distinguished cast.

Oct 5. Baliol Holloway in Shakespeare's **Richard III** directed by Andrew Leigh at Old Vic.

—Mr Holloway's closing scenes, like Kean's, are the most brilliant... His onslaught and overthrow are a great piece of work, almost lifting one out of one's seat. JAMES AGATE *Sunday Times*

Oct 8. Ruth Draper in her one-woman show at Garrick.

Oct 19. Miriam Lewes as Arkadina, John Gielgud as Konstantin and Valerie Taylor as Nina in Anton Chekhov's **The Seagull** directed by A E Filmer at Little. The critic of *Outlook* said Gielgud was unequalled as an English interpreter of Russian drama.
—John Gielgud, as Konstantin, acted with an overwhelming intensity and bitterness; it was a fine piece of gloomy introspection. LIONEL GRANT *Theatre World*

Oct 25. Phoenix Society. Ion Swinley in Christopher Marlowe's **Doctor Faustus** directed by Allan Wade at New Oxford. One critic thought that Ernest Thesiger's Mephistopheles looked like a maiden from Balham. John Gielgud played the Good Angel.

Oct 26. Baliol Holloway as Petruchio and Edith Evans as Kate in Shakespeare's **The Taming of the Shrew** directed by Andrew Leigh at Old Vic. Kate, in her lecture on the duties wives owed their husbands, gently mocked Petruchio.

Oct 28. Wilfred Temple and Olive Groves in **Lionel and Clarissa** directed by Nigel Playfair at Lyric, Hammersmith. Libretto by Isaac Bickerstaff. Music by Charles Dibdin re-arranged by Alfred Reynolds. Lottie Venne as Ward. Nigel Playfair as Col. Oldboy. Charming revival of an opera which had been a huge success at Covent Garden in 1768.
—It's another triumph for the eighteenth century for there is not a single contemporary musical to touch it. *Truth*
—Lottie Venne – a charming old ward figure in black and gold brocade, stepped down, as it were, from a cabinet of priceless Dresden china. Acting in Excelsis! *Theatre World*

Nov 11. Evelyn Laye, Mary Leigh and Jack Hobbs in **Betty in Mayfair** directed by Fred J Blackman at Adelphi. Book by J Hastings Turner. Music by H Fraser-Simson. Lyrics by Harry Graham. Musical adaptation of J Hastings Turner's *The Lilies of the Field*. The vicar's twin daughters come up to London in search of a beau. Laye and Leigh played the wins. Leigh had the better role. Hobbs was cast as the inarticulate young man. Many critics found the show "a welcome contrast to the almost all-pervading noise and fatuousness" of the modern American musical.

Nov 16. Sara Allgood as Juno, Arthur Sinclair as Boyle and Sydney Morgan as Joxer in Sean O'Casey's **Juno and the Paycock** directed by J B Fagan at Royalty. O'Casey's masterpiece was so successful in Dublin in 1924 that the run had to be extended for a second week, the first time an Abbey production had run longer than a week. Its success persuaded the 44-year-old playwright to give up his labouring job and earn his living from writing alone. The play ("tainted with bitter memory" and staged less than a year after the Republican ceasefire) begins in farce and ends in tragedy. The action is set at the end of the Civil War when the Diehards (hard-line Republicans) refused to accept the 1922 treaty and turned on their ex-comrades whom they believed had betrayed them. "Haven't I done enough for Ireland?" asks Johnny Boyle, who lost a hip and an arm in the Easter Rising. "No man can do enough for Ireland!" is the chilling response. He is dragged off to be shot. "Captain" Jack Boyle and Joker Daly are one of the best loved music hall acts. There were critics who dismissed the play ("a sordid, squalid, photographic melodrama") but the majority recognised the greatness of the play and the performance.
—Mr O'Casey mixes the ludicrous with the horrible and the mixture comes as a shock. One day he will divide his moods and do better things. *Illustrated London News*

Nov 17. Gilbert Childs, Anita Wilson and Davy Burnaby in **The Co-optimists** at His Majesty's. 11th New programme. The Co-optimists, a Pierrot troupe who had turned the old style seaside show into a sophisticated West End entertainment, had in five years become a national institution. The most original sketch was a married couple's quarrel staged as though it were taking place in a boxing ring.

Nov 19. Ellen Terry made her last appearance in Walter de la Mare's **Crossings** directed by Stephen Thomas at Lyric, Hammersmith. Terry played a Ghost.

Nov 23. Mary Clare and Frederick Cooper in Arnold Ridley's **The Ghost Train** directed by Holman Clark at St Martin's. Six people are stranded in the cold, wet and miserable waiting room of a remote country railway station, which is said to be haunted by the ghosts of a train smash. A silly ass, who is obviously not the prize idiot he looks, turns out to be a detective. The villains are Bolshevik gunrunners. The play was famous for the noise of the train, "so loud it almost kills you." The sound effect was achieved by using a drum, a thunder-sheet, a cylinder of compressed air and a garden roller. Richard Bird succeeded Frederick Cooper.

Dec 6. The Stage Society. Robert Farquharson in Anton Chekhov's **Ivanoff** directed by Theodore Komisarjevsky at Duke of York's. Translation by Marion Fell.

Dec 23. Norman V Norman as Henry and Sybil Thorndike as Katharine and E Lyall

Swete as Wolsey in Shakespeare's **Henry VIII** directed by Lewis Casson at Empire. Designs by Charles Ricketts.
—Miss Thorndike was magnificent in her stillness and grief and still a queen. Altogether a beautiful moving performance and almost entirely free from the mannerisms that sometimes detract from her acting. *Era*

1926

Jan 16. Robert Farquharson as Vanya, Henry C Hewitt as Astrov and Jean Forbes-Robertson as Sonia in Anton Chekhov's **Uncle Vanya** directed by Theodore Komisarjevsky at Barnes. The production made Sonia the leading role.

Jan 26. Tallulah Bankhead in Patrick Hastings's **Scotch Mist** directed by Basil Dean at St Martin's. Bankhead was cast as a woman who drives men mad. The Bishop of London denounced the play from the pulpit turning what many critics had described as one of the worst plays ever written into a *succès de scandale*.
—Although his [Patrick Hastings's] dialogue was terse and sharpened with caustic humour, none of his characters ever seemed to come alive. BASIL DEAN

Feb 1. Bernard Shaw double-bill: Esme Percy and Florence Jackson in **The Man of Destiny** and Esme Percy in **Don Juan in Hell** at Regent.

Feb 3. Allan Prior in Sigmund Romberg's musical **The Student Prince** at His Majesty's. Book and lyrics by Dorothy Donnelly. Based on R Bleichmann's version of William Meyer Forster's *Old Heidelberg*. Prince falls in love with a waitress and, to everybody's surprise, they don't get married. Hit songs: "The Drinking Song", "Deep in My Heart's Desire" and "Overhead the Moon is Beaming." The show did not repeat its New York success.
—Light-opera singers should not resemble rival railway engines letting off steam. JAMES AGATE *Sunday Times*

Feb 14. Rupert Harvey, Mercia Swinburne, William Stack and Gwladys Black-Roberts in James Joyce's **Exiles** directed by W G Fay at Regent. The exiles know all about the bitterness, the loneliness and the self-destructive jealousy of love. Way ahead of its time (theatrically at least), unfailingly honest, it probed and searched into motives, which were rightly blurred. Joyce had said in 1913 he didn't think an audience would be able to follow it or take it in.

Feb 16. Mary Sheridan as Olga, Beatrix Thomson as Irina, Margaret Swallow as Masha, Ion Swinley as Vershinin and John Gielgud as Tusenbach in Anton Chekhov's **The Three Sisters** directed by Theodore Komisarjevsky at Barnes. Komisarjevsky cut out all references to the Baron being ugly and insisted that Gielgud should play him as a romantic hero.

Mar 6. Shakespeare Memorial Theatre destroyed by fire.

Apr 10. Riverside Nights, a revue about Hammersmith and its environs by A P Herbert and Nigel Playfair, at Lyric, Hammersmith. Music by Frederic Austin and Alfred Reynolds. High spots: Ashley Duke's skit on modern Russian ballet and Elsa Lanchester singing "Please Sell No More Drink to My Father."

Apr 14. Fred Astaire and Adele Astaire in George and Ira Gershwin's musical **Lady, Be Good** directed by Felix Edwardes at Empire. Book by Guy Bolton and Fred Thompson. "Fred and Adele have only to appear," said *The Sketch*, "and everyone is blissfully happy." The songs included "Fascinating Rhythm", "Hang on to Me", and "Lady, Be Good".

Apr 27. Dennis Eadie in Jules Romains's **Doctor Knock** translated by Harley Granville Barker and directed by Peter Godfrey at Royalty. An old and familiar joke at the expense of doctors and their gullible patients. The fraudulent Knock sees medicine as his passport to influence and power. Relying on a mesmeric personality and pseudo-medical jargon, he easily persuades a whole community that they are sick and quickly reaps the considerable financial rewards of mass hypochondria. Eadie has great fun in a role created in Paris by Louis Jouvet, but what the production needed, according to *The Times*, "to complete an excellent dish was a sprinkling of absurdity, a pinch of extravagance."

Apr 28. Claude Rains as Khelestakov and Charles Laughton as Osip in Nikolai Gogol's **The Government Inspector** directed by Theodore Komisarjevsky at Barnes. The farce was acted with stylised absurdity on a spinning roundabout.

Apr 29. Spinelly, Ernest Thesiger, Hermione Baddeley and Léonide Massine in **Cochran's Revue** directed by Frank Collins at London Pavilion. Book by Ronald Jeans. Music by Pat Thayer. Choreography by Léonide Massine.
— "Spi" is not beautiful, her dancing is ordinary, her singing voice is barely more than a squeak, yet she has that priceless gift of a most enveloping and delightful stage personality. Her's is disarming, cheeky gaiety, coupled with an irresistible chic which enables her, when she

1926 World Premieres
Dublin
   Sean O'Casey's *The Plough and the Stars*
New York
   Eugene O'Neill's *The Great God Brown*
   Paul Green's *In Abraham's Bosom*
Moscow
   Mikhail Bulgakov's *The White Guard.*
Budapest
   Ferenc Molnar's *The Play's the Thing*

Births
Queen Elizabeth II

Dario Fo, Italian, actor, playwright
Hugh Leonard, Irish playwright
Peter Shaffer British playwright

Deaths
Sir Squire Bancroft (*b.*1841), British actor-manager

Honours
Dame
   Madge Kendal, British actor

History
General Strike in England

is on stage, to obliterate a whole host of more beautiful and (technically) more accomplished performers. *Theatre World*

May 1. Leslie Banks, Franklin Dyall, Dorothy Dickson, Nigel Bruce and Gordon Harker in Edgar Wallace's **The Ringer** directed by Gerald du Maurier at Wyndham's. A crook play in which the Scottish police-doctor turns out to be the crook.

May 12. Sara Allgood, Maire O'Neill, Kathleen Drago, Arthur Sinclair, Sydney Morgan and J A O'Rourke in Sean O'Casey's **The Plough and the Stars** directed by J B Fagan at Fortune. The first performance was at Abbey Theatre, Dublin on 8 February 1926. O'Casey offered a slice of Dublin tenement life and a timely reminder that far more people had died of malnutrition and consumption than had been killed in the war. The words of the Speaker recalled the terrifying speeches of Padraic Pearse: "Bloodshed is a cleansing and sanctifying thing and the nation that regards it as the final horror has lost its manhood... We must be ready to pour out the same red wine in the same sacrifice, for without shedding of blood there is no redemption." On the fourth night in Dublin there were riots, the audience reacting angrily to O'Casey's unflattering portrayal of the Irish during the months leading up to the Easter Rising of 1916. What the rioters objected to (apart from the Tricolour being brought into a public house and the appearance of a prostitute on stage) was that O'Casey sided with the victims rather than the heroes. There had been objections to the language during rehearsal from various members of the company and the Board of Governors. W B Yeats, director of the Abbey, anticipating a disturbance, had prepared a speech, which he had already sent to the newspapers: "You have disgraced yourselves again. Is this to be an ever-recurring celebration of the arrival of Irish genius? Synge first and then O'Casey. The news of the happenings of the past few minutes will go from country to country. Dublin has once more rocked the cradle of the genius. From such a scene in this theatre went forth the fame of Synge. Equally the fame of O'Casey is born here tonight. This is his apotheosis."
—These actors and actresses, of course, start off in England with an immense advantage for the English are easily ravished by the Irish voice. Half the members of the Critics' Circle will this week be blithering about the charm of it, although Miss O'Neill carefully assumes a Dublin adenoidy voice specially to let them hear how ugly that voice can be. ST JOHN ERVINE *Observer*

Jun 9. Jane Cowl in Noël Coward's **Easy Virtue** directed by Basil Dean at Duke of York's. Coward attempted to recreate a typical drawing-room drama of the late Victorian period in modern dress. A young man, in his early twenties, marries a woman who is 15 years his senior and far more intelligent than he is. His wealthy upper-middle-class family give her a frosty reception which gets even frostier when they discover she was involved in an unsavoury sex scandal.
—[Jane Cowl] has poise, and pace, and she delivers the second-act tirade as such things ought to be delivered, while her sullens at the end are magnificent. JAMES AGATE *Sunday Times*

Jun 12. Irene Vanbrugh, Marie Löhr and Edith Evans in Somerset Maugham's **Caroline** directed by Athole Stewart at Playhouse. "The glitter is brilliant," said *The Times*, "the polish exquisite and the performances faultless." Lilian Braithwaite took over from Vanbrugh.

Jun 15. Sybil Thorndike in Clemence Dane's **Granite** directed by Lewis Casson at Ambassadors. Grand Guignol. Farmer's wife says she is willing to sell her soul to the devil and finds herself in the arms of an escaped convict.

Jun 21. Yvonne Printemps and Sacha Guitry in Sacha Guitry's **Mozart** directed by Sacha Guitry at Gaiety. Music by Reynaldo Hahn. At the age of 20 Mozart set out to write *Don Juan*; but he needed to get some experience from the ladies first. Printemps played Mozart.
—It would be impossible to praise too highly the perfection and finesse of Mlle Printemps's acting... The most significant thing about her performance is the way in which we are made to feel we are in the presence of genius. JAMES AGATE *Sunday Times*

Jun 30. Tom Walls, Ralph Lynn, Robertson Hare, Mary Brough and Winifred Shotter in Ben Travers's **Rookery Nook** directed by Tom Walls at Aldwych. Farce. A pretty young girl in her pyjamas runs away from her bullying German stepfather and takes shelter in a house, which a recently married young man has hired for the summer. How is he going to explain her presence and the fact that she slept in his bed to his wife, sister-in-law, daily woman and neighbours?

Jul 5. Parade at His Majesty's. Choreography by Léonide Massine. Music by Erik Satie. Book by Jean Cocteau. Designs by Pablo Picasso. "Etonne-moi!" said Diaghilev. "Be vulgar!" said Cocteau. The poet Guillaume Apollinaire coined a new word to describe *Parade* – sur-realisme. The audience had booed and hissed its Paris premiere.

Aug 12. Nicholas Hannen in John Galsworthy's **Escape** directed by Leon M Lion at Ambassadors. Nine episodes in the life of a convict who has escaped from Dartmoor. Each character he meets reacts according to the circumstance in his or her life.

Aug 24. Madge Titheradge, Herbert Marshall, Francis Lister, Ada King and Lady Tree in Noël Coward's **The Queen Was In Her Parlour** directed by Basil Dean at St Martin's. Ruritanian, romantic costume melodrama.
—It is impossible not to feel that Mr Coward wrote the play with his tongue in his cheek. ALAN PARSONS *Daily Mail*

Aug 31. Dorothy Dickson, Laddie Cliff, John Kirby and Allen Kearns in George and Ira Gershwin's musical **Tip-Toes** directed by William Ritter at Winter Garden. Book by Guy Bolton and Fred Thompson. Tip-Toes (the heroine's name) is a poor vaudeville artiste who discovers the poor boy she loves is actually a rich glue magnate. Songs included "That Certain Feeling" and "Looking for a Boy."

Sep 6. Edmund Gwenn as Samuel Pepys and Yvonne Arnaud as Mrs Pepys in J. B Fagan's **And So To Bed** directed by J B Fagan at Queen's. Charles 11 catches Pepys with Mrs. Knight. Arnaud's French accent enchanted.
—She [Yvonne Arnaud] gives what is probably the most fascinating and clever display of acting to be seen on the London stage at the present moment. Whether expressing anger or tenderness, laughter or sadness, she is equally perfect. H M WALBROOK *Play Pictorial*

Sep 14. Edna Best and Noël Coward in Margaret Kennedy and Basil Dean's dramatisation of Margaret Kennedy's novel, **The Constant Nymph** directed by Basil Dean at New. Dean had promised the role of the musical genius to Gielgud, but he only got it because Coward fell ill three weeks after the opening night and had to withdraw from the cast.

Sep 30. Edith Evans and Charles Carson in Henrik Ibsen's **Rosmersholm** directed by H K Ayliff at Kingsway.
—In accepting an invitation to sit through two and a half hours' unrelieved gloom makes one thank Providence that one has not been invited to spend the week-end at Rosmersholm, for at Rosmersholm no one has ever been known to smile, a fact which when mentioned on the stage hardly surprised the audience. *Theatre World*

Oct 5. Maisie Gay, Herbert Mundin and Anton Dolin in **The Charlot Show of 1926** directed by Frank Collins at Prince of Wales. Revue. Book by Ronald Jeans, Donovan Parsons and Rowland Leigh. Music by Noël Gay and Dick Addinsell. Ballet by Anton Dolin. Maisie Gay had a big success playing a faded soubrette.
—Masie Gay is one of the best low comediennes we have and can be counted on to convulse audiences whatever the type of revue, but her methods are best suited to a small theatre. *Theatre World*

Oct 6. Jean Forbes-Robertson in **Berkeley Square** by John L Balderston in collaboration with J C Squire directed by Frank Birch at St Martin's. Two people in different centuries meet and fall in love. She lives in 1926. He lives in 1786.

Oct 21. W H Berry, Alice Delysia, Edmund Willard and George Grossmith in **Prince Charming** directed by William Mollison at Palace. Music and lyrics by Arthur Wimperis and Laurie Wylie. Additional numbers by Russell Bennett and Jack Waller. Old-fashioned romantic musical. King finds the woman (Winnie Melville) he wants to marry is already married to a sailor (John Clarke). Delysia played the vamp. High spot: the company singing the patriotic "Swords and Sabres".

Nov 3. Cedric Hardwicke, Frank Vosper and Ralph Richardson in Eden and Adelaide Phillpotts's **Yellow Sands** directed by H K Ayliff at Haymarket. The authors, in their homely, very English way, come down firmly on the side of basic human goodness, within the social order, as it is. In the year of the General Strike, with millions of people out of work, what the socialist (Frank Vosper) had to say made a lot of sense.

Dec 1. Cicely Courtneidge, Jack Hulbert and Phyllis Dare in Richard Rodgers and Lorenz Hart's musical **Lido Lady** directed by Jack Hulbert at Gaiety. Book by Ronald Jeans. In order to win the woman he loves the hero has to knock out the world's welterweight boxing champion. Hulbert excelled as dancer and comic.

Dec 11. Philip Desborough as Horner, Isabel Jeans as Margery and Athene Seyler as Lady Fidget in Wycherley's **The Country Wife** directed by Allan Wade at Everyman.
—The present performance, lacking all but a few patches of the most necessary veneer, leaves little impression but of prolix licentiousness. *The Times*

Dec 12. Marda Vanne, Peter Earle and Colin Keith-Johnston in D H Lawrence's **The Widowing of Mrs Holroyd** directed by Esme Percy at Kingsway. Attracted by his good looks and big muscles, Mrs Holroyd marries a miner, only to discover he is a low-minded brute, drunkard and coward. Another miner, a decent chap, asks her to come away with him to Spain. The very next day her husband dies in the pit. Mrs Holroyd sees his death as a judgement on her and feels she has murdered him because she wished him dead.

Dec 12. Jean Forbes-Robertson and Lawrence Anderson in Shakespeare's **Romeo and Juliet** at Strand. Robert Loraine as Mercutio. Ethel Harper as Nurse. D A Clarke-Smith as Friar.

Dec 23. Ivor Novello as Liliom and Fay Compton as Julie in Ferenc Molnar's **Liliom** directed by Theodore Komisarjevsky at Duke of York's. Adaptation by Osmond Shillingford and Anthony Ellis. A fair-ground barker, a big bully, dies in a brawl and goes to heaven. Novello was hopelessly miscast. Charles Laughton (making his stage debut as a pickpocket) was much more convincing. The play would have more success when Rodgers and Hammerstein turned it into a musical called *Carousel*.

Dec 24. Henry Ainley and Sybil Thorndike in Shakespeare's **Macbeth** directed by Lewis Casson at Prince's.
—It is hard to believe that this Lady Macbeth could incite a man to commit petty larceny, let alone murder. *Theatre World*
—In the sleep-walking scene she spoke in a dull, flat voice, sometimes breaking into a wail of utter misery. I have never known wretchedness presented on the stage as she presented it. GORDON GROSSE *Playgoing*

1927

Jan 10. Florence Mills in **Blackbirds (second edition)** at London Pavilion. Mills sang "I Ain't Got Nobody But You". The high spot was the Black Bottom. *Theatre*

1927 World Premieres
New York
Oscar Hammerstein and Jerome Kern's *Show Boat*
Berlin
Ernst Toller's *Hoppla! Wir Leben!*

Births
Gunter Grass, German playwright
Peter Nichols, British playwright
Neil Simon, American playwright
Kenneth Tynan, British critic

Deaths
Isadora Duncan (*b.*1878), American dancer

Notes
—Harley Granville Barker's *Prefaces to Shakespeare* published
—Arts Theatre opened as a club theatre

History
—Trotsky expelled from Communist party
—Charles Lindberg's solo flight across Atlantic
—John Gutzon Borgium sculpted giant presidential figures on Mount Rushmore
—Premiere of *The Jazz Man* (first talkie)

World said that "the demonstration of this grotesque dance should result in its exclusion from the ballroom for all time."

Jan 19. Esme Percy as Professor Higgins and Gwen Ffrangcon-Davies as Eliza Doolittle in Shaw's **Pygmalion** directed by Esme Percy at Kingsway.

Jan 20. Edith Evans as Mrs Sullen, George Hayes as Archer, Nigel Playfair as Gibbet and Miles Malleson as Scrub in George Farquhar's **The Beaux Stratagem** directed by Nigel Playfair at Lyric, Hammersmith. The production confirmed Evans's reputation.
—Nobody who has seen Miss Evans in this and other plays during the last year or two will deny that here is our greatest actress in either comedy or tragedy. *Theatre World*

Feb 14. Raymond Huntley in **Dracula** at Little. Hamilton Deane's adaptation of Bram Stoker's novel was directed by Hamilton Deane who also played Van Helsing. Uniformed nurses were in attendance for the faint-hearted. (Blood transfusions, free of charge?) The stage-struck Stoker (who had worked for Henry Irving in the box office of the Lyceum Theatre) had a nightmare in 1890, produced, so he said, by a dinner of dressed crab. Seven years later, having done his research, he published the most famous Gothic horror story of them all. The novel was described as "a kind of

Gladys Cooper in The Letter

incestuous, necrophiliac, oral-anal-sadistic all-in male wrestling." The play ran for 391 performances. It transferred to New York, acquiring a co-author, John L Balderston. Bela Lugosi, who played the lead, went on to make the film version, the top-grossing movie of 1931.

Feb 16. Marie Tempest in Noël Coward's **The Marquise** directed by W Graham Browne at Criterion. Two fathers, the best of friends, want their children to marry each other, but the girl is in love with her father's secretary and the boy is in love with a dancer in Paris. The comedy, set in the 18th century, acted like a translation from the French. Coward was the first to admit the play was tenuous, frivolous and the third act, weak.

Feb 24. Gladys Cooper, Leslie Faber, Nigel Bruce and Clare Harris in Somerset Maugham's **The Letter** directed by Gerald du Maurier at Playhouse. Based on a real-life murder in Kuala Lumpur in 1911. Wife, jealous of her lover's Chinese mistress, shoots him dead and faces a charge of murder. (Wives, east of Suez, between the wars, had very little else to do all day but have affairs and shoot their lovers.) "What have I done?" she cries. She claims he tried to rape her. "You've done what any woman would have done in your place." The role was specially written for Gladys Cooper and recreated on film by Bette Davis.
—Posterity will endorse my view, which is that Gladys Cooper's performance in *The Letter* will be remembered and acclaimed from generation to generation. EDGAR WALLACE

Feb 27. Charles Laughton in Benn W Levy's adaptation of Hugh Walpole's novel, **The Man with Red Hair** directed by Theodore Komisarjevsky at Little. Grand Guignol. The man was a murderer who killed to revenge his ugliness. Laughton turned Walpole's two-pence coloured villain into something truly horrible. *Theatre World* likened him to a whiff of poisonous gas. *The Observer* said he was "a gargoyle of obscene desires."
—Mr Laughton has made so subtle, so revoltingly brilliant a study of sadistic obsession that the man, and through him the play, is well-nigh intolerable. *The Times*

Mar 15. Nicholas Hannen and Peter Gill in Miles Malleson's **The Fanatics** directed by Miles Malleson at Ambassadors. Malleson argued that couples intending to get married should live together first to find out if they are compatible.
—*The Fanatics* will cause a good deal of talk. Indeed it is a question whether the stage is the place for such a frank discussion on sex and marriage. *Daily News*
—It struck me as among the most poisonous rubbish I have ever listened to. H M WALBROOK *Play Pictorial*

Mar 29. Henry Oscar in Reginald Berkeley's **The White Chateau** directed by Raymond Massey at Everyman. Six episodes in the life of a chateau. Hailed as the sanest anti-war play that had yet been produced. Transferred to St Martin's.

Apr 4. The Forum Theatre Guild. Jean Forbes-Robertson as Leah in S Ansky's **The Dybbuk** directed by Robert Atkins at Royalty. Translation by Henry G Alsberg and Winifred Katzin. Yiddish play set in a Jewish village in Russia in the 1840s. A dybbuk is a vagrant soul, which finding neither rest nor harbour, passes into the body of a living being until it has attained purity. A father chooses a rich son for his daughter, Leah, unmindful of the promise he made to his best friend, now dead, that their respective unborn children should marry when they grew up. A young student, who is in love with her, dies when he discovers she is already betrothed. On the wedding day (in which both bride and groom are being forced to marry against their will) the student's spirit returns and possesses her body. Atkins's production did not do justice to the play. Some of the critics thought that Forbes-Robertson was not equal to the tragedy and pathos.
—Miss Jean Forbes-Robertson confirmed me in my belief that we have the great English actress of the future. ST JOHN ERVINE *Observer*

Apr 6. Fay Compton and Leon Quartermaine in Somerset Maugham's **The Constant Wife** directed by Basil Dean at Strand. Constance, married for 15 years, has known about her husband's affair but has preferred to turn a blind eye. She is no more in love with him than he is in love with her. As she sees it, wives are parasites and at best merely inconvenient ornaments, so she doesn't feel she has the right to complain or reproach him for his unfaithfulness, so long as he continues to provide for her. She turns interior decorator (as Maugham's wife had done) and makes a fortune. Once she has economic freedom, she is quick to claim sexual independence and pay him back in kind. When the husband suggests that he could be her lover, the idea does not appeal. "My dear," she says, "no one can make yesterday's cold mutton into tomorrow's lamb cutlets." The comedy had been a big success in New York in 1926 with Ethel Barrymore and C Aubrey Smith; but it failed in London. The critics disliked its cynicism. On the first night the front row of the pit had been occupied by the back row of the stalls. The pitites refused to give up their seats. At the curtain call Compton mistook a call for silence as a personal affront and thanked "the civil members of the audience for their kind reception." This was greeted with boos.
—Somerset Maugham has made his anaemic puppets dance most divertingly, but they are only puppets, and you really cannot take them seriously. *Daily News*

Apr 7. Harry Welchman, Edith Day and Gene Gerrard in Sigmund Romberg's musical **The Desert Song** directed by Laurence Schwab at Drury Lane. Book and lyrics by Oscar Hammerstein, Otto Harbach and Frank Mandel. Son of a French general places himself at the head of a band of brigands for purely honourable motives.

Apr 11. Katherine Revner in Anne Nichols's **Abie's Irish Rose** directed by Anne Nichols at Apollo. Originally called *Marriage in Triplicate*. Jewish boy marries Irish girl in New York City.
—The whole play indeed is ingenuous, unsophisticated, and so free from pretentiousness as almost to disarm criticism. *The Times*

Apr 19. Derek Oldham, Winnie Melville, Mark Lester, Norah Blaney and H A Saintsbury in **The Vagabond King** directed by Richard Boleslavsky at Winter Garden. Musical based on Justin Huntly McCarthy's *If I Were King*. Book and lyrics by W H Post and Brian Hooker. Music by Rudolph Friml. Oldham was cast as the vagabond, who escapes the guillotine and becomes king for a day. Saintsbury was Louis XI. Rousing songs.
—*The Vagabond King* puts the last dab of whitewash on the character of Francois Villon – and does it to the strains of tuneful music. The result is quite irresistible. There in no vagabond king; it is a kingly vagabond. *The Times*

Apr 19. Ellis Jeffreys, Ronald Squire, Valerie Taylor and Edmond Breon in Frederick Lonsdale's **On Approval** directed by Tom Walls at Fortune. Two couples decide to have a trial marriage in the wilds of Scotland. The snobbish, selfish, conceited, ill-natured Lord Bristol and the spoiled, bad-tempered Mrs Wislack deserve each other. Lonsdale's cynical little comment on the aristocracy was very much an actors' piece, relying for its comedy on rudeness.

Apr 19. Mae West in New York was found guilty of indecent behaviour for appearing in **Sex**, a play she had written.

Apr 21. Angela Baddeley and Deering Wells in Allen Harker and F R Pryor's **Marigold** directed by Norman Page at Kingsway. A wee Scots lass runs away to Edinburgh to see the Queen and misses the Queen because she falls in love with a handsome Scots officer. Quaint, wholesome, crinolined entertainment for old-fashioned playgoers.

May 20. Jessie Matthews, Sonnie Hale, Douglas Byng, Edythe Baker and Max Wall in Lorenz Hart and Richard Rodgers's revue **One Dam Thing After Another** directed by Frank Collins at London Pavilion. Book by Ronald Jeans. Matthews sang "My Heart Stood Still" and "My Lucky Star." Wall's eccentric dancing was a big success.

May 27. Harry Hutchinson. Arthur Sinclair and Eileen Carey in Sean O'Casey's **The Shadow of a Gunman** directed by Arthur Sinclair at Court. First performance in England: a realistic study of Irish tenement life, in all its squalid poverty, played out against the background of the Troubles. A girl sacrifices herself for the man she loves – a futile gesture, made even more futile by the fact that the poet, for whom she dies, is not a gunman at all. O'Casey's message is loud and clear: "I'm a Nationalist right enough; I believe in the freedom of Ireland, an' that England has no right to be here, but I draw the line when I hear the gunmen blowin' about dying for the people, when it's the people that are dyin' for the gunmen. With all due respect to the gunmen, I don't want them to die for me." When the Abbey Theatre had played in New York in 1923 there were 250 policemen in the stalls to stop rioting. In London the audience laughed so often in the wrong places that they practically ruined the play. They were "criminally unintelligent," said one critic. The play was acted in a double bill with Sara Allgood in J M Synge's **Riders to the Sea**.

May 30. Tallulah Bankhead in R Bernauer and R Oesterreicher's **The Garden of Eden** adapted by Avery Hopwood and directed by William Mollison at Lyric. Bankhead stripped off her wedding dress in front of the guests of honour. "A masterpiece of dull stupidity," was one critic's comment. "Never have I listened to such a string of banalities of theatrical clichés," said Edgar Wallace.

Jun 2. Wilfred Shine, Miriam Lewes and Ernest Thesiger in **When Crummles Played** at Lyric, Hammersmith. Nigel Playfair adaptation of Dickens' *Nicholas Nickleby* included George Lillo's *George Branwell* or *The London Merchant*. Hermione Baddeley played The Infant Phenomenon.

Jun 14. Adrianne Allen, Gillian Lind, Allan Jeayes and Raymond Massey in August Strindberg's **The Spook Sonata** directed by J B Fagan at Globe. 80-year-old malevolent cripple, a robber of souls, plays havoc with people's lives and destinies until his mask is ripped off and he himself is exposed for a liar, a thief and a murderer.

Jun 26. Tom Douglas and Gillian Lind in Theodore Dresier's novel, **An American Tragedy**, adapted by Patrick Kearney and directed by Raymond Massey at Apollo. Based on a New York murder case. Young man leaves his pregnant girlfriend to drown. The girl's part was crudely written and the pathos was forced.

Jul 4. Tom Walls, Ralph Lynn, Robertson Hare, Mary Brough and Winifred Shotter in Ben Travers's **Thark** directed by Tom Walls at Aldwych. The first two acts were bedroom farce without a bedroom. The third act was haunted house comedy with a bedroom. The final scene, with an elderly gent sharing a four-poster with his nephew, was straight music hall. "The jokes are suggestive," said *The Daily Mail*, "but they are never ugly."

Aug 17. Jeanne de Casalis and Paul Cavanagh in Edgar C Middleton's **Potiphar's Wife** directed by Norman Loring at Globe. Flighty wife attempts to seduce her chauffeur. He tells her that he doesn't find her attractive and she flies into a rage and accuses him of having raped her.

Sep 7. Fred Kerr in Frederick Lonsdale's **The High Road** directed by Tom Walls at Shaftesbury. The peerage is shocked when one of their members wants to marry an actress. They are even more shocked when her father prefers his daughter to be an actress rather than to marry into the peerage.

Sep 8. Louise Brown and Roy Royston in **The Girl Friend** directed by William Mollison at Palace. Musical adaptation of P Bartholomew and Otto Harbach's *Kitty's Kisses* by R P Weston and Bert Lee. Music and lyrics by Con Conrad, Gus Kahn, Richard Rodgers and Lorenz Hart. Emma Haig and George Gee were a big hit with their eccentric dancing. The songs included "Mountain Greenery" and "Blue Room." The main surprise was that Irish actress Sarah Allgood, famous for her roles in the plays of Sean O'Casey, should be wasting her time in a fatuous role in a poor musical comedy.

Sep 11. Helen Haye, Ursula Jeans and Frank Lawton in John Van Druten's **Chance Acquaintance** directed by Henry Kendall at Strand. Girl meets boy in a hotel lobby. It's then a question of finding somewhere to spend the night. She takes the initiative.

Sep 14. Lilian Braithwaite and Denys Blakelock in Sidney Howard's **The Silver Cord** directed by Sidney Howard at St Martin's. Ruthless, possessive mother won't let go of her sons.

Sep 21. Gertrude Lawrence, John Kirby and Claude Hulbert in George and Ira Gershwin's musical **Oh, Kay!** directed by William Ritter at His Majesty's. Book by Guy Bolton and P G Wodehouse. Kirby played a bootlegger turned butler. Songs included "Clap Yo' Hands" and "Someone To Watch Over Me".
—[Gertrude Lawrence] has all the command of voice that is the especial gift of a born mimic. She is a brilliant comedienne; but it seems to me she relies just a little too much upon "clowning" her part. *Morning Post*

Sep 29. Edith Evans and Frederick Leister in Georges Berr and Louis Verneuil's **The Lady-in-Law** directed by Leon M Lion at Wyndham's. According to one critic, the best acting came from the audience who, from time to time, pretended they were enjoying themselves.

Oct 25. Nina Boucicault in Noël Coward's **Home Chat** directed by Basil Dean at Duke of York's. Marital infidelity. Coward was booed by stalls and gallery during his curtain call. "We expected better," said a voice. "So did I," replied Coward.

Nov 3. Ivy Tresmand, Stanley Holloway, Sydney Howard and Alice Morley in Vincent Youmans' **Hit the Deck!** directed by William Mollison at London Hippodrome. American musical. Lyrics by Clifford Grey and Leo Robin. Adapted from the play *Shore Leave* by Herbert Osborne. English version by R P Weston and Bert Lee. A sailor is going to marry a girl until he finds out she is an heiress. Tresmand and Holloway sang "Sometimes I'm Happy". Morley sang the hit song, the Negro spiritual, "Hallelujah!"

Nov 16. Edith Evans as Millamant and Godfrey Tearle as Mirabell in William Congreve's **The Way of the World** directed by Nigel Playfair at Wyndham's. "There has never been on or off the stage a woman so sublime as Millamant," said Playfair. The play was fantasticated: "a rattling, jaunty, jigging, almost jazzing musical," said *The Times*. Margaret Yarde was accused of making Lady Wishfort too farcical. "Why, in heaven's name, shouldn't she?" asked Playfair.
—Edith Evans alone strikes the true key-note. She is superb and gives reality to the artificiality of the period. Dorothy Green presents Mrs Marwood as she might have been played in the days of Kean and Kemble. Godfrey Tearle showed how Mirabell would be played in a modern melodramatic manner. *Theatre World*

Nov 16. Charles Laughton in Arnold Bennett and Edward Knoblock's **Mr Prohack** directed by Theodore Komisarjevsky at Court. Senior treasury official comes into a quarter of a million pounds. The comedy came from the contrast between the man's public parsimony and his private recklessness. Laughton made up to look like Bennett.

Nov 23. Margaret Bannerman and Leon Quartermaine in Arthur Wing Pinero's

Trelawny of the "Wells" at Globe. Bannerman seemed more at home in Cavendish Square than she did at the Wells,
—It is as it was when it was first written one of the most fragrant pieces of sentiment in the theatre. Its charm doesn't fade at all. *Era*

Nov 24. Ivor Novello and Frances Doble in Noël Coward's **Sirocco** directed by Basil Dean at Daly's. English wife in Italy makes love to a local lad on the floor of a bistro. The scene was punctuated with catcalls from the gallery. The audience hooted, booed, hissed and shrieked their displeasure during the curtain call. Coward faced the barrage. Someone in the audience yelled for Doble. She stepped forward and said, "Ladies and gentlemen, this is the happiest moment of my life." 'Sirocco' in theatrical circles became a synonym for disaster.

Dec 1. Cicely Courtneidge and Jack Hulbert in **Clowns in Clover** directed by Jack Hulbert at Adelphi. Revue. Book by Ronald Jeans. Music by Noël Gay. Lyrics by Donovan Parsons. Courtneidge burlesqued a French music hall singer who could neither sing nor dance.

Dec 12. Athene Seyler, Leslie Banks, Nicholas Hannen, Hilda Trevelyan and Alison Leggatt in H W Gribbles' **March Hares** directed by Nicholas Hannen at Ambassadors. Banks played a man who has no idea that women fancied him.

Dec 21. Jean Forbes-Robertson in **Peter Pan** at Gaiety. She would play Peter every year until 1934. For many she was the best Peter, vigorous yet fey, hovering perfectly between the joy and sadness of boyhood. William Luff was Captain Hook.

1928

Jan 9. Frank Randell as Mr Zero in Elmer Rice's **The Adding Machine** directed by W G Fay at Court. Mr Zero is found guilty of murder and is sent to the electric chair.

Jan 16. Robert Loraine, Miriam Lewes and Edmund Gwenn in August Strindberg's **The Dance of Death** directed by Robert Loraine at Apollo.
—This is not food for babes. It could not possibly be a popular success. It is too sombre, too harrowing in arts, too brutal altogether. *Daily Express*

Jan 24. Noël Coward, Zena Dare, Raymond Massey and Ursula Jeans in S N Behrman's **The Second Man** directed by Basil Dean at Playhouse. Ménage a quatre: poor poet, rich widow, rich scientist and fluffy flapper.
—[Noël Coward] is a self-conscious actor, with a set of small tricks and grimaces that sometimes rob him of expressiveness; but it is a real pleasure to observe his intelligence at work on niceties of dialogue. *Daily Telegraph*

Feb 6. Eric Maturin and Mary Merrall in Shakespeare's **Macbeth** directed by H K Ayliff at Court. Modern dress production with Jocks and Tommies firing rifles at each other. Maturin in khaki was a colloquial Macbeth. *The Morning Post* said, "The soliloquies were bashed to pieces." Lady Macbeth wore a cocktail dress and took drugs. Lady Macduff and the children were murdered at tea-time. Laurence Olivier was a lively Malcolm.

Feb 12. Frank Lawton and Kathleen O'Regan in John Van Druten's **Young Woodley** directed by Basil Dean at Savoy. Woodley, a 17-year-old house prefect, a sensitive and reticent lad, writes poetry and finds sex "beastly." He falls in love with the housemaster's unhappily married young wife. The housemaster, who thinks writing poetry is unhealthy, catches them kissing. His wife threatens to leave him if he gets the boy expelled, saying she was to blame. The badly constructed third act then gets very melodramatic with the boy going berserk, having beastly sex with a local girl and attempting

1928 World Premieres
New York
  Eugene O'Neill's *Strange Interlude*
  Ben Hecht and Charles
    MacArthur's *The Front Page*
  Sophie Treadwell's *Machinal*
Berlin
  Bertolt Brecht's *The Threepenny Opera*
Paris
  Jean Cocteau's *Les Enfants Terribles*

Births
Edward Albee, American playwright
David Mercer, British playwright

Deaths
Hermann Sudermann (*b.*1857), German playwright
Ellen Terry (*b.*1848), British actor
Little Tich (*b.*1868), British comedian

Notes
—Visit of Moscow Arts Theatre
—Visit of Diaghilev's Ballets Russes
—Gate Theatre founded

History
—Sir Alexander Fleming discovered penicillin
—First Mickey Mouse cartoon

Macbeth (Eric Maturin) confronts the ghost of Banquo in Dunsinane in 1928

to stab an obnoxious prefect. The play was initially banned by the Censor and was first performed in New York in 1925. Three years later it was staged for one night by The Stage Society, a Sunday night club. Critics and audiences could not understand why the Censor had banned the play. The production transferred to the Arts Theatre Club where the censor saw it and he, too, wondered why he had banned it. The boy and the wife were guilty of nothing more than a kiss. The ban was revoked and the production transferred to the Savoy Theatre where it had a long run. Frank Lawton's overwhelming success ruined his career. He was forever connected with Woodley.
—[John Van Druten's] play is limited but within its limits is beautiful and true, having sentiment that does the word honour and a freshness which in the sordid squalor that besets a great part of the theatre, is like a spring wind. *The Times*
—It is, at the heart of it, an exquisitely delicate, sincere and beautiful treatment of adolescent love. *Morning Post*

Feb 14. Frederick Ranalow as Macheath in John Gay's **The Beggar's Opera** directed by Nigel Playfair at Lyric, Hammersmith.

Feb 14. Eric Portman and Jean Forbes-Robertson in Shakespeare's **Romeo and Juliet** directed by Andrew Leigh at Old Vic. The lovers lack dramatic force. Ernest Milton as Mercutio.

Feb 27. Charles Laughton as Mr Crispin in Benn W Levy's adaptation of Hugh Walpole's **The Man with Red Hair** directed by Theodore Komisarjevsky at Little. The play was inferior to the novel, but Laughton's sadistic performance was recognised as a brilliant piece of character acting.

Mar 6. Genevieve Tobin and all-American cast in Bayard Veiller's **The Trial of Mary Duggan** directed by Guthrie McClintic at Queen's. Nobody was ever in any doubt that Duggan was innocent.
—The acting, though it is for the most part nothing more than slick realism, is all excellent of its kind. *Daily Telegraph*

Mar 12. Ernest Milton as Palamon and Eric Portman as Arcite in Shakespeare and Fletcher's **Two Noble Kinsmen** directed by Andrew Leigh at Old Vic. First performance since 17th century. The actors played with a light touch which avoided burlesque.

Mar 22. Jessie Matthews, Sonnie Hale, Tilly Losch and Douglas Byng in Noël Coward's **This Year of Grace!** directed by Frank Collins at London Pavilion. Revue. Coward wrote the book, the lyrics and the music. High spots: "Dance, Dance, Dance, Little Lady" and Matthews and Hale singing "A Room with a View."
—I must be careful with my superlatives, so I will say only this, that *This Year of Grace* is the most amusing, the most brilliant, the cleverest, the daintiest, the most exquisite, the most fanciful, the most graceful, the happiest, the most ironical, the jolliest, the most kaleidoscopic, then loveliest, the most magnificent, the neatest and nicest, the most opulent, the pithiest, the quickest, the richest, the most superb and tasteful, the most uberous, the most versatile, the wittiest – St John Ervine *Observer*

Apr 2. Laurence Olivier in Alfred, Lord Tennyson's **Harold** directed by H K Ayliff at Court. The production was in modern dress. Harold, the last of the Saxon kings, loves Edith but the Church forbids him to marry. Published in 1876, this was the play's first performance. Many thought it would be its last. "The piece contains a good deal of history, a good deal of tedium," said *The Daily Mail*. St John Ervine in *The Observer* recognised Olivier's promise: "He has the makings of a considerable actor in him."
—Laurence Olivier's Harold is quick in action, musical in voice, responsive to warlike and romantic mood. *The Times*

Apr 2. Joan Bourdelle as Lorelei Lee in Anita Loos's **Gentlemen Prefer Blondes** directed by John Emerson at Prince of Wales. Loos and Emerson described their adaptation as "a play without hero or heroine, love story or plots." Lorelei, a shrewd, vulgar, young American gold-digger, never opened her mouth without saying a mouthful. Ernest Thesiger played Henry Spoffard.

—He must be a blasé narrow-minded Pharisee who could and would not laugh at these cartoons. J T GRIEN *Sketch*

Apr 15. Mrs Patrick Campbell as Mrs Alving and John Gielgud as Oswald in Henrik Ibsen's **Ghosts** directed by Peter Godfrey at Arts. Matinees only. James Agate said Campbell was like the Lord Mayor's coach with nothing in it.

Apr 18. Jill Esmond Moore, Herbert Lomas and Felix Aylmer in John Drinkwater's **Bird in Hand** directed by John Drinkwater at Royalty. Squire's son wants to marry village innkeeper's daughter but dad does not believe girls should marry above their station.

Apr 27. Piccadilly Theatre opened with Evelyn Laye in Jerome Kern's musical **Blue Eyes** directed by John Harwood. Book and lyrics by Guy Bolton and Graham John. The critics, as an act of charity, concentrated on the building rather than the show.

Apr 30. Scott Sunderland as Petruchio and Eileen Beldon as Katharine in Shakespeare's **The Taming of the Shrew** directed by H K Ayliff at Court. Modern dress production. The star turn was Ralph Richardson as Tranio (Petruchio's cockney chauffeur) trying to get the car to start.

May 3. Cedric Hardwicke, Howett Worster, Edith Day and Marie Burke in Oscar Hammerstein and Jerome Kern's musical **Show Boat** directed by Felix Edwardes at Drury Lane. Milestone in the history of musical theatre. It was the first musical to merge a traditional showbiz story with serious drama. Edna Ferber's complex romantic plot traces the lives of a family of showboat performers over four decades, from the 1880s to the 1920s, and dealt with social conditions, racial tensions, marital discord, alcoholism and miscegenation. The strength of the show (Hammerstein and Kern's answer to Gershwin's *Porgy and Bess*) is the score and its sophisticated musical structure. Hit songs included "Can't Help Lovin' Dat Man" and "Why Do I Love You?" High spot: Paul Robeson singing "Ol' Man River".
—The stalls and boxes were full of prominent people, but the enthusiasm came mainly from the gallery. The show wants only more humour – and more of Paul Robeson. *Daily Express*

May 14. Ernest Milton in Shakespeare's **King Lear** directed by Andrew Leigh at Old Vic. Jean Forbes-Robertson as Cordelia. Eric Portman as Edmund. Prosaic performances and poor elocution.

May 15. Charles Laughton as Hercule Poirot in Michael Morton's adaptation of Agatha Christie's **Alibi** directed by Gerald du Maurier at Prince of Wales.
—Mr Charles Laughton, with very little from the text, makes a personality out of the fat and sentimental-like ratiocinator. His Poirot is an admirable comedy sketch. *The Times*

May 16. Philip Merivale and Isabel Jeans in Robert E Sherwood's **The Road to Rome** directed by William A Brady at Strand. Portrait of Hannibal. Anti-war play.
—Miss Isabel Jeans is absolutely charming until she tries to vamp Hannibal. Philip Merivale is a mournful, philosophic, rather stolid Hannibal. *Morning Post*

May 29. Hartley Power, George Relph, Lewin Mannering and Mercia Swinburne in Edgar Wallace's **The Squeaker** directed by Campbell Gullan at Apollo. Scotland Yard drama. The squeaker got shot.

Jun 26. Tom Walls, Ralph Lynn, Robertson Hare, Mary Brough and Winifred Shotter in Ben Travers's **Plunder** directed by Tom Walls at Aldwych. A parody of the detective genre and the weakest and most laboured of the Aldwych farces. Two fortune-hunters rob an unscrupulous housekeeper of £40,000-worth of jewellery. Somewhat surprisingly for a farce somebody actually gets killed during the night of the bungled burglary.

Jul 18. Nicholas Hannen and Marda Vanne in Monckton Hoffe's **Many Waters** directed by Monckton Hoffe at Ambassadors. Many waters cannot quench love.

Aug 13. Jane Henry and Henry Kendall in Ian Hay and P G Wodehouse's **A Damsel in Distress** directed by Nicholas Hannen at New. P G Wodehouse's novel of the same name, first published in 1919, was made into a silent film in 1920 and then into a play, which ran for 242 performances and follows her to her ancestral home disguised as a footman. George Gershwin wrote music and lyrics for a Hollywood film in 1937, which he never saw because he had died suddenly of a brain tumour.
—It is the sort of play that no child need be afraid to take his parents to. The characters move in a world of sunshine and champagne; they live in castles and lunch at Claridge's, and keep butlers carefully trained to drop their "h's." *Play Pictorial*

Aug 16. Brian Aherne as Young Marlow, Marie Ney as Miss Hardcastle and Nigel Playfair as Tony Lumpkin in Oliver Goldsmith's **She Stoops to Conquer** directed by Nigel Playfair at Lyric, Hammersmith. The comedy was acted as if it were by Sheridan and the production steered clear of all traditional horseplay and gags.

Aug 21. Tallulah Bankhead and Leslie Howard in Jacques Deval's **Her Cardboard Lover** directed by Leslie Howard at Lyric. Adaptation by Valerie Wyngate and P G Wodehouse. Bankhead appeared in her undies and pyjamas.
—They love to see me in my underwear. That sort of thing makes a four week run certain. TALLULAH BANKHEAD *quoted by* HANNEN SWAFFER *Daily Express*
—In the eyes of the gallery she can do no wrong. They would be perfectly content if she merely came on and recited *The Wreck of the Hesperus* in that hoarse emotional voice of hers. *The Times*

Sep 18. Yvonne Arnaud, Ronald Squire and Leslie Faber in Harry Graham's adaptation of Siegfried Geyer's **By Candle Light** directed by Leslie Faber at Prince of Wales. Mistress and maid, master and servant, all swap roles. Transferred to Criterion.
— Leslie Faber, as the baron, waiting on Ronald Squire, as the miserably embarrassed valet, is one of the chief delights... Miss Arnaud's performance places her right in the front rank. What an exquisite actress! In turn provocative, alluring, demure and roguish. *Theatre World*

Sep 19. Robert Farquharson as Count Phalen and Matheson Lang as Tsar Paul 1 in **Such Men Are Dangerous** directed by Matheson Lang and Reginald Denham at Duke of York's. Ashley Dukes' adaptation of Alfred Neumann's *The Patriot*. Lang tried hard to raise the plot – a conspiracy to dethrone the Tsar – above the level of melodrama.

Oct 5. Ivor Novello, Lilian Braithwaite and Lily Elsie in H E S Davidson's **The Truth Game** directed by W Graham Browne at Globe. Young widow stands to forfeit her fortune if she remarries. Viola Tree scored a big success as a gawky, devastatingly honest 34-year-old virgin with no looks, no tact, no manners and no taste but with the ability to laugh at herself. H E S Davidson was the *nom de plume* of Novello. Many critics thought it was time he got rid of his pseudo-romantic complex.

Oct 24. James Dale as Mr Puff in Richard Brinsley Sheridan's **The Critic** directed by Nigel Playfair at Lyric, Hammersmith. Great fun.

Nov 8. Fred Astaire, Adele Astaire and Leslie Henson in Ira and George Gershwin's musical **Funny Face** directed by Felix Edwardes at Princes. Book by Fred Thompson and Paul Gerrard Smith. The easy-going grace of the Astaires made them ideal interpreters of Gershwin's music. During the second week a night watchman accidentally blew up the theatre whilst searching for a gas leak with a lighted match. The show transferred to Winter Garden.

Dec 4. Gerald du Maurier and Ursula Jeans in Ferenc Molnar's **The Play's the Thing** adapted by Frederick Lonsdale and directed by Gerald du Maurier at St James's. Young musician and his two librettists descend unannounced on their leading lady. The musician, who is in love with her, overhears her entertaining another man in her bedroom. The cleverer of the two librettists, wishing to save the lad any unnecessary heartache, writes down the overheard dialogue and persuades the couple to re-enact the scene and pretend they were rehearsing a play by Sardou.
—A dull play, curiously lacking in sparkle and lightness. *Daily Telegraph*
—Poor stuff and no acting could make much of it. *Daily News*

Dec 10. Laurence Oliver as Captain Stanhope, George Zucco as Osborne and Maurice Evans as Lt Raleigh in R C Sherriff's **Journey's End** directed by James Whale at Apollo. Presented by Stage Society. The Unknown Soldier was the hero of World War 1. On 21 March 1918 (the day the play ends) the British lost 38,000 men. The war killed 10,000,000 people. "There must be no squeamishness about losses," said Field Marshal Haig, Commander of the British forces. *Journey's End* was the first play about the Great War to achieve West End success. It ran for nearly 600 performances and was produced all over the world. Sherriff, who had served in the war, vividly recreated what life and death were like in the front-line trenches. His tribute to the stoicism and quiet courage of the officer class was an authentic document of the time, written in the public school idiom of the Edwardian era. The officers "put up a good show", even when they know they haven't a fighting chance. The men stick it out because "it is the only thing a decent man can do". The life expectancy of a 2nd Lieutenant, straight out of school, was 15 days.
—Superficially it may seem photographic rather than dramatic – but in the end one realises that it has fulfilled itself far better than any trashy melodrama has or could have done. *Morning Post*
—This play is stark realism, and at the same time great drama. I cannot remember an evening where I had so continued a catch in the throat. *Daily Mail*

Dec 15. Charles Laughton, Mary Clare and Madeleine Carroll in Cosmo Hamilton and F C Reilly's adaptation of Charles Dickens's **Mr Pickwick** directed by Basil Dean at Haymarket. Eliot Makeham as Sam Weller stole the show.

Dec 19. Helen Ford in Barty Conners's **The Patsy** directed by Gordon D Parker at Apollo. The ugly duckling of the family buys a book, *How to Develop a Personality*, and goes hunting for men. The American comedienne Helen Ford scored a big success.
—The curtain went up five times to cheers at the end of the first act; six times to louder cheers at the end of the second; and nine times to still louder cheers at the end of the third. *Morning Post*

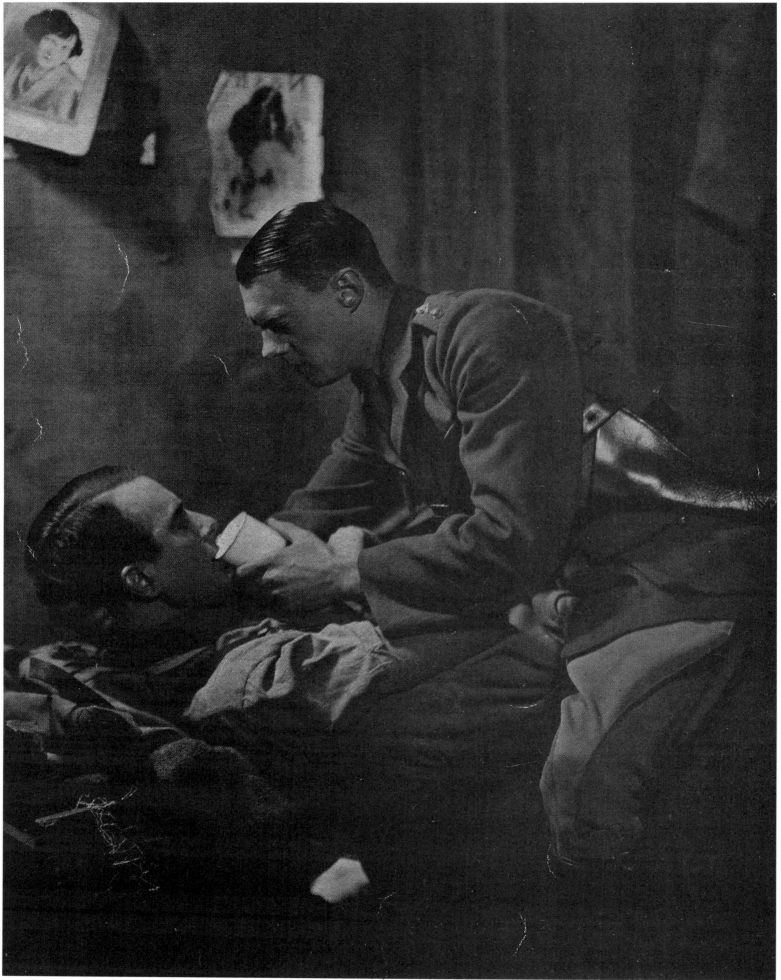

Colin Clive and Melville Cooper in Journey's End

1929

Jan 5. Edith Evans as Florence Nightingale and Eille Norwood as Lord Palmerston in Reginald Berkeley's **The Lady With A Lamp** directed by Leslie Banks and Edith Evans at Arts. The play was based on Lytton Strachey's essay. Berkeley introduced a love story. Nightingale rejects the man she loves so that she can do good works in the Crimea. Transferred to Garrick.

Jan 21. Colin Clive as Captain Stanhope in R C Sherriff's **Journey's End** directed by James Whale at Savoy. Clive landed the leading role because Laurence Olivier who had created it was already committed to appearing in *Beau Geste*. 594 performances.

Jan 22. Esme Percy in Alicia Ramsey's **Byron** directed by Esme Percy at Lyric.
—Never was seen, outside Madame Tussaud's, such a collection of lifeless puppets bearing the names of famous men and women. *Daily Telegraph*

Jan 30. Laurence Olivier, Jack Hawkins, Robin Irvine, Madeleine Carroll and Marie Löhr in Basil Dean and Charlton Mann's adaptation of P C Wren's novel, **Beau Geste** directed by Basil Dean at His Majesty's. Dean's technically impressive but interminable production (which on the first night did not finish until 11.45) was spectacle and nothing else. The critics dismissed it as fifth-form entertainment.

Feb 8. Gladys Cooper, Mary Jerrold, Richard Bird and Sebastian Smith in Somerset Maugham's **The Sacred Flame** directed by Raymond Massey at Playhouse. Maugham

attempted to write in a more formal and artificial manner. The result was verbose and mawkish sentimentality. The Bishop of London said it was the most immoral drama in London and box office takings immediately went up.
—Altogether a play that will appeal to women more than to men, for there is a tremendous amount of conversation with very little action, which spells weariness to a large number of playgoers. *Theatre World*

Feb 11. Bobby Howes and Binnie Hale in **Mr Cinders** directed by George D Parker at Adelphi. Musical comedy. Book by Clifford Grey and Greatrex Newman. Additional lyrics by Leo Robin. Music by Vivian Ellis and Richard Myers. Inversion of popular fairy-tale. Mr Cinders has two ugly brothers. Rich girl masquerades as parlour maid. Hit song: "Spread a Little Happiness". Hannen Swaffer thought it "the best musical in years." He was alone among the critics to think so.

Mar 5. Sybil Thorndike as Barbara, Baliol Holloway as Undershaft, Lewis Casson as Adolphus Cusins, Gordon Harker as Bill Walker and Margaret Scudmore as Lady Britomart in Bernard Shaw's **Major Barbara** directed by Leon M Lion at Wyndham's.
—[Sybil Thorndike] has an ecstatic quality, a sort of pleasant fanaticism, which can blast a poor part out of existence, but is very effective in a good part. *Daily Telegraph*.

Mar 27. Jessie Matthews, Sonnie Hale, Douglas Byng and Tilly Losch in Charles B Cochran's **Wake Up and Dream** directed by Felix Edwardes under the personal supervision of Charles B Cochran at London Pavilion. Book by John Hastings Turner. Music and lyrics by Cole Porter. Spectacular: high spots included the San Francisco Gold Rush of 1849 and the ballet *Coppelia* as seen from the wings of the Old Empire Theatre. Porter's best number was "Let's Do It".

Edith Evans and Cedric Hardwicke in The Apple Cart

1929 World Premieres

New York
Elmer Rice's *Street Scene*
Kurt Weill's *Happy End*
Paris
Jean Giraudoux's *Amphitryon 38*
Paul Claudel's *The Satin Slipper*
Warsaw
Bernard Shaw's *The Apple Cart*
Moscow
Vladimir Mayakovsky's *The Bed Bug*
Saint-Trod, Belgium
Michel de Ghelderode's *Pantagleize*

Births

Brian Friel, Irish playwright
Heiner Muller, German playwright
John Osborne, British playwright

Deaths

Sergei Diaghilev (*b.*1872), Russian impresario
Hugo Hoffmannsthal (*b.*1874), Austrian playwright
Henry Arthur Jones (*b.*1851), British playwright
Lily Langtry (*b.*1852), British actor

Honours
Knight
Philip Ben Greet, British actor-manager

History
—St Valentine's Day massacre
—New York stock market crashed
—Japan invaded Manchuria

Notes
—Kurt Weill – Bertolt Brecht's *Happy End*, hurriedly staged to cash in on the huge success of *The Threepenny Opera*, was a complete fiasco at the Berlin premiere. Helene Weigel, Brecht's wife, hijacked Act 3 to shout communist propaganda. There was booing and a near riot. The show closed two days later. Brecht (who had only provided the songs) washed his hands of it and it wasn't seen again in Germany for thirty years.
—Malvern Festival founded by Barry Jackson
—Harcourt Williams artistic director at Old Vic

Apr 4. Evelyn Laye and Howett Worster in **The New Moon** directed by Felix Edwardes at Drury Lane. Book by Oscar Hammerstein II and Laurence Schwab. Music by Sigmund Romberg. Romantic musical set in New Orleans in the 18th century. *Theatre World* said it was a "treacly admixture of all the saccharine valses of the past twenty years lumped together."

Apr 10. Theatre Guild of New York. Frank Wilson as Porgy, Evelyn Ellis as Bess, Percy Verwayne as Sporting Life, Georgette Harvey as Maria in Dorothy and Dubose Heyward's **Porgy** directed by Rouben Mamoulian at His Majesty's. A vivid picture of life in Catfish Row, a poor tenement in Charleston, South Carolina. The big crowds, the sound and the lighting effects were brilliantly orchestrated by Mamoulian. James Agate said he had never seen a finer ensemble. Alan Parsons in *The Daily Mail* said it was a masterpiece of Negro life. The patois gave West End audiences a bit of difficulty.
—For vitality, sweeping, pulsating vitality *Porgy* is almost unique. As a play it is neither very good nor very bad; as a production it is almost flawless. *Theatre World*

Apr 25. Anthony Ireland, Brian Aherne and Ernest Milton in Patrick Hamilton's **Rope** directed by Reginald Denham at Ambassadors. Hamilton always denied that the play was based on the Leopold and Loeb murder case in America. Nobody believed him. The homoeroticism, implicit in the text and stage directions, was kept under wraps. The leading role was not the murderers, but their friend, a deeply embittered, amoral homosexual, who was wounded in the Great War. He quickly sussed them out. Ernest Milton seemed to be in a different and more serious play than the other actors; especially in a long harangue when he slammed society for condemning murder but condoning war.

Apr 29. Sybil Thorndike and Lewis Casson in Clemence Dane's **Mariners** directed by Leon M Lion and Lewis Casson at Wyndham's. Termagant wife makes her husband's life a misery, but when he dies, she dies, too, from exposure on his grave. She loved him after all.

May 7. Tom Walls, Ralph Lynn, Robertson Hare, Mary Brough and Winifred Shotter in Ben Travers' **A Cup of Kindness** directed by Tom Walls at Aldwych. Farcical family feud between the Tutts and the Ramsbottoms. Walls was on form as an intoxicated rogue.

May 8. Mrs Patrick Campbell in G B Stern's **The Matriarch** directed by Frank Vernon at Royalty. Adaptation of Stern's epic novel, *The Tents of Israel*. The matriarch tyrannised her children and grandchildren. Campbell's comeback after a long absence was a personal triumph; but her monumental performance destroyed the balance of the play.

Jun 4. New York Theatre Guild. Lynn Fontanne and Alfred Lunt in G Sil-Vara's **Caprice**, adapted and directed by Philip Moeller at St James's. A witty trifle was stylishly acted. Fontanne's performance was highly praised.
—[Lynn Fontanne] made an instantaneous appeal to her audience: she has good looks, great

acting technique, a musical voice with a wide range of intonation, a sense of humour, and she uses her hands quite beautifully. *Daily Mail*

Jun 19. Lewis Casson and Edmund Gwenn in John Galsworthy's **Exiled** directed by Leon M Lion at Wyndham's. Struggle between Capital and Labour.
—The picture of England as it is today is sketched with that truthfulness of observation which made Galsworthy's great reputation. HANNEN SWAFFER *Sunday Express*

Jun 21. Frank Vosper, Nora Swinburne, Sara Allgood, Muriel Aked and Frederick Leister in Frank Vosper's **Murder on the Second Floor** directed by Frank Vosper at Lyric. Young author imagines the guests in his mother's boarding house are characters in the detective melodrama he is writing.

Jul 2. Marie Tempest, Henry Ainley and Ursula Jeans in St John Ervine's **The First Mrs Fraser** directed by W Graham Browne at Haymarket. A scintillating light comedy of manners. The second Mrs Fraser, a deeply unpleasant vulgar woman, wants a divorce. Her husband seeks advice from his first wife. The play marked the return of Ainley to the stage after a two-year illness.
—*The First Mrs Fraser* is, in every department, a triumph of brains and its arrival definitely restores the English comedy stage to its former eminence. *Theatre World*

Jul 18. Peggy Wood, George Metaxa and Ivy St Helier in Noël Coward's operetta **Bitter Sweet** directed by Noël Coward at His Majesty's. Coward made theatrical history. For the first time on the London stage one man had written the book and the music of a musical play and also directed it. Hit songs: "If Love Were All", "I'll See You Again" and "Ziegeuner".
—I do not think he has genius but it is talent which comes very close to it. *Daily News*
—The dancing was excellent, though too many members of the company suggested by their accents that recruiting for this production had taken place in and about Blackpool. JAMES AGATE *Sunday Times*

Jul 27. Oscar Asche as Falstaff and Robert Atkins as Ford in Shakespeare's **The Merry Wives of Windsor** directed by Oscar Asche at Apollo. Modern dress production slated for being a grotesque burlesque and illegitimate travesty.

Sep 14. John Gielgud and Adele Dixon in Shakespeare's **Romeo and Juliet** directed by Harcourt Williams at Old Vic. Donald Wolfit as Mercutio. Harcourt Williams, stop-watch in hand, was determined that the production would be what the Chorus said it was – two hours long. The actors gabbled and such was the pace the audience and critics complained they couldn't keep up.

Sep 17. Cedric Hardwicke as King Magnus and Edith Evans as his mistress in Bernard Shaw's **The Apple Cart** directed by H K Ayliff transferred from the Malvern Festival to Queen's. Shaw wrote of the indifference of the public to politics, the dwindling prestige of the House of Commons, the corrupting influence of big business and the Americanisation of England. His "political extravaganza" foreshadowed the abdication crisis in 1936. The socialist cabinet wants the king to shut up and keep his opinions to himself. They threaten to resign if he does not. The king, who has no intention of being a mere puppet, calls their bluff, threatening to abdicate and stand for parliament.
—Mr Shaw is the greatest mind which has done honour to the English theatre in the last three hundred years. JAMES AGATE *The Sunday Times*
—Let me say at once that it is one of the most brilliant plays Bernard Shaw has written. *Daily News*
—Today was a great event in the history of English theatre. HANNEN SWAFFER *Sunday Express*
—To produce such a piece of high farce, fantastic wisdom, high discourse, at the age of seventy-three, is a feat of which men half the age of Mr Shaw might be envious. ST JOHN ERVINE *Observer*
—Mr Cedric Hardwicke's performance as the King is superb in its quietness, dignity and force of intellect. *Evening Standard*
—Edith Evans treats us to a superb exhibition of imperious vanity. *Daily Chronicle*

Sep 17. Mary Newcomb and Leslie Banks in Temple Thurston's **Emma Hamilton** directed by Leslie Banks at New. George Romney (1734–1802) was infatuated with Emma and painted her many times. The play had too much sentimentality and Nelson took far too long to arrive on stage.
—[Mary Newcomb] was frequently inaudible and seemed to rely far too often on glances galleryward for her appeal. *Daily Chronicle*

Sep 18. Owen Nares, Cathleen Nesbitt, Gordon Harker and Alfred Drayton in Edgar Wallace's **The Calendar** directed by Edgar Wallace at Wyndham's. Racing melodrama. The hero is a poor judge of horses and women. *Theatre World* thought it was far and away his best play.

Sep 19. Matheson Lang and Peggy Ashcroft in Ashley Dukes's adaptation of Leon Feuchtwanger's **Jew Suss** directed by Matheson Lang and Reginald Denham at Duke of York's. Historical romance. The sincerity and integrity of Ashcroft's acting was thrown into high relief by what *The Times* described as "the lavish emotional display of Matheson Lang, all magnetic eyes and thrilling tremolo."

Sep 23. Lucille La Verne as Shylock and Virginia Pemberton as Portia in Shakespeare's **The Merchant of Venice** directed by E Lyall Swete at Little.
—The truth is that, having set herself an impossible task, she has made a credible attempt to perform it; but why any actress should be so handicap herself, heaven knows. *The Times*

Sep 25. Miriam Lewes as Arkadin in Anton Chekhov's **The Seagull** directed by A E Filmer at Fortune. Valerie Taylor as Nina. Glen Byam Shaw as Konstantin. Martin Lewis as Trigorin.
—Until I see a better performance I shall regard this actress's Madame Arkadin as perfect. JAMES AGATE *Sunday Times*

Oct 10. Harry Fox in Richard Rodgers and Lorenz Hart's adaptation of Mark Twain's **A Yankee at the Court of King Arthur** directed by David Miller at Daly's. Witty, vulgar and completely fatuous.
—Without exception it is the worst America has ever sent us – and that's saying something. It is quite impossible to understand why Harry Fox should have been brought from America to be leading man. He cannot sing – much – and he does not dance, I can only imagine he cannot do that, either. He does little but display an excellent set of teeth. This he did so consistently that I almost searched my programme for acknowledgements to his dentist. *Theatre World*

Oct 11. Charles Laughton, Barry Fitzgerald, Beatrix Lehmann, Una O'Connor and Ian Hunter in Sean O'Casey's **The Silver Tassie** designed by Augustus John and directed by Raymond Massey at Apollo. Yeats's rejection of O'Casey's great anti-war play led to a rift between O'Casey and the Abbey Theatre, doing irreparable harm to both playwright and theatre. Laughton was miscast as the Dublin football hero, who wins the silver Tassie (a cup) three times before going to the War and losing his legs. The play, based on Wilfred Owen's poem, *Disabled*, is notable for the expressionistic choral second act when the front-line soldiers parody the language of the liturgy. The use of Christian ritual for satirical purposes (and the strong anti-religious feeling throughout) caused deep offence in Dublin when the play was eventually performed there in 1935.

Oct 14. Ivor Novello, Lilian Braithwaite and Benita Hume in Ivor Novello's **Symphony in Two Flats** directed by Raymond Massey at New. Composer struggles to finish his symphony before he is completely blind. "An extravagantly unpersuasive story," said *The Times*. It ran for five months, before transferring to New York, and then had a long tour.

Oct 21. Ronald Squire, Yvonne Arnaud, Mabel Sealby and Athole Stewart in Frederick Lonsdale's **Canaries Sometimes Sing** directed by Athole Stewart at Globe. Canaries only sing when they have a mate.
—Lonsdale has little respect for consistency in his character drawing and never hesitates to sacrifice a character to a situation. The acting throughout is superb. *Daily Telegraph*
—*Canaries Sometimes Sing* will appeal very strongly to "smart" audiences, but I am inclined to wonder if a continual flow of wit and cynicism is all that the general playgoer requires for his entertainment. *Theatre World*

Nov 5. Madeleine Carroll, Eric Portman, Frank Lawton and Horace Hodges in John Galsworthy's **The Roof** directed by Basil Dean at Vaudeville. Galsworthy's last play observed the behaviour of people in a hotel, room by room, before during and after a fire in a small Paris Hotel. The critics thought the play "a damp squib". Galsworthy decided he would write no more plays.

Nov 18. John Gielgud in Shakespeare's **Richard II** directed by Harcourt Williams at Old Vic.
—His playing of the abdication scene will live in my mind as one of the great things I have witnessed in the theatre. HARCOURT WILLIAMS

Nov 28. Frank Cellier and Angela Baddeley as Sir Peter and Lady Teazle in Richard Brinsley Sheridan's **The School for Scandal** directed by Frank Cellier at Kingsway. Cellier was not the usual grumpy old man approaching senility but a graceful and debonair cavalier carrying his fifty years with ease.

Dec 9. John Gielgud as Oberon, Adele Dixon as Titania, Leslie French as Puck, Gyles Isham as Bottom, Martita Hunt as Helena, Donald Wolfit as Demetrius and Wendy Toye as Moth in Shakespeare's **A Midsummer Night's Dream** directed by Harcourt Williams at Old Vic.
—[Harcourt Williams] has taken this sorely used thing of loveliness and laughter and put it straight were it belongs into the very heart of moonstruck Yorkshire. IVOR BROWN *Manchester Guardian*

Dec 10. Marie Ney, Henry Oscar, Owen Ryenold and Muriel Aked in Frank Vosper's **People Like Us** directed by Frank Vosper at Arts. Performance for club members only. Suburban wife incites her lover to kill her degenerate husband. The Lord Chamberlain initially banned the play because it was based on the notorious Frederick Bywaters/Edith Thompson murder trial in 1923. He was forced to relent when a newspaper published the text. Vosper got the play's title from Beverley Nichols, the only journalist to interview Mrs Thompson's father after she had been condemned to death. The first thing the old man had said was: "To think that such a thing could happen to people like us." Transferred to Strand.

1930–1939

1930

Jan 29. Nigel Playfair as the Dean in Arthur Wing Pinero's **Dandy Dick** directed by Nigel Playfair at Lyric Hammersmith. Marie Löhr was unexpectedly cast as Georgina Tidman, "the daisy of the Turf."
—Marie Löhr combined in a perfectly astounding way the horsiness of the race-course with the feminine charm of the boudoir. *Theatre World*

Feb 1. Edna Best and Herbert Marshall as a bigamous couple in A A Milne's **Michael and Mary**. Directed by Charles Hopkins at St James's. "A brilliant partnership," said the *Times*. "The best thing Milne has done for the stage," said *The Daily Mail*.

Mar 5. Tallulah Bankhead and Glen Byam Shaw in Alexander Dumas fils's **The Lady of the Camellias** directed by Nigel Playfair at Garrick.
—I am afraid I must judge the whole performance to have been a brave and gallant effort to cope with a part which the actress carried insufficient guns. JAMES AGATE *Sunday Times*
—Miss Bankhead's monotony of delivery (which in contemporary plays is part of her personal appeal) and certain pervasive modernity of manner and style tell against her. But make no mistake about it, she is worth seeing. W A DARLINGTON *Daily Telegraph*

Mar 11. The Intimate Revue at Duchess had a catastrophic first night and closed the same night.

Mar 17. John Gielgud and Martita Hunt in Shakespeare's **Macbeth** directed by Harcourt Williams at Old Vic. James Agate went round in the middle of the performance to tell Gielgud that he wouldn't be up to acting the rest of the play. Harcourt Williams thought it was the best thing Gielgud had done at the Vic.
—The young actor, in my judgement, easily outdistanced all his predecessors, and revealed a promise, which, when, as we all expect, it comes to complete fulfilment, must be what we have long waited for – an actor acknowledged national supremacy in the greatest Shakespearian roles. ALAN PARSONS *Daily Mail*

Mar 20. Gwen Ffrangcon-Davis as Nora and Henry Oscar as Torvald in Henrik Ibsen's **A Doll's House** directed by Henry Oscar at Arts. Harcourt Williams as Dr Rank. Frederick Lloyd as Krogstad. Transferred to Criterion.
—It destroyed the idea, that has become general, of Nora being out of date, of our having dealt with and done with her rebellion. Why, he [Ibsen] sounds like the last word in modernity. J T GRIEN *Illustrated London News*

Mar 28. Dennis King as D'Artagnan and Arthur Wontner as Richelieu in a spectacular musical version of Alexandre Dumas's **The Three Musketeers** directed by Felix Edwardes at Drury Lane. Music by Rudolph Friml. Lyrics by Clifford Grey. Book by William Anthony McGuire.
—No one with theatre in his blood can resist the extraordinary theatricalism of the Drury Lane scene. *The Times*

Apr 2. Charles Laughton and Emlyn Williams in Edgar Wallace's **On the Spot** directed by Edgar Wallace at Wyndham's. Gangster thriller dedicated to the Chief Commissioner and the Deputy Commissioner of Chicago Police Department, "who are daily dealing effectively with situations more incredible and more fantastic than any I have depicted."
—I have never seen a more repulsive creature on the stage than Pirelli, whom Mr Charles Laughton, acting with all his usual brilliance, made an oily, smirking, dangerous animal. W A DARLINGTON *Daily Telegraph*

Apr 28. John Gielgud in Shakespeare's **Hamlet** in its entirety directed by Harcourt Williams at Old Vic. Donald Wolfit as Claudius. Martita Hunt as Gertrude. Adele Dixon as Ophelia. Harcourt Williams as Ghost. Gielgud at twenty-six was the youngest Hamlet in living memory.
—I have no hesitation whatsoever in saying that it is the high watermark of English Shakespearian acting of our time. JAMES AGATE *Sunday Times*
—The performance puts him beyond the range of the arriving actors; he is in the first rank. IVOR BROWN *Observer*

May 19. Paul Robeson in Shakespeare's **Othello** directed by Ellen Van Volkenburg at Savoy. Maurice Browne as Iago. Peggy Ashcroft as Desdemona. Sybil Thorndike as Emilia. Ralph Richardson as Roderigo. A small number of black people attended the performance. One editor walked out after the third act saying he did not like being near coloured people. The critics were divided: some found Robeson great, magnificent, remarkable; others found him disappointingly prosaic and genteel.
—Robeson endows Othello with an inferiority complex which is incongruous. *Time and Tide*
—The part of Shakespeare's Moor was not written for a coloured actor of any kind. E A BAUGHAN *Daily News*
—The production did Mr Robeson enormous disservice in the matter of the lighting which robbed his features of all expressiveness, and turned his face into a black, unintelligible mask. JAMES AGATE *Sunday Times*

Jun 2. Alexander Moissi in Shakespeare's **Hamlet** at Globe. Acted in German. Moissi, who confessed that he seldom felt the same way about Hamlet from perform-

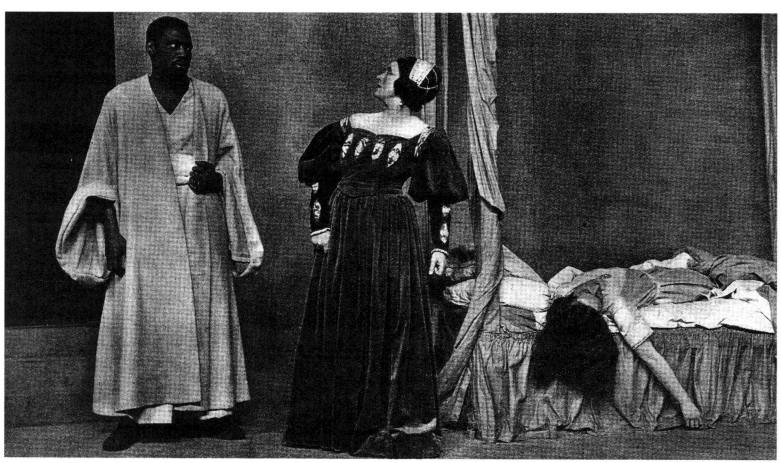

Paul Robeson, Sybil Thorndike and Peggy Ashcroft in Othello

ance to performance, was the sweet Prince of Goethe's imagination. The play was so ruthlessly trimmed that it became scenes from *Hamlet*.
—Herr Moissi is an actor who believes very strongly that the part is made for the actor and not the actor for the part. *Daily Telegraph*

Jun 10. Ludmilla Pitoëff as Jeanne and Georges Pitoëff as the Dauphin in Bernard Shaw's **Sainte Jeanne** at Comedy. Acted in French. *The Times* thought Shaw's epilogue worked better in French than it had done in English.

Jun 11. Edith Evans and Godfrey Tearle in George Farquhar's **The Beaux's Stratagem** directed by Nigel Playfair at Royalty.
—The picture she [Edith Evans] presents is as enchanting as her mastery of the character is brilliant. HAROLD HOBSON *Observer*

Jun 14. Ludmilla Pitoëff in Alexandre Dumas fils's **La Dame Aux Camelias** at Globe. Acted in French.

Jun 26. Gerald du Maurier, Celia Johnson and Gladys Cooper in **Cynara** by H M Harwood and R Gore Browne directed by Gerald du Maurier at Playhouse. Shop girl enjoys a brief affair with a married middle-aged barrister and then commits suicide.

June 30. Herbert Marshall, Edna Best, Irene Vanbrugh and Colin Clive in Ferenc Molnar's **The Swan** directed by Gilbert Miller at St James's. Princess falls in love with her young brother's handsome tutor and then uses him as a decoy to catch a Crown Prince. Molner's sophisticated, witty and stylish fairy tale cleverly denied the audience's expectations. The princess marries the prince, not the tutor.
—Mr Colin Clive lends the tutor such intense virility and capacity for emotion that he disturbs the whole balance of the play and emerges as its hero. *Daily Telegraph*

Jul 2. Owen Nares and Jeanne de Casilis in Sacha Guitry's **Désiré**, directed by Owen Nares and D A Clarke-Smith at New. Adapted by John Leslie Frith. No sex, please, we're French.

Jul 7. John Gielgud as John Worthing, Anthony Ireland as Algernon Moncrieff and Mabel Terry-Lewis as Lady Bracknell in Oscar Wilde's **The Importance of Being Earnest** directed by Nigel Playfair at Lyric, Hammersmith. The production was designed in black and white so as to recall Aubrey Beardsley.
—He confirms the impression that deepens with every performance that he is a young man with a very great future. MONICA EWER *Daily Herald*
—Mr Gielgud is totally unfitted for the part, not because he is a tragic actor, but because he is a serious one. JAMES AGATE *Sunday Times*

Jul 8. André Van Gyseghem, Lesley Wareing, Frederick Piper, Edith Sharpe and Donald Wolfit in Karel Capek's **The Macropulos Case** directed by A R Whatmore at Arts. This grim bedroom farce was too absurd for tragedy, but not quite horrific enough for Grand Guignol. The femme fatale turned out to be over three hundred years old.

Sep 1. Baliol Holloway in Shakespeare's **Richard III** directed by Baliol Holloway at New.

Sep 2. Martin Harvey, Edmund Gwenn and Judith Anderson in Bernard Shaw's **The Devil's Disciple** directed by Martin Harvey at Savoy. *The Times* thought Harvey swaggered over much in the opening act.

Sep 4. Beatrice Lillie, Henry Kendall, Florence Desmond, Dora Vladimorova and Anton Dolin in **Charlot's Masquerade** directed by Andre Charlot at Cambridge. Revue. Book by Ronald Jean. Lyrics by Rowland Leigh. High spots included Beatrice Lillie singing on skates and a sketch showing the effect of Negro spirituals on fashionable Mayfair society. A ballet based on Edgar Allan Poe's *The Masque of Red Death* was not nearly macabre enough.

Sep 9. Erin O'Brien-Moore, Mary Servoss, David Landau, Mary Grew, Margaret Moffatt, Stanley Viven and Leonard Sachs in Elmer Rice's **Street Scene** directed by Elmer Rice at Globe. Rice's Impressionistic slice of New York tenement life on a hot summer's day made a vivid commentary on the Depression years and the American Dream.
—London is not partial to plays of the lower depths – that is London of society; the pit and gallery are another story. The former do not want to plunge into the sordidness and misery of the poor; musical comedy and bed-room scenes are its venue. J T GRIEN *Sketch*

Sep 17. Claude Hulbert and Sophie Tucker in Vivian Ellis's **Follow a Star** directed by Jack Hulbert at Winter Garden. Book by Douglas Furber and Dion Titheradge.
—There can be no half measures when dealing with Sophie Tucker's performance. Either you are a "Soph" fan or you are not, but even those in the latter category must conceded that she is the most dynamic personality expert America has yet exported. *Theatre World*

Sep 23. Cedric Hardwicke as Edward Moulton-Barrett, Gwen Ffrangcon-Davies as

Elizabeth Barrett and Scott Sunderland as Robert Browning in Rudolf Besier's **The Barretts of Wimpole Street** directed by H K Ayliff at Queen's. Barretts' descendents took strong exception to the portrayal of Barrett lusting after his daughter.
—Mr Hardwicke is one of our finest actors, but the dice were too heavily loaded against him. Mr Besier will not allow Edward Moulton-Barrett the tiniest fragment of sympathy. *Daily Mail*
—I feel strongly that the form of autobiographical drama is a dramatic outrage, an offence against the amenities of our social life ... Whether the story is true or false, it should not be allowed upon our stage. SYDNEY W CARROLL *Daily Telegraph*

Sep 24. Noël Coward, Gertrude Lawrence, Laurence Olivier and Adrianne Alien in Noël Coward's **Private Lives** directed by Noël Coward at Phoenix. Verbal and physical sparring in a 1930s cocktail-and-pyjama world: two divorcees meet again for the first time on their honeymoon and decide to ditch their spouses. "There is no need to be nasty," says Amanda. "Yes, there is!" retorts Elyot. Coward wrote the play as a vehicle for himself and Lawrence. The comedy, all brittle staccato rudeness, is dangerously thin but this has never interfered with its success.
—Noël Coward is the play-boy of the London stage. He has raised flippancy to the plain of genius. *News Chronicle*
—Mr Coward's genius consists in this, that he catches admirably the conversational tone of the day, the fool-bom jests of the wise, the world-weary banter of the modish restaurant's most privileged table. JAMES AGATE *Sunday Times*
—Mr Coward's great gift as a dramatist is that his dialogue has the rhythm of life, and the rhythm of modern life is more broken and much quicker than that of twenty years ago. He understands, too, that it is important that a joke on the stage should be spontaneous than perfect. *New Statesman*
—It is the most adroit play that Noël Coward has fashioned. It is testimony to his skill that the whole thing passes off so lightly and entertainingly. On paper his dialogue looks abrupt, thin and scrappy. Yet its brevity and rapidity give the effect of extreme brilliance. A E WILSON *Star*

Sep 25. Edith Evans in H R Barbor's **Delilah** directed by Edith Evans at Prince of Wales. John Langdon as Samson. Delilah was a bore.

Sep 30. Ronald Squire, Marie Löhr, Jack Hawkins, Peggy Ashcroft and William Fox in Somerset Maugham's **The Breadwinner** directed by Athole Stewart at Vaudeville. Middle-aged stockbroker, having lost all his money and bored with his family, decides to leave home. The family is deeply shocked. They don't like him, they don't respect him, but they do expect him to provide for them "They're a dreary lot, that war generation," says one Bright Young Thing. "Well, don't forget that except for the war, there would have been a lot more of them," says another. Many critics objected to the statement: "Don't you know that since the war the amateurs have entirely driven the professionals out of business. No girl can make a decent living now by prostitution."

Oct 6. John Gielgud as Prospero in Shakespeare's **The Tempest** directed by Harcourt Williams at Old Vic. Ralph Richardson as Caliban. Gielgud looked like a Doge painted by an old Master. Leslie French was the first male actor in 100 years to play Ariel. The role was usually acted by a girl

Oct 8. Raymond Massey, Alice Delysia, Martita Hunt, Sebastian Shaw and Donald Wolfit in Benn W Levy's adaptation of Marcel Pagnol's **Topaze** directed by Reginald Denham at New. A cynical fantasia on the theme that honesty is the worst policy. Topaze, an innocent teacher, is taken in hand by a worldly woman. This popular French play flopped in London. The translation and performances were blamed.

Oct 9. Glen Byam Shaw, Angela Baddeley, Athene Seyler, Anthony Ireland, George Hayes, Iris Baker and Adele Dixon in John Dryden's **Marriage a La Mode** directed by Nigel Playfair at Lyric, Hammersmith. *Theatreworld* said Seyler's affected Melantha was 'the very whirlwind of boisterous mischief."

Oct 18. Jean Forbes-Robertson and Ernest Milton in Henrik Ibsen's **Little Eyolf** directed by Michael Orme at Arts.
—[Jean Forbes-Robertson's] power to communicate the emotion of the part, to enter into its intellectual subtlety and, above all, to establish a unity between herself and her audience, is beyond question. *The Times*

Oct 22. Roy Graham in C K Munro's **Mr Eno, His Birth, Death and Life** at Arts. Mr Eno was a failure, a waste product, a slave to a contraption of steel and iron. Munro's ironic comedy was written in eight stylised scenes. The gaps between the scenes made it difficult for some audiences to concentrate.

Nov 26. Amy Veness. Margaretta Scott, Violet Fairbrother, Henry Kendall and Veronica Turnleigh in Emlyn Williams's **A Murder Has Been Arranged** directed by Emlyn Williams at St James's. A ghost story told in the manner of Pirandello, rather than in the manner of Edgar Wallace, was, inevitably, more likely to appeal to theatre aficionados rather than to the general public in search of a thriller.

Dec 3. Jessie Matthews and Sonnie Hale in Richard Rodgers and Lorenz Hart's

Gertrude Lawrence and Noel Coward in
Private Lives

1930 World Premieres

New York
Moss Hart and Edna Ferber's *Once in a Lifetime*
Marc Connelly's *Green Pastures*
Milan
Luigi Pirandello's *As You Desire Me*
Edinburgh
James Bridie's *The Anatomist*
Paris
Jean Cocteau's *La Voix Humaine*

Births
John Arden, British playwright
A R Gurney, American playwright
Peter Hall, British director
Harold Pinter, British playwright
Stephen Sondheim, American composer, lyricist

Deaths
A Conan Doyle (*b.*1859), British novelist, playwright
D H Lawrence (*b.*1885), British novelist, playwright

Notes
—The following six theatres opened: Phoenix, Cambridge, Prince Edward, Whitehall, Adelphi, Leicester Square

History
—Nazis gained in German elections
—Mahatma Gandhi led Salt March in India
—Pluto discovered by astronomers
—Cyclotron invented

musical **Ever Green** directed by Frank Collins at Adelphi. Musical. Book by Benn W V Levy. The spectacle was lavish. Matthews wore a gigantic headdress of net, spangle and ostrich feathers, which measured 15 feet in height and 25 feet across, and comprised 150 large tails and more than 500 feathers of a smaller size. Matthews and Hale "danced on the ceiling" round a chandelier that grew upwards.

Dec 17. Frederick Burtwell as Toad, Ivor Barnard as Rat and Richard Goolden as Mole in A A Milne's **Toad of Toad Hall** directed by Frank Cellier at Lyric. An adaptation of Kenneth Grahame's *The Wind in the Willows*. Goolden would go on playing Mole practically every Christmas for the rest of his life.

Dec 22. John Mills and Arthur P Bell in Brandon Thomas's **Charley's Aunt**, directed by Amy Brandon at New. At twenty-one Mills was the youngest actor ever to play Lord Fancourt Babberley on the West End stage.

1931

Jan 6. Sadler's Wells reopened with Shakespeare's **Twelfth Night** directed by Harcourt Williams. John Gielgud as Malvolio. Dorothy Green as Viola. Joan Harben as Olivia. Ralph Richardson as Sir Toby Belch. Leslie French as Feste. Gielgud was handicapped by having to play his prison scene in what seemed to be a sound-proof sentry box.

Jan 22. Yvonne Arnaud and Frank Cellier in J B Fagan's **The Improper Duchess** directed by J B Fagan. Satire on American commercialism. Arnaud's charm, grace and sparkle were irresistible.

Feb 3. Mary Ellis and Basil Sydney in Eugene O'Neill's **Strange Interlude** directed by Philip Moeller at Gate. A woman's lover dies in World War I. She marries another man, only to find there is a history of insanity in his family. She aborts their child, turning to a doctor to impregnate her. They fall in love. Meanwhile an old childhood friend remains constantly at her side, ready to do anything, but make physical love to her. She lives off the three men for the rest of their lives. The audience hears the characters' inner thoughts as they speak with the other characters on the stage. The thoughts are not asides directed to the audience, but rather part of the continuing conversation. The thoughts are not heard by the other characters.
—The truth is *Strange Interlude* would be a vastly improved play if it were short of its last two acts. It would be even better if Mr O'Neill throughout had left rather more to the imagination. *Era*
—It is sufficiently original to appeal to any adult who is not dead from the neck up ... Good fun, of course, but you can have too much of a good thing. *Illustrated London News*
—Miss Mary Ellis's skill in the part cannot prevent Nina from being an exceedingly tiresome woman ... We may be sorry for her during one, two, three or even five acts – from 6pm to 8pm. After nine acts (with dinner interval) from 6 to 8 and then from 9 to 11 one may be forgiven, for finding her intolerable. RICHARD JENNINGS *Spectator*

Feb 24. George Merritt as Ephraim, Norman Shelley as Peter, Flora Robson as Abbie, Arthur Coullet as Simeon and Eric Portman as Eben in Eugene O'Neill's **Desire Under the Elms** directed by Peter Godfrey at Gate. The drama, built on classical lines, is deeply flawed and ends not in Greek Tragedy but in romantic nonsense. It is impossible to believe that Abbie who has been cast as the villainess (whore, thief and murderer) has been redeemed by love. It is also impossible to believe that Eben, having learned that she has killed their baby, would not have murdered her. Instead he loves her so much that he is willing to go to the gallows with her.

—Mr O'Neill is an impulsive, emotional writer with more vitality than discretion and with more emotion than intellect. *The Times*
—Miss Robson keeps a wonderful firm hold in the part which shows great judgment, since Mr O'Neill is apt to let his emotions run away with them. IVOR BROWN *Observer*

Mar 3. Godfrey Tearle in Shakespeare's **Hamlet** directed by Charles La Trobe at Haymarket. Tearle took over at 24 hours' notice when Henry Ainley fell ill. Fay Compton played Ophelia.

Mar 17. Jean Forbes-Robertson in Henrik Ibsen's **Hedda Gabler** at Arts. Walter Piers as Tesman. Walter Hudd as Lovbörg. Transferred to Fortune.
—Miss Forbes-Robertson is an actress very much in the tradition of Duse. That is to say she has very little power of subduing herself to a part but a very great power of subduing a part to the demands of her own personality. *Daily Telegraph*
—Miss Forbes-Robertson suggests by her icy calm the streak of insanity as the explanation of Hedda's depression. A E WILSON *Star*

Mar 19. Eve in **Cochrane's 1931 Revue** directed by Frank Collins at London Pavilion. Book and music by Noël Coward. Eve was a contortionist and the audience had to sit through 25 boring items before she appeared.

Mar 29. W E C Jenkins as Melchior, Leonard Sachs as Moritz and Eric Knight as Otto in Frank Wedekind's **Spring Awakening** presented by The Sunday Theatre Club at the Grafton. German adolescents try to come to terms with their sexuality in a repressive, middle-class society. The text, first published in 1891, included scenes of flagellation, rape, eroticism in the lavatory, communal masturbation in prison, homosexual love, abortion, madness, death-wish, and suicide. The play wasn't produced in Germany until 1906 (by Max Reinhardt) and then only in a highly cut version.

Mar 30. Miriam Lewes as Mrs Warren, Rosalinde Fuller as Vivie and Wilfrid Lawson as Sir George Crofts in Bernard Shaw's **Mrs Warren's Profession** directed by Charles Macdona at Court. The ban was finally lifted.
—Vivie, far from suggesting the austere intellectuality of chambers in Chancery, looks as if she might at any minute join her mother in the can-can. *Era*

Apr 6. Fay Compton, Francis Lederer and Martita Hunt in C L Antony's **Autumn Crocus** directed by Basil Dean at Lyric. Antony was the *nom de plume* for Dodie Smith. English schoolmistress falls in love with a Tyrolean inn-keeper, only to find that he is already married. This simple-hearted, improbable romance, with its quiet comedy and gentle pathos, was enhanced by Compton's bitter-sweet wistfulness and Lederer's charm and good looks. Such was its success, the management had to put an additional 35 seats into the stalls.

Apr 8. Clifford Mollison and Lea Seidl in **White Horse Inn** directed by Erik Charell at London Coliseum. Musical. Book and lyrics by Harry Graham. Music by Ralph Benatzky and Robert Stoltz. The £50,000 spectacular was designed by Erik Charrell. (Kollosal said the critics.) The foyers in Berlin had been made to resemble the corridors of an inn in the Tyrol. The programme sellers were dressed as Tyrolean peasants. The big surprise was that the waiter was really a waiter and didn't turn out to be a prince in disguise. Frederick Leicester as the Emperor did most of the acting.

Apr 9. Francis L Sullivan as Hercule Poirot in Agatha Christie's **Black Coffee** directed by D A Clarke-Smith at St Martin's. Sullivan brought zest, veracity and a charming bedside manner to the Belgian detective.

Apr 22. Henry Ainley in Shakespeare's **Hamlet** at Haymarket. Gwen Ffrangcon-Davies as Ophelia. Irene Vanbrugh as Gertrude.
—In place of an interpretation of Hamlet we had a display of executive virtuosity and bravura declamation which instead of revealing the character, blinded us to it. JAMES AGATE *Sunday Times*

May 1. Marie Ney, Henry Mollison and John Mills in John Van Druten's **London Wall** directed by Auriol Lee at Duke of York's. Slice-of-life drama is set in a typical London solicitor's office.

May 11. Paul Robeson in Eugene O'Neill's **The Hairy Ape** directed by James Light at Ambassadors. "A comedy of modern and ancient life." A simplistic story is told in a series of expressionistic yet realistic tableaux, which contrasted the brutal and brutalising existence of the poor with the vacuous existence of the rich. Yank, a stoker on a luxury liner, is rejected by Man and Ape. (The ape, said O'Neill, is a symbol of man who has lost the old harmony with Nature, which he used to have as an animal and has not yet acquired another and more spiritual one.) The play was denounced in 1922 as socialist propaganda and therefore subversive and un-American. Robeson exulted in his physical strength. The production came to an abrupt end after five performances when doctors warned him that if he went on shouting he would permanently injure his voice.
—A fitting background for Paul Robeson's magnificent voice, gestures and physique. Subtlety

1931 World Premieres

New York

Eugene O'Neill's *Mourning Becomes Electra*

Elmer Rice's *Councillor-in-Law*

Ira and George Gershwin's *Of Thee I Sing*

Robert E Sherwood's *Reunion in Vienna*

Berlin

Odon von Horvath's *Tales from the Vienna Woods*

Carl Zuckmayer's *The Captain from Kopenik*

Paris

Jean Giraudoux's *Judith*

André Obey's *Noah*

Births

Peter Barnes, British playwright

Rolf Hochhhuth, German playwright

Charles Wood, British playwright

Deaths

Arthur Schnitzler (*b.*1862), Austrian playwright

Honours

Dame

Sybil Thorndike, British actor

History

—Spain declared a republic

—Japan occupied Manchuria

—Sir Oswald Mosley founded British Socialist Party

—Empire State Building erected

---

you do not expect from him, but there is a simple grandeur in his acting that is a relief from over-refined West End traditions. *Theatre World*

May 14. John Gielgud as Inigo Jollifant, Edward Chapman as Jess Oakroyd, Adele Dixon as Susie Dean and Edith Sharpe as Elizabeth Trant in J B Priestley's **The Good Companions** directed by Julian Wylie at His Majesty's. Adaptation of the novel by J B Priestley and Edward Knoblock. Music by Richard Addinsell. Lyrics by Harry Graham and Frank Eyton. The only people who would seem not to have read the novel were the critics who were disconcerted to find that the audience greeted the characters as if they were long-lost friends. There were also those who felt that Gielgud, after his brilliant seasons at the Old Vic, should be doing something more taxing and a little less dinky-do than playing a romantic juvenile lead in a West End show.

May 27. Margaret Rawlings as Salome, John Clements as Jokanaan, Robert Speaight as Herod, Flora Robson as Herodias and Esmond Knight as Young Syrian in Oscar Wilde's **Salome** adapted by Constance Lambert and directed by Peter Godfrey at Gate.

Jun 22. Compagnie de Quinze de Theatre du Vieux-Columbier, Paris, at Arts. Auguste Bovério in André Obey's **Noé** directed by Jean Copeau. Jean Villard was Sem. Michel Saint-Denis played the elephant. Imaginative, austere, intellectual and disarmingly simple, it was acted in tandem with André Obey's **Pour Lucrece**, which

was based on Shakespeare's *The Rape of Lucrece*. Transferred to Ambassadors.

—As a work of art the thing is flawless and unique. JAMES AGATE *Sunday Times*

Aug 3. Mary Grew in Sophie Treadwell's **The Life Machine** directed by Henry Oscar for six private performances at Arts Theatre. Treadwell, playwright, journalist (war correspondent in World War I), novelist, producer and sometime actor and director, was one of the newspaper reporters who witnessed the murder trial of Ruth Snyder and Judd Grey. The trial became the inspiration for her expressionistic play, a feminist tract on the lot of women in a world run by men. It was a damning report on the dehumanising experience of modern society. Premiered in New York in 1928, the London premiere was delayed by the Lord Chamberlain who objected to the intimate details of a wedding night, talk of abortion and a homosexual pick-up in a speakeasy. The West End management advertised the production with a lurid poster, some tantalising quotes from the critics and an announcement that it was 'for adults only'. Audiences expecting a cheap thrill were bitterly disappointed. Transferred to the Garrick

Aug 10. A W Baskcomb, Mary Clare, Basil Foster, Jane Baxter and Clive Currie in **The Midshipmaid**, "a naval manoeuvre" by Ian Hay and Stephen King-Hall directed by Campbell Gullan at Shaftesbury. Farce aboard ship with amateur theatricals in honour of a visiting VIP. Baskcomb provided the most fun, playing the euphonium and reciting Longfellow with his eyes shut.

Aug 17. Evelyn Herbert and Robert Halliday alternated with Adrienne Bruno and Esmond Knight in **Waltzes from Vienna** directed by Hassard Short at Alhambra. The story was based on the life and music of Johann Strauss, father and son. Strauss doesn't want his son to follow a music career and suffer as he had done. The climax was the first public performance of "The Blue Danube".

Aug 18. Cathleen Nesbitt, Emlyn Williams, Gordon Harker and Finlay Currie in Edgar Wallace's **The Case of the Frightened Lady** directed by Edgar Wallace at Wyndham's. Classic 1930s detective thriller with a truly unexpected and chilling denouement. The lady is frightened because she is being forced to marry a madman. Williams, excellent, was a subtle homicide. Harker's police-sergeant provided the light relief.

Sep 3. Elena Miramovo, Ursula Jeans, Ivor Barnard, Hugh Williams, Lyn Harding, Ernest Milton, Harold Scott and George Merritt in Vicki Baum's **Grand Hotel** adapted by Edward Knoblock and directed by Raymond Massey at Adelphi. Vicki Baum worked as a parlour maid for six months in a Berlin hotel whilst researching her novel, which was published in 1929 and follows the fates of the hotel's clientele and staff after the Wall Street Crash when time is running out for them all.

—I feel as if I had been investigating an ant-hill rather than visiting a play. *Daily Telegraph*

Finlay Currie, Emlyn Williams, Cathleen Nesbitt, W Cronin Wilson, Gordon Harker and Joyce Kennedy in *The Case of the Frightened Lady*

Sep 15. Robert Speaight in Shakespeare's **King John** directed by Harcourt Williams at Sadler's Wells. Phyllis Thomas as Constance. Ralph Richardson as the Bastard buttressed the production with his panache.

Sep 18. Edith Evans, Eric Portman, Roland Culver, Diana Wynyard, James Dale, Miles Malleson and O B Clarence in William Congreve's **The Old Bachelor** directed by Nigel Playfair at Lyric, Hammersmith. Evans spoke both the prologue and the epilogue, which had been spoken in the original 1693 production by the two most famous actresses of the day, Mrs Bracegirdle and Mrs Barry, respectively.

Sep 19. Gladys Cooper in Somerset Maugham's **The Painted Veil** adapted by Bartlett Cormack and directed by Lewis Casson at Playhouse. Husband discovers his wife in the arms of another man. He says he will forgive her if she comes with him to cholera-ridden Mei Tan-Fu.

Sep 30. Phyllis Neilson-Terry in Ferdinand Bruckner's **Elizabeth of England**, adapted by Ashley Dukes and directed by Heinz Hilpert at Cambridge. Based on Lytton Strachey's *Elizabeth and Essex*. Matheson Lang as Philip of Spain. Frank Vosper as Francis Bacon. Long, dull and pretentious it was redeemed by the second act and a striking scene which showed simultaneously Philip at the Escorial reacting to the news of the Armada's defeat and Elizabeth in St Paul's Cathedral giving thanks for the victory.

Oct 5. Joan Maude as Salome, Laurence Anderson as Jokanaan, Robert Farquharson as Herod, Nancy Price as Herodias and Robert Donat as Young Syrian in Oscar Wilde's **Salome** directed by Nancy Prince at Savoy. Choreography by Ninette de Valois.
—There is nothing voluptuous, sadistic or passionate in her interpretation of the part. She [Joan Maude] appears just a nice little High School girl slightly offended because John the Baptist refused to partner her in a tennis tournament. *Illustrated London News*
—There is nothing more dreadful than the sight of a girl who is naturally good in the grip of an evil passion which she cannot control. That was the character I tried to play. It would have been easy to make Salome a common vamp – but how crude and how untrue! JOAN MAUDE

Oct 6. Barry Jones in Robert E Sherwood's **The Queen's Husband** directed by Maurice Colbourne at Ambassadors. Ruritanian royalty. The king, the last of a long line of nonentities, routs a military dictator and rescues his daughter from an arranged marriage. Grace Lane played the icy queen.
—Barry Jones as the king played the negative virtues of diffidence and self-effacement for all they were worth and scored a personal success. *Era*

Oct 7. Henry Ainley as Dr Robert Knox in James Bridie's **The Anatomist** directed by Tyrone Guthrie at Westminster. The Edinburgh surgeon dissected corpses brought to him by body-snatchers without asking where they came from. The play concentrated on drawing room comedy, love scenes and tiffs rather than the charnel house and only got down to the real subject matter when Knox argues that a murdered prostitute serves the community far better dead than she did when she was alive. Ainley was a flamboyant, over-bearing and repellent Knox. J A Rourke and Harry Hutchinson played Burke and Hare, the body-snatchers. Flora Robson made her name as the prostitute. Bridie said that she gave a performance of such beauty that she burst the play into two.

Oct 12. Edna Best, Herbert Marshall, May Whitty and Cyril Raymond in Frederick Lonsdale's **There's Always Juliet** directed by Auriol Lee at Apollo. Waspish romance between a debonair American architect and a bad-tempered, shallow woman.
—Ena Best and Herbert Marshall are the West End's most adored couple; the romance of their personal relationship goes to the heart of the crowd without fail in a play of clean and sincere sentiment like this. *Era*

Oct 13. Mary Clare, Edward Sinclair, Una O'Connor and Fred Groves in Noël Coward's **Cavalcade** directed by Noël Coward at Drury Lane. The patriotic pageant covered the first thirty years of the 20th century in a series of large tableaux depicting such national events as the Boer War, the sinking of the *Titanic*, World War I and Armistice Night. These events alternated with domestic scenes, which followed the fortunes and misfortunes of two families, one upper class, the other lower class. There were visits to the music hall, seaside, society balls and nightclubs. The scene which made the most impact was the one with the silent crowds, dressed in deepest black, mourning the death of Queen Victoria. Coward described the first night as one of the most agonising nights he had spent in the theatre. One of the six hydraulic lifts jammed and there was a hiatus of four-and-a-half minutes. The hiatus took the edge off the performance; but not off the audience's enthusiasm. "I hope that this play will make you think that in spite of the troubled times we are living in, it's still pretty exciting to be English," said Coward in his curtain speech and instantly regretted it, feeling he had cheapened the play. Two weeks later King George V and the royal family attended a performance and there were even more patriotic fervour.
—Drury Lane has come into its own again – our national theatre has a theme worthy of itself. ALAN PARSONS *Daily Mail*
—It is sensational. It is staggering. IVOR BROWN *Observer*

Nov 15. Frank Vosper, John Gielgud, Carol Goodner, Margaret Webster, Jessica Tandy, Marjorie Gabain, Roger Livesey and Finlay Currie in Ronald Mackenzie's **Musical Chairs** directed by Theodore Komisarjevsky at Arts. Tragi-comedy in the Russian manner is set among the oil fields of Poland. Gielgud played a cynical, consumptive pianist whose fiancée had died during the bombing of Düsseldorf in an air raid in which he had participated. James Agate said it was the best first play written by an English playwright during the last forty years. Transferred to Criterion in 1932.
—Mr Gielgud was a wonderfully convincing mixture of nervous exasperation and real emotion. DESMOND MCCARTHY *New Statesman and Nation*

Nov 30. Ralph Richardson in Shakespeare's **Henry V** directed by Harcourt Williams at Old Vic. Richardson was a cold bath king.
—He shied at the part from the beginning, but as soon as he got into his stride, his virility, his humour and his steel-true emotion gave us a hero worthy of the name. HARCOURT WILLIAMS *Old Vic Saga*

Dec 16. Baliol Holloway and Oscar Asche alternated Falstaff in Shakespeare's **The Merry Wives of Windsor** directed by Baliol Holloway at Duchess.

Dec 17. Gracie Fields in **Walk This Way!** at Winter Garden. Revue written and directed by Archie Pitt. Lyrics and music by Gordon Courtney. Fields was at her funniest as coloratura soprano who broke into ribald laughter whenever the pathos of her aria became too much for her.

1932

Jan 3. Jean Cadell and Francis L Sullivan in **1066 and All That** directed by Esme Church at Arts. Adaptation by Michael Watts from the book by W C Sellar and R J Yeatman. Music by Kate Coates. Naïve burlesque of history: its naivety was for sophisticated audiences, who were treated as if they were pupils in a classroom. Cadell played Queen Elizabeth I. Sullivan played Alfred the Great, Brutus, Philip of Spain and assorted wicked barons.

Jan 19. Jack Hawkins and Frances Doble in Anthony Kimmins's **While Parents Sleep** directed by Nigel Playfair at Royalty. Boisterous humour, coarse language and a breezy likeable performance by Hawkins. "He acted with the abandon of a distressed auctioneer," said Ivor Brown in *The Observer*. Transferred to Garrick.

Jan 30. Evelyn Laye, George Robey and W H Berry in **Helen!** directed by Max Reinhardt, designed by Oliver Messel and choreographed by Léonide Massine at Adelphi. Opera bouffe based on Offenbach's *La Belle Hélène* by Meilhac and Halévy with additions by A P Herbert. Not since the heyday of the Diaghilev Ballet had London seen anything to compare with the scenery, costumes and décor. Helen's bedroom, all in white, was stunning.

Feb 9. Gerald du Maurier in Edgar Wallace's **The Green Pack** directed by Edgar Wallace at Wyndham's. Gold prospectors in Portuguese West Africa. Franklin Dyall played the villain. Du Maurier's quiet incisiveness, perfect timing and ironical humour were invaluable.

Feb 10. Frank Vosper as Henry VIII and Angela Baddeley as Katheryn Howard in Clifford Bax's **The Rose without a Thorn** directed by Frank Birch and produced by the People's National Theatre at Duchess.
—Here, too, is the best Henry the modern stage has seen or is likely to see. There is no doubt that Mr Vosper's Henry is a genuine Holbein. Nature and art have given the actor the little eyes, the cruel dilettante-ish mouth, the muffin-like jowl, and the four square Tudor head. JAMES AGATE *Sunday Times*
—The true national theatre should be built by the people for the people. The theatre should be endowed by every citizen and be within the financial reach of every citizen … Help to build it. NANCY PRICE

Mar 4. Peggy Wood and Francis Lederer in **The Cat and the Fiddle** directed by William Mollison at Palace. Musical comedy. Book by Otto Harbach. Music by Jerome Kern. Highbrow composer falls in love with composer of popular American music. Peggy Wood sang "She Didn't Say Yes." Delysia was cast as a jealous leading lady.

Mar 9. Frederick Piper as Tobias and Henry Ainley as Archangel Raphael in James Bridie's **Tobias and the Angel** directed by Evan John at Westminster. Tobias grows in wisdom yet remains the same timid youth. Bridie offered platitudes, anachronisms colloquialisms, childish humour and moralising. James Agate thought its lack of brevity spoiled an otherwise enchanting play. *The Times* said Ainley's majestic Archangel was "the quintessence of all the better public schools of Persia."

Mar 22. Olive Blakeney in Elmer Rice's **See Naples and Die** directed by Bernard Nedell at Little. Satire at the expense of English, American and German tourists.

Mar 23. Ivor Novello and Ursula Jeans in Ivor Novello's **I Lived With You** directed by Auriol Lee at Prince of Wales. Russian Prince meets typist in Hampton Court maze.
—Mr Novello acted the Dark Prince with all his nice desire and ability to please. IVOR BROWN *Observer*

Mar 30. Gladys Cooper and Ronald Squire in Harrison Owen's **Dr Pygmalion** directed by Gerald du Maurier at Playhouse. A cynical and attractive doctor revives his patients by pretending to be in love with them.
—It is an actors' play par excellence and so long as they coruscate – as they do during the whole evening – the matter is secondary to the manner. J T GREIN *Sketch*

Mar 31. Gwen Ffrangcon-Davies as Prue Sarn and Robert Donat as Gideon in Edward Lewis's adaptation of Mary Webb's **Precious Bane** directed by Campbell Gullan at St Martin's. Ffrangcon-Davies showed no sign of Prue's hair-lip.

Apr 1. Frank Vosper, John Gielgud, Carol Goodner, Dorice Ford, Amy Veness, Jack Livesey and Finlay Currie in Rodney Ackland's **Musical Chairs** directed by Theodore Komisarjevsky at Criterion. James Agate said it was a small masterpiece.

Apr 4. Ernest Milton in Shakespeare's **Othello** directed by Ernest Milton at Old Vic. Henry Oscar as Iago. Athene Seyler as Emelia. Flora Robson as Bianca. Milton rolled his eyes to an absurd degree.

Apr 9. Tilly Losch as the Nun in Karl Vollmoeller's **The Miracle** directed by Max Reinhardt at Lyceum. Wordless mystery spectacle by Karl Vollmoeller. Music by Englebert Humperdinck. Scenery by Professor Strand. Costumes by Oliver Messel. Dances and ensembles by Léonide Massine who played Spielmann who lures the Nun into the wicked world. The dignity, poise, beauty and immobility of Lady Diana Manners as Madonna was much admired; but the revival did not repeat the success of the original production in 1911.
—Miss Tilly Losch stands out pre-eminently, her performance of the Nun being one of the most delicate, perceptive and brilliantly executed things ever seen in London. JAMES AGATE *Sunday Times*

Apr 14. Anny Ahlers and Heddle Nash in **The Dubarry** directed by Felix Edwardes at His Majesty's. Musical. Book by Paul Knepler and J M Willeminski. English version by Rowland Leigh and Desmond Carter. Music by Carl Millocker. Lyrics by Rowland Leigh. Dubarry discards her poet lover in order to become King Louis XV's mistress. 398 performances.

Apr 23. Stratford Memorial Theatre reopened with Shakespeare's **Henry IV Parts 1 and 2.** One critic likened the new building to a jam factory.

Apr 25. Cedric Hardwicke as Shotover, Edith Evans as Lady Utterword, Margaret Chatwin as Mrs Hushabye, Eileen Beldon as Ellie, Wilfrid Lawson as Mangan, O B Clarence as Manzini Dunn and Leon Quartermaine as Hector Hushabye in Bernard Shaw's **Heartbreak House** at Queen's directed by H K Ayliff.
—Cedric Hardwicke's Captain Shotover with a face as intensely virile as the Moses in Michelangelo is a great comedy success. *Era*
—Miss Evans is herself worthy of the brilliant first act and much too good for the rest of it. *New Statesman and Nation*
—As an allegory, as a sermon, as a satire, the play has not a leg to stand on; or rather, it can never stand on the same leg for long. But as a comedy, it will do very well. There is more than enough wit to set off the *longuers*. PETER FLEMING *Spectator*

Apr 28. Ernest Milton as Shylock and Mary Newcomb as Portia in Shakespeare's **The Merchant of Venice** directed by Henry Oscar at St James's.

May 17. Flora Robson, William Fox, Marie Ney and Richard Bird in J B Priestley's **Dangerous Corner** directed by Tyrone Guthrie at Lyric. Priestley rejected the ordinary conception of time and assumed the possibility that there was a split in the time process so that from any given moment there were two alternative series of events ready to be set in motion. A chance remark about a cigarette box in Act 1 triggers off a series of hysterical self-revelations. In the third act the action goes back to the beginning and this time the Pandora box is not opened and the dangerous corner is avoided. Written in a week, when he was 32 years old, Priestley dismissed it as "merely an ingenious box of tricks" and said he doubted if he would walk half a mile to see the finest production in the world.

May 20. Ellis Jeffreys, Mary Ellis, Ian Hunter and Barry Jones in Arthur Wing Pinero's **A Cold June** directed by Basil Dean at Duchess. June takes advantage of two elderly gentlemen who believe they are her father. The critics gave June a cold reception and the play ran for only 19 performances.

May 23. Ivor Novello, Benita Hume and Lilian Braithwaite in Ivor Novello's **Party** directed by Athole Stewart at Strand. The party is given by a popular young actress after a fashionable first night.

1932 World Premieres
New York
Cole Porter's *Gay Divorce*
George S Kaufman and Edna Ferber's *Dinner at Eight*
Boston
Bernard Shaw's *Too True to Be Good*
Berlin
Bertolt Brecht's *Mother*

Births
Athol Fugard, South African playwright
Peter O'Toole, British actor
Arnold Wesker, British playwright

Deaths
Edgar Wallace (b. 1875), British playwright

Lady Augusta Gregory (b. 1852) Irish playwright, director

Honours
Nobel Prize for Literature
John Galsworthy, novelist, playwright

History
—14 million unemployed in USA
—Great Hunger March
—F D Roosevelt President USA
—Opening of Sydney Harbour Bridge
—Charles Lindbergh's baby kidnapped
—Thomas Beecham founded London Philharmonia
—BBC opened its new London headquarters

—One trembles to think what would be said of Mr Novello's plays, if anyone else had written them. JAMES AGATE *Sunday Times*

May 24. Jean Forbes-Robertson as Viola, Arthur Wontner as Malvolio, Phyllis Neilson-Terry as Olivia, Robert Atkins as Sir Toby Belch and John Laurie as Feste in Shakespeare's **Twelfth Night** directed by Robert Atkins at New. The production had a black and white setting.

May 24. Arthur Fear in Johann Strauss's **Casanova** at London Coliseum directed by Erik Charell. English book by Harry Graham. The finale was a revolving panorama of Venice at carnival time.

Jun. The Crazy Gang at the London Palladium. Flanagan and Allen, Nervo and Knox, Naughton and Gold and Eddie Gray appeared together for the first time in a series of "crazy bills" which continued until December. Flanagan and Allen sang "Underneath the Arches".

Jun 30. Edith Evans in Edward Knoblock and Beverley Nichols's **Evensong** directed by Athole Stewart at Queen's. Audiences presumed that the ageing prima donna, a dominating, selfish, possessive and finally tragic woman, was a portrait of Nellie Melba. The play removed much of the novel's bitterness.

Jul 19. Colin Clive, Phyllis Konstam and Leon M Lion in John Galsworthy's **Escape** directed by Leon M Lion at Garrick. Clive gave the episodes in the convict's flight across Dartmoor its impetus and tension. The production began a season of three plays by Galsworthy.
—Galsworthy stands in the present age for all that is best and sanest in the idealism which brings the vision of a better world. He stands for cleanness of view and for courageous expression. Nobody can see one of his plays without being profoundly moved or remain quite the same afterwards. C E *quoted on flyer*

Aug 16. Gertrude Lawrence, Gerald du Maurier and May Whitty in John Van Druten's **Behold, We Live** directed by Auriol Lee at St James's. Man prevents a girl from committing suicide. They fall in love and then he dies. What the audience enjoyed most was the sight of Whitty and Lawrence blowing soap bubbles.

Aug 22. Colin Clive and Oliver Raphael in John Galsworthy's **Loyalties** directed by Leon M Lion at Garrick.
—It is a little hard and those who come after him that whoever plays De Levis Mr Milton [who created the role in 1922] will always receive good notices the next morning. *The Times*

Aug 31. Sydney Howard, Angela Baddeley, Harold French, Connie Ediss and Austin Melford in Avery Hopwood and Wilson Collison's **Night of the Garter** revised by Austin Melford and directed by Leslie Henson at Strand. Farce.
—Mr Howard stands a rock-like figure. He never bustles. When he moves it is with the deliberate dignity of an elderly elephant suffering from foot trouble. Nothing funnier has been seen on the stage for a long time. *Illustrated London News*

Sep 13. Bernard Shaw's **Too True To Be Good** directed by H K Ayliff at New. Ernest Thesiger as Microbe. Leonora Corbett as Patient. Margaret Halstan as Elderly Lady. Donald Wolfit as Doctor. Ellen Pollock as Nurse. Cedric Hardwicke as Burglar. Scott Sunderland as Col Tallboys. Walter Hudd as Private Meek (an affectionate caricature of T E Lawrence). Ralph Richardson as Sgt Fielding. H K Ayliff as The Elder. "I must preach and preach," said Shaw, "no matter how late the hour and how short the day, no matter whether I've nothing to say." The Sergeant had the most prophetic lines on the folly of War and the Wrath to Come. The actors gave robust music hall performances. The rambling "political extravaganza" ran only six weeks in the West End, proof, it was argued, for the need of a National Theatre.

—Irritated, yes, violently and frequently – by the infantile clowning of the opening act that are as unpleasant as they are silly – but never bored, not for a single moment. ALAN PARSONS *Daily Mail*

—With extreme gusto and customary eloquence Mr Shaw exploits his favourite characters and flogs his pet donkeys brilliantly. *Sketch*

Sep 16. Words and Music a revue written and directed by Noël Coward at Adelphi. Songs included "Mad About the Boy" and "Mad Dogs and Englishmen".

Sep 27. Rodney Ackland's **Strange Orchestra** directed by John Gielgud at Embassy. Blowsy slattern, who has three grown-up children by three different fathers, lets out rooms to jobless, sponging, young lodgers, who can't pay the rent. The characters are a silly, tiresome, neurotic lot, looking for happiness and frightened of what life holds out for them. One young woman who is about to go blind decides to have a fling with a charmer who turns out to be an absolute rotter. Two newly-weds turn tragedy into farce when they fail to commit suicide. "Who are these people? Does Gladys Cooper know them?" asked Mrs Patrick Campbell, who was to have played the slattern. But she argued with the director, quarrelled with the author and walked out of the rehearsal. Gielgud modelled his production on Komisarjevsky.

Sep 29. Colin Clive, Leon M Lion, Margaretta Scott and Lawrence Hanray in John Galsworthy's **Justice** directed by Leon M Lion at Garrick. Clive was too virile.

—He is completely miscast for instead of the weak character of Galsworthy's imagination he gave us a desperate looking ruffian capable of holding up a troop train. W A DARLINGTON *Daily Telegraph*

Oct 7. Jessica Tandy and Joyce Bland in Christa Winsloe's **Children in Uniform** directed by Leontine Sagan at Duchess. English adaptation by Barbara Burnham. The play, set in a girls' boarding school, was a protest against Prussian repression. One of the girls has an infatuation for her teacher. Cathleen Nesbitt was the headmistress, a tyrannical disciplinarian. Sagan's film version was superior.

Nov 1. Cedric Hardwicke, Louise Hampton, Flora Robson and Ralph Richardson in Somerset Maugham's **For Services Rendered** directed by H K Ayliff at Globe. Maugham's outburst against a nation which had forgotten its war heroes, was a damning tirade against the incompetence, vanity, greed and stupidity of an Establishment, which seemed intent on leading the nation into another war. The play concentrated on the women left behind, bereft of any eligible men to marry. West End audiences thought the subject too bleak and stayed away.

Nov 7. Sacha Guitry and Madeleine Renaud in a season of three plays by Sacha Guitry acted in French at Cambridge: **La Jalousie, La Pelerine Ecoissaise** and **Desire**. Theatregoers were offered charming, frothy, feather-light, old-fashioned soufflés. "They have no inner or dramatic value," said *The Illustrated London News*. "They are a string of light and bright conversations held together by a mere soupcon of plot."

Nov 8. Ronald Squire, Nigel Bruce, Isabel Jeans, Joan Barry in Benn W Levy's **Springtime for Henry** directed by Benn W Levy at Apollo. Farcical romance. The prudish gallerites were outraged when a man went into the bedroom of his best friend's wife.

Nov 21. Baliol Holloway and Francis L Sullivan in Hugh Walpole's **The Cathedral** directed by André van Gyseghem at New. Holloway was the histrionic, arrogant and volatile Archdeacon. Sullivan was the calm, smooth and sly Canon.

Dec 1. Edna Best, Herbert Marshall, Louis Hayward and Mary Jerrold in Rose Franken's **Another Language** directed by Auriol Lee at Strand. Popular American comedy: a mother continues to rule her three sons long after they are married.

Dec 12. Edward Chapman in James Bridie's **Jonah and the Whale** directed by Henry Oscar at Westminster. Jonah, who is inside the whale's stomach, has a bellyful from the whale, who lectures him on natural history.

—While Dr James Bridie is content to be merely flippant, he is tolerably amusing; but when he seeks to touch Shavian depths he is grounded in the shallows of futility. *Illustrated London News*

Dec 20. Sydney Fairbrother, Margaretta Scott, Harold Warrender, Alexander Field and Sam Livesey in Dion Boucicault's **The Streets of London** directed by Maxwell Wray at Ambassadors. This very funny and way-over-top burlesque of Victorian melodrama was a travesty of Boucicault. The audience had a good time, hissing and booing the villains and cheering the hero and heroine.

1933

Jan 2. Anthony Ireland, George Merritt, Robert Douglas and Celia Johnson in Anthony Armstrong's **Ten Minute Alibi** directed by Sinclair Hill at Embassy. Clas-

sic 1930s murder thriller. Suave Latin American plans to have a quick affair with the heroine in Paris and then ditch her. "My God, Sevilla, you are a swine!" says the wimpish young barrister who will do anything to save the girl he loves even though she doesn't love him. He dreams up the perfect murder with a watertight alibi and then puts it into action. The audience witnesses first the dream and then the reality when things go wrong. The only question is whether he will get away with it? Rave reviews: "A rattling good thriller," said *The Evening News*. "A spanking good crook play," said *The Sunday Dispatch*. Transferred to Haymarket.

Jan 5. Ellis Jeffreys, Lilian Braithwaite and Martita Hunt in Ivor Novello's **Fresh Fields** directed by Athole Stewart at Criterion. English aristocracy meets Australian *nouveaux riches*.

—Novello never bothers his head about life. All his characters are, in one way or another, caricatures. *The Daily Telegraph*

Jan 6. Irene Vanbrugh, Jane Baxter, Margaret Vines, Mabel Terry-Lewis, Edie Martin, Laura Cowie, Lyn Harding, Carol Goodner, Basil Sydney and Susan Richmond in George S Kaufman and Edna Ferber's **Dinner at Eight** directed by George S Kaufman at Palace. American satire on the vulgar American rich falling over themselves to meet the English aristocracy. There were a number of interlocking stories and solo turns involving adultery, a crooked deal, a knifing, a heart attack, bigamy and suicide. The social-climbing hostess was so busy socialising that she didn't notice that her husband was bankrupt and that her daughter was having an affair with a burned-out, ageing movie star. Her husband had fallen prey to a business shark, whose sluttish wife was having an affair with their doctor. Meanwhile the servants (butler, maid and chauffeur) were having their own sordid love-triangle.

—There are scenes written with a slash and brilliance and racy, let-it-go invective none of our English dramatists seems nowadays to have the fire for. They afford acting opportunities, magnificently taken by an almost entirely English cast. *Morning Post*

Jan 25. Frank Vosper, Hugh Williams, Catherine Lacey and Herbert Lomas in Mordaunt Shairp's **The Green Bay Tree** directed by Milton Rosmer at St Martin's. Young man is adopted by a rich homosexual and introduced to a life of luxury.

Feb 2. John Gielgud in Gordon Daviot's **Richard of Bordeaux** directed by John Gielgud at New. Gwen Ffrangcon-Davies as Anne of Bohemia.

—In my opinion he [John Gielgud] is now the first of English actors. DESMOND MACCARTHY *New Statesman and Nation*

—Nothing to equal it can be seen today on the English stage. SYDNEY W CARROLL *Daily Telegraph*

—Mr Gielgud's performance is a marvellous combination of vacillation, nobility and embittered disillusion, finely restrained even in his most passionate outbursts. This is genuinely great acting which has the power to thrill in its intensity. HAROLD CONWAY *Daily Mail*

Feb 23. Charles Victor, Richard Caldicot and Olive Milbourne in Moss Hart and George S Kaufman's **Once in a Lifetime** directed by Herbert M Prentice at Queen's. Three small-time vaudeville artists decide to break into the film business. Topical caricature at the expense of Hollywood and the coming of sound.

Mar 1. Marie Ney in Dorothy Massingham and Murray Macdonald's **The Lake** directed by Tyrone Guthrie at Arts. Mother pushes her daughter into a loveless marriage. Massingham died a fortnight after the production opened. Transferred to Westminster

Mar 13. Paul Robeson as Jim Harris and Flora Robson as Ellie in Eugene O'Neill's **All God's Chillun' Got Wings** directed by Andre van Gyseghem at Embassy. A Negro marrying a white woman was anathema to American theatre audiences. In 1924 and at its premiere in New York the Klu Klux Klan had threatened to burn down the theatre. In London the Embassy Theatre was so poor it could only afford to pay Robeson £10 and when O'Neill's agent demanded £100 royalties in advance it was Robeson who had to write the cheque. His dignity and pathos were much admired; but the play belonged to Robson. The production transferred to Piccadilly for six weeks only, Robeson having committed to film *The Emperor Jones*.

—I have seldom known two performances fuse so perfectly; Miss Robson's emotional power and her uncanny skill with which she stripped bare the meagre soul of the wretched Ellie was almost more than one could bear at such close range. Such a technically superb performance found a perfect foil in Robeson's sincerity. ANDRE VAN GYSEGHEM *quoted by* MARY SETON *in her biography of Paul Robeson*

Apr 20. Alfred Sangster as Rev Patrick Bronte, Lydia Sherwood as Charlotte, Dorothy Black as Emily, Helena Pickard as Anne and Denys Blakelock as Branwell in Alfred Sangster's **The Brontes** directed by Henry Cass at Royalty. The production's high point was the acting of Dorothy Black and Emily's death-scene in particular. The other sisters were not so well cast.

—Miss Black's Emily is magnificent in its suggestion of genius and high passion with really nothing but her personality to do it with. *Morning Post*

Apr 25. Douglas Byng, Frances Day and Edward Chapman in **How D'You Do?** directed by Andre Charlot at Comedy. Revue Book by Arthur Macrae. Music by Ord Hamilton. Byng appeared as Boadicea, Queen of the Obsceni.

May 16. Cedric Hardwicke, Edith Evans, Louise Hampton and Barry K Barnes in René Fauchois's **The Late Christopher Bean** adapted by Emlyn Williams and directed by Gilbert Miller at St James's. Satire on human greed. Artist who died in misery and poverty is hailed a genius and the paintings he left to the family maid are now worth a fortune.
—Miss Evans's picture of Gwenny the maid, voluble, lachrymose, ignorant, generous, and true-hearted, must rank as one of the best things she has ever done. *Daily Telegraph*

May 19. Mary Ellis in Oscar Hammerstein and Jerome Kern's musical **Music in the Air** directed by C B Cochran at His Majesty's. Ellis, who was known primarily as an actress, surprised everybody with her singing. The songs included "I've Told Every Little Star", "And Love was Born" and "The Song is You."

May 26. Diana Wynyard as Charlotte, Beatrice Lehmann as Emily, Thea Holme as Anne and Emlyn Williams as Branwell in Clemence Dane's **Wild Decembers** directed by Benn W Levy at Apollo. Many critics thought Dane's play about the Brontes was better than Alfred Sangster's version but it suffered at the box office from coming into the West End so soon after it.

Jun 14. Ivor Novello, Fay Compton and Zena Dare in Ivor Novello's **Proscenium** directed by Athole Stewart at Globe. 40-year-old actress marries a 28-year-old man, the son of an old flame who died in the war. Novello played both men. "Novellette" said the wags.

Jul 5. The Open Air Theatre opened in Regent's Park with a season of plays by Shakespeare directed by Robert Atkins with regular changes in the cast: **A Midsummer Night's Dream**. Phyllis Neilson-Terry, Jack Hawkins and Jean Forbes-Robertson played Oberon. Jessica Tandy as Titania. Robert Atkins as Bottom. Margaretta Scott as Hermia. Agnes Lauchlan as Helena. Leslie French as Puck. Basil Gill and Ion Swinley as Theseus. John Laurie as Lysander.
— [Leslie French] is the perfect Puck, boy eternal, yet somehow communicating to the after-dinner of a faun with admirable impishness. IVOR BROWN *Observer*

Twelfth Night. Nigel Playfair as Malvolio. Phyllis Neilson-Terry and Margareta Scott alternated Olivia and Viola. The dungeon scene was omitted.

As You Like It. Phyllis Neilson-Terry as Rosalind. Jack Hawkins as Orlando. Ion Swinley as Jaques.
—The capers of Mr George Grossmith as a Black and Tan Touchstone are funny from the wriggling of his waist to the witch-like waving of his fingers … a brilliant piece of work possessing a classic humour. M WILLSON DISHER *Daily Mail*

The Tempest. John Drinkwater as Prospero. Robert Atkins as Caliban. Leslie French as Ariel.
—Mr John Drinkwater gave Prospero a dignity that was ladylike rather than stately and in his speaking of the verse sometimes seemed to be striving to impose on it a rhythm alien from its own. *The Times*

Sep 5. Sybil Thorndike, Haidee Wright and Martita Hunt in John Van Druten's **The Distaff Side** directed by Auriol Lee at Apollo. The tyranny of matriarchy: a comedy about six women over three generations.
—The author leaves the moral to you. He is content to "photograph". So you must not ask for a well defined plot, only for delicate portraiture. M WILLSON DISHER *Daily Mail*
—Gone are the old mannerisms, she [Sybil Thorndike] plays with a restraint and a quality of understanding that she has never approached before. W F *Morning Post*

Sep 14. Ralph Richardson in Somerset Maugham's **Sheppey** directed by John Gielgud at Wyndham's. Modern morality play, rooted in the 1929 slump and its aftermath. Sheppey is a barber who wins £8,500 in the Irish sweepstake and decides to give it all to the poor. He says he wants to live like Jesus and brings

John Gielgud, Gwen Ffrangcon Davies, Barbara Dillon and Francis Lister in Richard of Bordeaux

1933 World Premieres
Madrid
 Federico Garcia Lorca's *Blood Wedding*
New York
 Jack Kirkland's *Tobacco Road*
 T S Eliot's *Sweeney Agonistes*
 Maxwell Anderson's *Both Your Houses*
Pittsburgh
 Eugene O'Neill's *Ah, Wilderness!*
Paris
 Jacques Deval's *Tovarich*

Births
Michael Frayn, British playwright

Joe Orton, British playwright
David Storey, British playwright

Deaths
J B Fagan (*b.*1873), British director, playwright
John Galsworthy (*b.*1867), British playwright

History
—Adolf Hitler became German Chancellor
—Roosevelt's New Deal
—Prohibition repealed in US

—[Robert Donat's] first appearance as the brilliant and ungovernable consumptive fairly set the stage alight. IVOR BROWN *Manchester Guardian*

Oct 3. Miss Josephine Baker at Prince Edward. Revue.
—Josephine Baker has it all – class, talent and ding-dong. WALTER WINCHELL

Oct 6. Gertrude Lawrence in Cole Porter's **Nymph Errant** directed by Charles B Cochran at Adelphi. A play with music by Romney Brent from the novel by James Laver. Designs by Doris Zinkeisen. The heroine dances through Europe and Asia –Paris, Vienna, Athens, Smyrna, Turkey – with any number of admirers. She remains, much to her irritation, unmolested – even in a harem – and returns to England still a virgin.
—There is no other English actress who combines grace, wit, humour, elegance and that rare gift of turning words into luminous darts in such an ensemble of all the qualities that make a great comedienne. This time it is not the play: it is the actress that's the thing. J T GRIEN *Illustrated London News*

Oct 9. Athene Seyler as Ranevsky and Charles Laughton as Lophapin in Anton Chekhov's **The Cherry Orchard** directed by Tyrone Guthrie at Old Vic. Laughton put on a Yorkshire accent. James Agate said he was superb.

Oct 18. Robert Harris, Celia Johnson and Mackenzie Ward in Merton Hodge's **The Wind and the Rain** directed by Auriol Lee at St Martin's. Touching comedy about life among medical students in Edinburgh.

Nov 2. Fred Astaire and Claire Luce in Cole Porter's musical **The Gay Divorce** directed by Felix Edwardes at Palace. Book by Dwight Taylor. Astaire sang "Night and Day".

Nov 7. Charles Laughton as Henry, Flora Robson as Queen Katharine and Robert Farquharson as Cardinal Wolsey in Shakespeare's **Henry VIII** directed by Tyrone Guthrie at Sadler's Wells. Marius Goring as Cardinal Compelus, Nicholas Hannen as Buckingham, Athene Seyler as Old Lady. James Mason as Cromwell. Laughton's performance was a disappointment after the success he had had in Alexander Korda's film, *The Private Life of Henry VIII*. Audiences presumed, wrongly, that the Henry in the film and the play would be the same person.

a prostitute and a thief into his home. His wife is very distressed. (Christianity, after all, is not something you actually practise.) His daughter and her fiancé want him certified mad so that they can have the money. The play wasn't a success. Maugham felt he was no longer in touch with public taste and never wrote for the theatre again.
—Once again he shows a rare understanding of human goodness, and a rare restraint in expressing it; Mr Richardson is again the perfect interpreter of a dramatist's subtler intentions, and in a part, too, which requires a nice adjustment between humour and deep feeling. DESMOND MCCARTHY *New Statesman and Nation*

Sep 19. Robert Donat, Sophie Stewart and Ernest Thesiger in James Bridie's **The Sleeping Clergyman** directed by A K Ayliff transferred from Malvern Festival to Piccadilly. A study of heredity over three generations, designed to prove you cannot produce genius by eugenics. When the critics complained about the last act, Bridie retorted: "All this nonsense about last acts. Only God can write last acts, and he seldom does."

Charles Laughton, Flora Robson, Robert Farquhar and Marius Goring in Henry VIII

Nov 25. Nicholas Hannen as Prime Minister in Bernard Shaw's **On the Rocks** directed by Lewis Casson at Winter Garden. The big surprise was that Shaw should still be writing when he was seventy-seven. A national crisis, with hordes of unemployed, leads to a cynical argument in favour of dictatorship. The PM is heading for a breakdown, brought on, he thinks, by overwork. His doctor points out that it is the very reverse – an acute want of mental exercise – and packs him off to a clinic. The PM, an obvious humbug, prefers making speeches to actually doing anything. The first act makes some easy political jokes and gives little indication of the quality of the second. The PM returns rejuvenated and embarks on wholesale nationalization, offering the nation "platonic communism".
—He is just as adept as ever at leading his audience along one line of argument, and then puncturing the whole affair with a sudden shaft of wit. *Irish Times*
—All the flood-lit mediocrity which bores us on the political stage of real life is here transmuted into a sparkling farce of ideas. *Morning Post*
—Why has GBS become so consistently malicious to the Labour Party, and so uncritically bitter towards the liberal belief in parliamentary democracy and personal freedom of the intellectual?... The critics of future generations, if they notice *On the Rocks*, will cite it as a picture of British society in catastrophic decadence, portrayed by an aged cynic who has outlived his genius. BEATRICE WEBB

Nov 28. Edmund Gwenn in J B Priestley's **Laburnum Grove**, directed by Cedric Hardwicke at Duchess. Priestley's immoral comedy was a morality play set in the aftermath of the Depression. Gwenn played an amiable suburban forger.

Nov 30. Jean Forbes-Robertson in Alexandre Dumas fils's **The Lady of the Camellias** directed by Peter Godfrey as Gate.
—[Jean Forbes-Robertson] gave a performance of beauty and quiet dignity. It seemed to me practically flawless; it was only now and again that she lapsed into Peter-pannish mannerisms entirely unsuited to anything but Barrie's play. *Era*

Dec 8. Elisabeth Bergner made her London debut in Margaret Kennedy's **Escape Me Never** directed by Theodore Komisarjevsky at Apollo. Hugh Sinclair and Griffith Jones played the two brothers the heroine falls in love with. Bergner's husky English made her performance even more appealing.
—Elisabeth Bergner's conquest of the audience was certain from the moment she enters. It was the triumph of an artist of great charm and undeniable grace. A E WILSON *Star*

Dec 14. Charles Laughton as Angelo and Flora Robson as Isabella in Shakespeare's **Measure for Measure** directed by Tyrone Guthrie at Old Vic. Guthrie thought the actors were too far removed from the incense-laden sexuality Shakespeare had in mind.
—Laughton was not angelic but a cunning oleaginous monster whose cruelty and lubricity could have surprised no one, least of all himself. TYRONE GUTHRIE *A Life in the Theatre*

Dec 21. Marie Tempest in H M Harwood's **The Old Folks at Home** directed by H M Harwood and W Graham-Browne at Queen's. A mother engineers adultery between her daughter (Nora Swinburne) and a novelist (Frank Allenby) on the principle that "many a marriage has been saved by unsuccessful infidelity." *The Times* described the atmosphere as "not too wholesome."

Dec 23. Ralph Richardson, Jean Forbes-Robertson and Marie Löhr in J M Barrie's **Peter Pan** directed by Lichfield Owen at Palladium.

1934

Jan 3. Lynn Fontanne, Alfred Lunt and Cecil Parker in Robert E Sherwood's **Reunion in Vienna** directed by Alfred Lunt at Lyric. Two former lovers take up where they left off, only to decide it best to part.
—High comedy acting of exquisite quality. W A DARLINGTON *The Daily Telegraph*
—Every gesture is timed, every inflexion studied, every glance measured – with the result that a delightful effect of complete spontaneity is attained. H M WALBROOK *Play Pictorial*

Jan 8. Charles Laughton as Prospero in Shakespeare's **The Tempest** directed by Tyrone Guthrie at Old Vic. Elsa Lanchester as Ariel. Laughton should have played Caliban.

Jan 18. Lady Tree as Mrs Malaprop, Jack Livesey as Captain Absolute, Baliol Holloway as Sir Anthony Absolute, Lesley Wareing as Lydia Languish, John Laurie as Faulkland, Joyce Carey as Julia Melville and Frank Cellier as Bob Acres in Richard Brinsley Sheridan's **The Rivals** directed by Baliol Holloway at Ambassadors.

Jan 25. Leslie Banks, Gillian Lind and Henry Caine in W P Lipscombe and R J Minney's **Clive of India** directed by Campbell Gullan at Wyndham's. Clive, who had saved the empire on many occasions, is impeached for treason. Laurence Irving's sets were much admired.

Jan 27. Godfrey Tearle in Shakespeare's **Henry V** directed by Stanley Bell at Alhambra. Yvonne Arnaud as Princess. The text was ruthlessly cut. The production relied on spectacle and Tearle's physique and Englishness.

Jan 31. Joyce Bland, Ian Hunter and Isabel Jeans in Emlyn Williams's **Spring 1600** directed by John Gielgud at Shaftesbury. Country girl comes to London. She turns boy actor and works with Richard Burbage, the most famous actor of his day and creator of Shakespeare's Richard III, Hamlet, Othello and Lear.

Feb 5. Athene Seyler as Lady Bracknell, Roger Livesey as John Worthing, George Curzon as Algernon Moncrieff, Flora Robson as Gwendolen, Ursula Jeans as Cecily, Elsa Lanchester as Miss Prism, Charles Laughton as Chasuble and James Mason as Merriman in Oscar Wilde's **The Importance of Being Earnest** directed by Tyrone Guthrie at Old Vic. Guthrie in his biography said his direction was galumphing and that Chasuble "a devastating, brilliant and outrageous lampoon" appeared to be the leading part. Harold Hobson said Laughton was "pre-eminently unfrockable."

Feb 16. Yvonne Printemps and Noël Coward in Noël Coward's **Conversation Piece** directed by Noël Coward at His Majesty's. French duke (Coward) in exile in Brighton tries to pass off a girl (Printemps) he picked up in the gutter as his ward so that she will marry a rich man and he can inherit a fortune. Printemps sang "I'll Follow My Secret Heart". Coward had written the role especially for her.
—If you cannot afford a ticket for this show any other way, sell your wife's jewellery or your children's schoolbooks. You will never regret the sacrifice. W A DARLINGTON *Daily Telegraph*
—In spite of the fact that her English began and ended with 'Good morning', 'Yes' and 'No', she contrived to enchant the public, the critics, the supporting cast, the orchestra, and even the stage hands. It is also an uninhibited tribute to her that by the end of the London and New York runs, most of the company spoke fluent French. NOËL COWARD *Present Indicative*

Mar 7. People's National Theatre. Nancy Price in C E Bechhofer Roberts and C S Forester's **Nurse Cavel** directed by Frank Birch at Vaudeville. Sincere but lifeless.

Apr 2. Charles Laughton and Flora Robson in Shakespeare's **Macbeth** directed by Tyrone Guthrie at Old Vic. *The Daily Mail* did not believe that Shakespeare had intended Macbeth to be a petulant, sulky schoolboy. James Bridie thought Robson acted Lady Macbeth like a schoolgirl in a Dalcroze school in love with her headmistress.
—Mr Laughton was never within measurable distance of any kind of grandeur, and his performance beginning on the ground knew no heights from which to topple. JAMES AGATE *Sunday Times*
—Never mind, dear, I'm sure you did your best. And I'm sure that one day you may be quite a good Macbeth. LILIAN BAYLIS *quoted by* TYRONE GUTHRIE *A Life in the Theatre*

Apr 2. Malcolm Keene as plaintiff and Frances Doble as his wife in Ward Dorane's **Libel!** directed by Leon M Lion at Playhouse. Baronet, who is accused of having no right to his title, learns that his son is illegitimate. Nigel Playfair and Leon Lion played the opposing counsels.

Apr 9. Oscar Hammerstein and Jerome Kern's **Three Sisters** directed by Jerome Kern and Oscar Hammerstein and choreographed by Ralph Reader at Drury Lane. Musical set in rural England pre- and post-World War I. One sister (Victoria Hopper) ran off with a gypsy (Esmond Knight) who deserted her for a busker (Albert Burdon). Another sister (Adele Dixon) married into the peerage (Richard Dolman). The eldest sister (Charlotte Greenwood) married a village policeman (Stanley Holloway). High spot was the spectacle of the crowds on Derby Day.

Apr 10. The Birmingham Repertory Company. Hugh Miller in Elmer Rice's **Counsellor-at-Law** directed by Herbert Prentice at Piccadilly. Charles Victor as detective. Edie Martin as counsellor's mother. Elspeth Duxberry as secretary. Part slice-of-life drama, part modern morality play, the action is set in a suite of offices in a skyscraper on Fifth Avenue in New York in 1931 in the aftermath of the Wall Street Crash. Brilliant Jewish lawyer from the East Side had risen to the top of his profession by taking the sensational cases his colleagues would prefer not to touch. His career is suddenly in jeopardy when it is discovered that he had connived at perjury to save a young criminal from a life sentence. Communist agitator accuses him of working for crooked bourgeois politicians and pimping for corporations that feed on the blood and sweat of the workers. Will he jump out of the window? Miller gave the lawyer the swiftness, the energy and the theatricality that he requires. The role was created by Paul Muni on stage in New York and played by John Barrymore on screen.

Apr 15. Donald Wolfit as Holvard Solness in Henrik Ibsen's **The Master Builder** directed by Donald Wolfit at Westminster. Margaret Webster as Hilda Wangel. Margaret Rutherford as Mrs Solness.
—Mr Wolfit's acting was sound and vigorous – perhaps too vigorous. *Era*

Apr 24. Florence Desmond and Nelson Keys in **Why Not Tonight?** a revue by Her-

1934 World Premieres
Madrid
Federico Garcia Lorca's *Yerma*
Paris
Jean Cocteau's *The Infernal Machine*
New York
Lillian Hellman's *The Children's Hour*
Cole Porter's *Anything Goes*
Dallas
Bernard Shaw's *Village Wooing*

Births
Alan Bennett, British playwright
Edward Bond, British playwright
Maggie Smith, British actor
Ian Richardson, British actor
Wole Soyinka, Nigerian playwright

Deaths
Arthur Wing Pinero (*b.*1855), British playwright

William Poel (*b.*1852), British director

Honours
Nobel Prize for Literature:
Luigi Pirandello

Notes
—W Bridges Adams resigned from Stratford. Ben Iden Payne succeeded
—John Christie founded Glyndebourne

History
—Adolf Hitler became Reichsführer
—Night of the Long Knives
—Start of Stalin's purges in the Soviet Union
—Bonnie and Clyde shot dead
—John Dillinger shot dead
—Discovery of nuclear fission

bert Farjeon and directed by J A and R J Tomson at Palace. Desmond was the foremost impersonator of the day. Her targets included Greta Garbo, Tallulah Bankhead and Katharine Hepburn.

Apr 25. Ina Claire, Laurence Olivier and Frank Cellier in S N Berhman's **Biography** directed by Noël Coward at Globe. American comedy did not repeat its Broadway success. Olivier blamed Coward's direction.

May. The Open Air Theatre Season included Bernard Shaw's **Androcles and the Lion** (Nigel Playfair as The Emperor, Andrew Leigh as Androcles), John Milton's **Comus** (Clifford Evans as Comus) and three plays by Shakespeare: **Romeo and Juliet** (Griffith Jones and Margaretta Scott), **As You Like It** (Anna Neagle and Jack Hawkins) and **A Midsummer Night's Dream** (Leslie French as Puck).

May 25. Felix Aylmer, May Whitty, Harcourt Williams, Maurice Evans, Marius Goring and Joyce Bland in Harley Granville Barker's **The Voysey Inheritance** directed by Harley Granville Barker and Harcourt Williams at Sadler's Wells. Transferred to Shaftesbury.

May 26. The Comedie Française in a season of plays at Cambridge Theatre. Albert Lambert in Sophocles's **Oedipe Roi**. Albert Lambert and Vera Korene in Jean Racine's **Le Cid**. Albert Lambert in Molière's **Le Misanthrope**. Albert Lambert as valet and Victor Monteuil in Victor Hugo's **Ruy-Blas**.
—In spite of what seems to our ears excessive rhetoric it [*Ruy Blas*] remains a remarkable melodrama which works up – too slowly for our habits today – into a superbly effective climax in which the valet kills his master. *New Statesman and Nation*
—They [the Comédie Francaise] are in fact genuinely old fashioned, and not in the least afraid of an occasional shabbiness... all the old gestures with a really astonishing lack of self-consciousness. *The Times*

May 27. Edith Evans as the Duchess of Marlborough in Norman Ginsbury's **Viceroy Sarah** directed by Tyrone Guthrie at Arts. Intrigue at the court of Queen Anne between the Duchess and Mrs Masham. Barbara Everest played the gouty Queen. Doris Fordred was Mrs Masham.

Jun 8. Gwen Ffrangcon-Davies as Mary Stuart and Laurence Olivier as Bothwell in Gordon Daviot's **Queen of Scots** directed by John Gielgud at New. The critics admired Olivier's virility and praised his ferocity and dash, but thought him more Hollywood than Holyrood.
—I don't believe that a Scottish noble could have so many of the attributes and mannerisms of Clark Gable. *Evening News*

Jun 19. Sybil Thorndike and Arthur Wontner in Bernard Shaw's **Village Wooing** directed by Bernard Shaw at Little. Shaw described his amusing and touching one-acter as an unladylike comedieta for two voices and three conversations. He wrote it while he and his wife were travelling aboard a cruise ship in 1933. It was premiered in Texas in 1934 and played by two men, which is somewhat strange since one of the roles is a woman. A young schoolmaster, the future playwright, Christopher Fry, directed the first performance in England at Tunbridge Wells. The hero, a self-sufficient, self-absorbed "writing machine" has neither the strength nor the courage to resist a woman's determination. The role was said to be a posthumous portrait of Lytton Strachey. Village Wooing was acted with John Galsworthy's **The Little Man** with Finlay Currie and Robert Speaight directed by Nancy Price.

Jul 4. John Gielgud. Jack Hawkins and Stephen Haggard in Ronald Mackenzie's **The Maitlands** directed by Theodore Komisarjevsky at Wyndham's. The Maitlands live in a dreary seaside town in reduced circumstances in the post-slump years. They long to escape the boredom and pettiness of their existence. Gielgud thought it a brittle piece of work, full of observation and bitter wit, with an unnerving quality of theatrical effectiveness, which, in his opinion, was not explored to the full in the performances they gave. The play was booed on the first night and only cheered when the audience was informed the playwright had died in a car crash in the South France. (The car was driven by his mistress, Diana Rowan-Robins, who survived the accident and attended the first night.)

Jul 17. Charles Carson as King Edward III and Phyllis Neilson-Terry as Queen in Bernard Shaw's **The Six of Calais** directed by Maxwell Wray at Open Air Theatre. On 4 August 1347 Edward agreed to lift the year-long siege of Calais if six burghers would lay down their lives. Shaw felt that he had improved on Froissart, claiming that "the old snob" had got the story all wrong because he didn't understand women. His Edward III is a big cry-baby. The debate has no intellectual content and there is no pity for the poor burghers. There's more characterisation in Rodin's sculpture. Greer Garson played a court lady.

Sep 5. Ivor Novello, Edna Best, Fay Compton, Zena Dare and Robert Andrews in Ivor Novello's **Murder in Mayfair** directed by Leontine Sagan at Globe. Novello played a French pianist who is suspected of murder.

Sep 10. Walter Reynolds's **Young England** directed by Lyn Perring at Victoria Palace. Reynolds's naïve and stilted melodrama was produced in all seriousness, but the situations and dialogue were so ridiculous that the show caught the public's fancy and became a huge box office success. Theatregoers returned again and again to cheer the heroine, boo the villain and to laugh, gag and rag the show with their whistles and ribald comments. The scoffers outnumbered the serious members of the audience. The actors gave in and played to the gallery. The unhappy 84-year-old author would regularly attend performances.

Sep 13. Ralph Richardson, Beatrix Lehmann and Edward Irwin in J B Priestley's **Eden End** directed by Irene Hentschel at Duchess. English middle-class family drama set in 1912 allowed the playwright full rein for his irony about a better, saner and cleaner world coming in the future. Priestley thought it was his best play. Richardson played a larger-than-life, alcoholic actor.
—The best shorter part I ever had was that in *Eden End*. I was given wonderful jokes all set to music – what more could one ask? RALPH RICHARDSON *quoted by Sunday Times*

Sep 28. Tily Losch and Florence Desmond in **Streamline** directed by Charles B Cochran at Palace. Book and lyrics by A P Herbert. Book by Ronald Jeans. Music by Vivian Ellis. Witty revue: high spot was a brilliant pastiche of Gilbert and Sullivan.

Oct 1. Jean Forbes-Robertson as the Unknown Woman in Luigi Pirandello's **As You Desire Me** directed by Peter Godfrey at Royalty. Intellectual thriller. Pirandello developed his familiar theme that we are nothing more or less than what we seem to be to others. An Italian wife goes missing, following her rape and abduction by the Germans during World War I. A decadent Berlin cabaret artist, who is mistaken for the wife, seizes a chance for a new life and assumes the character of the missing woman. The audience is kept in suspense as to whether she is the real wife or not. Her ex-lover, as an act of revenge, produces a mad woman and says she is the real wife. She could well be; but even if she were genuine, she would still be an impostor, for she in no way resembles the wife they all remember. The Unknown Woman ("I am a body without a name") was created by Marta Abba in Milan in 1930 and played by Greta Garbo on screen in 1932.

Oct 3. Douglas Byng, John Tilley, June, Walter Crisham and Doris Hare in **Hi Diddle Diddle** directed by Andre Charlot at Comedy. Revue. Byng sang Cole Porter's "Miss Otis Regrets".

Oct 5. Marion Lorne, Gordon Harker and Godfrey Tearle in Walter Hackett's **Hyde Park Corner** directed by Walter Hackett and Thomas Reynolds at Apollo. Murder, melodrama and farce: "clues pop out of every ash-tray" said *The Times*.

Oct 15. Maurice Evans in Shakespeare's **Richard II** directed by Henry Cass at Old Vic. Abraham Sofaer as Bolingbroke. Evans gave his lines a sardonic edge.

Oct 23. Marie Tempest, George Zucco, Laurence Olivier and Mary Merrall in Edna Ferber and George S Kaufman's **Theatre Royal** directed by Noël Coward at Lyric. The comedy was a joke at the expense of America's most famous theatrical family, the Drew-Barrymore dynasty, known as "the royal family of Broadway." Ethel Barrymore was not amused and threatened legal action.

Nov 14. John Gielgud in Shakespeare's **Hamlet** directed by John Gielgud at New. Jessica Tandy as Ophelia. Laura Cowie as Gertrude. Frank Vosper as Claudius. George Howe as Polonius. Glen Byam Shaw as Laertes. Jack Hawkins as Horatio.

John Gielgud as Hamlet

Anthony Quayle as Guildenstern. Richard Ainley as Rosencrantz. George Devine as First Player. Alec Guinness as Osric.
—Altogether the best production of Hamlet I have ever seen or am ever likely to see. RAYMOND MORTIMER *New Statesman and Nation*
—As acting nothing to equal it can be seen on the English stage. SYDNEY W CARROLL *Daily Telegraph.*

Nov 20. Mary Newcombe in Bernard Shaw's **Saint Joan** directed by Henry Cass at Sadler's Wells. Cecil Trouncer as Inquisitor. Abraham Sofaer as Cauchon. Maurice Evans as Dauphin. Felix Aylmer as Warwick. Leo Genn as Dunois. Alan Webb as Ladvenu.

Nov 21. Flora Robson and Robert Donat in James Bridie and Claud Gurney's **Mary Read** directed by Tyrone Guthrie at His Majesty's. Mary Read, masquerading as a man, turns dragoon and pirate. Bridie wrote the role for Robson who wanted a change from the frustrated spinster roles she was usually asked to play.
—Her [Flora Robson's] dash and zest and dare-devilry and faith and courage, and ringing voice and – at the right time – feminine tenderness and sacrifice, roused the audience to such a pitch of enthusiasm at the finish that the rest of the company forgot all about themselves and just joined in – one of the rarest of all tributes. *Morning Post*

Nov 23. Charles Carson and Donald Wolfit in Denis Johnston's **The Moon in the Yellow River** directed by Fred O'Donovan at Haymarket. Irish workers attempt to destroy an electric power station. Wolfit was more convincing as a revolutionary than Carson was.

Nov 28. Esme Percy, Louise Hampton, Andrew Leigh, Roger Livesey and Fabia Drake in S I Hsiung's **Lady Precious Stream** directed by Nancy Price and S I Hsiung at Little. A picturesque fairy tale was acted according to the conventions of Chinese theatre without scenery

Dec 19. Frances Day and Arthur Riscoe in Vivian Ellis's musical **Jill, Darling!** directed by William Mollison at Saville. Book by Marriott Edgar and Desmond Carter. John Mills and Louise Brown sang the show-stopping "I'm on a See-Saw."

Dec 20. Blackbirds of 1935 at Coliseum. Harlem Rhapsody. All-black revue written and directed by Lew Leslie. Book by Lew Leslie and Dorothy Fields. Music by Irving Berlin, George Gershwin and Jimmy McHugh. The energy the cast brought to their dancing and singing had a terrific impact.

—Perhaps the most remarkable quality of her [Valaida's] singing, which is so great that when in the course of one of her songs last night she appeared to swoon the audience did not know whether to applaud the actress or to keep a sympathetic silence. *The Times*

1935

Jan 2. Diana Churchill, Richard Bird and Ellen Pollock in Michael Egan's **The Dominant Sex** directed by John Fernald at Shaftesbury. Sexual equality between husband and wife is impossible. Three acts of domestic conflict: the man wins the argument with a knock-out blow, much to the woman's delight.

Jan 22. Gwen Ffrangcon-Davies as Elizabeth Barrett, Scott Sunderland as Robert Browning in Rudolf Besier's **The Barretts of Wimpole Street** directed by H K Ayliff at Piccadilly.

Jan 30. Wendy Hiller, Cathleen Nesbitt, Beatrice Varley and Julien Mitchell in Ronald Gow and Walter Greenwood adaptation of Walter Greenwood's novel **Love on the Dole** directed by Reginald Bach at Garrick. The play, set in a Lancashire town during the Depression, was a major turning point in Hiller's career. Her sincerity, charm and emotional strength were much praised and her success in London and New York led to Bernard Shaw asking her to play Eliza Doolittle in Anthony Asquith's film version of *Pygmalion*.

Feb 12. Irene Vanbrugh as the Duchess of Marlborough, Barbara Everest as Queen Anne and Olga Lindo as Mrs Masham in Norman Ginsbury's **Viceroy Sarah** directed by Tyrone Guthrie and Murray Macdonald at Whitehall. Court intrigue.

Feb 28. Comedian George Robey as Falstaff in Shakespeare's **Henry IV Part 1** directed by Robert Atkins at His Majesty's. John Drinkwater as Henry. Patrick Waddington as Hal.
—A superb Falstaff, oozing humour in a rich flow and owing nothing to slapstick. ALAN BOTT *The Tatler*
—His humour is never exaggerated, never tinged with mere burlesque. He speaks actual Shakespeare but with a naturalness that would make those who do not know imagine the lines were "gags" of his own. *Morning Post*

Mar 13. Mabel Terry-Lewis, Veronica Turnleigh, Dorothy Holmes-Gore, Basil Bartlett, S J Warmington and Henrietta Watson in Richard Pryce's adaptation of Richard Oke's novel **Frolic Wind** directed by John Wyse at Royalty. Weekend house party. Those who hadn't read the novel had a difficult time following the play.
—I shall make no bones about the acting and say straight out that as a mosaic it is in a different class from anything else to be seen in London. JAMES AGATE *Sunday Times*

Mar 20. Ralph Richardson in J B Priestley's **Cornelius** directed by Basil Dean at Duchess. Cornelius is a businessman who thinks there are more important things in life than aluminium. Priestley wrote his allegory on the decline of capitalism especially for Richardson.

Mar 27. Richard Ainley in **Everyman** directed by Robert Atkins at Ambassadors. Marie Ney as Knowledge. Tilly Losch as the Angel. Pamela Stanley as Good Deeds. The Prologue and Epilogue were spoken by Ben Greet.

Apr 3. Jean Cadell, Mary Jerrold, Edith Evans in Rodney Ackland's adaptation of Hugh Walpole's novel **The Old Ladies** directed by John Gielgud at New. The script, a canny mixture of the ordinary and the macabre, was based on the physical, mental and financial horrors of old age. Three poor and lonely old ladies live in three bed-sitters in a large 18th-century country house in a Cathedral town. One of the women, silly and easily frightened, who has a poor heart condition, owns a most beautiful piece of amber, her most treasured possession. A wicked, greedy, half-crazy old gypsy is determined to possess it. Evans was a frightening gypsy.
—The Agatha Payne of Edith Evans might have stepped out of a nightmare. A swollen, bloated figure with purple cheeks and bolting eyes she waddles round the house like a huge toad. *Illustrated London News*

Apr 11. Stephen Haggard in John Galsworthy's **Justice** directed by Leon M Lion at Playhouse. Haggard was praised but the cast was uneven and the play no longer made the impact it once did.

Apr 24. Cedric Hardwicke and Eugenie Leontovich in Jacques Deval's **Tovarich** translated by Robert Sherwood and directed by Gilbert Miller at Lyric. Two Russian exiles in Paris, a former prince and an archduchess, take service in the home of a wealthy banker as valet and lady's maid.
—I don't want to make use of superlatives, but her [Eugenie Leontovich] performance of the Archduchess, by no means an actress-proof part, is one I shall never forget. Anybody with even a rudimentary knowledge of acting must realise that here is an artist of the very first rank. She is the Pavlova of the stage. VERNON WOODHOUSE *Bystander*

1935 World Premieres
New York
Clifford Odets's *Awake and Sing*
Clifford Odets's *Waiting for Lefty*
George Gershwin's *Porgy and Bess*
Robert E Sherwood's *Petrified Forest*
Sidney Kingsley's *Dead End*
Maxwell Anderson's *Winterset*
Bernard Shaw's *The Simpleton of the Unexpected Isle*
Paris
Jean Giraudoux's *La Guerre de Troie N'Aua Pas Lieu*
Barcelona
Garcia Lorca's *Donna Rosita*
Canterbury
T S Eliot's *Murder in the Cathedral*

Warsaw
Witold Gombrowicz's *Princess Ivona*

Births
Trevor Griffith, British playwright

Honours
Knight
Seymour Hicks, actor-manager

History
—Persecution of Jews in Germany
—Italy invaded Abyssinia

Apr 29. Maurice Evans in Shakespeare's **Hamlet** in its entirety directed by Henry Cass at Old Vic. Abraham Sofaer as Claudius. Dorothy Green as Gertrude. Vivienne Bennett as Ophelia. Alec Clunes as Laertes. Evans was compared to John Gielgud and, inevitably, suffered from the comparison.

May 1. Pamela Stanley as Queen Victoria and Vincent Price as Prince Albert in Laurence Housman's **Victoria Regina** directed by Norman Marshall at Gate.

May 2. Ivor Novello and Mary Ellis in Ivor Novello's musical **Glamorous Night** directed by Leontine Sagan at Drury Lane. Lyrics by Christopher Hassall. The cast included Jack Buchanan, Ivy St Helier and Fred Emney. "I lift my hat to Mr Novello," said *The Observer*. "He can wade through tosh with the straightest of faces." *The Daily Telegraph* described the show as "Glamorous nonsense."

May 15. Jeanne de Casalis, Frank Cellier and Vivien Leigh in Carl Sternheim's **The Mask of Virtue** in aversion by Ashley Dukes directed by Maxwell Wray at Ambassadors. Jilted mistress in Paris, circa 1760, schemes to humiliate a proud marquis by luring him into a marriage with a demure, sweet young girl, who is actually a prostitute. Leigh's charm, dignity, grace and ravishing beauty were universally acclaimed. Alexander Korda signed her up immediately with a £50,000 film contract.

May 28. Marie Tempest's Jubilee celebrated at Drury Lane in the presence of King George V and Queen Mary.

May 31. May Whitty, Emlyn Williams, Angela Baddeley, Kathleen Harrison and Basil Radford in Emlyn William's **Night Must Fall** directed by Miles Malleson at Duchess Not the usual who-dun-it?, but rather a when-will-he-do-it-again? "It's just a thriller," wrote Whitty to her daughter, "and it won't run." The production ran for 435 performances, and she went on to repeat her role in the 1937 movie, which launched the 72-year-old actress's successful career in Hollywood. Williams freely admitted to being obsessed by the macabre and the abnormal. The story was based on several real-life cases. Initially the pageboy and victim were mother and son, but he quickly realised that a West End audience would find absolute truth too shocking. Williams based the physical characteristics and idiom of the page boy on his long-time Welsh lover, Festinog ("Fess") Griffiths, who had been 20 years old when they first met. He wore Fess's shoes on stage.
—The art of Emlyn Williams as an actor of semi-sane youths, half-crazed with vanity and driven to crime by relentless egoism, is unique in its power of mesmeric fascination. He cannot be described as good-looking, but there is a weird wild Celtic beauty in his aspect which suggests a magic mystic pool in the Welsh hills. SYDNEY W CARROLL *Daily Telegraph*

Jun 14. Adele Dixon and Sydney Howard in Cole Porter's musical **Anything Goes** directed by Frank Collins at Palace. Book by Guy Bolton and P G Wodehouse. Stowaway on ocean liner persuades a beautiful girl, who is engaged to an English lord (a typical silly ass) to marry him instead. He is helped in his endeavours by a notorious evangelist turned nightclub singer and a hoodlum disguised as a clergyman. Songs included "You're The Top", "I Get A Kick Out of You", "All Through the Night" and "Blow, Gabriel, Blow".

Jun 17. Dublin's Gate Theatre. Micheal Mac Liammoir in Shakespeare's **Hamlet** directed by Hilton Edwards at Westminster. *The Observer* said that Mac Liammoir hadn't an ounce of melancholy in him. *The Times* complained that the actors spoke to the audience rather than each other. Hilton Edwards, playing Claudius, made the strongest impact.

Laurence Olivier and Edith Evans and John Gielgud in Romeo and Juliet

Robert Speaight in Murder in the Cathedral

Jul 2. John Gielgud in André Obey's **Noah** directed by Michel Saint-Denis at New. Biblical pantomime for adult children. Arthur Wilmurt's translation did not do justice to Obey's quaint naïvety and poetry.
—Mr Gielgud's Noah, with his six-hundred-year-old body so swaddled and hirsute as to make summer's nights seem a dreadful thought, is a prodigious mixture of Lear, Job, Tolstoy, and the Old Man of the Sea plagued with a Load of Mischief. IVOR BROWN *Observer*

Jul 15. Flora Robson and Oscar Homolka in W O Somin's **Close Quarters** adapted by Gilbert Lennox and directed by Irene Hentschel at Haymarket. There were just two people in the cast, husband and wife, both communists, and one of them was responsible for a political murder. But which one?

Aug 21. Lilian Braithwaite, Isabel Jeans, Heather Thatcher and Robert Andrews in Ivor Novello's **Full House** directed by Leslie Henson at Haymarket. Jeans put Thatcher across her knee and spanked her. "Puerile," said *The Daily Mail*. "Very cheap stuff," said *The Daily Telegraph*.

Sep 17. Lucie Mannheim and Cecil Parker in Bruno Frank's **Nina**, directed by Owen Nares at Criterion. Mannheim played two roles: an elegant, sophisticated international film star and her vulgar understudy.

Oct 1. Group Theatre Season. John Moody in T S Eliot's **Sweeney Agonistes** directed by Rupert Doone at Westminster. Music by William Alwyn.

—T S Eliot's *Sweeney Agonistes* defies description and calls for little attention. It is dull and pretentious, and as far as I was concerned – despite the explanatory note on the programme – quite pointless. GEORGE W BISHOP *Daily Telegraph*

Oct 1. Baliol Holloway, Anthony Quayle and Athene Seyler in Thomas Otway's **The Soldier's Fortune** directed by Baliol Holloway at Ambassadors. The soldiers return from the wars in Flanders. The first revival in two centuries of this cynical, bitter comedy of whoring, drunken brawling and murder. "If the play were performed in modern dress, it would be quite impossible and rather unpleasant," said Athene Seyler, who played Lady Dunce, the flighty wife of a dirty, nauseous old man. Seyler was adorable.
—It would be idle to pretend that any historical purpose is served by this revival. It is just a clever and amusing comedy. Had it been written by Mr Noël Coward about 1935 Mayfair, I cannot think what the Lord Chancellor would have said. *Theatre World*

Oct 11. Stephen Haggard, Jean Cadell and Catherine Lacey in James Bridie's **The Black Eye** directed by H K Ayliff at Shaftesbury. "Mr Bridie," said *The Times*, "has written an entirely meaningless and an entirely delightful play." Haggard was cast as a gambler, who, with the help of an ex-convict, won £8,500 and saved the family from disaster. During the scene changes he stepped out of the play to address the audience directly. His performance was a shrewd mixture of arrogance and humility.

Oct 15. Marion Lorne and Edwin Styles in Walter Hackett's **Espionage** directed by Walter Hackett and Tom Reynolds at Apollo. Spies on board the Orient Express.

Oct 17. John Gielgud, Peggy Ashcroft and Laurence Olivier in Shakespeare's **Romeo and Juliet** at New. Gielgud and Olivier alternated Romeo and Mercutio. Gielgud's production, definitive until the 1950s, was highly commended for its freshness, speed, continuity and youth. Ashcroft made no secret that she thought Olivier was the best Romeo and Gielgud the best Mercutio. Olivier's Romeo was dismissed because he did not act or speak like Gielgud did. The contrast between classical and naturalistic acting jarred and he was accused of being a ranting, prose Romeo lacking in poetry and tenderness. James Agate in *The Sunday Times*, having pulled Olivier's performance to bits, then said that he was the most moving Romeo he had seen.
—Mr Gielgud seems to me almost the perfect Romeo. J G BERGEL *Evening News*
—Mr Laurence Olivier can play many parts: Romeo is not one of them. He has neither the tone nor the compass and his blank verse is the blankest I have ever heard. STEPHEN WILLIAMS *Evening Standard*
—Mr Gielgud's own vital, courageous Mercutio is an outstanding performance – less bitter than most; his Queen Mab speech was exquisite and his death scene a wonderful suggestion of disillusioned chivalry. P L MANNOCK *Daily Herald*
—His [Laurence Olivier] Mercutio is a good example of bravura. Gaiety, whimsicality and ferocity are fused into one mood. *Daily Mail*
—[Peggy Ashcroft] does more than make Shakespeare's expression of Juliet's thoughts seem natural; she makes it inevitable. PETER FLEMING *Spectator*

Oct 30. Fay Compton, Owen Nares and Marie Löhr in **Call It A Day** by C L Anthony directed by Basil Dean. 24 hours in the life of a London middle-class family. C L Anthony was Dodie Smith's pseudonym.
—What it did exemplify to the nth degree was Dodie's unique gift for skilful juxtaposition of the unexpected, the ineptitudes, the frictions, laughter and tears of family life and, above all, its humanity. BASIL DEAN *Mind's Eye*

Nov 1. Robert Speaight as Thomas a Becket in T S Eliot's **Murder in the Cathedral** directed by E Martin Browne at Mercury. Originally performed at Canterbury Cathedral. Speaight, rich in spiritual vitality, spoke the verse and prose with clarity and dignity.

Nov 2. Marie Tempest, A E Matthews, Una Venning, Margaret Rutherford, Rex Harrison, Cyril Raymond, Ursula Jeans and Sybil Thorndike in Robert Morley's **Short Story** directed by Tyrone Guthrie.
—Young Mr Morley ought to be permanently on his knees backstage, thanking God for his cast. STEPHEN WILLIAMS *Evening Standard*

Nov 8. Jessica Tandy and Harold Warrender in St John Ervine's **Anthony and Anna** directed by Irene Hentschel at Whitehall. Anthony, who earns his living by being a professional guest in the homes of the rich, falls in love with Anna but he won't marry her unless her millionaire father (Morris Harvey) gives him a big settlement. The father won't give him any money until he gets a proper job.

Dec 12. Flora Robson in Wilfrid Grantham's **Mary Tudor** directed by Peter Creswell at Playhouse. Joyce Bland as Queen Elizabeth. Marius Goring as Philip of Spain. Lawrence Anderson as Bishop Gardiner. Grantham wrote a romantic whitewash rather than a psychological portrait. There was no indication that 300 people had been burned by her warrant. The role offered Robson few dramatic opportunities.
—Miss Robson proves once again that she is one of the best of our emotional actresses. It is to be regretted that her choice of plays is not likely to bring this fact to the knowledge of a wider public. *Illustrated London News*

Dec 20. Rosalinde Fuller and Leslie French in **Fritzi** directed by John Wyse at His Majesty's. Musical comedy. Book by Sydney Blow and Edward Royce. Lyrics by Arthur Stanley. Music by Carl Tucker. A gamine marries a famous man in the theatre. Rosalinde French had all the best songs, including a mock-heroic ballad, "My Lord, the Carriage Waits".

1936

Jan 6. Noël Coward and Gertrude Lawrence in Noël Coward's **Tonight at 8.30** directed by Noël Coward at Phoenix. Coward wrote the one-act plays as acting, singing and dancing vehicles for himself and Lawrence. **Family Album**: Victorian family, in deep mourning for their hateful papa, get tipsy and a wake turns into a sing-song. **The Astonished Heart**: A psychiatrist's obsession for his mistress leads to him jumping out of the window. **Red Peppers**: Two dead common music hall artistes, squabble in their squalid dressing room and perform two tacky routines.

Jan 13. Noël Coward and Gertrude Lawrence in Noël Coward's **Tonight at 8.30** directed by Noël Coward at Phoenix. Three more one-act plays. **Hands Across the Sea**: Scatterbrained hostess mistakes two colonials for somebody else. **Fumed Oak**: A browbeaten husband gives his ghastly family a piece of his mind before he walks out on them. **Shadow Play**: Musical fantasy. An unhappy wife takes an overdose of

sleeping tablets and whilst hallucinating, relives past happy moments she shared with her husband. The two programmes played in repertoire.

Jan 29. Noël Coward and Gertrude Lawrence in Noël Coward's **Tonight at 8.30** directed by Noël Coward at Phoenix. **We Were Dancing** replaced *Family Album*.
—If by careful writing, acting and producing I can do a little towards reinstating it [the one-act play] in its rightful place, I shall have achieved one of my more sentimental ambitions. NOËL COWARD *in a programme note*

Jan 30. Geoffrey Wincott as Dog and Robert Eddison as Poet in W H Auden and Christopher Isherwood's **The Dog Beneath the Skin** directed by John Moody at Westminster. Music by Herbert Murrill. A poetic, symbolic satirical revue in which the dog turns out to be a long-lost baronet.
—This eclectic revue, admirably written and entertaining, is a manifesto of youth, a call to crusade against reactionary powers that make modern life a travesty of the poet's ideal. *Observer*

Jan 30. Seymour Hicks and Margaretta Scott in Seymour Hicks's **The Man in Dress Clothes** directed by Seymour Hicks at Victoria Palace.

Feb 2. Frank Pettingell and Claire Luce in **Follow the Sun** directed by Frank Collins at Adelphi. Revue. Book by Ronald Jeans and John Hastings Turner. Music by Arthur Schwartz. Lyrics by Howard Dietz and Desmond Carter. Irene Eisinger (dressed as the Madonna) sang "The Three Holy Kings" in words by Heine to music by Herr Ruth. Frederick Ashton choreographed "The First Shoot", a mock ballet of men and pheasants to music by William Walton. The Cuban dancers stole the show.

Feb 5. Sara Allgood and Roger Livesey in James Bridie's **Storm in a Teacup** directed by W G Fay at Royalty. Adaptation of Bruno Frank's *Sturm in Wasserglass*. A Scottish streetwalker is unable to renew her dog licence, so the Provost condemns the dog to be destroyed. Transferred to Haymarket.

Feb 18. Romney Brent in John Cecil Holm and George Abbott's **Three Men on a Horse** directed by Alex Yokel at Wyndham's. American farce. Writer of greetings card verses earns forty dollars a week. On his way home, as a hobby, he plays the horses, and wins a fortune; but he never actually bets, instinctively feeling that if he were to play for real he would lose. His fortune is only on paper. One day, drunk in a New York bar, he gets picked up by three professional gamblers, who realizing they are on to a good thing, kidnap him.

Feb 21. Mary Clare and Griffith Jones in Rodney Ackland's **After October** directed by A R Whatmore at Arts. A boarding house in Hampstead is full of failed Bohemians. Ex-Gaiety girl is up to her eyes in debt. Her son, a playwright, is in love with the lodger, who is trying to ward off the attentions of a boring ex-pat. Her eldest daughter works as a dance hostess in Paris and has just married a Frenchman. Her youngest daughter is having an unhappy affair with her boss. Other characters include a very grand amateur thespian, a strange intruder and a comic servant. They all pin their hopes on the playwright's play being a zonking success. It is a resounding flop. The critics dubbed Ackland the English Chekhov. Transferred to Criterion.

Feb 27. Celia Johnson as Elizabeth Bennett, Hugh Williams as Mr Darcy, Barbara Everest as Mrs Bennett, Athole Stewart as Mr Bennett, Dorothy Hyson as Jane Bennett, Leueen MacGrath as Lydia Bennett, Lionel Watts as Mr Collins, Eva Moore as Lady Catherine de Bourgh and Anthony Quayle as Mr Wickham in Jane Austen's **Pride and Prejudice** adapted by Helen Jerome and directed by Gilbert Miller at St James's. The décor by Rex Whistler was an essential part of the production's success. Watts played Collins for outright farce; but that's how he is written.
—Every true Janeite has his own idea of Elizabeth and it may not agree with Miss Johnson's portrait, but every Janeite who is not stony hearted will rejoice in a substitute so alive, so unforced, so intelligent and unaffected. *The Times*

Mar 2. Lydia Lopokova and Geoffrey Edwards in Henrik Ibsen's **The Doll's House** directed by Michael Orme at Criterion. The critical opinion was that Lopokova was a lovely dancer but only a fair actress.

Mar 5. Jean Forbes-Robertson as Rebecca West and John Laurie as Rosmer in Henrik Ibsen's **Rosmersholm** directed by Irene Hentschel at Criterion.
—Her [Jean Forbes-Robertson] austerity and her power to communicate passion without display has returned. To each word and each phrase she gives a perfect lucidity; nothing is squandered, nothing done for effect. *The Times*

Mar 9. Jean Forbes-Robertson in Henrik Ibsen's **Hedda Gabler** directed by Irene Hentechel at Criterion. Walter Piers as George Tesman. D A Clarke-Smith as Judge Brack. John Laurie as Lövborg.

Mar 12. D A Clarke Smith as Solness and Lydia Lopokova as Hilda Wangel in Henrik Ibsen's **The Master Builder** directed by Irene Hentshel at Criterion.
—Lydia Lopokova is more at home on those cloud-capped towers of symbolism than amid the homely bric-a-brac of *A Doll's House*. *Sketch*

1936 World Premieres
New York
Hart and Kaufman's *You Can't Take It With You*
Rodgers and Hart's *On Your Toes*
Robert E Sherwood's *Idiot's Delight*
Robert E Sherwood's *Tovarich*
Clare Boothe Luce's *The Women*
Moscow
Mikhailm Bulgakov's *Molière*
Vienna
Bernard Shaw's *The Millionairess*

Births
Albert Finney, British actor
Vaclav Havel, Polish playwright
Simon Gray, British playwright
Glenda Jackson, British actor
David Rudkin, British playwright

Deaths
Oscar Asche (*b.*1871), British actor-manager
Ben Greet (*b.*1857), British actor-manager
Maxim Gorky (*b.*1868), Russian playwright

Federico Garcia Lorca (*b.*1898), Spanish playwright
Luigi Pirandello (*b.*1867), Italian playwright

Notes
—London, it is said, is the only civilised city without a National theatre. But surely a nation receives the theatre it deserves – and happens to want. The English have never taken their playgoing seriously. The theatre of London has always been, and will always be, a means of enjoyment and recreation. It may be deplorable, although frankly, I cannot see why, but there it is. David Fairweather *Theatre World*

History
—King George V died.
—Accession and abdication of King Edward VIII
—Accession of King George VI
—Start of Spanish Civil War
—Crystal Palace burned down
—*Queen Mary*'s maiden voyage

Mar 19. Keneth Kent as Napoleon in R C Sherriff and Jeanne de Casalis's **St Helena** directed by Henry Cass at Daly's. The once Great Emperor descends further and further into his dotage. Incredibly tedious, it transferred to the Old Vic only because of the enthusiasm of Winston Churchill.

Mar 31. Frank Vosper and Marie Ney in Frank Vosper's adaptation of Agatha Christie's **Love From A Stranger** directed by Frank Vosper at New. Woman wins £20,000 in a sweepstake, falls in love, and marries. Is her husband a murderer? Transferred to Queen's.

Apr 1. Nelson Keys, Ivy St Helier and Dorothy Dickson in Herbert Farjeon's **Spread It Abroad** directed by C Denis Freeman at Saville. Revue. High spot: Ivy St Helier drinking absinthe brought Degas's painting to life.

Apr 8. Vivien Leigh as Jenny Mere, Isabel Jeans as La Gambosi, Ivor Novello as Lord George Hell and Marius Goring as Amor in Max Beerbohm's **The Happy Hypocrite**, adapted by Clemence Dane and directed by Maurice Colbourne at His Majesty's. Novello's public did not want to see him as an ugly debauched Regency rake.

Apr 14. Nancy Price, Stephen Haggard, Ellis Irving and Robert Newton in Mazo de la Roche's **Whiteoaks** directed by Nancy Price and Frank Birch at Little. Price's magnificent centenarian dominated the production. To whom would she leave her fortune? Haggard was splendid as a shy, clumsy, highly-strung lad. Transferred to Playhouse.

Apr 23. Wyndham Goldie as Charles Parnell, Margaret Rawlings as Mrs O'Shea and Arthur Young as Prime Minister Gladstone in Elsie T Schauffler's **Parnell** directed by Norman Marshall at Gate. The Irish MP is hounded out of political life because of his affair with Kitty O'Shea, a married woman whose husband won't divorce her and who insists that she pays him to stay out of her bed. Initially the play was banned because of complaints by the ancestors of Captain O'Shea. Schauffler died just before the production opened. Transferred to New.

May 4. Cyril Cusack in Eugene O'Neill's **Ah, Wilderness!** at Westminster. O'Neill's purpose had been to write a play true to the spirit of the American small town at the turn of the 20th century. Written in 1933, during the Great Depression, he looked back to a happier era, nostalgic for the idyllic childhood he had never had. O'Neill's only comedy – sentimental, heart-warming and wish-fulfilling – is an affectionate portrait of adolescent immaturity. The young and earnest hero is 17, the same age O'Neill was in 1906. The writing had autobiographical truth, though the truth was much distorted and softened. The play was an antidote to *Long Day's Journey into Night*.

May 5. Noël Coward and Gertrude Lawrence in **Tonight at 8.30** directed by Noël Coward at Phoenix. **Ways and Means** was added to the repertoire and was the weakest of them all.

May 12. Eric Portman as Lord Byron, Mary Glynne as Augusta Leigh and Mabel

Edith Evans and John Gielgud in The Seagull

Terry-Lewis as Lady Melbourne in Catherine Turney's **Bitter Harvest** directed by Stephen Thomas at St Martin's. Byron's affair with his half-sister was treated with such tact and discretion that the audience was led to presume there hadn't been any sex. The censor still wanted to ban it. *The Sunday Times* dismissed the play as "a quagmire of milk pudding."

May 18. Noël Coward and Gertrude Lawrence in Noël Coward's **Tonight at 8.30** directed by Noël Coward at Phoenix. **Still Life** was added to the repertoire and was the best. It was made into a film in 1945 and retitled *Brief Encounter*. Directed by David Lean and starring Celia Johnson and Trevor Howard, it became a classic of British cinema.
—The play is a tiny masterpiece of economical writing, and is beautifully acted.
George W Bishop *Sunday Times*

May 20. Anton Chekhov's **The Seagull** directed by Theodore Komisarjevsky at New. When Chekhov was asked how he would like his play performed he replied he would like it performed as well as possible. Komisarjevsky's production was by common consent one of the great productions of the 1930s, praised for its meticulous detail and fine ensemble work by a distinguished cast. Edith Evans as Arkadina. Stephen Haggard as Constantin. Peggy Ashcroft as Nina. John Gielgud as Trigorin. Frederick Lloyd as Sorin. George Devine as Shamrayef. Clare Harris as Paulina. Martita Hunt as Masha. Leon Quartermaine as Dorn. Ivor Barnard as Medevedenko. Alec Guinness as a workman.

June 23. People's Theatre. Edmund Willard as Tramp and Esmond Knight as Parasite in Karel and Josef Capek's **The Insect Play** directed by Nancy Price at Playhouse.

Jul 8. Barbara Vernon, Shaun Glenville and Clifford Mollison in Vincent Youmans's **No! No! Nanette** directed by William Mollison at Hippodrome. Book and lyrics by Frank Mandel, Otto Harbach and Irving Caesar. The musical was acted twice nightly at speed and in a much broader manner than it had been in the 1920s.

Jul 11. Nicholas Brothers and The Four Bobs in **Blackbirds of 1936** directed by Lew Leslie at Gaiety. Rhapsody of blue notes and black rhythm. Revue conceived and staged by Lew Leslie. Music and lyrics by Johnny Mercer and Rube Bloom. 14-year-old Harold Nicholas was the hit of the show.

Aug 6. Ralph Richardson in Barré Lyndon's **The Amazing Dr Clutterhouse** directed by Claud Gurney at Haymarket. The doctor's hobby was criminal research.

He infiltrated the underworld and became the leader of a gang who carried out the biggest fur robbery of the century.

Aug 13. George Benson in Eleanor and Herbert Farjeon's musical **The Two Bouquets** directed by Maxwell Wray at Ambassadors. Gentle, good-natured guying of the Victorians: satirical songs and sentimental tum-te-tum tunes. Benson's "Masher"–with his moustache, prodigious smile and dashing French phrases – was the hit of the show.

Sep 2. Leslie Henson in **Swing Along** directed by Leslie Henson and Herbert Bryan. Musical comedy. Book by Guy Bolton, Fred Thompson and Douglas Furber. Music by Martin Broones. Lyrics by Graham John. Funniest moments: Henson about to be assassinated and Richard Hearne getting entangled with his trombone.

Sep 11. Dorothy Dickson and Ivor Novello in Ivor Novello's musical **Careless Rapture** directed by Leontine Sagan at Drury Lane. Lyrics by Christopher Hassell. Known in the theatrical profession as "Careless Rupture".

Sep 28. John Martin Harvey in Sophocles's **Oedipus Rex** translated by Gilbert Murray and directed by W Bridges-Adams at Covent Garden. Miriam Lewes as Jocasta. Baliol Holloway as Creon. J Fisher White as Teiresias. Franklin Dyall as Messenger. Recreation of Max Reinhardt's 1912 production.
—His [Martin Harvey] performance has a light and fire quite astonishing in a man of his years. W A DARLINGTON *Daily Telegraph*
—Sir John Martin Harvey may not have the physical size for Oedipus but mentally and spiritually he sizes it up beautifully. JAMES AGATE *Sunday Times*

Sep 29. Robert Morley in Leslie and Sewell Stokes's **Oscar Wilde** directed by Norman Marshall at Gate. John Bryning as Lord Alfred Douglas. Reginald Beckwith as Frank Harris. The Lord Chamberlain refused a licence and so the play had to be produced in private club theatre. Some critics thought the subject matter "left a slightly unpleasant taste in the mouth." The most surprising criticism was that the actual trials lacked drama. Douglas never saw the production. He told the authors it would be too painful an experience for him to attend a performance.
—Mr Robert Morley achieves a remarkable likeness to Wilde's portrait and speaks his lines with acceptable character. But the play is little but a précis of notorious facts which seem to emphasise the sordid at the expense of the significant. HAROLD HOBSON *Observer*

Oct 6. Michael Redgrave as Horner, Ruth Gordon as Margery Pinchwife, Edith Evans as Lady Fidget and James Dale as Mr Pinchwife in William Wycherley's **The Country Wife** designed by Oliver Messel and directed by Tyrone Guthrie at Old Vic. Richard Goolden as Jasper Fidget. Ernest Thesiger as Sparkish. Alec Clunes as Mr Harcourt. Iris Hoey as Dainty Fidget. Ursula Jeans as Alithea. Kate Cutler as Lady Squeamish. Eileen Peel as Mrs Squeamish. Freda Jackson as Lucy. First performance since the end of the 18th century. Nobody was shocked, except for *The Daily Telegraph* critic who did not think the Old Vic should be putting on a coarse play which had no educational value and wondered why it should be exempted from entertainment taxes. Earl of Lytton, Chairman of the Old Vic Governors, justified its inclusion in the repertoire, arguing: "The play is a caricature of the loose morals of the Restoration period. Its immoral plot is so preposterous as to be ridiculous and the coarseness of its dialogue is redeemed by its wit." Edith Evans got the biggest laugh of the evening when she said, "Nay, Fy! Let us not be smutty."
—It is impossible to imagine any other actress tackling this character with such wit and hoydenish charm, such shy, awkward grace and such a delicate suggestion of growing, yet essentially innocent slyness. I would rate this as one of the few great performances of comedy the contemporary stage has seen. AUDREY WILLIAMSON *on Ruth Gordon Old Vic Drama*

Oct 14. Donald Wolfit and Eugenie Leontovich in Shakespeare's **Antony and Cleopatra** directed by Theodore Komisarjevsky at New. Leon Quartermaine as Enobarbus. Leonvich had great difficulty with Shakespeare's language and verse. Charles Morgan in *The Times* recorded phonetically the Russian actress's delivery of three famous lines thus:

O weederdee degarlano devar
Desolderspo lees falln: yong boisenguls
Alefelnow wimen.

What she meant to say was:

O wither'd is the garland of the war,
The soldier's pole is fall'n; young boys and girls
Are level with men.

Oct 30. Robert Speaight as Thomas Becket in T S Eliot's **Murder in the Cathedral** directed by E Martin Brown at Duchess. Following a 41-week run at the Mercury Theatre the production transferred to the West End.
—This is the one great play by a contemporary dramatist now to be seen in England. *The Times*

—He has re-animated a literary form which in England has been dead or dormant for nearly three hundred years, and in doing so he has found himself anew as a poet, only with an added ease, lucidity and objectiveness. *Spectator*

Nov 6. Trevor Howard, Guy Middleton, Rex Harrison, Roland Culver, Kay Hammond, Robert Flemyng and Jessica Tandy in Terence Rattigan's **French Without Tears** directed by Harold French at Criterion. Six young men, destined for the diplomatic service, are trying to learn French at a crammer in France. (The play's title comes from a popular primer of the period.) They are distracted by a young woman who has a gift for making men fall in love with her. Hailed as a "masterpiece of frivolity", the play brought 23-year-old Rattigan instant fame. 1,030 performances.
—A brilliant, witty comedy, gay, witty, thoroughly contemporary without being unpleasantly modern. *Morning Post*
—This is not a play. It is not anything. It is nothing … It is not witty. It has no plot. It is almost without characterisation. JAMES AGATE, *The Sunday Times*
—It has no conceivable relation to British Drama and is a depressing commentary on West End theatre. *Daily Herald*
—I think it is a bit more serious than anyone has ever allowed. I regard it as a comedy of mood and character. It's not simply a lot of young men romping around. TERENCE RATTIGAN

Nov 10. Edith Evans as Rosalind and Michael Redgrave as Orlando in Shakespeare's **As You Like It** directed by Esmé Church at Old Vic. James Dale was Jacques. Alec Guinness played Le Beau and William. The action was played out in a Watteauesque setting. Evans had been considered told old to be playing Rosalind in 1936 when she was 38. Now at 48, she was irresistible, despite a costume which did her no favours, and she was acclaimed as the definitive Rosalind of her generation. Alan Dent in *The News Chronicle* said she turned the whole audience into one Orlando. Redgrave fell under her spell on stage and off.

Nov 12. Valerie Taylor and Ursula Jeans in Lillian Hellman's **The Children's Hour** directed by Norman Marshall and Reginald Beckwith at Gate. Based on a true 1810 Scottish legal case, it was banned in a number of American cities and in London on account of its lesbianism. Its real subject, however, was the destructive power of gossip. The reputation of two teachers and the boarding school they have founded are destroyed when one of the pupils (Mavis Edwards) falsely accuses them of being lovers. The girl's grandmother (Mary Merrall) alerts the other parents who withdraw their children. The teachers decide to brazen it out in court and lose. The twist is that the accusation does have some truth.

Nov 12. Frederick Leister and P Kynaston Reeves in Ian Hay's adaptation of his novel **The Housemaster** directed by Herbert Bryan at Apollo. Conflict between lovable old-fashioned housemaster and an odious headmaster with modern ideas.

Dec 1. Nicholas Hannen as Trebell and Catherine Lacey as Amy in a revised version of Harley Granville Barker's **Waste** directed by Harley Granville Barker and Michael Macowan at Westminster. The critics thought that the fault with the play was not that it was out of date but that Barker had not treated the subject dramatically enough.

Dec 14. Elizabeth Bergner in J M Barrie's **The Boy David** directed by Theodore Komisarjevsky at His Majesty's. David was a sexless child. Nobody believed he had killed a bear and a lion. But then he hadn't. God had. Barrie wrote David for Bergner and thought her performance the best ever given in a play by him.
—*David* exploits her naïvety, her charm, her other worldliness but it is Mr Godfrey Tearle who dominates the play. *Sunday Times*
—Miss Berger has still to show us what she can do with a great role. ALAN BOTT *Bystander*

Dec 26. Charles Laughton and Elsa Lanchester in J M Barrie's **Peter Pan** directed by Stephen Thomas at London Palladium. Laughton had recently starred in *Mutiny on the Bounty* and Barrie feared that Captain Hook might become Captain Bligh and frighten the children. So anxious was Laughton not to offend the playwright that he went to the other extreme and was far too pleasant. *The Times* said that would be pleasant to dine with this portly pirate after a morning's murder and to take afternoon-tea with him after a little plank-walking.

1937

Jan 8. Laurence Olivier in Shakespeare's **Hamlet** in its entirety directed by Tyrone Guthrie at Old Vic. Francis L Sullivan as Claudius. Dorothy Dix as Gertrude. George Howe as Polonius. Cherry Cottrell as Ophelia. Michael Redgrave as Laertes. Robert Newton as Horatio. Marius Goring as First Player. Alec Guinness as Osric. Guthrie and Olivier were influenced by Dr Ernest Jones, the President of the International Psycho-Analytical Association, who saw Hamlet as having an Oedipus complex. Olivier's performance was admired for its naturalism, speed, intelligence, grace, sardonic humour and tenderness.

1937 World Premieres
New York
John Steinbeck's *Of Mice and Men*
Clifford Odets' *Golden Boy*
Marc Blitzstein's *The Cradle Will Rock*
Maxwell Anderson's *High Tor*
Paris
Jean Anouilh's *Traveller Without Luggage*

Births
Steven Berkoff, British actor, playwright, director
Tom Courtenay, British actor
David Hockney, British painter, designer
Arthur Kopit, American playwright
Vanessa Redgrave, British actor
Tom Stoppard, British playwright
Lanford Wilson, American playwright

Deaths
J M Barrie (*b.*1860), British playwright
Lilian Baylis (*b.*1874), British manager and founder of Old Vic
John Drinkwater (*b.*1882), British playwright
Johnston Forbes-Robertson (*b.*1858), British actor
George Gershwin (*b.*1898), American composer
Annie Horniman (*b.*1860), British manager

History
—Pablo Picasso's *Guernica* at Paris Exhibition
—Joe Louis won World Heavyweight Boxing Championship
—Billy Butlin opened holiday camp

—Mr Olivier does not speak poetry badly. He does not speak it at all. JAMES AGATE *The Sunday Times*

Jan 17. The Repertory Players. Gerald Savory's **George and Margaret** directed by Richard Bird at Strand. Irene Handl made her debut as the maid. Transferred to Wyndham's. 799 performances.

Jan 17. Margot Fonteyn's debut in **Giselle** at Sadler's Wells.

Feb 2. Nelson Keys and Binnie Hale in A P Herbert's musical **Home and Beauty** directed by John Murray Anderson at Adelphi. Choreography by Frederick Ashton. Revue. Hale sang "A Nice Cup of Tea".

Feb 5. Vera Zorina in Richard Rodgers and Lorenz Hart's musical **On Your Toes** directed by Leslie Henson at Palace. Music teacher, a former child hoofer on the vaudeville stage, is led astray by a sexy Russian ballerina, much to the rage of her jealous lover, who attempts to murder him. The story and the parody of Mikhail Fokine's *Scheherzade* (tawdry Arabian Nights kitsch) were inspired by the visit of Diaghilev's Ballets Russes to the US. Initially conceived as a film project for Fred Astaire it was the first Broadway musical to blend jazz and classical music and the first Broadway musical to be about dance and dancers and to integrate dance and plot. It was also the first time the word "choreography" was used in billing in a musical. George Balanchine's *Slaughter on Tenth Avenue* was one of the high spots. Songs included "It's Got To Be Love", "There's a Small Hotel" and "The Heart Is Quicker Than The Eye".

Feb 11. Edith Evans and Michael Redgrave in Shakespeare's **As You Like It** directed by Esmé Church transferred from Old Vic to New.

Feb 23. Jessica Tandy as Viola, Laurence Olivier as Sir Toby Belch and Alec Guinness as Sir Andrew Aguecheek in Shakespeare's **Twelfth Night** directed by Tyrone Guthrie at Old Vic. Jill Esmond as Olivia. Leo Genn as Orsino. Marius Goring as Feste. Ivy St Helier as Maria.
—A baddish, immature production of mine with Olivier outrageously amusing as Sir Toby and a very young Alec Guinness less outrageous and more amusing as Sir Andrew. TYRONE GUTHRIE *A Life in the Theatre*

Feb 25. Joyce Barbour, Jane Baxter, Ronald Ward, Nigel Patrick and Noël Howlett in Gerald Savory's **George and Margaret** directed by Richard Bird at Strand. Irene Handl had a hit in her debut as a tongue-tied maid. George and Margaret never appeared. 799 performances.

Feb 26. William Devlin in W H Auden and Christopher Isherwood's **The Ascent of F6** directed by Rupert Doone at Mercury. Music by Benjamin Britten. Written in a mixture of prose and poetry, the play, part fairy tale, part political statement, described a journey of self-discovery, which led to salvation on a demon-haunted mountain. Transferred to Little.

Mar 23. Edith Evans and Leslie Banks in Shakespeare's **The Taming of the Shrew** designed by Doris Zinkeisen and directed by Claud Gurney at New. Director and designer took enormous liberties. Petruchio and Kate rode off to their honeymoon on a pantomime horse. Evans spoke the homily to wives so beautifully that she threw into relief the shallowness of all that had gone before.

Apr 6. Laurence Olivier in Shakespeare's **Henry V** directed by Tyrone Guthrie at Old Vic. Marius Goring as Chorus. Jessica Tandy as Princess. Patriotic revival to celebrate King George VI's coronation. Olivier, a pacifist, initially, wasn't too keen on all the jingoism. However, come World War 2, he would regularly be invited to declaim the "Once more into the breech" rallying cry and give "God for Harry, England and Saint George!" the full over-the-top theatrical works. He would go on to film *Henry V*, its release timed to coincide with the Allies' invasion of Europe in 1944.
—With the minimum of heroic gestures and a clear avoidance of rant he contrives steadily to impress the mind with the image of a heroic character. *The Times*

May 2. The Incorporated Stage Society. Francis James as the Stranger and Wanda Rotha in August Strindberg's **The Road to Damascus Part I** directed by Carl H Jaffé and Ossia Trilling at Westminster. A spiritual autobiography.

May 19. Hedley Briggs, Rosalind Atkinson and Nigel Stock in Jack Kirkland's **Tobacco Road** directed by Norman Marshall at Gate. Based on Erskine Caldwell's novel about the physical and moral degeneracy of white labour on a derelict plantation in Georgia in 1933.
—It saddens a gloomy evening to see such brilliant acting expended on the dustbin appeal of this squalid story... How much better all this skill would have been employed by giving a good rousing performance of *Charley's Aunt*. *The Times*

May 26. John Gielgud and Emlyn Williams in Emlyn Williams's **He Was Born Gay** directed by John Gielgud at Queen's. Marie Antoinette's son is alive and well in England disguised as a music master. The improbable romantic fiction was not helped by the addition of two farcical claimants to the throne.

Jun 2. Catherine Lacey and Eric Berry in Elmer Rice's **Judgment Day** directed by Murray Macdonald at Strand. Three prisoners are on trial in South-Eastern Europe on a charge of the attempted assassination of a dictator. Berry was outstanding.
—His [Eric Berry's] long denunciation of the fascist régime – the finest speech in the play, written in Rice's most urgent and rhythmic prose – was notable for its fire, its emotional feeling and its clear and musical qualities of diction. AUDREY WILLIAMSON, *Theatre of Two Decades*

Jun 8. Robert Speaight as Thomas Becket in T S Eliot's **Murder in the Cathedral** directed by E Martin Browne at Old Vic. The production returned to London, following a long tour.
—Mr Speaight as Becket has become more liturgical than ever; and presuming a little on the undeniable perfection of his elocution is often, especially in the now famous sermon, draggingly slow. *The Times*

Aug 26. Jean Forbes-Robertson, Raymond Huntley, Barbara Everest, Mervyn Johns, Rosemary Scott and Eileen Erskine in J B Priestley's **Time and the Conways** directed by Irene Hentschel at Duchess. The most successful of Priestley's Time plays records a family chronicle set in the North of England between the wars. First act takes place during a birthday party in 1919. Second act leaps forward twenty years and gives a glimpse of the unhappy marriages and financial ruin which awaits them all. ("If this is all life is, what's the use? Better to die before Time gets to work on you.") Third act returns to the party and their bright hopes for the future.
—The play's major theme is conveyed so delicately and with such little display that many will enjoy the first-class entertainment without grasping its full significance. Those who do grasp it will be haunted by it long after they have left the theatre. *Spectator*
—Individually and collectively they make up a concatenation of intention and display of achievement which has no parallel on the London stage at the moment. JAMES AGATE *Sunday Times*

Sep 1. Ivor Novello, Dorothy Dickson and Marie Löhr in Ivor Novello's musical **Crest of the Wave** directed by Leontine Sagan at Drury Lane. Lyrics by Christopher Hassall. English Earl goes to Hollywood and fails to make good. The spectacle included a train crash. James Agate in *The Sunday Times* dismissed the show as "sheer, unadulterated tosh."
—[Ivor Novello] continues to fill Drury Lane with a consistency that no other author, actor or manager has been able to achieve. ALAN BOTT *Tatler*

Sep 1. The Crazy Gang in **London Rhapsody** directed by Gordon Black and Charles Henry at Palladium. The revue, described as "a symphony of a great city", was surprisingly elegant. The gang was in a more serious vein than usual. Cast as flowergirls on the steps of Eros they sang "Six Broken Blossoms".

Sep 6. John Gielgud in Shakespeare's **Richard II** directed by John Gielgud at Queen's. Michael Redgrave as Bolingbroke. Peggy Ashcroft as Queen.
— [John Gielgud] has never shown a finer sensibility to beauty, his voice has never displayed so wide a range. ALAN DENT *Manchester Guardian*

Sep 21. Robert Morley as Henry Higgins and Diana Wynyard as Eliza Doolittle in Bernard Shaw's **Pygmalion** directed by Tyrone Guthrie at Old Vic. Wynyard was never believable as a cockney; she was a lady from the very start. Jay Laurier was Alfred Doolittle.

—Robert Morley's Higgins is heavy, but has the right touch of irresponsibility – rather like a slightly intoxicated elephant. *Sunday Times*

Sep 22. Eileen Beldon, Lewis Casson, William Fox and Wilfrid Lawson in J B Priestley's **I Have Been Here Before** directed by Lewis Cason at Royalty. The third of Priestley's Time plays and the least successful. At a pub on the Yorkshire moors, a man, his wife and her schoolmaster-lover find themselves helplessly trapped in a recurring cycle of events. A mysterious German professor, a Jewish exile, seems to know what is going to happen. Can the trio break the spell and so avert the disaster?
—There is actually more of myself in this play than any I have written, and even though it so obviously lacks humour, I would not hesitate to choose it as my most representative play. J B PRIESTLEY
—As the husband, Mr Wilfrid Lawson gives a remarkable performance. It is a brilliant study of a hag-ridden man, haunted by half-remembered dreams of a previous tragedy. Mr Lawson has long been considered, by the few, one of our best actors. It is likely he will now be acclaimed by the many. *Illustrated London News*

Oct 12. Emlyn Williams and Marie Ney in Shakespeare's **Measure for Measure** directed by Tyrone Guthrie at Old Vic. Williams, a very young and sensual Angelo, wore an elegant blonde wig and a flowing grey gown. Jay Laurier turned Pompey into a musical hall turn, reinforcing the idea that Shakespeare's clowns should be played by contemporary clowns.

Oct 19. Arthur Margetson in **The Laughing Cavalier** directed by William Mollison at Adelphi. Musical. Book and lyrics by Reginald Arkell and Stafford Byrne. Music by Wainwright Morgan. John Garrick as Franz Hals. Margetson looked exactly like the celebrated portrait by Frans Hals.

Nov 1. The People's Theatre. Esmond Knight as Orphée and Eileen Peel as Eurydice in Jean Cocteau's **Orphée** translated and directed by Carl Wildman at Playhouse.
—[Jean Cocteau] applies puerile magic to the most serious occasions, the most tragic and universal emotions, and distils from it a rapid, prestidigitatory, and extremely rarefied poetry. *The Times*

Nov 2. Emlyn Williams in Shakespeare's **Richard III** directed by Tyrone Guthrie at Old Vic. Williams acted as if he were playing the Demon King in a jolly melodrama. Many critics thought it was his best performance.
—He does not exult in his physical and spiritual deformity, he weighs it and analyses it with cold, dispassionate curiosity of a scientist examining microbes. STEPHEN WILLIAMS *Evening Standard*

Nov 19. Beatrix Lehmann, Laura Cowie, Robert Harris, Reginald Tate and Mark Dignam in Eugene O'Neill's **Mourning Becomes Electra** directed by Michael Macowan at Westminster. Epic tale of murder and revenge is set at the end of the American Civil War in New England, bastion of Yankee Puritanism. Based on Aeschylus's *Oresteia*, O'Neill combined Greek tragedy and Freudian psychology. Members of the House of Mannon are punished merely for being born and are doomed to an unending cycle of violence. Wife poisons her husband on his return from the war, so that she can marry her seafaring lover. Her daughter, who had incestuous feelings for her father and has always been jealous of her mother's sexual prowess, persuades her weak-willed brother (who has incestuous feelings for his mother) to kill the lover. "A great occasion," said *The Sunday Times*. "Theatrical event of the first magnitude," said *The Daily Telegraph*. The commercial success of the production (which lasted four-and-a-half hours) surprised everybody.

Nov 23. Edith Evans, Owen Nares and David Horne in St John Ervine's **Robert's Wife** directed by Murray Macdonald at Globe. A clash between private and professional lives: a wife's behaviour stands to wreck her husband's chances of becoming Dean.

Nov 25. John Gielgud as Joseph Surface, Leon Quartermaine as Sir Peter Teazle, Peggy Ashcroft as Lady Teazle and Athene Seyler as Mrs Candour in Richard Brinsley Sheridan's **The School for Scandal** directed by Tyrone Guthrie at Queen's. Michael Redgrave as Charles Surface. Dorothy Green as Lady Sneerwell. Harcourt Williams as Rowley. Alec Guinness as Snake. The production was thought to be something of a scandal. There was so much bowing, skipping and pirouetting that many critics felt they were assisting at a performance by *Les Ballets Russes*.

Nov 26. Laurence Olivier and Judith Anderson in Shakespeare's **Macbeth** directed by Michel Saint-Denis at Old Vic. Vivien Leigh said: "You hear Macbeth's first line, then Larry's make-up comes on, then Banquo comes on, then Larry comes on." Transferred to New.
—Sometimes he still misses the full music of Shakespearian verse but his speaking has gained in rhythm and strength, and his attack upon the part itself, his nervous intensity, his dignity of movement and swiftness of thought, above all his tracing of the precise deterioration in a man not naturally evil gives to his performance a rare consistency and power. *The Times*

Dec 7. Sybil Thorndike as Hecuba in Euripides's **The Trojan Women** translated by Gilbert Murray and directed by Lewis Casson at Adelphi. Margaret Rawlings as Helen. Timely revival produced under the auspices of the League of Nations Union. Thorndike and Casson had fire and lucidity but the chorus was very weak.

Dec 16. Lupino Lane in Noel Gay's musical **Me and My Girl** directed by Lupino Lane at Victoria Palace. Book by Arthur Rose and Douglas Furber. Bright and breezy. Cheeky Cockney lad becomes an earl and remains true to his girl. The costermongers teach the county how to do "The Lambeth Walk" and soon the whole country was doing it. 1,646 performances.
While dictators rage and statesmen talk
All Europe dances to the Lambeth Walk
Times leader

Dec 27. Robert Helpmann as Oberon, Vivien Leigh as Titania and Ralph Richardson as Bottom in Shakespeare's **A Midsummer Night's Dream** directed by Tyrone Guthrie, at Old Vic. Agnes Lauchlan as Helena. Alexis France as Hermia. Stephen Murray as Lysander. Anthony Quayle as Demetrius. A lovely Victorian tuppence-coloured dream designed by Oliver Messel and choreographed by Ninette de Valois in the Taglioni tradition to music by Mendelssohn and played by a full orchestra. The fairies in white muslin flew through groves of green canvas. Helpmann, a classical dancer, making his first appearance on the legitimate stage, spoke the verse better than anyone else. Leigh was an exquisite, doll-like fairy. Puck was played by a child, Gordon Miller.
—Not in my entire theatrical life have I attended a performance so charged with magic. AUDREY WILLIAMSON *Old Vic Drama*
—Helpmann as Oberon, looking like some strange, sinister stag-beetle, was indeed a spirit of another sort. His speech and movement, as one would expect, were beautiful. HARCOURT WILLIAMS *Old Vic Saga*

1938

Jan 19. Beatrix Lehmann as Lavinia, Laura Cowie as Christine, Mark Dignam as Ezra and Robert Harris as Orin in Eugene O'Neill's **Mourning Becomes Electra** directed by Michael Macowan transferred to New. "It is," said *The Observer*, "a play no intelligent playgoer can afford to miss."

Jan 25. Donald Wolfit in Ben Jonson's **Volpone** directed by Michael Macowan at Westminster. Alan Wheatley as Mosca. First performance of the play since 1785. Macowan cut the sub-plot of Sir Politick and Lady Would-Be. He emphasised the animal symbolism by turning the judges into owls. Wolfit, a foxy fox, would return to the role with even greater success in 1940.
—Mr Donald Wolfit, delighting in the rogue's richness of imagery and sultry splendour of thought, is able to suggest not only the foxiness of the fox but the spectacle of the fox endowed with a powerful mind. *The Times*

Jan 26. Hermione Baddeley, Cyril Ritchard and George Benson in Herbert Farjeon's **Nine Sharp** directed by Hedley Briggs at Little. Many critics thought the best revue they had ever seen and the Little Theatre, because of its intimacy, the perfect for revue. The Little would be bombed during World War 2.
—When she [Hermione Baddeley] has given to a part all it can take, she goes on to give twice as much again, and yet – such is the paradox of the actress's personality – we would not talk for a moment of over-acting. J C TREWIN *The Turbulent Thirties*

Jan 28. Gwen Ffrangcon-Davies as Olga, Carol Goodner as Masha, Peggy Ashcroft as Irina and John Gielgud as Vershinin in Anton Chekhov's **Three Sisters** designed by Motley and directed by Michel Saint-Denis at Queen's. Michael Redgrave as Tusenbach. Glen Byam Shaw as Solyony. George Devine as Andrey. Leon Quartermaine as Kuligin. Angela Baddeley as Natasha. Alec Guinness as Fedotik. Harry Andrews as Roddey. The beautifully orchestrated production was one of the finest examples of ensemble playing yet seen in England. Gielgud made up to look like the contemporary portraits of Stanislavsky's Vershinin.
—One should not fling the word 'masterpiece' carelessly about but I am using such terms with all the deliberation and consideration. For this is a masterpiece as a dramatic conception, and in the manner of presentation and acting; nothing that I have seen in the theatre for many years has so profoundly moved me; and so burned itself into my memory. A E WILSON *Star*
—Anyone who fails to see this production will miss one of the greatest intellectual and aesthetic pleasures the modern theatre can afford. RUPERT HART-DAVIS *Spectator*

Feb 8. Ralph Richardson as Othello and Laurence Olivier as Iago in Shakespeare's **Othello** directed by Tyrone Guthrie at Old Vic. Curigwen Lewis as Desdemona. Anthony Quayle as Cassio. Martita Hunt as Emilia. Olivier and Guthrie were full of theories about the subconscious love Iago had for Othello, but Richardson did not want to be party to any homosexual interpretation and so the production didn't work.

Feb 10. Godfrey Tearle in Merton Hodge's **The Island** directed by Glen Byam Shaw

Peggy Ashcroft, John Gielgud, Carol Goodner and Gwen Ffrancgon-Davies in Three Sisters

at Comedy. There was nothing to do on the island except to play bridge, badminton, bagatelle and have affairs.

Feb 20. The Stage Society. Basil C Langton and Joan Miller in Clifford Odets's **Awake and Sing!** directed by Leon M Lion and Guy Glover at Vaudeville. Awake and sing, ye that dwell in the dust. Isaiah 26.19. A characteristic work of The Group Theatre: Odets's naturalistic American drama, set in the Bronx during the Depression years, was a Marxist wake-up call to a disaffected lower-middle class Jewish family to get off their backsides and do something with their lives.

—His merit is to write about animated people with animation and to give actors effective lines in simple stereotyped situations. IVOR BROWN *Observer*

Mar 16. Peggy Wood, Fritzi Massary, Irene Vanbrugh and Griffith Jones in Noël Coward's **Operette** directed by Noël Coward at His Majesty's. Edwardian Gaiety Girl achieves overnight stardom and sacrifices love for career. Coward thought the show was over-written and under-composed. The most memorable song was "The Stately Homes of England." The casting of the German Jewish singer Massary helped her to get out of Germany and escape the gas chambers.

—Mme Fritzi Massary is a bravurista of the highest order; and one of her gestures reduces English notion of acting to the likeness of a milk pudding with a grating of nutmeg. JAMES AGATE *Sunday Times*

Mar 22. Raymond Massey and Tamara Geva in Robert E Sherwood's **Idiot's Delight** directed by Raymond Massey at Apollo. American song and dance man and phoney Russian countess, stranded in the Italian Alps, decide to have a fling just as World War 2 is about to begin.

—Mr Sherwood's play is neither a discussion of war nor an examination of human beings in the stress of war; it is rather mob oratory, a shouted protest, a scream of rage. *The Times*

Mar 29. Harcourt Williams as William of Sens in Dorothy L Sayers's **The Zeal of Thy House** directed by Harcourt Williams and Frank Napier at Westminster. William of Sens designed and built the greater part of Canterbury Cathedral. William and his aristocratic mistress (Marie Ney) were in a builder's cradle having sex when the rope snapped. He fell to the ground. Was he punished by God for his scandalous behaviour or was he punished by the Devil for building a cathedral?

Apr 8. Felix Aylmer, Oscar Homolka and Beatrice Varley in Karel Capek's **Power and Glory** directed by Claud Gurney at Savoy. Doctor in a totalitarian state discovers a cure for a plague but refuses to share his knowledge until nations agree not to fight any more.

Apr 19. Laurence Olivier in Shakespeare's **Coriolanus** directed by Lewis Casson at Old Vic. Sybil Thorndike as Volumnia. Cecil Trouncer as Memenius Agrippa. Olivier's Fascist dictator was a study in arrested development, full of sardonic humour and soaring insolence. The scenes with his mother were acted with great tenderness. His spectacularly ostentatious death-fall had the audience on its feet, cheering wildly. He threw himself down a staircase in a complete somersault, rolled over three times on his side, and crashed to his death just short of the footlights.

—There is no doubt in my mind that the only sign of a great actor in the making in England today is Mr Olivier. *John O'London's Weekly*

Apr 21. John Gielgud as Shylock and Peggy Ashcroft as Portia in Shakespeare's **The**

1938 World Premieres
New York
    Robert E Sherwood's *Abe Lincoln in Illinois*
    Richard Rodgers and Lorenz Hart's *The Boys from Syracuse*
    Olsen and Johnson's *Hellzapoppin*
Princeton
    Thornton Wilder's *Our Town*
Paris
    Jean Cocteau's *Les Parents Terribles*
    Jean Anouilh's *Thieves Carnival*
Vienna
    Bernard Shaw's *Geneva*

Births
    Caryl Churchill, British playwright

John Guare, American playwright
Derek Jacobi, British actor
Diana Rigg, British actor

Deaths
Karel Capek (*b.*1890), Czech playwright
Odon von Horvath (*b.*1901), Austrian-Hungarian playwright

History
—Germany annexed Austria
—IRA bombings in England
—Discovery of nylon in US
—Orson Welles broadcasted *The War of the Worlds* and caused panic throughout the US

Merchant of Venice directed by John Gielgud and Glen Byam Shaw at Queen's. Leon Quartermaine as Antonio. Harry Andrews as Salerio. Richard Ainley as Bassanio. Glen Byam Shaw as Gratiano. Alec Guinness as Lorenzo. Angela Baddeley as Nerissa. There were those, Laurence Olivier amongst them, who rated Shylock as one of Gielgud's best performances; but they were in the minority. Gielgud thought he had failed.

Apr 27. The People's Theatre. Edmund Willard as Tramp and Robert Helpmann as butterfly, cricket and ant in Karel and Josef Capek's **The Insect Play** directed by Nancy Price at Duke of York's.

Apr 27. Robertson Hare, Alfred Drayton and Olga Lindo in Ben Travers's **Banana Ridge** directed by Gardner Davies at Strand. Paternity farce in the Malayan jungle.

May 17. Lynn Fontanne as Alkmena and Alfred Lunt as Jupiter in Jean Giraudoux's **Amphitryon 38**, adapted by S N Behrman and directed by Bretaigne Windust at Lyric. Zeus seduces Alkmena by disguising himself as her husband. Giraudoux worked out that thirty-seven authors had already used the legend, hence his title. The heroine's originality (for a bedroom farce) is that she genuinely does prefer married love to adultery. She commits adultery (without knowing it) and keeps her virtue intact, the envy of every bourgeois married woman in the audience, who had ever wanted to have an affair, but only so long as her bourgeois husband didn't find out and she didn't lose her bourgeois respectability. The acting, much admired, was on a higher plane than the play. Sydney Greenstreet played a trumpeter.
—They are more like musicians than actors in the way they linger over a phrase, an intonation, a gesture, as if they can hardly bear to let it go. W A DARLINGTON *Daily Telegraph*

May 23. Centenary of Henry Irving's birth celebrated at Lyceum.

May 26. Jessica Tandy, Reginald Tate and Raymond Huntley in Norman Macowan's **Glorious Morning** directed by Claud Gurney at Duchess. Girl, living in a totalitarian state, dies for her religious convictions.

May 31. Zena Dare, Roger Livesey, Arthur Sinclair, Joyce Carey and Margaret Rutherford in M J Farrell and John Perry's **Spring Meeting** directed by John Gielgud at Ambassadors. Aunt Bijou, a fussy, absurd old maid, has a secret knowledge of the turf. The role made Rutherford a star, but she was always unhappy when the audience laughed. She thought of Bijou as a tragic figure.
—It was Margaret Rutherford's triumph that while making a devastating figure of fun she gave her at the same time an extraordinary sympathy. ERIC KEOWN *Punch*

Jun 10. Nora Swinburne and Cecil Parker in Peter Blackmore's **Lot's Wife** directed by Cecil Parker at Whitehall. Modern Asia Minor: Mrs Lot does not turn into a pillar of salt and is able to join her lover.

Jun 20. Irene Vanbrugh's Jubilee celebrated at His Majesty's.

Jun 21. Luther Adler in Clifford Odets' **Golden Boy** directed by Harold Clurman at St James's. Violinist, during the American Depression, turns boxer and sells out for fame and fortune. (Odets, a member of the politically active Group Theatre, also sold out – in his case to Hollywood.) The play did not make as much comment on a competitive society and the American dream as, perhaps, the sub-title, "a modern allegory", and the reputation of The Group Theatre might have led audiences to expect.

Jul 19. The Open Air Theatre's season included Gladys Cooper in Aristophanes' **Lysistrata**, Jack Hawkins in Goethe's **Faust** and Jean Forbes-Robertson as Oberon in Shakespeare's **A Midsummer Night's Dream**.

Aug 17. Adele Dixon, Ralph Reader, Frances Day and Stanley Lupino in **The Fleet's Lit Up** directed by George Black and assisted by Charles Henry at Hippodrome. Plotless naval frolic by Guy Bolton, Eric Thompson and Bert Lee. Music by Vivian Ellis.
—[Stanley Lupino] has never been more broadly boisterous, though his jokes grazed the knuckle more often than was necessary. *Theatre World*
—Having almost every conceivable fault and no merits that I can discern, it will probably run a year. For if there is one thing on which the British public dotes it is poverty of ideas richly dressed. JAMES AGATE *Sunday Times*

Aug 31. Richard Hearne, Leslie Henson and Fred Emney in Douglas Furber's **Running Riot** at Gaiety. Musical comedy: incomprehensible plot, half-hearted satire on the movies and an indifferent Chinese ballet by Frederick Ashton.

Sep 1. Godfrey Tearle, Leo Genn, Anthony Ireland, Marda Vanne, Margaret Rawlings and Felix Aylmer in Charles Morgan's **The Flashing Stream** directed by Peter Cresswell at Lyric. Love and mathematics on a British Island in the Atlantic: the commander of an experimental unit refuses to admit to any error when his figures are held in doubt and his position jeopardised. The woman he loves, a greater mathematician than he, comes to his rescue. "Intellectual treat of the year," said *The Sunday Dispatch*. James Agate said it was the best play since Huxley's *The World of Light*.
—Its dialogue is persuasive, but inclined to be high flown; its incidental humours are apt but inclined to be stilted. ALAN BOTT *Tatler*

Sep 13. Seymour Hicks in James Bridie's **The Last Trump** directed by H K Ayliff at Duke of York's. An unscrupulous businessman, who is about to ruin the Highlands with his electric power scheme, is tricked into thinking the end of the world is about to happen.

Sep 14. Marie Tempest, John Gielgud, Leon Quartermaine, Valerie Taylor, Nan Munro, John Justin, Muriel Pavlow, Kate Cutler and Angela Baddeley in Dodie Smith's **Dear Octopus** directed by Glen Byam Shaw with Dodie Smith at Queen's. Three generations celebrate a couple's golden wedding anniversary. Smith's affectionate tribute to "that British institution, the family", and its homely and comforting philosophy about accepting middle and old age, was tailored to pre-war West End requirements. This meant that its basic weakness was not its sentimentality but its lack of depth and bite.

Sep 16. Ivor Novello in Shakespeare's **Henry V** directed by Lewis Casson at Drury Lane. Gwen Ffrangcon-Davies as Chorus. Dorothy Dickson as Katharine. 1938 was the year of the Munich crisis and the public wanted romanticism not jingoism. Novello lacked physique and virility.
—Mr Novello plays the King with far more zest and poetry than his more serious admirers could have anticipated. ALAN DENT *Manchester Guardian*.

Sep 20. Sybil Thorndike as Miss Moffat, Emlyn Williams as Morgan Evans and Kathleen Harrison as Mrs Watty in Emlyn Williams's **The Corn is Green** directed by Emlyn Williams at Duchess. Pit boy wins a scholarship to Oxford with the help of a brusque, business-like, socialist schoolmarm. Thorndike had the two qualities absolutely essential to the role – unbounded vitality and complete unsentimentality.
—Mr Williams plays the role as if he were living rather than acting it. *Illustrated London News*
—Not for years has Dame Sybil had a part that gave her better scope for her special gift of interpreting devotion. W A DARLINGTON *Daily Telegraph*
—It has all the great dramatic virtues of looking facts in the face and not sneaking off with sentimental side-issue and – as most plays do – beginning on one subject to please yourself and ending on another to please everybody else. HARLEY GRANVILLE BARKER *in a letter to Emlyn Williams*

Sep 21. First production of The London Mask Theatre Company, whose policy was "distinguished plays at popular prices." Robert Harris as Troilus and Ruth Lodge as Cressida in a modern-dress production of Shakespeare's **Troilus and Cressida** directed by Michael Macowan at Westminster. Max Adrian as Pandarus. Robert Speaight as Ulysses. Harry Andrews as Diomedes. Michael Denison as Paris. Stephen Murray's Thersites was a railing, intellectual communist.
—Our object in forming the company is to provide London with a theatre not only less expensive than the ordinary West End playhouse, but one that will produce plays of genuine merit, that is to say the sort of plays which intelligent playgoers can be sure they are not wasting both time and money in going to see. MICHAEL MACOWAN, *artistic director*

Sep 23. Leslie Banks and Constance Cummings in James Hilton's **Goodbye Mr Chips** directed by Murray Macdonald at Shaftesbury. Adaptation by James Hilton and Barbara Burnham.
—Mr Chips had a beautiful nature but not as beautiful as Mr Banks' interpretation of it. *Illustrated London News*

Oct 6. Michael Redgrave, Peggy Ashcroft, George Devine, Stephen Haggard, George Hayes, Glen Byam Shaw, Marius Goring and James Donald in Mikhail Bulgakov's **The White Guard** adapted by Rodney Ackland and directed by Michel

John Gielgud, Una Venning, John Justin, Jean Ormonde, Angela Baddeley, Nan Munro, Kate Cutler, Leon Quartermaine, Madge Compton, Pat Sylvester, Sylvia Hammond, Felix Irwin and Marie Tempest in **Dear Brutus**

Saint-Denis at Phoenix. One of Stalin's favourite plays. In 1918 the bourgeois military class – White Russians in the Ukraine – put up a desperate and futile fight against the Bolsheviks. But whom and what were they defending? The White cause was finished; there was nothing to fight for. Bulgakov described the horrors of the civil war mainly through one family and their friends. Stanislavsky, fearing the original title was politically too risky for the Moscow Arts Theatre, re-titled the play *The Days of the Turbins*. At the end, as in Chekhov's *The Cherry Orchard*, the wiping away of the old regime and the coming of the new was clearly meant to be seen as something positive and good. Yet such a reading is not inherent in the text, but rather seemed to have been tacked on for the benefit of the censor. The timing of the production was not ideal, coming, as it did, after the Munich Conference, The public stayed away and the play was withdrawn after only three weeks.

—Miss Peggy Ashcroft gave an exquisite performance of something which got no nearer to Russia than the handbag department of Harridges. JAMES AGATE *Sunday Times*

Oct 11. Beatrice Varley, Lloyd Pearson, Muriel George, Frank Pettingell, Raymond Huntley and Patricia Hayes in J B Priestley's **When We Are Married** directed by Basil Dean at St Martin's. Priestley's best loved and most enduring play is a farce set in Yorkshire. Three very respectable couples, celebrating their silver wedding, discover that, because of a clerical error, they have never been married. Priestley took over the role of the photographer when Pettingell (who had a big success in the role) was involved in a car accident. Basil Dean said of Priestley's performance that he was only an amateur photographer. The critics admired the characterisation but were patronising about the play. *When We Are Married* was the first play to be televised from a theatre.

Oct 11. Alec Guinness in Shakespeare's **Hamlet** directed by Tyrone Guthrie in its entirety and in modern dress at Old Vic. Andrew Cruickshank as Claudius. Veronica Turnleigh as Gertrude. Hermione Hannen as Ophelia. O B Clarence as Polonius. Visually the most striking scene was Ophelia's funeral in a downpour of rain, the mourners carrying open umbrellas. "I was," said Guinness, "but a pale shadow of Gielgud with some fustian trimmings, encouraged by Guthrie."

Oct 14. Elizabeth Allen, Frank Lawton, Marie Löhr, Marjorie Fielding, Clive Morton and Glynis Johns in Esther McCracken's **Quiet Wedding** directed by Maurice Browne assisted by Marjorie Morris at Wyndham's. English domestic comedy. The title was ironic.

Oct 25. Francis L Sullivan in Leslie and Sewell Stokes's **Oscar Wilde** directed by Ronald Adam at Arts. Peter Osborn as Lord Alfred Douglas. The playwrights, not approving of the interpretation, asked for their names to be removed from the programme and all advertisements. *The Sunday Times* thought Sullivan was far more successful than Robert Morley had been in suggesting the human tragedy behind the brilliant façade.

Nov 4. The People's Theatre. Edmund Willard as Simon Eyre, Harold Warrender as the shoemaker and Hedley Briggs as Firk in Thomas Dekker's **The Shoemaker's Holiday** directed by Nancy Price at Playhouse.

Nov 17. Basil Sydney as Sir Thomas More and Julien Mitchell as Thomas Cromwell in Morna Stuart's **Traitor's Gate** directed by Leslie French at Duke of York's. The high spot was the scene between More and Cromwell. The play was far too talky for West End audiences,

Nov 22. Allison Leggatt, Donald Eccles, Arthur Ridley, Ernest Thesiger, Alexander Knox, Cecil Trouncer and Walter Hudd in Bernard Shaw's **Geneva** directed by H K Ayliff transferred from Malvern Festival to Saville. The theme was the ineffectiveness of the League of Nations. The third act was best. Three dictators, Herr Battler, Signor Bombardone and General Flanco (Hitler, Mussolini and Franco), find themselves in the dock at the International Court of The Hague. Shaw pleaded that there could never be world peace until nations were above nationalism and patriotism; however, since the human race did not like each other, the chances of internationalism succeeding were nil. Cecil Trouncer, as the bombastic Bomardone, had all the best lines.

—I am neither omniscient nor omnipotent, and the utmost I or any other playwright can do is to extract comedy and tragedy from the existing situation and wait and see what will become of it. GEORGE BERNARD SHAW

Nov 24. Jack Hulbert and Cicely Courtneidge in Vivien Ellis's **Under Your Hat** directed by Jack Hulbert at Palace. Two married film stars track down spies who have stolen a vital carburettor. The high spot was the burlesque number, "The Empire Depends Upon You".

Dec 1. Peggy Ashcroft as Viola, George Hayes as Malvolio, Esmond Knight as Orsino, George Devine as Sir Toby Belch and Michael Redgrave as Sir Andrew Aguecheek in Shakespeare's **Twelfth Night** directed by Michel Saint-Denis at Phoenix. The production was much criticised for cutting away all the traditional business and putting nothing in its place, when, in fact, what Saint-Denis had done was to reproduce Jacques Copeau's famous 1914 production.

Dec 6. Anthony Quayle as Jack Absolute, Ellen Compton as Mrs Malaprop, Lewis Casson as Sir Anthony Absolute, Hermione Hannen as Lydia, André Morel as Faulkland, Meriel Forbes as Julia and Andrew Cruickshank as Sir Lucius Trigger in Richard Brinsley Sheridan's **The Rivals** directed by Esmé Church at Old Vic. Alec Guinness's Bob Acres was likeable, eccentric and real.

Dec 26. Griffith Jones as Marco Polo in Eugene O'Neill's **Marco Millions** directed by Michael Macowan at Westminster. A rambling and tedious satire on obsessive commercialism. Marco Polo is the eternal businessman. Since The London Mask Theatre Company simply did not have the financial resources to produce the play O'Neill described in his stage directions, Macowan cut all the pageantry and relied on a simple and suggestive presentation.

Dec 26. Robert Helpmann as Oberon and Dorothy Tyson as Titania in Shakespeare's **A Midsummer Night's Dream** directed by Tyrone Guthrie. A rare vision: a revival of last year's highly successful Victorian production designed by Oliver Messel and choreographed by Ninette de Valois. Edward Chapman as Bottom. John Mills as Puck. Anthony Nicholls as Lysander. Harry Andrews as Demetrius. Ruth Wyn Owen as Hermia. Peggy Livesey as Helena.
—The ballets have all their original freshness and that sureness of timing which makes them seem part of some lovely gliding hallucination. *The Times*

1939

Jan 19. Beatrix Lehmann in Max Cato's **They Walk Alone** directed by Berthold Viertel at Shaftesbury. Melodrama. A maidservant strangles young men and plays the church organ at midnight.

Jan 24. John Mills as Young Marlow, Ursula Jeans as Kate Hardcastle, Edward Chapman as Mr Hardcastle, Margaret Yarde as Mrs Hardcastle, Pamela Brown as Miss Neville, Anthony Nicholls as Hastings and George Benson as Tony Lumpkin in Oliver Goldsmith's **She Stoops to Conquer** directed by Tyrone Guthrie and Frank Napier at Old Vic.
—Nothing could surpass Mills's nerve-wracked bashfulness and tongued-tied constraint as the speechless lover. AUDREY WILLIAMSON *Old Vic Drama*

Jan 25. Diana Wynyard, Anton Walbrook, Rex Harrison and Alan Webb in Noël Coward's **Design for Living** directed by Harold French at Haymarket. The "three-sided erotic hotchpotch" was set in Paris, London and New York. The play "has been liked and disliked and hated and admired," said its author, "but never sufficiently loved by any but its three leading actors." Written specifically for himself and the American husband and wife team, Lynn Fontanne and Alfred Lunt, it was first performed on Broadway in 1933. "We managed," said Coward, "to give the worst performances of our careers every night together for months and managed to be very good." The West End premiere was delayed five years due to the Lord Chamberlain raising objections to a ménage a trois, which embraced homosexuality and bisexuality. Coward described the trio as "glib, over-articulate, amoral creatures," essentially "cheap, second-rate little opportunists, ready to sacrifice anything, however sacred, to the excitement of the moment." *The Sunday Express* thought the play "a rather unhealthy piece of impertinence and all too rarely funny." Many critics regretted that they hadn't seen Fontanne, Lunt and Coward in the leading roles.

Jan 27. Cyril Cusack as Christy, Pamela Gibson as Pegeen and Maire O'Neill as Widow Quinn in J M Synge's **The Playboy of the Western World** directed by John Chandos at Mercury.
—The play is nicely acted by Mr Cyril Cusack, but seems to take rather less pleasure than he should in the power of his own tongue. *The Times*

Jan 31. Milton Rosmer, Gwen Ffrangcon-Davies and Dennis Arundell in Patrick Hamilton's **Gaslight** directed by Gardner Davies at Apollo. Compelling pastiche Victorian melodrama: a man systematically drives his wife insane. Hamilton didn't let the audience off the hook with the rising and falling gaslight.

Jan 31. John Gielgud as John Worthing, Ronald Ward as Algernon, Edith Evans as Lady Bracknell, Joyce Carey as Gwendolen, Margaret Rutherford as Miss Prism, Angela Baddeley as Cecily and David Horne as Chasuble in eight special matinees of Oscar Wilde's **The Importance of Being Earnest** directed by John Gielgud at Globe. Gielgud's performance was hailed as a masterpiece of artificial acting and his production was hailed as the most subtle treatment of the play anybody could remember. For many people, even for those who never saw it, the production has remained the definitive one, immortalised by Edith Evans's delivery of "A handbag!" which is, probably, the most quoted and imitated phrase in British theatre. Gielgud had a perfect understanding of the author's philosophy, namely that we should treat all the trivial things of life seriously and all the serious things of life with sincere and studied triviality. "You must not indulge yourself in caricature," he said. "You must play it with your tongue in your cheek like a solemn charade."

1939 World Premieres

New York
William Saroyan's The *Time of Your Life*
Cole Porter's *Du Barry Was A Lady*
Kaufman and Hart's *The Man Who Came to Dinner*
Lilian Hellman's *Little Foxes*
Philip Barry's *The Philadelphia Story*
Robert Sherwood's *No Time for Comedy*

Paris
Jean Giraudoux's *Ondine*

Malvern
Bernard Shaw's *In Good King Charles's Days*

Births

Alan Ayckbourn, British playwright
Ian McKellen, British actor

Deaths

Frank Benson (*b.*1858), British actor-manager
Ernst Toller (*b.*1893), German playwright
W B Yeats (*b.*1865), Irish playwright

Honours

Dame
Marie Tempest, actor
Knight
Max Beerbohm, critic
Academy Award for best screenplay
Bernard Shaw for *Pygmalion* (directed by Anthony Asquith, starring Leslie Howard, Wendy Hiller and Wilfrid Lawson)

Notes

—Gaiety Theatre closed down
—Dame Myra Hess organised lunchtime chamber concerts at National Gallery
—Performances of *The Cherry Orchard, Les Parents Terribles* were announced but cancelled due to the outbreak of war.

History

—Germany invaded Poland
—Second World War started
—Italy invaded Albania
—USSR invaded Finland

Feb 17. Stephen Haggard, Barry Jones, Max Adrian, Stephen Murray and Ruth Lodge in Bernard Shaw's **The Doctor's Dilemma** at Westminster. Haggard had Dubedat's charm, cheek and genius.

Feb 21. Roger Livesey, Edward Chapman, Ursula Jeans and Nora Nicholson in Henrik Ibsen's **The Enemy of the People** directed by Tyrone Guthrie at Old Vic. The headline in *The Times* was "Ibsen's Tremendous Metaphor for Sewage" which didn't help the Box Office. The returns were the lowest the Old Vic could remember.

Feb 22. Ralph Richardson and Edna Best in J B Priestley's **Johnson Over Jordan** directed by Basil Dean at New. Modern morality play offered three phases in the life after death of a 50-year-old businessman: *1)* at the office, an expressionistic nightmare, *2)* at a nightclub, acted in sinister masks, *3)* at an inn, and all very sentimental. Richardson was perfect casting for Johnson. The play divided critics and public and was withdrawn after only 16 nights, only to get an instant reprieve and transfer to Saville.
—What's the use of my wasting my time writing like plays like this? For two pins I'll never write another play in my life. J B PRIESTLEY *Sunday Pictorial*

Feb 22. Official visit of the Comedie Française. The season included Molière's **L'école des maris**, Alfred de Musset's **Le Chandelier**, Jean Francois Regnard's **Le Légataire Universal** and Alfred de Musset's **A quoi revent les jeunes Filles**.
— [M. Ledoux in *Légataire Univeral*;] played with an extravagance that in less gifted hands would have been intolerable, his coughs were as piercing as sirens, his legs revolved beneath him, suspicion, avarice, fear, love of power, and sly lasciviousness exuded from his rheumy eyes and flappy cheeks – a more ferocious caricature of old age could not be imagined. *New Statesman and Nation*

Mar 1. Alexander Knox, Constance Cummings, Patrick Barr and Irene Vanbrugh in Benn W Levy's **The Jealous God** directed by Ben W Levy at Lyric. What is the proper reaction in the event of war: pacifism or participation?

Mar 2. Louise Hampton in Karel Capek's **The Mother** adapted and directed by Miles Malleson at Garrick. The invasion of a small European country by a fascist state forces the mother's four sons to choose between her and Mother Country. One by one they go off to war and death. The dead were still able to commune with the living. With World War 2 just about to start, Capek's harrowing tragedy was particularly timely.
—Louise Hampton as the mother draws pity out of anguish but saves the audience from the embarrassment of pain. It is her best performance to date; but then, it is her best opportunity to date. HERBERT FARJEON *Bystander*

Mar 8. Vic Oliver, Frances Day and Max Wall in George Black's **Black and Blue** directed by Robert Nesbitt at London Hippodrome. Twice-nightly revue billed as an intimate musical rag.
—[Frances Day] is the ideal revue artist. She has everything for the part: glamour, comedy, high spirits, a mischievous sense of burlesque and the ability to make men of all ages sit up and take notice. *The Times*

Ralph Richardson (second left) in the nightclub in Johnson Over Jourdan

Mar 19. The Incorporated Stage Society. David Markham as Bridegroom, Vera Lindsay as Bride, Martita Hunt as Mother and Selma Vaz Dias as Death in Fedirico Garcia Lorca's **Marriage of Blood** directed by Michel Saint-Denis at Savoy. The story was inspired by a newspaper account of a bride, who on her wedding day, ran off with her former lover, a married man. The Bride ("a woman on fire") explains her action by likening her virginal Bridegroom to "a single drop of water" and her lover to "a dark big river."

Mar 21. Michael Redgrave, Helen Haye, Catherine Lacey and Henzie Raeburn in T S Eliot's **The Family Reunion** directed by E Martin Browne at Westminster. Eliot's Modern Greek tragedy, based on the legend of Orestes, is set in an English drawing-room. Harry, returning home after eight years, is a man possessed, contaminated by some terrible disease and locked in some unspeakable horror he cannot either understand or escape. The curse on his family cannot be expiated until Harry knows what he has to expiate. (He may or he may not have murdered his wife.) Eliot thought Harry was an insufferable prig. "The play has a magnificent compulsion," said *The Times*. "A great achievement," said *The New Statesman and Nation*. Elliott was his own best critic: "The deepest flaw of all was the failure of adjustment between the Greek story and the modern situation. I should have either stuck closer to Aeschylus or else taken a great deal more liberty with his myth."

Mar 23. Ivor Novello, Mary Ellis, Roma Beaumont and Olive Gilbert in Ivor Novello's musical **The Dancing Years** directed by Leontine Sagan at Drury Lane. Lyrics by Christopher Hassall. The anti-Nazi sentiments were removed. Ellis played a prima donna. Novello played a composer. The songs included "Waltz of My Heart" and "My Dearest Dear". Beaumont stopped the show when she sang "Primrose". "In every way Ivor Novello's best work for the theatre," said *The Daily Sketch*. "A triumph of craftsmanship", said *The Daily Telegraph*.

Apr 12. John Mills, Niall MacGinnis and Clare Luce in John Steinbeck's **Of Mice and Men** directed by Norman Marshall at Gate. Originally called *Something That Happened* and conceived as a play in novella form, it was set during the American Depression when up to 15 million people were out of work and the American Dream had gone sour. George and Lennie are two migrant labourers in California. Lennie, a huge, mentally retarded man, is unable to take care of himself and is easily frightened. Essentially kind, he doesn't know his own strength and accidentally kills the things he loves best. George, his minder, never stops complaining about having to look after him, but he needs Lennie as much as Lennie needs him. A powerful and moving production moved to a strong climax when George kills Lennie before the lynch-mob can kill him. Transferred to Apollo.

—If John Mills, whom I have seen in a short space of time in revue, musical comedy, farce and classic comedy, is not one of the most versatile actors of the day, then I have no notion what acting is. A E WILSON *Star*

Apr 20. Karen Peterson, Emily Ross, Mary Alice Collins, Claire Carleton and Effie Afton in Claire Boothe Luce's **The Women** directed by Gilbert Miller with assistance of Lewis Allen at Lyric. Wisecracking American comedy. The special gimmick was that there wasn't a man in sight. The sentimental bits were hard to take. The moralising about swallowing one's pride ("it's a luxury no woman in love can afford") was at a woman's magazine level, but when the women were being their sour, cynical, spoiled, bitchy selves, the comedy had a splendid High Camp vulgarity.

Apr 21. Cyril Ritchard, Hermione Baddeley, Joyce Grenfell and George Benson in Herbert Farjeon's **The Little Revue** at Little. Grenfell's monologues, gentle but deadly in their accuracy, were recognised as the best things of their kind since Ruth Draper.

Apr 23. Robertson Hare and Alfred Drayton in Ben Travers's **Spotted Dick** directed by Ralph Lynn at Strand. Farce. Hare appeared without his trousers crying "O, Purgatory! O, Pandemonium!".

Jun 19. Royal Theatre Company of Greece at His Majesty's Catina Paxinou in Sophocles's **Electra** directed by Rondiris. Helen Papadaki as Clytemnestra. Acted in Greek.
—Madame Paxinou needs no other variety than her voice and the astonishingly expressiveness of her body. She proved again and again a majestic actress with that magnetism and above all that discipline, which in any mood draws an audience to her and holds it in unfailing expectancy. *The Times*

Jun 20. Robert Eddison in Shakespeare's **Pericles** directed by Robert Atkins in Regent's Park.

Jun 21. Catherine Lacey, Robert Harris and Martin Walker in Terence Rattigan's **After the Dance** directed by Michael Macowan at St James's. An attack on the Bright Young Things of the 1920s and Noël Coward in particular.

Jun 27. Alec Guinness in W H Auden and Christopher Isherwood's **The Ascent of F 6** directed by Rupert Doone at Old Vic. Guinness, as the leader of the expedition, emphasised the character's psychological likeness to T E Lawrence, a role he would play twenty-one years later in Terence Rattigan's *Ross*.

John Mills and Nial MacGinniss in **Of Mice and Men**

—The play is full, of challenge and sensitive perception but leaves at the end an impression of work, which, though, brilliantly written, lacks unity for the plain reason that its implications have not been fully thought out, selected and assembled. *The Times*

Jun 28. John Gielgud in Shakespeare's **Hamlet** at Lyceum. Fay Compton as Ophelia. Laura Cowie as Gertrude. Jack Hawkins as Claudius and Ghost. George Howe as Polonius. Harry Andrews as Laertes. Glen Byam Shaw as Horatio. Transferred to Elsinore.

Jul 1. Lyceum closed down.

Jul 5. Margaretta Scott, John Clements and Frederick Valk in Sidney Howard's **Alien Corn** directed by Henry Cass at Wyndham's. Chekhovian pastiche: two unhappy love affairs on an American campus.

Jul 20. Harcourt Williams as Faustus and Frank Napier as Mephistopheles in Dorothy L Sayers's **The Devil to Pay** directed by Harcourt Williams transferred from Canterbury to His Majesty's. Faustus is in Purgatory. The verse was not equal to the drama.
—Mr Napier repeats his extraordinary skilful performance which ranges from guttersnipe impudence to utter misery. *The Times*
—The piece should be acted in one of two ways – either by rank amateurs or by blazing geniuses. What it will not stand is professional competence. JAMES AGATE *Sunday Times*

Aug 7. Leslie French and Robert Eddison in J M Bridie's **Tobias and the Angel** directed by Robert Atkins at Open Air Theatre, Regent's Park. French's Tobias was impish, roguish, and good humoured. Eddison's archangel, travelling incognito, had dignity and charm.

Aug 16. John Gielgud's production of Oscar Wilde's **The Importance of Being Earnest** revived at Globe with the following changes of cast: Jack Hawkins as Algernon, Gwen Ffrangcon-Davies as Gwendolen and George Howe as Chasuble.

Sep 2. All theatres closed on outbreak of war.

Sep 14. Some theatres reopened.

Oct 2. The Old Vic moved to Streatham Hill for a season: Robert Donat and Constance Cummings in Shakespeare's **Romeo and Juliet** directed by Murray Macdonald. *The Times* found Donat wonderfully romantic. *The Daily Telegraph* said he didn't look romantic at all.

Oct 3. Old Vic at Streatham Hill. Robert Donat as Old Croaker in Oliver Goldsmith's **The Good Natur'd Man** directed by Tyrone Guthrie.

Oct 4. Old Vic at Streatham Hill. Robert Donat as Dick Dudgeon, Stewart Granger as Pastor Anderson and André Morell as General Burgoyne in Bernard Shaw's **The Devil's Disciple** directed by Esmé Church.
—Looking boyishly Byronic, he [Robert Donat] had the right kind of hard intellectual mischief which saves the romantic drama from being merely romantic. IVOR BROWN *Manchester Guardian*

Oct 10. Old Vic at Streatham Hill. Constance Cummings in Bernard Shaw's **Saint Joan** directed by Esmé Church. Andrew Cruickshank as Warwick. Hubert Harben as Inquisitor. André Morell as Bishop of Beauvais. Stewart Granger as Dunois. Max Adrian was a sly, effeminate, mean and malicious Dauphin.
—Her [Celia Johnson] gallantry has more the flourish of a Peter Pan out to discomfort pirates than that of a great patriot and soldier set on a mission she believes divine. *The Times*

Oct 10. Robert Harris, Stephen Murray, Jean Cadell, Catherine Lacey and Michael Denison in J B Priestley's **Music at Night** directed by Michael Macowan at Westminster. The three acts are represented by the three movements of a concerto during which the characters revealed their innermost secrets.

Oct 11. Flanagan and Allen, Nervo and Knox, Naughton and Gold in **The Little Dog Laughed** directed by George Black at Palladium.

Nov 1. Noël Howlett, Irene Brown, Arthur Macrae and Jane Baxter in Gerald Savory's **George and Margaret** at Piccadilly. Irene Handl made her name as the maid. "Flippant and trivial it may be," said *The Times*, "but it is brilliantly and unfailingly true to its standards of flippancy and triviality."

Nov 14. Vic Oliver, Pat Kirkwood and Roma Beaumont in **Black Velvet** directed by Robert Nesbitt under the personal supervision of George Black at London Hippodrome. Revue.

Nov 15. Gordon Harker in Frank Harvey's **Saloon Bar** directed by Richard Bird at Wyndham's. Harker was in his element in this effective mixture of crook play and cockney wit.

Nov 21. Jill Esmond, Eric Berry and George Relph in Elmer Rice's **Judgment Day** directed by Murray Macdonald at Phoenix. Timely revival of the 1937 production.

Dec 7. Marius Goring as Pip, Yvonne Mitchell as Estella, Martita Hunt as Miss Havisham and Alec Guinness as Herbert Pocket in Charles Dickens's **Great Expectations** adapted by Alec Guinness and directed by George Devine at Rudolph Steiner Hall. Martita Hunt and Alec Guinness repeated their definitive performances in David Lean's 1946 classic film.

Dec 12. Mary Clare and Mary Merrall in Edward Percy and Reginald Denham's **Ladies in Retirement** directed by Reginald Denham at St James's. The play was not a who-done-it? but a will-she-get-away-with-it? A paid companion-housekeeper strangles her wealthy employer, a retired chorus girl, who is living off the money she got from her former lovers. The murderess wants the money in order to buy a home for her poor sisters. The story was based on a true French murder case of the late 19th century.

Dec 20. Beatrice Lillie, Fred Emney, Adele Dixon and Bobby Howes in **All Clear** directed by Harold French at Queen's. Revue. Beatrice Lillie, in her role of world-weary diva with a taste for jewellery, sang Noël Coward's "Weary of it All".

Dec 21. Sydney Howard, Vera Pearce, Arthur Riscoe and Richard Hearne in Douglas Furber's **Shephard's Pie** at Princes. Revue. High spot: Hearne wrestling with a trombone.

Dec 23. Diana Wynyard, Anton Walbrook and Alan Webb in Noël Coward's **Design for Living** directed by Noël Coward at Savoy.

Dec 23. Max Miller, Bebe Daniels and Ben Lyons in **Haw Haw!** directed by George Black at Holborn Empire. Broad comedy. Broad comedy sketches.

Cecil Parker, Margaret Rutherford, Fay Compton and Kay Hammond in Blithe Spirit

1940–1949

1940

Jan 11. Stanley Lupino and Florence Desmond in **Funny Side Up** directed by Stanley Lupino at His Majesty's. Twice-nightly revue.
—She [Florence Desmond] is an actress who can play the fool with gusto and then turn round on her heel and remind the audience that she can act. *The Times*

Jan 12. Edward Chapman and Diana Churchill in Hugh Mills and Wells Root's **As You Are** directed by Claud Gurney at Aldwych. Domestic warfare plus a gadget which revolutionises the manufacture of ladies' underwear. Transferred to Whitehall.

Jan 24. Beatrix Lehmann as Abbie, Mark Dignam as Ephraim and Stephen Murray as Eben in Eugene O'Neill's **Desire under the Elms** directed by Henry Cass at Westminster. Land-greed, lust and murder in New England in 1850. First public performance following a 15-year ban.
—The Westminster is now almost the only theatre in London not given over to frivolous nit-wittery. PHILIP PAGE *Daily Mail*

Feb-Mar. Lunchtime Shakespeare at Kingsway. The performance lasted an hour and Donald Wolfit acted scenes from Shakespeare's plays. He played Othello, Shylock, Malvolio, Hamlet, Benedict and Petruchio. His finest comedy performance was as Ben Jonson's Volpone.
—To launch such a season as this at such a moment is a splendidly brave, if not hazardous thing to do, and that there are circumstances when even mediocrity deserves a pat on the back. PHILIP PAGE *Daily Mail*
—It is surprising how much of the plays can be given in the short space of an hour, and how few of the finest passages are missed. *Theatre World*
—Mr Wolfit turns the whole play [Macbeth] into a ranting, roaring, Saturday night melodrama, full of sound and fury but signifying nothing of the play's pity and melancholy. JAMES AGATE *Sunday Times*
—Mr Wolfit sustains a performance [Macbeth] unwavering in its excitement and its hold upon the mighty line. J C TREWIN *Observer*
—A soft-spoken, touchingly simple Moor [Othello] who at the very height of his frenzy suggests that he is listening to his own voice. He is never formidable. *The Times*
—[Othello] Mr Wolfit is not among the very small number of actors who can black their faces and retain their dignity. His first act the other night only wanted a banjo to suggest Margate. JAMES AGATE *Sunday Times*

Feb 9. Evelyn Laye, Clifford Mollison, Martyn Green, Doris Hare and James Hayter in **Lights Up**, a revue by Ronald Jeans directed by Charles B Cochran at Savoy. Music by Noel Gay. Laye sang "With A Song in My Heart".

Feb 21. Angela Baddeley and Godfrey Tearle in Emlyn Williams's **The Light of Heart** directed by Emlyn Williams at Apollo. Aged alcoholic actor, living in squalor, takes to the bottle just before the first night of his return to the stage in *King Lear*. Megs Jenkins played a stage-struck gallery girl. When Tearle left the cast Williams rewrote the role for himself.

Mar 5. Michael Redgrave as Macheath, Audrey Mildmay as Polly and Linda Gray as Lucy in John Gay's **The Beggar's Opera** directed by John Gielgud at Haymarket. Gielgud, inspired by the early drawings of George Cruickshank, gave Gay a Dickensian update. Redgrave in his first singing role was not up to the singing. Gielgud thought his performance lacked humour and breadth. *The Bystander* thought there was too much Gielgud and too little Gay.

Mar 7. Edith Evans, Peggy Ashcroft and Alec Guinness in Clemence Dane's **Cousin Muriel** directed by Norman Marshall at Globe. Evans was miscast as Muriel, a liar, forger, cheat and kleptomaniac. Guinness played her son unfairly tarred with the same brush. Ashcroft played the girl he wanted to marry.

Mar 19. Jessie Matthews and Sonnie Hale in **Come Out to Play** directed by Sonnie Hale at Phoenix. Song, dance, comedy Show.

Mar 20. Derek Oldham, Nita Croft and Hal Bryan in **White Horse Inn** directed by Prince Littler at Coliseum. Musical. Book and lyrics by Harry Graham. Music by Ralph Benatzky and Robert Stoltz. Twice daily. Dairy maids and real water, real doves and real goats.

Apr 3. Barbara Mullen, Eric Portman and Albert Lieven in Aimee Stuart's **Jeannie** directed by Irene Hentschell at Wyndham's. Young Scottish woman has to choose between a romantic count and a stolid middle-aged Yorkshire man.

Apr 5. Celia Johnson as Rebecca, Owen Nares as Maxim de Winter and Margaret Rutherford as Mrs Danvers in Daphne du Maurier's **Rebecca** directed by George Devine at Queen's. The production opened at the same time as the release of Alfred Hitchcock's film. Rutherford, unexpectedly cast as the sinister housekeeper, generated uncanny menace. The run was curtailed when the theatre was bombed.

Cathleen Nesbitt, Fay Compton, John Gielgud and Jessica Tandy in **King Lear**

Apr 11. **New Faces** directed by Hedley Briggs at Comedy. Revue. Judy Campbell sang "A Nightingale Sang in Berkeley Square" and "Paris is Not the Same".

Apr 15. John Gielgud in Shakespeare's **King Lear** directed by Lewis Casson and Harley Granville Barker at Old Vic. Fay Compton as Regan. Cathleen Nesbitt as Goneril. Jessica Tandy as Cordelia. Jack Hawkins as Edmund. Robert Harris as Edgar. Stephen Haggard as Fool. Lewis Casson as Kent. Andrew Cruickshank as Cornwall. "Lear should be an oak," said Barker to Gielgud. "You'll never be that, but we might make something of you as an ash."
—The Olympian grandeur, the frets, the rages, the madness lit with savage irony and broken in upon by spiritual illumination – all these phases of the part he succeeded in treating as though they were a spontaneous product of the mind, but the simplicities of the end he surrounded with a stillness of beauty which is rarely achieved on the stage. *The Times*

Apr 17. Leslie Henson, Binnie Hale, Cyril Ritchard, Stanley Holloway, Carroll Gibbons and Patricia Burke in **Up and Doing** directed by Leslie Henson and Robert Nesbitt at Saville. Revue. High spot was a send-up of striptease with enormous ostrich feathers.

Apr 23. Mary Alice Collins, Meriel Forbes, Tucker McGuire, Gwynne Whitby and Kathleen Boutall in Clare Booth Luce's **The Women** directed by Peter Mather at Strand. Cynical and acrid American comedy: The women's conversation is all about men; and there's not a man to be seen.

May 9. Ernest Thesiger, Irene Vanbrugh, Herbert Lomas and Cecil Trouncer in Bernard Shaw's **In Good King Charles's Days** directed by H K Ayliff transferred from Malvern Festival to New. Subtitled *A True History That Never Happened*. Isaac Newton is interrupted in his studies by a number of visitors, including the king, the king's brother James, George Fox, the founder of the Quakers, and the painter Godfrey Knellner. They sit around and chat about anything that comes into Shaw's head: science, religion, the arts, astronomy, the Church, the age of the earth. The king's two mistresses, (the Duchess of Portsmouth, the Duchess of Cleveland) and Nell Gwynn, drop in to relieve the intellectual tension and provide a bit of sexual bickering. Shaw, 83 years old, said his intention was to rehabilitate the reputation of Charles II. He portrayed the king (Ernest Thesiger might have sat for Sir Peter Lely) as a shrewd politician, a man of taste and, contrary to public opinion, the best of husbands.
—The characters are mature and brilliantly drawn, each full of his own idiosyncrasy, each stamped with the ineradicable lines of life ... The skill with which GBS seizes on the essential characteristics of these men and women is extraordinary. ST JOHN ERVINE *Bernard Shaw: His Life, Works and Friends*

1940 World Premieres

New York
Robert E Sherwood's *There Shall Be No Night*
Rodgers and Hart's *Pal Joey*
James Thurber's *The Male Animal*

Paris
Jean Anouilh's *Leocadia*

Births

Trevor Nunn, British director

Deaths

Mikhail Bulgakov (b. 1891), Russian playwright, novelist
Vsevold Meyerhold, Russian actor and director, tortured and murdered in prison

Notes

—ENSA (The Entertainment National Service Association also known as "Every Night Something Awful") organised tours
—The Windmill Theatre never closed

History

—Winston Churchill became Prime Minister
—Evacuation of Dunkirk
—Battle of Britain
—Italy declared war on Britain
—Trotsky assassinated in Mexico

—Mr Thesiger is too powerful a personality to make a plausible Charles. He fails to suggest gusto; and the melancholy too often is petulance, the wit a sneer. But he is always an intelligent actor. DESMOND MCCARTHY *New Statesman and Nation*

May 22. Hermione Gingold, Madge Elliott, Robert Helpmann and Peter Ustinov in **Swinging the Gate** directed by Norman Marshall at Ambassadors. Revue. Gingold played a Bacchante on Streatham Common. Ustinov gave an impression of a Bach recital in Huddersfield.

May 29. John Gielgud as Prospero in Shakespeare's **The Tempest** directed by George Devine and Marius Goring at Old Vic. Goring as Ariel. Jack Hawkins as Caliban. Jessica Tandy as Miranda. Alec Guinness as Ferdinand. Gielgud's Renaissance Prospero, virile, scholarly and lightly bearded, looked as if he had just stepped out of El Greco's *The Agony in the Garden*.

Jul 2. Lyn Harding, Rosalinde Fuller, Dennis Noble and Jerry Verno in revival of **Chu Chin Chow** directed by Robert Atkins at Palace. Not as spectacular as the 1916 production.

Jul 18. Robertson Hare and Alfred Drayton in Vernon Sylvaine's **Women Aren't Angels** directed by Richard Bird at Strand. Farce. Hare wore a kilt, which, to nobody's surprise, regularly fell down.

Jul 24. Robert Donat as Dick Dugeon, Roger Livesey as Pastor Anderson and Milton Rosmer as General Burgoyne in Bernard Shaw's **The Devil's Disciple** directed by Milton Rosmer at Piccadilly. Donat stormed the barn.

July 27. Francis L Sullivan as Bottom in Shakespeare's **A Midsummer Night's Dream** directed by Robert Atkins at the Open Air Theatre.

Jul 30. Michael Redgrave, Frederick Valk, Selma Vaz Dias, Bernard Miles, Fredda Brilliant and Rosalind Atkinson in Robert Ardrey's **Thunder Rock** directed by Herbert Marshall at Globe. Embittered isolationist retires to a lighthouse where he meets the ghosts of a group of immigrants who were shipwrecked in a storm in the 19th century. They give him the will to return to society and face up to the war. Ardrey's propaganda parable, written when Britain was in danger of being invaded by the Nazis, was designed to bring America into World War 2. "A tonic to the mind and a bath to the spirit," said Alan Dent in *The News Chronicle*.

Jul 31. Leslie Banks, Alastair Sim and Gillian Lind in Geoffrey Kerr's **Cottage to Let** directed by Richard Bird at Wyndham's. First spy-thriller of the war. Sim played a Nazi agent intent on kidnapping a famous scientist. He was foiled by a 14-year-old evacuee (child actor George Cole).

Sep 5. Peter Glenville as Oedipus and Jeanne de Casalis as Jocasta in Jean Cocteau's **The Infernal Machine** designed by Oliver Messel and directed by Charlotte Frances at Arts. English version by Carl Wildman. Cocteau rewrote the classical legend to show that modern life was grotesque, decadent and banal. De Casilis was most at ease when Cocteau was being least serious. "No classical tragedy can bear so much sprightly modernistic decoration," said *The Times*, "without suffering some abatement of tragic temper."

Sep 9. Bombing of London began in earnest.
—The management is not liable for the safety of the audience in any consequence arising from acts of war. In the event of an air-raid warning during the performance, the audience will be informed from the stage, and those who so desire will be conducted by attendants to the vaults under the theatre, or to other shelters of which there are four within a few

yards of the theatre – but the Play will go on. *Note in Westminster Theatre programme*

Oct 28. Edith Evans, Dorothy Dickson, Joyce Grenfell, George Benson and Peter Ustinov in **Diversion** devised by Herbert Farjeon and directed by George Benson at Wyndham's. Revue. Matinees only. Evans appeared as Elizabeth 1. Ustinov appeared as a raddled Austro-Hungarian prima donna called Madame Liselotte Beethoven-Finck.

Dec 23. Lunchtime Shakespeare at Strand. Donald Wolfit as Falstaff in Shakespeare's **The Merry Wives of Windsor**. Irene and Violet Vanbrugh as the wives. Both actresses were in their seventies. The sub-plot was cut and the play lasted an hour and a quarter. It was a great success.

Dec 24. Jean Forbes-Robertson and Andre van Gysenghem in John L Balderston and J C Squire's **Berkeley Square** directed by Andre van Gysenghem at Vaudeville. Forbes Robertson acted the girl with exquisite, mystic sensibility.

1941

Jan 1. Edith Evans, Dorothy Dickson, Joyce Grenfell, Bernard Miles, Peter Ustinov, Walter Crisham, Vida Hope and Derek Bogaerde (later known as Dirk Bogarde) in Herbert Farjeon's **Diversion 2** directed by Walter Crisham at Wyndham's. Revue. Ustinov imitated three different directors tackling *King Lear*: the continental with a sense of mission, the Communist doctrinaire and the semi-precious. "An oasis of pungency in a theatre-starved city," said *The Daily Herald*.
—Like a high explosive bomb, Miss Grenfell leaves no institution she touches quite the same. GRAHAM GREENE *Spectator*

Jan. The one-hour lunch-time performances of Shakespeare at Strand made Donald Wolfit a national figure. He played scenes from Shakespeare's plays and his roles included Touchstone, Othello, Richard III, Hamlet, Shylock, Petruchio, Othello, Bottom and Giovanni in *'Tis Pity She's A Whore*.
—Mr Donald Wolfit's Hamlet has always been interesting. It strikes me as being more tense, and, at times, madder than ever. All that he occasionally lacks is poetic value. *Daily Mail*

Jan 20. John Gielgud, Margaret Rawlings, Muriel Pavlow, Roger Livesey, Leon Quartermaine, Ronald Ward and George Howe in Dodie Smith's **Dear Brutus** directed by John Gielgud at Globe. Matinees only. Wartime audiences found the whimsy hard to take. Gielgud (who played the painter who meets the child he had always wanted but never had) didn't feel he was as good as George du Maurier who had created the role.
—To the notorious and unremunerative part of Dearth, Mr Gielgud has devoted his immense talent – nobody could make it more plausible. GRAHAM GREENE *Spectator*

Feb 25. Cyril Cusack in Robert Ardrey's **Thunder Rock** directed by Charlotte Frances at St Martin's.

Mar 5. Max Miller, Florence Desmond and Vera Lynn in George Black's **Apple Sauce** directed by Charles Henry at Palladium. Revue. Vera Lynn, billed as "Radio's Sweet Singer of Sweet Songs", would become the Forces' sweetheart.
—Miss Vera Lynn's singing may be a trifle sugary to a sophisticated palate but they are of a kind that simple sailors and soldiers home on leave like to hum. *The Times*

Mar 27. Diana Wynyard, Rex Harrison, Lilli Palmer and Elizabeth Welch in S N Behrman's **No Time for Comedy** directed by Harold French at Haymarket. The slanging match between two women over a suave, boorish charmer made for slick, glossy, mechanical comedy.

May 5. Bobby Howes, Arthur Riscoe, Vera Pearce and Richard Hearne in **Shephard's Pie** directed by Douglas Furber at Princes. Revue. Howes sang "If I Only Had Wings". Hearne danced the Lancers single-handed. Riscoe gave an imitation of Hitler.

May 19. Old Vic damaged during an air raid.

May 20. Leslie Henson, Binnie Hale, Stanley Holloway and Cyril Ritchard in **Up and Doing** directed by Leslie Henson and Robert Nesbitt at Saville. Revue. "Rattling bouncing nonsense," said *The Times*. The sketch which got the biggest laugh was a send-up of striptease.

Jun 5. Hermione Baddeley, Hermione Gingold, Walter Crisham, Henry Kendall and Wilfred Hyde-White in **Rise Above It** directed by Henry Kendall at Comedy. Revue. Lyrics and music by Leslie Julian Jones. Baddeley and Gingold together for the first time. The most popular sketch was Queeries, a send-up of war-time concert parties, "one of the major horrors of modern warfare."

1941 World Premieres

New York

Lillian Hellman's *Watch on the Rhine.*

Joseph Kesselring's *Arsenic and Old Lace*

Moss Hart, Ira Gershwin and Kurt Weill's *Lady in the Dark*

Zurich

Bertolt Brecht's *Mother Courage*

Notes

—The Commons declined to approve the government's proposal to permit entertainments on Sundays for the benefit of the Services and industrial workers.

History

—Germany invaded Soviet Union
—Japan bombed Pearl Harbor
—USA declared war on Japan
—All Jews in Germany required to wear yellow star
—Premiere of Orson Welles's film, *Citizen Kane*

Jul 2. Fay Compton, Kay Hammond, Cecil Parker and Margaret Rutherford in Noël Coward's **Blithe Spirit** directed by Noël Coward at Piccadilly. The daily prospect of imminent death concentrated the mind. Coward's light comedy, one of his most popular plays, was written in five days at the height of the Blitz and produced six weeks later. It ran for four and a half years and 1,997 performances, a record then for a straight play. On the first night there were cries of "Rubbish!" Graham Greene thought the play "a weary exhibition of bad taste." The Church disapproved of its flippancy but *Blithe Spirit's* phenomenal success was precisely because it did take a flippant view of mortality and because it also held out a hope of life after death and reunion with loved ones. Coward always took great pride in the fact that he had made no corrections and that only two lines of the original script were ultimately cut. The situation, with first one dead wife and then two dead wives, is excellent, but it would have been a better play had he been more ruthless. The comedy is over-long, repetitive and short on witty lines. Madame Arcati, the eccentric, bicycle-riding medium (based on the novelist and playwright, Clemence Dane) is one of those roles which is forever identified with one actress. Rutherford's definitive performance is preserved in Anthony Asquith's film and it comes as a surprise to learn that she had initially turned down the role, which had been written specially for her. She was a believer in spiritualism and did not wish to mock mediums. The part of the sexy first wife, sly, wicked, irresponsible and incorrigibly selfish, was created by Kay Hammond whose diaphanous performance is also preserved on film. Coward never liked Asquith's film, dismissing it as "a coloured photograph."

—If there are suggestions of bad taste, they are swamped by the delicious fun of it all, by the immaculate production and by fine performances. PHILIP PAGE *Daily Mail*

Jul 7. Ernest Milton and Sybil Thorndike in **King John** directed by Tyrone Guthrie and Lewis Casson at New. The English and French kings wrangling over Angiers reminded wartime audiences of Hitler and Stalin.

Jul 16. Sybil Thorndike in Euripides's **Medea** directed by Lewis Casson at New. The production toured the Welsh mining villages.

—Dame Sybil has the russet majesty of a tremendous oak through which the winds of tragedy are sighing. IVOR BROWN *Observer*

Jul 18. Madge Elliott, Betty Ann Davies, Charles Hawtrey, Joan Swinstead and Ernest Thesiger in **The New Ambassadors Revue** directed by Cyril Ritchard at Ambassadors.

Jul 22. Marjorie Fielding, George Thorpe, Frank Cellier, Michael Wilding and Glynis Johns in Esther McCracken's **Quiet Week-end** directed by Richard Bird at Wyndham's. Sequel to McCracken's *Quiet Wedding*. 1059 performances.

—Its real charm lies in the contrast it presents to the life most of us are forced to live these days. This glimpse of a very human and typically English family week-ending it at their cottage in the country in peace-time has an appeal of almost fairy-tale quality. To see it is to vow never again to take the simple pleasures of life for granted. *Theatre World*

—Miss Glynis Johns has considerable talent but she needs to pay attention to her voice. What is now a forgivable mannerism may develop into a serious handicap. *New Statesman and Nation*

Jul 22. Jerry Verno as Ali-Baba in Oscar Asche's **Chu Chin Chow** directed by Robert Atkins at Palace.

July 24. Stanley Lupino, Pat Kirkwood and Sally Gray in Stanley Lupino's musical **Lady Behave** directed by Stanley Lupino at His Majesty's. Lyrics by Frank Eyton. Music by Edward Horan. Pre-war musical comedy set in a nightclub in Hollywood. High spot: Judy Campbell singing "Ordinary Man."

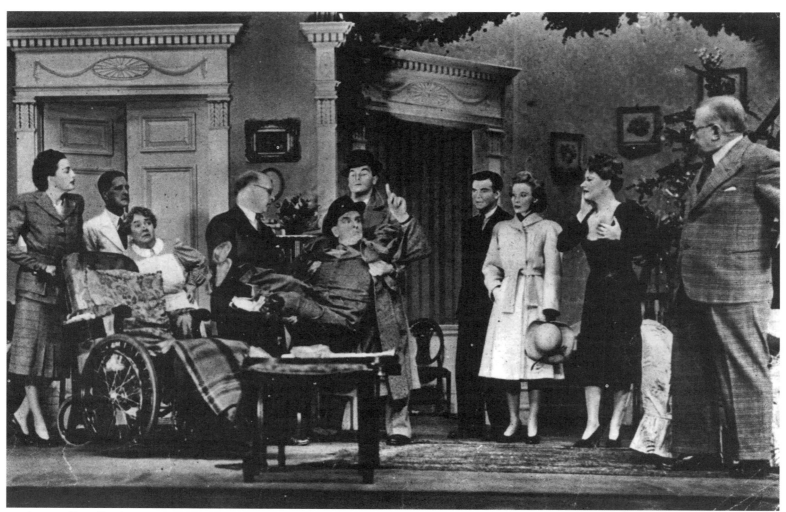

Coral Browne (far Left) and Robert Morley (being carried) in **The Man Who Came to Dinner**

Aug 1. Mary Clare, Nellie Bowman and Joan Kemp-Welch in Edward Percy and Reginald Denham's **Ladies in Retirement** directed by Mary Clare at St Martin's.

Aug 21. Sydney Howard, Arthur Riscoe, Vera Pearce and Richard Hearne in Douglas Furber's **Fun and Games** directed by Douglas Furber and Frank Collins at Princes. Revue.

Aug 28. Athene Seyler as Ranevesky and James Dale as Lopahin in Anton Chekhov's **The Cherry Orchard** directed by Tyrone Guthrie at New. Walter Hudd as Trofimov, Nicholas Hannen as Gaev. Rosalind Atkinson as Varya. Olive Layton as Anya. O B Clarence as Firs. James Donald as Yasha.
—It is a mark of Chekhov's genius that *The Cherry Orchard* can be enjoyed by Russian audiences as wild farce while English interpretation prefers sentimental comedy. *New Statesman and Nation*
—A very lovely performance by an actress [Athene Seyler] who has style at her finger tips and can catch the radiance of laughter shot with tears. AUDREY WILLIAMSON *Old Vic Drama*

Sep 21. Yvonne Arnaud in Marjorie Sharp's **The Nutmeg Tree** directed by Irene Hentschel at Lyric. Mother saves her 21-year-old daughter from an unsuitable marriage.
—No one will wish to pursue the question of probability when under the spell of Yvonne Arnaud's infectious chuckle and delicious humour. *Theatre World*

Oct 29. James Mason and Peggy Bryan in A J Cronin's **Jupiter Laughs** directed by James Mason at New. Embittered doctor is insufferably arrogant and callous in his relations with women. The girl he once loved was blown to bits by TNT in his laboratory. He goes off to China to do missionary work.

Nov 19. Vic Oliver in James Hadley Chase's **Get a Load of This** directed by Robert Nesbitt at London Hippodrome. A mixture of drug trafficking and lavish floor shows.

Nov 20. Richard Bird and Ann Todd in Kenneth Horne's **Love in a Mist** directed by Richard Bird at St Martin's. Farce. Bride and groom stranded in a bungalow on Exmoor fight for the only bed when another couple arrives.

Dec 4. Robert Morley and Coral Browne in George S Kaufman and Moss Hart's **The Man Who Came To Dinner** directed by Marcel Varnel at Savoy. Classic 1930s wisecracking American farce. Sheridan Whiteside, a popular writer and broadcaster, slips on an icy porch in the Mid-West, breaks a leg, and quarters himself on the unfortunate family. His visitors include Noël Coward, Harpo Marx, cockroaches, penguins, choirboys and 21 Chinese students. Whiteside, a selfish, petty, obnoxious monster, will do anything to ensure his secretary does not marry a local journalist. His long-suffering nurse, the endless butt of his rudeness and insults, decides to leave the profession. "I became a nurse because all my life, ever since I was a little girl, I was filled with the idea of serving a suffering humanity. After one month with you, Mr Whiteside, I am going to work in a munitions factory. From now on anything I can do to help exterminate the human race will fill me with the greatest pleasure." Sheridan Whiteside was based on drama critic Alexander Woollcott and the play is dedicated to him.

Dec 10. Emlyn Williams and Angela Baddeley in Emlyn Williams's **The Morning Star** directed by Emlyn Williams at Globe. Tribute to the courage and humour of Cockneys during the London Blitz. Williams seemed ill at ease. Gladys Henson, playing a charwoman, had the best role and the best notices. "She has," said *Theatre World*, "that rare gift of being able to make you laugh most when nearest to tears."

Dec 17. Bebe Daniels, Ben Lyon, Tommy Trinder, Anne Ziegler and Webster Booth in George Black's **Gangway** directed by Robert Nesbitt at London Palladium. Revue. Woe betide any latecomer when Trinder was on stage

Dec 18. Edith Evans, Marian Spencer and Muriel Pavlow in John Van Druten's **Old Acquaintance** directed by William Armstrong at Apollo. Two novelists: one, financially successful; the other artistically so.
—The world he [John van Druten] presents seems far away and long ago. Perhaps a recent series of explosions in the Pacific Ocean has blown some of them up; that would be no pity. IVOR BROWN *Punch*

Dec 23. Gordon Harker in Vernon Sylvaine's **Warn That Man** directed by Richard Bird at Garrick. Cockney stage doorkeeper tracks down Fifth Columnists.

Dec 24. Alastair Sim as Captain Hook in **Peter Pan** directed by Cecil King at Adelphi. Barbara Mullen as Peter. Joan Greenwood as Wendy. Sim, avuncular and balefully comic, was absolutely determined not to frighten the children.

Dec 24. Donald Wolfit as Bottom in Shakespeare's **A Midsummer Night's Dream** directed by Donald Wolfit at Strand.

Dec 26. Florence Desmond and Arthur Askey in Emil Littler's **Jack and Jill** directed by Frank Adey at Palace. Pantomime.

1942

Jan 6. Donald Wolfit Shakespeare Season at Strand and St James's included **The Merchant of Venice**, **Richard III** and **Hamlet**.
—Mr Donald Wolfit might be well advised to leave Hamlet alone. It is a part which he does credibly but not memorably. *The Times*
—His final "A horse! A horse! A horse! My kingdom for a horse!" is agony made vocal. JAMES AGATE *Sunday Times*

Mar 3. Donald Wolfit in Ben Jonson's **Volpone** directed by Donald Wolfit at St James's.
—Wolfit achieves Elizabethan gusto, pride, wit and fox-like subtlety of a high order; his Volpone, both sensual and miserly, is monumental. AUDREY WILLIAMSON *Theatre of Two Decades*

Mar 4. Cyril Cusack as Dubedat and Vivien Leigh as Jennifer in Bernard Shaw's **The Doctor's Dilemma** directed by Irene Hentschel at Haymarket. The commercial success was due to Leigh's success in *Gone with the Wind*. She looked like a portrait painted by John Singer Sargent. Cusack had a drink problem and John Gielgud replaced him.

Mar 14. Ivor Novello and Muriel Barron in Ivor Novello's musical **The Dancing Years** directed by Leontine Sagan at Adelphi. Lyrics by Christopher Hassell. Nostalgia for a pre-war world that had gone forever. Songs included "Waltz of My Heart", "I Can Give You the Starlight" and "My Life Belongs to You."
—Almost alone among our theatre men he [Ivor Novello] is able to devise shows that will fill the enormous playhouse, and he seems to be able to do it at will. *Daily Telegraph*
—In every way *The Dancing Years* is Ivor Novello's best work for the theatre. *Daily Sketch*

Mar 17. Richard Tauber as Franz Schubert in Rodney Ackland's **Blossom Time** directed by Robert Nesbitt at Lyric. Romantic escapism in Old Vienna. Schubert is in love and sings his own songs. Tauber could act as well as sing.

Mar 26. Constance Cummings and John Clements in Samson Raphaelson's **Skylark** directed by Benn W Levy and William Armstrong at Duchess. Husband pursues business career at expense of his wife.

Apr 1. Sylvia Cecil, Malcolm Keen, Sonnie Hale and Elsie Randolph in **The Maid of the Mountains** directed by Emil Littler at Coliseum. Musical. Book by Frederick Lonsdale. Music by Harold Fraser-Simpson. Lyrics by Harry Graham.

Apr 16. Jack Hulbert and Cicely Courtneidge in **Full Swing** directed by Jack Hulbert at Palace. Musical comedy by Arthur Macrae, Archie Menzies and Jack Hulbert. The sequel to *Under the Hat* offered the actors numerous opportunities for disguise.
—There is no comedian alive [Jack Hulbert] who can make the helplessness of a good man struggling with adversity more amusing. *The Times*

Apr 22. Diana Wynyard and Anton Walbrook in Lillian Hellman's **The Watch on the Rhine** directed by Emlyn Williams at Aldwych. Propaganda piece to get the Americans involved in the war in Europe. Daughter returns home after twenty years with her German husband, who is an important member of the Anti-Fascist underground movement. Her rich, Liberal family, dominated by an abrasively witty and selfish matriarch (Athene Seyler) has to be shocked out of their ignorance and insularity.

Apr 30. Leslie Henson, Stanley Holloway and Douglas Byng in **Fine and Dandy** devised by Jack Shepard and Robert Nesbitt at Saville. Revue. The biggest laugh was a skit on the BBC's Brains Trust, a popular radio show.

May 19. Robert Helpmann in his ballet version of **Hamlet** at Sadler's Wells. Music by Tchaikovsky. Design by Leslie Hurry. Margot Fonteyn as Ophelia. Hamlet's life is seen in flashback, at the moment of his death, taking as its starting point the legend: "For in that sleep of death what dreams may come." Not everybody thought it a striking success. "One can scarcely call it 'ballet'," said *The Dancing Times*.
—Robert Helpmann is choreographer, but it is mime, tableaux, and drama rather than ballet; so that it might be said that Robert Helpmann devised it, brilliantly combining beauty with a penetrating psychology, imagination with professional stagecraft. *Queen*
—It is to be hoped that having made this experiment the Wells will remember that when we go to see them we go to see dancing. *The Dancing Times*
—It is a first-rate piece of imaginative theatre, excitingly assembled, brilliantly decorated and appropriately tuned. IVOR BROWN *Observer*

May 20. Alec Clunes started his tenure as artistic director of the Arts Theatre with

John Gielgud and Gwen Ffrangcon-Davies in Macbeth

Lilly Kann and Julian Somers in his production of Clifford Odets's **Awake and Sing**. Jewish poverty in the Bronx. Richard Attenborough played the boy who wants to create a brave new Marxist world, a role created on Broadway by John Garfield. Transferred to Cambridge.

Jun 4. Hermione Baddeley, Hermione Gingold, Naughton Wayne and Walter Crisham and Elizabeth Welsh in **Sky High** directed by Walter Crisham at Phoenix. Revue. The high spot was Baddeley and Gingold as two mermaids in search of naval prey. Elizabeth Welsh sang "Jungle, Hold My Man".

Jun 24. Wanda Rotha as Sadie Thompson and G H Mulcaster as the Rev. Davidson in Somerset Maugham's **Rain** directed by Reginald Long at St Martin's. Plenty of hysterical frenzy from Rotha, but not nearly enough rain from the stage management. Mulcaster was inadequate.

Jul 6. Phyllis Dixey in **All's Fair** directed by Alfred Esdaile at Whitehall. Continuous revue from 2.00 to 9.00. Dixey, billed as "England's Queen of Glamour", went on to become a wartime phenomenon. Her shows, an astute combination of gentility, striptease and profit, were hugely popular with servicemen.

Jul 8. John Gielgud and Gwen Ffrangcon-Davies in Shakespeare's **Macbeth** directed by John Gielgud at Piccadilly. "I have the wrong face for Macbeth," said Gielgud. "The whole point about Macbeth is that he doesn't look like a man who sees ghosts. But I look as if I see ghosts all the time."
—Mr Gielgud can, we know, speak blank verse very finely; but often in this production one seemed to be listening to a cruel skit in a revue upon his mannerisms. ROGER MARVELL *New Statesman and Nation*

Jul 22. Frederick Valk in Shakespeare's **Othello** directed by Julius Gellner at New. Hermione Hannen as Desdemona. Freda Jackson as Emilia. Many critics thought that Valk, despite his Polish accent and unintelligibility, was the best Othello London had seen since Tomasso Salvini's savage performance, which had caused a sensation in 1875. Bernard Miles's volatile Iago was half-matador, half-Machiavelli.
—Valk's faults include insufficient pathos and excessive bulk. He is slow and German, the buffalo rather than the tiger. Not by any means an ideal Othello. But I repeat, all things considered, the best I have seen. JAMES AGATE *Sunday Times*

Jul 30. Linden Travers, Hartley Power, Robert Newton and Mary Clare in James Handley Chase's **No Orchids for Miss Blandish**, adapted and directed by Robert Nesbitt at Prince of Wales. Twice nightly at 5.15 and 7.45. Blandish was surrounded by hoodlums and degenerates. *The Times* thought that the non-squeamish would probably enjoy the brutality.

Aug 6. Jessie Matthews and Richard Hearne in Jerome Kern's musical **Wild Rose** devised and staged by Robert Nesbitt at Princes. Book and lyrics by Guy Bolton and Clifford Grey. A Cinderella story: a dishwasher becomes a famous dancer.
—Lovely melodies and a production of lavish, pre-war proportions are ingredients guaranteed to bring welcome forgetfulness of grim realities. *Theatre World*

Aug 13. Adrianne Allen, Phyllis Calvert, Kathleen Harrison, Jack Watling, Leslie Dwyer and George Cole in Terence Rattigan's **Flare Path** directed by Anthony Asquith at Apollo. Rattigan, an air-gunner in the RAF during the war, based his first serious play on his experiences at Biggin Hill. The scenes which made the most impact were those in which the characters watched the planes taking off and the scenes when they counted them as they returned.
—I was very much moved by the play. It is a masterpiece of understatement. But we are rather good at that, aren't we? WINSTON CHURCHILL *quoted by Daily Sketch*

Sep 3. John Mills and Bernard Miles in Mary Hayley Bell's **Men in Shadow** directed by John Mills and Bernard Miles at Vaudeville. English saboteurs, hiding in a loft of a disused mill in Occupied France, are infiltrated by a Nazi spy.

Sep 16. Evelyn Laye in Gustave Kerker's musical **Belle of New York** directed by Rodney Ackland at Coliseum. Musical. Book and lyrics by Hugh Morton. The singers hadn't got the pitch of the house on the first night.

Sep 17. Hugh Sinclair and Pamela Brown in Rose Franken's **Claudia** directed by William Armstrong at St Martin's. Claudia has a mother fixation. Her husband behaves with saintly fortitude.

Sep 30. Ivor Sheridan as Chopin in **Waltz without End** directed by Jack Buchanan at Cambridge. The show tried to do for Chopin what *Lilac Time* had done for Schubert, but Chopin's music doesn't lend itself to musical comedy.

Oct 6. Max Adrian, John Ruddock and Noël Willman in Peter Ustinov's **The House of Regrets** directed by Alec Clunes at Arts. Ustinov was nineteen when he wrote his tragi-comedy about Russian exiles living in West Kensington. Critics, who had seen his monologues at the Players' Theatre, thought he should have played all the roles.

Oct 8. Leslie Banks, Michael Redgrave, Walter Fitzgerald and Hugh Burden in Patrick Hamilton's **The Duke in Darkness** directed by Michael Redgrave at St James's. Verbose battle of wits in 16th century France. Who can fool whom and for how long? The Duke (Leslie Banks), imprisoned by his enemy for some fifteen years, has for the last five years been feigning madness as part of his plan to escape (a longterm policy). Redgrave played the Duke's crazed servant, a virtuoso exhibition of maudlin hysterics. Despite good notices the play failed. Redgrave thought it was too sombre for the times.

Oct 14. John Gielgud, Cyril Ritchard, Edith Evans, Gwen Ffrangcon-Davies, Peggy Ashcroft, Jean Cadell and J H Roberts in Oscar Wilde's **The Importance of Being Earnest** directed by John Gielgud at Phoenix.
—Miss Edith Evans as Lady Bracknell is the Koh-i-noor of this bediamonded and fine de siecle fairy tale. IVOR BROWN *Observer*

Oct 21. Fay Compton in Lillian Hellman's **The Little Foxes** directed by Emlyn Williams at Piccadilly. Classic melodrama, an indictment of American greed and racism. Hellman's took her title from the Book of Solomon: "Take us the foxes, the little foxes, that spoil the vines; for our vines have tender grapes." The characters, rich, vulgar, cynical, middle-aged opportunists, are willing to lie, steal, cheat, starve and even murder those who stand in their way. Two brothers want to sign a contract with a Chicago dealer to build a factory; but in order to clinch the deal they need their sister's husband's money. The brothers are no match for their sister. Mary Merrall played the abused wife and Richard Attenborough was her obnoxious son. The production suffered from arriving after William Wyler's definitive film version with Bette Davis in the role created by Tallulah Bankhead on Broadway.

Oct 22. Frances Day and Arthur Riscoe in Cole Porter's musical **Du Barry Was a Lady** directed by Richard Bird at His Majesty's. Book by Herbert Fields and B G De Sylva. Costumes by Berkeley Sutcliffe. Lavatory attendant in American night club dreams he is Louis XV and all his friends are members of the French court. Hit songs: "Do I love You?", "Friendship", and "Did You Evah?" Transferred to Phoenix.

Nov 7. Tommy Trinder in **Best Bib and Tucker** directed by George Black at Palladium. Revue. Trinder appeared in drag as Carmen Miranda.

Nov 12. Isabel Jeans, Ronald Squire and Barry Jones in Somerset Maugham's **Home and Beauty** directed by Val Gielgud at Playhouse. "However well served," said *The Times*, "flat champagne remains flat."

Nov 19. Bobby Howes, Joyce Barbour and Pat Kirkwood in Cole Porter's musical **Let's Face It** directed by George Black at London Hippodrome. Lyrics by Dorothy Fields. High spot was Howes singing and miming the seven ages of a recruit.
—It has no pretensions to style or wit, for though Mr Cole Porter has written the songs, the singers do not succeed in making their meaning clear, and the comedy for the most part is a happy-go-lucky affair. *The Times*

Dec 16. Owen Nares, Constance Cummings and Hartley Power in Robert E Sherwood's **The Petrified Forest** directed by Norman Marshall at Globe. The subject matter is the collapse of the individual, the rise of chauvinism and the threat of communism. The action is set in a God-forsaken gas station/diner in the wilds of Arizona during the Depression era. A failed poet is looking for something worth dying for. He finds it in a woman who reads Villon and dreams of escaping to Paris to become a painter. He makes out a will in her favour and then begs a notorious gangster to shoot him. The two men complement each other; both are ossified as the Petrified Forest. The poet belongs to a vanishing race ("I am one of the intellectuals!") The gangster ("the last great apostle of rugged individualism") is on the run after a massacre in Oklahoma City. The big surprise was that the role, which launched Humphrey Bogart's Hollywood career and typecast him as a gangster, should be so small. Sherwood's dialogue was long-winded and pretentious.
—The trouble with me is that I start with a big message and end up with nothing but good entertainment. I lost control of the idea. ROBERT E SHERWOOD

Dec 23. Lilian Braithwaite, Mary Jerrold and Naughton Wayne in Joseph Kesselring's **Arsenic and Old Lace** directed by Marcel Varnel at Strand. Two sweet maiden old ladies help lonely old gentlemen to find lasting peace with the help of their homemade elderberry wine laced with arsenic. Their brother, who is as mad as they are, thinks he is Teddy Roosevelt and is building the Panama Canal in the cellar and burying the corpses, under the impression they are Canal workers who have died of Yellow Fever. "Insanity," observes the aunts' nephew, "doesn't run in this family, it practically gallops." The nephew has a mad brother who has killed twelve people and has brought home a corpse to bury. He's on the run from the police and he's had plastic surgery and now looks like Boris Karloff. (On Broadway – nice touch this – he was actually played by Boris Karloff.) Legend has it that Kesselring wrote the comedy as a serious thriller and that the producers (Howard Lindsay and Russell Crowse) turned it into a farce. It was so successful – it ran on Broadway for 1,444 performances – that the release of the Frank Capra-Cary Grant film, made in 1941, had to be delayed, for contractual reasons, until 1944.

Dec 24. Alastair Sim as Captain Hook and Ann Todd as Peter in **Peter Pan** directed by Cecil King at Winter Garden.

1943

Jan 25. Donald Wolfit in Shakespeare's **King Lear** at St James's directed by Donald Wolfit.
—The best and maddest Lear we have ever set eyes on. ALAN DENT *Punch*

Jan 27. Donald Wolfit as Malvolio in Shakespeare's **Twelfth Night** directed by Donald Wolfit at St James's.

Feb 11. Michael Redgrave, Valerie Taylor, Ronald Squire in Ivan Turgenev's **A Month in the Country** adapted and directed by Emlyn Williams at St James's. The elegant, delicate production was over-dressed by Cecil Beaton. Taylor played Natalia on one note of brittle artificiality.

Feb 16. Frederick Valk as Shylock in Shakespeare's **The Merchant of Venice** directed by Esmé Church at New. Kay Bannerman as Portia. Valk had tremendous power and the speech, which began "Hath not a Jew eyes?" inevitably in 1943 became a rallying cry for all Jews against the Nazis. The rest of the play was pure fairy tale.

Mar 4. Madge Elliott and Cyril Ritchard in Franz Lehar's **The Merry Widow** directed by Jack Hylton at His Majesty's. Book by Victor Leon and Leo Stein, lyrics by George Groves as Baron Popoff, lyrics by Adrian Ross.
—Neither Miss Madge Elliott nor Mr Cyril Ritchard is sufficiently adept in the art of a former day to give the romance of Sonia and her harum-scarum prince the light, easy touch it requires. Both seem to bring to it the wrong kind of sophistication. *The Times*

Mar 11. Richard Attenborough as Pinkie, Dulcie Gray as Rose and Hermione Baddeley as Ida in Graham Greene's **Brighton Rock** directed by Richard Bird at Garrick. Greene's novel, a first-rate thriller set in a 1930s Brighton (a purgatory of gang-warfare, protection rackets and violence), is a psychological study of a Catholic mind. Pinkie, the 17-year-old, baby-faced gangster, is possessed by evil. ("A Catholic," said Greene, "is more capable of evil than anyone; because he believes in God, he is more in touch with the devil than other people.") Greene didn't like the stage version. There was an excellent film in 1947, directed by John Boulting, for which he wrote the screenplay. There were memorable repeat performances by Attenborough and by Baddeley as the beery, blowsy, brassy Ida, part avenging angel, part amateur detective.

Mar 12. Jimmy Nervo and Teddy Knox in **It's Foolish But It's Fun** directed by Frank C Marshall at Coliseum. Comedy, ballet and musical numbers.

Mar 16. Sonia Dresdel as Hedda, Walter Hudd as Tesman and Elwyn Brook-Jones as Judge Brack in Henrik Ibsen's **Hedda Gabler** directed by Walter Hudd at Mercury. Transferred to Westminster.
—Miss Sonia Dresdel is a coloratura, brilliant in her own way: she whispers too often and throws away lines in a piece where every syllable tells. But her movement and expression have the quick and radiant quality of a great player. IVOR BROWN *Observer*

Mar 18. Robert Donat as Captain Shotover, Isabel Jeans as Lady Utterword, Edith Evans as Hesione Hushabye and Deborah Kerr as Ellie in Bernard Shaw's **Heartbreak House** directed by John Burrell at Cambridge. Michael Relph's set owed its inspiration to James Tissot. Donat's make-up was inspired by Michelangelo's Ezekiel. Shaw didn't find him convincing as an old man and thought he should have played Hector. When Donat fell ill, Mervyn Johns took over. John Laurie took over from Johns.
—Miss Edith Evans is deliciously entertaining as she treats the coquetries of the heroine with her now famous rising inflection of absurdity ... Deborah Kerr plays the part with unfaltering sincerity which saves it from its own longueurs. *The Times*

Mar 18. Sid Field in **Strike a New Note** directed by Robert Nesbitt at Prince of Wales. Revue. Field, a versatile cockney comic, the last of the great music hall artists, became a star overnight with his golf lesson. Jerry Desmonde was his straight man.

Mar 24. Joan White and Ronald Ward in Jerome Chodorov and Joseph Fields's **Junior Miss** directed by Marcel Varnel at Saville. Based on the Sally Benson stories which appeared in The New Yorker. Sally had a lively and adolescent romantic imagination.

Mar 30. Lupino Lane in Noël Gay's musical **La-Di-Da-Di-Da** directed by Lupino Lane at Victoria Palace. An elaborate cabaret brought a story of missing necklaces to a complete standstill.

Apr 8. John Gielgud as Valentine, Rosalie Crutchley as Angelica, Yvonne Arnaud as Mrs Frail and Angela Baddeley as Miss Prue in William Congreve's **Love for Love** designed by Rex Whistler and directed by John Gielgud at Phoenix. Leslie Banks as Tattle. Cecil Trouncer as Sir Samson. Marian Spencer as Mrs Foresight. Leon Quartermaine as Scandal. Miles Malleson as Foresight. Gielgud in Valentine's feigned madness looked as if he had stepped out of Robert Smirk's famous 18th-century painting.
—John Gielgud's brilliant production, with a cast unequalled in London, easily sails past the censor. It is at once the naughtiest and most civilised play in town. ERNEST BETTS *Daily Express*

Apr 13. Herbert Lomas in John Drinkwater's **Abraham Lincoln** directed by Tyrone Guthrie at Playhouse. A war leader employs means which he abhors to achieve noble ends. Timely, potent revival. Lomas, tough yet compassionate, played Abe with an English North Country accent.

Apr 17. Gwyneth Lascelles and Bruce Carfax in Oscar Hammerstein and Jerome Kern's musical version of Edna Ferber's **Show Boat** directed by James Moran at Stoll. Mr Jetsam sang "Ol' Man River."

Apr 21. Googie Withers, John Clements, Raymond Huntley, Ada Reeve and A E

Richard Attenborough in Brighton Rock

1943 World Premieres

New York
Richard Rodgers and Oscar Hammerstein's *Oklahoma!*
John Van Druten's *The Voice of the Turtle*

Zurich
Bertolt Brecht's *Galileo*
Bertolt Brecht's *The Good Woman of Setzuan*

Paris
Paul Claudel's *The Satin Slippers*
Jean-Paul Sartre's *The Flies*

Dublin
Sean O'Casey's *Red Roses for Me*

Biel, Switzerland
Fritz Hochwälder's *The Strong Are Lonely*

Births

Richard Eyre, British director

Mike Leigh, British playwright, stage and film director
Sam Shepard, American playwright

Deaths

Stephen Haggard (*b.*1911), British actor
Lorenz Hart (*b.*1895), American lyricist
Leslie Howard (*b.*1893), British actor

Notes

—James Bridie founded The Citizens Theatre in Glasgow

History

—Germans surrender at Stalingrad
—Rome declared open city
—Italy surrendered to Allies
—Benito Mussolini deposed

Matthews in J B Priestley's **They Came to a City** directed by Irene Hentschel at Globe. Sermon on Utopian socialism. The city reflects the beliefs and prejudices of the people who visit it.

Apr 29. Noël Coward, Judy Campbell and Joyce Carey in Noël Coward's **Present Laughter** directed by Noël Coward at Haymarket. Coward wrote the bravura central role of a philandering, egotistical matinee idol "advancing with every reluctance into middle age" for himself. Cole Lesley, Coward's lover, said in his biography that the role gave a good, if exaggerated, idea of what he was like. The most memorable moment was his blistering lecture to a budding Left-Wing playwright from Uckfield, played by James Donald.
—The dialogue throughout has the effervescence of light, heady wine. *Evening Standard*

Apr 30. Noël Coward, Judy Campbell, James Donald and Joyce Carey in Noël Coward's **This Happy Breed** directed by Noël Coward at Haymarket. Coward's sentimental chronicle of an ordinary suburban lower middle-class family's life in Clapham in the inter-war years was a tribute to the lower orders, who knew their place and didn't have ideas above their station. Written in 1939 during the Phoney War, it was a bit of "proud-to-be-British" propaganda. The head of the household was the mouthpiece for the status quo and the oft-reiterated message that "there are worse things than being ordinary." Coward was accused of being patronising, a charge he denied, saying that the play was written from personal experience and without the faintest condescension. He would go on to repeat his patriotic theme – 'The old girl's got stamina and it is up to ordinary people like us to keep it steady' – in his film, *In Which We Serve*.
—Here, for the first time in his brilliant career, we have him writing with sympathy, understanding, and admiration of the common man. *Daily Telegraph*

Jun 1. Donald Wolfit in Molière's **The Imaginary Invalid** directed by Donald Wolfit at Westminster. Adaptation by F Anstey. Rosalind Iden as the maid.

Jun 8. Lewis Casson and Paul Scofield in John Steinbeck's adaptation of his novel **The Moon is Down** directed by Basil C Langton at Whitehall. Patriotic propaganda. Scofield played a young miner sentenced to death in Nazi-occupied Norway.

Jun 10. Hermione Gingold and Walter Crisham in **Sweet and Low** directed by Charles Hickman at Ambassadors. Revue. High spots included Gingold as a Wagnerian heroine who has lost her Siegfried and Gingold as a Duchess explaining English pantomime to an American marine (Bonar Colleano).

Jun 25. Beatrix Lehmann as Mrs Alving in Henrik Ibsen's **Ghosts** directed by Dennis Arundell at Duke of York's. John Carol as Oswald. Edward Byrne as Pastor Manders.
—She is less a tragic heroine than the luckless heroine of a thriller and the quality of the tension throughout the evening is that of a thriller which obstinately refuses to thrill. *The Times*

June 29. Donald Wolfit and Rosalind Iden in Henrik Ibsen's **The Master Builder** directed by Donald Wolfit at Westminster. Wolfit's make-up reminded James Agate of an amiable gorilla and a seaside phrenologist.
—[Donald Wolfit] begins the play with admirable speed, but a hanging on to syllables in the last scene suggests he has not yet successfully thrown off the Shakespearean manner. *Theatre World*

Jul 27. Alec Clunes as Sir Harry Wilder and Avice Landone as Lurewell in George Farquhar's **The Constant Couple** directed by Alec Clunes at Arts. A libertine is faced with a choice between murder and matrimony. Clunes brought a light and easy touch to the comedy.

Aug 3. Alastair Sim, Walter Fitzgerald and Sophie Stewart in James Bridie's **Mr Bolfry** directed by Alastair Sim at Westminster. Two servicemen, one a cockney (Alfie Bass) the other an intellectual (Ronald Millar) are billeted on a Calvinistic minister in the Western Highlands. They and the minister's niece (Sheila Brownrigg) are exasperated by his refusal to live and let live. Their exasperation reaches its pitch when they are caught drinking tea on Sunday afternoon and told they have broken the Fourth Commandment. Unable to compete in argument, they decide that night to raise the devil to argue for them. And to their surprise he comes – in top hat with and looking strangely like a Scottish clergyman. The big scene between the minister (Alastair Sim) and the devil (Walter Fitzgerald) disappointed. Transferred to Playhouse.
—Mr Alastair Sim, bodeful as the Wrath of God, over sin in the highlands, gives a magnificent performance in triumph and collapse. IVOR BROWN *Observer*

Aug 3. Denys Blakelock in Arthur Wing Pinero's **The Magistrate** directed by Alec Clunes at Arts. Harold Lang played the magistrate's step-son.
—The shrewdness with which it mocks Victorianism will be something of a revelation to a playgoing generation brought up on the easy and fundamentally false Victorian burlesques of the past decade. *The Times*

Aug 18. Edith Day, Evelyn Laye and Dennis Noble in Oscar Hammerstein and Sigmund Romberg's musical **Sunny River** directed by Maxwell Wray at Piccadilly. Musical. New Orleans in 1806. Costumes by Doris Zinkeisen. Songs included "Along the Winding Road" and "My Girl and I."

Sep 1. David Horne and Iris Hoey in Roland Pertwee's **Pink String and Sealing Wax** directed by William Armstrong at Duke of York's. Victorian domestic comedy included a strict father, murder and suicide.

Sep 22. Coral Browne, Sally Gray and Max Bacon in Joseph Fields and Jerome Chodorov's **My Sister Eileen** directed by Marcel Varnel at Savoy. Farce based on Ruth McKenney's short stories which appeared in *The New Yorker*. Two inexperienced sisters in Greenwich Village, New York: one is plain and intelligent; the other is a ravishing dumb blonde. A series of slapstick incidents are constantly interrupted by explosions made by engineers who are dynamiting the subway.

Sep 23. Jack Hulbert and Cicely Courtneidge in **Something in the Air** directed by Jack Hulbert at Palace. Book by Arthur Macrae. Music by Manning Sherwin. Lyrics by Harold Purcell and May Kester. Same old spy formula allowed Hulbert and Courtneidge to appear in more disguises. Ronald Shiner played a sergeant.

Oct 15. Robertson Hare, Catherine Lacey, Basil Radford and Joyce Heron in Ben Travers's **She Follows Me About** directed by Ben Travers at Garrick. Farce. Hare was a parson on locum at a seaside town. His trousers came down far too early and he had few chances thereafter to be funny.

Oct 19. Peggy Ashcroft in Rodney Ackland's **Dark River** directed by Rodney Ackland at Whitehall. This mock Chekhovian piece, set during the Spanish Civil War, was all futile longings and gratuitous gloom. Ashcroft played a woman torn between an ineffectual husband and an over-earnest architect. "How unhappy I could be with neither," said one wag. Ashcroft's charm and sincerity couldn't save the play.

Nov 4. Bebe Daniels, Richard Hearne and Max Wall in Cole Porter's musical **Panama Hattie** directed by William Mollison at Piccadilly. Book by Herbert Fields and B G De Sylva. Hattie stops the Panama Canal from being blown up.

Nov 9. Mary Ellis in Ivor Novello's musical **Arc de Triomphe** directed by Leontine Sagan at Phoenix. A singer of genius has to choose between love and career. Ellis (in her role of diva playing in an opera about Joan of Arc) sang a patriotic aria, "France Will Rise Again". Olive Gilbert, who was still appearing in Novello's *The Dancing Years* at the Adelphi, would come over to the Phoenix every night to bolster the singing in the opera section.

Nov 10. 150 American soldiers in Irving Berlin's **This Is The Army** at Palladium. Berlin sang the song he had sung during World War 1: "Oh, How I Hate to Get Up in the Morning." Two thirds of the tickets were sold to raise funds for the British Services Charity Committee. The others were given to Allied servicemen free.

Nov 16. Martita Hunt as Mrs Cheveley, Roland Culver as Lord Goring, Irene Vanbrugh as Lady Markby and Esme Percy as Earl of Caversham in Oscar Wilde's **An Ideal Husband** directed by Jack Minster at Westminster.

Nov 17. Terence de Marney and Linden Travers in Agatha Christie's **Ten Little Niggers** directed by Irene Hentschel at St James's. Ten people, who have escaped punishment for murder, are invited to a deserted house on an island by a host they have never met. They are murdered one by one. The ending is patently absurd. "I thought I had killed you," says the heroine. "Thank goodness a woman can't shoot straight," says the hero. The lethal nursery rhyme is so lethal (politically incorrect) these days that it is no longer taught in schools. The title was changed to *Ten Little Indians* (which wasn't any better) and then to *Ten Little Redskins* (which also wasn't any better) and finally to its present title, *And Then There Was None*. The rhyme was based on an 1869 song by G W Moore which was based on an 1864 song by Septimus Winner. The island was inspired by Burgh Island off the Devon Coast.

Nov 23. Trevor Howard as Plume and Helen Cherry as Sylvia in George Farquhar's **The Recruiting Officer** directed by Alec Clunes at Arts. The production – the first in London in 113 years – burlesqued the artificiality and added boisterous songs. Howard was a light-hearted, insolent charmer. Elwyn Brook-Jones played his exuberant recruiting sergeant.

Dec 13. Lynn Fontanne and Alfred Lunt in Robert E Sherwood's **There Shall Be No Night** directed by Alfred Lunt at Aldwych. Wartime tragedy. When the play was produced In New York the story was about Russia invading Finland. But by the time it reached London, the war had moved on, and the story was about Nazis invading Greece.

Dec 22. Baliol Holloway as Captain Hook and Glynis Johns as Peter in J M Barrie's **Peter Pan** directed by Cecil King at Cambridge.

Dec 24. Michael Wilding, Hugh McDermott, Eugene Deckers, Jane Baxter, Ronald Squire and Brenda Bruce in Terence Rattigan's **While the Sun Shines** directed by Anthony Asquith at Globe. Wartime escapism. Earl is about to marry a Lady when an American serviceman and a French serviceman fall in love with her. Much of the comedy came from the fact that the aristocratic characters were in the ranks and not officers. *The Manchester Guardian* thought it had "the inspired lucidity of P G Wodehouse". *The Times* thought it was "a little masterpiece of tingling impertinence." 1,153 performances.

1944

Jan 26. Gladys Henson and Richard Burton in Emlyn Williams's **The Druid's Rest** directed by Emlyn Williams at St Martin's. In a Welsh village at the turn of the 20th century, a young boy thinks a stranger might be a notorious murderer. 14-year-old Brynmor Thomas, making his first stage appearance, had a big success.

Feb 3. Robert Beatty, Joyce Barbour and Meriel Forbes in Reginald Beckwith's **A Soldier for Christmas** directed by Norman Marshall at Wyndham's. Canadian soldier charms an English family. Transferred to Vaudeville.

Feb 10. Stephen Murray and John Wyse in J B Priestley's **Desert Highway** directed by Michael Macowan at Playhouse. Tank crew stranded in the Syrian Desert have a debate on war. The second act had a flashback to the 8th century BC.

Feb 11. Robert Helpmann in Shakespeare's **Hamlet** at Old Vic designed by Leslie Hurry and directed by Tyrone Guthrie and Michael Benthall. Pamela Brown as Ophelia. Basil Sydney as Claudius. Margot Grahame as Gertrude. Dennis Price as Horatio. The very idea of a dancer playing Hamlet surprised a number of critics. (It only remained, said one of them, for Donald Wolfit to dance *Swan Lake*.) But audiences, who were expecting disaster, were surprised just how good Helpmann was. Slight, white-faced, tousle-haired, he beat a devil's tattoo on the players' drum. Eager, intelligent and exciting, he excelled in the neurotic and pitiful aspects of the character.
—Mr Helpmann looked like Hamlet and acted like Hamlet but he could not speak like Hamlet. STEPHEN WILLIAMS *Evening News*

Feb 17. Hermione Gingold and Henry Kendall in **Sweeter and Lower** directed by Charles Hickman at Ambassadors. Revue. Gingold's malicious lampoon of Helpmann's Hamlet was one of the high spots.

Mar 11. Donald Wolfit in Shakespeare's **King Lear** directed by Donald Wolfit at Scala. James Agate, in the *Sunday Times*, said his performance was the greatest piece of Shakespearean acting he had seen. "I was in no mood to deny it," said Wolfit. Richard Goolden's sad Fool was deliberately humourless.
—Mr Wolfit created a Lear of outstanding majesty, grandeur and pathos ... His was an emotional tour-de-force lit by a perpetually active intelligence which flatly contradicted Lamb's contention that Lear should never be acted. *Times*

Mar 15. Sonia Dredel and John Bryning in Joan Morgan's **This Was A Woman**

directed by Henry Kendall at Comedy. The woman wrecks her daughter's marriage and murders her husband. Her lover rejects her and her son exposes her. There was only one thing to do in the circumstances: jump from a high window and kill herself.

Mar 29. Michael Redgrave, Beatrix Lehmann and Ena Burrill in Thomas Job's **Uncle Harry** directed by William Armstrong and Michael Redgrave at Garrick. Harry is a mild and inoffensive man, whose life is made a misery by his sisters. He murders one of them and intends to let the other hang for his crime. She accepts the sentence, preferring that he should go on living and suffer in the same way that the Ancient Mariner had suffered. Redgrave has his first commercial success, but he found Harry an unnerving role to act during a long run.
—At the end of the performance I felt fit for nothing. It was a year of hurly-burly, Benzedrine and colonic irrigations: illnesses real and imaginary. MICHAEL REDGRAVE *In My Mind's Eye*

Mar 30. Evelyn Dall, Daphne Barker, Jack Billings and Leigh Stafford in Cole Porter's musical **Something for the Boys** directed by Frank P Adey at Coliseum. Musical. Three long-lost heiresses arrive at a Texan ranch where army manoeuvres are taking place.
—Mr Cole Porter has temporarily mislaid the knack of writing the song which is an immediate and resounding success. He is for the moment no more than a clever imitator of himself. *The Times*

Apr 5. Pat Taylor, Bernard Clifton, Elizabeth French, and Leo Franklyn in **Lilac Domino** directed by Jack Hylton at Her Majesty's. Music by Charles Culliver. Lyrics by R B Smith. Book by H B Smith. Melodious and workmanlike revival.

Apr 24. Ivor Novello was sentenced to eight weeks imprisonment on a fuel conspiracy charge which was reduced to four weeks on appeal.

Apr 25. Frank Cellier, Marjorie Fielding, George Thorpe and Jeanne Stuart in Esther McCracken's **Quiet Weekend** directed by Richard Bird at Wyndham's.

May 10. Dorothy Dickson, Ernest Thesiger and Esmond Knight in Eric Linklater's **Crisis in Heaven** directed by John Gielgud at Lyric. Sardonic allegory about love and war with Helen of Troy, Voltaire, Florence Nightingale and others participating.
—It is not sufficiently witty; it is not at all poetic; indeed it is as little entertaining as a dull sermon. *The Times*

Donald Wolfit as King Lear

Laurence Olivier in Richard III

1944 World Premieres
New York
Philip Yordan's *Anna Lucasta*
Mary Chase's *Harvey*
John Van Druten's *I Remember Mama*
Chicago
Tennessee Williams's *The Glass Menagerie*
Paris
Jean Anouilh's *Antigone*
Jean-Paul Sartre's *Huis Clos*

Deaths
Martin Harvey (*b.*1863), British actor-manager
Jean Giraudoux (*b.*1882), French playwright

History
—Normandy invasion (D-Day landings)
—Attempt to assassinate Hitler failed
—Paris liberated

May 24. Daria Bayan, Henry Wendon, Dennis Noble and Jerry Verno in Johann Strauss's **A Night in Venice** at Phoenix. Book by Lesley Storm. Lyrics by Dudley Glass. Venice at carnival time.

Jun 15. Jack Buchanan, Coral Browne, Athene Seyler, Austin Trevor, James Dale and Frances Rowe in Frederick Lonsdale's **The Last of Mrs Cheyney** directed by Tyrone Guthrie at Savoy. The action was put back from 1925 to 1906. Browne was an elegant and languorous thief.

Aug 1. Ralph Lynn and Enid Stamp-Taylor in E Vivian Tidmarsh's **Is Your Honeymoon Really Necessary?** directed by Ralph Lynn at Duke of York's. Bedroom farce.

Aug 30. Robert Harris, Elizabeth Allan and Jean Cadell in James Gow and Arnaud d'Usseau's **Tomorrow the World** directed by Marcel Varnel at Aldwych. Nice American family has to cope with a nasty young Nazi. *The Sunday Dispatch* described 14-year-old David O'Brien's performance of a fanatical member of the former Hitler Youth Movement as "the most astonishing acting achievement of 1944."

Aug 31. Ralph Richardson in Henrik Ibsen's **Peer Gynt** directed by Tyrone Guthrie and Robert Helpmann at New. Sybil Thorndike as Aase. Laurence Olivier as the Button-Moulder.
—Here is the actor's dream fulfilled: to be always on the stage and never to stop talking. But great occasions require heroic response; certainly on Thursday the response was forthcoming. JAMES AGATE *Sunday Times*
—Mr Ralph Richardson and Mr Tyrone Guthrie respond nobly – the first with a performance as virile and cogent as any in his record; the second with a production which clarifies many of Ibsen's cloudy symbols and warms heart and mind. J C TREWIN *Observer*

Sep 5. Ralph Richardson, Margaret Leighton, Laurence Olivier, Nicholas Hannen and Sybil Thorndike in Bernard Shaw's **Arms and the Man** directed by John Burrell at New. Olivier thought Sergius a humbug, a buffoon, a blackguard, a coward, "a bloody awful part" until Guthrie said he would never succeed in the role until he learned to love Sergius. Olivier, spurred and moustached, was high camp.

Sep 6. Roger Livesey, Michael Shepley, Hugh Burden and Ursula Jeans in Peter Ustinov's **The Banbury Nose** directed by Norman Marshall at Wyndham's. The story of four generations is told in reverse, starting in 1944 and making its way back to 1884. The actors got younger and younger. It was a conceit that gave an ordinary family saga more depth than it in fact had.
—[Peter Ustinov] the greatest master of stage-craft at present working in the British theatre. JAMES AGATE *Sunday Times*

Sep 13. Laurence Olivier in Shakespeare's **Richard III** directed by John Burrell at New. Ralph Richardson as Buckingham. If there was one role more than any other which established Olivier's greatness then it was Richard III, a huge success with the public, the critics and the profession. The performance, much imitated, has passed into theatrical consciousness and is preserved on film. John Gielgud, with characteristic generosity, presented Olivier with the sword Edmund Kean had used in the same role.
—As he made his way downstage very slowly and with odd interpretations in his progress he seemed malignity incarnate. All the complications of Richard's character – its cruelty, its ambition, its sardonic humour seemed implicit in his expression and his walk, so that when he at last reached the front of the stage and began his speech, all that he had to say of his evil purpose seemed to us in the audience less like a revelation than a confirmation of something we had already been told. W A DARLINGTON *Daily Telegraph*

Sep 25. Philip Friend, Iris Hoey, Dorothy Hyson and Malcolm Keen in Roland Pertwee's **Pink String and Sealing Wax** directed by William Armstrong revived at Phoenix.

Oct 2. Carole Lynn in Ronald Gow's **Jenny Jones** directed by Hugh Miller at Hippodrome. Music by Harry Parr Davies, lyrics by Harold Purcell. Life in a Welsh village. Musical adaptation of the stories of Rhys Davies.

Oct 3. Tommy Trinder, Cairoli Brothers, Elizabeth Welch and the Dagenham Girl Pipers in George Black's **Happy and Glorious** directed by Robert Nesbit at Palladium. Revue. Trinder burlesqued Frank Sinatra.

Oct 4. Fay Compton in Esther McCracken's **No Medals** directed by Richard Bird at Vaudeville. Tribute to the unsung mothers of wartime England.

Oct 11. John Gielgud, Yvonne Arnaud, Leslie Banks, Cecil Trouncer and Rosalie Crutchley in Somerset Maugham's **The Circle** directed by William Armstrong at Haymarket. A civilised, witty, cruel and cynical entertainment.
—What an actor this is! He can poise a line like a foil and put it home with the most delicate turn of the wrist. He matches Mr Maugham's irony – and even the Theatre Royal, Haymarket, in grace. LIONEL HALE *Manchester Guardian*
—Miss Yvonne Arnaud's Lady Kitty – more Arnaud than Maugham – happily combines fading orchid with blown rose. *Observer*

Oct 12. John Gielgud, Rosalie Crutchley, Leslie Banks, Yvonne Arnaud, Miles Malleson, Cecil Trouncer, Leon Quartermaine, Marian Spencer, Max Adrian, Angela Baddeley in William Congreve's **Love for Love** set by Rex Whistler and directed by John Gielgud at Haymarket.
—John Gielgud's brilliant production, with a cast unequalled in London, easily sails past the censor. It is at once the naughtiest and most civilised play in town. ERNEST BETTS *Daily Express*

Oct 12. Alastair Sim, Angela Baddeley and Wilfred Hyde-White in James Bridie's **It Depends What You Mean** directed by Alastair Sim at Westminster. Army chaplain organises a Brains Trust at which a WRAC wants to know whether the team thinks marriage is a good idea. The platform becomes a scene of disorder as husband, wife and lover wash their dirty linen in public. Sim's hilarious performance as the harassed chaplain is preserved on film.
—The partnership of James Bridie and Alastair Sim is a marriage of true minds and just the kind of union which our theatre needs. IVOR BROWN *Observer*

Oct 13. John Gielgud in Shakespeare's **Hamlet** directed by George Rylands at Haymarket. Peggy Ashcroft as Ophelia. Leslie Banks as Claudius. Marian Spencer as Gertrude. Miles Malleson as Polonius. Leon Quartermaine as Ghost.
—Gielgud's Hamlet is one of the great performances of our time and perhaps of all time. W A DARLINGTON *New York Times*

Nov 1. Kay Hammond and John Clements in Noël Coward's **Private Lives** directed by John Clements at Apollo.
—There must be a kind of butterfly immortality about these quite useless but altogether diverting characters. To renew their acquaintance is like the offer of a glass of bubbling champagne after years of flat beer. *Theatre World*

Nov 23. Denys Blakelock, Derek Blomfield, Avice Landone, David Bird and Bill Shine in Arthur Wing Pinero's **The Magistrate** directed by Alec Clunes at St Martin's
—Denys Blakelock is an endearing blend of squirrel and mountain goat. J C TREWIN *Observer*

Nov 30. Sid Field in George Black's **Strike It Again** directed by Alec Shanks at Prince of Wales. Revue. Field played a photographer: "Show me your teeth. No, don't take them out."

Dec 20. Alfred Lunt and Lynn Fontanne in Terence Rattigan's **Love in Idleness** directed by Alfred Lunt at Lyric. Priggish son nearly wrecks the happiness of his mother when he forces her to choose between him and her lover. Some critics thought it was Rattigan's best play. "A most satisfying and dazzling piece of theatre," said *The Evening Standard*. "A riot of laughter, almost every remark was greeted with anything from a titter to a deafening guffaw," said *The Daily Mail*.

1945

Jan 4. George Gee in Philip King's **See How They Run** directed by Henry Kendall at Comedy. A country vicarage full of real and bogus clergy in wartime has farcical possibilities. The vicar is married to an actress who decides to have dinner with a soldier, a former boyfriend, who gets out of his uniform and into the vicar's clothes... Three doodlebugs fell on the West End during the first night. George Gee complained they ruined three of his best laughs. Joan Hickson played the mad maid. Joan Sanderson played the tweedy spinster. 589 performances

Jan 10. Clive Brook, Nora Swinburne and Ronald Ward in Daphne du Maurier's **The Years Between** directed by Irene Hentschel at Wyndham's. Man, presumed dead in World War 2, returns just as his wife is about to remarry. The Government knew he was alive; he was a spy working in Europe.

Jan 16. Ralph Richardson as Vanya, Laurence Olivier as Astrov, Margaret Leighton

1945 World Premieres
New York
Richard Rodgers and Oscar
Hammerstein's *Carousel*
Paris
Albert Camus's *Caligula*
Jean Giraudoux's *The Mad Woman
of Chaillot*
Buenos Aires
Federico Garcia Lorca's *The House of
Bernada Alba*
Naples
Eduardo de Filippo's *Napoli
Milionaria*

Births
August Wilson, American playwright

Deaths
Josef Capek (*b.*1887), Czech
playwright

Georg Kaiser (*b.*1878), German
playwright

Notes
—Premiere of Laurence Olivier's film
of *Henry V*
—Premiere of Noël Coward's film of
Brief Encounter

History
—World War 2 ended in Europe
—Atomic bombs dropped on
Hiroshima and Nagasaki
—Death of Franklin D Roosevelt
—Nuremberg War Crimes Trials
began
—Benito Mussolini shot
—Charles de Gaulle President of
France
—George Orwell's *Animal Farm*
published

as Yelena, Harcourt Williams as Professor, Joyce Redman as Sonya, Sybil Thorndike as Marina and George Relph as Telyegin in Anton Chekhov's **Uncle Vanya** directed by John Burrell at New. Some critics thought that Richardson and Olivier should have swapped roles.
—Mr Ralph Richardson is the perfect compound of absurdity and pathos. *The Times*
—It is a great relief to have the doctor [Laurence Olivier] played straight and not turned into a vodka-swilling character all shaggy, maudlin, super-Chekhovian charm. IVOR BROWN *Observer*

Jan 25. John Gielgud as Oberon, Peggy Ashcroft as Titania, Leslie Banks as Bottom, Max Adrian as Puck and Miles Malleson as Quince in Shakespeare's **A Midsummer Night's Dream** directed by Nevill Coghill at Haymarket. Gielgud with his greenish face looked so grim and sinister that the critics likened him to Julius Caesar's ghost, Hamlet's father, the Demon King, a misfit and a Roman centurion. He changed his make-up after the first night. The little duet, especially choreographed for Oberon and Titania by Frederick Ashton, was not greatly appreciated.
—Mr Gielgud and Miss Ashcroft did a ballroom dance. One, two, three, one two three. Just as I hoped they were going to do a rumba, it degenerated into a minuet. BEVERLEY BAXTER *Evening News*

Mar 1. Evelyn Laye, Esmond Knight and Charles Goldner in Oscar Strauss's **Three Waltzes** directed by Norman Marshall at Princes. Book and lyrics by Diana Morgan and Robert MacDermot. The operetta was set in three periods: Victorian, Edwardian and Georgian.

Mar 7. Mark Dignam and Cicely Paget-Bowman as Priest and Priestess in Bernard Shaw's **The Simpleton of the Unexpected Isles** directed by Judith Furse at Arts. Allegorical political fantasy and satire on the British Empire. The characters are mere mouthpieces. Easily the most appealing is the impotent, weak-minded clergyman simpleton (Peter Jones), who having had his communal sexual fling, chooses to return home to the land of Gilbert and Sullivan and "Jerusalem." The play ends with the arrival of an Angel (Bill Shine) announcing Judgement Day. ("Well, I'll be damned!") Those who cannot justify their existence, simply disappear. The Bank of England, the House of Commons, the Exchequer, the medical profession, a Westminster Abbey congregation and one million novel readers are among those who disappear. Shaw wrote the play in 1935 when he was 79 years old. The kindest review likened him to a dignified monkey shying coconuts at a bewildered couple.

Mar 8. Ruth Naylor, Cyril Ritchard and Irene Ambrus in Johann Strauss's **Gay Rosalind** choreographed by Wendy Toye and directed by Leontine Sagan and Bernard Delfont at Palace. English adaptation of the Max Reinhardt and E W Korngold version of *Die Fleidermaus*. Book by Austin Melford and Rudolf Bernauer. Lyrics by Sam Heppner. The emphasis was on spectacle rather than virtuoso singing.

Mar 22. Barry Morse in Irwin Shaw's **The Assassin** directed by Marcel Varnel at Savoy. Underground movement in Algiers at the time of the Allied invasion. Adventure and a bit of philosophy.

Apr 11. Keneth Kent in Edward Percy's **The Shop at Sly Corner** directed by Henry Kendall at St Martin's. Antique dealer murders his blackmailer who threatens to tell the daughter that he is a fence. Edward Percy was the pen-name of Edward Percy Smith, the MP. "Should MPs write plays?" asked *The Evening Standard*.

Apr 12. Diana Wynyard, Herbert Lomas and Megs Jenkins in Emlyn Williams's **The Wind of Heaven** directed by William Armstrong at St James's. Jesus (in the person of a child) returns to a mid-19th century Welsh mountain village where all the children have drowned.

Apr 18. Peggy Ashcroft as Duchess, John Gielgud as Ferdinand, Cecil Trouncer as Bosola and Leon Quartermaine as Cardinal in John Webster's **The Duchess of Malfi** directed by George Rylands at Haymarket. Audiences, who had just been made aware of the atrocities committed by the Nazis at Auschwitz and other concentration camps, found the tortures the Duchess suffered more decorative than horrible. Gielgud offered a Freudian interpretation for Ferdinand's paranoid objection to his sister's marriage. Ferdinand wanted to marry her himself.
—Something more than plaintiveness, however touching, is wanted if "I am Duchess of Malfi still" is not to sound like "I am little Miss Muffet." JAMES AGATE *Sunday Times*
—Gielgud's Ferdinand was a performance of dazzling virtuosity. Every young actor should see it and go home and weep in sheer desperation. BEVERLEY NICHOLS *Sunday Chronicle*

Apr 21. Ivor Novello, Roma Beaumont, Muriel Barron, and Margaret Rutherford in Ivor Novello's musical **Perchance to Dream** staged by William Newman and directed by Jack Minster at London Hippodrome. The action was set in three periods: Regency, Victorian and 1930s. Novello played a highwayman, a choirmaster and a modern young man. Olive Gilbert sang the hit song, "We'll Gather Lilacs in the Spring". 1,017 performances.
—All the songs gain much by the rapture with which Mr Novello listens to them. *The Times*

May 8. VE Day.

May 16. Vivien Leigh as Sabina in Thornton Wilder's **The Skin of Our Teeth** directed by Laurence Olivier at Phoenix. Cecil Parker and Joan Young as Mr and Mrs Antrobus. Ena Burrill as the Fortune-Teller. Wilder's idiosyncratic comic-strip history of the world is a mixture of highbrow tomfoolery, anachronisms and stage mishaps. He wrote the allegory (which won him his third Pulitzer Prize) on the eve of America's entry into World War 2. The world, he said, is an awful place and mankind constantly has to pick itself up and begin all over again. Mr and Mrs Antrobus and their two children live simultaneously in pre-historic times and in 20th century New Jersey. The end of the world is always nigh, but whatever the disaster – Ice Age, Flood, Plagues, Earthquakes and World War – the human race always survives. "I hate this play," says Sabina, the sexy maid. Many critics agreed with her. Sabina was created by Tallulah Bankhead on Broadway in 1942. Agate thought Vivien Leigh's performance was "an enchanting piece of nonsense-cum-allure, half dab-chick, half dragon-fly." Olivier revived the production in 1948 when he and Vivien Leigh led the Old Vic Company in a ten-month tour of Australia and New Zealand. Olivier played Mr Antrobus.

Jun 6. Michael Redgrave and Karel Stepanek in S N Behrman's adaptation of Franz Werfel's **Jakobowsky and The Colonel** directed by Michael Redgrave at Piccadilly. Esme Percy as the Tragic Gentleman. Jacobowsky, heroic, yet ridiculous, is the eternal refugee. His tenacity for life is matched by his resourcefulness and his ingenious improvisation.
—One of the finest of the new plays we have seen, certainly the best import from America during the war years. TED WILLIS *Daily Worker*

Jun 7. Peter Pears and Joan Cross in Benjamin Britten's opera **Peter Grimes** conducted by Reginald Goodall at Sadler's Wells. Montagu Slater's libretto was based on George Crabbe's poem, *The Borough*, published in 1810.

Jun 21. Anne Ziegler and Webster Booth in **Sweet Yesterday** directed by Jack Hulbert at Adelphi. Book by Philip Leaver. Music by Kenneth Leslie-Smith. Lyrics by James Dyrenforth and Max Kester. Intrigue and espionage lead up to the Battle of Waterloo.

Jun 27. John Mills in Mary Hayley Bell's **Duet for Two Hands** directed by Anthony Pelissier and John Mills at Lyric. Young poet, having had both hands amputated, acquires a new pair grafted from a corpse to his living stumps. The hands once belonged to a murderer. The play was a popular West End mixture of Grand Guignol and whimsy.

Jul 2. Official visit of the Comédie Française at New. Pierre Dux, Mony Daimes and Jean Desaily in Beaumarchais's **Le Barbier de Seville**. Pierre Dux in Molière's **L'Impromptu de Versailles**. Paul Deiber and Jean Yonnel in Victor Hugo's **Ruy Blas**. Jean Yonnel and Louis Seigner in Molière's **Tartuffe**. Marie Bell and Jacques Dacqmine in Racine's **Phèdre**. The Old Vic and the Comédie Française swapped theatres during the visit.

Jul 12. Robert Donat and Marjorie Rhodes in Walter Greenwood's **The Cure for Love** directed by H K Ayliff at Westminster. Lancashire comedy. The cure for love is marriage.
—Donat acts beautifully: in a sense all too beautifully; his profile may be set in Salford but belongs to Ancient Rome. IVOR BROWN *Observer*

Jul 18. Robert Morley as the Prince Regent and Wendy Hiller as his daughter Charlotte in Norman Ginsbury's **The First Gentleman** directed by Norman Marshall at New. The author didn't like what Morley had done to his text and brought an injunction. The judge sided with Morley.
—Mr Morley passes the first test of a star, which is that he can play his hand in act one and then replay it in acts two and three without ever losing our interest. IVOR BROWN *Observer*

Aug 6. Atom bomb dropped on Hiroshima.

Aug 9. Atom bomb dropped on Nagasaki.

Aug 14. VJ Day.

Aug 21. Isabel Jeans as Mrs Erlynne, Dorothy Hyson as Lady Windermere, Griffith Jones as Lord Darlington. Geoffrey Toone as Lord Windermere and Athene Seyler as the Duchess of Berwick in Oscar Wilde's **Lady Windermere's Fan** directed by John Gielgud at Haymarket. In the years following the end of World War 2 rationing continued and the public still needed coupons to buy clothes. Cecil Beaton's magnificent costumes and scenery were therefore a special treat; but the actors never quite lived up to their sumptuous surroundings.

Aug 22. Cyril Ritchard, Madge Elliott, Joyce Grenfell and Graham Payn in Noël Coward's revue **Sigh No More** directed by Noël Coward at Piccadilly. Payn sang "Matelot". Grenfell stopped the show as a gawky, toothy schoolgirl gloating over her family's misfortunes.
—You cannot dress up pre-war jokes in their peacetime feathers without seeming out of date. *New York Times*

Aug 28. Emrys Jones and Margaretta Scott in John Patrick's **The Hasty Heart** directed by Murray Macdonald at Aldwych. Young Scots soldier in a convalescent ward in a British military hospital in Burma is shortly to die and doesn't know it.

Sep 25. Edith Evans as Mrs Malaprop, Anthony Quayle as Captain Absolute, Audrey Fildes as Lydia Languish, Morland Graham as Sir Anthony Absolute and Reginald Beckwith as Bob Acres in Richard Brinsley Sheridan's **The Rivals** directed by Edith Evans and William Armstrong at Criterion. Peter Cushing as Faulkland, Jean Wilson as Julia. Oliver Messel's décor was the production's only real success.
—But even the grotesque magnificence of Edith Evans as Mrs Malaprop could not raise the revival above mere competence. BEVERLEY BAXTER *Evening Standard*

Sep 26. Ralph Richardson as Falstaff, Laurence Olivier as Hotspur and Justice Shallow, Nicholas Hannen as King Henry, Michael Warre as Prince Hal, Joyce Redman as Doll Tearsheet, Sybil Thorndike as Mistress Quickly and Margaret Leighton as Lady Percy in Shakespeare's **Henry IV Parts 1 and 2** directed by John Burrell at New. Richardson was the most natural, the most human, the greatest Falstaff in living memory. "He had everything the part wants," said James Agate, "the exuberance, the mischief, the gusto." The performance, universally praised, put him among the great actors. Olivier had two roles and was transformed from a virile, hot-tempered, passionate, stammering soldier into a feeble quavering scarecrow of an old man.
—This was the least vulgar, least sensual and least clownish of Falstaffs, the most dignified, the most thoughtful and the most gentlemanly. He had gusto, mischief and exuberance, but no grossness. RICHARD FINDLATER *These Our Actors*

Oct 11. Robert Speaight in Ronald Duncan's **This Way to The Tomb** directed by E Martin Browne at Mercury. Verse play combined the temptation of Father Antony in the 14th century with an attack on present-day materialism in religion. The result was an over-wordy mixture of dull sincerity and forced satire. Transferred to Garrick.

Oct 18. Double-bill at New. Laurence Olivier as Oedipus in Sophocles's **Oedipus Rex** directed by Michel Saint-Denis and as Mr Puff in Richard Brinsley Sheridan's **The Critic** directed by Miles Malleson. Most critics felt a tragedy should not have been followed by a burlesque, forgetting, perhaps, that was exactly what the Ancient Greeks did in their theatres. Oedipus's cry of agony, worthy of Edvard Munch, is remembered to this day, even by people who never heard it. Sybil Thorndike as Jocasta.
—[Oedipus] One of those performances in which blood and electricity are somehow mixed. It pulls down lightening from the sky. It is as awesome, dwarfing and appalling as one of nature's angriest displays. JAMES MASON BROWN *Saturday Review of Literature*
—[Puff] His rattling volubility, and his trick of throwing snuff into the air and catching it in his nostrils, kept the comedy spinning. AUDREY WILLIAMSON *Old Vic Drama*

Nov 9. Marie Ney as Hecuba and Eileen Herlie as Andromache in Euripides's **The Trojan Women** directed by Greta Douglas at Lyric, Hammersmith. Modern dress production. Andromache dominated the action rather than Hecuba. The Greek tragedy was acted in a double-bill with Thornton Wilder's **The Happy Journey To Trenton and Camden** with Joan Young and Alexander Archdale directed by Eric Crozier.

Nov 22. Sonia Dresdel and Mary Hinton in Somerset Maugham's **The Sacred Flame** directed by Geoffrey Wardwell at St Martin's. A nurse accuses a woman of murdering her husband. The sex-starved nurse's motives are highly suspect.

Nov 22. Cicely Courtneidge, Cyril Raymond, Hartley Powers and Thorley Walters in Arthur Macrae's **Under the Counter** directed by Jack Hulbert. Music by Manning Sherwin. Lyrics by Harold Purcell. Blackmarket comedy.

Dorothy Hyson and Isabel Jeans in **Lady Windermere's Fan**

Dec 6. Andrew Cruickshank as Richard Burbage in Emlyn Williams's **Spring 1600** directed by Emlyn Williams at Lyric, Hammersmith. Jessica Spencer played the girl who disguises herself as a boy and lands the role of Viola at the premiere of *Twelfth Night* at the Globe Theatre.

Dec 18. Ronald Shiner in R F Delderfield's **Worm's Eye View** directed by Ronald Shiner at Whitehall. Aircraftmen are living in a billet which is run by an awful landlady and her awful son. The comedy relied for its enormous success on Shiner's bright and breezy persona. Transferred to Comedy Theatre in 1950.

1946

Feb 14. Walter Crisham, Frederick Valk and Margaret Johnston in William Saroyan's **The Time of Your Life** directed by Peter Glenville at Lyric, Hammersmith. Customers in a San Francisco honky-tonk live out their lives and dreams in public. This production by The Group Theatre, and rooted in the years of the American Depression, preached a sentimental left-wing message of brotherliness and revolution. The action is held together (there is no story as such) by a rich drunk, who patronises the joint, distributing largesse and philosophy ("Money is the guiltiest thing in the world".) The drunk, a man who believes in dreams rather than statistics, is "the Christian conscience in a world, which has no conscience at all". A brutal policeman (a symbol of interference and harassment in ordinary people's lives) is shot dead.

Feb 19. Cecil Trouncer, Edith Sharpe and Robert Flemyng in Warren Chetham Strode's **The Guinea Pig** directed by Jack Minster at Criterion. Working class boy (Derek Blomfield) wins scholarship to public school.

Feb 26. Kieron O'Hanrahan, Eddie Byrne, Alex Dignam and Tristan Rawson in Sean O'Casey's **Red Roses for Me** directed by Ria Mooney at Embassy. Dublin's poor are given the full expressionistic treatment with sentimental mimes, rhetorical fantasy and a chorus of Roman Catholic women. Transferred to Lyric, Hammersmith, then to New and then to Wyndham's.

Mar 7. John Hargreaves, Halina Victoria and Janet Hamilton-Smith in **Song of Norway** directed by Charles Hickman at Palace. Operetta based on the life and music of Edvard Grieg. Book by Homer Curran. Choreography by Robert Helpmann and Pauline Grant.

Mar 20. Max Wall and Avril Angers in **Make It a Date** at Duchess. Revue. Music by Edward Horan and Arthur Young. Directed by Leigh Stafford and Marianne Davis. The funniest items were provided by Wall, who was seen first as an unusual pianist and then as an incompetent conjurer bungling his act under the critical gaze of a nasty little child.

Apr 11. Jack Hulbert and Bobby Howes in **Here Come the Boys** at Saville. Revue. Music by Manning Sherwin. Lyrics by Harold Purcell. Sketches by Max Fester.
—Mr Hulbert is in charge, dancing and singing with that amateur charm which his highly polished professionalism has enabled him to carry through the years from the Cambridge Footlights. *The Times*

Apr 24. Beatrice Lillie, Walter Crisham, George Benson and Joyce Grenfell in **Better Late** directed by Norman Marshall at Garrick. Mediocre revue was only partly redeemed by Lillie singing some of her most popular songs.

Apr 30. Marc Connelly in Thornton Wilder's **Our Town** directed by Jed Harris at New. One of the most popular American dramas, premiered in 1936, describes a bittersweet cycle of daily life in a typical American small town in New Hampshire at the beginning of the 20th century. The action deliberately concentrates on the humdrum and trivial. Wilder, who was more interested in veracity than reality, introduced a revolutionary style of theatre. "I am not an innovator," he wrote, "but a rediscoverer of forgotten goods and I hope a remover of obtrusive bric-a-brac." Feeling that a set stifled the life in a drama by narrowing the action to one moment in time and place, he wrote a play to be produced without scenery and props, relying on two kitchen tables, a number of wooden chairs, a ladder, a couple of trellises, the occasional sound effect and the actors' mime.

May 2. Valerie White and Jack Allen in Ronald Millar's **Frieda** directed by Irene Hentschel at Westminster. British officer brings home German girl who helped him after he had escaped from a POW camp. She gets a such a poor reception that she contemplates suicide.

May 3. Freda Jackson in Joan Temple's **No Room at the Inn** directed by Anthony Hawtrey at Embassy. Some of the children, who were evacuated during the war, were treated appallingly. Social workers often couldn't do anything about it, since there were often no other billets available. Jackson was cast as a drunken, sluttish bully who finally got her come-uppance. Transferred to Winter Garden.

1946 World Premieres
New York
Eugene O'Neill's *The Iceman Cometh*
Irving Berlin's *Annie Get Your Gun*
Garson Kanin's *Born Yesterday*
Lillian Hellman's *Another Part of the Forest*
Paris
Jean-Paul Sartre's *The Respectable Prostitute*
Naples
Eduardo de Filippo's *Filumena*

Births
Howard Barker, British playwright
Christopher Hampton, British playwright
Cameron Mackintosh, British impresario

Deaths
Harley Granville Barker (b.1877), British playwright, actor, director, critic
Gerhart Hauptmann (b.1862), German playwright

Notes
—Sir Barry Jackson appointed director and reopened Memorial Theatre with Peter Brook's *Love's Labour's Lost*

History
—Iron Curtain descended – Cold War began
—UNESCO established
—Chinese Civil war resumed
—Britain blockaded ports to prevent illegal entry of Jews to Palestine

May 8. Eileen Herlie as Alcestis, Sebastian Shaw as Heracles and John Justin as Admetus in Maurice J Valency's **The Thracian Horses** directed by Sebastian Shaw and Murray Macdonald at Lyric, Hammersmith. Satire on Greek heroes and gods: Alcestis is absolutely furious when Admetus (her husband) and Heracles bring her back from the underworld.
—Eileen Herlie plays Alcestis with an accomplished ease which enables her to pass from graceful devotion to languid exhibitionism and still surprise us with the fury of a celebrated Greek beauty deprived of her triumph. *The Times*

May 9. Hermione Gingold and Henry Kendall in Alan Melville's **Sweetest and Lowest** directed by Charles Hickman at Ambassadors. Revue. Music by Charles Zwar. High spot: Gingold mocking Coward's wartime service.

May 14. John Clements, Kay Hammond and Robert Eddison in Margaret Luce's **The Kingmaker** directed by John Clements at St James's. England during the Wars of the Roses. Clements was the kingmaker, the Earl of Warwick. Eddison had the better role of the Duke of York, the future Edward IV. James Agate said the play should have been called The Warwicks of Wimpole Street. *The Times* said it was "medieval pageantry, written in cliché and spoken in Wardour Street English".

May 23. Angela Baddeley, Frank Cellier and Emlyn Williams in Terence Rattigan's **The Winslow Boy** directed by Glen Byam Shaw at Lyric. A young cadet, falsely accused of having stolen a five shilling postal order, is expelled from the Royal Naval College. (The story was based on the Archer-Shere case of 1910–1912.) The theme was not so much justice as the rights of the individual. Rattigan managed to wave the flag whilst at the same time knocking the Establishment. The message was spelled out: "If ever the time comes that the House of Commons has so much on its mind that it cannot find time to discuss Ronnie Winslow and his bally postal order, this country will be a far poorer place than it is now." The play's most famous scene is the boy's cross-examination by the best advocate in the country, the cold and supercilious Sir Robert Morton (incisively played by Emlyn Williams), who having brutally reduced the boy (Michael Newell) to tears, announces: "The boy is plainly innocent. I accept the brief." The play was a major turning-point in Rattigan's career. Frank Cellier's performance as the father was highly praised. So, too, was Kathleen Harrison's as the maid. (The boy was killed at Ypres in World War I; he was 19 years old.)

Jun 4. Frederick Valk, Ernest Milton, James Donald, Elizabeth Sellars and Alec Guinness in Feodor Dostoevsky's **The Brothers Karamazov** adapted by Alec Guinness and directed by Peter Brook at Lyric, Hammersmith. Despite the brilliance of the production, and the acting of Valk in particular, the selected episodes from the novel did not add up to a play.

Jun 11. Sybil Thorndike as Clytemnestra, Ann Casson as Electra, Basil C Langton as Orestes, Lewis Casson as Shepherd, Esmond Knight as Messenger in Euripides's **Electra** directed by Lewis Casson at King's, Hammersmith.

Jun 26. John Gielgud as Raskolnikoff, Audrey Fildes as Sonia, Edith Evans as Katerina and Peter Ustinov as Petrovitch, the Police Chief in Fydor Dostoievsky's **Crime and Punishment** adapted by Rodney Ackland, designed by Paul Sheriff and directed by Anthony Quayle at New. Ustinov thought Gielgud was far too neurotic and wondered why the Police Chief did not arrest him immediately.
—Gielgud's performance as the murderer is an astonishing feat, rising to moments of sheer epileptic frenzy. ERNEST BETTS *Daily Express*
—Peter Ustinov's detective: an astonishing characterisation, even if this jumpy, nail-biting satyr is hardly the Parfiri Petrovitch of the book. *Theatre World*

Clive Morton, Michael Newell, Emlyn Williams, Madge Compton, Jack Watling, Frank Cellier and Angela Baddeley, The Winslow Boy

Jul 16. Beatrix Lehmann, Betty Ann Davies, Alec Guinness and Donald Pleasance in Jean-Paul Sartre's **Huis Clos** ("Vicious Circle") directed by Peter Brook at Arts. Existentialist melodrama, famous for its definition, "Hell is other people." The central weakness is that what "the three damned souls" have done on earth is far too explicit and not nearly interesting enough. The play's strength is that they know that they are trapped together for eternity. The most electrifying moment was when Guinness was hammering at the door and the door unexpectedly opened. The possibility of getting out of that claustrophobic room actually existed – but the inmates were too afraid to take it.

Jul 17. Carole Lynn in **Big Ben** directed by Wendy Toye at Adelphi. Book by A P Herbert. Music by Vivian Ellis. Shop girl stands for parliament and falls in love with a candidate of another party. The political satire had no cutting edge.

Jul 23. Patricia Plunkett in Elsa Shelley's **Pick-Up Girl** directed by Peter Cotes at Prince of Wales. Juvenile Court determines to save a 15-year-old girl from a life of prostitution. The play, competently written, occasionally tedious, but never sensational, was recognised an important social document. There was a strong performance by Joan Miller as the girl's mother. Ernest Jay was cast as a patient, tolerant and humane judge. Transferred to Casino.

Jul 24. John Clements, Robert Eddison, Kay Hammond, Moira Lister and David

Peel in John Dryden's **Marriage à la Mode** designed by Laurence Irving and directed by John Clements at St James's. The romantic frolic and epigrammatic intrigue was prettily designed and wittily acted. The duel was fought to music as if the duellists were in a ballet.

Aug 14. Constance Cummings, Patricia Burke, Basil Radford and Naughton Wayne in Benn W Levy's **Clutterbuck** directed by Benn W Levy at Wyndham's. Two married couples on board a pleasure cruise are confronted with past affairs.

Sep 2. Glynis Johns and Derek Farr in Kenneth Horne's **Fools Rush In** directed by Richard Bird at Fortune. Bride refuses to get married on her wedding day. Joyce Barbour played her mother.

Sep 3. Antony Eustrel in John Milton's **The Masque Comus** directed by Leslie French assisted by Seymour Hicks at Coliseum. Music by Handel and Henry Lawes. The Masque (originally premiered in 1664 at Ludlow Castle, Shropshire) was given the full musical comedy treatment. Robert Helpmann's 1939 dramatic ballet version in which he had starred with Margot Fonteyn was vastly superior.

Sep 3. A E Matthews and Mary Jerrold in Frederick Lonsdale's **But For The Grace of God** directed by Leslie Armstrong at St James's. The cure for blackmail is murder. During the run Hugh McDermott and Michael Gough fought each other so con-

John Gielgud (far left) and Peter Ustinov (fourth right in top hat) in **Crime and Punishment**

vincingly that McDermott broke a wrist and a finger. Gough fractured three ribs, broke a chest bone and put his knee out of joint.

Sep 4. Eileen Herlie and James Donald in Jean Cocteau's **The Eagle Has Two Heads** adapted by Ronald Duncan and directed by Murray Macdonald at Lyric, Hammersmith. The Queen, celebrating the anniversary of the king's death, is dining all alone, tête-à-tête with his ghost, when through the window staggers a wounded revolutionary poet, the living image of the dead king. He has come to assassinate her and, this being Cocteau, the Queen is more than willing to embrace Death. Written in 1946, it felt like a 19th-century Romantic French drama, a combination of *The Prisoner of Zenda* and *Tristam and Isolde*. It should have been an opera. The role made Herlie a star over night.
—Herlie's acting has at times an almost lustral quality which can wash from the play the dust and smirch of melodramatic routine. J C TREWIN *Observer*
—A performance of remarkable stamina by Miss Eileen Herlie who talks and talks and talks, but is most eloquent, perhaps, in that one enormous scream. HAROLD HOBSON *Sunday Times*

Sep 24. Laurence Olivier in Shakespeare's **King Lear** directed by Laurence Olivier at New. Margaret Leighton as Regan. Pamela Brown as Goneril. Joyce Redman as Cordelia. Michael Warre as Edgar. George Relph as Gloucester. Alec Guinness as Fool. Nicholas Hannen as Kent. Peter Copley as Edmund. Harry Andrews as Cornwall. The production was notable for the unexpected humour of the abdication scene and the king's total lack of senility. The Fool, trimmed to just twelve lines of speech, was one of Guinness's favourite roles.
—Olivier is a player of unparalleled animal powers miraculously crossed with a player of extreme technical cuteness. KENNETH TYNAN *He that Plays The King*

Sep 29. Nigel Patrick, Maurice Denham and Michael Hordern in K B Woolard's **Morning Departure** directed by Maurice Colbourne at Adelphi. Submarine strikes a mine and sinks fifteen fathoms deep. The crew wait to be rescued.

Oct 1. Ralph Richardson in J B Priestley's **An Inspector Calls** directed by Basil Dean at New. This modern morality play, a socialist tract against capitalist greed, was an Edwardian swan song set in 1912 and, arguably, the best stage detective story since Sophocles's *Oedipus Rex*. The Russians were the first to produce the play. A complacent, confident, selfish society's bourgeois values are about to be shattered, first by the *Titanic* disaster and then by the Great War. A family is celebrating their

daughter's engagement when a detective arrives to tell them that a girl has died. One by one they are all implicated. The predictability of the plot, once it is set in motion, is its great strength; and the irony is not any the less telling for being laboured. Richardson as the mysterious inspector struck exactly the right balance between the mundane and the celestial. The play, underestimated by the critics, had a short run.
—No other actor of his or subsequential generation has this peculiar quality of inviting you to look beyond the ordinary to what is extraordinary. BASIL DEAN *Mind's Eye*

Oct 11. Sid Field in Dick Hurran and Phil Park's **Piccadilly Hayride** directed by Alec Shanks at Prince of Wales. Revue. Field played a refined cinema organist and a gormless lad learning snooker. The bent cue went right through the cloth and the table.
—Mr Field is our greatest comic and he never utters a dirty line. BEVERLEY BAXTER *Evening Standard*

Oct 16. Robert Donat as Benedict and Renee Acherson as Beatrice in Shakespeare's **Much Ado About Nothing** directed by Fabia Drake at Aldwych. Jay Laurier as Dogberry. Asherson was miscast.
—Mr Donat himself was admirable, humorous, inventive, clear-spoken and able to give new charm to the most familiar and oft-cited lines. IVOR BROWN, *Observer*

Oct 24. Ralph Richardson in Edmond Rostand's **Cyrano de Bergerac** translated by Brian Hooker and directed by Tyrone Guthrie at New. Margaret Leighton as Roxane. Michael Warre as Christian. Alec Guinness as de Guiche.
—As Cyrano, Mr Ralph Richardson abundantly succeeds; he is not a natural romantic but he is a great actor. His air of solid common sense is at odds with Cyrano's pride and panache. IVOR BROWN *Observer*

Nov 20. Paul Scofield, Hermione Hannen and Joan White in Christopher Fry's **A Phoenix Too Frequent** directed by Noël Willman at Arts. This witty, poetic one-act satire on the false heroics of Love was inspired by Petronius's tale of a widow who was wooed by a young soldier over the tomb of her dead husband. Fry's imagery was sensuous and the denouement was happily cynical.

Nov 21. Coral Browne in Somerset Maugham's **Lady Frederick** directed by Murray Macdonald at Savoy. The play was put back to the 1880s. Browne played the scene when she disillusions her young lover with dyes, powder puff and rouge pot for high comedy.

Dec 19. Mary Martin in Noël Coward's musical **Pacific 1860** directed by Noël Coward at Drury Lane. Prima donna is forced to choose between love and career. Sumptuous dullness.
—The piece is not worthy of the occasion, the theatre and the genius – I use the word advisedly – of the author. *The Times*

Dec 20. Godfrey Tearle and Edith Evans in Shakespeare's **Antony and Cleopatra** directed by Glen Byam Shaw at Piccadilly. Anthony Quayle as Enobarbus. Evans was 57 years old.
—Edith Evans gave us a Cleopatra who was really Lady Bracknell cruelly starved of cucumber sandwiches. KENNETH TYNAN *He That Plays the King*

1947

Jan 1. Frederick Valk, Valerie White and Jane Henderson in Henrik Ibsen's **The Master Builder** directed by Peter Ashmore at Arts.
—Valk's Solness is a magnificent struggle between this fine actor's great energy and power and his imperfect rhythm of English speech. HAROLD HOBSON *Sunday Times*
—His [Valk's] performance in this great part is of a vitality and sheer power which no other actor in England could begin to match. ALAN DENT *News Chronicle*

Jan 14. Ralph Richardson as Face, George Relph as Subtle, Joyce Redman as Dol Common, Nicholas Hannen as Sir Epicure Mammon, Alec Guinness as Abel Drugger and Margaret Leighton as Dame Pliant in Ben Jonson's **The Alchemist** directed by John Burrell at New. Richardson, said *Theatre World*, "reels off the mumbo-jumbo with classic authenticity and Rabelaisian good humour."
—Drugger used to be Garrick's part, but, Mr Guinness having now appropriated it, I name him the best living English character-actor. But not, while Mr Valk is here, the best actor in England. KENNETH TYNAN *He That Plays the King*

Jan 23. Hartley Power and Yolande Donlan in Garson Kanin's **Born Yesterday** directed by Laurence Olivier at Garrick. American satire on corruption and the seductiveness of dumb blondes. Ex-chorus girl (Yolande Donlan) gets an education in democracy from a journalist (William Kemp) and realizes that her lover (a racketeer played by Hartley Power) is no good. The dialogue was racy in the Damon Runyon manner. The production was a triumph for Donlan, who was hailed as a superb actress and "the most charming nitwit who ever looked out of the pages of *The New Yorker*." The role had been created on Broadway by Judy Holliday who also appeared in the film version.

Jan 29. Yvonne Arnaud, Ronald Squire, Irene Browne and Charles Victor in S N Behrman's adaptation of Somerset Maugham's **Jane** directed by Richard Bird at Aldwych. Jane is a dowdy Liverpudlian widow who marries a young architect and becomes the rage of London.

Feb 11. Julian Somers, Owen Holder, Harry Quashie, Basil Gordon and Peter Doughty in William Douglas Home's **Now Barabbas** directed by Colin Chandler at Bolton. The demoralisation and monotony of prison life was based on Home's own experience. He had been sent to prison whilst serving as an officer during the war. He had, on grounds of conscience, refused to obey an order. Transferred to Vaudeville.

Feb 18. Michael Gwynn, Frances Rowe, Joan Haythorne and Geoffrey Dunn in Bernard Shaw's **Back to Methuselah** directed by Noël Willman at Arts. Nine hours spread over four evenings.

Feb 23. Alec Guinness in Shakespeare's **Richard II** directed by Ralph Richardson at New. Harry Andrews as Bolingbroke.
—It was a performance of which I am still ashamed – a partly plagiarised, third-rate imitation of Gielgud's definitive Richard, at the same theatre in 1937. ALEC GUINNESS *Blessings in Disguise*

Mar 6. Robert Helpmann, Margaret Rawlings, Roderick Lovell and Martita Hunt in John Webster's **The White Devil** directed by Michael Benthall at Duchess. Sadism and sensuality by the Tussaud Laureate.
—Robert Helpmann is not only a first rate ballet dancer, but he is very much at home as an actor in the picturesque stuff – he displays sardonic humour and utters many purple passages with superb relish and dies horrifically. A E WILSON *Star*
—Margaret Rawlings, resplendent of voice and figure, sometimes seems to be listening to the sound of her own performance. PHILIP HOPE-WALLACE *Manchester Guardian*

Mar 26. Jack Hawkins in Shakespeare's **Othello** directed by Peter Powell at Piccadilly. Anthony Quayle as Iago. Elizabeth Kentish as Desdemona. Fay Compton as Emilia. Hawkins was far too young and far too mild.

Apr 5. Beatrice Varley, Dirk Bogarde and Kenneth More in Michael Clayton Hutton's **Power with Glory** directed by Chloë Gibson at Fortune. The impact of murder on an ordinary working class family.
—I had a great success in the third act where I screamed my head off. That's why I got the notices. DIRK BOGARDE

Apr 15. Clive Brook, Irene Worth and Michael Shepley in Ferenc Molnar's **The Play's the Thing** directed by Clive Brook at Lyric, Hammersmith. Transferred to St James's.
—Herr Molnar has not the wit that his whimsically arranged situations require. *The Times*

Apr 16. Noël Coward and Moira Lister in Noël Coward's **Present Laughter** directed by Noël Coward at Haymarket. Robert Eddison was very funny as the left-wing playwright from Uckfield.
—Mr Coward himself plays the lead with an occasional excess of bounce and grin but for the most part with unapproachable dexterity. LIONEL HALE *Daily Mail*
—Occasionally one has the uncomfortable feeling that Mr Coward is laughing at us when all the time we thought we were laughing at him and at the fantastic, hysterical and amoral characters. *Theatre World*

Apr 17. Crazy Gang in **Together Again** directed by Jack Hylton at Victoria Palace.

Apr 26. Lizabeth Webb and Georges Guétary in A P Herbert and Vivian Ellis's musical **Bless the Bride** directed by Wendy Toye at Adelphi. Sweet Victorian English miss on her wedding day falls in love with a French actor. They elope to Paris on the eve of the Franco-Prussian War. He is killed. Very pretty, very sentimental, very nostalgic, and very, very English. Hit song: "This is My Lovely Day".

Apr 30. Harold Keel and Betty Jane Watson in Richard Rodgers and Oscar Hammerstein's musical **Oklahoma!** directed by Rouben Mamoulian at Drury Lane. Rivalry of a cowboy and a cowhand for a cowgirl. Landmark in American musicals. Premiered in 1943, it set new standards, notably in its integration of dance to further plot and characterisation. For 18 years it held the record for the longest-running musical in Broadway history. One of the high spots was Agnes de Mille's choreography for the 15-minute ballet which closed the first act. London had seen nothing like it and was bowled over by its speed, drive and dynamism. The wonderful score included "Oh, What A Beautiful Mornin'", "The Surrey with the Fringe on Top" "I Can't Say No" and "People Will Say We're in Love". 1,343 performances

May 10. Laurel and Hardy at London Palladium.

May 28. John Carol, Nigel Stock and Andre Morrell in Reginald Beckwith's **Boys in Brown** directed by Norman Marshall at Arts. "How would Harrow and Eton fare," asks the paternalistic Governor of a Borstal Institution, "if their intake was drawn from failures and no-goods?"

May 30. Robert Morley and Peggy Ashcroft in Robert Morley and Noël Langley's **Edward, My Son** directed by Peter Ashmore at His Majesty's. Edward, the worthless son of a crooked newspaper magnate, is never seen. The play covered a period of twenty-eight years from 1919 to 1949, tracing the rise of the father through arson, blackmail and murder, to the peerage, and the descent of his wife, through neglect and disillusionment, to alcoholism. Ashcroft's role was so unlike the sweet romantic heroines the public had identified her with for so long that her performance took everybody by surprise.
—Whenever she appeared this clever and unstable comedy took on a depth and texture which its horrifying implications demanded. *New Statesman and Nation*

Jun 5. Leslie Banks and Sophie Stewart in Howard Lindsay and Russel Crouse's **Life With Father** directed by Murray Macdonald at Savoy. 19th-century home life based on Clarence Day's *New Yorker* recollections. The play needed American actors.

Jun 7. Dolores Gray and Bill Johnson in Irving Berlin's musical **Annie Get Your Gun** directed by Helen Tamiris and Charles Hickman at Coliseum. Book by Herbert and Dorothy Fields. Annie Oakley is the best shot in the world ("Anything You Can Do, I Can Do Better") but she has to learn that she can't get a man with a gun. The only way Frank Butler will ever marry her is if she is second best to him. "There's No Business Like Show Business" became the theatrical profession's hymn. The 23-year-old Dolores Gray stopped the show with "Doin' What Comes Naturally". The curtain-calls went on for half an hour. When the audience learned it was Gray's birthday they sang Happy Birthday.

Jun 17. Robert Helpmann, Ernest Milton and Audrey Fildes in Leonid Andreyev's **He Who Gets Slapped** directed by Tyrone Guthrie at Duchess. Aristocrat, who has been betrayed by his friend and his wife, becomes a clown. The circus is a symbol of a world in miniature. An equestrienne in a ballet skirt symbolises Virtue. A baron masquerades as Vice.
—Guthrie's touch is extremely ingenious but the words tend to get lost in the general brouhaha. *Observer*

Jun 18. Alec Clunes as Professor Higgins and Brenda Bruce as Eliza Doolittle in Bernard Shaw's **Pygmalion** directed by Peter Ashmore at Lyric, Hammersmith. Mervyn Johns as Doolittle.

Jun 19. Robert Donat, Margaret Leighton and Francis Lister in James Bridie's **A Sleeping Clergyman** with Francis Lister directed by H K Ayliff at Criterion. Seduction, murder, blackmail and tuberculosis: a study of heredity over three generations. Donat returned to the two roles he had played in 1933.

Jul 8. Gordon Heath and Evelyn Ellis in Arnaud d'Usseau and James Gow's **Deep Are the Roots** directed by Daphne Rye at Wyndham's. Racial prejudice in the Southern states. Much-decorated black soldier returns to the white home where he was brought up. He rejects the white daughter's offer of marriage because he knows it won't work.

Jul 9. Margaret Sullivan, Wendell Corey and Audrey Christie in John Van Druten's **The Voice of the Turtle** directed by John Van Druten at Piccadilly. Wartime romantic comedy. Turtle-doves are noted for their soft cooing and affection for mate and young. Out-of-work actress spends a weekend with a soldier on leave who has been stood up by her best friend. Will they go to bed? Will she allow herself to fall in love? Wry, charming and unpretentious, it was immensely popular when it was first produced in New York in 1943 when it ran for 1,557 performances. The London critics could not understand its Broadway success and it failed in London.

Jul 22. Bernard Lee, Beatrice Varley, Elspeth March and Ralph Michael in Noël Coward's **Peace in Our Time** directed by Noël Coward and Alan Webb at Lyric. Coward imagined the Battle of Britain lost and the nation conquered but not defeated. Written in the patriotic idiom of *This Happy Breed*, it came too soon after the war to

have box office appeal. The line, which got the biggest laugh, was when the publican refused to serve the local prostitute: "It's not because you're a tart but because you've been selling yourself to the enemy."
—It was like watching 36 very competent swimmers paddling about in six inches of water.
ALAN DENT *News Chronicle*

Jul 30. Alastair Sim, George Cole and Jane Aird in James Bridie's **Dr Angelus** directed by Alastair Sim at Phoenix. Burlesque thriller based on Dr Pritchard, the last man to be hanged in public in 1865. The Glaswegian doctor had murdered his wife and his mother-in-law. A colleague knew he was poisoning them but didn't inform the police because he thought it would have been unprofessional to do so. Sim was a most avuncular hypocrite.

Aug 15. Lewis Casson and Sybil Thorndike in J B Priestley's **The Linden Tree** directed by Michael Macowan at Duchess. Everley Gregg as housekeeper. Professor of History refuses to retire at 65 much to the fury of the Vice-Chancellor, the chagrin of his wife and his family and the indifference of his students.

Aug 24. First Edinburgh Festival opened.

Aug 27. A E Matthews, Marjorie Fielding, Peter Coke and Michael Shepley in William Douglas Home's **The Chiltern Hundreds** directed by Colin Chandler at Vaudeville. One of the losers in the Labour landslide of 1945 is an aristocrat whose family has been sending a Tory candidate to Parliament for 200 uninterrupted years. The Labour candidate, having been elected, is promptly dispatched to the House of Lords which leads to a by-election. The aristocrat decides to stand, second time round, as the Labour candidate. The family butler, a stout Tory, is appalled and stands as the Conservative candidate. Naturally, the butler wins. The comedy, a big

Betty Jane Watson and Harold Keel in **Oklahoma!**

1947 World Premieres
New York
Tennessee Williams's *A Streetcar Named Desire*
Arthur Miller's *All My Sons*
Columbus, Ohio
Eugene O'Neill's *A Moon for the Misbegotten*
Paris
Jean Genet's *The Maids*
Jean Anouilh's *L'invitation au Chateau*
Jean-Paul Sartre's *Les Mains Sales*

Births
Stephen Daldry, British director
David Hare, British playwright
David Mamet, American playwright
Jonathan Pryce, British actor

Willy Russell, British dramatist, songwriter

Deaths
James Agate (*b.*1877), British critic
Luigi Chiarelli (*b.*1880), Italian playwright

Honours
Knights
Laurence Olivier, actor
Ralph Richardson, actor

History
—Independence of India and Pakistan
—House Un-American Activities Committee began hearings
—Dead Sea Scrolls found in Palestine

hit, was inspired by the political activities of Home's father's butler. The satire was very gentle. The real subject was keeping the upper classes and their servants in their proper places. 79-year-old A E Matthews, who was as eccentric as the dotty, rabbit-shooting Wodehousian old buffer he was playing, blundered through the play with his blunderbuss making numerous entrances and exits.

Sep 3. Mary Ellis and Anthony Ireland in Noël Coward's **Point Valaine** directed by Peter Glenville at Embassy. This melodrama, set in the West Indies, was first produced in America in 1934, with Alfred Lunt and Lynn Fontanne, when it was not a success. Ten years later it repeated its failure in London. Coward recognised that the story and characters were "neither big enough for tragedy nor light enough for comedy."

Sep 4. Joyce Grenfell, Elizabeth Welch and Max Adrian in **Tuppence Coloured** directed by Laurier Lister at Lyric, Hammersmith. Revue. Transferred to Globe. Grenfell satirized a number of extremely silly women. Welch sang "La Vie en rose."

Oct 3. James Donald and Rosamund John in Bernard Shaw's **You Never Can Tell** directed by Peter Ashmore at Wyndham's. D A Clarke-Smith as the father. Harcourt Williams as the waiter. Ernest Thesiger as the solicitor.

Oct 21. Patrick J Kelly and Beryl Seton in **Finian's Rainbow** directed by James Gelb at Palace. Musical. Book by E Y Harburg and Fred Saidy. Lyrics by E Y Harburg. Music by Burton Lane. Choreography by Michael Kidd. How Are Things in Glocca Morra? Finian arrives in Missitucky with his daughter and a crock of gold he stole from the little people. Alfie Bass played the Leprechaun. The musical did not repeat its Broadway success.

Oct 29. The American Negro Theatre. Hilda Simms, Frederick O'Neal and Earle Hyman in Philip Yordan's **Anna Lucasta** directed by Walter Thompson Ash at His Majesty's. Prostitute marries nice young man, who doesn't care about her past. Yordan had originally written a story of Polish immigrant life in Pennsylvania, but when no Broadway producer was interested in Polish immigrants he rewrote it for the American Negro Theatre. The actors made a big impression in New York and London.
—The full-blooded acting is, oh such a wonderful change from the over-civilised histrionics we have been watching lately. LEONARD MOSLEY *Express*

Nov 4. Trevor Howard as Petruchio and Patricia Burke as Kate in Shakespeare's **The Taming of the Shrew** directed by John Burrell at Old Vic. Bernard Miles' Christopher Sly, the drunken tinker, dominated the production.
—Trevor Howard plays in the manner of a dashing young pirate, a gallant with a twinkle, which softens his outrageous conduct. ERIC KEOWN *Punch*

Nov 10. Ruth Draper at Criterion.

Nov 18. Jack Buchanan, Coral Browne, Austin Trevor and Heather Thatcher in Frederick Lonsdale's **Canaries Sometimes Sing** directed by Norman Marshall at Garrick. Husbands exchange wives. A once fashionable comedy of the late 1920s had dated. It seemed to *The Times* "no longer a brilliant display of bad manners but a facile and strangely vulgar piece of stage craft."

Dec 3. Celia Johnson in Bernard Shaw's **Saint Joan** directed by John Burrell at New. John Clements as Dunois. Bernard Miles as Inquisitor. Mark Dignam as Cauchon. Harry Andrews as Warwick. Alec Guinness as the Dauphin.
—For all her sincerity, she [Celia Johnson] is at no point suited, not in voice, presence or weight. This is no fault of hers, but her acting fails to redeem it. T C WORSLEY *New Statesman and Nation*

—Mr Alec Guinness's Dauphin is a triumph. It suggests a sharp-nosed, half-witted schoolgirl in its red stockings and its yellow smock, and it replies to all the bullying it encounters with a flouncing and sulky resentment that is endearing as well as comic. HAROLD HOBSON *Sunday Times*

Dec 18. Michael Redgrave and Ena Burrill in Shakespeare's **Macbeth** directed by Norris Houghton at Aldwych. Many critics complained about Paul Sherriff's distracting design.
—Speeches and phrases of incomparable beauty are hurled out in martial rage. IVOR BROWN
—I have never known any Macbeth begin worse or finish better. ALAN DENT *News Chronicle*

1948

Jan 5. Mickey Rooney at Palladium. Rooney was not a success and cut his engagement short.

Jan 24. Mae West in Mae West's **Diamond Lil** directed by William Mollison at Prince of Wales. Twice nightly at 6.10 and 8.35. Comic melodrama of the gay nineties proved to be an ornate and shoddy vehicle for West's husky, voluptuous, hip-swaying, brassy caricature of sex. Asked about the men in her life, she memorably replied, "It's not the men in my life that counts, but the life in my men."

Jan 28. Cyril Ritchard as Lord Foppington and Madge Elliott is Berinthia in John Vanbrugh's **The Relapse** directed by Anthony Quayle at Phoenix. Jessie Evans as Hoyden. Esmond Knight as Fashion. Audrey Fildes as Amanda. Hamlyn Benson as Sir Tunbelly Clumsey.
—Mr Cyril Ritchard's Foppington pirouettes perilously near the borderline between musical comedy and comedy, but there is no resisting the effervescence of his high spirits. *The Times*

Feb 2. Danny Kaye at Palladium. The audience yelled and cheered. Kaye was the most sensationally successful single performer to appear in London in living memory. His act included such songs as "Anatole of France" and "Minnie the Moocher".

Feb 3. Alec Guinness in Nikolai Gogol's **The Government Inspector** directed by John Burrell at New. Bernard Miles as the Mayor. Harry Andrews as Osip. The costumes and heavy make-up turned the actors into marionettes.
—In his role Alec Guinness is immaculately funny. If his performance is Chaplinesque in its puffed-up elegance, Bernard Miles' blundering mayor is Hogarthian in its grossness: the very contrast of their comedy is a joy. CECIL WILSON *Daily Mail*

Feb 5. Gladys Cooper, Andrew Cruickshank and Francis Lister in Peter Ustinov's **The Indifferent Shepherd** directed by Norman Marshall at Criterion. A clash between two priests: one is a good man, despised, patronised and spineless; the other is of doubtful character but a first-rate cleric. Cooper played the latter's unhappy wife. She did not always know Ustinov's lines and provided her own, which varied from performance to performance.
—There has rarely been an actress who exuded more animal health, even in old age, or who was more fatally attractive, her deep and lovely voice cajoling and cruel, or both at once. PETER USTINOV *Dear Me*

Feb 19. Joseph O'Connor, Arthur Hambling and Geoffrey Dunn in Bridget Boland's **Cockpit** directed by Michael Macowan at Playhouse. During the chaos of post-war Europe, a German provincial theatre is filled with refugees from concentration camps and prisons. Macowan created the illusion that the Playhouse audiences were all refugees.

Mar 2. Mady Christians in John Van Druten's **I Remember Mama** directed by Mady Christians at Aldwych. Humorous incidents in the life of a Norwegian-American family in San Francisco. Mady Christians' grace, beauty, dignity and simple naturalness were much admired.

Mar 10. Alec Clunes and Sheila Manahan in Christopher Fry's **The Lady's Not For Burning** directed by Jack Hawkins at Arts. In the small market town of Cool Clary in the year 1400 they believe they have a witch and a murderer in their midst. Their religious upbringing, superstition and fear of damnation, purgatory and hell, lead them inevitably to take the witch much more seriously than the murderer. They are not prepared to hang Thomas Mendip, the self-confessed criminal, but they are prepared to burn Jennet Jourdemayne as a witch on the flimsiest of evidence. The irony is that she, who wishes to live, is to be condemned to death; while he, who wants to die, is to be condemned to more life. Fry, preoccupied with the mysteries, perplexities and contradictions of life and death, is insistent on the Christian values of hope, compassion and love. He comes firmly down on the side of life and his belief in the kindness of God and men.
—Mr. Christopher Fry is a poet, the most brilliant and fertile, in my judgment, that has appeared since Auden ... no one who enjoys poetry and the clash and thunder of rhetoric should miss *The Lady's Not for Burning*. T C WORSLEY *New Statesman and Nation*

1948 World Premieres

New York
Cole Porter's *Kiss Me Kate*
Tennessee Williams's *Summer and Smoke*
Maxwell Anderson's *Anne of a Thousand Days*

Northfield, Minnesota
Bertolt Brecht's *The Caucasian Chalk Circle*

Paris
Paul Claudel's *Partage du Midi*
Jean Anouilh's *Ardèle*
Jean Genet's *Deathwatch*

Zurich
Bertolt Brecht's *Mr Puntila and His Man Matti*

Births
David Edgar, British playwright
Andrew Lloyd Webber, British composer

Deaths
Seymour Hicks (*b.*1871), British actor-manager
Matheson Lang (*b.*1877), British actor-manager

History
—Gandhi assassinated
—Soviet blockade of West Berlin
—Apartheid official policy in South Africa
—National Health Service introduced in UK

Notes
—Aldeburgh Festival established
—Anthony Quayle artistic director of Memorial Theatre
—Company of Four at Lyric

Mar 20. Yolande Donlan and Ronald Simpson in Clifford Odets's **Rocket to the Moon** directed by Peter Cotes at St Martin's. Male menopausal tragi-comedy. Forty-year-old dentist, unhappily married, falls in love with his secretary, but is unable to leave his wife. The English accents didn't help the play.

Mar 23. Denys Blakelock and Joan Young in Arthur Wing Pinero's **Dandy Dick** designed by Cecil Beaton and directed by Athene Seyler at Arts.

Mar 29. Margaret Rutherford and George Howe in John Dighton's **The Happiest Days of Your Life** directed by Richard Bird at Apollo. Ministerial blunder leads to girls' school being billeted on boys' school. Rutherford's definitive performance as the headmistress is preserved on film.

Mar 31. John Clements in Shakespeare's **Coriolanus** directed by E Martin Browne at Old Vic. Rosalind Atkinson as Volumnia. Most critics felt that Alec Guinness as Memenius had stolen the play
—[Memenius] is in some ways the best part, but I protest strongly the use of the hateful phrase, "stealing the play" when a good actor has a good opportunity and takes it properly. Actors who steal plays should be drummed off the stage. Theft is not part of their craft and Guinness gives a beautiful loyal performance "in support". IVOR BROWN *Observer*

Apr 21. Peter Ustinov, Joan Greenwood and Denholm Elliott in Ingmar Bergman's **Frenzy** adapted by Peter Ustinov and directed by Murray Macdonald at St Martin's. Ustinov was chilling as a mad, tormented, sadistic pervert who debauches a 19-year-old girl.

Apr 29. Two operas by Gian Carlo Menotti at Cambridge. Marie Powers in **The Medium** and Maria d'Attili in **The Telephone**. The medium loses her grip. Scared by the forces she has unleashed, she inadvertently, murders her mute servant.

May 11. Joseph Calleia and Margalo Gillmore in Arthur Miller's **All My Sons** directed by Warren Jenkins at Lyric, Hammersmith. Award-winning drama, modelled on Greek classical tragedy. American manufacturer during the war knowingly allowed defective engines to be shipped to the United States Air Force. 21 pilots died. He let his partner go to prison, denying his complicity. He argues that it was business and what he did was for the family. The American business community, sensitive to charges that they had made their fortunes out of the Second World War, denounced the play as a smear on their profession and accused Miller of being a communist. Calleia was likened by one critic to a small-town Macbeth. Transferred to Globe.

Jun 2. Yvonne Arnaud and Charles Victor in Arthur Macrae's **Traveller's Joy** directed by Richard Bird at Criterion. Government currency restrictions for people travelling abroad have led to rich holidaymakers finding themselves short of cash. Some, whilst staying in a luxury hotel, are reduced to petty criminality.
—Yvonne Arnaud, whose English grows deliciously worse and worse, manages by her inimitable giggles and squeaks to make the comedy much funnier than it really is. CECIL WILSON *Daily Mail*

Jun 3. Clive Brook and Pamela Brown in Aldous Huxley's **The Gioconda Smile** directed by Peter Glenville at New. Psychological thriller: woman poisons a man's wife in order to marry him. When he rejects her, she plans to get him arrested for the murder. Melodrama plus a bit of philosophy.

Jun 18. Yolande Donlan as Lucrece in Noël Langley's **Cage Me A Peacock** designed by Berkeley Sutcliffe and directed by Charles Hickman at Strand. Music by Eve Lynd. Frolics in Ancient Rome plus a witty satire on the Lucrece legend. Linda Gray as Cassandra. Simon Lack as Tarquin.

Jul 6. Kathleen Michael, Clive Morton, Robert Flemyng and Miles Malleson in Frank Vosper's **People Like Us** directed by Murray Macdonald at Wyndham's. There was a disclaimer in the programme to the effect that the characters were entirely fictitious but everybody knew the play was based on the sensational Edith Bywaters/Frederick Thompson murder trial. It was Mrs Bywaters' sexually and murderously explicit letters which had made the trial so sensational. Kathleen Michael had a big success as the over-sexed suburban wife who tells her lover, after he has committed the murder she incited, that she had not meant him to do it.

Jul 25. Basil Dignam, Denholm Elliott and Ferdy Mayne in Arthur Schnitzler's **The Green Cockatoo** directed by Michael Warre at Lyric, Hammersmith. Sunday night production. One-act play set in a public house in the slums of Paris on the eve of the storming of the Bastille. The landlord engages actors to play criminals for the benefit of an aristocratic audience looking for a cheap thrill. Can you tell the difference between a real murderer and an actor playing a murderer? Which is more real: the drama in the pub or the drama in the street? Or to put the question another way, what would you bet on the chances of the aristocrats present, on this day of all days, the 14 July 1789, living long enough to be guillotined?

Jul 28. Helen Hayes as Amanda, Frances Heflin as Laura, Phil Brown as Tom and Hugh McDermott as the Gentleman Caller in Tennessee Williams's **The Glass Menagerie** directed by John Gielgud at Haymarket. Williams' first stage success was based on a poignant and cruel incident, which had happened to his sister. Tom brings home a friend from the shoe factory where he works as a clerk. His mother had asked him to bring a gentleman caller for his painfully shy sister, who has retreated into a world of her own and is as fragile as her glass menagerie. The friend turns out to be the boy she had secretly admired at high school. Against all expectation, he succeeds in drawing her out – only for her to learn that he is already engaged to be married. Williams won The New York Drama Critics Award and the Pulitzer Prize. Hayes got better notices than the play. Williams in his *Memoirs* recorded how much he loathed her "pancake performance" and "her whole bag of tricks."
—The play itself is a bitter disappointment. It's like being offered a fine poem and given whimsical doggerel instead and fobbed off with two ounces of sugar candy. ALAN DENT *News Chronicle*
—Miss Hayes flutters and flutes triumphantly through this part, with the absolute assurance of the master artist who convinces us that it could only have been like this. T C WORSLEY *New Statesman and Nation*

Aug 4. Basil Sydney, Joyce Redman and Michael Gough in Jean-Paul Sartre's **Crime Passionel** (*Les Mains Sales*) directed by Peter Glenville transferred from Lyric, Hammersmith, to Garrick. French political thriller and philosophical tragedy: intellectual bourgeois anarchist finds that he cannot pull the trigger in cold blood; but when he mistakenly thinks his wife is having an affair with a fellow anarchist he has no difficulty in killing him. Thus do political assassinations become crimes passionelles.

Aug 26. Angela Baddeley and Jessica Spencer in J B Priestley's **Eden End** directed by Michael Macowan at Duchess. A woman returns home, unexpectedly, after eight years, her marriage and career in tatters. She presumes she can continue where she left off. Her sister, who sacrificed her life to look after their mother and father, deeply resents her arrival. The play is set in 1912 when nobody on stage knows that it is curtains for Edwardian England. ("There is a better world coming ... saner, cleaner ...") Priestley plugged the period cross-references so relentlessly that it was difficult for the pathos to have its proper impact.

Sep 2. Francis Lister and Constance Cummings in Sacha Guitry's **Don't Listen, Ladies!** directed by William Armstrong at St James. French farce adapted by Guy Bolton and Stephen Powys. Art dealer has trouble dealing with two wives.

Sep 8. Eric Portman and Mary Ellis in Terence Rattigan's **Playbill** directed by Peter Glenville at Phoenix. Two one-act plays. **The Browning Version** was based on an actual incident from Rattigan's boyhood. He wrote the role of the failed public schoolteacher for John Gielgud, who turned it down, tactlessly remarking that he didn't think his public wanted to see him in anything second-rate. (He later acted the play on American television with great success.) The play has two fine scenes. The first is when the pupil gives the teacher a present of a book and the teacher breaks down. The second is when the teacher's wife wilfully misinterprets the boy's gift as a bribe. **Harlequinade** was a poor farce at the expense of tacky touring companies and two self-centred actors, actor and wife team, who were still playing Romeo and Juliet in their late forties.
—Mr Eric Portman as the schoolmaster gives one of the brilliant performances of the year. He keeps and holds very exactly the details of the personality, the tics of speech and the uncontrollable jerks of mannerism which a life-time has stamped on the mask. T C WORSLEY *New Statesman and Nation*

Sep 19. Jane Baxter as Viola, Harry Andrews as Malvolio and Cedric Hardwicke as Sir Toby Belch in Shakespeare's **Twelfth Night** directed by Alec Guinness at New. Robert Eddison's melancholy Feste stole the notices.

Sep 29. Gordon Harker in Frank Harvey's **Saloon Bar** directed by Richard Bird at Garrick. Harker revived one of his best Cockney roles.

Sep 29. Eileen Herlie in Euripides's **Medea** freely adapted by Robinson Jeffers, designed by Leslie Hurry and directed by John Gielgud at Globe. Cathleen Nesbitt as Nurse. Herlie looked magnificent but she needed to turn down the volume.
—There's no nonsense about under-acting with Miss Herlie. Her eyes blaze, her voice thunders. She does not so much speak daggers as a whole armoury of broadswords. HAROLD HOBSON *Sunday Times.*
—Eileen Herlie's Medea is one of the greatest tragic performances seen in an English theatre (in over forty years). She redeems completely a vulgar and abbreviated version of the tragedy by a dramatic exhibition of Asiatic revenge and hatred that terrifies while it enthrals, a classic purity of diction, a maturity of technique, a passion and a pathos no other actress could surpass. SIDNEY W CARROLL *in a letter to The Sunday Times*

Oct 1. Comédie Française at Cambridge. Jean Yonnel as Orestes and Annie Ducaux as Andromache in Racine's **Andromache**. Beautifully spoken but without fire.

Oct 7. Cedric Hardwicke in Christopher Marlowe's **Dr Faustus** directed by John Burrell at New. Robert Eddison, a gaunt, melancholy, handsome and beautifully spoken Mephistopheles, was the more impressive figure.

Oct 13. Flora Robson and Richard Leech in Bernard Shaw's **Captain Brassbound's Conversion** directed by John Counsell at Lyric, Hammersmith. Robson, usually cast in strong emotional roles, acted with an unexpectedly light and charming touch.

Oct 21. Harry Andrews as Mirabell and Faith Brook as Millamant in William Congreve's **The Way of the World** directed by John Burrell at New. Edith Evans as Lady Wishfort looked like an old peeled wall and behaved like a battleship on the offensive after its ammunition was spent. She resembled a preposterous caricature of Queen Elizabeth.

Nov 2. Alastair Sim as Dr Knox in James Bridie's **The Anatomist** directed by Alastair Sim at Westminster. Sim had just been elected Rector of Edinburgh University and this may have accounted for his tentative performance. He played up the comedy and underplayed the villainy. He didn't sport an eye-patch. He wasn't the barnstorming tenor Bridie had imagined and which Henry Ainley had acted in 1931, but Bridie was won over to his interpretation.

Nov 3. Anton Walbrook as Ekdal, Fay Compton as his wife, Mai Zetterling as his daughter, Robert Harris as Gregers Werle, Walter Fitzgerald as Dr Relling and Miles Malleson as Old Ekdal in Henrik Ibsen's **The Wild Duck** directed by Michael Benthall at St Martin's. Zetterling, the 22-year-old Swedish film star, was heartbreaking: she looked no more than fourteen and her broken English intensified the pathos of the baffled child.
—Never have I seen a grown actress who could catch more surely the eager innocence, the mingled grace and clumsiness of childhood. W A DARLINGTON *Daily Telegraph*
—*The Wild Duck* is as exquisitely comic as it is exquisitely pathetic. ANTHONY COOKMAN *Tatler*

Nov 4. Leslie Banks, Irene Worth and Cecil Trouncer in J B Priestley's **Home is Tomorrow** directed by Michael Macowan at Cambridge. A wordy, pedestrian debate on the problems of international harmony takes place on a Caribbean island administered by UNO.

Nov 17. Hermione Gingold and Walter Crisham in **Slings and Arrows** devised by Hermione Gingold and Charles Hickman at Comedy. Revue. Gingold mocked Eileen Herlie's Medea: "O Euripides, how are thou translated!"

Eileen Herlie in Medea

Nov 24. John Gielgud, Sybil Thorndike and David Horne in St John Hankin's **The Return of the Prodigal** directed by Peter Glenville at Globe. The major mistake was to let Cecil Beaton loose on his favourite period. The play was lost in all the theatrical plumage. The production cut out Hankin's bitter denouncement of society, a key speech.

Nov 25. Edith Evans as Ranevsky, Robert Eddison as Trofimov, Mark Dignam as Lopahin, Cedric Hardwicke as Gaev, Harry Andrews as Erihodov and Pauline Jameson as Dunyasha in Anton Chekhov's **The Cherry Orchard** designed by Tanya Moiseiwitsch and directed by Hugh Hunt at New.
— [Edith Evans] is indeed rather like a great Parisian actress playing an imaginary Madame Ravensky with infinite sparkling perceptiveness but without that quality of ease and naturalness, which signifies the identification of player and part. *The Times*

Nov 26. Diana Churchill, Elizabeth Welch and Max Adrian in **Oranges and Lemons** directed by Laurier Lister at Lyric. Revue.

Dec 15. Gertrude Lawrence and Michael Gough in Daphne du Maurier's **September Tide** directed by Irene Hentschel at Aldwych. Artificial, clichéd and novelettish, its success was due entirely to Gertrude Lawrence who was making her return to the London stage after a twelve-year absence. Dressed by Molyneux and trailing 1930s theatrical glamour and behaviour, she was cast as a widow, who lived in Cornwall and had old-fashioned ideas about morality. She and her son-in-law, an artist, became attracted to each other and one stormy night, they were left all on their own. Du Maurier didn't want there to be any physical expression of their love and declared that anybody who thought there had been had a filthy mind. The reason for this no-sex-please-we're-British reticence was that the widow was a disguised portrait of Ellen Doubleday, with whom she was having a passionate friendship. After the production had opened, Du Maurier became obsessed with Gertrude Lawrence and entered into another passionate friendship.

1949

Jan 5. Sid Field and Athene Seyler in Mary Chase's **Harvey** directed by Anthony Quayle at Prince of Wales. Lovable dipsomaniac is accompanied by an invisible six-foot white rabbit called Harvey. Music hall comedian Field, who was making his first appearance in a straight play, introduced a lot of extraneous music hall comic business. Joe E Brown played the role when Field left the cast.

Jan 20. Laurence Olivier and Vivien Leigh as Sir Peter and Lady Teazle in Richard Brinsley Sheridan's **The School for Scandal** directed by Laurence Olivier at New.
—The acting is stylised to such a pitch that I felt on occasion I was at a ballet rather than a serious comedy and as a result Sir Laurence achieved decorative effect at the expense of dramatic power. W A DARLINGTON *Daily Telegraph*

Jan 24. Michael Redgrave and Freda Jackson in August Strindberg's **The Father** directed by Dennis Arundell at Duchess. First performance in 20 years. The critics compared Redgrave unfavourably with Robert Loraine, many forgetting that Loraine had cut the play. Redgrave gave the full version and was truer to Strindberg.
—Many playgoers (myself included) regretted the lack of sound and fury. The fuse was laid with infinite skill, but there was – so it seemed – no explosion: the actor fizzled, instead of flaring with the necessary violence. RICHARD FINDLATER *Michael Redgrave Actor*

Feb 1. Ralph Richardson, Peggy Ashcroft and James Donald in Ruth and August Goetz's **The Heiress** directed by John Gielgud at Haymarket. Battle between a commonplace girl and her sardonic father develops when she is courted by an adventurer who is interested only in her money. Henry James always longed to be a successful playwright, but his success came only after his death when his novels were adapted for stage and screen. Goetz's adaptation of *Washington Square*, however, trivialised a great novella, removing its subtlety and, without the author's brilliant ironic commentary, all the audience was left with was the melodrama.
—Ralph Richardson plays the father with that unobtrusive certainty of touch which makes him an actor at once easy to appreciate and difficult to anatomize. W A DARLINGTON *Daily Telegraph*
—Of Miss Peggy Ashcroft's Catherine one hesitates to speak simply because everything one says must be inadequate. For her performance all superlatives are pale and feeble things. HAROLD HOBSON *Sunday Times*

Feb 10. Vivien Leigh as Antigone, George Relph as Creon and Laurence Olivier as Chorus in Jean Anouilh's **Antigone** directed by Laurence Olivier at New. Greek tragedy is dressed in white tie and tails. When the play was first produced in Occupied France during World War 2 in 1942 the French saw in it their own struggle against the Germans. Anouilh is at his best when he discards Sophocles, as in the splendid twist he gives the story of Eteocles and Polynices, who were "a pair of blackguards and they died like cheap gangsters." In death they were so mutilated that Anouilh's Creon could not tell them apart and so gave the State funeral to the prettier of the two carcasses. Antigone's gesture is therefore even more futile; but the whole point, during the war, was that

Hugh Stewart, Thomas Heathcote, Vivien Leigh, George Relph, Michael Reddington, Laurence Olivier, Helen Beck and Eileen Beldon in Antigone

1949 World Premieres

New York
Arthur Miller's *Death of a Salesman*
Richard Rogers and Oscar
  Hammerstein's *South Pacific*
Edinburgh
T S Eliot's *The Cocktail Party*
Paris
Albert Camus' *Les Justes*

Deaths

Philip Barry (*b.*1896), American
  playwright
Maurice Maeterlinck (*b.*1862),
  Belgian poet, playwright

Honours

Laurence Olivier's film of *Henry V*
  won five Oscars

Notes

—The National Theatre Bill was
  passed through both Houses of
  Parliament without a division.
  By this act the government was
  empowered to contribute up to £1
  million towards the building. The
  date of its implementation however
  was left to the discretion of the
  Chancellor of the Exchequer

History

—NATO Alliance formed
—Mao Zedong declared People's
  Republic of China
—Creation of West and East
  Germany
—Republic of Ireland formed
—George Orwell's *1984* published

it didn't matter how small the gesture was so long as the Germans were defied.
—Miss Vivien Leigh's Antigone has the appeal of an exquisite carved statuette. Mute and helpless, she commands the pathos of the part but when vehemence of argument is called for she has not all the power that splendid defiance requires. *The Times*

Feb 11. Alec Guinness, Sophie Stewart, John Laurie and John Gregson in J Lee-Thompson and Dudley Leslie's **The Human Touch** directed by Peter Ashmore at Savoy. Dr James Young, the first anaesthetist to use chloroform, had to battle in 1847 against professional, lay and religious prejudice. The authors were heavy-handed.

Feb 23. Sybil Thorndike, Mary Merrall and Lewis Casson in Margery Sharp's **The Foolish Gentlewoman** directed by Michael Macowan at Duchess. Scatterbrained old lady tries to make amends to a woman she tricked out of marriage 35 years earlier,

but the woman, a mean, bitter, dried-up spinster, doesn't want her money. She wants her friendship.

Feb 24. John Lewis as Franz Schubert and Celia Lipton as Lili in **Lilac Time** directed by Pat Hillyard at His Majesty's. Book by A M Willner and Heinz Reichert. English adaptation and lyrics by Adrian Ross. Lewis's tongue-tied Schubert lacked volume.

Mar 7. William Sylvester and Sheila Burrell in Howard Richardson and William Berney's **Dark of The Moon** directed by Peter Brook at Lyric, Hammersmith. Witch boy of the Smokey Mountains turns human and seeks the love of no-good Barbara Allen. If he can keep her faithful he can remain mortal. The inventive and erotic production with its immense vitality, square dances and revivalist hymns, was a triumph for Brook. Transferred to Ambassadors.

Mar 17. Paul Scofield as Alexander the Great in Terence Rattigan's **Adventure Story** directed by Peter Glenville at St James's. Gwen Ffrangcon-Davies as the Queen Mother of the Persians. Rattigan said his play "lacked the language of the poet and the perception of the philosopher."
—Mr Paul Scofield is a young actor graced with the most enviable array of gifts: an excellent presence, fine looks, a musical voice and that indefinable magnetism which can by itself take an audience. T C WORSLEY *New Statesman and Nation*

Mar 23. Edith Evans, Peter Finch and Felix Aylmer in James Bridie's **Daphne Laureola** directed by Murray Macdonald at Wyndham's. A rich and unhappy woman longs to be wanton, but has the misfortune to be a dyed-in-the-wool Puritan. Evans, charming and funny, burst into song during a long, drunken monologue.
—[Edith Evans] is now at the height of her powers. This play will be revived many times in the future and we who have seen Edith Evans in it will long bore the less fortunate with our comparisons. T C WORSLEY *New Statesman and Nation*

Apr 14. Philip Hanna and Patricia Hughes in Alan Jay Lerner and Frederick Loewe's musical **Brigadoon** directed by Robert Lewis at His Majesty's. Choreography by Agnes de Mille. Synthetic Scottish village appears out of the mist every two hundred years. An American falls in love with a highland lassie. Noelle Gordon had a big success with two comic songs.

Claire Bloom, Nora Nicholson, John Gielgud, Pamela Brown, David Evans, Harcourt Williams, Richard Burton and Richard Leech in *The Lady's Not for Burning*

Paul Muni, Katharine Alexander, Kevin McCarthy and Frank Maxwell in Death of a Salesman

Apr 28. Stewart Granger, Jean Simmons, Sonia Dresdel, Harold Scott, Frederick Valk and Mary Clare in Leo Tolstoy's **The Power of Darkness** adapted and directed by Peter Glenville at Lyric.
—Much talent, money, energy have been expended; but neither talent, nor money, nor energy are enough to get at the secret of this elemental drama when they are combined only with the genteelest realistic approach. J C WORSLEY *New Statesman and Nation*

May 3. Flora Robson in Lesley Storm's **Black Chiffon** directed by Charles Hickman at Westminster. Rich woman on impulse steals a black chiffon nightdress. Robson's ability to play women at the end of their tether was legendary and she transformed a mundane script.

May 5. John Clements as Archer, Kay Hammond as Mrs Sullen and Robert Eddison as Aimwell in George Farquhar's **The Beaux's Stratagem** directed by John Clements at Phoenix. Clements's comic gravity was contrasted with Eddison's foppish levity. Hammond languished, drawled and lisped. She was especially delightful when Mrs Sullen was about to be ravished by Archer. "Help! Help! Help!" she cried, her voice getting softer and softer. Transferred to Lyric.

May 11. John Gielgud, Pamela Brown, Harcourt Williams, Nora Nicholson, Richard Burton, Claire Bloom, David Evans, Richard Leech, Peter Bull, Eliot Makeham and Esme Percy in Christopher Fry's **The Lady's Not For Burning** directed by John Gielgud and Esme Percy at Globe. Scenery and costumes by Oliver Messel. Gielgud acted and directed this romantic, medieval, metaphysical frolic as if it were a first cousin to an artificial comedy. The verse glittered in the second act duet, notable for its lyric beauty and wit. Gielgud thought that the production had been too beautiful and that if he had worn modern battle-dress, Fry's message might have been clearer.
—From the moment the curtain rises on *The Lady's Not For Burning,* we are launched into a sea of dazzling verbal invention which never for a moment flags. *New Statesman*
— [Christopher Fry] is without doubt one of the brightest hopes in British theatre. A poet and a wit, he is also that even rarer creature, a man of rich and abundant fancy with an ironic sense of humour. *Punch*
—Gielgud, letting loose his vocal music with a new and ringing vigour, played Mendip with unexpected virility of approach: this was a transformed Gielgud, dirt-encrusted, black with scorn, robust rather than picaresque. AUDREY WILLIAMSON *Theatre of Two Decades*

May 18. Renée Houston, Ronald Frankau and Muriel Smith in Cecil Landeau's **Sauce Tartare** directed by Cecil Landeau at Cambridge. Revue.

May 20. Wendy Hiller and Robert Harris in Ronald Gow's adaptation of H G Wells' **Ann Veronica** directed by Peter Ashmore at Piccadilly. Ann Veronica was one of the key figures in the suffragette movement. The Edwardian period was guyed and Cyril Ritchard behaved as if he were appearing in a revue.

Jun 7. Peter Ustinov, Brenda Bruce, Robin Bailey, Mollie Urquhart and Peter Jones in Eric Linklater's **Love in Albania** directed by Peter Ustinov at Lyric, Hammersmith. Ustinov played a military policeman, a picaresque buffoon, who was looking for his long-lost daughter. Transferred to St James's.
—Peter Ustinov's Sergeant is a work of art, a chef d'œuvre of comic invention. *Theatre World*

Jul 12. Raymond Huntley, Stephen Murray, Catherine Lacey and Beatrice Varley in William Dinner and William Morum's **The Late Edwina Black** directed by Chloë Gibson at Ambassadors. Who murdered Edwina? Her husband? Her companion? Or her maid?

Jul 15. Maria d'Attili and George Tozzi in A P Herbert and Vivian Ellis's musical **Tough at the Top** directed by Wendy Toye at Adelphi. Ruritanian nonsense: princess falls in love with a world champion boxer who likes poetry. The décor by Oliver Messel was the best thing about it.

Jul 28. Paul Muni, Katharine Alexander and Kevin McCarthy in Arthur Miller's **Death of a Salesman** directed by Elia Kazan at Phoenix. Willy Loman, a little man who remained little all his life, is a parable on the American Dream after the Dream has gone sour and life is nothing more than a race to the junkyard. It is a play of memory, but there are no flashbacks, only daydreams. The action is happening in Loman's mind. (At one point Miller was going to call the play *The Inside of His Head*.) Loman, who has lost touch with reality and gone slightly crazy, is contemplating suicide. When *Death of a Salesman* was first produced, such was its effect on audiences, that Bernard Gimbel, head of one of New York's largest department stores, immediately gave orders that none of his employees was to be fired for being over-age. *The Evening Standard* said it was the best Russian play since Chekhov. *The Times* called it a masterpiece. Arthur Miller thought Paul Muni wasn't right: he found him too studied, too technical, and his performance having little real inner life.

understand its Broadway success. Leigh's performance is fortunately preserved in Elia Kazan's film. Colleano's foul-mouthed, virile Stanley Kowalski was highly praised for his charm and intelligence. On the first night 150 disappointed galleryites unable to get seats attempted to storm the theatre and were ejected. Acting Blanche finally tipped Leigh into madness.
—After two hours of tedium, the play crackles into a burst of violence. Now and then good writing glimmers but little to explain the Broadway reputation and run. J C TREWIN *Illustrated London News*

Oct 10. Frances Day in Bernard Shaw's **Buoyant Billions** directed by Esme Percy transferred from Malvern Festival to Princes. A comedy of no manners and, for a play by Shaw, surprisingly brief. Young man (Denholm Elliott) wants to take up world-bettering as a profession.

Oct 11. Michael Redgrave as Berowne and Baliol Holloway as Don Armado in Shakespeare's **Love's Labour's Lost** directed by Hugh Hunt at New. The comic roles fared better than the romantic ones. Mark Dignam was Holofernes. George Benson was Costard. Miles Malleson's lovable curate was for many critics the definitive Sir Nathaniel. Paul Rogers took over from Holloway.

Oct 18. Michael Redgrave as Young Marlow, Diana Churchill as Kate Hardcastle, Miles Malleson as Mr Hardcastle, Angela Baddeley as Mrs Hardcastle, Nigel Stock as Tony Lumpkin, Michael Aldridge as Hastings and Yvonne Mitchell as Constance in Oliver Goldsmith's **She Stoops to Conquer** directed by Michael Benthall at New. Alan Barlow's décor was inspired by Thomas Rowlandson. The actors wore grotesque make-ups and there was a lot of horseplay. Redgrave adopted a stutter on the letter M so that "Madam, will you marry me?" would give him particular difficulty. Eric Keown, writing in *Punch*, said his performance "puts him among the great stage stammerers."

Oct 26. Constance Cummings in Rodney Ackland's adaptation of Somerset Maugham's **Before the Party** directed by Benn W Levy at St Martin's. Wife announces that her husband had not died from malaria as everybody had thought, but that she had cut his throat. Maugham left it at that. Ackland ill-advisedly provided a second act.

Nov 29. Hermione Gingold and Hermione Baddeley in Noël Coward's **Fumed Oak** and **Fallen Angels** directed by Willard Stoker at Ambassadors. The actresses turned the play into an extended revue sketch, much to the fury of Coward.

Nov 30. Angela Baddeley as Natalia and Michael Redgrave as Rakitin in Turgenev's **A Month in the Country** directed by Michel Saint-Denis at New. Yvonne Mitchell as Verotchka. Mark Dignam as doctor. Baddeley played Natalia for comedy. Redgrave was thought by some to be too chilly and diffident and the more romantic performance he had given in 1943 was generally preferred.
—But with the exception of Mr Redgrave the acting strikes me in this production as suffering from an excess of expressive emphasis. It catches the manner but not the heart of the characters. T C WORSLEY *New Statesman and Nation*

Dec 1. Margaret Leighton, Hugh Sinclair, Anthony Forwood, Robert Beatty and Wilfred Hyde-White in Philip Barry's **The Philadelphia Story** directed by Harold French at Duchess. Barry's high society comedy was a great success on Broadway in 1939; but it was never that good and its success was due entirely to Katharine Hepburn. The play's reputation rests on the 1940 George Cukor film, which starred Hepburn, Cary Grant and James Stewart, the definitive casting. The heroine, a spoiled heiress, is variously described – much to her mortification – as a virgin goddess, a prig and a perennial spinster – is about to enter a disastrous second marriage, having failed to consummate the first. The biggest laugh is when the heiress discovers that a journalist hadn't take advantage of her when she was blotto and they had both taken a swim in the nude. "Why?" she asks haughtily. "Was I so darned unattractive?"

Ivor Novello in King's Rhapsody

—I believe that the common man is as apt a subject for tragedy in its highest sense as kings are. ARTHUR MILLER
—This play seems to lay the soul of America bare, thrown across the footlights, flat in your face, all the hopes, fears, frustrations, inhibitions, and terrible yearnings of a nation. *Daily Express*

Aug 31. Mervyn Johns and Thora Hird in Jack Kirkland's **Tobacco Road** based on Erskine Caldwell's novel, adapted by Rodney Ackland and directed by Robert Henderson at Playhouse. The play was lambasted by practically every American critic. Yet it went on to be a big box office success.

Sep 15. Ivor Novello, Vanessa Lee, Phyllis Dare and Zena Dare in Ivor Novello's musical **King's Rhapsody** directed by Murray Macdonald at Palace. The mixture as before: Ruritanian nonsense, lavish spectacle, champagne and sugar. The king takes an interest in social reform and has to abdicate in favour of his son. Songs included "If This Were Love" and "Some Day My Heart Will Awake". 842 performances.
—Mr Ivor Novello has pulled out most of the known stops in the organ of easy sentiment. *Punch*

Oct 4. Isabel Jeans as Arkadina, Paul Scofield as Konstantin, Mai Zetterling as Nina, Nicholas Hannen as Dorn and Ian Hunter as Trigorin in Anton Chekhov's **The Seagull** directed by Irene Hentschel at Lyric, Hammersmith. Zetterling's lack of English worried many critics and the production was compared unfavourably to Komisarjevsky's 1936 production. Scofield was accused of being flat, stiff and dull.
—This scene [the last] properly played should be heart-rending; but with Miss Zetterling's monotonous enunciation and Mr Scofield's reserved blankness the whole effect is sadly muzzled. T C WORSLEY *New Statesman and Nation*

Oct 10. Vivien Leigh as Blanche Dubois, Bonar Colleano as Stanley Kowalski, Renee Asherson as Stella and Bernard Braden as Harold Mitchell in Tennessee Williams's **A Streetcar Named Desire** directed by Laurence Olivier at Aldwych. Blanche DuBois, a faded Southern Belle, a frightened and pathetic figure, given to self-dramatisation, sees herself as a heroine in a play by Alexander Dumas. "I don't want realism," she declares, "I want magic." Destitute, she comes to New Orleans to stay with her sister and attempts to break up her sister's marriage. The husband, a primitive brute, takes a terrible revenge, drags up her sordid past, destroys the illusions of her suitor and rapes her. The play was violently condemned. The censor wouldn't allow any reference to homosexuality. The House of Commons thought it lewd and salacious. The rape scene was toned down, but many critics still found the play shoddy and couldn't

Vivien Leigh in A Streetcar Named Desire

1950–1959

1950

Jan 17. Miles Malleson as Harpagon in his free adaptation of Molière's **The Miser** directed by Tyrone Guthrie at New. Malleson softened the satire. "C'est magnifique," said Eric Keown in *Punch*, "mais ce n'est pas Molière."
—Mr Malleson has replaced the comic monster with a great overgrown baby who will not share his toys. A V Cookman *Tatler*

Jan 18. Laurence Olivier in Christopher Fry's **Venus Observed** directed by Laurence Olivier at St James's. The second in Fry's quartet of seasonal comedies. Duke (Laurence Olivier), seeking an end to affairs-without-end, asks his son (Denholm Elliott) to take on the role of Paris and choose a wife for him from three of his former mistresses during an eclipse of the sun. The choice lies between incendiary Rosabel (Valerie Taylor), vulgar Jessie (Brenda de Banzie) and Home Counties Hilda (Rachel Kempson). Son and father are distracted by the unexpected return of a beautiful 25-year-old (Heather Stannard) from America. The play's pleasure was the self-conscious virtuosity of the language; but the shimmering phrases were skating on thin ice. George Relph's embezzling agent was delightful.

Jan 19. Richard Burton and Mary Jerrold in Christopher Fry's **The Boy with a Cart** directed by John Gielgud at Lyric, Hammersmith. Shepherd boy wheels his elderly mother in a cart to a site where God had instructed him to build a church. Acted in a double bill with J M Barrie's **Shall We Join the Ladies?** Burton's performance as the boy led Anthony Quayle to cast him as Hal in The Stratford Memorial season of *Henry IV Parts 1 and 2* and *Henry V*.

Jan 26. Margaret Rutherford, Paul Scofield and Claire Bloom in Jean Anouilh's **Ring Round the Moon**, a charade with music translated by Christopher Fry, designed by Oliver Messel and directed by Peter Brook at Globe. Anouilh's elegant, exquisite and fragile *pièce rose*, set in pre-World War 1 France, was given a memorable production. Scofield played identical twins. Cold, egotistical Hugo, who is jealous of his tender-hearted brother's infatuation for a multi-millionaire's daughter (Audrey Fildes), hires a beautiful ballet dancer (Claire Bloom) to come to the ball and be the centre of attention. The idea is to distract Frederic and so put an end to the romance and prevent the marriage. Instead she falls in love with Hugo. The supporting characters, extravagantly artificial, included a wheelchair-bound, eccentric aunt (Margaret Rutherford), her faded companion (Daphne Newton), a silly, vulgar mother (Mona Washbourne), a lepidopterist (William Mervyn), a crumbling butler (David Horne) and a millionaire (Cecil Trouncer) who tears up all his money, only to find he is twice as rich as was before. Marjorie Stewart and Richard Wattis as the millionaire's mistress and secretary danced an ostentatious tango.
—The poet's pen turns the French dialogue into coloured but not too highly figured English speech. The result is an enchanting little fairy tale of laughing, Musset-like grace, its sentiment masked by cool, brittle, elegant mockery. *The Times*

Feb 2. Michael Redgrave in Shakespeare's **Hamlet** directed by Hugh Hunt at New. Yvonne Mitchell as Ophelia. Mark Dignam as Claudius. Wanda Rotha as Gertrude.
—Few interpretations of the play in the last twenty years have been so intelligent. Philip Hope Wallace *Manchester Guardian*

Mar 1. Frederick Valk in Henrik Ibsen's **John Gabriel Borkman** directed by Frith Banbury at Arts.
—Actors from the centre of Europe have one great advantage over ours: they can grunt and shout as no English actor can; but they have to carry the invincible handicap of a foreign intonation. T C Worsley *New Statesman and Nation*

Mar 2. Ronald Squire, Michael Gough, Glynis Johns and Kenneth More in Frederick Lonsdale's **The Way Things Go** directed by Anthony Pelissier at Phoenix. American heiress sets her sights on marrying an unwilling member of a bankrupt British family.

Mar 7. Ralph Richardson in R C Sherriff's **Home at Seven** directed by Murray Macdonald at Wyndham's. Middle-class bank clerk cannot account for the last twenty-four hours and believes he may have committed a murder.
—Sir Ralph is the Wordsworth of our actors in that he sees poetry in the commonplace. Harold Hobson *Sunday Times*

Mar 9. Alastair Sim, Megs Jenkins, Gordon McLeod and George Cole in James Bridie's **Mr Gillie** directed by Alastair Sim at Garrick. The life of an obscure Scottish schoolmaster is seen in flashback. The celestial powers rank him with Abraham Lincoln.

Mar 28. Jane Baxter, Herbert Lomas and Bryan Forbes in Wynyard Browne's **The Holly and the Ivy** directed by Frith Banbury at Lyric, Hammersmith. Domestic problems at the vicarage over Christmas. The vicar proves unexpectedly understanding about his family's failings. Transferred to Duchess.

1950 World Premieres
New York
William Inge's *Come Back Little Sheba*
Frank Loesser's *Guys and Dolls*
Tennessee Williams's *The Rose Tattoo*
Clifford Odets' *The Country Girl*
Carson McCuller's *The Member of the Wedding*
Paris
Eugene Ionesco's *The Bald Prima Donna*
Jean Anouilh's *The Rehearsal*
Max Ophuls's film of Arthur Schnitzler's *La Ronde*

Deaths
Harry Lauder (*b.*1870), Scottish singer, comedian
Sid Field (*b.*1904), British comedian
Kurt Weill (*b.*1900), German composer
Bernard Shaw (*b.*1856), Anglo-Irish playwright

Notes
—Schnitzler allowed Max Ophuls to make a film in 1950 and it is on the film that *La Ronde's* reputation largely rests. Its enormous international success was due to the elegance and wit of the director and the stylish acting of an all-star cast, which included Simone Signoret, Serge Reggiani, Simone Simon, Daniel Gelin, Danielle Darrieux, Jean Louis-Barrault, Isa Miranda, Gerard Philipe and Anton Walbrook as the ringmaster-narrator, a character not in the play. The scene with Danielle Darrieux and Daniel Gelin playing a married woman and a young man in bed together had a Freudian twist for cinemagoers who knew that in real life they were mother and son. The film (though far more romantic than the play) was banned in New York and other American cities. Four more films followed, none of them any good. Theatregoers had to wait until 1982 when the ban was lifted. There were three immediate productions, all of them disappointing.

History
—Outbreak of war between United Nations and North Korea
—First successful kidney transplant
—Arrest of Klaus Fuchs for selling atom bomb secrets
—Paul Robeson's passport revoked

Apr 27. Douglas Byng, Muriel Smith, Bob Monkhouse and Joan Heal in **Sauce Piquante** directed by Cecil Landeau at Cambridge. Revue. Audrey Hepburn made her debut.

May 3. Rex Harrison, Margaret Leighton, Ian Hunter, Alison Leggatt, Gladys Boot, Robin Bailey and Donald Houston in T S Eliot's **The Cocktail Party** directed by E Martin Browne at New. Classic ingredients of sin, guilt and expiation are explored within a Christian cycle of death and rebirth. Husband and wife, who have been deceiving each other and themselves, find salvation in reconciliation. The husband's young mistress finds salvation in atonement and crucifixion. The wife's young lover ends up in Hollywood, which is crucifixion of another sort. Rex Harrison played the Unidentified Guest (the role memorably created by Alec Guinness at the Edinburgh Festival), and was found wanting.
—That Mr Rex Harrison is miscast goes without saying. Mr Guinness was rigid, decisive, imperial; Mr Harrison is soft, tentative, engaging; Mr Guinness commanded his way through; Mr Harrison charms his way along. T C Worsley *New Statesman and Nation*

May 23. Eric Portman in Dorothy and Campbell Christie's **His Excellency** directed by Charles Hickman at Princes. New Governor, a down-to-earth, honest, pig-headed, ex-trade unionist, determines to shake things up in the colony.

Jun 7. Iva Withers as Julie Jordan and Stephen Douglass as Billy Bigelow in Richard Rodgers and Oscar Hammerstein II's musical **Carousel** choreographed by Agnes de Mille and designed by Miles White and directed by Rouben Mamoulian at Drury Lane. Based on Ferenc Molnar's *Liliom*. In Molnar's play, the hero commits suicide after a botched robbery. In Purgatory he is given a second chance and allowed to return to earth for one day and redeem himself by performing a good deed. He botches his second chance and is damned forever. The musical, set in a small New England fishing village towards the end of the 19th century, provides a sentimental ending in which both wife and daughter testify that his beatings never hurt them. This is followed by an uplifting reprise of "You'll Never Walk Alone". Songs include "If I Love You, "You're A Queer One, Julie Jordan", "June is Bustin' Out All Over" and "When I Marry Mr Snow". Many critics compared *Carousel* to *Oklahoma!* and found it wanting.
—May not appeal to those who demand the mixture as before or who wince at the mawkishly sentimental. *Sphere*

Jun 8. Alec Clunes and Margaret Rawlings in Shakespeare's **Macbeth** directed by Alec Clunes at Arts. Clunes never felt he got it right and Michael Hordern as Macduff was the only actor to get good notices.

Jul 10. Frank Sinatra at London Palladium. Mass hysteria. The police grappled with 800 banner-carrying members of the Frank Sinatra fan club. He sang 15 songs, mainly soulful ballads. *The Illustrated London News* thought that he had "nothing to offer but a slow amplified gargling and cooing." Max Wall was on the supporting variety bill.

—His technique is interesting. He sings from the hips; his hands spread wide in a constant gesture of despair, when they are not clutching his heart or pressing his diaphragm, his eyes are dilated with sentiment or something. MAURICE WILTSHIRE *Daily Mail*

—He gave me the sensation of having been forcibly fed with treacle; I hope it will wear off soon. W A DARLINGTON *Daily Telegraph*

Jun 14. Ronald Shiner, Bernard Lee, William Hartnell, Nigel Stock and John Gregson in Hugh Hastings's **Seagulls over Sorrento** directed by Wallace Douglas at Apollo. Group of volunteers in a disused wartime naval fortress in Scapa dream of Sorrento while they are carrying out secret peace-time radar experiments. Ronald Shiner was the life and soul of the fortress. 1463 performances.

Jul 19. Tyrone Power in Thomas Heggen and Joshua Logan's **Mister Roberts** directed by Joshua Logan at Coliseum. Based on Thomas Heggen's novel. Naval inactivity in a remote Pacific backwater during World War 2 leads to sadism and sentimentality. English audiences were surprised by the lack of discipline in the American navy. Tyrone Power as the lead was not as convincing as Henry Fonda was in the film. Jackie Cooper (former child film star, who played the Kid in Charlie Chaplin's *The Kid*) had the comic role.

July 28. Bud Abbott and Lou Costello at London Palladium. Traditional music hall business and quick repartee. Max Bygraves on the bill.

Aug 2. Robin Bailey, Henry Hewitt, E J Kennedy and Michael Golden in Roger MacDougall's **The Gentle Gunman** directed by Roy Rich at Arts. Thriller plus political debate: an Irish gunman is forced to recognise the futility of violence and reject terrorism.

Aug 9. Diana Wynyard and James Donald in Denis Cannan's **Captain Carvallo** directed by Laurence Olivier at St James's. Officer (James Donald) in the invading army arrives at a farmhouse and demands to be put up for the night. Members of the Resistance (Peter Finch and Richard Goolden) have orders to kill him, but liking the fellow, they plan to save his life with the aid of the padre's wife (Diana Wynyard).

Aug 22. Signe Hasso as Rebecca, Robert Harris as Rosmer, Edward Chapman as Kroll and George Coulouris as Ulric Brendel in Henrik Ibsen's **Rosmersholm** directed by Michael Macowan at St Martin's. Hasso was too lightweight.

—Her Rebecca was polished and beautiful but her strength seemed a matter of manners and habit rather than of character, cultivated and innate. *Theatre World*

Aug 23. Robert Morley, Joan Tetzel and David Tomlinson in André Roussin's **The Little Hut** designed by Oliver Messel and directed by Peter Brook. Husband, wife and lover are shipwrecked on a desert island. Husband and lover agree to share the wife.

—In the third act immorality is capped by snobbishness, and the curtain falls on downright vulgarity; I was embarrassed and so were many people round me; maybe the Censor needs a new pair of glasses. *News Chronicle*

Aug 29. Eileen Herlie, Leslie Banks, Marie Ney and Ronald Ward in Arthur Wing Pinero's **The Second Mrs Tanqueray** directed by Murray Macdonald at Haymarket.

—Miss Herlie seems to have discarded the author's hints. There's no volatility, nothing of the mercurial about her playing. T C WORSLEY *New Statesman and Nation*

Aug 31. Brenda Bruce, Hugh Burden and Anthony Marlowe in Somerset Maugham's **Home and Beauty** directed by Roy Rich at Arts. Transferred to St Martin's.

Sep 7. Emlyn Williams and Diana Churchill in Emlyn Williams's **Accolade** directed by Glen Byam Shaw at Aldwych. Writer's double life is exposed just after he has accepted a knighthood.

Sep 12. Colin Morris's **Reluctant Heroes** directed by Frank Dermody at Whitehall. National Service farce. Wally Patch as the sergeant. Larry Noble, Dermot Walsh and Brian Rix as the rookies.

Oct 11. John Mills in Tyrone Guthrie's **Top of the Ladder** directed by Tyrone Guthrie at St. James's. German expressionism with Freudian additions. Business tycoon on his death-bed re-enacts key moments in his banal life. The role was as long as Hamlet. John Mills's *tour de force* was not enough to save the play.

—In my opinion, it is not wise for authors to direct their own work…I learned this painfully when, having produced my own play, I was assured by many discriminating friends, that I had spoiled the play by failing to cut obvious and repetitious passages. TYRONE GUTHRIE *A Life in the Theatre*

Mai Zetterling and Dirk Bogarde in Point of Departure

Oct 12. Michael Denison and Dulcie Gray in Jan de Hartog's **The Fourposter** directed by Peter Ashmore at Ambassadors. Two-hander comedy: six scenes of marriage from 1902 to 1950 were set in the same bedroom. The bed stayed the same, but the furnishings changed as the couple got richer.

Oct 13. Carol Raye, Peter Graves and Olga Lindo in **Dear Miss Phoebe** directed by Charles Hickman at Phoenix. Musical based on J M Barrie's *Quality Street*. Music by Harry Parr Davies. Lyrics by Christopher Hassall. Songs included "Marry" and "Carry Me Home."

Oct 24. Robert Flemyng, Athene Seyler and Roland Culver in Terence Rattigan's **Who is Sylvia?** directed by Anthony Quayle at Criterion. Wife stays with her husband despite his succession of mistresses, who always looked so alike you could hardly tell them apart. The comedy was less serious than Rattigan had originally intended. The story was based on his parents and, since they were both still alive, he had felt obliged to tone it down. Diane Hart played Sylvia's three incarnations.
—This play has neither the exuberance of inexperience nor the technique of a tired master. It was assembled not written. BEVERLEY BAXTER *Evening Standard*
—High comedy needs a philosophic touch, and the idea was too thin, too worn, and too obvious to stand it. *Manchester Guardian*

Nov 1. Mai Zetterling and Dirk Bogarde in Jean Anouilh's **Point of Departure** directed by Peter Ashmore at Lyric, Hammersmith. This reworking of the Orpheus and Eurydice myth was written in 1941 at the height of the war when the death of loved ones was a daily possibility. It had Anouilh's familiar themes: the sordidness of life and the corruption of innocence. Orpheus (a street musician) meets Eurydice (a young actress) in a seedy provincial railway station buffet. They fall in love and run away to a shabby hotel in Marseilles. She dies in a road accident. The messenger of Death (Stephen Murray) argues that death is preferable to life. Orpheus's old dad (an untalented harpist, down on his luck) has a long monologue, a virtuoso argument in favour of the sensual life, which Hugh Griffith delivered with great style. Transferred to Duke of York's.
—A great deal of acting goes on and some of it is very good acting, as the acting of acting, but it is for the most part strictly irrelevant to the play. T C WORSLEY *New Statesman and Nation*

Nov 14. Old Vic reopened with Shakespeare's **Twelfth Night** directed by Hugh Hunt. Peggy Ashcroft as Viola. Paul Rogers as Malvolio. Leo McKern as Feste. Ursula Jeans as Olivia. Alec Clunes as Orsino. Roger Livesey as Sir Toby Belch. Robert Eddison as Sir Andrew Aguecheek. Pauline Jameson as Maria. The inhabitants of Illyria indulged in *commedia dell'arte* antics.
—As for Miss Ashcroft, she is nearly as perfect as makes no matter: delicately impassioned, speaking beautifully, and boyish without the slightest trace of mixed hockey. ERIC KEOWN *Punch*

Dec 14. Sophie Stewart, Muriel Aked, Eleanor Macready and Perlita Neilson in Aimée Stuart's **Lace on Her Petticoat** directed by Willard Stoker at Ambassadors. Friendship between a marquis's daughter and a milliner's daughter in the 19th century is sacrificed because of class distinctions.

Dec 18. Roger Livesey as Justice Overdone, Alec Clunes as Humphrey Waspe, Mark Dignam as Zeal-of-the-Land and Robert Eddison as Bartholomew Cokes in Ben Jonson's **Bartholomew Fair** directed by George Devine at Old Vic. Slice of Jacobean life – bawdy, raucous and crude. Crime is a great leveller: everybody, from pimp to religious fanatic, from cutpurse to the magistrate's wife, is tarred with the same brush.

1951

Jan 17. Jean Forbes-Robertson in Henrik Ibsen's **Hedda Gabler** directed by Roy Rich at Arts. Eric Berry as Tesman. Campbell Singer as Judge Brack. The emphasis was on flippant comedy and malicious irony. *The Bystander* suspected Forbes-Robertson was "taking the mickey out of Hedda."
—Hedda Gabler is an arch bitch; and it is this bitchiness above everything else that Miss Forbes-Robertson lays bare. T C WORSLEY *New Statesman and Nation*

Jan 26. Elizabeth Bergner and A E Matthews in Molière's **The Gay Invalid** directed by Michael Langham at Garrick. Matthews did little beyond sit around and make frequent visits to the lavatory.

Jan 30. Alec Clunes in Shakespeare's **Henry V** directed by Glen Byam Shaw at Old Vic. Clunes toned down the rhetoric to play a very human Henry. Roger Livesey was a hail-fellow-well-met Chorus. Robert Eddison was a lively Pistol. Dorothy Tutin was a delightful Princess of France. Douglas Wilmer was a very sick King of France. Paul Rogers was far too exaggerated as the Dauphin. The Duke of Orleans's remark that "these British are shrewdly out of beef" was so topical that it got a big laugh. Argentina had just stopped exporting beef to Britain.

Jan 31. Kathleen Harrison, Marjorie Fielding, Frederick Leister and Peter Hammond in John Galsworthy's **The Silver Box** directed by Frith Banbury at Lyric, Hammersmith. Harrison was deeply moving as the charwoman.

Feb 7. Patricia Neway, Marie Powers, Gloria Lane and Norman Kelley in Gian-Carlo Menotti's **The Consul** directed and conducted by Gian-Carlo Menotti at Cambridge. Opera aimed at the general theatregoing public, but this moving Middle-European political drama did not repeat the success it had had in New York and Laurence Olivier who had backed it lost money.

Feb 14. John Clements and Kay Hammond in Bernard Shaw's **Man and Superman** directed by John Clements at New. Clements played John Tanner with enormous gusto and eloquence. "I wish that I had a car that would go as fast as you can talk," said his chauffeur (Michael Medwin). Hammond's drawling Ann Whitefield was a delicious boa constrictor. At certain performances the *Don Juan in Hell* scene was acted.

Feb 15. Martita Hunt in Jean Giraudoux's **The Mad Woman of Chaillot** directed by Robert Speaight at St James's. Marius Goring as Rag-Picker. Mad woman saves Paris from profiteers and speculators by inviting them all to her house and flushing them down the sewer. Written in 1943 and produced in Paris in 1945, French audiences were quick to draw a parallel between the profiteers and the Nazi invaders. Martita Hunt had scored a big success in New York. The play flopped in London. The poor translation and pedestrian production were blamed.

Mar 1. Ronald Squire, Marie Löhr, Alan Webb, Basil Radford, Denys Blakelock, Virginia McKenna and Ronald Howard in John Whiting's **A Penny For A Song** designed by Emett and directed by Peter Brook at Haymarket. Written at a time of great personal happiness, the comedy is an affectionate portrait of the unflappable English gentry muddling through life in their eccentric, amateur English way. Sir Timothy Bellboys (Alan Webb) in 1802 thinks the best way to deal with the invasion of Napoleon Bonaparte is for him to impersonate the Emperor and order the French army to retreat. He buys a military costume and a French phrase book. Mistaking an army exercise for the real thing, he is arrested by the local home guard. "It is rarely necessary," said Whiting, "to embroider the finer lunacies of the English at war." When two cannon balls roll into the garden, the reaction is merely to suggest somebody should shut the gate. The historical references were true. Several people in different parts of the country were arrested under the impression they were Bonaparte. The play was not a success.
—This is not a play, a comedy or even a farce. It is a superbly mounted and well acted rag – fifth form, without the excuse of adolescence. BEVERLEY BAXTER *Evening Standard*

Mar 7. Danny Kaye at London Palladium. A big success again.

Mar 8. Bill Johnson and Patricia Morison in Cole Porter's **Kiss Me Kate** directed by Sam Spewack at Coliseum. Book by Sam and Bella Spewack. Porter's masterpiece was the first musical in which he made a conscious effort to integrate songs and story. The action is set on-stage and back-stage during a performance of a musical version of *The Taming of the Shrew*. The situation of the wisecracking and quarrelling actors playing the wisecracking and quarrelling Kate and Petruchio was based on the off-stage quarrelling of the famous Broadway husband-and-wife team, Alfred Lunt and Lynn Fontanne. Audiences, who did not know *The Shrew*, were surprised to learn just how much of Shakespeare's original dialogue had been retained. Porter's lyric for Kate's final song lifts Shakespeare's soliloquy almost word for word. Julie Wilson sang "Always True To You in My Fashion" and stopped the show.
—Infants now rocking in their cradles will very likely grow up to regret they were born too late to enjoy the heyday of the American musical. *Tatler*

Mar 13. Peggy Ashcroft in Sophocles's **Electra** directed by Michel Saint-Denis at Old Vic. Robert Eddison as Orestes. Catherine Lacey as Clytemnestra. Acted in a double-bill with Anton Chekhov's **The Wedding** with Leo McKern, Paul Rogers and Dorothy Tutin, directed by George Devine.
—Miss Ashcroft can tear the heart out of you with a whisper, and her immense sensibility is matched to the profundity of Electra's grief. ERIC KEOWN *Punch*

Apr 1. Judy Garland's debut at London Palladium. Huge success.

Apr 17. Edith Evans, Sybil Thorndike, Kathleen Harrison and Wendy Hiller in N C Hunter's **Waters of the Moon** directed by Frith Banbury at Haymarket. Shallow, inconsiderate rich woman sweeps into poor middle-class guest house in a dull provincial backwater and upsets everybody. Hunter's model was Chekhov and most critics slammed it as being sub-Chekhov and not worthy of so talented a cast.
—One has the uneasy sensation that almost all the dramatic effects had been better managed by some other dramatist. PHILIP HOPE-WALLACE *Time and Tide*
—Dame Edith gives a dazzling performance as Dame Edith. She is, as all know, fabulous. She lifts the whole thing out of the decent, ordinary range in which it is written, and by doing so in a sense splits it right down the middle. T C WORSLEY *New Statesman and Nation*

May 3. Celia Johnson as Olga, Margaret Leighton as Masha, Renee Asherson as Irina, Ralph Richardson as Vershinin, Diana Churchill as Natasha, Eric Porter as Solyoni and Harcourt Williams as Cheboutikin in Anton Chekhov's **Three Sisters** directed by Peter Ashmore at Aldwych. The production was a big disappointment. The play never came alive; its haunting sadness and pervading humour were lost.

May 10. Laurence Olivier and Vivien Leigh in Bernard Shaw's **Caesar and Cleopatra** directed by Michael Benthall at St James's. Robert Helpmann as Apollodorus. Wilfred Hyde-White as Brittanus. The play was acted in tandem with Shakespeare's *Antony and Cleopatra*. Leigh had already played Cleopatra with great success in the Alexander Korda film opposite Claude Rains.
—[Laurence Olivier] is a steely stage personality and it gives a terrifying edge to all Caesar's intellectual magnanimities and gentle philosophising. *The Times*

May 11. Laurence Olivier and Vivien Leigh in Shakespeare's **Antony and Cleopatra** directed by Michael Benthall at St James's. Norman Wooland as Enobarbus. Robert Helpmann as Octavius Caesar. John Gielgud thought Leigh, sensual, wily, treacherous, was outstanding. Harold Hobson thought Olivier's Antony was more showy but less impressive than his Caesar. Olivier thought Antony was an absolute twerp whom Cleopatra had firmly by the balls.
—Sir Laurence is a lightweight, charming and somewhat too dry Antony who certainly does not overload the lover's sighs. PHILIP HOPE-WALLACE *Manchester Guardian*

May 15. Leonard White, Denholm Elliott, Stanley Baker and Hugh Pryse in Christopher Fry's **A Sleep of Prisoners** directed by Michael Macowan at St Thomas's Church, Regent Street. Verse drama. Four prisoners of war in a church dream they are God, Cain, Abel, Joab, Absalom, Shadrac, Meshac and Abednego.

May 17. Alec Guinness in Shakespeare's **Hamlet** directed by Alec Guinness and Frank Hauser at New. Lydia Sherwood as Gertrude. Walter Fitzgerald as Claudius. Ingrid Burke as Ophelia. Alan Webb as Polonius. Robert Shaw as Rosencrantz. Kenneth Tynan as First Player. Guinness's indecisive performance was not helped on the first night when the lighting went wrong and scenes, which should have been played in the dark, were acted in a blaze of light and vice versa. The gallery booed. "This is the worst production of Hamlet I have ever seen," said Beverley Baxter in *The Evening Standard* and went on to say that Tynan was so bad that he would never be heard of again. Tynan became *The Evening Standard*'s theatre critic and Baxter lost his job.
—It is the custom of genius to do things in a big way, and the cropper that Mr Guinness came on Thursday night was truly monumental. HAROLD HOBSON *Sunday Times*

May 23. Peter Ustinov in Peter Ustinov's **The Love of Four Colonels** directed by John Fernald at Wyndham's. Four colonels of the Allied control – a Frenchman, an American, a Russian and an Englishman – are whisked to the castle of Sleeping Beauty and provided with a miniature stage. The colonels in turn enact a scene with their ideal woman in the periods they find most appropriate for their emotions. The four scenes were satires on Molière, Shakespeare, the American gangster film and Chekhov. Moira Lister was each colonel's ideal. Peter Ustinov was the bad fairy.
—The only difficulty is that as actor he steals the show from himself as playwright. Each of his little sketches is so dazzlingly vivid that it makes the rest of each of them seem a little dowdy. T C WORSLEY *New Statesman and Nation*

May 24. Dora Bryan, Joan Heal and Ian Carmichael in **The Lyric Revue** directed by William Chappell at Lyric, Hammersmith. Funniest sketch had Heal stuck in a sedan chair.

Jun 3. The York Cycle of Mystery Plays at York. The first revival since 1572.

Jun 27. John Gielgud as Leontes, Diana Wynyard as Hermione and Flora Robson

as Paulina in Shakespeare's **The Winter's Tale** directed by Peter Brook at Phoenix. There was no doubt that this Leontes had drunk and seen the spider. Gielgud's success made the play more popular than it had been for a very long time and the production broke all records.
—It is a virtuoso performance, theatrically expert in conception and execution and the verse is spoken with subtle lucidity and delicate balance. RICHARD FINDLATER *Tribune*

Jun 28. Joyce Grenfell, Elizabeth Welch, Max Adrian and Desmond Walter-Ellis in **Penny Plain** devised and directed by Laurier Lister at St Martin's. Grenfell was very funny refusing to come into the garden and listening to her favourite author, but the revue as a whole disappointed.

Jul 6. Godfrey Tearle, Mary Kerridge and Sebastian Shaw in Arthur Wing Pinero's **His House in Order** directed by John Counsell at New. A good solid revival. Kerridge was the wife who is treated abominably by her husband's family, who compare her unfavourably with his first wife. Tearle played her only friend, a compassionate and wise man. Brian Oulton and Joan Haythorne were the odious and icy relatives.

July 13. H M The Queen laid the Foundation Stone of the National Theatre to the living memory of William Shakespeare on a site adjoining the Festival Hall.

Jul 26. Fay Compton in Jean Cocteau's **Intimate Relations** (*Les Parents Terribles*) directed by Judith Furse at Arts and then transferred to Strand. Mother, besotted with her 22-year-old son, refuses to accept that he has grown up and becomes hysterical when she learns that he has fallen in love with a young woman. His father isn't pleased, either, for the woman is his mistress. The play, written in eight days whilst under the influence of opium, was first performed in 1938. Its incestuous theme caused a sensation. The actors in Paris were expelled from the theatre, following a series of stink bombs, tear gas and claques invading the stage. They transferred to another theatre where its highly successful run was interrupted only by the outbreak of World War 2.

Aug 30. Isabel Jeans, Ronald Squire, George Relph and Nicholas Phipps in Jean Anouilh's **Ardèle** directed by Anthony Pelissier at Vaudeville. Ardele, a hunchback, shocks her family by marrying a hunchback.

Sep 5. Michael Hordern in John Whiting's **Saint's Day** at Arts directed by Stephen Murray. 33-year-old Whiting won the Festival of Britain's play competition. He had written it immediately after the dropping of the first atom bomb and had thought of it as a technical exercise, never thinking it would be produced. The action is set on the 25th January, the anniversary of St. Paul's conversion. Famous 83-year-old poet and pamphleteer, having been driven into exile by his fellow artists 25 years earlier, is invited to a dinner in London to celebrate his greatness and to wipe out the memory of hatred and violence which had been inflicted on him by his peers. The critics disliked the play. The theatrical profession – led by Peter Ustinov, Christopher Fry, Alec Clunes, Peter Brook, John Gielgud, Peggy Ashcroft, Tyrone Guthrie and George Devine – wrote a letter to *The Times* supporting the author, saying: "Its passion and its unbroken tension are the product of a new and extraordinary theatrical mind."
—It is a wild play; a maddening play; a botched play, if you like, but one that that has undeniable dark power. J C TREWIN *Illustrated London News*
—I really do not think that theatre is just a place where people should laugh and cry. JOHN WHITING

Sep 24. Donald Wolfit in Christopher Marlowe's **Tamburlaine** directed by Tyrone Guthrie at Old Vic. Performed for the first time in 300 years. "A savage oratorio," said Guthrie. Barbaric splendour and bloody spectacle: one atrocity after another, unrelieved cruelty, gruesome tortures, and interminably long. Strong support from Jill Balcon as Zenocrate and Margaret Rawlings as a conquered queen who has been driven mad.
—Mr Donald Wolfit is the very man for Tamburlaine. His voice has the widest range of any actor on the stage today. He has the force and the power. T C WORSLEY *New Statesman and Nation*
—[Donald Wolfit] can strike terror from lines that, in the text, are the merest fee-fi-fo-fum. J C TREWIN *Illustrated London News*

Oct 16. John Mills in André Roussin's **Figure of Fun** directed by Peter Ashmore at Aldwych. In the second act the audience discovered that Mills was playing an actor and what they had just been watching was a French comedy which replicated his marital problems in real life.

Oct 17. Betty Paul, Leslie Henson and Jessie Royce Landis in J B Fagan's **And So To Bed** directed by Wendy Toye at New. Music and lyrics by Vivian Ellis. Samuel Pepys played a supporting role to his clever wife. Keith Michell was King Charles II.

Oct 18. Orson Welles in Shakespeare's **Othello** directed by Orson Welles at St James's. Gudrun Ure as Desdemona. Peter Finch as Iago said, "I hate Othello" in much the same way that some people might say, "I hate tea."

—The folly of the chief actor's trying also to do the production is continually illustrated throughout. T C WORSLEY *New Statesman and Nation*
—When all is said Mr Welles remains something of a genius and a great guy if not a great Othello. PHILIP HOPE-WALLACE *Time and Tide*

Oct 29. Emlyn Williams as **Charles Dickens** at Lyric, Hammersmith. Williams stood at Dickens's lectern and gave dramatic readings from the novels: a *tour de force*.

Nov 1. Mary Martin and Wilbur Evans in Richard Rodgers and Oscar Hammerstein's musical **South Pacific** directed by Joshua Logan at Drury Lane. Pulitzer Prize winner for Drama. The book was based on James Michener's *Tales of the South Pacific* and narrated two romances on an island during World War 2. A young US Navy nurse falls in love with a middle-aged French plantation owner but balks at the idea of marrying a man who had married a Polynesian woman and had two children by her. A young lieutenant falls in love with a native girl, but worries what the folks back home will think of a native bride. The plea for racial tolerance and mixed marriages caused problems for the musical when it toured the Southern States in the US in early 1950s. Expectations in London were too high and it was regarded as a retrograde step after *Oklahoma!* The score included "Some Enchanted Evening", "I'm Gonna To Wash That Man Right Out of My Hair" and "There's Nothing Like a Dame."
—South Soporific. Alas, some not entirely enchanted evening. *Daily Express*
—We might have welcomed it twice as loudly if we had not been told from New York that it is four times as good as it is. J C TREWIN *Illustrated London News*

Nov 21. Eric Portman as Marshal and Charles Goldner as Prime Minister in Peter Ustinov's **The Moment of Truth** directed by John Fernald at Adelphi. The Fall of France and the trial of Marshal Petain were revisited. Petain negotiated the armistice-oldner played Pierre Laval, who openly collaborated with the Germans. The play was originally called *King Lear's Photographer*.

Nov 22. Margaret Johnston as Miss Alma and William Sylvester as John Buchanan in Tennessee Williams's **Summer and Smoke** directed by Peter Glenville at Lyric, Hammersmith. Allegorical drama representing the conflict of body and soul. Alma, a minister's daughter, has loved the boy next door since they were children. He is a handsome, manly wastrel who spends his time drinking, whoring and gambling. Alma, sexually repressed and prematurely spinsterish, rejects his overtures. She comes across as a portrait of the young Blanche DuBois – the heroine of *A Streetcar Named Desire* – before she had turned to prostitution and become dependent on the kindness of strangers. Johnson was beautiful, sad, and delicate. Sylvester was insolent and charming. Transferred to Duchess.

Nov 29. Gladys Cooper, Angela Baddeley, Judy Campbell and Richard Leech in Noël Coward's **Relative Values** directed by Noël Coward at Savoy. Earl decides to marry a film star, who turns out to be the sister of his mother's personal maid.

Dec 1. Peter Pears as Captain Vere, Frederick Dalberg as Claggart and Theodor Uppman as Billy in Benjamin Britten's opera **Billy Budd** directed by Basil Coleman at Sadler's Wells. Book E M Forster and Eric Crozier.

Dec 5. Donald Wolfit as Lord Ogleby in George Colman and David Garrick's **The Clandestine Marriage** directed by Tyrone Guthrie at Old Vic. Rare revival of the 1766 comedy. Ogleby, a Restoration fop, has great style and recalls a bygone age: "Beauty is to me a religion in which I was born and bred a bigot and would die a martyr." The best scene was the one where he proposes to a young lady under the impression that she is encouraging him whereas she merely wants to confide in him that she has married a young man.

Dec 13. Yvonne Arnaud, Joyce Redman, Michael Gough, Esme Percy and Laurence Naismith in Jean Anouilh's **Colombe** directed by Peter Brook at New. Julien

Joyce Redmond, John Stratton, Esme Percy, Vernon Greeves, Yvonne Arnaud, Rosalind Atkinson and David Horne in Colombe

(Michael Gough) goes off to do his national service, leaving his sweet, innocent young wife (Joyce Redman) and their baby in the care of his mother, a famous actress. Colombe's naïvety is a protection against the crude advances of a poet, an actor and the theatre manager, but not against the charms of Julien's wastrel half-brother. Julien returns, forcing his brother to kiss him on the lips. "Kiss me as you kiss her. I want to know what it is like." A priggish idealist, he expects Colombe to live a life of self-denial, poverty and boredom and to be the Colombe he imagines her to be rather than the Colombe she really is. He expects her to love him, merely because he loves her. His mother accuses him of being far more selfish than she has ever been. Yvonne Arnaud played the *monstre sacré* (a tragedienne to rival Sarah Bernhardt) for too much comedy.

1952

Jan 2. John Laurie, Robin Bailey, Judith Furse, Maxine Audley and Wyndham Goldie in Jean Anouilh's **Thieves Carnival** translated by Lucienne Hill and directed by Roy Rich at Arts. French pickpockets, thieves and English aristocrats on the Riviera: a frothy, flimsy harlequinade.

Jan 11. The Shakespeare Memorial Theatre Company. John Gielgud as Benedict and Diana Wynyard as Beatrice in Shakespeare's **Much Ado about Nothing** directed by John Gielgud at Phoenix. Paul Scofield as Don Pedro. Lewis Casson as Leonato. Dorothy Tutin as Hero. Robert Hardy as Claudio. George Rose as Dogberry. John Moffatt as Verges. John Whiting as Sexton. The merry war was acted with the lightest of touches. The definitive *Much Ado* of the 1950s.
—Mr Gielgud shows once more that it is nonsense to regard him as a tragedian who jokes with difficulty. The truth is that he turns his minor failings as a tragedian, his natural hauteur and air of remoteness, into comic virtues. *The Times*

Jan 29. Alec Clunes as Moses and Mark Dignam as Pharaoh in Christopher Fry's **The Firstborn** directed by John Fernald at Winter Garden. Old Testament drama in verse. Moses ("a stone in Israel's sling") returns to Egypt to deliver his people.
—There were flame and thunder in the speaking. For years I had not heard such eloquence as this in a London theatre; Clunes's command of the difficult vocal line barely faltered. It chilled the heart. J C Trewin *Alec Clunes*

Jan 30. Marcel Marceau at Arts. The French mime's first visit to London.

Jan 30. Ronald Squire, Peter Finch and Rachel Kempson in Samuel Taylor's **The Happy Time** based on a novel by Robert Fontaine and directed by George Devine at St. James's. Growing up in a family of womanisers in Ottawa in the 1920s: a young boy's sentimental education begins when he steals the maid's nightdress so that he can see her in the nude.

Feb 27. Anthony Sharp's dramatisation of Thomas Love Peacock's **Nightmare Abbey** directed by John Fernald at Westminster. The literary satire worked better on stage than anybody could have imagined. Alan McNaughton was the lovesick Scythrop Glowry, a Shelley-like figure, torn between two women. Geoffrey Dunn was The Hon. Mr Listless, too frightened to exert himself for fear it will be too exhausting. Charles Lloyd Pack was Mr Glowry, a disillusioned widower who likes people to be happy in a melancholy way. Valerie Hanson was Marionetta, a blooming and accomplished young minx.

Mar 4. Isabel Jeans and Dirk Bogarde in Noël Coward's **The Vortex** directed by Michael Macowan at Lyric, Hammersmith. Jeans was elegant and witty as the mother who was having an affair with a man no older than her son. Bogarde, cast in Coward's role of the neurotic, piano-drumming, drug-taking son was compared to Coward and found wanting. Transferred to Criterion.

Mar 6. Peggy Ashcroft, Kenneth More and Roland Culver in Terence Rattigan's **The Deep Blue Sea** directed by Frith Banbury at Duchess. The story of an older married woman, obsessed with a younger man, who does not return her love, was a disguised dramatization of Rattigan's relationship with his lover, Ken Morgan, who did commit suicide. There was a splendid moment when the lover gives his suicidal mistress a shilling to feed the gas meter–"Just in case I'm late for dinner." The play made Kenneth More a star and he went on playing variations on the role ever after. Ashcroft was beautifully understated.
—Peggy Ashcroft never forces. A dimming of the eyes, a barely perceptible catch in the voice, an audience is at her feet. No one can so move with sorrow-in-stillness. J C Trewin *Illustrated London News*
—In Kenneth More we have acquired an actor who may become our best retort to Marlon Brando, with the same doubting proviso: can he do anything else? Kenneth Tynan *Evening Standard*

Raymond Francis, Kenneth More and Peggy Ashcroft in The Deep Blue Sea

1952 World Premieres
Paris
Eugene Ionesco's *The Chairs*
Jean Anouilh's *The Waltz of the Toreadors*
Zurich
Friedrich Dürrenmatt's *The Marriage of Mississippi*
New York
George Axelrod's *The Seven Year Itch*
Joseph Kramm's *The Shrike*

Births
Stephen Poliakoff, British playwright

Deaths
Ferenc Molnar (*b.*1878), Hungarian playwright

Vesta Tilley (*b.*1864), British music hall singer

Notes
Royal Court, closed since 1932, re-opened

History
—Death of King George VI
—Accession of Queen Elizabeth II
—UK and US tested hydrogen bomb
—Eisenhower elected US President
—Mau Mau rebellion in Kenya
—First contraceptive pill

Mar 14. Alec Clunes and Maxine Audley in George Farquhar's **The Constant Couple** directed by Alec Clunes at Winter Garden. "What business has a woman with virtue?" asks Sir Harry Wildair, recently returned to London in 1699 and out to conquer the ladies of the Town. For him the pleasure is the means and the end. Clunes was in great form, especially when he was full of burgundy.

Mar 15. Billie Worth, Anton Walbrook and Jeff Warren in Irving Berlin's **Call Me Madam** directed by Richard Bird at Coliseum. Musical. Book by Howard Lindsay and Russell Crouse. The US sends an oil heiress as its ambassador to Lichtenton. The authors insisted that their character had nothing to do with President Truman's appointment of Perle Mesta as the US ambassador to Luxembourg. "You're Just in Love" stopped the show nightly and had to be reprised six times before the audience would go home. Walbrook was wasted.

Apr 2. Mary Morris in Jennette Dowling and Francis Letton's **The Young Elizabeth** directed by Charles Hickman at New. Morris was a spirited, heartless, impulsive future Queen. Peggy Thorpe-Bates was a bigoted, pitiable, bloody Mary Tudor. Margaretta Scott was a dignified Katherine Parr. The authors presumed too much on the audience's knowledge of Tudor history.

Apr 3. Michael Redgrave, Googie Withers and Sam Wanamaker in Clifford Odets's **Winter Journey** directed by Sam Wanamaker at St James's. Sentimental backstage melodrama about a famous actor making a comeback. Will he be able to remember his lines? Will he be able to remain sober? Will his wife louse things up? Will the young director be able to see him through the out-of-town run and the first night? The happy ending did not ring true. The improvisation in the opening scene was genuine.
—[The improvisation] had a most useful effect for me of making me wonder each night whether I would be able to succeed in the scene, which was exactly the feeling I needed before going on for the first scene of the play. MICHAEL REDGRAVE *The Actor's Ways and Means*

Apr 8. Richard Burton, Noël Willman and Esmond Knight in Emanuel Robles's **Montserrat** adapted by Lillian Hellman and directed by Noël Willman and Nigel Green at Lyric, Hammersmith. In Venezuela, at the beginning of the 19th century, Montserrat had helped a revolutionary escape and refuses to say where he is hiding. His Colonel orders six innocent people to be brought in from the streets and swears he will shoot them, unless Montserrat tells him. One by one they are shot. The question is how long will it be before Montserrat cracks? Willman as the insolent sadist had more acting opportunities than Burton did as the silent martyr.

Apr 23. Diana Churchill and Alec Guinness in Sam Spewack's **Under the Sycamore Tree** designed by Oliver Messel and directed by Peter Glenville at Aldwych. Satirical fable set in an ant colony, where, thanks to the brilliance of the chief scientist, the ants were able to share the benefits of mankind without enduring his hardships. Guinness played seven roles in a series of revue turns: scientist, Harley Street doctor, engineer, psychiatrist, Prince Consort, drooling father and a doddering elder statesman.

Jun 18. Hermione Baddeley in Rodney Ackland's **The Pink Room or The Escapists** directed by Frith Banbury at Lyric, Hammersmith. Wartime drinking club in West End is frequented by bohemians and servicemen. Hammered by the critics, Ackland never wrote another original work again.

Jun 19. Emrys James and Jane Baxter in Frederick Knott's **Dial M for Murder** directed by John Fernald at Westminster. Husband blackmails an old school acquaintance into murdering his unfaithful wife. Andrew Cruickshank was the detective. Hitchcock turned the play into a successful film.

Jun 27. Katharine Hepburn as Epifania Ognisanti Di Parega in Bernard Shaw's **The Millionairess** directed by Michael Benthall at New. Robert Helpmann as the Egyptian doctor. Shaw wrote his didactic farce on the power of money in 1934 when he was 78. The heroine is one of nature's bosses: pampered, spoiled, resilient, ruthless and resourceful, she has neither moral decency nor a sense of humour. The speech on the power of marriage is a modern companion piece for Kate's final soliloquy in Shakespeare's *The Taming of the Shrew*. The play relies entirely on the authority, energy and sexiness of the actress who plays her. Hepburn played unashamedly to the gallery.

Jul 3. Flora Robson in William Archibald's **The Innocents** directed by Peter Glenville at Her Majesty's. Adaptation of Henry James's *The Turn of the Screw*. Victorian governess discovers the children in her charge have been thoroughly corrupted. 13-year-old Jeremy Spenser and 12-year-old Carol Wolveridge were the possessed children. Barbara Everest was the housekeeper. Jo Mielziner's gloomy décor and lighting provided the necessary ghostly atmosphere.

Jul 10. Dora Bryan, Ian Carmichael and Joan Heal in. **The Globe Revue** directed by William Chappell at Globe. High spot: Noël Coward's song, "Bad Times Are Just Around the Corner".

Aug 21. Hugh Williams Coral Browne, Wilfred Hyde-White and Joyce Redman in Louis Verneuil's **Affairs of State** directed by Roy Rich at Cambridge. American senator is in love with his best friend's wife. His best friend arranges a marriage of convenience for him with a schoolteacher.

Sep 2. Pamela Brown, Paul Scofield, Virginia McKenna, Marjorie Fielding and Michael Goodliffe in Charles Morgan's **The River Line** directed by Michael Macowan at Lyric, Hammersmith. Young American learns that that the man he shot in World War 2 was not a spy and that he was half-brother to the woman he loves. Transferred to Strand.

Sep 3. Emlyn Williams as Charles Dickens in **Bleak House** at Ambassadors. One man show. Williams acted all the roles.

Sep 12. Alfred Lunt and Lynn Fontanne in Noël Coward's **Quadrille** directed by Noël Coward at Phoenix. Scenery and costumes by Cecil Beaton. It was *Private Lives* all over again, this time in Victoria costume. Middle-aged philanderer (Griffith Jones) runs off with a railway magnate's wife (Marian Spencer). Their respective partners (Lunt and Fontanne) chase after them, bring them home, and then elope themselves the following year. The play's success was due to the American stars' acting rather than to Coward's script.

Sep 15. Alan Badel and Claire Bloom in Shakespeare's **Romeo and Juliet** directed by Hugh Hunt at Old Vic. Peter Finch as Mercutio. Athene Seyler as Nurse. Kenneth Tynan said that Bloom's Juliet was the best he had seen, omitting to mention she was the only Juliet he had seen.

Sep 25. Jean Carson in Hugh Martin's musical **Love from Judy** directed by Charles Hickman at Saville. Musical based on Eric Maschwitz and Jean Webster's *Daddy Long Legs*. Lyrics by Hugh Martin and Jack Grey. The story was sentimental. Berkeley Sutcliffe's décor was pretty. The music was unmemorable and the lyrics were banal. Carson scored a success as the orphan.

Sep 29. **Betty Hutton** at Palladium. "I'm not meant to be a good singer," she said, "only a loud one."

Oct 7. Claude Hulbert in Oscar Wilde's **Lord Arthur Savile's Crime** adapted by Constance Cox and directed by Jack Hulbert at Royal Court. The style was much nearer to Ben Travers and P G Wodehouse than it was to Wilde. Hulbert played Lord Arthur as a dim-witted relation of Bertie Wooster.

Oct 9. William Warfield and Leontyne Price in George Gershwin's **Porgy and Bess** directed by Richard Bird at Stoll. Book based on a play by Dorothy and Dubose Heyward's play. Lyrics by Ira Gershwin and DuBose Heyward. The musical was a dramatic portrait of the life of a black community in a crumbling tenement mansion on the waterfront in Charleston, South Carolina. Gershwin drew his inspiration from jazz, blues, spirituals, street cries and classical music. When *Porgy and Bess* was premiered in 1935 the American music and drama critics were divided about its merits and unable to decide whether they were watching a musical or an opera. Having taken 17 years to reach London, the Musicians' Union then tried to stop the American conductor (Alexandre Smallens) from conducting. The vitality, the energy and the acting of the singers made a big impression. The score included "Summertime", "It Ain't Necessarily So", "I Got Plenty o' Nuttin'" and "Bess, You is My Woman Now".

Oct 23. David Markham in Oscar Wilde's **Lord Arthur Savile's Crime** adapted by Basil Dawson and St John Clowes and directed by Stephen Murray at Arts. Two versions of Wilde's short story opening within sixteen days of each other were not good for the box-office. This production was preferred because it felt much more like a play by Wilde. Walter Hudd made the most impact as the imperturbable butler pouring out poison.

Oct 28. Maurice Chevalier at London Hippodrome. The French entertainer always managed to create an atmosphere of cabaret intimacy even in large venues. His repertoire included such old favourites as "Valentine", "Louise", "Place Pigalle" and "Paris, Je T'Aime".

Nov 8. Maria Callas made her London debut in Bellini's **Norma** at the Royal Opera House, Covent Garden.

Nov 19. Jack Warner, Bonar Colleano and Gordon Harker in Ted Willis and Jan Read's **The Blue Lamp** at London Hippodrome. The attempt to stage the highly popular 1950 film failed at the box office. Harker played the Jack Warner role of the shot policeman. Colleano played the Dirk Bogarde role of gunman. Warner was promoted to Chief Inspector.

Nov 20. Fay Compton in Jean Cocteau's **The Holy Terrors** directed by John Fernald at Arts. The holy terrors are actors, husband and wife. She commits suicide when her son marries.

Nov 25. Richard Attenborough as the Detective in Agatha Christie's **The Mousetrap** directed by Peter Cotes at Ambassadors. 8 people are stranded in a snowbound house. One of them is a killer. Transferred to St Martin's and still running well into the 21st century.
—There is not enough cheese in this mousetrap. STEPHEN WILLIAMS *Evening News*

Dec 17. Leslie Phillips and Geraldine McEwan in Arthur Watkyn's **For Better, For Worse** directed by John Counsell at Comedy. Cosy English comedy about two newly-weds living in a one-room flat and the domestic disasters they suffer.

Dec 18. Yvonne Arnaud and Charles Goldner in Alan Melville's **Dear Charles** directed by Murray Macdonald at New. Three grown-up children learn their mother

has never been married and each of them has a different father. Since two them wish to marry, she feels it is her duty now to be married and summons the three fathers.

Dec 19. Mark Dignam in **Maria Martin or The Murder in the Old Red Barn** directed by Alec Clunes at Arts. Burlesque of Victorian melodrama interspersed with songs. Dignam was a splendid villain to boo.

Dec 24. Paul Scofield in Shakespeare's **Richard II** directed by John Gielgud at Lyric, Hammersmith. Eric Porter as Bolingbroke. Herbert Lomas as John of Gaunt. Scofield's performance would probably have been even better had he been given a freer hand and had he not been directed by the greatest Richard of his generation.

Dec 25. Anthony Twite in Alfred Jarry's **Ubu Roi** translated by Barbara Wright and directed by Willam Jay at Irving. First performance in English. The actors wore masks and behaved like marionettes. Jay read out the stage directions. *Theatre World* reported that "On the second night a crapulous person in the small audience had a word the translator had not used and this he bawled two or three times before going out and slamming the door."

1953

Jan 18. Danny Kaye at Palace. His original engagement of six weeks was extended to fourteen

Jan 20. Nigel Patrick and Phyllis Calvert in Roger MacDougall's **Escapade** directed by John Fernald at St James's. Pacifist tract. Sixteen-year-old schoolboy steals a plane and flies to Vienna with his manifesto saying that he does not want to kill the children of any other school.

Feb 4. Donald Wolfit in Sophocles's **Oedipus The King** and **Oedipus in Exile** directed by Donald Wolfit at King's, Hammersmith. It was the first time in the history of the English theatre that the two plays had been acted in the same programme. The performance was heavy-going. Rosalind Iden's Electra looked as if she had just

Mairhi Russell, Paul Scofield, Pamela Brown, John Gielgud and Pauline Jameson in *The Way of the World*

Maria Charles, Anne Rogers, Julia Hunt and Joan Gadson in The Boy Friend

come out of a beauty salon. The soldiers needed more substantial clothing and the palace door needed oiling.

Feb 11. Bobby Howes and Sally Ann Howes in Alan Jay Lerner and Frederick Loewe's **Paint Your Wagon** directed by Richard Bird at Her Majesty's. Choreography by Agnes de Mille. A noisy boisterous musical set during the Gold Rush. Songs included "Wanderin' Star", "I Talk to the Trees" and "They Call the Wind Maria".

Feb 12. Clive Brook as Lord Illingworth, Isabel Jeans as Mrs Alonby and Nora Swinburne as Mrs Arbuthnot in Oscar Wilde's **A Woman of No Importance** designed by Loudon Sainthill and directed by Michael Benthall at Savoy. Athene Seyler as Lady Hunstanton. Jean Cadell as Caroline Pontefract. Frances Hyland as Hester Worsley. Peter Barkworth as Gerald Arbuthnot. An unnamed adaptor (later identified as Paul Dehn) cut the play ruthlessly, added his own epigrams ("Nothing should be rewritten but the classics") and changed the ending. Part of the entertainment was guessing which were Dehn's witticisms and which were Wilde's.
—The revival, it may be thought, is fully justified merely by the presence of Miss Isabel Jeans, in crimson bustle, as the outrageous Mrs Alonby; she indeed does contrive to make her every utterance and her big set pieces upon marriage in the second act sound like the purest gold of high comedy. PHILIP HOPE-WALLACE *Sunday Times*

Feb 19. John Gielgud as Mirabell, Pamela Brown as Millamant and Margaret Rutherford as Lady Wishfort in William Congreve's **The Way of the World** directed by John Gielgud at Lyric, Hammersmith. Eileen Herlie as Mrs Marwood. Eric Porter as Fainall. Paul Scofield as Witwoud. Richard Wordsworth as Petulant. Pauline Jameson as Mrs Fainall. Brewster Mason as Sir Wilfull. Rutherford was the definitive Lady Wishfort. "The soul of Cleopatra," said Kenneth Tynan, "had somehow got trapped into the corporate shape of an entire lacrosse team."

Feb 26. Wilfrid Lawson and Beatrix Lehmann in August Strindberg's **The Father** directed by Peter Cotes at Arts. Lawson, gruff and tight-lipped, was utterly compelling up to the end of the second act.

Feb 28. Anna Neagle in **The Glorious Days** directed by Robert Nesbitt at Palace. Musical. Book by Robert Nesbitt. Music by Henry Parr Davies. Lyrics by Harold Purcell. Neagle played four roles: Nell Gwynn, Queen Victoria, a World War I comedy star and a service woman during the London Blitz.

Mar 23. Johnnie Ray at Palladium. Ray sang and wept. Hysteria on stage and in the auditorium. Exhausting.

Mar 31. Robert Donat as Thomas à Becket in T S Eliot's **Murder in the Cathedral** directed by Robert Helpmann at Old Vic. Donat, returning to the theatre after an absence of six years and still very ill, wondered if he would last the performance. (Two oxygen machines were in the wings.) He had a noble bearing and an inner radiance. His diction, notably in the sermon, was much admired. The four knights' transition from snarling Gestapo to caricatures of Englishmen debating was funny while it lasted; but so broad and so out of key with rest of the play that the audience were unable to settle down for to the final moving moments.

Apr 6. Donald Wolfit in E Temple Thurston's **The Wandering Jew** directed by Donald Wolfit at King's Hammersmith. Wolfit spoke the turgid prose as if it were blank verse.

Apr 14. Anne Rogers in Sandy Wilson's **The Boy Friend** directed by Vida Hope at The Players. The pastiche 1920s musical was a masterpiece of nostalgia. Millionaire's daughter (Anne Rogers) at a finishing school on the Riviera falls in love with a messenger boy (Anthony Hayes), who turns out to be a millionaire. Joan Sterndale Ben-

1953 World Premieres

New York
Arthur Miller's *The Crucible*
Tennessee Williams's *Camino Real*
William Inge's *Picnic*
Cole Porter's *Can Can*

Paris
Samuel Beckett's *Waiting for Godot*
Jean Anouilh's *The Lark*
Jean Giraudoux's *The Duel of Angels*
Jean-Paul Sartre's *Kean*

Edinburgh
T S Eliot's *The Confidential Clerk*

Births

Frank McGuinness, Irish playwright

Deaths

Ugo Betti (b.1892), Italian playwright
Eugene O'Neill (b.1888), American playwright
Godfrey Tearle (b.1884), British actor
Dylan Thomas (b. 1914), Welsh poet, playwright

Honours

Knight
John Gielgud, actor, director

Notes

—Joan Littlewood made her base at Theatre Royal Stratford East from 1953–1964
—Stratford Festival, Ontario, Canada, opened with Shakespeare's *All's Well That Ends Well* with Alec Guinness as King and Irene Worth as Helen directed by the artistic director, Tyrone Guthrie
—Michael Benthall, artistic director, at Old Vic, started a five-year plan to complete all Shakespeare's plays
—John Gielgud arrested for importuning.

History

—Coronation of Queen Elizabeth
—Edmund Hilary and Sherpa Tenzing conquered Everest
—Death of Stalin
—Korean War ended

---

nett played the headmistress. The temptation to burlesque the period was resisted. Rogers's demure heroine was always perfectly in period – in voice, dress, mannerisms – even when she was acknowledging the audience's applause. The costumes – the short skirts, cloche hats, cami-knickers and the men's swimwear – were hilarious. The songs included "I Could Be Happy With You" and "A Room in Bloomsbury". Maria Charles was hilarious in "It's Never Too Late To Fall In Love." Transferred to Embassy and then Wyndham's and ran for five years.

Apr 16. Eric Portman and Dorothy Tutin in Graham Greene's **The Living Room** directed by Peter Glenville at Wyndham's. A young woman is in love with a married man, who is old enough to be her father, but she cannot bear the thought of leaving him. She turns first to her lover, a psychologist, then to her uncle, a priest. Both fail her.

May 6. Paul Rogers as Henry, Gwen Ffrangcon-Davies as Queen Katharine and Alexander Knox as Wolsey in Shakespeare's **King Henry VIII** directed by Tyrone Guthrie at the Old Vic. At the Gala Performance, in the presence of H M The Queen, in honour of the coronation, Archbishop Cranmer's patriotic speech at the christening of Elizabeth I was constantly interrupted by applause.

May 7. Noël Coward as King Magnus in Bernard Shaw's **The Apple Cart** directed by Michael Macowan at Haymarket. Laurence Naismith as Prime Minister. George Rose as Boanerges. Margaret Leighton as the king's mistress was as extravagant as the huge chaise-longue Loudon Sainthill had designed for her private apartment.
—Shaw, even in his dotage, had a consuming interest in power politics; whereas Mr Coward, beyond an occasional kindly wink at the British Empire, is unable to convey any interest in politics at all. KENNETH TYNAN *Evening Standard*

May 15. John Gielgud as Jaffier and Paul Scofield as Pierre in Thomas Otway's **Venice Preserv'd** designed by Leslie Hurry and directed by Peter Brook at Lyric, Hammersmith. Eileen Herlie as Belvidera. Pamela Brown as Aquilina. Richard Wordsworth as Antonio. The play, which had once held the stage for a century and a half, was now a collector's item. The play was based on an actual plot against the Venetian Senate in 1618. The high-blown and largely empty rhetoric owed more to the French classical tradition than it did to English theatre. The play's critical success was not matched by the box office returns.

May 28. Vivian Blaine as Miss Adelaide, Sam Levene as Nathan Detroit, Jerry Wayne as Sky Masterson and Lizabeth Webb as Sister Sarah in Frank Loesser's **Guys and Dolls** directed by Arthur Lewis at Coliseum and based on the American production of George S Kaufman. Book by Jo Swerling and Abe Burrows. Choreographed by Michael Kidd. Set and lighting by Jo Mielziner. This landmark in American music theatre was premiered in New York in 1950, when it ran for 1,200 performances. The script, sentimental and witty, is based on Damon Runyon's *The Idyll of Miss Sarah Brown* and the characters of Runyon's short stories. The tales are satires on the low life of petty crooks in and around Broadway. The bums, broads, touts, pickpockets, showgirls, gangsters (many based on real-life gangsters whom Runyon knew personally) are immortalised by their whimsical nicknames and idiosyncratic language. Life, for them, is one big crap game. Nathan Detroit, who runs the oldest established float-

ing crap game in New York, bets Sky Masterson that he can't seduce a Salvation Army lass, the prudish, all-buttoned-up Sister Sarah. Songs included "I've Never Been in Love", "Take Back Your Mink", "Sue Me", "Luck Be a Lady Tonight". Stubby Kaye as Nicely Nicely Johnson stopped the show at every performance with "Sit Down, Sit Down, You're Rocking the Boat". The show, amazingly, was booed by the gallery on the first night.
—The show remains fascinating in its exoticism, in its originality, in its verve. ANTHONY COOKMAN *Tatler*
—It may displease those who imagine that sex is another nasty American invention. IAIN HAMILTON *Spectator*
—An interminable, an overwhelming, and in the end, intolerable bore. HAROLD HOBSON *Sunday Times*

Jun 22. **Dean Martin and Jerry Lewis** at London Palladium. Lewis practised lunacy, both visual and vocal, to a degree where it became an art. Martin was on hand to bring a touch of sanity to their act and to check his exuberance.

Jul 7. Diana Lynn, Robert Flemyng and Biff McGuire in F Hugh Herbert's **The Moon is Blue** directed by F Hugh Herbert at Duke of York's. Shockingly naïve twenty-year-old is picked up by a young architect. Her frankness disarms him. The only play in London ever to have got an X certificate.

Aug 5. Helen Haye as the Dowager Empress of Russia and Mary Kerridge as Anna Brown in Marcelle Maurette's **Anastasia** adapted by Guy Bolton and directed by John Counsell at St James's. Will Anna Brown be able to persuade the Dowager Empress that she is her granddaughter?

Aug 6. Jane Baxter, Ronald Squire, Marie Löhr and Marjorie Fielding in Frederick Lonsdale's **Aren't We All?** directed by Roland Culver at Haymarket. A wife (Jane Baxter) catches her husband (Ronald Howard) in the arms of another woman and is shocked. Putting the 1923 play back to 1914 didn't help; it still wasn't worth reviving.

Aug 24. Isabelle Cooley in Philip Yordan's **Anna Lucasta** directed by Frederick O'Neal and Ken Freeman at Prince of Wales. A coloured family cheats a white man by marrying him off to a prostitute. The crude melodrama was poorly acted.

Sep 8. Mai Zetterling as Nora and Mogens Wieth as Torvald in Henrik Ibsen's **The Doll's House** directed by Peter Ashmore at Lyric, Hammersmith. The casting of two Norwegian actors gave the production an extra weight. Weith's patronising manner, his narrow-minded and his stodginess were exactly right.
—Miss Mai Zetterling so extravagantly exaggerates her early childishness that in her final demonstration of maturity she seems to be a totally different person. ERIC KEOWN *Punch*

Sep 14. Richard Burton in Shakespeare's **Hamlet** directed by Michael Benthall at Old Vic. Burton chopped up the verse and kept the audience guessing whether Hamlet was mad or merely pretending. (Burton always said he had played him as a raving maniac.) The Ghost was so visible that it was amazing that Gertrude (a deathly-white Fay Compton) couldn't see him. Michael Hordern played Polonius for laughs all the time. Claire Bloom's mad scene was one of the better moments. John Gielgud, foremost Hamlet of his generation, went backstage, intending to take Burton out to dinner and made one of his classic *faux pas*. "Shall I go ahead or wait until you're better – I mean ready?"
—Burton is a rugger-playing Hamlet – an uncomplicated prince determined to revenge the murder of his father. He plays the part with dash, attack and verve, not pausing to worry about psychology. DAVID LEWIN *Daily Express*

Sep 15. Claire Bloom as Helena and Fay Compton as the Countess in Shakespeare's **All's Well that Ends Well** designed by Osbert Lancaster and directed by Michael Benthall at Old Vic. John Neville was Bertram. The production kept the unpleasantness of the story at bay. Bloom was adorable. Michael Hordern's cowardly Parolles did on one occasion actually draw his sword with a flourish – but only to clean his nails.

Sep 16. Paul Rogers, Isabel Jeans, Margaret Leighton, Denholm Elliott and Alan Webb in T S Eliot's **The Confidential Clerk** directed by E Martin Browne transferred from Edinburgh Festival to Lyric. The clerk realizes that the girl he has fallen in love with is his half-sister. Eliot was quoted as saying that if he had meant to say something else, he would have done so – and just as obscurely. He also pointed out that if you had something to say it was much easier to say in comedy than in tragedy. People took tragedy seriously on the surface; but they took comedy lightly on the surface and seriously underneath.

Oct 8. Valerie Hobson and Herbert Lom in Richard Rodgers and Oscar Hammerstein's **The King and I** directed by John van Druten under the supervision of Jerome Whyte at Drury Lane. Settings and lighting by Jo Mielziner. Costumes designed by Irene Sharaff. Choreography by Jerome Robbins. The musical was based on the film, *Anna and the King of Siam*, starring Irene Dunne and Rex Harrison, which was

Peggy Ashcroft in Antony and Cleopatra

....

based on the novel by Margaret Landon, which was based on the memoirs of Mrs Anna Leonowens, English governess to the 82 (*sic*) children of King Mongkut in the 1880s. Lom concentrated on the acting, leaving the singing to Muriel Smith. Hobson had the breeding but not the voice, which barely reached the auditorium. The songs included "Hello, Young Lover", "I Whistle a Happy Tune", "Getting to Know You" and "Shall We Dance?" The high spot was Robbins' interpretation of *Uncle Tom's Cabin*.
—The principal parts are taken by Valerie Hobson and Herbert Lom. Their performances will not get past anyone who knows what acting is. Harold Hobson *Sunday Times*
—It is all so childish and as drama not worth a pair of Siamese pins. *Daily Express*

Oct 27. Michael Hordern as John, Richard Burton as Bastard and Fay Compton as Constance in Shakespeare's **King John** directed by George Devine at Old Vic. A dull history lesson and a lot of ranting.

Oct 28. Patricia Jessel in Agatha Christie's **Witness for the Prosecution** directed by Wallace Douglas at Winter Garden. Old Bailey drama.

Nov 4. Michael Redgrave and Peggy Ashcroft in Shakespeare's **Antony and Cleopatra** directed by Glen Byam Shaw transferred from Stratford to Palace. Ashcroft, though physically and temperamentally wrong, succeeded beyond most critics' expectations, except for Kenneth Tynan who dismissed her as a "Cleopatra from Sloane Square." Pale-faced and red-wigged, she was certainly no Egyptian dish, no gypsy, either; she was rather a wily Greek, cunning, witty, sadistic and passionate.

Nov 5. Laurence Olivier and Vivien Leigh in Terence Rattigan's **The Sleeping Prince** directed by Laurence Olivier at Phoenix. American chorus girl in London at the time of the 1911 coronation is invited by the Prince Regent of the Carpathian Legation to pass the evening with him. It was generally felt that Olivier was wasting his time. Rattigan had written his "fairy tale" especially for the coronation, but the production was delayed because of Leigh's illness. Martita Hunt, playing a Grand Duchess, had the best lines and walked off with the play.
—Mr Rattigan, of course, is an old hand at keeping this kind of nonsense bubbling. But this time his invention seems to have petered out somewhere about the middle of the second act. Beneath his facade of froth he shows only froth. Milton Shulman *Evening Standard*

Nov 26. John Gielgud, Ralph Richardson, Sybil Thorndike and Irene Worth in N C Hunter's **A Day by the Sea** directed by John Gielgud at Haymarket. Hunter's melancholy mood piece offered wistful, gentle, bitter studies of loneliness, frustration, lost opportunities and unfulfilled ambitions. The writing was very much in the Chek-

hovian idiom and blatantly so when a little girl walked on carrying a dead thrush. Gielgud was cast as a failed diplomat who proposed twenty years too late to a woman (Irene Worth), who already had had two disastrous marriages and wasn't keen to have another. An unhappy spinster (Megs Jenkins) waited in vain for a drunken doctor (Richardson) to propose to her. The ensemble acting of the all-star cast was admired far more than the play was.

Dec 10. Pamela Brown, Gladys Cooper and Paul Scofield in Wynyard Browne's **A Question of Fact** directed by Frith Banbury at Piccadilly. A young classics master returns from his honeymoon to learn that his father was hung for murder and that the defence had put forward a plea of insanity. Is he a fit person to educate the minds of his pupils? Is he a fit person to have children?

Dec 23. Hermione Baddeley, Ian Carmichael and Dora Bryan in **At the Lyric** directed by William Chappell at Lyric, Hammersmith. Revue.

1954

Jan 1. Sam Wanamaker, Renee Asherson, Frederick Valk, George Coulouris and Diane Cilento in Clifford Odets's **The Big Knife** directed by Sam Wanamaker at Westminster. Overwrought Hollywood drama transferred to Duke of York's.

Jan 10. Mary Ellis in Noël Coward's **After the Ball** directed by Robert Helpmann at Globe. Musical adaptation of Oscar Wilde's *Lady Windermere's Fan*. The songs merely accentuated the bathos and melodrama. Helpmann said there should have been either more Coward and less Wilde or more Wilde and less Coward.

Feb 10. John Mills in Brandon Thomas's **Charley's Aunt** directed by John Gielgud at New. Mills was unflagging in energy and unfailing in comic resource, but the joke never seemed less than laboured. Gielgud made the mistake of directing Thomas's farce as if it were a comedy by Wilde.

Feb 18. Michael Gough, Michael Goodliffe, Laurence Naismith and Faith Brook in Charles Morgan's **The Burning Glass** directed by Michael Macowan at Apollo. A scientist is not convinced that his invention is to the country's good and is willing to concede the use of its power only in an extreme military emergency. Discussion gave way to melodrama: abduction, threats of war and suicides. Gough, as a young man with adultery and treachery on his mind, went through some extraordinary tantrums. The most convincing performance was by Naismith as the Prime Minister

Feb 23. Richard Burton in Shakespeare's **Coriolanus** directed by Michael Benthall at Old Vic. Fay Compton as Volumnia. Burton had all the attributes of the role save one – true harshness.

Mar 12. Dorothy Tutin as Sally Bowles in John Van Druten's **I Am A Camera** directed by John Van Druten at New. Based on Christopher Isherwood's Berlin stories. The camera is Isherwood (Michael Gwynn), who befriends Sally in 1930s Berlin and records faithfully what he sees. ("No Leica," said a New York critic.) The uninhibited and wanton Sally, with her long cigarette holder and her painted green nails, is never as sophisticated as she thinks she is. One of the key scenes is when a German (Robert Cartland) confesses to being a Jew and she fails even to begin to appreciate what such an admission means.
—Dorothy Tutin takes full advantage of the naïve charm that can go with amorality. Every bob of her head, every quasi-regal gesture of her arm is spellbinding, and she is at her best in brief moments of regret. Anthony Hartley *Spectator*

Mar 31. Harold Lang and Carol Bruce in Richard Rodgers and Lorenz Hart's musical **Pal Joey** directed by Neil Hartley at Princes. Book by John O'Hara based on his series of fictional letters published in *The New Yorker*. Rodgers said it was a show with long pants and, of the 25 musicals he had written, it was his favourite. Brooks Atkinson in *The New York Times*, famously asked, "Can you draw sweet water from a foul well?" Broadway audiences in 1940 weren't quite ready for a cynical and sordid musical about a wealthy married society woman taking a fancy to a young nightclub singer and buying him a nightclub (for which he pays her back in kind). The authors would have to wait for a revival in 1952 before the musical got its proper appreciation. Hart, a closet homosexual and frequenter of cheap bars, identified with the ambitious and amoral Joey, a selfish and callous womaniser. The weakness of O'Hara's book was the feeble blackmailing plot. There were four songs satirising tacky nightclub dance routines, which was at least two too many. Carol Bruce's poise and timing were perfect for the show's most memorable number: "Bewitched, Bothered and Bewildered".

Apr 8. Robert Flemying in John Whiting's **Marching Song** directed by Frith Banbury at St Martin's. An unidentified European country needs a scapegoat for losing the war. Who better then than their general who has just been released by the victors? However, the politicians do not want a trial, with the inevitable washing of dirty linen in public, and suggest he might like to commit suicide instead.

1954 World Premieres
New York
Maxwell Anderson's *The Bad Seed*
Dublin
Brendan Behan's *The Quare Fellow*
Paris
Eugene Ionesco's *Amédée*
Arthur Adamov's *Ping Pong*

Births
Harvey Fierstein, American
playwright

Deaths
Frederick Lonsdale (b.1881), British
playwright

Timberlake Wertenbaker, Anglo-
French-American playwright
George Robey (b.1869), British music
hall comedian

Notes
—Dylan Thomas's *Under Milk Wood*
broadcast

History
—Vietnam divided into North and
South
—Roger Bannister ran first four-
minute mile
—Racial segregation in US schools
declared illegal

Apr 13. Michael Hordern as Prospero in Shakespeare's **The Tempest** directed by Robert Helpmann at Old Vic. Richard Burton as Caliban. John Neville as Ferdinand and Claire Bloom as Miranda. *The Times* refused to review the production until Robert Hardy (who was playing Ariel) put on more clothes.

Apr 14. Alec Guinness in Bridget Boland's **The Prisoner** directed by Noël Willman at Globe. Noël Willman as the Interrogator. Wilfrid Lawson as the Warder. This timely and disturbing duel of wits between the Roman Catholic Church and the Communist Party had its roots in the recent trials of Cardinal Midszenty of Hungary and Cardinal Stepinac of Yugoslavia. A much-loved cardinal, a wartime hero of the Resistance, is arrested on a false charge of treason. The interrogator's task is to deface the national monument by extorting a public confession and discrediting man and Church. Guinness skilfully charted the prisoner's physical and mental deterioration, revealing not only the man's deep despair but also his arrogance and lack of humanity.

Apr 22. Eli Wallach and William Sylvester in John Patrick's **The Teahouse of the August Moon** directed by Robert Lewis at Her Majesty's. Satire on America's attempt to spread democracy in the Far East. Sylvester was the Captain who goes all native. Wallach was the interpreter who takes Uncle Sam for a ride. The play should have been a musical.

Apr 29. Joan Heal, Ronnie Stevens, Joan Sims, Geoffrey Hibbert and Dilys Laye in **Intimacy at 8.30** directed by Michael Charnley at Criterion. Revue. High spots included Hibbert's judge hankering after a sordid case, Stevens's Barber of Charing Cross Road and Heal as a society woman visiting the coal mines in overalls designed by Dior.

Apr 30. Edith Evans in Christopher Fry's **The Dark is Light Enough** directed by Peter Brook at Aldwych. The third of Fry's seasonal plays was set in winter during the Hungarian Revolution in 1848. Evans played a Countess, who entertained the most worthless characters, including her deserter son-in-law (James Donald). The cast included Margaret Johnston, Hugh Griffith, Peter Barkworth and John Moffatt.
—There is no other living dramatist with such a command of the English language. His verse-prose makes the dialogue of ordinary plays shrivel like raisins. BEVERLEY BAXTER *Evening Standard*

May 21. Gwen Ffrangcon-Davies as Ranevsky, Trevor Howard as Lopahin, Esme Percy as Gaev, Pauline Jameson as Varya, Robert Eddison as Epihodoff and Patience Collier as Charlotta, in Anton Chekhov's **The Cherry Orchard** directed by John Gielgud at Lyric, Hammersmith. The contrast between the uncle and the aunt, who are so childlike and the younger generation, who are so serious, was amusingly underlined. Esme Percy was the definitive Gaev.

Jun 2. Joyce Grenfell Requests the Pleasure directed by Laurier Lister at Fortune. Revue. She was joined by dancers, Beryl, Kaye, Paddy Stone and Irving Davies. Her character sketches were witty and accurate. When it came to playing gauche, toothy, gushing, hockey-sticks women, Grenfell had no rival. High spot: the daughter telling her parents to accept old age at 40 and to stop going round enjoying themselves.
—In wit, humour, grace and pathos it is like nothing else in London. HAROLD HOBSON *Sunday Times*

Jul 20. Agnes Bernelle as Salome and Frank Thring as Herod in Oscar Wilde's **Salome** directed by Frederick Farley at St. Martin's. Australian actor Thring, bloated, voluptuous and lascivious, looked like one of Aubrey Beardsley's more grotesque drawings. Some critics thought his performance was "the lustiest exhibition of old ham."

Jul 20. Ralph Michael as the Father, Mary Morris as the Step-Daughter, Marda

Vanne as the Mother and Reginald Tate as the Producer in Luigi Pirandello's **Six Characters in Search of an Author** directed by Royston Morley at Arts. Intellectual debate on illusion and reality. But what is reality? Do the characters of the imagination exist any less vitally than the actors? Six characters, abandoned by their author, suspended in limbo, invade a theatre during a rehearsal, searching for a director and actors capable of responding to their tragedy truthfully rather than in a crude and theatrical manner. The story they have to tell is melodrama – lechery, guilt, hate, incest, prostitution, drowning and murder. But can truth make good theatre? The director tries to re-arrange their lives into a coherent piece of theatre. Transferred to St James's.

Jul 27. Wilfrid Lawson and Joan Miller in Edmund Morris's **The Wooden Dish** directed by Joseph Losey at Phoenix. Wife wants to put her husband's old father into an old people's home. Heartbreaking performance by Lawson.

Jul 28. Jane Wenham, Joan Plowright and Patricia Routledge in Richard Brinsley Sheridan's **The Duenna** directed by Lionel Harris at Westminster. Music by Julian Slade. Gerald Cross, playing a Portuguese Jewish rogue, overacted and was very funny when he was tricked into marrying the Duenna (Joyce Carey). Sheridan's comic operetta with music by Thomas Linley had enjoyed seventy-five nights when first produced in 1775.

Aug 5. Julian Slade and Dorothy Reynolds's **Salad Days** directed by Denis Carey at Vaudeville. This naïve, whimsical, amateurish and terribly English musical/revue, which was about a magic piano that could make people dance, was originally staged by the Bristol Old Vic as a Christmas entertainment. It amazingly transferred to London and, even more amazingly, ran for 2,289 performances. Catchiest tune was "Oh Look At Me I'm Dancing."
—Those best qualified to enjoy *Salad Days* at the Vaudeville would be an aunt, an uncle and some fond relative of the cast. MILTON SHULMAN *Evening Standard*

Aug 31. Brian Rix, Basil Lord and John Slater in John Chapman's **Dry Rot** directed by Wallace Douglas at Whitehall. Farce. Swindle at the local racecourse.

Sep 8. Peggy Ashcroft in Henrik Ibsen's **Hedda Gabler** directed by Peter Ashmore at Lyric, Hammersmith. George Devine as George Tesman. Alan Badel as Lovborg. Micheal Mac Liammoir as Brack. Rachel Kempson as Mrs Elvsted. Audiences, expecting to see tragedy and Ibsenite gloom, found instead a brilliant high comedy. Hedda, socially and sexually frustrated, achingly bored, constantly shivered, as if

Edith Evans and Margaret Johnson in *The Dark is Light Enough*

159

Siobahn McKenna in Saint Joan
....

Oct 20. Ingrid Bergman in Paul Claudel's **Joan of Arc at the Stake** translated by Dennis Arrundell and directed by Roberto Rossellini at Stoll. Music by A Honegger. Oratorio, drama, ballet and mime. Cast of 100. Choir of 50. The staging was elaborate but static. Bergman's sincerity was obvious but Joan was a bore and there was too much symbolism. The production was preceded by Ballet Rambert in **Giselle**.

Nov 3. Michael Gough and Yvonne Mitchell in Ruth and Augustus Goetz's adaptation of Andre Gide's **The Immoralist** directed by Peter Hall at Arts. Homosexual archaeologist, who prefers the company of Arab boys to women, marries and dashes off to Biskra, where his behavior confuses his wife. The happy ending was false to Gide's novel. There was a scene-stealing performance by Wolfe Morris as an insolent, lazy, thieving, perverted Arab boy, a role created on Broadway by James Dean.

Nov 4. Ruth Gordon, Sam Levene, Eileen Herlie, Arthur Hill, Alec McCowen, Rosamund Greenwood, Lee Montagu and Prunella Scales in Thornton Wilder's **The Matchmaker** directed by Tyrone Guthrie at Haymarket. Mean-minded, elderly store-owner (Sam Levene) wants to get married and employs as matchmaker (Ruth Gordon), an impoverished, bossy, scheming Irish widow. She has matrimonial designs on him herself. Wilder slightly modified his earlier play, *The Merchant of Yonkers* (1938), which was based on a Viennese comedy, *Einen Jux will er sich Machen* (1842) by Johann Nestroy, which was based on John Oxenford's *A Day Well Spent* (1835). Asked what the play was about, Wilder said it was about the aspirations of the young for a fuller, freer participation in life. "Don't sit quietly at home wishing you were out having lots of adventures – have adventures." The play, alternating broad farce and homely homilies, parodied the stock company plays of Wilder's boyhood.

Nov 17. Jimmy Edwards, Tony Hancock and Joan Turner in Frank Muir and Denis Norden's **Talk of the Town** directed by Alec Shanks at Adelphi. Revue. High spots included Edwards as a skittish judge and as a lighthouse keeper and Hancock as a transatlantic crooner.

Nov 29. **An Evening with Beatrice Lillie** at Globe. Noel Coward had said that Lillie was the funniest woman in the world. The first half of the programme was a series of poor revue sketches. The joke at the expense of Japanese theatre was interminable. The second half was cabaret. The songs (apart from "You're rotten to the core, Maude") were indifferent. It was the inconsequential things Lillie did with her accessories – a fur wrap, a handkerchief, a wineglass and a necklace – which were funny.

Dec 2. Paul Scofield, Margaret Rutherford and Mary Ure in Jean Anouilh's **Time Remembered** directed by William Chappell at Lyric, Hammersmith. Melancholy Duke (Paul Scofield) remembers a three-day romance with the beautiful Leocadia, who died tragically in the Isadora Duncan manner with the aid of a scarf getting trapped in the wheel of a car. His eccentric aunt (Margaret Rutherford) ensures that the precious souvenirs of the happy affair shall not be forgotten by importing them and having them permanently at hand. The streets of Paris are faithfully reconstructed in her back garden; even the people who crossed their lives join the paid staff in a bid to recapture the atmosphere. The Duke keeps up the appearance of being in love. His aunt, fearing for his life, takes the fantasy one step further and invites a pretty milliner (Mary Ure), who is the living image of Leocadia, to come and play Leocadia. The end is obvious. The aunt, instead of preserving her nephew's love, kills it. Anouilh failed to repeat the success he had had with *Ring Round the Moon*. Transferred to New.

Dec 14. Margaret Lockwood in Agatha Christie's **Spider's Web** directed by Wallace Douglas at Savoy. Comedy thriller without thrills. Lockwood showed an unexpected gift for comedy.

1955

Jan 18. John Neville in Shakespeare's **Richard II** directed by Michael Benthall at Old Vic. Eric Porter as Bolingbroke. Meredith Edwards as Gaunt. Virginia McKenna as Queen. The poet-king showed off to his girl friends, Bushy, Bagot and Green.

Feb 16. Peggy Mount in Philip King and Falkland Cary's **Sailor, Beware!** directed by Melville Gillam at Strand. Peggy Mount became a star overnight as the definitive mother-in-law from hell. There was a memorable moment in the last act, when, having not stopped nagging for one minute, she said, "I have tried to be quiet, God knows I have tried."

Feb 17. Patrick McGoohan, Olga Lindo and Frank Lawton in Philip King's **Serious Charge** directed by Martin Landau at Garrick. A loutish lad (Anthony Wager) falsely accuses a vicar (Patrick McGoohan) of having interfered with him.

Feb 23. Pat Kirkwood and Shani Wallis in Leonard Bernstein's musical **Wonderful Town** directed by Richard Bird at Princes. Book by Joseph Fields and Jerome Cho-

---

unable ever to get warm. Ashcroft's Hedda, totally unsympathetic and calculating evil, was lethal in her irony. Transferred to Westminster. King Haakon awarded Ashcroft the King's Gold Medal when the production visited Oslo.

—In future I shall set no limits on this actress's dramatic powers. CECIL WILSON *Daily Mail*
—It is curious to have to register that an English actress has shown the Norwegian public how Hedda should be played. *Aftenpost, Norway.*

Sep 22. Eric Portman and Margaret Leighton in Terence Rattigan's **Separate Tables** directed by Peter Glenville at St James's. Two one-act plays set in the same boarding house. The supporting actors played the same characters in both plays. Only the leading actors changed their roles. Portman played a blunt, hard-hitting, hard-drinking Yorkshireman and a bogus major who is arrested for indecent behavior in the cinema. Leighton played an elegant woman of the world and a poor crushed creature, unable to escape her mother's clutches. The second play was the best, its homosexuality kept well and truly under covers.

—He is now without question the master playwright of our day. His great strength is his strange, almost clinical gift of laying bare the hidden afflictions of the heart and the bad humours that cripple human behaviour. MAURICE WILTSHIRE *Daily Mail*

Sep 29. Siobhan McKenna in Bernard Shaw's **Saint Joan** directed by John Fernald at Arts. Kenneth Williams as the Dauphin. Peter Wyngarde as Dunois. Douglas Wilmer as Warwick. Charles Lloyd Pack as the Inquisitor. David Marsh as de Stogumber. McKenna, more like a nun than a soldier, was the most saintly, the most profoundly religious of Joans; her Irishness helped. Kenneth Tynan said it was "the richest portrait of saintliness since Renée Falconetti shaved her head for Carl Dreyer's 1928 film, *La Passion de Jeanne d'Arc*". Transferred to St Martin's.

Oct 5. Rex Harrison, Lilli Palmer, Athene Seyler and Wilfrid Lawson in John Van Druten's **Bell, Book and Candle** directed by Rex Harrison at Phoenix. Witchcraft in Knightsbridge.

Oct 14. Irene Hilda, Edmund Hockridge, Alfred Marks, Gillian Lynne and George Gee in Cole Porter's **Can-Can** directed by Abe Burrows at Coliseum. Book by Abe Burrows. Choreography by Michael Kidd. Settings and lighting by Jo Mielziner. Costumes by Motley. Montmartre in the naughty nineties. A judge is keen to stamp out all immorality until he falls in love with a madam who runs a café. The musical was a big disappointment. Hilda sang Porter's only good number, "I Love Paris."

—But this just isn't Paris and those slick tunes go so oddly with the can-can. MAURICE WILTSHIRE *Daily Mail*

1955 World Premieres
New York
Arthur Miller's *A View from The Bridge* (one-act version)
Tennessee Williams's *Cat on a Hot Tin Roof*
William Inge's *Bus Stop*
Melbourne
Ray Lawler's *Summer of the Seventeenth Doll*
Paris
Jean-Paul Sartre's *Nekrassov*

Births
Sebastien Barry, Irish playwright, novelist, poet

Deaths
Paul Claudel (*b.*1868), French playwright

Robert E Sherwood, (*b.*1896) American playwright

Notes
—Premiere of Laurence Olivier's film of *Richard III*

History
—Warsaw Pact formed
—Riots in Algeria and Morocco against the French
—Juan Peron overthrown in Argentina
—Ruth Ellis hanged
—Commercial TV started in Britain

dorov based on their play, *My Sister Eileen*. Lyrics by Betty Comden and Adolph Green. The casting made nonsense of the story. Kirkwood was no wallflower and Wallis didn't look the sort of girl to have men running after her. Wittiest songs: "One Hundred Easy Ways to Lose a Man" and "Wrong Note Rag".

Mar 9. Stephen Murray, Helena Hughes and Susan Richards in Eugene Ionesco's **The Lesson** directed by Peter Hall at Arts. Classic of the Theatre of the Absurd. An aged professor of philology gets so carried away with his own words that he rapes and kills his pupils. Acted in a double bill with André Obey's **Sacrifice to the Wind**, translated by John Whiting and directed by Stephen Murray.

Mar 9. John Neville as Orlando and Virginia McKenna as Rosalind in Shakespeare's

As You Like It directed by Robert Helpmann at Old Vic. Eric Porter as Jacques. Paul Rogers as Touchstone. McKenna's tomboy was a charmer.

Mar 30. Clare Austin, Zena Walker, Lyndon Brook and Denholm Elliott in Julien Green's **South** directed by Peter Hall at Arts. Shortly before the outbreak of the American Civil War, young man (Lyndon Brook) of rigid religious principles fails to recognise an officer's love for him and precipitates a tragedy. Denholm Elliott was very moving as the officer who provokes a duel in order to get himself killed.

Apr 4. Maurice Chevalier at Palace.

Apr 14. Diana Wynyard in Maxwell Anderson's **Bad Seed** directed by Frith Banbury at Aldwych. Golden-haired child with an angelic smile has inherited her granny's murderous genes. Carol Wolveridge as the child was so convincingly evil that when she took her curtain call the audience, still in a state of shock, failed to clap her.

Apr 19. Diana Churchill, Bernard Lee and Richard Carlyle in Joseph Hayes's **The Desperate Hours** directed by Howard Erskine at London Hippodrome. Three trigger-happy escaped convicts take a family hostage.

Apr 20. Alfred Drake, Doretta Morrow and Joan Diener in **Kismet** directed by Albert Marre and Mervyn Nelson at Stoll. Adaptation of Alexander Borodin's *Prince Igor*. Book by Charles Lederer and Luther Davis. Music and lyrics by Robert Wright and George Forrest. Poet-beggar becomes an Emir and father-in-law to the Caliph. Hit song: "Stranger in Paradise".

Apr 21. Benny Hill and Tommy Cooper in **Paris by Night** directed by Dick Hurran at Prince of Wales. Billed inaccurately as a *Folies Bergère* revue, Cooper's inept conjuring was the show's one classy music hall act.

Apr 28. Paul Rogers as Falstaff, Robert Hardy as Prince Hal and Eric Porter as King Henry in Shakespeare's **Henry IV Parts 1 and 2** directed by Douglas Seale at Old Vic. Rogers was the best Falstaff and Paul Daneman was the funniest Justice Shallow in the 1950s.

John Gielgud, Richard Easton, Timothy Harlow, Helen Cherry, Judith Stott, Peggy Ashcroft and Moira Lister in **Much Ado About Nothing**

Timothy Bateson, Paul Daneman , Peter Bull and Peter Woodthorpe in Waiting for Godot

May 11. Dorothy Tutin as Joan of Arc in Jean Anouilh's **The Lark** directed by Peter Brook at Lyric, Hammersmith. Donald Pleasance as Dauphin. Leo McKern as Promoter. Michael Goodliffe as Inquisitor. Laurence Naismith as Cauchon. Coming so soon after Siobhan McKenna's Joan, the production did not escape unfavourable comparison. Tutin's sophisticated Joan didn't look as if she had ever worked on the land.

May 12. Ronald Shiner, George Rose and Nigel Stock in Sam and Bella Spewack's **My Three Angels** directed by Wallace Douglas at Lyric. Adaptation of Albert Husson's *Cusine des Anges*. Two murderers and an embezzler escape from prison in French Guiana in 1910 and act as fairy godfathers to a family.

May 18. Nigel Patrick and Elizabeth Sellars in Liam O'Brien's **The Remarkable Mr Pennypacker** directed by John Fernald at New. Pennypacker was a bigamist.

May 21. Emlyn Williams in **Dylan Thomas Growing Up** at Globe. One-man show. Williams did not pretend to be the poet. He was Thomas only in so far as he spoke in the first person.

May 23. Danny Kaye at Palladium.

May 24. Celia Johnson, Wilfred Hyde-White and Anna Massey in William Douglas Home's **The Reluctant Debutante** directed by Jack Minster at Cambridge. Mother worries what her daughter may be doing when she stays out all night with a notorious playboy. Her fears are unfounded.

Jun 2. Michael Redgrave as Hector in Jean Giraudoux's **Tiger at the Gates** translated by Christopher Fry and directed by Harold Clurman at Apollo. Walter Fitzgerald as Ulysses. Barbara Jefford as Andromache. Leueen MacGrath as Cassandra. Nicholas Hannen as Priam. John Laurie as Dmokos. Catherine Lacey as Hecuba. Giraudoux, writing shortly before World War 2, preached a pacifist message in the face of jingoistic sentiments. Which is the worse cowardice? To appear cowardly to others and make sure of peace? Or to be cowardly in your own eyes and let loose a war? The vivid description of Helen and Paris making love on board ship was worthy of Chaucer. Diane Cilento was a sly, languorous, husky-voiced Helen. The high water mark was a meeting between Hector and Ulysses on the eve of the war when peace was won only to be lost in the same breath. Kenneth Tynan in *The Observer* said the play was a masterpiece and "the highest peak in the mountain-range of modern literature."
—He [Michael Redgrave] speaks the lines brilliantly. There is a mind at work behind what he says. Although the part is classical, he keeps the human being alive and responsive inside the classical formalities. The dimensions of his acting are big, but the humanity is warm and simple. BROOKS ATKINSON *New York Times*

Jun 16. Orson Welles as Captain Ahab in his adaptation and production of Herman Melville's **Moby Dick** at Duke of York's. Patrick McGoohan as Starbuck. Gordon Jackson as Ishmael. There are no half measures about Ahab. "I'd strike the sun, if it insulted me," he says. The production's gimmick was to stay in rehearsal throughout. But Moby Dick without the whale didn't make much sense. Pip, the mad Negro cabin boy, was played by Joan Plowright.

Jun 21. The Shakespeare Memorial Theatre Company. John Gielgud as Benedict and Peggy Ashcroft as Beatrice in a revival of John Gielgud's production of Shakespeare's **Much Ado About Nothing** at Palace. The raillery was in good hands. A star had clearly danced when Ashcroft was born. "Kill, Claudio!" got a laugh, which was the fault of the audience rather than the actors. George Devine was a fruity-voiced Dogberry.

Jun 26. The Shakespeare Memorial Theatre Company. John Gielgud in Shakespeare's **King Lear** directed by George Devine at Palace. Claire Bloom as Cordelia. Helen Cherry as Goneril. Moira Lister as Regan. David O'Brien as Fool. George Devine as Gloucester. Harold Lang as Edmund. Richard Easton as Edgar. Gielgud played Lear as if he were playing Gloucester. Isamu Noguchi's designs would have been more appropriate for a ballet by Martha Graham. There were Martian soldiers, Japanese swords, triangular shapes (apt to move about the stage) and an artist's giant palate for Kent's stocks which looked like a lavatory seat. Lear was fantastically dressed in a costume whose holes got larger and larger. The headline in *The Daily Sketch* was: Lear looks like a Gruyère cheese.

Aug 3. Peter Woodthorpe as Estragon, Paul Daneman as Vladimir, Timothy Bateson as Lucky, Peter Bull as Pozzo and Michael Walker as the Boy in Samuel Beckett's **Waiting for Godot** directed by Peter Hall at Arts. Tragi-comedy in two acts, famously described by Vivian Mercer as a play in which nothing happens twice. Two tramps blather about nothing in particular. Bernard Levin thought it "a remarkable piece of twaddle". Audiences hurled insults at the actors: "Rubbish! Disgusting! Take it off!"
—Go and see *Waiting for Godot*. At worst you will discover a curiosity, a four-leaved clover, a black tulip; at the best, something that will securely lodge in the corner of your mind for as long as you live. HAROLD HOBSON *Sunday Times*

—*Waiting for Godot* is a play to send the rationalist out of his mind and induce tooth-gnashing among people who would take Lewis Carroll's Red Queen and Lear's nonsense exchanges with the food as the easiest stuff in the world. PHILIP HOPE-WALLACE *Manchester Guardian*
—It is superb as a serious frolic for highbrows; but in the regular workaday theatre it has no conceivable place at all. No management would ask the ordinary playgoer to face it. W A DARLINGTON *Daily Telegraph*
—Another of those plays that tries to lift superficiality to significance through obscurity. MILTON SHULMAN *Evening Standard*
—It forced me to re-examine the rules which have hitherto governed the drama; and having done so, to pronounce them not elastic enough. KENNETH TYNAN *Observer*

Aug 31. Dora Bryan in Vivian Ellis's musical **Water Gypsies** directed by Charles Hickman at Winter Garden. Book and lyrics by A P Herbert. Barges and bargees. Hit song: Bryan singing "Why did you call me Lilly?"

Sep 6. Clive Brook, Mai Zetterling, Helen Haye and Valerie Taylor in Marcel Aymé's **The Count of Clérambard** translated by Norman Denny and directed by Murray Macdonald at Garrick. A very French anti-clerical piece got a very English treatment. The count (Clive Brook) having had a conversion and turned saint, wants his son to marry the local prostitute (Mai Zetterling) and the rest of the family to renounce what little they have and preach the gospel to the poor from a caravan. Alec McCowen as the weak, ineffectual son was very amusing.

Sep 8. Thelma Ruby, Kenneth Williams and Betty Warren in Sandy Wilson's musical **The Buccaneer** directed by William Chappell at Lyric, Hammersmith. An earlier piece than *The Boy Friend* and not so good: a children's newspaper, threatened by the American horror comic market, is bought by a wealthy mother for her son. Kenneth Williams was the son, the ultimate precocious brat. The catchiest song was "Good Clean Fun".

Sep 9. Alexander Knox, Leo McKern, Yvonne Mitchell and Esme Percy in Ugo Betti's **The Burnt Flower-Bed** translated by Henry Reed and directed by Peter Hall at Arts. Political drama. A totalitarian state, having decided to come to terms with the people across the frontier, seeks out their ex-Dictator and asks him to help them find a basis for peace – or so it seems.

Sep 13. Edwige Feuillère in Alexandre Dumas's **La Dame aux Camélias** directed by Edwige Feuillere at Duke of York's. A dated vehicle, which belongs to the school of consumption for heroines so popular in the 19th century, before the invention of the lift shaft, as a convenient form of tragic exit. Feuillere did not erase memories of Greta Garbo in George Cukor's 1937 film.

Sep 28. Binnie Hale, Paul Daneman, Alfie Bass, Denis Martin and Joyce Blair in **The Punch Revue** devised and directed by Vida Hope at Duke of York's. The best sketch was Paul Dehn's burlesque of the Old Vic. The presence of a good Shakespearean actor, Paul Daneman, helped enormously. Binnie Hale did impersonations of Beatrice Lillie, Marlene Dietrich and Yvonne Arnaud and sang W H Auden's torch song, "O Tell Me The Truth About Love."

Oct 13. Max Wall, Joy Nichols and Edmund Hockridge in **Pajama Game** directed by Robert E Griffith at Coliseum. Musical. Book by George Abbott and Richard Bissell based on Richard Bissell's novel, *Seven-and-a-half-cents*. Music and lyrics by Richard Adler and Jerry Ross. Workers in a pyjama factory want a raise. When the dishonest boss stalls for time, they threaten to go on strike. Two people fall in love. He's on the side of the management whilst she's in the union. Hit song: "Hernando's Hideaway". Dancer gamine Elizabeth Seal stole the show.

Oct 26. Irene Worth, Leo McKern and Gwen Watford in Ugo Betti's **The Queen and the Rebels** translated by Henry Reed and directed by Frank Hauser at Haymarket. Revolutionaries are looking for the Queen, who has eluded them for the last five years. Believing her to be one of a number of travellers, they delay them all at the frontier to interrogate them. A prostitute recognizes the Queen in a shrivelled, petrified peasant. Seeing a chance to make some money, she plans her death, only to have a change of heart at the last minute and help her to escape. She pretends to be the Queen and so convincing is her performance that she cannot make the Revolutionaries believe that she is only a prostitute. *Tour de force* by Irene Worth.

Nov 3. Robert Dhéry's **La Plume de ma tante** at Garrick. A delightful and original French revue. Lunatic fantasies and hilarious mime included: a singer, inexplicably, on horseback; an imaginary lion, which strikes panic into the hearts of the whole cast; a ludicrous striptease, which begins with the hat, the overcoat and the gloves; a tenor being bowled over by a girl on a swing and having to sing the lyric from the floor. Dhéry was very funny as a waiter extracting bits of cork from a customer's wineglass.

Nov 9. Dirk Bogarde and Geraldine McEwan in Ugo Betti's **Summertime** directed by Peter Hall at Apollo. In the mountains of Northern Italy at the turn of the 20th century a boy fails to realize that the girl next door has grown up. The girl has one summer's day to open his eyes. Nigel Stock played the boy when Bogarde left the cast.

Nov 15. Donald Wolfit and Ernest Milton in Fritz Hochwälder's **The Strong are Lonely** directed by Margaret Webster at Piccadilly. Jesuit fathers in Paraguay are accused of having unlawfully acquired wealth and enslaved Indians. Wolfit and Milton upstaged each other for the greater glory of God.

Dec 8. Paul Scofield in Shakespeare's **Hamlet** directed by Peter Brook at Phoenix. Diana Wynyard as Gertrude. Alec Clunes as Claudius. Mary Ure as Ophelia. Ernest Thesiger as Polonius. Richard Johnson as Laertes. The company came to London following their enormous success in Moscow. Tired, they were not at their best on the first night.

Dec 13. Richard Burton in Shakespeare's **Henry V** directed by Michael Benthall at Old Vic. John Neville as Chorus. Zena Walker as Katherine. John Wood as Dauphin. Dudley Jones as Fluellen. The rhetoric went for a burton. He was at his best in the play's quieter moments. *The News Chronicle* thought that "this splendid actor lacks nothing a good actor should have except inches."

Dec 14. Mona Washbourne, Nan Munro, Marda Vanne and Margaret Vines in Paul Osborn's **Morning's at Seven** directed by Jack Minster at Comedy. Four sisters and their families sit in an American backyard and chat about their problems for three acts.

Dec 16. Margaret McCourt, Richard Palmer and Mavis Sage in Angela Ainley Jeans's **Listen to the Wind** directed by Peter Hall at Arts. Music and lyrics by Vivian Ellis. A play for children and grownups about three Victorian children and their adventures in the Kingdom of the Winds. The show had considerable charm. The song was "When I Grow Up". Ronald Barker played a gypsy and Miriam Karlin was hilariously vulgar as a mermaid.

Dec 19. Marcia Ashton, Gordon Heath, Anthony Newley and Gilbert Vernon in John Cranko's **Cranks** directed by John Cranko at New Watergate. Surrealistic revue.

Dec 21. Emlyn Williams, Angela Baddeley, Michael Gough, Dorothy Tutin, George Relph and Laurence Hardy in Henrik Ibsen's **The Wild Duck** directed by Murray Macdonald at Saville. Williams's Hjalmar had a Dickensian pomposity. "I must grapple alone," he said. The idea of Hjalmar "grappling" with anything was amusing. Gough was a very neurotic Gregers Werle. Tutin was a very convincing child. The Saville was too big a theatre for so intimate a play.

Dec 22. Frankie Howerd in Brandon Thomas's **Charley's Aunt** directed by William Chappell at Globe. By no stretch of the imagination was Howerd either a lord or an Oxford undergraduate.

1956

Feb 9. Bill Owen as Mack the Knife in Bertolt Brecht's **The Threepenny Opera**, directed by Sam Wanamaker at Royal Court. Music by Kurt Weill. Daphne Anderson as Polly Peachum. Georgia Brown as Lucy. George A Cooper as Tiger Brown. Warren Mitchell as Crookfinger Jake. The opera (premiered in Berlin in 1928) had taken a long time to reach London. Brecht set John Gay's 1728 pastoral, *The Beggar's Opera*, in an imaginary Edwardian era. In 1933 it was officially denounced as a prime example of Degenerate Art. Two years later, with Jewish persecution on the increase, Brecht and Weill were forced to flee from Germany. Bill Owen modelled himself on James Cagney; his music hall training stood him in good stead. Transferred to Aldwych.
—I do not go to the theatre to be instructed in the elements of Marxist science or sanitary engineering. I am not prepared to be bored to satisfy anybody's itch to teach. *Punch*

Feb 21. Richard Burton and John Neville alternated Othello and Iago in Shakespeare's **Othello** directed by Michael Benthall at Old Vic. Rosemary Harris as Desdemona. Wendy Hiller as Emilia. Burton was a sad, brooding, plausible, intelligent Iago for whom, surprisingly, the audience could feel some pity. Neville's spiv Iago was so obviously evil that nobody would have applied the word "honest" to him. Neville, too light-weight, did not have the physique for Othello.
—A drab squabble between the Chocolate Soldier and the Vagabond King. KENNETH TYNAN *Observer*
—Burton beats Neville – but Othello beats them both. *Evening Standard headline*

Feb 23. John Clements as Sir Anthony Absolute, Kay Hammond as Lydia Languish, Laurence Harvey as Captain Jack Absolute and Athene Seyler as Mrs Malaprop in

Richard Brinsley Sheridan's **The Rivals** directed by William Chappell at Saville. Paul Daneman as Faulkland. The high spot of this stylish revival came when Lydia discovered that the two rivals were one and the same person. Harvey was very funny trying to play two different characters at the same time, changing his voice and hiding behind his father.

Mar 21. Hugh Griffith as General St Pé in Jean Anouilh's **The Waltz of the Toreadors** directed by Peter Hall at Arts. The General remembers his past campaigns vividly, though these were rarely of a military kind. Griffith's performance never degenerated into farce, even though farce was going on around him all the time. His mistress (Brenda Bruce) and his bedridden wife (Beatrix Lehmann) both decided to commit suicide at the same time, one out of a window, the other on a railway line. Lehmann did not play the wife's harangue for the frightening, revolting tirade it should have been.

Apr 3. John Neville and Rosemary Harris in Shakespeare's **Troilus and Cressida** directed by Tyrone Guthrie at the Old Vic. Updated to World War 1. Rarely has the play been so accessible. The Greeks were monocled, heel-clicking Prussians. The Trojans were English. Derek Francis's Agamemnon bore a striking resemblance to the Kaiser. Paul Rogers's Pandarus, with his topper, spats, cane, gloves and moustache, was an ageing Edwardian dandy, who sang for Wendy Hiller's Helen, a gaiety girl. With the help of his binoculars, he was able to point out the returning troops to Cressida as if they were horses in the paddock at Ascot. The final image was of a sad, lonely and diseased old man sitting on a much-labeled suitcase. Charles Gray's Achilles was an odious, blasé, cigarette-smoking individual, who always seemed to have only just got out of bed. Jeremy Brett's Patroclus (his boyfriend), invariably by his side, was a pathetic figure. Thersites was a disgruntled, knickerbockered, socialist press photographer. Cressida was a coquette. Her departure for the Greek camp was very funny. She wept profusely. "But be not tempted," Troilus pleaded. "Do you think I will?" she asked coyly, getting into a becoming dress, putting on a ridiculous hat and seizing the prettiest muff she could lay her hands on.

Apr 4. Philip Bond as Billy Budd and Leo McKern as Claggart in **The Good Sailor** directed by Frith Banbury at Lyric, Hammersmith. Louis A Coxe and Robert Chapman's dramatisation of Herman Melville's novel offered a bit of philosophy and rather too much blank verse. Billy is a beautiful young man with a stammer. Everybody likes him, except the evil Master of Arms Claggart, who falsely accuses him of mutiny. The lad, at a loss for words, strikes out and kills him. The Commanding Officer is happy to see him dead. A court-martial acquits the boy. But England is at war and therefore cannot risk anything which might be misconstrued as mutiny. (There had been mutinies at Spithead and the Nore the previous year.) So Billy is hanged. McKern kept Claggart the right side of melodrama. Sean Connery was one of the sailors.

Apr 5. Paul Scofield as the Priest and Harry H Corbett as the Policeman in Denis Cannan and Pierre Bost's adaptation of Graham Greene's **The Power and the Glory**, directed by Peter Brook at Phoenix. The last priest in Mexico in the 1930s is on the run. All the other priests have been shot. He's not a good man. But a bad priest is better than no priest at all. Scofield, shabby, face deeply lined, was unrecognizable; only the occasional quaver in the voice gave his identity away.
—I don't often go to see things more than once. I was floored by his performance. It was wonderful. LAURENCE OLIVIER *Confessions of an Actor*

Apr 9. Michael Gwynne as John Proctor, Rosalie Crutchley as Elizabeth Proctor, Mary Ure as Abigail, John Welsh as Parris, Kenneth Haigh as Rev Hale, George Devine as Deputy Governor Danforth and Joan Plowright as Mary Warren in Arthur Miller's **The Crucible** directed by George Devine assisted by Tony Richardson at Royal Court. The gripping storyline was based on the notorious witchcraft trials in Salem in 1692. The most memorable scene is the one when Proctor, having finally confessed to having seen witches in order to save his life, refuses to have the confession nailed to the church door and tears it up. Asked why, he replies: "Because it is my name. How may I live without my name?" The play was inspired by Senator Joe McCarthy's witch-hunt of communists. In 1956 Miller appeared before the House Un-American Activities Committee and refused to name names.

Apr 11. Edith Evans, Peggy Ashcroft and Felix Aylmer in Enid Bagnold's **The Chalk Garden** directed by John Gielgud at Haymarket. A governess has just spent 15 years in prison as a reprieved murderer. Did she do it? The contrast between the witty, eccentric artificiality of Evans as the employer and the moving reality of Ashcroft as the governess gave the play an extra dimension. The language was very flowery. Kenneth Tynan said, somewhat rashly, that it was the best artificial play since Congreve's *The Way of the World*. George Rose fussed around endearingly as a camp manservant The role of the governess was also played by Pamela Brown and Gwen Ffrangcon-Davies. Gladys Cooper, who had created the eccentric lady on Broadway, took over from Evans.

Apr 25. Vivien Leigh and Ronald Lewis in Noël Coward's **South Sea Bubble** directed by William Chappell at Lyric. A personable native leads a lady up the jungle path to his beach hut and from which she only escapes by bashing him over the head with a bottle. The actors spoke their lines terribly fast.

May 2. Alec Guinness, Irene Worth, Martita Hunt and Frank Pettingell in Georges Feydeau's **Hotel Paradiso**, directed by Peter Glenville at Winter Garden. French farce. Kenneth Williams and Billie Whitelaw had cameo roles. Guinness (in a performance notable for its physical dexterity) played Boniface, a meek, down-trodden husband, who decides to have sex in a shady hotel with Mme Cot, the wife of his best friend. They never get to bed and are arrested during a raid by the police. Asked for their names, with great presence of mind, Boniface tells the inspector he is Cot just as Mme Cot, with equal presence of mind, is telling them she is Mme Boniface. The production had a terrific pace and led to the National Theatre inviting Jacques Charon of the Comédie Française to stage Feydeau's *A Flea in Her Ear.*

May 8. Kenneth Haigh as Jimmy Porter in John Osborne's **Look Back in Anger** with Mary Ure, Alan Bates, Helena Hughes and John Welsh directed by Tony Richardson at Royal Court. The English Stage Company's first success established the Royal Court as the place for new plays. The West End theatre was never the same again. Noël Coward and Terence Rattigan were banished. Drawing-rooms and French windows were out. Ironing boards and kitchen sinks were in. Jimmy Porter, first of the angry young men, spokesman for the disillusioned post-war generation, a master of rhetoric and insult, became a cult figure. He was self-absorbed, self-disgusted and self-pitying. His shrill, bitter, misogynous tirades were memorably delivered by Kenneth Haigh. Members of the audience hurled abuse at the stage and often left as noisily as possible, slamming the door, which led directly to the street.
—A forcible-feeble little piece that will add nothing at all to the reputation of the English Stage Company. *Illustrated London News*
—It aims at being a despairing cry but achieves only the stature of a self-pitying snivel. MILTON SHULMAN *Evening Standard*
—I doubt if I could love anyone who did not wish to see *Look Back in Anger*. It is the best young play of its decade. KENNETH TYNAN *Observer*
—A performance of *Look Back* without persistent laughter is like an opera without arias. JOHN OSBORNE

1956 World Premieres
New York
Alan J Lerner and Frederick Loewe's *My Fair Lady*
Leonard Bernstein's *Candide*
Paris
Jean Anouilh's *Poor Bitois*
Stockholm
Eugene O'Neill's *Long Day's Journey Into Night*
Zurich
Friedrich Dürrenmatt's *The Visit of the Old Lady*

Births
Martin Crimp, British playwright
Tony Kushner, American playwright

Deaths
Andre Charlot (*b.*1882), British impresario
Bertolt Brecht (*b.*1898), German playwright

Notes
—Foundation of the English Stage Company
—BBC began using new transmitter at Crystal Palace
—Decline of cinema attendances
—Rock 'n' roll music era started

History
—Nikita Khrushchev denounced Stalin
—Popular uprising in Hungary crushed
—CND march to Aldermaston

May 17. Peter Ustinov in Peter Ustinov's **Romanoff and Juliet** directed by Denis Carey at Piccadilly. Ustinov played the wily Prime Minister of a fictitious country in Europe. He spent his time scuttling between the American and Russian embassies and was amusingly evasive as to whose side he was actually on. ("You only have to strike oil to be invaded tomorrow," he said. "The English have been here often on the grounds that we were not fit to govern ourselves.") Frederick Valk as the Russian ambassador had a fine speech on the Revolution. Michael David and Katy Vail were the young lovers.
—It can be said that of Mr Ustinov that he takes the theatre very lightly and offers charades with himself as compère rather than plays with himself as strenuous author-dramatist. BEVERLEY BAXTER *Evening Standard*

Mary Ure, Alan Bates, Helena Hughes and Kenneth Haigh in Look Back in Anger

Leslie Caron and Estelle Winwood in Gigi

....

May 23. Leslie Caron as Gigi and Tony Britton as Gaston in Colette and Anita Loos's **Gigi** directed by Peter Hall at New. A reluctant coquette is about to be launched in Paris at the turn of the 20th century. The comedy scenes with Estelle Winwood's shrewd courtesan were the most rewarding. Caron's appealing gamine performance is preserved in the Alan J Lerner and Frederick Loewe musical film, *Gigi*.

May 24. Maxwell Shaw, Gerald Dynevor and Dudley Foster in Brendan Behan's **The Quare Fellow** directed by Joan Littlewood at Stratford East. A convincing argument for abolishing hanging felt like extracts from a prisoner's notebook. Behan had been to prison. "I didn't write this play," he said, "the lags wrote it."

May 31. Geraldine Page, Sam Wanamaker and Wilfrid Lawson in N Richard Nash's **The Rainmaker** directed by Sam Wanamaker and Jack Minster at St Martin's. A stranger arrives from nowhere in the middle of a drought and says he can produce rain for one hundred dollars. The words "The Method" were in blazing lights outside the theatre in letters bigger than the title of the play. Nash's comedy was an excellent vehicle for Method actors.

Jun 5. Ron Moody, Thelma Ruby, Hugh Paddick and Jimmy Thompson in Peter Myers's **For Amusement Only** directed by Michael Charnley at Apollo. Revue. Music by Ronald Cass and John Pritchett. The format was tired and unoriginal. High spot: Thompson's send-up of Liberace.

Jun 7. Paul Scofield, Sybil Thorndike, Gwen Ffrangcon-Davies, Nora Nicholson and Patience Collier in T S Eliot's **The Family Reunion** directed and designed by Peter Brook at Phoenix. A typical 1930s West End murder mystery play, except it wasn't "a story of crime and punishment, but of sin and expiation." Scofield was a tired overwrought aristocrat. Brook wisely left the furies outside the French windows in the cold.
—Though Mr Eliot can lower the dramatic temperature, he can never raise it; and this is why the theatre, an impure assembly that loves strong emotions, must ultimately reject him. He is glacial, a theatrical Jack Frost; at the first breath of warmth, he melts and vanishes. This has-been, would-be masterpiece is magnificently revived by Peter Brook. KENNETH TYNAN *Observer*

Jun 13. Lloyd Nolan in Herman Wouk's **The Caine Mutiny Court Martial** with

David Knight, Esmond Knight, Nigel Stock and Vivian Matalon directed by Lloyd Nolan at Hippodrome. Commander is relieved of his command while at sea. Nolan had played the part for two years on Broadway; unfortunately for him, London had already seen the movie with Humphrey Bogart.

Jun 14. Joyce Barbour and George Benson in **Jubilee Girl** directed by George Hall and Casper Wrede at Victoria Palace. Musical. Book and lyrics by Robin Fordyce and David Rodgers. Music by Alexander Kevin. Victorian romp. Emancipated woman falls for an English aristocrat. Fenella Fielding, playing a retired Russian ballerina, sang "I Can Always Go Back to the Stage", and stole the notices.

Jul 16. Joseph O'Connor and Moira Shearer in Bernard Shaw's **Major Barbara** directed by John Moody at the Old Vic. O'Connor had Undershaft's energy and authority, but Shearer lacked Barbara's religious fervor.

Aug 2. Diana Wynyard as Arkadina, Hugh Williams as Trigorin, Lyndon Brook as Konstantin, Perlita Neilson as Nina, Nicholas Hannen as Dorn, John Bennett as Medvedenko and Jill Bennett as Masha in Anton Chekhov's **The Seagull** directed by Michael Macowan at Saville. George Relph was delightful as old Sorin, his face clouding with sadness at the thought of opportunities for sex not taken.

Aug 23. Barry Nelson in Ira Levin's **No Time for Sergeants** directed by Emmett Rogers at Her Majesty's. Hillbilly in the American Air Force harasses sergeants and drives psychiatrists up the wall. Generals, in an effort to be rid of him, find themselves awarding posthumous awards to living persons at dead of night in the middle of a forest.

Aug 27. First visit of Berliner Ensemble. Helene Weigel in Bertolt Brecht's **Mother Courage and her Children**, directed by Erich Engel and Bertolt Brecht at Palace. One of the most famous images of 20th century theatre is Wangel dragging Courage's cart round the stage. Brecht wrote his epic of the Thirty Years War in 1938 shortly before the signing of the pact between Hitler's Germany and Stalin's USSR. Courage, camp-follower, small-trader, parasite, actively wants war because war is her livelihood. She is a great survivor. (Audiences had to be great survivors, too, in order to sit through three hours of didactics on warmongering and capitalism in German.) There were two unforgettable scenes: Courage haggling too long to save her son's life and her dumb daughter (Angelika Hurwicz) climbing a roof to beat a drum to warn the sleeping town of the advancing army. The Berliner Ensemble's season included Bertolt Brecht's **Trumpets and Drums** and **The Caucasian Chalk Circle**.

Aug 30. Alastair Sim as the Devil and Duncan Macrae as the Minister in James Bridie's **Mr Bolfry** with Sophie Stewart, George Cole, Annette Crosbie, Owen Holder and Eileen Moore directed by Alastair Sim at Aldwych. A Scottish minister debates with the Devil. Macrae, acting opposite Sim, very wisely underplayed.
—Alastair Sim loads every line with his own suave and sinister enjoyment of its sophistic effectiveness. *The Times*

Sep 5. Ralph Richardson in Shakespeare's **Timon of Athens** directed by Michael Benthall at Old Vic. There was no cursing, no fury, only irony. Dudley Jones, as Apemantus, the stone-throwing philosopher, made more impact.

Sep 19. Lillian Hellman's **The Children's Hour** directed by Graham Evans at Arts. Clare Austin and Margot Van der Burgh played the teachers. Patricia Healey played the child who accuses the teachers of being lesbians. Nobody understood why the Lord Chamberlain was still banning the play.

Sep 20. Donald Houston as the Narrator, William Squire as Captain Cat and Diana Maddox as Polly Garter in Dylan Thomas's **Under Milk Wood** directed by Edward Burnham and Douglas Cleverdon at New. Thomas's radio play worked far better on stage than anybody could have imagined. "Wildly comic," said *The Sunday Times*. "Thick, bawdy and beautiful," said *The Daily Sketch*. "Masterpiece," said *The News Chronicle*.

Oct 4. Anthony Ireland as Colenso Ridgeon in Bernard Shaw's **The Doctor's Dilemma** directed by Julian Amyes at Saville. Paul Daneman as Dubedat. Ann Todd as Mrs Dubedat. Michael Hordern, humming, hawing and misquoting Shakespeare, was very funny as Sir Ralph Bloomfield, a colossal humbug, who is so boring that he sends even himself to sleep.

Oct 11. Anthony Quayle, Megs Jenkins, Michael Gwynn, Mary Ure, Ian Bannen and Brian Bedford in Arthur Miller's **A View from the Bridge** directed and designed by Peter Brook at Comedy. Longshoreman is in love with his niece. Insanely jealous, he invents the lie that the young illegal Italian immigrant she loves is homosexual and comes to believe it and even tries to prove it by kissing the boy on the lips in front of the girl. The Lord Chamberlain had banned the play on account of the references to incest and homosexuality and so the theatre had to be turned into The New Watergate Theatre Club in order for audiences to be able to see it. Quayle was as inarticulate as the Actors Studio could have wished.

Ian Bannen, Brian Bedford, Mary Ure, Megs Jenkins and Anthony Quayle in A View from the Bridge

—*A View from the Bridge* is a "must" for those wanting a red-blooded play that kicks you mercilessly in the emotional solar plexus. MILTON SHULMAN *Evening Standard*

Oct 31. Peggy Ashcroft in Bertolt Brecht's **The Good Woman of Setzuan** directed by George Devine at Royal Court. This Marxist parable about the difficulties of being good in a wicked world was the first full-scale production of a Brecht play in English. The good woman, a prostitute, realising her kindness and generosity will be her financial ruin, invents a ruthless male cousin to protect her business interests, only to find she has to impersonate him. Ashcroft was more convincing as the man than she was as the prostitute. Kenneth Tynan said that nothing tougher had been heard since Montgomery last harangued the troops.

Nov 6. A double bill by Eugene Ionesco directed by Peter Wood at Arts. **The Bald Prima Donna** with Robert Eddison, Barbara Leake, Jessie Evans, Michael Bates and Jill Bennett explored the banalities of conversation and came to the conclusion that language was quite useless as a means of communication. **The New Tenant**: a man (Robert Eddison) wants all his treasured possessions around him. For forty minutes the audience watched two removal men cluttering up the set with furniture and burying him alive. The garrulous caretaker (Jessie Evans) drove many members of the audience out of their minds and out of the theatre.

Nov 7. John Gielgud in Noël Coward's **Nude with Violin** directed by Noël Coward at Globe. Famous painter is found to be a complete fraud after his death. He never painted anything in his life. Gielgud played the dead man's resourceful valet, a role which was later acted by Robert Helpmann and then Michael Wilding. Coward got a terrible press which didn't make a scrap of difference to the box office receipts.

Nov 8. Tyrone Power as Dick Dudgeon, David Langton as Pastor Anderson, Zena Walker as the Pastor's wife and Noël Willman as General Burgoyne in Bernard Shaw's **The Devil's Disciple** directed by Noël Willman at Winter Garden. Power was much happier with the action than with the Shavian dialogue. Willman, wonderfully dry, relished the wit when Dudgeon requested to be shot rather than hanged. "Now there, you talk like a civilian, if you will excuse me saying so. Have you any idea of the average marksmanship of the army of His Majesty King George the Third?"

Nov 15. Robert Morley and Ian Wallace in Harold Rome's **Fanny** directed by William Hammerstein at Drury Lane. Book by S R Behrman and Joshua Logan based on Marcel Pagnol's trilogy. Since Morley was the most English of actors and he couldn't sing or dance, his casting as a Frenchman in a musical was inexplicable. He was most effective on his death-bed.

Nov 16. The Madeleine Renaud-Jean Louis Barrault Company in Georges Feydeau's **Occupe Toi d'Amelia** at Piccadilly. One of the great farces of *La Belle Époque* with one of the funniest second act bedroom scenes. Renaud was the cocotte. Barrault had the tiny role of a government official with a limp. Jean Desailly was hilarious as the harassed lover. This production, a lesson in timing, style and stamina, was the start of Feydeau's popularity in Britain.

Nov 29. George Voskovec and Perlita Neilson in Frances Goodrich and Albert Hackett's dramatisation of **The Diary of Anne Frank** directed by Frith Banbury at Phoenix. Eight Amsterdam Jews hide in an attic from the Nazis from 1942 until 1944 when they are betrayed and taken to the concentration camps. The play's impact came precisely because it was not fiction.

Dec 6. John Clements as Mirabell and Kay Hammond as Millamant in William Congreve's **The Way of the World** directed by John Clements at Saville. Margaret Rutherford, reprising her definitive Lady Wishfort and looking like an enormous red beetle, was both funny and terrifying.

Dec 12. Robert Helpmann as Shylock and Irene Worth as Portia in Shakespeare's **The Merchant of Venice** directed by Michael Benthall at Old Vic. The quality of mercy was somewhat over-strained when Helpmann sharpened his knife on the sole of his boot in the courtroom.

Dec 12. Laurence Harvey as Horner, Diana Churchill as Lady Fidget, Joan Plowright as Margery Pinchwife and George Devine as Mr Pinchwife in William Wycherley's **The Country Wife** directed by George Devine at Royal Court. The production, a surprising choice for which the English Stage Company, as home of the kitchen sink, lacked the necessary style and manners. Most of the company looked as if they had just got into costume for Christmas. John Moffatt, who was cast as the fop Sparkish, was the only actor who really knew how to play Restoration comedy.

Dec 13. Alec Clunes and Denholm Elliott in Leo Lehman's **Who Cares?** directed by Basil Dean at Fortune. Young man escapes from behind the Iron Curtain to find that the British take freedom for granted.

1957

Jan 2. Michael Flanders and Donald Swann in their 'after dinner farrago', **At the Drop of a Hat** at Fortune. Cabaret, witty and informal. The bespectacled Swann sat at the piano and played his own music. The bearded Flanders sat in his wheelchair and sang his own songs.

Jan 22. Keith Michell as Proteus and Barbara Jefford as Julia in Shakespeare's **The Two Gentleman of Verona** directed by Michael Langham at Old Vic. Set in the early 19th century, Michell, looking very Byronic, got a big laugh on the line, "If man were constant, he were perfect." Robert Helpmann was Launce. Crab, his mongrel, was played by a golden Labrador.

Feb 5. Geraldine McEwan, Bertice Reading and John Hall in Carson McCullers's **The Member of the Wedding** directed by Tony Richardson at Royal Court. McEwan was miscast as the gawky, crop-haired, freakish 12-year-old, who wants to join her brother on his honeymoon.

Mar 4. Edwige Feuillère at Palace in a season of plays which included Alexandre Dumas's **La Dame aux Camélias**, Racine's **Phèdre**, Henri Becque's **La Parisienne** and Prosper Merimée's **Le Carrosse de Saint-Sacrement.** The Becque and the Merimée comedies, acted in a double bill, were very slight and not really worth bringing to London.

Mar 7. Bonar Colleano, Sally Ann Howes and Sam Wanamaker in Michael V Gazzo's **A Hatful of Rain** directed by Sam Wanamaker at Princes. Drug addict is at the mercy of a gruesome trio of dope-peddlers. Actors Studio set pieces for Method actors.

Mar 28. Belita, Bill Kerr and Betty Paul in Richard Adler and Jerry Ross's musical **Damn Yankees** directed by George Abbott at Coliseum. Book by George Abbott and Douglass Wallop. Dances and musical numbers by Bob Fosse. Middle-aged baseball fan sells his soul to the devil in order to become the greatest baseball player in the world and lead his hometown to victory. Apart from the vigorous male chorus work, led by Robin Hunter, and one likeable number, "You've Got to have Heart", the show disappointed. Belita didn't get any fun out of a girl doing a striptease and knowing all the while she was doing it very badly.

Apr 2. Samuel Beckett double-bill acted in French directed by Roger Blin at Royal Court. Roger Blin as Hamm and Jean Martin as Clov in **Fin de Partie**. Deryk Mendel in **Acte Sans Paroles.**
—It is a rather horrible evening. As symbols the characters are too grotesque to carry the drama on to so many varied levels of meaning as were found in *Waiting for Godot*. *The Times*

Apr 8. Tennessee Williams's **Camino Real** directed by Peter Hall at Phoenix. Set in a hot South American plaza, this sprawling and unfocused pageant was an artistic success on Broadway (i.e. it lost a lot of money). It was Williams's first commercial failure. In Camino Real (the price of admission is desperation) people are liable to be beaten up by the military police and carted off by the street cleaners in refuse bins. It's no good trying to escape, because if you are in Camino Real, you're already dead. It's a port of transit where historical and fictional personalities meet. An impoverished Casanova (Harry Andrews) courts a faded Marguerite Gautier (Diana Wynyard). Lord Byron (Robert Hardy) passes through. Don Quixote drops off to dream and doesn't wake until the end of the play. Kilroy (Denholm Elliott), a bewildered innocent, manages, despite his daily humiliation and corruption, to

retain his idealism. He falls for a young prostitute (Elizabeth Seal), who believes that, no matter how many times she has sex, she gets her virginity back with every new moon.
—When all is said and done it is possible that many of us would prefer to this piece of elevated mystification a good average musical comedy. *The Times*

Apr 9. **Victor Borge**, pianist and comedian, at Palace. "I do no requests," he said, "unless, of course, I am asked."

Apr 10. Laurence Olivier as Archie Rice in John Osborne's **The Entertainer** with Brenda de Banzie, Dorothy Tutin, George Relph and Richard Pasco directed by Tony Richardson at Royal Court. The very idea of Laurence Olivier appearing at the Court, and as a fifth-rate music hall comedian reduced to appearing in a twice-nightly nude show, came as a shock to a public brought up on Laurence Oliver, classical actor. His courage in risking his reputation paid off handsomely. Archie Rice was one of his best roles and one of his most popular successes, a major turning point in his career. Set in 1956 (the year of the Suez crisis), Britain, like the music hall, was on its last legs. "Don't clap too hard, lady, it's an old building!" Archie camped about on stage to get a titter out of his mutton-like audience and he camped about at home to hide his true feelings. Brenda de Banzie as his wife was deeply moving when she discovered her father-in-law (George Relph) tucking into the cake she had bought for her soldier son on his return from the war in Egypt. Relph's old man was a reminder of the elegance of the Edwardian age. Transferred to Palace.
—You will not see more magnificent acting than this anywhere in the world. HAROLD HOBSON *Sunday Times*
—It's no great play but no bad evening either. PHILIP HOPE-WALLACE *Manchester Guardian*

Apr 15. **Danny Kaye** at London Palladium.

Apr 22. Selma Vaz Dias and Hazel Penwarden in Jean Genet's **The Balcony** directed by Peter Zadek at Arts. A revolution rages outside a House of Illusions (a brothel) where the only thing that is feared is reality. Genet hated the production, claiming that Zadek and the actors had vulgarised the play and that his characters had been transformed into such grotesque and disgusting clowns that he didn't recognize them. When he tried to interrupt rehearsals the theatre barred his entrance.

Apr 25. Elizabeth Sellars and Tim Seely in Robert Anderson's **Tea and Sympathy** directed by John Fernald at Comedy. Eighteen-year-old American schoolboy is caught swimming in the nude with a master who is suspected of being a homosexual. Everybody presumes the worst. The wife of his housemaster goes to bed with him to prove he is a man. Written at the height of McCarthyism, the play was about persecution rather than about homosexuality; and since Anderson had studiously avoided saying anything that might have offended anybody, the Lord Chamberlain needn't have bothered to ban it and audiences wouldn't have had to be members of The New Watergate Theatre Club to see it.

Apr 30. June Jago, Ray Lawler and Kenneth Warren in Ray Lawler's **Summer of the Seventeenth Doll** directed by John Sumner at New. First Australian play to become internationally famous. For the last sixteen years two sugar-cane cutters have been working five months of the year and shacking up with the same two women for the rest of the year. This year one of the women has gone and got married and a substitute has had to be found.

May 14. George Devine and Joan Plowright in Eugene Ionesco's **The Chairs** directed by Tony Richardson at Royal Court. Described as a tragic farce, it premiered in Paris in 1952, when it failed. Two old people live in a lighthouse. The man has a message for mankind and has engaged a professional orator to speak for him. He invites everybody he has known (and not known) to hear the message. The couple engages in polite conversation with the imaginary guests whilst filling the stage with chairs. The orator turns out to be dumb. There was a strange fascination in watching a stage being filled with chairs, except that there were not really enough chairs.

May 30. Paul Scofield and Megs Jenkins in Rodney Ackland's **Dead Secret** directed by Frith Banbury at Piccadilly. Middle-aged, middle-class Edwardian businessman is accused of murder. Famous barrister offers to defend him if he can be convinced he is innocent, but the accused shows himself to be so lacking in any human feeling that the barrister is revolted and declines to accept the case.

Jun 11. Vivien Leigh is led from the House of Lords after she has protested against the destruction of the St James's Theatre to make way for an office block.

Jun 17. Kurfurstendamm Theatre Company of Berlin directed by Oscar Fritz Schuh at Sadler's Wells. The repertoire included August Strindberg's **The Dream Play** and two plays by Georg Buchner: **Wozzeck** with Bruno Dallansky and **Leonce und Lena** with Maximallan Schell and Marion Degler. Ernst Schröder played the magistrate in Heinrich Von Kleist's **The Broken Jug** and Maximallan Schell played the lead in G E Lessing's **Philotas**. Comparisons were made with the recent visit of the Berliner Ensemble and the company was found wanting.

1957 World Premieres

New York
Eugene O'Neill's *A Moon for the Misbegotten*
Tennessee Williams's *Orpheus Descending*
Leonard Bernstein's *West Side Story*

Stockholm
Eugene O'Neill's *A Touch of the Poet*
Eugene O'Neill's *Hughie*

Warsaw
Bertolt Brecht's *The Good Soldier Schweik*

Lyons
Arthur Adamov's *Paolo Paoli*

Births

Robert Lepage, theatre artist, director, playwright, designer, actor

Deaths

John Van Druten (*b.*1901), American playwright

Honours

Knight
Donald Wolfit, actor-manager

Notes

—The Chancellor of the Exchequer abolished entertainment tax on living theatre.
—Gaiety Theatre destroyed.

History

—Common Market established
—Sputnik launched by Russians
—Federal troops forced integration of schools in Little Rock
—Mao said, "Let a thousand flowers bloom."
—Harold Macmillan Prime Minister

Jul 1. Laurence Olivier in Shakespeare's **Titus Andronicus** directed by Peter Brook at Stoll. Vivien Leigh as Lavinia. Anthony Quayle as Aaron. Maxine Audley as Tamora. Rarely performed, the play proved to be a supper of horrors, an unnerving night of the long knives. Olivier, in Titus's rashness, rage and craziness, underlined the Lear-like parallels. Brook, by cutting and rearranging the text, sought to persuade audiences they were watching Roman tragedy and not Grand Guignol. Audiences fainted at every performance and extra St John's Ambulance volunteers had to be called in.
— As Lavinia, Vivien Leigh receives the news that she is about to be ravished on her husband's corpse with little more than mild annoyance of one who would have preferred foam rubber. KENNETH TYNAN *Observer*

Aug 21. Kenneth Williams and Maggie Smith in Bamber Gascoigne's **Share My Lettuce** directed by Eleanor Fazan at Lyric, Hammersmith. Surreal revue. Williams was in lettuce green. Smith was in orange.
—Mr Williams assumes a stage personality which is elegant, faintly macabre and immensely funny, a curious blend of music hall fairy and the awful child. *The Times*

Sep 8. Joyce Grenfell at Lyric, Hammersmith. William Blezard at the piano. Music by Richard Addinsell. Her first one-woman show, a programme of her monologues and songs, included a harassed nursery school teacher trying to cope with a naughty boy, which would become one of her most popular character sketches.

Sep 14. Marcel Marceau, the French mime, at Cambridge. Two programmes featuring his creation, Bip, in a variety of situations. The "David and Goliath" sketch in which he changes from one character to the other at lightning speed was hilarious. "The Ages of Man", in which he goes from youth to old age in a matter of seconds, was deeply moving.

Sep 17. Robert Helpmann in Jean Paul Sartre's **Nekrassov** directed by George Devine at Royal Court. Political satire. Helpmann played "the crook of the century" who rashly assumed the identity of the famous Nekrassov. Roddy McMillan was the police inspector. George Benson was the honest reporter. Harry H Corbett was the egoistical editor. Felix Felton was the bloated capitalist accused of being a communist. Percy Cartwright was the cry-baby mayor. The play, sloppily written and uncertainly directed, wasn't easy to follow.

Sep 18. John Neville in Shakespeare's **Hamlet** (First Quarto) directed by Michael Benthall at Old Vic. Neville, the idol of the bobby soxers, was a Prince without either irony, ferocity or humour. Coral Browne was a maternal, voluptuous, conscience-ridden Queen. Judi Dench, in her first professional job as Ophelia, was over publicised and her acting came in for a great deal of flack from the critics.
—Ophelia is played by a girl called Judi Dench whose first professional performance this only too obviously is. But she goes mad quite nicely and her talent will be shown to better advantage when she acquires some technique to go with it. THOMAS WISEMAN *Evening Standard*

Oct 16. Judy Garland at Dominion. "Welcome back!" they cried. It was an emotional evening. The programme included "The Man That Got Away" from *A Star is Born* and "A Couple of Swells" from *Easter Parade*. She stayed in her tramp costume to close the show. She sat on the stage, dangling her feet in the orchestra pit, surrounded by flowers. "Sing anything, Judy!" they cried. The applause was tumultuous throughout.

Nov 14. Janet Blair in Jule Styne's musical **Bells Are Ringing** directed by Gerald Freedman at Coliseum. Book and lyrics by Betty Comden and Adolph Green. Blair (in a role written for Judy Holliday) stopped the show when she sang, "I'm going back to where I can be me at the Bonjour Tristesse Brassiere." But it was a bit too late to have any effect. The show was stopping anyway. It was the last number.

Nov 21. Ralph Richardson and Celia Johnson in Robert Bolt's **Flowering Cherry** directed by Frith Banbury at Haymarket. Cherry hankers after an orchard. (If Chekhov hadn't been there before him Bolt would, no doubt, have called his play *The Cherry Orchard*.) Cherry's whole life has been built on lies. When his wife discovers there is no truth, not even in his daydreaming, she walks out on him. Richardson never lost the audience's sympathy, not even when Cherry was stealing money from his wife's purse.
—No actor is more interesting to watch. Even when he plays a dull man, that dull man is never permitted a dull moment. KENNETH TYNAN *Observer*

Nov 26. Ruth Ford, Zachary Scott and Bertice Reading in William Faulkner's **Requiem for a Nun** directed by Tony Richardson at Royal Court. An illiterate black prostitute murders a white child, whilst acting as her nurse. She kills her because she can't bear to see the girl suffer any more at the hands of her sluttish mother. Faulkner wrote the play for Ruth Ford, his wife. Already produced in Berlin and Paris, the London production was its English premiere.

Dec 5. John Gielgud in Shakespeare's **The Tempest** directed by Peter Brook transferred from Stratford to Drury Lane. Alec Clunes as Caliban. Brian Bedford as Ariel. The audience was audibly hushed by Gielgud's incomparably speaking of the Epilogue.
—Bodily inexpressive and manually gauche, he [John Gielgud] is perhaps the finest actor, from the neck up, in the world today. His face is all rigour and pain; his voice is all 'cello and woodwind; the rest of him is totem-pole. But he speaks the great passages perfectly, and always looks full of thinking. KENNETH TYNAN *Observer*

Dec 12. John Clements, Kay Hammond, Constance Cummings and Richard Attenborough in Benn W Levy's **The Rape of the Belt** directed by John Clements at Piccadilly. Weak little joke at the expense of Heracles and the 9th Labour.

Dec 20. Margaret Lockwood as Peter and her daughter Julia Lockwood as Wendy in J M Barrie's **Peter Pan** directed by Hugh Miller at Scala. Michael Warre as Captain Hook.

Dec 23. Frankie Howerd as Bottom in Shakespeare's **A Midsummer Night's Dream** directed by Michael Benthall at Old Vic. Derek Godfrey as Oberon. Joyce Redman as Titania. Coral Browne as Helena. Howerd always looked as if he wanted to throw Shakespeare overboard and ad-lib.

Dec 26. Joan Greenwood in Aristophanes' **Lysistrata**, directed by Minos Volanakis transferred from Oxford Playhouse to Royal Court. The women of Athens and Sparta take a reluctant oath to have no sex with their husbands and lovers until the war, which has been going on for twenty years, ends. One scene surpasses even the notorious "China" scene in William Wycherley's *The Country Wife* with its double-entendres. But what many people had feared was found to be true. The famously vulgar farce, premiered in 411 BC, wasn't as funny as all that. The joke didn't last the whole evening and the underlying seriousness failed to have any impact. The emphasis was on dreary song and dance. Greenwood looked like some delicate Greek sculpture and got as many laughs from the way she moved her exquisite arms as she did by what she was saying. Constance Cummings played Lysistrata at Oxford.

1958

Jan 29. Ian Bannen as Hickey in Eugene O'Neill's **The Iceman Cometh** with Lee Montague, Patrick Magee, Tony Church, Michael Bryant, Jack MacGowran, Vivian Matalon and Prunella Scales directed by Peter Wood at Arts. The action is set in Harry Hope's bar, a shabby, derelict place, based on a waterfront saloon O'Neill used to frequent. The year is 1912, the year O'Neill tried to commit suicide. The characters are down-and-outs, bums, whores, drunkards, slobs and parasites, all in a permanent stupor. Hickey comes twice a year and blows all his money. He's a great guy for cheering everybody up. But this time it's different. He has seen the light and is a reformed character and he wants to reform them. The play closes with his arrest for the murder of his wife and everybody returning to their pipe dreams.

Jan 30. Kim Stanley as Maggie, Paul Massie as Brick and Leo McKern as Big Daddy in Tennessee Williams's **Cat On A Hot Tin Roof** directed by Peter Hall at Comedy. Father is dying of cancer and doesn't know it. His son is a homosexual and won't admit it. (Audiences had to be members of The New Watergate Theatre Club to see the play because of the homosexuality.) Stanley sustained her long monologue in act one, but McKern and Massie were not up to their big scene.

Laurence Olivier and Vivien Leigh in **Titus Andronicus**

—Mr Peter Hall, the young genius whose touch so far has been all magic, has produced it on a level veering between hysteria and amateur; his sense of the playwright's rhythms is faulty, his mechanics – such as noises off – ludicrous and his handling of the actors has produced some of the most aggressively mediocre performances you could hope to see. DEREK MONSEY *Sunday Express*
—Paul Massie is callow and absurdly unprepared for a searching test like Brick. KENNETH TYNAN *Observer*
— [Paul Massie] catches the attention and extorts the admiration of the whole house. HAROLD HOBSON *Sunday Times*

Feb 5. John Gielgud in Graham Greene's **The Potting Shed** directed by Michael Macowan at Globe. Journalist discovers that when he was 14 years old he hanged himself in the potting shed. His uncle (Redmond Phillips), a Roman Catholic priest, had prayed to God, offering to give up what he loved most – his faith – if He would bring the boy back to life.

Feb 20. Norman Wisdom in Frank Loesser's musical **Where's Charley?** directed by William Chappell at Palace. Book by George Abbott based on Brandon Thomas's *Charley's Aunt*. Wisdom was surprisingly true to the original, except when he stopped the show to sing "Once in Love with Amy" and did an incongruous music hall act.

Apr 7. Liberace at London Palladium. He admitted his appeal was to women over 63. One critic described his performance as "gushing treacle, like an explosion in a molasses factory."

Apr 9. Michael Hordern and Maurice Denham in John Mortimer's **Dock Brief** directed by Stuart Burge at Lyric, Hammersmith. Duologue between a man accused of murdering his wife and the barrister chosen to defend him. They rehearse the scene in the cell, which they are later to re-enact in court. The mild murderer (who killed his wife because she was always so cheery) gets a reprieve, not because the barrister proved his innocence, but because the Home Office decided that the defence had been so appallingly incompetent, that it wouldn't have been fair to hang him. Hordern, sitting all alone, thinking of all the things he might have said on behalf of his client, was heartbreaking. Acted in a double bill with John Mortimer's **What Shall We Tell Caroline?**

Apr 17. Alastair Sim and George Cole in William Golding's **The Brass Butterfly** directed by Alastair Sim at Garrick. Roman Emperor is visited by an inventor, who, two thousand years ahead of his time, has invented a steamboat, a pressure cooker, a printing press and an explosive. The Emperor, a gourmet, is interested only in the pressure cooker. He sees the other inventions as merely harmless labour saving devices, until the explosive goes off, conveniently killing his best enemy.

Apr 23. Paul Scofield in **Expresso Bongo** directed by William Chappell at Saville. Musical. Book by Wolf Mankowitz and Julian More. Music by David Heneker and Monty Norman. Lyrics by Julian More, David Heneker and Monty Norman. Bongo (James Kenney) is a moronic youth, who plays the tom-toms and hasn't any talent. He ends up in Majorca, kept by an aging film star. Scofield delivered the agent's caustic and cynical asides with charm. The show's high spot was a send-up of a quasi-religious number.

Apr 24. Vivien Leigh as Paola and Claire Bloom as Lucile in Jean Giraudoux's **Duel of Angels** translated by Christopher Fry and directed by Jean Louis-Barrault at Apollo. Giraudoux died before he finished the play. Lucile, a magistrate's wife who lives in Aix-en-Provence in 1868, refuses to talk to those whose morals offend her. The notorious Paola dopes her and while she is unconscious, gets the

1958 World Premieres
New York
Tennessee Williams's *Suddenly Last Summer*
Zurich
Max Frisch's *The Fire Raisers*

Deaths
Yvonne Arnaud (*b.*1892), British actor
Harold Brighouse (*b.*1882), British playwright

History
—Military coup in Iraq
—Silicon chip invented in USA
—Introduction of stereo recordings
—Race riots in Notting Hill
—Manchester United football team in Munich air crash

local procuress (Freda Jackson) to put her to bed and make it look as if she has had sex with a man. Lucile falls for the ruse. Dreadfully distressed, she thinks of killing herself, until she comes round to the idea that her "seducer" (Peter Wyngarde) should kill himself. Paola's husband challenges the "seducer" to a duel on Lucile's behalf and kills him. When Lucile learns that she hasn't been seduced, she kills herself, but dies letting her husband think she has been. Bloom looked lovely. Leigh was splendid. "What a disaster it is to lie down a martyr and rise a virgin," she rasped.

Apr 30. Rex Harrison as Professor Higgins, Julie Andrews as Eliza Doolittle and Stanley Holloway as Doolittle in Alan Jay Lerner and Frederick Loewe's **My Fair Lady** choreographed by Hanya Holm, set by Oliver Smith and directed by Moss Hart at Drury Lane. Musical adaptation of Bernard Shaw's *Pygmalion*. The transition from Shaw's dialogue to song was so smooth that the music and the lyrics seemed inseparable from the play. An essential part of the production's success was due to Harrison's definitive performance as the "delightfully rude" Professor Higgins. He spoke his lyrics: "Why Can't A Woman Be More Like A Man" and "I've Grown Accustomed to Her Face". There was genuine excitement when Eliza finally triumphed and burst into song: "The Rain in Spain Stays Mainly in the Plain". Holloway had a big success with two music hall numbers: "With a Little Bit of Luck" and "Get Me to the Church on Time". Cecil Beaton's stunning costumes for the ladies at Ascot, limited to three colours (black, white and grey) were witty send-ups of the period. 2281 performances.

May 5. Johnny Ray at London Palladium. "Mr Ray has only to snap his fingers and shake his head," said *The Daily Telegraph*, "and the ensuing paroxysms of delight make one fear for the safety of the roof."

May 8. Margaret Leighton and Jeremy Brett in Terence Rattigan's **Variation on a Theme** directed by John Gielgud at Globe. Birmingham typist, who has already married four rich men, is about to marry her fifth when a ballet dancer arrives. He is clearly on the make. She is dying of consumption and should be going into a sanatorium; but she loves him more than life itself. Norman Hartnell, who designed her extraordinary clothes, seemed to be under the misapprehension that Leighton was acting in a High Comedy.

May 13. John Gielgud as Cardinal Wolsey, Edith Evans as Queen Katharine and Harry Andrews as Henry in Shakespeare's **Henry VIII** directed by Michael Benthall at Old Vic. The actors were ill at ease. Gielgud lacked Wolsey's vulgarity. Andrews didn't look right. The high point was Evans's exquisite death-scene.

May 15. Moscow Arts Theatre first visit to Britain in a season of plays by Anton Chekhov – **The Cherry Orchard**, **The Three Sisters** and **Uncle Vanya** – at Sadler's Wells was a major event. All three productions by Victor J Stanitsyn had a huge impact on the British acting profession. The company's teamwork and their technical expertise (in recreating dawn breaking, for instance) made a memorable impression. Leonid Gubanov's Trofimoff was unexpectedly virile, an eternal student who really did believe in Russia's future.
—This is not verbal acting like ours, but total acting. KENNETH TYNAN *Observer*
—It is usually a white fib to assert that good acting penetrates the language barrier; but this is the simple truth for once. ANTHONY COOKMAN *Tatler*

May 19. Willoughby Gray, Beatrix Lehmann, Richard Pearson, John Slater and John Stratton in Harold Pinter's **The Birthday Party** directed by Peter Wood at Lyric, Hammersmith. The setting is a seedy seaside boarding house. Stanley, a dirty, slovenly concert party pianist, is in hiding. Why he is in hiding and who the two men are and why they have come to get him is never made clear. "Vintage Hitchcock thriller edited by a cross-eyed studio janitor with a lawn mower," said *The Spectator*. "Wallows in symbols and revels in obscurity," said *The Daily Telegraph*. "An insane, pointless play," said the Lord Chamberlain. The play closed at the end of its first week.
—What all this means only Mr Pinter knows, for his characters speak in non-sequiturs, half-gibberish and lunatic ravings. *Manchester Guardian*
—I am willing to risk whatever reputation I have as a judge of plays by saying that *The*

Birthday Party is not a Fourth, not even a Second, but a First; and that Mr Pinter, on the evidence of this work, possesses the most original, disturbing, and arresting talent in theatrical London. HAROLD HOBSON *Sunday Times*

May 27. Avis Bunnage, Frances Cuka and Murray Melvin in Shelagh Delaney's **A Taste of Honey** directed by Joan Littlewood at Stratford East. Delaney saw Terence Rattigan's *Variation on a Theme* on tour. It was the first play she had never seen. "I can do better than that," she said. Schoolgirl (Frances Cuka) lives with her mother (Avis Bunnage), a tart, who has never shown her any love and is always going away with men friends, leaving her to fend for herself. She meets a black sailor (Jimmie Moore) and becomes pregnant by him. She invites a gay art student (Murray Melvin) to share her room. Transferred to Wyndham's.

May 28. Charles Laughton in Jane Arden's **The Party** with Joyce Redman, Elsa Lanchester, Ann Lynn and Albert Finney directed by Charles Laughton at New. 17-year-old (Ann Lynn) is so ashamed of her alcoholic father that she persuades her mother to delay his return so that she can have her birthday party without him. The heart-to-heart scene between her dad and her boyfriend gave Laughton (back in the West End after a 22-year absence) and Finney (in his West End debut) the most opportunities.

Jul 10. Dora Bryan, Daniel Massey, George Rose and Janie Marden in Arthur Macrae's **Living for Pleasure** directed by William Chappell at Garrick. Revue. Music by Richard Addinsell. High spot: Bryan in a hotel bedroom getting undressed when the Spectre de la Rose leaps in through the window and she becomes his reluctant partner in a *pas de deux*.

Jul 14. Frank Finlay and Anthony Valentine in Arnold Wesker's **Chicken Soup with Barley** directed by John Dexter at Royal Court. Jewish boy loses his faith in communism following Russia's invasion of Hungary.

Jul 16. Roland Culver, Adrianne Allen, Michael Bryant, Brian Bedford and Juliet Mills in Peter Shaffer's **Five Finger Exercise** directed by John Gielgud at Comedy. Young German tutor longs for a happy home, something he never had in Nazi Germany. He looks forward to the day when he can become a British subject. The tutor is unaware that the pupil's mother and brother want to go to bed with him and unconsciously, refuses them both. They get nasty and he tries to commit suicide. Bryant's tutor was brilliantly observed. Bedford had the more showy part of the son.
—By the end one knows that Mr Shaffer may easily become a master of the theatre. HAROLD HOBSON *Sunday Times*

Jul 17. Elizabeth Seal and Keith Michell in **Irma la Douce** directed by Peter Brook at Lyric. Musical. Book and lyrics by Alexandre Breffort. English book and lyrics by Julian More, David Heneker and Monty Norman. Music by Marguerite Monnot. Prostitute falls in love with a law-student but in order to keep him she has to continue working. Fed up with her innumerable admirers, he decides that there will be only two men in her life: himself and an elderly protector. She acquiesces, never guessing that the old gentleman with the beard and spectacles is the student in disguise. Worn out doing two jobs, he decides to kill the old man, only to find he is accused of murder and deported. Seal singing "Dis-Donc, Dis-Donc" was enchanting.

Sep 6. Emlyn Williams in **A Boy Growing Up** at Globe. Amusing one-man show based on the stories of Dylan Thomas, covering a ten-year period from seven to seventeen.

Sep 10. Beatrice Lillie in Jerome Lawrence and Robert E Lee's adaptation of Patrick Dennis's **Auntie Mame** directed by Jack Minster at Adelphi. Florence Desmond played Mame's best friend. Lillie's first appearance in a straight play felt like a revue without the music and won the *Plays and Players* Award for Damp Squib of the Year.

Sep 16. Beatrix Lehmann, Patricia Neal and Philip Bond in Tennessee Williams's **Suddenly Last Summer** directed by Herbert Machiz at Arts. Hothouse theatrics included lust, greed, incest, paedophilia and cannibalism. Wealthy Mrs Venables wants to protect her dead son's memory and moral character. He was a poet and a pederast. She had always accompanied him on his travels, acting as his procuress, until she suffered a stroke and lost her looks. Her young and pretty niece took over her role. But, by then he was 40 and had gotten old and had to go down market for his pleasures, picking up the homeless, the hungry and the naked boys on the beach. They murdered him and ate him. The shock drove the niece insane. Mrs Venables intends to bribe a lobotomist to cut the hideous story out of her brain. (Williams's sister had had a lobotomy.) Acted in a double bill with Williams's **Something Unspoken** with Beatrix Lehmann and Beryl Measor.

Sep 17. Irene Worth as Mary Stuart and Catherine Lacey as Queen Elizabeth in Friedrich Schiller's **Mary Stuart** translated by Stephen Spender and adapted and directed by Peter Wood at Old Vic. Wood had made so many efforts to tidy up the text that when The Düsseldorf Company (who had brought their own production of Mary Stuart to London), saw his production, they didn't recognize Schiller's play.

Sep 24. Gwen Ffrangcon-Davies, Anthony Quayle, Alan Bates and Ian Bannen in Eugene O'Neill's **Long Day's Journey Into Night** directed by José Quintero at Globe. The most powerful and acrimonious of all 20th century family dramas, written in blood and tears, was an act of exorcism and so autobiographical, that O'Neill didn't want it published until 25 years after his death. He never wanted it staged. His widow ignored his wishes and it was produced three years after his death in New York in 1956 when it won a posthumous Pulitzer Prize. The action is 36 years of marriage compressed into a single day. The Tyrone family, haunted by their collective guilt, can neither forget nor forgive. They blame each other, for what they are: miser, morphine-addict, wastrel, and consumptive. The script's great weakness – its inordinate length (three-and-a-quarter-hours) and its endless repetition – is, in performance, paradoxically, its greatest strength. The knife is turned in the same wound over and over again. James Tyrone is a portrait of James O'Neill, Eugene's father, the Irishborn American actor, who could have been a great classical actor to rank with Edwin Booth. Instead he had "the good bad luck" to find a gold mine in *The Count of Monte Cristo* and was trapped in it for a quarter of a century, his public not wanting to see him in anything else. He acted the Count some 6,000 times, mainly in one night stands up and down the country.

Sep 25. Paul Rogers, Anna Massey, William Squire, Eileen Peel and Alec McCowen in T S Eliot's **The Elder Statesman** directed by E Martin Browne transferred to London from Edinburgh Festival to Cambridge Theatre. The statesman has had to retire from public life on his doctor's orders. He needs rest and quiet; but he does not get either, until "two spectres from his past" prompt a confession to his daughter. Browne directed the actors as if they were in a play by Sophocles.
—*The Elder Statesman* is a zombie play designed for the living dead. Occasionally across the pallid mortuary scene flits an ironic joke or a haunting phrase but the smell of formaldehyde hangs heavy in the air. ALAN BRIEN *Spectator*

Sep 30. Wilfrid Lawson, Alan Dobie, Frances Cuka in John Arden's **Live Like Pigs** directed by George Devine and Anthony Page at Royal Court. Nomads, put against their will into a brand new flat on a housing estate, proceed to turn it into a slum.

The neighbours turn nasty. Nigel Davenport and Anna Manahan had a hilarious sex scene.

Oct 2. Bertice Reading as Mrs Yajnavalkya, Fenella Fielding as Lady Parvula de Panzoust and Geoffrey Dunn as Cardinal Pirelli in Sandy Wilson's **Valmouth** directed by Vida Hope at Lyric, Hammersmith. High Church/High Camp musical based on Ronald Firbank's novel. The characters – hothouse flowers, esoterically absurd, steeped in religious and sexual eccentricities – were wittily costumed by Tony Walton. The lyrics for Parvula and Pirelli out Firbanked Firbank. Fenella Fielding, exquisitely mannered, was a past mistress with the innuendo.

Oct 14. Howard Goorney, Avis Bunnage and Murray Melvin in Brendan Behan's **The Hostage** directed by Joan Littlewood at Stratford East. A sprawling and uninhibited Irish play about Anglo-Irish relations in which a member of the IRA is caught and sentenced to death. The IRA kidnaps a cockney national serviceman and holds him as a hostage in a whorehouse. Behan was the laziest of writers and when he couldn't think of anything to say Littlewood would throw in a song and a jig.
—Certainly, it is the most preposterous comic and unnerving evening in London. ALAN BRIEN *Spectator*

Oct 28. Patrick Magee in Samuel Beckett's **Krapp's Last Tape** directed by Donald McWhinnie and George Devine at Royal Court. A 69-year-old man sits at a harshly lit desk, surrounded by darkness and spools of tapes, listening to his 39-year-old self on a tape-recorder. The depth of his bitterness and desolation is bottomless. His heart aches for the woman he rejected to pursue a career as a writer. The 55-minute monologue, especially written for Patrick Magee, was acted in a double bill with Beckett's **End Game** with George Devine and Jack MacGowran. The Lord Chamberlain refused to pass Hamm's blasphemy, "The bastard! He doesn't exist." Beckett reluctantly agreed to change bastard to swine.

Nov 6. John Fraser, Judith Stott and Alan Dobie in Jeremy Kingston's **No Concern of Mine** directed by Adrian Brown at Westminster. Two young men and a girl in their twenties share a sordid basement flat in Bayswater and wonder what they are going to do with their lives.

Alan Bates, Gwen Ffrangcon-Davies and Anthony Quayle in Long Day's Journey into Night

Jets v Sharks in **West Side Story**. George Chakiris is the tall guy on right.

Nov 12. Flora Robson as Mrs Alving, Michael Hordern as Pastor Manders and Ronald Lewis as Oswald in Henrik Ibsen's **Ghosts** directed by John Fernald at Old Vic. Hordern played for so many laughs that it made Manders' earlier relationship with Mrs Alving seem more and more unlikely.

Nov 26. Joan Miler, John Slater, Andrée Melly and Lloyd Reckford in Ted Willis's **Hot Summer Night** directed by Peter Cotes at New. Trade unionist finds he is not as liberal as he had thought he was when his daughter falls in love with a black guy.

Dec 2. Hugh Williams, Celia Johnson and Joan Greenwood in Hugh and Margaret Williams's **The Grass is Greener** directed by Jack Minster at St Martin's. Wife goes off for the week-end with an American oil millionaire. Husband wonders what to do.

Dec 4. Earle Hyman and Soraya Rafat in Erroll John's **Moon on a Rainbow Shawl** directed by Frith Banbury at Royal Court. Shanty town drama: a pregnant West Indian woman is deserted by her lover. He thinks England is the Promised Land. The play won first prize in the *Observer* competition. *Plays and Players* voted it (and *Auntie Mame*) "the damp squib of the year."
—The author's compassion rings as true as his attempted lyricism rings false. *The Times*

Dec 12. Marlys Watters as Maria, Don McKay as Tony, Chita Rivera as Anita, Ken Le Roy as Bernardo and George Chakiris as Riff in Leonard Bernstein's musical **West Side Story** directed and choreographed by Jerome Robbins at Her Majesty's. Book by Arthur Laurents. Lyrics by Stephen Sondheim. Scenic production by Oliver Smith. Costumes designed by Irene Sharaff. Co-choreographed by Peter Gennaro. Lighting by Joe Davis. The story line is based on Shakespeare's *Romeo and Juliet* and updated to the 20th century. The Capulets and Montagues become two feuding street gangs, New Yorkers versus Puerto Ricans. In one respect Laurents's book actually improves on Shakespeare. In the play Romeo doesn't know that Juliet is still alive because the postman fails to deliver a letter. In the musical Tony (the Romeo character) learns that Maria (the Juliet character) is dead and the source is impeccable. Anita, Maria's best friend, deliberately gives the wrong information as an act of revenge after she has been raped by the Jets. Bernstein's operatic score

was wonderfully varied. Hit number followed hit number: "Something's Coming", "Maria", "Tonight", "America", "Cool", "One Hand, One Heart", "I Feel Pretty", "A Boy Like That", the ballet "Somewhere", and "Gee Officer, Krupke" (in which the delinquents explain how they came to be "sociologically sick"). Jerome Robbins's exhilaratingly energetic choreography was fully integrated, developing plot and character, and managing a skilful balance between reality and poetry, aggression and sentimentality. It is hard to believe that the Academy, faced with a choice between this landmark American musical and *The Music Man*, chose *The Music Man* as the best musical in 1957. But many Americans felt that the violence of the subject matter was inappropriate for a musical and it wasn't until *West Side Story* was made into a movie that it really succeeded.

Dec 18. Tommy Steele as Buttons in Richard Rodgers and Oscar Hammerstein's musical **Cinderella** designed by Loudon Sainthill and directed by Freddie Carpenter at Coliseum. Yana as Cinders. Jimmy Edwards as King. Betty Marsden as Fairy Godmother. Kenneth Williams and Ted Durante as Ugly Sisters

1959

Jan 7. Robert Shaw and Peter O'Toole in Willis Hall's **The Long and the Short and the Tall** with Bryan Pringle, Alfred Lynch, Edward Judd and Kenji Takaki directed by Lindsay Anderson at Royal Court. Reconnaissance patrol in the Malayan jungle in World War 2 is cut off from the rest of the battalion. They capture a Japanese soldier. Some are prepared to forget the Geneva Convention and kill him. The key role is the loud-mouthed, trouble-making Private Bamforth, the biggest shower since the Flood and up to every dodge and skive in the book. He doesn't go a bundle on this death and glory stuff; yet, when the crunch comes, he is the only one who is prepared to make a stand for the Jap's life. Bamforth was Willis Hall's Jimmy Porter. 25-year-old Peter O'Toole made his London debut in a role which had been ear-marked for Albert Finney who had fallen ill just as Lindsay Anderson was about to go into rehearsal.

Jan 15. Lea Padovani and Sam Wanamaker in Tennessee Williams's **The Rose Tattoo**

1959 World Premieres

New York

Richard Rogers and Oscar Hammerstein's *The Sound of Music*

Lorraine Hansbury's *Raisin' in the Sun*

Jack Gelber's *The Connection*

Spoleto

Tennessee Williams's *Sweet Bird of Youth*

Paris

Jean-Paul Sartre's *Altona*

Jean Anouilh's *Becket*

Jean Genet's *The Blacks*

Berlin

Edward Albee's *The Zoo Story*

Deaths

Maxwell Anderson (*b.* 1888), American playwright

Grock (*b.* 1880), Swiss clown

Laurence Houseman (*b.* 1865), British playwright

Honours

Knight

Michael Redgrave

Notes

—Jerome Robbins ballet season in London

History

—Formation of European Free Trade Association.

—Cuban Revolution. Castro came to power

—First photograph of the dark side of the moon

directed by Sam Wanamaker at New. Serafina Delle Rose keeps the memory of her dead husband precious with an urn full of his ashes. It isn't until she smashes the urn (having learned of his infidelity) that she is able to come out of mourning and release her own and her fifteen-year-old daughter's long pent-up sexual energy.

Jan 27. The 59 Theatre Company, founded by Michael Elliott, opened with Georg Buchner's **Danton's Death** translated and adapted by James Maxwell and directed by Casper Wrede at Lyric, Hammersmith. A revolutionary play by a young revolutionary who died young. Written in 1835 it was not performed until 1903 in Berlin. Patrick Wymark roared as Danton. Harold Lang whined as Robespierre. There was too much verbiage. The play badly needed cutting.

Jan 27. Sandy Wilson's **Valmouth** transferred to the Saville. Mrs Yarjnavalkya was played by Cleo Lane.

Jan 29. Denholm Elliott in Jean Anouilh's **Traveller Without Luggage** directed by Peter Hall at Arts. Young soldier returns from World War I having lost his memory. His family instantly recognizes him but he does not recognize them. They remember how he had pushed his best friend downstairs and crippled him for life; how he had raped the fifteen-year-old kitchen maid; how he used to kill animals for fun; and how he had taken his brother's wife for his mistress. They cannot remember when he was happy or when he did a kind or good action. Horrified by all that he hears he does not admit to being their son and starts a new life. The curtain-raiser was **Madame de ...** Anouilh's adaptation of Louis de Vilmorin's long-short story about some earrings. A wry and somewhat heavy tragic-comic soufflé

Feb 10. Shelagh Delaney's **The Taste of Honey** transferred to Wyndham's.
—It is uncommonly alive and kicking blend of maturity and immaturity (not to mention maternity) of penny dreadful and comic strip, down-to-earth slum drama and airy slapstick, alternating glib cross-talk with moments of sheer poetry. CECIL WILSON *Daily Mail*

Feb 17. Miriam Karlin, Barbara Windsor, James Booth, Toni Palmer, Yootha Joyce, Wallace Eaton and George Sewell in Frank Norman and Lionel Bart's **Fings Ain't Wot They Used T'Be** directed by Joan Littlewood at Stratford East. Crooks, gamblers and tarts: no story, just a slice of bawdy life in Joan Littlewood's characteristic shamboloic manner plus one catchy tune. James Booth played a gangling, fast-talking and good-humoured ponce.

Mar 3. Mai Zetterling, Michael Gough and Lyndon Brook in August Strindberg's **Creditors** directed by Casper Wrede at Lyric, Hammersmith. A merciless ex-husband systematically sets about destroying the lives of two people. Acted in a double bill with Molière's **The Cheats of Scapin** with Harold Lang as Scapin directed by Peter Dews. The more Patrick Wymark asked Scapin, "What in the devil was he doing in the boat?" the funnier it got.

Mar 18. Michael Hordern in Arthur Wing Pinero's **The Magistrate** directed by Douglas Seale at Old Vic. Barrie Ingham played the magistrate's step-son. Jack May's tired dandy looked just the sort of chap who would be shoved onto an unsafe balcony and made to stand in the pouring rain.

Apr 8. Patrick McGoohan in Henrik Ibsen's **Brand** translated by Michael Meyer and directed by Michael Elliott for 59 Theatre Company at Lyric, Hammersmith. The company continued its policy – as *The Times* critic put it – of giving the public not what it is supposed to want, but what it ought to want, and, surprisingly, it had a box office success. Ibsen's epic poem, written in 1865, was designed to be read not

performed. A Lutheran pastor worships the harsh, unforgiving God of the Old Testament. He never compromises and refuses to come to his mother's deathbed. He won't allow his wife to grieve over their dead baby and forces her to give the baby's christening clothes (the only mementos she has) to a greedy and ungrateful gypsy. "You are hard, Brand," says somebody. "God's love is hard" he replies. The villagers at the beginning see in Brand the priest they need. Later when he has led them up the mountain path, they stone him. "Brand dies a saint," said Bernard Shaw, "having caused more intense suffering by his saintliness than the most talented sinner could have possibly done with twice his opportunities."
—Mr Patrick McGoohan is magnificent throughout in a part which is pitched on a single note. *The Times*

Apr 23. Nigel Patrick, Coral Browne and Judith Stott in Samuel Taylor and Cornelia Otis Skinner's **The Pleasure of His Company** directed by Nigel Patrick at Haymarket. Father returns after an absence of fifteen years to upset his daughter's wedding plans.

Apr 29. Barbara Jefford and Hugh Griffith in Percy Bysshe Shelley's **The Cenci** designed by Leslie Hurry and directed by Michael Benthall at Old Vic. The only drama came when the heroine realized that there had been no need to murder her father because there was already a warrant out for his death.

Apr 30. Denis Quilley as Candide, Mary Costa as Cunegonde and Laurence Naismith as Dr Pangloss in Leonard Bernstein's musical **Candide** directed by Robert Lewis at Saville. Lyrics by Richard Wilbur. Book by Lillian Hellman based on Voltaire's picaresque and philosophical novel (written in 1758) and inspired by the great Lisbon earthquake in 1755. "There is more of me in that piece than anything else I've done," said Bernstein. It opened on Broadway in 1956 and ran for only 73 performances, one of Broadway's most famous failures. Audiences, who came expecting a musical, found an opera bouffe. The show also proved too sophisticated for West End audiences.

May 5. Dennis Lotis in John Osborne's musical **The World of Paul Slickey** directed by John Osborne at Palace. Music by Christopher Whelen. Choreography by Kenneth Macmillan. Satire on Fleet Street. Some members of the audience, not satisfied with booing in the theatre, went round to the stage door and booed Osborne in the street as well. The flop was front-page news. Osborne was quoted as saying that he had had the worst notices since Judas Iscariot.

May 28. Mermaid, the first theatre to be built in the precinct of the city in 300 years, opened with a musical, **Lock Up Your Daughters**, an adaptation of Henry Fielding's *Rape Upon Rape* by Bernard Miles and directed by Peter Coe. Music by Laurie Johnson. Lyrics by Lionel Bart. Hy Hazell sang "When does the ravishing begin?" The production was meant to be delightfully improper (and often was) but no amount of feigned bawdy could hide the fact that the reason why Fielding's comedy hadn't been revived for so long was that it wasn't any good.

Jun 18. Ralph Richardson, Paul Scofield and Phyllis Calvert in Graham Greene's **The Complaisant Lover** directed by John Gielgud at Globe. "Marriage is a damn boring condition," says a husband, "and boredom is not a good reason for divorce." Richardson was most moving when the husband learns that his wife is unfaithful. Sobbing, he sank into a chair – inadvertently choosing (a brilliant stroke, this) the chair with his "trick" cushion. He sat there, his whole body shaking, while the cushion played its silly tune.

Jun 30. Joan Plowright as Beattie Bryant in Arnold Wesker's **Roots** directed by John Dexter at Royal Court. The second play in Wesker's trilogy was a major turning-point in Plowright's career. Beattie returns home to her family after a three-year stay in London, bringing her boyfriend's Marxist ideas with her and finds the family hasn't a clue what she is talking about. The characters spend their time making real tea, eating real food, sweeping real dust, washing real dishes in real water and just sitting around. The high spot was when Beattie tried to share the joys of classical music with her mother (Gwen Nelson).
—This is by far the best and most faithful play about working class life that has appeared for a long time. WALTER ALLEN *New Statesman*
—Joan Plowright is to my mind one of the most accomplished, quite the most interesting and easily the most versatile of our younger leading actresses. W A DARLINGTON *Daily Telegraph*

Jul 8. Queen's Theatre reopened with John Gielgud in **Ages of Man**, a one-man show, based on George Rylands's Shakespeare anthology. Gielgud had always believed that if you got the verse right, you would then get the sense. He was incomparable in the great laments: Henry VI, Clarence, John of Gaunt and particularly Richard II when he was as moved as the audience and wept buckets. The recital would become a regular stand-by over the next ten years, winning him acclaim all over the world.

Jul 29. Vivien Leigh in Noël Coward's **Look After Lulu!** directed by Tony Richardson at Royal Court. Based on Georges Feydeau's *Occupe Toi D'Amelie*. Leigh was a fetching Lulu. Max Adrian wore his uniform (and his striped underwear) with style. Michael Bates had a scene-stealing cameo as a policeman.

Alfred Lynch, Peter O'Toole, Robert Shaw, Kenji Takaki and Bryan Pringle in The Long and the Short and the Tall

Aug 4. Earle Hyman, Juanita Moore, Kim Hamilton and Olga James in Lorraine Hansbury's **A Raisin' in the Sun** directed by Lloyd Richards at Adelphilack working-class family, living in a Chicago ghetto in the 1950s, comes into an inheritance of $10,000. The 35-year-old son wants to buy a liquor store and is prepared to grovel to get it. His wife wants to buy a house. His younger sister wants to complete her education and become a doctor. The mother buys a house in a white neighbourhood. The whites want to buy them out. Hansberry's own middle-class family had moved into a white district in the 1930s and met with terrible hostility. They were finally evicted. Her father, a successful real-estate broker, took their case to court and won. 29-year-old Hansberry (1930–1965) was the first black female author to have her work staged on Broadway. Premiered in New York in 1959 and starring Sidney Poitier, it was voted best play of the year by the New York Critics' Circle and ran for 530 performances. In London it ran for 78.

Aug 12. Michael Redgrave, Flora Robson and Beatrix Lehmann in Michael Redgrave's adaptation of Henry James's **The Aspern Papers** directed by Basil Dean at Queen's. Literary detective admits there is no baseness he would not commit to get hold of a famous American poet's love letters, though he does balk at marrying a plain, dowdy, sexless woman who is years older than himself. One of the poet's many mistresses is miraculously still alive. It's miraculous because the poet died seventy years ago. She sees right through him the moment he appears and decides to make him pay through the nose. Lehmann sat bolt upright in her chair, still the grand lady, who had had society at her feet. "Don't try and pay me compliments," she growled. "I've been spoiled."

Sep 6. Robert Stephens, John Briggs, Charles Kay and Alfred Lynch in Arnold Wesker's **The Kitchen** directed by John Dexter produced without décor at Royal Court. The kitchen is a microcosm for the world.

Sep 15. Richard Harris, Ronald Fraser, Wendy Craig and Isabel Dean in J P Donleavy's **The Ginger Man** directed by Philip Wiseman at Fortune. "Do you think God will ever forgive the Catholics?" Donleavy asked. There was no plot, just a lot of bawdy, blasphemous, boring, anti-Irish rant in a prose-poetry which exhausted Harris and audience equally.

Sep 23. Kenneth Williams and Fenella Fielding in **Pieces of Eight** directed by Paddy Stone at Apollo. Revue mainly written by Peter Cook. Williams had a sketch by Harold Pinter in which he played a newspaper vendor spouting boring and obvious inanities.

Sep 30. Douglas Wilmer and Patricia Kneale in Friedrich Dürrenmatt's **The Marriage of Mr Mississippi** directed by Clifford Williams at Arts. Police prosecutor poisons his wife and marries a woman who has poisoned her husband. Obscure Swiss allegory.

Oct 6. Robert Shaw, Paul Rogers, Percy Herbert and Dudley Foster in Beverley Cross's **Once More River** directed by Guy Hamilton at Duke of York's. Looting, mutiny and lynching aboard a rotting cargo boat.

Oct 13. Fay Compton as Lady Bracknell, John Justin as John Worthing, Alec McCowen as Algernon Moncrieff, Barbara Jefford as Gwendolen, Judi Dench as Cecily and Miles Malleson as Chasuble in Oscar Wilde's **The Importance of Being Earnest** at the Old Vic. Fay Compton forgot her lines and was prompted not only from the prompt corner but also from the auditorium.

Oct 19. Daniel Massey, Dilys Laye and Martin Miller in **Make Me an Offer** directed by Joan Littlewood at Stratford East. Musical. Book by Wolf Mankowitz. Lyrics and music by Monty Norman and David Heneker. The action was set in Portobello Market "where business is business and honesty is a luxury no man with a family can afford." Transferred to New.

Oct 22. Ian Bannen in John Arden's **Serjeant Musgrave's Dance** with Colin Blakely, James Bree, Alan Dobie, Frank Finlay and Freda Jackson directed by Lindsay Anderson at Royal Court. Arden preached an anti-Establishment, anti-military, anti-colonial, anti-war message. The action, realistic but not naturalistic, was set in the Victorian era. The text, a mixture of verse, prose and song, had the sinewy strength of an old ballad. A northern mining town is in the grip of a strike. The mayor presumes that the serjeant and his soldiers are on a recruiting mission and thinks he might be able to break the strike by unloading the agitators on the army. But, unbeknown to him, the soldiers are deserters. The mad serjeant brought up on the Bible (an eye for an eye) and Queen's Regulations, intends to kill twenty-five innocent citizens as an act of retribution for the twenty-five innocent people the British army had killed abroad. They had come to teach the town a lesson. But it is the soldiers who have to learn, in harsh and uncompromising terms, that violence cannot be cured with violence. The story was inspired by a specific atrocity by the British army in Cyprus.
—It is not the principal function of the theatre to strengthen peace, to improve morals and establish a good social system. Churches, international associations and political parties already exist for those purposes. It is the duty of theatre, not to make men better but to render them harmlessly happy. HAROLD HOBSON *Sunday Times*
—I think it is something short of a great play. But wild horses wouldn't have dragged me from my seat before the end. PHILIP HOPE-WALLACE *Manchester Guardian*

Nov 17. Gary Raymond and Tsai Chin in Paul Osborn's **The World of Suzie Wong**, directed by Peter Coe at Prince of Wales. Based on novel by Richard Mason. Penniless artist meets prostitute in Hong Kong. Sometimes referred to as "The World of Wuzy Song", it really should have been a musical.

Nov 18. Peggy Ashcroft as Rebecca West in Henrik Ibsen's **Rosmersholm** directed by George Devine at Royal Court. Eric Porter as Rosmer. Mark Dignam as Mr Kroll. Alan Dobie as Ulric Brendel. There were those who thought Ashcroft should have hammed it up but she had taken her cue from the line: "Nobody could accuse me of being too emotional." Transferred to Comedy.

Dec 14. Bernard Miles as Long John Silver in Robert Louis Stevenson's **Treasure Island** directed by Peter Coe at Mermaid. Miles, too bland, too genial and lacking in cruelty, was not Stevenson's pirate. Anybody wanting the real thing would have had to have seen Robert Newton's definitive performance in the 1950 film.

Dec 22. Graham Crowden, Douglas Wilmer, George Benson, Alison Leggatt and Gwen Nelson in N F Simpson's **One Way Pendulum** directed by William Gaskill at Royal Court. A man teaches speak-your-weight machines to sing the Hallelujah Chorus. Another man reconstructs the Old Bailey in his living room with a do-it-yourself kit. A daily woman comes to help with eating the food. Simpson built his play entirely on non-sequiteurs.

1960–1969

1960

Jan 27. Albert Finney in Harry Cookson's **Lily White Boys** with Georgia Brown, Shirley Ann Field and Willoughby Goddard directed by Lindsay Anderson at Royal Court. Songs by Christopher Logue. Satire on the Establishment. Three Teddy Boys give up juvenile delinquency to earn bigger money in business.

Feb 11. Lionel Bart's **Fings Ain't Wot They Used T'Be** transferred to Garrick.

Feb 25. William Peacock in Shakespeare's **Henry V** directed by Julius Gellner at Mermaid. Modern battle dress. The soldiers sang "Roll Out the Barrel". Agincourt became El Alamein.

Mar 2. Harold Pinter double-bill at Royal Court. **The Dumb Waiter** with Nicholas Selby and George Tovey directed by James Roose-Evans. Two hired assassins, wait nervously for their victim, only to find the victim is themselves. **The Room** with Vivien Merchant, Thomas Baptiste and Michael Caine, directed by Anthony Page. Working-class housewife is visited by a blind Negro, who asks her to come home.

Mar 7. Compagnie Marie Bell at Savoy in three plays by Jean Racine: **Phèdre**, **Bérénice** and **Britannicus**. The French tragedienne, acting in a tradition which went right back to Sarah Bernhardt, was at her best as Agrippine in *Britannicus*, the most exciting of the three productions. Robert Hirsch was Nero. Bell, staggering about the stage, sweeping up stairs and leaning against pillars, was at her hammiest when she played Bérénice, described by one critic as pure jambon.

Mar 16. Andrew Cruickshank in Jerome Lawrence and Robert E Lee's **Inherit the Wind** directed by Terence Kilburn at St Martin's. The play was based on the "Monkey Trial" in 1925. A schoolmaster is arrested for reading Darwin's *Origin of Species* to his class. Lawyer Clarence Darrow argues that the trial is not about Christianity versus Atheism but about whether a man is to be allowed to think for himself and whether education should be left in the hands of bigots. Cruickshank's Darrow did not have the acting opportunities Orson Welles's Darrow had in the film, *Compulsion*.

Mar 24. Yau Shan Tung, Yama Saki, Tim Herbert and Sonya Hana in Richard Rodgers and Oscar Hammerstein II's musical **Flower Drum Song** at Palace directed by Jerome Whyte. Book by Oscar Hammerstein and Joseph Fields based on novel by C Y Lee. Christmas in San Francisco's Chinatown. Some unenchanted evening: flat, naïve production with amateurish performances.

Apr 21. Inia Waita in Frank Loesser's **The Most Happy Fella** directed by Jerome Eskow at Coliseum. Musical based on Sidney Howard's 1924 play, *They Knew What They Wanted*. Shy middle-aged Italian, courting a waitress (Helena Scott) by post, thinks he will have more chance of success if he encloses a photograph of his handsome young foreman. Hit songs: "Standing on the Corner" and "Big D".

Apr 27. Donald Pleasence as Davies, Alan Bates as Mick and Peter Woodthorpe as Aston in Harold Pinter's **The Caretaker** directed by Donald McWhinnie at Arts. Tramp, befriended by one brother and humiliated by the other, stupidly, switches his allegiance to the bully and finds himself rejected by both. Peter Woodthorpe's mentally handicapped brother had a riveting monologue describing his experiences in hospital. Transferred to Duchess. Pinter took over from Bates four weeks.

—Mr Pinter's work literally fascinates; but one hopes he will move on. JOHN ROSSELLI *Guardian*

—Had *Waiting for Godot* never been written this piece would be judged masterly. As it is it appeared to be excessively derivative almost to the point of parody. PATRICK GIBBS *Daily Telegraph*

Peter Woodthorpe, Donald Pleasance and Alan Bates in The Caretaker

1960 World Premieres

New York
Tennessee Williams's *Period of Adjustment*

Berlin
Edward Albee's *Death of Bessie Smith*

Paris
Eugene Ionesco's *Rhinoceros*

Deaths

Oscar Hammerstein II (*b.*1895), American lyric-writer
A E Matthews (*b.*1869), British actor

Honours

Dame
Flora Robson, actor

Notes

—Foundation stone of NT laid by the Queen Mother on a site adjacent to the Festival Hall
—Peter Hall artistic director of the Shakespeare Memorial Theatre

History

—Sharpeville massacre in South Africa
—Trial of D H Lawrence's *Lady Chatterley's Lover*
—Adolf Eichmann, Nazi war criminal, tried and executed.

—It is written with an original and unmistakable sense of theatre and is impeccably acted and directed. NOËL COWARD *Sunday Times*

Apr 28. Laurence Olivier in Eugene Ionesco's **Rhinoceros** directed by Orson Welles at Royal Court. One man refuses to follow the herd and does not become a rhinoceros. The play did not repeat its continental success. Transferred to Strand.

May 12. Alec Guinness as T E Lawrence in Terence Rattigan's **Ross** directed by Glen Byam Shaw at Haymarket. Why did Lawrence of Arabia become an anonymous private in the Air Force? Rattigan offered two solutions – the deaths of the bodyguards he loved and being buggered by the Turks whilst in captivity. Guinness bore a striking resemblance to Lawrence; though it was difficult to believe in him as a man of action.
—There is not a single moment of his performance, which is not both calculated and intelligent. Somehow, however, the calculation is too apparent. He is neither Lawrence, nor Ross, nor Shaw, but an outstanding actor keeping a little aloof from the legend which he impersonates. ALAN PRYCE-JONES *Observer*

Jun 7. Frank Finlay, Kathleen Michael, Cherry Morris and David Saire in Arnold Wesker's Trilogy – **Chicken Soup with Barley, I'm Talking About Jerusalem** and **Roots** – at Royal Court directed by John Dexter. The Odyssey of a Jewish family traced the political disillusionment and the betrayal of the idealistic Left from the Civil War in Spain to Russia's invasion of Hungary. The family attempted to emulate William Morris's ideals in Norfolk.

Jun 16. Bernard Miles in Bertolt Brecht's **The Life of Galileo** adapted by Charles Laughton and directed by Bernard Miles at Mermaid. Lacklustre, rustic, painfully slow and terribly tedious. Laughton had played Galileo in New York.

Jun 23. Royalty Theatre opened with Alfred Lunt and Lynn Fontanne in Friedrich Dürrenmatt's **The Visit** directed by Peter Brook. The richest woman in the world returns to the god-forsaken town of her birth. She arrives in a sedan-chair, carried by two ex-murderers. She is accompanied by her latest husband, two violinists (whom she has blinded and castrated), a former magistrate (now her butler), a panther, plus a coffin. At the celebratory dinner in her honour, she offers the citizens a billion marks in exchange for the life of their mayor, who had seduced her when she was seventeen years old and deserted her when she became pregnant. She knows the citizens cannot afford to refuse. The town is bankrupt. She made them bankrupt. The performance never lived up to the play's fame and the meeting between the former lovers proved an anti-climax.

Jun 30. Ron Moody as Fagin in Lionel Bart's **Oliver!** directed by Peter Coe at New. Georgia Brown as Nancy. Danny Sewell as Bill Sikes. Paul Whitsun-Jones as Mr Bumble. Keith Hamshere as Oliver. Martin Horsey as Artful Dodger. Fagin was sentimentalized too much; but the musical's broad humour and broad pathos complemented Dickens perfectly. The production (with the help of Sean Kenny's huge, timbered and adaptable revolving set) was as fine an example of Victorian melodrama as anybody could wish. The murder of Nancy near the misty, murky Thames was particularly effective. The score had an engaging tuneful music-hall verve. High spots: the boys singing "Food, Glorious Food", Moody singing "You've Got to Pick A Pocket or Two", Brown singing "As Long As He Needs Me" and the whole company led by Horsey singing the catchy, show-stopping "Consider Yourself." 2618 performances.
—Perhaps here at last is that British musical for which we have been waiting with Messianic patience for so long. FELIX BARKER *Evening News*
—A truly wonderful Fagin impersonated by Ron Moody as a Jewish Santa Claus, with touches of Popeye, Peter Sellers and Grock, a dustbin Boris Goudonov, a kitchen-sink Rasputin. ROBERT MULLER *Daily Mail*

Jul 1. Paul Scofield in Robert Bolt's **A Man for All Seasons**, directed by Noël Willman at Globe. Written in the wake of the Berliner Ensemble's first London season, Bolt attempted to do for Sir Thomas More what Brecht had done for Galileo. More refuses to sanction the king's divorce. His resistance is entirely passive. He puts his trust in the law and presumes silence cannot be equated with treason; but his silence reverberates louder than any condemnation. Scofield, dry, cynical, civilized, was not at his best on the first night and made a far greater impact in the film version. Leo McKern as The Common Man popped up in various guises: steward, boatman, jailor, foreman of the jury and executioner. The result, immensely worthy, but never tragic, was always much nearer to the costume dramas of the 1930s than it was to Brecht.
—The chronicle for all its cynical power is dramatically bloodless until the climax. HAROLD CONWAY *Daily Sketch*

Jul 28. Diane Cilento and Leon Peers in a double-bill of Anton Chekhov's **The Proposal** and August Strindberg's **Miss Julie** directed by Leila Blake at Lyric, Hammersmith. Strindberg got more laughs than Chekhov. In the circumstances it might have made more sense to have played *Miss Julie* for farce and *The Proposal* straight.

Aug 24. Barbara Ferris, Amelia Bayntun, Fanny Carby, Frank Coda and Roy Kinnear in Stephen Lewis's **Sparrers Can't Sing** directed by Joan Littlewood at Stratford East. There was no story, just a day in the lives of various people in the East End. Littlewood turned down an offer of a transfer to the West End because she was tired of constantly having to rebuild the company.

Aug 25. Two American plays at the Arts. Edward Albee's **The Zoo** with Kenneth Haigh and Peter Sallis directed by Donald Howarth. A sad and frightening tale about a man losing a dog's friendship. Tennessee Williams's **This Property is Condemned** with Marcia Stillman and Ralph Williams directed by Henry Kaplan. A simple-minded 15-year-old girl dresses up in her dead sister's finery and lives the life of a prostitute among the railroad men.

Sep 1. Judith Anderson as Arkadina, Tom Courtenay as Konstantin and Ann Bell as Nina in Anton Chekhov's **The Seagull** directed by John Fernald at Old Vic. Tony Britton as Trigorin. Ralph Michael as Dorn. Cyril Luckham as Sorin. Courtenay riveted attention. He might have been playing Oswald in Ibsen's *Ghosts*.

Sep 5. Le Compagnie Roger Planchon in a free adaptation of Alexandre Dumas's **Les Trois Mousquetaires** directed by Roger Planchon transferred from the Edinburgh Festival to Piccadilly. A poor send-up of the swashbuckling era and not a patch on Christian-Jacque's *Fanfan la Tulipe* with Gérard Philipe.

Sep 13. Albert Finney, George A Cooper, Mona Washbourne and Ann Beach in Keith Waterhouse and Willis Hall's **Billy Liar** directed by Lindsay Anderson at Cambridge. Kitchen-sink drama, whose roots went right back to the Lancashire comedies of Stanley Houghton and Harold Brighouse. Billy has three girl friends and is engaged to two of them. High spot was the solo in which he put a bamboo cane to various uses: cigarette holder, crutch, mashie, mace and finally, most moving of all, rifle for the Last Post. The play was a major turning-point in Albert Finney's career. The film was a major turning point in Tom Courtenay's career.

Sep 17. Sybil Thorndike, Marie Löhr, Lewis Casson, Maureen Delany, Una Venning, Nora Nicholson, Mary Clare, Graham Payn and William Hutt in Noël Coward's **Waiting in the Wings** directed by Margaret Webster at Duke of York's. Set in a home for retired actresses, the play was sentimental, generous and occasionally cruel. It was the most serious play Coward had written in years, and underrated.

Sep 28. John Gielgud and Ralph Richardson in Enid Bagnold's **The Last Joke** with Robert Flemyng, Anna Massey and Ernest Thesiger directed by Glen Byam Shaw at Phoenix. It acted like an early play by Anouilh and was fatally uncertain whether it was a *pièce rose* or a *pièce noir*. The production pleased nobody, the author least of all.

Sep 29. John Neville, Charles Kay and Fulton Mackay in Russell Braddon's **Naked Island** directed by Edward Burnham at Arts. A number of disparate POWs are in the notorious Changi Jail during World War 2. The horrors of working on the infamous railway has united them, but the closer the Allies get to winning the war, the more likely is it that their guards will murder them. Brian Currah's set was based on Ronald Searle's drawings.

Oct 4. John Stride and Judi Dench in Shakespeare's **Romeo and Juliet** directed by Franco Zeffirelli at Old Vic. Peggy Mount as Nurse. Alec McCowen as Mercutio. Major Shakespearian production was notable for its Italianate zest and physicality but not for its verse speaking. The balcony scene was touching, humorous and real. Benvolio (Peter Ellis) was in love with Romeo.
—Judi Dench's Juliet is a matter of fact young girl from beginning to end. And like a young girl experiencing tragedy for the first time her reaction contains an element of consciously simulated emotion, as if Juliet had seen too many films. ROBERT WRIGHT *Star*

John Stride and Judi Dench in Romeo and Juliet

Oct 12. Siobhan McKenna, Donal Donnelly, Eithne Dunne and Brian O'Higgins in J M Synge's **The Playboy of the Western World** directed by Shelagh Richards at Piccadilly. "An enchanting experience," said Milton Shulman in *The Evening Standard*, "even if the Irish does floor you." McKenna put out a lighted match with her bare foot – to the audible pain of the audience.

Oct 13. Rex Harrison in Anton Chekhov's **Platonov** directed by George Devine and John Blatchley at Royal Court. The 72-year-old play – a portrait of an amoral, self-destructive and anti-Semitic society in provincial Russia in the 1880s – had never been performed before in England. Platonov is a schoolteacher, a malicious scoundrel and weak-willed wastrel, who rails against bourgeois mediocrity. Women throw themselves at him, but he has no desire to be a Don Juan and declares his mission in life is to tell women how stupid they are. The production was a wild, unwieldy, crude mixture of tragedy, comedy, melodrama, farce and much nearer to Ostrovsky than Chekhov. Some actors, unable to check the audience's laughter in the wrong places, gave up the fight and played for as many laughs as they could get. Harrison's performance was burlesque.

Oct 31. Micheal Mac Liammoir in **The Importance of Being Oscar** at Apollo following its premiere at the Dublin Festival. The one-man show was a tribute of one Irishman to another: Mac Liammoir wore a green carnation and bore a strong physical resemblance to Oscar Wilde but he did not attempt to be Wilde. The recital included a long extract from *De Profundis*. He acted Herod's speech from *Salome* in French.

Nov 3. Anthony Quayle and Celia Johnson in Francois Billetdoux's **Chin Chin** directed by Harold Sackler at Wyndham's. Over-blown and episodic one-act play traced the degradation of an English woman and an Italian man whose respective partners are having an affair.

Nov 8. Judi Dench as Kate Hardcastle, Peggy Mount as Mrs Hardcastle and Tommy Steele as Tony Lumpkin in Oliver Goldsmith's **She Stoops to Conquer** directed by Douglas Seale at Old Vic. Dench, kittenish, pert, high-spirited, was irresistible.

Nov 10. Wendy Hiller, Diana Wynyard, Coral Browne and Ian Bannen in Lillian Hellman's **Toys in the Attic** directed by John Dexter at Piccadilly. Boredom and incest in New Orleans. Hellman's play was a cross between a Chekhov still-life and a Tennessee Williams melodrama. Two sisters have cared so long for their reckless younger brother that they don't take kindly either to his marriage or to his sudden wealth. It might have been better with an American cast. The English accents jarred.

Dec 15. The Stratford-on-Avon Company moved into Aldwych, its London base, and opened with John Webster's **The Duchess of Malfi** directed by Donald McWhinnie. Peggy Ashcroft was magnificent in theDuchess's death scene. Max Adrian's Cardinal was not so much High Church as High Camp. Eric Porter's Ferdinand was coarse and melodramatic.

Dec 19. Dorothy Tutin as Viola and Geraldine McEwan as Olivia in Shakespeare's **Twelfth Night** directed by Peter Hall transferred from Stratford to Aldwych. Eric Porter as Malvolio. Patrick Wymark as Sir Toby Belch. Richard Johnson as Sir Andrew Aguecheek. Dressed in Caroline costume, Viola looked as if she had just stepped out of the popular Civil War painting, "When did you last see your father?" Tutin was enchanting. McEwan was a squeaky-voiced minx. Max Adrian's infinitely sad clown cast an enormous shadow over the whole production.

Dec 20. Alec McCowen as Oberon and Gwen Watford as Titania in Shakespeare's **A Midsummer Night's Dream** directed by Michael Langham at Old Vic. Douglas Campbell as Bottom. Barbara Leigh-Hunt as Helena. Judi Dench was a volatile Hermia. Nobody was surprised that Puck frightened the village maidens. Tom Courtenay's Puck could have been mistaken for Caliban.

1961

Jan 12. Stratford-on-Avon Company. Leslie Caron, Richard Johnson, Gwen Ffrangcon-Davies and Eric Porter in Jean Giraudoux's **Ondine** directed by Peter Hall at Aldwych. Part fairy tale, part romance, part pantomime, part masque, part bore, Ondine is a water sprite, who falls in love with a knight-errant and she loves him so much that her love is the death of him. She does not understand what mortals are like and foolishly makes a pact with her uncle that if ever he should prove unfaithful to her, he will be killed. Giraudoux described Ondine as "the most human person who ever lived because she was human by choice." Caron was a radiant, ethereal sprite. Porter was very funny as the Lord Chamberlain.

Jan 18. **Three** directed by Donald McWhinnie at Arts. Triple bill. Emlyn Williams, Wendy Craig and Alison Leggatt in John Mortimer's **Lunch Hour**. A couple come to a seedy hotel to have sex but never get as far as taking off their coats. Emlyn Williams, Wendy Craig, Richard Briers and Alsion Leggatt in N F Simpson's **The Form**. Non sequiturs. Briers played a man who had a passion for taking photographs of Tower Bridge from every conceivable angle in all kinds of weather. Emlyn Williams, Alison Leggatt and Richard Briers in Harold Pinter's **A Slight Ache**. Who is the match seller? And what does he want? He might be death, conscience or even lost youth.
Mr Williams and Miss Leggatt act with great self-possession but only in isolated moments do they throw any light on the characters they represent. *The Times*

Jan 24. Barry Foster, Robert Ayres, Harry Towb and Susan Hampshire in J P Donleavy's **Fairy Tales of New York** directed by Philip Wiseman at Comedy. Four overextended sketches, set in a mortician's parlor, an executive suite, a boxing ring and a night club, offered humour, sadness and poetry in a manner which recalled William Saroyan's plays.

Feb 20. Stratford-on-Avon Company. Richard Johnson as Urbain Grandier and Dorothy Tutin as Sister Jeanne in John Whiting's **The Devils** directed by Peter Wood at Aldwych. Suspected diabolism in 17th-century France. This vast, sprawling drama, based on Aldous Huxley's *The Devils of Loudon*, recalled the worst excesses of Jacobean theatre. The exorcism, the hysteria and the torture were painful to watch. Grandier was young, handsome, ambitious and lecherous. Jeanne, a hunchback, let her imagination run riot and accused him of seducing her and the other nuns in the convent. The authorities used the accusation to send Grandier to the stake. Max Adrian acted Father Barre (never happier than when he is hunting for witches) for farce. "A masterpiece," said T C Worsley in *The Financial Times*.
—For those with adequate stomachs, the production can hardly be overpraised.
ROBERT MULLER *Daily Mail*
—A powerful dramatic spectacle, a play of depth, force, terror and beauty. ROBERT MULLER *Daily Mail*

Feb 21. Mary Ure as Beatrice, Robert Shaw as de Flores and Jeremy Brett as Alsemero in Thomas Middleton and William Rowley's **The Changeling** directed by Tony Richardson at Royal Court. The unobtrusive performances lacked grandeur and guts.

Mar 9. Anna Massey and Janina Faye in William Gibson's **The Miracle Worker** directed by Peter Coe at Royalty. Based on the true story of the childhood of the blind and deaf Helen Keller. That moment, when the girl at last realises that what she has always thought to be just a game with fingers is actually an alphabet and a means of communicating, was very moving. High spot was the free-for-all, no-holds-barred fight between the two actresses, which went on for six minutes.

Peter Cook, Jonathan Miller, Dudley Moore and Alan Bennett in Beyond the Fringe

1961 World Premieres

New York

Samuel Beckett's *Happy Days*

Tennessee Williams's *The Night of the Iguana*

Edward Albee's *The American Dream*

Zurich

Max Frisch's *Andorra*

Deaths

Moss Hart (*b.*1904), American playwright, director

Barry Jackson (*b.*1879), British director

George Kaufman (*b.*1889), American playwright

Notes

—Joan Littlewood left Theatre workshop

—Shakespeare Memorial Theatre changed its name to Royal Shakespeare Theatre

—The Coliseum became a cinema from 1961–1967.

History

—John F Kennedy US President

—Yuri Gagarin first man in space

—Berlin Wall erected

—South Africa a republic

—Rudolf Nureyev defected to the West

Mar 15. Margaret Leighton as Ellida in Henrik Ibsen's **The Lady From The Sea** directed by Glen Byam Shaw at Queen's. Vanessa Redgrave as Boletta. Andrew Cruickshank as Dr Wangel. John Neville as the Stranger. Leighton, amphibian, distracted and noticeably wan, was particularly impressive when Ellida is finally forced to choose between the land and the sea. Pasco was delightful as the earnest artist, especially in his half-proposal of marriage when he has no idea how selfish he is being. Redgrave's gauche sincerity was touching.

—The play cries out for acting in the grand manner and the grand manner we certainly get from Margaret Leighton under Glen Byam Shaw's forceful, precise and excellently judged production. Indeed Miss Leighton pulls out every stop she knows and makes Ellida into Blanch DuBois of the Fjords, a Camille choking on dreams of fresh water. ROBERT MULLER *Daily Mail*

Mar 16. Van Johnson in Meredith Willson's musical **The Music Man** directed by Robert Merriman at Adelphi and based on original production by Morton Da Costa. A fast-talking, self-centred salesman's commodity is music. The rousing "Seventy-Six Trombones" stopped the show. The film was better; but then it had Robert Preston who had created the lead role on Broadway.

Mar 19. Dorothy Tutin, Max Adrian, Richard Johnson and John Barton in **The Hollow Crown** at Aldwych (RSC). Entertainment by and about the Kings and Queens of England devised by John Barton.

Apr 6. Phyllis Calvert, Alan Badel, Maggie Smith, Diana Churchill and Robert Hardy in Jean Anouilh's **The Rehearsal** directed by John Hale at Globe. A brilliantly witty and nasty comedy of manners. Five decadent aristocrats are rehearsing Marivaux's *La Double Inconstance*. The Countess does not mind her husband having mistresses (she has her lovers) but she won't put up with his affair with a déclassée governess, who offers selfless love. French audiences could hardly tell when Marivaux's dialogue finished and Anouilh's began.

Apr 8. Wakefield Mystery Plays directed by Colin Ellis and Sally Miles at Mermaid. Eighteen of the original thirty-two plays were acted in a way which attempted to capture the performances which would have been given by amateur actors in the 15th century. The result was some of the worst acting London had seen.

Apr 19. Claire Bloom, Basil Sydney, Kenneth Haigh, Nigel Stock and Diane Cilento in Jean-Paul Sartre's **Altona** directed by John Berry at Royal Court. Can a former Nazi torturer go on living in the knowledge of what he did in World War 2? His eldest son has locked himself in his room where he confesses his crimes to crabs. The characters remained mouthpieces.

May 10. Alan Bennett, Peter Cook, Jonathan Miller and Dudley Moore in **Beyond the Fringe** directed by Eleanor Fazan transferred from Edinburgh Festival to Fortune. Revue was never the same again, killed stone dead at a stroke. The Oxford and Cambridge graduates kick-started a wave of satire in *That Was the Week That Was*, *Private Eye* and Peter Cook's Establishment Club. 1,184 performances. Kenneth Tynan said it was "the funniest revue London has seen since the Allies dropped the bomb on Hiroshima." 1184 performances.

—A revue so brilliant, so adult, hard-boiled, accurate, merciless, witty, unexpected, alive, exhilarating, cleansing, right, true and good. I shall go and see it once a month for the rest of my life. If I live to be a hundred. BERNARD LEVIN *Daily Express*

May 18. Jean Bayless and Roger Dann in Richard Rodgers and Oscar Hammerstein II's **The Sound of Music** directed by Jerome Whyte at Palace. Book by Howard Lindsay and Russell Crouse based on Maria Augusta Trapp's autobiography, *The Trapp Family Singers*. A boisterous postulant becomes governess to the seven children of a widowed naval officer and the end result is old-fashioned, sentimental claptrap:

a schmaltzy mixture of nuns, children and Nazis. The musical (aka "The Sound of Mucus" and "The Sound of Money") has never been popular with critics – an over-ripe, soggy old plum said *The Daily Mail* – but it has always been hugely popular with audiences. Hit songs included "The Sound of Music", "Maria", "My Favourite Things", "Sixteen Going On Seventeen" and "Edelweiss". Constance Shacklock sang "Climb Every Mountain" and "Do-Re-Mi" stopped the show. The original production ran for 1,435 performances on Broadway and 2,385 performances in London.

May 30. Felicia Okoli, Rashidi Onikoyi and Bloke Modisane in Jean Genet's **The Blacks** designed by Andre Acquart and directed by Roger Blin at Royal Court. A sermon on the foolishness of racial prejudice was acted by an all-black cast. Those playing whites wore white masks. Blin did not speak English and chose the actors for their looks. The accents were difficult to follow, but it looked good and Genet was delighted:

—The staging that you have perfected, I tell you, has given my play an extraordinary force which from time to time frightens me a bit. JEAN GENET

Jun 11. Christopher Plummer as King Henry and Eric Porter as Thomas Becket in Jean Anouilh's **Becket or The Honour of God** translated by Lucienne Hill and directed by Peter Hall at Aldwych (RSC). "I created," said Anouilh, "the king I wanted and the ambiguous Becket I needed." Henry claims that Becket is the only man he can trust and makes him his Primate. Becket immediately realizes that if he becomes Archbishop he can no longer be his friend; but Henry does not see this, until it is too late. Plummer, in the king's more emotional (and homosexual) moments gave an uncanny imitation of Laurence Olivier. There was a memorable scene with the two men on horseback on a windy plain. Patrick Wymark was a disarmingly wily King of France. Tranferred to Globe.

Jun 15. Chita Rivera and Peter Marshall in **Bye Bye Birdie** directed by Tony Mordente at Her Majesty's from the original American production of Gower Champion. Musical. Book by Michael Stewart. Music by Charles Strouse. Lyrics by Lee Adams. Birdie (Marty Wilde), rock 'n roll idol, makes his farewell appearance before doing his national service. The show was a send-up of Elvis Presley and a kick in the teeth for American Mothers. High spot was Angela Baddeley's Jewish mom crawling across the kitchen floor to put her head in the gas oven.

Jun 27. Harry Landis, Robert Stephens and Alison Bayley in Arnold Wesker's **The Kitchen** directed by John Dexter at Royal Court. A typical working day in a large restaurant's kitchen turned out to be a *cri de coeur* for peaceful co-existence. The lunch-hour rush, with chefs and waitresses working at a furious pace, was brilliantly orchestrated.

Jul 4. Victor Borge at Saville.

Jul 20. Anthony Newley and Anna Quayle in Leslie Bricusse and Anthony Newley's **Stop The World I Want To Get Off** directed by Anthony Newley at Queen's. Modern morality play set in a circus tent. Newley sang "What Kind of Fool Am I?" Quayle played the women in his life: English rose, Russian football player, German domestic, and American cutie.

Jul 26. Annette Crosbie, Davy Kaye and Hugh Sullivan in Sean O'Casey's **The Bishop's Bonfire** directed by Frank Dunlop at Mermaid. A touch of poetry, a bit of blasphemy, a fair whack of anti-Catholic propaganda, a great deal of knockabout and a lot of boredom.

Jul 27. Albert Finney in John Osborne's **Luther** directed by Tony Richardson at Royal Court. The sale of indulgences in 1517 led Luther to nail his thesis ("The just shall live by faith alone") to the cathedral door and trigger the Reformation. Johann Tetzel (Peter Bull), the most infamous and successful vendor, offered indulgences not only for sins already committed but also for sins which would be committed in the future. He was even willing to sell indulgences for the dead. The Pope needed the money to fund the building of Rome's St Peter's basilica. Albert Finney was riveting. Transferred to Phoenix.

—No finer Luther could be imagined than the clod, the lump, the infinitely vulnerable Everyman presented by Albert Finney, who looks, in his moments of pallor and lip gnawing doubt, like a reincarnation of the young Irving, fattened up for some cannibal feast. KENNETH TYNAN *Observer*

Aug 2. Brian Rix, Leo Franklyn and Basil Lord in Ray Cooney and Tony Hilton's **One for the Pot** directed by Henry Kendall at Whitehall. Farce. Not everybody's cup of tea. Rix played three brothers.

Aug 22. Sammy Davis Jr at Prince of Wales. A great singer and a great mimic, but he got a bad press. His impersonations of Jimmy Stewart, Humphrey Bogart and Jerry Lewis were uncanny. The critics found him exhausting, overpowering, narcissistic and sentimental.

Aug 23. Ronnie Stevens, Joan Sims and Millicent Martin in **The Lord Chamberlain**

Regrets directed by Eleanor Fazan at Saville. The revue was dull, crude and camp. The Empire Loyalists objected to one sketch and made a disturbance. Many suspected the disturbance had been planted by the management for publicity purposes

Sep 7. John Wood, Stephanie Voss and Peter Gilmore in **The Fantasticks** directed by Word Baker at Apollo. Book and lyrics by Tom Jones. Music by Harvey Schmidt. A sentimental and absurdly twee cornucopia of stage conventions based on Edmond Rostand's play. John Wood was very funny as an outrageously hammy Shakespearian actor. The show's long-running success in New York was not repeated in London.

Sep 13. Vanessa Redgrave and Derek Godfrey in Shakespeare's **The Taming of the Shrew** directed by Maurice Daniels at Aldwych (RSC). The production was the most original and subtle reading of the text in living memory. Katherine falls in love with Petruchio on sight and, in the incident where she is forced to acknowledge that the sun is the moon, she is in on the joke from the very start.

Oct 12. Max Bygraves in **Do Re Mi** directed by Bernard Gersten at Prince of Wales. Book by Garson Kanin. Music by Jule Styne. Lyrics by Betty Comden and Adolph Green. The musical marked Bygraves's acting debut and whenever he was in any doubt as how to play a scene or say a line he sent it up. A dreadful amateurism hung over the whole production.

Oct 24. Two plays by Edward Albee directed by Peter Yates at Royal Court. Gene Anderson in **The Death of Bessie Smith,** a story of racial prejudice and racial injustice. Mavis Villiers in **The American Dream,** a comedy of non-sequiturs.

Nov 1. Roger Livesey as Shotover, Judy Campbell as Hesione, Dulcie Gray as Lady Utterword, Michael Denison as Hector and Perlita Neilson as Ellie in Bernard Shaw's **Heartbreak House** directed by Frank Hauser transferred from The Oxford Playhouse to Wyndham's. George Benson hadn't had such a good role as Boss Mangan in years and was splendid. Donald Eccles's elderly Mazzini Dunn was charming: "Would you believe it," he says, "that a lot of women have flirted with me because I am quite safe. But they get tired of me for the same reason."

Nov 7. Aeschylus's **The Oresteia** directed by Minos Volanakis at Old Vic. Catherine Lacey's Clytemnestra lacked stature. Yvonne Mitchell's Electra was disturbingly modern. Ronald Lewis's Orestes made no impression. Ruth Meyer's Cassandra and the female chorus came out best.

Dec 4. Peggy Ashcroft as Ranevsky and George Murcell as Lopahin in Anton Chekhov's **The Cherry Orchard** directed by Michel Saint-Denis at Aldwych (RSC). It was an all-crying, all-kissing production and the third act was brilliantly performed. Ranavesky is incapable of listening, even when her world is toppling about her. "What am I to do?" she cries. Lopahin keeps telling her. Roy Dotrice's senile retainer was the most Russian performance. "What am I going to do with you, eh?" he asked Gaev, adopting a tone more suitable for a little boy. John Gielgud's Gaev was delightful as he tried to rise above it. Dench was a charming, excitable child-like Anya. Ian Holm's ugly Trofimov was a far cry from the virile Trofimov in the Moscow Arts Theatre's production.

Dec 21. Alfred Marks in Max Frisch's **The Fire Raisers** directed by Lindsay Anderson at Royal Court. Frisch issued a solemn warning that if nations continue to see the danger and take no steps to avert it, then they cannot blame Fate for their destruction. A wealthy and ruthless business man allows into his house two people whom he suspects of being fire raisers when the whole city is in flames. He innocently believes that he will be saved if he makes friends with them. Marks exuded false bonhomie. Colin Blakely and James Booth as the firemen were figures of farce, but not any the less scary for that. Blakely and Booth also appeared in the curtain-raiser: *Box and Cox,* the 1847 farce by J Maddison Morton.

1962

Feb 9. The Stratford Ontario Company in two operas by Gilbert and Sullivan directed by Tyrone Guthrie at Her Majesty's: **HMS Pinafore** and **The Pirates of Penzance.**

Feb 10. Vanessa Redgrave and Ian Bannen in Shakespeare's **As You Like It** transferred from Stratford to Aldwych (RSC). Redgrave, "more than common tall", was a radiant, high-spirited, enchanting, loveable and for many theatregoers the definitive Rosalind of the second half of the 20th century. Max Adrian, "wrapped in a humorous sadness", was a subtle and beautifully spoken Jacques. Rosalind Knight was a witty and pert Celia.
—Oh, wonderful, wonderful, most wonderful... this is not acting at all but living, being loved. If the word enchantment has any meaning, it is here. BERNARD LEVIN *Daily Express*

Feb 20. David Tomlinson and Patrick Cargill in Marc Camoletti's **Boeing Boeing**

1962 World Premieres
New York
Edward Albee's *Who's Afraid of Virginia Woolf?*
Spoleto
Tennessee Williams's *The Milk Train Doesn't Stop Here Any More*
Zurich
Friedrich Dürrenmatt's *The Physicists*
Paris
Eugene Ionesco's *Exit the King*

Deaths
Michel de Ghelrode (*b.*1898), Belgian playwright

Notes
—Laurence Olivier appointed Director of National Theatre
—Gilbert and Sullivan operettas out of copyright
—Coventry Cathedral consecrated

History
—Cuban Missile Crisis
—Nelson Mandela jailed

adapted by Beverley Cross and directed by Jack Minster at Apollo. French farce with seven doors and three fiancées. The girls are air hostesses. 2,035 performances.

Feb 27. Bob Monkhouse in Neil Simon's **Come Blow Your Horn** directed by Cy Enfield at Prince of Wales. 19-year-old Michael Crawford made his West End debut as a gangling, open-mouthed youngster, who runs away from home to join his playboy brother, who provides him with a girl as a twenty-first birthday present. At first he is embarrassed ("'Why couldn't he get me socks like everybody else?'") but it's not long before he puts his brother's feats in the shade.

Feb 28. An Evening with Yves Montand at Saville. Popular French actor and singer, probably best known to English audiences for his performance in H G Cluzot's *Le Salaire de la Peur* (*Wages of Fear*). The high spot of his one-man show was Jacques Prévert's dramatic poem, *Barbara.*
—Montand's gift consists of a throatily masculine baritone voice, an expressively mobile face and body, and an air of casual virility that can curl the toes of every properly nourished female in the house. *Time*

Mar 27. Rita Tushingham, Julian Glover, Philip Locke and James Bolan in Ann Jellicoe's **The Knack** directed by Ann Jellicoe and Keith Johnstone at Royal Court. The message was very simple. Girls never get raped unless they want to be raped. A little less symbolism and a bit more realism might have helped.

Mar 29. Patsy Byrne in Bertolt Brecht's **The Caucasian Chalk Circle** directed by William Gaskill at Aldwych (RSC). Who is the rightful mother? The one who gave birth? Or the one who looked after the child? The production drew freely on Chinese theatre and the crowded cabin scene was a straight crib from the Marx Brothers' *A Night at the Opera.* Hugh Griffith enjoyed himself hugely as the judge. Russell Hunter was amusing as a drunken Orthodox priest, uncertain whether he is blessing a marriage or a deathbed. Michael Flanders was a dull narrator.

Apr 5. Ralph Richardson and Anna Massey as Sir Peter and Lady Teazle in Sheridan's **The School for Scandal** directed by John Gielgud at Haymarket. John Neville and Daniel Massey as Joseph and Charles Surface. Margaret Rutherford's Mrs Candour (lapping up the scandal) got the production off to a spanking start. Laurence Naismith carried off "the auction of the family portraits" scene with great charm. Cast changes included John Gielgud as a very smooth Joseph Surface and Geraldine McEwan as Lady Teazle.
—Sir John makes every sentence seem to carry twice its weight by phrasing it so perfectly. It is the very model of how the language should be spoken. T C WORSLEY *Financial Times*

Apr 27. John Kelland, Frank Finlay and Corin Redgrave in Arnold Wesker's **Chips with Everything** directed by John Dexter at Royal Court. The most authentic picture of National Service yet seen on stage. "We'll break you,' says the corporal, "because it's our job." The public school boy (John Kelland) is officer material, but he prefers, as his own personal gesture against Society, to remain in the ranks. The officers accuse him of slumming and turn down his request. The ORs misunderstand the gesture. His efforts to make friends with a working class boy (Colin Campbell) fail. Wesker loaded the dice against the officer class. The odious Squadron Leader (Martin Boddey) says he would gladly give a million men in exchange for one Javelin fighter. The tragedy of Smiler Wingate (a moving performance by Ronald Lacey) was that he made no gesture. He smiled in spite of himself: "I'm not smiling, sir,' he said. "I was born like that." The production's physical high spot was the excellently timed and mimed stealing of the coke behind a wire fence.
—This is the Left-wing drama's first real breakthrough, the first anti-Establishment play of which the establishment has cause to be afraid. If there is a better play in London I haven't seen it. This is something to be discussed and re-discussed, admired, feared. HAROLD HOBSON *Sunday Times*
—*Chips* remains the most outspoken and explicit challenge so far from a young left-wing playwright to our assumptions about social progress. ALAN BRIEN SUNDAY *Telegraph*

Chips with Everything

May 8. Amelia Bayntun and Bob Grant in Lionel Bart's musical **Blitz** directed by Lionel Bart and Eleanor Fazan at Adelphi. Nostalgia for World War 2, evacuees, wailing sirens, bombs falling, people sleeping in the underground and Vera Lynn singing. The heroine goes blind but her boy friend stands by her. The songs – especially "Who's This Geezer, Hitler?" and "Petticoat Lane" – were catchy, but the audience came out of the theatre singing the sets. Designer Sean Kenny reproduced the London Blitz in a brilliant transformation scene. Noël Coward said the show was twice as long as the actual Blitz and not nearly so funny.

May 9. Nicol Williamson and Robert Lang in Maxim Gorky's **The Lower Depths** directed by Toby Robertson at New Arts Club (RSC). The production was full of actors imitating Toby Robertson. Wilfred Lawson's sly Louka was splendid; though, as usual, somewhat nerve-wracking, since the audience was never quite certain that he knew where he was in the text.

May 10. Two plays by Peter Shaffer directed by Peter Wood at Globe. Maggie Smith, Douglas Livingstone and Terry Scully in **The Private Ear**. A shy young man's possible relationship with extrovert girl is spoiled by his friend exposing her for the frivolous person she is. **The Public Eye**, with Kenneth Williams, Maggie Smith and Richard Pearson, was the better of the two plays, not least because of Williams's performance as a bizarre private detective.

May 16. Geraldine McEwan and Giles Cooper's **Everything in the Garden** directed by Peter Coe transferred to Duke of York's. Suburban housewife takes to high class prostitution. Her husband is outraged until he learns that the income is tax free.

May 17. Patricia Routledge, Bernard Cribbins, Joyce Blair and Terence Cooper in Rick Sesoyan's musical, **Little Mary Sunshine** directed by Paddy Stone at Comedy. Send-up of *Rose Marie* and tatty touring shows.

May 19. Final performance of The Crazy Gang's farewell show **Young at Heart** at Victoria Palace.

May 25. **Black and White Minstrel Show** at Victoria Palace ran for the next ten years. The blacked-up cast went through the motions to their pre-recorded voices. 4,344 performances.

May 29. Alastair Sim in Shakespeare's **The Tempest** directed by Oliver Neville at Old Vic. Sim always seemed surprised that his magic actually worked. Ariel never entered from the side he expected. His Prospero was a kindly schoolmaster, admonishing his naughty pupils; and nowhere more disgracefully so than in his delivery of the Epilogue.

Jun 7. David Rudkin's **Afore Night Come** directed by Clifford Williams at New Arts (RSC). Casual labourers in a pear orchard in the Black Country are joined by three outsiders: a student (Roger Croucher), a Teddy Boy (Henley Thomas) and an Irish tramp (Gerry Duggan). The labourers are a crude, ignorant, superstitious lot. The tramp is an educated, garrulous, sick, filthy old man, who has a poet's gift for language. The labourers don't like him because he's Irish and they blame him for the poor harvest. The ritual sacrifice, which takes place beneath the drenching poisonous sprays of a pest-control helicopter, is as nasty as anything in Jacobean drama. 25-year-old Rudkin (who had worked as a fruit picker in a Worcestershire orchard when he was a student) was hailed as a major new writer. *The Times* said the play was a masterpiece. Kenneth Tynan said it was the most striking debut since *Look Back in Anger*. The Lord Chamberlain found the level of violence and whiff of homosexuality between student and tractor driver (Peter McEnery) unacceptable. Audiences had to pay three guineas to become members of the Arts Theatre Club.
—David Rudkin is a born playwright and poet, and his imagination, like so many young poets in the past, is often grisly as well as beautiful. ROGER GELLERT *New Statesman*

Jun 13. Bernard Braden, Collin Wilcox, Neil McCallum and Betty McDowell in Tennessee Williams's **Period of Adjustment**, directed by Roger Graef at Royal Court. Williams's only comedy on the theme of "Love is a very difficult occupation – you have to work at it." Neil McCallum took it too seriously. Transferred to Wyndham's.

Jun 18. Harold Pinter's **The Collection** directed by Peter Hall at Aldwych (RSC). Husband (Kenneth Haigh) accuses his wife (Barbara Murray) of having slept with "a pansy boy" in Leeds. The boy (John Ronane) denies it and then admits it. The wife admits she slept with him to her husband but denies it to the pansy's elderly boyfriend (Michael Hordern) saying her husband has made it all up. Finally, nobody admits anything. Acted in a double-bill with August Strindberg's **Playing with Fire** with Kenneth Haigh, Sheila Allen and Colin Jeavons directed by John Blatchley.

Jun 21. Elaine Stritch in Noël Coward's **Sail Away** directed by Noël Coward at Savoy. Old-fashioned musical. High spot: the long-legged, gravel-voiced Stritch singing "Why Do the Wrong People Travel?"

Jul 3. Chichester Festival Theatre opened with Francis Beaumont and John Fletcher's **The Chances**, directed by Laurence Olivier, who had written off to sixty stars, asking them whether, if there were the parts for them, they would be willing to appear at Chichester with him. Everybody said yes. The cast included Keith Michell, John Neville, Joan Plowright, Athene Seyler and Kathleen Harrison. The play was not worth reviving.

Aug 1. Marius Goring, Gwen Ffrangcon-Davies, Michael Gwynn, Mark Eden, Judi Dench and Newton Blick in John Whiting's **A Penny for a Song** directed by Colin Graham at Aldwych. The comedy was considerably revised and most critics thought Whiting had spoiled his play. The young man (Mark Eden) was no longer a blind soldier, but an angry young man who was deeply involved in the issues of the day and constantly quoting from Thomas Paine's *The Rights of Man*. Goring was miscast as Sir Timothy Bellboys who dresses up as Napoleon and intends to order the French army home. The best performance came from James Bree who played the fixated firefighter, who has had a passion for all things inflammatory ever since his undergraduate days when his future wife caught fire and he had to extinguish her.

Aug 20. Dora Bryan in **Gentlemen Prefer Blondes** directed by Henry Kaplan at Princes. Musical. Book by Joseph Fields and Anita Loos. Music by Jule Styne. Lyrics by Leo Rabin. Faced with the impossible task of following Marilyn Monroe's screen performance, Bryan played Lorelei on her own Lancashire terms. The production was tatty in the extreme.

Sep 4. Leonard Rossiter, Donal Donnelly and Pauline Delaney in Sean O'Casey's **Red Roses for Me** directed by Julius Gellner at Mermaid. Rossiter played one of O'Casey's most appealing characters, Brennan o' the Moor, the miserly yet kindly landlord, who is obsessed with the soundness of the Bank of Ireland.

Sep 11. Ian Richardson, Alec McCowen and Diana Rigg in Shakespeare's **The Comedy of Errors** directed by Clifford Williams at Aldwych (RSC). The fantisticated production drew freely on masque, pantomime and music hall. The critics began to take the play more seriously for the first time.

Sep 19. Sheila Hancock and Edward Woodward in Charles Dwyer's **The Rattle of a Simple Man** directed by Donald McWhinnie at Garrick. Mancunian, up for the Cup, goes back to a prostitute's basement flat and they have a long chat. A one-act, two-hand play was spread over three acts. Woodward's Mancunian had the ring of truth; Hancock's prostitute was pure fiction.

Sep 26. Leo McKern as Peer in Henrik Ibsen's **Peer Gynt** translated by Michael Meyer directed by Michael Elliott and designed by Richard Negri at Old Vic. Catherine Lacey as Aase. Dilys Hamlett as Solveig. Wilfred Lawson as the Button-

Moulder. One of the great productions of the 1960s. McKern's magnificent performance carried the audience through the four hours. "Life is a terrible price to pay for birth." The scene where Peer converts his mother's death-bed into a sledge and drives her into heaven was superb.
—Ibsen's great morality play is quite literally the experience of a life time. Forty scenes might sound a lot, but they pass rapidly. PHILIP HOPE-WALLACE *Guardian*

Oct 9. Derek Godfrey as Henry and Alan Dobie as Thomas Becket in Christopher Fry's **Curtmantle** directed by Stuart Burge at Aldwych (RSC). Primate and King addressed each other as if they were debating at the Oxford Union. Jean Anouilh's *Becket*, one of the RSC's biggest successes, may have been less historically accurate than Fry's version, but his play had a far better feel for history than Fry's had.

Oct 15. Ian Holm and Dorothy Tutin in Shakespeare's **Troilus and Cressida** directed by John Barton at Aldwych (RSC). Michael Hordern as Ulysses. Patrick Allen as Achilles. Gordon Gostelow as Thersites. The action was played out in a sandpit. Holm was very boyish. Tutin was very shallow. This Cressida wanted to be false so that she would become famous. Max Adrian's Pandarus treated the lovers as if they were pussycats. "You must be witty", he said to Troilus, worried that he would bore Cressida to death. The fights were magnificent spectacle.

Nov 1. Brenda Bruce in Samuel Beckett's **Happy Days** directed by George Devine at Royal Court. Hypnotic *tour de force* for some, diabolically dull for others.

Nov 28. Leo McKern as Subtle, Lee Montagu as Face and Priscilla Morgan as Dol Common in Ben Jonson's **The Alchemist** directed by Tyrone Guthrie at Old Vic. There were so many modern colloquial expressions and references to such things as Lyons Corner House, travellers' cheques and flick knives that many people felt they weren't watching Jonson at all. Charles Gray's physically repulsive Sir Epicure Mammon was modelled on Toulouse-Lautrec's portrait of Oscar Wilde at the time of his trials. Gray was hilarious.

Dec 4. Andrew Cruickshank and Mary Miller in August Strindberg's **The Master Builder** at Arts. Cruickshank resisted the temptation to give a star performance and the play was the duller for it.

Dec 5. Laurence Olivier in David Turner's **Semi-Detached** directed by Tony Richardson at Saville. This cheap, crude rep play should have stayed in rep. The irony was that the charabanc parties, who might have liked it, were put off because Olivier was in it, whilst those people who wanted to see Olivier were appalled by the vulgarity. The role of the North Country insurance man should have been played by Leonard Rossiter, who had created the role at Belgrade Theatre, Coventry, with great success.

Dec 9. Edward Bond's **The Pope's Wedding** directed by Keith Johnstone at Royal Court. Production without décor. Jealous husband comes to believe a hermit (who lives in a kennel) is his wife's father and kills him.
—I wouldn't care to be inside the author's head on a dark night ... Mr Bond is an original. We shall hear more of him. BERNARD LEVIN *Daily Mail*

Dec 12. Paul Scofield in Shakespeare's **King Lear** directed by Peter Brook transferred from Stratford to Aldwych (RSC). Irene Worth as Goneril. Pauline Jameson as Regan. Diana Rigg as Cordelia. John Laurie as Gloucester. Alec McCowen as Fool. The most startling innovation was that Goneril was given just cause to complain about Lear's 100 knights. They really did treat her home as if it were an inn and finally broke the place up. Scofield, grizzled and robust, was a great Lear and deeply moving in his scenes with Cordelia and Gloucester. Alec McCowen was a great Fool. James Booth's Edmund was a spiv out of *Fings Aint Wot They Used T'Be*. Cornwall, memorably, put out Gloucester's eyes with the spur on his boot.
—[Paul Scofield] possesses as few other Lears I have seen the ability to make the pathos of old age utterly convincing, terrible and touching, without a hint of sentimentality.
PHILIP HOPE-WALLACE *Guardian*
—The best all round performance of this tremendous play in modern times. W A DARLINGTON *Daily Telegraph*

1963

Jan 9. Cyril Cusack, Michael Hordern, Irene Worth and Alan Webb in Friedrich Dürrenmatt's **The Physicists** directed by Peter Brook at Aldwych (RSC). Bleak black comedy. Three famous physicists, in the pay of their respective countries' secret service, are feigning madness in a Swiss sanatorium. Their task is to abduct a genius. Webb was made up to look like Einstein. Cusack carried the brunt of the play's debate on moral responsibility. To whom is the physicist responsible? Is it to a power? Or is it to science? Or is it to humanity?

Jan 23. Michael Caine, Barry Foster, Liz Fraser, Michael Bryant and Denys Graham

1963 World Premieres
New York
Dale Wasserman's *One Flew Over the Cuckoo's Nest*
Berlin
Rolf Hochhuth's *The Representative*

Births
Neil LaBute, American playwright and screenwriter

Deaths
Jean Cocteau (*b.*1899), French poet, playwright, novelist, film maker, designer
Charles Laughton (*b.*1899), British actor

Max Miller (*b.*1895), British comedian
Clifford Odets (*b.*1906), American playwright
John Whiting (*b.*1915), British playwright

History
—Race riots in Alabama
—Martin Luther King's "I Have A Dream" speech
—President John F Kennedy assassinated
—Harold Macmillan resigned
—Great Train Robbery in UK
—The Beatles became internationally known

in James Saunders's **Next Time I'll Sing To You** directed by Shirley Butler at New Arts. Based on Raleigh Trevelyan's novel about Jimmy Mason, the Hermit of Great Canfield, Essex, who cut himself off from the world for forty years. A prolonged debate about the very nature of existence: stimulating, digressive, bawdy, funny, pretentious, poetic, music-hallish. Transferred to Criterion.
—For me, it is simply a kind of diarrhoea of the cerebrum and when one begins to discern the spiritual overtones, it positively palls. CHARLES MAROWITZ *Plays and Players*

Jan 31. Spike Milligan in **The Bed Sitting Room** written, directed and designed by John Antrobus and Spike Milligan at Mermaid. This shambolic and carelessly writ-

ten post-atomic comedy had one or two moments of inspired lunacy, but Milligan was generally inaudible and unfunny. Transferred to Duke of York's.

Feb 7. Peter O'Toole, Harry Andrews and Mary Miller in Bertolt Brecht's **Baal** directed by William Gaskill at Phoenix. Baal, vagabond, braggart, poet, tramp and drunk, behaves like a depraved animal and destroys everybody with whom he comes in contact. His degradation was given a romantic staging and the action was punctuated with songs.
—I find it quite unutterably boring. But I have not the right temperament to revel in Teutonic gloom. W A DARLINGTON *Daily Telegraph*

Feb 12. Norman Rodway in Hugh Leonard's adaptation of James Joyce's **Stephen D** directed by Jim Fitzgerald, transferred from Dublin Festival to St Martin's. High spot was a long sermon on hell, which was so long that even the preacher (Gerard Healy) looked at his watch. "Do you intend to become a Protestant?" he asked Stephen. "I said I had lost my faith," replied Stephen, "not my self respect." The picture of hell was so awful that the only thing an audience could do was laugh in self-defence.

Feb 27. Maggie Smith in Jean Kerr's **Mary, Mary** directed by Joseph Anthony at Queen's. Wise-cracking American comedy which recalled the sophisticated screwball films of the 1930s. Smith was enchanting. Felix Barker in *The Evening News* described her performance as "a hilarious, incomparable display of high comedy acting."

Mar 6. Bernard Miles and Marjorie Rhodes as the parents in Bill Naughton's **All in Good Time** directed by Josephine Wilson at Mermaid. Sensitive, young man (John Pickles) fails to consummate his marriage. His wife (Lois Daine) is philosophical: "What you never have, you never miss." It is their families who are outraged. Transferred to Phoenix.

Mar 7. Richard Harris in Nikolai Gogol's **The Diary of A Madman** directed by

Frank Finlay and Peter O'Toole in Hamlet

Lindsay Anderson at Royal Court. Solo performance. Harris didn't have the authority to carry the audience.

Mar 19. Ann Beach, Murray Melvin, Brian Murphy, George Sewell and Victor Spinetti in **Oh! What a Lovely War** by Charles Chilton and directed by Joan Littlewood at Stratford East. Memorable anti-war propaganda and one of the great theatrical successes of the 1960s, it offered "songs, battles and some jokes" within an end-of-pier framework. Behind the actors a news panel screen flashed famous World War I posters and photographs of the men in the trenches. Most devastating were the constant reminders of the appalling statistics: "Battle of the Somme. British lose 65,000 men in the first three hours. Gain, Nil." ("Don't worry," says a nurse, comforting a wounded soldier, "we'll have you back in the firing line within a week.") The French soldiers – lambs for the slaughter – march into No Man's Land baa-ing like sheep. Field Marshal Earl Haig, commander-in-chief, was not squeamish about using the men as cannon fodder, confident that Britain would eventually win, because they had more men to lose than the Germans. He put himself in the hands of God and prayed for victory before the Americans arrived. The most moving scene of all was the one when the British and German soldiers exchanged Christmas presents. The music hall songs, the recruiting songs ("We don't want to lose you, but we think you ought to go") and the barrack-room ballads were heartbreaking. Victor Spinetti memorably recreated a bayonet drill sergeant's parade ground gibberish. Transferred to Wyndham's.
—The most brilliantly imagined political comment of our theatre in all the years since the second war. PHILIP HOPE-WALLACE *Guardian*
—It is deeply emotional and coldly factual, and it provides rare and brilliant theatre. DAVID NATHAN *Daily Herald*
—My one serious complaint is that the devices for conveying an anti-war message are as evidently contrived, as intellectually false and as artificially immoral as the devices used during the war to convey a patriotic message. MILTON SHULMAN *Evening Standard*

Mar 21. Tommy Steele as Kipps in **Half a Sixpence** directed by John Dexter at Cambridge. Musical. Book by Beverley Cross based on H G Wells' novel. Music and lyrics by David Heneker. Steele could do the sentimental bits ("she's too far above me, she'd laugh – not half she would") but he was happiest when he was bashing out a music hall number like "Flash, Bang, Wallop".

Mar 28. Warren Berlinger and Billy de Wolfe in Frank Loesser's musical **How To Succeed in Business Without Really Trying** choreographed by Bob Fosse and directed by Abe Burrows at Princes. Book by Abe Burrows, Jack Weinstock and Willie Gilbert. Gentle satire on corporate ethics follows the spectacular and unstoppable rise of a conniver supreme from window-washer to President of the Board. Berlinger was a likeable rogue; the mock-innocent grin to the audience, following every back-stabbing coup, was particularly endearing.

Apr 10. **Maurice Chevalier** at Saville. His repertoire included such old favourites as "Place Pigalle", "Valentine" and "Louise" as well as "Thank Heavens for Little Girls" and "I'm Glad I'm Not Young Any More" from his recent success in the Alan Lerner and Frederick Loewe film, *Gigi*.

Apr 23. Shakespeare's 400th birthday. Kenneth Tynan suggested that the best way to celebrate it would be to have nobody stage Shakespeare's plays for a year.

Apr 24. Edward de Souza and Rosemary Martin in Noël Coward's **Private Lives** directed by James Roose-Evans at Hampstead. Modest start in Coward's renaissance, but it was a mistake to update the play to the 1960s. Transferred to Duke of York's.

Apr 29. Madeleine Delavaivre and Jacques François in Georges Feydeau's **Le Systéme Ribadier** and Alfred de Musset's **Un Caprice** directed by Jacques François at Piccadilly. Ribadier's system is to hypnotise his wife every time he wants to go and see his mistress.

May 23. James Donald as Colenso Ridgeon and Anna Massey as Mrs Dubedat in Bernard Shaw's **The Doctor's Dilemma** directed by Donald McWhinnie at Haymarket. "Life does not cease to be funny when people die, any more than it ceases to be serious when people laugh." Wilfred Hyde-White as BB mumbled and mistimed his lines. The best performance was by Brian Bedford as Dubedat.

May 30. Leonard Bernstein's **On the Town** directed by Joe Layton at Prince of Wales. Book and lyrics by Betty Comden and Adolph Green. Landmark in American musicals, but with no names and not a patch on the definitive film version, the production closed after only six weeks.

Jun 17. Mayfair Theatre opened with Ralph Richardson, Barbara Jefford, Megs Jenkins and Michael O'Sullivan in Luigi Pirandello's **Six Characters in Search of an Author** directed by Michael Ball. Reality, illusion and incest for the discriminating playgoer. Jefford was superb as the brazen, arrogant step-daughter.
—Sir Ralph has now developed a style so idiosyncratic and personal that one is sometimes frightened that he is going to exercise it in the blue, as it were, with only passing reference to

the character he happens to be acting. But here the style and the character fit to perfection. T C WORSLEY *Financial Times*

Jun 18. Burgess Meredith and Jack MacGowran in Eugene O'Neill's **Hughie** directed by Fred Sadoff at Duchess. The first act was made up of isolated quotes. "Plenty of platitude," said *The Evening News*. "Perfectly ghastly evening," said *The Daily Mail*. The second act was better. Hughie is dead. He was a night clerk in a fleabag New York hotel, who had recently died. His friend makes out that Hughie was a bum, who needed him; but the friend is the bum, shooting a line, and, without that line to shoot, he would be as dead as Hughie.
—The paradox about Eugene O'Neill was, and is, that he was a writer of genius who couldn't write. W A DARLINGTON *Daily Telegraph*

Jun 19. John Neville and Margaret Courtenay in Bill Naughton's **Alfie** directed by Donald McWhinie at Mermaid. "The average man in his heart knows how rotten he is; he doesn't want to keep being reminded of it with somebody good round him." Alfie was a jaunty, breezy, irrepressible cockney spiv, unpleasant yet winning, and a true professional, when it came to being heartless. ("Catch 'em young. You gotta to 'elp yourself. Love has a way of going off like yesterday's milk.") Neville's unexpected casting was a revelation, vocally and physically.

Jul 1. Laurence Olivier as Astrov, Michael Redgrave as Vanya, Joan Greenwood as Ilyena, Joan Plowright as Sonia, André Morell as Serebtyakov, Fay Compton as Voynitsky, Lewis Casson as Waffles and Sybil Thorndike as Marina in Anton Chekhov's **Uncle Vanya** directed by Laurence Olivier transferred from Chichester Festival to Old Vic. One of the great Chekhovian productions, its greatness lying in the fine ensemble playing of its highly distinguished cast. Astrov – his feelings blunted by the banality of life in a provincial backwater – was one of Olivier's favourite roles.

Jul 4. Harry Secombe in **Pickwick** directed by Peter Coe at Saville. Musical. Book by Wolf Mankowitz. Music by Cyril Ornadel. Lyrics by Leslie Bricusse. It looked like Dickens, but it didn't feel like Dickens. The score never really recreated the Victorian Music Hall vulgarity it aimed at. Secombe looked as if he had come straight out of a Phiz drawing and got two rounds of applause for just doing a cartwheel. Anton Rogers, as Jingle, came nearest to capturing the spirit of the original novel.

Jul 9. Michael Denison, Dulcie Gray and Keith Baxter in Elizabeth Hart's adaptation of E M Forster's **Where Angels Fear To Tread** directed by Glen Byam Shaw transferred from New Arts to St Martin's. The old-fashioned production, the stilted dialogue and the performances were all out of a 1920s and 1930s theatrical scrapbook.

Jul 16. Derek Godfrey as Macheath in John Gay's **The Beggar's Opera** directed by Peter Wood at Aldwych (RSC). Ronald Radd as Peachum. Doris Hare as Mrs Peachum. Virginia McKenna as Lucy Lockit. The production owed a bit too much to Bertolt Brecht and Joan Littlewood. The prisoners improvised with wooden crates and rags. The songs weren't well sung and the acting, with the exception of Dorothy Tutin's Polly Peachum, was not good. High spot was designer Sean Kenny transforming the prison into a ship sailing to Australia.

Sep 3. **Martha Graham Dance Company** at Prince of Wales. A major theatrical experience. Graham's ballets were like danced plays: powerful, erotic, inexorably bleak and tragic, full of stunning angular images. Outstanding was *Night Journey*, the story of Jocasta and Oedipus, and *Circe*, a brilliant picture of hell.

Sep 4. Charles Boyer in Terence Rattigan's **Man and Boy** directed by Michael Benthall at Queen's. One of the world's great financiers (variously described as the "savior and mystery man of Europe" and the "biggest crook who ever lived") is in serious trouble. The play, inspired by Krueger's fall in the 1930s, had the makings of tragedy, but Rattigan's script constantly belittled the theme. Boyer's swindler and confidence trickster was a charmer. Barry Justice played his son he so shamefully exploits.

Sep 12. Alec Guinness, Googie Withers and Eileen Atkins in Eugene Ionesco's **Exit the King** directed by George Devine at Royal Court. A fairy tale for grown-ups. "You are going to die in an hour-and-a-half," says the Queen to the King. "You are going to die at the end of the show." The ceremony – a journey from his material kingdom to his spiritual one – took various stages from farce to tragedy, from degradation and pain to grandeur. Guinness had a splendid speech when the King (in his role of Everyman), wide-eyed with fear, desperately tries to think of any means to perpetuate his name after his death. Whenever the audience was getting particularly restless, Ionesco would remind them that it was wonderful to be able to feel bored, if the alternative was to be dead or dying.

Sep 25. Alec McCowen, Alan Webb and Ian Richardson in Rolf Hochhuth's **The Representative** directed by Clifford Williams at Aldwych (RSC). Half documentary, half play, Hochhuth condemned Pope Pius XII for failing to condemn the Final Solution during World War 2. It felt more like an illustrated lecture than a play. The production ended on that iconic newsreel image of a bulldozer bulldozing the naked, dead bodies, as if they were just so much manure.

Alec Guinness and Googie Withers in Exit the King

Sep 30. Joan Plowright in Bernard Shaw's **Saint Joan** directed by John Dexter transferred from Chichester Festival to Old Vic (NT). Plowright, sturdy, down-to-earth, spoke with tremendous passion and sincerity. Robert Lang's Bishop of Beauvais was no villain, but genuinely worried by the girl's presumption.
—The result is holy innocence that is most moving without being mawkish and most certainly without being arrogant. BERNARD LEVIN *Daily Mail*

Oct 3. Frankie Howerd, Kenneth Connor, Jon Pertwee, Robertson Hare and Eddie Gray in Stephen Sondheim's musical **A Funny Thing Happened on the Way to the Forum** directed by George Abbott at Strand. Book by Burt Shevelove and Larry Gelbart based on the plays of Plautus. The opening number, "Comedy Tonight" promised much, but the promise was only truly realized in "Everybody Ought To Have A Maid," the nearest the production came to a genuine show-stopper. The book owed much to the crude campery and verbal and physical knockabout of the music hall. ("Don't you lower your voice to me," said a harem floozy to her eunuch bodyguard.) Sondheim's lyrics had literacy and wit. Howerd scored the biggest success of his career and this led to his TV series, *Up Pompeii*.

Oct 22. The inaugural production of the National Theatre Company at Old Vic. Peter O'Toole in Shakespeare's **Hamlet**, directed by Laurence Olivier. Michael Redgrave as Claudius. Diana Wynyard as Gertrude. Rosemary Harris as Ophelia. Max Adrian as Polonius. Derek Jacobi as Laertes. Robert Stephens as Horatio. Olivier, in a programme note, linked Hamlet to Jimmy Porter. O'Toole entered from underneath the stage. The first thing the audience saw was a blonde wig, then a wracked and pained face and, finally, a tall, thin body. It was obvious right from the start, that he wasn't the Prince for the job.
—If you want to know what it's like to be lonely, really lonely, try playing Hamlet. PETER O'TOOLE *quoted by Barry Norman Daily Mail*

Nov 13. Donald Pleasence, Charles Gray and Ronald Lewis in Jean Anouilh's **Poor Bitos** directed by Shirley Butler at New Arts. Anouilh originally said he wouldn't allow the play to be produced outside of France, arguing that one didn't wash one's dirty linen abroad. Bitos, a public prosecutor in a small provincial backwater, is ruthlessly killing off those Frenchmen who collaborated with the Germans during World War 2. The local aristocracy decides to teach him a lesson and invites him to a fancy dress dinner at which they will all be dressed as French Revolutionaries. Bitos, cast in the role of Robespierre, has a demented soliloquy (a *tour de force* by Pleasence) in which he gets carried away by the idea of "a government run by a machinery of nonentities." Charles Gray's Saint-Just was the eternal bully, cynical, corrupt and vicious.

Nov 28. Edith Evans in Robert Bolt's **Gentle Jack** directed by Noël Willman at Queen's. Evans was a modern Queen Elizabeth. Kenneth Williams was a God of Lust, more pansy than Pan. Both actors were miscast and the play, a pagan rite, disappeared up its symbolism and obscurity.

Dec 3. Susannah York, James Donald and Wendy Hiller in Christopher Taylor's adaptation of Henry James's **The Wings of the Dove** directed by Frith Banbury at Lyric. American girl persuades her poor lover to propose to a dying heiress in the hope that she will accept and marry him. The idea is that when the heiress is dead they will then be rich enough to marry. The heiress's essential goodness thwarts their plan. Designer Loudon Sainthill provided a high-ceiling palazzo for a literate, civilized and stylish bit of theatre.

Dec 4. Donald Wolfit, Flora Robson and Margaret Rawlings in Henrik Ibsen's **John Gabriel Borkman** directed by David Ross at Duchess. Stodgy melodrama. "I thought I was wading in glue," said Bernard Levin in *The Daily Mail*. "The heaviest thing to descend on London since the Chiswick flyover," said Herbert Kretzmer in *The Daily Express*.

Maggie Smith and Lyn Redgrave in The Recruiting Officer

Dec 9. Marie Kean in Samuel Beckett's **Happy Days** directed by Jack MacGowran at Stratford East. Vivid moments of terror and desolation.

Dec 10. Maggie Smith as Silvia, Robert Stephens as Captain Plume and Laurence Olivier as Captain Brazen in George Farquhar's **The Recruiting Officer** directed by William Gaskill at Old Vic (NT). The officers share their beds with women and men. Brazen and Plume are much addicted to kissing each other and on their first encounter, it was only after a particularly long and warm embrace that Brazen actually asked Plume his name. Maggie Smith was enchanting when she donned breeches. Gaskill's production was a major turning point in how Restoration and post-Restoration was acted. The period costumes actually looked as if they had been worn and the men's boots were caked in mud.

1964

Jan 7. Michael Redgrave as Mr Hobson, Joan Plowright as Maggie Hobson and Frank Finlay as Willie Mossop in Harold Brighouse's **Hobson's Choice** directed by John Dexter at Old Vic (NT). The proposal scene was sheer delight. Maggie's

two moments of sentimentality were doubly moving for being so rare: firstly, when she kept a solitary flower to press in her Bible and secondly, when she refused to exchange her brass wedding ring for something grander. Redgrave, far too gentle to be the bullying father, was at his best, sitting sadly on the sofa, getting no comfort whatsoever from Mossop.

Jan 11. The War of the Roses directed by Peter Hall and John Barton at Aldwych (RSC). One of the great Shakespearian productions was drawn from the three parts of *Henry VI* and *Richard III*. The trilogy was the RSC's answer to Joan Littlewood's *Oh! What a Lovely War* and it lasted nearly ten hours: a marathon for actors and audiences alike. The excessive carnage acted like a Greek tragedy. David Warner allowed the audience to laugh at King Henry's naïvety and Christian goodness. Ashcroft's Margaret held the trilogy together, developing from an 18-year-old wanton to a crazy old witch, every facet of her character brutally and pitifully revealed. Margaret's ranting in *Richard III* made far more sense than it usually did when the play was acted on its own. Ian Holm's Richard III was not allowed to dominate the action. Instead *The War of the Roses* dominated him. The magnificent Machiavellian villain was not part of the Hall-Barton design.

Jan 14. Trevor Howard and Joyce Redman in August Strindberg's **The Father**

Uta Hagen and Arthur Hill in Who's Afraid of Virginia Woolf?

1964 World Premieres
New York
Arthur Miller's *After the Fall*
Joseph Stein, Jerry Block and
    Sheldon Harwick's *Fiddler on the
    Roof*
Jerry Herman and Michael Stewart's
    Hello, Dolly!
Edward Albee's *Tiny Alice*
James Baldwin's *Blues for Mr Charlie*
Dublin
Brian Friel's *Philadelphia, Here I
    Come*

Births
Patrick Marber, British playwright
Deaths
Brendan Behan (*b*.1923) Irish
    playwright

Ben Hecht (*b*.1894) American
    playwright
Sean O'Casey (*b*.1880) Irish
    playwright
Cole Porter (*b*.1892) American
    composer

Notes
—Peter Daubeny's World Theatre
    season begins a ten year season
—*My Fair Lady* won 8 Oscars
    including best picture and Rex
    Harrison for best actor

History
—Civil Rights Bill in USA
—Nelson Mandela sentenced to life
    imprisonment

directed by Casper Wrede at Piccadilly. "Curse you, woman – and all your sex!" cries the Captain (voicing Strindberg's own feelings). Howard, hoarse and coarse, modelled his performance on Wilfred Lawson's. His wife was conceived in terms of a 19th-century villainess. "I have never," she said, "been able to look at a man without feeling superior." The production resisted actually throwing the burning lamp in Redman's face.

Jan 28. Tom Courtenay, Cyril Cusack, Diana Wynyard and Colin Blakely in Max Frisch's **Andorra** directed by Lindsay Anderson at Old Vic (NT). Grim reminder of what the Nazis did to the Jews. A young man accepts that he is a Jew at the very moment it is proved he is definitely not a Jew.

Feb 8. Uta Hagen and Arthur Hill in Edward Albee's **Who's Afraid of Virginia Woolf?** directed by Alan Schneider at Piccadilly. Albee's dance of death is a harrowing long night's journey into day. George and Martha have been married for 23 years. He is an unsuccessful history lecturer at a New England university. She is the daughter of the Dean. Their marriage is total war and there is no limit to their sadomasochism. "You're disgusting!" screams a smooth young man who doesn't want to get involved. "I disgust me!" she retorts. Hagen and Hill were excellently matched, the loud blousy vulgarity of the wife contrasting with the needling vulgarity of the husband.
—For showy acting, Uta Hagen is superb as the wife – a piece of all-round-the-clock acting with range, attack and technical resource almost brandished contemptuously under our noses: magnificent. PHILIP HOPE-WALLACE *Guardian*
—I prize his [Edward Albee] vivid theatricality, his corrosive use of language, his marvellous insight into certain human relationships, and his basic compassion. ALAN SCHNEIDER

Feb 12. Joan Greenwood in Henrik Ibsen's **Hedda Gabler** directed by Minos Volanakis at New Arts. George Cole as Tesman. André Morell as Judge Brack. Maurice Good as Lovborg. Greenwood had the cold, aristocratic elegance that in another age would have taken Hedda straight to the guillotine.

Mar 12. Anton Chekhov's **The Seagull** directed by Tony Richardson at Queen's. Peggy Ashcroft's Ranevesky was bored, vulgar and insensitive. Vanessa Redgrave's Nina, having made comparatively little of the first two acts, succeeded with the difficult last act. Paul Rogers's Sorin, a chuckling, affected dandy, was delightful when he was trying to persuade Arkadina to give her son (Peter McEnery) a proper allowance. Peter Finch's self-effacing Trigorin was conceived in the light of Nina's disillusionment at finding him so very ordinary, rather than as the much sought-after literary lion. Richardson directed the tantrums over horses and flowers in the second act with wit.

Mar 17. Comédie Française at Aldwych. Louis Seigner and Jacques Charon in Molière's **Tartuffe** directed by Louis Seigner and Jacques Charon. Robert Hirsch in Georges Feydeau's **Un Fil à la Patte** directed by Jacques Charon. Hirsch's seedy, physically repulsive amateur songwriter was hilarious, especially when he was forced at pistol point to remove his trousers on a landing of a block of flats.

Mar 30. The Schiller Company in two plays at Aldwych. Klaus Kammer and Martin Held and in Max Frisch's **Andorra** directed by Fritz Kortner. An indictment and penance for the atrocities the Germans committed during World War 2. Held and Krammer as father and son were very moving. What gave the play an added dimension were the glib apologies from a number of witnesses for their actions and inactions. Klaus Kammer and Karin Remsing in Goethe's **Clavigo** directed by Willi Schmidt. Young man breaks off his engagement fearing the marriage will ruin his future career.

Apr 6. Kenneth Haigh, Michael Gwynn, Victor Maddern, Andrew Ray and Genevieve Ward in Albert Camus's **Caligula** directed by Peter Coe at Phoenix. Caligula, tyrant and transvestite, is encouraged to murderous excess by the Roman senate in order that he will bring about his own downfall. Haigh whipped himself into virtuoso rages, but Camus's pretentious philosophizing and endless aphorisms kept getting in his way.

Apr 7. Double bill at Old Vic (NT). Rosemary Harris, Billie Whitelaw and Robert Stephens in Samuel Beckett's **Play** directed by George Devine. Colin Blakeley and John Stride in Sophocles's **Philoctetes** directed by William Gaskill. The interval, which separated the two plays, was longer than the Beckett (which was so short that the actors went through it twice.) It still lasted under twenty minutes. The three actors, stuck Ali Baba fashion in three urns, gabbled their lines in a flat, clipped, ratatatat manner. The lighting operator had to time his cues so that the actor was lit as he spoke. It was a relief to come to the Sophocles.

Apr 21. Laurence Olivier in Shakespeare's **Othello** directed by John Dexter at Old Vic (NT). Frank Finlay as Iago. Maggie Smith as Desdemona. Derek Jacobi as Cassio. Joyce Redman as Emilia. Olivier not only looked like a black man, but he walked and talked like one. The transition from Christian nobility to barbaric fury was sudden and his disintegration was terrifying. The only actor who could have been equal to playing Iago opposite Olivier's Othello would have been Olivier himself.
—The power, passion, verisimilitude and pathos of Sir Laurence's performance are things which will be spoken of with wonder for a long time to come. PHILIP HOPE-WALLACE *Guardian*
—There is a kind of bad acting of which only a great actor is capable. I find Sir Laurence Olivier's Othello the most prodigious and perverse example of this in a decade. ALAN BRIEN *Sunday Telegraph*.

May 6. Madge Ryan and Dudley Sutton in Joe Orton's **Entertaining Mr Sloane** directed by Patrick Dromgoole at New Arts. Orton (variously described as the Oscar Wilde of the welfare state, the Douanier Rousseau of the criminal suburbs, and the Grandma Moses of the rubbish dump) had his first commercial success. The black comedy, written at a time when homosexual offenders were still going to prison, is a knowing mixture of sexual innuendo, suburban artifice and gratuitous violence. Sloane (a Joe Orton clone in black leather) is a rapacious, egotistical, amoral thug who kicks an old man to death. He is then blackmailed by the man's middle-aged son and daughter, who promise not to tell the police so long as they can both continue to employ his carnal services. Sutton was barely on stage before his trousers came off. Ryan's blowsy, affected landlady was a revue turn. The script was an outrageous mixture of violence, sex and bad taste. With hindsight it is not surprising that Orton should have been murdered by his lover, Kenneth Halliwell. Transferred to Wyndham's.
—I feel as if snakes have been writhing round my feet. W A DARLINGTON *Daily Telegraph*
—A play to make a man pull his trousers up. SEAN O'CASEY

May 12. Greek Art Theatre Company at Aldwych in Aristophanes's **The Birds** directed by Karolos Koun. Written in 414 BC, the play combines religious ceremony and satire. The production's huge success was directly attributable to Koun's imaginative handling of the Chorus. You didn't need to understand a word of Greek in order to enjoy the performance. The pleasure came from the singing, the dancing and watching the actors being birds. The pettiness of the quarrelling gods was accentuated by their huge carnival heads and tiny bodies.

May 26. Moscow Arts Theatre at Aldwych in Mikhail Bulgakov's adaptation of Nikoli Gogol's **Dead Souls** (the original Constantin Stanislavsky production) and Anton Chekhov's **The Cherry Orchard** directed by Victor Y Stanistin.

Jun 9. Michael Redgrave and Maggie Smith in Henrik Ibsen's **The Master Builder** directed by Peter Wood at Old Vic (NT). The surprise was that Redgrave should play Solness so young and that Smith should find so much comedy in Hilde Wangel; sadly, they failed to generate any sexual excitement. Celia Johnson, as Solness's wife, had that cold, duty-like quality; her confession that she loved her dolls more than her children was the production's high spot. It was Johnson's wide-eyed fear, which gave the fatal climb off-stage its huge tension on stage. When Olivier took over Solness from Redgrave, Maggie Smith and Joan Plowright alternated Hilde. It was during this production that Olivier's paralyzing stage-fright began and would continue until 1970.

Jun 18. Newton Blick, Doris Hare, Bryan Pringle, Janet Suzman, Brewster Mason and Patrick Magee in Harold Pinter's **The Birthday Party** directed by Harold Pinter at Aldwych (RSC). Magee was a sadistic and sinister thug. The tearing of the newspaper into equal strips was riveting.

Jun 25. David Rudkin's **Afore Night Come** directed by Clifford Williams transferred to Aldwych (RSC).

Jul 9. Patrick Magee and Jack MacGowran in Samuel Beckett's **Endgame** directed by Donald McWhinnie at Aldwych (RSC).

—The grave error of most people approaching Mr Beckett's work is that they seek for meanings that are not contained in the text. They seek symbols, they seek hidden, subtle meanings that aren't there at all. JACK MACGOWRAN *in a programme note*
—Mr Beckett's plays may be static but they are not sterile and this one is alive and vigorous throughout, coached in rhythmic, allusive, fresh and ear-catching prose. BERNARD LEVIN *Daily Mail*

Aug 19. Laurence Harvey and Elizabeth Larner in Alan Jay Lerner and Frederick Loewe's musical **Camelot** designed by John Truscott and directed by Robert Helpmann at Drury Lane. Based on T H White's *The Once and Future King.* Harvey talked his way through the songs in the Rex Harrison manner. It was of this show that people said you came out whistling the scenery.
—As Guinevere Miss Elizabeth Larner raises insipidity to the status of a new art form. BERNARD LEVIN *Daily Mail*

Aug 20. Patrick Magee as de Sade and Glenda Jackson as Charlotte Corday in Peter Weiss's **The Persecution and Assassination of Marat as performed by the Inmates of the Asylum of Charenton under the direction of the Marquis de Sade** directed by Peter Brook at Aldwych (RSC). "I haven't seen the play," the wags used to say, "but I've read the title." Between 1797 and 1811 the Director of the Charenton Asylum established regular theatrical entertainments in his clinic as part of the therapeutic treatment of his patients. Sade, an inmate from 1803 until his death, became the resident playwright and director. The performances were attended by fashionable Paris society who came to gawp. Brook rehearsed the cast for two months, beginning with workshops on madness. Jackson was convinced they were all going loony. *Marat/Sade* was not a rewarding evening for the actors. They were merely Brook's puppets. In the curtain-call the actors used to stand in character, staring at the audience, waiting for them to leave first. People in the front row used to get embarrassed and apologise to the "lunatics" and explain they had trains to catch and sneak out.
—Everything about this play is designed to crack the spectator on the jaw, then douse him with ice-cold water, then force him to assess intelligently what has happened to him, then give him a kick in the balls, then bring him to his senses again. PETER BROOK

Sep 9. Nicol Williamson in John Osborne's **Inadmissible Evidence** directed by Anthony Page at Royal Court. Harassed solicitor, "irredeemably mediocre", up to his eyes in domestic and professional troubles, is on the verge of a nervous breakdown. He knows from his own experience, that marriage, by its very nature, is already grounds for divorce for many people. Clients, employees, mistresses and his wife gradually draw away from him, until finally he has nobody, except the Law Society at his heels. Osborne admitted that writing the play had left him permanently despoiled. It had all his familiar rage, contempt and sarcasm and Williamson, in a long and gruelling part, was excellent. He won the Plays and Players award for best actor, based on the voting of the London theatre critics.
—[Nicol Williamson] This twenty-seven-year-old, pouting, delinquent cherub produced the face to match the torment below the surface. He's much too young, but no matter. He is old within. JOHN OSBORNE

Oct 1. The RSC celebrated Christopher Marlowe's 400th birthday with Clifford Williams's production of **The Jew of Malta** at Aldwych. Unable to decide whether to take Barabas seriously or to send him up, Clive Revill tried to do both.

Oct 27. Edith Evans, Maggie Smith, Roland Culver, Robert Stephens, Robert Lang, Derek Jacobi and Lynn Redgrave in Noël Coward's **Hay Fever** directed by Noël Coward at Old Vic (NT). Evans knew how to play Judith Bliss, but she was too old and hadn't the energy. Her casting affected the comedy. It was difficult to laugh at Judith's endless references to her "old" age. The best performance was by Maggie Smith as Myra, who "goes around using sex as a sort of shrimping-net". She got a round when she came on and then immediately got another just for the sexy way she looked the man who had opened the door up and down. Smith enhanced the most ordinary line ("This haddock is disgusting"). Redgrave, playing a lisping, silly, gauche cry-baby, with clunking necklace, was very funny.
—I'm thrilled and flattered and frankly a little flabbergasted that the National Theatre should have had the curious perceptiveness to choose a very early play of mine, and to give it a cast that could easily play the Albanian telephone directory. NOËL COWARD

Oct 29. David Warner, Donald Sinden, Brenda Bruce, Patsy Byrne and Nicholas Selby in Henry Living's **Eh?** directed by Peter Hall at Aldwych (RSC). Farce. A boiler man, an anarchic innocent, drives everybody up the wall with his honesty. The long-legged, tight-suited Warner looked like an animated maypole. The star turn was the boiler (designed by John Bury) which belched steam and made splendid noises.

Nov 18. Bruce Forsyth in **Little Me** choreographed by Bob Fosse and directed by Arthur Lewis at Cambridge. Musical. Book by Neil Simon. Music by Cy Coleman. Lyrics by Carolyn Leigh. Based on novel by Patrick Dennis. Satire on show biz. Anybody expecting to see Belle Poitrine's salacious memories lifted directly from the printed page on to the stage was bound to be in for a big disappointment. The musical was only on nodding terms with Patrick Dennis's amusing spoof. Bruce Forsyth played all the men in Belle Poitrine's life: blue-eyed aristocrat; an old man à la

Robert Stephens and Colin Blakely in The Royal Hunt of the Sun

Scrooge; a French cabaret artist; a German film director; a short-sighted American soldier; and a dying European Prince. His characterizations extended no further than throwing on yet another costume and yet another wig. The show's high spot was Bob Fosse's choreography. Sven Swenson was a very stylish, sexy dancer.

Nov 23. **Marlene Dietrich** at Queen's. Encased in fur, still unbelievably glamorous, she was everybody's idea of a *femme fatale*, and drew applause by merely standing there. She sang "The Boys in the Back Room", "Falling in Love", "Lola" and "The Laziest Girl in Town". The high spot was the incomparable and deeply moving "Where Have All the Flowers Gone?" Burt Bacharach's orchestrations were excellent throughout.

Dec 2. Spike Milligan, Joan Greenwood and Bill Owen in **Son of Oblomov** directed by Frank Dunlop at Comedy. Freely adapted from a play by Riccardo Aragno and based on Goncharov's novel. Milligan's ad-libbing was always hit and miss. His excuse for ad-libbing was because the original play was "diabolical"; the real reason was that he couldn't act. Greenwood was wasted.
—Hilarious hotchpotch of free association, extravagant usual goonery and brusque (if hardly Brechtian) alienation. *The Times*

Dec 8. Robert Stephens as Atahuallpa and Colin Blakely as Pizarro in Peter Shaffer's **The Royal Hunt of the Sun** designed by Michael Annals and directed by John Dexter and Desmond O'Donovan transferred from Chichester to Old Vic (NT). Pizarro's conquest of Peru was not just a search for gold, but a search for God, a search for belief, a search for the meaning of death. The play opened with the death of Atahuallpa. His people gather round his corpse. They are not alarmed because they know he is immortal. They start to pray to the Sun, his father. The Incas wore beautiful ceremonial masks and at the end of each prayer they turned round to face the audience, waiting for the Sun to give Atahuallpa back his life. Only gradually does it dawn on them that their god has failed them and that Atahuallpa really is dead. Stephens had a memorable first entrance when the huge stage sun opened to reveal him standing there, a noble and striking figure, superbly costumed. The spectacle of the Spaniards on the march and the choreographed fights always had more impact than the script.

—A third seeing confirms and strengthens my belief that no greater play has been written and produced in our language in our lifetime. BERNARD LEVIN *Daily Mail*

—Peter Shaffer's *The Royal Hunt of the Sun* is an intellectual spectacular, a de Mille epic for educated audiences, an eye-dazzling, ear-buzzing, button-holing blend of *Ben Hur*, *The King and I* and *The Devils*. ALAN BRIEN *Sunday Telegraph*.

Dec 22. Kenneth More and Millicent Martin in **Our Man Crichton** directed by Clifford Williams at Shaftesbury. Musical based on J M Barrie's *The Admirable Crichton*. Book and Lyrics by Herbert Kretzmer. Music by David Lee. More couldn't sing and should have done the play instead.

Dec 30. Alfred Lynch as Estragon, Nicol Williamson as Vladimir, Jack MacGowran as Lucky and Paul Curran as Pozzo in Samuel Beckett's **Waiting for Godot** directed by Anthony Page at Royal Court. Ten years after its premiere the play was hailed as a masterpiece. "Nothing happens," says one tramp. "I've been better entertained," says the other. The audience laughed uneasily.

—This is a play full of implications and every important statement may be taken at three or four levels. But the actor has only to find the dominant ones because he does so does not mean the other levels will be lost. All that matters is the laugh and the tear. SAMUEL BECKETT *at rehearsals quoted by* KENNETH PEARSON *Sunday Times*

1965

Jan 19. Colin Blakely as John Proctor, Joyce Redman as Goodwife Proctor and Robert Lang as the Reverend Hale in Arthur Miller's **The Crucible** directed by Laurence Olivier at Old Vic (NT). The hysteria and the violence make twice their impact for being found beneath a calm, unemotional Puritan front. There is a frightening scene when Proctor's wife lies to save his life and everybody knows and can see that she is lying, except the Deputy Governor.

Feb 16. Maggie Smith as Beatrice and Robert Stephens as Benedict in Shakespeare's **Much Ado About Nothing** directed by Franco Zeffirelli at Old Vic (NT). Albert Finney as Don Pedro. Ian McKellen as Claudio. Smith, blonde, bedraggled and slatternly, looked as if she had just got out of bed. Her lips were smeared with lipstick and her hair needed a good brush.

Mar 11. Bettina Jonic in Bertolt Brecht and Kurt Weill's **Happy End** directed by Michael Geliot at Royal Court A romance between a Chicago gangster and a Salvation Army lieutenant sounds familiar but *Happy End* predates Guys and Dolls by 20 years and it even predates Damon Runyon's *The Idyll of Miss Sarah Brown* on which *Guys and Dolls* was based. The true source is Bernard Shaw's *Major Barbara* and Edward Sheldon's *Salvation Nell*. The Salvation Army rejects the lieutenant: "You may be a poor sinner but you are not the kind of poor sinner we want." The show had a Marxist message: "Robbing a bank is no greater a crime than owning one. Blasting open a safe is nothing – We've got to blast open the big gang that keeps the safe locked."

Mar 16. Robert Eddison, Rosalind Atkinson and Sonia Dresdel in Luigi Pirandello's **Right You Are If You Think You Are** directed by Robin Midgley at Mermaid. The puzzle centres on the identity of a man's wife. Is she his first wife? Or is she really his second wife pretending to be his first wife? Who is lying? Who is mad? The wife says, "I am whoever you think I am."

Mar 17. John Osborne's **Inadmissible Evidence** directed by Anthony Page transferred to Wyndham's.

Mar 22. Theatre de France at Aldwych. Genevieve Page, Jean Louis-Barrault and Jean Desailly in Jean Racine's **Andromaque**.

—If ever there was a performance to convince British audiences that Racine's greatness is no academic myth it is Mlle Page's mighty projection of uncontrollable passion and complex inner turmoil through the iron severities of the language. *The Times*

Mar 24. Mark Eden and Siân Phillips in Tennessee Williams's **The Night of the Iguana** directed by Philip Wiseman at Savoy. Episcopalian priest, defrocked for heresy and fornicating, becomes a tour guide and takes a party of Baptist women round Mexico. He has just seduced a teenager and is on the verge of a breakdown. A 40-year-old spinster from New England and her 97-year-old grandfather are destitute and travel from one hotel to another paying as they go with her watercolours and his recitals of his poetry. The film with Richard Burton and Deborah Kerr had just been released, which didn't help either the actors or the box office.

Mar 26. Theatre de France in a double-bill at Aldwych. Jean-Louis Barrault in Eugene Ionesco's **Le Pieton de l'air**, directed by Jean-Louis Barrault. A dream-like fantasy about death. Madeleine Renaud and Jean Desailly in Georges Feydeau's **Mais n'te promene donc pas toute nue!** directed by Jean-Louis Barrault. Crude music hall sketch: politician's wife, who wanders about her apartment all day in the flimsiest

1965 World Premieres
New York
  Neil Simon's *The Odd Couple*
Johannesburg
  Athol Fugard's *Hello and Goodbye*
Berlin
  Peter Weiss's *The Investigation*
Moscow
  Aleksei Arbuzov's *The Promise*

Deaths
T S Eliot (*b.*1888), British poet, playwright

Somerset Maugham (*b.*1874), British playwright, novelist

Notes
—First Commonwealth Festival of Arts held in Britain

History
—Death of Winston Churchill
—Malcolm X shot dead
—War between India and Pakistan
—Unilateral declaration of independence by Rhodesia

of night dresses, gets stung on the bottom by a wasp and begs her husband to remove the sting and when he declines, thinks nothing of asking two complete strangers.

Apr 1. Theatre de France at Aldwych. Jean-Louis Barrault and Genevieve Page in Paul Claudel's **Le Soulier de Satin** directed by Jean-Louis Barrault. A woman surrenders a slipper to the Virgin Mary with a prayer to the effect that should she ever prove unfaithful she should limp ever after.

Apr 3. Theatre de France at Aldwych. Madeleine Renaud and Jean-Louis Barrault in Samuel Beckett's **Oh! Les beaux jours** directed by Roger Blin. Barrault described the play as "a hymn to life".

Apr 6. Catherine Lacey as Mrs Alving, Leonard Rossiter as Pastor Manders and Barry Warren as Oswald in Henrik Ibsen's **Ghosts** directed by Adrian Rendle at Stratford East. Rossiter walked the tightrope in the first two acts, managing to be both funny and real; but in the third act defeated him and he became merely a comic character and played to almost continuous laughter

—Leonard Rossiter's Pastor Manders is one of the funniest and most savage portraits of a hypocrite I have ever seen. ALAN BRIEN *Sunday Telegraph*

Apr 8. Compagnie de Giovani at Aldwych. Romola Valli and Rossella Falk in Luigi Pirandello's **Six Characters in Search of an Author** directed by Georgio De Lullo. The most startling innovation was to remind audiences that the six characters are also played by actors. Valli and Falk, as father and stepdaughter, had tremendous power: her contemptuous laughter was the perfect complement for his nauseating, humiliating self-disgust.

Apr 12. Greek Art Theatre Company in Aeschylus's **The Persians** directed by Karolos Koun at Aldwych. Premiered in 472 BC, eight years after the Battle of Salamis, in which the whole army had been destroyed and with it the flower of Persian youth. Aeschylus wrote with a mixture of compassion for the vanquished and pride for the victors. The magnificent production was epic enough to fill the theatre at Dionysus. The grief-stricken figures in their stylized movement looked as if they had stepped off a Grecian urn. Their anguish was overwhelming. The Chorus, vocally and physically, reached its height in the raising of the dead King Darius. The company also revived their production of Aristophanes' **The Birds**.

Apr 17. Ken Dodd in **Doddy's Here** at London Palladium. The last of the great vaudeville comedians.

Apr 19. Derek Fowlds, Ann Holloway and Richard Brooke in Frank Wedekind's **Spring Awakening** directed by Desmond O'Donovan at Royal Court. First English production. The Lord Chamberlain refused to allow the actors playing the boys to kiss, embrace and caress. He banned any mention of penis and vagina, and insisted that the masturbation scene was cut.

Apr 21. Nigel Patrick as Gary Essendine in Noël Coward's **Present Laughter** directed by Nigel Patrick at Queen's. Richard Briers had his funny moments as the author from Uckfield, but it wasn't until Garry Essendine was blowing his top, betraying every confidence, that the production actually came to life.

Apr 26. Habimah National Theatre at Aldwych. Eva Lion in Salomon Anski's **Dybbuk** directed by I Yakhtangov at Aldwych. Museum piece in slow motion.

May 3. Al Freeman, Jr. and Beverley Todd in James Baldwin's **Blues for Mister Charlie** directed by Burgess Meredith at Aldwych. White storekeeper kills young Negro and is acquitted by racially-prejudiced court. Members of British National Party gate-crashed the theatre.

—The great and memorable effect of the play lies in the pity and the compassion of its utter, its unqualified, its complete hopelessness. HAROLD HOBSON *Sunday Times*

May 4. Margaret Rutherford and Sidney James in George S Kaufman and Howard

Teichmann's **The Solid Gold Cadillac** directed by Arthur Lewis at Saville. The satire at the expense of corruption in big business was slim. Rutherford was miscast as a small investor who turns up at a shareholders' meeting and embarrasses the board of directors by asking questions about their salaries.

May 6. Dorothy Tutin as Queen Victoria in **Portrait of a Queen** directed by Val May at Vaudeville. Derek Waring as Prince Albert. The script was drawn from Victoria's private letters and diaries.

May 10. Michael Hordern in John Whiting's **Saint's Day** at Stratford East, directed by David Jones. Hordern returned to the role he had created in 1951 and the play still didn't work.

May 12. Madge Ryan in Bertolt Brecht's **Mother Courage and Her Children** directed by William Gaskill at Old Vic (NT). Lyn Redgrave as the dumb daughter.
—One day perhaps a producer will come along prepared to jettison all the Brechtian paraphernalia and produce his plays as if they were plays and not textbooks. B A Young *Financial Times*

May 18. Actors' Studio Theatre at Aldwych. George C Scott, Kim Stanley and Sandy Dennis in Anton Chekhov's **The Three Sisters** directed by Lee Strasberg. Four hours of boredom, a morass of self-indulgence, and a travesty of a masterpiece.

May 27. Ian Holm in **Henry V** directed by John Barton and Trevor Nunn at Aldwych (RSC). The production was once part of the whole history cycle at Stratford and this explained how Shakespeare's most patriotic jingoistic play had come to resemble an anti-war tract on the lines of Bertolt Brecht's *Mother Courage*. Holm, singularly lacking in charm, took his cue from the French Princess, who described Henry as being "created with a stubborn outside, with an aspect of iron".

Jun 2. Yvonne Arnaud Theatre opened with Ingrid Bergman, Michael Redgrave, Max Adrian, Fay Compton, Daniel Massey and Jennifer Hilary in Ivan Turgenev's **A Month in the Country** directed by Michael Redgrave.

Jun 3. Paul Rogers, Ian Holm, John Normington, Terence Rigby, Vivien Merchant and Michael Bryant in Harold Pinter's **The Homecoming** designed by John Bury and directed by Peter Hall at Aldwych (RSC). The action was set in a hanger. Teddy brings his wife home to introduce her to his family for the first time. His father, who hasn't had a whore in the house since his wife died, instantly recognises "a dirty tart" when he sees one. Members of the audience presumed he has made an embarrassing mistake. They soon found out there is no mistake and that Ruth will fill the gap left by the dead mother and be mother, whore and Madonna to the whole family.
—One of the best overall productions the Royal Shakespeare Company has given us in a long time and one of the most striking new plays ever. JOHN RUSSELL TAYLOR *Plays and Players*
—The play blithely plumbs the depths of human degradation and is assuredly not for all tastes. ERIC SHORTER *Daily Telegraph*

Jun 17. Beryl Reid and Eileen Atkins in Frank Marcus's **The Killing of Sister George** directed by Val May at Duke of York's. Sister George is a favourite character in a popular radio serial. The BBC decides "to kill her off" in order to boost their listening figures. Her death is timed to coincide with Road Safety Week. The sacking of the actress coincides with the break-up of her relationship. The plot is given a nasty twist when the producer (Lally Bowers) arrives on the day of George's "funeral" to offer the actress (Beryl Reid) the part of a cow in a new children's serial; and then to add injury to insult, walks off with her partner (Eileen Atkins). Reid, a revue artiste and music hall comedienne, making her first West End appearance as an actress, was very funny and very moving.

Jun 30. Maximilian Schell as Alfred Redl in John Osborne's **A Patriot for Me** directed by Anthony Page at Royal Court. The action is set between 1890–1913. A railway clerk's son becomes one of the Austro-Hungarian Royal Imperial Army's most distinguished officers. A brilliant career finds him head of the secret service from which position he betrays his country to the Russians, not for any ideological reason, but merely to pay his debts and to keep himself and his numerous boyfriends in style. He seems to have slept with the whole army, officers and other ranks. Laurence Olivier said that had he been twenty years younger he would have given up the National Theatre to play Redl. In the event, no other English actor evidently being willing to play a homosexual in 1965, the role went to Maximilian Schell. Osborne wrote Baron Von Epp especially for George Devine but he only got to play the part after Anthony Page had offered the role to Micheal Mac Liammoir, Noël Coward and John Gielgud and they had all turned it down. The Baron presides over a drag ball, which was the main reason for the Lord Chamberlain banning the play. (The English Stage Company turned the Royal Court into a club and played to full houses.) Maximilian Schell was dull. Devine had a heart attack towards the end of the run.

Jul 15. Roy Dotrice, Patrick Magee, Ian Richardson and Glenda Jackson in Bertolt

Brecht's **Puntila and His Servant Matti** directed by Michel Saint-Denis at Aldwych (RSC). This farcical allegory on class conflict and satire on paternalistic, a crude bit of Communist pamphleteering, was dismissed by most critics as "tiring claptrap" and "merciless rubbish."

Aug 3. Alec McCowen and Peter Cushing in Ben Travers's **Thark** directed by Ray Cooney at Garrick. The actors played it as a 1920s period piece on their own comedic terms and did not give pale imitations of Tom Walls and Ralph Lynn.

Aug 8. D H Lawrence's **A Collier's Friday Night** directed by Peter Gill at Royal Court. Lawrence, writing in 1913, said: "I believe that just as an audience was found in Russia for Chekhov so an audience might be found in England for some of my stuff, if there was a man to whip them in." That man fifty years on was Peter Gill, meticulous in his detail.

Aug 9. The Berliner Ensemble at Old Vic with four plays by Brecht: **The Resistible Rise of Arturo Ui, Coriolanus, The Threepenny Opera** and **The Days of the Commune**. Ekkehard Schall's Chaplinque Ui/Hitler, ranting and raving to a background of jazz and machine-gun fire, was a brilliant comic characterisation. Wolf Kaiser was equally memorable as Mack the Knife, an immensely stylish villain in Brecht's update of Gay's operas to the Edwardian era.

Sep 22. Alastair Sim, Dora Bryan, George Cole, Kenneth Haigh, June Ritchie, Athene Seyler and James Bolam in Bernard Shaw's **Too True To Be Good** directed by Frank Dunlop at Garrick. Cole as the sergeant had the best lines and what he had to say about war and destruction were easily the most heartfelt things in the production. The rest of the play was pretty heavy going.

Sep 23. Ingrid Bergman, Michael Redgrave, Emlyn Williams, Fay Compton, Jeremy Brett and Joanna Dunham in Ivan Turgenev's **A Month in the Country** directed by Michael Redgrave at Cambridge. The best play Chekhov did not write. Bergman in her more lyrical moments recalled the radiance of Greta Garbo in *Camille*, but she tended to rob her more vicious lines of their sting by playing them for comedy.
—Truth to say, she was not at the top of her form, but in most people's opinion and in mine it simply didn't matter. Her capacious good nature shone through everything she did. She was a lovely paradox: a very private person whose whole personality was on display. MICHAEL REDGRAVE *In My Mind's Eye*

Sep 30. John Gielgud, Claire Bloom, Roland Culver, Yvonne Mitchell, Angela Baddeley, Richard Pasco and Edward Atienza in Anton Chekhov's **Ivanov** directed by John Gielgud at Phoenix. Ivanov, weak, indolent, self-centred, lets everything slide. Edward Atienza was a loveable old bore, one moment relishing the idea of doing something shabby like marrying a rich widow for her money and the next despairing at the very thought, Yvonne Mitchell as the unloved Anna, dying of consumption, had an unexpected sense of humour.

Oct 6. Hermione Gingold in Arthur Kopit's **Oh Dad, Poor Dad, Mama's Hung You in the Closet and I'm Feeling So Sad** directed by Charles Forsythe at Piccadilly. This bizarre, black comedy, a send-up of a Tennessee Williams drama, was not so much Grand Guignol as Grande Gingold.

Oct 12. Albert Finney, Robert Stephens, Frank Wylie and Geraldine McEwan in John Arden's **Armstrong's Last Goodnight** directed by John Dexter and William Gaskill at Old Vic (NT). Written in mock 16th-century Scots it was difficult to know what was going on.

Oct 12. Claudia McNeil in James Baldwin's **The Amen Corner** directed by Lloyd Richards transferred from Edinburgh Festival to Saville. Baldwin traced the decline and fall of Sister Margaret of The Holy Rollers, an evangelical sect.

Oct 20. John Stride and Geraldine McEwan in William Congreve's **Love for Love** directed by Peter Wood at Old Vic (NT). Wood cut the usual Restoration paraphernalia of fans, curtsies, bowing and general affectation to the very minimum and played out the heartless and vulgar intrigue against a Hogarthian background. Lila de Nobili's superb sets looked lived in. Wood's realism was carried to such extremes that Stride and McEwan didn't wear any make-up. Colin Blakeley was delightful as the simple sailor whose entire vocabulary is drawn from nautical terms. Lynn Redgrave was a big, wholesome Miss Prue. Joyce Redman's Mrs Frail was a tiny galleon in full sail, all eyebrows and oeillade. Laurence Olivier, who played Tattle, the faded and effeminate beau who is unable to keep a secret, was very funny when, to his horror, he found himself married to Frail.

Nov 3. Dennis Waterman, Barbara Ferris, Ronald Pickup and Tony Selby in Edward Bond's **Saved** directed by William Gaskill at Royal Court. The Lord Chamberlain banned this exhibition of ignorance, apathy, sadism, lust and crude language. The performances were for club members only. Many people left during the interval. The most revolting thing was the brutal stoning to death of a baby in a pram. There were

Mary Martin and Loring Smith in Hello Dolly!

cries of "Revolting! Dreadful!" from the audience and uproar in the press. Laurence Olivier in *The Observer* came to the play's defence, saying "the grown-ups of this country should have the courage to look at it".

—Only those with strong stomachs and a highly cultivated sense of tolerance should venture to Royal Court. MILTON SHULMAN *Evening Standard*

—Will supply valuable ammunition to those who attack modern theatre as half-baked, gratuitously violent and squalid. Why on earth did the theatre accept it? *The Times*

—There comes a point when both life and art are irretrievably debased, and Edward Bond's play in this production is well past that point. J W LAMBERT *Sunday Times*

—If such things are really going on in South London they are properly the concern of the police and the magistrates rather than audiences of theatres even the Royal Court. B A YOUNG *Financial Times*

Nov 10. Alfred Marks, John Alderton, Melvyn Hayes and Ruth Dunning in Bill Naughton's **Spring and Port Wine** directed by Allan Davis at Mermaid.

Nov 17. Robert Stephens as Tom Wrench and Louise Purnell as Trelawny in Arthur Wing Pinero's **Trelawny of the "Wells"** directed by Desmond O'Donovan at Old Vic (NT). A rightly unashamedly sentimental performance, a glossary of stage tricks and conventions, lovingly recreated

Nov 24. Peter Brook's production of Peter Weiss's **Marat/Sade** returned to Aldwych (RSC). Patrick Magee as Sade.

Dec 1. Gwen Ffrangcon-Davies, Anna Massey, Ian McShane and George Baker in Tennessee Williams's The **Glass Menagerie** directed by Vivian Matalon at Haymarket. Young man brings home a gentleman-caller for his crippled sister, only to

discover too late that he is already engaged to another girl. Beautifully acted and hauntingly sad.

Dec 2. Mary Martin in Jerry Herman's musical **Hello, Dolly!** at Drury Lane. Book by Michael Stewart based on Thornton Wilder's *The Matchmaker*. Choreography and direction by Gower Champion. The production was notable for its style and wit. Martin, dressed in dazzling red, stopped the show when she sang the title song.

Dec 9. Ian Cuthbertson, Ronald Pickup, John Castle, Victor Henry, Sebastian Shaw and Frances Cuka in John Arden's **Sergeant Musgrave's Dance** directed by Jane Howell at Royal Court. Cuthbertson's swart and sardonic sergeant towered over everybody.

Dec 15. Joe Brown, Anna Neagle, Derek Nimmo and Hy Hazell in **Charlie Girl** directed by Wallace Douglas at Adelphi. Musical. Book by Hugh and Margaret Williams with Ray Cooney. Music and lyrics by David Heneker and John Taylor. This vacuous piece of cardboard was mounted strictly for the coach trade. Nimmo hogged away and gave his usual silly ass performance. Brown was a very poor man's Tommy Steele. Lambasted by the critics it broke all records. Bernard Levin described it as "Somewhere between perfectly frightful and dead 'orrible." 2202 performances.

Dec 22. David Warner in Shakespeare's **Hamlet** directed by Peter Hall at Aldwych (RSC). Hamlet was a drop-out student. Janet Suzman was a butch Ophelia. "The language," said Philip Hope-Wallace in *The Guardian*, "is treated in the most prosaic, flat and unprofitable manner whenever possible."

1966

Jan 12. Ralph Richardson, Harry Andrews, Judy Campbell and Keith Baxter in Bernard Shaw's **You Never Can Tell** directed by Glen Byam Shaw at Theatre Royal, Haymarket. The casting of Richardson as the affable and philosophical waiter threw the production off balance. The audience longed for Richardson to come ambling back.

Jan 19. Paul Scofield as Khlestakov in Gogol's **The Government Inspector** directed by Peter Hall at Aldwych (RSC). Paul Rogers as the Mayor. Khlestakov was in high heaven when he was being royally entertained by the Mayor. He sat there, a drink and cigar in hand, the tired dandy, affected, effete, and amazed to find everybody so gullible. His pretensions were farcical. Scofield deployed a wide variety of accents which often changed in mid-sentence. The production was notable for its gallery of grotesques. The characters, cruelly observed in all their grubbiness, were straight out of the Russian cartoonists of the period. David Warner's postmaster looked like something left over from the French Revolution.

Jan 26. Alec Guinness and Anthony Quayle in Arthur Miller's **Incident in Vichy** directed by Peter Wood at Phoenix. Jews were being rounded up and dispatched to the concentration camps. The doctor, the poet, the communist, the businessman, the actor, the aristocrat, etc, were not so much characters as spokespersons. Miller's premise was that the Germans only did what the rest of the world had wanted them to do. Guinness was cast as the only gentile, a dilettante Austrian prince who had been arrested by mistake. He gave up his life that a Jew might live.

Feb 8. Albert Finney, John Stride, Geraldine McEwan and Edward Hardwicke in Georges Feydeau's **A Flea in Her Ear** translated by John Mortimer and directed by Jacques Charon at Old Vic (NT). Bourgeois husband and a bordello hall porter look exactly alike. Finney played both roles. McEwan as his wife, her eyes darting hither and thither, was in fine form and never more so than when she adopted a patronising tone to the hall porter: "We've had quite enough of this," she said, thinking her husband was pretending to be a hall porter. The second act in the bordello with all the frantic coming and going was hilarious. Hardwicke, as a young man with a cleft palate, was a memorable creation.

Mar 8. Albert Finney and Maggie Smith in August Strindberg's **Miss Julie** directed by Michael Elliott transferred from Chichester Festival to Old Vic (NT). Julie, beautiful, refined, educated, a victim of her frustration, class and hereditary, recklessly throws herself at her father's valet. She taunts, goads and insults him until she finally, gets what she wants, only to be humiliated. Maggie Smith, no aristocrat, was at her best when pleading with the cook, babbling on about starting a hotel at Lake Como, pathetically searching for a way out. Strindberg played in a double-bill with Peter Shaffer's **Black Comedy** directed by John Dexter. Young sculptor and his fiancée are expecting a visit from a millionaire art collector when a fuse blows and plunges them into darkness. The action takes place in the dark. But so that the audience can see what is going on, the stage is brilliantly illuminated. When the lights are on, as far as the characters on stage are concerned, the action is taking place in the dark. When the lights are off, the action is taking place in the light. Shaffer got the idea from a famous scene in Peking Opera in which two warriors fight in the dark with all the lights on. Louise Purnell (with her grating debbie voice) and Derek Jacobi (carting furniture in and out of his flat) were very funny.

Mar 28. Compagnia dei Giovani at Aldwych. Romolo Valli and Rosella Falk in Luigi Pirandello's **The Rules of the Game** directed by Giorgio de Lullo. Sardonic comedy of manners written in 1918, anticipates Anouilh's *pieces noires*. Husband, wife and lover play their civilised game up to the hilt. Valli was smooth and witty as the seemingly complacent husband, who bides his time and very neatly side-steps the death-trap set for him by his wife. He agrees to fight the duel she has forced on him, only insisting her lover be his second. Then at the very last minute, he withdraws, leaving the lover forced to take his place (the rules of the game) and fight on the disadvantageous terms of an unconditional duel he himself had insisted on. The lover is killed. The production was highly stylized. The glossy, elegant surface of Pier Luigi Pizzi's striking cubist set suited Falk's edgy send-up of a femme fatale.

Mar 31. Compagnia dei Giovani at Aldwych in Luigi Pirandello's **Six Characters in Search of an Author**.

Apr 11. John Castle in Harley Granville-Barker's **The Voysey Inheritance** at Royal Court directed by Jane Howell. The play (a major discovery) survived the miscasting and a painfully slow production.

Apr 12. The National Theatre of Greece at Aldwych. Katina Paxinou in Euripides's **Hecuba** and Alexis Minotis in Sophocles's **Oedipus** and **Oedipus at Colonus** directed by Alexis Minotis. The eloquent and formidable Paxinou, a superb technician, was monumental in her grief.
—[Katina Paxinou] can conjure up low notes from the depths of Hades. FELIX BARKER *Evening News*

1966 World Premieres
New York
John Kander, Fred Ebb and Joe Masteroff's *Cabaret*
Edward Albee's *A Delicate Balance*
Neil Simon, Cy Coleman and Dorothy Fields' *Sweet Charity*
Edinburgh
Tom Stoppard's *Rosencrantz and Guildenstern Are Dead*

Births
Mark Ravenhill, British playwright

Deaths
George Devine (*b.*1910), British actor, director, theatre manager
Edward Gordon Craig (*b.*1872), British director, designer, theorist
Wilfred Lawson (*b.*1900), British actor
Ada Reeve (*b.*1874), British music hall artiste

History
—Indira Gandhi became Indian Prime Minister
—Cultural Revolution in China
—First lunar soft landing

Apr 13. Barbra Streisand as Broadway comedienne and singer Fanny Brice in Jule Styne's musical **Funny Girl** directed by Lawrence Kasha at Prince of Wales. Book by Isobel Lennard. Lyrics by Bob Merrill. Streisand was described as "a great original" by *The Sunday Express* and likened by one critic to a sea-sick ferret. She was very larky with lots of funny faces and angular movements. High spot was the debunking of vaudeville and the Ziegfield Follies. The show was always more about Streisand than it was about Fanny Brice.
—She has the definitive voice of the age. She also has a beautiful pair of legs. And the most famous and prominent nose since Cleopatra. ROBIN DOUGLAS-HOME *Sunday Express*

Apr 14. Noël Coward, Irene Worth and Lilli Palmer in Noël Coward's **Suite in Three Keys** directed by Vivian Matalon at Queen's. Three plays set in a Swiss hotel. **Song at Twilight**: Famous author (Noël Coward), an insufferable old man, is accused of "complacent cruelty and moral cowardice" by his ex-mistress (Lili Palmer), who has a bundle of letters he wrote to his boyfriend, which she says she is going to hand over to a Harvard Professor, who is about to write his biography. The story – a muted plea for a change in the homosexual laws – had its roots in Somerset Maugham and his boy friend, Gerald Haxton. **Shadows of the Evening**: Man (Noël Coward) learns that he is going to die. His mistress (Lili Palmer) and his wife (Irene Worth) decide to call a truce, but he finds the strain of pretending he is not gong to die too much and argues that it would be better for all three of them to face up to the truth. **Come into the Garden, Maud**: American millionaire (Noël Coward) finally ditches his ghastly wife (Irene Worth) in favour of an Italian princess (Lili Palmer). Coward was 66, frail and having difficulty remembering his lines. He was to have taken the trilogy to New York with Margaret Leighton (his original choice) instead of Lilli Palmer but he was too ill and the play was not produced on Broadway until after his death. Hume Cronyn, Jessica Tandy and Anne Baxter appeared in a truncated version in New York in 1974.

Apr 20. Mona Washbourne, Sheila Hancock, Jack Hedley, Michael Crawford, James Cossins and June Ritchie in Bill MacIlwraith's **The Anniversary** directed by Patrick Dromgoole at Duke of York's. Vicious black comedy: a relentless and exhausting torrent of crude insults. Washbourne, cast against type as the mother from hell, was a one-eyed monster, a grotesque black widow, a selfish, mean, petty, malevolent blackmailer, ready to gobble up her three sons.

Apr 25. Polish People's Theatre at Aldwych in Stanislav Wyspanski's **The Wedding** and Fydor Dostoyevsky's **Crime and Punishment** and Adam Hanusziewicz's **The Columbus Boys** directed by Adam Hanuszkiewicz.

Apr 26. Joyce Redman as Mrs Boyle and Colin Blakely as Captain Boyle in Sean O'Casey's **Juno and the Paycock** directed by Laurence Olivier at Old Vic. Frank Finlay as Joxer Dally. It was O'Casey's death which prompted the National to revive the play. Olivier had seen Dublin's Abbey Theatre's actors in 1925 when they came to London and he still had vivid memories of the production which he incorporated into his own. Madge Ryan's over-the-top performance as Mrs Managan rocked the boat.

May 5. Vanessa Redgrave in Jay Presson Allen's **The Prime of Miss Jean Brodie**, based on Muriel Spark's novel directed by Peter Wood at Wyndham's. Brodie teaches in a private school in Scotland in the 1930s. "Give me a girl at an impressionable age and she is mine for life!" Her teaching methods are not popular with the Headmistress. Vickery Turner didn't look like a sixteen-year-old and so her love affair with the art master was robbed of any shock it might have had.
—She is described by other characters as ridiculous and magnificent. Miss Redgrave's performance certainly justifies the description; but like all her work it is lived from line to line. *The Times*

May 9. Leningrad Gorki Theatre at Aldwych. Innokenti Smoktunovsky as Prince Mishkin in Fydor Dostoyevsky's **The Idiot** adapted and directed by Georgi Tovstonogov. "It's like a novel – old-fashioned nonsense," said one of the characters pre-

Vanessa Redgrave in *The Prime of Miss Jean Brodie*. Left-hand side, anti-clockwise, Vickery Turner, Olivia Hussey, Jane Carr and Alison Blair as the Brodie set

sciently. The acting was better than the production which was played out against dreary drab tabs. Mishkin, sincere and honest, innocently brings disaster to all those who come in contact with him. Smoktunovsky (best known to London audiences for his Hamlet in the Russian film) acted with great sensitivity and subtly, but some members of the audience were just as heartless as the people on stage and actually found the Prince's madness funny. Tatyana Doronmna smouldered glamorously, almost operatically, as Filipovna.

—He is manifestly a great actor. He is so inside the poor beguiled character that he asserts complete authority without appearing to try. FELIX BARKER *Evening News*

Jun 2. Fenella Fielding in Victorien Sardou and Emil de Najac's **Let's Get A Divorce** directed by Robin Midgley at Mermaid. Sardou wrote *Divorçons* at the height of the controversial Divorce Bill of the 1880s. Here is the familiar ménage a trois, except the role of husband and lover has been reversed. The husband is sexy; the lover is the bore. Fielding was very funny when she was criticizing her husband for his lack of passion, romance and adventure. Transferred to Comedy.

Jun 9. Peggy Ashcroft and George Baker in Margaret Duras's **Days in the Trees** directed by John Schlesinger at Aldwych (RSC). Rich old lady indulges her gigolo son. The play was boring at a realistic and a symbolic level. Harold Hobson, champion of Duras's work in England, complained that Ashcroft's performance had entirely reversed the play's political meaning.

Jun 15. Donald Sinden and Barbara Ferris in Terence Frisby's **There's A Girl in My Soup** directed by Robert Chetwyn at Globe. A middle-aged gourmet and a kooky nineteen-year-old discover the incompatibility of age and youth.

Jul 18. Hermione Baddeley and Andree Melly in Frank Marcus's **The Killing of Sister George** directed by Val May at St Martin's.

Jul 21. Max Wall in Alfred Jarry's **Ubu** designed by David Hockney and directed by Iain Cuthbertson at Royal Court. 70 years after the riots in Paris at the Paris premiere, Jarry's notorious play got its first British professional staging, Ubu, grotesque, hideous, stupid, brutal, murders the King of Poland and seizes the throne for a reign of terror. Wall, miscast, ad-libbed. The production was completely innocuous. Jarry would have disowned it.

Sep 14. Two one-act plays by Bernard Shaw at Mermaid. **O'Flaherty V.C.** directed by Peter Gill. Ian McKellen was the World War I soldier who begins to think for himself and sees the war clearly for what it is. **The Man of Destiny** directed by Robert Kidd. Ian McKellen was an arrogant Bonaparte. Siân Phillips's Strange Lady was strangely lacking in vivacity.

Sep 22. Joss Ackland, Paul Eddington, Willoughby Goodard and Thelma Ruby in David Heneker's musical **Jorrocks** directed by Val May at New. Book by Beverley

Alec Guinness and Simone Signoret in Macbeth
....

Cross based on the novels of R C Surtees. The unspeakable in full pursuit of the uneatable. Songs in praise of fox-hunting.

Oct 6. Ralph Richardson as Sir Anthony Absolute, Daniel Massey as Captain Jack Absolute, Margaret Rutherford as Mrs Malaprop , Marilyn Taylerson as Lydia Languish and Keith Baxter as Bob Acres in Richard Brinsley Sheridan's **The Rivals** directed by Glen Byam Shaw at Haymarket. Rutherford seemed somewhat tentative at first, as if she were not quite sure of her lines; but as the play went on, it became obvious that she was suffering from exhaustion.

Oct 12. Jack Klugman and Victor Spinetti in Neil Simon's **The Odd Couple** directed by Harvey Medlinsky at Queen's. Two men, in the throes of divorce, decide to set up flat together. The comedy springs entirely from their domestic quarrels. The queer thing about the play is that it is not queer. It should be, of course.

Oct 13. US directed by Peter Brook at Aldwych. Text by Denis Cannan adapted by Michael Kustow and Michael Scott. Lyrics by Adrian Mitchell. Music by Richard Peaslee. Potted history and wake-up call on the war in Vietnam: a series of tableaux, news flashes, poems, press conferences, letters, songs of protest, interviews and discussions. The dice were deliberately loaded. Glenda Jackson had a very long speech, which turned on the very people who had supported the play and hoped that what was happening in Vietnam would happen in England. The production opened with an actor miming a Buddhist monk setting himself alight. The audience was far more shocked when a butterfly was burned alive.
—*US* cannot be neglected by anyone who takes a serious interest in theatre and its relation to the world we live in. If you miss it, you will live to regret it. MICHAEL BILLINGTON *Plays and Players*

Oct 13. Coral Browne as Mrs Erlynne, Isabel Jeans as the Duchess of Berwick, Wilfred Hyde-White as Lord Augustus, Juliet Mills as Lady Windermere and Ronald Lewis as Lord Darlington in Oscar Wilde's **Lady Windermere's Fan** directed by Anthony Quayle at Phoenix. The serious side of the play was often as funny as the epigrams. Coral Browne, the scarlet woman *par excellence*, looked very much like "an edition de luxe of a wicked French novel meant especially for an English market". Designer Cecil Beaton emphasised Lord Darlington's decadence by giving him Moorish apartments.

Oct 20. Alec Guinness and Simone Signoret in Shakespeare's **Macbeth** directed by William Gaskill at Royal Court. Staged in a bare box and brilliantly lit throughout, the production was so uncompromisingly Brechtian that most critics were completely alienated. Guinness's performance was not helped by the film actress's French-American accent and her unfamiliarity with Shakespeare's language and rhythm. The notices were so bad that Gaskill threatened to ban the critics from all future productions at the Royal Court. There was a blazing row in the Press and calls for Gaskill's resignation. Finally, he was forced to retract.
—It must have taken a great deal of work to persuade Alec Guinness to give a performance so totally colourless as this. B A YOUNG *Financial Times*

Oct 25. John Clements, Bill Fraser and Michael Aldridge in Jean Anouilh's **The Fighting Cock** directed by Norman Marshall transferred from Chichester Festival to Duke of York's. General despises what his country has become and wants to lead her back to a life of austerity, discipline and hard work. The irony is that he, who would teach others what Honour and Love mean, has failed abysmally in both areas.

Nov 1. Michael Bates, Sheila Ballantine, Kenneth Cranham, Gerry Duggan and Simon Ward in Joe Orton's **Loot** directed by Charles Marowitz at Criterion. A modern classic of bad taste embraced Roman Catholicism, murder, homosexuality, bank robbery, corruption and death. A mother's dead body is taken out if its coffin and shoved in a cupboard so that her son can hide stolen money in its place. It's a theme, observed Orton, "which less skilfully handled, might cause offence." The comic absurdity is developed with Wildean wit. The best jokes are at the expense of the police. (The production followed the first British police inquiry into corruption in its own ranks.) Inspector Truscott of Scotland Yard (who pretends to be an official from the Water Board, a disguise which doesn't fool anybody) is one of the great comic policemen, fit to stand in the ranks with Dogberry in *Much Ado About Nothing* and Peter Sellers's accident-prone Inspector Clouseau in *The Pink Panther* films. Michael Bates scored a big success. Truscott was created by Kenneth Williams (gross miscasting) in 1965 when the production got no further than Golders Green.
—The most genuinely quick-witted, pungent and sprightly entertainment by a new young British playwright for a decade. ALAN BRIEN *Sunday Telegraph*
—I have a lot of vices, but false modesty is not one of them. The best thing about *Loot* is the quality of the writing. *Joe Orton*

Nov 2. Paul Scofield and Patrick Magee in Charles Dyer's **Staircase** directed by Peter Hall at Aldwych. Two ageing homosexual barbers bicker. Scofield was a sneering, sadistic egoist. Magee was his masochistic flabby punch-bag. The roles were reversible.
—Mr Scofield, blanched and desperate, runs through the whole repertoire of male effeminacy without once approaching theatrical cliché. *The Times*

Nov 17. David Waller, John Hurt, Sheila Allen, Sebastian Shaw and Helen Fraser in David Mercer's **Belcher's Luck** directed by David Jones at Aldwych. Class warfare was given the full melodrama: greed, lust, madness and murder. The embittered Belcher, a boozing, glutinous fornicator, takes malicious pleasure in humiliating and taunting his master. His philosophy is that, "They're here to rule and we're here to screw them for all we can get." He wants his rights. He wants his master's estate. He foolishly underestimates the opposition.

1967

Jan 17. Judi Dench, Ian McKellen and Ian McShane in Aleksei Arbuzov's **The Promise** translated by Ariadne Nicolaeff and directed by Frank Hauser at Fortune. In World War 2, during the siege of Leningrad, which lasted 900 days, 600,000 died, most from starvation and cold. It was the hardest winter for 100 years. People lived on a handful of bread a day. Arbuznov followed the fortunes of three young people from the idealistic optimism in their teens to the bitter disillusionment in their thirties in the post-Stalin era. The production was a major turning point in the careers of Dench, McKellen and McShane.
—In ten year's time I expect them to dominate our theatre. PETER LEWIS *Daily Mail*.

Jan 31. Leo McKern, Zia Mohyeddin and Leonard Rossiter in Ben Jonson's **Volpone** directed by Frank Hauser at Garrick. The actors made heavy farce of the plot.

Feb 16. Topol in Jerry Block's musical **Fiddler on the Roof** directed and choreographed by Jerome Robbins at Her Majesty's. Book by Joseph Stein based on stories by Sholem Aleichem. Lyrics by Sheldon Harnick. The breakdown of Jewish observances, traditions and customs. ("Without our traditions," says the milkman, "our life would be as shaky as a fiddler on the roof.") Who would have thought the repression, harassment and exile of impoverished Jews in the Ukraine in 1905 in Tsarist Russia could be turned into a Broadway hit musical? Topol sang "If I Was A Rich Man". 2030 performances.

Feb 21. Laurence Olivier, Geraldine McEwan and Robert Stephens in August Strindberg's **The Dance of Death** directed by Glen Byam Shaw at Old Vic (NT). Twenty years of marriage is twenty years of hell. Isolated and abandoned, the couple exists only to torment each other. Olivier, coarse and arrogant, was ferocious in his triumph over his wife and her lover: "I'm not dead yet, I tell you!" He was also very funny when he was describing how he very nearly pushed his wife off the pier, an incident which was based on an incident in the playwright's own life. McEwan, too young, was nearer to Feydeau than she was to Strindberg.

—Olivier's Edgar is a masterly creation of snarling venom, vulgarity and self-pity shot through with shafts of alarming politeness that indicate yet nastier behaviour is in the offing.
JEREMY KINGSTON *Punch*

Feb 23. Bridget Turner in Arnold Wesker's **Roots** directed by Jane Howell at Royal Court. The attention to the realistic detail of everyday living – eating, cooking, washing-up, cleaning – meant that a very short play lasted nearly three hours. Gwen Nelson in the original 1959 production repeated her excellent performance of the mother.

Mar 13. Nicol Williamson in Nikolai Gogol's **The Diary of a Madman** directed by Anthony Page at Duchess. Poor, paranoid clerk comes to believe he is the King of Spain. A snarling *tour de force*.

Mar 16. Mike Pratt, Judy Parfitt and Anne Dyson in D H Lawrence's **The Daugh-**ter-in-Law directed by Peter Gill at Royal Court. "How is a woman," asks the daughter-in-law, "ever to have a husband when all the men belong to their mothers?" Her mother-in-law, surprisingly, agrees with her, but blames the men. Rediscovered in 1967 and universally praised, it seemed extraordinary that a drama of such quality should have remained unperformed. Lawrence's working class dramas, way ahead of their time, were a deliberate reaction against the plays of Shaw, Galsworthy and Granville-Barker.

Mar 29. Michael Hordern, Celia Johnson, Richard Briers and Jennifer Hilary in Alan Ayckbourn's **Relatively Speaking** directed by Nigel Patrick at Duke of York's. Comedy of mistaken identities and spiraling misunderstandings has everybody at cross-purposes

Apr 3. Comédie Française at Aldwych. Jacques Destoop as Le Cid, Claude Winter as Chimene and Genieve Casile as Infanta in Corneille's **Le Cid** directed by Paul-Emile Deiber. Love and honour: a sumptuous, static mausoleum piece, rigidly formal of movement and gesture. Destop was a beefy, hammy hero.

—These ravishingly dressed actors do everything perfectly, except engage one's emotions.
MILTON SHULMAN *Evening Standard*

Apr 6. Comédie Française at Aldwych. Claude Winter and Jacques Toja in Marivaux's **Le Jeu de L'Amour et du Hasard** directed by Maurice Escande. The production had an aristocratic, fragile, porcelain elegance. It was acted in a double-bill with Georges

Avril Elgar, Glenda Jackson, Jack Shepherd and Marianne Faithfull in **Three Sisters**

1967 World Premieres
New York
　Rochelle Owens's *Futz*
　Galt MacDermott's *Hair*
　LeRoi Jones's *Slave Ship*

Births
Joe Penhall, British playwright

Deaths
Jean Cadell (*b*.1884), British actor
Balliol Holloway (*b*.1883), British
　actor
Frank Lawton (*b*.1904), British actor
Vivien Leigh (*b*.1913), British actor
Duncan Macrae (*b*.1905), Scottish
　actor

Paul Muni (*b*.1896), American actor
Joe Orton (*b*.1933), British
　playwright
Claude Rains (*b*.1889), British actor
Elmer Rice (*b*.1892), American
　playwright

Notes
—First British colour TV broadcast

History
—Arab-Israel Six-Day War
—Civil war in Nigeria
—Che Guevara killed
—First human heart transplant

Feydeau's **Feu La Mere de Madame** with Jacques Charon and Micheline Boudet directed by Jacques Charon. This cheap, crude and vulgar vaudeville sketch was the farce that Feydeau himself predicted The Comédie Française would perform after his death. Charon was the husband, who went to a fancy dress ball dressed as Louis XIV and returned home very late to face the music, a sad, tired, bedraggled, drenched figure with a hangover.

Apr 10. Noh Theatre of Japan in two programmes of classical Noh plays and Kyogen comedies at Aldwych: **The Robe of Feathers**, **The Ground Spider**, **The Chrysanthemum Child**, **The Mosquito Wrestlers** and **Romance of Genji, Lady Aoi**. The oldest living drama in the world, performed almost exactly as it was centuries ago, preserved intact by the continuous handing-down of the tradition within the family. "The main aim of Noh is to depict grace, dignity and beauty wherever it may be found." Gorgeous costumes, striking masks, stately measured entrances, highly stylised gestures, accompanied by harsh, unfamiliar vocal sounds. A mysterious, infinitely remote, religious ritual: a formal, aristocratic ceremony, at once austere and solemn, alien, forbidding and repetitive, incredibly slow, yet quite beautiful. The mime is so economical that at times there seems to be almost nothing happening. It is, in fact, a largely static performance. The singers kneel. The stage-hands sit on stage with their hands, monk-like, in their cassocks. The leading role is given to a kimono which lies at the front of the stage, symbolising a sick woman. The audience behaved as if they were in church. The most accessible play was *Aoi No Ue* (*Lady Aoi*), an exciting exorcism with rattling beads, incessant chanting and the constant beating of the drum.

Apr 11. John Stride and Edward Petherbridge in Tom Stoppard's **Rosencrantz and Guildenstern Are Dead** directed by Derek Goldby at Old Vic (NT). Graham Crowden as The Player. A huge success on the fringe at the 1966 Edinburgh Festival. Hamlet's chums are caught up in events they don't understand. They don't even know who they are. Which of them, for instance, is Rosencrantz? And what is the game? And what are the rules? There are no rules, except that they must die. "Eternity is a terrible thought. Where is it all going to end?" Stoppard's *jeu d'esprit*, a mixture of parody and allegory, was full of puns and word play. Larky and pretentious, comic and sad, it was great fun, bringing back memories of Vladimir and Estragon in Samuel Beckett's *Waiting for Godot*.
—As a first stage play, it is an amazing piece of work. IRVING WARDLE *The Times*
—A single idea is developed without imagination and in language of tedious brutality. HILARY SPURLING *Spectator*.
—The most important event in the British professional theatre of the last nine years. HAROLD HOBSON *Sunday Times*

Apr 18. Avril Elgar, Glenda Jackson and Marianne Faithfull, Michael Gwynn, John Shepherd and George Cole in Anton Chekhov's **Three Sisters** directed by William Gaskill at Royal Court. Jackson was a harsh, forbidding and not very passionate Masha. Faithfull amazed everybody with her emotional power.
—William Gaskill's production, surprisingly orthodox, seems to have confused a funereal pace with a Slavic mood of despair. MILTON SHULMAN *Evening Standard*

Apr 19. Googie Withers, Ian Carmichael, Moira Lister, Hugh Williams, Raymond Huntley and Alec Clunes in Bernard Shaw's **Getting Married** directed by Frank Dunlop at Strand. A wordy seminar on marriage and divorce makes a bride (Perlita Neilson) realize what she is letting herself in for and she refuses to go through with the wedding service.

Apr 24. Bremen Theatre at Aldwych in Frank Wedekind's **Spring Awakening** directed by Peter Zadek. Bruno Ganz as Moritz, Vadim Glowna as Melchial. Zadek threatened to withdraw the production if the censor did not allow the actors to flagellate, masturbate and rape. The censor relented at the eleventh hour. The production – inferior to the Royal Court's – was simplified realism; everything was reduced to

the absolute minimum. The actors were a bit old to be playing schoolboys.

May 8. Greek Art Theatre Company at Aldwych in Aristophanes' **The Frogs** and **The Birds** and Aeschylus's **The Persians** both directed by Karolos Koun.

May 17. Euripides' trilogy – **Hecuba**, **Electra** and **Orestes** – directed by Bernard Miles at Mermaid. The Trojan War was set within a World War 1 context. Jack Lindsay's banal and bathetic translation was a barrier to any tragic response.

May 22. Piccolo Theatre of Milan at Aldwych. Ferruccio Soleri as Arlecchino in Carlo Goldoni's **The Servant of Two Masters** directed by Giorgio Strehler. The Piccolo Theatre had been seen at the 1956 Edinburgh Festival when Marcello Moretti had given a dazzling performance in the role of the servant who serves two masters dinner at the same time. Without him the *commedia dell'arte* business didn't seem as funny.

May 29. Theatre of the Balustrade of Prague at Aldwych. Jan Preucil as Joseph K in Franz Kafka's **The Trial** and Alfred Jarry's **King Ubu** both directed by Jan Grossman. *The Trial* was an urban, expressionistic, acrobatic phantasmagoria with spooky organ music and a swirling complex of steel. Joseph K somersaulted backwards to his garrotting.
—I am not interested in the philosophy of the absurd, but I want to create its gestures. JAN GROSSMAN

Jun 14. Peggy Ashcroft as Mrs Alving, David Waller as Pastor Manders and John Castle as Oswald in Henrik Ibsen's **Ghosts** directed by Alan Bridges at Aldwych (RSC). Ashcroft subtly conveyed the cost of having kept the syphilitic truth from her son for so long, but the big emotional scene leading to the fatal dose of morphine was less than harrowing.

Jun 29. Robert Hardy as Sir Harry Wildair in George Farquhar's **The Constant Couple** directed by Richard Cottrell at New. Mounted on the cheap, seriously undercast and lacking in pace, the intrigues, infidelities, hypocrisy and impertinences had no panache.

Jul 3. Derek Smith, Brenda Bruce, Barbara Jefford, Roland Curram and Derek Godfrey in Jules Feiffer's **Little Murders** designed by Ralph Koltai and directed by Christopher Morahan at Aldwych (RSC). New Yorkers are under siege. There have been 345 murders in six months and not one of them has been solved. The play was a satire on American conformity, police inefficiency, male virility, art, parenthood, religious sects, cant and clichés.
—One of the most devastating hatchet jobs on civilisation ever done. FELIX BARKER *Evening News*

Jul 4. John Shepherd in David Storey's **The Restoration of Arnold Middleton** directed by Robert Kidd at Royal Court. History master has sex with his mother-in-law.

Jul 4. Joan Plowright, Jeanne Watts and Louise Purnell in Anton Chekhov's **Three Sisters** directed by Laurence Olivier at Old Vic (NT). Plowright, superbly out of sorts, clipping her lines, gave Masha the right edge.

Jul 20. Joe Melia and Zena Walker in Peter Nichols's **A Day in the Death of Joe Egg** directed by Michael Blakemore at Comedy. The play was based on Nichols's experience of having to cope day in, day out with a severely brain-damaged child. Initially, no management had wanted to stage it, thinking it wasn't right to make a comedy out of tragedy. How (and the question is asked during the performance) do you describe such a life without provoking a sudden stampede to the exit doors? Nichols' solution was to have the characters step out of the play to address the audience directly and to act out revue sketches, which allowed for easy jokes at the expense of medics and clerics and unpalatable truths to be openly expressed. Joe Egg is the nickname the parents give the child, a silent, passive girl, capable only of moaning.

Jul 27. Donald Pleasence in Robert Shaw's **The Man in the Glass Booth** directed by Harold Pinter at St Martin's. Is the man a Nazi war criminal pretending to be a Jew? Or is he a Jew pretending to be a Nazi war criminal? The bullet-proof glass protects him in the same way that a glass booth had protected Adolf Eichmann in 1962 during his trial for organising the extermination of six million Jews. The denouement was melodrama. The man was not a war criminal. He wanted to atone for the guilt of the German people.
—Donald Pleasence plays him with superb sadistic timing: subtly grading his delivery between Berlin and the Bronx, and stunning his victims with violently unpredictable changes of mood. IRVING WARDLE *The Times*

Aug 17. Donald Sinden as Sir Novelty Fashion and Janet Suzman as Berinthia in John Vanbrugh's **The Relapse** directed by Trevor Nunn at Aldwych (RSC). Sir Novelty, over-wigged and overdressed, rarely let anybody finish what they were saying. Sinden's timing of the expletives ("Stap me vitals", "Strike me dumb", "Strike me

Gordon Jackson and Alec Guinness in Wise Child

speechless" etc) was perfect. Nunn saw an affinity between Vanbrugh and Cyril Tourneur, but the quartet of lovers came across as much nearer to Noël Coward.

Aug 21. The National Youth Theatre in Peter Terson's **Zigger Zagger** directed by Michael Croft at Jeanette Cochrane. Young hooligan has to learn that "there is more to life than a football match". The NYT always has had the advantage of sheer numbers and they easily filled a football stand full of supporters to shout and sing their heads off. Terson loaded the dice against Society and "law and order" so much that he seemed to be on the side of the thugs.

Sep 7. Ralph Richardson as Shylock and Angela Thorne as Portia in Shakespeare's **The Merchant of Venice** directed by Glen Byam Shaw at Haymarket. Dreary beyond belief; a tacky touring production, unworthy of the West End.

Sep 20. Donal Donnelly and Patrick Bedford in Brian Friel's **Philadelphia Here I Come** directed by Hilton Edwards at Lyric. 25-year-old Irish man, about to emigrate to America, is in two minds as to whether to go. The outcome is always in doubt and the play ends before he leaves. The man is played by two actors: Donnelly played his sensitive public self. Bedford played his brash private self, voicing the witticisms he thinks but never says.

Oct 3. Jeremy Brett as Orlando and Ronald Pickup as Rosalind in an all-male version of Shakespeare's **As You Like It** directed by Clifford Williams at Old Vic (NT). Charles Kay as Celia. Derek Jacobi as Touchstone. Robert Stephens as Jacques. Richard Kay as Phoebe. Anthony Hopkins as Audrey. The comedy was sexless and duller and unfunnier for it.

Oct 5. Lila Kedrova as Ranevsky and Patrick Wymark as Lopahin in Anton Chekhov's **The Cherry Orchard** directed by Richard Cottrell at Queen's. Kedrova emphasized Ranevsky's childishness. She was incapable of understanding what Lopahin was talking about when he suggested that she should sell their orchard to pay her mounting debts. The cherry orchard was her life, her youth, her happiness. "If it is to be sold," she said, "sell me with it." There was a memorable bit of comic business – perfect Chekhov – when, weeping profusely, she emptied all the contents of her handbag (a typical woman's handbag) into her lap to find her lover's letter and the audience found themselves laughing and crying at the same time.

Oct 10. Alec Guinness in Simon Gray's **Wise Child** directed by John Dexter at Wyndham's. A murderous black comedy, written in the Joe Orton manner, was set in a seedy boarding house run by a homosexual hotelier (Gordon Jackson) with a religious bent. Guinness played a criminal on the run who in order to elude the police had disguised himself as a mother with a grown-up son (Simon Ward). He had two voices, one gruff, the other genteel. It was a bit like watching Magwitch in drag.

Oct 11. Juliet Prowse as Charity in Cy Coleman's musical **Sweet Charity** conceived staged and choreographed by Bob Fosse in New York and directed in London by Lawrence Carr and Robert Linden at Prince of Wales. Book by Neil Simon based on Federico Fellini's film *Cabiria*. Lyrics by Dorothy Fields. Charity (created by Gwen Verdon in New York in 1966), is a dance hall hostess, who, fatally, trusts men. Prowse was a long-legged, gawky, exuberant redhead. She, Josephine Blake and Paula Kelly sang the mordant "Big Spender" and stopped the show. Bob Fosse's witty choreography for "Rich Man's Frug" also stopped the show.

Oct 18. Fenella Fielding and Edward Woodward in Henry James's **The High Bid** directed by Bernard Miles at Mermaid. A rarity, an actual play by Henry James as opposed to an adaptation of one his novels. American widow helps a captain to see his baronial home through her eyes.

Oct 24. Myfanwy Jenn and Bill Wallis in Richard Ingrams and John Wells's **Mrs Wilson's Diary** directed by Joan Littlewood at Criterion. This affectionate lampoon of Prime Minister Harold Wilson, based on articles in *Private Eye*, was a mixture of undergraduate revue and music hall comedy. Wilson made his entrance as Batman. The Lord Chamberlain wanted savage cuts and it took three months of negotiations before he would agree to licence the play.

Nov 9. John Clements as Captain Shotover, Irene Worth as Hesione Hushabye, Diana Churchill as Lady Utterword and Sarah Badel as Ellie Dunn in Bernard Shaw's **Heartbreak House** directed by John Clements transferred from Chichester Festival to Lyric. In its black pessimism and its tirade against mankind, the production was closer to *King Lear* than *The Cherry Orchard*. Irene Worth played Hesione with tremendous aplomb, a gorgeous, witty, stylish, sensual woman with a splendid Edwardian bust.

Nov 20. Phyllis Calvert as Mrs Arbuthnot and Tony Britton as Lord Illingworth in Oscar Wilde's **A Woman of No Importance** directed by Malcolm Farquhar at Vaudeville. Laboured and slow. The headline in the *Sunday Times* was "Wilde turkey served up cold."

Nov 21. John Gielgud as Orgon and Robert Stephens as Tartuffe in Molière's **Tartuffe** directed by Tyrone Guthrie at Old Vic (NT). Richard Wilbur's rhyming couplets did a disservice to Molière, constantly getting in the way of the seriousness of the comedy. Stephens's Tartuffe was a very crude and very vulgar country yokel. It was a great disappointment that Gielgud was not playing the role.

Nov 29. Sandy Wilson's **The Boy Friend** directed by Sandy Wilson at Comedy. Not a patch on the original production.

Dec 5. Harry Secombe as D'Artagnan in **The Four Musketeers** directed by Peter Coe at Drury Lane. Musical. Book by Michael Pertwee. Music by Laurie Johnson. Lyrics by Herbert Kretzmer. Sean Kenny's massive set, a cross between a commando assault course and a Minotaur's labyrinth, did all manner of strange arabesques and took over the show completely. Aubrey Woods played Richelieu and accompanied the fracas on an old piano.

Dec 7. Richard Todd, Cicely Courtneidge, Jack Hulbert, Joyce Carey and Lally Bowers in Dodie Smith's **Dear Octopus** directed by Frith Banbury at Haymarket. Courtneidge, good for the box office, was too consciously comic to be good for the play.

1968

Jan 4. Paul Scofield and Vivien Merchant in Shakespeare's **Macbeth** directed by Peter Hall at Aldwych. Hall emphasised the Christian imagery, opening with a witch holding a cross upside down and pouring blood on it. Scofield's verse speaking came in for a great deal of criticism. Philip Hope-Wallace in *The Guardian* thought the actors, with the exception of Ian Richardson's Malcolm, "had nearly all been infected by Scofield's habit of putting full stops in the verse every three or four words."

Jan 16. Colin Blakely in Ben Jonson's **Volpone** directed by Tyrone Guthrie at Old Vic (NT). The production began with Volpone taking his ablutions and his communion in gold. The "vultures" were dressed and behaved as "birds of prey". Frank Wylie took no relish in either Mosca's wit or his cunning.

Feb 9. Isabel Jeans as Lady Bracknell, John Standing as Algernon Moncrieff, Daniel Massey as John Worthing, Flora Robson as Miss Prism, Robert Eddison as Chasuble, Pauline Collins as Cecily and Helen Weir as Gwendolen in Oscar Wilde's **The Importance of Being Earnest** directed by Robert Chetwyn at Haymarket.
—With brilliant inspiration, they [Flora Robson and Robert Eddison] play as an elderly Heloise and Abelard. Gleaming at each other like pale-eyed impassioned sheep, they languish and swoon in panting, tragic infatuation. Beside their lust, the leads indeed seem trivial. RICHARD BRYDEN *Observer*

Feb 14. Celia Johnson, Roland Culver and Prunella Scales in Noël Coward's **Hay Fever** directed by Murray Macdonald at Duke of York's. The set and the business were borrowed from Coward's 1964 production at the National Theatre. Johnson was miscast.

Feb 21. Ian McKellen and James Bolam in Peter Shaffer's **The White Lies** and **Black Comedy** directed by Peter Wood at Lyric.

Feb 28. Judi Dench as Sally Bowles in Fred Ebb and John Kander's musical **Cabaret** directed by Hal Prince at Palace. Book by Joe Masteroff based on John Van Druten's play of Christopher Isherwood's stories. Sally Bowles, with her green nail polish, green eye-shadow, false eyelashes, pale skin, red lips and helmet hair-cut, was the star

1968 World Premieres
New York
Arthur Miller's *The Price*
Mart Crowley's *The Boys in the Band*
Howard Sackler's *The Great White Hope*
Arthur Kopit's *Indians*
David Rabe's *The Basic Training of Pavlo Hummel*

Deaths
Tallulah Bankhead (*b.*1903), American actor
Bud Flanagan (*b.*1896), British comedian
John Steinbeck (*b.*1902), American playwright and novelist
Donald Wolfit (*b.*1902), British actor

Honours
Knights
John Clements, actor, director and manager
Robert Helpmann, dancer, choreographer, actor, director

Notes
—Trevor Nunn became artistic director of the RSC

History
—Robert Kennedy assassinated
—Martin Luther King assassinated
—Russia invaded Czechoslovakia
—Students' protests throughout Europe
—Enoch Powell's "Rivers of Blood" speech

attraction of the Kit Kat Klub, a familiar icon of decadence, Berlin-style 1929/30. Barry Dennen was an outrageous, sexually ambiguous, tacky and crude Master of Ceremonies.
—Miss Dench does her best, but really wickedness is not in her. Instead of aphrodisiac cooking, she offers us the wholesomeness of whole-meal bread. This is good for our soul but not for the play. HAROLD HOBSON *Sunday Times*
—Her performance suggests the thwarted fantasies of a Pinner secretary. IRVING WARDLE *The Times*

Feb 29. D H Lawrence trilogy at Royal Court directed by Peter Gill began with Victor Henry, Anne Dyson and Susan Williamson in **A Collier's Friday Night**. It was like watching an adaptation of *Sons and Lovers*. The play was written between 1907–8. The novel was published in 1913. The relationships are exactly the same; even the dialogue was familiar. Whole chunks of the book were there.
—To make up for the lack of action director Peter Gill is painstaking with the domestic detail. Rarely have there been such long pauses between lines while tea is brewed, food is dished up, clothes are folded or they all just sit quietly. DAVID NATHAN *Sun*

Mar 7. Judy Parfitt, Victor Henry and Anne Dyson in D H Lawrence's **The Daughter-in-Law** directed by Peter Gill at Royal Court. Michael Billington in *The Times* thought it "a superb example of stage naturalism at its microscopic best."

Mar 12. Anthony May in Peter Terson's **Zigger Zagger** directed by Michael Croft at Strand.

Mar 14. Judy Parfit, Len Jones, Mark Jones and Anne Dyson in D H Lawrence's **The Widowing of Mrs Holroyd** directed by Peter Gill at Royal Court. Once again it was Gill's extraordinary attention to the actual physical details of life and death, which made the production so convincing. The ritual of laying out and washing the dead body had a powerful impact.

Mar 19. John Gielgud and Irene Worth in Seneca's **Oedipus** translated by Ted Hughes and David Anthony Turner and directed by Peter Brook at Old Vic (NT). Seneca's version is more brutal and more horrific than Sophocles's version. The actors in brown sweaters and brown slacks were already in place when the audience entered the auditorium. Some were in the auditorium, tied to the pillars like prisoners to the mast. (Latecomers used to ask them for programmes.) The cast on stage sat on small cubes while an enormous golden cube revolved hypnotically. Gielgud's Oedipus was magnificent when he realises that it was he who has brought destruction to Thebes and calls on all the diseases and terrors of mankind to join him in exile. At the end a golden seven-foot penis was dragged onto the stage and the company whooped it up, dancing and singing in the aisles. Coral Browne's comment on the phallus ("Nobody we know!") has passed into theatrical legend.
—He [Peter Brook] wouldn't let me be emotional. He made me stylised and he wouldn't allow me to let go. I'd been hoping I'd have a chance to rival Larry's Oedipus with all that screaming and howling. But Brook's Oedipus was so different, so staid, so stylised, so static. JOHN GIELGUD *quoted by* NICHOLAS DE JONGH *Guardian*

Mar 21. Wilfred Brambell, Jessie Evans and Kenneth J Warren in Geoffrey Chaucer's **Canterbury Tales** directed by Vlado Habnek at Phoenix. Adaptation by Nevill Coghill and Martin Starkie. Music by Richard Hill and John Hawkins. Lyrics by Nevill Coghill. The production included tales by the Miller, the Steward, the Priest, the Pardoner, the Merchant, and the Wife of Bath. Nicky Henson sang "I have a noble cock." Badly directed and badly acted, the production did a gross disservice to Chaucer's original and Nevill Coghill's famous translation. 2082 performances.

Mar 28. Michael Hordern as a failed inventor in Tom Stoppard's **Enter a Free Man** directed by Frith Banbury at St Martin's. The inventor's wife (Megs Jenkins) was philosophical: "Since he was going to be a failure anyway, he was better off failing at something he wanted to succeed in."

Apr 1. John Bowen's **Little Boxes** directed by Philip Grout at Duchess. Two plays. **The Coffee Lace** had June Jago, Sylvia Coleridge, Frank Middlemass, Maureen Pryor and Larry Noble as chorus boys and girls from the 1920s. Now retired, they live in dire poverty and, with the exception of their manager, they never leave the house because of a dreadful humiliation they once suffered on tour. **Trevor** described the frantic efforts of two girls (Angela Thorne and Anna Cropper) to hide from their parents that they are lesbians. They engage an out-of-work actor (David Cook) to pretend he is their respective boyfriend.

Apr 7. Marianne Faithful and Moira Redmond in Edward Bond's **Early Morning** directed by William Gaskill at Royal Court. Florence Nightingale accuses Queen Victoria of raping her. Disraeli and Albert plot the assassination of the Queen in order to establish a protectorate.

Apr 15. Theatre of the Balustrade of Prague at Aldwych. Jan Libicek in Alfred Jarry's **King Ubu** directed by Jan Grossman plus two programmes of mime by Ladislav Fialka: **The Clowns** and **The Fools**. "There is, nothing except for a brief burst of blasphemy, to shock Aunt Edna," said Harold Hobson in *The Sunday Times*. "Jarry's ghost is laid."

Apr 18. Alec McCowen in Peter Luke's adaptation of Fr Rolfe (Baron) Corvo's **Hadrian the Seventh** directed by Peter Dews at Mermaid. The embittered, lonely Rolfe, denied his rightful vocation as a priest, dreams of the papacy. McCowen's edgy and witty transition from impotent fury and biting sarcasm to smiling Papal paternalism was subtly judged.
—Alec McCowen gives a performance of scouring brilliance as Rolfe. He is a master of portrayals of warped and wounded men. He catches perfectly Rolfe's complexity – the satanic pride, the biting sarcasm, the shield of arrogance and lets the wounds show through. Peter Lewis *Daily Mail*

Apr 24. Keith Michell as Don Quixote and Bernard Spear as Sancho in **The Man From La Mancha** directed by Albert Marre at Piccadilly. Musical. Book by Dale Wasserman. Music by Mitch Leigh. Lyrics by Joe Darion. The theatre was gutted. The opening scene was very impressive. An enormous staircase descended, like a gangplank, from the flies. Down the stairs came the guard of the Inquisition and Cervantes. Joan Diener's performance was a collector's piece. She turned the musical into The Woman of La Mancha. Even in Don Quixote's finale, as he went up the stairs, the spotlight was on Diener. Against such formidable upstaging, Keith Michell hadn't a chance.

Apr 29. Théâtre de France in three plays at Aldwych. Edwige Feuillère and Jean Louis Barrault in Paul Claudel's **Partage du Midi** and Madeleine Renaud and Jean Desailly in Francois Billetdoux's **Il faut passer par les nuages** both directed by Jean-Louis Barrault. Dominique Paturel in Beaumarchais's **Le Barbier de Seville** directed by Jean-Pierre Grandval. It was Feuillère's performance in *Partage du Midi* that had persuaded Harold Hobson that she was the greatest actress in the world.

Apr 30. John Stride in Bertolt Brecht's **Edward II** directed by Frank Dunlop at Old Vic (NT). Edward proved unexpectedly strong in Brecht's cynical, tongue-in-cheek version of Christopher Marlowe's play. Charles Gray's Gaveston was a common Irish butcher's son. Geraldine McEwan's sad bewildered Queen became a grotesque and physically repulsive glutton.

May 20. Dublin's Abbey Theatre at Aldwych. Cyril Cusack in Dion Boucicault's **The Shaughraun** directed by Hugh Hunt. The old-fashioned romantic and melodramatic absurdities made for charming comedy. "Save my brother!" cries the heroine. "I'll do my best," promises the hero. Cyril Cusack played the Shaughraun, "the soul of every fair, the life of every funeral, the first fiddle at all weddings and patterns." He had easily the best comic situation when the Shaughraun sat up at his own wake to join the mourners in a drink. "I couldn't," he said, "refuse a drink out of respect to the corpse – long life to it."

May 23. Jill Bennett and Katharine Blake in John Osborne's **Time Present** directed by Anthony Page at Royal Court. A friendship between an out-of-work actress and a woman MP didn't prove very interesting.
—Politically and socially Mr Osborne may be a rebel; emotionally he is as reactionary as a Cheltenham colonel. David Nathan *Sun*

Jun 3. Royal Dramatic Theatre Company of Sweden at Aldwych. Gertrud Fridh in Ibsen's **Hedda Gabler** directed by Ingmar Bergman. Ingvar Kjellson as Tesman. Olof Widgren as Brack. Georg Arlin as Lovborg. Hedda was pregnant and Fridh mimed nausea. Bergman's cinematic production liberated Ibsen from its naturalism.

Jun 4. Sammy Davis, Jr, in a musical version of Clifford Odets's **Golden Boy** directed by Michael Thoma at London Palladium. The boxing story was no longer set in the Depression era, but acted out against a background of 1960's racial prejudice, race riots and Black Power. The new book by William Gibson preached aggressive, chip-on-shoulder, militant propaganda. Davis was too old to be convincing as the boy boxer.

Jun 10. Bunraku National Theatre in two traditional programmes at Aldwych. The Japanese puppeteers remained completely visible throughout. Three men worked each puppet. The performance was far less static and the stories were far more dramatic than the Noh plays.

Jun 17. Richard Briers and Ronnie Barker in Tom Stoppard's **The Real Inspector Hound** directed by Robert Chetwyn at Criterion. The best thing about this crude and over-rated send-up of an Agatha Christie country-house murder mystery was the amusing parody of the jargon critics adopt in their reviews. (Stoppard was a critic on a Bristol newspaper before he was a playwright.) The only trouble was that what the two critics were saying bore no relation to what they were watching. And no rep company, however bad, would have acted quite as badly as the actors did here.

Jul 3. Paul Scofield, Judy Parfitt, Joss Ackland and Claire Davidson in John Osborne's **Hotel in Amsterdam** directed by Anthony Page at Royal Court. Conversation piece and full of invective. The employees of a film magnate take a city break without telling him and then spend all their time talking about him. Scofield played the camp, slightly effeminate, possibly gay, second-rate film writer, managed a nice mixture of flippancy and vanity. The weak but engaging smile was absolutely right. The unseen, megalomaniac boss, described as "the biggest, most poisonous, voracious Machiavellian dinosaur in movies" was a portrait of Anthony Richardson, the stage and film director.

Sep 11. Victor Henry as Rimbaud and John Grillo as Verlaine in Christopher Hampton's **Total Eclipse** directed by Robert Kidd at Royal Court. There was compassion and humour, but no passion and no depravity. There were kisses but no nudity and Rimbaud didn't look 16.

Sep 26. Stage censorship was abolished.

Sep 27. Paul Nicholas, Oliver Tobias and Annabel Leventon in Galt MacDermot's **Hair** directed by Tom O'Horgan at Shaftesbury. Book and lyrics by Gerome Ragni and James Rado. This American Tribal Love-Rock Musical marked the end of the Lord Chamberlain's powers in the theatre. The audience couldn't wait for the actors to get their kit off. There was no book, no story and as a protest against the Vietnam War, with a plea for sexual, racial and verbal freedom thrown in, it was ineffective; its crudities and nudities were meaningless. The acting was amateurish. Anybody going to see the show for the nudes was in for a big disappointment because (a) it was all over before it had begun, and (b) it was so dark that nothing could be seen, anyway. ("The orgy that never was," was the headline in *The Evening News*.) The strength of the show was MacDermot's music and its highly insistent beat. The strength of the dancing was in its frenzied vitality. "A rocking raving sexcess," said *The Daily Mail*. "Idiotic and offensive," said *The Sun*. 1997 performaces.
—A complete bore. It was noisy, it was ugly and quite desperately unfunny. W A Darlington *Daily Telegraph*
—The effect was like being a voyeur at an orgy of Boy Scouts and Girl Guides. Milton Shulman *Evening Standard*

Oct 8. Geraldine McEwan, Robert Stephens and Robert Lang in Somerset Maugham's **Home and Beauty** directed by Frank Dunlop at Old Vic (NT). McEwan as "a dear little thing", who has done her bit during the war by marrying two DSOs, acted in a very affected manner, which was funny at first, but robbed the comedy of its sting.

Oct 30. John Standing, Isabel Jeans, Maureen O'Brien, Bill Fraser, Flora Robson, Robert Eddison, Angela Thorne and John Warner in Jean Anouilh's **Ring Round the Moon** translated by Christopher Fry and directed by Noël Willman at Haymarket. This *pièce rose* had thorns.

Oct 31. John Gielgud in Alan Bennett's **Forty Years On** directed by Patrick Garland at Apollo. The subject of this impudent charade was England and its decline in the 20th century. Bennett's satire was a mixture of parody and pastiche. The script, sentimental, cynical and affectionately shocking, had a strong lacing of schoolboy smut, puns, corny jokes and double entendres. The framework for the production was a Headmaster's retirement from a minor public school. High spots included a mini-sex talk by the housemaster, vulgar rugby songs by the boys, pastiche Wilde and lavatory humour. ("When people go to the lavatory for their humour, I know the writing is on the wall.") Bennett's verbal dexterity and his ability to misquote and turn well-known phrases inside out was much in evidence in the Headmaster's opening address, a potpourri of rhetoric, cliché, mumbo-jumbo and prayers.
—For me it is the funniest show of its kind since *Beyond the Fringe* and might easily become a habit. Philip Hope-Wallace *Guardian*

Hair

....

—John Gielgud plays Albion's headmaster, a fastidious, maudlin old spinster, and is at his most elegant, attenuated and mellow, like a Stradivarius playing Mozart.
BENEDICT NIGHTINGALE *New Statesman*

Nov 6. Alec Guinness and Eileen Atkins in T S Eliot's **The Cocktail Party** directed by Alec Guinness transferred from Chichester to Wyndham's. Eliot's tiresome mixture of social chatter and religious allegory turned out to be much easier than everybody had thought at its premiere eighteen years earlier. The second act – cold, dignified and artificial – was particularly good. Guinness wore a beard in Chichester and looked like a satanic Freud. He shaved it off when the production came to London.

—Guinness effaces himself almost totally. No other actor so firmly rejects any temptation to showiness. Yet in this poetic and mystical territory his command and authority are absolute.
PETER LEWIS *Daily Mail*

Dec 11. Michael Bryant, Gordon Jackson John Phillips and Alethea Charlton in John Hopkins's **This Story of Yours** directed by Christopher Morahan at Royal Court. A detective sergeant, brutalised by twenty years in the force, has a mental and moral breakdown. Whilst questioning a man accused of raping a young girl, he beats him to death, seeing in him a mirror of his own paedophiliac desires, homosexual temptations and innate violence.

Dec 12. John Colicos as Winston Churchill in Rolf Hochhuth's **Soldiers** directed by Clifford Williams at New. Ever since the National Theatre's Board had turned it down, the controversy had raged in the newspapers and on TV. Most of the people, who argued against it being staged, hadn't either read it or seen it. Hochhuth did not say Churchill was responsible for the Polish Prime Minister's death. Far more shocking was the revelation that Churchill had actively encouraged the Germans to bomb London in order to divert attention from the airfields. He did this in order to give the air force a vital breathing space. There was a remarkably convincing performance by Colicos.

1969

Jan 14. Peggy Ashcroft, Michael Hordern, Sheila Hancock and Elizabeth Spriggs in Edward Albee's **A Delicate Balance** directed by Peter Hall at Aldwych (RSC). An American family is visited by their best friends, who are fleeing from some unnamed terror. Paralysed by their fear they seek permanent sanctuary, thus testing friendship to the very limit. The play, densely packed, was verbose and elusive.

Feb 7. Kenneth Cranham and Adrienne Posta in Edward Bond's **Saved**, directed by William Gaskill, returned to Royal Court following the abolition of theatre censorship. Throat-grabbing, jangling, raw and poetic," said *The Financial Times*. "It offers an experience no serious playgoer should deny himself," said *The Daily Telegraph*.

Feb 11. Kenneth Nelson, Tom Aldredge and Leonard Frey in Mart Crowley's **The Boys in the Band** directed by Robert Moore at Wyndham's. Landmark in gay theatre: first play in which all the characters were openly homosexual. Michael throws a birthday party, which is interrupted by his old college room mate, who is so homophobic that everybody presumes he must be a closet gay. The guests are forced to play a juvenile truth game in which they have to phone somebody they once loved and who doesn't know they are gay and tell them they love them. "You are," says a friend, "a sad and pathetic man. You're a homosexual and you don't want to be." Michael, filled with self-loathing, retorts: "Show me a happy homosexual and I'll show you a gay corpse."

Feb 17. Nicol Williamson in Shakespeare's **Hamlet** directed by Tony Richardson at Round House. Marianne Faithfull as Ophelia. Judy Parfit as Gertrude. Anthony Hopkins as Claudius. Mark Dignam as Polonius. Michael Pennington as Laertes. Gordon Jackson as Horatio. Roger Livesey as Gravedigger. Williamson's Prince was a nasal, Northern, splenetic, self-flagellating, self-mocking post-graduate.

Feb 19. Peter Needham, Jack Shepherd, Gillian Martell and Nigel Hawthorne in Edward Bond's **Narrow Road to the Deep North** directed by Jane Howell at Royal Court. Atrocities by Japanese tyrants in the 17th century were juxtaposed with atrocities by British imperialists in the 19th century. The political parable was given the full Noh treatment and ended with a Buddhist priest disembowelling himself.

Feb 20. Ginger Rogers in Jerry Herman's musical **Mame** directed by Gene Saks and restaged by Lawrence Kasha at Drury Lane. Book by Jerome Lawrence and Robert E Lee based on Patrick Dennis's novel. Ginger Rogers was never a comedienne. She wasn't really a singer, either. And here she barely danced. The show's best number, "Mame", was a watered-down *Hello, Dolly!*.

Feb 25. Roy Dotrice as James Aubrey in **Brief Lives** adapted and created by Patrick Garland at Criterion. First seen on TV when Dotrice was voted Television Actor of the Year. Julia Trevelyan Oman's wonderful set provided the dirt, the clutter and the squalor in which Aubrey (1626–1697), biographer, antiquarian, scholar, pauper and gossip, lived. There is one anecdote, which nobody ever forgets. Edward de Vere, Earl of Oxford, while making a low bow to Queen Elizabeth I, happened to fart. He was so embarrassed and ashamed that he immediately left the country and did not return to the court for 7 years. The Queen welcomed him back. "It's all right," she said, "I've forgotten all about the fart."

Mar 4. Albert Salmi, Kate Reid, Harold Gray and Shepperd Strudwick in Arthur Miller's **The Price** directed by Arthur Miller at Duke of York's. The theme is Time and the price we put on it. The setting is an attic full of old furniture. The antagonists are two middle-aged brothers who haven't seen each other for many years. One is a doctor, highly successful and rich; the other is an unsuccessful cop, who sacrificed himself for his father's sake during the Depression. The brothers have come together to find out what an old Jewish dealer will offer for the furniture. The play asks which brother did right? Was it the one who stayed at home to look after his father or was it the one who left home and thought only of himself? The millionaire father was a liar and the son, who stayed home, knew it. The sacrifices he made, and which wrecked his education, were totally unnecessary.

Mar 5. Ralph Richardson, Coral Browne and Stanley Baxter in Joe Orton's **What The Butler Saw** directed by Robert Chetwyn at Queen's. Orton's unfinished Freud-

1969 World Premieres
New York
Kenneth Tynan's *Oh! Calcutta!*
Johannesburg
Athol Fugard's *Boseman and Lena*

Deaths
Witwold Gombowicz (*b.*1905), Polish playwright
Martita Hunt (*b.*1900), British actor
Frank Loesser (*b.*1910), American composer
Miles Malleson (*b.*1888), British actor, playwright
Eric Portman (*b.*1903), British actor

Honours
Knights
Lew Grade, impresario
Bernard Miles, actor

Dame
Anna Neagle, actor

Notes
—Samuel Beckett awarded Nobel Prize for Literature
—Royal Court decided to withdraw tickets from critics
—Edward Bond's *Saved* won award at Belgrade Festival

History
—Neil Armstrong first man on the moon
—Richard Nixon became US President
—Maiden flight of Concorde
—Woodstock Festival

ian black farce, a mixture of Wildean pastiche, bogus psychiatric language and puerile smut, was written shortly before he was murdered by his male lover. Set in a madhouse, the paranoia gathers its own momentum, catering for every predilection – transvestism, striptease, indecency, nymphomania, homosexuality, rape and phallic worship. The play was booed by the gallery and reviled by the critics. The mistake was to have given it a slap-up West End production with the wrong actors.
—It's the kinkiest play in town. MILTON SCHULMAN *Evening Standard*
—A sad business from which no one emerges with credit. *Daily Mail*
—Totally spoiled by gratuitous obscenity. HAROLD HOBSON *Sunday Times*
—*What the Butler Saw* will live to be accepted as a comedy classic of English literature. FRANK MARCUS *Sunday Telegraph*

Apr 14. Théâtre de la Cité at Aldwych. Francine Berge and Samy Frey in Racine's **Berenice** directed by Roger Planchon. The actors were too young and didn't have the guns.
—It is like watching a play performed by statues which come to life briefly and freeze back into their marble poses. It is beautiful. It is pure. It is cold. It is classical. PETER LEWIS *Daily Mail*

Apr 15. Elizabeth Seal, Richard Briers, Murray Melvin and Victor Spinetti in Georges Feydeau's **A Cat Among the Pigeons** directed by Jacques Charon at Prince of Wales. Not nearly as funny as the Comédie Française's production.

Apr 16. Polly James in Donald Harron and Norman Campbell's adaptation of L M Montgomery's **Anne of Green Gables** directed and choreographed by Alan Lund at New. A sentimental, homely, wholesome, old-fashioned Canadian musical for little girls.

Apr 17. Théâtre de la Cité at Aldwych. Jean Bouisse in Molière's **Georges Dandin** directed by Roger Planchon. There was more Planchon than Molière. The action was filled out with 17th-century peasant life. Dandin literally became the laughing stock of the farmyard. The peasants were straight out of Brueghel. Bouise's wonderfully lugubrious, oafish Dandin knew that it was his fault if his wife was unfaithful.

Apr 22. Bill Owen, Alan Bates, Brian Cox, James Bolam, Constance Chapman, Gabrielle Daye and Fulton Mackay in David Storey's **Celebration** directed by Lindsay Anderson at Royal Court. Three sons are raised by their working class parents to better things. They end up educated but unhappy in meaningless jobs.

Apr 30. Betty Grable in **Belle Starr** at Palace directed by Jerry Schafer. Book by Warren Douglas. Lyrics by Steve Allen, Warren Douglas and Jerry Schafer. Music by Steve Allen. A disastrous Wild West musical. Belle runs a whorehouse. The matronly Grable had little to do and only showed her famous legs once.

May 1. Robert Lang as Mirabell and Geraldine McEwan as Millamant in William Congreve's **The Way of the World** directed by Michael Langham at Old Vic (NT). Ironically, there was much more wit in Fainall's encounter with Mrs Marwood. John Moffatt, alone in the cast, knew how to play Congreve. Hazel Hughes's crude and vulgar Lady Wishfort was Widow Twankey transformed into a latter-day Queen Elizabeth I.

May 5. Negro Ensemble Company at Aldwych in Peter Weiss's **Song of the Lusitanian Bogey and God is a (guess what?)** directed by Michael Schultz.

May 7. Tom Courtenay and Juliet Mills in Oliver Goldsmith's **She Stoops to Con-**

Leonard Rossiter in The Resistible Rise of Arturo Ui

quer directed by Braham Murray at Garrick. The production was of a low rep standard. Courtenay, a natural for Tony Lumpkin, was cast as Marlow.

May 19. Greek Art Theatre at Aldwych. Nelly Angelidou in Aristophanes's **Lysistrata** directed by Karolos Koun. Jolly vulgarity and modern songs. The goddess of peace appeared in a bikini. The play, premiered in Athens in 411 BC, was still politically relevant to events in Greece at the time and, no doubt, one of the reasons for its revival.

Jun 2. Anna Magnani in Giovanni Verga's **La Lupa** directed by Franco Zeffirelli at Aldwych. Sicilian passion: the fatal love of an older woman for a younger man ends in murder. Magnani, returning to the theatre after an absence of 15 years, to everybody's surprise, avoided melodrama. Softly spoken, she prowled the stage and let Osvaldo Ruggiero do all the over-acting.

Jul 1. Leonard Rossiter in Bertolt Brecht's **The Resistible Rise of Arturo Ui** directed by Michael Blakemore at Saville. Initially no London management could be found willing to take the risk of bringing the play into the West End. Brecht was considered box-office poison and Rossiter wasn't a star. It took two years and two revivals before it reached London. Brecht equated Hitler and the Nazi Party with a mob of gangsters, riding to power on a wave of hysteria and terror. They played to a continuous round of machinegun-fire which sounded like ironic applause. Rossiter's Ui, a petty snarling, slimy, vicious hoodlum in an over-large raincoat, was brilliant caricature, which owed nothing to Charlie Chaplin and *The Great Dictator*. Highly stylised and grotesquely funny (though nevertheless frightening for that), he was a cartoon figure, constantly being galvanised into schizophrenic ranting and petulant rages. The most famous scene was when Ui, determined to improve his diction and deportment, went to an actor, an old-time ham, for private coaching and was transformed into a goose-stepping, Fascist-saluting Hitler.
—The star in question (a term that cannot be withheld after this performance) is Leonard Rossiter's whose account of Brecht's Chicago hoodlum Hitler is one of the most staggeringly examples of grotesque comedy I have ever seen. IRVING WARDLE *The Times*
—You could say I am at my best at strong characters with a manic streak. I like roles such as Hitler where you can go from outraged hysteria to assumed calm in seconds. I think I am better equipped to do that than most. LEONARD ROSSITER *quoted by* BYRON ROGERS *TV Times*

Jul 2. Peggy Ashcroft and David Waller in Harold Pinter's **Landscape** directed by

Peter Hall at Aldwych (RSC). Play for two voices: one coarse and brutal; the other, quiet and gentle. The two parallel monologues make one continuous bit of music. A couple sits at the opposite ends of a kitchen table in a country house. They are Beth, a housekeeper, and Duff, a chauffeur. She never looks at him. He looks at her practically all the time. They remain in their separate worlds. She has succeeded in blocking him out completely. She is lost in a reverie, remembering a time when she made love on a desolate beach on a beautiful autumn morning. But who was the man on the beach? Was he the master of the house? Is she grieving for his death? Did she make love with him while Duff was away? Or did she make love with him only after Duff had told her he had been unfaithful? Did Duff try to rape her? Was Duff, in fact, the man on the beach long, long ago? Played in a double bill with Harold Pinter's **Silence** with Norman Rodway, Frances Cuka and Anthony Bate. Both plays were like poems. The mundane was made poetic.

Jul 10. Maxine Audley, Paul Jones and Jeremy Clyde in Barry England's **Conduct Unbecoming** directed by Val May at Queen's. Courtroom drama set in India during the Raj when British officers treated the native women like pigs.

Aug 10. Joyce Blair and Sheila White in **Dames at Sea** directed and choreographed by Neal Kenyon at Duchess. Book and lyrics by George Haimsohn and Robin Miller. Music by Jim Wise. Affectionate spoof at the expense of cliché-ridden backstage stories, so popular in 1930s Hollywood musicals. "I've just got off the bus and I want to be a star," announces the heroine. And by the end of the day, she has graduated from chorus girl to leading lady.

Sep 10. Bernard Lloyd and Ben Kingsley in Sean O'Casey's **The Silver Tassie** directed by David Jones at Aldwych (RSC). The lack of Irish accents didn't help.

Sep 24. Ian McKellen alternated in Christopher Marlowe's **Edward II** and Shakespeare's **Richard II**, both directed by Toby Robertson at Mermaid. McKellen as Edward cried, screamed, wielded a huge sword, grovelled on the ground, and always went for the big vocal and physical effects. The final scene was heightened when the murderer Lightborn (Robert Eddison, excellent), having killed Edward, fell on top of him in such a way to imply cunnilingus, an additional piece of sensationalism which would, no doubt, have appealed to Marlowe. James Laurenson's Gaveston had charm. Timothy West's Mortimer was a good man corrupted by power. Transferred to Piccadilly.

Ian McKellen and James Laurenson in Edward II

—Mr McKellen is in fact a tremendous actor. No player of similar age has such lustre, such interior excitement, such spiritual grace. HAROLD HOBSON *Sunday Times*

Sep 29. Madeleine Renaud in Samuel Beckett's **Oh! Les Beaux Jours** at Royal Court directed by Roger Blin. A haunting and spellbinding performance.
—Flawlessly grounded between radiance and dismay the performance is totally free from easy pathos and shows Mme Renaud's characteristic faculty for transmitting brief decisive action through a body as fragile as a bird's. IRVING WARDLE *The Times*

Oct 2. Anthony Roberts in Burt Bacharach's musical **Promises, Promises** directed by Charles Blackwell at Prince of Wales. Book by Neil Simon, based on the screenplay for *The Apartment* by Billy Wilder and I A L Diamond. Lyrics by Hal David. Ambitious young man, in the hope of quick promotion, hires out his one-room flat to senior executives for one-night stands. Michael Bennett's choreography was witty and energetic.

Oct 16. Jim Dale in Peter Nichols's **National Health or Nurse Norton's Affair** directed by Michael Blakemore at Old Vic (NT). Morbid, crude, heartless and grotesque, this was the sick joke to end all sick jokes. The overworked nurses patronised the patients, treated them like babies and, most ghoulish of all, kept them alive long after they should have been dead. Jim Dale played an orderly, who turned out to be the devil in disguise, an ideal master of ceremonies for the worst bits of bad taste. Running parallel with the everyday hospital routine was a slushy woman's TV serial concerning a Scots house physician and a black nurse. Blakemore's production consolidated his position as one of the top directors.
—It had a pungency that Chekhov would have envied at times and it caught me between wind and water, half in tears and half with laughter. PHILIP HOPE-WALLACE *Guardian*

Oct 21. Bill Owen, T P McKenna and Martin Shaw in David Storey's **The Contractor** directed by Lindsay Anderson at Royal Court. The action was the mounting and dismantling of a wedding marquee in Yorkshire. The actors fleshed out the characters. Anderson directed the play with meticulous detail as if he were directing Chekhov. Riveting.

Nov 12. Frank Finlay in Dennis Potter's **Son of Man** directed by Robin Midgley transferred from Phoenix Theatre, Leicester, to Round House. Stephen Macdonald as Judas. The first modern drama portraying Christ to be seen in public since the end of censorship. It was originally performed on television, when Sylvia Clayton, writing in *The Daily Telegraph*, said that Potter's Christ "made the Beatitudes sound more like a political broadcast than a divine revelation."

Nov 13. Derek Godfrey, Geraldine McEwan, Edward Woodward and Jane Lapotaire in John Webster's **The White Devil** directed by Frank Dunlop at Old Vic (NT). A lascivious dream turns into a nightmare of intrigue, violence and revenge. Bracciano was strangled with a crucifix. The coup de theatre was saved till last when Vittoria and Zanche desperately plead with Flamineo to give them the two pistols he is brandishing. When they finally get the pistols they shoot him dead – a big shock. This was followed by an even bigger shock. The audience gasped out loud when they found that Flamineo wasn't dying at all and that he had merely tricked them. Designer Piero Gherardi's enormous white stone slabs provided a striking background.

Nov 27. Alan Howard in Cyril Tourneur's **The Revenger's Tragedy** directed by Trevor Nunn at Aldwych (RSC). The whole performance was a dance of death, a necrophiliac revel. The characters, drained of their colour, looked like twitching corpses. Matching sensation for sensation, savagery for savagery, pornography for pornography, the production was a *tour* (neur) *de force* played for laughs. Howard, in golden jock-strap and bare buttocks, stood out.

Dec 16. A Talent to Amuse, a tribute to Noël Coward by the profession for the profession on his 70th birthday directed by Wendy Toye, Nigel Patrick and Douglas Squire at Phoenix. One performance at midnight.

Dec 4. Anthony Jacobs in Peter Barnes's **Leonardo's Last Supper** directed by Charles Marowitz at Open Space, Tottenham Court Road. The space was turned into a gloomy, spooky charnel house with skeletons and bones. Cobwebs brushed the audience's faces as they groped their way to their seats by candlelight. Leonardo da Vinci has died; but just as the undertakers are about to prepare him for burial, he comes back to life again. His delight is not shared by the undertaker and his family. They need the money they will be paid for burying him. So they kill him. This gruesome, macabre and frightening tale was followed by Peter Barnes's **Noonday Demons**. A saint, living all alone in the desert, is disconcerted to find that he has been joined by another saint, who says Jesus has sent him. Both monks, suspecting the other is the devil, vie with each other in spirituality and self-sacrifice, trying to prove who the holy one is. Unable to resolve their argument, they fight to the death. Joe Melia played the religious fanatic as a camp Jewish music hall comedian.

1970–1979

1970

Jan 15. David Warner and Irene Worth in Edward Albee's **Tiny Alice** directed by Robin Phillips at Aldwych (RSC). A lay brother, good for a lay, goes through some sort of test, temptation and ritual sacrifice. The symbolism, the allegory, the re-working of the Christian story was so obscure that it negated against any dramatic appeal. Warner had a very long soliloquy when he became Christ on the cross crying out for proof of God.

Jan 20. Ian McKellen in Christopher Marlowe's **Edward II** and Shakespeare's **Richard II** transferred from Mermaid to Piccadilly.
—Nothing like this unrestrained recognition of a great actor has been seen in Britain since John Gielgud's Richard of Bordeaux. HAROLD HOBSON *Sunday Times*
—One of the greatest performances of our time, imaginative, intelligent and sympathetic. It would be mad not to go. B A YOUNG *Financial Times*

Jan 28. Jill Bennett, Richard O'Callaghan and Diana Dors in Donald Howarth's **Three Months Gone** directed by Ronald Eyre at Royal Court. Older woman and a younger man have Freudian fantasies. Diana Dors played a vulgar Mum with the aplomb of a modern-day Wife of Bath. Transferred to Duchess.

Feb 5. John Gielgud, Patrick Magee, Wendy Hiller and Martin Shaw in Peter Shaffer's **Battle of the Shrivings** directed by Peter Hall at Lyric. World-famous humanist, talks humanity all the time but finds that he is just as lacking in humanity as everybody else; perhaps even more so when his old friend, an ex-pupil and a famous poet, challenges him to a symbolic fight, saying that he will make him hate him. Since it is obvious that universal hate is a much easier philosophy than universal love, the outcome is never in any doubt. Gielgud in the Bertrand Russell role was much easier to listen to than Patrick Magee was in his role of the poet.

Feb 10. Michael Hordern in Shakespeare's **King Lear** directed by Toby Robertson at Old Vic. Frank Middlemass's Fool was very old, a mirror image of Lear.

Feb 12. Anthony Quayle and Keith Baxter in Anthony Shaffer's **Sleuth** directed by Clifford Williams at St Martin's. civilized Grand Guignol played by two consenting adults in private. Shaffer's intellectual thriller was a literary spoof of the country-house detective stories of the 1920s and 1930s, as written by Dorothy L Sayers, Agatha Christie and Margery Allingham. A writer of detective stories is so "obsessed with playing games and murder as a fine art" that he decides to give his wife's young lover a nasty fright. He stages a detective fiction in his own home. The humiliated lover (who considers "thrillers are the recreation of snobbish, life-hating, ignoble minds") takes his revenge. Baxter pulled such a fast one that the audience was completely taken in by his disguise. Carl Toms's cluttered set, full of Gothic atmospheric junk, played a major role. 2359 performances.

Feb 24. Paul Scofield as Vanya, Colin Blakely as Astrov and Anna Calder-Marshall as Sonya in Anton Chekhov's **Uncle Vanya** directed by Anthony Page at Royal Court. The best production of the play since the legendary production with Laurence Olivier and Michael Redgrave in 1963. Ronald Bryden in *The Observer* described Scofield's performance as "marvellous, deft, flawless in taste, endlessly inventive." The balance between the absurd and the pathetic was perfect.

Feb 26. Frank Finlay and Leslie Sands in David Mercer's **After Haggerty** directed by David Jones at Aldwych (RSC). A confrontation between a bigoted North Country railwayman and his theatre critic son.

Apr 8. Maggie Smith and Robert Stephens in George Farquhar's **The Beaux Stratagem** designed by Rene Allio and directed by William Gaskill at Old Vic (NT). The characters hanker after London in much the same way as the three sisters hanker after Moscow. The production did away with all the affectation once thought so essential in reviving 18th-century comedy. There was a subtle change of emphasis. The subject was clearly seen to be, not so much marriage, as divorce. Maggie Smith's performance made it abundantly clear that there was nothing funny in a lady of refined taste being married off to a lethargic, sottish husband.

Apr 27. Schiller Theatre at Aldwych. Carl Raddatz in Carl Zuckmayer's **The Captain of Kopenik** directed by Boleslaw Barlog. Martin Held in Samuel Beckett's **Krapp's Last Tape** directed by Samuel Beckett and in Schiller's **Intrigue and Love** directed by Hans Hollman.
—In directing Martin Held Beckett has come to grips with a force of nature and the result is an alliance between Apollo and Dionysus, a marvellous fusion of austerity and passion. HAROLD HOBSON *Sunday Times*
—I have no hesitation in saying that I cannot recall worse acting in forty years of theatregoing. This performance [*Intrigue and Love*] ought to be preserved as compulsory viewing for any director tempted to be self-indulgently clever. MARTIN ESSLIN *Plays and Players*

Apr 28. Laurence Olivier and Joan Plowright in Shakespeare's **The Merchant of**

1970 Premieres
Milan
Dario Fo's *The Accidental Death of an Anarchist*
New York
Robert Patrick's *Kennedy's Children*
Oxford
Samuel Beckett's *Breath*

Births
Martin McDonagh, British playwright

Deaths
Arthur Adamov (*b.*1908), French playwright
Alec Clunes (*b.*1912), British actor
Nancy Price (*b.*1880), British actor
Naughton Wayne (*b.*1901), British actor

Honours
Peerage
Laurence Olivier, actor
Knight
Noël Coward, playwright, composer, actor

Notes
—Giles Havergal, Philip Prowse and Robert David Macdonald artistic directors of The Glasgow Citizens

History
—Riots in Gdansk
—Gay Liberation Front held first demonstration

Venice directed by Jonathan Miller at Old Vic (NT). Set in the late 19th century, the most original touch was to play the trial scene in a private courtroom where the matter of the pound of flesh could be discussed calmly across the table. (A woman in distress in the upper circle interrupted the scene to complain that Laurence Olivier was a Shylock to put on such a horrible play and hadn't the Jews suffered enough under the Nazis, etc, etc.) Shylock's heart-rending sobs off-stage, after he had lost his case, were even more moving for the woman's interruption. Plowright played Portia as a brusque spinster, who is so desperate for a man that she will even marry a homosexual (Jeremy Brett's Bassanio looked like a flabby, young Oscar Wilde). Charles Kay was delightful as a doddery, absent-minded, short-sighted Arragon. Morocco was straight out of a seaside minstrel show.
—The actor [Laurence Olivier] gives one of the great Shakespearian performances of our time. J C TREWIN *Illustrated London News*
—Sir Laurence will not be remembered for his Shylock. Or if he is, he will be singularly unlucky. HAROLD HOBSON *Sunday Times*

May 4. Comédie Française at Aldwych. Micheline Boudet in Henri Becque's **La Navette**, directed by Jean Piat, gave a delightful, sophisticated comedy performance as a demimondaine manipulating three lovers. Molière's **Amphitryon**, with Jacques Toja and Genieve Casile, directed by Jean Meyer, was dominated by Robert Hirsch's servant. Georges Descrieres as Juan in Molière's **Dom Juan**, directed by Antoine Bourseiller, was upstaged by Jacques Charon playing his servant, Sgnarelle.

May 5. Michael Hordern in David Mercer's **Flint** directed by Christopher Morahan at Criterion. 70-year-old rebel vicar (an agnostic since the day he was ordained) makes love to a girl in the vestry during choir practice and inadvertently sets the church on fire. Vivien Merchant's outwardly spinsterish gentility hid unexpected passions.

May 17. Keith Michell and Diana Rigg in Ronald Millar's **Abelard and Heloise** directed by Robin Phillips at Wyndham's. A story of lust, flagellation and castration was based on Helen Waddell's novel and the letters of Abelard and Heloise. A 37-year-old virgin and a schoolgirl of seventeen-and-a-half fall in love in 1131. A chorus of eavesdropping monks and nuns remained on stage all the time whispering and breathing heavily. Rigg and Michell appeared briefly in the nude; the lighting was so dim they might as well have kept their clothes on.

May 18. Catania Stabile Theatre at Aldwych. Turi Ferro and Fioretta Mari in Luigi Pirnadello's **Liola**, directed by Turi Ferro and Francesco Contrafatto. This frivolous, Sicilian, cuckolding romp, written within a week, was definitely not for feminists. Liola was a peasant, who had fathered many unwanted children by many women. The women were reduced to mere sexual objects.
—The entire Catania Stable cast is notable chiefly for its uninhibited demonstration of all those exuberant mannerisms that Italians display when they are coping with intense emotions. MILTON SHULMAN *Evening Standard*

May 25. Moscow Art Theatre at Aldwych. A I Stepanova as Arkadina and O A Stritzenhov as Konstantin in Anton Chekhov's **The Seagull** directed by Boris Livanov. S A Yabokiev in Nikolai Pogdon's **Lenin – The Third Pathetique** directed by M N Kedrov. The Lenin play was boring, dutiful propaganda. The Chekhov, crude and restless, was not up to the standard of previous Chekhov productions by the Moscow Arts.
—How many people realise that his *Seagull* is really a play about two seagulls, the white one and the black one, Masha? BORIS LIVANOV

May 27. Raymond Massey in Robert Anderson's **I Never Sang For My Father**

Ralph Richardson and John Gielgud in Home

directed by Vivian Matalon at Duke of York's. Pages from an autobiography. The father was a mean, selfish old bore and his son (George Baker) didn't have the courage to resist his emotional blackmail. Catherine Lacey played the arthritic mother. Drab and depressing (without the compensation of being theatrical) the production was acted at a funereal pace.

Jun 16. Ronald Radd as Benjamin Franklin and Lewis Fiander as John Adams in **1776** directed by Peter H Hunt at New. Music and lyrics by Sherman Edwards. Book by Peter Stone. The debate, the postponements, the set-backs and ploys involved in the writing and signing of the Declaration of Independence seemed a most unlikely subject for a musical. There was in fact more book than songs. The most moving moment came in the second act, when, in order to appease South Carolina, the slavery clause was struck out because "it's a luxury we cannot afford". James Wilson decided to vote for Independence, not from conviction, but because he hadn't the courage to say no when everybody else was saying yes. The book and lyrics pandered overmuch to the public's enjoyment of sexual innuendo. Thomas Jefferson, evidently, wasn't able to write the Declaration until he had had a good shag first.

Jun 17. John Gielgud and Ralph Richardson in David Storey's **Home** directed by Lindsay Anderson at Royal Court. A key moment in both actors' careers did for them

what John Osborne's *The Entertainer* had done for Laurence Olivier, and brought them firmly into the mainstream. There was no story, no action, just two old gentlemen in an asylum chatting away about nothing in particular. The line between fact and fantasy was blurred. (The script must have been as difficult to learn as *Waiting for Godot* which it, initially, resembled.) The two men fall back on the same phrases time and time again. The emptiness Gielgud and Richardson found in repeated phrases such as "oh, dear", "how exciting", "really?" "by Jove" and "my word" was extraordinary. Transferred to Apollo.
—He has an ear as acute as Pinter's and a quality more genuinely human. J C TREWIN *Birmingham Post*
—Mr Storey seems to me a true original, sensitive and poetic, and constantly aware of a dramatist's responsibility towards his audience. B A YOUNG *Financial Times*

Jun 23. Donald Sinden, Judi Dench and Elizabeth Spriggs in Dion Boucicault's **London Assurance** directed by Ronald Eyre at Aldwych (RSC). Written in 1841 when he was twenty, Boucicault presumed that theatregoers would accept that a father does not recognize his own son. The comedy owed something to Sheridan's *The Rivals* and Goldsmith's *She Stoops to Conquer*. 63-year-old Sir Harcourt Courtly, a fop of the old school, courts a young woman and a mature, horsy, married member of the aristocracy. His joint-creaking morning toilette was a blatant crib from Lord Ogleby's toilette in Colman and Garrick's *The Clandestine Marriage*.

Jun 29. Maggie Smith as Hedda and Jeremy Brett as Tesman in Henrik Ibsen's **Hedda Gabler** directed by Ingmar Bergman at Cambridge (NT). The production, non-naturalistic and Strindbergian (first seen in the 1968 World Theatre Season) got in the way of the play. Bergman's insistence on having Hedda and Judge Brack eavesdropping on the action, when they were not meant to be on stage, added nothing. Smith, gaunt, icy, frigid, ironic, mordant, thin-lipped, was as blanched as Charles Adams's Morticia. Robert Stephens's Lovborg tried to put his hand up her skirt. The scenes she shared with John Moffatt's Brack were the best.
—Maggie Smith's Hedda in many ways resembles her Swedish counterpart, Gertrud Fridh, in looks and gesture. But she is more regal, more majestic, cooler. And she has in all her tragic frustration, the sense of humour and the timing of a born comedienne. Martin Eslin *Plays and Players*

Jul 2. Judi Dench in Shakespeare's **The Winter's Tale** directed by Trevor Nunn transferred from Stratford to Aldwych (RSC). The opening scenes, acted in a nursery with a rocking horse, blocks and toys, emphasised the innocence of the characters. Dench played Hermione and Perdita. In that magical moment, when the statue comes to life, the audience was far too busy watching how she was going to do it. (Three actresses were needed.) Hermione's faint in slow motion at her trial was stunning. The Bohemian scenes were a straight filch from *Hair*, giving the second half a much-needed lift. It was like watching a musical. The "flower power" could wittily be justified in the text.

Jul 16. Leonard Rossiter and Joseph O'Connor in Morris West's **The Heretic** directed by Morris West at Duke of York's. The Roman Catholic Church burnt Giordano Bruno. Rossiter's worst vocal and physical mannerisms were on display.
—Has there been such a grotesquerie since the hunchbacked Laughton swung from the gargoyles of Notre Dame? Felix Barker *Evening News*

Jul 21. Peggy Ashcroft in Gunter Grass's **The Plebeians Rehearse The Uprising** directed by David Jones at Aldwych (RSC). What did Brecht do during the abortive 1953 East German uprising? His refusal to commit himself, to speak out either against or for the regime, angered both workers and government who wanted his name on their manifestoes. The great man of the theatre, the number one communist playwright of his day, "the friend of the proletariat" was found to be only a communist because it was professionally expedient for him to be one. Without Russian support Brecht would have had no theatre. His commitment was only to Brecht and the Berliner Ensemble.

Jul 23. Patrick Cargill, Phyllis Calvert and Amanda Reiss in Noël Coward's **Blithe Spirit** directed by Nigel Patrick at Globe. Beryl Reid played Madame Arcati. The actors didn't have either the acidity, charm or the physical attractiveness.

Jul 27. Kenneth Tynan's **Oh! Calcutta!** directed by Clifford Williams at Round House. Or as they say in French: Oh, quell cul t'as! A puerile and singularly unfunny nude revue, but all the publicity paid off. The theatre, despite exorbitant prices, played to packed houses. The audience, however, remained lukewarm and niggardly in their laughter and applause. The production ended with members of the cast voicing their own and the audience's thoughts. "If the show closes," said one actor, "I'm going to throw my cock away. Who wrote this shit, anyway?" Clive Barnes said in *The New York Times* that *Oh! Calcutta* was the sort of show to give pornography a bad name. Transferred to Royalty. 3918 performances.

Aug 3. Alec McCowen, Dinsdale Landen and Charles Gray in Christopher Hampton's **The Philanthropist** directed by Robert Kidd at Royal Court. A philologist, intelligent, reliable, kind, safe and dull, leads a full yet empty life. Hampton modelled his witty, civilised and urbane conversation piece on Molière. He examined the philologist in the light of one defining trait, his chronic anxiety to please people and to do what they want. He never stops apologizing. "I am a man of no conviction," he confesses and then after a very long pause, adds, "at least I think I am." His literal mindedness and his weak and indecisive nature, lead him to handle relationships badly. He infuriates everybody. The opening scene, once seen, never forgotten, took the audience completely by surprise. A student shoots himself. Charles Gray played his familiar role of a shit of the first order.

Aug 5. Robert Morley in Alan Ayckbourn's **How the Other Half Loves** directed by Robin Midgley at Lyric. The actual mechanics were so much more interesting than the play. There were two separate homes, but they shared the same set. The action in both houses went on concurrently. The set was a mixture of both homes' furniture. It took the audience some time to fathom out what was happening. The best moment was when two separate dinners, taking place on two different days, were played at the same table simultaneously. Morley, looking more than ever like a great big sulky baby, walked through the production, pulling faces.

Aug 5. Judi Dench as Viola and Donald Sinden as Malvolio in Shakespeare's **Twelfth Night** directed by John Barton transferred from Stratford to Aldwych (RSC). There was a memorable bit of business when Malvolio looked at his watch and corrected the sundial. Elizabeth Spriggs's Maria was an old spinster, who was abominably treated by an unpleasant Sir Toby. Sir Andrew Aguecheek was a Scot with bagpipes.

Sep 17. Donald Pleasance, Barrie Foster and Stephanie Beacham in Harold Pinter's **The Party** and **The Basement** directed by James Hammerstein at Duchess. Adaptation of two television plays. Sexual frustration in both, but they did not have the impact they had had on television.

Sep 23. Ian Holm as Nelson and Zoe Caldwell as Emma Hamilton in Terence Rattigan's **A Bequest to the Nation** directed by Peter Glenville at Haymarket. Nelson played a supporting role to Emma, who was acted as the cartoonists of the day saw her: a fat, absurd woman making a fool of herself. Caldwell gave a performance of such exaggerated comic vulgarity that Emma remained a character in a play and never a real person. Nelson hated his wife (Leueen MacGrath) because she was so forgiving.

Oct 8. Eileen Atkins as Elizabeth I, Sarah Miles as Mary Stuart and Richard Pearson as Lord Cecil in Robert Bolt's **Vivat! Vivat Regina** directed by Peter Dews transferred from Chichester to Piccadilly. Three hours of talk rather than drama. Mary was a high squeaking Chinese doll. Elizabeth was a puffy butterfly.

Oct 19. Judi Dench, Brewster Mason, Richard Pasco, Elizabeth Spriggs and Michael Gambon in Bernard Shaw's **Major Barbara** directed by Clifford Williams at Aldwych (RSC). Excellently argued and constantly witty, Brewster Mason had the weight for Undershaft and was a persuasive villain.
—[Judi Dench] is adroit at using her hoarse croaking voice for making us think she is on the edge of virtuous tears. John Barber *Daily Telegraph*

Oct 27. Edward Woodward in Edmond Rostand's **Cyrano** directed by Patrick Garland at Cambridge. Not so much a translation, as nearly a complete re-write. Charles Kay was excellent as de Guiche.

Nov 5. Kenneth More in Terence Rattigan's **The Winslow Boy** directed by Frith Banbury at New. More, a first-rate light comedy player, was cast as the distinguished lawyer and lacked the severity the role needed. Peter Cellier, as the humourless, boring solicitor, gave the subtlest comedy performance.

Nov 12. John Woodvine, Vivien Merchant, David Parfitt, Timothy West and Lynn Farnleigh in James Joyce's **Exiles** directed by Harold Pinter at Mermaid. Joyce, unfailingly honest, probed and searched into motives, which were rightly blurred. He was way ahead of his time (theatrically at least). Ezra Pound had thought audiences wouldn't be able to follow his exploration of the bitterness, the loneliness and self-destructive jealousy of love. Merchant smouldered. Her stillness was an effective contrast to the highly-strung and sardonic performance by Woodvine.

Nov 13. Victor Henry and Tony Sher in Heathcote Williams's **AC/DC** directed by Nicholas Wright at Royal Court. Three hippies, two schizophrenics and explicit sex. The verbal energy was explosive.

Nov 17. Peggy Mount, Hugh Lloyd and Freda Jackson in J B Priestley's **When We Are Married** directed by Robert Chetwyn at Strand. Fred Emney turned the photographer into a drunken music hall act and added a duet at the piano for good measure.

1971

Jan 1. Alan Bates in Shakespeare's **Hamlet** directed by Anthony Page at Cambridge. Celia Johnson as Gertrude. Audiences might have been forgiven for taking Bates's unprincely Prince to be one of the soldiers. Denmark was a prison. The aluminium cell, with its tunnels and sliding panels, were more appropriate for science fiction and jarred with the Elizabethan costume.
—The actor's equipment, technically admirable, does not yet encompass a wide enough range of expression for Hamlet's spiritual outrage. John Barber *Daily Telegraph*

Jan 28. Alan Badel in Jean-Paul Sartre's **Kean** translated and directed by Frank Hauser at Globe. Kean is so preoccupied with acting the great parts of Shakespeare that he has no personality of his own. He only comes alive during a performance. Badel, acting out his debauchery, tantrums and genius in the coarsest fashion, gave an amusing display of bad acting. The high spot was when Kean breaks down on in the middle of the bedroom scene in *Othello*, having failed to cope with his own drunkenness, the gross incompetence of his leading lady, interruptions from the rowdy auditorium, and rude comments from his mistress in the Royal Box. Desdemona (Felicity Kendal) holding out her cushion, silently begging Kean to smother her, was very appealing.

Feb 3. Jim Dale and Anthony Hopkins in Fernando Arrabal's **The Architect and the Emperor of Assyria** directed by Victor Garcia at Old Vic (NT). A banal and crude comment on civilisation: "Did God go mad before or after the creation?" The tricksy production had jock straps, bare buttocks, a parachute, a fork-lift truck and

1971 World Premieres

New York
Edward Albee's *All Over*
Stephen Sondheim's *Follies*
John Guare's *The House of Blue Leaves*
David Rabe's *Sticks and Stones*

Births
Sarah Kane, British playwright
Connor McPherson, Irish playwright

Deaths
Gladys Cooper (*b.*1888), British actor
St John Ervine (b.1883), British playwright
Tyrone Guthrie (*b.*1900), British director

N C Hunter (*b.*1908), British playwright
Cecil Parker (*b.*1897), British actor
Michel Saint-Denis (*b.*1897), French director

Honours
Knight
Terence Rattigan, playwright
Dame
Agatha Christie, playwright

History
—President Amin overthrown

blinding spotlights. "Never," said Harold Hobson, "have there been so many lights with so little illumination."

Feb 18. Ingrid Bergman as Lady Cicely Waynflete in Bernard Shaw's **Captain Brassbound's Conversion** directed by Frith Banbury at Cambridge. Banbury made the mistake of taking the Boy's Own stuff far more seriously than Shaw did. Bergman was not a comedy actress. Constantly stumbling over her lines, it was often difficult to follow what she was saying. (John Gielgud once said she spoke five languages and acted badly in all of them.) Kenneth Williams carried on in his usual way, having long since given up acting and was content merely to project his over-familiar nasal persona.

Feb 24. Jeremy Kemp, Anna Massey and Simon Ward in Simon Gray's **Spoiled** directed by Stephen Hollis at Haymarket. Schoolmaster invites a gauche, sensitive, none-too-bright lad for the weekend to brush up his French. Since the boy hasn't a chance of passing the exam, his wife rightly suspects her husband's motives. Simon Ward was still playing young lads when he was 29.

Mar 9. Paul Scofield in Carl Zuckmayer's **The Captain of Kopenick** directed by Frank Dunlop at Old Vic (NT). An ex-convict cannot get a job without a permit and he cannot get a permit without a job. He spends most of his life in prison, until one day he buys himself a uniform and finds that instead of being treated as a doormat, he commands immediate respect and can now treat everybody else as a doormat. The characters are drawn in the broadest strokes. There is pastiche Dickens for a sentimental death scene; pastiche Wedekind for homosexual and lesbian perversions; pastiche Gorky for lower depths; pastiche music hall for lavatory jokes. The satire reflected a decadent, boorish, petty society, whose bullying, yet essentially servile, nature was such that it was not very difficult to see how the Nazis could come to power. (The Nazis banned the play.) The best moment was right at the end when the Kaiser himself turned what had been an utter fiasco into a ludicrous patriotic triumph for discipline and authority. Scofield's performance, a sad statement on human dignity, gave the farce its depth. He was the only real person on stage. The rest were merely types.

Apr 19. Royal Dramatic Theatre of Sweden at Aldwych. Malin Ek in August Strindberg's **The Dream Play** directed by Ingmar Bergman. A medley of memories, experience, free fancies, absurdities and improvisation in which time and space do not exist. The severity and sparseness of the production made it feel as if it had been mounted on the cheap. The dream should have been more dazzlingly theatrical; it could have done with some Fellini-like surrealism.

Apr 26. Schiller Theatre of Berlin at Aldwych. Christa Witsch in Witold Gombrowicz's **Yvonne, Princess of Burgundy** directed by Ernst Schröder. This tragic, callous and grotesque farce was written in 1934 and not produced for thirty years. The heir to the throne, bored with court life, proposes to the ugliest, smelliest, sullenest, most lethargic, most anaemic and lowliest person in the kingdom. The court presumes it is a joke in bad taste, until he goes ahead and marries her. Ivona's ugliness is a reflection of the court's moral ugliness. Her unsettling, passive and silent presence is a permanent and humiliating reproach, and it drives them to Shakespearian distraction, madness and murder. Ernst Schroder's stylized production underlined both the silliness and the cruelty. Christa Witsch's wide-eyed and frightened Ivona, was touchingly vulnerable.

Apr 28. Gladys Cooper and Joan Greenwood in Enid Bagnold's **The Chalk Garden** directed by William Chappell at Haymarket. Old-fashioned play revived for old-fashioned theatregoers. Cooper was shallow and she did not relish the highly mannered language as Edith Evans had done 15 years earlier. This chalk garden needed some potash and a little granular pest.

Apr 29. Schiller Theatre of Berlin in a Samuel Beckett double-bill directed by Samuel Beckett. Martin Held in **Krapp's Last Tape** and Ernst Schröder and Horst Bollmann in **End Game**.
—If I asked him [Samuel Beckett] any kind of psychological question about the character he never provided any information. But he was delightfully precise about the minutest of pauses. ERNEST SCHRÖDER quoted by RONALD HAYMAN *The Times*

May 6. Anthony Hopkins in Shakespeare's **Coriolanus** directed by Manfred Wekworth and Joachim Tenschert at Old Vic (NT). Margaret Tyzack as Volumnia. The Berliner Ensemble directors tried to impose their Brechtian-Marxist interpretation on the English actors with disastrous results. Coriolanus's contempt for the mob was played down.

May 11. Tom Eyen's **The Dirtiest Show in Town** directed by Tom Eyen at Duchess. A nude revue, which was far superior to *Oh! Calcutta*.

May 17. Nuria Espert Company at Aldwych. Nuria Espert and Julieta Serrano as the maids and Maria Paz Ballesteros as their mistress in Jean Genet's **The Maids** directed by Victor Garcia.
—Superficially the result is impressive, but – regrettably – it is also more than a little ridiculous. FELIX BARKER *Evening News*

May 26. Timothy West and Peter Davies in Oscar Wilde's **The Critic as Artist** adapted and directed by Charles Marowitz at Open Space. Wilde's intellectual discussion on Art and Life became a series of sexual manoeuvres. The actors were observed through gauze. The older man seduced the younger by the force of his intellect. The dialogue was civilised, but it was the underlying sexual ploys, with its hint of *fin de siècle* decadence, which gave the epigrams and the paradoxes their theatrical edge. West was a condescending, old quean whose egoism and petulance were finally pathetic.

Jun 1. Colin Blakely, Dorothy Tutin and Vivien Merchant in Harold Pinter's **Old Times** directed by Peter Hall at Aldwych (RSC). Husband and wife, living in the depths of the country, are visited by the wife's ex-roommate. The women haven't seen each other in twenty years but the husband is still jealous of their past friendship. The husband believes that he met his wife for the first time in a cinema. The guest is convinced it was she who met the wife there. Husband and guest vie with each other in their memories, fighting for the possession of the wife. The husband hasn't a chance; but then neither has the guest. The wife wins, as she had done in the past, by keeping her mouth shut. The clue to the play comes early on when the guest says, "There are things one remembers even though they may never have happened". The husband cannot forget or forgive his wife for having had a lesbian relationship.
—Peter Hall directs the comedy with a musician's ear for the value of each word and silence which exposes every layer of the text like the Perspex levels of a three-dimensional chessboard. RONALD BRYDEN *Observer*
—Harold Pinter's poetic, Proustian *Old Times* has the inscrutability of a mysterious picture and the tension of a good thriller. *Independent*

Jun 3. Michael Crawford in Anthony Marriott and Alistair Foot's **No Sex Please –We're British** directed by Allan Davis at Strand. Newly weds embarrassed by an unwanted consignment of mail-order pornography. Crawford's physical dexterity was impressive.

Jun 10. Alan Howard as Oberon and Sara Kestelman as Titania in Shakespeare's **A Midsummer Night's Dream** directed by Peter Brook transferred from Stratford to Aldwych (RSC). The wettest dream ever – far more erotic than *Oh! Calcutta* – was a major turning point in Shakespearian productions. The action was played out in a dazzlingly bright, white gymnasium. There was no forest and no fairies as such. (The fairies were assistant stage managers.) The colour was in the costume and Titania's enormous plume feather bed. John Kane's acrobatic Puck was much nearer to Harlequin than he was to Robin Goodfellow. The rude mechanicals were 20th century workers with cloth cap, hobnail boots, string vest, braces and sandwiches. When Bottom was transformed into an ass, he was given a clown's black squat nose and tiny mufflers. David Waller looked like yogi bear. Bottom's climax (the stage splattered from all sides by falling white paper plates) was the climax to the first half. *A Midsummer Night's Dream* has never been quite the same again.
—I wanted everybody to understand that it was the actors always playing and improvising, it was never a production fixed by a director in a certain way for the actors to obey. PETER BROOK quoted in an interview with Judith Cook in *Director's Theatre*
—Old lines whose familiarity had bored one for years came up fresh and comic or distressingly apt. JOHN BARBER *Daily Telegraph*

Jun 15. Paul Scofield, Joan Plowright and Edward Hardwicke in Luigi Pirandello's **The Rules of the Game** directed by Anthony Page at New (NT). The husband claims that he has drained himself of all emotion, a lie that Scofield's performance expertly exposed. The emotion was patently still there. The humiliated husband seethed with anger and the indifference was merely a mask. Scofield's seriousness was at odds with the artificial little comedy the rest of the cast was acting.

The cast of **Godspell**

Jun 23. Christopher Plummer and Geraldine McEwan in Jean Giraudoux's **Amphitryon 38** directed by Laurence Olivier at New (NT). Plummer, a striking physical presence, played the dull husband and the lecherous god. McEwan was the devoted, chaste wife, and nowhere was she more appealing than when she allowed herself to half-embrace her husband, believing he was Zeus in disguise, and feeling ever so naughty.

Jul 6. Peggy Ashcroft, Maurice Denham and Gordon Jackson in Marguerite Duras's **The Lovers of Viorne** directed by Jonathan Hale at Royal Court. A woman kills her deaf and dumb cousin, cuts up her body and drops the pieces, one by one, into passing trains from the railway bridge of her home town. Ashcroft's performance was notable for its extraordinary serenity under interrogation, as if the chilling events had nothing to do with her.

Jul 14. Alan Bates in Simon Gray's **Butley** directed by Harold Pinter at Criterion. University lecturer's hetero and homosexual marriages break up. Realizing he is on the way down, he determines to take everybody with him. Bates acted his long monologues with considerable charm and humour.

Jul 22. John Wood, Mary Rutherford, Alan Howard, Patrick Stewart, Sebastian Shaw and Sara Kestelman in Maxim Gorky's **Enemies** directed by David Jones at Aldwych (RSC). Gorky's impassioned plea for decent behaviour is ignored by the bosses who see the dangers of leniency all too clearly. If the men cease to beg and start to demand, the end result will be rioting and killing. Therefore anything that smacks of "socialism" and "liberalism" has to be ruthlessly stamped out. Fine ensemble work.

Jul 29. Andre Jobin, Cleo Laine, Lorna Dallas, Thomas Carey, Kenneth Nelson and Derek Royle in Jerome Kern and Oscar Hammerstein's musical **Show Boat** directed and choreographed by Wendy Toye at Adelphi. Cleo Laine sang "Can't Help Loving

That Man Of Mine" and "Bill" with such feeling that many people wished the story could just concentrate on her.

Aug 3. Christopher Plummer as Danton and Charles Kay as Robespierre in George Buchner's **Danton's Death** directed by Jonathan Miller at New (NT). Danton's vice was infinitely preferable to Robespierre's virtue. He loved life so much that, when he found the fun had gone out of it, he preferred to be guillotined rather than to guillotine. Robespierre was convinced that "Virtue must rule through Terror". Miller daringly presented the play as a museum piece – a relic of the past in glass cases.

Aug 4. Alec Guinness and Jeremy Brett in John Mortimer's **A Voyage Round My Father** directed by Ronald Eyre at Haymarket. Mortimer's father was a famous barrister who had been involved in some of the most salacious divorce case of his times. In middle-age he suddenly went blind. He refused to take any notice of his disability and carried on as if it did not exist. He was eccentric, egotistical and selfish. A master of rhetoric in the courtroom, he had fun obliterating the opposition with some highly theatrical ploys. He also enjoyed winding up his son and even tried to persuade his son's fiancée not to marry him, saying she could do so much better. The text, all bits and pieces, acted like some isolated pages from an unfinished biography. The most dramatic moment was when the fiancée asked why everybody went round pretending that the father wasn't blind, but the drama inherent in that question wasn't followed up. Guinness was at his best when the barrister was being most caustic.

Aug 5. Ian McKellen in Shakespeare's **Hamlet** at Cambridge directed by Robert Chetwyn. The prince was a university drop-out. The production was dull, tatty and Wagnerian in its length. The costumes embraced a whole range of periods, many of them looking like bits and pieces out of a school's theatrical wardrobe. The high spot was the "O what a rogue and peasant slave am I" soliloquy.

Aug 17. Ralph Richardson in John Osborne's **West of Suez** directed by Anthony

Page at Royal Court The action was set on an island among the sort of colonial Brits Somerset Maugham, Noël Coward and E M Forster used to write about. Richardson's presence and familiar vocal mannerisms gave the production an immediate lift. He was cast as a devious, tactless, patronising "old duffer" who had a special knack for upsetting his family. Transferred to Cambridge Theatre.

Sep 13. Alan Howard and John Wood in George Etherege's **The Man of Mode** directed by Terry Hands at Aldwych (RSC). Etherege's centuries of neglect was inexplicable. The production, up-dated to some vaguely modern period, had barely started before Howard was in the nude having a bath. Vivien Merchant played Lady Loveit as if she were an exotic sultry film star, left over from the 1940s. Her hammy delivery of so many of her worst lines, surprisingly, did not detract from their underlying seriousness. The young lovers (Helen Mirren and Terence Taplin) gave a ludicrous display of love for the benefit of their eavesdropping parents. John Wood's Sir Fopling Flutter was way over the top and very funny.

Sep 29. Harry Andrews in Edward Bond's **Lear** directed by William Gaskill at Royal Court. Lear is mad from start to finish. Cordelia does not appear. Bond concentrated on the horrors of war, an endless killing spree of unrelenting brutality. Lear dies whilst attempting to demolish a wall.
—He [Edward Bond] falls back on Fine Writing, a bald Celtic rhetoric of wind, tears, leaves, pain and pity, which is desolatingly unhelpful … .Harry Andrews, grand and forceful as he is, goes down fighting against the gloom and monotony of the role. JOHN HOLMSTROM
Plays and Players

Oct 7. John Wood, Vivien Merchant, T P McKenna and Estelle Kohler in James Joyce's **Exiles** directed by Harold Pinter transferred from Mermaid at Aldwych. A masterpiece was reaffirmed.

Oct 14. Kenneth More in Alan Bennett's **Getting On** directed by Patrick Garland at Queen's. It was not the play Bennett had written. Kenneth More brought all his charm to bear on the role of a socialist, who was so busy talking all the time that he didn't listen to anybody and had failed to notice his wife was having an affair. The charm didn't make sense. The other characters seemed to be talking and acting with

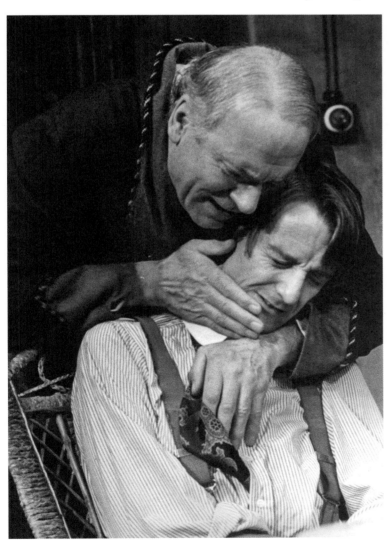

Laurence Olivier and Ronald Pickup in Long Day's Journey Into Night

quite a different person. He was presumably cast to make the seriousness more palatable to West End audiences; instead he merely made the play more trivial and the purple passages more awkward.

Nov 9. David Storey's **The Changing Room** directed by Lindsay Anderson at Royal Court. No story, just an authentic slice of North Country life, set in a rugby club on a wintry Saturday afternoon before, during and after a match. The cast was convincing as rugby players and when it came to full frontal nudity they gave *Oh! Calcutta* and *The Dirtiest Show In Town* a run for their money. Anderson had insisted that the actors shouldn't do anything so coy as to hide behind their towels. This was fine while they were at the Court enjoying an artistic success. However, once they transferred to the West End, they found they were acting to a completely different kind of audience who cheered every entrance, according to size of their penises. The actors (who had thought they were in a play and not a strip-show) started using their towels. There was talk of a film and one of the reasons it never got made was that Anderson insisted that the penises and buttocks should not be edited out by the censor.

Nov 17. David Essex in Stephen Schwartz's **Godspell** at Round House. The musical, conceived and directed by John Michael Tebelak, was based on the Gospel According to St Matthew. There were those who argued that the musical said Christianity was fun. There were others who argued that it merely made fun of Christianity. Godspell had the messy exuberance of Hair, the high-spirited naïvety of a primary school nativity play, and the larky sophistication of a university campus revue. The *commedia dell'arte* cast clowned, gagged, mimed, sang and generally mucked about. Their enjoyment was infectious. David Essex was a baby-face Jesus.

Nov 25. T P McKenna, Clement McCallin, Philip Locke and Barry Stanton in Jean Genet's **The Balcony** directed by Terry Hands at Aldwych (RSC). The brothel was a House of Illusions and Farrah's décor gave it a sordid, grotesque grandeur. The Bishop, the Judge, the General and the Chief of Police were turned into enormous carnival figures. The actors relished the erotic ritual. Helen Mirren played the general's filly.

Dec 16. Pablo Picasso's **Four Little Girls** directed by Charles Marowitz at Open Space. The space was converted into a farmyard and the audience sat on grassy mounds to watch a surrealistic mixture of poetic imagery and childhood fantasies and games. There were too many rhymes and jingles and not enough action. The cruelty and vindictiveness didn't lead anywhere and the actresses were too well developed to pass for little girls.

Dec 21. Laurence Olivier, Constance Cummings, Denis Quilley and Ronald Pickup in Eugene O'Neill's **Long Day's Journey Into Night** directed by Michael Blakemore at New (NT). O'Neill's four hours of unrelenting recriminations was revived because the National was strapped for cash and the cast was small. Olivier had put off playing James Tyrone because he didn't want to play an actor. The high spot was Tyrone's monologue when he talks of his childhood ("It was in those days that I learned to be a miser") and recalls with pride his early promise in the theatre. The surprise performance was by Quilley, who had spent so much of his theatrical career in trivia. He had at long last got a role worth acting: the elder brother who has a terrible drunken confession when he tells his consumptive younger brother that he had always wanted him to be a failure like himself.
—For a genuinely great actor to play a nearly great actor is the hardest feat of all. Olivier does it to perfection. MICHAEL BILLINGTON *Guardian*

1972

Jan 18. Elaine Stritch in Stephen Sondheim's **Company** directed by Harold Prince at Her Majesty's. Book by George Furth. Small American revue about marriage is made into a big American musical. A series of sketches are bound somewhat tenuously by a 35-year-old bachelor visiting his married friends and observing their unsatisfactory relationships. The lyrics were witty, cynical and trenchant. The abstract design, all chrome, glass, steel and elevators, dominated the production too much.

Jan 26. Albert Finney and Rachel Roberts in E A Whitehead's **Alpha Beta** directed by Anthony Page at Royal Court. Eleven years of marriage is good grounds for divorce.

Jan 26. Godspell transferred to Wyndham's.

Jan 31. Edward Albee's **All Over** directed by Peter Hall at Aldwych (RSC). Albee's best play since *Who's Afraid of Virginia Woolf?*. A famous man lies dying. His family, his mistress, his best friend gather. Who he is the audience never learns, for the characters are too busy talking about themselves. The syntax is as torturous as a Henry James novel; its very artificiality is its appeal. The individual and collective suffering are turned almost into a ritual and a series of arias becomes a litany of pain and acrimony. The ensemble was excellent: Angela Lansbury was the mistress. Peggy

Ashcroft was the wife. Sebastian Shaw was the best friend. David Waller was the son. David Markham was the doctor. Patience Collier was the nurse.

Feb 2. Michael Hordern and Diana Rigg in Tom Stoppard's **Jumpers** directed by Peter Wood at Old Vic (NT). Does God exist? Is man good, bad or indifferent? And what is so good about good anyway? A Professor of Moral Philosophy dictates at speed to his secretary, while his wife philanders with the Vice Chancellor and kills off his colleagues. The Professor, at the very moment that he discovers that he has inadvertently killed his beloved hare, inadvertently crushes his beloved tortoise to death. The production was a shapeless combination of philosophical gymnastics, intellectual farce and acrobatics. A J Ayer, foremost philosopher of his day, Professor of Logic at Oxford, and author of *Language, Truth and Logic*, enjoyed the play enormously. Laurence Olivier, the National Theatre's artistic director, fell asleep during a read-through by the author.

—Will make the cognoscenti squeal with laughter and leave those who think Wittgenstein is a lager beer not very amused. MILTON SHULMAN *Evening Standard*

Michael Hordern and Diana Rigg in **Jumpers**

1972 World Premieres
New York
Samuel Beckett's *Not I*
Tennessee Williams's *Small Craft Warnings*
Neil Simon's *The Sunshine Boys*
Cape Town
Athol Fugard's *Sizwi Bansi is Dead*

Deaths
Maurice Chevalier (*b.*1888), French music hall artist
Hetty King (*b.*1883), British music hall artist

Henri de Motherlant (*b.*1896), French novelist, playwright
Margaret Rutherford (*b.*1892), British actor

Notes
—John Betjamin Poet Laureate
—Tutankhamun Exhibition

History
—Bloody Sunday in Northern Ireland
—Massacre at Munich Olympics
—Watergate scandal began

—To fail to enjoy it is not actually a criminal offence but it is a sad evidence of illiteracy. HAROLD HOBSON *Sunday Times*

Feb 10. Joe Melia as Macheath in Bertolt Brecht and Kurt Weill's **The Threepenny Opera** directed by Peter Wood at Prince of Wales. "What keeps a man alive is hate and sin." With the wrong cast in the wrong theatre, it didn't look like a three-penny opera at all. It looked like a big musical. Melia looked like a small-time spiv. Vanessa Redgrave couldn't sing, couldn't dance and didn't act. She behaved as if she were in *The Boy Friend*. Barbara Windsor played Lucy on her own terms and stole the show. "I love you so much," she said to Macheath, "I'd rather see you hang than in the arms of another woman. Strange, isn't it?"

Mar 2. Leonard Rossiter, Jeremy Kemp and John Hurt in Harold Pinter's **The Caretaker** directed by Christopher Morahan at Mermaid. Rossiter, grotesque yet realistic, was wonderfully coherent in his incoherency and very funny.

Mar 9. John Gielgud and John Mills in Charles Wood's **Veterans** directed by Ronald Eyre at Royal Court. The veterans are two aging actors of the theatre on a film set in Turkey where they are shooting an epic. The gossipy, bitchy, camp script was a joke at Gielgud's expense and he gave a hilarious parody of himself, particularly so when he was put on a wooden box and left stranded there, not knowing what he had to do, trying to memorize his lines and having to cope with a blunt lighting man (played by a very funny Bob Hoskins).

Apr 3. Natal Theatre Workshop at Aldwych. Zulu Company in **Umabatha** directed by Pieter Scholtz. A Zulu version of *Macbeth*. The warriors, with feathers and shields, leaping, kicking, stomping, provided an exciting chorus line.

Apr 5. Donald Sinden and Judi Dench in Dion Boucicault's **London Assurance** transferred to New (RSC).

Apr 17. Nuria Espert Company at Aldwych. Nuria Espert in Frederico Garcia Lorca's **Yerma** directed by Victor Garcia. Naked bodies bounced, writhed and copulated on an enormous, undulating trampoline, which looked like a barren landscape, and was a powerful and sensual symbol for frustrated motherhood. Espert lay on her back with her naked legs lifted high in the air willing the unconceived child out of the terrible barren, wasteland of her own body.
—I have never seen anything so masterly as Yerma on the stage before ... it is not Lorca; it is better than Lorca; it is a triumph for Miss Espert and her company, for Mr Garcia and Mr Daubeny. HAROLD HOBSON *Sunday Times*

Apr 25. The Greek National Theatre at Aldwych in Aesychlus' **Oresteia** directed by Takis Mouzenides.
—For sheer blank tedium nothing in the World Theatre Season's record approaches this production. IRVING WARDLE *The Times*

May 3. Jorge Donn and Suzanne Farrell in Maurice Bejart's **Nijinksy Clown of God** at Coliseum. One of the major productions of the 1970s. A memorable moment, when Diaghilev (a huge, sinister, carnival, paper-mache figure) discovered that his favourite has married and behaved like an angry god, killing off Nijinsky's famous roles, one by one. Tchaikovsky's music disintegrated into jerky, electronic madness.

May 8. Eduardo De Filippo in Eduardo de Filippo's **Napoli Milionaria** directed by Eduardo de Filippo at Aldwych. Black market in post World War 2 Naples. De Filippo had the common touch as writer, actor and director and provided audiences with a genuine bit of popular theatre, mixing comedy and tragedy. He was very amusing when he was assisting at his own funeral. The kind policeman, knowing full well that he is shamming death, waits patiently for the satisfaction of seeing the "corpse" move.

May 11. Paul Curran and Louise Purnell as Sir Peter and Lady Teazle in Richard Brinsley Sheridan's **The School for Scandal** directed by Jonathan Miller at Old Vic (NT). Hogarthian production. Lady Sneerwell was discovered, not at her toilette, but on her toilet. Ronald Pickup's Joseph Surface behaved as if he were in a French bedroom farce.

May 15. The Kathakali Drama Company at Aldwych in **The Ramayana** and the **Mahabharata**. The appeal to uninitiated Western audiences was the colourful costumes, the heavily made-up faces and the sign language of hands and feet.

May 29. Cracow Stary Theatre at Aldwych. Fyodor Dostoyevsky's **The Possessed** was dramatised, designed and directed by Andrezj Wajda, who thought Albert Camus's 1959 adaptation was too conventional and wanted something more cosmic. Wajda's expressionistic production, a powerful mixture of melodrama and satire, was at times so grotesque as to be a parody of anarchism and nihilism. The clandestine meetings, the arson, the murders, the assassinations and the suicides, became more and more ruthless, more and more excessive, until all the leading protagonists, bar one, were driven out of their minds and into their graves. The nightmare was acted out in short, sharp scenes in a mud-spattered landscape. Black-hooded robed figures acted as stage managers. The action, visually stunning, was punctuated by amplified electronic grunts, whispers, vomiting and sexual ecstasy. Jan Nowicki was a sinister and malevolent Stravrogin, but there was nothing in his performance to suggest what his hold over the other characters was. Only once at the very beginning, in the opening hysterical confession, spoken at a terrific speed, was there any suggestion of that demoniac power which gripped all the characters. Wojciech Pszoniak hurled himself into the role of Yerkhovensky, the raving mad anarchist.
—*The Possessed* proved a weird and wonderful mixture of visual excitement and narrative obscurity with Middle European expressionism. FELIX BARKER *Evening News*

Jun 5. Tokyo's Kabuki Theatre at Sadler's Wells. First visit to London in two plays directed by Schochiki. Nakamura Shikan in **Kandehon Chushingura** (memorable for its long ritual suicide) and Nakamura Utaemon, Kabuki's greatest female impersonator, in **Sudmidagawa**. A mother's grieves over the loss of her child. There was much kneeling and self-abasement in gorgeous costumes with huge sleeves and trailing trouser legs. Movement was kept to the absolute minimum. The very slowness and sedateness increased the tension and pathos.

Jun 22. Emrys James as Shylock and Susan Fleetwood as Portia in Shakespeare's **The Merchant of Venice** directed by Terry Hands at Aldwych (RSC). A canine Shylock bared his teeth and barked. Launcelot Gobbo went mad.
—The only complaint is that Mr James reasonably Hebraic delivery is apt to slide into Welsh at moments of stress. IRVING WARDLE *The Times*

Jun 28. Jill Bennett as Hedda and Brian Cox as Lovborg in Ibsen's **Hedda Gabler** adapted by John Osborne and directed by Anthony Page at Royal Court. Hedda's mischief sprang from her boredom. She made passes at Mrs Elvsted. Denholm Elliott's Judge Brack was evil.
—As I see it, Hedda Gabler has her fun at the expense of others. She has a sharp wit but no authentic sense of humour. She is a bourgeois snob and a walking waste of human personality. JOHN OSBORNE

Jun 29. Gordon Gostelow in Maxim Gorky's **The Lower Depths** directed by David Jones at Aldwych (RSC). Powerful social commentary on a degrading, inhuman, filthy world, where death is the only relief. Gordon Gostelow's kind, tender Luka was an almost Christ-like figure, offering love, compassion, pity and hope.

Jul 4. Ralph Richardson and Peggy Ashcroft in William Douglas Home's **Lloyd George Knew My Father** directed by Robert Chetwyn at Savoy. Aristocrat threatens to kill herself if the planning authorities go ahead and build a road through her park. The comedy was so trivial that many people wondered what Richardson and Ashcroft were doing in it.

Jul 6. Denis Quilley in Ben Hecht and Charles MacArthur's **The Front Page** directed by Michael Blakemore at Old Vic (NT). White man shoots black policeman. The corrupt mayor and his corrupt sheriff, worried about the black vote, want him hanged. A senator, anxious to further his career, wants him reprieved. The action is seen mainly through the cynical and jaundiced eyes of the press who merely want a good story. The play – one of the National's biggest successes – manages to be all sorts of things at once: comedy, parody, indictment, melodrama, satire, social criticism, farce. The constant changes of mood spring a number of surprises – not least a suicide and that moment, in the middle of all the farce and wise-cracking, when it looked as if a man is actually going to be shot in cold blood. Denis Quilley was the ace-reporter. Maureen Lipman was the tart. David Bauer was the weak sheriff.

Aug 9. Paul Nicholas in Tim Rice and Andrew Lloyd Webber's musical **Jesus Christ Superstar** directed by Jim Sharman at Palace. Among the many innovations were a drunken Last Supper and a camp Pilate, The show, over-amplified, was at its worst in a squirm-making number like "Everything's Alright", which offered glib Hippie comfort. The crucifixion proved an anti-climax. Jesus rose rocket-like from the ground as if he was going to be blasted into outer space. Nicholas was a virile Jesus.

Paul Nicholas and Dana Gillespie in Jesus Christ Superstar

Dana Gillespie, as Mary, sang the show's hit song, "I Don't Know How To Love Him". Stephen Tate was a neurotic Judas, who might have come straight (or not so straight) from *The Boys in the Band*. John Parker gave the best performance as Pilate. "It is kitsch and vulgar, idiotic and amusing," said Jeremy Kingston in *Punch*. "Startling and nauseating," said John Barber in *The Daily Telegraph*." "Little for the card-carrying Christian," said Irving Wardle in *The Times*. The musical, nevertheless, had the blessing of Dr Ramsay and the Bishop of Southwark.

—Despite dreadful crudities of presentation, something near to Christianity occasionally leaps out. DR RAMSAY *Archbishop of Canterbury*

—There seems to me a good deal to object to: in particular the show's combination of shrill hysteria with tinselly showbiz vulgarity and its total failure to realise the dramatic potential of the original book. MICHAEL BILLINGTON *Guardian*

Aug 11. Tom Courtenay in Alan Ayckbourn's **Time and Time Again** directed by Eric Thompson at Comedy. The hero was a dazzlingly successful failure for whom nothing went right and yet he always came out on top. The first act set up the character and had him falling in love with somebody else's wife. The second act found him trying to pluck up courage to tell the husband.

Aug 31. Richard Pasco in T S Eliot's **Murder in the Cathedral** directed by Terry Hands at Aldwych (RSC). Something simpler and less clever would have served the text better. There were too many distractions. There was a ludicrous moment in the curtain calls when the company turned and bowed to the cross and the audience, presumably, applauded God.

Sep 6. Maggie Smith and Robert Stephens in Noël Coward's **Private Lives** directed by John Gielgud at Queen's. Smith, "jagged with sophistication" wore a 1930s hat with wit and gave her usual assured display of brittle high comedy technique. Her comic skills were much in evidence when she casually looked a man up and down and only after she had admired his accoutrements did she do a doubled-take, realising he was her ex-husband.

—Maggie Smith, who, pitching her performance somewhere midway between Tallulah Bankhead and Kenneth Williams, turns in a ravaging *tour de force* which, though undoubtedly the stuff theatregoers' memories are made of, is in fact curiously damaging to the play and most notably to the Elyot of Robert Stephens. SHERIDAN MORLEY *Punch*

Oct 4. Anthony Hopkins and Diana Rigg in Shakespeare's **Macbeth** directed by Michael Blakemore at Old Vic (NT). Hopkins had acquired so many of Laurence Olivier's inflections that it seemed as if he was Olivier's understudy. Lady Macbeth cracked up very early. She was all in by the coronation, her disintegration, brilliantly symbolized when she sank under the heavy weight of the coronation robes and had to be dragged up an endless flight of stairs. Later she turned into a deadly pale, highly rouged doll, looking more and more like Mary Queen of Scots gone to seed. Her sleepwalking took on a Noh-like grief.

Oct 19. Wendy Hiller as Queen Mary and Peter Barkworth as Bertie in Royce Ryton's **Crown Matrimonial** directed by Peter Dews at Haymarket. The abdication crisis in 1936 was seen entirely at a domestic level, through the eyes of members of the Royal Family. ("Well, really one might as well be in Romania.") Stammering George (Andrew Ray) was appalled at the idea of having to succeed his brother. The script was discreet, respectful, over-long and repetitive.

Nov 16. Lauren Bacall in **Applause** directed and choreographed by Ron Field at Her Majesty's. Book by Betty Comden and Adolph Green based on *All About Eve*. Music and lyrics by Charles Strouse and Lee Adams. The film, one of the best and wittiest films about showbiz, had an excellent script by Joseph L Mankiewicz and an unforgettable performance by Bette ("Fasten your safety belts; it's going to be a bumpy night") Davis. The musical's success was directly attributable to Bacall and the staging by Field and not to the music and lyrics. Angela Richards had the Anne Baxter role – a determined, ambitious, four-star bitch.

Nov 16. Gary Bond in Tim Rice and Andrew Lloyd Webber's musical **Joseph and the Amazing Technicolor Dreamcoat** directed by Frank Dunlop at Round House. Pop oratorio. Joseph was sold into slavery by his jealous brothers, but he came out on top because he was a great interpreter of dreams and had a flair for economic planning. He saved Egypt from famine. Rice and Webber's first musical success began in 1968 as a 15-minute cantata, written to be sung by a choir of junior-school children. The show, gradually expanded, until it made its first professional appearance at the 1972 Edinburgh Festival.

Nov 21. Peter Cook and Dudley Moore in **Behind the Fridge** at Cambridge. Nothing seemed to have happened since *Beyond the Fringe*. It was the same sort of juvenile undergraduate revue. The boys hadn't grown up. Moore was at his best in a parody of Kurt Weill and in his filmed appeal for a speech impediment fund. Cook was at his best as General Amin. They were particularly funny as Pete and Dud, talking about Women's Lib, while Dud did all the housework.

Dec 20. Jerome Savary's **Le Grand Magic Circus** at Round House. Modern *commedia dell'arte* relying on gags in the Goon/Helzapoppin/Marx Brothers/Monty Python manner. What dialogue there was largely sung and the rest was a mixture of French and broken English.

1973

Jan 1. The New Theatre is renamed The Albery as a tribute to the late Sir Bronson Albery.

Jan 16. Double bill by Samuel Beckett directed by Anthony Page at Royal Court. Billie Whitelaw in **Not I**. The stage is completely dark. A woman's voice begins speaking before the curtain rises and continues after it has come down. The audience sees only her mouth. She cannot stop talking. She has to get some horror out of her system. The monologue, rattled off at incredible speed and finished within fifteen minutes, is punctuated only by a scream, a hysterical laugh and the recurring "WHY? WHO? NO! SHE!" Whitelaw was riveting. Beckett thought Albert Finney in **Krapp's Last Tape** had about as much poetry as an ash-tray.

Feb 17. Gary Bond in Tim Rice and Andrew Lloyd Webber's **Joseph and his Amazing Technicolor Dreamcoat** directed by Frank Dunlop transferred to Albery. The additional prologue was a big mistake. The musical now ran forty minutes and wasn't as good as it had been at the Young Vic. Bond was charming and Paul Brooke, repeated his performances as God and chorus boy with huge abandon. Harold Hobson in *The Sunday Times* said it was "one of the most joyous entertainments we have ever seen".

Feb 20. Claire Bloom and Colin Blakely in Henrik Ibsen's **A Doll's House** directed by Patrick Garland at Criterion. Women's Lib rediscovered Ibsen. Bloom adopted the role of submissive wife to get her own way. Blakely played her complacent husband (whose masculine self-esteem takes such a battering) for the subtlest comedy.

Feb 22. Alec McCowen, Diana Rigg, Robert Eddison, Gillian Barge and Gawn Grainger in Molière's **Le Misanthrope** directed by John Dexter at Old Vic (NT). Translation by Tony Harrison. There was nothing funnier than Alceste raging – just as there was nothing sadder than Alceste begging Celemine to "try and pretend you're telling the truth and I'll try and pretend it's not a lie".

Mar 17. Eileen Atkins and Dinsdale Landen in Marguerite Duras's **Suzanna Andler** directed by Howard Sackler at Aldwych (RSC). The loneliness and pain of the unloved: Suzanna, indecisive, listless and preoccupied, is on the verge of a breakdown. Atkins had the tension of a Giacometti sculpture: a distraught, spectral-like figure in a large empty room.

Mar 22. June Jago as the mother, Patience Collier as the servant and Mia Farrow, Morag Hood, Helen Weir, Penelope Keith and Ann Firbank as the daughters of Federico Garcia Lorca's **The House of Bernada Alba** directed by Robin Phillips at Greenwich. Lorca described the play as "a photographic documentary". He completed it one month before the Spanish Civil War began in 1936 (the same year that he was murdered for his Republican sympathies and homosexuality). The play was not produced until 1945. It is set in the poorest part of rural Andalusia where "the worst punishment is to be born a woman." The peasants live in a society where women are ranked below land and oxen. Their job is to satisfy the sexual demands of their husbands and to raise male children. Women who lose their virginity outside of marriage pay a heavy price. They are either killed by their parents or stoned to death by the villagers. Bernarda Alba, who beats her five daughters into submission, expects them to mourn their dead father for eight years. Locked up and rotting away, their sexual frustration is symbolised by a stallion on heat off-stage kicking at the stable door, wanting to get out. The eldest daughter, 39 years old, is about to marry a man of 25, who is having sex with her youngest sister and is only marrying her because she has inherited her father's wealth. The actors were all far too English, except for Patience Collier who was so Spanish she looked like a foreigner.

Mar 26. Bochum Schauspielhaus from West Germany at Aldwych. Hans Fallada's **Little Man – What Now?** An inordinately long tract about a working-class couple being exploited by capitalists.

Apr 2. Nuria Espert Company at Aldwych. Nuria Espert in Federico Garcia Lorca's **Yerma** directed by Victor Garcia.

Apr 9. Burgtheater Vienna at Aldwych. Arthur Schnitzler's **Liebelei**, directed by

1973 World Premieres
New York
Stephen Sondheim's *A Little Night Music*
Cape Town
Athol Fugard's *The Island*

Deaths
W H Auden (*b.*1907), American poet, playwright
Hugh Beaumont (*b.*1908), British impresario
Noël Coward (*b.*1899), British playwright, composer, actor, director
William Inge (b.1933), American playwright
Jack Hawkins (*b.*1910), British actor
Laurence Harvey (*b.*1928), British actor

Notes
—Peter Daubeny's World Theatre celebrated its tenth and last season
—Peter Hall appointed next director of the National Theatre

History
—US withdrew from Vietnam
—Yom Kippur War
—Widespread industrial unrest in UK

Gerhard Klingenberg. A girl takes a liaison far too seriously. The story is romantic, yet realistic; the telling of it was cynical, yet sentimental.

Apr 12. Paul Scofield and Tom Conti in Christopher Hampton's **Savages** directed by Robert Kidd at Royal Court. The murder of a single diplomat hits the world's headlines and rouses international anger, whilst the systematic extermination of the Brazilian Indians is completely ignored. The public is more concerned about the extermination of the whale and the rhino. Scofield's performance – civilised, self-satisfied, affected – was witty satire which never degenerated into parody. Transferred to Comedy.

Apr 16. Comédie Française at Aldwych. Jacques Charon in Molière's **Le Malade Imaginaire** directed by Francis Perrin and **Le Médicin Volante** directed by Jean-Laurent Cochet. Robert Hirsch in Shakespeare's **Richard III** directed by Terry Hands. A typical RSC production – except it was in French. Hirsch, sick, demented and demoniac, was the best hunchback since Olivier.

Apr 30. Peppino de Filippo in Peppino de Filippo's **The Metamorphoses of a Wandering Minstrel** at Aldwych. Quaint, naïve, popular knockabout comedy in

Angela Lansbury in Gypsy

Peter Firth and Nicholas Clay in Equus

the *commedia dell'arte* manner. de Filippo was transformed into a statue of Caesar, a mustached baby in a high chair, a mad philosopher and a skeleton mummy.

May 7. Compagnia Dei Giovani and Morelli-Stoppa at Aldwych. Rossella Falk and Romolo Valli in Diego Fabbri's **La Bugiardi** and in Luigi Pirandello's **Right You Are, If You think You Are.**

May 10. Alec Guinness in Alan Bennett's **Habeas Corpus** directed by Ronald Eyre at Lyric. Sex and mortality, marriage and lust, frustration and despair: the farce was as English as John Betjeman (whom Bennett parodied) and as dirty as a seaside postcard by Donald McGill. Trousers were dropped and breasts were fondled. The production was acted out in a Magritte-like setting. Guinness's sly and lecherous GP had a little stop-start dance of death at the end, which the audience totally misunderstood.

May 21. Cracow Stary Theatre at Aldwych. Dostyevsky's **The Possessed** directed by Andrzej Wajda.

May 22. Coral Browne and Ian Holm in Edward Bond's **The Sea** directed by William Gaskill at Royal Court. Edwardian swan song with the lady of the manor, facing old age, knowing that she has wasted her life playing the bullying role the village expects of her. Ian Holm's mad draper was a Wellsian turn-of-the-century little man. His shop manner was perfect. There was a good scene when he broke down and crawled for custom. There was an even better scene when he started to cut velvet in a lunatic manner. Best of all was the funeral on the cliff top when her ladyship finds herself unable to compete with her companion in either hymn singing or a display of grief. Gillian Martell played the crushed companion, who so unexpectedly proved the stronger woman.

May 28. Royal Dramatic Theatre of Sweden at Aldwych. Max von Sydow as Gregers Werle, Ernst-Hugo Järegard as Hjalmar Ekdal and Lena Nyman as Hedvig in Henrik Ibsen's **The Wild Duck** directed by Ingmar Bergman. The brilliant, imaginative, cinematic production placed the loft firmly downstage. Bergman saw Werle and Ekdal as the opposite sides of the same coin. Von Sydow was very persuasive: a twitching, gangling, nervous, pathetic idealist bordering on lunacy

—I can't think of any other play so suffused with deep sympathy for everybody. Even the villain is treated with bitter affection. INGMAR BERGMAN

May 29. Angela Lansbury in **Gypsy** at Piccadilly. Book and direction by Arthur Laurents. Music by Jule Styne. Lyrics by Stephen Sondheim. The musical was based on the autobiography of Gypsy Rose Lee, the famous striptease artist, a classy elegant stripper, who didn't do anything as vulgar as actually strip. The book, a satire on tatty vaudeville and sleazy burlesque, follows the career of Gypsy's sister, Baby June (later June Havoc), in whose shadow the young Gypsy walked. The major role, however, is the mother, one of those aggressive, pushy, ruthless, over-ambitious, scheming, obsessive, domineering, headstrong, self-destructive, larger-than-life mothers. The role –one of music theatre's great roles – was specially written for Ethel Merman who didn't want Sondheim, a then-unknown composer, to write the score. Sondheim's lyrics inspired Jule Styne to write his best score. Lansbury singing "Rose's Turn" (a vivid and frightening picture of a woman unable to quit) was one of the finest bits of acting seen in a musical. Bonnie Langford was very funny as a precocious child dancing excruciating routines with nauseating professionalism.

June 4. **Umewaka Noh Troupe** at Aldwych in three traditional programmes.

Jun 19. Tim Curry as Frank-n-furter in Richard O'Brien's **Rocky Horror Show** directed by Jim Sharman at Theatre Upstairs. Rock 'n' roll horror based on the Frankenstein theme: mad mutants, tame transvestites, muscle-bound monsters, two virginal innocents, plus bondage and fishnet stockings. 2599 performances.
—It is far too joky to ever be accused of practising the corruption it pretends to preach. JACK TINKER *Daily Mail*

Jun 26. Richard Gere in Jim Jacobs and Warren Casey's **Grease** directed by Tom Moore at New London. The musical looked back to the late fifties, to the so-called "golden age of rock 'n' roll", and viewed the slobs, the morons, the creeps and the thugs with tongue-in-cheek nostalgia. A vulgar and tasteless era was lovingly recreated in all its vulgarity and tastelessness. Gere was particularly funny as a horny adolescent.

Tim Curry in The Rocky Horror Show

Jun 28. Robert Eddison, Geoffrey Chater and Kenneth Cranham in Howard Brenton's **Magnificence** directed by Max Stafford-Clark at Royal Court. Brenton's treatise in favour of anarchy argued revolution would never succeed so long as social protest remained so ineptly amateur.

Jul 4. Richard Briers, Bridget Turner, Michael Aldridge, Sheila Hancock, Anna Calder-Marshall and David Burke in Alan Ayckbourn's **Absurd Person Singular** directed by Eric Thompson at Criterion. Farcical tragedy is set over three Christmases in three different households in three different kitchens. Who would have thought suicidal despair could be so funny? A wife tries to jump out of the window, knife herself, hang herself and take an overdose of pills. The other people in the kitchen are so busy cleaning dirty ovens, unblocking sinks and mending faulty light fittings that none of them is aware that she is trying to kill herself. The second act is one of great second acts in English farce.

Jul 7. Richard Johnson and Janet Suzman in Shakespeare's **Antony and Cleopatra** directed by Trevor Nunn at Aldwych (RSC). Cleopatra has always had a bad press and Shakespeare, like everybody else, saw her through the biased, severe eyes of Rome, who loathed her because they were frightened of her. There was no indication of her intellectual powers at all. What was on offer was almost a parody of sexual obsession.

Jul 24. Jim Dale in **The Card** choreographed by Gillian Lynne and directed by Val May at Queen's. Musical. Book by Keith Waterhouse and Willis Hall based on Arnold Bennett's novel. Music and lyrics by Tony Hatch and Jackie Trent. The musical was shallow, repetitive and far too sentimental and pretty. Dale was most engaging when he was learning to dance.

Jul 26. Alec McCowen and Peter Firth in Peter Shaffer's **Equus** directed by John Dexter at Old Vic (NT). Psychological inquiry into why a 17-year-old semi-literate stable boy has blinded six horses. Can the psychiatrist restore the boy back to normality? If he takes away the pain, then what? ("Passion can be destroyed by a doctor. It cannot be recreated.") The psychiatrist, who, out of timidity, had settled for a pallid, provincial, hollow existence, is jealous of a boy who has known a passion more ferocious than he has felt in any second of his life. Firth's debut was striking. Claude Chargrin's mime for the actors playing the horses was particularly effective.

Aug 2. Martin Shaw as Dionysus, John Shrapnel as Pentheus and Constance Cummings as Argave in Euripides's **The Bacchae** directed by Roland Joffe at Old Vic (NT). Rewrite by Wole Soyinka: the Bacchae were now subversive slaves.

Sep 19. Ingrid Bergman in Somerset Maugham's **The Constant Wife** directed by John Gielgud at Albery. Bergman was far too nice for the cool, calculating revenge when the wife pays her husband back in kind for his infidelities. The text has far more acidity and irony than could be guessed from this revival. The viciousness had either been toned down or cut. Bergman, like the production, was strong on sentiment but weak on humor.

Sep 20. John Kani and Winston Ntshona in **Sizwe Bansi is Dead** devised by Athol Fugard, John Kani and Winston Ntosha at Royal Court Theatre Upstairs. The anti-Apartheid propaganda was based on personal experience. The social injustice, which denies a man dignity and identity merely because he is black, was spelled out in distressing terms. But the extraordinary thing was that so much of the performance should have been so funny.

Sep 25. Donald Sinden and Joan Greenwood in Terence Rattigan's **In Praise of Love** directed by John Dexter at Duchess. Rattigan says *le vice anglais* is not flagellation and pederasty but "our refusal to admit to an emotion." A wife tries to shield her selfish and boorish husband from the knowledge that she is dying. The irony is that he knows she is dying, but thinks she doesn't and so continues to be his usual brusque self for fear that if he changes the habits of a lifetime, she will guess she must be really ill. The play was based on the marriage of Rex Harrison and Kay Kendall, who died of leukaemia. They, like the characters in the play, kept up the pretence to the very end. Harrison, far from being upset by the play, decided he wanted to be in it. Rattigan turned it into a full-length piece, which was then performed in New York. Rattigan hated Harrison's self-indulgent performance.

Oct 3. John Mills, Michael Denison and Dulcie Gray in William Douglas Home's **At the End of the Day** directed by Robert Chetwyn at Savoy. A patronising political comedy at the expense of Harold Wilson and Harold Macmillan.

Oct 17. Alastair Sim and Patricia Routledge in Arthur Wing Pinero's **Dandy Dick** directed by John Clements transferred from Chichester to Garrick. The production was stale and Routledge was working so desperate for laughs it was grotesque.

Oct 22. Ben Kingsley and Janet Suzman in Athol Fugard's **Hello and Goodbye** directed by Peter Stevenson transferred from King's Head to Place. Highly emotional squalor in South Africa: half-crazed brother and his whorish sister ransack their tyrannical father's house in search of money.

Oct 22. Nicol Williamson in Shakespeare's **Coriolanus** directed by Trevor Nunn at Aldwych (RSC). Williamson was so erratic and so demented that it was never clear why the patricians should be so keen for him to be consul. The extended pause after his mother had gone down on her bended knees and begged him not to sack Rome was electrifying.

Oct 23. Leo McKern, Judi Dench and Edward Woodward in Ferenc Molnar's **The Wolf** directed by Frank Hauser at Apollo. Has a husband's insane jealousy of his wife any foundation or is it merely his fantasy? The second act allowed the audience to see into the wife's petty bourgeois mind. She imagines her lover returning in various guises. The romantic clichés, a parody of the worst sort of melodramatic theatre, should have been funny, but they weren't.

Oct 30. Paul Jones in Stephen Schwartz's **Pippin** directed and choreographed by Bob Fosse at Her Majesty's. Musical. Book by Roger O Hirson. Design by Tony Walton. Charlemagne's son, in his search for fulfilment, tries War, Sex, Revolution, Murder, Humanity, God, Love and Marriage. None of these things satisfies him. The music and the lyrics were never as witty and imaginative as the staging. Northern J Calloway, who played a devil-like figure and acted as compère, held the production together. He was elegant, witty and sexy; and he danced beautifully.

Oct 31. Joan Plowright, Frank Finlay and Laurence Olivier in Eduardo De Filippo's **Saturday, Sunday, Monday** directed by Franco Zeffirelli at Old Vic (NT). De Filippo had been quoted as saying that he wrote for the people in the street. The British actors were out of their depth with Italian neo-realism. The phony cod-Italian accents and the vast ballroom set didn't help. The most successful performance was by Frank Finlay, who judged the fine line between comedy and realism, especially in the second act, when he insulted his wife in front of the whole family and their friends.

Dec 12. Jenny Agutter, Faith Brook, Nigel Hawthorne, Alan Howard, Nicky Henson, Gayle Hunnicutt and Nicola Pagett in Peter Handke's **The Ride Across Lake Constance** directed by Michael Rudman transferred from Hampstead to Mayfair. Pretentious twaddle. The actors seemed to know what was going on. There was no interval, presumably, because had there been, nobody would have come back.

Dec 20. Laurence Olivier in Trevor Griffiths's **The Party** directed by John Dexter at Old Vic (NT). Elderly Glaswegian Trotskyite has an 18-minute monologue on the futility of forming a revolutionary party without the participation of the working-classes. This was Olivier's final stage performance.

Dec 21. Vanessa Redgrave, Jeremy Brett and John Stride in Noël Coward's **Design for Living** directed by Michael Blakemore at Phoenix. The *ménage à trois* is very exclusive: "It doesn't matter who loves who the most ... we all love each other a lot, far too much, and we've made a bloody mess of it." The original audience found the play unpleasant without being quite certain why. The present production was more explicit about the homosexuality; though not too explicit. The audience thought the trio were only pretending.

1974

Jan 1. John Wood in Arthur Conan Doyle and William Gillette's **Sherlock Holmes** directed by Frank Dunlop at Aldwych (RSC). The efforts to make the detective an almost tragic figure, by suggesting that he is so bored with his reputation and the criminal world that he longs to die, was unnecessary. The production tended to get bogged down in a complicated plot in which nobody was interested. There was an enchanting moment when a young lady (Mary Rutherford) dipped into her handbag and produced, as a token of her love for Holmes, a pipe! Wood's deadpan performance was spot on. Philip Locke's Moriarty was a worthy rival and their confrontation caught the absurdity of the genre perfectly.

Jan 2. John Kani and Winston Ntshona in Athol Fugard, John Kani and Winston Ntshona's **The Island** directed by Athol Fugard at Royal Court. The action is set on Robben Island, the notorious maximum-security jail, where Nelson Mandela was imprisoned. On a bare stage the actors mimed two political prisoners working in a quarry, digging, filling wheelbarrows, pushing them, and emptying them, a repetitive, totally useless, soul-destroying task. The sequence went on for 15 minutes, which some audiences found too long. But that was the whole point. (Think what it must have been like for real prisoners doing that day in, day out.) The prisoners performed Sophocles's *Antigone* as an act of defiance.

Jan 8. John Kani and Winston Ntshona in **Sizwe Bansi is Dead** directed by Athol Fugard at Royal Court.

1974 World Premieres
New York
Ntozakii Shange's *For Colored Girls Who Have Considered Suicide When the Rainbow is Enuf*
Milan
Dario Fo's *Can't Pay, Won't Pay*
Chicago
David Mamet's *Sexual Perversity in Chicago*
Nottingham
Howard Brenton's *The Churchill Play*

Deaths
Ernest Milton (*b.*1890), British actor
Marcel Pagnol (*b.*1896), French playwright

Notes
—Alexander Solzhenitsyn, deprived of Soviet citizenship, awarded Nobel Prize for Literature.
—English National Opera established at Coliseum

History
—President Nixon resigned
—Turkey invaded Cyprus
—First test-tube baby born

Lindsay Kemp in Flowers

Jan 9. Peter McEnery and Lynn Farleigh in David Rudkin's **Ashes** directed by Pam Brighton at Open Space. The story of a married couple who are unable to have a baby was Rudkin's contribution to World Population Year. The emotional impact was increased by the insistent attention to nauseating clinical detail.

Jan 22. Ben Kingsley and Yvonne Bryceland in Athol Fugard's **Statements After An Arrest Under The Immorality Act** directed by Athol Fugard at Royal Court. White teacher and black librarian have an affair in South Africa. The law forbids sexual contact between races.

Feb 14. Glenda Jackson, Susannah York and Vivien Merchant in Jean Genet's **The Maids** directed by Minos Volanakis at Greenwich. Sado-masochistic games of servility are played by two of society's outcasts. Merchant gave an entertaining parody of a pampered, spoiled lady, whose fantasies were as grotesque as the fantasies of her maids. The actresses waded ankle-deep in a carpet of fur.

Feb 14. Trevor Howard as General St Pé and Coral Browne as his wife in Jean Anouilh's **The Waltz of the Toreadors** directed by Peter Dews at Haymarket. The general, a compulsive womaniser, now an empty shell, is so afraid of life slipping by that he grabs at anything. The most arresting scene was when his sick wife rose from her invalid bed to tell him a few truths. "You're my thing, my object, my garbage bin!" she screamed and went on to say that she would never let him go. She would follow him right into the grave and on to the tombstone itself, never for one moment leaving his side.

Feb 20. Rex Harrison as Luigi Pirandello's **Henry IV** directed by Clifford Williams at Her Majesty's. It should have been an excellent showcase for Harrison, but the performance never materialized. There was no fury, no obsession, no poignancy and worst of all, no madness, feigned or otherwise.

Mar 4. Edward Fox in David Hare's **Knuckle** directed by Michael Blakemore at Comedy. Hare's parody of an American film thriller superimposed a Raymond Chandler/Mickey Spilane idiom on to the Home Counties. It remained a literary and cinematic joke.
—Now the trouble with theatrical parody is that when you are imitating something bad the result must either be hilariously funny or seem as bad as the original. Most of Mr Hare's dialogue, cleverly observed though it is, just seems bad. B A YOUNG *Financial Times*

Mar 5. John Gielgud as Prospero in Shakespeare's **The Tempest** directed by Peter Hall at Old Vic (NT). There was, surprisingly, very little vocal magic. The applause at the curtain-call was for the theatrical pleasure Gielgud had given in the past.

Mar 12. The Actors' Company. Ian McKellen as Astrov in Chekhov's **The Wood Demon** at Wimbledon directed by David Giles. Often thought of as a first draft for *Uncle Vanya*, it is a play in its own right, though much more diffuse and far lighter and happier than the later work. The two plays share the same characters, the same scenes and even occasionally the same dialogue. Here the Professor (Robert Eddison) and his young wife hold centre stage.

Mar 13. Maggie Smith in Charles Laurence's **Snap** directed by William Gaskill at Vaudeville. It was originally called *Clap*, since that was what it was about.

Mar 14. Claire Bloom as Blanche duBois and Martin Shaw as Stanley Kowalski in Tennessee Williams's **A Streetcar Named Desire** directed by Edwin Sherin at Piccadilly. Joss Ackland as Mitch. Morag Hood as Stella. Bloom ("a delicate beast") was good with the ambiguity: she was prim and proper, genteel and respectable, and yet, at the same time, a compulsive flirt.
—Her performance speaks with dazzling eloquence for all those who have seen a great light and beaten themselves insensitive against the window-pane trying to fly towards it.
JACK TINKER *Daily Mail*

Mar 26. The Actors' Company. Ian McKellen as Giovanni and Paola Dionisotti as Annabella in John Ford's **Tis Pity She's A Whore** directed by David Giles at Wimbledon. The action was updated to the Edwardian era. Dionisotti was a full-blooded, tempestuous wanton. McKellen, arrogant, reckless and jealous, was always near to hysteria. The final horror (the bandying of his sister's heart on the end of a sword) was but a continuation of the decadence, which had gone before. Edward Petherbridge's dilettante Soranzo was an elegant, cynical sensualist.

Mar 27. Lindsay Kemp's **Flowers** at Regent. Kemp's transvestite "pantomime for Jean Genet" was a homosexual's erotic dream. Mixing church and brothel images of death and sex, it produced a High Mass of masturbation fantasies, full of queer self-pity and camp self-indulgence.

Apr 4. Joan Plowright in J B Priestley's **Eden End** directed by Laurence Olivier at Old Vic (NT). Priestley had dated in a way, which made the characterization and the plotting seem a caricature of the English. Olivier's old-fashioned production didn't help.

Apr 9. Alan Bates in David Storey's **Life Class** directed by Lindsay Anderson at Royal Court. An art teacher stands by and watches his model being raped by one of his students. Transferred to Duke of York's.

Apr 16. The Actors' Company. John Woodvine and Sheila Reid in Georges Feydeau's **Ruling the Roost** directed by Richard Cottrell at Wimbledon. French farce. There's no love, only physical exhaustion. "Do you think I am here for my pleasure?" roars an outraged wife. She is merely in a man's arms because she wants to take her revenge on her husband. Meanwhile, he has only agreed to meet another woman because she is blackmailing him with threats of suicide. The very last thing he wants to do is to have sex with her.

May 1. Michael Crawford in **Billy** directed by Patrick Garland at Drury Lane. Musical based on Keith Waterhouse and Willis Hall's *Billy Liar*. Book by Dick Clement and Ian La Frenais. Music by John Barry. Lyrics by Don Black. Crawford played for sympathy and made Billy far nicer than he really was, reducing a compulsive liar to an adolescent whine.

May 15. Alec McCowen and Diana Rigg in Bernard Shaw's **Pygmalion** directed by John Dexter at New. Bob Hoskins as Doolittle. Rigg was a turn-of-the-century's cartoonist idea of a cockney flower girl. She played so hard for laughs her performance became a comic turn.

May 27. Derek Jacobi in Shakespeare's **Pericles** directed by Toby Robertson at Her

Tom Courtenay, Penelope Wilton, Felicity Kendal, Penelope Keith and Michael Gambon in *The Norman Conquests*

Majesty's. The whole action was set in a male brothel. The bored transvestites were often amusing but the setting didn't make the text any the easier to follow. The most striking performance was Harold Innocent's Bawd in black underwear and negligee.

May 28. Peter Firth as Melchior and Michael Kitchen as Moritz in Frank Wedekind's **Spring Awakening** directed by Bill Bryden at Old Vic (NT). Kitchen only came alive, ironically, when Moritz was dead. Beryl Reid was moving as the mother who cannot bring herself to tell her daughter the facts of life. Edvard Munch's famous painting, which was reproduced on the programme cover, said far more than Veronica Quilligan's performance. The audience was shocked by the communal masturbation.

Jun 8. Mike Pratt and Richard O'Brien in Sam Shepard's **Tooth of Crime** directed by Jim Sharman at Royal Court. This rock musical parody of the American gangster film was billed as a "three-round entertainment bout of the century." Mike Pratt played an ageing pop star who is on the skids and is being challenged by a newcomer (Richard O'Brien). The jargon was often impenetrable. "Not recommended for the squeamish," said *The Daily Express*.
—Jim Sharman's direction leaves the piece groaning along at a pace which would outrage any self-respecting snail. J W LAMBERT *Sunday Times*

Jun 10. John Wood in Tom Stoppard's **Travesties** directed by Peter Wood at Aldwych (RSC). A mixture of history and fantasy as seen through the eyes and faulty memory of a minor consular figure, who, in his old age, confuses his very minor role in a major political event with the major role he played in an amateur production of *The Importance of Being Earnest*. It was absolutely essential to have seen *The Importance* because most of the jokes came from the way Stoppard drifted in and out of Wilde. The play was an extraordinary juxtaposition of drawing-room epigram

and party-political rhetoric. The Russian Revolution and the Dada Revolution were observed side by side. Difficult, obscure, over-long, over-clever, it was very entertaining, largely due to the vitality of John Wood's stylish High Comedy performance as both the young and the old man.
—The serious people find the whole thing hopelessly frivolous, and people who really think they are going to see an empty comedy find the whole thing impossibly intellectual. And my object is to perform a marriage between the play of ideas and farce. TOM STOPPARD

Jul 2. Julie McKenzie in **Cole** directed by Alan Strachan and David Toguri at Mermaid. An entertainment by Benny Green and Alan Strachan based on the work and music of Cole Porter. The revue tried to do for Porter what *Cowardy Custard* had done for Noël Coward. It was not nearly so successful.

Jul 11. John Mills, Judi Dench and Christopher Gable in **The Good Companions** directed by Braham Murray and Christopher Selbie at Her Majesty's. Musical based on J B Priestley's novel. Book by Ronald Harwood. Lyrics by Johnny Mercer. Music by André Previn.
—The show has all the plastic deodorised anonymity of an airport lounge.
MICHAEL BILLINGTON *Guardian*
—John Mills, as a gnarled little Yorkshireman in a cloth cap, gets to do a tap dance to a reception that could easily seem a little fulsome if he had actually risen from the dead.
KENNETH HURREN *Spectator*

Aug 1. Tom Courtenay, Penelope Keith, Felicity Kendal, Michael Gambon, Bridget Turner and Mark Kingston in Alan Ayckbourn's **The Norman Conquests** at Globe. The trilogy's originality was that the action was not consecutive but parallel and simultaneous. **Table Manners** was set in the dining room. **Living Together** was set in the sitting room. **Round and Round and Round the Garden** was set in the garden. One play's exit was another play's entrance. The audience over three performances was able gradually to piece together the whole picture of what had happened during a family weekend in the country. Penelope Keith was a bossy, snobbish, self-centred, middle-class Englishwoman who cannot stop organising everybody. One of the funniest scenes was when she tried to convert an off-the-cuff meal into a social occasion with folded napkins and everybody sitting in their correct seat. Gambon managed to make dullness very appealing. There was something almost Chekhovian in his scene with Felicity Kendal when he cannot bring himself to propose because it doesn't occur to him that he might.

—Mr Ayckbourn, the Kingsley Amis of the stage, is the most remarkable British dramatist to have emerged since Harold Pinter – with whom he has more in common than may seem instantly probable. J W LAMBERT *Sunday Times*

—He is our greatest master of situation comedy today. B A YOUNG *Financial Times*

Aug 14. John Gielgud as Shakespeare in Edward Bond's **Bingo** directed by Jane Howell and John Dove at Royal Court. Subtitled "scenes of money and death". Bond (who didn't pretend to be historically accurate) said that Shakespeare was "so stupefied with all the suffering he had seen" that he committed suicide. Bond's Shakespeare, written-out and dying, brooded on the emptiness of his life and the irony that everybody (barring his family and himself) should find him serene and humane. Arthur Lowe, as a drunken Ben Jonson on the cadge, provided the only bit of light relief; yet even his short scene had the same bleakness, the same pessimism, the same cold hatred, which informed the rest of the play. The high spot was Shakespeare's description of the bear-baiting he had witnessed in London.

Aug 15. Bernard Hill as Lennon, Trevor Eve as McCartney, Philip Joseph as Harrison, Antony Sher as Starr in Willy Russell's **John, Paul, George and Ringo … and Bert** directed by Alan Dossor transferred from Liverpool's Everyman to Lyric. Robin Hooper as Brian Epstein. This quasi-musical documentary about the Beatles was a mixture of eulogy and dirge, praising the musical talent and lamenting the Myth and Big Business, which destroyed it. The story was told by Bert, the lad the Beatles dropped right at the beginning. The songs were sung by Barbara Dickson. George Costigan played Bert.

Aug 27. Ian Richardson and Norman Rodway in Maxim Gorky's **Summerfolk** directed by David Jones at Aldwych (RSC). The Russian Intelligentsia failed at the turn of the 20th century to give the country the lead it needed, because they were so preoccupied with their own futile, boring, petty lives. These "summerfolk" (the term was used as an insult) were tragically incapable of living properly; and though some of them did want to lead useful and meaningful lives, they did not know how to do so. The tragi-comedy was brilliantly directed and brilliantly acted by the whole company which included: Mike Gwilym (as angry young man), Estelle Kohler (as his sister, cool and remote), Margaret Tyzack (old enough to be his mother, who falls in love with him), Norman Rodway (as the compulsive gossip and drunk), Ian Richardson (as the burnt-out writer) and Susan Fleetwood (who behaved like a parody of a poetess but was, nevertheless, a poetess).

Sep 5. Ian McKellen in Christopher Marlowe's **Dr Faustus** directed by John Barton at Aldwych (RSC). Barton had no qualms about re-writing Marlowe. Emrys James as Mephistopheles had none of the usual overt theatrical magnificence, but was rather something quieter, smaller, and more academic. One of the most striking images was the use of Jennifer Carry's puppets for the Good and Bad Angels, all Seven Deadly Sins, and every "show", including even Helen.

Sep 18. Ian Richardson and Richard Pasco alternated Richard and Bolingbroke in Shakespeare's **Richard II** directed by John Barton at Aldwych (RSC). One of the more successful scenes, ironically, was the one, which has the whole cast throwing down their gages for Aumerle to pick up. Based though it is on historical fact, it usually plays to unwanted laughs; but not here where the lords queued up to throw down their gages, giving the challenges a formal ritual. Pasco had a strong declamatory style, as if he were constantly addressing a public meeting. Even in prison his lines became an illustrated lecturette, played directly to the audience. Richardson's Bolingbroke turned up in the prison disguised as the groom.

Oct 8. Eduardo de Filippo's **Saturday, Sunday, Monday** directed by Franco Zeffirelli transferred to Queen's.

Oct 22. Deborah Norton in Robert Patrick's **Kennedy's Children** directed by Clive Donner at King's Head. Five separate monologues, five horror stories leading to drugs, madness and death.

Nov 19. Ian McKellen in Frank Wedekind's **The Marquis of Keith** directed by Ronald Eyre at Aldwych (RSC). Indictment of the moral standards of Munich at the turn of the century when capitalists and crooks were working hand in glove. The Marquis, a self-centred confidence trickster, moved quickly from one swindle to another. McKellen played him as if he were Chaplin playing Hitler.

Nov 28. Dorothy Tutin as Maggie and Peter Egan as Shands in J M Barrie's **What**

Every Woman Knows directed by Clifford Williams at Albery. The most moving moment came after Shands had won his first election and Maggie knew she should release him from his marriage vow, but she couldn't bring herself to do it. Egan said the unexpectedly brutal line – "I wish I was fond of you" – without any brutality whatsoever, as a statement of fact, which made it even more brutal. Tutin had all of Maggie's courage, intelligence and humour

Dec 2. Max Wall as Archie Rice in John Osborne's **The Entertainer** directed by John Osborne at Greenwich. Archie Rice was a fifth-rate and unfunny comedian. Max Wall was a first-rate comedian and extremely funny. The casting robbed the play of its point.

Dec 10. An Evening with Hinge and Bracket at Mayfair. An original and amusing drag act. Hinge and Bracket (Perri St Claire and George Logan) were two elderly spinsters performing a musical repertoire in a village hall.

1975

Jan 9. Emrys James in Shakespeare's **King John** directed by John Barton at Aldwych (RSC). Barton had practically rewritten the play. The king was presented as a sinner in a Morality play, stalked by Death, stripped naked by the Holy Church and given a Last Supper. The Papal Legate was Death encased in pontifical robes. The wedding festivities gave way to war in a striking transformation scene with bride and groom continuing to dance in the smoke of battle. Ian McKellen was a far too noble Bastard.

Jan 28. Ralph Richardson, Peggy Ashcroft and Wendy Hiller in Henrik Ibsen's **John Gabriel Borkman** directed by Peter Hall at Old Vic (NT). Edvard Munch described Ibsen's penultimate play as "the most powerful winter landscape in Scandinavian art." Richardson was excellent with the poetry. Hiller's ramrod Mrs Borkman (a cross between Queen Mary and her role of Russian Princess in Agatha Christie's *Murder on the Orient Express*), acted in an older theatrical convention than Ashcroft.

—Sir Ralph is in my opinion the most extraordinary actor in the world. Other great players have a wide range; but he is the only one who can be at both ends of the range at the same time. HAROLD HOBSON *Sunday Times*

Feb 5. Nicol Williamson as Malvolio and Jane Lapotaire as Viola in Shakespeare's **Twelfth Night** directed by Peter Gill at Aldwych (RSC). Malvolio, chasing Olivia round the garden, resembled a frustrated vulture. Ron Pember's Feste was more Petticoat Lane than Illyria.

Feb 20. Paul Scofield as Prospero in Shakespeare's **The Tempest**, directed by John Harrison at Wyndham's. The subtleties of the isle were missing. There was no storm, no mystery, no harmony, no terror, no masque, no island, only a bare stage. But Prospero had a God-like potency; and nowhere more so than when he broke his staff. Scofield looked as if he might have sat for William Blake.

Feb 25. Colin Blakely as Captain Shotover, Anna Massey as Lady Utterword, Eileen Atkins as Hesione Hushabye and Paul Rogers as Boss Mangin in Bernard Shaw's **Heartbreak House** directed by John Schlesinger at Old Vic (NT). Kate Nelligan gently and touchingly guyed Ellie's fragile romantic innocence.

Mar 13. Peggy Ashcroft as Winnie in Samuel Beckett's **Happy Days** directed by Peter Hall at Old Vic (NT). Alan Webb as Willy. Ashcroft with her rouged cheeks and her silly hat might, momentarily, have been mistaken for a suburban housewife having a jolly day at the seaside; but a performance, begun in comedy, ended in ashen-panic-stricken terror as Winnie scanned the horizon and saw only approaching death.

—Peggy Ashcroft's Winnie is worth crawling over broken glass to see. JACK TINKER *Daily Mail*

—I suspect one of Beckett's main attractions to theatre folk is the opportunity he gives leading actors and actresses to indulge in uninterrupted monologues. MILTON SHULMAN *Evening Standard*

Mar 20. Irene Handl in Oscar Wilde's **The Importance of Being Earnest** directed by Jonathan Miller at Greenwich. Handl, famous for her cockney roles, played Lady Bracknell as a German Jewess. Dumpy, frumpish and cosy, she was no gorgon. "What Handl does to Lady Bracknell," said one critic, "is nothing to what the real Lady Bracknell would have done to Miss Handl." Miller had wanted to direct an all-male production at the National Theatre but the idea had been vetoed by Harold Pinter who was on the NT's board.

Apr 9. James Stewart in Mary Chase's **Harvey** directed by Anthony Quayle at Prince of Wales. Harvey is a six-foot white rabbit, visible only to its owner. The pleasure of seeing Stewart on stage was tempered by having to sit through Chase's sentimental farce, full of cardboard characters and laboured situations. Painfully slow, there was only one joke. James Thurber's *The Unicorn in the Garden* has the same twist and is more succinct.

1975 World Premieres
New York
  John Kander and Fred Ebb's *Chicago*
  James Kirkwood, Nicholas Dante,
    Marvin Hamlisch and Edward
    Kleban's *A Chorus Line*
Chicago
  David Mamet's *American Buffalo*
Dublin
  Brian Friel's *Volunteers*

Deaths
Josephine Baker (*b.*1906), singer
Pamela Brown (*b.*1917), British actor

Peter Daubeny (*b.*1921), British
  impresario
Marie Löhr (*b.*1899), British actor
Andre Obey (*b.*1892), French
  playwright
Thornton Wilder (*b.*1897), American
  playwright
P G Wodehouse (*b.*1881), British
  playwright

History
—Communists captured South
  Vietnam
—Pol Pot took over Cambodia
—General Franco died
—King Faisal assassinated

Apr 14. Marty Brill as Lenny Bruce in Julian Barry's **Lenny** directed by Jonathan R Yates at Criterion. Lenny Bruce was imprisoned for obscenity and found guilty of illegal possession of drugs. "All my humour is based on destruction and despair," he said; and so long as the quasi-documentary script stuck to his abrasive act and his pleadings in court, the production was fine. His pathetic defence, when he tries to argue his own case, was very moving.

Apr 15. Jean Simmons, Joss Ackland and Hermione Gingold in Stephen Sondheim's **A Little Night Music** directed by Harold Prince at Adelphi. Book by Hugh Wheeler based on Ingmar Bergman's film, *Smiles of a Summer's Night*. An elegant, civilised, sophisticated musical was played in waltz time, a tempo perfect for romantic happiness and romantic disillusionment. Harold Prince described the script as "whipped cream with knives." The score is almost entirely made up of interior monologues. The lyrics, full of innuendo and unexpected internal rhymes, are witty, cynical, sharp and complex. Simmons sang the haunting and heartbreaking "Send in the Clowns." Gingold (a formidable matriarch) sang "Liaisons" and knew how to deliver a line like, "To lose a lover or even a husband or two during the course of one's life can be vexing but to lose one's teeth is a catastrophe."

Apr 17. Beryl Reid, Malcolm McDowell and Ronald Fraser in Joe Orton's **Entertaining Mr Sloane** directed by Roger Croucher at Royal Court. McDowell had neither the verbal nor the sexual ambiguity. Fraser was miscast. Reid, pretending to a gentility she so painfully hadn't got, was very funny in the seduction scene. The production reeked of motherly incest. Transferred to Duke of York's.

Apr 22. David Hemmings as Bertie Wooster and Michael Aldridge as Jeeves in Andrew Lloyd Webber's musical **Jeeves** directed by Eric Thompson at Her Majesty's. Book by Alan Ayckbourn based on P G Wodehouse. A witless, disastrous travesty. "As close to the spirit of the original as Budeleigh Salterton is to Timbuctoo," said Michael Billington in *The Guardian*.

Apr 23. John Gielgud, Ralph Richardson, Michael Feast and Terence Rigby in Harold Pinter's **No Man's Land** directed by Peter Hall at Old Vic (NT). "What does it matter what it means," said Gielgud, "so long as the audience is held?" The action takes place in no man's land, which never moves, which never changes, which never grows older, but which remains forever, icy and silent. Hirst, a man of letters, rich, successful and dying, is a prisoner in his own home, guarded by two thuggish minders. Spooner, an unsuccessful and down-at-heel poet, having wormed his way into his house, is determined to stay. When Hirst collapsed, falling three times to the ground in quick succession, he was so convincing that the audience was genuinely worried that what they were actually witnessing was the death of a famous actor on stage. Transferred to Wyndham's.
— These two great actors are the best double-act since Laurel and Hardy. FRANK MARCUS *Sunday Telegraph*
—*No Man's Land* remains palpably the work of our best living playwright in its command of language and its power to erect a coherent structure in a twilight zone of confusion and dismay. IRVING WARDLE *The Times*

Apr 24. Michael Denison, Derek Griffiths, Val Pringle and Norman Beaton in **The Black Mikado** directed by Braham Murray at Cambridge. In this exuberant all-black version of Gilbert and Sullivan, the only Englishness that remained was Denison's Pooh-Bah. The most striking singer was Anita Tucker.

Apr 29. Alastair Sim as Lord Ogleby in George Colman and David Garrick's **The Clandestine Marriage** directed by Ian McKellen at Savoy. Sim repeated the performance he had given at Chichester nine years earlier. His facial reactions were far funnier than anything he said.

May 7. Jimmy Jewel and Alfred Marks in Neil Simon's **The Sunshine Boys** directed

by Danny Simon at Piccadilly. Two very old comedians, who haven't spoken to each other for eleven years, came together to do a television spectacular. The script, a tribute to the vaudeville comedian's art, was spiced with Simon's one-liners.

Jun 16. Daniel Massey and Judi Dench in Arthur Wing Pinero's **The Gay Lord Quex** directed by John Gielgud at Albery. There had been discussions about changing the title fearing that audiences might think Quex really was gay. Gielgud's production made Pinero's play more trivial than, perhaps, it was.
—As for Judi Dench she has the enviable talent of bestowing truth and poignancy on everything she touches. Surely, she is everybody's favourite actress. FRANK MARCUS *Sunday Telegraph*

Jul 16. Henry Fonda in David W Rintels's **Clarence Darrow** directed by John Houseman at Piccadilly. One man show, based on Irving Stone's *Clarence Darrow for The Defence*, which traced the life and career of the famous American lawyer, who fought so long and so successfully for the underprivileged. The script was not a play, not even an autobiography, just a collection of cuttings to make a statement about human liberty. There were no histrionics. Fonda, who had played so many honest, decent, good men with authority in the cinema, relied on Darrow's intellectual and moral integrity to hold and move an audience.

Jul 17. Glenda Jackson in Henrik Ibsen's **Hedda Gabler** directed by Trevor Nunn at Aldwych (RSC). Peter Eyre as Tesman. Patrick Stewart as Lövborg. Jackson's Hedda –sour, caustic, frigid, lesbian – was the finest since Peggy Ashcroft's. The sexual tension was always there and Timothy West's Judge Brack was an excellent sparring partner. The burning of Lovbörg's manuscript was an act of infanticide.

Jul 23. Richard Briers in Alan Ayckbourn's **Absent Friends** directed by Eric Thompson at Garrick. Three married couples come to cheer up an old friend whose fiancée has just died; but he doesn't need cheering up and depresses them by unwittingly reminding them how unsuccessful their marriages are. Pat Heywood was the most real. The funniest, the most Feydeau-like character was a chap, who just couldn't keep still. Ray Brooks had to make the most of the joke because there was nothing more to the role than fidgeting.

Jul 30. Alan Bates in Simon Gray's **Otherwise Engaged** directed by Harold Pinter at Queen's. A publisher refuses to get involved and remains totally indifferent. His bland, ironic and calculatedly negative response to every confidence and situation is so detached, that it raises rudeness to a high art. The role benefited enormously from Bates' wit, charm and persona. The other characters existed merely for his reactions.

Aug 13. Julian Curry as Angelo and Penelope Wilton as Isabella in Shakespeare's **Measure for Measure**, directed by Jonathan Miller at Greenwich. Set in a 1920s Vienna, it took a clinical look at two unattractive people who had kept so firm a rein on their emotions that it was perverse. There was hardly any emotion, not even in the seduction scene. Angelo coldly spelled out to Isabella precisely what he wanted in return for her brother's life. Isabella did not leap into the Duke's arms at the end but rushed straight back to the convent.

Aug 26. The Oxford Playhouse Company. Arthur Cox, Veronica Clifford and Bob Hoskins in Kurt Weill and Bertolt Brecht's musical **Happy End** at Lyric. Book by Dorothy Lane. The actors looked as if they were having a bash at something way outside their range.

Sep 2. Jack Shepherd, Helen Mirren and Anthony Sher in David Hare's **Teeth 'n Smiles** directed by David Hare at Royal Court. Lyrics by Tony Bicat. Music by Nick-Bicat. Rock group in Cambridge for May Ball: booze, drugs, arson and a great deal of foul language.

Sep 9. Diana Rigg in Tony Harrison's **Phaedra Britannica** an adaptation of Racine's *Phedre* directed by John Dexter at Old Vic (NT). Set in India, just before the Mutiny, the Victorian domesticity stifled the myth. The characters talked about "rude carnality" and "uncontrollable passions" but the production was curiously bloodless. The sheer horror was missing. There was no obscenity, no bestiality and no savagery. The epic language was at odds with the surroundings. Rigg underplayed. The story might just have been about any older married woman and any younger man, a novella pretending to tragedy. David Yelland, as the chaste Hippolyte, got the period and tone exactly right.

Sep 18. Mia Farrow in Harley Granville Barker's **The Marrying of Ann Leete** directed by David Jones at Aldwych (RSC). It looked at first as if the play might be a parody of a typical 18th-century comedy; yet the dialogue was strangely modern. There was a scene early on which was so enigmatic that it seemed to anticipate Harold Pinter. The vulgar wedding reception (a mixture of Hogarth and Chekhov) was meant to symbolize the end of the century and the coming revolution, but in performance the vulgarity was too caricatured to work.

Sep 25. Jonathan Pryce, Stephen Rea and Jimmy Jewel in Trevor Griffiths's

Estelle Kohler, Mia Farrow and Mike Gwilym in **The Marrying of Ann Leete**

Comedians directed by Richard Eyre transferred from Nottingham Playhouse to Old Vic. Six apprentice comedians have just completed a night school course in comedy. The most brilliant comedian (Jonathan Pryce) is, paradoxically, the least funny. His act is ugly, inhuman, terrifying. He is so bunged up with hate and pain that he silences laughter completely. Rea showed a splendid comic talent

Oct 12. Bette Davis on stage and screen at London Palladium. Davis showed clips from her old films and then answered questions from the audience. It was only slightly less squirm-making than it sounds. Toured England in 16 one-night stands,

Oct 23. Bernard Shaw's **Too True To Be Good**, directed by Clifford Williams at Aldwych (RSC). Ian McKellen as the clergyman turned gentleman-burglar. Judi Dench as the nurse. Shaw's jokes at the expense of the rich, doctors, sex and Lawrence of Arabia were not that funny. Williams tried to liven things up with some 1920s dance music.

Oct 28. Joan Plowright as Arkadina, Peter McEnery as Trigorin, Frank Grimes as Konstantin and Helen Mirren as Nina in Anton Chekhov's **The Seagull** directed by Lindsay Anderson at Lyric. The scene when Arkadina persuades Trigorin to come

back to Moscow with her was played for laughs. It was as if she were acting in one of her own tatty plays, a classic example of Life imitating Art. "Of course stay if you wish," she said, getting up off her knees and carefully dusting her skirt, a gesture, which wittily underlined that the performance she had just given was as shallow and empty and vulgar as any she had given in the theatre. McEnery was a very young Trigorin. The difficult last act dragged.

Oct 29. Stephen Rea as Christy Mahon and Susan Fleetwood as Peegan Mike in J M Synge's **The Playboy of the Western World** directed by Bill Bryden at Old Vic (NT). Rea, a natural for the playboy, was deeply moving when Christy's da returns and he stands to lose everything he has just won. Goaded and jeered at (a vicious scene) he thinks the only way to win back Pegeen's respect is to kill his da all over again. Susan Fleetwood made much of the long-delayed last line when she realizes she has lost the playboy for ever.

Nov 18. Tom Courtenay as John Clare in Edward Bond's **The Fool** directed by Peter Gill at Royal Court. The Northamptonshire peasant poet (1793–1864) was taken up and lionised, only to be discarded when his poetry started to express things the public didn't want to hear. Clare (who spent the last 23 years of his life in an asylum) was a peg on which Bond could hang a social comment about the way that the rich treat the poor. The peasant uprising provided a distressing scene in which an old parson was stripped of everything he had. The peasants would have stripped him of his flesh if they could have. The strength of Gill's production was its stark cruelty and violence. The weakness was its failure to come to grips with the subject matter.

Nov 20. Dorothy Tutin and Derek Jacobi in Ivan Turgenev's **A Month in the Country** directed by Toby Robertson at Albery. The romanticism (circa 1850) was underlined by bringing up the lights on the soliloquies and giving them a musical accompaniment. Petrovna's infatuation and jealousy were not acted in the grand manner. Tutin played the irritability, the spiky needling, the high spirits and her confusion, as to whether the tutor should stay or go, with full awareness of the comic possibilities. Timothy West was the doctor and his singularly unromantic proposal was very funny.

Dec 3. Max Wall in Samuel Beckett's **Krapp's Late Tape** directed by Patrick Magee at Greenwich. Wall, like other comedians before him – Buster Keaton and Bert Lahr – came to Beckett late in his career. Beckett had specifically asked for him.

Dec 4. Denholm Elliott in Graham Greene's **The Return of A J Raffles** directed by David Jones at Aldwych (RSC). A pointless, snobbish and childish exercise in Edwardian pastiche, with a bit of pornography thrown in, became a hymn to cricket, burglary and buggery. Elliot should have been good as the gentleman thief, but he ran all his lines together, effectively robbing them of their meaning and was upstaged by Paul Rogers as Edward VII.

Dec 9. Joan Plowright and John Moffatt in Ben Travers' **The Bed Before Yesterday** directed by Lindsay Anderson at Lyric. Travers was 89 and everybody wondered if he had taken an old play out of a bottom drawer and given it a dusting. The most amusing moment was the husband's consternation when his wife suddenly decided she liked sex. Plowright and Moffatt played their scenes in a way which made many people wish they had revived one of his original Aldwych farces instead.

Dec 9. Albert Finney in Shakespeare's **Hamlet** directed by Peter Hall at Old Vic (NT). Denis Quilley as Claudius. Angela Lansbury as Gertrude. Susan Fleetwood as Ophelia. Roland Culver as Polonius. The soliloquies were public statements. The house lights came up and the audience was addressed directly. In order that Finney should not look too old (he was 39) he was surrounded by even older actors. He wore a tracksuit. He was a rugger-playing Hamlet.
—Now in an age which puts a low value on grace, style and subtlety, Mr Finney is an appropriate enough choice. His voice is monotonously rasping and his mind does not respond to the text and his way of taking curtain-calls suggests an insufferable conceit. HAROLD HOBSON *Sunday Times*
—His timing is marvellous; he can detonate a famous phrase before you have time to duck away from it. ROBERT CUSHMAN *Observer*

1976

Jan 14. Frank Finlay and Dinsdale Landen in Ben Travers's **Plunder** directed by Michael Blakemore at Old Vic (NT). What works against the revivals of Travers's plays is that his farces were always rooted in the personalities and business of the original Aldwych team. Actors and directors no longer know how to play him. The night of the bungled burglary was genuinely funny; the surprise was that in a parody of the detective genre somebody actually gets killed.

Jan 15. Peter Brook directs **The IK** at Round House. Documentary drama by Denis Cannan and Colin Higgins based on Colin Turnbull's *The Mountain People*. The Iks are a starving Ugandan tribe. The production's intention was to draw world attention to their plight.

Jan 20. Alan Howard in Shakespeare's **Henry V** directed by Terry Hands at Aldwych (RSC). The rhetoric was exciting but what came across sharply, was the burden and responsibility of having constantly to galvanize himself into yet another rallying cry. The eloquence, the patriotism, the jingoism, the imperialism and the sheer courage were very much a PR job. Henry looked exhausted, as if he had not had a proper night's sleep for a very long time. His performance, rooted in his scene with the soldier Williams and the soliloquy, "Upon the king", allowed audiences to see Harry, "his ceremonies laid by, in his nakedness". The result was that the role was subtler, deeper and more tragic.

Jan 21. Juliet Prowse and Rock Hudson in Harvey Schmidt's **I Do! I Do!** directed by Lowell Purvis at Phoenix. Book and lyrics by Tom Jones based on Jan de Hartog's *The Four Poster*. Two-hander musical.
—Mr Hudson capitulates entirely to the beefcake nonentity of the script. Musically he gets through the routines with graceless accuracy. IRVING WARDLE *The Times*

1976 World Premieres
New York
 David Rabe's *Streamers*
 Stephen Sondheim's *Pacific Overtures*
Chicago
 David Mamet's *Sexual Perversity in Chicago*

Deaths
Agatha Christie (*b.*1891), British crime novelist, playwright
André Malraux (*b.*1901), French playwright
Sybil Thorndike (*b.*1882), British actor

Honours
Knight
 John Mills, actor

History
—Soweto massacre
—Death of MaoZedong
—Concorde began transatlantic flights

Jan 27. Trevor Griffiths's **Comedians** transferred to Wyndham's.

Jan 29. Alan Howard as Hal, Brewster Mason as Falstaff and Emrys James as Henry in **Henry IV Parts 1 and 2** directed by Terry Hands at Aldwych (RSC). The end was visually striking. The deliberate all-pervading drabness suddenly gave way to the dazzling, brightness of the coronation with Hal, body and face, encased in gold. Brewster Mason was the finest Falstaff since Paul Rogers, dry, mellow, smug and complacent, the aged roué, not burnt-out yet, deluded right up to the end.

Feb 5. Jane Asher, Stephen Moore and James Bolam in Christopher Hampton's **Treats** directed by Robert Kidd at Royal Court. The heroine has to choose between a weed and a bully.

Feb 24. Jill Bennett and Frank Finlay in John Osborne's **Watch it All Come Down** directed by Bill Bryden at Lyttelton (NT). The marriage break-up of a film director and a novelist takes place in a converted railway station. The whole cast got shot in a shower of bullets and breaking glass.

Mar 4. Adam Faith in Stephen Poliakoff's **City Sugar** directed by Hugh Thomas at Comedy. A sad commentary on pop audiences and their mindless values. The message was clear: "Stop buying... refuse to lap it up. "The person who spelled it out was, ironically, a DJ on a local radio station, a purveyor of all that was tawdry.

Mar 16. **Barry Humphries Housewife – Superstar** at Apollo. Chat show in drag had two main targets: vulgar Australians and docile audiences. The housewife was Edna Everage who harasses and bullies unfortunate people (and willing victims) into talking about their bathrooms. The best monologue was the drunken Australian cultural attaché: "Don't talk to me about culture," he said. "We've got culture up to our arseholes."

Mar 17. Glynis Johns and Louis Jourdan in Georges Feydeau's **13 Rue de L'Amour** directed by Peter Dews at Phoenix. Neither Johns (as respectable bourgeois wife) nor Jourdan (as smooth seducer) had the style, the pace and the blind panic that Feydeau needs.

Apr 2. Samuel Beckett celebrated his 70th birthday directing the Schiller Theatre in **Waiting for Godot** in German at Royal Court. Excellent performances by Horst Bollmann and Stefan Wigger. Perhaps the most extraordinary thing was that a play, which was once thought so difficult, even incomprehensible, should now be totally accessible.

Apr 19. **Shirley Maclaine** at Palace. Unashamed, old-fashioned show biz with fast-moving dance numbers and sentimental songs about hookers.

Apr 26. **La Grande Eugene** devised, directed and designed by Frantz Salieri at Round House. The best homosexual show since Lindsay Kemp's *Flowers*. Always blatantly explicit, the flamboyant camp vulgarity was a parody of transvestite cabaret, except, of course, that it was the very thing that it parodied. The targets were familiar – Marlene Dietrich, Josephine Baker, Kurt Weill's Berlin, American twenties musical, *Jesus Christ Superstar*.

Apr 28. Maxim Gorky's **The Zykovs** directed by David Jones at Aldwych (RSC). Father (Paul Rogers) and son (Mike Gwylm) both love the same young girl (Mia Farrow), who is fresh out of a convent. The girl marries the father and regrets it. The more interesting relationship is the one between the clever Sofia (Sheila Allen) and the Forest Warden (Norman Rodway). Gary Bond played a smug petty embezzler's humourless proposal for easy laughs. The last act felt as if it was never going to end with characters constantly making their final exits only, disconcertingly, to return.

Apr 28. Julie Walters and Richard Beckinsale in Mike Stott's **Funny Peculiar** directed by Alan Dossor at Garrick. Sexual frustration. Beckinsale ended up in plaster in a hospital bed having oral sex.

229

May 4. Millicent Martin, Julia McKenzie, David Kernan and Ned Sherrin in **Side by Side by Sondheim** directed by Ned Sherrin at Mermaid. The songs were dramatic monologues – clever, witty, and literate – but divorced from the shows they were written for, they didn't always work. Transferred to Wyndham's

May 6. Patrick Magee as Hamm and Stephen Rea as Clov in Samuel Beckett's **End-game** directed by Donald McWhinnie at Royal Court. "You're on earth, aren't you? There's no cure for that."
—Between them they prove what a musical advantage it is to hear Beckett played in the original Irish. PETER LEWIS *Daily Express*

May 12. Lee Remick and Keir Dullea in William Inge's **Bus Stop** directed by Vivian Matalon at Phoenix. A number of passengers are stranded at a Kansas diner during a snowstorm. A 21-year-old cowboy, naïve, bumptious, randy, finds it hard to believe a fifth-rate nightclub singer doesn't love him and is determined, despite her protestations, to carry her back, Petruchio-fashion, to his ranch. The singer was created by Kim Stanley on Broadway in 1955 and played on film by Marilyn Monroe.

May 19. Pauline Collins and John Alderton in Alan Ayckbourn's **Confusions** directed by Alan Strachan at Apollo. Five playlets. The cleverest was the quarrelling couples in a restaurant. The audience only heard what the waiter heard when he approached their respective tables. The most amusing took place during a washed-out village fete when a scoutmaster's fiancée inadvertently announced over the tannoy system that she was pregnant.

May 20. Three plays by Samuel Beckett directed by Samuel Beckett at Royal Court. Anna Massey, Penelope Wilton and Ronald Pickup up to their necks in three urns in **Play**. Patrick Magee's head of a man appears to be floating in space in **That Time**. Billie Whitelaw in **Footfalls**. A woman in distress, shrouded in dusty shawls, paces up and down a narrow strip of light, with heavy tread, seven steps to the left, seven steps

to the right. Whitelaw has given a vivid account in her biography, *Billie Whitelaw... Who He?*, of what it was like to be rehearsed by Beckett. When she suggested in rehearsal that if she went any slower, she would bore the audience to death, Beckett was unperturbed. "Bore them to death," he said. "Bore the pants off them."

May 25. Ian Holm, Norman Rodway, Bob Hoskins and Patrick Stewart in Eugene O'Neill's **The Iceman Cometh** directed by Howard Davies at Aldwych (RSC). Holm, who was playing Hickey, had a breakdown during a preview. The critics were not invited until June 20 when Alan Tilvern took over.

May 26. Martin Shaw and Helen Mirren in Sam Shepard's **Teeth 'n Smiles** directed by David Hare transferred to Wyndham's.

Jun 16. Tom Stoppard's **Dirty Linen** and **New-Found-Land** directed by Ed Berman at Arts. Committee of MPs look at the moral standards of MPs. Freudian slips, mixed metaphors, French and Italian clichés.

Jun 23. Anton Chekhov's **Three Sisters** directed by Jonathan Miller at Cambridge. Susan Engel as the overworked Olga. Janet Suzman as the bad-tempered Masha. Angela Down as Irene (who had already lost her bloom even before the play began). Sebastian Shaw as the cynical doctor. Peter Bayliss as the mentally disturbed Soliony. Peter Eyre's sensitive Toozenbach became a leading role.

Jul 7. Douglas Fairbanks Jr, Belinda Carroll and Wilfred Hyde White in Samuel Taylor's **The Pleasure of His Company** directed by Peter Dews at Haymarket. Fairbanks returned to London after a long absence to pay the superannuated playboy who comes home to celebrate his daughter's wedding.

Jul 13. Tom Conti as Dick Dudgeon in Bernard Shaw's **The Devil's Disciple** directed by Jack Gold at Aldwych (RSC). John Wood's aristocratic, supercilious, foppish

The final number in **A Chorus Line**: A reprise of 'One'

General Burgoyne looked as if he had stepped out of an 18th-century caricature by James Gillray. The sparring with Dudgeon was a fine example of High Comedy playing, nicely judged and nicely paced. The dry wit did not hide his seething anger at military and governmental incompetence.

Jul 17. Robert Morley and George Cole in Ben Travers's **Banana Ridge** directed by Val May at Savoy. Farce in the tropics: a woman accuses six men of being the father of her child.

Jul 22. A Chorus Line conceived, directed and choreographed by Michael Bennett at Drury Lane. Book by James Kirkwood and Nicholas Dante. Music by Marvin Hamlisch. Lyrics by Edward Kleban. The demeaning experience of a public audition. The director invites 26 dancers to talk about themselves. The confessions were based on taped interviews. The 26 are transformed into the uniformity and anonymity of the chorus line – so much so that the audience had difficulty recognizing them in the exhilarating finale.
—At a very conservative estimate *A Chorus Line* is the greatest thing to have happened to the American musical since *West Side Story* and the greatest thing to have happened at Drury Lane since *My Fair Lady*. SHERIDAN MORLEY *Punch*

Sep 8. John Wood in Anton Chekhov's **Ivanov** directed by David Jones at Aldwych (RSC). Grotesque comedy and nobody was quite as grotesque as John Wood's Ivanov. Worn-out, frustrated, a broken man, all too aware of his own futility, he was filled with self-loathing. His wife was dying of consumption; but he felt neither pity, nor love – only emptiness. Likened to Hamlet far too often, this Ivanov fussed, moaned, wallowed and whined with actorish affectation. The supporting roles were caricatured. The most successful were Norman Rodway's drunken sot, Patience Collier's ancient harridan and Sebastian Shaw's malicious count.

Sep 11. Cricot 2 Company of Cracow in **Dead Class** at Riverside. The actors were human sculptures grouped in and around five pews. They performed a macabre dance of death, orchestrated and conducted by Tudeusz Kantor, who remained on stage in the centre of the action.

Sep 23. Michael Crawford and Frances Cuka in Bernard Slade's **Same Time Next Year** directed by Eric Thompson at Prince of Wales. Husband and wife (who are not married to each other), improbably, have had a one-night stand in the same hotel every year for twenty-five years. The décor never changes. Woman's magazine stuff with jokes, but without Neil Simon's wit. The roles were created on Broadway by Charles Grodin and Ellen Burstyn.

Oct 4. Albert Finney in Christopher Marlowe's **Tamburlaine** directed by Peter Hall at Olivier (NT). Denis Quilley as Bajzeth. The £16m National Theatre finally opened after three postponements. The delays in construction caused a loss of £800,000, the advance ticket sales having to be refunded. The actors, who had rehearsed for six months, gave only fourteen performances. Marlowe's sick-making barbarity went on for over four hours in a very repetitive manner. Bajazeth's fall had more impact than Tamburlaine's rise.
—Marlowe has given Tamburlaine a macabre humour. Albert Finney, who speaks the verse both with an acute understanding of the pitiless fury of the man and the fine music of the poetry, catches the humour effectively. B A YOUNG *Financial Times*

Oct 4. Michael Gambon in Simon Gray's **Otherwise Engaged** directed by Harold Pinter transferred to Comedy.

Oct 6. Alec Guinness in **Yahoo**, an entertainment based on the life and writings of Jonathan Swift, directed by Alan Strachan at Queen's. Liberal quotations from *Gulliver's Travels* and *A Modest Proposal*. The performance was tantalizingly unrevealing of the man.

Oct 7. Peggy Ashcroft and Anthony Quayle in Aleksei Arbuzov's **Old World** directed by Terry Hands at Aldwych (RSC). A Baltic *Brief Encounter* between a director of a sanatorium and one of his more rebellious and eccentric patients. The play was episodic, banal and cheaply sentimental.

Oct 11. The Frontiers of Farce, a double-bill, directed by Peter Barnes at Old Vic. Leonard Rossiter in Georges Feydeau's **The Purging** was rooted in the reality of Feydeau's own loveless marriage. Rossiter was very funny when demonstrating an unbreakable chamber pot, he ended up in debris of porcelain; and he was even funnier when he went on to prove conclusively, pot by pot, that the whole set was flawed. Frank Wedekind's **The Singer** with Leonard Rossiter and Dilys Laye was not so good. Neither the director nor the cast had found a consistent style. The cynicism and the unexpected suicide suggested that it was a much nastier play than it appeared to be in performance.
—The lunatic frenzy by Mr Rossiter in his scene – some twenty minute with hardly a breath drawn – is a delight and wonder to behold, but the nervous energy in it is alarming. I hardly dare to wish the enterprise well, for with seven such performances a week Mr Rossiter will be dead before Christmas. BERNARD LEVIN *Sunday Times*

Oct 13. Googie Withers, John McCallum, Susan Hampshire and Martin Jarvis in Somerset Maugham's **The Circle** directed by Peter Dews at Haymarket. Bill Fraser made much of that comic, yet sad, moment when he claims that he, the lover, is the injured party and not the husband. Perhaps the most interesting character, because it reveals so much about Maugham, is the husband, who seems so charming but is, in fact, malicious.

Oct 14. Ondeko-Da at Round House. Demon Drummers from Japan. Their energy was staggering. Just when you believed that the drummer could not possibly go on any longer, not only did he proceed to go on much, much longer, but he then went into another gear and topped the previous effect; and if that were not enough, there was then an encore. The company run twenty miles a day, rain or shine. They have to be fit. The performance is a killer.

Oct 25. The Queen officially opened the National Theatre, despite the fact that the building was unfinished. Laurence Olivier welcomed her in the auditorium named after him. It was to be his first and last appearance on a National Theatre stage and saw Beryl Reid, Peggy Mount and Stephen Rea in Bill Bryden's embarrassingly unfunny production of Carlo Goldoni's **Il Campiello**.

Nov 11. Warren Mitchell in Johnny Speight's **The Thoughts of Chairman Alf, or Where England went wrong**, transferred from Stratford East, to Criterion. One-man show. Alf Garnett, working class Tory, Christian, patriot, bigot, fed on the audience's ignorance and prejudice. One of the nicest touches was the large poster in the foyer, which expressed Garnett's fury that he had won an award for comedy. Transferred to Whitehall.

Nov 17. Théâtre National Populaire. Roger Planchon as Tartuffe and Guy Trejan as Orgon in Molière's **Tartuffe** directed by Roger Planchon at Lyttelton. One of the great productions of the 20th century, liberating Molière from its Comèdie Française straightjacket in much the same way that the RSC had liberated Shakespeare from the traditional Old Vic performances. A series of tempestuous confrontations were played for real. Planchon (looking a bit like Molière) humanised Tartuffe. He was not some grotesque cipher of Hypocrisy. The play became his crucifixion. The seduction scene, when Orgon is hiding under the table, normally the biggest laugh of the play, was played for real and there was no laughter. Trejan's Orgon, patently a good man, had great dignity and yet he was capable of frightening anger with his daughter and, right at the end, it seemed as if he really would throttle Tartuffe. The actual sets were enormous, starting in the backyard, moving into the kitchen and then further and further into the house until, in the very last scene of all, it seemed as if the Orgon household was living under siege. The army had to break down the doors. Arlette Gilbert's Dorine looked ready to carry the banner in Delacroix's *Liberty Leading the People*.

Nov 23. Théâtre National Populaire. Pierre Marivaux's **La Dispute** directed by Patrice Chereau at Lyttelton. Pretentious narcissism with the actors splashing about in a very dirty pool and getting soiled.

Dec 9. Alan Howard, Norman Rodway, Jeremy Irons, Tim Wylton and Zoë Wanamaker in John O'Keefe's **Wild Oats** directed by Clifford Williams at Aldwych (RSC). There is so much good nature, such kindness, such humanity in the writing, even when O'Keefe is making silly jokes at the expense of the Quakers. First performed in 1791, it had been completely forgotten until the RSC revived it. Rover (Alan Howard) is a strolling vagabond player who has "the abominable habit of quotation" and drifts into Shakespeare (and other playwrights) on cue, delivering familiar and unfamiliar lines either straight or mangled. At times it seems as if he can only converse in quotation. Lady Amaranth (Lisa Harrow), tireless in her good works, angelic in her beauty, deportment, language and forever mouthing well-meaning platitudes, is both a parody of Quaker goody-goodness and also the genuine article. She takes the actors into her home and falls for Rover's gentle, generous heart and his wild whimsicality.

Dec 9. Leonard Rossiter in Molière's **Tartuffe** directed by David Thompson at Greenwich. Updated to the late Victorian era. Rossiter's devious, insinuating, sanctimonious snake in the grass looked like a relation of Pastor Manders. The termagant Dorine, the family servant and the direct descendent of the all-licensed fool, was transformed into the family governess.

1977

Jan 17. John Mills, Jill Bennett, Margaret Courtenay, Raymond Huntley and Ambrosine Phillpotts in Terence Rattigan's **Separate Tables** directed by Michael Blakemore at Apollo. The first play was never any good and had dated badly. Mills was genuinely moving as the bogus major in the second play. Margaret Courtenay rocked the boat a bit as the terrible mother as if she were auditioning for Lady Bracknell.

1977 World Premieres

New York

Tennessee Williams's *Vieux Carre*

Sam Shepard's *Curse of the Starving Classes.*

D L Coburn's *The Gin Game*

Chicago

David Mamet's *A Life in the Theatre*

Deaths

Edith Evans (*b.*1888), British actor

Terence Rattigan (*b.*1911), British playwright

Carl Zuckmayer (*b.*1896), German playwright

Honours

Knight

Peter Hall, director

History

—Steve Biko died in custody in South Africa

—Launch of Voyager mission

Jan 26. Stephen Rea in Odon Von Horvath's **Tales from the Vienna Woods** translated by Christopher Hampton and directed by Maximilian Schell at Olivier (NT). Constantly whirling in waltz time, it offered a panorama of working class life during the Depression years following the dissolution of the Austrian-Hungarian Empire following World War I. A disillusioned, vulgar, shoddy, amoral society, degraded and brutalized by poverty, is on the skids and about to embrace Hitler and Fascism. A naïve young girl rejects her fiancé, a middle-aged butcher and runs off with a shallow, gambling, lying wastrel. She has his baby and is rejected by him and her sottish father. 87-year-old Madoline Thomas's power and energy as the horrible old granny-murderer, was extraordinary.

Jan 31. **Flowers**, a pantomime for Jean Genet by Lindsay Kemp at Round House.

Feb 21. Lindsay Kemp in David Haughton's adaptation of Oscar Wilde's **Salome** at Round House. The Incredible Orlando as Herodias. Kemp's visual flair reeked of morbid, decaying perversion. The drum beat, the incense, the naked flames, the naked painted bodies, the flying angel, the ritual sacrifice, were fine. But once the actors started speaking snippets of Wilde's play in English and French, it was embarrassingly amateur. It would have been better to have had no Wilde at all. The magic returned with the killing of Jokanaan and the curtain call in slow motion.

Feb 22. Denis Quilley and Nigel Hawthorne in Peter Nichols's **Privates on Parade** directed by Michael Blakemore at Aldwych (RSC). Based on Nichols's national service experience with the British army in 1948 during the so-called state of emergency when he was a member of SADUSEA (Song and Dance Unit South East Asia) entertaining the troops and the natives. The pastiche songs (music by Denis King) included an excellent parody of Noël Coward ("Can you please tell us how we came to lose the peace?"). Quilley, as an outrageous pouf in drag, camped it up and had a field day with all the double-entendres.

Mar 3. Schaubuhne am Halleschen Ufer in Maxim Gorky's **Summerfolk** adapted by Botho Straus and directed by Peter Stein at Lyttelton.

Mar 16. Maria Aitken, Stephen Moore, Michael Kitchen, Polly Adams, Susan Littler and Derek Newark in Alan Ayckbourn's **Bedroom Farce** directed by Alan Ayckbourn and Peter Hall at Lyttelton (NT). Three bedrooms and four married couples. The fourth couple drifts in and out of the bedrooms, leaving emotional and physical destruction in their wake. High spot was Michael Gough and Joan Hickson in bed eating pilchards and reading *Tom Brown's Schooldays.*

Mar 22. Brian Cox, Ronald Pickup and Mark McManus in Shakespeare's **Julius Caesar** directed by John Schlesinger at Olivier (NT). John Gielgud's Caesar dominated the action in life and death. Michael Billington, writing in *The Guardian*, dismissed the conspiracy as "a gratuitous attempt to kill off the best-verse speaker on the English stage."

Mar 23. Glenda Jackson and Mona Washbourne in Hugh Whitemore's **Stevie** directed by Clifford Williams at Vaudeville. Sympathetic portrait of the poet Stevie Smith was based on her letters, verse and conversation. Jackson made no attempt to imitate her.

Apr 18. Alison Steadman in **Abigail's Party** devised by Mike Leigh at Hampstead. This satire on the marital miseries and the social mores of the under-educated and rising lower-middle-classes was originally a cult hit on television. The play was a collective improvisation by the cast, structured and refined by Leigh.

Apr 20. Colin Blakely, Rosemary Leach, Michael Gambon and Constance Chapman in Alan Ayckbourn's **Just Between Ourselves** directed by Alan Strachan at Queen's. Husband drives his wife round the bend. Ayckbourn's most serious play to date. It should have been at The National Theatre and *Bedroom Farce* should have been in the West End.

Apr 21. **The Passion** directed by Bill Bryden and Sebastian Graham-Jones at the National Theatre. A selection of plays from the York Mysteries was given a promenade production. Mark McManus as Jesus. Michael Gough as John the Baptist. Richard Johnson as Pilate. Ann Firbank as Mary. Oliver Cotton as Judas.

Apr 26. Paul Scofield in Ben Jonson's **Volpone** directed by Peter Hall at Olivier (NT). Ben Kingsley as Mosca. Scofield, detached, aloof, too intellectual, was physically so attractive, so manly, such a gentleman, so charming, that it was amazing that the young woman he was attempting to seduce didn't jump into bed with him immediately.

Apr 27. Donald Sinden in Shakespeare's **King Lear** directed by Trevor Nunn at Aldwych (RSC). The high spots were the scenes Sinden shared with Michael Williams, excellent as a very old Fool. The storm scene, with the two of them, standing in the pelting rain, absolutely drenched, was very moving. Lear inadvertently urinated over his hand, just before Gloucester kissed it, giving the line, "Let me wipe it first. It smells of mortality" a new interpretation. Michael Pennington made such a meal of Edgar's first soliloquy that he already seemed to be playing Mad Tom.

May 4. Ralph Richardson, Celia Johnson and Alan Webb in William Douglas Home's **The Kingfisher** directed by Lindsay Anderson at Lyric. A man, who has loved a woman in vain for forty years, proposes to her on the day of her husband's funeral. The play was originally intended for the National Theatre until the commercial managements complained that the heavily-subsidized National Theatre should not be staging commercial productions.

May 4. Eileen Atkins in Bernard Shaw's **Saint Joan** directed by John Dove at Old Vic. Robert Eddison's austere Inquisitor was a striking figure of authority. Emrys James's jolly Cauchon was more Friar Tuck than Bishop of Beauvais. Atkins's Joan was crazy Women's Lib.

May 12. Ian McDiarmid, Michael Pennington, Paul Morairty, Frances Viner and Bob Peck in David Edgar's **Destiny** directed by Ron Daniels at Aldwych (RSC). The rise of the National Front was traced from its beginnings, through the Enoch Powell "rivers of blood" speech, and on up to the 1970s.

May 25. Christopher Logue's **War Music** directed by Toby Robertson at Old Vic. Music by Donald Fraser. Based on Homer's *Iliad*, the production took a Maurice Bejart dance-and-spectacle approach to the re-telling of the story of the Trojan War. The visual side – the swirling smoke, the bronze figures, the huge shields and the stylized, frieze-like fights, choreographed by William Louther to the percussion of Gary Kettel – was so good, the script was superfluous. Rupert Fraser's Achilles, half-God, half-man, held classical poses with notable confidence.

May 27. Derek Jacobi in Shakespeare's **Hamlet** directed by Toby Robertson at Old Vic. Barbara Jefford as Gertrude. Suzanne Bertish as Ophelia. Affectionately known as *I, Hamlet.* (Jacobi had just finished the television epic of Robert Graves's *I Claudius*.) Hamlet spoke the "To be or not to be" directly to Ophelia. He practically rammed the recorder down Guildenstern's throat, and he very nearly raped his mother. Timothy West as Claudius, outwardly mild and genial, but given to uncontrollable bursts of temper, dominated the production.

Jun 7. Eric Bentley's **Are You Now or Have You Ever Been?** directed by Anton Rodgers at Bush. Senator McCarthy's notorious witch-hunts searching for communists arraigned many innocent citizens and officials. The script was an edited transcript of the actual testimonies given to the Un-American Activities Committee of the House of Representatives from 1947 to 1956. Those who appeared before the tribunal had to choose between informing on their friends and colleagues and going to gaol. Many invoked the First and Fifth Amendment. Many were blacklisted. Transferred to Mayfair.

Jun 15. Janet Suzman in Henrik Ibsen's **Hedda Gabler** directed by Keith Hack at Duke of York's. John Shrapnel as Torvald. Ian Bannen as Judge Brack. Jonathan Kent as Lövborg. Suzman's witty Hedda, vicious, self-destructive and thoroughly bored, looked like photographs of Sarah Bernhardt.

Jun 21. Judi Dench as Adriana and Roger Rees as Antipholus from Ephesus in Shakespeare's **The Comedy of Errors** directed by Trevor Nunn at Aldwych (RSC). The farce was turned into an exuberant, slapstick musical. Richard Griffiths turned the non-existent role of police officer into a major comic turn.

—[Judi Dench] demonstrating once more that she is a comic actress of consummate skill, perhaps the very best we have. BERNARD LEVIN *Sunday Times*

Jun 22. Ronald Pickup and Paul Scofield in Harley Granville Barker's **Madras House** directed by William Gaskill at Olivier (NT). Barker, discussing the role of women in society, is thematic, diffuse, inconclusive and ambivalent. There are times in the last two acts when he begins to be as verbose as Bernard Shaw. The conversation, intellectual, civilised and subtle, was always entertaining. Pickup played the leading role, a prig, who confesses to disliking men and despising women and finds the whole idea of companionship in marriage pretty artificial. Scofield had the comparatively small role of his father, a converted to Mohammedanism, who argues that a woman's place is in the home and that the idea of equality is absurd.

Jun 23. Deborah Kerr in Bernard Shaw's **Candida** directed by Michael Blakemore at Albery. Denis Quilley as Morrel. Patrick Ryecart as Marchbanks. Kerr was far too old.

Jun 27. Donald Sinden as Benedict and Judi Dench as Beatrice in Shakespeare's **Much Ado About Nothing** directed by John Barton at Aldwych (RSC). Set in 19th century India. Everybody says Beatrice is merry but Dench's Beatrice was patently unhappy. "I was born to speak all mirth and no matter," she said, fighting back her tears. Sinden acted with the audience and was at his funniest in the soliloquies. The Watch were Indians; but for the joke to work Indian actors should have been cast. A joke, in far worst taste, came when Claudio was made to believe that he was going to be forced to marry an Indian girl.
—They are simply two definitive performances operating in perfect partnership. IRVING WARDLE *The Times*
—Judi Dench plays Beatrice like a tragedienne in soubrette's clothing: an intelligent woman at daggers drawn with her own feelings. JOHN PETER *Sunday Times*

Jun 30. Steven Berkoff, Matthew Scurfield, David Delve, Anna Nygh and Barry Philips in Steven Berkoff's **East** at Greenwich. Berkoff transformed cockney-argot into high-flown, mock Elizabethan/Jacobean verse. The raucous, snarling, vicious and self-indulgent production was a verbal and physical assault course.

Jul 1. John Wood and Ian McKellen in Tom Stoppard's **Every Good Boy Deserves Favour** directed by Trevor Nunn at Royal Festival Hall. The music was performed by the London Symphony Orchestra conducted by André Previn. Two men share the same room in a mental hospital. One is a lunatic (Ian McKellen), who believes he is conducting an orchestra; the other (John Woodvine) is a dissident, who has been put in the hospital for political reasons. Previn's Prokofievan score was witty, moving and highly theatrical.

Jul 4. Glynis Johns in Terence Rattigan's **Cause Célèbre** directed by Robin Midgley at Her Majesty's. When he was a young man in his early twenties in 1935, Rattigan had thought a sensational murder trial would make a good play. Forty years later, when he was dying, he wrote it. 38-year-old Alma Rattenbury and her 17-year-old lover were accused of beating her elderly husband to death with a mallet. When the police arrived on the scene, they found her drunk, dancing in a pool of blood. Though she was totally innocent, she felt morally responsible, and tried to save the boy's life by confessing she had done it. In the witness box she soon discovered that it was her morality which was on trial. The general public was outraged that she should have made love in the same room as her sleeping six-year-old son. Everybody presumed (wrongly) that she must have been the dominating partner and that she had led the boy astray. The major flaw of the play was that Rattigan should tell so little about the boy. Glynis John's drunken solo was the sort of number you might have expected in a Broadway musical.

Jul 4. Barbara Jefford and John Turner in John Dryden's **All for Love** directed by Frank Hauser at Old Vic. The quasi-Restoration performance was given in full eighteenth century costume with a formal ballet divertissement. The blank verse was empty rhetoric. Robert Eddison's insidious grandee, in a towering peruke, was the most Restoration-looking figure. Physically and vocally he was magnificent. Nicholas Georgiadis's costumes were so rich they bankrupted Prospect Company.

Jul 5. Ian McKellen and Francesca Annis in Shakespeare's **Romeo and Juliet** directed by Trevor Nunn with Barry Kyle at Aldwych (RSC). McKellen should have played Mercutio.

Aug 1. Ian McKellen in Henrik Ibsen's **The Pillar of the Community** directed by John Barton at Aldwych (RSC). The unacceptable face of capitalism: blatant self-interest and ruthless opportunism are presented as acts of philanthropy. Judi Dench played the wholesome woman who brought a breath of fresh air to the community.

Aug 10. Jane Carr, Anne Heywood and John Rogan in Mary O'Malley's **Once A Catholic** directed by Mike Ockrent at Royal Court. Blasphemy, sex, spiteful nuns: painful and bitter memories of convent-school life were turned into comedy. Transferred to Wyndham's.

Sep 7. Alec Guinness in Alan Bennett's **The Old Country** directed by Clifford Williams at Queen's. Philby-like spy, who defected and has lived in Russia for the last fourteen years, is invited home. But what is the point of going back to the old country when the England he knew no longer exists? But he has no choice. He is part of an exchange for a Russian spy in England.

Sep 13. Ian McKellen and Judi Dench in Shakespeare's **Macbeth** directed by Trevor Nunn at Warehouse (RSC). The high spot was the banquet scene. Macbeth could

hardly speak when he saw the Ghost of Banquo. He became hysterical, screaming, demented, and dribbling with fear. There was, of course, no Ghost. As with the dagger, it was all in his mind. The scene which immediately followed was equally memorable. Lady Macbeth, the most human and the most frightened of Lady Macbeths, was unable to stop crying.
—If this is not great acting I don't know what is. MICHAEL BILLINGTON *Guardian*
—It will astonish me if the performance is matched by any in this actress's generation. J C TREWIN *Lady*.
—The best Shakespearian production I have ever seen. ROBERT CUSHMAN *Observer*
—I can see nothing in Ian McKellen other than ranting and twitching; and he speaks the verse with inexcusable coarseness. BERNARD LEVIN

Sep 19. Peggy Ashcroft as Winnie in Samuel Beckett's **Happy Days** directed by Peter Hall at Lyttelton (NT). There was an extraordinary moment at the end when it seemed as if Winnie's husband was actually going to shoot her.

Sep 20. Anna Manahan, Cyril Cusack and Susan Fleetwood in Sean O'Casey's **The Plough and the Stars** directed by Bill Bryden at Olivier (NT). The third act was the best with the looting and dying going on at the same time. Manahan was a splendid termagant and Bessie Burgess's unexpected death had real power. The low comedy of Fluther was in the capable hands of Cusack and Fleetwood managed to keep Norah Clitheroe's madness the right side of melodrama.

Sep 28. **Bubbling Brown Sugar** directed by Charles Augins at Royalty. Book by Loften Mitchell. 50 years of Harlem in one night. One hit song after another.

Oct 13. Nigel Hawthorne and Dai Bradley in Henri de Montherlant's **The Fire That Consumes** directed by Bernard Miles at Mermaid. Roman Catholic teacher is in love with one of his pupils.
—There is no trace of a cold Christian ascetic with a sensual flaw; patently he is a wolf in priest's clothing. His perceptive level of inner conflict is no more than that of a beer-drinking parson in a Methodist boarding school. PETER STOTHARD *Plays and Players*

Oct 19. Claire Bloom, Daniel Massey and Michael Aldridge in Henrik Ibsen's **Rosmersholm** directed by Clifford Williams at Haymarket. Rebecca and Rosmer are not as emancipated as they had thought. They are products of the 19th century and the truth about their relationship, so long suppressed, kills them. The production was awkwardly plotted and paced. The blinding passion was mere melodrama. The last act defeated the actors completely.

Oct 27. Arthur Lowe in J B Priestley's **Laburnum Grove** directed by Hugh Goldie at Duke of York's. Dull morality play set in the aftermath of the Depression. Lowe, the epitome of bourgeois respectability, jolts humdrum suburbia out of its smug complacency when he admits that he is a crook like everybody else. The social criticism tended to get lost.

Nov 2. Joan Plowright and Colin Blakely in Eduardo de Filippo's **Filumena** directed by Franco Zeffirelli at Lyric. Premiered in 1946, it remains the most performed of modern Italian plays. A 52-year-old womaniser is tricked into marriage when his 48-year-old mistress of 25-years standing pretends she is on her deathbed. He rages at her deception and refuses to support her three grown-up illegitimate children until she tells him that one of them is his. She then refuses to tell him which one is, knowing he will lavish his affection and money on that one at the expense of the other two.

Nov 7. Keith Michell as King Magnus in Bernard Shaw's **The Apple Cart** directed by Patrick Garland at Phoenix. A patriotic revival in the year of the Queen's jubilee celebrations. Nigel Stock was perfect for the Prime Minister. Penelope Keith was a surprising choice for the king's mistress and her fans felt badly cheated when they found out too late that she appeared in only one scene.

Nov 16. Albert Finney as Horner in William Wycherley's **The Country Wife** at Olivier (NT) directed by Peter Hall. Finney played horny Horner as a North Country boor with slurred speech. Hall, amazingly, thought the notorious "china" scene actually needed the embellishment of a phallic vase for the audience to get the sexual innuendo.

Nov 16. Alec McCowen and Dorothy Tutin in Shakespeare's **Antony and Cleopatra** directed by Toby Robertson at Old Vic. Both actors were miscast. Derek Jacobi played Octavius.

Nov 17. John Gielgud in Julian Mitchell's **Half-Life** directed by Waris Hussein at Cottesloe (NT). Arrogant professor of archaeology discovers that his whole existence, professionally and emotionally, has been built on a false premise. Fiercely denying he ever was a homosexual, he wonders what he has done with his life. He is determined the university shall not have a penny of his fortune when he dies. This civilised, witty West End play gave Gielgud opportunities to be devastatingly rude.

233

Dec 1. Kenneth Wilson, Anna Palk, Stephen Hoye and Glory Annen in David Mamet's **Sexual Perversity in Chicago** directed by Albert Takazauckas at Regent. A sad and cynical commentary on sexual mores and morality traces a relationship between a naïve office manager and a commercial illustrator. "You are trying to understand women," she tells him, "and I am confusing you with information." Certain national newspapers refused to carry advertisements, finding the title and the provocative poster offensive. Acted in a double bill with David Mamet's **Duck Variations** with Bernard Spear and Gordon Sterne. Two American Jews talk about ecology.

Dec 14. John Woodvine as Subtle, Ian McKellen as Face and Susan Drury as Dol Common in Ben Jonson's **The Alchemist** directed by Trevor Nunn at Aldwych (RSC). Nickolas Grace as Abel Drugger. Paul Brooke as Sir Epicure Mammon. The actors strained to keep the farce going. The gem was Roger Rees's zealous zealot, who climbed on chairs and harangued everybody at the drop of his Puritan hat.

Dec 21. Roy Hudd as Fagin in Lionel Bart's **Oliver!** directed by Robin Midgley and Larry Oaks at Albery. Marcus d'Amico was the best Oliver yet.

1978

Jan 3. Richard Johnson and Diana Rigg in Ferenc Molnar's **The Guardsman** directed by Peter Wood at Lyttelton (NT). Written in 1910, this Hungarian soufflé, with its tantalising sexual nuances, offers two sorts of acting: the acting actors indulge in on and off-stage; and the acting husbands, wives and lovers indulge in all the time. Who gives the more convincing performance? The husband disguised as the lover? Or the wife pretending she cannot see through the disguise? The answer was the wife. Rigg wore exquisite gowns.

Jan 8. Alec McCowen read **St Mark's Gospel** at Riverside Studios. McCowen had learned the whole gospel by heart and he told the good news with absolute conviction, compassion, wonder and, unexpectedly, a great deal of humour.

Jan 12. The new Riverside Studios opened with Judy Parfitt as Ranevskaya, Michael Elphick as Lopakhin, Stephen Rea as Trofimov and Julie Covington as Varya in Anton Chekhov's **The Cherry Orchard** directed by Peter Gill. Philip Locke as Gaev. George Howe as Firs. The production was much more realistic, much less sentimental and much more political than usual. The tramp's intrusion was electrifying, an unmistakeable death knell. Lopakhin, normally played for a philistine, a boor and a drunk, came across as the rightful heir to the orchard.

Jan 26. Ingrid Bergman and Wendy Hiller in N C Hunter's **Waters of the Moon** directed by Patrick Garland at Haymarket. Bergman, unexpectedly bubbly, brought charm and vitality to her role without ever denying that the spoiled and selfish character she was playing was an awful woman. Wendy Hiller was at her most ramrod and glacial.

Jan 27. Michael Pennington as Mirabell and Judi Dench as Millamant in William Congreve's **The Way of the World** directed by John Barton at Aldwych (RSC). Heroes and villains were indistinguishable. Dench, the least secure Millamant, used her affectations as a mask to hide her true feelings. The happy ending in which she "dwindles into a wife" was patently unhappy. The comic high spot was Beryl Reid's Lady Wishfort, a vulgar, overblown, crumbling harridan, stranded on a chaise longue. Struggling to get up in the most ungainly fashion, she observed, "There is nothing more alluring than a levée from a couch in some confusion".
—Her [Judi Dench] voice shines like a bubble of mercury in sunlight. It is a living Millamant, not for one moment the self-conscious exercise in cruelty we have often had as a substitute. J C TREWIN *Illustrated London News*

Jan 30. An Evening with **Quentin Crisp and His Cure For Freedom** at Duke of York's. The television adaptation of *The Naked Civil Servant* (with John Hurt) had made Crisp so famous that he could now fill a theatre with a one-man chat show. The major surprise was that his lecture should be so un-camp and totally un-shocking. Homosexuality was hardly mentioned.

Feb 14. Albert Finney as Lopakhin, Dorothy Tutin as Ranyevskaya, Ben Kingsley as Trofimov and Ralph Richardson as Firs in Anton Chekhov's **The Cherry Orchard** directed by Peter Hall at Olivier (NT). Susan Fleetwood as Varya. Robert Stephens as Gaev. Nicky Henson as Yepikhodov. Less than heartbreaking. It seemed wilful, artistically and financially, for The National to be reviving the play when Peter Gill at Riverside Studios had just done it so well.

Feb 22. Jeremy Irons, Simon Ward, Clive Francis, Barry Foster and Donald Gee in Simon Gray's **The Rear Column** directed by Harold Pinter at Globe. Five men in an outpost in the Congo in 1887 are without food and medicine. Facing attack, disease and death, they go berserk and resort to flogging, shooting and cannibalism.

1978 World Premieres
New York
Sam Shepard's *Buried Child*
Bob Fosse's *Dancin'*
Lanford Wilson's *The Fifth of July*
Marsha Norma's *Getting Out*

Luis Valdez's *Zoot Suit*

History
—P W Botha became South African Prime Minister

Feb 23. Don Warrington, James Aubrey, Trevor Jones, Glyn Jones and Don McKilip in David Rabe's **Streamers** directed by Leslie Lawton at Round House. The last play of a trilogy on the traumatic experience of Vietnam began with slashed wrists. The long sequence, in which the violence, sexual and psychic, escalated until it seemed as if everybody must be raped and murdered, was horrific, the stage awash with blood. Lawton's production, strongly cast and closely modelled on Mike Nichols's original in New York, had a tight grip on the hysterical action. Streamers are parachutes that fail to open.

Mar 2. John Gielgud in Julian Mitchell's **Half-Life** directed by Waris Hussein transferred to Duke of York's.

Mar 6. Tom Conti in Brian Clark's **Whose Life Is It Anyway?** directed by Michael Lindsay Hogg at Mermaid. Should the doctor or the patient decide whether a person lives or dies? A sculptor, totally paralysed and quite incurable, takes the "calm, rational decision" that he wants to die. Finding the hospital unwilling to agree, he takes them to the high court. The sculptor's sexual banter and abrasive flippancy suited Conti's stage persona perfectly and the pain wasn't any less real for all the comedy

Mar 6. Alan Howard as Henry and Helen Mirren as Margaret in Shakespeare's **Henry VI Parts 1 2 3** directed by Terry Hands at Aldwych (RSC). Alan Howard's efforts to be young and innocent often made him look merely simple. James Laurenson's extrovert Jack Cade was extremely likeable. Graham Crowden's Humphrey had authority. Anton Lesser, straight out of RADA, played the future Richard III as a psychopath at large, a baby-face, crookback prodigy. The most disturbing performance was given by a non-member of the company. An insane Irishman wandered on to the stage, armed with daffodils and it said much for the RSC productions in general that the audience took an embarrassing long time to realize that he was not meant to be in the play.

Apr 4. Phil Daniels in Nigel Williams's **Class Enemy** directed by Bill Alexander at Royal Court. Six foul-mouthed schoolboys in a London comprehensive are left to their own devices and decide to teach each other.
—Mr Williams's point, at the end of a horrendously violent, savagely written and generally very powerful play, seems to be that any society which can tolerate a class like 5K fully deserves the hooligans it breeds. SHERIDAN MORLEY *Punch*

Apr 5. Paul Eddington, Julia McKenzie and Benjamin Whitrow in Alan Ayckbourn's **Ten Times Table** directed by Alan Ayckbourn at Globe. Small market town council decides to celebrate its own equivalent of The Tolpuddle Martyrs. A committee is formed, which quickly divides into Marxist and Fascist factions. It looks as if instead of a pageant there will be a political rally and history will repeat itself and there will be another bloody massacre. The premise was so much funnier than the trivial and utterly predictable execution. The characters were stereotypical bores.

Apr 6. Alan Howard in Shakespeare's **Henry V** directed by Terry Hands revived at Aldwych (RSC).

Apr 12. Kate Nelligan and Julie Covington in David Hare's **Plenty** directed by David Hare at Lyttelton (NT). The English malaise – not speaking one's mind, keeping one's true feelings hidden, never saying anything that might offend – is considered a virtue. A former spy, intelligent, but abrasive, neurotic and unpredictable, is unable to conform to these standards. Her disillusionment and disintegration are seen within the context of the disillusionment and disintegration of England.
—The National production is extremely sumptuous. What better place to hurl subsidised abuse at the ruling class? TED WHITEHEAD *Spectator*

Apr 13. Peter McEnery in Paul Thompson's **The Lorenzaccio Story** directed by Ron Daniels at Donmar Warehouse. The death of democracy. Thompson took Alfred de Musset's play about aristocratic debauchery and Machiavellian intrigue and adapted it to make a commentary on the impotence of revolutions and revolutionaries. Lorenzaccio, a man of high political ideals, disguises himself as a debauchee in order to become the confidant of a duke he intended to murder. McEnery cut a striking figure: a mixture of modern punk and High Renaissance, a dangerous, witty, cynical, sensual, intelligent villain, the one person who might be able to save Florence.

Apr 24. Eileen Atkins as Viola in **Twelfth Night** directed by Toby Robertson at Old Vic. Robert Eddison's Feste was an aging hippie and his songs were given a Brechtian edge. Ronald Stevens's Sir Andrew Aguecheek was straight out of P G Wodehouse.

'Don't Cry for me Argentina.' Joss Ackland and Elaine Page in Evita

Apr 25. Michael Bryant in Henrik Ibsen's **Brand** directed by Christopher Morahan at Olivier (NT). Ibsen's epic poem was designed to be read, rather than staged. Pastor Brand, as icy and forbidding as the Norwegian fjords and mountains, does not believe in a merciful and kind God. "Was God humane to Christ?" he asks. His God is the Jehovah of the Old Testament, the God of Storm. Brand disdains all compromise and sacrifices. Ralph Koltai's set, a huge sheet of ice, cracked and heaved.

May 1. Timothy West, Gemma Jones and Michael Kitchen in Harold Pinter's **The Homecoming** directed by Kevin Billington at Garrick. "I bump into my characters," said Pinter. "They remain strangers … one doesn't know very much about other people." The production was set firmly in suburban reality. Timothy West's father was a frightening figure, who had long ceased to frighten anybody. Michael Kitchen was a sinister and patronising pimp given to casual violence.

May 3. Stratford Johns, Sheila Hancock and Andrea McArdle in **Annie** choreographed by Peter Gennaro and directed by Martin Charnin at Victoria Palace. Book by Thomas Meehan. Music by Charles Strouse. Lyrics by Martin Charnin. Little Orphan Annie first appeared in Harold Gray's cartoon strip in 1924. The musical is set during the Depression just before Roosevelt (with the help of Annie) thinks up a New Deal for America. Sheila Hancock, as the drink-sodden Irish schoolmarm who runs the orphanage, acted in the wicked witch pantomime tradition and there was a memorable moment when, having very calmly left her office, she had hysterics in the hallway.

May 12. Nicol Williamson in John Osborne's **Inadmissible Evidence** directed by John Osborne at Royal Court. Williamson returned to the role he had created fourteen years earlier to win the *Plays and Players* Award for Best Actor again. The text's misogyny continued to cause great offence in some feminist quarters.

May 22. Lila Kedrova and Jean Marais in Jean Cocteau's **Les Parents Terribles** directed by Jean Marais at Old Vic. Acted in French. This absurdly hysterical boulevard play, once banned on account of its incestuous theme, was given a museum production. Kedrova's possessive, suicidal mother was unashamedly melodramatic. Marais shuffled aimlessly about the stage when he was not standing absolutely rigid and staring out front.

May 31. Alan Howard in Shakespeare's **Coriolanus** directed by Terry Hands at Aldwych (RSC). Two memorable physical moments. The first was when Howard bestrode the Gates of Corioli like a colossus and his army marched into the city under his legs. The second was when at the end of the speech beginning, "You common cry of curs", he lifted a table high above his head, and held it there, until he hurled it down at the tribunes' feet on the line, "I banish you!" Easily, the most moving moment was the rejected Menenius (Graham Crowden) grovelling at Coriolanus' feet.

Jun 6. Albert Finney and Dorothy Tutin in Shakespeare's **Macbeth** directed by Peter Hall with John Russell Brown at Olivier (NT). Poorly acted and intolerably dull, only Tutin's sleepwalking impressed. The scenes with Hecate and the witches, normally cut because they are not thought to have been written by Shakespeare, were included; but, since they were absurdly cast, staged and sung, it would have been better to have omitted them altogether.
—These Macbeths are the most erotic ever. Bernard Levin *Sunday Times*
—He [Albert Finney] has the physical appearance of a professional boxer gone slightly to seed. Milton Shulman *Evening Standard*

Jun 14. John Woodvine and Ian McDiarmid in Tom Stoppard and André Previn's **Every Good Boy Deserves Favour** directed by Trevor Nunn and revived at Mermaid.

Jun 21. Elaine Page as Eva Peron in Tim Rice and Andrew Lloyd Webber's musical **Evita** directed by Harold Prince at Prince Edward. Showbiz story about a slut who became a saint and sang "Don't Cry For Me Argentina". ("Puccini would have adored her," said Lloyd Webber.) The score was a mixture of pop, rock, waltz, opera, Broadway musical, Kurt Weill, Latin and church music. Joss Ackland's Peron was a tailor's dummy. David Essex played Che Guevera; though what Che had to do with Eva was never made clear.
—She handles the changes from public to private manner with shocking immediacy and her voice fills the theatre like a whole brass band. Irving Wardle *The Times*

Jun 28. Dave King, Jack Shepherd and Michael Feast in David Mamet's **American Buffalo** directed by Bill Bryden at Cottesloe (NT). Premiered in 1975, it made David Mamet famous and swiftly confirmed itself as a modern American classic. Three small-time Chicago crooks plan to steal a man's coin collection, which includes the valuable nickel in the play's title. They are so inept that they never get past the planning stage. The comedy is expletive-ridden and expletive-driven. Mamet parodies the vernacular of an inarticulate underclass. The swearing becomes almost hypnotic in its rhythmic repetitions. The inarticulateness of the trio is such that at times, even they (let alone the audience) don't know what they are talking about.

Jun 29. Frances Viner and Tom Chadbon in Stanley Haughton's **Hindle Wakes** directed by Robert Kidd at Greenwich. Fanny doesn't think she should marry a

callow young man who was no more than her "little fancy". Alan's reaction got a big laugh: "Do you mean to say that you didn't care any more for me than a fellow cares for any girl that he happens to pick up? It sounds so jolly immoral."

Jul 3. Derek Jacobi and Eileen Atkins in Christopher Fry's **The Lady's Not For Burning** directed by George Baker at Old Vic. Plodding, unbewitching production.

Aug 15. Sylvia Miles in Tennessee Williams's **Vieux Carré** directed by Keith Hack at Piccadilly. Perversion, humiliation, destitution, mental breakdown, disease and death. It acted like a parody of Tennessee Williams.

Aug 22. Julie Covington in **The Seven Deadly Sins of Ordinary People**, an opera/ballet with lyrics by Bertolt Brecht and music by Kurt Weill conducted by Lionel Friend and directed by Michael Geliot at Coliseum. Such was Covington's power it made many people regret that she had not played Evita. The production was ruined by the choreography.

Aug 23. George Chakiris in Bob Hall and David Richmond's **The Passion of Dracula** directed by Clifford Williams at Queen's. Roy Dotrice as Van Helsing. Michael Feast as Mr Renfield. The first of two Dracula plays from New York to open within three weeks of each other. Thunder, howling dogs, organ music, swirling smoke, stilted dialogue, old-fashioned construction, poor acting, poor direction and a totally inadequate Dracula.

Sep 7. Dinsdale Landen in Bernard Shaw's **The Philanderer** directed by Christopher Morahan at Lyttelton (NT). The philanderer is smug; but Landen played him with such charm and wit that he was totally engaging.

Sep 13. Terence Stamp in Hamilton Deane and John L Balderston's dramatization of Bram Stoker's **Dracula** designed by Edward Gorey and directed by Dennis Rosa at Shaftesbury. This parody of the Gothic horror genre was also a parody of a performance that might have been given on Broadway when the play was premiered in 1927. Stamp, not a stage actor, was inadequate and too common. Nickolas Grace was too self-indulgent as Mr Renfield. Rupert Frazer was perfect for a stolid 1920s romantic juvenile lead.

Sep 21. **Bette Midler** at Palladium was dressed like a hooker and spent much of her act on her back. Brazen, eccentric, noisy, crude, Midler had star quality.

Sep 27. Robert Stephens in William Congreve's **The Double Dealer** directed by Peter Wood at Olivier (NT). Stephens was confused as to whether to play Maskwell for comedy or seriousness. Michael Bryant as Sir Paul Plyant made cuckoldry and married celibacy both comic and sad. Dorothy Tutin's breathless Lady Plyant–"Me affected? Moi!"–was funny, especially when, in a squeaky whisper, she told her lover that she had given his letter to her husband by mistake.

Oct 25. Billie Whitelaw and T P McKenna in Simon Gray's **Molly** directed by Stephen Hollis at Comedy. Adaptation of Gray's television play, *Death of a Teddy Bear*, based on the Alma Rattenbury trial. Married woman, who is having an affair with a working class lad (Anthony Allen) murders her impotent husband.

Nov 1. Tom Courtenay and Felcity Kendal in Michael Frayn's **Clouds** directed by Michael Rudman at Duke of York's. Three visiting journalists are driven round Cuba seeing what the Cuban government wants them to see. What they actually see and how they react depends largely on the mood they are in.

Nov 8. Diana Rigg and John Thaw in Tom Stoppard's **Night and Day** directed by Peter Wood at Phoenix. Three reporters fly to an emerging black African state on the brink of war. The subject was the freedom of the press and its blatant misuse. Maggie Smith took over from Diana Rigg. *Plays and Players* dismissed it as "a perplexing, partial, exhaustive but unsatisfying evening."

Nov 15. Daniel Massey, Penelope Wilton and Michael Gambon in Harold Pinter's **Betrayal** directed by Peter Hall at Lyttelton (NT). Husband, wife and her lover. Who is being unfaithful to whom? Who knows what? And how long have they known? Did the husband and the lover have an affair? Pinter begins the story in 1977 and takes it back to 1968.
—A woman's magazine romance that goes backwards until it disappears up its own pauses. Herbert Kertzmer *Daily Express*

Nov 29. H W Longfellow's **Hiawatha** directed by Michael Bogdanov at Young Vic (NT). The spectacle, full of visual flair and gentle humour, was far too good to be limited to the 6–12 year-old range the National Theatre recommended.

Nov 30. Andrew Cruickshank and Michael Bryant in John Galsworthy's **Strife** designed by John Bury and directed by Christopher Morahan at Olivier (NT). A well-made play *par excellence*, solid and emphatic, acted like a modern Greek tragedy. The opening tableau, before the play proper began, was a stunning *coup de theatre* with wheel, furnace, noise and smoke, all grinding to a halt. Cruickshank's boss was a perfect image of obduracy and pride, vividly enjoying what he blindly and frighteningly believes to be "a fair fight." Locked in mortal combat, ditched by their own kind, Cruickshank and Bryant (leader of the strike) went down blazing all guns.

Dec 14. Penelope Keith in Bernard Shaw's **The Millionairess** directed by Michael Lindsay Hogg at Haymarket. Ideal role for Keith but the poor old-fashioned production had only Charles Kay's tactful performance as the Egyptian doctor to commend it.

1979

Feb 6. Allan Love in **Tommy,** a musical by Pete Townsend and The Who devised and directed by Paul Tomlinson and John Hale at Queen's. Tommy's father came home from a POW camp at the end of World War 2 to discover his wife having sex with her lover. He murders him. 4-year-old Tommy was so traumatised by the event that he became blind, deaf and dumb. Bullied by his cousin and the local lads, buggered by his uncle, he, nevertheless, somehow, managed to become a pinball wizard by the age of 10. Townsend used the pinball as a metaphor for rock 'n' roll.

Feb 20. Eugene O'Neill's **The Long Voyage Home** directed by Bill Bryden at Cottesloe (NT). A blanket title for four one-act plays set on board a tramp steamer just before and during World War I and sharing the same characters. **The Moon of the Caribbees**: Rum, sing-song, whoring and a knifing. **Bound East for Cardiff**: Sailor hankers for dry land, a home, a wife and kids. He dies, complaining about having travelled all over the world and not seen it. **In the Zone**: The crew, suspecting a well-spoken chap (Jack Shepard) of being a German spy, tie him up, beat him up –only to discover that his suspicious little black box contains nothing but love letters. **The Long Voyage Home**: Swede (Mark McManus), who longs to go home (he hasn't been home in ten years) is drugged, robbed of all his money and press-ganged into service yet again.

Mar 7. Alison Steadman, Christopher Cazenove, Julian Fellowes and Robert Austin in Alan Ayckbourn's **Joking Apart** directed by Alan Ayckbourn at Globe. The action was spread over twelve years. The have-nots lose out in looks, heath, sex, at work, with their children, and even on the tennis court. "The tragedy of life is not that you lose, but that you almost win," says the most embittered of them all. "Some people are born not only with a silver spoon in their mouths but the whole canteen of cutlery." Marcia Warren was excellent as the clinically depressed vicar's wife, who becomes a drug-addict.

Mar 8. Ralph Richardson in Lev Tolstoy's **The Fruits of Enlightenment** directed by Christopher Morahan at Olivier (NT). A rich, eccentric, gullible, doddery old landowner's interest in spiritualism leads him to be tricked into signing a contract, which will allow the poor peasants to buy their land. He prefers to let the peasants have their land, rather than admit he has been fooled. The play, something of a Christmas charade, was originally performed by Tolstoy's family, friends and servants. It was the reality of starving millions, which gave the comedy its edge and poignancy.

Mar 21. Keith Michell as Sherlock Holmes in Paul Giovanni's **The Crucifer of Blood** directed by Paul Giovanni at Haymarket. The recycling of Conan Doyle's The Sign of Four altered the denouement completely. The melodrama, with two boats drifting silently in a Dickensian pea-souper, worked best.

Mar 22. Andre De Sheilds, Charlaine Woodard, Jozella Reed, Evan Bell and Annie Joe Edwards in **Aint Misbehavin'** staged by Arthur Faria and Richard Maltby at Her Majesty's. Anthology of songs Fats Waller wrote and/or recorded. Sexy Andre De Shelds performing "The Viper's Drag" was the hit of the show. The most uncomfortable moment was when the quintet sang, "What did I do to be so black and blue? I feel white inside but what's the good, 'cause I can't hide what is on my face."

Apr 18. Edward Fox in T S Eliot's **Family Reunion** directed by Michael Elliott transferred from Manchester to Round House. Fox looked insane; he could well have pushed his wife overboard. One of the more telling moments was when he remembered the school holidays and how his mother always contrived to make him feel so guilty that he never enjoyed coming home. The Eumenides were portrayed as huge carnival *auto-da-fé* clerics, hooded in white. The sound effects, which preceded their entrances, were unnerving. The London Underground trains, which always rocked the Round House to its foundations, made a valuable contribution.

Apr 24. Jonathan Pryce and Paola Dionisotti in Shakespeare's **The Taming of the Shrew** directed by Michael Bogdanov at Aldwych (RSC). Sophisticated slapstick comedy opened with a stunning *coup de theatre*. A drunk climbs on to the stage and pulls down the set. (Audience for a moment think it's a real drunk.) The drunk is transformed into Christopher Sly, who in turn is transformed into Petruchio. The hurly-burly, largely extempore, with crashing scenery, the washing of Sly and a mili-

1979 World Premieres
New York
 Stephen Sondheim's *Sweeney Todd*
 Brian Friel's *Faith Healer*
 Mark Medoff's *Children of a Lesser God*
 Lanford Wilson's *Talley's Folly*
 Tina Howe's *The Art of Dining*
Londonderry
 Brian Friel's *Aristocrats*

Deaths
 Joyce Grenfell (*b.*1910), British actor

Richard Rodgers (*b.*1902), American composer

Notes
—Globe Theatre site located
—First complete performance of Alban Berg's *Lulu*

History
—Margaret Thatcher became Prime Minister
—Ayatollah Khomeini declared Iran an Islamic republic

tary band, was so exhilarating, so hilarious, that it was a bit of an anti-climax when the actors started speaking Shakespeare's dialogue. The production was funny and painful. Jonathan Pryce's dirty, crude, larky brute was "a madcap ruffian, one half lunatic". It was his violent streak, his insane triumphing in Kate's misery that made this Petruchio so unnerving. Pryce's performance was an extension of the one he had given in *Comedians*. Dionsetti as Kate was much older than he was and this made her humiliation all the nastier. Other actresses have played that last famous soliloquy for irony but it has usually been a witty irony, not a heartbreaking irony. Her sarcasm became more and more embarrassing and Petruchio found that it was he who was humiliated and not his wife.

May 1. Leslie Sands, Harold Innocent, Alison Fiske, John Quayle and Phyllida Law in Somerset Maugham's **For Services Rendered** directed by Michael Rudman at Lyttelton (NT). Rather than toning down the melodramatic theatrics in the last act, Rudman encouraged the cast to go right over the top.

May 2. Patrick Stewart as Shylock and Lisa Harrow as Portia in Shakespeare's **The Merchant of Venice** directed by John Barton at Warehouse (RSC). The production, which owed a great deal to the Jonathan Miller/Laurence Olivier 1970 version, was set in roughly the same Victorian period and had the same intimate courtroom drama. Stewart's Jew was so mean he kept his cigarette stubs in a tin. Hilton McRae played Launcelot Gobbo as an articulate Harpo Marx.

May 3. Ian McKellen and Tom Bell in Martin Sherman's **Bent** directed by Robert Chetwyn at Royal Court. Up to half a million homosexuals were killed by the Nazis. A philandering, drunken homosexual is willing to do anything to stay alive: he beats up his dying boyfriend rather than admit he knows him. He fucks a dead 13-year-old girl to prove he is not queer. In Dachau, since homosexuals are treated the worst, he pretends that he is Jewish. He falls in love with a fellow prisoner. They spend their days moving stones, a routine, which has no other purpose than moving stones. The most memorable moment was when they made love without even touching. They stood apart and the lover took him through the sexual act verbally. Transferred to Comedy.

May 16. Vanessa Redgrave in Henrik Ibsen's **The Lady from the Sea** directed by Michael Elliott at Round House. Ever since she had played Bolette in the 1961 production with Margaret Leighton, Redgrave had wanted to play Ellida. The two roles are the same woman at different points in her life. Redgrave entered dripping wet. Ellida was so nervous, so frightened, and so uncertain of herself; and the more she talked, the wilder and the more unbalanced she became. Redgrave's performance was memorable for great cries of agony ("It's to him I belong"). Graham Crowden gave the weak and ineffectual husband a towering presence and matched her almost crazy intensity with his own crazed intensity. They were both on the brink of madness and liable to go under.

May 29. Michael Pennington and Richard Griffiths in Mikhail Bulgakov's **The White Guard** directed by Barry Kyle at Aldwych (RSC). It's 1918 and the Bolsheviks are coming. The ship is sinking and the rats are leaving as fast as they can. The bourgeois military class – White Russians in the Ukraine – put up a desperate, but futile fight. Whom are they defending? What are they defending? The White cause is finished. There is nothing to fight for. The people are against them. Bulgakov sees the horrors of the Civil War largely through one family and their friends. Stanislavsky, director of the Moscow Arts Theatre, fearing the original title was politically too risky, re-titled the play *The Days of the Turbins* and that was the title under which it was performed in Russia. At the end, as with *The Cherry Orchard*, the wiping away of the old regime and the coming of the new is meant to be seen as something positive. Yet such a reading is not inherent in the text, but rather seems to have been tacked on for the benefit of the censor.

Jun 7. Billie Whitelaw in Samuel Beckett's **Happy Days** directed by Samuel Beckett at Royal Court. Beckett's last work as a director. Whitelaw in her autobiography gave a vivid account of what it was like to rehearse with him. At one point he told her that he didn't think it was a very good play.

—The fact that almost any actress can play Winnie is less a tribute to Beckett's art than it is a symptom of the mass hypnosis that Beckett's plays exert on audiences and critics alike.
Milton Shulman *Evening Standard*

Jun 12. Yul Brynner and Virginia McKenna in Richard Rodgers and Oscar Hammerstein's **The King and I** directed by Yuriko at London Palladium. Perhaps the most cunning thing of all about the musical is that a romantic love story shouldn't have any romance between the two principals. Brynner had been playing the King of Siam for so long (nearly thirty years) that it seemed as if the King of Siam was playing Yul Brynner. The high spot was Jerome Robbins's choreography for "The Small House of Uncle Thomas" ballet, danced in Bangkok style.

Jun 15. Jane Lapotaire in Pam Gems's **Piaf** directed by Howard Davies at Warehouse (RSC). The 'little sparrow' from the gutter became the richest singer in the world, yet remained true to herself – a slut from the gutter, ugly, scraggy, and arthritic. Gems's documentary was relentlessly crude and directed and acted for maximum vulgarity. Lapotaire sang in French and English. Piaf's final disintegration was deeply moving.

Jun 20. Dorothy Tutin and John Wood in Arthur Schnitzler's **Undiscovered Country** directed by Peter Wood at Olivier (NT). Vienna at the turn of the century was an age when love was equated with deceit and betrayal. The characters, who lead unfulfilled and unrewarding lives, indulge in "adventures" and "squalid affairs" to pass the time and/or because everybody else is doing it. The production faltered badly in the third act's protracted joke about the tourist trade. Designer William Dudley provided a ravishing set.

Jul 6. Alan Howard and Glenda Jackson in Shakespeare's **Antony and Cleopatra** directed by Peter Brook at Aldwych (RSC). Howard was very Shakespearian. Jackson was very modern. The pace was so lethargic it seemed as if the production was going to last longer than the *Ring* cycle.

Jul 31. Jessica Tandy and Hume Cronyn in D L Coburn's **The Gin Game** directed by Mike Nichols at Lyric. Pulitzer Prize Winner. A lonely old widow and a lonely old widower, deserted by their respective children, spend their days playing cards on the ramshackle porch of a seedy nursing home. She wins every time, partly by strategy, partly by luck. The deck of cards is a metaphor for life.

Sep 3. Ian Richardson as Klestakov in Gogol's **The Government Inspector** directed by Toby Robertson at Old Vic. The production was dedicated to G A Tovstonogov and The Gorky Theatre Company in Leningrad. The actors, encouraged to caricature, were recognizable 19th-century cartoon figures. Barbara Jefford's handsome performance as the mayor's wife was enhanced by the audience being able to see her sexual fantasies of moustachioed guardsmen and horse-riding, whip-cracking Cossacks. Richardson was hilarious during Khlestkov's long drunken monologue. Staggering round the room he, at one point, inadvertently made an exit. "Where are you all?" he squeaked from the wings.

Felicity Kendal and Simon Callow in Amadeus

Sep 4. Moss Hart and George S Kaufman's **Once in a Lifetime** directed by Trevor Nunn at Aldwych (RSC). Three small-time vaudeville artists decide to break into the film business and jump on the new Talkies bandwagon. Everybody in the hotel lobby, where the producers and the stars gather, wants to get into the movies. This once highly topical caricature of Hollywood's incompetence and trash was too protracted and heavy-handed. The mixture of farcical silliness and supposed seriousness often seemed strangely at odds. In a play of endless cameos, the most delightful was Carmen du Sautoy's secretary, elegantly dressed in black, waving a long cigarette holder and slinking around, unable to remember any name from one minute to the next.

Sep 20. Warren Mitchell and Doreen Mantle in Arthur Miller's **Death of a Salesman** directed by Michael Rudman at Lyttelton (NT). Mitchell may not have been the fat walrus Miller wanted but in everything else he was Willy Loman; and he alone in the company kept a tight grip on his American accent. There were two memorable moments: the first was when Loman is given the sack and the second was when his pride will not let him accept a job from his friend.

Sep 25. Carol Channing in Michael Stewart and Jerry Herman's musical **Hello, Dolly!** directed by Lucia Victor at Drury Lane. Channing had been playing Dolly for so long that she now acted with the audience rather than with the other actors.

Oct 9. Maxim Gorky's **Children of the Sun** directed by Terry Hands at Aldwych (RSC). Political satire. The Russian bourgeoisie is blind to the suffering of the masses. Natasha Parry and John Shrapnel were richly absurd. Sinead Cusack was quite hysterical. Alan Howard was very enigmatic.

Oct 17. Richard Briers and Paul Eddington in Roger Hall's **Middle Age Spread** directed by Robert Kidd at Lyric. New Zealand male menopause-comedy. "Just for once in a while," says the husband to his wife, who is lying beside him, "would you come to bed not looking like your mother?"

Oct 18. Frances de La Tour in Shakespeare's **Hamlet** at Half Moon. Promenade production: tough, intelligent and abrasive.

Oct 23. Tony Britton as Professor Higgins and Liz Robertson as Eliza Doolittle in Alan Jay Lerner and Frederick Loewe's musical **My Fair Lady** directed by Robin Midgley at Adelphi. Anna Neagle as Mrs Higgins. Peter Bayliss as Doolittle. Handsome production and wisely not a carbon copy of the original.

Nov 2. Paul Scofield as Salieri and Simon Callow as Mozart in Peter Shaffer's **Amadeus** directed by Peter Hall at Olivier (NT). Shaffer's black opera was based on the legend that Antonio Salieri, composer to the court of Emperor Joseph II of Austria, had murdered Mozart. Furious with God for speaking though "the voice of an obscene child" rather than through him, who had given his life in His service, Salieri determined to neutralise His creature, starve him, reduce him to destitution, destroy his career and hasten his madness and death. He did everything but murder him. The great strength of the role is Saleiri's total awareness of his own mediocrity. The big shock of the evening was how boorish and vulgar Mozart was. His constant falsetto giggling was particularly irritating. "Have you heard Salieri's music?" he asked. "It's the sound of somebody who can't get it up." Opinions about the play differed wildly, ranging from appalling to masterpiece.
—Mr Shaffer works out his tremendous, his colossal, theme in language of great strength and deceptively obvious subtlety. BERNARD LEVIN *The Times*
—I thought the play as hollow as a strip-cartoon. B A YOUNG *Financial Times*
—Mozart is depicted in an offensive and banal way because he is seen through the eyes of a very, very bad dramatist indeed – perhaps the worst serious English dramatist since Drinkwater. JAMES FENTON *You Were Marvellous*

Nov 8. Denholm Elliott and Diane Cilento in August Strindberg's **The Father** directed by Charles Marowitz at Open Space. Margery Withers as Nurse. The production opened with three images: the father in his straightjacket; the daughter stabbing her portrait of him; his wife and the doctor making love. Later, there was the image of the three women, as avenging furies, advancing on the father with flaming torches.

Nov 20. Gloria Grahame as Amanda, Clive Arrindell as Tom, Veronica Roberts as Laura and Malcolm Ingram as the Gentleman Caller in Tennessee Williams's **The Glass Menagerie** directed by Peter James transferred from Sheffield to the Round House. Graham, never grotesque, surprisingly subtle, made it transparent that Amanda wanted the Gentleman Caller for herself and not for her daughter.

Nov 28. Nigel Hawthorne as Vanya, Ian Holm as Astrov and Maurice Denham as the Professor in Anton Chekhov's **Uncle Vanya** directed by Nancy Meckler at Hampstead. Alison Steadman as Sonya. Susan Littler as Yelena. The production took an unconscionable time to begin and to end, dragging the last scene out quite unnecessarily.

Nov 28. Alfred Lord Tennyson's **The Ancient Mariner** directed by Michael Bogdanov at Young Vic. Visually, the production was a *tour de force*; but vocally, it had none of the mesmeric authority of the original. The inventiveness failed when it came to staging the moral struggle and spiritual journey.

Dec 12. Robin Bailey, Barbara Ferris, Harold Innocent, Joan Sanderson, Mary Maddox, Leslie Sands and Pat Heywood in J B Priestley's **When We Are Married** directed by Robin Lefevre at Lyttelton (NT). Liz Smith as the maid looked as if she has stepped out of the pages of back numbers of *Punch*. The interlude in the second act, when the whole play comes to a standstill for a comic turn by the fiddly photographer, fell completely flat. This was partly because Peter Jeffrey didn't know what he was doing, but mainly because it had nothing to do with the play.

Dec 13. Stephen Moore as Hjalmar Ekdal in Henrik Ibsen's **The Wild Duck** directed by Christopher Morahan at Olivier (NT). Moore was too lightweight to be tragi-comic and so all the lies, the lethargy, the self-pity and the refusal to face reality, were muted and meant little. Michael Bryant's Gregers Werle was mentally and physically warped. Ralph Richardson's strange, wild grandfather with a flaming orange toupee was full-blown caricature. The advantage of having a child (Eva Griffith) to play Hedvig was great. The production also boasted live poultry.

1980–1989

Nana Pachusashvil and Ramaz Chkikvadze in Richard III (Russian)

1980

Jan 19. **The Greeks** directed by John Barton at Aldwych (RSC). Ten Greek plays, staged as a trilogy, were adapted by John Barton and Kenneth Cavender mainly from Euripides with additional material from Homer, Aeschylus and Sophocles. Barton attempted to superimpose a coherent and dramatic whole. The language was bathetic, flip and so unceasingly ironic that everything was turned into a joke. There were no heroes. The characters behaved like wild animals, snarling, raging and foaming. The result was melodrama. The gods, playing for laughs, turned tragedy into farce.

Jan 22. Stacy Keach in Eugene O'Neill's **Hughie** directed by Bill Bryden at Cottesloe (NT). The lost American dream and the existential emptiness of modern life: Hughie is a night clerk in a fleabag New York hotel where the inmates lose themselves in illusion because it is the only way they know how to survive. "Hughie," said O'Neill, "is an essence of all the night clerks I've known in bum hotels." It was the one play in a cycle of short plays that he didn't destroy.

Jan 23. Beryl Reid, Barry Foster, Peter Bowles and Jan Waters in Peter Nichols's **Born in the Garden** directed by Clifford Williams at Duke of York's. Who are the most disturbed? Is it the ones who stayed home or is it those who fled the nest? The action is set in an England in decline, a land of foreigners and unemployed, a modernized Britain, in which nothing works.

Jan 28. The Rustaveli Company of Georgia, USSR at the Round House. Ramaz Chkhikvadze in Shakespeare's **Richard III** designed by Mirian Shvelidze and directed by Robert Sturua. One of the great Shakespearean productions of the 20th century: romantic, poetic, clownish, a stylised dance of death to a catchy sentimental tune. The characters emerged from the jaws of hell. Chkhikvadze, silver-haired, overweight, corseted and grotesque, was a crazy, boar-like hunchback, who wore a Napoleonic military grey overcoat and only limped when it suited him. He was dogged by Death and a Court Jester who aped his every action. Edward IV (a crazy baby-faced, ugly, moustached cartoon pig) made his entrance with a zimmer-frame. The final image had Richard and Richmond fighting inside a map of England, their half-naked bodies protruding through the canvas. The English theatrical profession turned out in force. The applause went on for ten minutes.

Jan 29. Timothy West in **Beecham** directed by Patrick Garland at Apollo. Solo performance. The famous conductor's charm, levity, rudeness and lethal judgements on composers, conductors and singers alternated with potted biography and tantalizing brief extracts from the original Beecham recordings.

Mar 12. Leonard Rossiter and Prunella Scales in Michael Frayn's **Make and Break** directed by Michael Blakemore at Lyric, Hammersmith. Business takes over businessmen's lives to the exclusion of wives, children, sex, friendship and conversation. Perhaps, the most telling moment was a seduction scene when Rossiter removed his secretary's shoe and could not resist looking at the label inside the shoe to find out the name of the firm who had made it. Prunella Scales gave a beautifully subdued performance as the loyal secretary. Audiences who came expecting a combination of *The Fall and Rise of Reginald Perrin* and *Fawlty Towers* would have been disappointed by the play's seriousness. Transferred to Haymarket.
—He [Leonard Rossiter] portrayed obsession so brilliantly because obsession comes from underground, and he knew how to work underground. MICHAEL FRAYN

Mar 20. Paul Scofield as Othello, Michael Bryant as Iago and Felicity Kendal as Desdemona in Shakespeare's **Othello** directed by Peter Hall at Olivier (NT). Scofield, perplexed in the extreme but lacking in passion, was totally unbelievable as a black man. Iago was so insanely jealous that he was convinced everybody was sleeping with his wife.

Apr 2. Jonathan Pryce as Hamlet and Ghost in Shakespeare's **Hamlet** directed by Richard Eyre at Royal Court. Harriet Walter as Ophelia. Michael Elphick as Claudius. Jill Bennett as Gertrude. Geoffrey Chater as Polonius. The play was acted as a Jacobean revenge drama. The Ghost spoke through Hamlet. The epileptic fits and the strange voice, which seemed to come from his very bowels, were undeniably histrionic; but they did not help the actual meaning of the text. Highly strung and extremely energetic, Pryce was liable at any minute to erupt into terrifying violence. His attack on Ophelia was particularly nasty.
—If you want to see an actor wrestling vibrantly, wittily and honestly with a great role, then London offers nothing better. ROBERT CUSHMAN *Observer*

Apr 2. Anton Chekhov's **Three Sisters** directed by Trevor Nunn at Warehouse (RSC). One of the great Chekhovian productions. The villains were striking presences. Bob Peck's Solliony, with cigar and scent bottle, was a huge, towering figure. His proposal to Irena was a chilling threat. Griffith Jones as Chebutkin (who callously does nothing to stop the Baron from getting shot) was very vain, constantly combing his very full grey beard. Susan Tracy's Natasha was a vulgar bourgeois upstart, who takes cruel revenge on the sisters for their earlier condescension and gradually eases

them out of house and home. In the last act she hovered over them like a vulture. Emily Richard's Irena, much older than is usual, was unexpectedly cruel when she lets the Baron go off to his death without giving him the satisfaction of saying she loves him. Suzanne Bertish made Masha's haggard silences and cries of pain unashamedly theatrical. Edward Petherbridge actually made Vershinin's philosophizing interesting. Roger Rees, wearing large spectacles and sporting a moustache, was a gauche and intense Tusenbach. Timothy Spall's Andrei got uglier as the production went on. Olga's final speech was divided between the three sisters who hugged each other closely in a heart-rending, defiant finale.

Apr 12. Derek Newark, James Grant and Robert East in Harold Pinter's **The Hothouse** directed by Harold Pinter at Hampstead. The patients in a lunatic asylum massacre the staff. The play was written in 1958 just before *The Caretaker*, but it wasn't until 1979 that Pinter decided it was worth presenting on stage. He made a few cuts but no changes to the original script.

Apr 22. Ralph Richardson in David Storey's **Early Days** directed by Lindsay Anderson at Cottesloe (NT). A retired politician could have been Prime Minister but for an indiscreet interview. Richardson had difficulty remembering his lines.
—Richardson has a genius for jaunty sadness and ebullient despair ... This is vintage acting: the result of a lifetime's experience. MICHAEL BILLINGTON *Guardian*

Apr 30. Tom Courtenay and Freddie Jones in Ronald Harwood's **The Dresser** directed by Michael Elliott at Queen's. The last of the great actor-managers, incapable of abdicating, is leading a wartime company of "old men, cripples and nancy boys" on a grueling provincial tour. His wife tells him that he is a third-rate actor in a third-rate company and that she is sick, week after week, reading in the papers that her performance is not worthy of his talents. The most exciting sequence was watching stage staff and actors working their guts out to create the storm – a genuinely thrilling sound – only to have Lear stomp into the wings and ask, "Where was the storm?" The relationship between the actor and his dresser paralleled the relationship of Lear and the Fool. Harwood said the play was not about Donald Wolfit. Nobody believed him. Courtenay's dresser was camp, devoted, self-pitying and malicious.

May 7. John Woodvine in Shakespeare's **The Merry Wives of Windsor** directed by Trevor Nunn and John Caird at Barbican (RSC). This subdued and essentially serious production ended with the whole community turning on Falstaff in such a vicious manner that it was a re-run of his rejection by Henry V at the coronation.

May 13. Alec McCowen and Geraldine McEwan in Terence Rattigan's **The Browning Version** and **Harlequinade** directed by Michael Rudman at Lyttelton (NT). The best and the worst of Rattigan side by side.

Jun 3. Stephen Moore, Penelope Wilton, Selina Cadell, Michael Bryant and Simon Callow in Alan Ayckbourn's **Sisterly Feeling** directed by Alan Ayckbourn and Christopher Morahan at Olivier (NT). The action was dictated by a flick of the coin at the end of the first scene and the actress's own impulse at the end of the second scene. There were thus a possible four permutations. The characterization was glib and the actors drifted into caricature.

Jun 4. Susan Tracy and Fulton MacKay in Eugene O'Neill's **Anna Christie** directed by Jonathan Lynn at Warehouse (RSC). Young prostitute returns to the father she has not seen since he palmed her off on her cousins fifteen years earlier, when she was five. The play falls apart in the second act, when a shipwrecked Irish stoker comes aboard and instantly declares his love for Anna. The RSC provided a real pea-souper.

Jun 5. Charles Dickens's **Nicholas Nickleby** adapted by David Edgar designed by John Napier and Dermot Hayes and directed by Trevor Nunn and John Caird at Aldwych. RSC marathon: a total of eight hours and forty minutes spread over two evenings. It seemed as if nothing was going to be left out. Roger Rees's charming Nickleby was straight out of Phiz. David Threlfall's spastic Smike was deeply moving. Despite an excellent press, the production initially did such bad business that the upper circle was closed.
—I can think of few actors who are better at conveying through facial expressions alone, a frank acquaintance with grief. It was a good move to cast such an engaging actor in the part of young Nickleby not because his personality closely resembles that of the Dickens hero, but because a striking character was required to add savour to the original. JAMES FENTON *Sunday Times*

Jun 10. Julie Walters and Mark Kingston in Willy Russell's **Educating Rita** directed by Mike Ockrent at Warehouse (RSC). Twenty-six year-old hairdresser decides she wants to know everything and enrols on an Open University degree course. The irony is that she begins with a mind of her own and ends with a mind full of Eng Lit crit. Transferred to Piccadilly.

Jul 2. Denis Quilley as Sweeney Todd and Sheila Hancock as Mrs Lovett in Stephen Sondheim's musical **Sweeney Todd the Demon Barber of Fleet Street** a musical thriller at Drury Lane directed by Harold Prince. Book by Hugh Wheeler. The

Sheila Hancock and Denis Quilley in Sweeney Todd

Demon Barber of Fleet Street first appeared in a penny dreadful between 1846 and 1847 and even before the serialisation was complete, George Dibdin Pitt had turned it into a "blood tub" (a violent and sensational melodrama). Wheeler's book is based on Christopher Bond's play, which was first performed at the Theatre Royal, Stratford East. Todd was sentenced to deportation on a trumped-up charge by a malevolent Judge, who drove his wife to an early death and then stole his daughter. Todd, bitter and self-obsessed, is presented as a tragic figure who turns serial killer and takes a demented revenge on the whole of society. The story moves to a powerful close. The bodies pile up in a familiar Jacobean revenge manner and the finale, when Todd discovers that the woman he has just murdered is his wife, plays like the last act of *Rigoletto*. *Sweeney Todd* was premiered in New York in 1979 when it won 8 "Tony" awards, including best musical, but it was never popular with Broadway audiences. London, too, rejected Prince's overwhelming production. The musical needed a much smaller and grittier venue than Drury Lane.

Jul 15. David Schofield as John Merrick and Peter McEnery as Frederick Treves in Bernard Pomerance's **The Elephant Man** directed by Roland Rees at Lyttelton (NT). Merrick (1863–1890) was so obscenely deformed, that he could only earn his living as a freak in a circus. He was rescued by Treves, an eminent surgeon, a benevolent, enlightened man, who wanted to mould him in his own image. Pomerance's premise was that the medical profession and society, even in their humanity, exploited Merrick just as much as the circus had done and that in trying to make him normal like themselves, they destroyed him. The play had opened at The Hampstead Theatre in 1977 but had to go to New York first and win six awards before it was thought good enough to transfer to the National Theatre.

Jul 29. Roger Rees in Nikolai Erdman's **The Suicide** directed by Ron Daniels at Warehouse (RSC). With the prospect of two million out of work, the government might well have felt that 1980 wasn't quite the moment to be reviving a play about a man who is refused employment. Erdman's nerve-wracking farce, a political satire in the tradition of Gogol's *The Government Inspector*, attacked everybody: Marxists, intelligentsia, Church, whores, workers and non-workers. The play was banned in 1930 whilst still in rehearsal. The lazy, selfish, jobless Semyon (a parody of a typical Russian hero) is a nonentity whose life is so vile and so inhuman that he becomes suicidal. He is besieged by intellectuals, clergymen, butchers, *femmes fatales*, who all want his death to be a political gesture and they are furious, at the end of the play, to find that he is still alive. Rees was hilarious when he could not make up his mind whether to shoot himself in the heart or the head. But the laughter often froze. The line of demarcation between farce and tragedy was minimal. The haggard, unshaven Rees might so easily have been playing Raskolnikov.

Aug 12. Ben Kingsley in Bertolt Brecht's **Baal** directed by David Jones at Warehouse (RSC). Baal, the poet-genius, was a depraved animal. The production, acted and sung with characteristic Brechtian aggression, emphasised all that was sordid, ugly and brutal; the only relief was the back-projection which provided lyrical photographs of forest trees.

Aug 13. Michael Gambon in Bertolt Brecht's **The Life of Galileo** directed by John Dexter at Olivier (NT). Galileo's discovery that the earth was not the centre of the universe undermined the authority of Church and State. His recantation was seen as ironic; he renounced the truth but only so as to avoid torture and so that he could continue his research. Dexter was at his best with the more intimate moments and the final scene, when the manuscript of the *Discoursi* is smuggled across the border, went for absolutely nothing. The stagehands in their spotless white overalls moved

1980 World Premieres

San Francisco
Sam Shepard's *True West*
Londonderry
Brian Friel's *Translations*

Deaths

Cecil Beaton (*b.*1904), British
designer
David Mercer (*b.*1928), British
playwright
Ben Travers (*b.*1886), British
playwright

Kenneth Tynan (*b.*1927), British
critic

Notes

—Field Day Theatre Company
founded

History

—Iran-Iraq war
—US funded Contras in Nicaragua
—John Lennon murdered in New
York

—Don't trust the reviews. The spectacle is far worse than has hitherto been made out, a milestone in the history of coarse acting. JAMES FENTON *Sunday Times*

Sep 16. Peggy Ashcroft in Lillian Hellman's **Watch on the Rhine** directed by Mike Ockrent at Lyttelton (NT). This 1941 propaganda piece to get the Americans into World War 2, inevitably, no longer had the urgency which could make an audience ignore Hellman's glib mixture of comedy and melodrama.

Oct 1. Judi Dench as Juno and Norman Rodway as Captain Boyle in Sean O'Casey's **Juno and the Paycock** directed by Trevor Nunn at Aldwych (RSC). O'Casey's centenary. Rodway's pompous, selfish, lying sot was at his most frightening in his Lear-like anger with his daughter. The third act melodrama was played with such honesty that it ceased to be melodrama. One of the lines–"Has none of you any respect for the Irish people's National regard for the dead?"–got a big laugh, only for it to be quashed immediately by the retort: "Maybe, it's nearly time we had a little less respect for the dead and a little more regard for the living." Mrs Boyle repeated Mrs Tancred's great lament at the end: "Blessed Virgin, where were you when me darlin' son was riddled with bullets?"
—Judy Dench gives a performance that can only be termed great. *Stage*
—The most telling performance of the part [Juno] in living memory. J C TREWIN *Illustrated London News*

Oct 15. Joan Plowright and Colin Blakely in Alan Bennett's **Enjoy** directed by Ronald Eyre at Vaudeville. Disturbing satirical comedy about the way the old are treated and the way people react to death.
—The classic tug in Bennett between childhood Yorkshire and intellectual sophistication has never been better, or more daringly expressed. ROBERT CUSHMAN *Observer*

Oct 16. Howard Brenton's **The Romans in Britain** directed by Michael Bogdanov at Olivier (NT). The epic was variously described as puerile, hollow, banal, obscene, degrading, disgusting, lewd, hopelessly inept, artistically worthless and morally offensive. The simulated buggery was as explicit as the buggery in John Boorman's film, *Deliverance*. Sir Horace Cutler, leader of the GLC, wanted the National Theatre's grant to be cut. Mrs Mary Whitehouse, under Section 13 of the 1956 Sexual Offences Act, charged Bogdanov with procuring, and being party to, "the commission by a man of an act of gross indecency with another man." The Director of Public Prosecu-

quietly and unhurriedly about the stage. They were so visibly an integral part of the production they should have shared a curtain call with the actors. Gambon's unexpected casting and the impressive performance he gave was a major turning point in his career. "A new star is discovered" was the headline in *The Times*. The rest of the cast circled in his orbit.

Aug 13. Donald Sinden as Othello and Bob Peck as Iago in Shakespeare's **Othello** directed by Ronald Eyre at Barbican (RSC). Impossible to believe in Sinden, the most English of actors, could be a Moor. Peck was such a big man that he made even Sinden look small.

Sep 3. Peter O'Toole in Shakespeare's **Macbeth** directed by Bryan Forbes at Old Vic. Frances Tomelty as Lady Macbeth. When O'Toole came on after the murder of Duncan he was covered in so much blood, that the line, "I have done the deed," was so superfluous that he got a huge unwanted laugh. Brian Blessed's Banquo was the most solid, bluff, smiling ghost you ever did see and chased Macbeth round the banquet table. The production was terrible. The reviews were terrible. The box office business was excellent.
—The performance is not so much downright bad as heroically ludicrous. JOHN TINKER *Daily Mail*

Romans in Britain

tions declared the production did not contravene the Act and refused to prosecute. Mary Whitehouse, who had not seen the play, brought her own private prosecution, but the Attorney-General refused her leave to do so.

—This play is a nauseating load of rubbish from beginning to end. It is written in ludicrous pseudo-poetic yob-talk; such themes as it possesses are banal beyond belief; and the intended bravery of the acting company amounts to no more than an embarrassing exhibitionism. It is advertised as unsuitable for children. It is unsuitable for anyone. JAMES FENTON *Sunday Times*

Nov 11. Jonathan Pryce as Mick, Kenneth Cranham as Aston and Warren Mitchell as Davies in Harold Pinter's **The Caretaker** directed by Kenneth Ives at Lyttelton (NT). Pryce suggested that Mick was just as disturbed as his brother and that he had probably been through the same shock treatment and had come out worse.

1981

Jan 13. Anton Rodgers, Benjamin Whitrow, Billie Whitelaw and Eileen Atkins in Peter Nichols's **Passion Play** directed by Mike Ockrent at Aldwych (RSC). Marriage on the rocks. Husband and wife were played by four actors, two of them playing *alter egos*. The husband is a dull stick on the outside; inside he is an extrovert. His wife is outwardly self-possessed; inside she is haggard and grief-stricken. When the wife learns that her husband is having an affair, the audience watched Whitelaw taking it so calmly, while Atkins went all to pieces. The final curtain in the middle of a Christmas party had Whitelaw mingling with her guests, while Atkins was packing her bags and leaving the house.

Jan 22. Daniel Massey as John Tanner and Penelope Wilton as Ann Whitefield in Bernard Shaw's **Man and Superman** directed by Christopher Morahan at Olivier (NT). Basil Henson as the Statue. Michael Bryant as the Devil. There was a very funny moment when Tanner rashly challenges Ann to elope with him and to his horror, she accepts. Like Granville-Barker before him, Massey made up to look like Shaw. It gave the comedy an extra dimension and made the Don Juan act, which Shaw described as "totally extraneous", not so extraneous after all. The last act was all the sadder. Massey, eyes flashing, vigorous, eloquent, impudent, really did seem to be in the grip of the Life Force.

Jan 29. Maggie Smith as Virginia Woolf, Nicholas Pennell as Leonard Woolf and Patricia Conolly as Vita Sackville-West in Edna O'Brien's **Virginia** directed by Robin Phillips at Haymarket. Based on the writings of Virginia and Leonard Woolf. Audiences arriving at the theatre expecting to see Edward Albee's *Who's Afraid of Virginia Woolf?* were in for a big disappointment.

Feb 23. Rowan Atkinson at Globe. Undergraduate humour. High spots: the Devil's pep talk to the latest batch of inmates, a vindictive schoolmaster calling a register, a drunken father of the bride laying into his son-in-law in his toast at the wedding reception, and a camp actor illustrating a lecture on Elizabethan drama. Atkinson also managed to put on his bathing trunks without removing his trousers first.

Feb 26. Henderson Forsythe and Carlin Glynn in **The Best Little Whorehouse in Texas** directed by Peter Masterson and Tommy Tune at Drury Lane. Book by Larry L King and Peter Masterson. Music and lyrics by Carol Hall. Musical numbers staged by Tommy Tune. The story was based on fact. A watchdog TV programme did succeed in shutting down a much-loved brothel. The musical cast the television evangelist as villain and guyed his vigilante group, who carried tiny phallic torches.

Apr 1. Helen Mirren and Bob Hoskins in John Webster's **The Duchess of Malfi** directed by Adrian Noble transferred from Royal Exchange, Manchester, to Round House. It seemed very appropriate that Mirren and Hoskins should have come straight to Webster from their melodramatic gangster film, *The Long Good Friday*. Mike Gwilym's paranoid Ferdinand went completely bonkers and bit Bosola to death.

—It makes most modern drama look childish. In its technique and its taste this production is something of a prodigy; I would put my money on Mr Noble turning out the best classical director to appear since Trevor Nunn. ROBERT CUSHMAN *Observer*

Apr 14. Norman Beaton as Angelo, Stefan Kalipha as The Duke and Yvette Harris as Isabella in Shakespeare's **Measure for Measure** directed by Michael Rudman at Lyttelton (NT). All-black production was set in 20th-century Caribbean. Peter Straker's pimp dominated the stage.

May 5. Simon Callow and Hilton McRae in Christopher Hampton's **Total Eclipse** directed by David Hare at Lyric, Hammersmith. Callow put on pounds of flesh to play Verlaine. McRae's Rimbaud, charmless, offensive, callous and destructive, looked as if he had stepped out of Verlaine's poem: the angel-devil as schoolboy monster.

May 11. Elaine Page, Wayne Sleep, Paul Nicholas and Brian Blessed in Andrew Lloyd Webber's **Cats** choreographed by Gillian Lynne and directed by Trevor Nunn

1981 World Premieres
New York
Charles Fuller's *A Soldier's Story*
Manuel Puig's *The Kiss of the Spider Woman*
Stockholm
Ingmar Bergman's *Scenes from a Marriage*

Deaths
Jessie Matthews (*b.*1907), British singer, dancer

Notes
—London International Festival

History
—Ronald Reagan became US President
—First report of AIDS
—Prince Charles married Lady Diana Spencer
—Yorkshire Ripper at loose
—Bobby Sands on hunger strike
—First London Marathon

at New London. Musical based on T S Eliot's *Old Possum's Book of Practical Cats*. There was no story; it was essentially a dance show. The costumes made the cats all punk alley cats. But Eliot's cats are not punk. They belong to a pre-war generation, who looked back, nostalgically, to the Twenties, Edwardian and Victorian eras. They inhabit an upper middle-class, terribly British world of snobbery and condescension. The only cat who looked right was Bustopher Jones (Brian Blessed) in a fat fur coat and monocle. The hit number, Memory, had nothing to do with cats. The critics raved: "the cat's whiskers", "possum power", "in a word, purr-fect." Two days before the opening Judi Dench tore her Achilles tendon and was replaced by Elaine Page. *Cats* became the longest-running musical. Can 7 million London theatregoers be wrong?

—Smash hits don't come more smash than this one. SHERIDAN MORLEY *Punch*

May 14. **Quentin Crisp** at Mayfair.

Jun 11. Michael Crawford in Cy Coleman's musical **Barnum** directed by Peter

Elaine Paige in Cats

Coe at London Palladium. Book by Mark Bramble. Lyrics by Michael Stewart. Barnum's the name and hokum's the game. The story as told in the programme was far more interesting than the one acted on stage. What the show needed was a big top, not a theatre.

—If it is a musical with only one decent tune and a book with only one slim theme, then this is the triumph of hokum over mediocrity. JACK TINKER *Daily Mail*

Jun 14. Steven Berkoff and Linda Marlowe in Steven Berkoff's **Decadence** at New End. The caricature of the degeneracy of the aristocracy was as unrelenting as Swift and as gross as Grosz. For sheer brutality, facially, vocally and verbally, there was nobody to touch Berkoff. His contortions on the sofa were hilarious. Linda Marlowe gave a memorable description of the sexual pleasures of fox-hunting.

Jun 19. Alfred Lynch in Thomas Dekker's **The Shoemaker's Holiday** directed by John Dexter at Olivier (NT). Dexter concentrated on creating a real, living, workaday world. The banter, the slanging matches and the crude jokes had an authentic ring. Lynch's shoemaker (who became Lord Mayor of London) was patently a good man. Brenda Bruce, playing his wife, acted in a broader, pantomime key and came to look more and more like Queen Elizabeth I.

Jul 2. Frank Finlay as Salierei and Richard O'Callaghan as Mozart in Peter Shaffer's **Amadeus** directed by Peter Hall at Her Majesty's. Shaffer's play returned to London, laden with 5 Tony awards from New York where the leading roles had been played by Ian McKellen and Tim Curry. Mozart still had his shrill treble giggles, but his vulgarity had been toned down for West End audiences. Finlay's Salierei was a provincial.

—He [Peter Shaffer] keeps his middlebrow audience entertained and sends them off to dinner with the feeling that they have seen something serious, even stimulating. MARK AMORY *Spectator*

—Frank Finlay's Salierei may lack Paul Scofield's guile but he banishes camp pantomimic gestures for a vital and anguished rendition of jealousy. NICHOLAS DE JONGH *Guardian*

Jul 14. Vernel Bagneris, Topsy Chapman, Thais Clark, John Stell and Sylvia "Kuumba" Williams in **One Mo' Time!** written and directed by Vernel Bagneris at Cambridge. Fast, noisy, exuberant, witty, tuneful, it was the best show of its kind since *Aint Misbehavin'*. Set in a sleazy 1926 New Orleans vaudeville theatre, it offered twenty-seven hit numbers, interspersed with backstage bickering.

Jul 16. David Suchet as Shylock and Sinead Cusack as Portia in Shakespeare's **The Merchant of Venice** directed by John Barton at Aldwych (RSC). Barton's small-scale and excellent 1979 studio production was enlarged to fill a bigger theatre and seemed even better.

Jul 17. Barbara Leigh-Hunt, Richard Pasco and Alan Howard in Alexander Ostrovsky's **The Forest** directed by Adrian Noble at Warehouse (RSC). Rich and devious widow pretends to be a pious do-gooder, distributing largesse, when in fact she is totally incapable of parting with any of her money. Leigh-Hunt, clutching her cash-box to her bosom, was a figure of farce and far more of a comedian than the actors who descended on her estate. Transferred to Aldwych.

Jul 21. Simon Callow in Edward Bond's **Restoration** directed by Edward Bond at Royal Court. 18th century lord, who accidently-on-purpose kills his country-born wife (who is disguised as a Ghost), palms the murder off on his servant, who naïvely thinks the lord will get him reprieved. The theme was very simple: if gentlemen kept their promises, society would fall apart.

Jul 21. Michael Pennington, Norman Rodway and Dearbhla Molloy in Sean O'Casey's **The Shadow of a Gunman** directed by Michael Bogdanov at Warehouse (RSC). It was O'Casey's special skill to mix tragedy and farce. As he said: "The Irish people are very fond of turning a serious thing into a joke." Bogdanov was much better with the tragedy than he was with the musical hall turns, which didn't work because he had toned them down too much and taken them too seriously.

Jul 23. Maggie Steed, Alfred Molina and Sylvester McCoy in Dario Fo's **Can't Pay? Won't Pay!** adapted and directed by Robert Walker at Criterion. Housewives revolt against pay increases in the supermarkets. The anarchic farce (a mixture of Bertolt Brecht and Brian Rix) complemented the anti-poll tax protests in Britain and mocked the Pope, the Communist Party, the trade unions, and the police.

—This, however, is no gloomy agitprop. Fo-faced farce wears a broad smile and proceeds at breathtaking speed. MICHAEL BILLINGTON *Financial Times*

Jul 30. Edward Fox, Robin Bailey, James Grout and Prunella Scales in Simon Gray's **Quartermaine's Terms** directed by Harold Pinter at Queen's. Gray set the action in the staff room of a not very successful School of English for Foreigners and then deliberately invited comparison with Chekhov, blatantly so when one member of staff refused to go and see *The Cherry Orchard* on the grounds that she couldn't see how anybody could get comedy out of depression, gloom and suicide. Fox played the decent Quartermaine, a naïve and lonely bachelor, whom everybody ignored and

everybody used and who was finally sacked for incompetence. Fox movingly suggested a sad inner emptiness under the outward fatuity. Scales was cast as a spinster, who, unable to cope with her malevolent invalid mother, pushed her down the stairs to her death, and then turned to religion and drink.

Aug 6. Ian Bannen and Tony Doyle Brien Friel's **Translations** directed by Donald McWhinnie at Lyttleton (NT). The British army in Ireland in the 1830s carried out an ordinance survey and anglicised all the Gaelic place-names. The Hedge schools were to be replaced by the new national schools and the children were going to be taught not only English but in English. Friel got some delightful comedy out of the language barrier in a sentimental scene when an English officer (Shaun Scott) and his Irish fiancée (Anna Keaveney) were talking to each other in their own language without understanding what the other was saying. The audience was able to understand what they were saying because both actors spoke in English.

—A modern classic. It engages the intellect as well as the heart, and achieves a profound political and philosophical resonance through the detailed examination of individual lives. ERIC SHORTER *Daily Telegraph*

Aug 12. Daniel Massey and Michael Bryant in Pedro Calderon de la Barca's **The Mayor of Zulema** directed by Michael Bogdanov at Cottesloe (NT). A Spanish aristocrat rapes a young peasant and expects, since he is an officer and a gentleman, to be tried by a military tribunal, who will let him off, or, at the very worst, fine him some footling sum. There was an extraordinary scene when the girl's father, who has just been made mayor and now had the legal powers to exact his revenge, preferred to beg the aristocrat to marry his daughter, promising him a huge dowry. The aristocrat sat there, saying nothing, until, unable to contain himself any longer, he refused in an arrogant outburst. When the mayor then took the law into his own hands and had the rapist garrotted, the audience naturally expected the officer class to close ranks. But, in an unexpected fairy-tale ending, the king accepted that justice had been done and gave the mayor even greater power. Adrian Mitchell's translation with its stilted dialogue, cheap H J Byron rhymes and anachronistic swearing, was very entertaining.

Aug 20. Georgina Hale, Brenda Blethyn and Maria Charles in Nell Dunn's **Steaming** directed by Roger Smith transferred from Stratford East to Comedy. Set in a public Turkish bath there was no story. The women just talked. The language was coarse and the actresses were in the nude.

Aug 25. Trevor Eve and Elizabeth Quinn in Mark Medoff's **Children of a Lesser God** directed by Gordon Davidson at Mermaid. The relationship between a speech therapist and his incurably deaf and non-speaking pupil was in the wisecracking Neil Simon comedy vein with sign language. Trevor Eve as the therapist had to do all the talking; he spoke for them both, translating everything she said as she was saying it. The part was longer than Hamlet. The pupil argued that she didn't want to have anybody speaking for her and that a deaf person's language was better than a hearing person's language. Elizabeth Quinn was deaf and non-speaking in real life. Transferred to Albery.

Aug 27. Margaret Tyzack and Paul Eddington in Edward Albee's **Who's Afraid of Virginia Woolf?** directed by Nancy Meckler at Lyttelton (NT). Gladiatorial exhibitionism: Eddington, unexpectedly cast, proved unexpectedly good, his acting extending far beyond his normal range.

Sep 2. Alan Howard in C P Taylor's **Good** directed by Howard Davies at Warehouse (RSC). An academic writes a novel advocating euthanasia on humane grounds and finds himself actively participating in the extermination of the Jews. Taylor traces the various compromises "good" Germans made. A cafe quintet played incongruous sentimental music, guying the Germans' love of music and providing a fantasy world into which the "good" professor could retreat. When the band ended up playing in Auschwitz there was no longer a fantasy world into which a "good" German could retreat any more. Joe Melia played an acerbic psychiatrist.

—Congratulation to all, not least Mr Taylor, for somehow combining 'Holocaust' with 'Pennies from Heaven.' ROBERT CUSHMAN *Observer*

Sep 22. Michael Kitchen and Felicity Kendal in Tom Stoppard's **On the Razzle** directed by Peter Wood at Lyttelton (NT). Stoppard had gone back to Thornton Wilder's source, Johann Nestroy's *Einen Jux Will Er Sich Machen* (1842), which in its turn was based on John Oxenford's *A Day Well Spent* (1835). Not funny and heavily over-burdened with bad puns, it was *Hello, Dolly!* without the music and without Dolly Levi. Felicity Kendal was cast as a boy.

Sep 30. Simon Callow and Patrick Ryecart in J P Donleavy's **The Beastly Beatitudes of Balthazar B** directed by Ron Daniels at Duke of York's. Picaresque journey of two rich young men – one good, one bad – who travel a downward path. The script was witty, bawdy and blasphemous. Ryecart was the shy bewildered Balthazar, who is sent down from Trinity College, Dublin, trapped into marriage and disinherited, and yet, somehow, remains incorrupt and good. His friend, Beefy, grows up to be a notorious and flamboyant pervert. Asked why he tolerates him, Balthasar says he does so for his charm. Callow, in the nude and goggles, was outrageously Beefy.

Oct 27. Colin Blakely and Rosemary Harris in Arthur Miller's **All My Sons** directed by Michael Blakemore at Wyndham's. Blakely didn't bother too much with an American accent and gave such a totally understated performance that he didn't seem to be in the same production as Harris. That moment when she inadvertently lets slip that he had never been ill in his life was electrifying. Harris could have been acting in a Greek tragedy.

Nov 5. Rupert Everett and Joshua Le Touzel in Julian Mitchell's **Another Country** directed by Stuart Burge at Greenwich. The public schools in the 1930s were the perfect breeding ground for homosexual spies. The future ruling classes, outwardly a decent, civilised bunch, were corrupt in mind and body, supporting a brutal and repressive regime, many of them no longer believed in. The petty politics of school life mirrored the more serious scandals, blackmails and compromises of adult life. Rupert Everett, effete, elegant and scruffy, gave a witty, knowing performance. Threatened with a beating by the prefects, he threatens to give the housemaster all the names of the boys he has slept with. When he finds that he is denied his rightful place in the hierarchy, because he is a homosexual, he decides to take his revenge on society. Transferred to Queen's when Kenneth Branagh, straight out of RADA, replaced Le Touzel and made his West End debut as the young communist.
—The experience undergone by boys at the great public schools, their glories and disappointments, are so intense as to dominate their lives and to arrest their development. From these it results that the greater part of the ruling class remains adolescent, school-minded, self-conscious, cowardly, sentimental and in the last analysis homosexual. CYRIL CONNOLLY *Enemies of Promise*.
—Rupert Everett's performance is a remarkable fusion of intellectual strength and carnal indulgence. JACK TINKER *Daily Mail*

Nov 26. Rosemary Leach and David Swift in Helene Hanff's **84 Charing Cross Road** directed by James Roose-Evans at Ambassadors. A New Yorker's love affair with second-hand books and a London second-hand bookshop was told in a series of letters. Unlike Swift who was cast as the chief buyer of the shop (a caricature of punctured British reserve) Leach did not act out the letters.

Nov 28. Aeschylus's **Oresteia** in a version by Tony Harrison directed by Peter Hall at Olivier (NT). Music by Harrison Birtwistle. Masks by Jenny West. Movement by Stuart Hopps. The London premiere, 2,439 years late, was ridiculously scheduled for only 20 performances. Everyone was masked and dehumanised. The masks completely hid the faces. The actors were not identified insofar as to which role they played. The graceful, blanched-faced, Noh-like actor, who played Orestes, was far more effeminate than either his mother or his sister. The Chorus dominated the play. The actors had rehearsed for eighteen weeks to a metronome and spoke ninety-two crotchets to the minute. The four-pulse beat in every line produced the most exciting sound the London stage had heard since the Greeks brought *The Persians* to Peter Daubenay's World Theatre Seasons at the Aldwych in 1965. The jagged score and the gritty translation added enormously to the excitement. Audiences came out after five-and-half-hours, feeling they had been listening to a great piece of music. The production was one of the great productions of the 1980s, but many critics objected to the masks, claiming they muffled and blurred the voices
—One is left to fend off the beckoning arms of Morpheos. JACK TINKER *Daily Mail*
—It is hard to believe that such a mountain of extravagant effort should have produced such a mouse of a production. JOHN ELSOM *Listener*

Dec 10. Anthony Sher and Bob Hopkins in Sam Shepard's **True West** directed by John Schlesinger at Cottesloe (NT). In this variation on a Cain and Abel theme, an articulate, educated, clean-cut writer and his roughneck, belligerent, foul-mouthed brother, a professional thief, swap roles. ("I always wondered what it would be like to be you.") Shepard's unpleasant drama moved to a predictably violent close in which the writer strangled his brother. Except that he hadn't. Hopkins leapt up, there was a quick black-out, and that was it.

1982

Jan 11. Arthur Schnitzler's **La Ronde** directed by John Barton at Aldwych (RSC). Bitter cycle of plays about the disillusionment of sex without love in ten episodes: prostitute and soldier, soldier and maid, maid and young gentleman, young gentleman and young wife, wife and husband, husband and girl, girl and poet, poet and actress, actress and count, and count and prostitute. There was no sex in the text, only dots. It was the same anecdote ten times over, ten little plays about the hypocrisy of women and the callousness of men. The biggest laugh was when the actress said to the poet after a bit of love-making, "That's better than acting in stupid plays." The audience applauded enthusiastically.

Feb 11. Penelope Keith, Anthony Quayle and Trevor Peacock in Harold Brighouse's **Hobson's Choice** directed by Richard Eyre at Haymarket. Peacock, who only came

up to Keith's shoulder, was delightful, just standing there, awkward, stocky, having his coat done up as if he were a little boy.

Feb 23. Patricia Routledge, Paul Eddington, Nicky Henson, Roger Lloyd Pack and Michael Aldridge in Michael Frayn's **Noises Off** directed by Michael Blakemore at Lyric, Hammersmith. One of the best farces of the 20th century. The first act is set during the final rehearsal of a farce when everything goes wrong. The second act, played almost entirely in mime, occurs backstage during a matinee when tempers are frayed. The third act takes place, well into the run, when the performances, the scenery and all relationships have disintegrated. Transferred to Savoy and went through three casts and played over 1,000 performances.

Mar 2. Rupert Everett and Kenneth Branagh in Julian Mitchell's **Another Country** directed by Stuart Burge at Queen's.
—I doubt if the West End has ever seen such an impressive pair of debuts as those of Rupert Everett as Guy and Kenneth Branagh as Judd. MICHAEL COVENEY *Financial Times*

Mar 9. Julie Covington as Sister Sarah, Ian Charleson as Sky Masterton, Julia McKenzie as Miss Adelaide and Bob Hoskins as Nathan Detroit in Frank Loesser's musical **Guys and Dolls** directed by Richard Eyre at Olivier (NT). Laurence Olivier had always wanted to stage it at the National and was on the point of playing Nathan Detroit in 1970 when he fell ill and the production had to be indefinitely postponed. There were (and still are) some people who think that the National Theatre should not stage musicals. But classic musicals have as much right to the National Theatre's stage as classical plays. Damon Runyon's hoods and hoodlums were affectionately caricatured with cartoon-like costumes and given a romantic dream-wedding finale among wafting clouds of dry ice. John Gunter's towering Times Square set, with its bright gaudy neon signs and tiny shop fronts, created the perfect ambience. Charleson, too lightweight, too charming, seemed ill at ease when he was singing.
—It was felt in some purist circles that the National Theatre doing *Guys and Dolls* was as unseemly as a tipsy nun doing the can-can. MILTON SHULMAN *Standard*

Mar 11. Elizabeth Taylor in Lillian Hellman's **Little Foxes** directed by Austin Pendleton at Victoria Palace. Taylor had an accident and ended up in a wheelchair, which was doubly unfortunate, since a leading character in the play was already wheelchair-bound.
—You call this theatre? sneered a despondent colleague in the first interval. Indeed, I do, I told him. I certainly don't call it acting. To imagine there was a person in the stalls last night who had paid £25 a seat to see Elizabeth Taylor act is as foolish a notion as pretending anyone had gone there just to see Lillian Hellman's creaking old classic ... For the most part, as an actress, she teeters on the brink of competence. JACK TINKER *Daily Mail*

Apr 7. Andrew Lloyd Webber's **Song and Dance** at Palace. Marti Webb sang "Tell Me on Sunday" directed by John Caird. Wayne Sleep danced to Webber's Variations on Pagananini's A Minor Caprice No 24. Choreography by Anthony van Laast.

Apr 22. Patrick Drury in Heinrich Von Kleist's **The Prince of Homburg** directed by John Burgess at Cottesloe (NT). The Prince is court-martialled and sentenced to death for rank disobedience; but his premature attack on the enemy had led to the victory of the army. The Prince puts his trust in the Elector for a reprieve; but when none is forthcoming, he abases himself, willing to sacrifice love and honour to save his life. His brother officers rally round and draw up a petition—a petition that will make a reprieve even more impossible, since the Elector cannot brook any indiscipline in the army. Cunningly, the Elector offers the Prince a reprieve if the Prince himself thinks he has done no wrong. Naturally, the Prince, having begged to live, now insists that he must die. The play moves to its tragic finish, only at the last minute to have the Prince reprieved after all. But having provided a happy ending

1982 World Premieres
New York
  Harvey Fernstein's *Torch Song Trilogy*
  A B Gurney's *The Dining Room*
Chicago
  David Mamet's *Edmond*
San Francisco
  Sam Shepard's *Fool for Love*
New Haven
  Athol Fugard's *Master Harold and the Boys*

Deaths
Ingrid Bergman (*b.*1915), Swedish actor
Peter Weiss (*b.*1916), Czech playwright, novelist

Notes
—The prosecution of Howard Brenton's *Romans in Britain* for indecency was abandoned
—The D'Oyly Carte Opera Company closed

History
—UK unemployment reached 3 million
—Falklands War
—Israel withdrew from Sinai Peninsula
—First compact disc on sale.

Julia Mackenzie and Bob Hoskins in **Guys and Dolls**

Von Kleist asks the audience to wonder if the whole action has not been a dream; and then tantalizingly leaves the question unanswered.

Apr 28. Glenda Jackson and Georgina Hale in Robert David MacDonald's **Summit Conference** directed and designed by Philip Prowse at Apollo. The Third Reich is viewed through a fictional confrontation between the mistresses of Hitler and Mussolini. Jackson acted like an animated doll, constantly nodding and patting her immaculate hair. Hale acted like a cartoon figure, a caricature of a *poule de luxe*. Their seduction and humiliation of a German soldier (Gary Oldman) was a metaphor for the behaviour of the Nazis and Fascists during the war. The message was lost in all the kitsch.
—As Clara Petacci, Miss Hale spika da English like a beserk organ grinder and grimaces like his monkey. She is frequently inaudible and, when not, often unintelligible. When she keeps her mouth shut, though, she is a joy to watch. Miss Jackson turns Eva Braun into a North Country Scarlet O'Hara, all flat vowels and flounces. JOHN WALKER *Mail on Sunday*

May 12. Cheryl Campbell in Henrik Ibsen's **A Doll's House** directed by Adrian Noble at Pit (RSC). Campbell, screeching and screaming, became more and more melodramatic. Stephen Moore as Torvald got quieter and quieter. Marjorie Bland's Mrs Linde was a feminist with a touch of the Gregers Werle. The problem of what to do with the crucial letterbox, when the play is acted in the round, was not solved by having it off-stage. The final slamming of the door (which was said to have reverberated throughout Europe) barely penetrated the auditorium.

May 18. Michael Bryant as Vanya and Dinsdale Landen as Astrov in Chekhov's **Uncle Vanya** designed by John Bury and directed by Michael Bogdanov at Lyttelton (NT). The political content came over strongly. The set was a marquee; the furniture looked lost in the vast empty space. Landen's Astrov, far from being no longer the man he once, was seemed to be in his prime. Patti Love was a bossy Sonia.
—They wander around a setting which resembles some smart Art Déco Odeon furnished by Habitat. JACK TINKER *Daily Mail*

May 26. Tim Curry, Pamela Stephenson, George Cole and Annie Ross in Gilbert and Sullivan's **The Pirates of Penzance** choreographed by Graciela Daniele and directed by Wilford Leach at Drury Lane. Purists were shocked that a classic English operetta had been tampered with and orchestrated into a Broadway musical with electronic guitars and synthesizers. But for theatregoers, who had been bored rigid for so long by the stale, museum productions of D'Oyly Carte, Joseph Papp's exuberant interpretation was a revelation. The highly disciplined and very funny slapstick had style and enormous energy. Curry's Pirate King, bearded, bare-chested, big smile, flashing teeth, legs apart, sword raised high, had the camp handsomeness, vigour and humour to lead the company in its high-spirited, larky mugging. The eight actresses, who played the Major General's daughters, had all been carefully chosen for their plainness and were hilarious. Comediennes all, they skipped, gawked, galumphed, pulled faces and got quite hysterical when Frederick (Michael Praed), Presley-like, started to sing, "Oh, Is There Not One Maiden Breast". The frightened policemen, with their jerky, angular, toy-like movement, all dressed in blue, white spats and batons at the ready, stopped the show.

Jun 9. The Royal Shakespeare Company opened at the Barbican with Shakespeare's **Henry IV Parts 1 and 2** directed by Trevor Nunn. Joss Ackland as Falstaff. Gerard Murphy as Hal. Patrick Stewart as King Henry. Timothy Dalton as Hotspur. Only once was there any real laughter and this was when Falstaff claims that he has killed Hotspur – the one moment when there should have been no laughter.

Jun 10. Penelope Keith and John Turner in Bernard Shaw's **Captain Brassbound's Conversion** directed by Frank Hauser at Haymarket. The bossy, patronising, intimidating heroine was a perfect role for Keith.

Jun 21. Maria Aitken as Gilda, Gary Bond as Otto and Ian Ogilvy as Leo in Noël Coward's **Design for Living** directed by Alan Strachan at Greenwich. The production was tactful about the fact that Otto and Leo were much more in love with each other than they were with Gilda. Transferred to Globe.

Jul 5. Peggy Ashcroft as the Countess, Harriet Walter as Helena, Philip Franks as Bertram, Stephen Moore as Parolles, Geoffrey Hutchings as Lavache and Robert Eddison as Lafeu in Shakespeare's **All's Well that Ends Well** directed by Trevor Nunn at Barbican (RSC). Visually the production, set in World War I, was stunning. Designer John Gunter's adaptable glasshouse provided a handsome framework.

Jul 12. Ian MacDiarmid, William Hootkins, Judy Davis and Larry Lamb in Terry Johnson's **Insignificance** directed by Les Waters at Royal Court. A witty, sharp and unlikely encounter between Albert Einstein, Joe McCarthy, Marilyn Monroe and Joe Di Maggio in a New York hotel bedroom in 1953. Monroe (dressed as she appeared in *The Seven Year Itch*) explains the Theory of Relativity to Einstein with the aid of two toy trains and three lamps.

Aug 5. Donald Sinden as Vanya, Ronald Pickup as Astrov, Harry Andrews as Ser-

ebriakov, Frances de la Tour as Sonia and Sheila Gish as Elena in Anton Chekhov's **Uncle Vanya** directed by Christopher Fettes at Haymarket. There was too much acting and the action did not flow naturally. The most successful performance was by Sheila Gish, whose Elena, more sensitive than usual, really did seem to understand what Astrov was on about when he was talking about the conservation of the forests.

Aug 6. Edward Fox in Shakespeare's **Hamlet** directed by Terry Palmer at Young Vic. Full text and monotonous diction.

Aug 17. Anton Lesser in Shakespeare's **Hamlet** directed by Jonathan Miller at Warehouse (RSC). One of Miller's many farewells to the theatre. Lesser was not noble and there was no urgency.

Sep 1. Caryl Churchill's **Top Girls** directed by Max Stafford-Clark at Royal Court. Socialist-feminist critique of bourgeois-feminist values: the roles women play in society as daughters, mothers, wives, mistresses and the price they pay for competing in a man's world. Top girls from the past – Isabella Bird (Deborah Findlay as Victorian traveller), Lady Nijo (Lindsay Duncan as 13th-century Japanese courtesan turned Buddhist nun), Pope Joan (Selina Cadell) Breughel's Dull Gret (Carole Hayman as the woman who had led a female charge through hell) and Chaucer's Patient Griselda (Lesley Manville) – sat down to dine at a slowly revolving table.
—It is splendid to see the Royal Court back as its old form, presenting virile and topical subjects, seizing our times by the scruff of the neck and shaking out the cant. JOHN ELSOM *Mail on Sunday*
—The sharpest and most intelligent acting to be seen in London right now. BRYAN ROBERTSON *Spectator*

Sep 9. Leonard Rossiter in Luigi Pirandello's **The Rules of the Game** directed by Anthony Quayle at Haymarket. Rossiter suggested that all sorts of sinister and dangerous emotions were going on behind his imperturbable façade. The end of the third act found him just standing there in the satisfied knowledge that his wife's lover was dead.
—He was not an open oven-door giving out a general warmth, but a very concentrated burning glass. It was a very rare talent. I had the most enormous admiration. A great actor. ANTHONY QUAYLE

Sep 14. Pina Bausch's **1980** at Sadler's Wells. Performed by an international and multi-lingual cast, there were times when it seemed as if the performance could go on forever. But just when everybody was getting fed up, a catchy 1920s dance tune would strike up and the cast would snake in and out of the auditorium. Most of the audience stayed to cheer; but a great number decided to take an early departure.
—Four hours of gross and grotesque self-indulgence by Miss Bausch and her camp-followers. Total theatre? No, total boredom. MICHAEL DARVELL *What's On*

Sep 16. Judi Dench, Nigel Havers and Martin Jarvis in Oscar Wilde's **The Importance of Being Earnest** directed by Peter Hall at Lyttelton (RNT). Dench, unexpectedly cast as Lady Bracknell, was no gorgon. Immaculately preserved, she flirted openly with Algy, her hand on his knee. Jarvis was so earnest an Ernest that he might have been mistaken for an undertaker.
—This is probably the best acted Lady Bracknell there has ever been. (Edith Evans was a Happening.) And somehow, through sheer technical prowess, this uncompromising portrayal floods the auditorium with more warmth than has been generated by any actress since Miss Dench played O'Casey's Juno. ROBERT CUSHMAN *Observer*
—Her triumph is naturally based on the sureness and precision of her timing and technique but she also seems more real than the others without sacrificing an inch of the highly artificial style. MARK AMORY *Spectator*

Sep 22. Michael Bryant in Thomas Kyd's **The Spanish Tragedy** directed by Michael Bogdanov at Cottesloe (RNT). The revival was so successful it made everyone wonder why this crude, savage, gory story of love, murder and revenge, one of the biggest box office successes of its day (circa 1589), had suffered five centuries of neglect.

Sep 22. John Rawnsley as Rigoletto, Marie McLaughlin as Gilda and Arthur Davies as The Duke in Verdi's **Rigoletto** conducted by Mark Elder directed by Jonathan Miller at London Coliseum. One of the major productions of the decade paid homage to the Hollywood Mafioso gangster movies and *From Here To Eternity*. The tavern was turned into a bar, inspired by Edward Hopper's *Nighthawks*. There was an excellent joke when "La Donna E Mobile" was played on a jukebox.

Sep 23. Bill Patterson in Bertolt Brecht's **Schweyk in the Second World War** directed by Richard Eyre at Olivier (NT). Influenced by the original 1920s Erwin Pisqator epic production of Jaroslav Hasek's novel, there were enormous blowups of caricatures by the cartoonist, Low. The stage was dominated by huge carnival figures of Hitler, Goering, Himmler and Goebbels, all living in some private, smoky, ops-room hell. Schweyk is officially certified as an idiot; but, like all fools and clowns, he is remarkably sane and shrewd. He is built to survive arrest, beatings-up and even being sent to the Russian Front. He survives because he is willing to knuckle under.

He does as he is told; but the joke is that he collaborates in the most subversive way, disguising his seditious remarks in anecdotes and proverbs. Julia McKenzie sang her militant and sentimental songs so well that her absence in the second half became a major flaw. (The music was by Hanns Eisler who wrote in the Weill idiom.) The finale in a waste land of snow, with huge amounts of dry ice pouring on to the stage and into the auditorium, had the carnival figure of Hitler doing a little dance with Schweyk.

Oct 4. Tony Haygarth, Susan Fleetwood, Julie Legrand and Jim Norton in Alan Ayckbourn's **Way Up Stream** directed by Alan Ayckbourn at Lyttelton (NT). A typical Ayckbourn comedy on a real boat in real water turned unexpectedly symbolic when two strangers joined the quartet and took over the running of the boat completely. "Life," said somebody, "is a holiday from death." The production needed 6,000 gallons of water, which caused enormous problems, including a six-week delay and flooding. The cast get soaked during a downpour of rain. Mark Amory in *The Spectator* thought it was Ayckbourn's most interesting play in years.
—Ayckbourn, directing Ayckbourn, is up the creek without a paddle. ROBERT CUSHMAN *Observer*

Oct 14. Judi Dench in Harold Pinter's **A Kind of Alaska** directed by Peter Hall at Cottesloe (RNT). Case history: fifteen-year-old girl, who has been asleep for twenty-nine years, wakes up and wonders where she has been. Dench played her as if she were still fifteen years old. There was a distressing moment when she tried desperately (constantly smacking her face) to stop herself slipping back into those "crushing, punishing spaces".
—Judi Dench's ability to conjure up the soul and voice of a teenager in the body of a woman nearly fifty should win her just about every one of this winter's acting awards. SHERIDAN MORLEY *Punch*

Nov 16. Roger Rees and Felicity Kendal in Tom Stoppard's **The Real Thing** directed by Peter Wood at Strand. Written in Stoppard's witty vein, the opening scene had a husband confirming his wife's adultery. It turned out not to be the real thing, but a scene from a play. Nothing was ever as good again. What is a real play? Can an awful script, written by a political activist, be the real thing, merely because the playwright is trying to say something?
—Stoppard combines touches of Pirandello role-playing, Shavian badinage and Barbara Cartland gush in a play whose adroit twists manage to disguise its obviousness and whose wit compensates for its glib solution. MILTON SHULMAN *Standard*

Nov 16. Peter O'Toole and Lisa Harow in Bernard Shaw's **Man and Superman** directed by Patrick Dromgoole at Haymarket. O'Toole, rasping and slurring his lines, did not act with anybody on stage; he prowled the stage and acted with the audience.
—Say what you will, nobody sleeps while Peter O'Toole is on. JACK TINKER *Daily Mail*
—It is a dangerous performance for its élan and speed might shatter the play. But on the contrary it breathes into it the breath of life. HAROLD HOBSON *Times literary Supplement*

Nov 18. Billy McColl, Gerard Kelly, Iain Andrew, Nicholas Sherry and Elaine Collins in John Byrne's **The Slab Boys** directed by David Hayman at Royal Court. The trilogy – **The Slab Boys**, **Cuttin' a Rug** and **Still Life** – was premiered at Edinburgh in 1958. The Glaswegian accents were not as impenetrable as some had feared. The boys worked in a slab room of a carpet factory where the colours are mixed. Their story began in the late Fifties and ended in the cemetery in the early Seventies. McColl's wisecracking, frustrated, angry lad was a latter-day Jimmy Porter. His irony was venomous.

Nov 25. Paul Scofield as Oberon and Susan Fleetwood as Titania in Shakespeare's **A Midsummer Night's Dream** directed by Bill Bryden at Cottesloe (NT). The seating had been removed and the audience sat on the floor. Oberon and Titania were middle-aged and their fairy kingdom was full of grey spectral, aged figures.

Dec 16. Miles Anderson in J M Barrie's **Peter Pan** directed by John Caird and Trevor Nunn at Barbican (RSC). This new version used not only the play, but also excerpts from the novel, the film scenario, and unpublished material from the original manuscript. The result was the best *Peter Pan* in years and the truest to Barrie's strange and sickly vision; but three-and-half-hours was too much for adults, let alone children. The production was notable for casting a man as Peter Pan (Barrie's original intention) and for the inclusion of a Narrator (Stephen Moore). Anderson's Peter was eclipsed by Jane Carr's very funny Wendy, a precocious little girl behaving like a grown-up

1983

Feb 9. Griff Rhys-Jones in Brandon Thomas' **Charley's Aunt** directed by Peter James and Peter Wilson at Lyric, Hammersmith. Rhys Jones brought an aggressive, hefty manliness to the role. "I'm not going to marry Spettigue," he said, "I'd never

1983 World Premieres
New York
Neil Simon's *Brighton Beach Memoirs*

Deaths
Ralph Richardson (*b.*1902), British actor

Notes
—Ed Mirvish spent 2.5 million refurbishing Old Vic
—Peter Hall published his diaries

History
—Anti-nuclear rallies in Europe
—Reagan proposed Star Wars missile shield in space
—Global Warming effect demonstrated

be happy with a man like that." There was a splendid bit of business when he gulped down his wine in one gulp, only to remember he was meant to be a lady and spat it back into the glass. "I'm Charley's Aunt," he said. There followed a long pause. "From Brazil," he added. There was an even longer pause before he said, "where the nuts come from." The timing won him a round of applause.

Apr 6. Michael Gambon and Helen Mirren in Shakespeare's **Antony and Cleopatra** directed by Adrian Noble at Pit (RSC). Bob Peck as Enobarbus. The lovers adopted a conversational style. The verse rang hollow the moment they started to rant, Mirren looked like a 1940s nightclub hostess. Enobarbus's death was more moving than the death of either Antony or Cleopatra.
—Mike Gambon's Antony is a garbled mistake. NICHOLAS DE JONGH *Mail on Sunday*
—Only – and it is a big only – Bob Peck as Enobarbus gave us the full value of this tragedy seen through his eyes. ROSEMARY SAY *Sunday Telegraph*

Apr 11. Barbara Dickson in Willy Russell's **Blood Brothers** directed by Chris Bond and Danny Hiller at Lyric. A rich middle-class woman, unable to have any children of her own, buys a twin from a poor, working-class mother. The script was always on the point of making a comment on the "class system" but the deaths were not the result of class differences, only the result of the two boys loving the same girl. The show was simplistic and very sentimental. Dickson as the natural mum sang "Tell Me It's Not True". Andrew C Wandsworth and George Costigan played the twins. Transferred to the Phoenix and still running well into the 21st century.
—The most exciting thing to have happened to English musical theatre in years. SHERIDAN MORLEY *Punch*

Apr 12. Michael Hordern as Sir Anthony Absolute and Gerald McEwan as Mrs Malaprop in Richard Brinsley Sheridan's **The Rivals** designed by John Gunter and directed by Peter Wood at Olivier (NT). Bath's famous Royal Crescent was recreated in miniature. Mrs Malaprop (never for one moment an old weather-beaten she-dragon) chose her words with great care, constantly worried that she might be choosing the wrong word. McEwan was given a new malapropism for her final exit: "All men are Bavarians!" (Sheridan had written barbarians.) Hordern was always funny, especially when he was describing and drooling over Lydia Languish's physical accomplishments. He was even funny just sitting at a small table eating an egg for breakfast.

Apr 15. Ben Kingsley in Raymund Fitzsimons's **Edmund Kean** directed by Alison Sutcliffe at Lyric, Hammersmith. Bravura solo performance. The script was decidedly thin and Kingsley's execution of it was lightweight and distractingly camp. Jean-Paul Sartre had done a far better job in his play, *Kean*. Transferred to Haymarket.
—He [Ben Kingsley] is already more acclaimed than Kean ever was, and this splendid occasion can only add to his stature. DAVID ROPER *Daily Express*

Apr 18. Alexandra Mathie in Denise Deegan's **Daisy Pulls It Off** directed by David Gilmore at Globe. Affectionate jolly gym-slip-and-tie spoof of Angela Brazil's popular adventure novels for girls circa 1927. Daisy, an elementary school pupil, wins a scholarship to a public school and suffers at the hands of some beastly snobs, who detest games ("sure sign of a rotter") and frame her as a cheat, sneak and thief. But Daisy, morally and intellectually superior, absurdly good at everything (lessons, creative writing, hockey, singing, piano playing) triumphs. She even saves her arch enemy from certain death in a cliffhanging finale.

Apr 21. Helen Mirren in Thomas Middleton and Thomas Dekker's **The Roaring Girl** designed by Chris Dyer and directed by Barry Kyle at Barbican (RSC). The roaring girl ("I scorn to prostitute myself to a man, that can prostitute a man to me") wore men's breeches and carried a sword. The production was much more fun for the director and the designer than it was for the actors. The audience sat in stony silence. Since there was not much plot and no characterization, the emphasis was placed on recreating London's teeming street life: a thieving, whoring, shop-keeping Jacobean underworld to which the stupid gallants had come in search of tobacco, feathers and sex.

May 5. Derek Jacobi as Benedict and Sinead Cusack as Beatrice in Shakespeare's

Much Ado About Nothing directed by Terry Hands at Barbican (RSC). Jacobi put on a spaniel-like face, adopted a camp, whining voice and was particularly endearing when he expressed his surprise that Beatrice should love him. The comedy of the arbour scene was much enhanced by the repeated re-appearance of a little boy with a book.

May 5. Steven Berkoff in **West** at Warehouse. Classic fight between two gangs. The yoboes lurched and swore in rhythm. Berkoff's language, a mixture of cockney patter and Shakespearian parody, had its familiar hobnail-boot grandiloquence.

May 19. Peter Ustinov in Peter Ustinov's **Beethoven's Tenth** directed by Robert Chetwyn at Vaudeville. The great man comes back to earth to confront the leading authority on his work (Robin Bailey). He is given a hearing aid and hears his music for the very first time. The intellectual battle between the two men never materialized. The cast sat around, watching Ustinov parading his personality and mannerisms, trying to rescue his play.

May 25. Michael Gambon in Shakespeare's **King Lear** directed by Adrian Noble at Barbican (RSC). Many critics have noted how often Lear plays stooge to the Fool, but Noble must have been the first director to get the actors to play Act 1 Scene V as if it were a music-hall double act. At the end of the play Gambon acknowledged what the production and his own performance owed to Antony Sher's Fool by sharing his curtain-call with him. Sher's Fool was rooted in the traditions of the circus and the music hall. He was clown, comedian, ventriloquist's dummy, Grock, George Formby, Max Wall, et al, all rolled into one. There was a startling innovation when Lear, inadvertently in his madness, not even knowing that he had done it, actually killed the Fool. Jonathan Hyde's Edgar had a wonderful entrance, when he appeared for the first time as Mad Tom, erupting from the bowels of the stage, the boards breaking to let him through, a stark, naked, charred, ashen fiend, rising out of hell.
—Antony Sher deserves to be hailed as a genius. DAVID ROPER *Daily Express*

Jun 16. Ralph Richardson in Eduardo de Filippo's **Inner Voices** directed by Mike Ockrent at Lyttelton (NT). An eccentric old man is so disgusted with the world that he has given up speaking and communicates only through the bangs, the whistles and the fizzes of his fireworks. Only Richardson could carry on a conversation with a firework.

Jun 21. Frances de la Tour, Ian Bannen and Piers Ibbotson in Eugene O'Neill's **Moon for the Misbegotten** directed by David Leveaux at Riverside Studios. This powerful, heartbreaking, taxing tragic-comedy, a sequel to O'Neill's autobiographical *Long Day's Journey Into Night*, was written to show his "deep pity, forgiveness and understanding" for his elder brother, Jamie. The action is set in 1923, the year when Jamie, nearly blind and mad from too much alcohol, died of cerebral apoplexy. De la Tour, though physically not right, portrayed the aching loneliness of unrequited love most movingly. Bannen, physically and spiritually numbed, looked like a dead man walking behind his own coffin.

Jul 20. Anthony Sher in Molière's **Tartuffe** directed by Bill Alexander at Pit (RSC). There was only one thing wrong with Sher's hilariously outrageous performance and that was nobody, not even the infatuated, gullible Orgon, could possibly have been taken in by such a sanctimonious faker whose specious religious fervor was laid on with a trowel. Nigel Hawthorne acted Orgon in a more realistic key.
—What isn't at all tolerable is Antony Sher's playing of Tartuffe as if he is filming Carry on Rasputin. GILES GORDON *Spectator*
—If you want to see bravura acting, go and admire Sher; if you want to see feeling, intelligence and skill unobtrusively at work, go and enjoy that hardy perennial, Hawthorne. BENEDICT NIGHTINGALE *The Times*

Jul 21. Derek Jacobi in Edmond Rostand's **Cyrano** directed by Terry Hands at Barbican (RSC). Rostand was in love with theatre; and what could be more theatrical than the end of Act IV? Christian (Floyd Bevan) realizing that he is not loved for himself but for Cyrano's soul rushes recklessly into battle and just as Cyrano is about to confess to Roxane (Alice Krige) that he, Cyrano, wrote all those wonderful letters, Christian is killed and the confession dies in his throat. The tableau, which follows (with the gunfire, the smoke, the dying, the dead and Cyrano, on top of the coach, waving a lance, to which is tied Roxane's handkerchief) is the sort of glorious theatrical "curtain", which survives these days only in opera. Jacobi's Cyrano had such wit, irony, eloquence and pathos. His death scene was deeply moving.
—Only in the size of his nose does Derek Jacobi show any decorum. It is ungainly rather than grotesque. MILTON SHULMAN *Standard*

Aug 1. Jimmy Jewell and Geraldine McEwan in Moss Hart and George S Kaufman's **You Can't Take It With You** directed by Michael Bogdanov at Lyttelton (NT). The 1936 Pulitzer prize-winning play came directly out of the American experience of the Depression years. The whimsical sentimentality and folksy homespun philosophy touched a common nerve. The play has a household of crazy, cheerful, eccentric, incompetent dreamers. The non-conformist content and anti-capitalist message was far more caustic in Frank Capra's 1938 film adaptation starring James Stewart. Jimmy

Jewel (who had spent most of his theatrical life in vaudeville) did not have the experience to play the grandfather and to be able to carry the play and its philosophy.

Aug 8. Alan Bates as Alfred Redl in John Osborne's **A Patriot for Me** directed by Ronald Eyre transferred from Chichester Festival to Haymarket. Bates played the spy as if he were a character in a Simon Gray play. The scenes he shared with the Russian intelligence officer (George Murcell) were effective, establishing a relationship seen nowhere else in the play. The scene with Sophia (Sheila Gish), when he taunts her with the knowledge that he knows her lover (Anthony Head) far more intimately than she ever will, was acted for good old-fashioned melodrama.

Sep 1. Michael Gambon in Christopher Hampton's **Tales from Hollywood** directed by Peter Gill at Olivier (NT). Hampton imagined that Odon von Horvath (the author of *Tales from the Vienna Woods*) emigrated to America with all the other exiled European writers and artists who were lucky enough to escape the gas chambers. So instead of being killed, aged 36, in a freak accident, by a tree in the Champys Elysees in 1938, he drowns in a David Hockney Californian swimming pool in 1950. The cinema industry had no idea what to do with all these intellectuals, but as an act of charity they put them on their payroll. Hampton drew a parallel between Nazism in the 1930s in Germany and the McCarthy witch-hunts in the 1950s in America, when the writers had to make choices, which could lead either to compromise, betrayal, blacklisting, exile and extermination. Much the most enjoyable sections were the monologues when Gambon was just chatting to the audience in a dry and witty manner. The play was killed stone dead every time Brecht walked on, his every scene acted, as if he were in a play by Brecht.

Sep 5. Anthony Sher in Mikhail Bulgakov's **Molière** directed by Bill Alexander at Pit (RSC). Molière's life was played out as if it were a *commedia dell'arte* script. Molière licked the king's spurs but was destroyed just the same. The original Russian production, which had been in rehearsal for four years, was finally premiered in 1936, only to be quickly withdrawn after just seven performances. The parallels between Molière and Louis XIV and Bulgakov and Stalin were too obvious for comfort. There was a tremendous performance by Sher. John Carlisle, impressively regal as King Louis, was patently dangerous, even when he was being farcical.

Sep 7. Michael Pennington as Raskolnikov and Bill Patterson as Porfiry in Fyodor Dostoevsky's **Crime and Punishment** directed by Yuri Lyubimov at Lyric, Hammersmith. Lyubimov, artistic director of the Taganka Theatre, who did not speak English, recreated his Moscow production, which presumed the audience had read the novel and wouldn't mind if he ripped it apart and put it together again in his own patchwork fashion. He used sound, shafts of light, strobe lighting, musical effects and colour to reproduce a frenetic canvas and claustrophobic nightmare. The actors, totally subservient to the production, often played a secondary role to their own huge shadows which filled the back wall. A blood-stained door took on a life of its own and played many roles. Raskolnikov was a Christ-like figure. (Russian schoolchildren used to be taught that Raskolnikov was right to kill the old woman and that it was to be regretted that he had been caught by the police.) Pennington always had a spotlight on his face. Paterson's detective had a noose at the ready. The production was hailed as the most imaginative since Peter Brook's *A Midsummer Night's Dream*.
—The amount of detailed intelligence applied to the dialogue would be impressive in any circumstances; in a production directed through an interpreter it is extraordinary. ROBERT CUSHMAN *Observer*

Sep 13. Derek Jacobi in Shakespeare's **The Tempest** directed by Ron Daniels at Barbican (RSC). Jacobi's Prospero was not composed of harshness. The one magical moment was when he spoke the lines beginning, "Ye elves of hills, brooks, standing lakes and groves". Maria Björnson's permanent romantic shipwreck setting was not helpful either to the main action or for the Masque element. Bob Peck was a dreadlocked, repellent Caliban.

Sep 20. Hannah Gordon, Martin Shaw and John Stride in Clifford Odets's **The Country Girl** directed by Robin Lefevre at Apollo. The dialogue was so dated and so full of clichés as to be almost a parody of a 1940s melodrama. The actors, shouting at each other in a highly emphatic manner, moved crudely from big scene to big scene.

Sep 21. Trevor Ray, Derek Newark, Jack Shepherd, Tony Haygarth, Keith Johnson and John Tams in David Mamet's **Glengarry Glenn Ross** directed by Bill Bryden at Cottesloe (NT). A Chicago real estate office is axing sales staff. Four men, who are fighting to keep their jobs, have to close deals. But firstly they have to get the leads and the best leads are the prerogative of the young manager. Mamet springs a number of twists and wittily parodies their limited expletive vocabulary and their ability to be articulate and inarticulate at one and the same time.
—A play for the 1980s: a sardonic, scabrous and really rather brilliant study of a human piranha pool where the grimly Darwinian law is swallow or be swallowed. BENEDICT NIGHTINGALE *The Times*

Oct 12. Ellen Greene in **Little Shop of Horrors** directed by Howard Ashman at Comedy. Book and lyrics by Howard Ashman. Music by Alan Menken. The only reason for seeing the spoof horror movie musical was for the monster-plant, brilliantly designed, manipulated and acted. The plant had an insatiable hunger. "FEED ME!" it rasped, opening its monstrous hippopotamus-jaws. "CUT THE CRAP AND GIVE ME THE MEAT!" The bespectacled nonentity-hero fed him first with his own blood, then with his dentist, then with his boss, then with his dizzy girlfriend and finally with himself. At the end, the plant, which had been growing all through the show, filled the whole-stage, and then, in a stunning *coup de theatre*, with branches and leaves falling from the ceiling, it filled the whole theatre. Martin P Robinson (puppet-maker) Anthony B Asbury (manipulator) and Michael Leslie (voice) provided the show's only excitement.

Oct 26. Judi Dench and Michael Williams in Hugh Whitemore's **Pack of Lies** directed by Clifford Williams at Lyric. Plodding television play, which was said to be "more or less true", was based on the 1961 Portland Spy case. An ordinary suburban family is put under intolerable strain when their house is being used by MI5 as a base to spy on Peter and Helen Kroger. The family need never have been involved. MI5 already had all the information they required. Richard Vernon, very English, very upper crust, very tall, very pinstripe, very dry, was perfect casting for an Establishment figure taking advantage of the working classes.
—If you have a taste for first rate acting at the level to which Miss Dench aspires in its emotional integrity, the actress will be reason enough to visit the Lyric. But at the same time, in the less showy role, Mr Williams can match her in subtlety as the equally perplexed husband whose fears for his wife's health are expressed with such delicate restraint. ERIC SHORTER *Daily Telegraph*

Nov 7. Shared Experience. Holly Wilson, Nick Dunning, Sandra Voe and Philip Voss in two plays by Marivaux translated by Timberlake Wertenbaker, designed by Paul Dart and directed by Mike Alfreds at Lyric Studio, Hammersmith. **False Admissions (Les Fausses Confidences).** The action was played out all in black. Holly Wilson acted her scenes with cruel wit and looked as if she might have stepped out of painting by Fragonard. **Successful Stratagies (Heureux Stratageme).** The action was played out in a little white arbour with a creamy canopy, everything bright, light and pretty; but that did not make the pain any the less real. Sam Dale played Arlequin.

Nov 14. Bob Fosse's **Dancin'** at Drury Lane. Big disappointment. The show was noisy, cheap and vulgar. The choreography had none of Fosse's usual style, wit and invention. There was but one personality – Andre de la Roche – and he wasn't given enough to do.

Nov 24. John Kani in Athol Fugard's **Master Harold and the Boys** directed by Athol Fugard at Cottesloe (NT). Fugard's painful memory of his 15-year-old self spitting in a black servant's face. Kani played the servant, friend and father to the boy, a performance of great dignity and charm.

Nov 24. Omar Sharif, Debbie Arnold and Judy Campbell in Terence Rattigan's **The Sleeping Prince** directed by Peter Coe transferred from Chichester to Haymarket.
—The evening will give a great deal of pleasure to Aunt Edna's nieces. MARTIN HOYLE *Financial Times*

1984

Feb 3. Tom Wilkinson and Julie Covington in Michael Hastings's **Tom and Viv** directed by Max Stafford-Clark at Royal Court. Writing about T S Eliot's marriage, Hastings comes down firmly on the side of Viv, implying that she was far saner than anybody let on; that her doctors were incompetent; that Eliot abnegated his responsibilities; that many of the things she did were "jokes"; and that the tests to prove her insanity were ludicrous. Covington made Viv's dottiness amusing, sad and frightening.
—The portrait of Eliot is shamefully inadequate, giving little impression of the super-subtle mind or the travelled sophisticate, and none whatsoever of the introspective torments and spiritual achievements of the greatest religious poet of the century. JOHN BARBER *Daily Telegraph*

Mar 8. Leonard Rossiter in Joe Orton's **Loot** directed by Jonathan Lynn at Ambassadors. Rossiter, a mad gleam in his eye, had the exact measure of Inspector Truscott, who was never happier than when he was beating somebody up or kneeing them in the balls.

Mar 8. Vanessa Redgrave, Christopher Reeve and Wendy Hiller in **The Aspern Papers** directed by Frith Banbury at Haymarket. Adaptation by Michael Redgrave from story by Henry James. Reeve, with his handsome good looks, adopted a lady-killer's transparent glib charm. Redgrave, red-eyed, red-nosed, bedraggled, poor, and not a little distracted, looked as if she might have been a member of the Paris Commune.

Mar 13. Alan Bates and Charles Lloyd Pack in Harold Pinter's **One for the Road**

directed by Harold Pinter at Lyric Hammersmith. Political statement about physical and psychological torture. The interrogator sees himself as an Old Testament God whose business it is to keep the world clean. "I love death," he boasts." Sexual intercourse is nothing compared to it."

Mar 27. Andrew Lloyd Webber and Richard Stilgoe's musical **Starlight Express** designed by John Napier and directed by Trevor Nunn at Apollo Victoria. There was never any doubt that in a race between an electric train and a steam train, that steam would win. The plot was always subordinate to the machinery. A large part of the theatre was gutted and skate tracks were installed roller-coaster fashion in and around the stalls and up to the circle and back. The £2 million production was a tremendous technical achievement for John Napier. The set looked stunning and dangerous. 7,046 performances.
—There is nothing here that comes within a whisker of *Cats* or *Evita* for originality. DAVID ROPER *Daily Express*
—I prophesy this show will keep bankruptcy from the door for another decade or so. JACK TINKER *Daily Mail*

Apr 6. Glenda Jackson, John Phillips, Brian Cox, Edward Peterbridge and James Hazeldine in Eugene O'Neill's **Strange Interlude** directed by Keith Hack at Duke of York's. Five-hour marathon covered 30 years in a woman's life. Jackson, emotionally and intellectually confident, sidestepped the melodramatic pitfalls. Petherbridge, barbed, sterile and elegantly old-maidish, delivered the Jamesian ironies with a dry wit.
—The evening is long and little more than *Dynasty* dressed up as art. JACK TINKER *Daily Mail*

Apr 12. Ian McKellen as Pierre and Michael Pennington as Jaffeir in Thomas Otway's **Venice Preserv'd** directed by Peter Gill at Lyttelton (NT). The story was based on an actual plot against the Venetian Senate in 1618. Otway's characters, however, joined the conspiracy for personal rather than political reasons. The production was firmly rooted in Zoffany's famous portrait of Garrick and Mrs Cibber in the leading roles and the acting was in the heroic manner of that era.

Apr 25. George Orwell's **Animal Farm** directed by Peter Hall at Cottesloe (NT). Orwell's allegory worked much better as an animated cartoon; having actors dressed as animals merely spoiled it. The only time the production equalled the impact of the novel was right at the end when the actors removed their masks and the audience could not tell the difference between the humans and the pigs.

May 10. Peter O'Toole in Bernard Shaw's **Pygmalion** directed by Ray Cooney at Shaftesbury. Jackie Smith-Wood as Eliza Doolittle. John Thaw as Alfred Doolittle. O'Toole, hardly a confirmed bachelor, was far less tyrannical, selfish and arrogant than most Higginses. He took off his shoes and waved them in visitors' faces. His most endearing aspect was the very special relationship he had with his mother (Joyce Carey).
—The play could be called Pyg Meets Gal. But, by God, he [Peter O'Toole] has presence, and a charm before which tougher girls than Eliza might crumple. KENNETH HURREN *Mail on Sunday*
—This is a tottering achievement of considerable brilliance. SHERIDAN MORLEY *Punch*

May 22. Albert Finney in John Arden's **Serjeant Musgrave's Dance** directed by Albert Finney at Old Vic. The 1984 confrontation between miners and police made the revival particularly apposite, but Finney's performance and production had no energy whatsoever and his desperate effort to whip up the second act with some flag-waving was merely embarrassing. The Mayor was played as a *Punch* caricature. The constable was out of Max Sennett. Max Wall, as the bargee, didn't know what he was doing.

Jun 12. Natalia Makarova and Tim Flavin in Richard Rodgers and Lorenz Hart's musical **On Your Toes** choreographed by George Balanchine and directed by George Abbott at Palace. Famous classical ballerina is tempted into modern dance. With the wonderfully leggy Makarova in the leading role it was a case of life imitating art. The show was a tuneful, lively and occasionally witty museum piece. The famous *Slaughter on Tenth Avenue* ballet was a disappointment, having long been superseded by the Raymond Chandler/Micky Spillane spoof in the film, *Band Wagon*, incomparably danced by Fred Astaire and Cyd Charisse.

Jun 20. Rex Harrison and Claudette Colbert in Frederick Lonsdale's **Aren't We All?** directed by Clifford Williams at Haymarket. Harrison played the philandering, worldly-wise father-in-law with practised ease. Colbert brought charm to the role of an old flame. The production softened Lonsdale's cynicism.
—Rex Harrison delivers his lines which all too often verge on the negligent. During the languid peregrinations around the text he occasionally bumps into the odd phrase which even Frederick Lonsdale would recognise as his own. JACK TINKER *Daily Mail*

Jul 10. Harriet Walter and Alan Rickman in Aphra Behn's **Lucky Chance** directed by Jules Wright at Royal Court. The Women's Playhouse Trust's inaugural production was a historical curiosity, which had not been seen since its premiere in 1686

Starlight Express

....

when it was thought "too indecent to be ever represented again." Behn relied on farcical situations and bawdry, which was as vulgar as any of her contemporaries. Rickman's libertine played dice with an old man for his wife. The funniest scene had a young rake (Denis Lawson) urgently trying to persuade a husband, who was just about to consummate his marriage, that he was needed in the city, so that he (the rake) could bed her first.

—Why hasn't a writer condemned for a level of indecency rivalled only by Dryden been plundered before now by the gentlemen of the South Bank? Surely, it can't be because the author in question is female? Ros Asquith *City Limits*

Jul 19. Ian McKellen in Anton Chekhov's **Wild Honey** directed by Christopher Morahan at Lyttelton (NT). Michael Frayn's version treated Chekhov's Platonov as if it were a rough draft rather than a finished play. Re-writing, transposing and editing, he turned the melodrama into farce. Platonov is a Don Juan in the Russian manner, a compulsive womaniser for whom nothing goes right. The scene on the rail track at dead of night, when he is trying to deal with three women at the same time, is as funny as anything in Feydeau.

—His [Ian McKellen] Platonov manages to be both Chekhovian and Fraynian and still utterly true to life; it is a brilliant dual creation. Christopher Hudson *Standard*

Aug 2. Al Pacino, J J Johnston and Bruce MacVittie in David Mamet's **American Buffalo** directed by Arvin Brown at Duke of York's. Some critics have interpreted the play as an allegory on the American Dream. Three small-time crooks plan a robbery that never gets beyond the planning stage because of their incompetence. Pacino, the most extrovert of the trio, was so mannered, physically and vocally, that he seemed to be caricaturing a Method actor. Johnston and MacVittie, who didn't do nearly so much acting, gave better performances.

—But the tedium of the piece is a mere pinprick, a small vaccination, against the armoury of tricks, mannerisms and self-regard with which Mr Pacino bombards us throughout the evening. Jack Tinker *Daily Mail*

—How can such illiterate, inconsequential chatter sustain out interest for two hours.

Much of the talk is of people we never meet and most of it is unprintable. Eric Shorter *Daily Telegraph*

Aug 6. Lena Horne at Adelphi. Looking and sounding much younger than her years Horne sang with such intensity that each song became a personal manifesto.

Aug 8. Georgia Brown, James Laurenson and Clare Leach in **42nd Street** at Drury Lane. Musical. Book by Michael Stewart and Mark Bramble. Music by Harry Warren. Lyrics by Al Dubin. Stewart and Mark Bramble. Directed by Lucia Victor. Original direction and dances by Gower Champion. The musical, a hymn to show-biz, drew on films of the 1930s for its songs. The "Dames" number was given the full no-expenses-barred, Busby Berkeley, tinsel-and-glitter kitsch with mirrors.

Aug 12. Sandy Wilson's **The Boy Friend** directed by Christopher Hewett at Old Vic. Anna Quayle, hilarious as the headmistress, looked as if she had stepped out of an Erté fashion plate.

Aug 13. Paul Eddington in Alan Bennett's **40 Years On** directed by Patrick Garland at Queen's. A pale carbon copy of the original production. Stephen Fry played a junior master.

Aug 31. Brian Cox and Colum Convey in Ray Hutchinson's **Rat in the Skull** directed by Max Stafford-Clark at Royal Court. The story of Ireland is 400 years of hatred. A member of the RUC interrogates a young bomber. Hutchinson's theme is that there will never be any reconciliation between Catholics and Protestants because the heart will always rule the head. "The rat in the skull" is the nagging doubt shown by both sides that they may be wrong.

Sep 24. Barbara Ferris, Diane Langton, Marcia Warren and Barbara Young in Richard Harris's **Stepping Out** directed by Julia McKenzie at Duke of York's. Seven women and one man sign up for a weekly tap class in a London suburban church hall.

1984 World Premieres

New York
David Rabe's *Hurly Burly*
August Wilson's *Ma Rainey's Black Bottom*
Berlin
Joshua Sobol's *Ghetto*
Montreal
Michel Tremblay's *Albertine Five Times*
Leicester
Howard Brenton's *Bloody Poetry*

Deaths

Richard Burton (*b.*1925), British actor
Eduardo de Filippo (*b.*1900), Italian playwright, actor, director

Lillian Hellman (*b.*1905), American playwright
James Mason (*b.*1909), British actor
J B Priestley (*b.*1894), British playwright, novelist

Notes

—Jayne Torvill and Christopher Dean performing *Bolero* won Winter Olympic Gold Medal.

History

—Miners' strike
—Indira Gandhi assassinated
—IRA bomb attack on Conservative Conference in Brighton

Warren was amusingly awful and finally pathetic as a posh and insensitive member of the class.

Oct 4. Julie Walters and Ian Charleson in Sam Shepard's **Fool for Love** directed by Peter Gill at Cottesloe (NT). Cowboy stuntman travels 2,500 miles to see his girl friend who lives in a grubby motel on the edge of Mojave Desert. She knows he will walk out on her because he always does. Their sexual battle has been going on now for fifteen years, ever since they fooled around in high school. The actors, hurled themselves at each other, bashed their heads against the walls and gave Mamet's incestuous melodrama noisy, hysterical, door-slamming performances.

Oct 24. Donald Sinden and Michael Williams in Ray Cooney's **Two Into One** directed by Ray Cooney at Shaftesbury. A Member of Parliament is meant to be in the House of Commons working on a vice bill. He is in fact in a hotel intending to have sex with one of the Prime Minister's staff. First-rate farce for two natural farceurs.

Oct 31. James Aubrey, Fiona Shaw, Jane Gurnett and Valentine Pelka in Howard Brenton's **Bloody Poetry** directed by Roland Rees at Hampstead. The action covered the period when Byron and Shelley were with Mary Shelley and Claire Clairemont in Switzerland and Italy in 1816 and 1822. The British public back home would have been delighted to know how much these revolutionary poets-in-exile suffered. Aubrey's Byron was a debauchée in the grand Regency manner. Brenton said that the story of Shelley and Byron could have been one of the great love stories, if it had been up to Byron, but that Shelley wasn't willing.

Nov 2. Judi Dench in Bertolt Brecht's **Mother Courage** directed by Howard Davies at Barbican (RSC). Dench wearing a flaming urchin-red wig and long overcoat (which touched the ground) looked like the Artful Dodger and was far too young to be the mother of Zoë Wanamaker, Miles Anderson and Bruce Alexander, but the performance, nevertheless, was deeply moving
—Brecht wanted us to observe detachedly not become involved. Fat chance of that with any good actress, let alone Miss Dench, indisputably a great one. MICHAEL COVENEY *Financial Times*
—This is one of the finest Brechtian performances I have seen, dry but gripping, pitiless and unsympathetic but eloquent. JOHN PETER *Sunday Times*

Nov 6. Tom Baker, Hywel Bennett and Julia Watson in Oliver Goldsmith's **She Stoops to Conquer** directed by Giles Block at Lyttelton (NT). Dora Bryan's mud-spattered Mrs Hardcastle, complaining to Tony Lumpkin (Tony Haygarth) that she had been robbed of all her jewellery, was as crude and as funny as a Rowlandson caricature.

Nov 13. Maggie Smith as Millamant and Michael Jayston as Mirabell in William Congreve's **The Way of the World** directed by William Gaskill transferred from Chichester to Haymarket. Smith acted the famous proviso scene with unexpected seriousness and without any affectation, making it a sincere statement of love. Joan Plowright's northern good sense was totally at variance with Lady Wishfort's superannuated frippery. She ignored the comic possibilities of the toilette and the apprehensive anticipation of meeting a potential admirer. She also underplayed the rage and pathos.
—Maggie Smith, as Mrs Millamant, turns in a very showy performance. She affects a nasal twang in her voice and invests, brilliantly, a wide range of mincing, whimsical and above all calculated gestures which succeed in proving she can outplay all the others in the froth of sexual hide and seek. CHRISTOPHER EDWARDES *Spectator*

Nov 14. Glenda Jackson in Jean Racine's **Phedra** directed and designed by Philip Prowse at Old Vic. There was a memorable *coup de theatre* right at the end when,

accompanied by thunder and smoke, the scenery came tumbling down and horses fell from the sky; but nobody, with the exception of Robert Eddison (who delivered the oration to the dead Hippolytus) had any idea how to speak the verse. Jackson, far too modern, lacked passion, majesty and tragedy.

Dec 15. Ian McKellen as Coriolanus, Irene Worth as Volumnia and Greg Hicks as Aufidius in Shakespeare's **Coriolanus** directed by Peter Hal at Olivier (NT).150 years previously the great actor-managers could field a 200-strong crowd with no difficulty. The National Theatre, with a huge deficit, solved the problem of how to afford the crowds the play needs by getting the public to pay to sit on stage and then making them join in. McKellen found a great deal of unexpected humour in the text and delivered the famous line, "There is a world elsewhere" as a cheeky goodbye from the wings. His charismatic performance confirmed him as the leading actor of his generation.
—Until McKellen gets style and content, manner and matter, consistently in sync', that present eminence of his will, I fear, never become pre-eminence. BENEDICT NIGHTINGALE *New Statesman*

Jan 7. Daniel Massey and Judi Dench in Harley Granville Barker's **Waste** directed by John Barton at Pit (RSC). Amalgam of the two versions Barker wrote. Massey as Trebell remained likeable, without ever denying the man's heartlessness. Dench's Amy O'Connell played her opening scene as if she were acting in Wilde or Restoration Comedy. "I may flirt," she said, "making love is another matter."

Jan 19. Brian Glover as God, Karl Johnson as Jesus, Jack Sheperd as Satan, Robert Stephens as Herod and Pontius Pilate in **The Mysteries** directed by Bill Bryden at Cottesloe (NT). A major event: Medieval religious drama is revived for secular audiences. The jolly, tongue-in-cheek promenade production started with Adam and Eve and ended with Judgement Day. The text was drawn from the York, Wakefield, Chester and Coventry Cycles. The theatre was festooned with trade union banners and dart boards. The staging was an intellectual and a technical triumph.
—Rarely have I felt language in the theatre so consume the bowels, excite the senses and stimulate the imagination. GILES GORDON *Punch*

Jan 31. Rik Mayall in Nikolai Gogol's **The Government Inspector** directed by Richard Eyre at Olivier (NT). Mayall concentrated on comic business rather than content and some of the business, when he danced with the Mayor (Jim Broadbent) was very funny. His performance was hit and miss; he missed the pathos completely. John Gunter's setting was a mountain of paper-work.

Feb 4. Julie Walters and Ian Charleson in Sam Shepard's **Fool for Love** directed by Peter Gill transferred from the National to Lyric.
—A competent display of inflected British acting. But it is not raw, it is not foul. It is not passionate, and it is not powerful. It is, in short, a bit of a doddle, to sit through and not very funny. MICHAEL COVENEY *Financial Times*
—Shepard seem to go for intensity rather than formal coherence and balance, and the result, while possessed of moments of real power, is uneven and ultimately, unsatisfying. CHRISTOPHER EDWARDS *Spectator*

Feb 12. Robert Lindsay, Frank Thornton and Emma Thompson in **Me and My Girl** directed by Mike Ockrent at Adelphi. Musical. Book by L Arthur Rose and Douglas Furber. Music by Noel Gay. Big popular success. The book had been "improved" by Stephen Fry, but was still patronising. Lindsay may not have been a natural song-and-dance man, but he was immensely likeable as the cockney lad. Since the best thing about the show is "The Lambeth Walk" it was odd the revival didn't exploit it more. *Me and My Girl* ran for eight years.
—Mike Ockrent's cutesy production (complete with tap-dancing family portraits) cannot disguise the fact that the show is snobbish codswallop. MICHAEL BILLINGTON *Guardian*

Feb 28. Charlton Heston as Commander Queeg in Herman Wouk's **The Caine Mutiny Court-Martial** directed by Charlton Heston at Queen's. The crack-up was not remotely tragic and Ben Cross, as the Jewish lawyer, who is reprimanded for the vigour with which he destroys Queeg, displayed no such vigour. The cast was drawn from American and Canadian actors, who each had a brief moment on the witness stand. It was like watching a series of audition pieces. The unnecessary and embarrassing coda – a drunken party to celebrate Queeg's defeat – was so badly acted that it was difficult to know what was going on

Mar 22. Edward Hermann, Julie Covington and David Haigh in Michael Hastings's **Tom and Viv** directed by Max Stafford-Clarke returned to Royal Court following performances in New York.

Mar 27. Jonathan Kent and Sheila Gish in Arthur Schnitzler's **Intermezzo** directed by Christopher Fettes at Greenwich. Husband and wife, a conductor and an opera

1985 World Premieres

New York

William Hoffman's *As Is*

Neil Simon's *Biloxi Blues*

Larry Kramer's *The Normal Heart*

August Wilson's *Joe Turner Has Come and Gone*

George C Wolfe's *The Colored Museum*

Avignon

Peter Brook's *Mahabharata*

Dublin

Frank McGuinness's *Observe the Sons of Ulster Marching Towards the Somme*

Berlin

Botho Strauss's *The Park*

Deaths

Alex Arburzov (*b.*1908), Russian playwright

Michael Redgrave (*b.*1908), British actor

Orson Welles (*b.*1915), American actor, director

Notes

Simon Callow published *Being An Actor*

Alec Guinness published *Blessings in Disguise*

History

—Gorbachev succeeded as Party Leader in USSR

—First Live Aid Concert

—*Rainbow Warrior* sabotaged

---

singer, agree to separate and remain good friends. Kent went completely berserk in Act III and turned high comedy into heavy-going melodrama.

Apr 20. Wendy Morgan in Jean-Jacques Bernard's **Martine** translated by John Fowles and directed by Peter Hall at Lyttleton (NT). Premiered in 1922, the play was an early example of the drama of the unspoken. A farm girl falls in love with a soldier (Andrew C Wadsworth) on his return from National Service in Algeria. It was no more than "a pretty interlude" but on it, Martine built a false hope of marriage. The story was directed and acted with the greatest sensitivity.

—The theatre is above all the art of the unexpressed ... The theatre has no worse enemy than fine writing; it expresses and dilutes what it should only suggest. JEAN JACQUES-BERNARD

Apr 24. Liv Ullmann, Michael Gambon and Nicola Pagett in Harold Pinter's **Old Times** directed by David Jones at Haymarket. Ullmann looked perfect casting for the wife's friend; but in a play, which deals in lies and truth, her Scandinavian accent added an extra dimension it didn't need, making innocent remarks about London, Sicily, and even her vocabulary, suspect. Nevertheless, of the three actors, she alone suggested that she knew exactly what was going on beneath the surface text.

Apr 25. Antony Sher in Shakespeare's **Richard III** directed by Bill Alexander at Barbican (RSC). Sher on metal crutches (coated in black leather) certainly looked like a "bottled spider", but apart from his initial bounding agility, the performance yielded few surprises, except for the coronation when he crawled grotesquely to the throne.

—The most spectacular appropriation of the role by an English actor since Olivier. MICHAEL COVENEY *Financial Times*

—One of the great Shakespearian performances of our time. NIGEL WILLIAMSON *Tribune*

Apr 27. Shared Experience in **Pamela** pretended to stage Samuel Richardson's novel as if it were taking place in a rehearsal room during a run-through with half the cast missing. (One of them had been arrested and was on his way to prison). The only trouble with this arrangement was that the audience was far more interested in what was happening on the periphery of the acting area than in Pamela's fate. The distractions of actors chatting, smoking, knitting and even answering the phone upstaged the novel completely.

May 2. Anthony Hopkins in Howard Brenton and David Hare's **Pravda** directed by David Hare at Olivier (NT). The comedy was based on recent events at *The Times* and *The Guardian* with Robert Maxwell and Rupert Murdoch. South African businessman buys up newspapers and allows editorial freedom insofar as it does not affect his ambition or pocket. Thus there is no editorial freedom. "Why go to the trouble of producing a good newspaper when bad ones are so much easier? And they sell better." Hopkins' caricature of the magnate was a major turning-point in his career. The rasping Afrikaans accent and the angled stance of the body immediately established the character as a witty villain in the Richard III class. "Exploitation," he said, "that's what I like." The major weakness was that Hare didn't give him a worthy opponent.

—I think the piece may well be remembered for Mr Hopkins's portrait of naked power on the rampage. JOHN BARBER *Daily Telegraph*

May 21. Deborah Kerr in Emlyn Williams's **The Corn is Green** directed by Frith Banbury at Old Vic. George Winter played the pit boy who wins a scholarship to Oxford. There was nothing of the brusque, business-like, socialist schoolmarm about Kerr, who was always unfailingly gracious. Kerr didn't know her lines and Banbury stopped Emlyn Williams from coming to see the production.

Jun 28. Brian Cox and Colum Convey in Ron Hutchinson's **Rat in the Skull** directed by Max Stafford-Clark returned to the Royal Court.

Jun 28. Alan Howard in Stephen Poliakoff's **Breaking the Silence** directed by Ron Daniels at Mermaid. (RSC). Aristocratic Russian Jew behaves as if the Revolution has never taken place. Turned out of his mansion, he and his family and maid live in an imperial railway carriage. He is made examiner of telegraph poles, a job he totally ignores, and concentrates all his energies on his invention – the marrying of sound to film. The man has such arrogance, such selfishness and such crass stupidity that it is quite obvious that he will eventually be shot. As it happens, he isn't; though it isn't for want of trying on his part. Howard was so very theatrical that it came as a surprise to realise that his invention was a serious possibility rather than mere fantasy.

Jul 9. Lauren Bacall in Tennessee Williams's **Sweet Bird of Youth** directed by Harold Pinter at Haymarket. A famous film star takes flight after what she presumes has been the disastrous premiere of her latest picture and picks up a 29-year-old beach boy (Michael Beck). Burnt-out and in constant need of oxygen, alcohol, drugs and sex, she is totally unintimidated by the boy's crass attempt to blackmail her into getting him a career in movies. The casting of Bacall as the Princess suggested (even more so, since she alone was billed above the title) that she was playing the leading role and it was disconcerting for audiences to find that she was off stage for most of the second act.

—Casting an actress with the potent charisma of Lauren Bacall in Tennessee Williams's *Sweet Bird of Youth* is like using a diamond to cut plastic. KENNETH HURREN *Mail on Sunday*

Jul 15. London International Festival of Theatre included companies from Spain, Italy, China, USA, Yugoslavia, Canada, Poland, Holland and South Africa.

Jul 31. Martin Shaw in Alan Bleasdale's **Are You Lonesome Tonight?** directed by Robin Lefevre at Phoenix. Shaw played the old, bloated Elvis Presley. The young Elvis was played by Simon Bowman.

—As a psychodrama the show is an honourable failure. As a musical tribute, it's magnificent. ROS ATKINS *Observer*

Aug 1. Bob Peck and Michael Gambon in Alan Ayckbourn's **Chorus of Disapproval** directed by Alan Ayckbourn at Olivier (NT). The joke was at the expense of an amateur group staging *The Beggar's Opera*. The parallels between Ayckbourn and Gay were laboured. A bit-player (Bob Peck) suddenly finds he is playing Macheath on stage and off, loved by two women, who are wives of members of the company. Gambon was cast as a flamboyant Welsh director who was much more interested in amateur theatricals than he was in his wife.

Aug 1. Vanessa Redgrave and Jonathan Pryce in Anton Chekhov's **The Seagull** directed by Charles Sturridge at Queen's. When Arkadina says to Nina "You are bound to end up on the stage," the line is amusing because she is so insincere and patronising. When it was said in this revival, it was amusing because the audience knew Vanessa Redgrave was addressing her own daughter, Natasha (who has her mother's voice and mannerisms). Redgrave, who was not as actressy as she might have been, played Arkadina as the sort of woman who goes round slapping the servants about the head. She brought Trigorin (Jonathan Pryce) crashing to the floor with a rugger tackle. "Stay if you want," she said after a great deal of rough-and-tumble. Trigorin's resigned smile suggested that he had been through such incidents many times before. It was one of the biggest laughs of the evening when, having got up off the floor, he immediately took out his notebook to make notes.

Aug 13. Marc Blitzstein's **The Cradle Will Rock** directed by John Houseman at Old Vic. This famous example of musical agit-prop by the American Acting Company in the Brecht-Weill manner had a memorable first night in 1937 and needs to be understood within the context of the Thirties left-wing theatre and eighteen million unemployed. 48 years on the satire at the expense of the rich and the corruptibility of the police, church, press, universities and the arts was very dated and simplistic. Ideally, the strikes, lockouts and riots, should be performed to a 2,500-strong partisan audience of left-wing organisations in far grubbier surroundings than the plush Old Vic.

Sep 20. Simon Callow and Mark Rylance in Manuel Puig's **The Kiss of the Spiderwoman** directed by Simon Stokes at Bush. Outrageous homosexual shares an Argentinean prison cell with a political prisoner, a weedy, morose, heterosexual Marxist. Congress took place under the blankets. Callow, podgy and flouncing, gave a big performance in a small space.

—It would be hard for the possessor of so much flesh to be limp-wristed; he [Simon Callow] more than compensates by being limp-tongued. His verbal and emotional range are exhilarating. GILES GORDON *Observer*

Sep 30. Colm Wilkinson as Jean Valjean in Alain Boublil and Claude-Michel Schönberg's **Les Miserables** directed by Trevor Nunn and John Caird at Barbican (RSC). Rock musical based on Victor Hugo's novel was a triumph of spectacle over content. Visually, the most striking scene was when the two sections of John Napier's towering slum keeled over to form an enormous barricade right across the width of the Barbican stage. The romantic tableau of the dead was worthy of Eugene Delacroix. The boy Gavroche dies singing, counting the bullets as they hit him. The boy

Les Miserables

actor gave the sort of cute brat performance much beloved by cinema audiences in the 1930s. The critics generally were underwhelmed, finding the show banal, remote, witless and synthetic. Francis King in *The Sunday Telegraph* said that a literary mountain had been reduced to a mole-hill. Transferred to Palace and then to the Queen's and still running well into the 21st century.
—It leaves one curiously uninvolved. Despite the grandeur of the music, the courage of the intentions, *Les Miserables* has, sadly, been reduced to The Glums. JACK TINKER *Daily Mail*
—If I was the RSC I'd forget about the West End transfer and settle for a made-for-TV American mini-series instead. LYN GARDNER *City Limits*

Oct 1. Antony Sher in Harvey Fierstein's **Torch Song Trilogy** directed by Robert Allan Ackerman at Albery. Three plays lasting just under four hours: a gay Ring Cycle. Sher, in the role created by Fierstein on Broadway, gave a bravura performance as a Jewish drag quean who attempts to form a permanent relationship and win self-respect. Sentimental and trite, the trilogy played to a continuous round of loud applause from a very partisan gay audience.
—His [Anthony Sher] lighting transitions from raw emotion to waspish wit papers over the cracks in Mr Fierstein's text. MICHAEL BILLINGTON *Guardian*

Oct 23. Frances Barber as Marguerite Gautier and Nicholas Farrell as Armand Duval in Pam Gems' **Camille** directed by Ron Daniels at Comedy. Seen through post-feminist eyes, the story was far less sentimental than the one told by Dumas. Gems's style was far removed from the Greta Garbo-George Cukor film and much nearer to Bernard Shaw's *Mrs Warren's Profession*, especially when Camille was talking about her reasons for becoming a prostitute. The most striking innovation was the scene between Camille and Armand's father, who far from pleading with her, threatened to have her arrested as an undesirable. Frances Barber was never a lady and there was no death-bed reconciliation.

Nov 13. Peter Wood's production of William Congreve's **Love for Love** was revived at Lyttelton (NT) twenty years after its first performance. Stephen Moore was a singularly common and clumsy Valentine. Barry James as his servant was far more of a gent. The nicest person was Valentine's younger brother, an honest tar, who addressed everybody in a nautical way. Neil Daglish's sailor was a charmer: "If you like me and I like you," he said to Prue (Sally Dexter), "we may chance to swing in a hammock together."

Nov 28. Colin Stinton in David Mamet's **Edmond** directed by Richard Eyre at Royal Court. This disturbing 20th-century odyssey – a highly concentrated modern morality play lasting 75 minutes – gave a terrible picture of violence, paranoia and isolation. Edmond, a 37-year-old American Everyman, walks out on his wife and quickly learns the brutal ways of the city from pimps, whores, cardsharpers and neurotics. He pawns his wedding ring to buy a knife and it is not long before he, too, has murdered somebody. He ends up in prison, believing that he is in a safer place and continues to believe it, even after being sodomized by a hulking black guy.

Dec 4. Alan Bates in Peter Shaffer's **Yonadab** directed by Peter Hall at Olivier (NT). In the Bible, Yonadab plays a very peripheral part in the story of the rape of Tamara. His appearance is limited to two verses. In Dan Jacobson's witty novel and Shaffer's play he is the leading character – narrator, stage-manager and voyeur. He makes up for his own emotional vacuity by manipulating the emotions and lives of others. Bates, in a role which mixed modern colloquialisms and old-fashioned rhetoric, camped it up and indulged in a bit of Old Testament acting.

Dec 10. Sheila Hancock as Ranevskaya and Ian McKellen as Lopakhin in Anton Chekhov's **The Cherry Orchard** directed by Mike Alfreds at Cottesloe (NT). The production's major innovation was to act the version which was performed on the first night at the Moscow Arts Theatre. This meant that Act II ended rather than began with Charlotta's life-story. She was joined by Firs who recalled having been falsely arrested for being involved in a murder. Hancock's Ranevsky was often very moving. Roy Kinnear turned Simeonov-Pishhhick's panic when he thinks he has lost all his money into an extended revue turn.

Dec 11. Donald Sinden in **The Scarlet Pimpernel** directed by Nicholas Hytner transferred from Chichester to Her Majesty's. The script, based on an old prompt copy, was surprisingly dull. (The 1934 film with Leslie Howard as Sir Percy Blakeney was superior in every way.) Sinden, too much the buffoon, was not at his ease in the romantic scenes. Desmond Barrit, as the inn-keeper, out-hammed the hunchback of Notre Dame when he was cutting up a dead rat to put in Chauvelin's soup. Charles Kay's Chauvelin (who drank the soup with relish) was easily the most stylish actor, guying the melodramatic convention whilst remaining studiously in it.

1986

Jan 2. Lindsay Duncan, Alan Rickman, Juliet Stevenson, Fiona Shaw and Lesley Manville in Christopher Hampton's adaptation of Choderlos de Laclos **Les Liaisons Dangereuses** directed by Howard Davies at the Pit (RSC). Duncan's elegant, intelligent and witty Marquise de Merteuil was a monster of considerable charm, totally confident in her cruelty. The play ended with her looking forward to the 1790s wondering what the decade would bring. There wasn't any doubt in the audience's mind that she would be among the first to be guillotined. Rickman was a mumbling, dirty, charmless de Valmont. Bob Crowley's handsome design gave Laclos a high polish.

Jan 2. Ben Kingsley as Othello and David Suchet as Iago in Shakespeare's **Othello** directed by Terry Hands at Barbican (RSC). The play was Iago's tragedy. There had been Iagos in the past who have been in love with Othello but none of them had burst into tears when Othello asked him why he had behaved in the way he had. Suchet's Iago was a villain who would have liked to have been good. He was distraught when Othello killed himself.

Jan 23. Peter Jeffrey as Falstaff, Lindsay Duncan as Mistress Ford and Jane Dale as Mistress Page in Shakespeare's **The Merry Wives of Windsor** directed by Bill Alexander at Barbican (RSC). Set in the late 1950s, Meg Page was under the drier at the hairdressers when she read Falstaff's love letter. Falstaff, with his handle-bar moustache and his plus-fours, looked like a bogus wing-commander. Nicky Henson's Ford behaved like Humphrey Bogart in a *film noir*. He actually got into the buck-basket to look for Falstaff. Sheila Steafel, as a sozzled Mistress Quickly, spent much of her time, trying to negotiate the Barbican's revolving stage.

Feb 25. Steven Mackintosh in Neil Simon's **Brighton Beach Memoirs** directed by Michael Rudman at Lyttelton (NT). Autobiographical piece set just prior to World War 2. The production had the sentimental realism of a Norman Rockwell cover for *The Saturday Evening Post*. There were a number of critics who questioned whether the National Theatre should be staging a commercial Broadway play.

Mar 5. Bill Fraser, James Grout, Patricia Hayes, Brian Murphy, Patricia Routledge, Patsy Rowlands, Prunella Scales, Elizabeth Spriggs and Timothy West in J B Priestley's **When We Are Married** directed by Ronald Eyre at Whitehall. Spriggs, formidable in her bearing and looks, was so right for the part of the battleaxe that when her hen-pecked husband hit her, the audience applauded.

Mar 20. Martin Sheen in Larry Kramer's **The Normal Heart** directed by David Hayman at Royal Court. Who cares if a faggot dies? Documentary about Kramer's efforts to make gays and governments do something about the AIDS epidemic. Kramer fought a losing battle. The medical profession didn't want to know and the Mayor of New York (himself a homosexual) was too frightened to put up any money for fear of being thought to endorse homosexuality. Equally unresponsive were the gays themselves who did not care for Kramer's propaganda to restrict their promiscuous life style. Kramer was thrown out of the organisation he had founded. *The Normal Heart* was not a play as much as a political platform in which the audience was bombarded with facts. There was a moving account of the death of one victim whose body was put in a plastic bag and left with the garbage because nobody wished to touch it. Sheen matched the author's passion and anger when Kramer was arguing for "recognition of a culture that is not just sexual".

Mar 22. John Kavanagh, Anita Reeves, Alan Devlin and Paul Bentley in Gilbert and Sullivan's **H.M.S.Pinafore** directed by Joe Dowling and choreographed by Mavis Ascott at Old Vic. The production owed more to Hollywood's *Anchors Away* and Joseph Papp's *The Pirates of Penzance* than it did to D'Oyly Carte. Life on the ocean wave was very gay – "an ocean of fun," said *The Daily Mail*. All the sailors were in love with Ralph Rackstraw. The gormless sailors were transformed into Tiller Girls, a high kicking, high camp knock-out finale.

Mar 22. Jim Cartwright's **Road** directed by Simon Curtis at Royal Court Upstairs. Cartwright (a modern Henry Mayhew in jobless Britain) offered a series of monologues on the same bitter, constipated note that all girls are slags and that all men are brutes. Transferred Downstairs.

Mar 26. Eileen Atkins in a new version of Euripides's **Medea** by Jeremy Brooks directed by Toby Robertson at Young Vic. Atkins acted like an unhinged Greenham Common activist arguing a feminist cause and played her second scene with Jason with such obvious irony that it was absurd that Jason didn't notice.

Apr 14. Albert Finney, Kevin Anderson and Jeff Fahey in Lyle Kessler's **Orphans** directed by Gary Sinise at Hampstead. Finney, as the enigmatic gangster, turned father-figure, suggested all sorts of hidden violence beneath his calm, controlled exterior. Transferred to Apollo.

May 1. Anton Lesser and Juliet Stevenson in Shakespeare's **Troilus and Cressida**

1986 Premieres
New York
    Robert Harding's *Steel Magnolias*

Deaths
Jean Genet (*b.*1910), French novelist, playwright, poet

Notes
—Swan Theatre opened in Stratford with *The Two Noble Kinsmen*

History
—Chernobyl nuclear power disaster
—Mikhail Gorbachev introduced Glasnost and Perestroka
—US space shuttle *Challenger* exploded

directed by Howard Davies at Barbican (RSC). Cressida's arrival among the merry Greeks turned into a gang-bang. Thersites (Alun Armstrong) was played as the Good Soldier Schweik, a licensed Geordie clown, rather than as Shakespeare's bitter railer. The permanent set was a crumbling mansion, with a sweeping, romantic staircase and Achilles' tent, somewhat oddly, on the first floor.

May 7. George Hearn and Denis Quilley in Jerry Herman's **La Cage aux Folles** directed by Arthur Laurents at London Palladium. Book by Harvey Fierstein based on play by Jean Poiret. Over-rated gay cult French movie turned into an American musical suitable for the whole family. The Palladium was perfect for the bright vulgarity of the tacky drag numbers. The show presumed audiences had seen the film. The best moment in the film was when Albin was sitting in a chair trying (and failing) to be "a man" and merely getting more and more effeminate. The scene, funny and touching, was not nearly so effective when it was turned into a song. Hearn's big moment was the over-kill number, "I Am What I Am", a poor gay's "My Way". It was quite a surprise when the "all-female chorus" removed their wigs and costumes in the curtain call to discover there were actually two girls among them. They had all looked like boys.
—It seems a broader, cruder occasion, one that contrives simultaneously to mock and travesty the gay life and sentimentalise and patronise it. Never have I witnessed more squalling, squawking and gratuitous camping it up in a theatre. BENEDICT NIGHTINGALE *New Statesman*
—*La Cage aux Folles* has to be the straightest show to hit town in many a year. It is old-fashioned as mom's apple pie, as safe as houses, and warm as toast. JACK TINKER *Daily Mail*

May 14. Elaine Paige, Murray Head, Tommy Korberg and John Turner in **Chess**, a musical by Benny Anderssen, Tim Rice and Bjorn Ulvaeus directed by Trevor Nunn at Prince Edward. USSR and the USA play political games, though what the game was never clear. A checkerboard stage was used but the chess analogy was not developed. The most visible evidence of Michael Bennett's early departure from the production was the lack of choreographic invention.
—As tasteful as *Time*, as jolly as *Les Miserables* and as intelligent as *Mutiny*, the show, directed by Trevor Nunn, may well be due for a long run. Whether it deserves it, is another matter. FRANCIS KING *Sunday Telegraph*

May 28. Alec McCowen as the Unidentified Guest in T S Eliot's **The Cocktail Party** with Sheila Gish, Simon Ward, Rachel Kempson, Sheila Allen, Stephen Boxer and Robert Eddison directed by John Dexter at Phoenix. The tiresome cocktail chitter-chatter was accompanied by a pianist. McCowen was never anything more than a psychiatrist.

Jun 25. Robert Holman's **Making Noise Quietly** directed by John Dove at Bush Theatre. Three plays. **Being Friends** was a wartime meeting in a Kent field between a sickly gay novelist (Ronan Vibert) and a young Quaker (Jonathan Cullen), a conscientious objector, who wanted to be gay. **Lost** had a young naval officer (Jonathan Coy) calling on a family to tell them that their son has died in action in the Falklands. When the officer mentions that the boy died doing his duty for his country, the mother (Jean Boht) tartly replies that he should have put his duty to his parents before his country. **Making Noise Quietly**: A corporal (Paul Copley), whose wife has left him, is lumbered with her autistic child (Daniel Kipling), whom he loves yet brutally belts. A German Jewess (Helen Ryan) with whom he is having an affair decides to tame them both, beginning with the boy.

Jul 3. Paul Scofield and Howard Rollins in Herb Gardner's **I'm Not Rappoport** directed by Daniel Sullivan at Apollo. Ex-waiter and black boiler man share a park bench in Central Park. The waiter's greatest fear is not the muggers but his daughter, who wants to put him in a Home and threatens that if he doesn't agree, she will take him to court and produce evidence that he is physically and mentally incapable of looking after himself.

Jul 23. Faye Dunaway in Donald Freed's **Circe and Bravo** directed by Harold Pinter at Wyndham's. Pretentious thriller. First Lady is under house-arrest at Camp David. Is the secret serviceman there to stop her from committing suicide? Or is he there to drive her to committing suicide? It turns out he is there to press the button. The play was Dunaway's monologue: a self-indulgent and terribly boring *tour de force*. Stephen Jenn gave valuable support as a tight-lipped secret serviceman who finally removes his dark glasses (easily the most dramatic moment) to reveal a terrible weakling.

Jul 30. John Mills and Rosemary Harris in Brian Clark's **The Petition** directed by Peter Hall at Lyttelton (NT). Retired general discovers his wife has signed a petition to ban the bomb and intends to speak at a rally. Transferred to Wyndham's.

Aug 4. Jack Lemmon, Bethel Leslie, Peter Gallaghar and Kevin Spacey in Eugene O'Neill's **Long Day's Journey into Night** directed by Jonathan Miller at Haymarket. Miller managed to cut an hour out of a long day by the simple expedient of getting the actors to talk over each other. The major disadvantage of casting Lemmon was that the audience came expecting a comedy. When he started spouting Shakespeare it seemed as if James Tyrone had made the right decision to stick to *The Count of Monte Cristo*. Gallagher was excellent as the consumptive Edmund raging against his dad.

Aug 6. Michael Bryant, Sara Kestelman and Neil Daglish in Arthur Miller's **The American Clock** directed by Peter Wood at Cottesloe (NT). Inspired by Studs Terkels' *Hard Times*, Miller offered "a mosaic, a mural" rather than a play about the Depression years when 15 million out of a labour force of 50 million were unemployed. Punctuated with songs of the period, it ended surprisingly, on a note of nostalgia for a time – the only time in American history, apart from the Civil War – when war was real.

Sep 3. Julia McKenzie in Alan Ayckbourn's **A Woman in Mind** directed by Alan Ayckbourn at Vaudeville. Vicar's wife becomes more and more disorientated. The action takes place largely inside her head and builds to a comic-horrific climax in which her hallucinated ideal family turns nasty and clashes with her real family.

Sep 8. Glenda Jackson, Joan Plowright and Patricia Hayes in Frederico Garcia Lorca's **The House of Bernarda Alba** directed by Nuria Espert at Lyric, Hammersmith. Jackson could have been mistaken for the eldest daughter instead of the mother. The outstanding performances were by Julie Legrand, as the daughter who is courted only for her money, and Chloe Salaman as the hysterical cripple.

Sep 18. Eric Idle as Ko-Ko in Gilbert and Sullivan's **The Mikado** directed by Jonathan Miller at Coliseum (ENO). Miller updated the operetta to the 1920s and set the action in a hotel in St Moritz, which is a very long way from Titipu in time and place. The hotel ballroom, designed by Stefanos Lazaridis, all in white was so brilliantly lit that the audience was momentarily blinded when the curtain first went up. Richard Angas as the Mikado wore a suit big enough to contain at least six Sydney Greenstreets.

Michael Ball and Sarah Brightman in The Phantom at the Opera

Sep 18. Roger Lloyd Pack as Kafka in Alan Bennett's **Kafka's Dick** directed by Richard Eyre at Royal Court. Kafkaesque nightmare in which Kafka comes back to find that Brod, contrary to his instructions, has not burned his manuscripts, and that he is world-famous. It is a great relief to Kafka to find that he has been dreaming. Lloyd Pack, angular, gaunt, cringing, miserable, consumptive, was a wonderfully creepy caricature. There was an amusing Grosz-like caricature of his dad by Jim Broadbent, a vulgar bully, played with North Country invective: "My son," he said, "is a spent condom." Geoffrey Palmer was the prissy insurance man who knew everything about Kafka's life and nothing about his work.

Sep 24. Nigel Hawthorne in Arthur Wing Pinero's **The Magistrate** directed by Michael Rudman at Lyttelton (NT). Hawthorne was very funny when Posket is back in his office, having been chased all over North London by the police. Bruised and battered, his clothes horribly soiled, he conducts a "painful interview" with the arrested Colonel Lukyn. "I regret to see you in this terrible position," he said and proceeded to lecture him on morality, every single word a criticism of himself.
—The National Theatre is constipated by plays that provide nice, undemanding nights out to nice, undemanding people. LYN GARDNER *City Limits*

Oct 2. Vanessa Redgrave, Tom Wilkinson and Adrian Dunbar in Henrik Ibsen's **Ghosts** directed by David Thacker at Young Vic. Mrs Alving, with her progressive views, defending her right to read what she wants and her son's way of life, suited Redgrave perfectly. Pastor Manders was a great big baby, an ignorant, sexist bigot, constantly standing in judgment and getting it wrong every time. Wilkinson was totally believable without losing any of the comedy. There was a moment when Mrs Alving hugged him as she might hug a child.
—It is quite the most inventive and magnificent performance she [Vanessa Redgrave] has given in years. NICHOLAS DE JONGH *Guardian*

Oct 2. Brian Cox, Elizabeth Spriggs, Richard Garnett and Richard McCabe in Bernard Shaw's **Misalliance** directed by John Caird at Barbican (RSC). Mike Ford was very funny with his moral outrage and his half-digested socialism.

Oct 9. Michael Crawford and Sarah Brightman in Andrew Lloyd Webber's musical **The Phantom of the Opera** directed by Harold Prince at Her Majesty's. Lloyd Webber's most romantic and operatic score yet. Lyrics by Charles Hart, who was on record as saying that he wished he had had more time. Crawford, who was half-masked horizontally (not vertically as in the poster and programme design), was a haunting rather than a horrific phantom. The success of the show was Prince's spectacular staging. The most memorable image was the journey across the lake in the subterranean labyrinth beneath the opera house. Crawford sang "The Music of the Night". Brightman (a sweet, wide-eyed, innocent heroine) sang "All I Ask You" and "Wishing You Were Somehow Here Again". *Phantom of the Opera* is still running well into the 21st century.
—The work is unmitigated tosh. But it is tosh of a high order. JOHN BARBER *Daily Telegraph*
—[Michael Crawford] It is surely one of the great performances not only in a musical but on any stage and in any year. JACK TINKER *Daily Mail*
—Only those of a very cruel frame of mind would suggest the musical was at all autobiographical. DAVID SHANNON *Today*

Oct 21. Derek Jacobi as Alan Turning in Hugh Whitemore's **Breaking the Code** directed by Clifford Williams at Haymarket. Alan Turing broke the Enigma Code during the war (for which he got the OBE). He broke the law after the war (for which he nearly went to prison). Incredibly naïve, he incriminated himself, admitting to mutual masturbation with a lad of nineteen, it never occurring to him that he was doing anything criminal.

Nov 1. Maggie Smith as Jocasta and Lambert Wilson as Oedipus in Jean Cocteau's **Infernal Machine** translated and directed by Simon Callow at Lyric. Cocteau's reworking of the Oedipus legend belonged to that period of French theatre in the 1930s and 1940s when he, Giraudoux, Sartre and Anouilh were all re-telling the Greek myths and legends in their boulevard/intellectual way. Oedipus confides in Jocasta, on their wedding night, that he has always dreamed of making love to his mother. The enormity is put off for another night when Jocasta pleads a headache. The set was a huge flight of narrow, steep steps, such as even an Inca, living in Uxmal, might balk at climbing. Maggie Smith made her entrance, trailing a long scarf, which looked as if, at any minute, it might do an Isadora Duncan on her. The audience spent most of the first act worried that she and Robert Eddison (Tiresias) were going to fall off the set. Smith was very funny in her usual highly strung camp manner: "The people hate me, my clothes madden them, my nail polish maddens them, my mascara maddens them."

Nov 6. Simon Cadell in Will Evans and Valentine's **Tons of Money** directed by Alan Ayckbourn at Lyttelton (NT). Michael Gambon (as the hunch-backed butler) and Diane Bull (as the parlour maid) looked as if they had stepped out of a cartoon by H M Bateman and walked off with the play.
—It is difficult to understand why the National is continuing its faintly morbid habit of reviving – or half-reviving – plays that have respectfully passed away. SIMON CARR *Independent*

Dec 9. Julie Walters, Geraldine James, Sheila Reid and John Gordon Sinclair in Sharman Macdonald's **When I Was A Girl I Used To Scream and Shout** directed by Simon Stokes at Whitehall. 15-year-old girl decides that the only way to stop her mother abandoning her is to go to New Zealand with her boyfriend and get pregnant.

Dec 12. Anthony Hopkins in Shakespeare's **King Lear** directed by David Hare at Olivier (NT). Michael Bryant as Gloucester. Anna Massey as Goneril. Suzanne Bertish as Regan. Miranda Foster as Cordelia. Roshan Seth as Fool. Bill Nighy as Edgar. Hopkins thought he was a total disaster.

Dec 12. Brian Cox in John Whiting's **Penny for a Song** directed by Howard Davies at Barbican (RSC). Blind soldier journeys to London to ask King George III to stop the war. He is accompanied by a little boy on his way to Bethlehem to find Jesus. Nobody has told the soldier that the king is mad and the little boy that Jesus has died a long time ago.
—What exactly persuaded them [RSC] to train so many big guns on what is at best a Sunday school picnic of a play? JACK TINKER *Daily Mail*

1987

Jan 7. Maggie Smith, Anthony Andrews and Tim Piggott-Smith in Stephen Poliakoff's **Coming into Land** directed by Peter Hall at Lyttelton (NT). Polish housewife attempts to gain asylum in Britain.

Jan 12. Cheek by Jowl in Shakespeare's **Twelfth Night** directed by Declan Donnellan at Donmar. Not for purists. Andrew Aguecheek (Aden Gillett) was a Texan. Sir Toby suffered two heart-attacks. Gay Feste loved Orsino. Malvolio (Hugh Ross) was a stuffy gentleman's gentleman in a 1930s Hollywood screwball comedy, who took great encouragement from the fact that Fergie had married Prince Andrew. Wearing a safari jacket, short trousers, yellow stockings, cross-gartered, he brandished his bare legs and ended up rolling on the grass with Olivia. The production was without poetry and the sexual ambiguity was played up to the hilt.

Jan 19. Cheek by Jowl in Pierre Corneille's **The Cid** directed by Declan Donnellan at Donmar. The production kept a bemused distance from the tragic feud and its spiralling need for revenge. The dilemma of Chimena (Patricia Kerrigan) who wants her fiancé dead, yet alive, was acted, with each new twist in a complex plot, more and more, for high comedy. Corneille's familiar rhetoric was ditched and with it the passion and the pain. The performances were superficial

Jan 22. Desmond Barrit, Cyril Shaps and Ken Stott in John Cecil Holm and George Abbott's **Three Men on a Horse** directed by Jonathan Lynn at Cottesloe (NT). A meek greetings-card writer (Geoffrey Hutchings), who has a flair for picking winners at the races, is kidnapped by some small-time gangsters. At one point, it looked as if the gangsters (graduates of the Damon Runyon School for gamblers) might actually turn really nasty and kill him.

Feb 12. Michael Gambon, Elizabeth Bell, Suzanne Sylvester, Adrian Rawlins and Michael Simkins in Arthur Miller's **A View from the Bridge** directed by Alan Ayckbourn at Cottesloe (NT). Gambon, a massive, mesmerising Eddie Carbone, prowled the stage like a caged animal, thwarted in his sexual desires, ready to explode; yet he was always vulnerable and liable to crumble into tears at any moment. The kiss Eddie gave Rodolpho to prove "the guy ain't right" was electrifying, though not any less electrifying than the kiss he gave his niece.
—To Gambon the ultimate accolade –he is Eddie Carbone. ROBIN RAY *Punch*
—It shows Michael Gambon unequivocally shaking hands with greatness. MICHAEL BILLINGTON *Guardian*
—Who, 10 years ago would have credited Mr Gambon with a *tour de force* of such shattering power. JACK TINKER *Daily Mail*

Feb 25. Natasha Richardson, Trevor Eve, Stephen Rea and Angela Richards in Cole Porter's musical **High Society** directed by Richard Eyre at Victoria Palace. Book by Richard Eyre based on Philip Barry's *The Philadelphia Story* and the MGM film, *High Society*. It was not a swell party.

Mar 16. Michael Pennington as Hal and John Woodvine as Falstaff in Shakespeare's **Henrys IV Parts 1 and 2 and Henry V** directed by Michael Bogdanov at Old Vic. Hal was a yobo in jeans. Gadshill and Doll Tearsheet were skinheads. The Sherriff was a policeman. Pistol (sporting a T-shirt with the legend "Never mind the bollocks 'ere comes Pistol") was a Hal's Angel. The Chorus was a TV newscaster in sports jacket and flannels. The British army left for France, singing "Here we go!" "Fuck the Frogs!" was blazoned across banners and "Jerusalem" was played loudly over the amplifiers. It only needed Margaret Thatcher to appear and say, "Rejoice! Rejoice!"

Mar 21. Daniel Webb in Caryl Churchill's **Serious Money** directed by Max Stafford-

1987 Premieres
New York
Stephen Sondheim's *Into the Woods*
David Henry Hwang's *M Butterfly*
August Wilson's *The Piano Lesson*
Alfred Uhry's *Driving Miss Daisy*
Los Angeles
Lanford Wilson's *Burn This*

Deaths
Fred Astaire (*b.*1899), American dancer, actor
Dario Fo (*b.*1926), Italian playwright
Bob Fosse (*b.*1927), American choreographer, director
Emlyn Williams (*b.*1905), Welsh actor, playwright

Honours
Dame
Judi Dench, actor

Notes
—Theatre Museum opened
—Andrew Lloyd Webber's *Cats* won the Queen's Award for Export achievement.

History
—World population passed 5 billion
—IRA bomb Enniskillen
—Stock Exchange collapses (Black Monday)

Clark at Royal Court. This satire on city scandals, written in doggerel, relied for its laughs on four-letter words. Linda Bassett, her upper-class nose constantly puckered by the smell of corruption, played a smooth operator, who ended up as the city's watchdog. Webb's laconic performance was a dummy run for Arturo Ui. Transferred to Wyndham's.

Mar 26. Juliet Stevenson in Federico Garcia Lorca's **Yerma** directed by Di Trevis at Cottesloe (NT). Yerma thinks only of the baby-to-be, never of the husband. The sexual act disgusts her. The result is that she makes him impotent and herself yerma (the Spanish word for barren). When an old woman suggests she take a lover, she is horrified; she prefers to strangle her husband. Stevenson suggested the barren wasteland could so easily, if it were up to her, have been fertile. Roger Lloyd Pack, as her cadaverous husband, lived up to her description of "a man who looked as if he had never seen the light of day."

Apr 9. Anthony Hopkins and Judi Dench in Shakespeare's **Antony and Cleopatra** directed by Peter Hall at Olivier (NT). Who would have thought Judi Dench would play the Serpent of Old Nile? Nobody would have been amazed to see this Cleopatra hop forty paces in the market-place. Volatile, restless, witty, regal, vicious, dangerous, she, suddenly and totally unexpectedly, collapsed, ageing before the audience's eyes. Hopkins's Antony was very much the old dog who has had his day, the triple pillar of the world transformed into a bore. Michael Bryant spoke Enobarbus' description of the barge with exceptional freshness.
—It is not only the most intelligently-spoken Shakespeare I have heard in years but it also contains two performances from Judi Dench and Anthony Hopkins that, in their comprehensive humanity, rank with Ashcroft and Redgrave at Stratford many moons ago. MICHAEL BILLINGTON *Guardian*

Apr 30. Jeremy Irons in Shakespeare's **Richard II** directed by Barry Kyle at Barbican (RSC). Designer William Dudley provided a ravishingly beautiful, medieval picture based on a "Book of Hours", an ideal setting for the stylised grief of a poet-king. Irons had found far more poetry in Evelyn Waugh's prose (in his voice-overs for *Brideshead Revisited* on television) than he did in Shakespeare's verse. Even when made-up to look like Christ at his trial, he was strangely unmoving. Michael Kitchen's lightweight and very modern Bolingbroke belonged in a more traditional RSC production. His emphatic ironic delivery of practically every word made Bolingbroke far more affected than Richard. Brewster Mason's Gaunt, on his death-bed, was the healthiest-looking man in Christendom.

May 11. Roland Schafer and The Schaubuhne Company from West Berlin in Eugene O'Neill's **The Hairy Ape** directed by Peter Stein at Lyttelton (NT). The hairy ape is "a symbol of man who has lost all the harmony he used to have as an animal and has not yet acquired a new spiritual harmony." A stoker on a luxury liner is rejected by Man and Ape. His story is told in a series of expressionistic/realistic tableaux, which contrasted the brutal and brutalising existence of the poor with the vacuous existence of the rich. The play was denounced in 1922 as socialist propaganda and therefore subversive and un-American. Tucio Fanti's first act set of the luxury liner was designed so that it would seem the whole ship was on stage from the first class passenger deck right down to the hold. The passenger deck was so high up (practically in the flies) that people in the front stalls got a crick in the neck looking up. The most powerful of many striking images was the stokers feeding the voracious appetite of the roaring furnaces.

May 21. Michael Gambon in Alan Ayckbourn's **A Small Family Business** directed by Alan Ayckbourn at Olivier (NT). Satire on Thatcher's Britain when everybody is on the fiddle and shoplifting and bribery, blackmail and large-scale fraud are the norm. One man determines to run a decent, honest family furniture business. He

Masane Tsukayana and Komaki Kurihara in Macbeth

ends up taking on the role of Godfather. There was a creepy performance by Simon Cadell, totally unrecognizable as a weasel-like private investigator, who knows his worth and is eminently corruptible. His insidiousness was comically underlined by a crash of thunder every time he arrived at the front door. There was a particularly unpleasant scene when it seemed he might not only steal the cash but rape the wife as well. He was finally murdered in the bathroom. It took the audience a long time to realize that he really was dead and not just knocked-out. Some people still went on laughing. Alan Tagg's multiple set was one basic house, which served for all three different homes.
—A major playwright who possesses an unnerving and unflinching insight into the ways of the suburban world. JANE EDWARDES *Time Out*
—Confirms the playwright's status as our most ingenious stage craftsman. PETER KEMP *Independent*
—Perhaps now we can admit to a surfeit of Ayckbourn and put him out to grass where he belongs – in commercial places. NICHOLAS DE JONGH *Guardian*

Jun 23. Alan Bates in Simon Gray's **Melon** directed by Christopher Morahan at Haymarket. Suggested by Stuart Sutherland's book, *Breakdown*. High-flying, egotistical publisher, pathologically jealous, writhes on the floor, screaming and crying, when his wife refuses to identify her lover.

Jul 21. Diana Rigg, Julia McKenzie, Daniel Massey, Dolores Gray and David Healy in Stephen Sondheim's **Follies** directed by Mike Ockrent at Shaftesbury. Book by James Goldman. It took sixteen years for the musical to reach London. By then it had a completely new book and was less bleak and more optimistic. There were several new songs and musical sequences. The framework was still a reunion of ex-Follies girls - an eerie party, attended by chorus ghosts, heavily sequined and gloriously feathered. (The costumes were by Maria Björnson.) The show's climax was a tribute to Ziegfeld: a mixture of Broadway tinsel, chorus-girl charm and old-fashioned vaudeville. Dolores Gray stopped the show with an old trouper number, a defiant, "I'm Still Here!"

Aug 13. Michael Kitchen in Nick Dear's **The Art of Success** directed by Adrian

Noble at Pit (RSC). Nick Dear, relentlessly vulgar, used William Hogarth's life to make comments on sex, marriage, pornography, censorship and the artist as businessman. Kitchen gave a typical performance, the familiar whine getting lots of laughs. There were striking performances by Penny Downie as a Newgate murderess and by Dinah Stubb as a prostitute.
—*The Art of Success* began as a play about the political manipulation of art. Along the way it snowballed into a rather lurid comedy of sexual manners. At its core, though, is a debate about the nature of ambition, and the lengths to which one will go to succeed, and the degree of compromise one learns one will accept. NICK DEAR *Introduction Plays 1*

Sep 17. The Ninagawa Company from Japan with Masane Tsukayama and Komaki Kurihara in **Macbeth** directed by Yukio Ninagawa at Lyttelton (NT). The production, a series of arresting tableaux, was notable for its vocal and physical stylisation and its lush romantic Western score. The witches were beautiful drag queens. The acrobatic murder of Banquo took place under blossom and was observed through a transparent screen. The operatic grief of Macduff was played out in a hall of huge terracotta warriors in aggressive poses. Macbeth's fight with Macduff was staged in the Chinese Opera manner. Lady Macbeth was a screeching Geisha Girl who, on the night of the murder, got very drunk and behaved like a demented puppet on a string.

Sep 24. The Ninagawa Company from Japan with Tokusaburo Arashi as Medea and Masane Tsukayama as Jason in Euripides's **Medea** directed by Yukio Ninagawa at Lyttelton (NT). The all-male cast had a flamboyant theatricality. The exotic barbarity ended with Medea flying off in a dragon-winged chariot.
—We are trying to create something in between the styles of Russian theatre and European realism. We are trying to absorb from western culture and then create by criticising and breaking down what we have in traditional theatre. We are trying to create something totally new in the theatre. YUKIO NINAGAWA

Sep 30. Stephen Sondheim's musical **Pacific Overtures** directed by Keith Warner at Coliseum (ENO). Book by John Weidman. The action – America's determination to open up Japan to foreign trade – is dramatised from the Japanese point of view and written in a series of scenes rather than a continuous narrative. What should the Japanese do? Should they expel or accommodate the barbarians? The humour comes from the Shogun's ineffectuality to deal with the crisis and their reliance on the wiles of a samurai and a fisherman to foil the aggressors. The music becomes increasingly westernised as the British, the Dutch, the Russians and the French jump on the American bandwagon. There are witty pastiches of Sousa, Gilbert and Sullivan, Tchaikovsky and Offenbach. Described by Sondheim as "the most bizarre and unusual musical ever to be seen in a commercial setting" it was not a success in New York in 1976. It failed in London, too. It was meant to be a big money-earner for the cash-strapped English National Opera; but it proved too esoteric for ENO's regular audience and played to 30% capacity.

Oct 2. Maggie Smith and Margaret Tyzack in Peter Shaffer's **Lettice and Lovage** directed by Michael Blakemore at Globe. A perfectly serious theme – the greyness of life and the hideousness of modern buildings – was coated in West End whimsy. Shaffer explored the unlikely friendship between two mature women whose passion for schoolgirl charades nearly ends in decapitation. Smith played a tour-guide at the dullest stately home in England. Tyzack played the brusque, efficient personnel officer who fires her.
—When Maggie Smith performs she acts. Impeccably controlled, she shows she can detonate comedy with just a tilt of the head or momentarily heavy stare. PETER KEMP *Independent*
—She [Maggie Smith] is a civilised delight and so is the play. CHARLES OSBORNE *Daily Telegraph*

Oct 15. Tim Piggott-Smith in David Edgar's **Entertaining Strangers** directed by Peter Hall at Cottesloe (NT). It was specially written on a large scale (150+ parts) for the Dorset community and transferred to London as a promenade production. The Reverend Henry Mooule preaches a harsh and unforgiving doctrine, putting the lightest profanity on a par with murder. It takes a cholera epidemic to make him realize that the plague is not a punishment of God for the sins of his parish but the direct result of the appalling physical conditions in which the poor lived. Piggott-Smith hadn't had such a good role since he appeared as Merrick in *The Jewel in the Crown* on television. Judi Dench had the less rewarding role of Sarah Eldridge who ran the local brewery. The script, for fear of offending her descendents, did not acknowledge Eldridge had run the local brothel.

Nov 4. Jeremy Irons, David Troughton, Stephanie Beacham, Imogen Stubbs and Hugh Quarshie in Aphra Behn's **The Rover** directed by John Barton at Mermaid (RSC). Three high-born girls dress up as whores at carnival time and go off in search of husbands. The play was a crude feminist tract on the theme that "women should do as men do".

Nov 24. Richard Briers as Malvolio in Shakespeare's **Twelfth Night** directed by Kenneth Branagh at Riverside Studios. Set in a ruined graveyard in winter it only needed a few more crosses and tombs to be Highgate Cemetery. The box tree was a Christmas tree. A grandfather clock was permanently fixed at 7.50. Everybody was in mourning. The *mis-en-scene* had such a chilling effect on the comedy that there was no laughter. Briers had a splendid moment, when, his mouth tightly turned down, he informed the audience very grimly that he would smile.

Nov 25. Samuel Beckett's **Waiting for Godot** directed by Michael Rudman at Lyttelton (NT). Light-weight performances. Alec McCowen was a perky Vladimir. John Alderton was a singularly unlovable Estragon. Peter Wight was a surprisingly plump and well-fed Lucky. Terence Rigby was an unusually effete Pozzo.

Dec 5. Mark Rylance in Carlo Goldoni's **Countrymania** designed by Paul Dart and directed by Mike Alfreds at Olivier (NT). The comedy, based on the *Villeggiatura*, trilogy, was surprisingly dark for Goldoni, much nearer to Marivaux in style, and ended with three unhappy marriages. The characters are all bankrupt and marrying for dowries. Sian Thomas, as a woman, who had only her envy and her debts to recommend her, was particularly funny. The production lasted just under five hours – handsomely designed and acted at speed it didn't feel that long – but, inevitably, on weekdays it emptied the Olivier Theatre.

Dec 17. Imelda Staunton as Dorothy, Paul Greenwood as Scarecrow, John Bowe as Tinman and Jim Carter as Cowardly Lion in **The Wizard of Oz** designed by Mark Thompson and directed by Ian Judge at Barbican (RSC). Book by L Frank Baum. Music and lyrics by Harold Arlen and E Y Harburg. The Yellow Brick Road (and "Over the Rainbow") without Judy Garland is like *Hamlet* without the Prince of Denmark. To avoid comparisons with Margaret Hamilton's definitive Wicked Witch of the West, the RSC cast a man, Bille Brown, who played her as a camp-glamorous, Hollywood-star. The Muchkins were played by children, not dwarfs. Dilys Laye as the Witch of the North made the most impact.
—Was it really worth doing? Or was it in fact just a pointless, expensive exercise? CLIVE HIRSCHHORN *Daily Express*
—This is not so much a theatrical version of a film as a grovelling homage to a culture about which the British have a raging ambivalence. VICTORIA RADIN *New Statesman*

1988

Jan 21. Pauline Collins in Billy Russell's **Shirley Valentine** directed by Simon Callow at Vaudeville. Monologue. Plump 42-year-old, unhappily married, plucks up courage to go to Greece with a girl friend. She never returns. The script was sentimental only in the final stages.

Jan 28. Vanessa Redgrave, Timothy Dalton and Rudi Davies in Eugene O'Neill's **A Touch of the Poet** directed by David Thacker at Young Vic, Written in 1936, and premiered five years after his death in 1958 in Stockholm, it was the third play in a projected cycle of nine plays dealing with Irish immigrant experience in America from the Revolution to the Depression. (Only two works survive. O'Neill and his wife burned the other incomplete manuscripts.) A veteran of Wellington's Peninsula Campaign, who has fallen on hard times, runs a tawdry tavern near Boston in 1828. His military career was cut short when he shot dead a Spanish nobleman, who was the husband of the woman with whom he was having an affair. He still sees himself as an officer and a gentleman. The Americans see him as just another Irish immigrant. There is more than a touch of O'Neill in the hard-drinking and there is more than a touch of O'Neill's father in the brooding, embittered self-pity. O'Neill didn't think there were many actors up to the role. He had favoured either Spencer Tracy or Laurence Olivier. Dalton, out of his depth in the third act, imitated Olivier. Davies was impressive as the openly contemptuous daughter, but it was difficult to accept Redgrave as a stupid peasant woman.

Feb 3. Lindsay Duncan as Maggie the Cat, Ian Charleson as Brick and Eric Porter as Big Daddy in Tennessee Williams's **Cat on a Hot Tin Roof** directed by Howard Davies at the Lyttelton (NT). "Why can't exceptional friendship, real, real, deep, deep friendship between two men be respected as something clean and decent without being thought of as fairies?" asks Brick. Originally banned, and not seen in London for 32 years, the National Theatre revived the play just as Clause 28 of the Local Government Bill was about to go on the Statute Book. Clause 28 banned anything promoting homosexuality. The production used Williams's original third act, the one that had been rejected by the director Elia Kazan at its premiere in New York in 1955.

Feb 10. John Gielgud, Ray McAnnally and Rosemary Harris in Hugh Whitemore's **The Best of Friends** directed by James Roose-Evans at Apollo. A recital of letters masqueraded as a play. The friends were Sir Sydney Cockerell, Dame Laurentia McLachlan and Bernard Shaw. There was an excellent *coup de théâtre* when the first act ended with the death of the nun and Shaw writing a moving letter of condolence. The second act opened with the discovery that Shaw had made a terrible bloomer and that the nun is alive and well. Gielgud, returning to the West End stage after an

1988 World Premieres
New York
Wendy Wasserstein's *The Heidi Chronicles*
David Mamet's *Speed-the-Plow*

Notes
—Richard Eyre director of National Theatre

—National Theatre celebrates its 25th anniversary and is given the right to use the prefix Royal

History
—George Bush elected US President
—Mikhail Gorbachev elected Russian President
—Iran-Iraq War ended
—Lockerbie disaster

absence of eleven years, his charm and wit undiminished, had the least interesting role of Cockrell. There were times when he was remembering lines (and forgetting them, too) rather than speaking them.

Mar 8. Roger Rees, Felicity Kendal and Nigel Hawthorne in Tom Stoppard's **Hapgood** directed by Peter Wood at Aldwych. The British, American and Russian spy networks are all using twins. This very confusing metaphysical spy-thriller was Stoppard without puns and jokes.
—The physics in Hapgood is really not very new. Stoppard gives us physics circa 1928 couched in metaphors and rhetoric some 30 years old. Physics has moved on. TOM WILKIE *science correspondent Independent*
—His language has now succumbed to mere linguistics. The light breeziness of his earlier manner has turned to heavy weather. CHARLES OSBORNE *Daily Telegraph*
—Everything falls so flat it should have opened on Shrove Tuesday. KENNETH HURREN *Mail on Sunday*

Mar 11. Stephen Rea in Dion Boucicault's **The Shaughraun** directed by Howard Davies at Olivier (NT). Convict, having escaped from Australia, returns to Ireland to reclaim his inheritance. William Dudley was the first designer to use the Olivier's revolve and also its hydraulic machinery. The set turning, rising and falling, offering a variety of vistas, provided much of the evening's enjoyment. Rea's Shaughraun (vagabond poacher, fiddler, the soul of every fair and the life of every funeral) wore the traditional red coat and enjoyed his own wake along with everybody else.

Apr 2. Cheek by Jowl in Alexander Ostrovsky's **A Family Affair** directed by Declan Donnellan at Donmar. Donnellan's production was characteristically lively and Nick Dear's translation was characteristically vulgar. Lesley Sharp was very funny as an obnoxious daughter, keen to marry into the aristocracy. Timothy Walker was the oiliest of solicitors, who seemed to have washed his hair, his teeth and his clothes in grease. He ingratiated himself with everybody, including the audience, whom he greeted on every entrance with a weak 'hello' and every exit with a weak 'goodbye'. Marcia Warren was an amusingly inefficient matchmaker.

Apr 7. Rik Mayall, John Sessions, Stephen Fry and John Gordon Sinclair in Simon Gray's **Common Pursuit** directed by Simon Gray at Phoenix. The life of a small literary magazine and its five Cambridge founders. The play, which had already gone through a number of productions on both sides of the Atlantic, finally arrived in the West End with a cast of alternative comedians. Fry played a moral tutor who is murdered by rough trade.

Apr 21. Antony Sher in Shakespeare's **The Merchant of Venice** directed by Bill Alexander at Barbican (RSC). A Christian spat on some unidentified Jew. The spitting did not stop until the trial scene when Shylock had his revenge and spat on Antonio. Sher was a wild and exotic Shylock.
—Sher is the true chameleon actor of his generation. His Shylock is another of his fabulous alterations and surprises. NICOLAS DE JONGH *Guardian*
—As always, Antony Sher pulls out all the stops. CHARLES SPENCER *Daily Telegraph*

May 18. Anthony Sher in Cyril Tourneur's **The Revenger's Tragedy** directed by Di Trevis at Pit (RSC). The ghostly pavane by candlelight anticipated the macabre horrors to come. The plot sprung so many surprises that audiences were never certain who was going to be killed next. The finale, in which everybody is murdered one after another at lightening speed, even to the extent that murderers are being murdered as they murder, was acted for brilliant farce. Nicholas Farrell (as a bejewelled, naked, perfumed villain) was only fractionally less over the top than Sher.

May 24. Michael Gambon, Jonathan Pryce, Imelda Staunton and Greta Scacchi in Anton Chekhov's **Uncle Vanya** translated by Michael Frayn and directed by Michael Blakemore at Vaudeville. Gambon's Vanya was a mixture of slob, buffoon and bear. Pryce's Astrov was more persuasive as conservationist than as doctor. Staunton's Sonya was the finest since Joan Plowright. Scacchi turned Yelena into Marilyn Monroe.
—You can't do Uncle Vanya eight times a week for six weeks and remain sane. MICHAEL GAMBON quoted by Mel Gussow in *Gambon: A Life in Acting*

May 25. Penelope Keith and David Yelland in Terence Rattigan's **The Deep Blue**

Antony Sher as Shylock in The Merchant of Venice

Sea directed by Alan Strachan at Haymarket. It was difficult to believe that this couple had ever had an affair.

Jun 8. Wendy Hiller and Clarke Peters in Alfred Uhry's **Driving Miss Daisy** directed by Ron Lagomarsino at Apollo. Pulitzer Prize winner. Gentle, touching and fragmentary, it traced the changing relationship of a 72-year-old imperious, irascible Jewess and her black, racially patient chauffeur.

Jun 23. Alex Jennings as Glumov in Alexander Ostrovosky's **Too Clever By Half** adapted by Rodney Ackland, designed by Richard Hudson and directed by Richard Jones at Old Vic. Everything was askew. The stage was raked, the walls were slanted at an alarming angle, and the costumes and furniture were either too big or too small. The characters were grotesque in hair, teeth and limb. The actors had been chosen for their physiques rather than their acting talents. Gloumov, intelligent, malicious envious and poor, has two ambitions: one, was to get into the civil service; two, was to marry a rich woman. Chameleon-like he adopts a variety of roles, taking contemptuous advantage of a corrupt and gullible society. Jennings was excellent when Gloumov turns on his accusers and lashes out at their hypocrisy, pointing out that they all knew what they were doing and let him get away with it because they needed him.

Jun 29. Brian Cox in Shakespeare's **Titus Andronicus** directed by Deborah Warner at Pit (RSC). Cox, crusty and craggy, the best Titus since Olivier, was already in his dotage when the play started. Estelle Kohler's costumes make it difficult to take her Tamara seriously. Titus in his role of chef (*cordon noir*) made two pasties out of her dead sons. The audience roared with delight and applauded when she gobbled them up. The scene was made even more farcical by the arrival of the servants in a Hi-Ho Snow White and the Seven Dwarfs fashion, and the slices of pie being so very, very large.

Jun 29. Greek written and directed by Steven Berkoff at Wyndham's. Berkoff's re-working of the Oedipus legend ended with Oedipus deciding not to tear his eyes out and going back to live with mum, arguing that there were far worse things in the world today than having sex with your mother. Berkoff painted a picture of a septic isle, awash with chemicals and spunk, cankerous and rotten, a society living in rancid, perverted filth, up to its neck in shit, AIDS and child abuse. The violence and vulgarity of the rhetoric was unrelieved. There were some notable set-pieces, such as the description of the rats invading London and the Sphinx's long tirade against men (which was warmly applauded by feminists). The mimed fight and mimed family reunion were brilliantly orchestrated. Berkoff looked like Alf Garnett playing Hitler.

Jul 21. David Haigh as Captain Plume in George Farquhar's **The Recruiting Officer** directed by Max Stafford Clark at Royal Court. Haigh showed both the pleasant and unpleasant side of Plume, who pressed both men and women into service. Ron Cook, cast as the braggart Brazen who knows everybody, played him as an essentially lonely man who actually knows nobody. Jim Broadbent's Sergeant Kite, a professional bigamist, ranting, lying, pimping, bullying, swearing, whoring and drinking, looked like a caricature by James Gilray. Acted in repertoire with Timberlake Wertenbaker's *Our Country's Good*.

Aug 8. Rex Harrison and Edward Fox in J M Barrie's **The Admirable Crichton** directed by Frith Banbury at Haymarket. Fox, the most aristocratic of actors, was playing the butler and he took everything at a funereal pace. His performance, dry and humourless, was absurdly actorish in the third act. Harrison, playing the socialist peer, no longer had either the memory or the energy and ad-libbed. Margaret Courtenay as a formidable Edwardian mama gave the last act a lift. "I am a mother," she said in tones that recalled Lady Bracknell. It was enough to strike fear in every grown-up.

Aug 10. Gillian Barge, Zoë Wanamaker and Francesca Annis in Nicholas Wright's **Mrs Klein** directed by Peter Gill at Cottesloe (NT). Wright explored the relationship between analyst Melanie Klein and her daughter, her professional rival and implacable opponent.

Aug 25. Renaissance Theatre Company. Kenneth Branagh as Benedict and Samantha Bond as Beatrice in Shakespeare's **Much Ado about Nothing** directed by Judi Dench at Phoenix. Dench's directorial debut: the merry war was set in the Napoleonic era. Branagh and Bond were perfect foils for each other.

Aug 31. Renaissance Theatre Company. Tam Hoskyns as Rosalind and James Larkin as Orlando in Shakespeare's **As You Like It** directed by Geraldine McEwan at Phoenix. Kenneth Branagh's Touchstone was an Edwardian music hall comedian.

Sep 1. David Haigh, Jim Broadbent and Linda Bassett in Timberlake Wertenbaker's **Our Country's Good** directed by Max Stafford-Clark at Royal Court. Based on Thomas Keneally's *The Playmaker*, it told an unusual backstage story, which was set in the first penal colony in Australia in 1788/89 when all the actors were convicts. The Governor, who believed that theatre was an expression of civilisation, felt that it was his duty to educate the criminals. The officers under his command were not impressed by his humanity and did everything they could to stop the production, flogging and even hanging the cast. There was a good joke when the convicts, who were rehearsing Farquhar's *The Recruiting Officer*, complained that if they started doubling parts, the audience would become confused. It was funny because practically everybody in Wertenbaker's play was already playing two parts. The Royal Court audience, predictably, applauded the director when he snootily admonished them: "People who cannot pay attention should not go to the theatre." Acted in repertoire with George Farquhar's *The Recruiting Officer*.
—I wanted to explore the redemptive power of theatre. TIMBERLAKE WERTENBAKER
—But what makes the play work is its very assumption that drama has the capacity to change lives and liberate imaginations: in these crass times it is heartening to find someone standing up for the theatre's antique spiritual power. MICHAEL BILLINGTON *Guardian*

Sep 7. Renaissance Theatre Company. Kenneth Branagh in Shakespeare's **Hamlet** directed by Derek Jacobi at Phoenix. Elsinore was a police state. The "to be or not to be" soliloquy was addressed directly to Ophelia (Sophie Thompson).
—On the positive side Branagh has the virility of Olivier, the passion of Gielgud, the assurance of Guinness, to mention but three famous actors who have assuaged the role. On the negative side, he has not got the magnetism of Olivier, nor the mellifluous voice quality of Gielgud nor the intelligence of Guinness. MILTON SHULMAN *Evening Standard*

Sep 13. 66-year-old Mickey Rooney and 64-year-old Ann Miller in **Sugar Babies** directed and choreographed by Ernest O Flatt at Savoy. Hymn to the brashness and vulgarity of American burlesque. The old jokes and old routines were played absolutely straight.

Oct 4. Claire Higgins, Mick Ford, Penelope Wilton and Jill Baker in David Hare's **Secret Rapture** directed by Howard Davies at Lyttelton (NT). The political allegory was an attack on Thatcherism and its materialism and also a commentary on Socialism in its death-throes. Hare said he wanted to write about the intractability of goodness and how it can bring out the worst in all of us. The heroine (a character nobody has loved, except the author) was a woman of high principles who had a misplaced sense of duty. Compassionate, selfless and tolerant of evil, she never got angry and let everybody trample all over her. She allowed her small business to be taken over by corrupt capitalists who, predictably, destroyed it. She said she was not judgmental but she was always making people feel worthless. Sainthood is not an easy role to act and the play fell apart in the second act.

Oct 13. Tom Wilkinson as Thomas Stockman in Arthur Miller's version of Henrik Ibsen's **An Enemy of the People** directed by David Thacker at Young Vic. Ibsen's play was adapted to underline the evils of McCarthyism. The jokes at the expense of the moderates and the radicals were good, but Miller's insistence that Stockman should stay on and continue the heroic fight rang false. Wilkinson's performance had tremendous vigour and David Henry's villainous mayor was a formidable antagonist. Transferred to Playhouse.

Oct 13. Kathryn Hunter and Simon Burney in Maurice Valency's adaptation of Friedrich Dürrenmatt's **The Visit** produced by Theatre de Complicite at Almeida. The richest woman in the world offers a billion pounds to a bankrupt town in exchange for the murder of the man who seduced her when she was seventeen and deserted her when she was pregnant. Hunter, with her squat body, her fur-lined crutches, her high heels, her green trousers, her fur coat and her dark glasses, looked like an evil pixie. At her wedding she arrived with the longest train and moved across the stage with the slow determination of an armadillo.

Oct 20. Harold Pinter's **Mountain Language** at National Theatre. Platform performance. The military has decreed that the people, who live in the mountains, must not speak their native language any more. Four tiny scenes of brutality ended in death. The political statement was so short (18 minutes) the audience couldn't believe the play had ended.

Nov 3. Alec Guinness and Edward Herrmann in Lee Blessing's **A Walk in the Woods** directed by Ronald Eyre at Comedy. Soviet diplomat and American negotiator meet privately in a wood near Geneva to see if they can come to any agreement away from the conference table. This facile conversation piece on nuclear arms control came to the conclusion that since neither of the great powers was serious about reducing arms, the destruction of the world was inevitable and that the time up till then would be filled with interminable discussions, always ending in deadlock. The

final moments blatantly echoed *Waiting for Godot*. Guinness, relaxed and disarming, was never more in earnest than when he was being most frivolous.

Nov 16. Ian McKellen in Alan Ayckbourn's **Henceforward...** directed by Alan Ayckbourn at Vaudeville. The action was set in the future when vigilante groups are haunting the streets. People, living in no-go areas, barricade their windows with thick steel plates. McKellen was cast as a composer who is more interested in machines than people. Jane Asher's uncredited performance as the robot in the first act was so good that it was unfair that so few members of the audience realized she was playing the role. Serena Evans's silly girl was adorable.

Dec 1. Alan Bennett's **Single Spies** at Lyttelton (NT) was two plays. **An Englishman Abroad,** directed by Alan Bennett, was based on fact. Traitor Guy Burgess, in exile in Moscow, asks actress Coral Browne (who was touring in *Hamlet*) to take his measurements and buy him a suit from his tailors in Jermyn Street. **A Question of Fact**, directed by Simon Callow, imagined an encounter between Anthony Blunt and the Queen in the Long Gallery in Buckingham Palace shortly before his public exposure as a former spy. Prunella Scales's convincing impersonation of the Queen was notable for its humour, good sense and tact. Bennett caught Blunt's detachment, vanity and humourlessness perfectly.

Dec 2. Cheek by Jowl at Donmar Keith Bartlett in Sophocles's **Philoctetes** directed by Declan Donnelan. There were moments when Philoctetes was hopping around on one foot, using his bow as a crutch, which were pure Long John Silver. Neoptolemos (played by a very British, very clipped Paterson Joseph) was impressive in his decency and humanity.

Dec 13. Vanessa Redgrave and Jean-Marc Barr in Tennessee Williams's **Orpheus Descending** directed by Peter Hall at Haymarket. Xavier takes on the job of store clerk by day and stud by night. "I've lived in corruption," he says, "but I'm not corrupted." He hugs his guitar as he might hug a lover. Barr's performance was underestimated. Redgrave seemed to be giving an imitation of Melina Mercouri, and the more Italian she pretended to be, the more embarrassing she became. Paul Freeman (as her first husband's murderer) was a powerful and frightening figure, a dying man who refuses to die. The end was horrifying. He shoots Lady and screams that Xavier has murdered her. The Klu Klux Klan kill Xavier with blow-torches.
—It's blazing glory is Vanessa Redgrave – majestic and magical. Even when she is wrong, she is right. KENNETH HURREN *Mail on Sunday*

1989

Jan 10. James Laurenson in Lope de Vega's **Fuente Juveno** directed by Declan Donnellan at Cottesloe (NT). In 1476 the citizens of a village in Andalusia rose up against their feudal commander. 300 villagers, men, women and children, some as young as ten, under interrogation and torture, refused to say who had actually been responsible for his murder and with one voice replied that Fuente Juveno had killed him. The story is told in simple melodramatic terms, which allows Lope de Vega to develop two of his favourite themes. Firstly, that love, honour and revenge are not the prerogative of the nobility and secondly, that the morality of the peasant classes is often superior to that of the aristocrats who ruled them. The uprising was triggered when the commander imprisoned a groom on his wedding day and raped his bride.

Jan 11. Charles Kay and John Duttine in **The Women in Black** adapted by Stephen Mallatratt from the novel by Susan Hill and directed by Robert Herford at Lyric Theatre, Hammersmith. A highly effective spine-chilling ghost story proved a splendid exercise for the actors, the director, the designer (Michael Holt), the lighting designer (Kevin Sleep), the sound designer (Ron Mead) and of course, the audience, who were terrified out of their wits. "Go away!" they shouted when a shadowy figure reappeared at the back of the stage during the curtain-call. Transferred to the Strand and then to the Fortune and still running well into the 21st century.

Jan 25. Alfred Molina, Colin Stinton and Rebecca Pidgeon in David Mamet's **Speed-the-Plough** directed by Gregory Mosher at Lyttelton (NT). Second-rate satire on Hollywood. New head of production (Stinton) is brought a script by an old friend (Molina). The script is garbage, but commercial, and a top director is willing to direct it. Molina's body language was very funny.
—The thing about Hollywood is that you find yourself dealing with characters you would not normally want to be associated with. DAVID MAMET *quoted by* NEIL NORMAN *in the programme*

Feb 2. Juliet Stevenson in Henrik Ibsen's **Hedda Gabler** in a new version by Christopher Hampton directed by Howard Davies at Olivier (NT). Bob Crowley's absurdly large set with sweeping staircase, sweeping chimney (to belch out smoke when the manuscript is burnt) and a conservatoire (with glass to be shattered by bullet) was designed to fill the Olivier stage, but architecturally it didn't make sense, and would have been more appropriate for an operetta. Hedda was so rude and unpleasant that it was inconceivable that Tesman was not regretting the marriage as much as she was.

Mark Rylance as Hamlet

Hedda, having first taken careful aim at Brack, Thea and Tesman, shot herself in full view of the audience. The only surprise then was that Stevenson did not fall down the staircase. For what other purpose had the staircase been built?

Mar 7. Maggie Steed, Janine Duvitski, Stephanie Cole, Joley Richardson, Rosemary Harris and Jean Boht in Robert Harding's **Steel Magnolias** directed by Julia McKenzie at Lyric. Synthetic, provincial soap opera set in a beauty parlour in Louisiana.

Mar 16. Daniel Day-Lewis in Shakespeare's **Hamlet** directed by Richard Eyre at NT. Judi Dench as Gertrude. Michael Bryant was a brilliant Polonius. When Day-Lewis retired from the production early, having seen a ghost too many, Ian Charleson (who was dying from AIDS) took over and went on playing the role until his death. Jeremy Northam then played Hamlet.
—[Daniel Day-Lewis] is plaintive when he should have been sardonic, wide-eyed in his indignation when he should have been savage. He hurries into his soliloquies; and while odd phrases and lines strike home, he lacks a feeling for the flow of the verse. JOHN GROSS *Sunday Telegraph*
—Alas, poor Daniel Day-Lewis. SHAUN USHER *Daily Mail*

Mar 16. Ralph Fiennes as Henry, Anton Lesser as Richard, Penny Downie as Margaret in **The Plantagents** adapted from *Henry VI Parts 1,2,3* and *Richard III* directed by Adrian Noble at Barbican (RSC). The scene at the conference table was acted for high comedy with everybody wondering who was next for the chop. Hastings's head

was served up on a platter along with the sandwiches. Coronation day found Richard perched on his throne like an unfriendly chimpanzee. At Bosworth Richmond ran his spear through Richard's hump. Joanne Pearce's Joan of Arc in her slip and hair bands looked like a street urchin playing Peter Pan. Simon Dormandy's Richmond, a knight in shining armour, was straight out of *Where The Rainbow Ends*.

Apr 17. Ann Crumb and Michael Ball in Andrew Lloyd Webber's musical **Aspects of Love** directed by Trevor Nunn at Prince of Wales. Lyrics by Don Black and Charles Hart. 17-year-old boy falls in love with an actress who marries his old uncle. Fifteen years later he falls in love with their daughter and Love (as the song says) changes everything. David Garnett's novel was given the full West End miked treatment when what the story really needed was something more intimate.

Apr 20. Anthony Hopkins and G G Goel in David Henry Hwang's **M. Butterfly** directed by John Dexter at Shaftesbury. The true story was based on a French diplomat who had an affair with a star of the Chinese Opera for twenty years without realising that he was a man. The banal script did not become interesting until late in the second act when Butterfly took off all his make-up and stripped naked to reveal his true gender. The diplomat, claiming that he had known she was a man all the time, then dressed up as Butterfly and killed himself. The tragedy was meant to be grotesque; but it shouldn't have been so grotesque as to recall Denis Quilley in drag in Peter Nichols's *Privates on Parade*. Hopkins was strangely unmoving.
—What matters is Hopkins's failure to master even a semblance of infatuation. The evening's rare hints of sensuality come from Goel, who makes a strong professional debut. JIM HILEY *Listener*

Apr 27. Alex Jennings in Joshua Sobol's **Ghetto** directed by Nicholas Hytner at Olivier (NT). The ghetto was in Vilna and Sobol observed the activities of a theatre troupe. Jennings was cast as the smiling, boyish SS officer, a connoisseur of art, who carries a machine-gun in one hand and a saxophone in the other. He encourages the actors and watches with delight a satirical revue number based on Shylock's "I am a Jew" diatribe acted by a chorus of Hitlers. He then lines them up and just when they (and the audience) think he is going to shoot them, he gives them buns and jam. It is only when they are eating that he has them machine-gunned. There were interesting performances by Jonathan Cullen as a ventriloquist and Linda Kerr Scott as his dummy, who said what she thought.

May 8. Eileen Atkins in Virginia Woolf's **A Room of One's Own** adapted and directed by Patrick Garland at Hampstead. Woolf turned two lectures on Women and Fiction she had given in Cambridge in 1928 into an essay, which became an instant classic feminist text, quickly selling over ten thousand copies. She had once been refused entry to a university library, simply because she was a woman. She described the extraordinary difficulty the women had had in raising a mere £30,000 for Girton College. The money was only enough money for the bricks and mortar and left nothing for anything else. Intelligent, eloquent, urbane, slyly witty, Atkins could have been Virginia Woolf.

Jun 1. Dustin Hoffmann in Shakespeare's **The Merchant of Venice** directed by Peter Hall at Phoenix. Hall recommended the role of Shylock as "a wonderfully economic part for someone going into Shakespeare for the first time." Hoffmann, vocally and physically limited, was so unshowy, so low-keyed, that there was no performance. The depth he usually brought to his film roles was missing. The biggest laugh was when Portia (Geraldine James) asked if Antonio could have a surgeon and Shylock, with a shrug and a wink to the Duke, said he couldn't find it in the bond. The line got a round of applause.
—Hoffmann is a light-weight characterisation, small of stature, he allows himself to be not only physically but also dramatically overshadowed by both Antonio and Bassanio in the first scene which he plays non-assertively and smilingly against the lines. CHARLES OSBORNE *Daily Telegraph*
—[Dustin Hoffmann] is the smallest person on stage and yet he seems the biggest. That is real presence for you. MAUREEN PATON *Daily Express*

Jun 22. Steppenwolf Theatre Company. Gary Sinise as Tom Joad, Lois Smith as Ma Joad and Terry Kinney as Jim Casy, the preacher, in John Steinbeck's **The Grapes of Wrath** adapted and directed by Frank Galati at Lyttelton (NT). Steinbeck's unforgettable indictment of the American Depression years continues to haunt the imagination. In much the same way that a cart dominated Brecht's *Mother Courage* so the Joad's jalopy dominated Steppenwolf's production. The final scene with the rain beating down and Rose of Sharon giving birth to a stillborn child and then giving suck to a dying man had extraordinary power.

Jun 27. Jeremy Northam and David Burke as son and father in Harley Granville Barker's **The Voysey Inheritance** directed by Richard Eyre at Cottesloe (NT). The father despises his son's scruples. Eyre gave the play a handsome, intimate production, which matched Barker's detailed and witty stage directions. Northam was excellent. Burke, full of angry self-justification, was a persuasive Shavian rogue. Robert Swann managed to contain Major Booth Voysey, a caricature of a pompous, stupid, bullying, bristling, booming bore.

Miss Saigon, the spectacular metamorphosis of Madame Butterfly

Jul 4. Elaine Page, Bernard Cribbins and Howard McGillin in Cole Porter's musical **Anything Goes** directed by Jerry Zaks at Prince Edward. Original book by P G Wodehouse and Guy Bolton and Howard Lindsay and Russell Crouse. The new book by Timothy Crouse and John Weidman was as silly as the old, full of laboured jokes and situations. Michael Smuin's choreography stopped the show twice, but what the production really needed was Ethel Merman. The company's diction was simply not crisp enough to over-ride the noisy, non-period orchestrations.

Aug 3. Jim Broadbent in Georges Feydeau's **A Flea in Her Ear** directed by Richard Jones at Old Vic. The farce was turned into a study of sexual impotence you might find in Krafft-Ebing's case-studies in *Aberrations of Sexual Life*. The situation of an eminently respectable solicitor being mistaken for the hall-porter of an infamous brothel was turned into a nightmare. Feydeau, who prized realism above all else and wanted his actors to play in a simple, everyday style, which emphasized the tedious banality of the characters' lives, would have been appalled. The brothel scene was designed in a high-German expressionistic style. The result was a darker, sinister, madder, syphilitic play. Feydeau was acted as if he were Wedekind. Broadbent, who was more convincing as the stupid hall-porter than he was as the solicitor, stood in front of a drop-curtain (which looked like a stained mattress) and was subjected to the mocking laughter of an unseen audience. Even the curtain was raised in a provocative way – as if a woman was lifting her skirt.

Aug 9. Willard White and Ian McKellen in Shakespeare's **Othello** directed by Trevor Nunn at Young Vic (RSC). White's dignified, powerful, thoughtful performance was a remarkable achievement for an opera singer who had never acted in Shakespeare before. McKellen's hard-bitten, malign Iago, a Strindbergian sergeant-major, stiff-backed and North-Country accented, was obviously psychotic. Imogen Stubbs was a delightful Desdemona. Zoë Wanamaker was an attractive Emilia, who had married beneath her. It seemed most unlikely that Venetian Senate would have put Sean Baker's Cassio in charge of Cyprus. Nunn added one excellent extraneous joke:

the locked drawer of Desdemona's writing bureau does not hide, as Othello believes, Cassio's love letters, but a box of her favourite chocolates.
—McKellen's devilish, amoral Iago has brought a new dimension of paranoiac evil to the role. MILTON SHULMAN *Evening Standard*

Sep 7. Trevor Eve in Luigi Pirandello's **Man, Beast and Virtue** directed by William Gaskill at Cottesloe (NT). Schoolteacher has made his mistress, a married woman, pregnant. To save her reputation, the baby must seem to be her husband's. The difficulty is that the husband, a seafaring man (and bigamist) won't sleep with his wife on his rare visits home. Trevor Eve, as the desperate schoolteacher, gave a manic performance worthy of Feydeau.

Sep 14. Moscow Arts Theatre. Innokenti Smoktunovsky as Vanya and Oleg N Yefremov as Astrov in Chekhov's **Uncle Vanya** directed by Oleg Y Yefremov at Lyttelton (NT). The production was cinematic, naturalistic, symbolic, sombre and low-key. The set, wrapped in mist, was huge and included the whole estate.
—Elegiac and entertaining, forlorn and mellow, Chekhov's great tragic-comedy of torpor is, in this production, wonderfully vivified. PAUL TAYLOR *Independent*

Sep 18. Christian Robert as Dr Prospero in Bob Carlton's **Return to the Forbidden Planet** at Cambridge. Great Balls of Fire and rock 'n' roll. The cult hilt was based on the 1956 B movie, which was distantly related to Shakespeare's *The Tempest*. Prospero was a mad scientist. Ariel (Craig Thornber) was a robot on skates. Cookie, the spaceship's cook, has a crush on Miranda (Alison Harding). Devitt, a funky singer and guitarist, sang "Only the Lonely". *Time Out* advised their readers to wear earplugs and prepare to dance in the aisles. "Best rock and roll in town," said *The Daily Express*. "The space low of intergalactic drivel," said *The Guardian*.

Sep 20. Jonathan Pryce, Lea Salonga and Simon Bowman in Alain Boubil and Claude-Michel Schönberg's musical **Miss Saigon** designed by John Napier and directed by Nicholas Hytner at Drury Lane. Lyrics by Richard Maltby Jr and Alain

1989 World Premieres
New York
Tina Howe's *Approaching Zanzibar*

Deaths
Samuel Beckett (*b.*1906), Irish playwright
Daphne du Maurier (*b.*1907), British playwright, novelist
Anthony Quayle (*b.*1913), British actor, director

Laurence Olivier (*b.*1907), British actor, director
Armand Salacrou (*b.*1899), French playwright
Tommy Trinder (*b.*1909), British comedian

History
—Demolition of Berlin Wall
—Tiananmen Square demonstration and massacre
—Hillsborough Stadium disaster

Boubil. *Miss Saigon* was *Madam Butterfly* transferred to Vietnam but there were no acknowledgements to either John Luther Long or Puccini. The sound of helicopters as the house lights dimmed brought back memories of *Apocalypse Now!* The opening scene in a sleazy bar teeming with GIs and prostitutes was so old-fashioned it brought back memories of *The World of Suzie Wong*. There was always a chance the chorus might sing "There's Nothing Like A Dame". The strength of the book was that it took the sergeant's moral responsibility to his mistress and their child seriously. The show aspired to grand opera and in its more melodramatic moments when Good (with a revolver) and Evil (with a knife) confronted each other the production recalled 19th-century theatre. The big number was that frantic evacuation by helicopter from the American Embassy with the GIs in the compound and the girls outside the wire mesh, a scene to bring back memories of *The Killing Fields*. The march past with flying flags, twirling streamers and martial acrobatics was Chinese Opera. Pryce was a resourceful 20th-century Pandarus, trying to wangle an exit visa; he sees the prostitute and her child as his passport to America. Pryce had the show-stopping number, "The American Dream", a cynical hymn to materialism and Broadway kitsch. The Statue of Liberty arrived in a solid gold Cadillac. *Miss Saigon* ran for ten years.
—I did a lot of research and I found that people in Saigon at that time did, in fact, sing everything. Jonathan Pryce quoted by *Independent*

Sep 21. John Wood and Joanne Pearce in Henrik Ibsen's **The Master Builder** directed by Adrian Noble at Barbican (RSC). When Wood walked on in his top hat, carrying two enormous scrolls, he looked like Mr. Hyde (of Dr Jekyll fame). Never for one moment did he look like Solness, the master builder. Pearce's idealistic, egotistical Hilde Wangel was very much a modern young miss.

Oct 6. Dorothy Tutin in Stephen Sondheim's musical **A Little Night Music** directed by Ian Judge transferred from Chichester Festival to Piccadilly. Book by Hugh Wheeler. Tutin was stylish, witty and sensual. "Send in the Clowns" was the high spot. Lila Kedrova had great difficulty getting her words out.

Oct 9. Yukio Ninagawa Company in Matsuyo Akimoto's **Suicide for Love** at Lyttelton (NT). An adaptation of two puppet plays by Monzaemon Chikamatsu. Two suicide pacts: one comic, the other tragic. The knockabout comedy, set among reeds and bull-rushes, played out against a huge panda-faced moon, was hilarious. The tragedy, which took place in a raging blizzard and acted against a blood-red sun, was lyrical, beautifully lit and almost balletic. The geisha was strangled by her lover with a long red scarf.

Oct 12. Paul Hipp in Alan Janes's **Buddy** directed by Rob Bettinson at Victoria Palace. The musical life of Buddy Holly: the man, the music and the legend. Here was the acceptable face of rock 'n roll: no sex, no drugs, no booze. The show was nostalgic, not biographic. Hit songs included "That'll be the Day", "Well All Right" and "Peggy Sue." Paul Hipp was a very convincing lookalike.

Oct 17. Julia Ormond in Ödön von Horváth's **Faith, Hope and Charity (a little dance of death)** translated by Christopher Hampton and directed by Heribert Sasse at Lyric, Hammersmith. Bleak and bitter comment on a cynical society, which cheats, exploits, betrays and abandons its people whose only crime is to be poor and unemployed. "The best thing you can do is to go home and throw yourself out of the window," is the advice of one doctor. Set in the early 1930s and based on a true story, it begins with an out-of-work salesgirl trying to sell her body (after she is dead) to science in order to get some money to buy the permit she needs to get a job. The play ends with her suicide, when, of course, science will get her corpse for free. Sasse, who had produced the play in German in Berlin, got a remarkably convincing Germanic response from the English actors. George Grosz and Otto Dix would have recognised Pamela Cundell's underwear-retailer, fat, squat woman with a cigarette permanently dangling from her mouth. Horváth described his ninety-minute political tract as 'a little dance of death' and it was no surprise to learn that the Nazis had banned it even before it was performed. Ormond was outstanding: rebellious and vulnerable at the same time, her bright, brave, nervous little smile was heartbreaking.

Oct 18. Peter O'Toole in Keith Waterhouse's **Jeffrey Bernard is Unwell** directed by Ned Sherrin at Apollo. The script was based on the life and writings of Jeffrey Bernard, who, when he was not in hospital, spent his days in pub, betting-office and race-track, living for the most part in an alcoholic and diabetic coma. John Gunter's set re-created the Coach and Horses, as seen through Bernard's eyes. The pub, lurching all over the place, was as drunk as he was.

Oct 23. Nigel Hawthorne as C S Lewis and Jane Lapotaire as Joy Davidson in William Nicholson's **Shadowlands** directed by Elijah Moshinsky at Queen's. Oxford don, a confirmed bachelor, marries American poet, a marriage of convenience so she could live in England. She then dies of cancer.

Oct 25. Clarke Peters, Hugh Quarshie and Carol Woods-Coleman in August Wilson's **Ma Rainey's Black Bottom** directed by Howard Davies at Lyttelton (NT). Wilson's indictment of the economic exploitation of black performers in the 1920s was the latest in his series of plays covering black history. Rainey and her jug-band come to the studios to record "Black Bottom". The record company wants her to sing an up-dated jazzy version, aimed at a white market. She wants to sing her old Blues version and being Ma Rainey she gets her way.

Oct 31. Denholm Elliott and Samuel West in David Mamet's **A Life in the Theatre** directed by Bill Bryden at Haymarket. Mamet explores the relationship between an older and younger actor back stage and on stage. A ravaged-looking Elliott immediately and wittily established the vanity and insecurity of the older actor on the skids. What was missing was the sub-text, the undeclared homosexuality.

Nov 7. Katharine Schlesinger as Salome and Steven Berkoff as Herod in Oscar Wilde's **Salome** directed by Steven Berkoff at Lyttelton (NT). Wilde's study in sexual frustration was given the full hypnotic, narcotic treatment to a tinkling piano accompaniment. Everything was stylised, every movement was in slow motion and every line was clearly enunciated to the very last languorous syllable. Berkoff gave an extraordinary display of verbal gymnastics, matching Wilde's absurdly self-conscious, ornate language. Schlesinger mimed the dance of the seven veils and, without removing any clothing, persuaded a hushed audience that she was standing there totally naked. The audience on the seventh veil lent forwards to see better. The soldiers were turned into a chorus of Bright Young Things.
—For all its virtuosity and visual excellence, *Salome* seems hollow at heart and no amount of brilliance can disguise the inadequacies of the play itself Kate Kellaway *Observer*

Nov 28. Cheek by Jowl at Almeida. Sally Dexter in Declan Donnellan's **Lady Betty** with music by Paddy Cunneen directed by Declan Donnellan. A true story. When the hangman of Roscommon Gaol absconded in 1780 and nobody was willing to hang Captain Flynn, Betty (who was about to be hanged herself for the murder of her child) offered to hang him in return for her life. She became Roscommon's executioner for the next thirty years and never left the gaol. What gave Donnellan's production its bite was the ballad-like vigour of the text, the aggression of the actors, the harsh singing, the Irish dancing, and Dexter's passion as Betty.

Dec 7. Alex Jennings as Dorante in Pierre Corneille's **The Liar** translated by Ranjit Bolt and directed by Jonathan Miller at Old Vic. The comedy of amorous stratagems and mistaken identities set in Paris in 1643 was given a superficial production. Dorante is the consummate liar, a callow, young, provincial lawyer, in search of a good time, trying to pass himself off as a courtier.

1990–1999

1990

Jan 4. Glenda Jackson as Galactia, Kevin McNally as her lover, Ralph Nossek as Cardinal and Jonathan Hyde as Doge in Howard Barker's **Scenes from an Execution** directed by Ian McDiarmid at Almeida. Barker satirized the dangers of sponsorship for sponsor and sponsored alike. Galactia, the most brilliant painter in Venice, is commissioned by the Doge to paint the Battle of Lepanto, the greatest triumph in Venetian history. She refuses to celebrate the power and glory of military Christian might and paints what actually happened in all its violence and mutilation. Doge and Cardinal are not pleased, seeing her "screaming truth" as a calculated and obscene affront to the state.

Jan 26. Phil Daniels in Anthony Burgess's **A Clockwork Orange** written in collaboration with Ron Daniels and directed by Ron Daniels at Barbican (RSC). Not a patch on either the book or the Stanley Kubrick film.

Feb 6. Oliver Ford Davies, Richard Pasco, Michael Bryant and David Bamber in David Hare's **Racing Demons** directed by Richard Eyre at Cottesloe (NT). Debate on the Church of England and the reasons for its decline. The rector in a poor London borough neglects the spiritual needs of his parish. When his bishop decides to sack him the rector threatens to take the bishop to court for wrongful dismissal. The rector, a bad priest in the eyes of his superiors, is patently a good man. His bishop, steeped in the rituals of his office and fiercely outspoken against the ordination of women, is cast as the villain.
—Not since the epilogue to Shaw's *Saint Joan* have we had such a spirited debate about church versus state. It is in the very best sense a moral thriller. SHERIDAN MORLEY *Herald Tribune*

Feb 14. Michael Gambon and Peter Bowles in Alan Ayckbourn's **Man of the Moment** directed by Alan Ayckbourn at Globe. Modern morality play satirized the media's and the public's preference for villains rather than heroes. A television presenter engineers a meeting between a famous robber and a once-famous bank clerk who "had a go" and is now totally forgotten. His foolhardy bravery resulted in the terrible disfigurement of a beautiful bank clerk when the robber's gun went off in her face. The former criminal is now a best-selling author and TV personality, living in a luxurious villa in Spain. The bank clerk is beholden to him for without the disfigurement the clerk would never have married him.

Feb 23. Claire Bloom and Espen Skjonberg in Henrik Ibsen's **When We Dead Awaken** translated by David Rudkin and directed by Jonathan Kent at Almeida. World-famous sculptor feels guilty that he chose Fame rather than Happiness, Art rather than Life. The casting of a Norwegian actor who had difficulty with the English language was not a good idea.

Mar 15. Philip Quast and Maria Friedman in Stephen Sondheim's musical **Sunday in the Park with George** designed by Tom Cairns and directed by Steven Pimlott at Lyttelton (NT). Book by James Lapine. The stage is a living canvas based on Seurat's *Un Dimanche d'tete a L'ile de la Grande Jette*. The relationship between artist and his imagined mistress/model (wittily called Dot) is not nearly as interesting as the relationship between artist and canvas. Sondheim's score complements Seurat's pointillism. Critical reaction ranged from "a collector's item worthy of the National" and "well worth seeing twice" to "banal" and "undramatic and dull."
—Two and a half hours geared to actors playing statues and statues standing in for humans has something to say about the arid self-regard of the Sondheim phenomenon and its adherents. MARTIN HOYLE *Financial Times*
—It does not set the pulse racing, the heart dancing or the feet tapping. DAVID NATHAN *Jewish Chronicle*

Mar 21. An Evening with Peter Ustinov at Haymarket. Master raconteur and master mimic imitated all the voices and all the instruments in a parody of a Bach cantata.

May 23. Richard Harris in Luigi Pirandello's **Henry IV** directed by Val May at Wyndham's. "I'm so bloody bored with all this," said Henry and Harris meant it. There was no inter-action between him and the rest of the cast.
—Made up to look like Worzel Gummidge, the actor dispatches the character's facile philosophising energetically enough for most of the play's length, but to little effect. CHARLES OSBORNE *Daily Telegraph*

Sunday in the Park

1990 World Premieres
New York
John Guare's *Six Degrees of Separation*
August Wilson's *Two Trains Running*
Dublin
Brian Friel's *Dancing at Lughnasa*

Notes
—Financial crisis closed the Barbican from Nov 1990 to March 1991
—The Three Tenors in Rome

—Adrian Noble succeeded Terry Hands as artistic director of the RSC
—Fire destroyed Savoy Theatre
—West Yorkshire Playhouse, Leeds, opened

History
—Margaret Thatcher resigned
—Iraq invaded Kuwait
—Nelson Mandela released from prison
—Demolition of Berlin Wall
—Reunification of Germany

May 24. David Sumner, Sara Mair-Thomas and Paul Mooney in Lope de Vega's **Punishment Without Revenge** directed by Laurence Boswell at Gate. The Duke of Ferrara, a reformed libertine, returning from the Holy Wars, discovers that in his absence his young wife has been sleeping with his illegitimate son and determines to kill him. The question is how to do it without compromising his honour. Cunningly, he tricks his son into killing his wife and then has him executed for murder. The tragic irony is that the Duke loves his son far more than his wife.

May 31. Tom Wilkinson and Zoë Wanamaker in Arthur Miller's **The Crucible** directed by Howard Davies at Olivier (NT). Wilkinson, in a performance of great physical and moral strength, carried the play to its terrible conclusion. Oliver Cotton was the unloved Reverend Parris. David Burke was the Reverend Hale, disintegrating scene by scene, realising too late that the accuser is not always holy. Paul Shelley was an unexpectedly foppish Judge Danforth.

Jun 7. Rosalind Knight as the Magician in Pierre Corneille's **The Illusion** directed by Richard Jones at Old Vic. Designer Nigel Lowery played tricks with scenic perspective. The chief pleasures were the splendid visions and the amplified sound effects. The so-called 'marvels' put the actors in a very subordinate role. The soldier-braggart, whose conquests on the field of battle are as illusory as his conquests in bed, is one of the theatre's oldest jokes; but Phelim McDermott was not helped by putting him into red underwear and briefs made of chain-mail.

Jun 7. Natasha Richardson in Eugene O'Neill's **Anna Christie** directed by David Thacker at Young Vic. Chris Christopherson (John Woodvine) emerged as the leading tragic character, challenging that "dirty old devil, the sea" whom he blames for all his troubles. There was a thrilling moment when the strapping Irish stoker (David Herlihy) claims Anna as his bride. "Just an old-fashioned melodrama," said Kenneth Hurren in *The Mail on Sunday*. O'Neill wouldn't have denied it. "In moments of great stress," he said, "life copies melodrama."

Jun 20. James Laurenson and Josette Simon in Arthur Miller's **After the Fall** directed by Michael Blakemore at Cottesloe (NT). Miller re-worked his political and marital dilemmas. When the play was first produced many people objected to him washing his dirty linen in public. In order that nobody should think that the heroine was Marilyn Monroe, Blakemore cast a black actress. It didn't make her any less Monroe. Simon still sounded and behaved like Monroe. There were two sides to the character: the innocent, trusting, carefree side; and the crude, self-destructive side, ending in suicide. Simon was never able to reconcile the two sides and make them seem one person. It was also difficult to believe that this particular lawyer, however liberal, would be having an affair with a black woman in the 1950s.

Jul 11. John Malkovich and Juliet Stevenson in Lanford Wilson's **Burn This** directed by Robert Allan Ackerman at Lyric. Manhattan love affair moved to a predictable bust-up and then opted for an unlikely sentimental reunion. Malkovich, in a splendid long-haired black wig, gave a larger-than-life performance. Lou Liberatore as a gay flat-mate had the best lines.

Jul 19. The Cusack theatrical dynasty in a new version of Anton Chekhov's **Three Sisters** by Frank McGuinness directed by Adrian Noble transferred from The Gate Theatre, Dublin, to Royal Court. Sorcha as Olga. Niamh as Irina. Sinead as Masha. Cyril as Chebutykn. Barry Lynch as Tuzenbach. Nicky Henson as Vershinin. Irina (with her spectacles and her hair tied back severely) looked much older and far less attractive than Tuzenbach.

Jul 25. Ian McKellen in Shakespeare's **Richard III** directed by Richard Eyre at Lyttelton (NT). The action was updated to Mosley's black-shirted England. Richard in an army greatcoat spoke the opening soliloquy in the clipped tones of Sandhurst. He was a tense, bible-carrying officer, moving in for the kill with military intelligence and without humour (or indeed much of a limp.) He was a 20th-century mass-murderer, who took no theatrical delights in his villainy. The production only faltered when Richard, addressing the citizens of London

through a microphone, turned into Hitler, a straight crib from Bertolt Brecht's *Arturo Ui*.
—McKellen offers us not a charismatic Richard but a beautifully executed study of the banality of evil. MICHAEL BILLINGTON *Guardian*
—It's not subtle but neither was Hitler. MAUREEN PATON *Daily Express*
—For much of the time I felt that his performance would have been enhanced by being set to the music of Offenbach. CHARLES SPENCER *Daily Telegraph*

Jul 26. Brian Cox in Shakespeare's **King Lear** directed by Deborah Warner at Lyttelton (NT). The division of the kingdom was a hoot: a Christmas charade with Lear and his daughters in paper hats playing party games and the map of England cut up with scissors. Cox's Lear was old and foolish from the very beginning, a shuffling, bumbling, vulnerable little man, given to bouts of rage. The grubby costumes looked as if they have come out of a dustbin rather than a wardrobe. There was no adjustment to the Lyttelton's proscenium stage. Warner and her designer, Hildegard Bechtler, might have been working in a fringe studio.
—Cox is both wonderful and curiously dull. It is something to do with lack of spiritual and intellectual energy at the core of this production. MICHAEL COVENEY *Observer*

Jul 26. Iain Glen in Arthur Miller's **The Man Who Had All the Luck** directed by Paul Unwin at Young Vic. Miller has described the play as the obverse of the Book of Job. It flopped on Broadway in 1944, closing after only four performances. Adapted from an aborted novel, the setting was a small town in the Mid-west in the late 1930s and early 1940s. A nice, conscientious mechanic gets all that he wants. Everything falls into his lap; so much so that be becomes ashamed and afraid of his luck. He waits all his days for the catastrophe that never comes. He even wills the death of his unborn child and the bankruptcy of his business, so desperately does he want to be a failure like everybody else.

Aug 7. Derek Jacobi in Jean-Paul Sartre's **Kean or disorder and genius** based on a play by Alexandre Dumas, translated by Frank Hauser, and directed by Sam Mendes at Old Vic. The extravagant and absurd romanticism was camp rather than passionate. Sarah Woodward was the imperturbable Miss Danby, determined to marry Kean and put some order into his disordered life. Eleanor David was very stylish as the Danish ambassador's wife. The centrepiece was a benefit performance of the last act of *Othello* at Drury Lane, which began in farce (Desdemona forgetting her lines, begging to be smothered), moved to a stand-up row with the Prince of Wales in the royal box ("Everywhere else you are Prince but here I am King") and ended in unexpected pathos when Kean admitted that, outside of his roles, he did not exist.

Aug 8. Stephen Rea, Penelope Wilton, Oliver Cotton, Philip Voss and Stephen Moore in Trevor Griffiths's **Piano** directed by Howard Davies at Cottesloe (NT). Based on the first act of Anton Chekhov's *Platonov* and N Mikhalkov and A Adabashian's film, *Unfinished Piece for Mechanical Piano*. It acted more like a play by Maxim Gorky than a play by Chekhov. Platonov (acted with shaggy, manic charm by Stephen Rea), thrashed about helplessly in middle age, haranguing everybody, and most of all himself. The piano was played beautifully by a peasant to the shock and outrage of the ruling classes, until they discovered their hostess had played a little joke on them and the peasant couldn't really play. It was a mechanical piano. The political message was clear enough: peasants would play pianos in the future and the ruling classes would go.

Sep 19. Joan Collins, Keith Baxter, Sara Crowe and Edward Duke in Noël Coward's **Private Lives** directed by Tim Luscombe at Aldwych. Collins was acted off the stage by Crowe, who, at the time, was best known for her appearances in a cream-cheese TV commercial.

Sep 25. Julia McKenzie, Imelda Staunton, Patsy Rowlands, Clive Carter and Nicholas Parsons in Stephen Sondheim's musical **Into the Woods** directed by Richard Jones at Phoenix. Book by James Lapine. Set by Richard Hudson. Costumed by Sue Blane. The musical was unexpectedly bleak and dark. Four classic fairy tales – *Cinderella, Jack and the Beanstalk, Little Red Riding Hood* and *Rapunzel* – were held together by an original story about a baker and his barren wife, who are sent to find a red cape, a silver shoe, a cow, and a strand of yellow hair. The wolf is split open and the ugly sisters have their toes and heels cut off. People are trampled to death by a terrifying, unseen giant. It was perfectly Grimm, a far cry from the usual English traditional family Christmas pantomime, and not for the squeamish. Clive Carter was splendid as a carnal wolf ("Hello, Little Girl – There's no possible way to describe what you feel/ When you're talking to your meal") and he also played the priggish, philandering, hair-blown Prince ("I was brought up to be charming", he tells Cinderella, "not sincere"). Tessa Burbridge was very funny as Red Riding Hood, played as a precocious brat who makes a fur cape out of the wolf's skin. The biggest laugh and the biggest round of applause came when Nicholas Parsons (very smug in his role of Narrator) was about to be sacrificed to the giant and asked who was going to tell the story and the witch replied, "Some of us don't like the way you've been telling it." The applause was for the way Julia McKenzie delivered the line, many feeling she was not speaking in character but on behalf of the cast and the audience.

—It is an unmitigated triumph. A most marvellous marriage of incorrigible imagination, visual and vocal, and heavenly casting. JACK TINKER *Daily Mail*

—[Stephen Sondheim] is reviled by those who want the musical to stay nice and cosy and mindless, even if it dies on its feet. JIM HILEY *Listener*

—Rewrite fairy tales? Hell! There's more wit, drama, and more sexual ambiguity in your average Christmas pantomime. RHODA KOENIG *Punch*

Oct 25. Five Guys Named Moe directed and choreographed by Charles Augins at Stratford East. A celebration of Louis Jordan's music by Clarke Peters. The Moes were sung, danced and acted by five fast-talking, fast-moving, sassy dudes. Big Moe (Kenny Andrews) sang "What's The Use Of Getting Sober When You Are Going To Get Drunk Again?" Little Moe (Paul J Medford) liked women at least three times his size and fat. Four Eyed Moe (Clarke Peters), disguised as a fox disguised as a fowl, assured everybody that there was "nobody here but us chickens."

Oct 15. Abbey Theatre, Dublin. Rosaleen Linehan, Brid Ni Neachtain, Catherine Byrne, Stephen Dillane, Brid Brennan and Alec McCowen in Brian Friel's **Dancing at Lughnasa** directed by Patrick Mason at Lyttelton (NT). Dedicated to five brave women and based on Friel's early childhood experiences in a village in County Donegal in 1936 when he was seven-years-old and brought up by his mother and aunts. There was a memorable scene when the aunts' pent-up longing for men, sex, life itself was allowed to let rip in a dance, which was more primitive than any Harvest Festival dance to Lugh, the Celtic god.

—Rich with atmosphere, redolent with an admittedly equivocal nostalgia, this dramatically unresolved play has a heady appeal, unfolding like a slow smooch to the music of time. CLAIRE ARMISTEAD *Financial Times*

Nov 14. The Contemporary Legend Theatre from Taiwan, Republic of China. Vu Hsing-kuo and Wei Hai-ming in Lee Huci-min's **The Kingdom of Desire** directed by Wujing-iji at Lyttelton (NT). A Peking Opera adaptation of Shakespeare's *Macbeth* combined Chinese and Western theatrical traditions and presented a series of colourful tableaux, each scene sharply divided from the other by a drop of the curtain. The final battle scene, with an unseen advancing army terrifying Macbeth's troops, ended with Macbeth flipping down from a five-foot high platform and falling dead on his back.

Dec 11. The Redgrave theatrical dynasty in Anton Chekhov's **Three Sisters** directed by Robert Sturua at Queen's. Vanessa as Olga. Lynn as Masha. Jemma as Irena. Histrionic, volatile and raw, the actresses acted with a total lack of physical restraint. Lynn's strapping, chain-smoking Masha wore a big floppy hat and behaved as if she'd been to Moscow and Paris and had had a really good time. "I'll stay to lunch," she said, ready to gobble up Vershinin (Stuart Wilson). The production did not end with Olga's great anguished speech but with the sisters singing "Aupres de ma blonde!"

—Strident, cacophonous, clamorous, clashing, discordant, grating, harsh, jangling, jarring, loud, rasping, raucous, screeching, shrill, stridulant, stridulous, unmusical. There are times when only the thesaurus will do and *Three Sisters* is one of them. Not a single bunch of adjectives can exhaust the horrors of this much heralded Redgrave production. JOHN GROSS *Sunday Telegraph*

Dec 12. Griff Rhys Jones as Toad in Kenneth Grahame's **The Wind in the Willows** designed by Mark Thompson and directed by Nicholas Hytner at Olivier (NT). Alan Bennett's adaptation matched the good nature and affection of the original. Hytner's gentle and atmospheric production took advantage of the Olivier stage. The revolving centre circle and its drum, rising and falling, represented the meadow and its burrows. The outer revolving circle served for the river, road and railway-line. Mole was an old-fashioned Northern schoolboy, a perpetual student, heading for the Poly down the road. David Bamber caught Moley's innocence, goodness and sheer joy in his new-found friendship. Richard Briers's Rat was an ex-naval officer in blazer, who tucked his long tail in his pocket. Michael Bryant, totally unrecognisable and amazingly large, was Badger. The lugubrious, Tennyson-reading cart-horse, Albert (a Wolverhampton cousin of A A Milne's Eeyore, who liked his carrots in a cream sauce or diced in a little bouillon) was a Bennett creation.

Dec 17. The Reduced Shakespeare Company in **The Complete Works of William Shakespeare (abridged)** written and performed by Jess Borgeson, Adam Long and Reed Martin at Lilian Baylis Theatre. Fourth-form humour. Transferred to Criterion.

1991

Jan 3. Warren Mitchell, Nicholas Woodeson, Greg Hicks and Cherie Lunghi in Harold Pinter's **The Homecoming** directed by Peter Hall at Comedy. Many members of the audience thought Mitchell was playing Alf Garnett. The casting of Hicks added a new dimension because he was never convincing as a Doctor of Philosophy at an American university. When he and Lunghi (elegant, enigmatic as his wife) came down to breakfast in their pyjamas, nightdress and dressing gowns they looked like two Noël Coward characters that had strayed into the wrong play.

Greg Hicks, Cherie Lunghi and Warren Mitchell in The Homecoming

Jan 17. Cheryl Campbell, Bill Nighy and Martin Shaw in Harold Pinter's **Betrayal** directed by David Leveaux at Almeida. At the National at its premiere in 1979 the play had looked quite lost on a tiny revolve in the middle of the vast Lyttelton stage. In the intimacy of the Almeida in a spare, sharp production, it now seemed so much better.

Feb 4. Tony Harrison's **The Trackers of Oxyrhynchus** directed by Tony Harrison at Olivier (NT). Written in colloquial rhyming couplets, it was the biggest cock-up since Peter Brook directed Seneca's *Oedipus*. Two classical archaeologists digging at Oxyrhynchusis (one hundred miles south of modern Cairo) discover fragments of Sophocles's *Ichneutae*, which had not been seen since 450 BC. The men become so obsessed with the old drama that they are transmuted into it. There was an electrifying entrance when the crates, which contained the papyrus, burst open to reveal twelve actors in orange body-stockings, painted tails, ears, horns, golden clogs and enormous erections. The satyrs were the outstanding feature. (Mark Addy and Lawrence Evans were the most outstanding.) As befitted creatures that were half-men, half-goats, they were excellent hoofers and the clog dancing was as exhilarating and as slick as the tap dancing in *42nd Street*. The play became a political statement (delivered with passion by Barrie Rutter) about how once there had been no division between high and low theatre.

1991 World Premieres
New York
Tony Kushner's *Angels in America*
Santiago, Chile
Ariel Dorfman's *Death and the Maiden*

Deaths
Peggy Ashcroft (*b.* 1907), British actress

Max Frisch (*b.* 1911), Swiss playwright, novelist
Graham Greene (*b.* 1904), British novelist, playwright

History
—Civil War started in Yugoslavia
—Yeltsin became Russian President
—Disintegration of Soviet Union

The Trackers of Oxyrchynchus

Feb 20. David Suchet in Shakespeare's **Timon of Athens** directed by Trevor Nunn at Young Vic (RSC). Karl Marx's favourite play was revived with visual gags and gimmicks: outside television, the Press, microphones, telephones, intercom, sound-trailers, SAS, muggers, hikers, a helmeted motorcyclist messenger (who can't read) and bunny girls. Suchet's Timon was a well-meaning innocent, a generous and liberal benefactor, totally at ease with everybody, including the media. The scene when he entertains his former friends was presented as a small dinner party. He greeted his guests in a kitchen apron, pretending that he personally has cooked something special and then served water. Timon ended up in a car junk yard. Churlish Apemantus (Barry Foster) who joined him looked as if he had come straight from Cardboard City.

Mar 21. Ralph Fiennes and Simon Russell Beale in Shakespeare's **Love's Labour's Lost** directed by Terry Hands at Barbican (RSC). David Troughton's Holofernes was so pedantic he carried a thesaurus. Griffith Jones's Marcade looked like Ibsen.

Mar 21. Anton Lesser and John Carlisle in Richard Nelson's **Two Shakespearian Actors** directed by Roger Michell at Pit (RSC). English actor William Charles Macready and American actor Edwin Forrest were convinced they spoke the verse as Shakespeare intended and elected to play Macbeth on the same night. The story was based on a true incident in New York in 1849. Macready was booed off the stage before he had even begun. Two days later, when he made a second attempt to perform, a riot broke out and the theatre was burned to the ground. The militia was called out and people were killed.

Mar 27. Wilhelmina Fernandez and Sharon Benson shared the role of Carmen, Damon Evans and Michael Austin shared the role of Joe, and Gregg Baker played Husky Miller in Oscar Hammerstein's **Carmen Jones** directed by Simon Callow at Old Vic. Music by Bizet. The Broadway show had taken nearly fifty years to come to London. Prosper Merimee's story was updated to World War 2 and set among black servicemen. Carmen worked in a parachute factory. Escamillo was no longer a toreador, but a boxer. Carolyn Sebron as Frankie dominated the stage even when she had nothing to say and was just standing there in a white evening dress, looking Junoesque.

Apr 4. Linus Roache, Sally Dexter and Paterson Joseph in Tirso De Molina's **Last Days of Don Juan** translated by Nick Dear and directed by Danny Boyle at Barbican Pit (RSC). The play, written in an extraordinary variety of styles, rather oddly gave the most sophisticated speech to an uneducated girl. The script was relentlessly larky and racy. Dear didn't take the action seriously until the supernatural finale when Juan is invited to supper by a statue with a very firm handshake. Linus Roache never disguised Juan's evil nature.

Apr 4. Roger Allam as Benedict and Susan Fleetwood as Beatrice in Shakespeare's **Much Ado About Nothing** at directed by Bill Alexander at Barbican (RSC). Beatrice pressed everybody to death with her wit. Claudio looked as if he had just come in off the streets. The only aristocrat was a very melancholy Don Pedro (John Carlisle) who was so obviously in love with Claudio that it was a genuine surprise when he suddenly proposed to Beatrice.

Apr 22. The Oxford Stage Company. Pam Ferris in Anton Chekhov's **The Seagull** directed by Mike Alfreds at Lilian Baylis. Ferris's vulgar Arkadina behaved as if she had been a star of the music hall rather than the legitimate stage.

Apr 24. Simon Russell Beale in Christopher Marlowe's **Edward II** directed by Gerard Murphy at Barbican Pit (RSC). The gays in 1991 were threatening to "out" a gay member of the royal family. Nothing new. Kit Marlowe had done it 400 years previously. The historic Edward was a man of splendid physique and constitution, toughened by outdoor pursuits. It was said he enjoyed watching plays. Beale's king, weak, roly-poly and camp, enjoyed watching soft-porn. Murphy's production was notable for its outstanding codpieces. Nearly everybody in medieval England was gay, including Edward's murderer, who caressed and kissed the naked king, who had just emerged from the sewers. The naked Beale was not a pretty sight. ("Catastrophic miscasting," said Jack Tinker in *The Daily Mail*.) Mortimer was played for a smooth, brylcreamed English villain, such as you might find in a Hollywood movie.
—Beale plays the role as someone short, fat and stupid who hops about like a bloated frog.
MALCOLM RUTHERFORD *Financial Times*

Apr 25. James Laurenson as Anthony and Diana Rigg as Cleopatra in John Dryden's **All for Love** directed by Jonathan Kent at Almeida. The production – a lot of empty, stilted rhetoric in the Racine manner – was neoclassical without the decorum, yet boasted not one but two grand staircases. The lovers wandered round *en deshabille*:

he in a tracksuit, she in a négligé. Rigg, full of self-mockery, sexily modern, looked all set for "wild extravagances in public." Laurenson looked all in, a tired old rugby player at the end of an exhausting game in which he had been playing on the losing side. Miscast, he was at his best in rage, when he thinks Cleopatra and Donabella having been having an affair behind his back. Jane Down was dressed so formally, she looks as if she was about to be painted by Valesquez.

—*All for Love* is a turkey of a play. CHRISTOPHER EDWARDS *Spectator*

Apr 25. John Wood in Shakespeare's **King Lear** directed by Nicholas Hytner at Barbican (RSC). Wood didn't seem old enough to be giving up his kingdom. There was a good moment when it seemed as if he was going to throttle Goneril and instead embraced her. In the storm scene, there was no storm and he addressed the audience directly. Linda Kerr Scott's Fool was a repeat of the performance she had given as the Dummy in Joshua Sobol's *Ghetto* at the National Theatre.

—There are long disconcerting silences, frantic acceleration of pace and, most alarming of all, moments when he seems to be impersonating Max Wall. It's a technique that shows off the actor's virtuosity rather than illuminating the role. CHARLES SPENCER *Daily Telegraph*

May 2. Niamh Cusack as Nora Clitheroe and Judi Dench as Bessie Burgess in Sean O'Casey's **The Plough and the Stars** directed by Sam Mendes at Young Vic. Dench's Bessie Burgess, a coarse Protestant woman coarsened by drink, might have stepped out of a back number of *Punch*, especially when she was brawling in the pub and squabbling over a pram laden with loot. John Rogan's Peter Flynn, dressed in the green and gold of the Foresters, looked like something off a Christmas tree.

—How superbly Judi Dench invests Bessie Burgess with truculent, irrepressible life – a fierce, ravaged old bundle with a bibulous, mulberry-coloured nose, like oil well on fire. JOHN PETER *Sunday Times*

Jun 12. Ralph Fiennes and Amanda Root in Shakespeare's **Troilus and Cressida** directed by Sam Mendes at Barbican Pit (RSC). Simon Russell Beale's Thersites was a filthy camp rogue. Ciaran Hinds's Achilles, a sinister and deeply disturbed homosexual, was an unattractive, unheroic figure. Patroculus (Peterson Joseph) was his surprisingly gentle and vulnerable black lover. Alfred Burke was a doddery Nestor. Sally Dexter's sultry Helen and John Warnaby's dull Paris, were no longer the glamour pusses they had once been. Norman Rodway was Pandarus.

Jun 12. Jason Donovan in Tim Rice and Andrew Lloyd Webber's musical **Joseph and The Amazing Technicolor Dreamcoat** directed by Steven Pimlott at London Palladium. Van Lasst's choreography was off an Egyptian wall. The theatre was full of screaming kids, who behaved as if they were at a rock concert. Donovan in a loincloth looked as if he was wearing a nappy.

Jun 13. Desmond Barrit and Graham Turner in Shakespeare's **The Comedy of Errors** directed by Ian Judge at Barbican (RSC). Magritte met Dali. The action was played out on a chequerboard stage with eleven doors. There were moments when the action stopped, missed a heartbeat, and then carried on. Barrit and Turner played both sets of twins which had the advantage (or disadvantage, depending on your point of view) that the audience was as confused as the characters on stage.

Jun 15. Donald Pleasence as Davies, Colin Firth as the lobotomised Aston and Peter Howitt as Mick in Harold Pinter's **The Caretaker** directed by Harold Pinter at Comedy. Thirty-one years on Pleasence (rather than Davies, the tramp) was but a shadow of his former aggressive self: a frightened, frail old man, far more vulnerable and totally out of his depth in his confrontations with Mick.

Jun 27. Ian McKellen and Claire Higgens in Eduardo De Filippo's **Napoli Milionari** directed by Richard Eyre at Lyttelton (NT). Black-market in Naples during World War 2. A genuine piece of popular theatre in the Sean O'Casey manner, mixing comedy and tragedy. The accents were Liverpudlian.

Jul 4. Susan Fleetwood as Arkadina, Simon Russell Beale as Konstantin, Roger Allam as Trigorin, Amanda Root as Nina and Alfred Burke as Sorin in Anton Chekhov's **The Seagull** translated by Michael Frayn and directed by Terry Hands at Barbican (RSC). Inferior to Mike Alfred's production for the Oxford Stage Company. Beale played Konstantin as a common, irritable, physically unappealing nonentity, podgy and a bit camp. "I've more talent than the lot of you!" he screamed during his quarrel with Arkadina. "I don't acknowledge you!"

Aug 6. Vanessa Redgrave and Frances de la Tour in Martin Sherman's **When She Danced** directed by Robert Allan Ackerman at Globe. Isadora Duncan, always fatally attracted to genius, marries a larky, sexy, drunken and slightly crazy Russian poet who doesn't speak a word of English and is liable to hang himself from the chandelier. Redgrave (returning to a role she had played 25 years earlier in Karl Reiz's film) was radiant and the division between actress and role was blurred artistically and politically. Oleg Menshikov, a charismatic, extrovert young Russian actor, spoke in his own language and nobody on stage understood a word he was saying. It was part of the production's charm. Martin Sheen, straight out of RADA, was cast as a Greek pianist who longs to see Isadora dance. He never does. She just stands

there while he plays Chopin. Frances de la Tour played an interpreter who interprets too well and gets the sack.

—Redgrave's acting is hard, translucent and sculptural, painfully realistic but without a shred of exhibitionism or self-indulgence. JOHN PETER *Sunday Times*

Sep 4. Peter McEnery, Susan Fleetwood and George Anton in Sam Shepard's **Curse of the Starving Class** directed by Robin Lefevre at Barbican Pit (RSC). The production matched the bawling capital letters of Shepard's text. The most memorable passage was the description of an eagle picking up a cat in his talons and carrying him screaming into the sky. They fight like crazy, the cat tearing the eagle's chest out. The eagle tries to drop him, but the cat won't let go because he knows if he falls he'll die. They both come crashing down to earth.

Sep 5. Alex Jennings in Shakespeare's **Richard II** directed by Ron Daniels at Barbican (RSC). Uncertain of period, unimaginative in staging, ugly in design, lacking in colour, bleakly lit, the performances were dead. Jennings, unflatteringly costumed, was a prosaic king. It was hard to believe the common people took Anton Lesser's Bolingbroke to their hearts.

Sep 5. Alan Alda, Robert Sean Leonard and Jemma Redgrave in Thornton Wilder's **Our Town** directed by Robert Allan Ackerman at Shaftesbury. A rare London revival of an American classic, which is produced all the time in North America. Alda was far too bland as the Stage Manager and clearly frightened of being mawkish and folksy he cut out every "Know what I mean?" in Wilder's text. Leonard was charming as an all-American-turn-of-the-century gauche lad.

Sep 26. John Carlisle, Carol Royle and Nicola McAuliffe in Oscar Wilde's **A Woman of No Importance** directed and designed by Philip Prowse at Barbican (RSC). A black actress played the Jamesian heroine. (Presumably she was the illegitimate daughter of a white millionaire?) The casting made nonsense of her role. Mrs Arbuthnot would never have accepted her son marrying a black girl. Bosie Douglas put in an unexpected appearance in the first act.

Oct 1. David Calder and Paterson Joseph in Henrik Ibsen's **The Pretenders** directed by Danny Boyle at Barbican Pit (RSC). The epic saga needed an epic arena, not a pit. Set in 13th-century Norway, a time of civil unrest, Haakon looks to the future and sees a united Norway. Skule looks to the past and wants the status quo. Haakon believes he is king by Divine Right. Skule wants to believe he is the rightful king but is tormented by doubt. The high spot was the death scene of the wicked old Bishop (Alan MacNaughton) when he is still trying to cheat God. Deeply frightened of hell, he nevertheless perks up at the thought of leaving the country in "perpetual torment" and the two pretenders at each other's throats

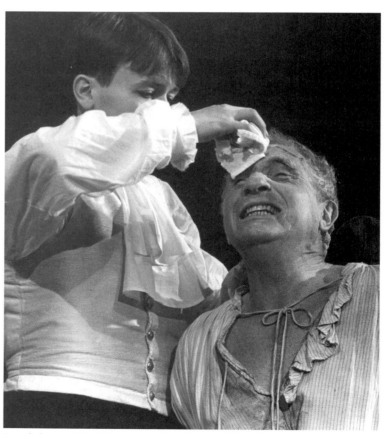

Daniel Flynn and Nigel Hawthorne in The Madness of King George

274

Oct 10. Michael Bryant, Richard Pasco and Alphonsia Emmanuel in David Hare's **Murmuring Judges** directed by Richard Eyre at Olivier (NT). The second of Hare's trilogy on the British Establishment was an attack on the legal system. (Murmuring judges means criticising the judiciary.) Disappointingly, there was nothing to compare on stage with the real life event of the Director of Public Prosecutions being arrested for importuning in King's Cross.
—Despite a few good jokes and the occasional satirical flourish, it is hard to avoid the suspicion that you would have a better time (and gain just as much insight) watching a few episodes of *The Bill*, *Rumpole of the Bailey* and *Porridge*. CHARLES SPENCER *Daily Telegraph*

Nov 14. Clive Owen and Eleanor David in Bernard Shaw's **The Philanderer** directed by Brian Cox at Hampstead. The philanderer finds that the fickleness of the women he loves is only equated by the infernal constancy of the women who love him. The production was all the better for including the missing fourth act, which had remained unpublished and unperformed for 40 years. The act was discarded because Lady Colin Campbell, (who had recently taken her husband to court for cruelty) advised Shaw that the public was not ready for a play which advocated divorce. The funniest scene was when a doctor (Jonathan Coy) learns that three diseases he has discovered do not exist and lashes out at his European rivals who have an unlimited supply of animals on which to experiment.

Nov 28. Nigel Hawthorne in Alan Bennett's **The Madness of George III** directed by Nicholas Hytner at Lyttelton (NT). The king had all the symptoms of madness but he was not mad. He suffered from porphyria, a painful illness of the nervous system. He was tied in a straight-jacket, strapped to a chair, gagged and blistered with glass. He was attended by a provincial clergyman, a strict disciplinarian turned medic. Charles Kay cut such a sinister a figure that it seemed as if the king was in the hands of a lunatic. The king's illness was played out within a political context, a battle between Pitt (Tory) and Fox (Whig) and the Prince Regent who wants to gain the throne. Hawthorne was magnificent. The king's humiliation and torture, compassionately handled, were as painful to watch as Lear's suffering.
—[Hawthorne] is at the top of his form and the only regret is that he met Bennett at the lower end of his. The play stands as a perversity among formidable works. MARK LAWSON *Independent*

Dec 4. Adrian Lester as Rosalind and Patrick Toomey as Orlando in Shakespeare's **As You Like It** directed by Declan Donnellan for Cheek by Jowl at Lyric, Hammersmith. The surprise was that the all-male production should be so non-homoerotic. The voice Lester adopted and his unflattering dress got in the way of his performance. There was only one line (Rosalind's "And I will satisfy you if ever I satisfy a man" addressed to Orlando) which got a laugh because of its sexual ambiguity. Jaques (Joe Dixon), an elegant, sensual, cigarette-smoking dandy, was the only character who was played as an overt homosexual. Tom Hollander's Celia stole the show.
—The most breathtakingly sensuous Rosalind since Vanessa Redgrave. IRVING WARDLE *Independent on Sunday*
—A jolting, intriguing production then, without quite sufficient magic, insight or sexual courage in its breaking of the gender barriers. NICHOLAS DE JONGH *Evening Standard*

1992

Jan 23. Marcus d'Amico, Sean Chapman and Henry Goodman in Tony Kushner's **Angels in America** directed by Declan Donnellan at Cottesloe (NT). Gay fantasia on a national theme. Panic-stricken Jewish young man, unable to cope with the fact that his lover has got AIDS, rushes off to Central Park to get infected. The two actors, standing on opposite sides of the stage, fully clothed, went through the actions. Meanwhile his lover, lying in a hospital bed, dying, is visited by two of his ancestors – one who had died of the plague in the 14th century, the other who had died of the pox in the Restoration era. An unhappily married Mormon, having denied his true sexuality, phones his mother at four AM to tell her he is gay. Roy Cohn (chief counsel to Senator McCarthy's Communist-hunting sub-committee) refuses to admit his homosexuality. "I'm not a homosexual. Homosexuals have no clout. Do I look like a person with no clout? I'm not a homosexual who sleeps with men. I am a heterosexual who makes bucks with men." Goodman's manic performance on the phone was a *tour de force* in the Steven Berkoff manner. Part Two followed in 1993.
—This is one play that's got its head up in the ozone layer. RHODA KOENIG *Punch*
—Declan Donnellan's production dances fleetfootedly around the cracks and the wisecracks in that extraordinary work which switches between the unflinching – though I flinched more than once – depiction of the horrors of AIDS, biting cynicism and tearing passion. DAVID NATHAN *Jewish Chronicle*
—Sprawling and over-written as it may be, it is a play of epic energy that gets American drama not just out of the closet but, thank God, out of the living-room as well. MICHAEL BILLINGTON *Guardian*

Jan 24. Donal McCann, Sinead Cusack and Ron Cook in Brian Friel's **Faith Healer** directed by Joe Dowling at Royal Court. An eloquent and elegiac allegory for the creative artist. An itinerant Irish faith healer – part showman, part charlatan, part priest

– tours outposts in Wales and Scotland in a series of one night stands in derelict halls. He possesses a gift for healing over which he has neither control nor understanding.

Jan 28. Patricia Routledge and Alan Bennett in Alan Bennett's **Talking Heads** directed by Alan Bennett at Comedy: **A Woman of No Importance**, **A Chip in the Sugar** and **A Lady of Letters**. These three monologues were originally written for television. The woman of no importance is a lonely middle-aged spinster, an office bore, smug and snobbish, and she is dying in a hospital bed. Routledge's beautifully understated performance was the best she had ever given either on stage or the small screen.

Jan 30. Alan Cumming in David Hirson's **La Bête** designed by Richard Hudson and directed by Richard Jones at Lyric, Hammersmith. Writing in rhyming couplets, Hirson parodied Molière. Cummings, camp, self-admiring and unrestrained, talked verbiage non-stop for twenty-five, nauseating minutes. It was enough to drive audiences up Hudson's skewwhiff walls.

Feb 11. Juliet Stevenson, Bill Paterson and Michael Byrne in Ariel Dorfman's **Death and the Maiden** directed by Lindsay Posner at Duke of York's. Fifteen years before the play begins a woman was tortured and raped whilst in prison. Her husband has just been appointed to an investigative commission to look into crimes of the old dictatorship. By chance, to their house comes a doctor whom she is convinced is the man who tortured her. She is determined to make him confess, threatening to shoot him if he does not confess. She tortures him as he tortured her. The man denies her charge, saying it wasn't him. The play worked at both a political and a thriller level. Has the woman made a dreadful mistake?

Feb 29. Ian McKellen as Vanya, Anthony Sher as Astrov, Janet McTeer as Yelena, Lesley Sharp as Sonia and Eric Porter as Serebryakov in Anton Chekhov's **Uncle Vanya** directed by Sean Mathias at Cottesloe (NT). No two performances were the same. The actors were allowed the freedom to move as they wished and not stick to any rigid pattern. Some of the acting was so muted as to be barely audible.

Mar 19. Paul Scofield as Captain Shotover, Vanessa Redgrave as Hesione Hushabye, Felicity Kendal as Ariadne Utterword, Daniel Massey as Hector Hushabye, Imogen Stubbs as Ellie Dunn, Oliver Ford Davies as Mazzini Dunn and Joe Melia as Burglar in Bernard Shaw's **Heartbreak House** directed by Trevor Nunn at Haymarket. Redgrave was a gorgeous woman, warm, sympathetic, witty and bare-foot. Kendal was comically silly on her first entrance when her family fails to recognise her. Staunton made Ellie's unlikely transition from impressionable romantic to calculating woman in a matter of hours believable. William Dudley's set was ship-shape.

Apr 30. Robert Stephens as Falstaff, Michael Maloney as Hal and Julian Glover as Henry in Shakespeare's **Henry IV Parts I and II** directed by Adrian Noble at Barbican (RSC). King Henry turned up at Eastcheap, disguised as the Grim Reaper. Falstaff was discovered sprawled on a vast red sofa, a huge hill of flesh, blasted with iniquity. What gave Stephens's performance its poignancy was that the actor was so frail that he had difficulty walking and had to be helped on and off the stage by the cast.
—I have not seen one in 30 years professional theatregoing who has given us a Falstaff to equal Robert Stephens. JACK TINKER *Daily Mail*

May 7. Richard Griffiths and Nicola Pagett in Luigi Pirandello's **Rules of the Game** directed by Jonathan Kent at Almeida. Griffiths's seeming complacency was unnerving. Pagett as his wife prowled and growled in a very Italianate, tigerish, Lulu-ish sort of way that most English actresses wouldn't dare attempt.

May 14. Jane Horrocks, Alison Steadman and Pete Postlethwaite in Jim Cartright's **The Rise and Fall of Little Voice** directed by Sam Mendes at Cottesloe (NT). A shy, silent, stay-at-home Lancashire lass can sing like Judy Garland, Shirley Bassey, Edith Piaf and Billie Holliday. She is exploited by her mum and a small-time agent. Steadman's mum was a wonderfully vulgar, boozy slattern. Transferred to Aldwych.
—The Rise and Fall of Little Voice is a cracker, original, hilarious and hauntingly sad. CHARLES OSBORNE *Daily Telegraph*

Jun 10. Peter Egan as Jimmy Porter in John Osborne's **Deja vu** directed by Tony Palmer at Comedy. Sequel to *Look Back in Anger*. "It has," said Jimmy Porter, "taken me half a lifetime to realise I was wrong about everything." Osborne banged on for three hours on one grating note. The production might have worked if Kenneth Haigh and Alan Bates had been able to repeat their original roles.

Jun 18. Stockard Channing, Paul Shelley and Adrian Lester in John Guare's **Six Degrees of Separation** directed by Phyllida Lloyd at Royal Court. Gay black hustler acquires enough knowledge and background information on three rich families in New York to gatecrash their homes and pretend to be Sidney Poitier's son and a friend of their children. The story was based on a black con man, who did exactly that. Guare found unexpected similarities between "the haves" and "the have-nots". The gullible Manhattan couple live like the hustler does, from hand-to-mouth; though, they are hustling on a higher plateau. The play's title is based on the statistical theory

Nancy Craine and Stephen Dillane in Angels in America. (Part Two: Perestroika.) 1993

1992 World Premieres
New York
Neil Simon's *Lost in Yonkers*
Dublin
Frank McGuinnness's *Someone Who'll Watch Over Me*

Deaths
Marlene Dietrich (*b*.1904), German singer, actress

History
—Prince and Princess of Wales agreed to separate
—Los Angeles police court cleared four policemen of beating Rodney King

that we all are related and that everyone in the world is just six people removed from any other person. The only problem is finding the right six people. Transferred to Comedy.

Jul 4. Alec McCowen, Stephen Rea and Hugh Quarshie in Frank McGuinness's **Someone To Watch Over Me** directed by Robin Lefevre at Hampstead. An American actor, an Irish journalist and an English lecturer share a cell in Beirut. This overrated hostage drama was not about Terry Waite, Brian Keernan and John McCartney, though it clearly drew on the audience's knowledge of their kidnapping. The play ended with the Irishman and Englishman combing each other's hair – a gesture emulating the Spartans who were mocked for the very same effeminacy and went on to win their greatest victory.

Jul 6. Druid Theatre Company in Vincent Woods' **At The Black Pig's Dyke** at Tricycle, Kilburn. The Dyke is an ancient mythical fortification between Ulster and the South of Ireland, a place where communities live under constant threat of intimidation and death. Will the murdering ever cease? Evidently not. What made the play special were the mummers (people in straw), performing dramas of heroes, death and resurrection.

Jul 9. Jeffery Kissoon as Oberon in Shakespeare's **A Midsummer Night's Dream** directed by Robert LePage at Olivier (NT). Set in a dirty pool, the main prop was an iron-bedstead in which were discovered the four lovers. Theseus and Hippoylta sat on the head-frame whilst the bed drifted in the pool. The slithering and glistening fairies wallowed in the mud. The production was dominated by Puck, played by Angela Laurier, a French contortionist, who could not cope with Shakespeare's language, so contortions were all the audience got. Lepage clearly thought she was the star of the show and gave her the final solo curtain.

Aug 13. Theatre de Complicite in Bruno Schulz's **Street of Crocodiles** directed by Simon McBurney at Cottesloe (NT). Outside the building could be heard the sound of marching Nazi feet. What followed – based on the stories of Schulz – was elusive,

fleeting, absurd, surreal, poetic, humorous, beautiful and multi-lingual. The action, played without interval, included memories of schooldays, family meals, picnics, shopping, birds in the attic, and a search for a dead father.

Aug 27. George Murphy as Oedipus, John Shrapnel as Creon, Philip Voss as Theseus, Joanne Pearce as Antigone and Electra in **The Thebans** directed by Adrian Noble at Barbican (RSC). Sophocles' Oedipus plays were neither conceived as a trilogy, nor were they written in the order they were acted. The message of all three, however, is the same: namely that it is best not to be born at all. It was a message which amused the first night audience enormously. Murphy in **Oedipus** played the bully-boy king as a peasant yobo. **Oedipus at Colonus**, celebrated for its lyric beauty, suffered because the play spends so much time repeating the story the audience had just seen. **Antigone**, morally and politically the most accessible and immediate of all Greek tragedies, suffered from having to be played in the same key as the other two plays. Pearce's Electra was both real and stylised. The Colonus chorus was masked, pot-bellied, hunch-backed and bulbous-cheeked. The gods appeared in the shape of helium balloons, an interpretation more appropriate for comedy.

Sep 11. Richard Pasco, Barbara Leigh-Hunt and Kenneth Cranham in J B Priestley's **An Inspector Calls** designed by Ian MacNeil and directed by Stephen Daldry at Lyttelton (NT). The action was set simultaneously in 1912 and in 1945 (the year it was written and the year of the general election, which led to a sensational landslide victory for Labour). The Birlings lived in a doll's house. The house was on stilts and situated in a vast blitzed landscape, a nightmarish no man's land, which was invaded by an army of Labour voters. There was a spectacular *coup de theatre* when the whole fabric came crashing down.

Sep 16. Diana Rigg and Tim Woodward in Euripides's **Medea** directed by Jonathan Kent at Almeida. "I was born unlucky and a woman," said Medea. "You need to be a clairvoyant to please your husband in bed," said the Chorus. Rigg was implacable. Jason went bananas.
—Diana Rigg confirms herself to be one of the great divas with a performance that deserves to be repeated all over the world. MAUREEN PATON *Daily Express*
—The role exploits all her talent for icy hauteur and irony, but transmutes it into fury and despair. This is the tragic performance she was born to give. MALCOLM RUTHERFORD *Evening Standard*

Sep 29. Harry Burton in Noël Coward's **Post Mortem** directed by Richard Stirling at King's Head. Though written shortly after Coward had appeared in R C Sherriff's *Journey's End* in Singapore in 1930, it only now received its first professional performance. Describing the play as confused, under-rehearsed and hysterical, Coward argued that it might have been better had he given more time to it and less vehemence. A soldier, who died in the trenches in World War 1, comes back as a ghost thirteen years later to find out if anybody has learned anything from the War or if they have slipped back into their illusions and false security. Coward vented his rage

An Inspector Calls

against journalists, Lady Bountifuls, society, the Church, Christianity and Christian Scientists.

Oct 8. Chita Rivera, Brent Carver and Anthony Crivello in John Kander and Fred Ebb's musical **Kiss of the Spider Woman** directed by Harold Prince at Shaftesbury. Book by Terrence McNally based on novel by Manuel Puig. Two men – a political activist and a gay sexual offender – share a cell in Latin America. The musical trivialised the novel and it was distasteful to watch tortured male prisoners walking across the stage being transformed into a chorus line.
—Everything combines in an occasion that melds the brutal and the camp into the quintessence of showbiz – and the best musical for a decade. KENNETH HURREN *Mail on Sunday*

Oct 22. Stephen Sondheim's musical **Assassins** directed by Sam Mendes at Donmar. Book by John Weidman. Seven people killed or attempted to kill the President of the United States. The setting was a garish fairground with the killers in their narrow booths/ dressing-rooms/coffins, each waiting for the moment which will make him famous. Sondheim took an ironic yet sympathetic line towards them. Henry Goodman was very funny as the crazy Charles Guiteau who wanted to be ambassador to France and killed William McKinley in 1901. He had an excellent number, "Look on the Bright Side", which alternated vaudeville and spiritual, and which he sang whilst mounting the steps of the scaffold which he climbed as if it were a catwalk.

Nov 2. Harold Pinter, Paul Eddington, Douglas Hodge and Gawn Grainger in Harold Pinter's **No Man's Land** directed by David Leveaux at Almeida. Eddington, who looked as if he has survived a lifetime of insults and deprivation, was a frail, wary-eyed old bird, deferential, ingratiating, yet capable of sudden flashes of arrogant superiority.

Nov 17. Martin Shaw as Lord Goring, David Yelland as Sir Robert Chiltern, Hannah Gordon as Lady Chiltern, Michael Denison as Lord Caversham, Dulcie Gray as Lady Markby and Anna Carteret as Mrs Cheveley in Oscar Wilde's **An Ideal Husband** directed by Peter Hall at Globe. The major innovation was to play the mistaken identities of Act III as if they were a scene from a farce by Feydeau. The real triumph, however, was the confident handling of the melodrama. Martin Shaw's portrait of Goring, a trivial, conceited, podgy dandy (who is a jolly good chap underneath) was modelled on photographs of Wilde. Shaw was not only witty in what he said but witty in his silent ironic comments directed to the audience and signalled by a weary and resigned raising of his eyebrows.

Dec 3. Ninagawna Company and Haruhiko Joh in Shakespeare's **The Tempest** at Barbican. The production was described as a rehearsal of a Noh play on Sado, the island to which the great Noh dramatist, Zeami, was banished in 1434. Shakespeare's characters had all been adapted to take on roles in a Noh play. Only Ariel and Caliban were seriously diminished. The Masque element was brilliantly executed in classical style, which was mesmerising in its elegance and slow motion. The isle was full of strange sounds: a fascinating combination of Oriental and Western music. The emotional intensity and musicality of Haruhiko Jo's delivery of the speech beginning, "Ye elves of hills, brooks, standing lakes and groves," transcended any language barrier. What made the soliloquy even more dramatic was that the actors, who had been sitting on the sidelines throughout, stood to listen. When Prospero said he was going to give up his Art, a frisson ran through the whole company, for without Prospero they would not exist. The frisson was again repeated during the beautifully spoken Epilogue.

Dec 3. Judi Dench, Michael Pennington and Jeremy Northam in Peter Shaffer's **The Gift of the Gorgon** directed by Peter Hall at Barbican Pit (RSC). A story of revenge in the Greek manner is turned into a characteristic Shafferian clash between Passion and Reason. Young professor at an American university writes to ask the widow of a famous English playwright if he might come and see her. The playwright had argued that to forgive the IRA terrorists was unforgivable and that the only response to terrorism was "to kill every terrorist we capture in proper rage and that way we can stay clean." The professor turned out to be the playwright's son, a life-long admirer of his father's works.

Dec 10. Michael Hayden as Billy Bigelow, Joanna Riding as Julie Jordan, Patricia Routledge as Nettie Fowler and Clive Rowe as Mr Snow in Richard Rodgers and Oscar Hammerstein's musical **Carousel** directed by Nicholas Hytner at Lyttelton (NT). Choreographer Kenneth Macmillan had died a month before the production opened. The choreography, which owed something to the spirit of Agnes de Mille, still needed working on.

Dec 12. Kenneth Branagh in Shakespeare's **Hamlet** directed by Adrian Noble at Barbican (RSC). Branagh's third attempt. The frenetic, impetuous Hamlet of 1988 had been transformed into a self-possessed, sober and princely young man. Jane Lapotaire as Gertrude. John Shrapnel as Claudius. David Bradley as Polonius. Designer Bob Crowley provided a surreal setting, which included a piano and discarded floral decorations littering the floor. Joanne Pearce's mad scene as Ophelia was one of the high

spots. Audiences would have to wait for Branagh's excellent film version in 1996 to see his best performance.
—He is undoubtedly the great Hamlet of our time. JACK TINKER *Daily Mail*
—Branagh has voices for every occasion, but they emerge as a theatrical mosaic, lacking any continuous emotional undercurrent. IRVING WARDLE *The Times*

1993

Jan 11. Maggie Steed and Peter Wingfield in Marivaux's **The Game of Love and Chance** designed by Paul Dart and directed by Mike Alfreds at Cottesloe (NT). Updated to the 1920s. Silvia and her maid change places so that Silvia can observe her suitor. But unbeknown to her, the suitor has decided to change places with his chauffeur so that he can observe her. The result is that they fall in love, each believing that the other is beneath them. Maggie Steed, old enough to be the suitor's mother, never behaved like a maid. Caroline Quentin and Marcello Magni were hilariously vulgar as the servants.

Jan 14. Simon Russell Beale in Shakespeare's **Richard III** directed by Sam Mendes at Donmar. Beale made lots of ugly, camp faces and practically every entrance was signalled by the barking of dogs. There was a good silly joke when Richard pretended he didn't know that Julius Caesar had built The Tower. There was a very nasty moment when Hastings's head was delivered in a brown parcel, tied with string, and he rammed his stick into the head.

Jan 21. David Healy, Zoë Wanamaker and Peter Davison in Arthur Miller's **The Last Yankee** directed by David Thacker at Young Vic. Two men meet in the waiting room of a mental institute. The fact that their wives are patients is due in no small measure to them.

Feb 5. Harold Pinter, Paul Eddington, Douglas Hodge and Gawn Grainger in Harold Pinter's **No Man's Land** directed by David Leveaux transferred to Comedy.
—Not even the coughers who haunt West End first nights can diminish Pinter's twilight masterpiece. MICHAEL BILLINGTON *Guardian*

Feb 22. Maggie Smith as Lady Bracknell, Alex Jennings as John Worthing and Richard E Grant as Algernon Moncrieff in Oscar Wilde's **The Importance of Being Earnest** directed by Nicholas Hytner at Aldwych. Maggie Smith solved the problem of how to say "a handbag!" by ignoring it completely and getting her big laugh on "The line is immaterial." Dressed all in grey, she was like some highly-strung bird. There was disapproval in every glance and fidget. "Style," says Lady Bracknell, "depends on the way the chin is worn. They are worn very high just at present." Smith wore her chin exceedingly high. The two men greeted each other with a kiss, which suggested, falsely, that Hytner was going to explore a Victorian gay sub-text and that the true meaning of being "earnest" and "bunburying" would be revealed.
—This, surely, is the role she [Maggie Smith] was born to play, and she lays into it with a relish and a precision that leaves the spectator helpless with admiration and laughter. CHARLES SPENCER *Daily Telegraph*
—Wilde was not writing a star vehicle for Lady Bracknell. In stealing the show, Dame Maggie's hyperactive performance subtly undermines it. MICHAEL BILLINGTON *Guardian*

Mar 3. Kirby Ward and Ruthie Henshall in George and Ira Gershwin's **Crazy for You** directed by Mike Ockrent at Prince Edward. Described as the new Gershwin musical, the original show had been completely reworked, given a new story, new dialogue and new songs. Too many numbers were just dragged in for the sake of it. The script by Ken Ludwig was ridiculous and meant to be, but that didn't necessarily excuse it. Some of the jokes ("Just because we didn't sell a ticket doesn't mean it was a failure") were clearly aimed at the profession. What Mike Ockrent's efficient production had going for it was Susan Stroman's witty and inventive choreography, which was danced with great energy by the whole company. "I Got Rhythm" and the Follies finale were a knock-out.

Mar 30. Roger Allam, Henry Goodman and Martin Smith in Cy Coleman's musical **City of Angels** directed by Michael Blakemore at Prince of Wales. Book by Larry Gelbart. Lyrics David Zippel. Award-winning Broadway musical was a parody of a Raymond Chandler 1940s *film noir*. Two stories ran concurrently: the *film noir* itself and the story of the author having to compromise in Hollywood. There was a splendid duet to end the first act with the gumshoe and his creator singing "You're Nothing without Me".

Mar 31. Richard McCabe and Nigel Cooke in Peter Whelan in **The School of Night** directed by Bill Alexander at Pit (RSC). What really happened to 29-year-old Christopher Marlowe, the well-known atheist and sodomite, on that fatal night in Deptford on 30 May 1593? Evidently he pretended that he was killed in a fight, passed off a dead man's body as his own and got a safe passage abroad. He was worried about what would happen to his future work when he was "dead". "Don't worry about that," said Shakespeare, "your plays can be performed under my name."

Rufus Sewell and Emma Fielding in Arcadia

Apr 13. Felicity Kendal, Bill Nighy, Harriet Walter, Emma Fielding, Rufus Sewell and Samuel West in Tom Stoppard's **Arcadia** directed by Trevor Nunn at Lyttelton (NT). There are two stories, which alternate and complement each other. The action is set in a large country house in 1809 and 1990. Designer Mark Thompson provided a beautiful Regency rotunda. A 20th-century academic and a historian are researching Lord Byron. The academic thinks that Byron had killed a poet. A 19th-century 13-year-old mathematical genius is exploring 'chaos mathematics' 180 years ahead of her time. (She only needs a modern high-speed computer to complete her findings.) Her mother is appalled by what Richard Noakes ("Culpability Noakes", the landscape architect) is doing to the park, turning classical order into Gothic chaos. Samuel West had no difficulty in persuading the audience that he, at least, understood quantum physics. *The Times* likened *Arcadia* to "a novel by Le Carre rewritten by Stephen Hawking in collaboration with Groucho Marx." 6,000 copies of the play were sold in the first three weeks.

—I have never left a new play more convinced that I'd just witnessed a masterpiece. CHARLES SPENCER *Daily Telegraph.*
—The snob hit of the season. NICHOLAS DE JONGH *Evening Standard*
—Too clever by about two-and-three-quarters. JACK TINKER *Daily Mail*

Jun 2. Alun Armstrong as Sweeney Todd and Julia McKenzie as Mrs Lovett in Stephen Sondheim's musical **Sweeney Todd** directed by Declan Donnellan at Cottesloe (NT). Denis Quilley (who had played Todd at the British premiere at Drury Lane in 1980) was now the Judge, who tried a bit of flagellation in order to curb his lusts. Hal Prince had cut this song in the original production. The tension was enormous when the Judge sat in the barber's chair for the first time and the audience waited for his throat to be cut. The production, lean and fluent, was razor-sharp.

Jun 3. James Larkin and Zara Turner in Brien Friel's **Translations** directed by Sam Mendes at Donmar. The British army in 1833 is engaged in mapping the whole of Ireland and in the process, standardising the language and translating all the place names into English. A lieutenant, a decent English soldier, loves Ireland and hates what the British are doing. He falls in love with a local girl. He doesn't speak any Irish; she doesn't speak any English. Their love scene was delightful.

Jun 13. Trevor Eve in John Osborne's **Inadmissible Evidence** directed by Di Trevis at Lyttelton (NT). The script, essentially a three-hour monologue, was exhausting for actor and audience alike. The vitriolic denunciation of all that the Swinging Sixties stood for was a combination of self-loathing and envy.

Jun 17. Kim Criswell, Kwame Kwei-Armah and Richard Dreyfus in Billy Russell's **Elegies for Angles, Punks and Raging Queens** directed by Billy Russell at Criterion Music by Janet Hood. The 33 short monologues in rhyming couplets, interspersed with eleven songs, were the theatrical equivalent of The Names Project AIDS Memorial Quilt. The most chilling was the one about the man who, having discovered he'd got AIDS, went down to the municipal baths and had sex with as many people as he could. The show lacked variety and weight and the doggerel trivialised the subject matter. The best laugh was provided by the crass playbill, which read: "With 33 dead characters on stage, *Elegies* easily outdoes Shakespeare at his tragic best, but unlike Shakespeare it plays out intense life and death dramas with the engaging vivacity and vigour of an intimate cabaret entertainment."

Jun 24. David Suchet and Lia Williams in David Mamet's **Oleanna** directed by Harold Pinter at Royal Court. Political correctness at American university: student, out of her depth, feeling she is not getting any help from her tutor and not happy with her grades, accuses him of being an elitist, sexist, self-serving pedant, who performs rather than teaches. She also accuses him of rape. The College accepts everything she says and he loses tenure, job and house. There was a memorable moment when he is speaking to his wife on the phone and she tells him not to call his wife "baby" and he lashes out at her. It felt as if the whole audience was egging him on. In the American production he actually did kick her. The audience hissed and booed the actress playing the student. Transferred to Duke of York's.

—Am I glad I no longer teach in an American university? You bet. BENEDICT NIGHTINGALE *The Times*

1993 World Premieres
New York
Tony Kushner's *Angels in America*
Alan Meakin and Howard Ashman's
Beauty and the Beast
David Mamet's *Oleanna*

Deaths
William Golding (*b*.1911), British
novelist, playwright

Sam Wanamaker (*b*.1919), American
actor, director and founder of
Shakespeare's Globe

History
—Bill Clinton US President
—Single market in Europe
—Siege of Waco

Jul 12. Patti LuPone and Kevin Anderson in Andrew Lloyd Webber's musical **Sunset Boulevard** directed by Trevor Nunn at Adelphi. Book and lyrics by Don Black and Christopher Hampton based on the Billy Wilder film whose special frisson had come from the fact that 50-year-old Gloria Swanson, who had been a great star of the silent era, was making her comeback and that the butler was played by Eric Von Stroheim, who had directed her in *Queen Kelly*. The musical stuck pretty close to the film; but, inevitably, without that frisson, *Sunset Boulevard* (synonymous with Hollywood) was but a shadow of its former self. LuPone was excellent in the final mad scene: grotesque, bejewelled, wigless and horribly old, she still persuaded you that she could have played Salome brilliantly in her heyday. The score sentimentalised and cheapened the lover. John Napier designed a Baroque mansion of ostentatious Randolph Hearstian vulgarity with a gilded, sweeping staircase. Anthony Powell's costumes were fit for a movie queen.
—Wilder's hard-boiled has become Lloyd Webber's soft-boiled. MALCOLM RUTHERFORD *Evening Standard*

Jul 13. Alison Steadman, Carmel McSharry and Aidan Gillen in Scott McPherson's **Marvin's Room** at Hampstead. McPherson had died of AIDS in November 1992. The surprise was that the play, though it was about dying, was not about AIDS.

Jul 15. Craig McLachlan and Debbie Gibson in Jim Jacobs and Warren Casey's **Grease** at Dominion. The 1973 musical, a nostalgic celebration of teenage sex in the late 1950s, was revised and had additional songs by B Gibb, J Farrar, L St Louis and S Simon. "A triumph of energy and group endeavour over good taste," said Steve Grant in *Time Out*.

Aug 26. Henry Goodman, Phoebe Nicholls, David de Keyser and Tim Potter in Terry Johnson's **Hysteria** directed by Phyllida Lloyd at Royal Court. Freud, 82 years old, dying and in great pain, asks to be put out of his misery. The doctor gives him the first of two lethal doses, warning him that he may hallucinate. Johnson's play (subtitled *Fragments of an Analysis of an Obsessional Neurosis*) was Freud's hallucination. Goodman as Freud was equally at home in the real and in the surreal world, equally skilful with the pathos and the slapstick.

Sep 2. Ian Holm, Anna Massey, Douglas Hodge, Michael Sheen and Claire Skinner in Harold Pinter's **Moonlight** directed by David Leveaux at Almeida. A former civil servant, brutal and loud-mouthed, is dying in his bed, refusing to go gently into the night. The scenes which worked best were those between Holm and Massey. When it came to malice and irony the wife won every time. She had had an affair with his mistress. Transferred to Comedy.
—Pinter seems to be dressed only in the tattered remains of his once formidable talent. CHARLES OSBORNE *Daily Telegraph*
—Pinter has written few more fascinating plays. For all its oddities and obscurities, Moonlight marks a genuine return to form. BENEDICT NIGHTINGALE *The Times*

Sep 16. Antony Sher in Tom Stoppard's **Travesties** directed by Adrian Noble at Barbican (RSC). Sher had to carry the play single-handed during the unnecessarily long opening monologue, a send-up of spoof memoirs. It was a relief when he could discard his mackintosh, his Wellington boots and his senility to play his younger, dapper Edwardian self. Witty, articulate, energetic, he and David Westhead (very stylish as Tzara) gave an amusing imitation of the way some actors carry on when they are acting in Wilde. Rebecca Saire expounded on socialism and did a striptease at the same time. The famous tea-scene from *The Importance of Being Earnest* was sung.
—This is a comedy that is almost calculated to keep your reactions oscillating between elation and exasperation. PAUL TAYLOR *Independent*

Oct 2. The David Hare Trilogy at National Theatre: **Racing Demons, Murmuring Judges** and **The Absence of War.** State of the nation in three institutions: Church, Judiciary and Politics. "The spectacle is bigger than the texts," said Malcolm Rutherford in *The Financial Times*. John Thaw played the Labour Leader in *The Absence of War.*
—Of the many daft things Neil Kinnock did must have done in his life by far the daftest was letting David Hare and his notebook into his private office during the 1992 election. IAN AITKEN *Guardian*

Patti LuPone in Sunset Boulevard

Oct 14. Antony Sher in Christopher Marlowe's **Tamburlaine** directed by Terry Hands at Barbican (RSC). The terror of the world's only regret is that there are not more lands to conquer. He would make God stoop if he could.
—It's a dangerous commanding performance from a dangerous commanding actor whose only limitation, apart from his lack of size, is that he is rarely able to achieve vocally what he can physically. CLIVE HIRSCHHORN *Sunday Express*
—Nature did not intend Antony Sher to play Tamburlaine. But Antony Sher, not for the first time, has said fiddle-di-dee to nature. JACK TINKER *Daily Mail*

Oct 15. Fiona Shaw in Sophie Treadwell's **Machinal** directed by Stephen Daldry at Lyttelton (NT). (Pronounced Mak'in-al, the term is French for "mechanical" or "automatic"). Lonely, highly-strung young woman marries "because that's what women do". Her story, told in nine selected episodes, ended with her in the electric chair. It was difficult to imagine Fiona Shaw being crushed by anybody or any system; miscast, she found herself playing a supporting role to Ian MacNeil's massive scenery and the machinery of the Lyttelton stage. The high spot was the first scene, where actions, voices and noises were brilliantly orchestrated to reproduce, in a highly stylised and exaggerated manner, the repetitions and banalities of office drudgery. The script sounded as if it had been written by Gertrude Stein. John Woodvine was the boring husband, who mistakenly believes he understands women.

Oct 25. Donald Sinden, Miriam Margolyes and David Essex in Oliver Goldsmith's **She Stoops to Conquer** directed by Peter Hall at Queen's. It was not a good idea to cast the leading characters with unknown and inexperienced actors and then cast the supporting parts with star names. In the same way that Mr Hardcastle loves everything that is old, so theatregoers loved Sinden's old-fashioned acting, his resonant voice, his grimaces, his mime and his rapport with the audience. Margolyes threw herself about the stage with great zeal, a miniature galleon in black and maroon. A little less slapstick would not have come amiss. In the 19th century Tony Lumpkin was perceived as the leading role and attracted many of the greatest actors of the day. Essex, twice as old as Lumpkin should have been, was miscast.

Nov 15. Steven Berkoff in Steven Berkoff's **One Man** at Garrick. Three monologues. The most arresting was the Millwall supporter and his rottweiler, the perfect music hall double act. Every police force in Europe would have recognised this burly, bullet-headed, swearing moron in his faded Union Jack T-Shirt: knocking back 30 lagers and ending up swimming in his own vomit – a surreal touch which was not to everybody's taste, and even less so when the dog lapped up the vomit. The rottweiler, also played by Berkoff, ran the show and dealt with all hecklers.

Nov 20. Stephan Dillane, Jason Isaacs, David Schofield and Joseph Mydell in Tony Kushner's **Angels in America** (Part Two: Perestroika) directed by Declan Donnellan at Cottesloe (NT) Kushner continued his gay fantasia on national themes. Even people with AIDS want to live. The play's episodic action sprawled all over the place. Characters wandered into each other's dreams. There were scenes in heaven:"Are you dead?" the hero (Stephen Dillane) asked his wife of his male lover. "No," she replied. "I've just had sex."

Dec 2. Ian McDiarmid and Emma Fielding in Molière's **The School for Wives** translated by Richard Wilbur and directed by Jonathan Kent at Almeida. The best production of a Molière play in English since John Dexter's *The Misanthrope* for the National in 1973. McDiarmid, mouth gaping wide, becoming more and more hysterical until his whole body was shaking, was hilarious as he listened to a young man, who not knowing who he was, confided that he had been with Agnes having eluded her guardian.

Dec 11. Derek Jacobi and Cheryl Campbell in Shakespeare's **Macbeth** directed by Adrian Noble at Barbican (RSC).
—He makes such an operatic meal of his soliloquies that instead of coming across as searingly honest and unsparing they sound like a case of someone trying to derive consolation from tuning in to the beautiful flexibilities of his own voice. PAUL TAYLOR *Independent*

1994

Jan 18. Stomp created and directed by Luke Cresswell and Steve McNicholas at Sadler's Wells. The rhythm was made from domestic utensils, brooms, buckets, drums, bins, tubes, mugs, newspapers, paper bags, lighters, and dustbin lids, anything that came to hand, including the kitchen sink. Transferred to Vaudeville in 1998 and still running well into the 21st century.

Jan 27. Zoë Wanamaker, Niall Buggy, Beatie Edney, David Haigh and Danny Webb in Terry Johnson's **Dead Funny** directed by Terry Johnson at Vaudeville. A group of friends come together to mourn the death of Benny Hill. Johnson used the familiar Benny Hill comic ingredients – big bosoms, knickers, custard pies, gay stereotypes and couples caught *in flagrante delicto* – to farcical and tragic ends

Feb 17. Christopher Fulford in Arnold Wesker's **The Kitchen** directed by Stephen Daldry at the Royal Court at Duke of York's. The kitchen, variously described as a public place, a battlefield, the United Nations and a madhouse, becomes a symbol for peaceful coexistence among all nations. A typical, mindless and soul-destroying working day was brilliantly choreographed and orchestrated to build to a memorable first act curtain. The theatre was gutted to accommodate the production. Fulford was excellent as the German cook who goes berserk with a cleaver.

Mar 14. Fiona Shaw and Susan Engels in Samuel Beckett's **Footfalls** directed by Deborah Warner at Garrick. Twice nightly. Beckett's stage directions were altered: instead of staying within a tiny strip, Shaw walked on a platform specially built round the dress circle. The Beckett estate withdrew performing rights and stopped the production going to Paris.
—Watching this attempt at roving realism is like seeing someone doodling on a Rembrandt. MICHAEL BILLINGTON *Guardian*
—Ludicrous homage to that misery guts Samuel Beckett. CHARLES SPENCER *Daily Telegraph*

Mar 17. Anton Lesser, Dora Bryan, Bob Peck, Trevor Peacock, Nicholas Woodeson and Emma Amos in Harold Pinter's **The Birthday Party** directed by Sam Mendes at Lyttelton (RNT). Lesser, snarling and unshaven, was a particularly nasty Stanley. Peck was a threatening presence. Bryan was very funny as Stanley's vacuous landlady, the over-motherly Meg. One of the biggest laughs was when Meg learns that there are actually shows in theatres where there is no dancing and no singing and she wonders what the actors do. Peacock was her husband, a kind chap, who made a sad attempt to save Stanley from the clutches of Goldberg and McCann. Tom Piper's tiny box set receded into the far distance, until it looked no bigger than a doll's house, and was then enveloped by the whole street, disappearing behind an anonymous suburban façade.

Mar 29. Mark Letheren and Shaun Dingwall in Jonathan Harvey's **Beautiful Thing** directed by Hettie Macdonald at Donmar. An urban fairy tale: two teenagers shared a bed, discovered they were gay. Mum (the abrasive Amelda Brown), after the initial shock, accepted it and the lads danced cheek-to-cheek and everybody was happy.

Mar 29. Helen Mirren and John Hurt in Ivan Turgenev's **A Month in the Country** directed by Bill Bryden at Albery. Mirren, who acted with too much awareness of the comic possibilities of the role, made it clear that Natalya had never loved Rakitin and cared little for his suffering. Their 'sickly consumptive affair' should never have been allowed to fester for four years. Her final leave-taking was breathtakingly humiliating. John Hurt gave a brilliant account of Rakitin.

1994 World Premieres
New York
Edward Albee's *Three Tall Women*

Deaths
John Osborne (*b.*1929), British playwright

History
—Democratic elections in South Africa
—Nelson Mandela President of South Africa
—Russia invaded Chechnya
—Ceasefire agreed in Ireland
—First woman priest ordained in UK

—The piece is a star vehicle and Mirren emerges from it as a whale of a star. IRVING WARDLE *Independent on Sunday*
—We all knew we were watching a major actress in her prime. BENEDICT NIGHTINGALE *The Times.*

Mar 31. John Sessions, David Bamber, Anthony Calf, Joe Duttine, Roger Frost and Kenneth Macdonald in Kevin Elyot's **My Night With Reg** directed by Roger Michell at Royal Court Upstairs. Sad gay comedy: Reg, who never appears, had slept with all the characters. So when Reg dies of AIDS, they are all at risk. Sessions was cast as a bottom-grabbing, globe-trotting, louche extrovert. Transferred to Criterion.

Apr 21. Alan Howard, Sheila Gish, Frances de la Tour, Jude Law and Lynsey Baxter in Jean Cocteau's **Les Parents Terribles** directed by Sean Mathias at Lyttelton (NT). The production took its cue from the fact that the family freely acknowledged that if they were characters in a play, everybody would find them too far-fetched. Mathias camped up the first act, directing it for a mixture of absurd melodrama and silly boulevard farce. This was very funny; but then he didn't know what to do with the serious scene between father and mistress in the second act and tried to play it completely straight. Inevitably, after all the preposterous nonsense that had gone before, the scene didn't work. Gish gave the mother (a grotesque, tearful, pathetic *monstre sacré*) the full-blown, operatic treatment. Stephen Brimson Lewis designed a palatial pigsty for her bedroom. The wardrobe poured out its contents and there was rubbish and dirty laundry everywhere.

May 26. Robert Stephens in Shakespeare's **King Lear** directed by Adrian Noble at Barbican (RSC). David Bradley as Gloucester. David Calder as Kent. Stephens didn't have the strength to carry Cordelia on to the stage and she has to be carried on for him by the soldiers. Who would have thought bookish, bespectacled, frightened Edgar (Simon Russell Beale) to have had so much brutality in him? He smashed Oswald's head in with a staff and attempted to strangle his brother. When he was disguised as Poor Tom, Beale was so caked in mud that he looked like a terracotta statue, a perfect subject for one of Lucien Freud's monumental nude portraits. Cornwall (Simon Dormandy) was a camp, public school bully, who made a pass at Edmund (Owen Teale).

Jun 2. Bob Peck and Tom Mannion in Githa Sowerby's **Rutherford and Son** directed by Katie Mitchell at Cottesloe (NT). Not seen since 1912 this bleak, solid North Country family drama was a major discovery, a 20th century classic. The tyrant father (Bob Peck), openly contemptuous of his children, did not invite sympathy. Only the women had the moral courage to stand up to him. His eldest daughter (Brid Brennan) has a magnificent tirade against her father at the end of the second act. His daughter-in-law (Phoebe Nicholls), at the end of the play, drove a hard bargain on behalf of her baby son in the knowledge that Rutherford in ten years time would be old and powerless.

Jun 16. James Bolam, William Armstrong, Anthony O'Donnell, Ron Cook, Keith Bartlett and Carl Proctor in David Mamet's **Glengarry Glen Ross** directed by Sam Mendes at Donmar. Moral bankruptcy and paranoia in Chicago: four salesmen in real estate fight meanly to keep their jobs. The American Dream is a nightmare. The actors were riveting. The production was confirmation, if confirmation were needed, of a modern masterpiece

Jun 16. Clare Higgins as Alexandra del Lago and Robert Knepper as Chance Wayne in Tennessee Williams's **Sweet Bird of Youth** directed by Richard Eyre at Lyttelton (NT). Designer Anthony Ward provided a wonderfully high-shuttered hotel bedroom for the opening scene. Higgins had all the faded glam, caustic camp wit, self-destruction and degradation Alexandra requires. She was splendid, especially when she lay down the sexual terms on which she was willing to help Chance: "When I say NOW, the answer must be not be later." One of the major weaknesses of the play is that Alexandra is off-stage for too much of the time. Knepper was not quite good enough to sustain the second act on his own.

Jun 29. Lindsay Duncan, Eddie Izzard and Danny Worters in David Mamet's **The Cryptogram** directed by Gregory Mosher at Ambassadors. A cryptogram is a piece of cryptographic writing written in cipher or in such a form or order that a key is required in order to know how to understand and put together the letters. The audience was left hanging in there, desperately trying to decipher the code. Mamet's dialogue acted like a parody of Mamet's highly stylised syntax with all those fractured

Helen Mirren and John Hurt in A Month in the Country

sentences. A young boy cannot get to sleep. He keeps hearing voices. He knows something is going on but he doesn't know what. The play, a memory of Mamet's childhood, was set in Chicago in 1959, the year his parents separated. He was 10 years old.

Jul 7. Alec McCowen in Shakespeare's **The Tempest** directed by Sam Mendes at Barbican (RSC). The production was dominated by Simon Russell Beale's Ariel. His hair was short, his face white, his feet bare and he wore lipstick. He was dressed in a smart, blue, Mao tunic suit, his arms stiffly by his side. Beale, quaint, camp, precise, eerily asexual, might have been a superciliously fourth-form prefect, a smug young cadet at junior military academy or, then, again, he might have been a lift-boy at a Grand Hotel. There was insolence in his studious politeness and the way he always looked Prospero straight in the eyes. It was very noticeable that the "sir" at the end of his sentences was always delayed. "Do you love me?" he asked his master in an arrogant manner, knowing full well that Prospero didn't love him. (At Stratford Ariel used to spit in Prospero's face on his final exit.) His exquisite singing of Shaun Davey's music was one of the chief pleasures. David Troughton's Caliban, bald, red-eyed, bare-chested, physically powerful, yet vulnerable, was a Bedlam lunatic out of Hogarth. David Bradley's Trinculo (in Little Titch's elongated shoes) was a ventriloquist, whose dummy was a miniature version of himself.

Jul 7. Judi Dench as Arkadina in Anton Chekhov's **The Seagull** directed by John Caird at Olivier (NT). Alan Cox as Konstantin. Helen McCrory, as Nina. Bill Nighy as Trigorin. Edward Petherbridge as Dorn. Rachel Power as Masha. Norman Rodway, as Sorin. Dench, dumpy, frumpy, bad-tempered, vulgar, and over-dressed, was the least sympathetic Arkadina. She had two moments of delicious absurdity: the first when she said she could play a girl of 15 and did an awkward little skip to prove it; the second when she bandaged her son's head as if it were a Christmas present. Dench must have been the first Arkadina to give Trigorin's penis a little pat and to enjoy an orgasm on stage.

Jul 12. John Gordon Sinclair and Ruthie Henshall in **She Loves Me** directed by Scott Ellis at Savoy. Book by Joe Masteroff based on play by Miklos Laszlo. Music by Jerry Block. Lyrics by Sheldon Harnick. The 1963 romantic musical comedy was inspired by *The Shop Around the Corner*, the Ernst Lubitsch film starring James Stewart and Maureen Sullivan, which in its turn was inspired by *Parfumerie* by the Hungarian writer Miklos Laszlo, which had been premiered in 1936. The film had also inspired the Judy Garland musical, *In The Good Old Summertime*. The story has a fragile, oldie worldly charm. Two pen-pals, unbeknownst to each other, are working in the same perfume shop in pre-war Budapest. In their letters they fall in love. In real life they take an instant dislike to each other. The music is charming and the lyrics are literate and witty. The performances were appealing. Hit song: "Vanilla Ice Cream".

Jul 25. Francesca Annis as Mrs Erlynne and Simon Dutton as Lord Darlington in Oscar Wilde's **Lady Windermere's Fan** directed and designed by Philip Prowse at Albery. The supporting cast was not asked to act. They were asked to model the sumptuous costumes. The play became a choreographed mannequin parade. Who was the woman all in white who circled the room continuously and was ignored by everybody? Presumably she was meant to be Mrs Erlynne's younger self. David Foxxe wore a green carnation and played Cecil Graham as a nasty caricature of Wilde, giving his epigrams a homosexual tartness.

Jul 26. Imelda Staunton in Bernard Shaw's **Saint Joan** directed by Gale Edwards at Strand. Ken Bones as Warwick. Peter Webster as Cauchon. Peter Jeffrey as Inquisitor. Jasper Britton as Dauphin. The cast stood around, giving very mechanical performances

Jul 30. Ian Kelly, Wendy Hewitt and Richard Stemp in Fanny Burney's **A Busy Day** directed by Alan Coveney at King's Head. Written in 1800, this was its first performance ever! A major discovery: a satire on the vulgarity and snobbery of both the nouveau riche and the aristocracy.

Aug 4. Margot Leicester, Henry Goodman and Ken Stott in Arthur Miller's **Broken Glass** directed by David Thacker at Lyttelton (NT). The play, set in 1938, relied on the audience's knowledge of the Holocaust and the ignorance of the Holocaust by the American characters on stage.

Aug 24. Peter Barkworth as Winslow's father and Simon Williams as the KC in Terence Rattigan's **The Winslow Boy** directed by Wyn Jones at Globe. Pedestrian revival. The scenes, which worked best, were those with the father. dryly humorous, and the one between the suffragette daughter (Eve Matheson) and her fiancé (Robin Hart), who is about to jilt her.

Sep 1. Rachel Weisz as Gilda, Clive Owen as Otto and Paul Rhys as Leo in Noël Coward's **Design for Living** directed by Sean Mathias at Donmar. "We all love each other a lot, far too much," says Leo, "and we've made a bloody mess of it." The 1930s glamour and veneer were removed. The three characters, predatory, volatile, totally selfish and totally irresponsible, were stripped to their underwear and revealed for what they were: vulgar, crude, mercurial and dead common. In the first act Coward's

play was unrecognisable. The actors humped against a bare brick wall. In the second and third acts, the actors caricatured Coward, clipping the lines in an absurdly exaggerated, staccato manner. "This is not Coward for the cowardly," said Jack Tinker in *The Daily Mail*. Transferred to Gielgud.

—The play's sexual politics can have never before been so honestly and powerfully presented. NICHOLAS DE JONGH *Evening Standard*

Oct 7. Tom Courtenay in **Moscow Stations** directed by Ian Brown at Garrick from The Traverse, Edinburgh. Solo performance: an adaptation by Stephen Mulrine of the cult novel, *Moscow to Petushki*, by the Russian dissident, Venedikt Yerofeev. The novel, set during the Brezhnev era, described a journey made by an intellectual dropout and a drunkard. He never got to Petushki. (Nobody ever did.) He died without ever having left Moscow. The journey was in his imagination.

Nov 4. The Globe Theatre changed its name to the Gielgud Theatre and opened with Stephen Dillane in Shakespeare's **Hamlet** directed by Peter Hall. Michael Pennington played the Ghost and Claudius. Donald Sinden was Polonius. Dillane was a modern, intelligent, ironic, shoulder-shrugging Hamlet, who spoke all his soliloquies out front. He wore a prop crown, spat at Ophelia, pretended to rape his mother, and took off all his clothes. The schoolgirls, sitting in the front row, couldn't believe their luck and gave him a standing ovation.

Nov 10. Mark Rylance and Michael Rudko in Sam Shepard's **True West** directed by Matthew Warchus at Donmar. The play is a vehicle for four terrific performances. Rylance and Rudko alternated the two lead roles giving the production an extra tension. ("I always wondered what'd be like to be you.") The second act was an orgy of destruction with Lee (a semi-literate thug) dismantling the typewriter (funny, at first), busting the phone with a golf club, and then demolishing the whole kitchen. The play ended with Austin (clean cut Ivy League and timid) trying to strangle Lee while their dotty mother clapped her hands – as if they were just naughty boys.

—*True West* strikes me as being enjoyable pulp melodrama rather than a work of art. CHARLES SPENCER *Daily Telegraph*

Nov 15. Maggie Smith, Frances de la Tour and Anastasia Hille in Edward Albee's **Three Tall Women** directed by Anthony Page at Wyndham's. In America Albee's return to form was hailed as the biggest comeback since Lazarus. "I wanted," he wrote in a programme note, "to write as objective a play as I could about a fictional character that resembled in every way, in every event, someone I knew well." That person was his adoptive mother, who rejected him when he was 18. He said the play was not an act of revenge and yet the 92-year-old lady was portrayed as a senile monster. The first act, practically a monologue, was about the miseries of old age, its indignities, humiliations, incontinence and loneliness. The old lady's ramblings, one minute lucid and sharp, the next muddled and pathetic, were occasionally interrupted by her companion and nurse and her lawyer. Maggie Smith, imperious, rouged, pale, frail, was both witty and distressing. In the second act the three actresses were recast as the 92-year-old's younger selves at different stages of her life: young (Hille), middle-aged (de la Tour) and old (Smith).

—*Three Tall Women* is a hard, sterile play, brutal but impersonal, almost cold: a useless passion. JOHN PETER *Sunday Times*

Nov 22. Penelope Wilton and Ian Holm in Harold Pinter's **Landscape** directed by Harold Pinter at Cottesloe (NT). The two parallel monologues make one continuous bit of music. Wilton was grave and lyrical. Holm seethed with anger, ready to burst.

Nov 28. Clive Francis as Scrooge in Charles Dickens's **A Christmas Carol** adapted by John Mortimer and directed by Ian Judge at Barbican (RSC). The story was given the same treatment that Trevor Nunn, John Caird and David Edgar had given *Nicholas Nickelby*. The most striking image was the terrible spectres of Ignorance and Want, symbolised by a little boy and a little girl, two wretched, abject children, ragged, hollow-eyed and starving. The Spirit of Christmas Yet to Come was an enormous Grim Reaper, towering over everybody. Francis looked as if he has stepped out of an illustration by "Phiz" rather than John Leech.

Dec 1. Theatre de Complicite in **Out Of A House Walked A Man...** directed by Simon McBurney at Lyttelton (NT) Based on the writings of Danil Kharms, the Russian Absurdist. Two high spots. The first was a *pas de deux*, danced by Kathryn Hunter and Marcello Magni, in which she played a corpse and he played a man trying to put her in a trunk. The second was when the whole back wall collapsed and a Niagara of manuscripts poured down on to the stage.

Dec 8. Jonathan Pryce as Fagin, Sally Dexter as Nancy and Miles Anderson as Bill Sikes in Lionel Bart's musical **Oliver!** directed by Sam Mendes at London Palladium. Book, music and lyrics freely adapted from Charles Dickens' *Oliver Twist*. Bart said that he thought his Fagin (a loveable rogue, who escapes at the end) was an improvement on Dickens. Pryce, tall, young, handsome, effete, was as genial and as stylish as the Pirate King in *The Pirates of Penzance*. There was no danger in his performance. The production had a clean, scrubbed look and could have done with a lot more squalor.

Anastasia Hille, Frances de la Tour and Maggie Smith in Three Tall Woman

Dec 14. Tom Hollander in **The Threepenny Opera** at Donmar. Book and lyrics by Bertolt Brecht translated by Robert David Macdonald. Music by Kurt Weill. New lyrics translated by Jeremy Sams. The show, dedicated to the poor and homeless, was radically rewritten. Updated to 2000, the London beggars were highly organised and threatening to disrupt the coronation of William V. The stage was encircled by surveillance cameras. The agit-prop lethality of the new lyrics gave the revival its incisiveness. Weill's music was as irresistible as ever. Mack the Knife was a small-time crook, a puny, long-haired, cockney spiv. Hollander acted him as if he were Pinkie in Graham Greene's *Brighton Rock*. His public execution was turned into a game show on television.

1995

Jan 17. John Neville and Gemma Jones in August Strindberg's **The Dance of Death** directed by Peter Stormare at Almeida. First major revival in 25 years. Neville and Jones danced with incisive humour in a jaunty production.

Jan 17. Kate Ashfield, Pip Donaghy and Dermot Kerrigan in Sarah Kane's **Blasted** directed by James MacDonald at Royal Court Upstairs. Kane was inspired by the atrocities in the war in Bosnia. The play, unremittingly bleak, was obsessed with death, sex and brutality. A dying, racist tabloid journalist raped his former girlfriend, an epileptic and mentally retarded vegetarian. He got his comeuppance when civil war broke out and he was raped and blinded by a soldier. The critics lambasted the play: "disgusting feast of filth ... nauseating dog's breakfast ... abject puerility ... like hanging your head down in a bucket of offal ... unadulterated brutality without any dramatic merit ... catalogue of lurid on-stage depravity." The Court hadn't had such a bad press since hooligans had stoned a baby in a pram in Edward Bond's *Saved*. Bond, Harold Pinter and Samuel Beckett were among Kane's supporters and praised her moral vision and fierce humanity; but Kane admitted that Macdonald's graphic production had even shocked her.
—If people don't think racism, sexism, abuse and violence are central in the world we live in, they live in a different world from me. JAMES MACDONALD

Jan 23. Theatre de Complicite. Lilo Baur in **The Three Lives of Lucie Cabrol** based on a story by John Berger adapted by Simon McBurney and Mark Wheatley and devised by the company at Shaftesbury. Lucie Cabrol was an ugly, dwarfish woman born in France in 1900. In her third life, she is murdered and becomes a ghost. It was only in death that she was, finally, able to marry the man she loved. The actors played birds, animals, bushes, trees and the land itself. There was an exhilarating scene when McBurney raced through an imagined countryside, made up entirely of chairs and planks which were constantly being rearranged by the company. The sheer physical and emotional power of the production was overwhelming.

Feb 9. Nigel Lindsay, Ray Winstone, Phil Daniels, Nicholas Day, David Barker-Jones and Tom Georgeson in Patrick Marber's **Dealer's Choice** directed by Patrick Marber at Cottesloe (NT). A major debut. It was not necessary to know anything about poker to enjoy Marber's sharp and witty script. Five compulsive gamblers are joined by a professional. The lesson is simple: play the man, not the cards. Georgeson had the ultimate deadpan poker face. The only thing he revealed was his seediness. Excellently acted, the play transferred to Vaudeville.

Feb 14. Rik Mayall and Stephen Fry in Simon Gray's **Cell Mates** directed by Simon Gray at Albery. George Blake, traitor, and Sean Bourke, petty criminal, were cell mates in Wormwood Scrubs. Bourke sprung Blake and invited him to Moscow for a holiday. Fry, who had a breakdown and disappeared after the first night, wrote a letter to *The Independent* saying he was not cut out for the theatre.
—Stephen Fry does his usual Stephen Fry impersonation of a superior manservant. NICHOLAS DE JONGH *Evening Standard*
—Stephen Fry's abrupt departure provides the most eloquent comment on his own performance. MICHAEL ARDITTI *Sunday Express*

Feb 17. Ralph Fiennes in Shakespeare's **Hamlet** directed by Jonathan Kent at Hackney Empire. Francesca Annis as Gertrude. Fiennes (straight from his big success in the film, *Schindler's List*) rattled through the "To be or not to be" soliloquy on the assumption it was a bore and better to get it out of the way as quickly as possible. Ophelia had no flowers in her mad scene; instead she had chopped off her hair and handed out strands, describing them as rosemary, fennel, columbine, etc.

1995 World Premieres

New York

Terence McNally's *Love! Valour! Compassion!*

Horton Foote's *Young Man from Atlanta*

Deaths

Max Frisch (*b.* 1911), Swiss playwright, novelist

Michael Hordern (*b.* 1911), British actor

Eugène Ionesco (*b.* 1909), Franco-Romanian playwright

Eric Porter (*b.* 1928), British actor

Robert Stephens (*b.* 1931), British actor

History

—Peace agreed in Bosnia

—Assassination of Rabin

—With Fiennes the play became the possession of a heroic actor. Blink and you could be watching Beerbohm Tree and Martin-Harvey. IRVING WARDLE *Independent on Sunday*

—So it is a mixed, yes-and-no evening: one that gives us in full measure Hamlet the fast moving thriller but all too little of the timeless tragedy of loss, alienation and rigorous intellectual self-examination. MICHAEL BILLINGTON *Guardian*

Feb 20. Rupert Graves, Rachel Weisz and Marcus d'Amico in Noël Coward's **Design for Living** directed by Sean Mathias at Gielgud. Mathias's randy production and ended with the trio making animal noises, as if they were performing Gyorgy Ligeti's *Aventures/Nouvelles Aventures*. Gilda said that the hormones in her body were working overtime and nobody watching Weisz's carnal performance doubted it for one minute. Graves, who would have been perfect for Leo, was cast as Otto.

—It will send Noël purists into severe decline from which they may never recover, for the implicitly bisexual theme of 1937 has now been made thoroughly explicit in a production that drags Coward out of the closet. MAUREEN PATON *Daily Express*

Feb 27. Felicity Kendal, Art Malik and Margaret Tyzack in Tom Stoppard's **Indian Ink** directed by Peter Wood at Aldwych. Set in two different continents in two different periods – India 1930s and England 1980s – the actions were acted concurrently. 40 years after Independence the Indians were more British than the Brits. A friendship develops between an English erotic poet who is dying of consumption and an Indian painter. The painter paints her twice: first, fully clothed, as a western artist might paint her; and then, at her insistence, in the nude, as an Indian, who had been brought up on the Kangra school of erotic art, might paint her.

Mar 16. Rosemary Harris in Euripides's **The Women of Troy** directed by Annie Castledine at Olivier (NT). Greek theatregoers back in 415 BC, who had come to see an interpretation of a familiar myth, found instead that they were being forced to confront the reality of their misdeeds. Two years earlier, the Greeks had destroyed the neutral city state of Melos, slaughtering all the men and taking the women back to their homes as slaves and concubines. Rosemary Harris hadn't the physical power for Hecuba. Jane Birkin, as Andromache, sounded as if she was appearing in a middle class, stiff-upper-lip British war film. Josette Bushell-Mingo's Cassandra was manic. The victors were Americans. Peter McEnery's Menelaus (in naval uniform) had a Southern drawl. Janie Dee's Helen was modelled on Marilyn Monroe. Philip Whitchurch's herald was a relation of Denis Hopper's nutty photographer in Francis Ford Coppola's *Apocalypse Now!* Leo Wringer's Poseidon wore high platform shoes. Robert Pickavance's Athene was a tacky and emaciated drag queen. The sound of helicopters filled the air.

Mar 30. Donal McCann in Sebastian Barry's **The Steward of Christendom** directed by Max Stafford Clark at Royal Court Upstairs. The struggle for Irish independence: set in the 1930s, it looks back to the surrender of Dublin Castle to Michael Collins in 1922. The former Chief Superintendent of the Dublin Metropolitan Police ends his days in a mental asylum. The character was based on Barry's great-grandfather. McCann's hypnotic performance was deeply moving.

—No piece of theatre yet seen on the Irish stage has presented the viewpoint of the Irish Catholic loyalist of eighty years ago with such acute sensitivity, with marvellous intellectual, historical and dramatic integrity ... This is a quite wonderful play which brilliantly re-opens a hitherto closed chapter of Irish history. It is lyrical and profound, extremely funny and extraordinarily observant; and above all it is hauntingly sad. This is one of the great Irish tragedies and all the more tragic because true. KEVIN MYERS *Irish Times*

Mar 30. Emma Fielding as Viola and Desmond Barrit as Malvolio in Shakespeare's **Twelfth Night** directed by Ian Judge at Barbican (RSC). Viola emerged from under a huge Hokusai-like wave. Malvolio, a lugubrious Welshman, pushed his lips this way and that in a frantic effort to force them into a smile. He arrived before his mistress, wrapped in his cloak which he opened (as a flasher might) to reveal yellow everywhere. Barrit's humourless and overweening turkeycock was transformed into a Brobdignagian wasp. Fielding was as charming as a Nicholas Hilliard miniature. Bille Brown's flaxen-haired Sir Andrew Aguecheek was a prancing child, a harmless, silly clodpole who had never ever grown up and was so unused to putting quill to paper that when he wrote his challenge, he covered himself in ink.

Mar 31. Ewen Bremner, James Cunningham, Susan Vidler and Malcolm Shields in Irvine Welsh's **Trainspotting** directed by Ian Brown at Bush. Welsh's novel has nothing to do with trainspotting and anoraks were advised to stay away. John Gross in *The Sunday Telegraph* likened the experience to "a sustained trawl through a sewer."

Apr 25. Juliet Stevenson and Simon Russell Beale in John Webster's **The Duchess of Malfi** directed by Philip Franks transferred from Greenwich to Wyndham's. No terror. Beale was much more of a Duchess than Stevenson was.

—Juliet Stevenson was born to play the Duchess of Malfi. What a pity she was out when she called. JACK TINKER *Daily Mail*

May 3. Catherine Byrne as Nora Clitheroe, Anita Reeves as Mrs Cogan, Aideen O'Kelly as Mrs Burgess and Eamon Morrissey as Fluther Good in Sean O'Casey's **The Plough and the Stars** directed by Joe Dowling at Garrick. A major Irish revival. Seventy years on after the premiere in Dublin audiences were still identifying with Nora's great outburst: "No woman gives a son or a husband to be killed – if they say it, they're lyin', lyin', lyin', against God, Nature, an' against themselves."

May 4. Michael Gambon and Lia Williams in David Hare's **Skylight** directed by Richard Eyre at Cottesloe (NT). Middle-aged widowed millionaire attempts to rekindle a relationship with a thirty-year-old feminist schoolteacher who had walked out on him. Hare's play was a scathing attack on right-wingers who sneer at teachers, social workers and probation officers who are left to pick up the government's mess. Gambon revealed a wounded vulnerability beneath a bullying, pompous, hectoring exterior. Transferred to Wyndham's.

—This wonderful new play is the first in which Hare has fully managed to integrate his bracing sense of anger at social fudge with his governing belief in the transforming power of love. MICHAEL COVENEY *Observer*

May 21. Judi Dench in Rodney Ackland's **Absolute Hell** directed by Anthony Page at Lyttelton (NT). Ackland's revised version of his 1952 play, *The Pink Room*. The action is set in a wartime drinking club in the West End of London in the weeks

Judi Dench in Absolute Hell

leading up to the 1945 general election and a landslide victory for Labour. The clientele are Bohemians and servicemen, a galaxy of lost souls, seedy, louche failures, who have buried their heads in the sand and are living for the moment, escaping reality in alcohol and sex. The owner, blowsy, generous, volatile, vulnerable, is liable to burst into tears and either offer drinks on the house or turf everybody out. Everything about Judi Dench's performance was so right: her wig, her tight-fitting dress, the way she walked, her bottom. (A whole paragraph could have been written about her bottom.)

May 29. Daniel Massey and Michael Pennington in Ronald Howard's **Taking Sides** directed by Harold Pinter at Criterion. Wilhelm Furtwangler (1886–1954), the great German conductor, worked with the Berliner Philharmonic throughout the whole Nazi period, including World War 2. Though he was denazified after the war and exonerated of any accusations of collusion in Nazi crimes, he was seriously compromised and the taint of collaboration never left him. Furtwangler argued that a single performance of a great masterpiece by Wagner and Beethoven was a stronger and more vital negation of the spirit of Buchenwald and Auschwitz than any words.

Jun 2. Michael Flatley and Jean Butler in **Riverdance** directed by John McColgan at Labatt's Apollo, Hammersmith. Music by Bill Whelan. The principal choreographer was Michael Flatley. The show was billed as "the hottest event on 160 legs with 3,5000 taps per minute." It had started as a seven-minute item at the Eurovision Song Contest in Dublin in 1994. The choreography drew on traditional Irish steps. The top part of the body remains absolutely rigid. The arms are held stiffly to the side. (The Catholic Church in times gone-by didn't want any dancing that might be considered sexy and lead to copulation.) The movement was concentrated in the lightening, crisscrossing, scissors-like movements of the feet and the back and side flicks of the legs. The steel capped shoes loudly amplified made a hell of a noise.

Jun 2. Fiona Shaw in Shakespeare's **Richard II** directed by Deborah Warner at Cottesloe (NT). The casting of a woman as Richard gave a new twist to his relationship with Henry Bolingbroke (David Threlfall) and made it seem as if they were childhood sweethearts, boy and girl. At the Coventry Lists Richard was in tears and practically fainted at the thought that Mowbray might kill Henry. When they met again outside Flint Castle, it was acted as a reunion of lovers. In the abdication scene they were like children playing with the crown. At the end when Henry learns that Richard is dead, he is grief-stricken. Shaw, hyperactive, never looked like a king (nor a queen for that matter). Threlfall never looked like a king, either. The action was played *en traverse* with the audience sitting in high-ranked pews.

Jul 11. Julie Christie, Leigh Lawson and Harriet Walter in Harold Pinter's **Old Times** directed by Lindy Davies at Wyndham's. Christie, smiling and aloof, was inscrutable: "You talk of me," she said, "as if I were dead."
—Time has not been kind to Harold Pinter's *Old Times* though any play which brings us back to Julie Christie after 30 years can't be all bad. SHERIDAN MORLEY *Spectator*

Jul 14. Tom Hollander in Jezz Butterworth's **Mojo** directed by Ian Rickson at Royal Court. Rising young rock n' roll star of the 1950s is abducted by a rival gang leader. Butterworth's mixture of violence and humour was in the Quentin Tarantino mould; there was a death scene straight out of *Reservoir Dogs*. The dialogue was out of David Mamet. Matt Bardock and Andy Serkis, high on drugs, all jitters and word-play, were a hilarious double-act.

Jul 27. Michael Gambon in Ben Jonson's **Volpone** directed by Matthew Warchus at Olivier (NT). Gambon looked as fleshy and sensual as a Beardsley drawing. When Volpone was not groping himself, he was usually groping Mosca, who was always ready for a bit of oral sex. Simon Russell Beale's Mosca was no elegant rascal but a low-born, dirty, droopy-drawered servant, a personification of sly, sweating servility.

Aug 10. Toby Stephens in Shakespeare's **Coriolanus** directed by David Thacker at Barbican (RSC). Caroline Blakiston as Volumnia. Updated to the Napoleonic era and acted out against a background of Delacroix's Liberty, Roberts was a charismatic upper-class, mummy's boy. Handsome, sexy, callow, bloody-minded, he snarled and blubbed away.
—That he has star quality is never in doubt; but it is still only a promise. ALASTAIR MACAULAY *Financial Times*

Sep 5. Iain Glen in Shakespeare's **Henry V** directed by Matthew Warchus at Barbican (RSC). Glen emphasised the bully-boy king in his chilling ultimatum to the citizens of Harfleur and in his order to kill all the French prisoners. Tony Britton played the Chorus as an elderly soldier who had fought in World War 2, his overcoat lined with medal ribbons and a poppy in his button-hole.

Sep 7. Anton Lesser, James Bolam, Sarah Woodward and Benjamin Whitrow in John O'Keeffe's **Wild Oats** directed by Jeremy Sams at Lyttelton (NT). Benjamin Whitrow played Ephraim Smooth, the Puritan spoilsport, a sanctified, sanctimonious poop, who oppressed the poor, leched after the farmer's bosomy daughter and –sacrilege!–trampled on the works of Shakespeare.

Sep 12. Zoë Wanamaker, Claire Skinner and Ben Walden in Tennessee Williams's **The Glass Menagerie** directed by Sam Mendes transferred from Donmar Warehouse to Comedy. Walden's emphatic delivery turned poetry into prose.

Sep 26. Judi Dench in Stephen Sondheim's musical **A Little Night Music** directed by Sean Mathias at Olivier (NT). Dench acted the bitter-sweet *Send in the Clowns* and was heartbreaking. Patricia Hodge as the humiliated wife sang "My Husband Is a Pig," a witty lyric which had been dropped from the original Harold Prince production.
—Judi Dench plays Desiree like it was one of the great character roles of modern theatre – as maybe it is – with an endearing shabby grandeur and incredible finesse. MICHAEL WHITE *Independent on Sunday*
—Judi Dench once more proves the intelligent musical is as much her domain as the intelligent play. JACK TINKER *Daily Mail*

Sep 28. Edward Albee's **Three Tall Women** directed by Anthony Page returned to Wyndham's with Maggie Smith, Sara Kestelman and Samantha Bond.

Oct 3. Harold Pinter and John Shrapnel in Harold Pinter's **The Hothouse** directed by David Jones at Comedy. The patients (lunatics and political dissidents) in a state-run rest home in England are known only by their numbers. The neurotic principal (played by a moustached Pinter), a bully and an idiot, is almost certainly a murderer and the father of a baby. His number two (played by a bespectacled Nazi-looking Shrapnell) is responsible for the massacre.

Oct 5. Rufus Sewell and Tony Doyle in Ron Hutchinson's **Rat in the Skull** directed by Stephen Daldry at Duke of York's. An indictment of interrogation technique became a microcosm of Ireland's 400-year-old Holy War. An Irish bomber is being detained under the Prevention of Terrorism Act and while he waits he has a long monologue full of ironic wit which would go down extremely well on the Northern Ireland comedy circuit. The moment, however, his interrogator from the Royal Ulster Constabulary arrives, he clams up. We know from the beginning that the Detective Inspector is going to beat him up; but the reason for the beating is totally unexpected and a splendid theatrical coup. He beats the man up so that the police case against him will fall apart and he will have to be set free.

Oct 10. Eddie Izzard at Shaftesbury. Cross-dresser, comic surrealist and language terrorist. His flights of fancy took him to a midnight queue of murderers outside a petrol station and over the Alps with Hannibal's elephants on skies. One section was done entirely in French and the audience had no problem.

Oct 13. James Wilby in John Osborne's **A Patriot For Me** directed by Peter Gill at Barbican (RSC). Gill's meticulous production was so meticulous that it went on for over four hours. Denis Quilley as the dowager was in full regalia, tiara, diamonds, feathers and long white gloves.

Oct 16. Leo McKern, Nicola McAuliffe and Graham Turner in Harold Brighouse's **Hobson's Choice** directed by Frank Hauser at Apollo. Turner's shy, awkward and unassuming Willie Mossop, the master shoemaker, was just right, but McKern didn't have the energy to drive the production; his Hobson was a crushed windbag from the very start. Kate Bassett in *The Times* described McAuliffe's bossy, hard-faced Maggie as "somewhere between a nascent Margaret Thatcher and a Salford Cilla Black."

Oct 17. Roger Allam as Mirabell and Fiona Shaw as Millamant in William Congreve's **The Way of the World** directed by Phyllida Lloyd at Lyttelton (NT). The first scene took place in a modern gay club. The idea that Mirabell and Fainall were bisexual was not developed. The last scene (when everybody is discussing private matters, both marital and financial), was, for some unexplained reason, staged in the street. Equally unbelievable was the way the family abandoned Lady Wishfort (Geraldine McEwan), who was last seen lolling in a stupor amongst the black plastic rubbish bags in the gutter.

Oct 24. Howard McGillin and Caroline O'Connor in Jerry Herman's musical **Mack and Mabel** directed by Paul Kerryson at Piccadilly. Book by Michael Stewart. Great score but poor book. Mack was Mack Sennett who made the Keystone Kops movies, classics of the silent cinema. Mabel was Mabel Normand whose career was shattered when a Hollywood producer was murdered and her name was dragged into the newspapers. Hit songs included "I Won't Send Roses" and "When Mabel Comes into the Room."

Oct 30. Lily Savage and Maggie Kirkpatrick in **Prisoner Cell Block H** directed by David McVicar at Queen's. Concept, music and lyrics by Don Battye and Peter Pinne from TV series. The cult Australian soap, set in a Melbourne jail, was absolute kitsch.
—To call this a terrible show is to miss the point. *Prisoner* is supposed to be bad. MAUREEN PATON *Daily Express*.

Nov 14. Diana Rigg in Bertolt Brecht's **Mother Courage** in a version by David Hare directed by Jonathan Kent at Olivier (RNT). Jonathan Bent and Jonathan Dove's music toned down the harsh realities. The play was still an epic bore.

—This is Brecht Without Tears: both a strangely emotionless production and an anodyne, de-politicised reading for all those who hate Brecht. MICHAEL BILLINGTON *Guardian*

Dec 13. Adrian Lester in Stephen Sondheim's musical **Company** directed by Sam Mendes at Donmar. Book by George Furth. A witty, smart and highly enjoyable production. The married friends of a 35-year-old bachelor decide to give him a surprise birthday party but, having learned of the surprise in advance, he doesn't turn up. Is the bachelor gay? The first time *Company* was staged in 1970 the subject was avoided. This time the subject was brought up and he admitted to having had gay relationships but said he was not gay. Lester was charming, sexy and funny. There was also plenty of power and pain in his last number, the ambiguously positive "Being Alive", when he declares he wants someone to hold him too close, someone to hurt him too deep, someone to pull him up short and put him through hell, someone, who like it or not, will want him to share a little a lot ... Sheila Gish sang "The Ladies Who Lunch." Anna Francolini rattled through "Another Hundred People". Sophie Thompson panicked wonderfully on her wedding day.

Dec 14. Adrian Scarborough and Simon Russell Beale in Tom Stoppard's **Rosencrantz and Guildenstern Are Dead** directed by Matthew Francis at Lyttelton (NT). They looked like Tweedledum and Tweedledee and behaved like Vladimir and Estragon. You couldn't imagine either of them being friends of Hamlet. Alan Howard gave a caricature of Alan Howard playing The Player King.

Dec 15. Paul Ireland, Peter Ireland, Gavin Marshall and Michaelle Gomez in Irvine Welsh's **Trainspotting** adapted and directed by Harry Gibson at Ambassadors. The in-yer-face cult novel, first published in 1993, described the life-giving/life-taking drug scene in Edinburgh and did it with uncompromising brutality. The script, a series of painful vignettes, looked at the sterile and wrecked lives of three junkies and one psychopath, an unending catalogue of abuse, partner-bashing, nausea, machismo, miscarriage, shagging and AIDS. The play opened with a man telling how he woke up one morning to find himself in a strange bed covered in excrement, vomit and sperm. Some people had difficulty with the Scottish accent. The production took the attitude that if you didn't understand what Gavin Marshall's psycho was saying, then that was your problem, because that was the way he spoke. Some of Welsh's set-pieces were so revolting that they had the young audience groaning out loud. Two scenes took place in public lavatories. The first had a junkie searching for a suppository he had dropped in an overflowing lavatory bowl. The second had a barmaid tampering with her customers' drinks with her tampon. The third loud groan went up when a nude junkie, having run out of veins, injected himself in his penis.

—Welsh is one of the few writers around with the guts to recognise the highs as well as the lows of drug experience. STEVE GRANT *Time Out*

—My best critics are probably the people in pubs and clubs. IRVINE WELSH

1996

Jan 2. Anastasia Hille in John Webster's **The Duchess of Malfi** directed by Declan Donnellan at Wyndham's. It had a glittering, anti-Catholic, in-your-face flamboyance. Hille's Duchess came across as a neurotic, voracious, hard-as-nails, cigarette-smoking bitch. Words like strumpet, hyena and screeching-owl (bandied by her enemies) were totally apposite. "I am the Duchess of Malfi still" was thrown away in the most off-hand and ironic way. There wasn't any poetry or pathos. Presented with a severed hand, she dropped it into a wastepaper basket. Scott Handy's wild-eyed Ferdinand attempted to bite off his doctor's ear. The Cardinal's mistress rammed her revolver up his Jacobean arse.

Feb 13. Ken Stott and Elizabeth McGovern in Molière's **The Misanthrope** directed by Lindsay Posner at Young Vic. Martin Crimp's hilarious update was set in present day London. Celimene was an iconic film star who appeared in movies just one step from pornography. She was a skin-deep femme fatale, surrounded by bullshitters. "I am beginning to find you morally and physically repulsive," said Alceste. "Come on," she replied, "I bet you say that to all the girls." Stott, who looked as if he had slept in his clothes, was fully aware of his humiliating lack of self-esteem and self-control but was still naïve enough to think Celimene would forsake showbiz and come and live with him in the suburbs.

Feb 16. Slava, the Czech clown in **Snowshow** at Hackney Empire. He tore up a love-letter. The letters turned into snowflakes. The flakes turned into a blizzard. With the aid of a wind-machine and masses and masses of little bits of paper, a raging, whirling, blinding snowstorm filled the whole auditorium and was as "sensational" as anything produced by the Victorian theatre. The audience was covered in paper. It took two industrial machines plus ten cleaners to clear up the mess after each show.

Feb 27. Peter Bowles in Noël Coward's **Present Laughter** directed by Richard Olivier at Aldwych. Bowles hammed. The play had no reason to be back in the West

1996 World Premieres

New York
August Wilson's *Seven Guitars*
Jonathan Larson's *Rent*
Gavion Glover and George C Wolfe's *Bring in 'Da Noise, Bring in 'Da Funk*

Paris
Yasmin Reza's *Art*

Deaths
George Abbot (*b.* 1887), American director, playwright and actor

Vivian Ellis (*b.* 1904), British composer
Evelyn Laye (*b.* 1900), British actor
Jack Tinker (*b.* 1938), British critic

History
—Divorce of Prince and Princess of Wales
—IRA resumed campaign in Northern Ireland
—Dunblaine killings
—O J Simpson trial begins

End, having been revived only three years previously with Tom Conti.

Mar 5. Druid Theatre Company at Royal Court Upstairs. Anna Manahan and Marie Mullen in Martin McDonagh's **The Beauty Queen of Leenane** directed by Garry Hynes. Leenane is a small town in Connemara in County Galway. A 70-year-old malign hypochondriac is given to emptying her enormous pot of urine down the kitchen sink. Her 40-year-old unmarried daughter, who punishes her with a diet of lumpy Complan and stale biscuits, gets an opportunity to escape to America with her new boyfriend. Vindictiveness turns to Synge-like brutality. The daughter refuses to part with the poker (with which she had murdered her mother), preferring, she says, to keep it for sentimental reasons.

Mar 5. Paul Keating and Kim Wilde in Peter Townsend's musical **The Who's Tommy** directed by Des McAnuff at Shaftesbury. Book by Peter Townsend and Des McAnuff. Tommy, blind, deaf, dumb and buggered, became a pinball wizard by the age of 10. Tommy had had many incarnations since his conception in 1969: album, concert (including The Met, New York), symphony, ballet and movie. The rock opera was premiered in New York in 1992 when it won five Tonys for score, direction choreography, design and lighting. It didn't have the same success in London.

—The old master work has been reduced to a piece of noisy, pretentious twaddle. JACK TINKER *Daily Mail*

Mar 6. Abbey Theatre, Dublin, at Barbican. Clive Geraghty, Peter Gowen, Sean Campion, Ronan Leahy, Robert Patterson, Gerard Byrne and Conor McDermottroe in Frank McGuinnes's **Observe the Sons of Ulster Marching Towards the Somme** directed by Patrick Mason. Memorial to the Ulster Protestants, who volunteered during World War I to fight for King and Empire and were slaughtered in Flanders. This modern Irish classic was fit to stand alongside such World War I classics as *Journey's End*, *All Quiet on the Western Front*, Stanley Kubrick's *Paths of Glory*, the poetry of Wilfred Owen and the paintings of Paul Nash and Stanley Spencer. First produced in 1985, and revived in 1995 to mark the IRA cease-fire, the production arrived in London just after the bombing had recommenced.

Mar 12. Paul Ireland in Irvine Welsh's **Trainspotting** directed by Harry Gibson transferred to Whitehall. Stomachs were churned. "As funny as a rubber truncheon," said John Gross in *The Sunday Telegraph*. "Seeing it," said Benedict Nightingale in *The Times*, "is like being asked to squelch barefoot through every bodily liquid known to man."

Mar 13. Stephen Sondheim's **Company** directed by Sam Mendes at New transferred from Donmar having won awards for best musical, best director, best actor (Adrian Lester) and best supporting actor (Sophie Thompson).

—The show is indispensable to civilised life. JOHN PETER *Sunday Times*

—The whole evening is as cool, polished and hollow as a designer vase. SARAH HEMMING *Financial Times*

Mar 26. Michael Ball and Maria Friedman in Stephen Sondheim's musical **Passion** directed by Jeremy Sams at Queen's. Book by James Lapine. Adaptation of a little known Italian film, Ettore Scola's *Passione d'Amore*, which was based on *Fosca*, a novel by Iginio Ugo Tarchetti, written in 1869. The passion had its full measure of 19th-century fatalism. The story line, a creepy variation on *Beauty and the Beast*, was gripping. Fosca, a plain and ugly woman, falls in love with a captain and dogs his every step. Persistently scorned, she constantly humiliates and degrades herself. Nevertheless, the captain finds himself more and more drawn to her. Given the opportunity to flee her company and rejoin his mistress, he returns immediately, realising that nobody has ever loved him as much as she has. Friedman was moving in her vulnerability and unnerving in her single-mindedness.

Mar 27. Dein Perry's **Tap Dogs** at Lyric. Seven macho Aussies in hob-nailed boots looked as if they have just come off a building site. Backed by drum and percussion, and occasionally blow-torches, they tapped, stamped, stomped, skidded, slid, scraped and pounded various amplified wooden, steel and wet surfaces with metal-plated precision for 75 minutes without interval.

Swan Lake

Apr 19. Ken Stott in Victor Hugo's **The Prince's Play** translated by Tony Harrison and directed by Richard Eyre at Olivier (NT). Victor Hugo's *Le Roi s'amuse*, best known today through Verdi's *Rigoletto*, was premiered in Paris in 1832 and banned the next day for political and moral reasons. Eyre transferred the melodrama and revolutionary sentiment to 19th century London. François I, king-in-waiting and wanton womaniser, was clearly identified with the House of Windsor. Anti-royalist, the play thus became a contribution to the on-going republican debate. The hunch-backed, all-licensed jester Rigoletto was turned into Scotty Scot, a Glaswegian music hall comedian, who made his entrance as a pantomime dame clog dancing. The production was not a patch on either Franco Zeffirelli's sumptuous Renaissance revival of the opera for the Royal Opera House or Jonathan Miller's brilliant Mafia update for English National Opera.

May 20. Philippa Williams and Cas Harkins in Sarah Kane's **Phaedra's Love**

directed by Sarah Kane at Gate. A disturbing, brutal and gory variation on a classical myth offering masturbation, rape and castration. Hippolytus, no virgin, was a masochistic, heartless, cynical slob who scoffed fries and hamburgers while watching TV and being orally satisfied by Phaedra. "I'm doomed," he said, "absolutely fucking doomed." His penis was grilled on a barbecue.

—It is not a reading that anyone could accuse of subtlety; but it is delivered with great punch and laced with black humour. SARAH HEMMING *Financial Times*

—The impression of a mind on the brink of breakdown is overpowering. It's not theatre that's required here, it's a psychiatrist. CHARLES SPENCER *Daily Telegraph*

Jun 5. Jim Broadbent, Brenda Blethyn, Jason Watkins, Imelda Staunton and Hugh Bonneville in Alan Bennett's **Habeas Corpus** directed by Sam Mendes at Donmar. Farcical sexual repulsion: "Show me a human body," says the doctor, "and I'll show you a cesspit."

Jun 11. Paul Scofield, Vanessa Redgrave and Eileen Atkins in Henrik Ibsen's **John Gabriel Borkman** directed by Richard Eyre at (NT). Scofield's booming, demonic, power-mad banker looked like Ibsen. Vocally and physically he was a formidable stage presence. Atkins and Redgrave were totally convincing as twins. Michael Bryant was delightful as the old clerk. The final scene was a big disappointment. There was no hill. The actors had to pretend to climb.

—He might be a mix of Faust, Prometheus, Napoleon on Elba and Milton's Lucifer given the passionate intensity with which he talks of industrial conquest and the rasping brutality with which he dismisses lesser mortals. A terrific performance. BENEDICT NIGHTINGALE *The Times*

Jun 12. Steven Berkoff in Shakespeare's **Coriolanus** directed by Steven Berkoff at Mermaid. Coriolanus was a strutting, shaven-headed, SS bully boy, ferocious one minute, camp the next. Berkoff brought back memories of Mosley, Mussolini, Roehm and the Kray Brothers. The highly drilled, Black Shirted, jackbooted ensemble of eight actors differentiated whose side they were on by the simple addition of either a worker's jacket or a pair of Mafioso dark glasses. The tribunes in their mackintoshes were members of the secret police. The army rode into battle on imaginary horses to the sound of the "Ride of the Valkyries". The gates of Corioli were prised open in mime.

Jul 10. Iain Glen, Juliette Caton and Jérôme Pradon in Alain Boubil and Claude-Michel Schonberg's musical **Martin Guerre** directed by Declan Donnellan at Prince Edward. The story, set in 16th century France, is probably best known through the French film starring Gerard Depardieu. Everybody in the cinema was kept in suspense right up to the very last moment of the trial as to whether the man really was Martin Guerre or an impostor. Nor was it clear in the film whether his wife knew if he was her husband or not. The whole point of the story was the ambiguity. In the musical she knew he was not Martin and fell in love with him

on sight. "The mega musical," said Richard Harrison in *The Times*, "has run out of puff."
—It's a show which you come out humming the songs, all right. But they are the songs from *Les Miserables*. BILL HAGHERTY *News of the World*

Jul 30. Alexandra Gilbreath in Henrik Ibsen's **Hedda Gabler** directed by Stephen Unwin at Donmar. With her hair brushed back Gilbreath was ready to stand in for Agnes Moorehead playing Mrs Danvers in Alfred Hitchcock's *Rebecca*. Caustic and cruel, she was always very much General Gabler's daughter. She sat, studying her face, a mirror in one hand and a pistol to her temple in the other.

Sep 11. Adam Cooper and Scott Ambler in Matthew Bourne's **Swan Lake** designed by Lez Brotherson at Piccadilly. One of the most radical and one of the most overt homoerotic interpretations, updated to the 1950s: Odette/Odile and the corps de ballet were male swans. They were never fey and definitely not camp. Cooper, a powerful and mesmeric swan, was equally spellbinding as a gate-crashing Odile (transformed into rough trade in leather plus whip), who cheekily chatted up the Queen Mother and all the girls, before dancing with the Prince. Shocked by the discovery of his true sexuality the Prince went mad and tried to rape his mother. Hospitalised in the palace, he was pecked to death by the swans, which appeared from under, over and through his bed, in a thrillingly nightmarish finale. One of the major theatrical events of the 1990s.

Sep 17. Alan Howard in **The Oedipus Plays** directed by Peter Hall at Olivier (NT). Colloquial translation by Ranjit Bolt. Everybody wore masks and everything was played out front. Greg Hicks, as the blind seer Tiresias, wore a skin-suit of peeling clay and was as emaciated as a Giacometti skeletal statue. Hicks's weird and androgynous Polynices was modelled on Elizabeth Frink's *The Fallen Warrior*.

Sep 21. Robert LePage's **The Seven Streams of Ota** at Lyttelton (NT). Ota is the delta on which Hiroshima stands. The epic story, lasting eight hours, was visually stunning and examined East-West relationships and culture. Lepage drew on many genres: opera, American comedy, Japanese puppets, French farce, satire, video, television, magic and a government film on what to do when the Atom Bomb drops.

Sep 25. Diana Rigg, David Suchet, Clare Holman and Lloyd Owen in Edward Albee's **Who's Afraid of Virginia Woolf?** directed by Howard Davies transferred from Almeida to Aldwych. Humiliate the Host? Hump the Hostess? Better still, Get the Guests. Rigg, loud, vulgar and blowsy, was high camp. "If you existed," she sneered, "I'd divorce you." Suchet, working in a drier key, was lethal in his sarcasm. The production was a genuine 24-carat ball-breaker.
—One of the most exhilarating and cathartic experiences the post-war theatre has to offer. PAUL TAYLOR *Independent*

Oct 1. James Kennedy, Antony Riding, Kate Ashfield, Andrew Clover and Robin Soans in Mark Ravenhill's **Shopping and F***ing** directed by Max Stafford-Clark at Ambassadors (home of Royal Court Upstairs in exile). Sexploitation, commercialism and violence: *Shopping* belonged to the *Trainspotting* School of Playwriting and offered a bleak picture of four f***ing losers in London's bed-sit land. A former druggie, can't cope with emotional dependency. He just wants sexual transactions, not personal relationships. A 14-year-old rent boy, who was abused by his step-father, is searching for a father-figure who will abuse him and knife him in the anus. The production toured England.
—This is an important first play: barbarous, compassionate, shocking and callously witty. JOHN PETER *Sunday Times*
—The play's impact is as short-lived as the pre-packed throwaway meals on which the characters survive. SARAH HEMMING *Financial Times*
—The play's harsh, neon-lit poetry, the savage humour and scenes of disgusting degradation throb in the memory like an unlanced boil. CHARLES SPENCER *Daily Telegraph*
—I can't wait to see how it goes down in Bury St Edmunds. JAMES CHRISTOPHER *Sunday Express*

Oct 2. Alison Steadman, Dawn French and Annette Badland as the wives and Roger Lloyd Pack, Gary Waldhorn and Paul Copley as the husbands in J B Priestley's **When We Are Married** directed by Jude Kelly transferred from Chichester Festival Theatre to Savoy. French's lack of stage experience showed. Leo McKern as the drunken photographer and Elizabeth Chadwick as the maid stole the notices.

Oct 15. Albert Finney, Tom Courtenay and Ken Stott in Yasmin Reza's **Art** directed by Matthew Warchus at Wyndham's. Serge (Tom Courtenay) proudly shows the abstract painting he has just acquired to Marc (Albert Finney). The painting is a white rectangle with barely visible white lines across it. Serge has paid Ffr200,000 for it. Marc thinks the painting rubbish and that Serge has been ripped off. Serge finds Marc's condescension and insensitivity deeply offensive. Their friend (Ken Stott) intervenes, attempting the role of arbitrator and peacemaker. The conflict gets nastier. There is a terrible moment when Serge offers Marc his felt tip pen and challenges him to destroy the painting. What was truly shocking was that there were so many members of the audience who actually found the idea of destroying the paint-

Tom Courtenay, Ken Stott and Albert Finney in Art

ing hilarious. "The snob hit of this autumn," said Sheridan Morley in *Punch*. "At last," said Nicholas de Jongh in *The Evening Standard*, "a true adult comedy." *Art* played over 2000 performances.
—If I'm who I am because I'm who I am and you're who you are because you're who you are, then I'm who I am and you're who you are. If, on the other hand, I'm who I am because you're who you are and if you're who you are because I'm who I am, then I'm not who I am and you're not who you are. YASMIN REZA

Oct 23. Smokey Joe's Café directed by Jerry Zaks at Prince of Wales. Award-wining Broadway tribute to songmakers Jerry Leiber and Mike Stoller, who were famously described as white guys with black souls. The high spots (in an exhilarating evening of high spots) included Delee Lively shimmying and Victor Trent Cook singing "I Who Have Nothing".

Oct 24. Janet McTeer and Owen Teale in Henrik Ibsen's **A Doll's House** translated by Frank McGuinness and directed by Antony Page at Playhouse. The idea that anybody could describe the uncommonly tall McTeer as little was absurd. Nevertheless, her highly-strung portrayal, rich in detail, was one of the great Noras of the century. Teale's Torvald was younger, sexier, and randier than usual. When he declared that his wife was not fit to be the mother of his children, the women in the audience laughed loudly.

Oct 31. Alun Armstrong in Arthur Miller's **Death of a Salesman** directed by David Thacker at Lyttelton (NT). The action was clearly happening in Willy Loman's mind. Mark Thompson's set was dominated by a huge flowering elm-tree with the trunk symbolically sliced so that there was a gap between its roots and branches. A broken-down Chevrolet was embedded in the revolving stage. A red-headed woman slept in a bed which was hung from the flies. The design was obtrusive. Armstrong's Loman looked as if he had been a failure all his mortgaged life. Colin Stinton, cast as Loman's boss, had the production's best scene when he brutally fires him, totally indifferent to the thirty-four years he had given to the firm and his father before him.

Nov 5. Teresa Banham as Susanna and Joseph Fiennes as Rafe in Peter Whelan's **The Herbal Bed** directed by Michael Attenborough at Pit (RSC). Wheelan's ecclesiastical courtroom drama was historical fiction based on fact. In Stratford-upon-Avon in 1613 Jack Lane publicly slandered Susanna Hall (Shakespeare's eldest daughter), accusing her of adultery with Rafe Smith. Could Susanna remain calm under cross-examination? Would Rafe crack and admit to fondling her?

Dec 17. Clarke Peters as Sky Masterson, Henry Goodman as Nathan Detroit, Joanna Riding as Sister Sarah, Imelda Staunton as Miss Adelaide and Clive Rowe as Nicely-Nicely Johnson in Frank Loesser's **Guys and Dolls** directed by Richard Eyre (NT). Revival of Eyre's highly successful 1982 production. Goodman's hyperactive Nathan was a small-time weasel who feared that at any minute that he was going to be either arrested or bumped off.

—In apparently flouting the principles of state-subsidised art Richard Eyre has concocted the best possible argument in its favour. MICHAEL COVENEY *Observer*

1997

Jan 7. Ruaidhri Conroy in Martin McDonagh's **The Cripple of Innishmaan** directed by Nicholas Hytner at Cottesloe (NT). Sweet, sensitive crippled lad hears that the famous film director Robert Flaherty is coming to the islands to make a documentary and is looking for actors. He discovers that Hollywood would prefer to employ a normal fellow, who can act crippled rather than a cripple who can't act.

Jan 23. David Bradley, Michael Sheen, Lindsay Duncan, Sam Kelly, Eddie Marsan and Keith Allen in Harold Pinter's **The Homecoming** directed by Roger Michell at Lyttelton (NT). Duncan, cool, sensual, enigmatic, had only to cross her legs for the tension to rise.

Jan 28. English Touring Theatre at Old Vic. Timothy West as Falstaff and Samuel West as Hal in Shakespeare's **Henry IV Parts 1 and 2** directed by Stephen Unwin. West, in a mellow and intimate performance, never got sentimental about the old rogue and never let the audience forget that Falstaff was a mean, selfish, lying, sponging, cowardly, bragging shit, who preyed on the poor, the weak and the defenceless, filling his pocket with bribes. The fact that West's son, Samuel, was playing Hal inevitably led to the conjecture that Falstaff must have been a surrogate father to Hal.

Feb 6. Ralph Fiennes, Harriet Walter, Oliver Ford Davies, Anthony O'Donnell, Bill Paterson, Rosemary McHale and Colin Tierney in Anton Chekhov's **Ivanov** directed by Jonathan Kent at Almeida. This was a major event. Chekhov's first full-length play, written when he was 27, was always considered the poor relation of his more famous masterpieces until Kent's excellent production, with David Hare's vigorous translation and the fine acting of a distinguished ensemble, proved otherwise. Fiennes really did look if he were dead on the inside. The second act party was played as if it was a farce by Gogol or Ostrovsky.

Feb 11. Peter Bowles, Eric Sykes, Carmen Silvera and Henry McGee in Molière's **The School for Wives** directed by Peter Hall at Piccadilly. Bowles mugged and postured so outrageously that when he came to the serious part it was impossible to take him seriously. Ranjit Bolt's anachronistic translation opted for vulgarity rather than wit.

Feb 12. Peter Gill's **Cardiff East** directed by Peter Gill at Cottesloe (NT). A day in the interlocking lives of a working-class community. Times are hard. Jobs are lost. Homes are broken. Fragmentary and impressionistic, realistic and gritty, the production was notable for two ensemble set pieces: the first, a collage of voices, immigrant and Welsh; the second, a mimed kaleidoscopic night out on the town. Two teenagers (Daniel Evans and Matthew Rhys) spent most of the time naked in bed together having a gay time. Key quote: "Feminism is for women with rich husbands or a university degree. It's too good for the working class."

Feb 12. Cliff Richard in **Heathcliff** directed by Frank Dunlop at Apollo, Hammersmith. Musical adaptation of Emily Bronte's *Wuthering Heights*. Book by Cliff Richard and Frank Dunlop. Lyrics by Tim Rice. Music by John Farrar. Helen Hobson as Cathy. The novel's dark, destructive and demonic forces were beyond Richard.

Feb 18. Douglas Henshall, Neil Stuke and Nicholas Woodeson in David Mamet's **American Buffalo** directed by Lindsay Posner at Young Vic. Henshall gave a highly entertaining and very physical performance as the volatile and paranoid Teach.

Mar 5. Rob Morrow and Matthew Wait in Naomi Wallace's adaptation of William Wharton's **Birdy** directed by Kevin Knight at Comedy. Cult psychological novel:

two guys are scarred by the horrors and traumas of war. Birdy, who has always had an affinity with birds and is obsessed with the idea of flying, comes to think of himself as a bird.

Mar 11. Maria Friedman in **Lady in the Dark** directed by Francesca Zambello at Lyttelton (NT). Book by Moss Hart. Lyrics by Ira Gershwin. Music by Kurt Weill. Highly successful fashion editor is seen in two alternating roles: as her austere, workaholic, business-suited self, and as the glamourpuss she imagines herself to be. Her fantasies are the musical part of the show, send-ups of various showbiz genres, including Gilbert and Sullivan. The best songs, "The Saga of Jenny" and "My Ship" come right at the end. James Dreyfus rattling off the 47 composers' names in "Tschaikowsky" (*sic*), a tongue-twisting revue number specially written for Danny Kaye, only made you wonder what Kaye had done on Broadway in 1941 to stop the show and make him a star overnight.

Mar 13. Simon Callow in Micheal Mac Liammoir's **The Importance of Being Oscar** directed by Patrick Garland at Savoy. One-man show based on Oscar Wilde's writings. The only green carnations in sight were those worn by the first night audience. The high spot was a long passage from *De Profundis*, the letter Wilde wrote in prison to Lord Alfred Douglas. The pain, the anger, the bitterness, all deeply felt, were expressed with dignity and without resource to histrionics.

Mar 14. Michael Pennington and Felicity Kendal in Harley Granville Barker's **Waste** directed by Peter Hall at Old Vic. Ideal revival for election year. Hall used Barker's 1926 re-write. The characters, scenes and actions were all the same, but every line of dialogue had been changed; and, in Hall's opinion, for the better.

Mar 23. Rupert Graves, Stephen Dillane and Andy Serkis in David Rabe's **Hurlyburly** directed by Wilson Milam at Old Vic. Two Hollywood casting directors share an apartment and their women. The result is paranoia and virulent nastiness.

Mar 26. Linda Bassett in Ayub Khan-Din's **East is East** directed by Kristine Landon Smith at Royal Court. Devout Muslim in Salford in 1970 refuses to accept that he is living in a different country, culture and time to his family. Bassett played his English-born wife.

Mar 27. Ian Holm in Shakespeare's **King Lear** directed by Richard Eyre at Cottesloe (NT). It has often been said that the play is too big for the stage; but as Eyre's lucid production proved it can be played at a domestic level and acted in a small space with the audience sitting either side of a narrow strip. Holm was a crop-haired, grizzled, crazy, little man given to ungovernable rage and obscene curses, who constantly blocked his ears, as if trying desperately to shut out truths he didn't want to hear. His cry, "I am bound upon a heel of fire" when he woke from a long sleep was tremendous. Michael Bryant's elderly Fool, no pretty knave, looked like a garden gnome. His jaunty footwork recalled the music hall of yesteryear.

Apr 2. Danny Webb and Patrick O'Kane in Ben Elton's **Popcorn** directed by Laurence Boswell at Apollo. Cult Hollywood film director, famous for his violent films, returns to his Beverly Hills home and is greeted by two notorious killers who tell him at gun-point that they are his greatest admirers and that his movies have been their inspiration. They want him to take the blame for their 57 murders. The killers, speaking directly to the television cameras, say they will not kill any of the hostages if the viewers turn off their sets immediately. The ratings immediately go up.

Apr 8. Siân Phillips in Pam Gems's **Marlene** directed by Sean Mathias at Lyric. A recreation of Marlene Dietrich's performance backstage and on-stage. The applause at the end was as much for Dietrich as Phillips's remarkable impersonation.

Apr 14. Michael Gambon and Alec McCowen in Stephen Churchett's **Tom and Clem** directed by Richard Wilson at Aldwych. Fictitious meeting during the 1945 Potsdam Conference between Tom Driberg, popular journalist and bon viveur, and Clement Atlee, who had just won a landslide victory for Labour.

Apr 16. Ian McShane as Crichton and Michael Denison as the Earl of Loam in J M Barrie's **The Admirable Crichton** directed by Michael Rudman at NT. The production (out of Douanier Rousseau) lacked social bite.

Apr 17. Gary Wilmot and Ann Crumb in Neil Simon's musical version of **The Goodbye Girl** directed by Bob Bettinson at Albery. Music by Marvin Hamlisch. Lyrics by Don Black. Wilmot was too cute for the abrasive egocentricity, and never for one minute did he convince that he was an actor. Having been asked to give the sort of ridiculously camp performance nobody would ever give as Richard III, he then had to sing a song about how one day he would play Richard as he should be played, and everybody was expected to take him seriously and be moved.

Apr 23. Phoebe Nicholls in Federico Garcia Lorca's **Doña Rosita, The Spinster** directed by Phyllida Lloyd at Almeida. Rosita is engaged to be married but her fiancé cannot marry her until he has made his fortune. He goes to South America asking her to wait until his return. Fifteen years later she is still waiting. He never comes back. Phoebe Nicholls did not age and she never looked like a spinster.

May 9. Felicity Kendal as Arkadina, Michael Pennington as Trigorin, Victoria Hamilton as Nina, Dominic West as Konstantin and David Yelland as Dorn in Anton Chekhov's **The Seagull** directed by Peter Hall at Old Vic. Pennington's Trigorin was so spineless and submissive that you wondered what Arkadina saw in him.

May 13. Alasdair Harvey and Julie-Alanah Brighten in **Beauty and the Beast** directed by Robert Jess Roth at Dominion. Musical. Book by Linda Woolverton. Music by Alan Menken. Lyrics by Howard Ashman and Tim Rice. The 1991 Disney full-length cartoon always did have the razzmatazz of a big Broadway show. Gaston, the beastly villain was far more beastly than the Beast. Burke Moses, as the strapping vain hunk with biceps and muscles to spare, was an amusing send-up of boorish, brainless machismo. The stage show had twice as many songs as the cartoon. The witty show-stopping number, "Be Our Guest", with the chorus as crockery, cutlery, kitchen utensils and napkins, was choreographed by Matt West in the Busby Berkeley manner on a staircase of saucers.

May 19. Julian Glover, Catherine Cusack and Stanley Townsend in Sebastian Barry's **Prayers of Sherkin** directed by John Dove at Old Vic. Three Manchester families in 1790, members of a Visionary sect, set sail for Ireland to found a New Jerusalem. They settled on the small and isolated island of Sherkin. One hundred years later only one family remains. The widowed father prays to the Lord to send a husband for his daughter and a wife for his son. The chances of his prayers being answered are nil.

May 27. Mark Rylance in Shakespeare's **Henry V** directed by Richard Oliver opened Shakespeare's Globe. Rylance, the gentlest of actors, not obvious casting, underplayed the jingoism and was deeply moving on the eve of the Battle of Agincourt.

May 29. Liza Walker, Clive Owen, Ciaran Hinds and Sally Dexter in Patrick Marber's **Closer** directed by Patrick Marber at Cottesloe (NT). Obscene conversations on the internet: a sexual quadrille in which everybody behaves badly and everybody gets hurt. Transferred to Vaudeville.

Jun 4. Jerry Lewis in **Damn Yankees** directed by Jack O'Brien at Adelphi. Musical. Book by George Abbott and Douglass Wallop. Words and music by Richard Alder and Jerry Ross. The show came to a halt in the second act for Lewis's ten-minute solo.

Jun 16. Ben Kingsley as Estragon and Alan Howard as Vladimir in Samuel Beckett's **Waiting for Godot** directed by Peter Hall at Old Vic. Denis Quilley as Pozzo. Greg Hicks's Lucky, a frail, exhausted old man, panting, dribbling, spitting, gibbering, was outstanding.

Jun 19. Niamh Cusack, Kerry Fox and Josette Simon in Jean Genet's **The Maids** directed by John Crowley at Donmar Warehouse. Prosaic, miscast and not erotic. It was difficult to believe Fox and Cusack were sisters. Cusack seemed to be a tweeny rather than a lady's maid. Simon had the hauteur as the mistress but she seemed to be acting in the maids' charade. The cross-casting might have made more sense in a different production.

Jun 24. Caroline Catz, Pearce Quigley, Lloyd Hutchinson, Tony Guilfoyle and Russell Barr in Mark Ravenhill's **Shopping and F***ing** directed by Max Stafford-Clark at Gielgud. Drugs, prostitution, simulated vomiting, loud music, simulated masturbation, neon lettering, simulated gay oral sex, microwave meals, telephone sex, simulated bottom-licking, shoplifting, casual violence, and simulated buggery. Some West End theatregoers were disturbed by the loud music. Ravenhill's overrated drama, originally produced at Ambassadors, remained a Fringe play in need of a twenty-something audience in a smaller and grubbier venue.
— What makes this play so dangerous to closed minds is its unnerving knack of opening our eyes to the horrors of our daily lives. JAMES CHRISTOPHER *Sunday Express*
—It may be the important play of the decade. *The Stage*
—Mark Ravenhill's debut play hits you like a punch in the solar plexus or even lower below the belt. JACK TINKER *Daily Mail*

Jul 4. Michael Pennington as Sir John Brute in John Vanbrugh's **The Provok'd Wife** directed by Lindsay Posner at Old Vic. Brute, a dirty, stupid, ugly, brawling, bragging sot, only married Lady Brute because she wouldn't sleep with him unless he did. She married him for his money. Marriage has driven him to debauchery and his barbarous usage of her has driven her to thoughts of infidelity. The high spot was when he was disguised as a woman and looked as if he had just escaped from Hogarth's Bedlam. He insisted his wife kiss him. Pennington, against all the odds, managed to make Brute, momentarily, a pathetic figure.

Jul 4. Kieran Ahern, Brendan Coyle, Julia Ford, Gerard Horan and Jim Norton in Conor McPherson's **The Weir** directed by Ian Rickson at Royal Court Upstairs. Haunting in more senses than one, a number of ghost stories were cleverly linked and

1997 World Premieres
New York
Elton John and Tim Rice's *The Lion King*
Peter Stone and Mauray Yeston's *Titanic*
Notes
—The original Globe theatre was built in 1598 and accidentally destroyed by fire on the 29 June 1613 when a canon was fired during a performance of *Henry VIII*. The ball landed in the thatched roof. Some people thought that the new building should have reopened with that play and an apology for the delay.

History
—Tony Blair elected Prime Minister
—China resumed control of Hong Kong
—Scientist cloned Dolly, the sheep
—Heaven Gate cult mass suicide
—Princess Diana killed in Paris car crash

gained immeasurably from their juxtaposition. The most horrific was the stranger in a graveyard who turns out to be a dead paedophile who wants to be buried in a little girl's grave. The actors were an excellent ensemble and play and production got rave notices: "Mesmeric," said *The Independent on Sunday*. "Marvellous," said *The Daily Telegraph*. "Enthralling," said *The Observer*. "Devastating," said *The Express*. "The most exciting evening in theatrical London," said *The Guardian*.

Jul 17. Martin McDonagh's **The Leenane Trilogy** directed by Gary Hynes at Royal Court. Daughter murders mother. Son murders father. Husband murders wife. It's a safe bet that two brothers will shortly blow each other's brains out. Leenane, a small town in Connemara in County Galway, is the murder capital of Europe. There doesn't seem much else for the townspeople to do. In **The Beauty Queen of Leenane** mother (Anna Manahan) and daughter (Marie Mullen) vie in cruelty. In **The Skull of Connemara** two men (Mick Lally and David Wilmot) have a manic time smashing skulls and bones to smithereens on a kitchen table. In **The Lonesome West** two brothers (Maeliosa Stafford and Brian F O'Byrne) compete to see who can confess to the worst crime.

Aug 5. Alan Bates in Simon Gray's **Life Support** directed by Harold Pinter at Haymarket. Popular travel writer, who hates travel, makes up his escapades in his hotel bedroom.

Aug 14. Richard Griffiths as Captain Shotover, Patricia Hodge as Lady Utterwood, Penelope Wilton as Hesione Hushabye and Emma Fielding as Ellie Dunn in Bernard Shaw's **Heartbreak House** directed by David Hare at Almeida. Shotover, inventor and prophet, warns the nation that they are heading for the rocks and that unless they learn to navigate they will perish. "Can't you think of something that will murder half of Europe in one bang?" asks his daughter.

Aug 22. David Harewood as Othello, Simon Russell Beale as Iago and Claire Skinner as Desdemona in Shakespeare's **Othello** directed by Sam Mendes at Cottesloe (NT). Updated to 1930s. Othello was a young chap. Iago was a vulgar, squat, crop-haired, bull-necked, chain-smoking, vicious, petty man, who had been, quite rightly, passed over. Desdemona listened to a 78 crackling recording of "The Willow Song" on a gramophone instead of singing it herself.

Aug 26. Alan Howard in Shakespeare's **King Lear** directed by Peter Hall at Old Vic. Lear had incestuous feelings for his daughters. It was difficult to imagine Victoria Hamilton's waif-like Cordelia leading the French army to victory. Stephen Noonan's skinhead Oswald was a perfect recruit for the National Front.

Aug 26. Nicholas Le Provost as the King and Geraldine Alexander as Evadne in Francis Beaumont and John Fletcher's **The Maid's Tragedy**, directed by Lucy Bailey at Shakespeare's Globe Theatre. The groundlings roared with laughter when the king was being murdered and crying out for pity.

Aug 27. Mark Rylance as Mr Allwit in Thomas Middleton's **A Chaste Maid in Cheapside** directed by Malcolm McKay at Shakespeare's Globe. A rambling, rollicking, bawdy slice of London life (circa 1613) is set during Lent when nobody is allowed to buy or sell flesh on pain of imprisonment. There were more doubles entendres than you would find in a *Carry On* film.

Sep 2. Robert Bowman and Thusitha Jayasundera in Shakespeare's **The Comedy of Errors** directed by Tim Supple at Young Vic (RSC). Acted in deadly earnest, a deliberate damper was put on the farce. The high spot was a moving reunion, a long and silent sequence, when the characters are invited, one by one, into the local priory by the abbess.

Sep 4. Rupert Penry-Jones in Arnold Wesker's **Chips with Everything** directed by Howard Davies at Lyttelton (NT). National Service. Rob Howell's design and Rick Fisher's lighting made it feel as if the whole action was taking place in a concentration camp.

Paul Rhys and John Wood in The Invention of Love

Sep 19. Ian McKellen in Henrik Ibsen's **An Enemy of the People** directed by Trevor Nunn at Olivier (NT). The final image of the Stockmann family, huddled together, high above the screaming mob, defiant to the last, determined to stay on against all the odds and re-educate the town, was heroic, but utterly unconvincing, a futile gesture, much more in keeping with the hero of Arthur Miller's adaptation, which was written in the era of the Senator McCarthy witch-hunts in the USA.

Sep 23. Caryl Churchill's **Blue Heart** directed by Max Stafford-Clark at Royal Court. Two plays. Bernard Gallagher, Valerie Lilley and Mary Macleod in **Heart's Desire** had to keep stopping and restarting. Sometimes they went back only a few lines; sometimes they spoke only part of the sentence; sometimes they repeated only the last word. More often than not they went right back to the beginning. The tape was rewound 27 times. **Blue Kettle** didn't work so well. The language gradually disintegrated and the words "blue" and "kettle" replaced all the nouns and verbs until, blue me, the audience was listening to a lot of kettle.

Oct 1. John Wood and Paul Rhys in Tom Stoppard's **The Invention of Love** directed by Richard Eyre at Cottesloe (NT). A E Housman fell in love with Moses Jackson, a hearty athlete and scientist, who never guessed Housman was "sweet" on him until his girlfriend told him. Wood (ravaged by age and grief) and Rhys (fresh-faced, quivering with youth and promise), cast respectively as the old and young Housman, complemented each other perfectly. The final imagined scene was between the introvert Housman and the extrovert Oscar Wilde. Wilde knew everybody and had lots of friends. Housman knew nobody and had only colleagues. Wilde ended up with two years' hard labour and an early death. Housman ended up with half a life, which was not as celibate as, perhaps, the play implied.

Oct 1. Monica Dolan in Shared Experience's adaptation of Charlotte Bronte's **Jane Eyre** directed by Polly Teale at Young Vic. It was like an erotic ballet. The movement was choreographed by Liz Ranken. Neil Warmington provided a Gothic setting: a sweeping, curving, dilapidated staircase backed by a sky of stormy clouds redolent of the Yorkshire Moors. The parallels between Jane and the demoniac Mrs Rochester were established from the very start by having Pooky Quesnel play Jane's *alter ego* and Mrs Rochester.

Oct 14. Edward Fox as Harold Macmillan in Hugh Whitemore's **Letter of Resignation** directed by Christopher Morahan at Comedy. The John Profumo/Christine Keeler scandal acted as a springboard for Whitemore's sympathetic portrait of the Prime Minister. Fox's impersonation of the Edwardian grandee in decline was amusing and touching.

Oct 15. The Ninagawa Company in Shuji Terayama's **Shintoku-Maru** directed by Yukio Ninagawa at Barbican. The story of a teenager (15-year-old Tatsuya Fuji-

nara) and his step-mother (Kayo Shiraishi) was told in a series of striking tableaux. Grotesque Fellini-like strolling players of varying sizes advanced downstage in slow motion. Screaming mothers searched for their lost children in hell.

Oct 21. Maggie Smith, Eileen Atkins and John Standing in Edward Albee's **A Delicate Balance** directed by Anthony Page at Haymarket. The balance between actor and actor, and actor and audience, is crucial. Audiences presumed Maggie Smith was playing the lead. She wasn't. Eileen Atkins should have been the fulcrum but was constantly upstaged.

Oct 25. Zoë Wanamaker as Electra and Marjorie Yates as Clytemnestra in a version of Sophocles's **Electra** by Frank McGuinness directed by David Leveaux at Donmar. Wanamaker, red hair cropped, feet bare, dressed in a grey trench coat, prowled the stage and wept inconsolably. Clytemnestra was a proud, handsome woman and not nearly as monstrous as her reputation. The chorus, represented by just three women, were refugees from Sarajevo.

Oct 27. Rupert Everett in Tennessee Williams's **The Milk Train Doesn't Stop Here Anymore** directed by Philip Prowse at Lyric, Hammersmith. Hermione Baddeley scored a big success in the original production in 1953. It closed three days later. It was revived the following year in a new version with Tallulah Bankhead who, deep into drugs and drink, no longer had the stamina to sustain the role. It was made into a film, *Boom!*, starring Elizabeth Taylor. Ruth Gordon was going to act it at the Royal Court but she didn't get past the first week of rehearsal. Williams went on rewriting the play until his death in 1965. He never got it right. There is no reason why Flora shouldn't be played by a man, but Everett simply wasn't good enough.
—I draw every character out of my multiple split personality. My heroines always express the climate of my interior world at the time those characters were created. If you write a play with a strong female role, it is likely to surface repeatedly since female stars of a certain age have a rough time finding vehicles suitable for their talents, personalities and public image.
Tennessee Williams

Nov 5. Michel Piccoli and Lucinda Childs in Marguerite Duras's **La Maladie de la Mort** directed and designed by Robert Wilson at Peacock. A man who has never known love pays a woman to spend seven nights with him. Wilson treated the actors as sculptures in an empty landscape.

Nov 6. Michael Sheen in Shakespeare's **Henry V** directed by Ron Daniels at Barbican (RSC). Modern dress production. Sheen's Tony Blairish king was just out of Sandhurst.

Nov 18. Ruthie Henshall, Ute Lemper, Henry Goodman and Nigel Planer in Fred

Ute Lemper in Chicago

Ebb and John Kander's musical **Chicago** directed by Walter Bobbie at Adelphi. Book by Fred Ebb and Bob Fosse based on 1926 comedy by Maurine Dallas Watkins. A bitter and cynical satire on American justice in which the guilty go free and the innocent get hanged. The criminals behave like movie stars. The bony, angular, high-kicking, long-legged and unbelievably thin Lemper led the company in the opening number, *All That Jazz*, the first of many show-stoppers. Ann Reinking's choreography was in the style of Bob Fosse.

Nov 19. Royal Court at Duke of York's. Richard Briers and Geraldine McEwan in Eugene Ionesco's **The Chairs** directed by Simon McBurney. Briers's mood swung from cry-baby to ferocious anger. McEwan, who looked like a haystack (as the text required she should) was too much the comedienne when she started flirting outrageously with the guests.

Nov 25. Antony Sher in Edmond Rostand's **Cyrano de Bergerac** directed by Gregory Doran at Lyric (RSC). Sher had Cyrano's intellect, poetry and self-pity, but not his physique, charm, warmth and panache. The production, too, lacked the necessary spectacle.

Dec 3. Siobhan Redmond as Bel-Imperia in Thomas Kyd's **The Spanish Tragedy** directed by Michael Boyd at Barbican Pit (RSC). Kyd's crude and gory story of love, murder and revenge was one of the biggest box office successes of the Elizabethan age. The most gripping scene comes towards the end when the Spanish court is watching a play, little realising that the murders they are witnessing are for real.

Dec 4. Alex Jennings in Shakespeare's **Hamlet** directed by Matthew Warchus at Barbican (RSC). Nine characters (including Fortinbras) were dropped. Scenes were interpolated and lines were redistributed. Hamlet was discovered pouring the ashes of his dead father on to the ground, while a home movie of his childhood was screened behind him. He then attended a party to celebrate his mother's marriage to his uncle and took Polaroid pictures of them necking. The Ghost turned up in evening dress for a chat. When Derbhle Crotty's Ophelia went mad; there weren't any flowers, just pills, which she dropped all over the place.

Dec 11. Leslie Phillips in Shakespeare's **The Merry Wives of Windsor** directed by Ian Judge at Barbican (RSC). Phillips, mellow and tweedy, hadn't got the physical bulk.

Dec 12. Julian Clary in **Special Delivery** at Vaudeville. One man show. Doubles entendres and buggery jokes.

Dec 15. Griff Rhys Jones in Ben Hecht and Charles MacArthur's **The Front Page** directed by Sam Mendes at Donmar Warehouse. The English accents got in the way.

Dec 16. Daniel Evans in J M Barrie's **Peter Pan** in a new version written and directed by John Caird and Trevor Nunn at Olivier (NT). Evans was a sad, vulnerable, asexual, Puckish, Welsh boyo. There was a particularly touching moment when he comes back to the nursery after a long absence to find that Wendy has grownup and is a mother. Ian McKellen's Captain Hook was a Charles II lookalike. Alec McCowen was the narrator.

Dec 17. Tom Hollander as Khlestakov in Nikolai Gogol's **The Government Inspector** directed by Jonathan Kent at Almeida. Set in Scotland, the characters, somewhat oddly, kept their Russian names. Hollander's blubbery, baby-voiced, wide-eyed pipsqueak in a ginger wig was the sort of naughty little boy you might find in an early 18th-century wood carving to illustrate a volume of nursery rhymes.

1998

Jan 15. Joanne Pearce as Imogen in Shakespeare's **Cymbeline** directed by Adrian Noble at Barbican (RSC). The cast wore pigtails, hobbled about in slippers and carried picturesque Japanese umbrellas. Battle scenes were staged in a quasi-oriental manner with flags, drum beats, and shadow play. The audience liked Guy Henry's Cloten so much that it was a big shock for those who didn't know the play to find that Cloten gets his head chopped off.

Feb 12. Alan Howard in Mikhail Bulgakov's **Flight** directed by Howard Davies at Olivier (NT). The satire was set during the Russian Civil War at the moment of the defeat of the White Army by the Red Army. Written in 1928, it was banned during Bulgakov's life time for being anti-Soviet.

Feb 24. Juliette Binoche in Luigi Pirandello's **Naked** directed by Jonathan Kent at Almeida. Nanny is having an affair with her employer and a naval officer when the baby in her charge dies in an accident. The employer sacks her and the naval officer deserts her. She turns to prostitution and then attempts to commit suicide.

Mar 3. Susannah York as Marguerite Gautier, Paola Dionisotti as the gypsy brothel-keeper and David Collings as Baron de Charlus in Tennessee William's **Camino Real** directed by Steven Pimlott at Young Vic (RSC). Pimlott rose to the challenge of two set pieces. The first is a fiesta of the dead inspired by Diego Rivera's mural *The Dream of a Sunday Afternoon in the Almeda Park*. The second is the frantic scramble to get away on a plane. Needless to say the plane crashes. You can't cheat Death when your number is up.

Mar 3. Jane Asher and Steven Pacey in Alan Ayckbourn's **Things We Do For Love** directed by Alan Ayckbourn at Gielgud. Ayckbourn's tragicomedy may not have been as dark as some of his most recent work, but that did not make the humiliations, the fights, the revenge any the less cruel and hurtful. The set was deliberately designed so that the audience could only see the actors' legs in the top floor flat, but how this gimmick actually served the play was not made clear.

Mar 5. Corin Redgrave, James Blake, Finbar Lynch, Sherri Parker Lee and Sandra

Dickinson in Tennessee Williams's **Not About Nightingales** directed by Trevor Nunn at Cottesloe (NT). World premiere. Written in 1938 when he was 27 it was based on events which had hit the headlines that year. The prisoners at Philadelphia County's model prison, fed up with a daily diet of meat balls and spaghetti, went on hunger strike. The Governor put the strikers into Klondyke (a small building, 50 feet long, 12 feet wide, and 8 feet high) which contained a bank of radiators. The windows were closed. The water was turned off. The heat was turned up. Four men died, baked to death, their hearts shrunk to half their normal size by dehydration. Staged as if the play were a black and white Warner Bros prison movie, everything was in monochrome; even the United States flag. The brutality was awesome. The jets of steam coming through the floor were lethal.

Mar 19. Liam Neeson as Oscar Wilde and Tom Hollander as Lord Alfred Douglas in David Hare's **Judas Kiss** directed by Richard Eyre at Playhouse. Two key moments in Oscar Wilde's life. The first was just before his arrest on a charge of gross indecency. The Law gave him time to catch the last train to Paris, but he chose to stay, stood trial, and was sentenced to two years hard labour. The second was in exile and poverty in Naples following his release from prison. Hollander (who had to stand on tiptoe to kiss Neeson) played Bosie Douglas for a shallow, feckless, selfish, petulant and repellent little boy, who saw himself as much a victim as Oscar and even claimed his suffering had been the greater.
—He [Liam Neeson] eschews all camp and he combines authority with relaxation. He has warmth and charm. But in both vice and gesture he has less theatricality than the lines he speaks; and he seems altogether more ordinary than the tragic Romantic and witty poseur Wilde elected to be. ALISTAIR MACAULAY *Financial Times*

Mar 23. Michael Williams in John Aubrey's **Brief Lives** adapted and directed by Patrick Garland at Duchess. Gossip. Solo performance. The basic fault with the script is that nothing is sustained and that there is too much talk about people whose names mean very little, if anything at all. Aubrey is not nearly as entertaining as Samuel Pepys and John Evelyn

Mar 25. Stephen Dillane, Linus Roache, Anastasia Hille and Jo McInnes in Anton Chekhov's **Uncle Vanya** directed by Katie Mitchell at Young Vic (RSC). Dilane and Roache were a bit young to be playing Vanya and Astrov. Hille's Yelena, looked as worn out as everybody else, having lost her youth and beauty nursing her sick, cantankerous husband. McInnes's Sonia underplayed the stoicism in the final moments. Mitchell's production, notable for its sound effects, benefited enormously from being performed in the round and with the audience at such close quarters. At times the conversations

Not About Nightingales

1998 World Premieres
New York
　Terrence McNally, Stephen Flaherty
　and Lynn Ahrens's *Ragtime*

History
—President Clinton impeachment
　trial
—America bombed Iraq
—US government approved Viagra

turned a 60th birthday party into a wake. Spacey was mesmeric.
—[Kevin Spacey] is an extraordinary actor because of his concentration and stillness, his flat but musically distinctive voice, an unassuming yet dominating presence and the dangerous satanic gleam that plays around his eyes. Michael Coveney *Daily Mail*

were so private that it was difficult to hear what was being said. Hille was the worst offender; but, despite numerous complaints, she made no attempt to raise her voice.

Mar 26. Michael Pennington and Elaine Page in Molière's The **Misanthrope** directed by Peter Hall at Piccadilly. Le Roi Soleil presented his bare bum to the audience. The only proper response to this would have been for the audience to reply in kind.

Apr 8. Michael Gambon and Eileen Atkins in Yasmina Reza's **The Unexpected Man** directed by Matthew Warchus at Barbican Pit. Two alternating interior monologues. Gambon (moroseness personified) remained seated for all but the last few minutes when he got up to quote Chekhov. Atkins, who had the less interesting role, was allowed to get up and wander around aimlessly. The tension came from wondering if they would ever talk to each other. They didn't.

Apr 17. Kevin Spacey in Eugene O'Neill's **The Iceman Cometh** directed by Howard Davies at Almeida. Triumph of ensemble work. Spacey brought a bright and breezy, salesman-like patter to Hicky. He was tough, shrewd, and slightly creepy. His evangelical smiles had no warmth. He looked right through the inmates and stripped them of the illusions that had made their lives bearable and

Apr 21. Adam Garcia in **Saturday Night Fever** choreographed and directed by Arlene Phillips at London Palladium. Stage adaptation by Norman Wexler based on the film, based on a story by Nik Cohn. Songs by the Bee Gees. The audience greeted Garcia with screams as if he were John Travolta reincarnated.

Apr 22. Desmond Barrit and David Tennant in Tom Stoppard's **The Real Inspector Hound** and Peter Shaffer's **Black Comedy** directed by Greg Doran at Comedy. Stoppard always said he wished he had thought of *Black Comedy* first.

Apr 28. George Grizzard and Carole Shelley in Jerome Kern and Oscar Hammerstein II's **Show Boat** directed by Harold Prince at Prince Edward Theatre. The production was culled from the original 1929 production, the subsequent London script, the 1946 Broadway version, and the 1936 film.

May 6. Stuart McQuarrie and Martin Marquez in Sarah Kane's **Cleansed** directed by James Macdonald at Royal Court. Social outcasts in a university were butchered and murdered. Limbs, tongues and penises were lopped, severed and transplanted. But somehow love survived. "Disgusting feast of filth!" said *The Daily Mail*.
—Watching Sarah Kane's *Cleansed* was one of the most repellent experiences of my theatregoing life. Nicholas de Jongh *Evening Standard*

May 7. Douglas Hodge, Lia Williams, Penelope Wilton and Bill Nighy in three

Kevin Spacey, Mark Strong and Tony Guilfoyle in The Iceman Cometh

plays by Harold Pinter at Donmar Warehouse. **A Kind of Alaska** directed by Karl Reisz. **The Collection** and **The Lover** directed by Joe Harmston. *The Lover* worked best. The fantasies that Richard and Sarah indulge to keep their marriage alive are, at first, amusing, then pathetic and finally, degrading. He pretends to be her lover; she pretends to be his whore. But since their role-play has become as sterile as their marriage, Richard deliberately, sadistically, sets out to destroy their fantasies by making them real. What begins in romantic Molnar-like comedy fashion ends in Strindbergian viciousness. Hodge and Williams were first-rate.

May 9. Bonnie Langford and Mark Wynter in Cy Coleman's musical **Sweet Charity** directed by Carol Metcalfe at Victoria Palace. Book by Neil Simon. Lyrics by Dorothy Fields. Badly directed and with a poor chorus line who couldn't do justice to Chet Walker's pastiche Fosse choreography, it looked like a shop-worn touring show which should never have come to London.

May 12. Jonathan Larson's **Rent** directed by Michael Greif at Shaftesbury Theatre. Larson, aged 35, earning his living as a waiter in a SoHo diner, finally got his rock opera staged with the financial help of an award from Stephen Sondheim. He had been working on the show since 1989. He died of an aortic aneurism a few hours before the final dress rehearsal. Rent went on to win the New York Drama Critics Circle Award, the Drama Desk Award, an Obie and a Tony. The story, an update of Puccini's *La Boheme*, set in New York's lower East End's Alphabet City, told a sordid tale of love, poverty, threats of eviction, drug addiction, AIDS and death. There was no spoken dialogue. The lyrics were colloquial and bellicose.
—Deep down there's nothing that couldn't have been written by our Mr Broadway colleagues, Ersatz and Schmaltz. ROBERT BUTLER *Independent on Sunday*
—This is saccharine, ghoulish stuff, made worse by its masquerade of gritty realism. SUSANNAH CLAPP *Observer*

May 14. Peter Bowles as Undershaft, Jemma Redgrave as Barbara and David Yelland as Cusins in Bernard Shaw's **Major Barbara** directed by Peter Hall at Old Vic. A play for New Labour. Bowles's charismatic arms manufacturer, beneficent and amiable on the surface, was thoroughly dangerous. He and Yelland, equally well cast, carried the debate in the last act to a triumphant conclusion.

May 20. Norbert Kentrup as Shylock in Shakespeare's **The Merchant of Venice** directed by Richard Olivier at Shakespeare's Globe. The groundlings behaved as if they were an Elizabethan audience and applauded Shylock's downfall. The biggest laugh was when Antonio insisted that Shylock became a Christian.

May 28. Sara Kestelman, David Burke and Matthew Marsh in Michael Frayn's **Copenhagen** directed by Michael Blakemore at Cottesloe (NT). In 1941 during World War 2 the German physicist Werner Heisenberg went to occupied Copenhagen to see his Danish counterpart, Nils Bohr, the most famous physicist in the world. They had been friends and colleagues since 1920 and had worked together on quantum mechanics. Nobody knows what they said. Frayn imagined what they might have said and the action was replayed more than once to provide a variety of questions. Did Heisenberg come on his own account or on behalf of the Nazis? Did he come to try and persuade Bohr to persuade the Allies to drop their nuclear programme if he promised to drop his nuclear programme?

Jun 5. Cheek by Jowl at Playhouse. Matthew MacFadyen as Benedict and Saskia Reeves as Beatrice in Shakespeare's **Much Ado About Nothing** directed by Declan Donnellan. Men were deceivers ever. The line is repeated often. The comedy is set in Edwardian times among the guffawing officer class, juvenile ex-public school boys, who have no idea how to conduct themselves and behave appallingly in church.

Jun 23. Colin Stinton, Zoë Wanamaker and Diana Quick in David Mamet's **The Old Neighbourhood** directed by Patrick Marber at Royal Court. Middle-aged man's marriage has just collapsed. He returns home to see his best mate, his sister and his former lover. Three separate autobiographical playlets were revised and joined together to make one very short, 80-minute play. They were written in Mamet's characteristic ruptured and discursive manner, but the over-all message was clear: life is too short, the world is a shit-hole and goodbye to love

Jun 25. Fiona Shaw in Jay Presson Allen's adaptation of Muriel Spark's **The Prime of Miss Jean Brodie** directed by Phyllida Lloyd at Lyttelton (NT). The newly revised adaptation was still flawed but, like the previous versions, worth seeing for the central performance. When Jean Brodie returns to Edinburgh from one of her many trips abroad, the girls blindfold her and lead her to a seat at the table. When the blindfold is removed she finds herself in a *tableau vivant* of Leonardo's *The Last Supper*, playing Jesus to the girls' adoring disciples.
—A second rate adaptation of a first rate novel by a living author should have no claims on the diminished resources of a great subsidised company. JOHN PETER *Sunday Times*

Jul 1. Marcus Lovett and Lottie Mayor in Andrew Lloyd Webber's musical **Whistle Down the Wind** directed by Gale Edwards at Aldwych. Lyrics by Jim Steinman. Three motherless Lancashire farm children mistake a murderer on the run for Jesus.

The modest 1961 British film was relocated to the Bible/racist belt of Louisiana in the 1950s. Lovett, who played the murderer, looked all set to sing in *Jesus Christ Superstar*. When Hayley Mills in the film told Alan Bates that she loved him, the lines did not have any sexual connotation whatsoever; but with a much older actress playing the role, the sexual element was inevitable.

Jul 14. Philip Schofield in Leslie Bricusse's musical **Doctor Dolittle** based on stories by Hugh Lofting and directed by Steven Pimlott at Labatt's Apollo. The songs were written so that Rex Harrison in the 1967 film could talk his way through them as he had done so successfully in *My Fair Lady*. Schofield played a supporting role to the animaltronics created by Jim Henson's Creature Shop.

Jul 15. Hugh Jackman and Josefina Gabrielle in Richard Rodgers and Oscar Hammerstein's musical **Oklahoma!** directed by Trevor Nunn at Olivier (NT). Curly strolled on to the stage to sing "O What A Beautiful Mornin'" as if it was the most natural thing in the world. Jackman had the voice, the physique, the looks, the naïvety, and the star quality for the role. Nunn took the book seriously and this was especially true of the portrayal of Jud (Shuler Hensley), who was no cardboard villain but a sad, mentally unbalanced, sexually frustrated figure.

Jul 16. Steppenwolf Theatre Company at Barbican. John Mahoney as Sheridan Whiteside in Moss Hart and George S Kaufman's **The Man Who Came To Dinner** directed by James Burrows. An excellent example of 1930s wisecracking American comedy. Sheridan Whiteside, a name-dropping, Falstaffian spoiled baby, who alienates everybody with his acerbic rudeness, is a major comic creation. John Mahoney was a Monty Woolley lookalike.

Sep 2. Alan Howard and Frances de la Tour in Edward Albee's **The Play About the Baby** directed by Howard Davies at Almeida. Boy meets Girl. The Boy (Rupert Penry-Jones) claims he always has a hard-on and promises his partner that he will do something that hasn't been done for three centuries and has been outlawed by three religions. Whatever it is that he does (off-stage), the girl doesn't like it.

Sep 9. Diana Rigg and Toby Stephens in Jean Racine's **Phedre** directed by Jonathan Kent for The Almeida at Albery. Rigg shielded her face from the light and hugged the walls, occasionally splashing her face with water from a tap. Stephens postured. Barbara Jefford, cast as Phedre's confidante, looked as if she had stepped out of an old theatre print and gave the most classical performance.
—Mr Stephens wearing black vinyl, High boots and flowing coat looks and sounds like a petulant West End clubber, refused entry to a gay fancy dress night. NICHOLAS DE JONGH *Evening Standard*

Sep 10. Nicole Kidman and Iain Glen in David Hare's **The Blue Room** directed by Sam Mendes at Donmar. Schnitzler's *La Ronde* was updated. Kidman took off her kit and put the Donmar on the international map.
—In this production you might just as well lie back and enjoy the sheer style or sexuality on display: it's pure theatrical Viagra. CHARLES SPENCER *Daily Telegraph*

Sep 10. Jonathan Cullen, Stephen Beresford, David Beames, Ian Redford and Declan Colan in Timberlake Wertenbaker's **Our Country's Good** directed by Max Stafford-Clark at Young Vic. Excellent revival. Penal Colony in Sydney in 1788. The Governor-in-Chief of New South Wales gives the go-ahead for a production of Farquhar's *The Recruiting Officer*: "The theatre is an expression of civilization. We belong to a great country, which has spawned great playwrights: Shakespeare, Marlowe, Jonson, and even in our own time, Sheridan. The convicts will be speaking a refined, literate language and expressing sentiments of a delicacy they are not used to. It will remind them that there is more to life than crime, punishment. And we, this colony of a few hundred, will be watching this together, for a few hours we will no longer be despised prisoners and hated gaolers. We will laugh, we may be moved, we may even think a little."

Sep 14. Lee Evans at Apollo. Brilliant stand-up comedian. His act fed on his fears and neuroses. The body language was hilariously frenetic.

Sep 22. Lesley Joseph and Kevin Colson in **Annie** directed by Martin Charnin at Victoria Palace. Musical Book by Thomas Meehan. Music by Charles Strouse. Lyrics by Martin Charnin. Lily Savage, a drag artist, took over at Christmas from Lesley Joseph and turned the gin-sodden Miss Hannigan, who runs the orphanage, into a pantomime dame (and a bit of a slag).

Sep 28. Geoffrey Hutchings as Sid James, Samantha Spiro as Barbara Windsor and Adam Godley as Kenneth Williams in Terry Johnson's **Cleo, Camping, Emmanuelle and Dick** directed by Terry Johnson at Lyttelton (NT). Johnson's first act was a very superior Carry On script (far too good for a Carry On film.) Sid James came across as an unhappy, dirty, old sod of whom it was said that what he admired most in women was himself. Barbara Windsor emerged as warm, compassionate and life-giving. Adam Godley, though far too tall, caught Kenneth Williams's caustic nasal drawl and facial mannerisms perfectly.

Oct 8. Judi Dench in Eduardo de Filippo's **Filumena** directed by Peter Hall at

Piccadilly. Dench has this ability to play roles for which, on paper at least, she is totally unsuitable, and play them brilliantly. So nobody was surprised when she was cast as a Neapolitan prostitute. Filumena, a survivor, humane, generous, and compassionate, has tremendous moral authority. Her triumph is movingly consolidated when her husband marries her again and promises to love all three sons equally. The performance, begun in broad comedy, ended in tears.

—Of all the great English actresses, Dench is the one you most instinctively warm to. CHARLES SPENCER *Daily Telegraph*

—This is yet another heartbreaking, compelling performance from Dench, our finest actress. GEORGIA BROWN *Mail on Sunday*

Oct 17. Hamish McColl and Sean Foley in Bertolt Brecht's **Mr Puntila and His Man Matti** directed by Kathryn Hunter at Almeida. Puntila is a huge role and McColl carried it off with manic, eye-popping aplomb. Foley, a first rate foil, had a wonderful and hilariously over-extended bit of mime when he couldn't make up his mind what to do and dithered interminably, spatially confused.

Oct 20. Alan Rickman and Helen Mirren in Shakespeare's **Antony and Cleopatra** directed by Sean Mathias at Olivier (NT). There was no chemistry between the actors. Rickman walked through the production.

Oct 20. Patrick O'Kane in Brian Friel's **Volunteers** directed by Mick Gordon at Gate. The auditorium had been converted into an archaeological site. The lighting remains on throughout and the audience sat on stone slabs round the dig. Five political prisoners, who have volunteered to work on the site, discover on their last day of digging that a Kangaroo Court has condemned them to capital punishment and that a series of "accidents" will take place during an organised riot on their return. Premiered at The Abbey in Dublin in 1975 when it wasn't well received. Revived in London it felt like a major play.

Oct 21. David Suchet as Salieri and Michael Sheen as Mozart in Peter Shaffer's **Amadeus** directed by Peter Hall at Old Vic. Suchet was a sleek cat, Sheen toned down the irritating falsetto giggling, once thought so essential to the role. He still had the sniggering, swaggering, juvenile vulgarity, the role required; but what made the performance special was the sadness and vulnerability.

Oct 28. William Houston and Jayne Ashbourne in Shakespeare's **Troilus and Cressida** directed by Michael Boyd at Barbican Pit (RSC). The Trojans were working-class Irish Catholics. The Greeks wore suits. Patroclus (Achilles's male lover) was played by an actress, so it seemed as if Achilles was having an affair with a lesbian. Helen was dressed up to look like a Virgin Mary statue. Paris was discovered under her skirts. Patroclus was shot by his own army. Achilles killed Hector without the help of his Myrmidons. Cressida's arrival in the Greek camp turned into a gang-rape in tango time.

Nov 4. Diana Rigg and Toby Stephens in Jean Racine's **Britannicus** directed by Jonathan Kent at Albery. Nero was at the very start of his highly successful career in murder, rape, robbery, chariot-racing, singing and buggery. He was so successful that he was dead by the time he was 31. Racine showed him as a 21-year-old boy still trying to break loose from his mother's apron strings. Rigg's Agrippina, elegant, brittle, chain-smoking, was the ultimate awful mum, desperate to maintain her hold on power and watching it slip away. Stephens's emperor was a sinister, nervous, baby-faced, psychopathic voyeur, liable to have hysterics at any minute.

—Diana Rigg here presents a lethally sophisticated Agrippina whose lofty derisiveness and arrogance remind you that this actress is a supreme mistress of high-comedy. PAUL TAYLOR *Independent*

Nov 4. Patrick Barlow and John Ramm in the National Theatre of Brent's production of Patrick Barlow's **Love Upon The Throne** directed by Martin Duncan at Comedy Theatre. The romance, courtship and matrimony of Prince Charles and Diana Spencer: the deliberate banality of the text and the deliberate ineptitude of the acting were very funny.

Nov 6. Clare Burt as the Witch and Frank Middlemass as the Narrator in Stephen Sondheim's musical **Into the Woods** directed by John Crowley at Donmar. Book by James Lapine. A chamber musical in a chamber theatre made sense, but the lyrics were still not always audible. Nick Holder and Sophie Thompson were very likeable as the baker and his wife. Damian Lewis doubled as the Prince and the carnal wolf.

—It is easy to admire Stephen Sondheim, much harder to love him. There is a cold calculation about his work, an ostentatious cleverness that holds the audience at a distance. CHARLES SPENCER *Daily Telegraph*

—It's a long haul evening and – as usual – there's not a single tune to hum on the way out. ROBERT GORE-LANGTON *Express*

Nov 19. Ewan McGregor in David Halliwell's **Little Malcolm and His Struggle Against the Eunuchs** directed by Denis Lawson at Hampstead. Malcolm, fatally weak-willed, lives out his fantasies but is too petrified to put them into action. McGregor's scruffy, bearded, great-coated baby-dictator was too impotent, too naïve, ever to be really dangerous. Transferred to Comedy.

Nov 19. John Gordon-Sinclair in Alan Bennett's **Kafka's Dick** directed by Peter Hall at Piccadilly. Jason Watkins struck the right farcical note as Brod. The last scene took place in heaven, a somewhat desperate attempt to give the production a lift.

Nov 24. Douglas Hodge, Imogen Stubbs and Anthony Calf in Harold Pinter's **Betrayal** directed by Trevor Nunn at Lyttelton (NT). Es Devlin's set (inspired by Rachel Whitehead's House) put an immediate damper on the play and the scene changes were cumbersome.

Nov 25. Greg Hicks as Herod and Emily Woof as Salome in Oscar Wilde's **Salome** directed by Mick Gordon at Riverside Studios. No poetry, no gaudy ornateness, no severed head, no voluptuousness, no Grand Guignol. Salome wore white jeans. Herod wore an eye-patch. Jokanaan was discovered atop a step-ladder.

Nov 27. The Improbable Theatre in Angela Carter's **Cinderella**, adapted and staged by Julian Crouch, Phelim McDermott, Lee Simpson and Neil Bartlett at Lyric, Hammersmith. The production drew on traditional pantomime, marionettes, origami and the Black Theatre of Prague but it was never as cruel as Grimm and Carter. The children in the audience clearly didn't want Cinders (Angela Clerkin) to marry the Prince. They wanted her to marry the sexually inexperienced Buttons (a delightful performance by Martin Freeman).

1999

Jan 2. Jeremy Northam, Sean Chapman and Andrew Woodall in Peter Gill's **Certain Young Men** directed by Peter Gill at Almeida. Gay relationships, gay culture and gay politics explored in brief duologues.

Jan 6. **The Colour of Justice** edited by Richard Norton-Taylor and directed by Nicholas Kent and Surian Fletcher-Jones at Tricycle. Black teenager was stabbed to death in an unprovoked racist attack by five white youths. The police investigation failed to provide sufficient evidence in court to convict. The text was based on the transcripts of the Stephen Lawrence public inquiry. Transferred to Victoria Palace.

Jan 7. Samuel Beckett's **Breath** at Arts. At 35 seconds, the shortest play in the history of drama. Better in the telling than in the seeing it was first performed in New York in 1969 in Kenneth Tynan's erotic revue, *Oh! Calcutta!*, where it was used as an incongruous prologue to the nudity which followed. Staged in a double bill with Edward Petherbridge in Beckett's **Krapp's Last Tape**, directed by Edward Petherbridge and David Hunt. 45 minutes of Krapp and 35 seconds of rubbish were not to everybody's taste.

Jan 11. Alison Steadman, Samantha Bond and Julia Sawalha in Shelagh Stephenson's **The Memory of Water** directed by Terry Johnson at Vaudeville. Three sisters meet for their mother's funeral. The eldest complains that if she had left the funeral arrangements to the other two their mother would have had to cremate herself.

Jan 18. Robert Lindsay in Shakespeare's **Richard III** directed by Elijah Moshinsky at Savoy (RSC). Lindsay, swirling an enormous black cloak, acted as he were the Demon King in pantomime.

Jan 20. Stephen Boxer as Angelo and Clare Holman as Isabella in Shakespeare's **Measure for Measure** directed by Michael Boyd at Barbican (RSC). Adrian Schiller's gum-chewing Lucio was the sort of guy who would offer a cigarette to a nun. Jimmy Chisholm's Pompey, who had green-eye shadow, rouged lips and a powdered face, was both flattered and taken-aback by the judiciary's compliment on his bum. There was a surreal moment when prisoners' heads appeared out of the ground and he watered them with his watering-can. Jake Nightingale's Abhorson, the executioner, looked as if he could apply for the post of butler to the Addams Family. Clare Holman's novice decided to kick the habit and marry the Duke.

Jan 26. Sheila Hancock and David Tennant in Maxim Gorky's **Vassa** directed by Howard Davies at Albery Theatre. Splendid black comedy written in 1910. Of the three versions this, the earliest, is easily the funniest. Vassa advocates that a mother's duty is always to her family and taking care of the family can never be wrong, even if it means embezzlement, bribery, forgery, blackmail and murder. She has two sons and she likes neither of them. Tennant was very funny as a snivelling, limping, self-pitying, impotent cripple whose wife is having an affair with his alcoholic uncle.

Jan 28. Frances de la Tour, Michael Feast and Michael Williams in Alexander Ostrovsky's **The Forest** directed by Anthony Page at Lyttelton (NT). De La Tour was far too sympathetic as the do-gooder who never does any good. Feast, playing her nephew, brandished a pistol in her face and stole her moneybox. Williams played a threadbare thespian, who specialises in comedy, bitterly complaining that he can't make a proper living because the acting profession has been invaded by retired civil servants, army officers and university students.

1999 Deaths

Lionel Bart (*b.* 1930), British composer
Sarah Kane (*b.* 1971), British
   playwright hanged herself

History

—President Clinton acquitted
—NATO bombed Yugoslavia
—Panama Canal handed back to
   Panama
—Columbine High School killings

Julian Bleach in Shockheaded Peter

Feb 9. Mark Little in Bob Becker's **Defending the Caveman** directed by David Gilmore at Apollo. Pseudo-anthropological lecture on the differences between the sexes.

Feb 10. David Westhead in Stephen Poliakoff's **Talk of the City** directed by Stephen Poliakoff at Young Vic (RSC). A man (Angus Wright), working for the BBC in the later 1930s, decides the best way to alert the nation to what the Nazis are doing to the Jews would be to recruit a song-and-dance man (David Westhead) to front the programme.

Feb 11. Geoffrey Hutchings and Emma Rice in Nick Darke's **The Riot** directed by Mike Shepherd at Cottesloe (NT). Joint production with Kneehigh. In 1896 in Newlyn, Cornwall, Mackerel fishermen, staunch Methodists, objected to Lowestoft fishermen working on Sundays and landing their fish on Mondays, thus lowering prices for the rest of the week. What began as a peaceful demonstration quickly disintegrated into violence.

Feb 17. Shockheaded Peter directed and designed by Julian Crouch and Phelim McDermott at Lyric Theatre, Hammersmith. Inspired by *Struwwelpeter*, which Heinrich Hoffman had written and illustrated for his 3-year-old son in 1844. Set within a Victorian toy theatre with pop-up scenery, puppets, marionettes and numerous small doors, the production was a facsimile of the original picture book and its colours. The master of ceremonies was played by the creepy, hammy and deadly funny Julian Bleach. Haunting Berlin cabaret style music was provided by The Tiger Lillies, led by the castrato crooner, Martyn Jacques, a sinister, white-faced, plumpish fellow in a bowler hat, screaming "DEAD! DEAD!".

Mar 4. Klaus Maria Brandauer in Esther Vilar's **Speer** directed by Klaus Maria Brandauer at Almeida. Speer was Hitler's chief architect and minister for war production during World War 2. Part interview, part interrogation, part debate, the dialogue was wooden, psychologically unconvincing and intellectually inferior to Michael Frayn's *Copenhagen*.

Mar 11. Ben Keaton, Joseph Alessi and Toby Sedgwick as the Marx Brothers in **Animal Crackers** directed by Emil Wolk and Gregory Hersov at King's Head. Book by George S Kaufman and Morrie Ryskind. Music and lyrics by Bert Kalmar and Harry Ruby. Hit Broadway musical in 1928 became one of the Marx Brothers best films, a compendium of some of their most famous visual and verbal gags.

Mar 15. Peter de Jersey and Sophie Okonedo in Shakespeare's **Troilus and Cressida** directed by Trevor Nunn at Olivier (NT). The Greeks were white actors in leather. The Trojans were black actors in flowing robes. With the exception of Roger Allam's Ulysses the acting was disappointing. David Bamber was a mincing, hand-flapping Pandarus.

Mar 17. Abbey Theatre Dublin at Lyttelton. Pat Kinevane, Peter O'Meara and Barbara Brennan in Dion Boucicault's **The Colleen Bawn** directed by Conall Morrison. The trouble with sending the play up is that it has diminishing returns.

Mar 18. Charles Dance in C P Taylor's **Good** directed by Michael Grandage at Donmar. Dance's "good" German remained something of a blank. Ian Gelder was more animated as his best friend, a Jewish doctor, who hates Jews, loves Germany, and doesn't want to leave.

Mar 22. Michael Pennington in Moises Kaufman's **Gross Indecency – The Three Trials of Oscar Wilde** directed by Moises Kaufman at Gielgud. The script was drawn from the original trial transcripts and *De Profundis*, with commentary from letters, newspapers and contemporary biographies. Pennington was a very smug Wilde.

Mar 22. Richard Dreyfuss and Marsha Mason in Neil Simon's **The Prisoner of Second Avenue** directed by David Taylor at Haymarket. 47-year-old executive gets the sack and has a complete mental breakdown. Dreyfuss relied too much on jaw-dropping mugging for his laughs.
—Never try to make comedy funny. Honesty will do nicely, thank you. Neil Simon *Rewrites, A Memoir*

Mar 25. Antony Sher as Leontes in Shakespeare's **The Winter's Tale** directed by Gregory Doran at Barbican (RSC). Leontes, a small, bearded, vulgar despot, was surrounded by tall courtiers and seemed to get smaller as the production progressed. His behaviour was so irrational that it was strange that nobody locked him up.

Apr 6. Dorothy Tutin and Joss Ackland in D L Coburn's **The Gin Game** directed by Frith Banbury at Savoy. In New York the audience behaved as if they were watching a tennis match and delightedly applauded every time she won. In London the production was much darker and far less sentimental.

Apr 6. Siobhan McCarthy, Jenny Galloway and Louise Plowright in Benny Andersson and Bjorn Ulvaeus's **Mamma Mia!** directed by Phyllida Lloyd at Prince Edward. Book by Catherine Johnson. This was the one musical where audiences went into the theatre singing the songs. The show was based round Abba's hit singles of the 1970s and 1980s. Girl (Lisa Stokke) on a Greek island is about to get married and would like to know who her dad was. She rifles through her mother's old diary and discovers she had had a fling with three men nine months before she was born. She invites them to the wedding. The naff way ABBA's songs were introduced was all part of the fun. Transferred to Prince of Wales and still running well into the 21st century.

Apr 7. Zuban Varla in Bernard-Marie Koltes's **Roberto Zucco** directed by James Macdonald at Barbican Pit (RSC) A murderer escapes from prison, strangles his mother, rapes a schoolgirl, shoots a policeman and kills a boy.

Apr 8. Sheila Gish and Rachel Weisz in Tennessee Williams's **Suddenly Last**

Summer directed by Sean Mathias at Comedy. The sculptured tropical garden designed by Tim Hatley was overwhelming. Gish, breathless, gasping, rasping, face lopsided, was a Grand Guignol monster, a Venus-flytrap in her own right.

Apr 13. Simon Russell Beale as Voltaire and Doctor Pangloss in a new version of Leonard Bernstein's musical **Candide** directed by John Caird at Olivier (NT). Lyrics by Richard Wilbur. Additional lyrics by Stephen Sondheim, John Latouche , Lillian Hellman, Dorothy Parker and Leonard Bernstein. Book adapted from Voltaire by Hugh Wheeler. Daniel Evans, sweet of disposition, unaffected in his simplicity, was a wide-eyed, open-mouthed, Candide. Alex Kelly, all pearls and rouge, hammed her way through Cunegonde's burlesque jewel song, "Glitter and Gay," relishing her shame and her jewellery.

Apr 15. Tony Guilfoyle as Frank Lloyd Wright in Robert Lepage and Ex Machina's **Geometry of Miracles** directed by Robert Lepage at Lyttelton. The subject was the great American architect, but told so obscurely, it might as well have been acted in Quebecois. Rodrigue Proteau, playing a naked, grunting, horned, horny Beelzebub, was a convincing devil, even if his relationship to Lloyd Wright was obscure.

Apr 20. Timothy West, Prunella Scales, Nigel Terry and Steven Pacey in Harold Pinter's **The Birthday Party** directed by Joe Harmston at Piccadilly. The line of demarcation between those who are to be locked up and those who do the locking up is thin. Pacey's unappealing, unwashed, myopic, pyjama-jacketed victim was just as much a bully as his tormentors.

Apr 27. Cate Blachett in David Hare's **Plenty** directed by Jonathan Kent at Albery. Blanchett, sensuous, leggy, exhibitionistic, was a classy psychiatric cabaret turn.
—She has a mesmerising stage presence, but it is an entirely histrionic one. She behaves like a ham: her upper class vowels sound like elocution exercises. SUSANNAH CLAPP *Observer*

May 7. Miranda Richardson and Glenne Headly in Wallace Shawn's **Aunt Dan & Lemon** directed by Tom Cairns at Almeida. Aunt Dan makes a passionate speech in defence of Henry Kissinger's actions during the Vietnam War.

May 13. Juliet Stevenson and Anton Lesser in Noël Coward's **Private Lives** directed by Philip Franks at Lyttelton (NT). No 1930s glamour, no cigarette-holders, no brylcreamed hair, no clipped tones, and no chemistry between the actors.

May 26. Danny Sapani as Brutus, Richard Bremmer as Cassius and Mark-Lewis Jones as Anthony in Shakespeare's **Julius Caesar** directed by Mark Rylance at Shakespeare's Globe. The fickle crowd was represented by just four actors, in baseball caps, T-shirts, jeans and trainers, who mingled with the groundlings.

May 27. Stephen Dillane and Jennifer Ehle in Tom Stoppard's **The Real Thing** directed by David Leveaux at Donmar. The characters run the full gamut of suspicion, jealousy, anger, guilt, remorse and humiliation. "I don't believe in behaving well," says the man, "I don't believe in debonair relationships. I believe in mess, tears, pain, self-abasement, loss of self-respect, nakedness."

Jun 3. Simon Russell Beale in Edward Bulwyer Lytton's **Money** directed by John Caird at Olivier (NT). A big success at its premiere in 1840, it was regularly revived throughout the 19th century. Beale, who played the poor relation who comes into the money (a role created by Macready), was so much more real than the caricatures that surrounded him.

Jun 16. Sheila Ferguson, Danny John-Jules and Sharon Benson in Mark Clements and Michael Vivian's **Soultrain** directed by Mark Clements at Victoria Palace. 45 classic soul songs. High spot: Benson singing "Cigarettes and Coffee".

Jun 17. Henry Goodman as Shylock and Derbhle Crotty as Portia in Shakespeare's **The Merchant of Venice** directed by Trevor Nunn at Cottesloe (NT). Set in the cafe society of the 1930s. Portia, languid, sophisticated, Fascist-glamorous, was a Noël Coward leading lady in a Gustav Klimt setting. Launcelot Gobbo (Andrew French) was played as a stand-up comedian at the Kit Kat Club. Forced to become a Christian, Shylock throws his skullcap into the scales, his pound of flesh.

Jun 28. Siobhan Redmond in Liz Lochhead's **Perfect Days** directed by John Tiffany at Vaudeville. 39-year-old Glaswegian celebrity hairdresser wants a baby. Who will give it her? Her ex-husband? The gay cutter who works in her hairdressing salon? Or her 26-year-old toyboy?

Jul 6. Charlton Heston and Lydia Clarke Heston in A R Gurney's **Love Letters** at Haymarket. Heston and his wife sat side by side behind an enormous desk and read their scripts, turning over the pages in unison. It was as exciting as being back at school on Speech Day listening to the Headmaster and the Deputy Headmistress droning on.

Jul 15. Michael Sheen as Jimmy Porter and Emma Fielding as Alison in John

Osborne's **Look Back in Anger** directed by Gregory Hersov at Lyttelton (NT). Less political and not as funny as it had once been.

Jul 27. Eddie Izzard in Julian Barry's **Lenny** directed by Peter Hall at Queen's. The trouble with casting Izzard as Lenny Bruce is that Bruce sounded like Izzard rather than the other way round.

Jul 30. Paul Shelley as Antony and Mark Rylance as Cleopatra in Shakespeare's **Antony and Cleopatra** directed by Giles Block at Shakespeare's Globe. Rylance, 39, the same age as Cleopatra, was a playful, wilful, restless, volatile, dangerous and wonderfully comic bare-footed gypsy in a black wig and sporting a bracelet on his ankle.

Aug 4. Patricia Routledge as Lady Bracknell, Alan Cox as Algernon Moncrieff and Adam Godley as John Worthing in Oscar Wilde's **The Importance of Being Earnest** directed by Christopher Morahan at Haymarket. Routledge was an upholstered, suburban steamroller disguised as stately galleon

Sep 3. Raymond Coulthard, Beverley Klein and, Michael Bryant in Maxim Gorky's **Summerfolk** in a new version by Nick Dear and directed by Trevor Nunn at Olivier (NT). Major revival. Using the full depth of the stage, there was always something going on in the furthest recesses. The canvas was enormous, yet always focused. Christopher Oram's birch tree setting, with its dappled cyclorama, was beautiful. Jasper Britton did the only thing a decent nihilist could do when his offer of marriage was refused – he shot himself.
—Gorky's problem was that he was not Chekhov. JOHN PETER *Sunday Times*

Sep 8. Stephanie Cole, Alec McCowen, Donald Sinden and Angela Thorne in Ronald Harwood's **Quartet** directed by Christopher Morahan at Albery. Four retired opera singers, living in an old people's home, wonder if singing at a private concert for the inmates is a good idea.

Sep 8. Keith Jochim as Richard Nixon and Tim Donoghue as Henry Kissinger in Russell Lee's **Nixon's Nixon** directed by Charles Towers at Bridewell. On the evening of 7 August 1974, facing certain impeachment and conviction, Nixon summoned his Secretary of State to the White House for a secret meeting. The next day he resigned. Lees's play was pure fiction and often very funny when the President, desperately trying to find ways of hanging on to the presidency, came to the conclusion that the best thing to do would be to pretend he was mad.

Sep 21. Leslie Ash and Graham Bickley in **The Pajama Game** directed by Simon Callow at Victoria Palace. Musical. Book by George Abbott and Richard Bissell. Music and lyrics by Richard Adler and Jerry Ross. Nobody believed the actors wanted to get into each other's pajamas.

Sep 24. Elton John and Tim Rice's musical **The Lion King** directed by Julie Taymor at Lyceum. Book by Roger Allers and Irene Mecchi. The Walt Disney cartoon turned into a Broadway musical. The most enchanting menagerie was played by humans and puppets: full-sized puppets, rod-puppets, shadow-puppets. The mechanics always remained visible. The magical effects and the clever use of fabrics and colour were a constant delight. Two giraffes crossed the stage (actors on stilts). A huge elephant (made out of wicker basket and cloth) lumbered down the aisle. Wooden gazelles leapt (on dancers' arms and heads). Paper birds flew (on the ends of poles). A cheetah prowled (visibly pushed on wheels). *The Lion King* is still running well into the 21st century.
—*The Lion King* is not a great work of art. But it is superlative entertainment and it puts most mega-musicals in the shade. JOHN GROSS *Sunday Telegraph*
—Its diverse visual brilliance is often betrayed by its Disneyfied verbal banality. MICHAEL BILLINGTON *Guardian*

Oct 1. Jude Law and Eve Best in John Ford's **'Tis Pity She's A Whore** directed by David Lan at Young Vic. Superficial performances.

Oct 11. Tara Fitzgerald as Antigone and Jonathan Hyde as Creon in Sophocles's **Antigone** directed by Declan Donnellan at Old Vic. "It must be nice to be king," said Antigone to Creon. "You can get away with murder." She played a supporting role to Creon. The chorus was a group of shaven-headed old men in black knickerbockers, played by drama students who had just graduated. They carried long staves and looked as if they were about to go off on a hike.

Oct 5. Ian McDiarmid in Christopher Marlowe's **The Jew of Malta** directed by Michael Grandage at Almeida. Witty and camp, McDiarmid established an immediate rapport with the audience when Barabas casually boasted, as if it were the most normal thing, to having poisoned whole convents, strangled friars and massacred armies.

Oct 5. Barbara Dickson in **Spend, Spend, Spend** directed by Jeremy Sams at Piccadilly. Musical. Book and lyrics by Steve Brown and Justin Greene. Music by Steve Brown. Yorkshire miner in 1961 won £152,319 on the pools. Asked what he was going to do with it, his wife famously replied that she was going to spend, spend, spend. Within four years she had blown the lot. The show's vulgarity was relentless.

Oct 26. Mel Raido in Terrence McNally's **Corpus Christi** directed by Stephen Henry at Pleasance. The story of Jesus was retold from a gay perspective. Set in Texas in the 1950s, Jesus was seduced by Judas (Stephen Billington) in the toilets of Pontius Pilate High School. Satan turned out to be James Dean. Premiered Off-Broadway in 1998 the police had to install airport-style bomb-detecting gates because of protests and threats by ultra-right wing religious groups, who threatened to burn down the theatre.
—This is the most remarkable and powerful Passion play I have ever seen. I was in tears. It blew me away. RICHARD HOLLOWAY *Bishop of Edinburgh.*

Oct 28. Nigel Hawthorne in Shakespeare's **King Lear** directed by Yukio Ninagawa at Barbican (RSC). During the storm Hawthorne was bombarded with rocks from the flies which hit the deck with hard, distracting thuds.

Nov 8. Jonny Lee Miller, Christopher Fulford, James Purefoy and Martin Marquez in Paul Corcoran's **Four Nights in Knaresborough** directed by Richard Wilson at Tricycle. The murder of Thomas a Becket was considered the greatest crime since the crucifixion. The knights, realising they had made the worst career move in history, took refuge in Knaresborough Castle where they were holed up for a whole year, waiting for a word from the king, which never came.

Nov 9. Edward Fox in William Douglas Home's **The Chiltern Hundreds** directed by Ray Cooney at Vaudeville Theatre. Fox's performance was a comic variation on his Harold Macmillan impersonation.

Nov 10. Helen Mirren and Anne-Marie Duff in Donald Margulies **Collected Stories** directed by Howard Davies at Haymarket. Student publishes her first novel which is based on her tutor's youthful love affair with a burnt-out poet. Who owns the story? Is it the person to whom it happened or is it the person who tells it?

Nov 10. Bette Bourne in Tim Fountain's **Resident Alien** directed by Mike Bradwell at Bush. Monologue based on the life and writings of Quentin Crisp who died at 90 just as he was about embark on a tour of Britain in his one-man show. Asked what he had attributed his longevity to, he had replied, "Bad luck!"

Dec 1. Aeschylus's **The Oresteia** directed by Katie Mitchell at Cottesloe (NT). The trilogy, translated by Ted Hughes was a punishing six hours. There were two sets of chorus. The first were be-medalled war-veterans, in wheelchairs, which were pushed around in the dark by nurses, who shone torches in their faces when they spoke. The second were the Furies, who wore tailored suits, surgical gloves, and stockings over their faces and looked like district nurses disguised as bank robbers. Clytemnestra (Anastasia Hille in floral printed dress and high heels) looking like Princess Diana as Eva Peron, addressed the chorus through a free-standing microphone. Orestes (Paul Hilton) was a guerrilla. Electra (Lilo Baur) was a schoolgirl in pigtails, white ankle socks and duffel coat. Cassandra (also played by Baur) was a hysterical child-bride, her face covered by a Magritte wedding veil.
—This is a genuine millennial *Oresteia.* Its moral values are those of the UN inspector; its art that of the Post-Modern and the multimedia practitioner. PETER STOTHARD *The Times*

Dec 2. Malcolm Storry as Volpone and Guy Henry as Mosca in Ben Jonson's **Volpone** directed by Lindsay Posner at Barbican Pit (RSC). Volpone was discovered in bed with his hermaphrodite, his dwarf and his eunuch.

Dec 7. Maggie Smith, Nicholas Farrell and Kevin McNally in Alan Bennett's **The Lady in the Van** directed by Nicholas Hytner at Queen's. Miss Shepherd, a cantankerous, dirty, smelly, incontinent, cranky tramp with delusions of grandeur, parked in Bennett's front garden for three months and stayed until her death, fifteen years later. He had mixed feelings about her. "One seldom was able to do her a good turn," he wrote, "without some thought of strangulation." There were two Bennetts on stage: the author who remains indoors and the author who connects with the outside world. McNally and Farrell were instantly recognisable Bennett look-alikes.
—*The Lady in the Van* is more of a display than a play, a vehicle for Maggie Smith to ride her inventive way to comic triumph. Bennett has concocted a soufflé all dressed up to resemble the square meal it is not. NICHOLAS DE JONGH *Evening Standard*

Dec 9. Simon Russell Beale and Zoë Wanamaker in Nick Stafford's **Battle Royal** directed by Howard Davies at Lyttelton (NT). George IV, who was already secretly married to Mrs Fitzherbert, only married Caroline of Brunswick to produce an heir, but the idea of making love to a dirty and unattractive woman repulsed him. Beale, though he was never as gross as Gillray's caricatures, occasionally behaved like a drag queen. Wanamaker's Caroline was far more sympathetic than Caroline was in real life.

Dec 15. Nicholas Monu in Biyi Bandele's adaptation of Aphra Behn's novel, **Oroonoko,** directed by Gregory Doran at Barbican Pit (RSC). Behn's novel (1678),

Maggie Smith in The Lady in the Van

the first in English literature to express sympathy for black slaves, was very popular with Abolitionists. In the novel, Oroonoko had his genitals, nose and ears hacked off. In Thomas Southerne's stage adaptation (1695) he committed suicide. In Bandele's play, he was shot dead by the most liberal white. The text was a passionate indictment of slavery and a reminder that it was black people who sold black people into the slave trade in the first instance.

Dec 16. Roy Fearon and Richard McCabe in Shakespeare's **Othello** directed by Michael Attenborough at Barbican Theatre (RSC). Fearon, the first black actor to play Othello at Stratford since Paul Robeson, was, at 31, too young. McCabe's Iago was a corpulent, sneering, dirty-minded, sexually impotent creep.

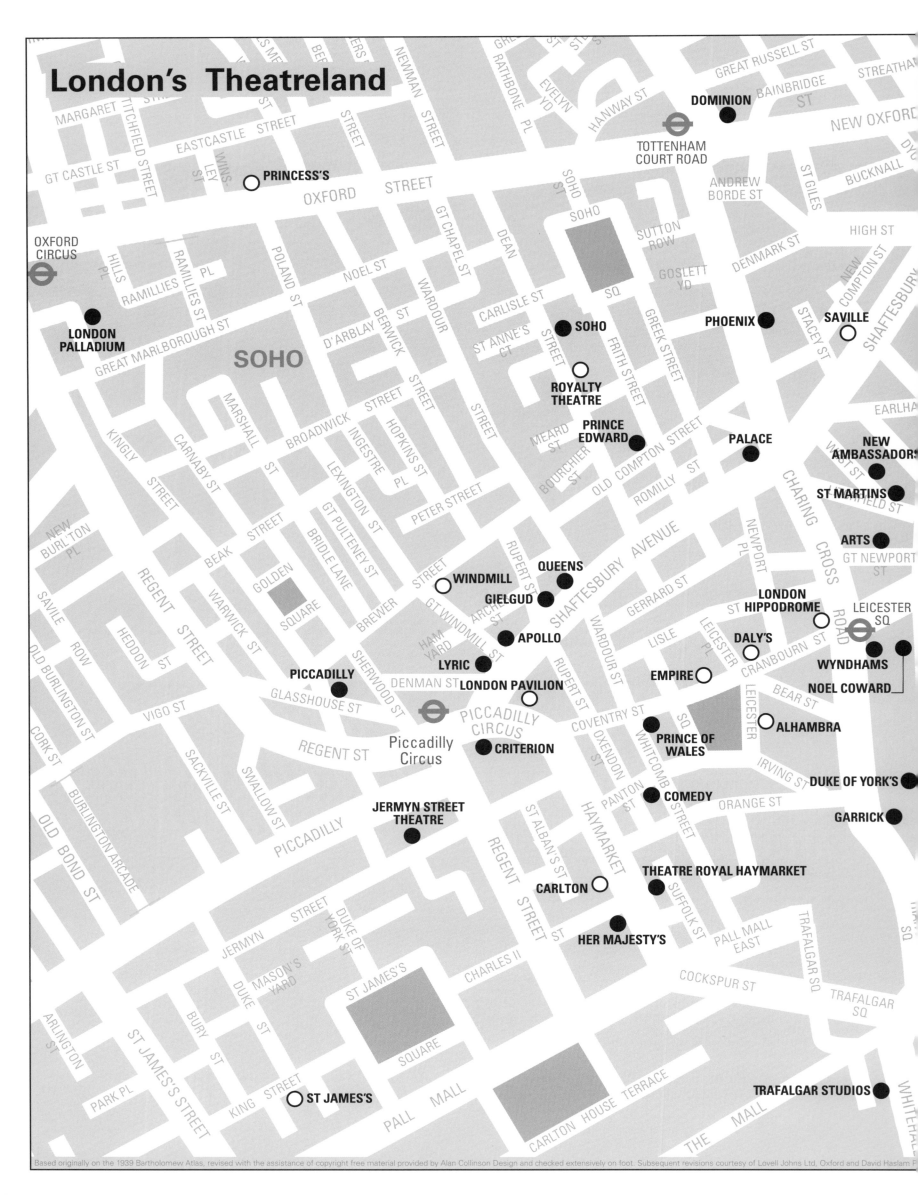

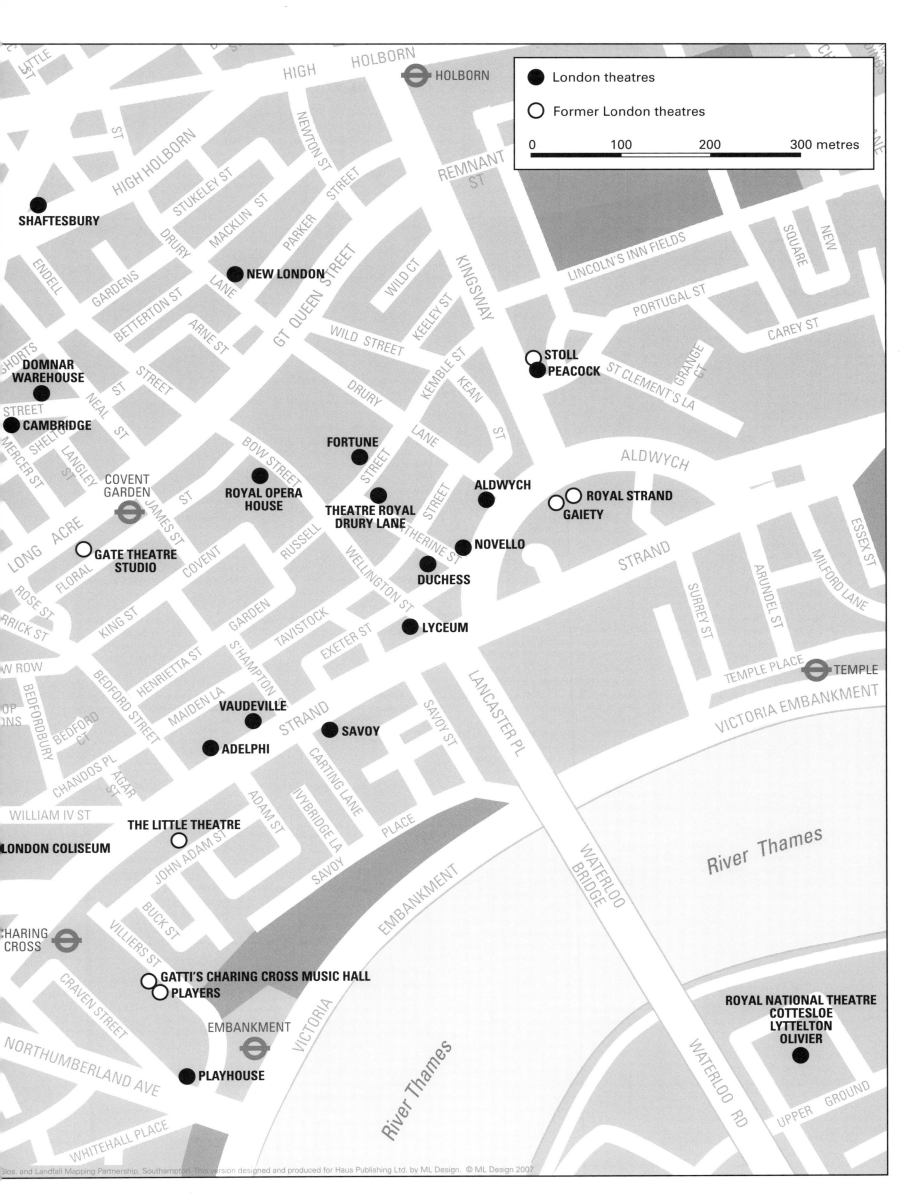

London theatres
○ **Former London theatres**

0   100   200   300 metres

HOLBORN

SHAFTESBURY

NEW LONDON

DOMNAR WAREHOUSE

CAMBRIDGE

STOLL
PEACOCK

FORTUNE

ROYAL OPERA HOUSE

ALDWYCH

ROYAL STRAND
GAIETY

COVENT GARDEN

THEATRE ROYAL DRURY LANE

NOVELLO

GATE THEATRE STUDIO

DUCHESS

ALDWYCH

STRAND

LYCEUM

TEMPLE

TEMPLE PLACE

VICTORIA EMBANKMENT

VAUDEVILLE

SAVOY

ADELPHI

River Thames

WILLIAM IV ST

THE LITTLE THEATRE

LONDON COLISEUM

CHARING CROSS

GATTI'S CHARING CROSS MUSIC HALL
PLAYERS

ROYAL NATIONAL THEATRE
COTTESLOE
LYTTELTON
OLIVIER

EMBANKMENT

PLAYHOUSE

NORTHUMBERLAND AVE

River Thames

WHITEHALL PLACE

WATERLOO RD

UPPER GROUND

Index of Theatres

London theatres in the 20th century past and present

Index of Names

This Index contains actors, authors, designers, directors, composers and choreographers.
NB For William Shakespeare please see under the titles of his individual plays in the Index of Titles.

Index of Titles

Picture credits

The author and publishers wish to express their thanks to the following sources of illustrative material and/or permission to reproduce it. They will make proper acknowledgements in future editions in the event that any omissions have occurred.

Getty Images: pp. 18, 100, 104, 132, 146, 147, 152, 156, 161, 162, 163, 167, 168, 174, 183, 192, 194, 200, 206, 211, 212, 228, 235, 238, 242, 244, 245. Lebrecht Music Collection: pp, 222, 301. Mander and Mitchenson: pp. 4, 8, 17, 46, 50, 88,89, 105, 111, 118, 119, 122, 134, 141, 145, 155, 156, 159, 160, 166, 173, 178, 179, 182, 188, 199, 203, 220, 222, 224, 225. Private Collections: pp. 2, 3, 6, 10, 15, 19, 20, 22, 25, 26, 28, 29, 32, 33, 38, 39, 40, 41, 42, 43, 47, 49, 51, 53, 54, 55, 58, 60. 61. 62, 64, 66, 69, 71, 72, 73, 75, 77, 82, 84, 85, 90, 94,95, 99, 103, 107, 126, 142, 208, 209, 272.Topham Picturepoint: pp. 12, 129, 137, 171, 176, 180, 186, 191, 201, 213, 216, 217, 218, 221, 230, 246, 249, 254, 257, 259, 261, 263, 265, 266, 270, 276, 277, 279, 280, 282, 284, 285, 288, 289, 290, 293, 294, 295, 296, 299.